SOCIAL SECURITY LEGISLATION 2007

VOLUME IV:
TAX CREDITS, CHILD TRUST FUNDS AND EMPLOYER-PAID SOCIAL SECURITY BENEFITS

AUSTRALIA
Law Book Co.
Sydney

CANADA and USA
Carswell
Toronto

HONG KONG
Sweet & Maxwell Asia

NEW ZEALAND
Brookers
Auckland

SINGAPORE and MALAYSIA
Sweet & Maxwell Asia
Singapore and Kuala Lumpur

SOCIAL SECURITY LEGISLATION 2007

General Editor
David Bonner, LL.B, LL.M

VOLUME IV: TAX CREDITS, CHILD TRUST FUNDS AND EMPLOYER-PAID SOCIAL SECURITY BENEFITS

Commentary By

Nick Wikeley, M.A. (Cantab)
Barrister, Professor of Law, University of Southampton
Deputy Social Security and Child Support Commissioner,
Deputy District Chairman, Appeal Tribunals

David W. Williams, LL.M., Ph.D., C.T.A.
Solicitor, Social Security and Child Support Commissioner,
Deputy Special Commissioner of Income Tax and
part-time Chairman of VAT and Duties Tribunal

Consultant Editor
Child Poverty Action Group

LONDON
SWEET & MAXWELL
2007

Published in 2007 by
Sweet & Maxwell Limited of
100 Avenue Road, Swiss Cottage,
London NW3 3PF
http://www.sweetandmaxwell.co.uk
Typeset by Servis Filmsetting Ltd, Manchester
Printed in Great Britain by MPG Books, Bodmin, Cornwall

No natural forests were destroyed to make this product.
Only farmed timber was used and re-planted.

A catalogue record for this book is
available from the British Library

ISBN 9781847032614

All rights reserved. Crown Copyright Material is reproduced with the permission of the Controller of HMSO and the Queen's Printer for Scotland.
 No part of this publication may be reproduced or transmitted in any form or by any means, or stored in any retrieval system of any nature without prior written permission, except for permitted fair dealing under the Copyright, Designs and Patents Act 1988, or in accordance with the terms of a licence issued by the Copyright Licensing Agency in respect of photocopying and/or reprographic reproduction. Application for permission for other use of copyright material including permission to reproduce extracts in other published works shall be made to the publishers. Full acknowledgment of author, publisher and source must be given.
 Application for permission for other use of copyright material controlled by the publisher shall be made to the publishers. Material is contained in this publication for which publishing permission has been sought, and for which copyright is acknowledged. Permission to reproduce such material cannot be granted by the publishers and application must be made to the copyright holder.

Commentators have asserted their moral rights under the Copyright, Designs and Patents Act 1988 to be identified as the authors of the commentary in this Volume.

©
Sweet & Maxwell Limited
2007

CHILD POVERTY ACTION GROUP

The Child Poverty Action Group (CPAG) is a charity, founded in 1965, which campaigns for the relief of poverty in the United Kingdom. It has a particular reputation in the field of welfare benefits law derived from its legal work, publications, training and parliamentary and policy work, and is widely recognised as the leading organisation for taking test cases on social security law.

CPAG is therefore ideally placed to act as Consultant Editor to this 4-volume work—**Social Security Legislation 2007**. CPAG is not responsible for the detail of what is contained in each volume, and the authors' views are not necessarily those of CPAG. The Consultant Editor's role is to act in an advisory capacity on the overall structure, focus and direction of the work.

For more information about CPAG, its rights and policy publications or training courses, its address is 94 White Lion Street, London, N1 9PF (telephone: 020 7837 7979—website: *http://www.cpag.org.uk*).

FOREWORD

The volumes which make up the Social Security Legislation with the accompanying commentary have become an indispensable part of the tribunal decision making process. I am glad to be able, once again, to commend them and their sister publications to all those who are involved in any way in administrative decision making or who might have cause to come before our tribunals. Once again we have at our disposal a readily available source of some of the most complex legislation in any jurisdiction with a clear exposition of its meaning and interpretation. I am grateful to all those who have taken the time and effort to compile these volumes and present them for publication.

His Honour Michael Harris
President of Appeals Tribunals

PREFACE

Tax Credits and Employer-Paid Social Security Benefits is Volume IV of what is now a four volume series: *Social Security Legislation 2007*. The companion volumes are Bonner, Hooker and White, *Volume I: Non Means Tested Benefits*; Wood, Poynter, Wikeley and Bonner, *Volume II: Income Support, Jobseeker's Allowance, State Pension Credit and the Social Fund*; and Rowland and White, *Volume III: Administration, Adjudication and the European Dimension*.

Each of the volumes in the series provides a legislative text, clearly showing the form and date of amendments, and commentary up to date to April 12, 2007.

The Tax Credits Act 2002, introducing Child Tax Credit (CTC) and Working Tax Credit (WTC), represented a radical shift for the benefits system. These tax credits require appeal tribunals, advisers and other practitioners to get to grips with concepts, in many ways drawn from the income tax system, which are radically different from traditional welfare state principles. As we explained in the Preface to the first edition of *Volume IV*, this was the prime reason for the launch of this new book. This volume, designed in the same format as its established companion volumes, covers CTC and WTC along with statutory sick pay (SSP), statutory maternity pay (SMP), statutory paternity pay (SPP) and statutory adoption pay (SAP). The common theme for these last four benefits is that they are all employer-paid social security benefits. But note that this volume is not entitled *Tax Credits and Inland Revenue-administered Social Security Benefits*, as Child Benefit and Guardian's Allowance, now the responsibility of HMRC (formerly the Revenue), remain in *Volume I: Non Means Tested Benefits*. This volume also includes the statutory provisions relating to the new child trust funds.

This volume includes not just the substantive law relating to CTC and WTC but also the various procedural regulations governing both claimants' responsibilities and the duties of HMRC in administering claims for these benefits. We also cover the procedural provisions governing appeals before both appeal tribunals and the Social Security Commissioners. We remain indebted to Mark Rowland, co-author of Volume III, for his permission to use his expert commentary here and for his generous assistance in this process.

The new tax credits have still to generate a significant body of case law. However, we have taken the opportunity in this year's fifth edition of *Volume IV* to bring the statutory text up to date, reflecting the various amendments made by regulations to the scope of WTC and CTC (as well as ironing out some wrinkles identified by some eagle-eyed readers). We have also expanded the commentary on key provisions in the light of the experience to date in hearing tax credits appeals. In addition, given that there has been considerable public interest in the issue of overpayments of tax credits, we have included the text of Inland Revenue Code of Practice 26 and leaflet WTC7 on Tax Credits penalties. The labours of the Tax Law Rewrite

Preface

project have also borne fruit again this year, so we have removed extracts from the Income and Corporation Taxes Act 1988 and inserted relevant provisions from the Income Tax Act 2007. We have in addition incorporated those provisions of the Work and Families Act 2006 relating to statutory maternity pay, paternity pay and adoption pay which are at the time of writing in force.

In the last edition we had to omit the index for reasons of reducing page length. Having listened carefully to the view of users, we are very pleased that Sweet & Maxwell have felt able to respond by reinstating it in this edition.

Users of the original three volumes in this series, and their predecessors, have over the years provided valuable comments which have invariably been helpful to the editors in ensuring that the selection of legislative material for inclusion and the commentary upon it reflect the sorts of difficulties encountered in practice. In doing so, readers have thus helped to shape the content of each of the volumes in the current series. We hope that readers will maintain that tradition. Please write to the General Editor of the series, Professor David Bonner, Faculty of Law, University of Leicester, University Road, Leicester, LE1 7RH, who will pass on any comments received to the appropriate commentator.

Our gratitude also goes to the President of the Social Security and Child Support Appeals Tribunal and his staff for continuing the tradition of help and encouragement.

June, 2007   Nick Wikeley
                                                                                  David Williams

CONTENTS

	Page
Foreword	vii
Preface	ix
Using this book, using legal authority and finding other sources of information	xv
Table of Cases	xxiii
Table of Social Security Commissioners' Decisions	xxix
Table of Abbreviations	xxxi

PART I
HM REVENUE AND CUSTOMS
TAX CREDITS AND SOCIAL SECURITY

	Paras
Taxes Management Act 1970	1.1
Social Security Contributions and Benefits Act 1992	1.30
Social Security Administration Act 1992	1.132
Social Security Act 1998	1.145
Social Security Contributions (Transfer of Functions, etc.) Act 1999	1.188
Tax Credits Act 2002	1.217
Employment Act 2002	1.378
Income Tax (Earnings and Pensions) Act 2003	1.406
Child Trust Funds Act 2004	1.527
Income Tax (Trading and Other Income) Act 2005	1.625
Commissioners for Revenue and Customs Act 2005	1.730
Income Tax Act 2007	1.749

PART II
TAX CREDITS

	Paras
Tax Credits Act 2002 (Commencement No.3 and Transitional Provisions and Savings) Order 2003	2.1
Tax Credits Act 2002 (Commencement No.4, Transitional Provisions and Savings) Order 2003	2.8
Tax Credits Act 2002 (Transitional Provisions) Order 2005	2.12
Working Tax Credit (Entitlement and Maximum Rate) Regulations 2002	2.19
Tax Credits (Definition and Calculation of Income) Regulations 2002	2.100
Child Tax Credit Regulations 2002	2.183
Tax Credits (Income Thresholds and Determination of Rates) Regulations 2002	2.215
Tax Credits (Claims and Notifications) Regulations 2002	2.270

Contents

	Paras
Tax Credits [(Payment by the Commissioners)] Regulations 2002	2.332
Tax Credits (Administrative Arrangements) Regulations 2002	2.360
The Tax Credits (Notice of Appeal) Regulations 2002	2.367
The Tax Credits (Appeals) (No.2) Regulations 2002	2.370
The Social Security Commissioners (Procedure) (Tax Credits Appeals) Regulations 2002	2.438
Tax Credits (Interest Rate) Regulations 2003	2.492
Tax Credits (Immigration) Regulations 2003	2.498
Tax Credits (Residence) Regulations 2003	2.515
Tax Credits (Official Error) Regulations 2003	2.534
Tax Credits (Provision of Information) (Functions Relating to Health) Regulations 2003	2.540
The Tax Credits (Polygamous Marriages) Regulations 2003	2.545
Tax Credits (Provision of Information) (Functions Relating to Health) (No.2) Regulations 2003	2.558
Tax Credits (Provision of Information) (Functions Relating to Employment and Training) Regulations 2003	2.562
Tax Credits Act 2002 (Child Tax Credit) (Transitional Provisions) Order 2003	2.566
Tax Credits (Provision of Information) (Evaluation and Statistical Studies) Regulations 2003	2.570
Tax Credits (Provision of Information) (Evaluation and Statistical Studies) (Northern Ireland) Regulations 2004	2.572
Tax Credits (Provision of Information) (Functions Relating to Health) (Scotland) Regulations 2004	2.574
Tax Credits (Provision of Information) (Functions Relating to Employment and Training) Regulations 2005	2.576
Tax Credits (Approval of Child Care Providers) Scheme 2005	2.578

PART III
STATUTORY SICK PAY

	Paras
Statutory Sick Pay (General) Regulations 1982	3.1
Statutory Sick Pay (Mariners, Airmen and Persons Abroad) Regulations 1982	3.44
Statutory Sick Pay (Medical Evidence) Regulations 1985	3.65
Statutory Sick Pay (National Health Service Employees) Regulations 1991	3.75
Statutory Sick Pay Percentage Threshold Order 1995	3.82
Statutory Sick Pay and Statutory Maternity Pay (Decisions) Regulations 1999	3.91

PART IV
STATUTORY MATERNITY PAY

	Paras
Statutory Maternity Pay (General) Regulations 1986	4.1
Statutory Maternity Pay (Medical Evidence) Regulations 1987	4.56

Contents

	Paras
Statutory Maternity Pay (Persons Abroad and Mariners) Regulations 1987	4.61
Statutory Maternity Pay (National Health Service Employees) Regulations 1991	4.73
Statutory Maternity Pay (Compensation of Employers) and Miscellaneous Amendment Regulations 1994	4.80
Statutory Maternity Pay (General) (Modification and Amendment) Regulations 2000	4.92

PART V
STATUTORY PATERNITY PAY AND STATUTORY ADOPTION PAY

	Paras
Statutory Paternity Pay and Statutory Adoption Pay (Weekly Rates) Regulations 2002	5.1
Statutory Paternity Pay and Statutory Adoption Pay (National Health Service Employees) Regulations 2002	5.8
Statutory Paternity Pay and Statutory Adoption Pay (Administration) Regulations 2002	5.16
Statutory Paternity Pay and Statutory Adoption Pay (Persons Abroad and Mariners) Regulations 2002	5.33
Statutory Paternity Pay and Statutory Adoption Pay (General) Regulations 2002	5.44
Social Security Contributions and Benefits Act 1992 (Application of Parts 12ZA and 12ZB to Adoptions from Overseas) Regulations 2003	5.96
Statutory Paternity Pay (Adoption) and Statutory Adoption Pay (Adoptions from Overseas) (Administration) Regulations 2003	5.103
Statutory Paternity Pay (Adoption) and Statutory Adoption Pay (Adoptions from Overseas) (Persons Abroad and Mariners) Regulations 2003	5.108
Statutory Paternity Pay (Adoption) and Statutory Adoption Pay (Adoptions from Overseas) (No.2) Regulations 2003	5.113

PART VI
CHILD TRUST FUNDS

	Paras
Child Trust Funds Act 2004 (Commencement No.1) Order 2004	6.1
Child Trust Funds Act 2004 (Commencement No.2) Order 2004	6.3
Child Trust Funds Regulations 2004	6.5
Child Trust Funds (Insurance Companies) Regulations 2004	6.50
The Child Trust Funds (Non-tax Appeals) Regulations 2005	6.59
General Commissioners (Jurisdiction and Procedure) (Amendment) Regulations 2005	6.65
Special Commissioners (Jurisdiction and Procedure) (Amendment) Regulations 2005	6.69
The Child Trust Funds (Appeals) Regulations 2005	6.73
The Social Security Commissioners (Procedure) (Child Trust Funds) Regulations 2005	6.118

Contents

PART VII
HMRC CODES OF PRACTICE AND GUIDANCE

	Paras
WTC 7—Tax Credits Penalties	7.1
COP 26—What Happens if we have Paid you too much Tax Credit?	7.25

USING THIS BOOK, USING LEGAL AUTHORITY AND FINDING OTHER SOURCES OF INFORMATION

Introduction

This book is not designed as an introduction to, or general textbook on, the law relating to social security. Inevitably some familiarity with the social security system has been assumed. This note is designed to assist readers who are not lawyers—and also those lawyers who are not familiar with this particular field of law—by identifying the sources of social security law and showing how to find them. Volume IV also deals with income tax law, and its version of this section contains additional comments about that.

Primary sources of social security law

Social security law is based on legislation, consisting of *Acts of Parliament*, which are primary legislation and are also known as statutes, and *statutory instruments*, which are secondary or delegated legislation made by ministers acting under powers conferred by primary legislation and are also known as regulations (or, occasionally, orders). Another source of the law lies in *judicial decisions*, made, in this context, principally by Social Security Commissioners who hear appeals from appeal tribunals although some decisions of the courts are also relevant. Such judicial decisions provide authoritative interpretation of the legislation. The precise mixture of the three sources differs from benefit to benefit.

The scope of this book and the status of the commentary

This book contains an up-to-date text of the principal statutes and statutory instruments relevant to the work of appeal tribunals and Commissioners. It also contains a commentary on that legislation, referring to relevant decisions of Commissioners and the courts. The commentary aims to help readers understand the legislation and its implications. The focus in decision-making, however, must remain on the actual words of the legislation as applied by the Commissioners and courts, because the commentary merely reflects the opinion of the commentator on what the law is.

Finding a particular section in a statute

Statutes consist of numbered sections (sometimes grouped in Parts, which may in turn be divided into Chapters) and they often have schedules at the end.

Suppose you wanted to find section 94 of the Social Security Contributions and Benefits Act 1992. Sometimes the word "section" is abbreviated to "s."; so you could refer to the Social Security Contributions and Benefits Act 1992, s.94.

To find this provision, you can use the contents pages to find where provisions of the Social Security Contributions and Benefits Act 1992 are printed. You can also use the running heads at the top of each page; the header on the left-hand page gives the name of the Act while the header on the right-hand page gives the year and chapter number (abbreviated "c.") as well as the section dealt with on that page. The chapter number simply indicates the order in the Parliamentary year of the statute; the Social Security Contributions and Benefits Act 1992 is chapter 4, meaning that it was the fourth statute to be passed by Parliament in 1992.

After the text of the section comes a note of the AMENDMENTS made to the provision, reference to relevant DEFINITIONS, and the commentary, which appears under the heading GENERAL NOTE. Where the section is re-enacted in consolidating legislation, that is, legislation drawing together all the amendments over time in a new statute, the DERIVATION, or source, of the provision is also given so that you can see where the provision originally appeared. This can be helpful in considering any decisions of Commissioners or the courts on the earlier form of the provision.

Finding a particular regulation

Statutory instruments consist of numbered regulations (or articles where the statutory instrument is in the form of an order rather than being a set of regulations) and, like statutes, they sometimes have schedules at the end.

Suppose you wanted to find regulation 26 of the Social Security (Incapacity for Work) (General) Regulations 1995. Sometimes the word "regulation" is abbreviated to "reg."; so you could refer to the Social Security (Incapacity for Work) (General) Regulations 1995, reg.26.

To find this provision, use the contents pages to find the Social Security (Incapacity for Work) (General) Regulations 1995. Then move forward within the regulations until you find the one you want. Again the running headers at the top of each page will assist you. The header on the right-hand page gives the statutory instrument number, that is the year of publication and the number, as in SI 1995/311, indicating that these regulations were the 311th statutory instrument made by Ministers and approved by Parliament in 1995.

As with statutes, after the text of the regulation comes a note of the AMENDMENTS made to the provision, reference to relevant DEFINITIONS, and the commentary which appears under the heading GENERAL NOTE Where the regulation is re-enacted in consolidating regulations, that is, legislation drawing together all the amendments made over time in a new set of regulations, the DERIVATION or source, of the provision is also given so that you can see where the provision originally appeared. This can be helpful in considering any decisions of Commissioners or the courts on the earlier form of the provision.

Commissioners' decisions

Both reported and unreported decisions of Commissioners are important sources of guidance on the interpretation and application of legislation relating to social security benefits and their administration. Where relevant, these are binding on both decision-makers and on tribunals. The binding nature of Commissioners' decisions is discussed below. A single Commissioner hears most appeals, though the Chief Commissioner does occasionally direct that three Commissioners sitting together should hear cases of special importance. This is then known as a Tribunal of Commissioners.

Reported decisions

About 40 to 50 decisions a year are selected to be "reported". Selection used to be a decision of the Chief Commissioner acting alone. Later he made his selection on advice from a committee of Commissioners, but, since 2002, selection of decisions to report has been the task of an Editorial committee chaired by the Chief Commissioner. Decisions are selected for reporting only if they are of general importance and command the assent of at least a majority of Commissioners. They are published in biennial bound volumes by The Stationery Office and in looseleaf form (contact Margaret Drummond, Print Solutions, Room B0202, Benton Park Road, Newcastle-upon- Tyne NE98 1YX (tel. 0191 225 5422)) and on the world wide web (*http://www.dwp.gov.uk/advisers/docs/commdecs/index.asp*) by the Department for Work and Pensions (replacing the DSS). They can also be accessed via the Commissioners' website (*http://www.osscsc.gov.uk*). These decisions are available in all tribunal venues and can be consulted in local social security offices, and some main libraries.

Reported decisions are renumbered with the initial letter "R" for "reported". *R(IB) 1/00* was the first decision on incapacity benefit to be reported in 2000. A decision of a Tribunal of Commissioners is often identified by adding a letter "T" in brackets after the reference, as in *R(IB) 2/99(T)*. Scottish decisions are not specifically identified as such.

Unreported decisions

Reported decisions are selected from a greater body of decisions in the cases dealt with by the Commissioners. Those not reported are known as unreported decisions but still have precedential value. Each Commissioner's decision is given a file number in the Commissioners' Office, which is a unique identification number. From 1997 cases have been registered consecutively by number within a calendar year, without a separate range of numbers for each benefit. Prior to 1995, there was a separate range of numbers for each benefit. So Commissioner's decision *CU/23/1992* is the 23rd case on unemployment benefit registered in 1992. The letters "CU" indicate that the decision is that of a Commissioner (C) and that the benefit in question is unemployment benefit (U). Between 1995 and 1997, there had been a change of approach, reflecting computerisation. The system of numbering consecutively within benefits in a particular year ceased. The lettering system remained the same, but the number after the letters, as in *CU/7328/1995*, indicated that this was the 7328th case on any benefit registered since the beginning of 1995.

Scottish decisions have an "S" after the "C" (e.g. *CSI/26/98*) and, until the Welsh office of the Commissioners was closed, Welsh decisions could be identified as having a "W" after the "C".

Until the end of 2001, some 100 decisions a year were "starred" because it was considered that they raised points of significance or interest and deserved wider circulation. They did not, however, acquire any enhanced precedential status from being starred. The practice of starring was discontinued from the start of 2002. Instead decisions that Commissioners believe should have wider currency are available on the Commissioners' website (*http://www.osscsc.gov.uk*). Some decisions are selected as of particular interest and highlighted for a time in the Most Recent Decisions part of the

Using this Book

Decisions section of that website. As with "starring", however, a decision does not gain enhanced precedential status through "highlighting".

Other sources of/on Commissioners' decisions

There are a number of other sources of valuable information or commentary on Commissioners' decisions, whether reported or unreported: see in particular publications such as the *Journal of Social Security Law*, CPAG's *Welfare Rights Bulletin*, *Legal Action* and the *Adviser*. As far as online resources go there is little to beat Rightsnet (*http://www.rightsnet.org.uk*). This site contains a wealth of resources for people working in the welfare benefits field but of special relevance in this context are the "Briefcase" area which contains summaries of Commissioners' Decisions (with links to the full decision on the Commissioners' website (*http://www.osscsc.gov.uk*)) and the Commissioners' Decisions section of the "Toolkit" area.

What does it mean to say that a case is binding?

Reference to decisions being binding means that where a similar point is raised in a later case before an adjudicating authority bound by the decision, that adjudicating authority must accept the interpretation of the law contained in the decision. So a Commissioner's decision explaining what a term in a particular regulation means, lays down the definition of that term in much the same way as if the term had been defined in the regulations themselves. The decision may also help in deciding what the same term means when it is used in a different set of regulations, provided that the term appears to have been used in a similar text.

Appeals to the Commissioners are now available only on points of law, but before April 1987 appeals were available on points of fact as well as law. Care should be taken in reading older decisions to appreciate that some were concerned with fact rather than law, though the reported decisions invariably contain points of general application. Relevant decisions of the Commissioners and the courts are explained in the commentary to the statutory provisions in this volume, together with guidance on their significant for decision-making in the tribunals. Users of the book should remember that it is the decision itself which is binding and not the explanation of it in the commentary; that is merely the opinion of the commentator.

Using Commissioners' decisions: the hierarchy of authority

Although the Chief Commissioner has directed that, so far as possible, reference should be made to reported decisions only, the legal position is that all decisions of Commissioners are binding on decision-makers and tribunals. Where there is a conflict, a decision of a Tribunal of Commissioners should be preferred to a decision of a single Commissioner and a reported decision should generally be preferred to an unreported decision (*R(I) 12/75(T)*), unless the unreported decision was the later decision and the Commissioner expressly decided not to follow the earlier reported decision (see the Northern Ireland decision, *R 1/00(FC)*). Decisions of Commissioners are not binding on other Commissioners. However, a single Commissioner will always follow a decision of a Tribunal of Commissioners and will generally follow a decision of another single

Commissioner (*R(I) 12/ 75(T)*). A Tribunal of Commissioners will generally follow a decision of another such Tribunal but is not bound to do so (*R(U) 4/88(T)*).

There are separate Commissioners in Northern Ireland considering legislation that is often indistinguishable from the legislation in Great Britain. Decisions of Northern Ireland Commissioners are not binding in Great Britain (*R(SB) 1/90(T)*) but are persuasive. Such decisions are included in the decisions published on the website of the Great Britain Commissioners but the selection of decisions to be reported is made by the Chief Commissioner in Northern Ireland. Looseleaf publication by The Stationery Office and on the world wide web by the Department for Social Development (*http://www.dsdni.gov.uk*) is separate from the publication of Great Britain decisions. So was the publication of bound volumes by The Stationery Office until 1999. From 2000, reported Northern Ireland decisions are included in the same bound volumes as reported decisions of Commissioners in Great Britain. References to decisions of Northern Ireland Commissioners can always be distinguished from references to decisions of Commissioners in Great Britain because the former are numbered differently with the letters identifying the type of benefit always being in brackets after the numbers, as in *C12/98(IS)*, which has been reported as *R1/00(IS)*. Unreported decisions of the Northern Ireland Commissioners can be found on the Department for Social development website at *http://www.dsdni.gov.uk*.

Using Commissioners' decisions at Tribunals and before the Commissioners

Decision-makers and claimants are entitled to assume that tribunals and Commissioners have immediate access to reported decisions of Commissioners and they need not provide copies, although it may sometimes be helpful to do so. However, where either a decision-maker or a claimant intends to rely on an unreported decision, it will be necessary to provide a copy of the decision to the tribunal or Commissioner. A copy of the decision should also be provided to the other party before the hearing because otherwise it may be necessary for there to be an adjournment to enable that party to take advice on the significance of the decision.

Decisions of the Courts

Decisions of the superior courts in Great Britain and Northern Ireland on questions of legal principle are almost invariably followed by decision-makers, tribunals and Commissioners, even when they are not strictly binding because the relevant court was in a different part of the United Kingdom or exercised a parallel—but not superior—jurisdiction (see the note to s.14 of the Social Security Act 1998 in Pt I of *Vol. III: Administration, Appeals and the European Dimension.*)

Decisions of the courts on social security matters are generally included among the reports of Commissioners' decisions. So, for example, *R(I) 1/00* contains Commissioner's decisions *CSI 12/98*, the decision of the Court of Session upholding the Commissioner's decision and the decision of the House of Lords in *Chief Adjudication Officer v Faulds*, reversing the decision of the Court of Session. Decisions issued in recent years by the higher courts in the United Kingdom (e.g., the High Court, the Court of Appeal, the Court of Session and the House of Lords) and some decisions of tribunals are also published free on the website of the British and Irish Legal Information Institute (*http://www.bailii.org*), often within hours of delivery. Some of them can also be found in the various series of law reports familiar to lawyers (in particular, in the *Law Reports*, the *Weekly Law Reports*, the *All England Law Reports*, the *Industrial Cases Reports* and the *Family Law Reports*. Sweet and Maxwell's online subscription service *Westlaw* is another valuable source (*http://www.westlaw.co.uk*), as is Smith Bernal's *Casetrack* (*http://www.casetrack.com*) and Lexis Nexis *Lexis* (*http://www.lexis.com*).

European Community Law

The European Community is part of the European Union. European Community Law affecting social security is covered in the third volume in this series: *Administration, Appeals and the European Dimension*.

The European Union has two courts: the Court of Justice of the European Communities, and the Court of First Instance. Decision-makers, tribunals and Commissioners are under a duty by reason of Article 10 (ex.5) of the EC Treaty to apply decisions of the Luxembourg courts, where relevant to cases before them, in preference to other authorities binding on them.

Decisions of the Court of Justice of the European Communities come in two parts: the Opinion of the Advocate General and the decision of the Court. It is the decision of the Court which is binding. The Court is assisted by hearing the Opinion of the Advocate General before itself coming to a conclusion on the issue before it. The Court does not always follow its Advocate General. Where it does, the Opinion of the Advocate General often elaborates the arguments in greater detail than the single collegiate judgment of the Court. No dissenting judgments appear in reports from the Court of Justice.

Decisions of the Luxembourg courts, together with legislation of the European Union, are published in English on the world wide web at *http://eur-lex.europa.eu/en/index.htm*.

The European Convention on Human Rights, the Strasbourg Court and the Human Rights Act 1998

The Court of Human Rights in Strasbourg is quite separate from the Luxembourg courts and serves a different purpose: interpreting and applying the European Convention on Human Rights, which is incorporated into United Kingdom law by the Human Rights Act 1998. From October 2, 2000, public authorities, including courts, Commissioners, tribunals and decision-makers (the Secretary of State) must act in accordance with the incorporated provisions of the Convention, unless statute prevents this. They must take into account the Strasbourg case law. They are required to interpret legislation, so far as is possible to do so, to give effect to the incorporated Convention rights. Any court or tribunal may declare secondary legislation incompatible with those rights and, in certain circumstances, invalidate it. Only the higher courts can declare a provision of primary legislation to be incompatible with those rights, but no court or tribunal can invalidate primary legislation.

Using this Book

The work of the Court and the impact of the Human Rights Act 1998 on social security are discussed in the third volume in this series: *Administration, Appeals and the European Dimension*.

Judgments of the Court of Human Rights are made by majority, and separate concurring or dissenting judgments are included with the decision of the majority where the Court is not unanimous.

Decisions of the Court of Human Rights are available on the world wide web at *http://www.echr.coe.int*.

Official guidance on Social Security Law

The law has been translated into a more civil servant friendly format. Prior to the decision-making and appeals changes made by the Social Security Act 1998, guidance on benefits and their administration was set out in the thirteen volume *Adjudication Officers Guide (AOG)* published by The Stationery Office. This has now been replaced by a fourteen volume *Decision Makers Guide (DMG)*. This is available on the world wide web at *http://www.dwp.gov.uk/publications/dwp/dmg/index.asp*.

The coverage of the DMG is as follows:

Volume 1	Decision Making and Appeals
Volume 2	International Subjects
Volume 3	Subjects Common to all Benefits
Volume 4	Jobseeker's Allowance and Income Support
Volume 5	Jobseeker's Allowance and Income Support
Volume 6	Jobseeker's Allowance and Income Support
Volume 7	Jobseeker's Allowance and Income Support
Volume 8	No longer issued
Volume 9	No longer issued
Volume 10	Benefits for Incapacity, Disability and Maternity
Volume 11	Industrial Injuries Benefits
Volume 12	Widow's Benefit and Retirement Pension
Volume 13	State Pension Credit
Volume 14	State Pension Credit

It should be noted that the DMG is not binding on tribunals and Commissioners; it is internal guidance for the use of decision-makers within the Department.

Child Benefit and Guardian's Allowance are now administered by HM Revenue and Customs, as are tax credits. A range of useful material can be found on its website at *http://www.hmrc.gov.uk/practitioners/index.shtml*.

Unofficial guidance on Social Security Law

There are a large number of guides. CPAG's *Welfare Benefits Handbook*, published annually each spring, is unrivalled as a practical and comprehensive introduction from the claimant's viewpoint.

TABLE OF CASES

AWG Group Ltd (formerly Anglian Water Plc) v Morrison; sub nom. Morrison v AWG Group Ltd (formerly Anglian Water Plc) [2006] EWCA Civ 6; [2006] 1 W.L.R. 1163; [2006] 1 All E.R. 967, CA (Civ Div) 1.160
Akewushola v Secretary of State for the Home Department; sub nom. Akewushola v Immigration Officer (Heathrow) [2000] 1 W.L.R. 2295; [2000] 2 All E.R. 148; [1999] Imm. A.R. 594; [1999] I.N.L.R. 433, CA (Civ Div) 2.429
Akram v Adam [2004] EWCA Civ 1601; [2005] 1 W.L.R. 2762; [2005] 1 All E.R. 741; [2005] C.P. Rep. 14; [2005] H.L.R. 14; [2005] L. & T.R. 9; [2004] 50 E.G. 84 (C.S.); (2005) 102(5) L.S.G. 28; (2004) 148 S.J.L.B. 1433; [2004] N.P.C. 182; [2005] 1 P. & C.R. DG13, CA 2.429
Alabaster v Woolwich Plc (C147/02) [2005] All E.R. (EC) 490; [2004] E.C.R. I-3101; [2004] 2 C.M.L.R. 9; [2004] C.E.C. 261; [2005] I.C.R. 695; [2004] I.R.L.R. 486, ECJ 1.63, 4.36
Alabaster v Woolwich Plc (Reference to ECJ) [2002] EWCA Civ 211; [2002] 1 C.M.L.R. 56; [2002] I.R.L.R. 420, CA (Civ Div) 1.63
Alabaster v Woolwich Plc; sub nom. Alabaster v Barclays Bank Plc (formerly Woolwich Plc) [2005] EWCA Civ 508; [2005] 2 C.M.L.R. 19; [2005] Eu. L.R. 824; [2005] I.C.R. 1246; [2005] I.R.L.R. 576, CA (Civ Div) 1.63, 4.36
Attorney General v Johnstone 10 T.C. 758 .... 1.317
Bangs v Connex South Eastern Ltd; sub nom. Connex South Eastern Ltd v Bangs [2005] EWCA Civ 14; [2005] 2 All E.R. 316; [2005] I.C.R. 763; [2005] I.R.L.R. 389; (2005) 149 S.J.L.B. 148, CA (Civ Div) 2.420
Barke v Seetec Business Technology Centre Ltd [2005] EWCA Civ 578; [2005] I.C.R. 1373; [2005] I.R.L.R. 633, CA (Civ Div) 2.420
Baron v Secretary of State for Social Services, reported as an Appendix to R(M) 6/86 ... 2.420
Bland v Chief Supplementary Benefit Officer [1983] 1 W.L.R. 262; [1983] 1 All E.R. 537; (1983) 127 S.J. 53, CA (Civ Div); also reported as R(SB) 12/83 .... 1.163, 1.166
Braintree DC v Thompson; sub nom. Thompson v Braintree DC [2005] EWCA Civ 178; [2005] H.L.R. 37; [2005] N.P.C. 35, CA (Civ Div) 1.160
Brodt v Wells General Commissioners [1987] S.T.C. 207; 60 T.C. 436, Ch D 1.312
Brown v Chief Adjudication Officer [1997] I.C.R. 266; [1997] I.R.L.R. 110; (1996) 93(42) L.S.G. 28; (1996) 140 S.J.L.B. 221, CA (Civ Div) 1.40
Butterfield (on behalf of James William Butterfield) (Deceased) v Secretary of State for Defence [2002] EWHC 2247, QBD (Admin) 2.315
Carpenter v Secretary of State for Work and Pensions; sub nom. Carpenter v Social Security Commissioner [2003] EWCA Civ 33; [2003] A.C.D. 52, CA (Civ Div) 2.415, 2.419
Cenlon Finance Co Ltd v Ellwood (Inspector of Taxes); sub nom. Tableau Holdings v Williams [1962] A.C. 782; [1962] 2 W.L.R. 871; [1962] 1 All E.R. 854; 40 T.C. 176; (1962) 41 A.T.C. 11; [1962] T.R. 1; (1962) 106 S.J. 280, HL 1.21
Centre Public d'Aide Sociale, Courcelles v Lebon (316/85) [1987] E.C.R. 2811; [1989] 1 C.M.L.R. 337, ECJ 1.540
Chief Adjudication Officer v Ellis, reported as the Appendix to R(IS) 22/95 .... 2.33
Clixby v Pountney [1968] Ch. 719; [1968] 2 W.L.R. 865; [1968] 1 All E.R. 802; 44 T.C. 575; (1967) 46 A.T.C. 398; [1967] T.R. 383; 117 N.L.J. 1343; (1968) 112 S.J. 16, Ch D 1.311
Cooke v Glenrose Fish Co [2004] I.C.R. 1188; [2004] I.R.L.R. 866, EAT 2.408, 2.429
Cooke v Secretary of State for Social Security; sub nom. Cooke v Social Security Commissioner [2001] EWCA Civ 734; [2002] 3 All E.R. 279, CA (Civ Div); reported as R(DLA) 6/01 .... 1.166
Customs and Excise Commissioners v Medway Draughting and Technical Services Ltd; Joined Cases Customs and Excise Commissioners v Adplates Offset Ltd [1989] S.T.C. 346; [1989] B.T.C. 5070; [1989] C.O.D. 497, QBD 1.312

Denson v Secretary of State for Work and Pensions. *See* R. (on the application of MH) v Special Educational Needs and Disability Tribunal.
E v Secretary of State for the Home Department; Joined Cases R v Secretary of State for the Home Department [2004] EWCA Civ 49; [2004] Q.B. 1044; [2004] 2 W.L.R. 1351; [2004] I.N.L.R. 268; [2004] B.L.G.R. 463; (2004) 101(7) L.S.G. 35; (2004) 148 S.J.L.B. 180, CA (Civ Div) 1.160
Eagil Trust Co v Pigott-Brown [1985] 3 All E.R. 119, CA (Civ Div) 2.420
Edwards (Inspector of Taxes) v Clinch [1982] A.C. 845; [1981] 3 W.L.R. 707; [1981] 3 All E.R. 543; [1981] S.T.C. 617; 56 T.C. 367; [1981] T.R. 393; (1981) 125 S.J. 762, HL...2.125
English v Emery Reimbold & Strick Ltd; Joined Cases DJ&C Withers (Farms) Ltd v Ambic Equipment Ltd; Verrechia (t/a Freightmaster Commercials) v Commissioner of Police of the Metropolis [2002] EWCA Civ 605; [2002] 1 W.L.R. 2409; [2002] 3 All E.R. 385; [2002] C.P.L.R. 520; [2003] I.R.L.R. 710; [2002] U.K.H.R.R. 957; (2002) 99(22) L.S.G. 34; (2002) 152 N.L.J. 758; (2002) 146 S.J.L.B. 123, CA (Civ Div) 2.420
Ensign Tankers (Leasing) Ltd v Stokes (Inspector of Taxes) [1992] 1 A.C. 655; [1992] 2 W.L.R. 469; [1992] 2 All E.R. 275; [1992] S.T.C. 226; 64 T.C. 617; [1992] S.T.I. 364; (1992) 89(17) L.S.G. 49; (1992) 136 S.J.L.B. 89, HL 2.141
Evans v Secretary of State for Social Security, reported as R(I) 5/94 ....2.415, 2.420
Fitzpatrick v Sterling Housing Association Ltd [2001] 1 A.C. 27; [1999] 3 W.L.R. 1113; [1999] 4 All E.R. 705; [2000] 1 F.L.R. 271; [1999] 2 F.L.R. 1027; [2000] 1 F.C.R. 21; [2000] U.K.H.R.R. 25; 7 B.H.R.C. 200; (2000) 32 H.L.R. 178; [2000] L. & T.R. 44; [2000] Fam. Law 14; [1999] E.G. 125 (C.S.); (1999) 96(43) L.S.G. 3; [1999] N.P.C. 127; (2000) 79 P. & C.R. D4, HL 5.58
Flannery v Halifax Estate Agencies Ltd (t/a Colleys Professional Services) [2000] 1 W.L.R. 377; [2000] 1 All E.R. 373; [2000] C.P. Rep. 18; [1999] B.L.R. 107; (1999) 11 Admin. L.R. 465; (1999) 15 Const. L.J. 313; (1999) 96(13) L.S.G. 32; (1999) 149 N.L.J. 284; [1999] N.P.C. 22, CA (Civ Div) 2.420
George Mitchell (Chesterhall) Ltd v Finney Lock Seeds Ltd [1983] 2 A.C. 803; [1983] 3 W.L.R. 163; [1983] 2 All E.R. 737; [1983] 2 Lloyd's Rep. 272; [1983] Com. L.R. 209, HL 1.160
Ghaidan v Godin-Mendoza; sub nom. Mendoza v Ghaidan; Ghaidan v Mendoza; Godin-Mendoza v Ghaidan [2004] UKHL 30; [2004] 2 A.C. 557; [2004] 3 W.L.R. 113; [2004] 3 All E.R. 411; [2004] 2 F.L.R. 600; [2004] 2 F.C.R. 481; [2004] H.R.L.R. 31; [2004] U.K.H.R.R. 827; 16 B.H.R.C. 671; [2004] H.L.R. 46; [2005] 1 P. & C.R. 18; [2005] L. & T.R. 3; [2004] 2 E.G.L.R. 132; [2004] Fam. Law 641; [2004] 27 E.G. 128 (C.S.); (2004) 101(27) L.S.G. 30; (2004) 154 N.L.J. 1013; (2004) 148 S.J.L.B. 792; [2004] N.P.C. 100; [2004] 2 P. & C.R. DG17, HL 5.58
Gillespie v Northern Health and Social Services Board (C342/93) [1996] All E.R. (EC) 284; [1996] E.C.R. I-475; [1996] 2 C.M.L.R. 969; [1996] I.C.R. 498; [1996] I.R.L.R. 214; (1996) 31 B.M.L.R. 65, ECJ 1.63
Gillies v Secretary of State for Work and Pensions; sub nom. Secretary of State for Work and Pensions v Gillies [2006] UKHL 2; [2006] 1 W.L.R. 781; [2006] 1 All E.R. 731; 2006 S.C. (H.L.) 71; 2006 S.L.T. 77; 2006 S.C.L.R. 276; [2006] I.C.R. 267; (2006) 9 C.C.L. Rep. 404; (2006) 103(9) L.S.G. 33; (2006) 150 S.J.L.B. 127; 2006 G.W.D. 3-66, HL...1.160, 2.391
Gladders v Prior (Inspector of Taxes) [2003] S.T.C. (S.C.D.) 245; [2003] S.T.I. 946, Sp Comm...1.312
Gray (Inspector of Taxes) v Matheson [1993] 1 W.L.R. 1130; [1993] S.T.C. 178; 65 T.C. 577; [1993] S.T.I. 214; (1993) 90(10) L.S.G. 36; (1993) 137 S.J.L.B. 46, Ch D 1.21
Great Western Railway Co v Bater (Surveyor of Taxes) [1922] 2 A.C. 1, HL 2.125
Grzelcyk (C184/99) [2001] E.C.R. I-6193 ....1.540
Harrison's Settlement, Re; sub nom. Harrison v Harrison; Joined Cases Ropner v Ropner; Ropner's Settlement, Re; Williams Will Trust, Re [1955] Ch. 260; [1955] 2 W.L.R. 256; [1955] 1 All E.R. 185; (1955) 99 S.J. 74, CA...................................2.427
Harrison's Share, Re, *See* Harrison's Settlement, Re.
Hatungimana v Secretary of State for the Home Department [2006] EWCA Civ 231, CA (Civ Div) 2.420
Hillenbrand v Inland Revenue Commissioners 1966 S.L.T. 213; 42 T.C. 617; (1966) 45 A.T.C. 224; [1966] T.R. 201, IH (1 Div) 1.311
Hinchy v Secretary of State for Work and Pensions [2005] UKHL 16; [2005] 1 W.L.R. 967; [2005] 2 All E.R. 129; (2005) 102(17) L.S.G. 32; (2005) 149 S.J.L.B. 299, HL 1.249, 1.277

Table of Cases

Hirvisari v Finland, unreported, 2001, ECHR 2.420
Hoppe v Germany (28422/95) [2003] 1 F.L.R. 384; [2003] 1 F.C.R. 176; (2004) 38
    E.H.R.R. 15; [2003] Fam. Law 159, ECHR 2.476
Hornal v Neuberger Products [1957] 1 Q.B. 247; [1956] 3 W.L.R. 1034; [1956] 3 All
    E.R. 970; (1956) 100 S.J. 915, CA 1.312
Hudson v Humbles 42 T.C. 380; (1965) 44 A.T.C. 124; [1965] T.R. 135; (1965) 109
    S.J. 315 .... 1.311
Inland Revenue Commissioners v Lysaght; sub nom. Lysaght v Inland Revenue
    Commissioners [1928] A.C. 234; [1928] All E.R. Rep. 575; 13 T.C. 511, HL 2.521
Jones v Leeming; sub nom. Leeming v Jones; Leeming v Jones (Inspector of Taxes)
    [1930] A.C. 415, HL 2.141
Kerr v Department for Social Development [2004] UKHL 23; [2004] 1 W.L.R. 1372;
    [2004] 4 All E.R. 385; [2004] N.I. 397, HL (NI); also reported as an Appendix to
    R1/04(SF) 1.329
King v United Kingdom (Admissibility) (No.2) (13881/02) [2004] S.T.C. 911; [2007]
    B.T.C. 74; 6 I.T.L. Rep. 872; [2004] S.T.I. 1117, ECHR 1.312
Krasniqi v Secretary of State for the Home Department [2006] EWCA Civ 391, CA
    (Civ Div) 1.163
Lawal v Northern Spirit Ltd [2003] UKHL 35; [2004] 1 All E.R. 187; [2003] I.C.R.
    856; [2003] I.R.L.R. 538; [2003] H.R.L.R. 29; [2003] U.K.H.R.R. 1024; (2003)
    100(28) L.S.G. 30; (2003) 153 N.L.J. 1005; (2003) 147 S.J.L.B. 783, HL 1.160
Leeves v Chief Adjudication Officer [1999] E.L.R. 90, CA (Civ Div) 2.152
Levene v Inland Revenue Commissioners [1928] A.C. 217; [1928] All E.R. Rep. 746;
    13 T.C. 486, HL 2.521
Locabail (UK) Ltd v Bayfield Properties Ltd (Leave to Appeal); Joined Cases Locabail
    (UK) Ltd v Waldorf Investment Corp (Leave to Appeal); Timmins v Gormley;
    Williams v Inspector of Taxes; R. v Bristol Betting and Gaming Licensing
    Committee Ex p. O'Callaghan [2000] Q.B. 451; [2000] 2 W.L.R. 870; [2000] 1 All
    E.R. 65; [2000] I.R.L.R. 96; [2000] H.R.L.R. 290; [2000] U.K.H.R.R. 300; 7
    B.H.R.C. 583; (1999) 149 N.L.J. 1793; [1999] N.P.C. 143, CA (Civ Div) 1.160
Martinez Sala v Freistaat Bayern (C85/96) [1998] E.C.R. I-2691, ECJ 1.540
Meyers v Adjudication Officer (C116/94) [1995] All E.R. (E.C.) 705; [1995] E.C.R. I-
    2131; [1996] 1 C.M.L.R. 461; [1995] I.R.L.R. 498, ECJ (4th Chamber) 1.273
Millar (David Cameron) v Dickson; Joined Cases Stewart v Heywood; Payne v
    Heywood; Tracey v Heywood; Marshall v Ritchie [2001] UKPC D 4; [2002] 1
    W.L.R. 1615; [2002] 3 All E.R. 1041; 2002 S.C. (P.C.) 30; 2001 S.L.T. 988; 2001
    S.C.C.R. 741; [2001] H.R.L.R. 59; [2001] U.K.H.R.R. 999; 2001 G.W.D. 26-
    1015, PC (Sc) 2.391
Miller v Secretary of State for Work and Pensions 2002 G.W.D. 25-861, IH (Ex Div) ... 2.476
Mooney v Secretary of State for Work and Pensions; sub nom. Mooney, Petitioner 2004
    S.L.T. 1141; 2004 G.W.D. 29-611, OH; also reported as R(DLA) 5/04 .... 1.163
Morrell v Secretary of State for Work and Pensions [2003] EWCA Civ 526, CA (Civ
    Div) 2.152
Moyna v Secretary of State for Work and Pensions; sub nom. Moyna v Secretary of State
    for Social Security [2003] UKHL 44; [2003] 1 W.L.R. 1929; [2003] 4 All E.R. 162;
    (2003) 73 B.M.L.R. 201, HL; also reported as R(DLA) 7/03 .... 1.160
Mulvey v Secretary of State for Social Security 1997 S.C. (H.L.) 105; 1997 S.L.T. 753;
    1997 S.C.L.R. 348; [1997] B.P.I.R. 696; 1997 G.W.D. 11-488, HL 1.555
Murrell v Secretary of State for Social Services, reported as an Appendix to R(I) 3/84 ... 1.160
Nethermere (St Neots) Ltd v Gardiner; sub nom. Nethermere (St Neots) Ltd v Taverna
    [1984] I.C.R. 612; [1984] I.R.L.R. 240; (1984) 81 L.S.G. 2147; (1984) 134 N.L.J.
    544, CA (Civ Div) 2.33
Nimmo v Alexander Cowan & Sons Ltd [1968] A.C. 107; [1967] 3 W.L.R. 1169;
    [1967] 3 All E.R. 187; 1967 S.C. (H.L.) 79; 1967 S.L.T. 277; 3 K.I.R. 277; (1967)
    111 S.J. 668, HL 1.329
Nu-Swift International Ltd v Mallinson [1979] I.C.R. 157; [1978] I.R.L.R. 537, EAT ... 1.59
PM v United Kingdom (6638/03) (Admissibility) [2005] S.T.I. 1480; (2004) 39
    E.H.R.R. SE21, ECHR 1.312
PM v United Kingdom (6638/03); sub nom. M v United Kingdom (6638/03) [2005]
    S.T.C. 1566; [2005] 3 F.C.R. 101; (2006) 42 E.H.R.R. 45; 18 B.H.R.C. 668; 7
    I.T.L. Rep. 970, ECHR 1.312
Porter v Magill; sub nom. Magill v Weeks; Magill v Porter; Joined Cases Weeks v Magill;
    Hartley v Magill; England v Magill; Phillips v Magill [2001] UKHL 67; [2002] 2

Table of Cases

A.C. 357; [2002] 2 W.L.R. 37; [2002] 1 All E.R. 465; [2002] H.R.L.R. 16; [2002] H.L.R. 16; [2002] B.L.G.R. 51; (2001) 151 N.L.J. 1886; [2001] N.P.C. 184, HL 1.160
Quinn v Department for Social Development [2004] NICA 22 .... 2.420
R (Iran) v Secretary of State for the Home Department; sub nom. R. (on the application of R) v Secretary of State for the Home Department; Joined Cases A (Afghanistan) v Secretary of State for the Home Department; M (Afghanistan) v Secretary of State for the Home Department; T (Afghanistan) v Secretary of State for the Home Department; T (Eritrea) v Secretary of State for the Home Department [2005] EWCA Civ 982; [2005] Imm. A.R. 535; [2005] I.N.L.R. 633, CA (Civ Div) 1.160
R. v Allen (Brian Roger) [2001] UKHL 45; [2002] 1 A.C. 509; [2001] 3 W.L.R. 843; [2001] 4 All E.R. 768; [2001] S.T.C. 1537; [2002] 1 Cr. App. R. 18; [2002] H.R.L.R. 4; 74 T.C. 263; [2001] B.T.C. 421; 4 I.T.L. Rep. 140; [2001] S.T.I. 1348, HL 1.312
R. v Barnet LBC Ex p. Shah (Nilish); Joined Cases Akbarali v Brent LBC; Abdullah v Shropshire CC; Shabpar v Barnet LBC; Shah (Jitendra) v Barnet LBC; Ablack v Inner London Education Authority; R. v Shropshire CC Ex p. Abdullah [1983] 2 A.C. 309; [1983] 2 W.L.R. 16; [1983] 1 All E.R. 226; 81 L.G.R. 305; (1983) 133 N.L.J. 61; (1983) 127 S.J. 36, HL 2.521
R. v Deputy Industrial Injuries Commissioner Ex p. Moore [1965] 1 Q.B. 456; [1965] 2 W.L.R. 89; [1965] 1 All E.R. 81; (1964) 108 S.J. 1030, CA; also reported as an Appendix to R(I) 4/65 .... 1.329
R. v Higher Education Funding Council Ex p. Institute of Dental Surgery [1994] 1 W.L.R. 242; [1994] 1 All E.R. 651; [1994] C.O.D. 147, DC 2.420
R. v Inland Revenue Commissioners Ex p. Knight [1973] S.T.C. 564 .... 1.312
R. v Medical Appeal Tribunal (Midland Region) Ex p. Cararrini [1966] 1 W.L.R. 883; (1966) 110 S.J. 509, DC; also reported as an Appendix to R(I) 13/65 .... 2.415
R. v Medical Appeal Tribunal (North Midland Region) Ex p. Hubble [1959] 2 Q.B. 408; [1959] 3 W.L.R. 456; [1959] 3 All E.R. 40; (1959) 103 S.J. 562, CA 1.329
R. v Secretary of State for the Home Department Ex p. Mehta; sub nom. Mehta v Secretary of State for the Home Department [1975] 1 W.L.R. 1087; [1975] 2 All E.R. 1084; (1975) 119 S.J. 475, CA (Civ Div) 2.436
R. v Secretary of State for the Home Department Ex p. Saleem; sub nom. R. v Immigration Appeal Tribunal Ex p. Saleem; Saleem v Secretary of State for the Home Department [2001] 1 W.L.R. 443; [2000] 4 All E.R. 814; [2000] Imm. A.R. 529; [2000] I.N.L.R. 413, CA (Civ Div) 2.374
R. v Social Security Commissioner Ex p. Bibi, unreported, May 23, 2000 .... 2.415
R. v Soneji (Kamlesh Kumar); sub nom. R. v Soneiji (Kamalesh Kumar); Joined Cases R. v Bullen (David Frederick) [2005] UKHL 49; [2006] 1 A.C. 340; [2005] 3 W.L.R. 303; [2005] 4 All E.R. 321; [2006] 2 Cr. App. R. 20; [2006] 1 Cr. App. R. (S.) 79; [2006] Crim. L.R. 167; (2005) 102(31) L.S.G. 26; (2005) 155 N.L.J. 1315; (2005) 149 S.J.L.B. 924, HL 1.160
R. (on the application of Asha Foundation) v Millennium Commission [2003] EWCA Civ 88; [2003] A.C.D. 50; (2003) 100(11) L.S.G. 31, CA (Civ Div) 2.420
R. (on the application of Begum (Anayet)) v Social Security Commissioners [2002] EWHC 401, QBD (Admin) 1.163
R. (on the application of Bidar) v Ealing LBC (C209/03) [2005] Q.B. 812; [2005] 2 W.L.R. 1078; [2005] All E.R. (EC) 687; [2005] E.C.R. I-2119; [2005] 2 C.M.L.R. 3; [2005] C.E.C. 607; [2005] E.L.R. 404, ECJ 1.540, 1.541
R. (on the application of MH) v Special Educational Needs and Disability Tribunal; sub nom. H v Special Educational Needs and Disability Tribunal [2004] EWCA Civ 770; [2004] B.L.G.R. 844; [2004] E.L.R. 424; (2004) 101(29) L.S.G. 29; (2004) 148 S.J.L.B. 792, CA (Civ Div) 2.380
R. (on the application of Roberts) v Parole Board; sub nom. Roberts v Parole Board [2005] UKHL 45; [2005] 2 A.C. 738; [2005] 3 W.L.R. 152; [2006] 1 All E.R. 39; [2005] H.R.L.R. 38; [2005] U.K.H.R.R. 939; (2005) 155 N.L.J. 1096, HL 2.400
R. (on the application of Thompson) v Law Society [2004] EWCA Civ 167; [2004] 1 W.L.R. 2522; [2004] 2 All E.R. 113; (2004) 101(13) L.S.G. 35; (2004) 154 N.L.J. 307; (2004) 148 S.J.L.B. 265, CA (Civ Div) 2.476
Ransom (Inspector of Taxes) v Higgs; sub nom. Dickinson v Kilmorie (Aldridge) Downes; Joined Cases Motley (Inspector of Taxes) v Higgs Settlement Trustees; Dickinson (Inspector of Taxes) v Downes; Grant (Inspector of Taxes) v Downes

Table of Cases

Settlement Trustees; Kilmorie (Aldridge) Ltd v Dickinson (Inspector of Taxes); Motley v Higgs Trustees; Restorick v Godber, Parry [1974] 1 W.L.R. 1594; [1974] 3 All E.R. 949; [1974] S.T.C. 539; [1974] T.R. 281; (1974) 118 S.J. 849, HL 2.141
Reina v Landeskreditbank Baden-Wurttemberg (C65/81) [1982] E.C.R. 33; [1982] 1 C.M.L.R. 744, ECJ (3rd Chamber) 1.540
Revenue and Customs Commissioners v Thorn Baker Ltd, unreported, July 14, 2006 .. 1.120
Rowland v Boyle (Inspector of Taxes); sub nom. Chartered Accountant v Inspector of Taxes [2003] EWHC 781; [2003] S.T.C. 855; 75 T.C. 693; [2003] B.T.C. 359; [2003] S.T.I. 885, Ch D...1.312
Rydqvist v Secretary of State for Work and Pensions [2002] EWCA Civ 947; [2002] 1 W.L.R. 3343; [2002] I.C.R. 1383; (2002) 146 S.J.L.B. 247, CA (Civ Div)............. 2.398
Scorer (Inspector of Taxes) v Olin Energy Systems Ltd; sub nom. Olin Energy Systems Ltd v Scorer (Inspector of Taxes) [1985] A.C. 645; [1985] 2 W.L.R. 668; [1985] 2 All E.R. 375; [1985] S.T.C. 218; (1985) 82 L.S.G. 1943; (1985) 129 S.J. 248, HL.. 1.21
Secretary of State for Defence v Pensions Appeal Tribunals (England and Wales); sub nom. R. (on the application of Secretary of State for Defence) v President of the Pensions Appeal Tribunals [2004] EWHC 141; [2004] 2 All E.R. 159, QBD (Admin) 2.429
Secretary of State for Work and Pensions v Cunningham, 2005 1 S.C. 19; 2004 S.L.T. 1007; 2004 G.W.D. 25-546, IH (Ex Div); also reported as R(DLA) 7/04 .... 1.160, 2.391
Sharkey v De Cross (Inspector of Taxes); sub nom. Sharkey v Revenue and Customs Commissioners; Sharkey v De Croos (Inspector of Taxes) [2006] EWHC 300; [2006] S.T.C. 2026; 77 T.C. 484; [2006] S.T.I. 455, Ch D 1.312
Shilton v Wilmshurst (Inspector of Taxes) [1991] 1 A.C. 684; [1991] 2 W.L.R. 530; [1991] 3 All E.R. 148; [1991] S.T.C. 88; 64 T.C. 78; (1991) 135 S.J. 250, HL........ 2.34
South Buckinghamshire DC v Porter (No.2); sub nom. South Buckinghamshire DC v Secretary of State for Transport, Local Government and the Regions [2004] UKHL 33; [2004] 1 W.L.R. 1953; [2004] 4 All E.R. 775; [2005] 1 P. & C.R. 6; [2004] 4 P.L.R. 50; [2004] 28 E.G. 177 (C.S.); (2004) 101(31) L.S.G. 25; (2004) 148 S.J.L.B. 825; [2004] N.P.C. 108, HL 2.420
Stansby v Datapulse Plc; sub nom. Stansby v Datapulse Plc [2003] EWCA Civ 1951; [2004] I.C.R. 523; [2004] I.R.L.R. 466; [2004] U.K.H.R.R. 340; (2004) 101(6) L.S.G. 32; (2004) 148 S.J.L.B. 145, CA (Civ Div) 1.160
Taylor Gordon & Co Ltd (t/a Plan Personnel) v Timmons [2004] I.R.L.R. 180; (2003) 100(44) L.S.G. 32, EAT... 1.31, 1.191
W v L [1974] Q.B. 711; [1973] 3 W.L.R. 859; [1973] 3 All E.R. 884; 72 L.G.R. 36; (1973) 4 Fam. Law 134; (1973) 117 S.J. 775, CA (Civ Div).................................2.96
Whelan v Chief Adjudication Officer; *Independent*, November 14, 1994, CA (Civ Div) ..2.195
White v Chief Adjudication Officer [1986] 2 All E.R. 905; (1986) 83 L.S.G. 1319; (1986) 130 S.J. 448, CA (Civ Div) 2.491
Zalewska v Department for Social Development, unreported, May 9, 2007, CA (NI)....2.526

TABLE OF COMMISSIONERS' DECISIONS

CA/4297/2004	2.420
CCR/3396/2000	2.418
CCS/2064/1999	2.436
CCS/6302/1999	2.374
CCS/1626/2002	2.420
CCS/3749/2003	1.329
CCS/3757/2004	2.394
CCS/2288/2005	2.374
CDLA/1389/1997	2.425
CDLA/3680/1997	2.415
CDLA/5793/1997	2.420
CDLA/1552/1998	2.415
CDLA/1347/1999	2.396, 2.400
CDLA/5419/1999	2.420
CDLA/7980/1999	1.160
CDLA/557/2001	2.415
CDLA/572/2001	2.421
CDLA/4895/2001	2.435
CDLA/2748/2002	2.407
CDLA/5574/2002	2.471
CDLA/1807/2003	2.420
CDLA/2462/2003	2.410
CDLA/1685/2004	1.157
CDLA/2014/2004	1.329
CDLA/145/2006	2.407
CDWA/3123/1997	2.90, 2.91
CF/6923/1999	1.157
CFC/1537/1995	2.194, 2.195
CG/2973/2004	2.374, 2.429
CH/2484/2005	1.162
CH/2553/2005	2.420
CI/141/1987	2.427
CI/3887/1999	2.427
CI/1021/2001	1.329
CI/3596/2001	1.161
CI/1814/2005	1.160
CIB/3013/1997	2.425
CIB/4497/1998	2.418
CIB/303/1999	2.374, 2.429
CIB/2620/2000	2.391
CIB/4791/2001	2.451, 2.452
CIB/2751/2002	2.409
CIB/4751/2002	2.417
CIB/460/2003	2.369
CIB/1009/2004	2.415
CIB/2058/2004	2.415
CIB/4253/2004	2.394
CIS/49/1991	2.195
CIS/2132/1998	2.420
CIS/5321/1998	1.329
CIS/2428/1999	1.155
CIS/1753/2000	2.410
CIS/2292/2000	2.415
CIS/1952/2001	2.452
CIS/2345/2001	2.418, 2.420
CIS/4248/2001	2.396
CIS/4533/2001	1.157
CIS/995/2004	1.234, 1.278, 2.274, 2.276
CIS/1363/2005	2.380, 2.404
CIS/2559/2005	2.526
CIS/2680/2005	2.526
CIS/3573/2005	2.526
CPC/2920/2005	2.526
CS/343/1994	3.425
CS/1753/2000	1.160
CS/1952/2001	2.449
CS/3202/2002	2.409
CSDLA/71/1999	2.436, 2.450
CSDLA/536/1999	2.435, 2.449
CSDLA/551/1999	2.420
CSDLA/101/2000	2.486
CSDLA/300/2000	2.455
CSDLA/1207/2000	2.454
CSDLA/2/2001	2.465
CSDLA/866/2002	2.394, 2.415
CSIB/439/2004	2.424.2
CSIB/404/2005	2.408
CSIS/48/1992	1.233
CST/76/2006	2.79
CSTC/326/2003	1.229
CSTC/76/2006	2.56
CTC/2090/2004	1.238, 1.329, 2.372
CTC/2576/2004	1.283
CTC/3059/2004	1.238
CTC/3543/2004	1.238
CTC/3864/2004	1.238
CTC/4390/2004	1.283, 2.372
CTC/643/2005	2.56
CTC/1629/2005	1.238
CTC/2612/2005	2.372
CTC/2662/2005	1.287
CTC/1594/2006	1.316
CTC/2103/2006	2.36
CTC/2113/2006	2.128, 2.219
CTC/3981/2006	1.283
R(A) 1/72	2.420
R(A) 1/82	1.160
R(A) 4/89	2.400
R(A) 2/92	2.96, 2.97
R(A) 2/06	2.372
R(CS) 4/04	2.380
R(DLA) 2/98	2.369
R(DLA) 2/01	1.155
R(DLA) 6/01	1.166
R(DLA) 2/03	1.155
R(DLA) 7/03	1.160

Table of Commissioner's Decisions

R(DLA) 5/04	1.163	R(M) 1/89	2.424.1, 2.471
R(DLA) 7/04	1.160, 2.391	R(M) 2/89	2.89
R(DLA) 3/05	2.374	R(M) 1/96	2.420
R(DLA) 3/06	2.411	R(S) 11/51	2.88
R(DLA) 5/06	2.391	R(S) 24/54	3.5
R(F) 2/79	2.194	R(S) 1/72	3.5
R(F) 2/81	2.194	R(S) 4/82	1.329
R(FC) 2/90	1.159, 1.266	R(S) 8/85	2.491
R(FC) 1/92	2.36	R(S) 4/93	3.5
R(FIS) 1/86	2.34	R(SB) 17/81	1.238
R(I) 4/65	1.329	R(SB) 12/83	1.163, 1.166
R(I) 13/65	2.415	R(SB) 19/83	2.374
R(I) 14/74	2.427	R(SB) 55/83	2.374
R(I) 3/84	1.160	R(SB) 19/93	2.429
R(I) 5/94	2.415, 2.420	R(SSP) 1/85	3.12
R(I) 4/02	2.420	R(SSP) 1/86	1.121
R(I) 3/03	2.420	R(SSP) 1/89	3.37
R(IB) 6/03	2.415, 2.419	R(TC) 1/05	2.380
R(IB) 7/05	1.329	R(U) 3/88	2.415
R(IS) 12/92	1.266		
R(IS) 22/95	2.33	**Northern Ireland**	
R(IS) 11/99	1.329, 2.418, 2.420, 2.435, 2.455	C6/05-06(IS)	2.526
		R2/01(IB)	2.420
R(IS) 5/04	2.420	R3/01(IB)	2.420
R(IS) 17/04	1.329	R1/02(IB)	1.329, 2.396
R(M) 2/78	2.420	R3/02(IB)	2.420, 2.471
R(M) 1/85	2.521	R1/04(SF)	1.329
R(M) 6/86	2.420	R2/04(DLA)	2.420
R(M) 1/87	2.436	R3/04(IB)	2.396

TABLE OF ABBREVIATIONS USED IN THIS SERIES

2002 Act	Tax Credits Act 2002
AA	Attendance Allowance
A.C.	Appeal Cases
A.C.D.	Administrative Court Digest
ADHD	Attention Deficit Hyperactivity Disorder
Adjudication Regulations	Social Security (Adjudication) Regulations 1986
Admin.L.R.	Administrative Law Reports
All E.R.	All England Law Reports (Butterworths)
All E.R. (EC)	All England Law Reports European Cases
AMA	Adjudicating Medical Authority
AO	Adjudication Officer
AOG	*Adjudication Officers' Guide*
Attendance Allowance Regulations	Social Security (Attendance Allowance) Regulations 1991
BAMS	Benefits Agency Medical Service
B.H.R.C.	Butterworths Human Rights Cases
B.L.G.R.	Butterworths Local Government Reports
Blue Books	*The Law Relating to Social Security*, Vols 1–11
B.M.L.R.	Butterworths Medico-Legal Reports
B.P.I.R.	Bankruptcy and Personal Insolvency Reports
B.T.C.	British Tax Cases
CAA 2001	Capital Allowance Act 2001
CAB	Citizens Advice Bureau
CAO	Chief Adjudication Officer
CBA	Child Benefit Act 1975
CBJSA	Contribution-based Jobseeker's Allowance
C.C.L. Rep.	Community Care Law Reports
CCM	Claimant Compliance Manual
CCN	New Tax Credits Claimant Compliance Manual
C.E.C.	European Community Cases
CERA	Cortical Evoked Response Audiogram
Ch.	Chancery Law Reports
Child Benefit Regulations	Child Benefit (General) Regulations 2006
Claims and Payments Regulations 1979	Social Security (Claims and Payments) Regulations 1979

xxxi

Table of Abbreviations used in this Series

Claims and Payments Regulations 1987	Social Security (Claims and Payments) Regulations 1987
C.M.L.R.	Common Market Law Reports
C.O.D.	Crown Office Digest
Commissioners Procedure Regulations	Social Security Commissioners (Procedure) Regulations 1999
Computation of Earnings Regulations 1978	Social Security Benefit (Computation of Earnings) Regulations 1978
Computation of Earnings Regulations 1996	Social Security Benefit (Computation of Earnings) Regulations 1996
Const.L.J.	Construction Law Journal
Council Tax Benefit Regulations	Council Tax Benefit (General) Regulations 1992 (SI 1992/1814)
CP	Carer Premium
CPAG	Child Poverty Action Group
C.P.L.R.	Civil Practice Law Reports
CPR	Civil Procedure Rules
C.P.Rep.	Civil Procedure Reports
Cr.App.R.	Criminal Appeal Reports
Cr.App.R.(S)	Criminal Appeal Reports (Sentencing)
CRCA	Commissioners for Revenue and Customs Act 2005
Crim.L.R.	Criminal Law Review
Crim.L.R.	Criminal Law Review
CRU	Compensation Recovery Unit
CSA 1995	Child Support Act 1995
CS(NI)O	Child Support (Northern Ireland) Order 1995
CSO	Child Support Officer
CSPSSA	Child Support, Pensions and Social Security Act 2000
CTC	Child Tax Credit
DAT	Disability Appeal Tribunal
DCP	Disabled Child Premium
Decisions and Appeals Regulations 1999	Social Security and Child Support (Decision and Appeals) Regulations 1999
Dependency Regulations	Social Security Benefit (Dependency) Regulations 1977
Disability Working Allowance Regulations	Disabnility Working Allowance (General) Regulations 1991
DLA	Disability Living Allowance
DLADAA 1991	Disability Living Allowance and Disability Allowance Act 1991
DM	Decision Maker
DMA	Decision-making and Appeals
DMG	*Decision-Makers Guide*
DMP	Delegated Medical Practitioner

Table of Abbreviations used in this Series

DPTC	Disabled Person's Tax Credit
DSDNI	Department for Social Development, Northern Ireland
DSS	Department of Social Security
DTI	Department of Trade and Industry
DWA	Disability Working Allowance
DWP	Department for Work and Pensions
EAA	Extrinsic Allergic Alveolitis
ECHR	European Court of Human Rights
E.C.R.	European Court Reports
ECSMA Agreement	European Convention on Social and Medical Assistance
EEA	European Economic Area
E.G.	Estates Gazette
E.H.R.R.	European Human Rights Reports
E.L.R.	Education Law Reports
EMA	Education Maintenance Allowance
EMO	Examining Medical Officer
EMP	Examining Medical Practitioner
ERA	Evoked Response Audiometry
ERA 1996	Employment Rights Act 1996
ER(NI)O	Employers Rights (Northern Ireland) Order 1996
Eur. L. Rev.	European Law Review
FA	Finance Act
Fam.Law	Family Law
Family Credit Regulations	Family Credit (General) Regulations 1987
FAS	Financial Assistance Scheme
FIS	Family Income Supplement
Fixing and Adjustment of Rates (Amendment) Regulations 1998	Child Benefit and Social Security (Fixing and Adjustment of Rates) (Amendment) Regulations 1998
Fixing and Adjustment of Rates Regulations 1976	Child Benefit and Social Security (Fixing and Adjustment of Rates) Regulations 1976
F.L.R.	Family Law Reports
GA Regulations	Social Security (Guardian's Allowance) Regulations 1975
General Benefit Regulations	Social Security (General Benefit) Regulations 1982
General Regulations	Statutory Maternity Pay (General) Regulations 1986
G.P.	General Practitioner
Graduated Retirement Benefit Regulations 2005	Social Security (Graduated Retirement Benefit) Regulations 2005
GRP	Graduated Retirement Pension
G.W.D.	Green's Weekly Digest

Table of Abbreviations used in this Series

HASSASSA	Health and Social Services and Social Security Adjudication Act 1983
HCD	House of Commons Debates
HCWA	House of Commons Written Answers
H.L.R.	Housing Law Reports
HMRC	Her Majesty's Revenue and Customs
HNCIP	(Housewives') Non-Contributory Invalidity Pension
Hospital In-Patients Regulations	Social Security (Hospital In-Patients) Regulations 1975
Housing Benefit Regulations	Housing Benefit (General) Regulations 1987 (SI 1987/1971)
HPP	Higher Pensioner Premium
HRA 1998	Human Rights Act 1998
H.R.L.R.	Human Rights Law Reports
HSE	Health and Safety Executive
IB	Incapactity Benefit
IB Regulations	Social Security (Incapacity Benefit) Regulations 1994
IBS	Irritable Bowel Syndrome
ICA	Invalid Care Allowance
I.C.R.	Industrial Cases Reports
ICTA	Income and Corporation Taxes Act 1988
IIAC	Industrial Injuries Advisory Council
I.L.J.	Industrial Law Journal
Imm.A.R.	Immigration Appeals Reports
Incapacity for Work Regulations	Social Security (Incapacity for Work) (General) Regulations 1995
Income Support Regulations	Income Support (General) Regulations 1987
Increases for Dependents Regulations	Social Security Benefit (Dependency) Regulations 1977
IND	Immigration and Nationality Directorate of the Home Office
I.N.L.R	Immigration and Nationality Law Reports
Invalid Care Allowance Regulations	Social Security (Invalid Care Allowance) Regulations 1976
IPPR	Institute of Public Policy Research
I.R.L.R.	Industrial Relations Law Reports
IS	Income Support
ISAs	Individual Savings Accounts
ITA	Income Tax Act 2007
ITEPA	Income Tax (Earnings and Pensions) Act 2003
ITTOIA	Income Tax (Trading and Other Income Act 2005)
ITS	Independent Tribunal Service
IWA	Social Security (Incapacity for Work) Act 1994

Table of Abbreviations used in this Series

IW (Dependants) Regs	Social Security (Incapacity for Work) (Dependants) Regulations
IW (General) Regulations	Social Security (Incapacity for Work) (General) Regulations 1995
IW (Transitional) Regulations	Social Security (Incapacity for Work) (Transitional) Regulations 1995
IVB	Invalidity Benefit
J.P.	Justice of the Peace
JSA	Jobseeker's Allowance
JSA 1995	Jobseekers Act 1995
JSA Regulations	Jobseeker's Allowance Regulations 1996
JSA (Transitional) Regulations	Jobseeker's Allowance (Transitional) Regulations 1996
JS(NI)O	Jobseekers (Northern Ireland) Act 1995
J.S.W.F.L.	Journal of Social Welfare and Family Law
J.S.W.L.	Journal of Social Welfare Law
J.S.S.L.	Journal of Social Security Law
K.I.R.	Knights Industrial Reports
LEL	Lower Earnings Limit
Ll.L.Report	Lloyds' Law Report
Lloyd's Rep.	Lloyd's Law Reports
L.S.G.	Law Society Gazette
LTAHAW	Living Together As Husband And Wife
L.&T.R.	Landlord and Tenant Reports
MA	Maternity Allowance
MAF	Medical Assessment Framework
MAT	Medical Appeal Tribunal
Maternity Benefit Regulations	Social Security (Maternity Benefit) Regulations 1975
Medical Evidence Regulations	Social Security (Medical Evidence) Regulations 1976
NCIP	Non-Contributory Invalidity Pension
NDPD	Notes on the Diagnosis of Prescribed Diseases
NI	National Insurance
N.I.	Northern Ireland Law Reports
NIC	National Insurance Contribution
N.L.J.	New Law Journal
N.P.C.	New Property Cases
Ogus, Barendt and Wikeley	A. Ogus, E. Barendt and N. Wikeley, *The Law of Social Security* (4th ed., Butterworths, 1995)
OPA	Overseas Pensions Act 1973
OPB	One Parent Benefit
OPSSAT	Office of the President of the Social Security Appeals Tribunal

Table of Abbreviations used in this Series

Overlapping Benefits Regulations	Social Security (Overlapping Benefits) Regulations 1979
Overpayments Regulations	Social Security (Payments on account, Overpayments and Recovery) Regulations
P.	Probate, Divorce and Admiralty
PAYE	Pay as You Earn
PCA	Personal Capability Assessment
P.&C.R.	Property, Planning & Compensation Reports
P.D.	Practice Direction
PD	Prescribed Disease
PPF	Pension Protection Fund
Pens.L.R.	Pension Law Reports
Persons Abroad Regulations	Social Security Benefit (Persons Abroad) Regulations 1975
Persons Residing Together Regulations	Social Security Benefit (Persons Residing Together) Regulations 1977
PIE	Period of Interruption of Employment
PILON	Pay in Lieu of Notice
PIW	Period of Incapacity for Work
P.L.R.	Planning Law Reports
Polygamous Marriage Regulations	Social Security and Family Allowances (Polygamous Marriages) Regulations 1975 (SI 1975/561)
PPF	Pension Protection Fund
Prescribed Diseases Regulations	Social Security (Industrial Injuries) (Prescribed Diseases) Regulations 1985
PTA	Pure Tone Audiometry
Q.B.	Queen's Bench
Recoupment Regulations	Social Security (Recoupment) Regulations 1990
REA	Reduced Earnings Allowance
RMO	Regional Medical Officer
RSI	Repetitive Strain Injury
R.T.R.	Road Traffic Reports
SAP	Statutory Adoption Pay
SAYE	Save As You Earn
S.C.	Session Cases
S.C.(H.L.)	Session Cases (House of Lords)
S.C.(P.C.)	Session Cases (Privy Council)
S.C.C.R.	Scottish Criminal Case Reports
S.C.L.R.	Scottish Civil Law Reports
SDA	Severe Disablement Allowance
SDP	Severe Disability Premium
SERPS	State Earnings-Related Pension Scheme
Severe Disablement Allowance	Social Security (Severe Disablement Regulations Allowance) Regulations 1984

Using this Book

S.J.	Solicitors' Journal
S.J.L.B.	Solicitors' Journal Law Brief
S.L.T.	Scots Law Times
SMP	Statutory Maternity Pay
SPC	State Pension Credit
SPCA	State Pension Credit Act 2002
SPCA(NI)	State Pension Credit Act (Northern Ireland) 2002
SPP	Statutory Paternity Pay
SPP and SAP (Administration) Regulations 2002	Statutory Paternity Pay and Statutory Adoption Pay (Administration) Regulations 2002
SPP and SAP (General) Regulations 2002	Statutory Paternity Pay and Statutory Adoption Pay (General) Regulations 2002
SPP and SAP (National Health Service Employees) Regulations 2002	Statutory Paternity Pay and Statutory Adoption Pay (National Health Service Employees) Regulations 2002
SPP and SAP (Weekly Rates) Regulations 2002	Statutory Paternity Pay and Statutory Adoption Pay (Weekly Rates) Regulations 2002
SSA	Social Security Act
SSAA	Social Security Administration Act 1992*
SSAC	Social Security Advisory Committee
SSAT	Social Security Appeal Tribunal
SSCBA	Social Security Contributions and Benefits Act 1992*
SSCB(NI)	Social Security Contributions and Benefits (Northern Ireland) Act 1992
SS(CP)A	Social Security (Consequential Provisions) Act 1992
SSHBA	Social Security and Housing Benefits Act 1982
SS(MP)A	Social Security (Miscellaneous Provisions) Act 1977
SSP	Statutory Sick Pay
SSPA	Social Security Pensions Act 1975
S.T.C.	Simon's Tax Cases
S.T.C. (S.C.D.)	Simon's Tax Cases: Special Commissioners Decisions
STIB	Short-term Incapacity Benefit
S.T.I.	Simon's Tax Intelligence
TC	Tax Cases
TCA	Tax Credits Act
TC (Claims and Notifications) Regs	Tax Credit (Claims and Notifications) Regulations 2002
TCGA	Taxation of Chargeable Gains Act 1992
TCTM	Tax Credits Technical Manual
TMA	Taxes Management Act 1970
U.K.H.R.R.	United Kingdom Human Rights Reports

Using this Book

Unemployment, Sickness and Invalidity Benefit Regs	Social Security (Unemployment, Sickness and Invalidity Benefit) Regulations 1983
USI Regulations	Social Security (Unemployment, Sickness and Invalidity Benefit) Regulations 1983
VERA 1992	Vehicle Excise and Registration Act 1992
WFTC	Working Family Tax Credit
White Paper	Jobseeker's Allowance, Cm.2687 (October 1994)
Widow's Benefit and Retirement Pensions Regulations	Social Security (Widow's Benefit and Retirement Pensions) Regulations 1979
Wikeley, Annotations	N. Wikeley, "Annotations to Jobseekers Act 1995 (c.18)" in *Current Law Statutes Annotated* (1995)
Wikeley, Ogus and Barendt	Wikeley, Ogus and Barendt, *The Law of Social Security* (5th ed., Butterworths, 2002)
W.L.R.	Weekly Law Reports
Workmen's Compensation Acts	Workmen's Compensation Acts 1925 to 1945
WRPA	Welfare Reform and Pensions Act 1999
WRP(NI)O	Welfare Reform and Pensions (Northern Ireland) Order 1999
WTC	Working Tax Credit
WTC (Entitlement and Maximum Rate) Regulations 2002	Working Tax Credit (Entitlement and Maximum Rate) Regulations 2002
W.T.L.R.	Wills & Trusts Law Reports

---

* Where the context makes it seem more appropriate, these could also be referred to as Contributions and Benefits Act 1992, Administration Act 1992 (AA 1992).

PART I

HM REVENUE AND CUSTOMS
TAX CREDITS AND SOCIAL SECURITY

Taxes Management Act 1970

(1970 c.9)

ARRANGEMENT OF SELECTED SECTIONS

Part I

Administration

1.	Responsibility for certain taxes	1.1

Part II

Returns of Income and Gains

Income tax

- 8. Personal return
- 9. Returns to include self-assessment
- 9ZA. Amendment of personal or trustee return by taxpayer
- 9ZB. Correction of personal or trustee return by Revenue
- 9A. Notice of enquiry
- 9B. Amendment of return by taxpayer during enquiry
- 9C. Amendment of self-assessment during enquiry to prevent loss of tax

Records

- 12B. Records to be kept for purposes of returns

Part IV

Assessments and Claims

- 28A. Completion of enquiry into personal or trustee return
- 29. Assessment where loss of tax discovered

Relief for excessive assessments

- 32. Double assessment
- 33. Error or mistake

Taxes Management Act 1970

Time-limits

34. Ordinary time-limit of six years
35. Time limit: income removed after year for which they are assessible
36. Fraudulent or negligent conduct

Part V

Appeals and Other Proceedings

Proceedings before Commissioners

54. Settling of appeals by agreement

Part X

Penalties, etc.

105. Evidence in cases of fraud and wilful default

Part XI

Miscellaneous and Supplemental

Documents

112. Loss, destruction or damage to assessments, returns, etc.
114. Want of form or errors not to invalidate assessments, etc.

Interpretation

118. Interpretation

Introduction and General Note

1.2 The TMA 1970 was a consolidation measure, but it has been extensively and repeatedly amended since 1970. Only two sections apply directly to tax credits: s.1 (read to include tax credits) and s.54. For the express application of s.54, see Tax Credits (Appeals) Regulations 2002, reg.3. But TCA 2002 refers to several other sections. Set out below are the key sections of the TMA 1970 that apply for the purposes of the income tax assessments, alongside which tax credit calculations will be made in most cases.

In addition, the selection includes other provisions setting out the power of HMRC to investigate and deal with income tax assessments, the scope for a taxpayer to amend a self-assessment or request an amendment of an assessment, and formal sections dealing with evidence and documentation.

(1970 c.9)

As s.1 indicates, this Act also deals with assessments and administration of capital gains tax and corporation tax, but all provisions relating only to those taxes have been excluded from this selection, as have provisions dealing with other taxes or past taxes.

PART I

ADMINISTRATION

[¹Responsibility for certain taxes

1. The Commissioners for Her Majesty's Revenue and Customs shall be responsible for the collection and management of—
  (a) income tax,
  (b) corporation tax, and
  (c) capital gains tax.]

AMENDMENT

1. Commissioners for Revenue and Customs Act 2005, s.50 and Sch.4, para.12 (April 18, 2005).

PART II

RETURNS OF INCOME AND GAINS

Income tax

Personal return

8.—(1) For the purpose of establishing the amounts in which a person is chargeable to income tax and capital gains tax for a year of assessment, . . . he may be required by a notice given to him by an officer of the Board—
  (a) to make and deliver to the officer, on or before the day mentioned in subsection (1A) below, a return containing such information as may reasonably be required in pursuance of the notice, and
  (b) to deliver with the return such accounts, statements and documents, relating to information contained in the return, as may reasonably be so required.
(1A) The day referred to in subsection (1) above is—
  (a) the 31st January next following the year of assessment, or
  (b) where the notice under this section is given after the 31st October next following the year, the last day of the period of three months beginning with the day on which the notice is given.
(1AA) For the purposes of subsection (1) above—
  (a) the amounts in which a person is chargeable to income tax and capital gains tax are net amounts, that is to say, amounts which take into

Taxes Management Act 1970

account any relief or allowance a claim for which is included in the return; and

(b) the amount payable by a person by way of income tax is the difference between the amount in which he is chargeable to income tax and the aggregate amount of any income tax deducted at source and any tax credits to which section 231 of the principal Act applies.

(1B) In the case of a person who carries on a trade, profession, or business in partnership with one or more other persons, a return under this section shall include each amount which, in any relevant statement, is stated to be equal to his share of any income, loss, tax, credit or charge for the period in respect of which the statement is made.

(1C) In subsection (1B) above "relevant statement" means a statement which, as respects the partnership, falls to be made under section 12AB of this Act for a period which includes, or includes any part of, the year of assessment or its basis period.

(2) Every return under this section shall include a declaration by the person making the return to the effect that the return is to the best of his knowledge correct and complete.

(3) A notice under this section may require different information, accounts and statements for different periods or in relation to different descriptions of source of income.

(4) Notices under this section may require different information, accounts and statements in relation to different descriptions of person.

(5) In this section and sections 8A, 9 and 12AA of this Act, any reference to income tax deducted at source is a reference to income tax deducted or treated as deducted from any income or treated as paid on any income.

Returns to include self-assessment

1.5   **9.**—(1) Subject to subsections (1A) and (2) below, every return under section 8 or 8A of this Act shall include a self-assessment, that is to say—

(a) an assessment of the amounts in which, on the basis of the information contained in the return and taking into account any relief or allowance a claim for which is included in the return, the person making the return is chargeable to income tax and capital gains tax for the year of assessment; and

(b) an assessment of the amount payable by him by way of income tax, that is to say, the difference between the amount in which he is assessedto income tax under paragraph (a) above and the aggregate amount of any income tax deducted at source and any tax credits to which [² section 7 of ITTOIA 2005] applies

but nothing in this subsection shall enable a self-assessment to show as repayable any income tax treated as deducted or paid by virtue of sections [¹ . . .] 246D(1) [¹ . . .] of the principal Act or section 626 of ITEPA.

(1A) The tax to be assessed on a person by a self-assessment shall not include any tax which, under Chapter I or IV of Part XIV of the principal Act or under section 394(2) of ITEPA 2003, is charged on the administrator of a scheme (within the meaning of section 658A of that Act) and is assessable by the Board in accordance with that section.

(2) A person shall not be required to comply with subsection (1) above if he makes and delivers his return for a year of assessment—

(a) on or before the 30th September next following the year; or

(b) where the notice under section 8 or 8A of this Act is given after the 31st July next following the year, within the period of two months beginning with the day on which the notice is given.

(3) Where, in making and delivering a return, a person does not comply with subsection (1) above, an officer of the Board shall, if subsection (2) above applies, and may in any other case—
  (a) make the assessment on his behalf on the basis of the information contained in the return; and
  (b) send him a copy of the assessment so made;
and references . . . in this Act to a person's self-assessment include references to an assessment made on a person's behalf under this subsection.

(3A) An assessment under subsection (3) above is treated for the purposes of this Act as a self-assessment and as included in the return.

(4) Subject to subsection (5) below—
  (a) at any time before the end of the period of nine months beginning with the day on which a person's return is delivered, an officer of the Board may by notice to that person so amend that person's self-assessment as to correct any obvious errors or mistakes in the return (whether errors of principle, arithmetical mistakes or otherwise); and
  (b) at any time before the end of the period of twelve months beginning with the filing date, a person may by notice to an officer of the Board so amend his self-assessment as to give effect to any amendments to his return which he has notified to such an officer.

(5) No amendment of a self-assessment may be made under subsection (4) above at any time during the period—
  (a) beginning with the day on which an officer of the Board gives notice of his intention to enquire into the return; and
  (b) ending with the day on which the officer's enquiries into the return are completed.

(6) In this section and section 9A of this Act "the filing date" means the day mentioned in section 8(1A) or, as the case may be, section 8A(1A) of this Act.

AMENDMENTS

1. ITTOIA 2005, Sch.3.
2. ITTOIA 2005, s.882 and Sch.1, para.361 (April 6, 2005).

Amendment of personal or trustee return by taxpayer

9ZA.—(1) A person may amend his return under section 8 or 8A of this Act by notice to an officer of the Board.

(2) An amendment may not be made more than 12 months after the filing date.

(3) In this section "the filing date" means the day mentioned in section 8(1A) or, as the case may be, section 8A(1A) of this Act.

Correction of personal or trustee return by Revenue

9ZB.—(1) An officer of the Board may amend a return under section 8 or 8A of this Act so as to correct obvious errors or omissions in the return (whether errors of principle, arithmetical mistakes or otherwise).

(2) A correction under this section is made by notice to the person whose return it is.

(3) No such correction may be made more than nine months after—

(a) the day on which the return was delivered, or
(b) if the correction is required in consequence of an amendment of the return under section 9ZA of this Act, the day on which that amendment was made.

(4) A correction under this section is of no effect if the person whose return it is gives notice rejecting the correction.

(5) Notice of rejection under subsection (4) above must be given—
(a) to the officer of the Board by whom the notice of correction was given,
(b) before the end of the period of 30 days beginning with the date of issue of the notice of correction.

Notice of enquiry

1.8 **9A.**—(1) An officer of the Board may enquire into a return under section 8 or 8A of this Act if he gives notice of his intention to do so ("notice of enquiry")—
(a) to the person whose return it is ("the taxpayer"),
(b) within the time allowed.

(2) The time allowed is—
(a) if the return was delivered on or before the filing date, up to the end of the period of twelve months after the filing date;
(b) if the return was delivered after the filing date, up to and including the quarter day next following the first anniversary of the day on which the return was delivered;
(c) if the return is amended under section 9ZA of this Act, up to and including the quarter day next following the first anniversary of the day on which the amendment was made.

For this purpose, the quarter days are 31st January, 30th April, 31st July and 31st October.

(3) A return which has been the subject of one notice of enquiry may not be the subject of another, except one given in consequence of an amendment (or another amendment) of the return under section 9ZA of this Act.

(4) An enquiry extends to anything contained in the return, or required to be contained in the return, including any claim or election included in the return, subject to the following limitation.

Amendment of return by taxpayer during enquiry

1.9 **9B.**—(1) This section applies if a return is amended under section 9ZA of this Act (amendment of personal or trustee return by taxpayer) at a time when an enquiry is in progress into the return.

(2) The amendment does not restrict the scope of the enquiry but may be taken into account (together with any matters arising) in the enquiry.

(3) So far as the amendment affects the amount stated in the self-assessment included in the return as the amount of tax payable, it does not take effect while the enquiry is in progress and—
(a) if the officer states in the closure notice that he has taken the amendment into account and that—
(i) the amendment has been taken into account in formulating the amendments contained in the notice, or
(ii) his conclusion is that the amendment is incorrect, the amendment shall not take effect;

(b) otherwise, the amendment takes effect when the closure notice is issued.

(4) For the purposes of this section the period during which an enquiry is in progress is the whole of the period—
  (a) beginning with the day on which notice of enquiry is given; and
  (b) ending with the day on which the enquiry is completed.

Amendment of self-assessment during enquiry to prevent loss of tax

9C.—(1) This section applies where an enquiry is in progress into a return as a result of notice of enquiry by an officer of the Board under section 9A(1) of this Act.

(2) If the officer forms the opinion—
  (a) that the amount stated in the self-assessment contained in the return as the amount of tax payable is insufficient; and
  (b) that unless the assessment is immediately amended there is likely to be a loss of tax to the Crown,
he may by notice to the taxpayer amend the assessment to make good the deficiency.

(3) In the case of an enquiry which under section 9A(5) of this Act is limited to matters arising from an amendment of the return, subsection (2) above only applies so far as the deficiency is attributable to the amendment.

(4) For the purposes of this section the period during which an enquiry is in progress is the whole of the period—
  (a) beginning with the day on which notice of enquiry is given, and
  (b) ending with the day on which the enquiry is completed.

Records

Records to be kept for purposes of returns

12B.—(1) Any person who may be required by a notice under section 8, 8A, or 12AA of this Act (or under any of those sections as extended by section 12 of this Act) to make and deliver a return for a year of assessment or other period shall—
  (a) keep all such records as may be requisite for the purpose of enabling him to make and deliver a correct and complete return for the year or period; and
  (b) preserve those records until the end of the relevant day, that is to say, the day mentioned in subsection (2) below or, where a return is required by a notice given on or before that day, whichever of that day and the following is the latest, namely—
    (i) where enquiries into the return or any amendment of the return are made by an officer of the Board, the day on which, by virtue of section 28A(1) or 28B(1) of this Act, those enquiries are treated as completed; and
    (ii) where no enquiries into the return or any amendment of the return are so made, the day on which such an officer no longer has power to make such enquiries.

(2) The day referred to in subsection (1) above is—
  (a) in the case of a person carrying on a trade, profession or business alone or in partnership or a company, the fifth anniversary of the

31st January next following the year of assessment or (as the case may be) the sixth anniversary of the end of the period;
(b) in any other case, the first anniversary of 31st January next following the year of assessment or, where a return is delivered by the person concerned after that date, the quarter day next following the first anniversary of the day on which the return is delivered;

and the quarter days for the purposes of this subsection are 31st January, 30th April, 31st July and 31st October.

(2A) Any person who—
(a) is required, by such a notice as is mentioned in subsection (1) above given at any time after the end of the day mentioned in subsection (2) above, to make and deliver a return for a year of assessment or other period; and
(b) has in his possession at that time any records which may be requisite for the purpose of enabling him to make and deliver a correct and complete return for the year or period,

shall preserve those records until the end of the relevant day, that is to say, the day which, if the notice had been given on or before the day mentioned in subsection (2) above, would have been the relevant day for the purposes of subsection (1) above.

(3) In the case of a person carrying on a trade, profession or business alone or in partnership—
(a) the records required to be kept and preserved under subsection (1) or (2A) above shall include records of the following, namely—
  (i) all amounts received and expended in the course of the trade, profession or business and the matters in respect of which the receipts and expenditure take place, and
  (ii) in the case of a trade involving dealing in goods, all sales and purchases of goods made in the course of the trade; and
(b) the duty under that subsection shall include a duty to preserve until the end of the relevant day all supporting documents relating to such items as are mentioned in paragraph (a)(i) or (ii) above.

(4) Except in the case of records falling within subsection (4A) below, the duty under subsection (1) or (2A) above to preserve records may be discharged by the preservation of the information contained in them; and where information is so preserved a copy of any document forming part of the records shall be admissible in evidence in any proceedings before the Commissioners to the same extent as the records themselves.

(4A) The records which fall within this subsection are—
(a) any statement in writing such as is mentioned in—
  (i) subsection (1) of section 234 of the principal Act (amount of qualifying distribution and tax credit); or
  (ii) subsection (1) of section 352 of that Act (gross amount, tax deducted, and actual amount paid, in certain cases where payments are made under deduction of tax), which is furnished by the company or person there mentioned, whether after the making of a request or otherwise;
(b) any certificate or other record (however described) which is required by regulations under section 566(1) of the principal Act to be given to a sub-contractor (within the meaning of Chapter IV of Part XIII of that Act) on the making of a payment to which section 559 of that Act (deductions on account of tax) applies;

(1970 c.9, s.12B)

(c) any such record as may be requisite for making a correct and complete claim in respect of, or otherwise requisite for making a correct and complete return so far as relating to, an amount of tax—
   (i) which has been paid under the laws of a territory outside the United Kingdom, or
   (ii) which would have been payable under the law of such a territory but for a relief to which section 788(5) of the principal Act (relief for promoting development and relief contemplated by double taxation arrangements) applies.

(5) Subject to subsections (5A) and (5B) below any person who fails to comply with subsection (1) or (2A) above in relation to a year of assessment or accounting period shall be liable to a penalty not exceeding £3,000.

(5A) Subsection (5) above does not apply where the records which the person fails to keep or preserve are records which might have been requisite only for the purposes of claims, elections or notices which are not included in the return.

(5B) Subsection (5) above also does not apply where—
(a) the records which the person fails to keep or preserve are records falling within paragraph (a) of subsection (4A) above; and
(b) an officer of the Board is satisfied that any facts which he reasonably requires to be proved, and which would have been proved by the records, are proved by other documentary evidence furnished to him.

(6) For the purposes of this section—
(a) a person engaged in the letting of property shall be treated as carrying on a trade; and
(b) "supporting documents" includes accounts, books, deeds, contracts, vouchers and receipts.

PART IV

ASSESSMENT AND CLAIMS

Completion of enquiry into personal or trustee return

28A.—(1) An enquiry under section 9A(1) of this Act is completed when an officer of the Board by notice (a "closure notice") informs the taxpayer that he has completed his enquiries and states his conclusions. In this section "the taxpayer" means the person to whom notice of enquiry was given.

(2) A closure notice must either—
(a) state that in the officer's opinion no amendment of the return is required; or
(b) make the amendments of the return required to give effect to his conclusions.

(3) A closure notice takes effect when it is issued.

(4) The taxpayer may apply to the Commissioners for a direction requiring an officer of the Board to issue a closure notice within a specified period.

(5) Any such application shall be heard and determined in the same way as an appeal.

(6) The Commissioners hearing the application shall give the direction applied for unless they are satisfied that there are reasonable grounds for not issuing a closure notice within a specified period.

Taxes Management Act 1970

Assessment where loss of tax discovered

1.13   **29.**—(1) If an officer of the Board or the Board discover, as regards any person (the taxpayer) and a year of assessment—
(a) that income which ought to have been assessed to income tax, or chargeable gains which ought to have been assessed to capital gains tax, have not been assessed, or
(b) that an assessment to tax is or has become insufficient, or
(c) that any relief which has been given is or has become excessive,
the officer or, as the case may be, the Board may, subject to subsections (2) and (3) below, make an assessment in the amount, or the further amount, which ought in his or their opinion to be charged in order to make good to the Crown the loss of tax.

(2) Where—
(a) the taxpayer has made and delivered a return under section 8 or 8A of this Act in respect of the relevant chargeable period, and
(b) the situation mentioned in subsection (1) above is attributable to an error or mistake in the return as to the basis on which his liability ought to have been computed,
the taxpayer shall not be assessed under that subsection in respect of the year of assessment there mentioned if the return was in fact made on the basis or in accordance with the practice generally prevailing at the time when it was made.

(3) Where the taxpayer has made and delivered a return under section 8 or 8A of this Act in respect of the relevant year of assessment, he shall not be assessed under subsection (1) above—
(a) in respect of the year of assessment mentioned in that subsection; and
(b) in the case of a return under section 8 or 8A, in the same capacity as that in which he made and delivered the return,
unless one of the two conditions mentioned below is fulfilled.

(4) The first condition is that the situation mentioned in subsection (1) above is attributable to fraudulent or negligent conduct on the part of the taxpayer or a person acting on his behalf.

(5) The second condition is that at the time when an officer of the Board—
(a) ceased to be entitled to give notice of his intention to enquire into the taxpayer's return under section 8 or 8A of this Act in respect of the relevant year of assessment; or
(b) informed the taxpayer that he had completed his enquiries into that return,
the officer could not have been reasonably expected, on the basis of the information made available to him before that time, to be aware of the situation mentioned in subsection (1) above.

(6) For the purposes of subsection (5) above, information is made available to an officer of the Board if—
(a) it is contained in the taxpayer's return under section 8 or 8A of this Act in respect of the relevant year of assessment (the return), or in any accounts, statements or documents accompanying the return;
(b) it is contained in any claim made as regards the relevant year of assessment by the taxpayer acting in the same capacity as that in which he made the return, or in any accounts, statements or documents accompanying any such claim;

(c) it is contained in any documents, accounts or particulars which, for the purposes of any enquiries into the return or any such claim by an officer of the Board, are produced or furnished by the taxpayer to the officer, whether in pursuance of a notice under section 19A of this Act or otherwise; or

(d) it is information the existence of which, and the relevance of which as regards the situation mentioned in subsection (1) above—
  (i) could reasonably be expected to be inferred by an officer of the Board from information falling within paragraphs (a)–(c) above; or
  (ii) are notified in writing by the taxpayer to an officer of the Board.

(7) In subsection (6) above—

(a) any reference to the taxpayer's return under section 8 or 8A of this Act in respect of the relevant year of assessment includes—
  (i) a reference to any return of his under that section for either of the two immediately preceding year of assessment; and
  (ii) where the return is under section 8 and the taxpayer carries on a trade, profession or business in partnership, a reference to any partnership return with respect to the partnership for the relevant year of assessment or either of those periods; and

(b) any reference in paragraphs (b) to (d) to the taxpayer includes a reference to a person acting on his behalf.

(8) An objection to the making of an assessment under this section on the ground that neither of the two conditions mentioned above is fulfilled shall not be made otherwise than on an appeal against the assessment.

(9) Any reference in this section to the relevant year of assessment is a reference to—

(a) in the case of the situation mentioned in paragraph (a) or (b) of subsection (1) above, the chargeable period mentioned in that subsection; and

(b) in the case of the situation mentioned in paragraph (c) of that subsection, the year of assessment in respect of which the claim was made.

(10) In this section "profits"—

(a) in relation to income tax, means income,

(b) in relation to capital gains tax, means chargeable gains, and

(c) in relation to corporation tax, means profits as computed for the purposes of that tax.

Relief for excessive assessments

Double assessment

32.—(1) If on a claim made to the Board it appears to their satisfaction that a person has been assessed to tax more than once for the same cause and for the same chargeable period . . ., they shall direct the whole, or such part of any assessment as appears to be an overcharge, to be vacated, and thereupon the same shall be vacated accordingly.

(2) An appeal on a claim under this section shall lie to any of the bodies of Commissioners having jurisdiction to hear an appeal against the assessment, or the later of the assessments, to which the claim relates.

1.14

Error or mistake

1.15　**33.**—(1) If a person who has paid income tax or capital gains tax under an assessment (whether a self assessment or otherwise) alleges that the assessment was excessive by reason of some error or mistake in a return, he may by notice in writing at any time not later than 5 years after the 31st January next following the year of assessment to which the return relates, make a claim to the Board for relief.

(2) On receiving the claim the Board shall inquire into the matter and shall, subject to the provisions of this section, give by way of repayment such relief . . . in respect of the error or mistake as is reasonable and just:

Provided that no relief shall be given under this section in respect of an error or mistake as to the basis on which the liability of the claimant ought to have been computed where the return was in fact made on the basis or in accordance with the practice generally prevailing at the time when the return was made.

(2A) No relief shall be given under this section in respect of—
(a) an error or mistake as to the basis on which the liability of the claimant ought to have been computed where the return was in fact made on the basis or in accordance with the practice generally prevailing at the time when it was made; or
(b) an error or mistake in a claim which is included in the return.

(3) In determining the claim the Board shall have regard to all the relevant circumstances of the case, and in particular shall consider whether the granting of relief would result in the exclusion from charge to tax of any part of the profits of the claimant, and for this purpose the Boardmay take into consideration the liability of the claimant and assessments made on him in respect of chargeable periods other than that to which the claim relates.

(4) If any appeal is brought from the decision of the Board on the claim the Special Commissioners shall hear and determine the appeal in accordance with the principles to be followed by the Board in determining claims under this section; and neither the appellant nor the Board shall be entitled to appeal under section 56A of this Act against the determination of the Special Commissioners except on a point of law arising in connection with the computation of profits.

(5) In this section, "profits"—
(a) in relation to income tax, means income; and
(b) in relation to capital gains tax, means chargeable gains; and
(c) in relation to corporation tax, means profits as computed for the purposes of that tax.

Time limits

Ordinary time-limit of six years

1.16　**34.**—(1) Subject to the following provisions of this Act, and to any other provisions of the Taxes Acts allowing a longer period in any particular class of case, an assessment to income tax or capital gains tax may be made at any time not later than five years after the 31st January next following the year of assessment to which it relates.

(1970 c.9, s.34)

(2) An objection to the making of any assessment on the ground that the time-limit for making it has expired shall only be made on an appeal against the assessment.

[¹Time limit: income received after year for which they are assessable

35.—(1) Where income to which this section applies is received in a year of assessment subsequent to that for which it is assessable, an assessment to income tax as respects that income may be made at any time within six years after the year of assessment in which it is received.

(2) This section applies to—
(a) employment income
(b) pension income, and
(c) social security income.]

AMENDMENT

1. Finance Act 2004, s.92 (April 6, 2004).

Fraudulent or negligent conduct

36.—(1) An assessment on any person (in this section referred to as "the person in default") for the purpose of making good to the Crown a loss of income tax or capital gains tax attributable to his fraudulent or negligent conduct or the fraudulent or negligent conduct of a person acting on his behalf may be made at any time not later than 20 years after the 31st January next following the year of assessment the year of assessment to which it relates.

(2) Where the person in default carried on a trade, profession or business with one or more other persons at any time in the period for which the assessment is made, an assessment in respect of the profits or gains of the trade, profession or business for the purpose mentioned in subsection (1) above may be made not only on the person in default but also on his partner or any of his partners.

(3) If the person on whom the assessment is made so requires, in determining the amount of the tax to be charged for any chargeable period in any assessment made for the purpose mentioned in subsection (1) above, effect shall be given to any relief or allowance to which he would have been entitled for that chargeable period on a claim or application made within the time allowed by the Taxes Acts.

(3A) In subsection (3) above, "claim or application" does not include an election under section 257BA of the principal Act (elections as to transfer of married couple's allowance).

(4) Any act or omission such as is mentioned in section 98B below on the part of a grouping (as defined in that section) or member of a grouping shall be deemed for the purposes of subsection (1) above to be the act or omission of each member of the grouping.

Proceedings before the Commissioners

Setting of appeals by agreement

1.19
54.—(1) Subject to the provisions of this section, where a person gives notice of appeal and, before the appeal is determined by the [¹appeal tribunal], the [¹officer of the Board] and the appellant come to an agreement, whether in writing or otherwise, that the [¹. . .] decision under appeal should be treated as upheld without variation, or as varied in a particular manner or as discharged or cancelled, the like consequences shall ensue for all purposes as would have ensued if, at the time when the agreement was come to, the [¹ appeal tribunal] had determined the appeal and had upheld the [¹. . .] decision without variation, had varied it in that manner or had discharged or cancelled it, as the case may be.

(2) Subsection (1) of this section shall not apply where, within thirty days from the date when the agreement was come to, the appellant gives notice in writing to the [¹ officer of the Board] that he desires to repudiate or resile from the agreement.

[²(3) Where an agreement is not in writing—
(a) the preceding provisions of this section shall not apply unless the Board give notice, in such form and manner as they consider appropriate, to the appellant of the terms agreed between the officer of the Board and the appellant; and
(b) the references in those preceding provisions to the time when the agreement was come to shall be construed as references to the date of that notice.]

(3) Where an agreement is not in writing—
(a) the preceding provisions of this section shall not apply unless the fact that an agreement was come to, and the terms agreed, are confirmed by notice in writing given by the [³officer of the Board] to the appellant or by the appellant to the [³officer of the Board]; and
(b) the references in the said preceding provisions to the time when the agreement was come to shall be construed as references to the time of the giving of the said notice of confirmation.

(4) Where—
(a) a person who has given a notice of appeal notifies the [¹officer of the Board], whether orally or in writing, that he desires not to proceed with the appeal; and
(b) thirty days have elapsed since the giving of the notification without the [¹officer of the Board] giving to the appellant notice in writing indicating that he is unwilling that the appeal should be treated as withdrawn,
the preceding provisions of this section shall have effect as if, at the date of the appellant's notification, the appellant and the [¹officer of the Board] had come to an agreement, orally or in writing, as the case may be, that the [¹. . .] decision under appeal should be upheld without variation.

(1970 c.9, s.54)

(5) The references in this section to an agreement being come to with an appellant and the giving of notice or notification to or by an appellant include references to an agreement being come to with, and the giving of notice or notification to or by, a person acting on behalf of the appellant in relation to the appeal.

[[1](6) In subsection (1) "appeal tribunal" means an appeal tribunal constituted—
  (a) in Great Britain, under Chapter 1 of Part 1 of the Social Security Act 1998 (social security appeals: Great Britain), and
  (b) in Northern Ireland, under Chapter 1 of Part 2 of the Social Security (Northern Ireland) Order 1998 (social security appeals: Northern Ireland).]

MODIFICATIONS

1. Modifications applying to both tax credit cases and child trust fund cases by virtue of reg.3 of the Tax Credits (Appeals) Regulations 2002 (SI 2002/2926) and reg.4 of the Child Trust Funds (Non-tax Appeals) Regulations 2005 (SI 2005/191).
2. Modifications applying only to tax credit cases by virtue of reg.3 of the Tax Credits (Appeals) Regulations 2002 (SI 2002/2926).
3. Modifications applying only to child trust fund cases by virtue of reg.4 of the Child Trust Funds (Non-tax Appeals) Regulations 2005 (SI 2005/191).

DEFINITIONS

"appeal tribunal"—see subs.(6).
"the Board"—see s.67 of the Tax Credits Act 2002 but note that the functions of the Board have now been transferred to the Commissioners for Her Majesty's Revenue and Customs (Commissioners for Revenue and Customs Act 2005, s.5(2)).

GENERAL NOTE

By virtue of reg.3 of the Tax Credits (Appeals) Regulations 2002, this section is applied in this modified form to those tax credit appeals which, by virtue of s.63 of the Tax Credits Act 2002, lie to an appeal tribunal or a Social Security Commissioner. Regulation 4 of the Child Trust Funds (Non-tax Appeals) Regulations 2005 applies the section to child trust fund appeals with the same modifications, save in subs.(3) where the amendments have the effect that notice is to be given by an officer of the Board (now an officer of Revenue and Customs) rather than the Board.

This section is central to the way that HMRC deals with direct tax and tax credit appeals. (To date it does not have the same power to settle when acting in indirect taxes). It is also widely used in settling disputes about underpayments and penalties. In February 2005, this was emphasised by Treasury Ministers in a House of Commons Written Answer: "Where possible the Department aims to settle an appeal by agreement with the appellant." (HCWA, HCD, February 8, 2005, col.1400W).

For application to tax credit penalties, see the note to s.31. For the HMRC published practices in dealing with tax credits settlements see the Codes of Practice published at the end of this work.

Subs.(1)
This allows the parties to compromise an appeal and reach an agreement that is as final as a decision of a tribunal. Indeed, it is more final because, not actually being a decision of a tribunal, there can be no appeal to a Commissioner. Note that the agreement must be reached before the appeal tribunal determines the appeal. Therefore, this sort of agreement cannot put an end to an appeal before a Social Security Commissioner, notwithstanding the definition of "tax credit appeal" in reg.2 of the Tax Credits (Appeals) Regulations 2002, although a Commissioner or Legal Officer would no doubt have regard to any agreement when deciding whether or not to allow

1.20

1.21

an appeal to be withdrawn under reg.21 of the Social Security Commissioners (Procedure) (Tax Credits Appeals) Regulations 2002. If a Commissioner sets aside a decision of an appeal tribunal and refers the case to another tribunal, it again becomes possible for an agreement to be made.

The effect of an agreement is to prevent an officer of Revenue and Customs from making any further decision in respect of the same issue and the same period (*Cenlon Finance Co Ltd v Ellwood* [1961] Ch.50). However, an officer is not barred from making a new decision if it is discovered that the agreement was based on incorrect information supplied by the appellant (*Gray v Matheson* [1993] 1 W.L.R. 1130). It is suggested that an officer is also not barred from making a decision under s.18 of the Tax Credits Act 2000 if the agreement related to a s.14 decision and it may also not be inappropriate to revise, under, says s.15 or s.16, an agreed award, depending on what exactly had been the scope of the agreement. In the context of tax credit cases there will not often be any doubt as to the scope of the agreement but where there was more than one issue between the parties—perhaps where the amount of earnings from self-employment is in dispute—the test is whether, looking objectively at all the relevant circumstances (including, in particular, the issues raised by the appellant and all the material known to have been in the possession of Her Majesty's Revenue and Customs), a reasonable man would conclude that the officer had accepted all the appellant's contentions (*Scorer v Olin Energy Systems Ltd* [1984] 1 W.L.R. 675). If the agreement is not in writing, see subs.(3).

Subs.(2)

1.22 This provides a 30-day cooling-off period for an appellant (but not an officer of Revenue and Customs) and may be particularly relevant in the light of subs.(5). It could give rise to delay if a hearing date is cancelled in the light of an agreement from which an appellant later resiles. On the other hand, the delay is no greater than can arise in a social security case where the Secretary of State makes a new decision, causing an appeal to lapse under s.9(6) of the Social Security Act 1998 but generating a new right of appeal.

Subs.(3)

1.23 If an agreement is not in writing, Her Majesty's Revenue and Customs must set out in writing their understanding of the agreement and give the appellant 30 days to object. This ensures a reasonable degree of certainty as to the terms of the agreement. The appellant is not required expressly to accept the written version.

Subs.(4)

1.24 There is no provision in the Tax Credits (Appeals) (No.2) Regulations 2002 allowing an appellant to withdraw an appeal by giving notice to the clerk to the tribunal (compare reg.40 of the Social Security and Child Support (Decisions and Appeals) Regulations 1999). Instead, an appellant may give notice of his desire to abandon the appeal to the officer of Revenue and Customs and the officer has 30 days in which to object. If the officer signifies agreement within the 30 days, subss.(1)–(3) will be brought into operation, as will be the case if the officer does nothing for 30 days. If the officer objects within the 30 days, the appeal proceeds. Presumably that means that any attempt to withdraw an appeal is ineffective for 30 days unless the officer consents. This provision applies only to appeals. Regulation 13 of the 2002 Regulations permits the unilateral withdrawal of an application for a direction or penalty proceedings where a tribunal has a first instance jurisdiction.

Subs.(5)

1.25 By virtue of this subsection, an agreement under subs.(1) may be entered into by an appellant's representative. However, such an agreement may be repudiated by the appellant under subs.(2).

(1970 c. 9, s. 105)

Part X

Penalties, etc.

Evidence in cases of fraud or wilful default

105.—(1) Statements made or documents produced by or on behalf of a person shall not be inadmissible in any such proceedings as are mentioned in subsection (2) below by reason only that it has been drawn to his attention that—
  (a) pecuniary settlements may be accepted instead of a penalty being determined, or proceedings being instituted, in relation to any tax, and
  (b) though no undertaking can be given as to whether or not the Board will accept such a settlement in the case of any particular person, it is the practice of the Board to be influenced by the fact that a person has made a full confession of any fraudulent conduct to which he had been a party and has given full facilities for investigation,

and that he was or may have been induced thereby to make the statements or produce the documents.

(2) The proceedings mentioned in subsection (1) above are—
  (a) any criminal proceedings against the person in question for any form of fraudulent conduct in connection with or in relation to tax; and
  (b) any proceedings against him for the recovery of any tax due from him and
  (c) any proceedings for a penalty or on appeal against the determination of a penalty.

Part XI

Miscellaneous and Supplemental

Documents

Loss, destruction or damage to assessments, returns, etc.

112.—(1) Where any assessment to tax, or any duplicate of assessment to tax, or any return or other document relating to tax, has been lost or destroyed, or been so defaced or damaged as to be illegible or otherwise useless, the Commissioners, inspectors, collectors and other officers having powers in relation to tax may, notwithstanding anything in any enactment to the contrary, do all such acts and things as they might have done, and all acts and things done under or in pursuance of this section shall be as valid and effectual for all purposes as they would have been, if the assessment or duplicate of assessment had not been made, or the return or other document had not been made or furnished or required to be made or furnished.

Provided that, where any person who is charged with tax in consequence or by virtue of any act or thing done under or in pursuance of this section proves to the satisfaction of the Commissioners having jurisdiction in the case that he has already paid any tax for the same chargeable periodin respect of the subject matter and on the account in respect of and on which he is so charged, relief shall be given to the extent to which the liability of that person has been discharged by the payment so made either by abatement from the charge or by repayment, as the case may require.

(2) In this section, "the Commissioners" means, as the case may require, either the Board or the General or Special Commissioners concerned.

(3) The references in subsection (1) above to assessments to tax include references to determinations of penalties; and in its application to such determinations the proviso to that subsection shall have effect with the appropriate modifications.

Want of form or errors not to invalidate assessments, etc.

1.28   **114.**—(1) An assessment or determination, warrant or other proceeding which purports to be made in pursuance of any provision of the Taxes Acts shall not be quashed, or deemed to be void or voidable, for want of form, or be affected by reason of a mistake, defect or omission therein, if the same is in substance and effect in conformity with or according to the intent and meaning of the Taxes Acts, and if the person or property charged or intended to be charged or affected thereby is designated therein according to common intent and understanding.

(2) An assessment or determination shall not be impeached or affected—
   (a) by reason of a mistake therein as to—
      (i) the name or surname of a person liable, or
      (ii) the description of any profits or property, or
      (iii) the amount of the tax charged, or
   (b) by reason of any variance between the notice and the assessment or determination.

Interpretation

Interpretation

1.29   **118.**—(1) In this Act, unless the context otherwise requires—
"Act" includes an Act of the Parliament of Northern Ireland; and "enactment" shall be construed accordingly;
"the Board" means the Commissioners of Inland Revenue;
"body of persons" means any body politic, corporate or collegiate, and any company, fraternity, fellowship and society of persons, whether corporate or not corporate;
[¹. . .]
"chargeable gain" has the same meaning as in the 1992 Act;
"chargeable period" means a year of assessment or a company's accounting period;
"collector" means any collector of taxes;
"company" has the meaning given by section 832(1) of the principal Act (with section 468 of that Act) . . .;
"the General Commissioners Regulations" means the General Commissioners (Jurisdiction and Procedure) Regulations 1994;

"incapacitated person" means any infant, person of unsound mind, lunatic, idiot or insane person;

"infant", in relation to Scotland, except in section 73 of this Act, means a person under legal disability by reason of nonage, and, in the saidsection 73, means a person under the age of 18 years;

"inspector" means any inspector of taxes;

"ITEPA 2003" means the Income Tax (Earnings and Pensions) Act 2003;

[2"ITTOIA 2005" means the Income Tax (Trading and Other Income) Act 2005];

"partnership return" has the meaning given by section 12AA(10A) of this Act;

"the principal Act" means the Income and Corporation Taxes Act 1988;

"the relevant trustees", in relation to a settlement, shall be construed in accordance with section 7(9) of this Act;

"return" includes any statement or declaration under the Taxes Acts;

"the Special Commissioners Regulations" means the Special Commissioners (Jurisdiction and Procedure) Regulations 1994;

"successor", in relation to a person who is required to make and deliver, or has made and delivered, a partnership return, and "predecessor" and "successor", in relation to the successor of such a person, shall be construed in accordance with section 12AA(11) of this Act;

"tax", where neither income tax nor capital gains tax nor corporation tax . . . is specified, means any of those taxes except that in sections 20, 20A, 20B, 20C and 20D it does not include development land tax;

"the Taxes Acts" means this Act and—

(a) the Tax Acts . . .; and
(b) the Taxation of Chargeable Gains Act 1992 and all other enactments relating to capital gains tax;

"the 1992 Act" means the Taxation of Chargeable Gains Act 1992;

"trade" includes every trade, manufacture, adventure or concern in the nature of trade.

(2) For the purposes of this Act, a person shall be deemed not to have failed to do anything required to be done within a limited time if he did it within such further time, if any, as the Board or the Commissioners or officer concerned may have allowed; and where a person had a reasonable excuse for not doing anything required to be done he shall be deemed not to have failed to do it unless the excuse ceased and, after the excuse ceased, he shall be deemed not to have failed to do it if he did it without unreasonable delay after the excuse had ceased: . . .

(3) For the purposes of section 36 and Part X of this Act, an assessment made in the partnership name and the tax charged in such an assessment shall, according to the law in Scotland as well as according to the law elsewhere in the United Kingdom, be deemed to be respectively an assessment made on the partners and tax charged on and payable by them.

(4) For the purposes of this Act, the amount of tax covered by any assessment shall not be deemed to be finally determined until that assessment can no longer be varied, whether by any Commissioners on appeal or by the order of any court.

AMENDMENTS

1. Words repealed by FA 2003, Sch.43.
2. ITOIA 2005, s.882 and Sch.1, para.380 (April 6, 2005).

Social Security Contributions and Benefits Act 1992

Social Security Contributions and Benefits Act 1992

(1992 c.4)

Sections Reproduced

Part XI

Statutory Sick Pay

Employer's liability

1.30 151. Employer's liability

The qualifying conditions

152. Period of incapacity for work
153. Period of entitlement
154. Qualifying days

Limitations on entitlement, etc.

155. Limitations on entitlement
156. Notification of incapacity for work

Rates of payment, etc.

157. Rates of payment
158. Recovery by employers of amounts paid by way of statutory sick pay (*repealed*)
159. Power to substitute provisions for section 158(2) (*repealed*)
159A. Power to provide for recovery by employers of sums paid by way of statutory sick pay

Miscellaneous

160. Relationship with benefits and other payments, etc.
161. Crown employment—Part XI
162. Special classes of persons
163. Interpretation of Part XI and supplementary provisions

Part XII

Statutory Maternity Pay

164. Statutory maternity pay—entitlement and liability to pay
165. The maternity pay period
166. Rate of statutory maternity pay
167. Funding of employers' liabilities in respect of statutory maternity pay

168.	Relationship with benefits and other payments, etc.
169.	Crown employment—Part XII
170.	Special classes of persons
171.	Interpretation of Part XII and supplementary provisions

Part XIIZA

Statutory Paternity Pay

171ZA.	Entitlement: birth
171ZB.	Entitlement: adoption
171ZC.	Entitlement: general
171ZD.	Liability to make payments
171ZE.	Rate and period of pay
171ZF.	Restrictions on contracting out
171ZG.	Relationship with contractual remuneration
171ZH.	Crown employment—Part XIIZA
171ZI.	Special classes of person
171ZJ.	Part XIIZA: supplementary
171ZK.	Power to apply Part XIIZA to adoption cases not involving placement

Part XIIZB

Statutory Adoption Pay

171ZL.	Entitlement
171ZM.	Liability to make payments
171ZN.	Rate and period of pay
171ZO.	Restrictions on contracting out
171ZP.	Relationship with benefits and other payments, etc.
171ZQ.	Crown employment—Part XIIZB
171ZR.	Special classes of person
171ZS.	Part XIIZB: supplementary
171ZT.	Power to apply Part XIIZB to adoption cases not involving placement

Part XIII

General

Interpretation

172.	Application of Act in relation to territorial waters
173.	Age
174.	References to Acts

Schedules

Schedule 11—Circumstances in which periods of entitlement to statutory sick pay do not arise

Schedule 12—Relationship of statutory sick pay with benefits and other payments, etc.
Schedule 13—Relationship of statutory maternity pay with benefits and other payments, etc.

PART XI

STATUTORY SICK PAY

GENERAL NOTE

1.31   Statutory sick pay (SSP) was originally introduced in April 1983 by the Social Security and Housing Benefits Act 1982. The main primary legislation is now to be found in Pt XI, annotated here; there are also various sets of regulations, principally the SSP (General) Regulations 1982 (SI 1982/894), which are contained in Pt III of this volume. Section 151(1) of the SSCBA 1992 provides that an employer is liable to pay to an employee for any day of incapacity for work in relation to the employee's contract of service with that employer, where the day in question is a qualifying day (see s.154) which forms part of a period of incapacity to work (see s.152) and falls within a period of entitlement as between that employer and that employee (s.153 and Sch.11). Incapacity must be duly notified to the employer, and SSP may be withheld in the event of non-existent or late notification (see s.156). Those who are self-employed (who by definition lack an employer) and those who are unemployed are excluded from entitlement to SSP. Some employees are also excluded from SSP. Section 153(3) and Sch.11 prevent the requisite period of entitlement arising as between employer and employees in various types of case (e.g. low earners, women at a certain stage of pregnancy, some persons affected by trade disputes).

SSP is payable at a weekly rate. The daily rate will depend on the number of qualifying days in the week (see s.157). SSP is not payable in respect of the first three qualifying days (or "waiting days") in any period of entitlement (see s.155(1)). SSP cannot be paid in kind or by the provision of board and lodging or other services or facilities (SSP (General) Regulations 1982 (SI 1982/894), reg.8). Any day of incapacity for work in relation to a contract of service which falls within a period of entitlement to SSP precludes concurrent entitlement to incapacity benefit (Sch.12, para.1). Employees reach their maximum entitlement to SSP as against any one employer in any one period of entitlement when they have been entitled in that period to 28 times the appropriate weekly rate of SSP (see s.155(4)). This is typically after 28 weeks of continuous incapacity. If the person remains incapacitated after that, he or she must look to incapacity benefit or, failing that, a means-tested benefit.

At the start of the SSP scheme in 1983, employers were able to recoup the entire amount paid from the National Insurance contributions and the PAYE tax that they were required to collect and account for to the Inland Revenue. The initial effect of SSP was thus to transfer the cost of administration from the State to the employer. The Statutory Sick Pay Act 1991 limited employers to recouping 80 per cent of the cost of SSP payments, but "small employers" were still able to claim full reimbursement. This was followed by the Statutory Sick Pay Act 1994, which abolished employers' general right to recover (some of) the costs of SSP. The special rules for reimbursing small employers were then repealed (although they remain for the purposes of SMP). Instead, in principle any employer—not just small employers—can recover the costs of SSP payments under the Percentage Threshold Scheme. However, this reimbursement is only available where the employer's expenditure on SSP exceeds 13 per cent of their gross National Insurance contributions liability—in other words, only where there is an epidemic of illness in the workforce (see further Statutory Sick Pay Threshold Order 1995 (SI 1995/512)).

In certain circumstances, where an employer does not, or because of insolvency, cannot, discharge their statutory liability to pay SSP, that liability became that of the Board of Inland Revenue (s.151(6), SSP (General) Regulations 1982 (SI 1982/894), regs 9A–9C). This liability was transferred from the Secretary of State to the Board of the Inland Revenue with effect from April 1, 1999, under the Social Security Contributions (Transfer of Functions, etc.) Act 1999, s.1(2) and Sch.2, along with those functions under SSP (General) Regulations 1982, regs 10 and 14.

The arrangements for resolving disputes about entitlement to SSP were changed with effect from April 1, 1999. Before that date, certain questions could be referred to an AO, thus opening up the usual channels of appeal to SSATs, Commissioners and ultimately the courts. Since that date the Social Security Contributions (Transfer of Functions, etc.) Act 1999 and the Statutory Sick Pay and Statutory Maternity Pay (Decisions) Regulations 1999 (SI 1999/776) have replaced the AO with an officer of the Board in Inland Revenue. Consequently, decision-making and appeals are now governed by Pt II of the 1999 Act, with the right of appeal lying to the tax appeal Commissioners. An employment tribunal has no jurisdiction under the Employment Rights Act 1996 to entertain an employee's complaint that SSP has not been paid: (per Mr Recorder Luba Q.C. in *Taylor Gordon & Co Ltd v Timmons* ([2004] I.R.L.R. 180, at para.43)).

Employer's liability

Employer's liability

151.—(1) Where an employee has a day of incapacity for work in relation to his contract of service with an employer, that employer shall, if the conditions set out in sections 152 to 154 below are satisfied, be liable to make him, in accordance with the following provisions of this Part of this Act, a payment (to be known as "statutory sick pay") in respect of that day.

(2) Any agreement shall be void to the extent that it purports—
(a) to exclude, limit or otherwise modify any provision of this Part of this Act; or
(b) to require an employee to contribute (whether directly or indirectly) towards any costs incurred by his employer under this Part of this Act.

(3) For the avoidance of doubt, any agreement between an employer and an employee authorising any deductions from statutory sick pay which the employer is liable to pay to the employee in respect of any period shall not be void by virtue of subsection (2)(a) above if the employer—
(a) is authorised by that or another agreement to make the same deductions from any contractual remuneration which he is liable to pay in respect of the same period, or
(b) would be so authorised if he were liable to pay contractual remuneration in respect of that period.

(4) For the purposes of this Part of this Act [¹a day of incapacity for work in relation to a contract of service means a day on which] the employee concerned is, or is deemed in accordance with regulations to be, incapable by reason of some specific disease or bodily or mental disablement of doing work which he can reasonably be expected to do under that contract.

(5) In any case where an employee has more than one contract of service with the same employer the provisions of this Part of this Act shall, except in such cases as may be prescribed and subject to the following provisions of this Part of this Act, have effect as if the employer were a different employer in relation to each contract of service.

1.32

Social Security Contributions and Benefits Act 1992

(6) Circumstances may be prescribed in which, notwithstanding the provisions of subsections (1) to (5) above, the liability to make payments of statutory sick pay is to be a liability of the [²Commissioners of Inland Revenue].

[²(7) Regulations under subsection (6) above must be made with the concurrence of the Commissioners of Inland Revenue.]

AMENDMENTS

1. Social Security (Incapacity for Work) Act 1994, s.11(1) and Sch.1, para.34 (April 13, 1995).
2. Social Security Contributions (Transfer of Functions, etc.) Act 1999, s.1(1) and Sch.1, para.9 (April 1, 1999).

DEFINITIONS

"contract of service"—see s.163(1).
"employee"—*ibid.* and SSP (General) Regulations 1982, reg.16.
"employer"—see s.163(1).
"prescribed"—*ibid.*

GENERAL NOTE

Subss. (1)–(3)

1.33   The general liability on employers to pay SSP—where the qualifying conditions are fulfilled by the employee—is set out in subs.(1). Employers cannot contract out of this liability (subs.(2), but note the qualification in subs.(3)).

Subs. (4)

1.34   For the purposes of SSP, a day of incapacity for work in relation to any contract of service may arise in either of two ways. The first is where the employee is actually incapable by reason of some specific disease or bodily or mental disablement of doing work which he or she can reasonably be expected to do under that contract. On "incapable of work" and "by reason of some specific disease or bodily or mental disablement", see the annotations to SSCBA 1992, s.171B(2) in Vol.I to this series. The second, and alternative, possibility is where the employee, although not actually incapable, falls within the protection of regulations which deem a day to be one of incapacity for work. On deemed incapacity, see SSP (General) Regulations 1982 (SI 1982/894), reg.2.

Subs. (5)

1.35   This contemplates that an employee who has more than one contract of service with the same employer could get SSP in respect of each contract of service, where the eligibility conditions were satisfied with respect to each contract. This provision is modified by SSP (General) Regulations 1982 (SI 1982/894), reg.21.

Subs. (6)

1.36   See SSP (General) Regulations 1982 (SI 1982/894), regs 9A–9C and see also General Note to Pt XI of this Act, above.

The qualifying conditions

Period of incapacity for work

1.37   **152.**—(1) The first condition is that the day in question forms part of a period of incapacity for work.

(2) In this Part of this Act "period of incapacity for work" means any period of four or more consecutive days, each of which is a day of incapacity for work in relation to the contract of service in question.

(3) Any two periods of incapacity for work which are separated by a period of not more than 8 weeks shall be treated as a single period of incapacity for work.

(4) The Secretary of State may by regulations direct that a larger number of weeks specified in the regulations shall be substituted for the number of weeks for the time being specified in subsection (3) above.

(5) No day of the week shall be disregarded in calculating any period of consecutive days for the purposes of this section.

(6) A day may be a day of incapacity for work in relation to a contract of service, and so form part of a period of incapacity for work, notwithstanding that—

(a) it falls before the making of the contract or after the contract expires or is brought to an end; or

(b) it is not a day on which the employee concerned would be required by that contract to be available for work.

DEFINITIONS

"contract of service"—see s.163(1).
"employee"—*ibid.* and SSP (General) Regulations 1982, reg.16.
"period of incapacity for work"—see subs.(2).
"week"—see s.163(1).

GENERAL NOTE

Liability to pay SSP can only arise if the qualifying day which is one of incapacity for work also forms part of a period of incapacity for work (subs.(1)). A period of incapacity for work is formed by any period of four or more consecutive days of incapacity for work in relation to the contract of service in question (subs.(2)). Every day of the week counts for determining periods of consecutive days (subs.(4)). Any two periods of incapacity "link" to form a single period where they are not separated by more than eight weeks, counting the separation period from the end of the "first" period. Note that under subs.(5), a day can still be one of incapacity for work in relation to the contract of service and thus be part of a period of incapacity for work where it is not one on which the contract would require the employee to be available for work, or where it falls before the contract was made or after it expires or is otherwise brought to an end.

1.38

Period of entitlement

153.—(1) The second condition is that the day in question falls within a period which is, as between the employee and his employer, a period of entitlement.

1.39

(2) For the purposes of this Part of this Act a period of entitlement, as between an employee and his employer, is a period beginning with the commencement of a period of incapacity for work and ending with whichever of the following first occurs—

(a) the termination of that period of incapacity for work;

(b) the day on which the employee reaches, as against the employer concerned, his maximum entitlement to statutory sick pay (determined in accordance with section 155 below);

(c) the day on which the employee's contract of service with the employer concerned expires or is brought to an end;

Social Security Contributions and Benefits Act 1992

(d) in the case of an employee who is, or has been, pregnant, the day immediately preceding the beginning of the disqualifying period.

(3) Schedule 11 to this Act has effect for the purpose of specifying circumstances in which a period of entitlement does not arise in relation to a particular period of incapacity for work.

(4) A period of entitlement as between an employee and an employer of his may also be, or form part of, a period of entitlement as between him and another employer of his.

(5) The Secretary of State may by regulations—
(a) specify circumstances in which, for the purpose of determining whether an employee's maximum entitlement to statutory sick pay has been reached in a period of entitlement as between him and an employer of his, days falling within a previous period of entitlement as between the employee and any person who is or has in the past been an employer of his are to be counted; and
(b) direct that in prescribed circumstances an employer shall provide a person who is about to leave his employment, or who has been employed by him in the past, with a statement in the prescribed form containing such information as may be prescribed in relation to any entitlement of the employee to statutory sick pay.

(6) Regulations may provide, in relation to prescribed cases, for a period of entitlement to end otherwise than in accordance with subsection (2) above.

(7) In a case where the employee's contract of service first takes effect on a day which falls within a period of incapacity for work, the period of entitlement begins with that day.

(8) In a case where the employee's contract of service first takes effect between two periods of incapacity for work which by virtue of section 152(3) above are treated as one, the period of entitlement begins with the first day of the second of those periods.

(9) In any case where, otherwise than by virtue of section 6(1)(b) above, an employee's earnings under a contract of service in respect of the day on which the contract takes effect do not attract a liability to pay secondary Class 1 contributions, subsections (7) and (8) above shall have effect as if for any reference to the contract first taking effect there were substituteda reference to the first day in respect of which the employee's earnings attract such a liability.

(10) Regulations shall make provision as to an employer's liability under this Part of this Act to pay statutory sick pay to an employee in any case where the employer's contract of service with that employee has been brought to an end by the employer solely, or mainly, for the purpose of avoiding liability for statutory sick pay.

(11) Subsection (2)(d) above does not apply in relation to an employee who has been pregnant if her pregnancy terminated, before the beginning of the disqualifying period, otherwise than by confinement.

(12) In this section—
"confinement" is to be construed in accordance with section 171(1) below;
"disqualifying period" means—
(a) in relation to a woman entitled to statutory maternity pay, the maternity pay period; and
(b) in relation to a woman entitled to maternity allowance, the maternity allowance period;

(1992 c.4, s.153)

"maternity allowance period" has the meaning assigned to it by section 35(2) above; and
"maternity pay period" has the meaning assigned to it by section 165(1) below.

DEFINITIONS

"confinement"—see subs.(12).
"contract of service"—see s.163(1).
"disqualifying period"—see subs.(12).
"employee"—see s.163(1) and SSP (General) Regulations 1982, reg.16.
"employer"—*ibid.*
"maternity allowance"—*ibid.*
"maternity allowance period"—subs.(12).
"maternity pay period"—*ibid.*
"period of incapacity for work"—see s.163(1).
"prescribed"—see *ibid.*
"week"—see *ibid.*

GENERAL NOTE

Subss. (1) and (2)
There can be no liability to pay SSP unless the qualifying day, being one of incapacity for work forming part of a period of incapacity for work, also falls within a period of entitlement as between the employee and his employer (subs.(1)). Such a period of entitlement generally begins on the first day of a period of incapacity for work (subs.(2)), but note the modifications effected by subs.(7), (8), and (9). A period of entitlement ends with whichever of the circumstances set out in subs.(2)(a)–(d) first occurs. Note that subs.2(d) does not apply in the circumstances set out in subs.(11).

The position of "regular casual" workers was dealt with by the Court of Appeal in *Brown v Chief Adjudication Officer* [1997] I.R.L.R. 110. So long as such workers have worked continuously for a period of three months, or for a series of periods totalling three months in aggregate and not separated by more than eight weeks, they become entitled to the minimum periods of notice provided for by s.86 of Employment Rights Act 1996, and their contract of employment will not terminate unless it is frustrated or is terminated by their employer. See further the commentary to Sch.11, para.2 below.

Subs. (3)
In the circumstances set out in Sch.11 below, no period of entitlement arises with respect to the particular period of incapacity for work there referred to, thus excluding certain employees from SSP in respect of that period of incapacity for work.

Subs. (4)
An employee may have a period of entitlement with more than one employer at the same time, albeit that the length of the period with each is not coterminous.

Subs. (5)
See SSP (General) Regulations 1982 (SI 1982/894), reg.3A.

Subs. (6)
See SSP (General) Regulations 1982 (SI 1982/894), reg.3 dealing with prisoners, pregnant women entitled neither to SMP nor to maternity allowance, and setting a maximum three-year limit on any one period of entitlement.

Subs. (10)
See SSP (General) Regulations 1982 (SI 1982/894), reg.4.

1.40

1.41

1.42

1.43

1.44

1.45

Qualifying days

1.46 **154.**—(1) The third condition is that the day in question is a qualifying day.

(2) The days which are for the purposes of this Part of this Act to be qualifying days as between an employee and an employer of his (that is to say, those days of the week on which he is required by his contract of service with that employer to be available for work or which are chosen to reflect the terms of that contract) shall be such day or days as may, subject to regulations, be agreed between the employee and his employer or, failing such agreement, determined in accordance with regulations.

(3) In any case where qualifying days are determined by agreement between an employee and his employer there shall, in each week (beginning with Sunday), be at least one qualifying day.

(4) A day which is a qualifying day as between an employee and an employer of his may also be a qualifying day as between him and another employer of his.

DEFINITIONS

"contract of service"—see s.163(1).
"employee"—*ibid.* and SSP (General) Regulations 1982, reg.16.
"employer"—see s.163(1).
"week"—*ibid.*

GENERAL NOTE

1.47 In order to attract SSP liability, the day of incapacity which forms part of a period of incapacity for work and falls within a period of entitlement must also be a qualifying day (subs.(1)). Under subs.(2) an employer and employee are permitted a degree of freedom to determine by agreement which days of the week will for them rank as such, although subs.(3) stipulates that such agreements must specify at least one qualifying day per week. Furthermore SSP (General) Regulations 1982 (SI 1982/894), reg.5(3) renders ineffective an agreement treating as qualifying days any day identified expressly or otherwise by reference to it being a day of incapacity for work in relation to the employee's contract of service with an employer, or by reference to a period of incapacity for work or to a period of entitlement. Where there is no agreement on qualifying days or the only agreement is one rendered ineffective by reg.5(3), qualifying days are determined in accordance with SSP (General) Regulations 1982, reg.5(2).

Limitations on entitlement, etc.

Limitations on entitlement

1.48 **155.**—(1) Statutory sick pay shall not be payable for the first three qualifying days in any period of entitlement.

(2) An employee shall not be entitled, as against any one employer, to an aggregate amount of statutory sick pay in respect of any one period of entitlement which exceeds his maximum entitlement.

(3) The maximum entitlement as against any one employer is reached on the day on which the amount to which the employee has become entitled by way of statutory sick pay during the period of entitlement in question first reaches or passes the entitlement limit.

(4) The entitlement limit is an amount equal to 28 times [¹the weekly rate applicable in accordance with] section 157 below.

(1992 c.4, s.155)

(5) Regulations may make provision for calculating the entitlement limit in any case where an employee's entitlement to statutory sick pay is calculated by reference to different weekly rates in the same period of entitlement.

AMENDMENT

1. Social Security (Incapacity for Work) Act 1994, s.8 (April 6, 1995).

DEFINITIONS

"employee"—see s.163(1) and SSP (General) Regulations 1982, reg.16.
"employer"—see s.163(1).
"period of entitlement"—*ibid.*
"qualifying day"—*ibid.*

Notification of incapacity for work

156.—(1) Regulations shall prescribe the manner in which, and the time within which, notice of any day of incapacity for work is to be given by or on behalf of an employee to his employer.

(2) An employer who would, apart from this section, be liable to pay an amount of statutory sick pay to an employee in respect of a qualifying day (the "day in question") shall be entitled to withhold payment of that amount if—
 (a) the day in question is one in respect of which he has not been duly notified in accordance with regulations under subsection (1) above; or
 (b) he has not been so notified in respect of any of the first three qualifying days in a period of entitlement (a "waiting day") and the day in question is the first qualifying day in that period of entitlement in respect of which the employer is not entitled to withhold payment—
  (i) by virtue of paragraph (a) above; or
  (ii) in respect of an earlier waiting day by virtue of this paragraph.

(3) Where an employer withholds any amount of statutory sick pay under this section—
 (a) the period of entitlement in question shall not be affected; and
 (b) for the purposes of calculating his maximum entitlement in accordance with section 155 above the employee shall not be taken to have become entitled to the amount so withheld.

1.49

Rates of payment, etc.

Rates of payment

157.—(1) Statutory sick pay shall be payable by an employer at the weekly rate of [²£72.55].

(2) The Secretary of State may by order—
[¹(a) amend subsection (1) above so as to substitute different provision as to the weekly rate or rates of statutory sick pay; and]
 (b) make such consequential amendments as appear to him to be required of any provision contained in this Part of this Act.

(3) The amount of statutory sick pay payable by any one employer in respect of any day shall be the weekly rate applicable on that day divided by the number of days which are, in the week (beginning with Sunday) in which that day falls, qualifying days as between that employer and the employee concerned.

1.50

Amendments

1. Social Security (Incapacity for Work) Act 1994, s.8 (April 6, 1995).
2. Social Security Benefits Up-rating Order 2007 (SI 2007/688), art.9 (April 6, 2007).

Recovery by employers of amounts paid by way of statutory sick pay

1.51   158. [¹ . . .]

Amendment

1. Statutory Sick Pay Percentage Threshold Order 1995 (SI 1995/512), reg.5(a) (April 6, 1995).

Power to substitute provisions for section 158(2)

1.52   159. [¹ . . .]

Amendment

1. Statutory Sick Pay Percentage Threshold Order 1995 (SI 1995/512), reg.5(a) (April 6, 1995).

[¹Power to provide for recovery by employers of sums paid by way of statutory sick pay

1.53   **159A.**—(1) The Secretary of State may by order provide for the recovery by employers, in accordance with the order, of the amount (if any) by which their payments of, or liability incurred for, statutory sick pay in any period exceeds the specified percentage of the amount of their liability for contributions payments in respect of the corresponding period.

(2) An order under subsection (1) above may include provision—
  (a) as to the periods by reference to which the calculation referred to above is to be made;
  (b) for amounts which would otherwise be recoverable but which do not exceed the specified minimum for recovery not to be recoverable;
  (c) for the rounding up or down of any fraction of a pound which would otherwise result from a calculation made in accordance with the order; and
  (d) for any deduction from contributions payments made in accordance with the order to be disregarded for such purposes as may be specified,
and may repeal sections 158 and 159 above and make any amendments of other enactments which are consequential on the repeal of those sections.

(3) In this section—
"contributions payments" means payments which a person is required by or under any enactment to make in discharge of any liability of his as an employer in respect of primary or secondary Class 1 contributions; and
"specified" means specified in or determined in accordance with an order under subsection (1).

(4) The Secretary of State may by regulations make such transitional and consequential provision, and such savings, as he considers necessary or expedient for or in connection with the coming into force of any order under subsection (1) above.]

Amendment

1. Statutory Sick Pay Act 1994, s.3 (February 10, 1994).

(1992 c.4, s.160)

Miscellaneous

Relationship with benefits and other payments, etc.

160. Schedule 12 to this Act has effect with respect to the relationship between statutory sick pay and certain benefits and payments.

1.54

Crown employment—Part XI

161.—(1) Subject to subsection (2) below, the provisions of this Part of this Act apply in relation to persons employed by or under the Crown as they apply in relation to persons employed otherwise than by or under the Crown.

(2) The provisions of this Part of this Act do not apply in relation to persons serving as members of Her Majesty's forces, in their capacity as such.

(3) For the purposes of this section Her Majesty's forces shall be taken to consist of such establishments and organisations as may be prescribed [[1]by regulations made by the Secretary of State with the concurrence of the Treasury], being establishments and organisations in which persons serve under the control of the Defence Council.

1.55

AMENDMENT

1. Social Security Contributions (Transfer of Functions, etc.) Act 1999, s.1(1) and Sch.1, para.10 (April 1, 1999).

Special classes of persons

162.—(1) The Secretary of State [[1]may with the concurrence of the Treasury] make regulations modifying this Part of this Act in such manner as he thinks proper in their application to any person who is, has been or is to be—

(a) employed on board any ship, vessel, hovercraft or aircraft;
(b) outside Great Britain at any prescribed time or in any prescribed circumstances; or
(c) in prescribed employment in connection with continental shelf opeations, as defined in section 120(2) above.

(2) Regulations under subsection (1) above may in particular provide—

(a) for any provision of this Part of this Act to apply to any such person, notwithstanding that it would not otherwise apply;
(b) for any such provision not to apply to any such person, notwithstanding that it would otherwise apply;
(c) for excepting any such person from the application of any such provision where he neither is domiciled nor has a place of residence in any part of Great Britain;
(d) for the taking of evidence, for the purposes of the determination of any question arising under any such provision, in a country or territory outside Great Britain, by a British consular official or such other person as may be determined in accordance with the regulations.

1.56

AMENDMENT

1. Social Security Contributions (Transfer of Functions, etc.) Act 1999, s.1(1) and Sch.1, para.11 (April 1, 1999).

Interpretation of Part XI and supplementary provisions

1.57 163.—(1) In this Part of this Act—
"contract of service" (except in paragraph (a) of the definition below of "employee") includes any arrangement providing for the terms of appointment of an employee;
"employee" means a person who is—
(a) gainfully employed in Great Britain either under a contract of service or in an office (including elective office) with [4 general earnings (as defined by section 7 of the Income Tax (Earnings and Pensions) Act 2003)];
[5. . .]
but subject to regulations, which may provide for cases where any such person is not to be treated as an employee for the purposes of this Part of this Act and for cases where any person who would not otherwise be an employee for those purposes is to be treated as an employee for those purposes;
[5"employer", in relation to an employee and a contract of service of his, means a person who—
(a) under section 6 above is liable to pay secondary Class 1 contributions in relation to any earnings of the employee under the contract, or
(b) would be liable to pay such contributions but for—
   (i) the condition in section 6(1)(b), or
   (ii) the employee being under the age of 16:]
"period of entitlement" has the meaning given by section 153 above;
"period of incapacity for work" has the meaning given by section 152 above;
[1. . .]
"prescribed" means prescribed by regulations;
"qualifying day" has the meaning given by section 154 above;
"week" means any period of seven days.

(2) For the purposes of this Part of this Act an employee's normal weekly earnings shall, subject to subsection (4) below, be taken to be the average weekly earnings which in the relevant period have been paid to him or paid for his benefit under his contract of service with the employer in question.

(3) For the purposes of subsection (2) above, the expressions "earnings" and "relevant period" shall have the meaning given to them by regulations.

(4) In such cases as may be prescribed an employee's normal weekly earnings shall be calculated in accordance with regulations.

(5) Without prejudice to any other power to make regulations under this Part of this Act, regulations may specify cases in which, for the purposes of this Part of this Act or such of its provisions as may be prescribed—
(a) two or more employers are to be treated as one;
(b) two or more contracts of service in respect of which the same person is an employee are to be treated as one.

(6) Where, in consequence of the establishment of one or more National Health Service trusts under [6the National Health Service Act 2006, the National Health Service (Wales) Act 2006] or the National Health Service (Scotland) Act 1978, a person's contract of employment is treated by a scheme under [6any of those Acts] as divided so as to constitute two or more contracts, [3or where an order [6paragraph 26(1) of Schedule 3 to the National Health Service Act 2006] provides that a person's contract of

employment is so divided,] regulations may make provision enabling him to elect for all of those contracts to be treated as one contract for the purposes of this Part of this Act or of such provisions of this Part of this Act as may be prescribed; and any such regulations may prescribe—
  (a) the conditions that must be satisfied if a person is to be entitled to make such an election;
  (b) the manner in which, and the time within which, such an election is to be made;
  (c) the persons to whom, and the manner in which, notice of such an election is to be given;
  (d) the information which a person who makes such an election is to provide, and the persons to whom, and the time within which, he is to provide it;
  (e) the time for which such an election is to have effect;
  (f) which one of the person's employers under the two or more contracts is to be regarded for the purposes of statutory sick pay as his employer under the one contract;
and the powers conferred by this subsection are without prejudice to any other power to make regulations under this Part of this Act.

(7) Regulations may provide for periods of work which begin on one day and finish on the following day to be treated, for the purposes of this Part of this Act, as falling solely within one or other of those days.

AMENDMENTS

1. Jobseekers Act 1995, s.41(5) and Sch.3 (April 1, 1996).
2. Social Security Act 1998, s.86 and Sch.7, para.74 (April 6, 1999).
3. Health Act 1999 (Supplementary, Consequential etc. Provisions) Order 2000 (SI 2000/90), Art.3(1) and Sch.1, para.27 (February 8, 2000).
4. Income Tax (Earnings and Pensions) Act 2003, s.722 and Sch.6, para.181 (April 6, 2003).
5. Employment Equality (Age) Regulations 2006 (SI 2006/1031), reg.49(1) and Sch.8, para.9 (October 1, 2006).
6. National Health Service (Consequential Provisions) Act 2006, s.2 and Sch.1, para.147 (March 1, 2007).

PART XII

STATUTORY MATERNITY PAY

Statutory maternity pay—entitlement and liability to pay

164.—(1) Where a woman who is or has been an employee satisfies the conditions set out in this section, she shall be entitled, in accordance with the following provisions of this Part of this Act, to payments to be known as "statutory maternity pay".

(2) The conditions mentioned in subsection (1) above are—
  (a) that she has been in employed earner's employment with an employer for a continuous period of at least 26 weeks ending with the week immediately preceding the 14th week before the expectedweek of confinement but has ceased to work for him, [3 . . .];

1.58

(b) that her normal weekly earnings for the period of eight weeks ending with the week immediately preceding the 14th week before the expected week of confinement are not less than the lower earnings limit in force under section 5(1)(a) above immediately before the commencement of the 14th week before the expected week of confinement; and

(c) that she has become pregnant and has reached, or been confined before reaching, the commencement of the 11th week before the expected week of confinement.

(3) The liability to make payments of statutory maternity pay to a woman is a liability of any person of whom she has been an employee as mentioned in subsection (2)(a) above.

[³(4) A woman shall be entitled to payments of statutory maternity pay only if—

(a) she gives the person who will be liable to pay it notice of the date from which she expects his liability to pay her statutory maternity pay to begin; and

(b) the notice is given at least 28 days before that date or, if that is not reasonably practicable, as soon as is reasonably practicable.]

(5) The notice shall be in writing if the person who is liable to pay the woman statutory maternity pay so requests.

(6) Any agreement shall be void to the extent that it purports—

(a) to exclude, limit or otherwise modify any provision of this Part of this Act; or

(b) to require an employee or former employee to contribute (whether directly or indirectly) towards any costs incurred by her employer or former employer under this Part of this Act.

(7) For the avoidance of doubt, any agreement between an employer and an employee authorising any deductions from statutory maternity pay which the employer is liable to pay to the employee in respect of any period shall not be void by virtue of subsection (6)(a) above if the employer—

(a) is authorised by that or another agreement to make the same deductions from any contractual remuneration which he is liable to pay in respect of the same period; or

(b) would be so authorised if he were liable to pay contractual remuneration in respect of that period.

(8) Regulations shall make provision as to a former employer's liability to pay statutory maternity pay to a woman in any case where the former employer's contract of service with her has been brought to an end by the former employer solely, or mainly, for the purpose of avoiding liability for statutory maternity pay.

(9) The Secretary of State may by regulations—

(a) specify circumstances in which, notwithstanding subsections (1) to (8) above, there is to be no liability to pay statutory maternity pay in respect of a week;

(b) specify circumstances in which, notwithstanding subsections (1) to (8) above, the liability to make payments of statutory maternity pay is to be a liability [²of the Commissioners of Inland Revenue];

(c) specify in what circumstances employment is to be treated as continuous for the purposes of this Part of this Act;

(d) provide that a woman is to be treated as being employed for a continuous period of at least 26 weeks where—

(1992 c.4, s.164)

    (i) she has been employed by the same employer for at least 26 weeks under two or more separate contracts of service; and
    (ii) those contracts were not continuous;
  (e) provide that any of the provisions specified in subsection (10) below shall have effect subject to prescribed modifications [³in such cases as may be prescribed]
[³(ea) provide that subsection (4) above shall not have effect, or shall have effect subject to prescribed modifications, in such cases as may be prescribed;]
  (f) provide for amounts earned by a woman under separate contracts of service with the same employer to be aggregated for the purposes of this Part of this Act; and
  (g) provide that—
    (i) the amount of a woman's earnings for any period; or
    (ii) the amount of her earnings to be treated as comprised in any payment made to her or for her benefit,
shall be calculated or estimated in such manner and on such basis as may be prescribed and that for that purpose payments of a particular class or description made or falling to be made to or by a woman shall, to such extent as may be prescribed, be disregarded or, as the case may be, be deducted from the amount of her earnings.

(10) The provisions mentioned in subsection (9)(e) above are—
(a) subsection (2)(a) and (b) above; and
(b) [⁴section 166(1) and (2)], [¹. . .] below.

[²(11) Any regulations under subsection (9) above which are made by virtue of paragraph (b) of that subsection must be made with the concurrence of the Commissioners of Inland Revenue.]

AMENDMENTS

1. Maternity Allowance and Statutory Maternity Pay Regulations 1994 (SI 1994/1230), reg.6 (October 16, 1994).
2. Social Security Contributions (Transfer of Functions, etc.) Act 1999, s.1(1) and Sch.1, para.12 (April 1, 1999).
3. Employment Act 2002, s.20 (April 6, 2003).
4. Employment Act 2002, s.53 and Sch.7, para.6 (April 6, 2003).

DEFINITIONS

  "confined"—see s.171(1).
  "confinement"—see *ibid.*
  "earnings"—see *ibid.* and reg.20 of the Statutory Maternity Pay (General) Regulations 1986.
  "employee"—see s.171 and reg.17 of the Statutory Maternity Pay (General) Regulations 1986.
  "employed earner"—see s.2.
  "employer"—see s.171(1).
  "modifications"—see *ibid.*
  "normal weekly earnings"—see s.171(4).
  "prescribed"—see s.171(1).
  "week"—see *ibid.*

GENERAL NOTE

Statutory Maternity Pay (SMP) provides an income for employees and former employees during a period of maternity leave. In order to qualify for SMP a woman

1.59

must have worked for an employer for 26 weeks continuously into the week (known as the qualifying week) preceding the 14th week before the expected date of her confinement (subs.(2)(a)). Part III of the SMP (General) Regulations 1986 (SI 1986/1960) defines the concept of continuous employment. The woman must also have been earning during the last eight weeks of her employment an amount at least equal to the lower earnings limit for contribution purposes (subs.(2)(b)). She must, moreover, have become pregnant and have reached (or given birth before reaching) the start of the 11th week before the expected week of confinement (subs.(2)(c)). The further requirement that she must actually have left that employment because of her pregnancy or confinement was repealed by the Employment Act 2002. This repeal itself effectively supersedes reg.2 of the Statutory Maternity Pay (General) (Modification and Amendment) Regulations 2000 (SI 2000/2883), which modified the original version of subs.(2)(a) of the Act in relation to pregnant women who were dismissed or whose employment was otherwise terminated without consent.

Where a woman leaves her employment earlier than 11 weeks before the expected week of confinement she loses her entitlement to SMP (unless she has given birth), but if her employer has dismissed her solely or mainly for the purpose of avoiding the liability to pay SMP she will remain entitled. This applies even if she has been working for that employer for only a short period, so long as it is at least eight continuous weeks (see reg.3 of the SMP (General) Regulations 1986 (SI 1986/1960)). If a woman qualifies for SMP from more than one employer she is entitled to receive it from each of them (*ibid.*, reg.18).

It is a precondition of entitlement to SMP that the woman has given notice of her intention to leave by reason of pregnancy or confinement at least 28 days (21 days before the Employment Act 2002) before leaving, unless it is not reasonably practicable to do so and she gives it thereafter as soon as it is reasonably practicable to do so (subs.(4); see further SMP (General) Regulations 1986 (SI 1986/1960), reg.23). This would be so if the baby arrives unexpectedly early, but may also extend to a woman who did not know of the notice requirement and had not been put on inquiry about it. (That was the position taken by the Employment Appeal Tribunal in *Nu-Swift International Ltd v Mallison* [1979] I.C.R. 157 in relation to maternity pay.) The notice must be in writing if the employer so requests (subs.(5)).

A woman is not entitled to SMP if at any time during the maternity pay period (on which see s.165) she is imprisoned or sentenced to imprisonment (other than suspended). SMP is lost for the remainder of the period whether or not she is imprisoned for the whole period (see reg.9 of the SMP (General) Regulations 1986 (SI 1986/1960)).

The liability to pay SMP rests with the employer (subs.(3)). In certain circumstances, where an employer does not, or because of insolvency, cannot discharge his liability to pay SMP, that liability is discharged by the Board, now HMRC (at least since April 1, 1999; see subs.(9)(b), SMP (General) Regulations 1986 (SI 1986/1960), reg.7 and Social Security Contributions (Transfer of Functions, etc.) Act 1999, s.1(2) and Sch.2.; the same applies to the Secretary of State's functions under SMP (General) Regulations, regs 25, 30 and 31).

SMP, therefore, like SSP, is administered by the employer whilst HMRC is responsible for the resolution of certain disputes about entitlement. Until April 1, 1999, this was achieved by enabling the reference of certain questions to an AO, thereby opening up the usual channels of appeal to SSATs, Commissioners and the courts. With effect from April 1, 1999, the Social Security Contributions (Transfer of Functions, etc.) Act 1999, and the Statutory Sick Pay and Statutory Maternity Pay (Decisions) Regulations 1999 (SI 1999/776) replaced the role of AO with that of an officer of the Board of Inland Revenue (now HMRC). Consequently decision-making and appeals relating to SMP are governed by Pt II of the 1999 Act, with the right of appeal lying to the tax appeal Commissioners.

(1992 c.4, s.165)

The maternity pay period

165.—(1) Statutory maternity pay shall be payable, subject to the provisions of this Part of this Act, in respect of each week during a prescribed period ("the maternity pay period") of a duration not exceeding [²52 weeks].

[³(2) Subject to subsections (3) and (7), the maternity pay period shall begin with the 11th week before the expected week of confinement.

(3) Cases may be prescribed in which the first day of the period is to be a prescribed day after the beginning of the 11th week before the expected week of confinement, but not later than the day immediately following the day on which she is confined.]

(4) [³Except in such cases as may be prescribed,] statutory maternity pay shall not be payable to a woman by a person in respect of any week during any part of which she works under a contract of service with him.

(5) It is immaterial for the purposes of subsection (4) above whether the work referred to in that subsection is work under a contract of service which existed immediately before the maternity pay period or a contract of service which did not so exist.

(6) Except in such cases as may be prescribed, statutory maternity pay shall not be payable to a woman in respect of any week after she has been confined and during any part of which she works for any employer who is not liable to pay her statutory maternity pay.

(7) Regulations may provide that this section shall have effect subject to prescribed modifications in relation—
 (a) to cases in which a woman has been confined before the 11th week before the expected week of confinement; and
 (b) to cases in which—
  (i) a woman is confined[¹ at any time after the end of the week immediately preceding the 11th week] before the expected week of confinement; and
  (ii) the maternity pay period has not then commenced for her.

[³(8) In subsections (1), (4) and (6) "week" means a period of seven days beginning with the day of the week on which the maternity pay period begins.]

AMENDMENTS

1. Maternity Allowance and Statutory Maternity Pay Regulations 1994 (SI 1994/1230), reg.3 (October 16, 1994).
2. Employment Act 2002, s.18 (April 6, 2003).
3. Work and Families Act 2006, s.1 (October 1, 2006).
4. Work and Families Act 2006, s.11 and Sch.1, para.7 (October 1, 2006).

DEFINITIONS

 "confined"—see s.171(1).
 "confinement"—*ibid.*
 "employer"—*ibid.*
 "maternity pay period"—*ibid.*
 "modifications"—*ibid.*
 "prescribed"—*ibid.*
 "week"—*ibid.*

GENERAL NOTE

SMP is now payable for a period of 39 weeks (previously 26 weeks as a result of the Employment Act 2002, in force in April 2003, before which the maximum period was 18 weeks). As a general rule, the maternity pay period begins with the 11th week before the expected week of confinement (subs.(2)). Regulations provide for this period to be varied when the woman gives birth early (see SMP (General) Regulations 1986 (SI 1986/1960), reg.2).

The normal rule under subs.(4) that a woman is not entitled to receive SMP for any week in which she works for the employer who is liable to pay her SMP has now been relaxed. A woman may now work for her employer for a maximum of 10 days without losing entitlement to SMP (see reg.9A of the SMP (General) Regulations 1986 (SI 1986/1960)). A woman is not entitled to SMP if she works for another employer after her confinement (subs.(6)) unless she had worked for two or more employers up to her qualifying week, one of whom was not liable to pay her SMP, and it is now that employer for whom she is working after confinement (see reg.8 of the SMP (General) Regulations 1986 (SI 1986/1960)). But where she works for a new employer after her confinement, even if she works only briefly, she loses her entitlement for the remainder of the maternity pay period. Apparently there is no restriction on working for another employer before confinement.

[[1]Rate of statutory maternity pay

1.62   **166.**—(1) Statutory maternity pay shall be payable to a woman—
   (a) at the earnings-related rate, in respect of the first six weeks in respect of which it is payable; and
   (b) at whichever is the lower of the earnings-related rate and such weekly rate as may be prescribed, in respect of the remaining portion of the maternity pay period.

[[2](1A) In subsection (1) "week" means any period of seven days.]

(2) The earnings-related rate is a weekly rate equivalent to 90 per cent of a woman's normal weekly earnings for the period of eight weeks immediately preceding the 14th week before the expected week of confinement.

(3) The weekly rate prescribed under subsection (1)(b) above must not be less than the weekly rate of statutory sick pay for the time being specifiedin section 157(1) above or, if two or more such rates are for the time being so specified, the higher or highest of those rates.]

[[2](4) Where for any purpose of this Part of this Act or of regulations it is necessary to calculate the daily rate of statutory maternity pay, the amount payable by way of statutory maternity pay for any day shall be taken as one seventh of the weekly rate.]

AMENDMENTS

1. Employment Act 2002, s.19 (April 6, 2003).
2. Work and Families Act 2006, s.11 and Sch.1, para.8 (October 1, 2006).

DEFINITIONS

"confinement"—see s.171(1).
"maternity pay period"—*ibid.*
"normal weekly earnings"—*ibid.*
"prescribed"—*ibid.*
"week—*ibid.*

GENERAL NOTE

1.63   A new s.166 was substituted by s.19 of the Employment Act 2002. This preserved the pre-existing position so far as the rate of payment for the first six weeks of the maternity pay period is concerned. During this initial period SMP is paid at the earnings-related rate of 90 per cent of the woman's average weekly earnings in the eight weeks preceding the qualifying week (subss.(1)(a) and (2)). Thereafter, SMP is paid at either the standard prescribed rate (£112.75 per week in 2007/08) or the earnings-related rate, whichever is the lower (subs.(1)(b)), for the balance of 20 weeks. Previously the balance of the maternity pay period was just 12 weeks, but the then lower rate was always payable, irrespective of whether the earnings-related rate was lower.

There remains an important issue relating to the SMP earnings calculation and the extent to which this takes into account pay rises. As a result of the decision of the European Court of Justice in *Gillespie v Northern Health and Social Services Board* [1996] I.R.L.R. 214, the earnings calculation for SMP purposes must take into account any pay rise which is backdated into the "relevant period" (on the meaning of which see SSCBA 1992, s.171(4) and (5) and SMP (General) Regulations 1986 (SI 1986/1960, reg.21)). The *Gillespie* decision led to a limited amendment to the relevant regulations (SMP (General) Regulations 1986, reg.21(7), inserted by the SMP (General) Amendment Regulations 1996 (SI 1996/1335)). The question remains whether a woman on maternity leave should receive the benefit of any pay rise which has been implemented after the qualifying week and before the end of paid maternity leave. The original reg.21(7), it was argued, failed to give full effect to the ruling in *Gillespie* by limiting it to cases in which the pay increase is backdated into the relevant period. The Court of Appeal referred a series of questions on this point to the European Court of Justice in *Alabaster v Woolwich plc* [2002] EWCA Civ. 211; [2002] 1 C.M.L.R. 56; [2002] I.R.L.R. 420. On the request for a preliminary ruling, the ECJ ruled as follows:

> "Article 119 of the Treaty must be interpreted as requiring that, in so far as the pay received by the worker during her maternity leave is determined, at least in part, on the basis of the pay she earned before her maternity leave began, any pay rise awarded between the beginning of the period covered by the reference pay and the end of the maternity leave must be included in the elements of pay taken into account in calculating the amount of such pay. This requirement is not limited to cases where the pay rise is back-dated to the period covered by the reference pay."

Alabaster v Woolwich plc and Secretary of State for Social Security Case C-147/02 [2004] I.R.L.R. 486, para.50.

A new reg.21(7) was subsequently inserted with effect from April 6, 2005, to ensure that a woman's entitlement (or potential entitlement) to statutory maternity pay reflects any pay rise that the woman would have received, but for her maternity leave, and which is effective at any time between the start of the period used to calculate her entitlement and the end of her maternity leave. See further Statutory Maternity Pay (General) (Amendment) Regulations 2005 (SI 2005/729), reg.3. A month later (May 3, 2005), the Court of Appeal delivered its judgment following the decision of the ECJ: see *Alabaster v Barclays Bank PLC and the Secretary of State for Social Security* [2005] EWCA Civ 508. The Court of Appeal held that in order to give effect to the appellant's rights under EU law it was necessary to disapply those parts of Equal Pay Act 1970 s.1 which imposed the requirement for a male comparator.

[¹Funding of employers' liabilities in respect of statutory maternity pay

167.—(1) Regulations shall make provision for the payment by employers of statutory maternity pay to be funded by the Commissioners of Inland Revenue to such extent as may be prescribed.

(2) Regulations under subsection (1) shall—
(a) make provision for a person who has made a payment of statutory maternity pay to be entitled, except in prescribed circumstances, to recover an amount equal to the sum of—

1.64

(i) the aggregate of such of those payments as qualify for small employers' relief; and

(ii) an amount equal to 92 per cent of the aggregate of such of those payments as do not so qualify; and

(b) include provision for a person who has made a payment of statutory maternity pay qualifying for small employers' relief to be entitled, except in prescribed circumstances, to recover an additional amount, determined in such manner as may be prescribed—

(i) by reference to secondary Class 1 contributions paid in respect of statutory maternity pay;

(ii) by reference to secondary Class 1 contributions paid in respect of statutory sick pay; or

(iii) by reference to the aggregate of secondary Class 1 contributions paid in respect of statutory maternity pay and secondary Class 1 contributions paid in respect of statutory sick pay.

(3) For the purposes of this section a payment of statutory maternity pay which a person is liable to make to a woman qualifies for small employers' relief if, in relation to that woman's maternity pay period, the person liable to make the payment is a small employer.

(4) For the purposes of this section "small employer", in relation to a woman's maternity pay period, shall have the meaning assigned to it by regulations, and, without prejudice to the generality of the foregoing, any such regulations—

(a) may define that expression by reference to the amount of a person's contributions payments for any prescribed period; and

(b) if they do so, may in that connection make provision for the amount of those payments for that prescribed period—

(i) to be determined without regard to any deductions that may be made from them under this section or under any other enactment or instrument; and

(ii) in prescribed circumstances, to be adjusted, estimated or otherwise attributed to him by reference to their amount in any other prescribed period.

(5) Regulations under subsection (1) may, in particular, make provision—

(a) for funding in advance as well as in arrear;

(b) for funding, or the recovery of amounts due under provision made by virtue of subsection (2)(b), by means of deductions from such amounts for which employers are accountable to the Commissioners of Inland Revenue as may be prescribed, or otherwise;

(c) for the recovery by the Commissioners of Inland Revenue of any sums overpaid to employers under the regulations.

(6) Where in accordance with any provision of regulations under subsection (1) an amount has been deducted from an employer's contributions payments, the amount so deducted shall (except in such cases as may be prescribed) be treated for the purposes of any provision made by or under any enactment in relation to primary or secondary Class 1 contributions—

(a) as having been paid (on such date as may be determined in accordance with the regulations); and

(b) as having been received by the Commissioners of Inland Revenue, towards discharging the employer's liability in respect of such contributions.

(7) Regulations under this section must be made with the concurrence of the Commissioners of Inland Revenue.

(8) In this section, "contributions payments", in relation to an employer, means any payments which the employer is required, by or under any enactment, to make in discharge of any liability in respect of primary or secondary Class 1 contributions.]

AMENDMENT

1. Employment Act 2002, s.21 (April 6, 2003).

DEFINITIONS

"contributions payments"—see subs.(8).
"employer"—see s.171(1).
"maternity pay period"—*ibid.*
"prescribed"—*ibid.*

GENERAL NOTE

The new s.167, substituted by s.21 of the Employment Act 2002, is different from its predecessor in two main respects. First, it allows regulations to be made which enable employers to recover SMP from tax and other payments due to HMRC (see subs.(5)(b) and now Statutory Maternity Pay (Compensation of Employers) and Miscellaneous Amendment Regulations 1994 (SI 1994/1882), reg.6), and not just from payments of national insurance contributions, as was previously the case. Secondly, as with the tax credits regime, it provides for regulations to be made enabling employers to apply to HMRC for advance funding (*ibid.*, reg.5). Formerly employers could only deduct, in arrears, the amount of SMP payments from contributions payments due to the Revenue.

1.65

Relationship with benefits and other payments, etc.

168. Schedule 13 to this Act has effect with respect to the relationship between statutory maternity pay and certain benefits and payments.

1.66

GENERAL NOTE

As a general rule, entitlement to SMP precludes any entitlement to maternity allowance, SSP or incapacity benefit for the same period. Where SMP is paid, it is treated as going towards the employer's contractual obligation (if any) to pay maternity pay for the same period. If a woman receives maternity allowance because she does not earn enough to qualify for SMP, but then receives a backdated pay increase, making her then entitled to SMP, the employer is required to meet the difference between the maternity allowance paid and the SMP due (SMP (General) Regulations 1986 (SI 1986/1960), reg.21B).

1.67

Crown employment—Part XII

169. The provisions of this Part of this Act apply in relation to women employed by or under the Crown as they apply in relation to women employed otherwise than by or under the Crown.

1.68

Special classes of persons

170.—(1) The Secretary of State may [¹with the concurrence of the Treasury] make regulations modifying this Part of this Act in such manner as he thinks proper in their application to any person who is, has been or is to be—

  (a) employed on board any ship, vessel, hovercraft or aircraft;

1.69

(b) outside Great Britain at any prescribed time or in any prescribed circumstances; or

(c) in prescribed employment in connection with continental shelf operations, as defined in section 120(2) above.

(2) Regulations under subsection (1) above may in particular provide—

(a) for any provision of this Part of this Act to apply to any such person, notwithstanding that it would not otherwise apply;

(b) for any such provision not to apply to any such person, notwithstanding that it would otherwise apply;

(c) for excepting any such person from the application of any such provision where he neither is domiciled nor has a place of residence in any part of Great Britain;

(d) for the taking of evidence, for the purposes of the determination of any question arising under any such provision, in a country or territory outside Great Britain, by a British consular official or such other person as may be determined in accordance with the regulations.

AMENDMENT

1. Social Security Contributions (Transfer of Functions, etc.) Act 1999, s.1(1) and Sch.1, para.14 (April 1, 1999).

DEFINITIONS

"Great Britain"—see s.172(a).
"prescribed"—see s.171(1).

Interpretation of Part XII and supplementary provisions

1.70   **171.**—(1) In this Part of this Act—
"confinement" means—
(a) labour resulting in the issue of a living child; or
(b) labour after [¹24 weeks] of pregnancy resulting in the issue of a child whether alive or dead;
and "confined" shall be construed accordingly; and where a woman's labour begun on one day results in the issue of a child on another day she shall be taken to be confined on the day of the issue of the childor, if labour results in the issue of twins or a greater number of children, she shall be taken to be confined on the day of the issue of the last of them;
"dismissed" is to be construed in accordance with [³Part X of the Employment Rights Act 1996];
"employee" means a woman who is—
(a) gainfully employed in Great Britain either under a contract of service or in an office (including elective office) with [⁵ general earnings (as defined by section 7 of the Income Tax (Earnings and Pensions) Act 2003)]
[⁷. . .]
but subject to regulations [⁴made with the concurrence of [⁵Her Majesty's Revenue and Customs] which may provide for cases where any such woman is not to be treated as an employee for the purposes of this Part of this Act and for cases where a woman who would not otherwise be an employee for those purposes is to be treated as an employee for those purposes;
[⁷"employer", in relation to a woman who is an employee, means a person who—

(a) under section 6 above is liable to pay secondary Class 1 contributions in relation to any of her earnings; or
(b) would be liable to pay such contributions but for—
   (i) the condition in section 6(1)(b), or
   (ii) the employee being under the age of 16;]

"maternity pay period" has the meaning assigned to it by section 165(1) above;

"modifications" includes additions, omissions and amendments, and related expressions shall be construed accordingly;

"prescribed" means specified in or determined in accordance with regulations;

[8. . .]

[8(1A) In this Part, except section 165(1), (4) and (6), section 166(1) and paragraph 3(2) of Schedule 13, "week" means a period of 7 days beginning with Sunday or such other period as may be prescribed in relation to any particular case or class of case.]

(2) Without prejudice to any other power to make regulations under this Part of this Act, regulations may specify cases in which, for the purposes of this Part of this Act or of such provisions of this Part of this Act as may be prescribed—
(a) two or more employers are to be treated as one;
(b) two or more contracts of service in respect of which the same woman is an employee are to be treated as one.

(3) Where, in consequence of the establishment of one or more National Health Service trusts [9the National Health Service Act 2006, the National Health Service (Wales) Act 2006] or the National Health Service (Scotland) Act 1978, a woman's contract of employment is treated by a scheme under [9any of those Acts] as divided so as to constitute two or more contracts, [2or where an order under [9paragraph 26(1) of Schedule 3 to the National Health Service Act 2006] provides that a woman's contract of employment is so divided,] regulations may make provision enabling her to elect for all of those contracts to be treated as one contract for the purposes of this Part of this Act or of such provisions of this Part of this Act as may be prescribed; and any such regulations may prescribe—
(a) the conditions that must be satisfied if a woman is to be entitled to make such an election;
(b) the manner in which, and the time within which, such an election is to be made;
(c) the persons to whom, and the manner in which, notice of such an election is to be given;
(d) the information which a woman who makes such an election is to provide, and the persons to whom, and the time within which, she is to provide it;
(e) the time for which such an election is to have effect;
(f) which one of the woman's employers under the two or more contracts is to be regarded for the purposes of statutory maternity pay as her employer under the one contract;

and the powers conferred by this subsection are without prejudice to any other power to make regulations under this Part of this Act.

(4) For the purposes of this Part of this Act a woman's normal weekly earnings shall, subject to subsection (6) below, be taken to be the average

weekly earnings which in the relevant period have been paid to her or paid for her benefit under the contract of service with the employer in question.

(5) For the purposes of subsection (4) above "earnings" and "relevant period" shall have the meanings given to them by regulations.

(6) In such cases as may be prescribed a woman's normal weekly earnings shall be calculatedin accordance with regulations.

[4(7) Regulations under any of subsections (2) to (6) above must be made with the concurrence of the Commissioners of Inland Revenue.]

AMENDMENTS

1. Still-Birth (Definition) Act 1992, s.2 (October 1, 1992).
2. Health Act 1999 (Supplementary, Consequential etc. Provisions) Order 2000, Art.3, Sch.1, para.27 (SI 2000/90) (February 8, 2000).
3. Employment Rights Act 1996, s.240 and Sch.1, para.51(5) (August 23, 1996).
4. Social Security Contributions (Transfer of Functions, etc.) Act 1999, s.1(1) and Sch.1, para.15 (April 1, 1999).
5. Income Tax (Earnings and Pensions) Act 2003, s.722 and Sch.6, para.182 (April 6, 2003).
6. Commissioners for Revenue and Customs Act 2005, s.50 and Sch.4, para.43 (April 18, 2005).
7. Employment Equality (Age) Regulations 2006 (SI 2006/1031), reg.49(1) and Sch.8, para.10 (October 1, 2006).
8. Work and Families Act 2006, s.11 and Sch.1, para.9 (October 1, 2006).
9. National Health Service (Consequential Provisions) Act 2006, s.2 and Sch.1, para.148 (March 1, 2007).

[1PART XIIZA

STATUTORY PATERNITY PAY

AMENDMENT

1. Part XIIZA was inserted by the Employment Act 2002, s.2 (December 8, 2002).

GENERAL NOTE

1.71 Part XIIZA of the SSCBA 1992 was inserted by the Employment Act 2002. The 2002 Act followed the Employment Relations Act 1999, which itself included a number of "family friendly" employment measures (e.g. new rights to 13 weeks' unpaid parental leave and to unpaid time off to deal with family crises). The ordinary period of maternity leave was also increased in 1999 from 14 to 18 weeks (this period was extended to 26 weeks in April 2003 by other provisions in the Employment Act 2002), along with several other reforms designed to simplify the notoriously complex rules governing maternity leave and pay. A further review was announced in the 2000 Budget statement, which led to the publication of a Green Paper, *Work and Parents: Competitiveness and Choice* (DTI, December 2000). The Government's decisions on that review were announced at or around the time of the 2001 Budget statement, and were followed by the issue of three further consultation documents on the frameworks for maternity, paternity and adoption leave and pay. In November 2001 the DTI published a summary of responses to these various papers in the *Government's Response on Simplification of Maternity Leave, Paternity Leave and Adoption Leave.*

The Government's proposals were then brought forward in the Bill which became the Employment Act 2002. Part I of the 2002 Act dealt with statutory leave and pay. Thus, s.1 introduced a right to paternity leave in the Employment Rights Act 1996 (inserting ss.80A–80E), while s.2 inserted this Pt XIIZA into the SSCBA 1992 to make provision for statutory paternity pay (SPP). Sections 3 and 4 dealt with adoption leave and statutory adoption pay (SAP) respectively (on the latter see SSCBA 1992, Pt XIIZB). The procedural provisions relating to SPP and SAP were contained in ss.5–16 of the 2002 Act. (The 2002 Act also included measures to establish statutory minimum dismissal, disciplinary and grievance procedures and changes to employment tribunal procedures.)

The amendments made by c.1 of Pt I of the Employment Act 2002 relating to paternity and adoption, including the insertion of Pt XIIZA into the SSCBA 1992, came into force on December 8, 2002 (Employment Act 2002 (Commencement No.3 and Transitional and Saving Provisions) Order 2002, art.2(2) and Sch.1, Pt II). However, art.3 and Sch.3, para.1 of the same Order provide that Pt XIIZA shall have effect only in relation to a person who satisfies the prescribed conditions of entitlement in respect of a child who is either (a) born on or after April 6, 2003 (or whose expected week of birth begins on or after that date); or (b) matched for the purposes of adoption with a person who is notified of having been matched on or after April 6, 2003 (or placed for adoption on or after that date).

SPP is payable for a two week period only (SSCBA 1992, s.171ZE(2)). Such paid paternity leave must be taken in a single block within the first eight weeks after the child's birth (SSCBA 1992, s.171ZE(3)). There are, in fact, two forms of SPP, known in the regulations (the Statutory Paternity Pay and Statutory Adoption Pay (General) Regulations 2002 (SI 2002/2822)) as SPP (birth) and SPP (adoption), although these terms do not appear in the primary legislation. The principal eligibility criteria for SPP (birth) are set out in SSCBA 1992, s.171ZA and for SPP (adoption) in s.171ZB. Entitlement to SPP (birth) arises in respect of children born on or after April 6, 2003, or whose expected week of birth begins on or after that date (SPP and SAP (General) Regulations 2002, reg.3(1)(a); see also (Employment Act 2002 (Commencement No.3 and Transitional and Saving Provisions) Order 2002, art.3 and Sch.3). Similarly, entitlement to SPP (adoption) arises where the adoptive parent is notified of having been matched on or after April 6, 2003 or the child is placed for adoption on or after that date (SPP and SAP (General) Regulations 2002, reg.3(1)(b)). Section 171ZC contains general conditions of entitlement (e.g. as to giving the requisite notice to the employer). Section 171ZD places the liability to make payments of SPP on employers (the recovery mechanisms are the same as for SMP), while s.17ZE, with the associated regulations, deals with matters such as the rate and period of pay. Although paid for a shorter period than SMP, SPP is paid at the same rate as SMP. Sections 171ZF–171ZK make provision for various types of special cases and matters of interpretation, etc.

Entitlement: birth

171ZA.—(1) Where a person satisfies the conditions in subsection (2) below, he shall be entitled in accordance with the following provisions of this Part to payments to be known as "statutory paternity pay".

(2) The conditions are—
(a) that he satisfies prescribed conditions—
   (i) as to relationship with a newborn child; and
   (ii) as to relationship with the child's mother;
(b) that he has been in employed earner's employment with an employer for a continuous period of at least 26 weeks ending with the relevant week;
(c) that his normal weekly earnings for the period of eight weeks ending with the relevant week are not less than the lower earnings limit in force under section 5(1)(a) above at the end of the relevant week; and
(d) that he has been in employed earner's employment with the employer by reference to whom the condition in para.(b) above is satisfied for

1.72

a continuous period beginning with the end of the relevant week and ending with the day on which the child is born.

(3) The references in subsection (2) above to the relevant week are to the week immediately preceding the 14th week before the expected week of the child's birth.

(4) A person's entitlement to statutory paternity pay under this section shall not be affected by the birth, or expected birth, of more than one child as a result of the same pregnancy.

(5) In this section, "newborn child" includes a child stillborn after 24 weeks of pregnancy.

DEFINITIONS

"employer"—see s.171ZJ(1).
"newborn child"—see subs.(5).
"prescribed"—see s.171ZJ(1).
"the relevant week"—see subs.(3).
"week"—see s.171ZJ(5).

GENERAL NOTE

Subs. (2) (a)

1.73 The entitlement conditions referred to in subs.(2)(a) are those prescribed in regs 4(2)(b) and (c) of the Paternity and Adoption Leave Regulations 2002 (SI 2002/2788), which are incorporated by the cross-reference in reg.4 of the SPP and SAP (General) Regulations 2002 (SI 2002/2822). These requirements are that the employee is, first, either (i) the father of the child, or (ii) married to or the partner of the child's mother, but not the child's father (reg.4(2)(b)); and, secondly, has, or expects to have (i) responsibility for the upbringing of the child (if he is the child's father); or (ii) the main responsibility (apart from any responsibility of the mother) for the upbringing of the child (if he is the mother's husband or partner but not the child's father) (reg.4(2)(c)).

Subs. (2) (b)

1.74 On the extended meaning of continuous employment, see SPP and SAP (General) Regulations 2002, regs 33–37.

Subs. (2) (c)

1.75 The minimum threshold requirement that the claimant's earnings are not less than the National Insurance lower earnings limit necessarily excludes those fathers on very low incomes, and typically in part-time work, from SPP. Arguably this is the group of men whose families are most at risk of social exclusion and thus most in need of support such as SPP. The problem is exacerbated by the fact that the National Insurance scheme, unlike the income tax system, does not aggregate earnings from e.g. two part-time jobs with different employers. (But note the special case of associated employers: see SPP and SAP (General) Regulations 2002, reg.38.) Women who do not meet the lower earnings limit requirement do not qualify for SMP (SSCBA 1992, s.164(2)(b)) but may qualify for maternity allowance (SSCBA 1992, s.35—see Vol.I of this series). There is, at present, no such alternative form of income maintenance for fathers in a similar position. This was the one aspect in relation to this part of the Employment Act 2002 which caused considerable disquiet amongst Government back-benchers during the Standing Committee debates on the Bill (Standing Committee F, January 10, 2002, cols 333–360). The minister promised members that the DWP and Department of Health were actively considering how to provide support for low-wage adoptive parents with some form of support equivalent to maternity allowance.

Subs.(2)(b)–(d)
The entitlement conditions are modified if a person fails to meet the conditions set out in subs.(2)(b)–(d) because the child's birth occurred earlier than the 14th week before the expected week of the birth: see SPP and SAP (General) Regulations 2002, reg.5. This modification is in exercise of the regulation-making powers under s.171ZC(3)(a).

Subs.(4)
Thus, SPP is not paid for twice as long in the case of a father of twins.

Entitlement: adoption

171ZB.—(1) Where a person satisfies the conditions in subsection (2) below, he shall be entitled in accordance with the following provisions of this Part to payments to be known as "statutory paternity pay".
 (2) The conditions are—
 (a) that he satisfies prescribed conditions—
  (i) as to relationship with a child who is placed for adoption under the law of any part of the United Kingdom, and
  (ii) as to relationship with a person with whom the child is so placed for adoption;
 (b) that he has been in employed earner's employment with an employer for a continuous period of at least 26 weeks ending with the relevant week;
 (c) that his normal weekly earnings for the period of 8 weeks ending with the relevant week are not less than the lower earnings limit in force under section 5(1)(a) at the end of the relevant week;
 (d) that he has been in employed earner's employment with the employer by reference to whom the condition in paragraph (b) above is satisfied for a continuous period beginning with the end of the relevant week and ending with the day on which the child is placed for adoption; and
 (e) where he is a person with whom the child is placed for adoption, that he has elected to receive statutory paternity pay.
 (3) The references in subsection (2) to the relevant week are to the week in which the adopter is notified of being matched with the child for the purposes of adoption.
 (4) A person may not elect to receive statutory paternity pay if he has elected in accordance with section 171ZL below to receive statutory adoption pay.
 (5) Regulations may make provision about elections for the purposes of subsection (2)(e) above.
 (6) A person's entitlement to statutory paternity pay under this section shall not be affected by the placement for adoption of more than one child as part of the same arrangement.
 (7) In this section, "adopter", in relation to a person who satisfies the condition under subsection (2)(a)(ii) above, means the person by reference to whom he satisfies that condition.

DEFINITIONS
 "adopter"—see subs.(7).
 "employer"—see s.171ZJ(1).
 "normal weekly earnings"—see s.171ZJ(6).

"prescribed"—see s.171ZJ(1).
"the relevant week"—see subs.(3).
"week"—see s.171ZJ(5).

General Note

1.78   The conditions prescribed under subs.(2)(a) are, first, that the claimant is married to or the partner of a child's adopter (or in a case where there are two adopters, married to or the partner of the other adopter) and, secondly, has, or expects to have, the main responsibility for the upbringing of the child (apart from the responsibility of the child's adopter, or in a case where there two adopters, together with the other adopter): SPP and SAP (General) Regulations 2002 (SI 2002/ 2822), reg.11. Note that, unusually, reg.11 specifically includes same-sex partners. "Partner" is defined by reg.11(2) as meaning a person (excluding certain defined relatives) "who lives with the adopter and the child in an enduring family relationship", irrespective of whether the relationship between the adults is heterosexual or same-sex in nature.

Entitlement: general

1.79   **171ZC.**—(1) A person shall be entitled to payments of statutory paternity pay in respect of any period only if—
  (a) he gives the person who will be liable to pay it notice of the date from which he expects the liability to pay him statutory paternity pay to begin; and
  (b) the notice is given at least 28 days before that date or, if that is not reasonably practicable, as soon as is reasonably practicable.
(2) The notice shall be in writing if the person who is liable to pay the statutory paternity pay so requests.
(3) The Secretary of State may by regulations—
  (a) provide that subsection (2)(b), (c) or (d) of section 171ZA or 171ZB above shall have effect subject to prescribed modifications in such cases as may be prescribed;
  (b) provide that subsection (1) above shall not have effect, or shall have effect subject to prescribed modifications, in such cases as may be prescribed;
  (c) impose requirements about evidence of entitlement;
  (d) specify in what circumstances employment is to be treated as continuous for the purposes of section 171ZA or 171ZB above;
  (e) provide that a person is to be treated for the purposes of section 171ZA or 171ZB above as being employed for a continuous period of at least 26 weeks where—
    (i) he has been employed by the same employer for at least 26 weeks under two or more separate contracts of service; and
    (ii) those contracts were not continuous;
  (f) provide for amounts earned by a person under separate contracts of service with the same employer to be aggregated for the purposes of section 171ZA or 171ZB above;
  (g) provide that—
    (i) the amount of a person's earnings for any period; or
    (ii) the amount of his earnings to be treated as comprised in any payment made to him or for his benefit,
shall be calculated or estimated for the purposes of section 171ZA or 171ZB above in such manner and on such basis as may be prescribed and that for that purpose payments of a particular class or description made or

falling to be made to or by a person shall, to such extent as may be prescribed, be disregarded or, as the case may be, be deducted from the amount of his earnings.

DEFINITIONS

"employer"—see s.171ZJ(1).
"modifications"—see *ibid.*
"prescribed"—see *ibid.*
"week"—see s.171ZJ(5).

GENERAL NOTE

See further regs 6 and 7 of the SPP and SAP (General) Regulations 2002 (SI 2002/2822) on the period of payment and notice requirements for SPP (birth). The requirements relating to evidence of entitlement are in reg.9. The equivalent provisions for SPP (adoption) are in regs 12, 13 and 15.

1.80

Liability to make payments

171ZD.—(1) The liability to make payments of statutory paternity pay under section 171ZA or 171ZB above is a liability of any person of whom the person entitled to the payments has been an employee as mentioned in subsection (2)(b) and (d) of that section.

1.81

(2) Regulations shall make provision as to a former employer's liability to pay statutory paternity pay to a person in any case where the former employee's contract of service with him has been brought to an end by the former employer solely, or mainly, for the purpose of avoiding liability for statutory paternity pay.

(3) The Secretary of State may, with the concurrence of the Board, by regulations specify circumstances in which, notwithstanding this section, liability to make payments of statutory paternity pay is to be a liability of the Board.

DEFINITIONS

"the Board"—see s.171ZJ(1).
"employer"—see *ibid.*

GENERAL NOTE

This section, placing the liability to make payments of SPP on employers, follows the same approach as the provisions governing SMP (ss.164(3) and (8)). Note that there is no liability to pay SPP in respect of any week during which the claimant either is entitled to SSP or is detained in custody (or sentenced to imprisonment): SPP and SAP (General) Regulations 2002 (SI 2002/2822), reg.18. Similarly, there is no liability to pay SPP in the week that the person entitled dies.

1.82

The rules governing the funding of SPP and employers' responsibilities in connection with SPP payments are contained in the SPP and SAP (Administration) Regulations 2002 (SI 2002/2820). The special circumstances in which the Board is liable to pay SPP under subs.(3) are set out in SPP and SAP (General) Regulations 2002, reg.43.

Rate and period of pay

171ZE.—(1) Statutory paternity pay shall be payable at such fixed or earnings-related weekly rate as may be prescribed by regulations, which may prescribe different kinds of rate for different cases.

1.83

(2) Statutory paternity pay shall be payable in respect of—
   (a) a period of two consecutive weeks within the qualifying period beginning on such date within that period as the person entitled may choose in accordance with regulations; or
   (b) if regulations permit the person entitled to choose to receive statutory paternity pay in respect of—
      (i) a period of a week, or
      (ii) two non-consecutive periods of a week,
   such week or weeks within the qualifying period as he may choose in accordance with regulations.

(3) For the purposes of subsection (2) above, the qualifying period shall be determined in accordance with regulations, which shall secure that it is a period of at least 56 days beginning—
   (a) in the case of a person to whom the conditions in section 171ZA(2) above apply, with the date of the child's birth, and
   (b) in the case of a person to whom the conditions in section 171ZB(2) above apply, with the date of the child's placement for adoption.

(4) Statutory paternity pay shall not be payable to a person in respect of a statutory pay week if it is not his purpose at the beginning of the week—
   (a) to care for the child by reference to whom he satisfies the condition in sub-paragraph (i) of section 171ZA(2)(a) or 171ZB(2)(a) above; or
   (b) to support the person by reference to whom he satisfies the condition in sub-paragraph (ii) of that provision.

(5) A person shall not be liable to pay statutory paternity pay to another in respect of a statutory pay week during any part of which the other works under a contract of service with him.

(6) It is immaterial for the purposes of subsection (5) above whether the work referred to in that subsection is work under a contract of service which existed immediately before the statutory pay week or a contract of service which did not so exist.

(7) Except in such cases as may be prescribed, statutory paternity pay shall not be payable to a person in respect of a statutory pay week during any part of which he works for any employer who is not liable to pay him statutory paternity pay.

(8) The Secretary of State may by regulations specify circumstances in which there is to be no liability to pay statutory paternity pay in respect of a statutory pay week.

(9) Where more than one child is born as a result of the same pregnancy, the reference in subsection (3)(a) to the date of the child's birth shall be read as a reference to the date of birth of the first child born as a result of the pregnancy.

(10) Where more than one child is placed for adoption as part of the same arrangement, the reference in subsection (3)(b) to the date of the child's placement shall be read as a reference to the date of placement of the first child to be placed as part of the arrangement.

[[1](10A) Where for any purpose of this Part of this Act or of regulations it is necessary to calculate the daily rate of ordinary statutory paternity pay, the amount payable by way of ordinary statutory paternity pay for any day shall be taken as one seventh of the weekly rate.]

(11) In this section—

"statutory pay week", in relation to a person entitled to statutory paternity pay, means a week chosen by him as a week in respect of which statutory paternity pay shall be payable;
"week" means any period of seven days.

AMENDMENT

1. Work and Families Act 2006 s.11 and Sch.1, para.16(1) and (3) (October 1, 2006).

DEFINITIONS

"employer"—see s.171ZJ(1).
"statutory pay week"—see subs.(11).
"week"—see *ibid*.

GENERAL NOTE

The weekly rate of SPP for 2005–06 is the lesser of £106.00 and 90 per cent of normal weekly earnings (on which see SPP and SAP (General) Regulations 2002 (SI 2002/2822), reg.40): SPP and SAP (Weekly Rates) Regulations 2002 (SI 2002/2818), reg.2.

The qualifying period for SPP (birth), i.e. the period within which the SPP period must occur, is the period of 56 days from the date of the child's birth (SPP and SAP (General) Regulations 2002, reg.8). For SPP (adoption), the 56 days runs from the date of the child's placement for adoption: see reg.14.

Regulation 18 of the SPP and SAP (General) Regulations 2002, made under para.(8), sets out the circumstances in which there is no liability to pay SPP (where SSP is payable, or the person has died or is in legal custody).

The rules governing the time for paying SPP are set out in reg.42 of the SPP and SAP (General) Regulations 2002. SPP may be paid in the same way as ordinary remuneration but must not include payment in kind or by way of board and lodging: reg.41.

1.84

Restrictions on contracting out

171ZF.—(1) Any agreement shall be void to the extent that it purports—
(a) to exclude, limit or otherwise modify any provision of this Part of this Act; or
(b) to require an employee or former employee to contribute (whether directly or indirectly) towards any costs incurred by his employer or former employer under this Part of this Act.

(2) For the avoidance of doubt, any agreement between an employer and an employee authorising any deductions from statutory paternity pay which the employer is liable to pay to the employee in respect of any period shall not be void by virtue of subsection (1)(a) above if the employer—
(a) is authorised by that or another agreement to make the same deductions from any contractual remuneration which he is liable to pay in respect of the same period; or
(b) would be so authorised if he were liable to pay contractual remuneration in respect of that period.

1.85

DEFINITION

"employer"—see s.171ZJ(1).

GENERAL NOTE

These restrictions on contracting out follow the equivalent provisions for SSP (s.151(2)–(3)) and SMP (s.164(6)–(7)).

1.86

Relationship with contractual remuneration

1.87 **171ZG.**—(1) Subject to subsections (2) and (3) below, any entitlement to statutory paternity pay shall not affect any right of a person in relation to remuneration under any contract of service ("contractual remuneration").

(2) Subject to subsection (3) below—
(a) any contractual remuneration paid to a person by an employer of his in respect of any period shall go towards discharging any liability of that employer to pay statutory paternity pay to him in respect of that period; and
(b) any statutory paternity pay paid by an employer to a person who is an employee of his in respect of any period shall go towards discharging any liability of that employer to pay contractual remuneration to him in respect of that period.

(3) Regulations may make provision as to payments which are, and those which are not, to be treated as contractual remuneration for the purposes of subsections (1) and (2) above.

DEFINITIONS

"contractual remuneration"—see subs.(1).
"employer"—see s.171ZJ(1).

GENERAL NOTE

1.88 This section mirrors Sch.12, para.2, the equivalent provision in relation to SSP, and Sch.13, para.3, which governs SMP to the same effect. The basic principle is that entitlement to SPP does not affect a claimant's rights to any contractual remuneration (subs.(1)), subject to the significant exception that any payment of contractual remuneration can be regarded as the discharge of SPP liability and vice versa (subs.(2)). Regulations made under subs.(3) provide that the payments to be treated as contractual remuneration are sums payable under a contract of service (a) by way of remuneration, (b) for incapacity for work due to sickness or injury, or (c) by reason of the birth or adoption of a child (SPP and SAP (General) Regulations 2002 (SI 2002/2822), reg.19).

Crown employment—Part XIIZA

1.89 **171ZH.** The provisions of this Part of this Act apply in relation to persons employed by or under the Crown as they apply in relation to persons employed otherwise than by or under the Crown.

GENERAL NOTE

1.90 This mirrors s.169, the equivalent provision for SMP.

Special classes of person

1.91 **171ZI.**—(1) The Secretary of State may with the concurrence of the Treasury make regulations modifying any provision of this Part of this Act in such manner as he thinks proper in its application to any person who is, has been or is to be—
(a) employed on board any ship, vessel, hovercraft or aircraft;
(b) outside Great Britain at any prescribed time or in any prescribed circumstances; or
(c) in prescribed employment in connection with continental shelf operations, as defined in section 120(2) above.

(1992 c.4, s.171ZI)

(2) Regulations under subsection (1) above may, in particular, provide—
(a) for any provision of this Part of this Act to apply to any such person, notwithstanding that it would not otherwise apply;
(b) for any such provision not to apply to any such person, notwithstanding that it would otherwise apply;
(c) for excepting any such person from the application of any such provision where he neither is domiciled nor has a place of residence in any part of Great Britain;
(d) for the taking of evidence, for the purposes of the determination of any question arising under any such provision, in a country or territory outside Great Britain, by a British consular official or such other person as may be determined in accordance with the regulations.

DEFINITIONS

"Great Britain"—see s.172(a).
"prescribed"—see s.171ZJ(1).

GENERAL NOTE

This enabling provision is in the same terms as s.162, which applies to SSP. See further the Statutory Paternity Pay and Statutory Adoption Pay (Persons Abroad and Mariners) Regulations 2002 (SI 2002/2821).

1.92

Part XIIZA: supplementary

171ZJ.—(1) In this Part of this Act—
"the Board" means the Commissioners of Inland Revenue;
[²"employer", in relation to a person who is an employee, means a person who—
(a) under section 6 above is, liable to pay secondary Class 1 contributions in relation to any of the earnings of the person who is an employee; or
(b) would be liable to pay such contributions but for—
  (i) the condition in section 6(1)(b), or
  (ii) the employee being under the age of 16;]
"modifications" includes additions, omissions and amendments, and related expressions are to be read accordingly;
"prescribed" means prescribed by regulations.
(2) In this Part of this Act, "employee" means a person who is—
(a) gainfully employed in Great Britain either under a contract of service or in an office (including elective office) with [¹general earnings (as defined by section 7 of the Income Tax (Earnings and Pensions) Act 2003)]
[². . .]
(3) Regulations may provide—
(a) for cases where a person who falls within the definition in subsection (2) above is not to be treated as an employee for the purposes of this Part of this Act; and
(b) for cases where a person who would not otherwise be an employee for the purposes of this Part of this Act is to be treated as an employee for those purposes.
(4) Without prejudice to any other power to make regulations under this Part of this Act, regulations may specify cases in which, for the purposes of this Part of this Act or of such provisions of this Part of this Act as may be prescribed—

1.93

(a) two or more employers are to be treated as one;
(b) two or more contracts of service in respect of which the same person is an employee are to be treated as one.

(5) In this Part, except section 171ZE, "week" means a period of seven days beginning with Sunday or such other period as may be prescribed in relation to any particular case or class of cases.

(6) For the purposes of this Part of this Act, a person's normal weekly earnings shall, subject to subsection (8) below, be taken to be the average weekly earnings which in the relevant period have been paid to him or paid for his benefit under the contract of service with the employer in question.

(7) For the purposes of subsection (6) above, "earnings" and "relevant period" shall have the meanings given to them by regulations.

(8) In such cases as may be prescribed, a person's normal weekly earnings shall be calculated in accordance with regulations.

(9) Where—
(a) in consequence of the establishment of one or more National Health Service trusts under [³the National Health Service Act 2006, the National Health Service (Wales) Act 2006], or the National Health Service (Scotland) Act 1978 a person's contract of employment is treated by a scheme under [³any of those Acts] as divided so as to constitute two or more contracts; or
(b) an order under [³paragraph 26(1) of Schedule 3 to the National Health Service Act 2006] provides that a person's contract of employment is so divided;

regulations may make provision enabling the person to elect for all of those contracts to be treated as one contract for the purposes of this Part of this Act or such provisions of this Part of this Act as may be prescribed.

(10) Regulations under subsection (9) above may prescribe—
(a) the conditions that must be satisfied if a person is to be entitled to make such an election;
(b) the manner in which, and the time within which, such an election is to be made;
(c) the persons to whom, and the manner in which, notice of such an election is to be given;
(d) the information which a person who makes such an election is to provide, and the persons to whom, and the time within which, he is to provide it;
(e) the time for which such an election is to have effect;
(f) which one of the person's employers under two or more contracts is to be regarded for the purposes of statutory paternity pay as his employer under the contract.

(11) The powers under subsections (9) and (10) are without prejudice to any other power to make regulations under this Part of this Act.

(12) Regulations under any of subsections (4) to (10) above must be made with the concurrence of the Board.

AMENDMENTS

1. Income Tax (Earnings and Pensions) Act 2003, s.722 and Sch.6, para.183 (April 6, 2003).
2. Employment Equality (Age) Regulations 2006 (SI 2006/1031) reg.49(1) and Sch.8, Pt 1, para.11(2) (October 1, 2006).

(1992 c.4, s.171ZJ)

3. National Health Service (Consequential Provisions) Act 2006, s.2 and Sch.1, para.149 (March 1, 2007).

General Note

"*Earnings*": The definition and enabling power under subss.(6) and (7) should be read with reg.39 of the SPP and SAP (General) Regulations 2002 (SI 2002/2822), which defines this term.

"*Employee*": The definition under subs.(2) is modified by regulations made under subs.(3). Thus those who are treated as employed earners under the Social Security (Categorisation of Earners) Regulations 1978 (SI 1978/1689) are also treated as employees for the purpose of SPP: SPP and SAP (General) Regulations 2002, reg.32(1). Apprentices are also covered (reg.32(2)). Employed earners who do not meet the residence or presence requirements under the rules governing National Insurance contributions are excluded from the definition of employee for these purposes (reg.32(3)). Continuous employment is dealt with by regs 33–37. Employment with more than one employer (subs.(4)) is covered by reg.38.

"*National Health Service trusts*": The special position of NHS employees with more than one contract of employment (e.g. with different NHS trusts) is dealt with by the SPP and SAP (National Health Service Employees) Regulations 2002 (SI 2002/2819). These regulations enable such employees to elect to treat two or more such contracts as one contract of employment.

"*Normal weekly earnings*": The definition and enabling power under subss.(6) and (7) should be read with reg.40 of the SPP and SAP (General) Regulations 2002, which defines this term.

1.94

Power to apply Part XIIZA to adoption cases not involving placement

171ZK.—The Secretary of State may by regulations provide for this Part to have effect in relation to cases which involve adoption, but not the placement of a child for adoption under the law of any part of the United Kingdom, with such modifications as the regulations may prescribe.

1.95

Definitions

"modifications"—see s.171ZJ(1).
"United Kingdom"—see s.172(b).

General Note

See further the Social Security Contributions and Benefits Act 1992 (Application of Pts 12ZA and 12ZB to Adoptions from Overseas) Regulations 2003 (SI 2003/499) and the Statutory Paternity Pay (Adoption) and Statutory Adoption Pay (Adoptions from Overseas) (No.2) Regulations 2003 (SI 2003/1194).

1.96

[¹Part XIIZB

Statutory Adoption Pay

Amendment

1. Part XIIZB was inserted by the Employment Act 2002, s.4 (December 8, 2002).

General Note

Part XIIZB of the SSCBA 1992 was inserted by the Employment Act 2002. On the background to the introduction of statutory adoption pay (SAP), see the General

1.97

Note to Pt XIIZA on statutory paternity pay (SPP), introduced at the same time. The amendments made by c.1 of Pt I of the Employment Act 2002 relating to paternity and adoption, including the insertion of Pt XIIZB into the SSCBA 1992, came into force on December 8, 2002 (Employment Act 2002 (Commencement No.3 and Transitional and Saving Provisions) Order 2002, art.2(2) and Sch.1, Pt 2). However, art.3 and Sch.3, para.2 of the same Order provide that Pt XIIZB shall have effect only in relation to a person with whom a child is, or is expected to be placed for adoption on or after April 6, 2003.

Adoptive parents have a right under employment legislation to 26 weeks' ordinary adoption leave with the option of 26 weeks' additional adoption leave, mirroring the arrangements now in place for maternity leave. SAP is payable for 26 weeks (SSCBA 1992, s.171ZN(2)), as with SMP (but unlike the mere two weeks for SPP). The rules governing entitlement to SAP are set out in SSCBA 1992, s.171ZL: employees must have completed 26 weeks' service with their employer by the time they are matched with the child to be adopted and their earnings, on average, must be at least equal to the lower earnings limit for the purpose of National Insurance contributions. The liability to make payments of SAP is placed on employers (SSCBA 1992, s.171ZM), with the recovery arrangements being as for SMP. Provision for various types of special cases and for matters of interpretation is to be found in SSCBA 1992, ss.171ZO–171ZT.

Entitlement

1.98   **171ZL.**—(1) Where a person who is, or has been, an employee satisfies the conditions in subsection (2) below, he shall be entitled in accordance with the following provisions of this Part to payments to be known as "statutory adoption pay".

(2) The conditions are—
  (a) that he is a person with whom a child is, or is expected to be, placed for adoption under the law of any part of the United Kingdom;
  (b) that he has been in employed earner's employment with an employer for a continuous period of at least 26 weeks ending with the relevant week;
  (c) that he has ceased to work for the employer;
  (d) that his normal weekly earnings for the period of 8 weeks ending with the relevant week are not less than the lower earnings limit in force under section 5(1)(a) at the end of the relevant week; and
  (e) that he has elected to receive statutory adoption pay.

(3) The references in subsection (2)(b) and (d) above to the relevant week are to the week in which the person is notified that he has been matched with the child for the purposes of adoption.

(4) A person may not elect to receive statutory adoption pay if—
  (a) he has elected in accordance with section 171ZB above to receive statutory paternity pay, or
[¹(b) he falls within subsection (4A);
(4A) A person falls within this subsection if—
  (a) the child is, or is expected to be, placed for adoption with him as a member of a couple;
  (b) the other member of the couple is a person to whom the conditions in subsection (2) above apply; and
  (c) the other member of the couple has elected to receive statutory adoption pay.

(4B) For the purposes of subsection (4A), a person is a member of a couple if—

(1992 c.4, s.171ZL)

(a) in the case of an adoption or expected adoption under the law of England and Wales, he is a member of a couple within the meaning of section 144(4) of the Adoption and Children Act 2002;

(b) in the case of an adoption or an expected adoption under the law of Scotland or of Northern Ireland, he is a member of a married couple.]

(5) A person's entitlement to statutory adoption pay shall not be affectedby the placement, or expected placement, for adoption of more than one childas part of the same arrangement.

(6) A person shall be entitled to payments of statutory adoption pay only if—

(a) he gives the person who will be liable to pay it notice of the date from which he expects the liability to pay him statutory adoption pay to begin; and

(b) the notice is given at least 28 days before that date or, if that is not reasonably practicable, as soon as is reasonably practicable.

(7) The notice shall be in writing if the person who is liable to pay the statutory adoption pay so requests.

(8) The Secretary of State may by regulations—

(a) provide that subsection (2)(b), (c) or (d) above shall have effect subject to prescribed modifications in such cases as may be prescribed;

(b) provide that subsection (6) above shall not have effect, or shall have effect subject to prescribed modifications, in such cases as may be prescribed;

(c) impose requirements about evidence of entitlement;

(d) specify in what circumstances employment is to be treated as continuous for the purposes of this section;

(e) provide that a person is to be treated for the purposes of this section as being employed for a continuous period of at least 26 weeks where—

(i) he has been employed by the same employer for at least 26 weeks under two or more separate contracts of service; and

(ii) those contracts were not continuous;

(f) provide for amounts earned by a person under separate contracts of service with the same employer to be aggregated for the purposes of this section;

(g) provide that—

(i) the amount of a person's earnings for any period; or

(ii) the amount of his earnings to be treated as comprised in any payment made to him or for his benefit;

shall be calculated or estimated for the purposes of this section in such manner and on such basis as may be prescribed and that for that purpose payments of a particular class or description made or falling to be made to or by a person shall, to such extent as may be prescribed, be disregarded or, as the case may be, be deducted from the amount of his earnings;

(h) make provision about elections for statutory adoption pay.

AMENDMENT

1. Adoption and Children Act 2002 (Consequential Amendment to Statutory Adoption Pay) Order 2006 (SI 2006/2012), art.3 (October 1, 2006).

DEFINITIONS

"employee"—see s.171ZS(2).
"employer"—see s.171ZS(1).

> "modifications"—see *ibid*.
> "normal weekly earnings"—see s.171ZS(6).
> "prescribed"—see s.171ZS(1).
> "relevant week"—see subs.(3).
> "United Kingdom"—see s.172(b).
> "week"—see s.171ZS(5).

General Note

1.99   This section sets out the qualifying conditions for receipt of SAP. A person is entitled to SAP if he or she meets each of five conditions (subs.(2)). First, the claimant must have an approved match with the child. Secondly, the person must be an employee who has satisfied the service qualification of continuous service with the same employer for at least 26 weeks by the week in which the approved match is made. Thirdly, the person must have actually stopped working for that employer (see also s.171ZN(3) (and (4)). Fourthly, the employee's average weekly earnings must be not less than the lower earnings limit for National Insurance contributions. Finally, the person must have elected to receive SAP, which requires that he or she provide the employer with an appropriate notification (see subss.(6) and (7); see also reg.23 of the SPP and SAP (General) Regulations 2002 (SI 2002/2822)) and evidence of entitlement (SPP and SAP (General) Regs 2002, reg.24).

SAP is available to an adoptive parent of a child newly placed for adoption, whether the child is being adopted within the United Kingdom or from overseas. There are, however, some slight differences in the provisions for SAP for domestic and overseas adoptions respectively: see further SSCBA 1992, s.171ZT. It is also important to note that entitlement to SAP arises only for children who are newly placed for adoption. It is therefore not possible to receive SAP for a step-family adoption or where the child is adopted by his or her existing foster carers.

Liability to make payments

1.100   **171ZM.**—(1) The liability to make payments of statutory adoption pay is a liability of any person of whom the person entitled to the payments has been an employee as mentioned in section 171ZL(2)(b) above.

(2) Regulations shall make provision as to a former employer's liability to pay statutory adoption pay to a person in any case where the former employee's contract of service with him has been brought to an end by the former employer solely, or mainly, for the purpose of avoiding liability for statutory adoption pay.

(3) The Secretary of State may, with the concurrence of the Board, by regulations specify circumstances in which, notwithstanding this section, liability to make payments of statutory adoption pay is to be a liability of the Board.

Definitions

> "the Board"—see s.171ZS(1).
> "employee"—see s.171ZS(2).
> "employer"—see s.171ZS(1).

General Note

1.101   This section, placing the liability to make payments of SAP on employers, follows the same approach as the provisions governing SMP (ss.164(3) and (8)) and SPP (s.171ZD). Note that there is no liability to pay SAP in respect of any week during which the claimant either is entitled to SSP or is detained in custody (or sentenced to imprisonment): SPP and SAP (General) Regulations 2002 (SI 2002/2822), reg.27 (but note that, unlike with SPP, there are exceptions to the latter preclusionary rule: reg.27(2)). As with SPP, however, there is no liability to pay SAP in the week that the person entitled dies.

The rules governing the funding of SAP and employers' responsibilities in connection with SAP payments are contained in the SPP and SAP (Administration) Regulations 2002 (SI 2002/2820). The special circumstances in which HMRC is liable to pay SAP under subs.(3) are set out in SPP and SAP (General) Regulations 2002, regs 43 and 44 (the latter applying solely to SAP and not SPP).

Rate and period of pay

171ZN.—(1) Statutory adoption pay shall be payable at such fixed or earnings-related weekly rate as the Secretary of State may prescribe by regulations, which may prescribe different kinds of rate for different cases.

(2) Statutory adoption pay shall be payable, subject to the provisions of this Part of this Act, in respect of each week during a prescribed period ("the adoption pay period") of a duration not exceeding [¹52 weeks].

(3) [¹Except in such cases as may be prescribed,] a person shall not be liable to pay statutory adoption pay to another in respect of any week during any part of which the other works under a contract of service with him.

(4) It is immaterial for the purposes of subsection (3) above whether the work referred to in that subsection is work under a contract of service which existed immediately before the adoption pay period or a contract of service which did not so exist.

(5) Except in such cases as may be prescribed, statutory adoption pay shall not be payable to a person in respect of any week during any part of which he works for any employer who is not liable to pay him statutiory adoption pay.

(6) The Secretary of State may by regulations specify circumstances in which there is to be no liability to pay statutory adoption pay in respect of a week.

[²(6A) Where for any purpose of this Part of this Act or of regulations it is necessary to calculate the daily rate of statutory adoption pay, the amount payable by way of statutory adoption pay for any day shall be taken as one seventh of the weekly rate.]

(7) In subsection (2) above, "week" means any period of seven days.

(8) In subsection (3), (5) and (6) above, "week" means a period of seven days beginning with the day of the week on which the adoption pay period begins.

AMENDMENTS

1. Work and Families Act 2006, s.2 (October 1, 2006).
2. Work and Families Act 2006, s.11 and Sch.1, para.21 (October 1, 2006).

DEFINITIONS

"adoption pay period"—see subs.(2).
"employer"—see s.171ZS(1).
"prescribed"—see *ibid*.
"week"—see subss.(7) and (8).

GENERAL NOTE

This section provides that SAP is payable for a period of up to 52 weeks (the "adoption pay period" under subs.(2)). The rate of SAP is the same as that for SMP, namely

Social Security Contributions and Benefits Act 1992

(from April 2007) the lesser of £112.75 a week or 90 per cent of the employee's average weekly earnings: SPP and SAP (Weekly Rates) Regulations 2002 (SI 2002/2818), reg.3. More detailed rules relating to the adoption pay period are set out in regs 21 and 22 of the SPP and SAP (General) Regulations 2002 (SI 2002/2822).

Restrictions on contracting out

1.104   **171ZO.**—(1) Any agreement shall be void to the extent that it purports—
(a) to exclude, limit or otherwise modify any provision of this Part of this Act; or
(b) to require an employee or former employee to contribute (whether directly or indirectly) towards any costs incurred by his employer or former employer under this Part of this Act.

(2) For the avoidance of doubt, any agreement between an employer and an employee authorising any deductions from statutory adoption pay which the employer is liable to pay to the employee in respect of any period shall not be void by virtue of subsection (1)(a) above if the employer—
(a) is authorised by that or another agreement to make the same deductions from any contractual remuneration which he is liable to pay in respect of the same period; or
(b) would be so authorised if he were liable to pay contractual remuneration in respect of that period.

DEFINITIONS

"employee"—see s.171ZS(2).
"employer"—see s.171ZS(1).

GENERAL NOTE

1.105   These restrictions on contracting out are in the same terms as the equivalent provisions for SSP (s.151(2)–(3)), SMP (s.164(6)–(7)) and SPP (s.171ZF). See also SPP and SAP (General) Regulations 2002 (SI 2002/2822), reg.30.

Relationship with benefits and other payments etc.

1.106   **171ZP.**—(1) Except as may be prescribed, a day which falls within the adoption pay period shall not be treated as a day of incapacity for work for the purposes of determining, for this Act, whether it forms part of a period of incapacity for work for the purposes of incapacity benefit.

(2) Regulations may provide that in prescribed circumstances a day which falls within the adoption pay period shall be treated as a day of incapacity for work for the purposes of determining entitlement to the higher rate of short-term incapacity benefit or to long-term incapacity benefit.

(3) Regulations may provide that an amount equal to a person's statutory adoption pay for a period shall be deducted from any such benefit in respect of the same period and a person shall be entitled to such benefit only if there is a balance after the deduction and, if there is such a balance, at a weekly rate equal to it.

(4) Subject to subsections (5) and (6) below, any entitlement to statutory adoption pay shall not affect any right of a person in relation to remuneration under any contract of service ("contractual remuneration").

(5) Subject to subsection (6) below—
(a) any contractual remuneration paid to a person by an employer of his in respect of a week in the adoption pay period shall go towards

discharging any liability of that employer to pay statutory adoption pay to him in respect of that week; and

(b) any statutory adoption pay paid by an employer to a person who is an employee of his in respect of a week in the adoption pay period shall go towards discharging any liability of that employer to pay contractual remuneration to him in respect of that week.

(6) Regulations may make provision as to payments which are, and those which are not, to be treated as contractual remuneration for the purposes of subsections (4) and (5) above.

(7) In subsection (5) above, "week" means a period of seven days beginning with the day of the week on which the adoption pay period begins.

DEFINITIONS

"adoption pay period"—see s.171ZN(2).
"contractual remuneration"—see subs.(4).
"employee"—see s.171ZS(2).
"employer"—see s.171ZS(1).
"prescribed"—see *ibid.*
"week"—see subs.(7).

GENERAL NOTE

The basic principle is that entitlement to SAP does not affect a claimant's rights to any contractual remuneration (subs.(4)), subject to the significant exception that any payment of contractual remuneration can be regarded as the discharge of SAP liability and vice versa (subs.(5)). Regulations made under subs.(6) provide that the payments to be treated as contractual remuneration are sums payable under a contract of service (a) by way of remuneration, (b) for incapacity for work due to sickness or injury or (c) by reason of the adoption of a child (SPP and SAP (General) Regulations 2002 (SI 2002/2822), reg.28).

1.107

Crown employment—Part XIIZB

171ZQ. The provisions of this Part of this Act apply in relation to persons employed by or under the Crown as they apply in relation to persons employed otherwise than by or under the Crown.

1.108

GENERAL NOTE

This mirrors s.169, the equivalent provision for SMP, and s.171ZH, which deals with SPP.

1.109

Special classes of person

171ZR.—(1) The Secretary of State may with the concurrence of the Treasury make regulations modifying any provision of this Part of this Act in such manner as he thinks proper in its application to any person who is, has been or is to be—

(a) employed on board any ship, vessel, hovercraft or aircraft;
(b) outside Great Britain at any prescribed time or in any prescribed circumstances; or
(c) in prescribed employment in connection with continental shelf operations, as defined in section 120(2) above.

(2) Regulations under subsection (1) above may, in particular, provide—

(a) for any provision of this Part of this Act to apply to any such person, notwithstanding that it would not otherwise apply;

1.110

(b) for any such provision not to apply to any such person, notwithstanding that it would otherwise apply;

(c) for excepting any such person from the application of any such provision where he neither is domiciled nor has a place of residence in any part of Great Britain;

(d) for the taking of evidence, for the purposes of the determination of any question arising under any such provision, in a country or territory outside Great Britain, by a British consular official or such other person as may be determined in accordance with the regulations.

DEFINITIONS

"Great Britain"—see s.172(a).
"prescribed"—see s.171ZS(1).

GENERAL NOTE

1.111 This enabling provision is in the same terms as s.162, which applies to SSP, and s.17ZI, which deals with SPP. See further the Statutory Paternity Pay and Statutory Adoption Pay (Persons Abroad and Mariners) Regulations 2002 (SI 2002/2821).

Part XIIZB: supplementary

1.112 **171ZS.**—(1) In this Part of this Act—
"adoption pay period" has the meaning given by section 171ZN(2) above;
"the Board" means the Commissioners of Inland Revenue;
[²"employer", in relation to a person who is an employee, means a person who—
(a) under section 6 above is liable to pay secondary Class 1 contributions in relation to any of the earnings of the person who is an employee; or
(b) would be liable to pay such contributions but for—
 (i) the condition in section 6(1)(b), or
 (ii) the employee being under the age of 16;]
"modifications" includes additions, omissions and amendments, and related expressions are to be read accordingly;
"prescribed" means prescribed by regulations.
(2) In this Part of this Act, "employee" means a person who is—
(a) gainfully employed in Great Britain either under a contract of service or in an office (including elective office) with [¹general earnings (as defined by section 7 of the Income Tax (Earnings and Pensions) Act 2003)]
[². . .]
(3) Regulations may provide—
(a) for cases where a person who falls within the definition in sub-section (2) above is not to be treated as an employee for the purposes of this Part of this Act; and
(b) for cases where a person who would not otherwise be an employee for the purposes of this Part of this Act is to be treated as an employee for those purposes.
(4) Without prejudice to any other power to make regulations under this Part of this Act, regulations may specify cases in which, for the purposes of this Part of this Act or of such provisions of this Part of this Act as may be prescribed—
(a) two or more employers are to be treated as one;

(b) two or more contracts of service in respect of which the same person is an employee are to be treated as one.

(5) In this Part, except sections 171ZN and 171ZP, "week" means a period of seven days beginning with Sunday or such other period as may be prescribed in relation to any particular case or class of cases.

(6) For the purposes of this Part of this Act, a person's normal weekly earnings shall, subject to subsection (8) below, be taken to be the average weekly earnings which in the relevant period have been paid to him or paid for his benefit under the contract of service with the employer in question.

(7) For the purposes of subsection (6) above, "earnings" and "relevant period" shall have the meanings given to them by regulations.

(8) In such cases as may be prescribed, a person's normal weekly earnings shall be calculated in accordance with regulations.

(9) Where—
(a) in consequence of the establishment of one or more National Health Service trusts under [3the National Health Service Act 2006, the National Health Service (Wales) Act 2006] or the National Health Service (Scotland) Act 1978, a person's contract of employment is treated by a scheme under [3any of those Acts] as divided so as to constitute two or more contracts; or
(b) an order under [3paragraph 26(1) of Schedule 3 to the National Health Service Act 2006] provides that a person's contract of employment is so divided;

regulations may make provision enabling the person to elect for all of those contracts to be treated as one contract for the purposes of this Part of this Act or such provisions of this Part of this Act as may be prescribed.

(10) Regulations under subsection (9) above may prescribe—
(a) the conditions that must be satisfied if a person is to be entitled to make such an election;
(b) the manner in which, and the time within which, such an election is to be made;
(c) the persons to whom, and the manner in which, notice of such an election is to be given;
(d) the information which a person who makes such an election is to provide, and the persons to whom, and the time within which, he is to provide it;
(e) the time for which such an election is to have effect;
(f) which one of the person's employers under two or more contracts is to be regarded for the purposes of statutory adoption pay as his employer under the contract.

(11) The powers under subsections (9) and (10) are without prejudice to any other power to make regulations under this Part of this Act.

(12) Regulations under any of subsections (4) to (10) above must be made with the concurrence of the Board.

AMENDMENTS

1. Income Tax (Earnings and Pensions) Act 2003, s.722 and Sch.6, para.184 (April 6, 2003).

2. Employment Equality (Age) Regulations 2006 (SI 2006/1031), reg.49(1) and Sch.8, Pt 1, para.12 (October 1, 2006).

3. National Health Service (Consequential Provisions) Act 2006, s.2 and Sch.1, para.150 (March 1, 2007).

DEFINITIONS

"Earnings": see General Note to s.171ZJ.
"Employee": see General Note to s.171ZJ.
"National Health Service trusts": see General Note to s.171ZJ.
"Normal weekly earnings": see General Note to s.171ZJ.

Power to apply Part XIIZB to adoption cases not involving placement

1.113   **171ZT.** The Secretary of State may by regulations provide for this Part to have effect in relation to cases which involve adoption, but not the placement of a child for adoption under the law of any part of the United Kingdom, with such modifications as the regulations may prescribe.

GENERAL NOTE

1.114   See further the Social Security Contributions and Benefits Act 1992 (Application of Pts 12ZA and 12ZB to Adoptions from Overseas) Regulations 2003 (SI 2003/499) and the Statutory Paternity Pay (Adoption) and Statutory Adoption Pay (Adoptions from Overseas) (No.2) Regulations 2003 (SI 2003/1194).

PART XIII

GENERAL

Interpretation

Application of Act in relation to territorial waters

1.115   **172.** In this Act—
(a) any reference to Great Britain includes a reference to the territorial waters of the United Kingdom adjacent to Great Britain;
(b) any reference to the United Kingdom includes a reference to the territorial waters of the United Kingdom.

Age

1.116   **173.** For the purposes of this Act a person—
(a) is over or under a particular age if he has or, as the case may be, has not attained that age; and
(b) is between two particular ages if he has attained the first but not the second;
and in Scotland (as in England and Wales) the time at which a person attains a particular age expressed in years is the commencement of the relevant anniversary of the date of his birth.

References to Acts

1.117   **174.** In this Act—
"the 1975 Act" means the Social Security Act 1975;
"the 1986 Act" means the Social Security Act 1986;

(1992 c.4, s.174)

"the Administration Act" means the Social Security Administration Act 1992;

"the Consequential Provisions Act" means the Social Security (Consequential Provisions) Act 1992;

"the Northern Ireland Contributions and Benefits Act" means the Social Security Contributions and Benefits (Northern Ireland) Act 1992;

"the Old Cases Act" means the Industrial Injuries and Diseases (Old Cases) Act 1975; and

"the Pensions Act" means the [¹ Pensions Schemes Act 1993].

AMENDMENT

1. Pension Schemes Act 1993, s.190 and Sch.8, para.41 (February 7, 1994).

Section 153(3)   SCHEDULE 11

CIRCUMSTANCES IN WHICH PERIODS OF ENTITLEMENT TO STATUTORY SICK PAY DO NOT ARISE

1. A period of entitlement does not arise in relation to a particular period of incapacity for work in any of the circumstances set out in para.2 below or in such other circumstances as may be prescribed.

[⁴1A. Regulations made under paragraph 1 must be made with the concurrence of the Treasury.]

2. The circumstances are that—
   (a) [⁶...]
   (b) [⁵...];
   (c) at the relevant date the employee's normal weekly earnings are less than the lower earnings limit then in force under section 5(1)(a) above;
   [¹(d) in the period of 57 days ending immediately before the relevant date the employee had at least one day on which—
      (i) he was entitled to incapacity benefit (or would have been so entitled had he satisfied the contribution conditions mentioned in section 30A(2)(a) above); or
      (ii) [³...]
      (iii) he was entitled to a severe disablement allowance;]
   (e) [¹...]
   (f) the employee has done no work for his employer under his contract of service;
   (g) on the relevant date there is [²...] a stoppage of work due to a trade dispute at the employee's place of employment;
   (h) the employee is, or has been, pregnant and the relevant date falls within the disqualifying period (within the meaning of section 153(12) above).

3. In this Schedule, "relevant date" means the date on which a period of entitlement would begin in accordance with section 153 above if this Schedule did not prevent it arising.

4. [⁵...]

5. [¹...]

[⁷5A. —(1) Paragraph 2(d)(i) above does not apply if, at the relevant date, the employee is over pensionable age and is not entitled to incapacity benefit.

(2) Paragraph 2(d)(i) above ceases to apply if, at any time after the relevant date, the employee is over pensionable age and is not entitled to incapacity benefit.

(3) In this paragraph "pensionable age" has the meaning given by the rules in paragraph 1 of Schedule 4 to the Pensions Act 1995.]

6. For the purposes of paragraph 2(f) above, if an employee enters into a contract of service which is to take effect not more than eight weeks after the date on which a previous contract of service entered into by him with the same employer ceased to have effect, the two contracts shall be treated as one.

7. Paragraph 2(g) above does not apply in the case of an employee who proves that at no time on or before the relevant date did he have a direct interest in the trade dispute in question.

8. Paragraph 2(h) above does not apply in relation to an employee who has been pregnant if her pregnancy terminated, before the beginning of the disqualifying period, otherwise than by confinement (as defined for the purposes of statutory maternity pay in section 171(1) above).

1.118

Social Security Contributions and Benefits Act 1992

AMENDMENTS

1. Social Security (Incapacity for Work) Act 1994, s.11(1) and Sch.1, para.43 (April 6, 1995).
2. Jobseekers Act 1995, s.41(5) and Sch.3 (October 7, 1996).
3. Social Security Act 1998, s.73 (April 6, 1999).
4. Social Security Contributions (Transfer of Functions, etc.) Act 1999, s.1(1) and Sch.1, para.20 (April 1, 1999).
5. Fixed-term Employees (Prevention of Less Favourable Treatment) Regulations 2002 (SI 2002/2034), reg.11 and Sch.2, para.1 (October 1, 2002).
6. Employment Equality (Age) Regulations 2006 (SI 2006/1031), reg.49(1) and Sch.8, Pt 1, para.13(1) (October 1, 2006).
7. Employment Equality (Age) (Consequential Amendments) Regulations 2007 (SI 2007/825), reg.2 (April 6, 2007).

DEFINITIONS

"contract of service"—see s.163(1).
"disqualifying period"—see s.153(12).
"employee"—see s.163(1) and SSP (General) Regulations 1982, reg.16.
"employer"—see s.163(1).
"period of entitlement"—see *ibid.*
"period of incapacity for work"—see s.163(1).
"prescribed"—see *ibid.*
"relevant date"—see para.(3).

GENERAL NOTE

Para.1

1.119 The general rule, stated here, is that no period of entitlement to SSP can arise in any of the circumstances set out in para.2 or in such circumstances as are prescribed by regulations. The relevant regulation is reg.3 of the SSP (General) Regulations 1986 (SI 1982/894), which excludes prisoners and women entitled neither to SMP nor to maternity allowance who have reached a particular stage in their pregnancy or have been confined before reaching that stage.

Para.2

1.120 This sets out the categories of persons for whom a period of entitlement does not arise for the purposes of para.1, and so who are excluded from the scope of SSP. The "relevant date" is the date on which a period of entitlement would otherwise begin were it not for the provisions of this Schedule (para.3). Thus the relevant date will usually be the first day of incapacity for work in the period of incapacity for work in question (s.153(2), but note the modifying provisions in (7), (8) and (9)). Those persons who are excluded from SSP by virtue of this paragraph may be able to claim incapacity benefit or, in the case of pregnant women, SMP or maternity allowance. The particular exclusions are:

(1) employees whose earnings are below the National Insurance lower earnings limit (sub-para.2(c));

(2) claimants whose day of incapacity links back to a recent entitlement to incapacity benefit (sub-para.2(d)). But note also para.5A, which ensures that employees who cannot return to incapacity benefit as they are now over pensionable age, but who would have returned to IB rather than becoming entitled to SSP had they been under pensionable age, are now entitled to SSP;

(3) employees who have yet to start work under the contract of service (sub-para.2(f), but note the linking rule in para.6);

(4) employees who are subject to a stoppage of work due to a trade dispute at their place of employment (sub-para.2(g), but note the exception in para.7);

(5) employees who are or have been pregnant and where the relevant date falls within the disqualifying period for persons entitled to SMP or maternity allowance (sub-para.2(h), but note the exception in para.8).

In addition, under the original para.(2)(b), employees with a contract of service for a specified period of not more than 3 months were excluded from entitlement to SSP. This exclusion was repealed by the Fixed-term Employees (Prevention of Less Favourable Treatment) Regulations 2002 (SI 2002/2034) as from October 1, 2002. The effect of this amendment was considered by Lewison J in *Commissioners for HMRC v Thorn Baker Ltd* [2006] EWHC 2190 (Ch), who held that the 2002 Regulations had no impact on employees working under fixed-term contracts who were agency workers. The effect of that decision is that SSP is not payable to agency workers whose contract with the agency is for a specified period of 3 months or less. The Court of Appeal has dismissed HMRC's appeal ([2007] EWCA Civ 626).

Para.7

The effect of the wording of this exception is that if the employee has at some time before the relevant date had a direct interest in the trade dispute, he or she cannot take advantage of this provision and so is caught by the exclusion in sub-para.2(g): see *R(SSP)1/86*.

1.121

Section 160 SCHEDULE 12

Relationship of Statutory Sick Pay with Benefits and Other Payments, etc.

The general principle

1. Any day which—
(a) is a day of incapacity for work in relation to any contract of service; and
(b) falls within a period of entitlement (whether or not it is also a qualifying day);
shall not be treated for the purposes of this Act as a day of incapacity for work for the purposes of determining whether a period is [¹ . . .] [² a period of incapacity for work for the purposes of incapacity benefit].

1.122

Contractual remuneration

2.—(1) Subject to sub-paragraphs (2) and (3) below, any entitlement to statutory sick pay shall not affect any right of an employee in relation to remuneration under any contract of service ("contractual remuneration").
(2) Subject to sub-para.(3) below—
(a) any contractual remuneration paid to an employee by an employer of his in respect of a day of incapacity for work shall go towards discharging any liability of that employer to pay statutory sick pay to that employee in respect of that day; and
(b) any statutory sick pay paid by an employer to an employee of his in respect of a day of incapacity for work shall go towards discharging any liability of that employer to pay contractual remuneration to that employee in respect of that day.
(3) Regulations may make provision as to payments which are, and those which are not, to be treated as contractual remuneration for the purposes of sub-paragraph (1) or (2) above.

1.123

[²*Incapacity benefit*

3.—(1) This paragraph and paragraph 4 below have effect to exclude, where a period of entitlement as between an employee and an employer of his comes to an end, the provisions by virtue of which short-term incapacity benefit is not paid for the first three days.
(2) If the first day immediately following the day on which the period of entitlement came to an end—
(a) is a day of incapacity for work in relation to that employee; and
(b) is not a day in relation to which paragraph 1 above applies by reason of any entitlement as between the employee and another employer,

1.124

that day shall, except in prescribed cases, be or form part of a period of incapacity for work notwithstanding section 30C(1)(b) above (by virtue of which a period of incapacity for work must be at least 4 days long).

(3) Where each of the first two consecutive days, or the first three consecutive days, following the day on which the period of entitlement came to an end is a day to which paragraph (a) and (b) of sub-paragraph (2) above apply, that sub-paragraph has effect in relation to the second day or, as the case may be, in relation to the second and third days, as it has effect in relation to the first.

4.—(1) Where a period of entitlement as between an employee and an employer of his comes to an end, section 30A(3) above (exclusion of benefit for first three days of period) does not apply in relation to any day which—

    (a) is or forms part of a period of incapacity for work (whether by virtue of paragraph 3 above or otherwise); and

    (b) falls within the period of 57 days immediately following the day on which the period of entitlement came to an end.

(2) Where sub-paragraph (1) above applies in relation to a day, section 30A(3) above does not apply in relation to any later day in the same period of incapacity for work.]

[²Incapacity benefit for widows and widowers

1.125   **5.** Paragraph 1 above does not apply for the purpose of determining whether the conditions specified in section 40(3) or (4) or section 41(2) or (3) above are satisfied.]

Unemployability supplement

1.126   **6.** Paragraph 1 above does not apply in relation to paragraph 3 of Schedule 7 to this Act and accordingly the references in paragraph 3 of that Schedule to a period of interruption of employment shall be construed as if the provisions re-enacted in this Part of this Act had not been enacted.

AMENDMENTS

1. Jobseekers Act 1995, s.41(5) and Sch.3, para.1 (October 7, 1996).
2. Social Security (Incapacity for Work) Act 1994, s.11(1) and Sch.1, para.44 (April 13, 1995).

GENERAL NOTE

Para. 1

1.127   No day which falls within a period of entitlement for the purposes of SSP (whether or not it is a qualifying day) can count as a day of incapacity for the purposes of establishing entitlement to incapacity benefit.

Paras 3 and 4

1.128   These paragraphs assist certain persons, not caught by para.1, who have days of incapacity subsequent to the end of a period of entitlement, to qualify for incapacity benefit by not applying the normal rules, e.g. on waiting days. See further SSP (General) Regulations 1982 (SI 1982/894), reg.12.

Section 168   SCHEDULE 13

RELATIONSHIP OF STATUTORY MATERNITY PAY WITH BENEFITS AND OTHER PAYMENTS, ETC.

The general principle

1.129   [²**1.** Except as may be prescribed, a day which falls within the maternity pay period shall not be treated as a day of incapacity for work for the purposes of determining, for this Act, whether it forms part of a period of incapacity for work for the purposes of incapacity benefit.]

(1992 c.4, Sch.13)

[¹Incapacity benefit

2.—(1) Regulations may provide that in prescribed circumstances a day which falls within the maternity pay period shall be treated as a day of incapacity for work for the purpose of determining entitlement to the higher rate of short-term incapacity benefit or to long-term incapacity benefit.

(2) Regulations may provide that an amount equal to a woman's statutory maternity pay for a period shall be deducted from any such benefit in respect of the same period and a woman shall be entitled to such benefit only if there is a balance after the deduction and, if there is such a balance, at a weekly rate equal to it.]

Contractual remuneration

3.—(1) Subject to sub-paragraphs (2) and (3) below, any entitlement to statutory maternity pay shall not affect any right of a woman in relation to remuneration under any contract of service ("contractual remuneration").

(2) Subject to sub-paragraph (3) below—
   (a) any contractual remuneration paid to a woman by an employer of hers in respect of a week in the maternity pay period shall go towards discharging any liability of that employer to pay statutory maternity pay to her in respect of that week; and
   (b) any statutory maternity pay paid by an employer to a woman who is an employee of his in respect of a week in the maternity pay period shall go towards discharging any liability of that employer to pay contractual remuneration to her in respect of that week.

[³(2A) In sub-paragraph (2) "week" means a period of seven days beginning with the day of the week on which the maternity pay period begins.]

(3) Regulations may make provision as to payments which are, and those which are not, to be treated as contractual remuneration for the purposes of sub-paragraphs (1) and (2) above.

AMENDMENTS

1. Social Security (Incapacity for Work) Act 1994, s.11(1) and Sch.1, para.45(3) (April 6, 1995).
2. Jobseekers Act 1995, s.41(4) and Sch.2, para.37 (October 7, 1996).
3. Work and Families Act 2006, s.11 and Sch.1, para.23 (October 1, 2006).

Social Security Administration Act 1992

(1992 c.5)

SECTIONS REPRODUCED

PART I

CLAIMS FOR PAYMENTS AND GENERAL ADMINISTRATION OF BENEFIT

Statutory sick pay

14.   Duties of employees, etc. in relation to statutory sick pay

Statutory maternity pay

15.   Duties of women etc. in relation to statutory maternity pay

Social Security Administration Act 1992

PART VI

ENFORCEMENT

113A. Statutory sick pay and statutory maternity pay: breach of regulations
113B. Statutory sick pay and statutory maternity pay: fraud and negligence

PART VII

INFORMATION

Information held by tax authorities

122. Supply of information held by tax authorities for fraud prevention and verification
122A. Supply of information by Inland Revenue for purposes of contributions

Statutory sick pay and other benefits

129. Disclosure by Secretary of State for purpose of determination of period of entitlement to statutory sick pay
130. Duties of employers—statutory sick pay and claims for other benefits

Statutory maternity pay and other benefits

131. Disclosure by Secretary of State for purpose of determination of period of entitlement to statutory maternity pay
132. Duties of employers—statutory maternity pay and claims for other benefits

PART I

CLAIMS FOR AND PAYMENTS AND GENERAL ADMINISTRATION OF BENEFIT

Statutory Sick Pay

Duties of employees etc. in relation to statutory sick pay

1.133   **14.**—(1) Any employee who claims to be entitled to statutory sick pay from his employer shall, if so required by his employer, provide such information as may reasonably be required for the purpose of determining the duration of the period of entitlement in question or whether a period of entitlement exists as between them.
(2) The Secretary of State may by regulations direct—
(a) that medical information required under subsection (1) above shall, in such cases as may be prescribed, be provided in a prescribed form;
(b) that an employee shall not be required under subsection (1) above to provide medical information in respect of such days as may be prescribed in a period of incapacity for work.

(3) Where an employee asks an employer of his to provide him with a written statement, in respect of a period before the request is made, of one or more of the following—
(a) the days within that period which the employer regards as days in respect of which he is liable to pay statutory sick pay to that employee;
(b) the reasons why the employer does not so regard the other days in that period;
(c) the employer's opinion as to the amount of statutory sick pay to which the employee is entitled in respect of each of those days,
the employer shall, to the extent to which the request was reasonable, comply with it within a reasonable time.

Statutory maternity pay

Duties of women etc. in relation to statutory maternity pay

15.—(1) A woman shall provide the person who is liable to pay her statutory maternity pay—
(a) with evidence as to her pregnancy and the expected date of confinement in such form and at such time as may be prescribed; and
(b) where she commences work after her confinement but within the maternity pay period, with such additional information as may be prescribed.

[[1](1A) Any regulations for the purposes of subsection (1) above must be made with the concurrence of the Inland Revenue.]

(2) Where a woman asks an employer or former employer of hers to provide her with a written statement, in respect of a period before the request is made, of one or more of the following—
(a) the weeks within that period which he regards as weeks in respect of which he is liable to pay statutory maternity pay to the woman;
(b) the reasons why he does not so regard the other weeks in that period; and
(c) his opinion as to the amount of statutory maternity pay to which the woman is entitled in respect of each of the weeks in respect of which he regards himself as liable to make a payment;
the employer or former employer shall, to the extent to which the request was reasonable, comply with it within a reasonable time.

AMENDMENT

1. Social Security Contributions (Transfer of Functions, etc.) Act 1999, s.2 and Sch.3, para.43.

PART VI

ENFORCEMENT

[1Statutory sick pay and statutory maternity pay: breach of regulations

113A.—(1) Where a person fails to produce any document or record, or provide any information, in accordance with—

Social Security Administration Act 1992

(a) regulations under section 5(1)(i) and (5), so far as relating to statutory sick pay or statutory maternity pay,
(b) regulations under section 130 or 132, or
(c) regulations under section 153(5)(b) of the Contributions and Benefits Act,

that person is liable to the penalties mentioned in subsection (2).

(2) The penalties are—
(a) a penalty not exceeding £300, and
(b) if the failure continues after a penalty is imposed under paragraph (a), a further penalty or penalties not exceeding £60 for each day on which the failure continues after the day on which the penalty under that paragraph was imposed (but excluding any day for which a penalty under this paragraph has already been imposed).

(3) Where a person fails to maintain a record in accordance with regulations under section 130 or 132, he is liable to a penalty not exceeding £3,000.

(4) No penalty may be imposed under subsection (1) at any time after the failure concerned has been remedied.

(5) But subsection (4) does not apply to the imposition of a penalty under subsection (2)(a) in respect of a failure to produce any document or record in accordance with regulations under section 130(5) or 132(4).

(6) Where, in the case of any employee, an employer refuses or repeatedly fails to make payments of statutory sick pay or statutory maternity pay in accordance with any regulations under section 5, the employer is liable to a penalty not exceeding £3,000.

(7) Section 118(2) of the Taxes Management Act 1970 (extra time for compliance etc) applies for the purposes of subsections (1), (3) and (6) as it applies for the purposes of that Act.

(8) Schedule 1 to the Employment Act 2002 (penalties relating to statutory paternity pay and statutory adoption pay: procedures and appeals) applies in relation to penalties imposed under this section (with the modifications set out in subsection (9)).

(9) That Schedule applies as if—
(a) references to a penalty under section 11 or 12 of that Act were to a penalty under this section,
(b) in paragraph 1(2), the reference to section 11(2)(a) of that Act were to subsection (2)(a) of this section, and
(c) the provisions of the Taxes Management Act 1970 having effect in relation to an appeal mentioned in paragraph 3(2) of that Schedule did not include section 50(9) of that Act.]

AMENDMENT

1. National Insurance Contributions and Statutory Payments Act 2004, s.9(5) (April 6, 2005).

GENERAL NOTE

1.136   This provision brings in a compliance regime based on civil penalties, as with the administration of tax. Section 113A provides for civil penalties for failures to keep records, to produce records, to provide information or to pay either statutory sick pay or statutory maternity pay. The appeals procedures for such penalties are governed by Sch.1 to the Employment Act 2002 (see ss.113A(8) and (9)). Section

113B below is concerned with breaches by commission, and provides for penalties in cases of fraud or negligence which involve employers making incorrect statements or declarations, producing incorrect documents or records, making incorrect payments of statutory sick pay and statutory maternity pay and receiving incorrect advances of statutory maternity pay. HMRC has stated that penalties will be reserved for "serious situations such as where there has been a deliberate manipulation of the schemes, where a failure has continued after we have put the employer right and where the employer has failed to pay after the appeal period against a formal decision on liability" (*Regulatory Impact Assessment*, Annex E, para.7).

[¹Statutory sick pay and statutory maternity pay: fraud and negligence

113B.—(1) Where a person fraudulently or negligently—
(a) makes any incorrect statement or declaration in connection with establishing entitlement to statutory sick pay or statutory maternity pay, or
(b) produces any incorrect document or record or provides any incorrect information of a kind mentioned in—
  (i) regulations under section 5(1)(i) and (5), so far as relating to statutory sick pay or statutory maternity pay,
  (ii) regulations under section 130 or 132, or
  (iii) regulations under section 153(5)(b) of the Contributions and Benefits Act,
he is liable to a penalty not exceeding £3,000.

(2) Where an employer fraudulently or negligently makes an incorrect payment of statutory sick pay or statutory maternity pay, he is liable to a penalty not exceeding £3,000.

(3) Where an employer fraudulently or negligently receives an overpayment in pursuance of regulations under section 167 of the Contributions and Benefits Act (statutory maternity pay: advance payments to employers), he is liable to a penalty not exceeding £3,000.

(4) Schedule 1 to the Employment Act 2002 (penalties relating to statutory paternity pay and statutory adoption pay: procedures and appeals) applies in relation to penalties imposed under this section (with the modifications set out in subsection (5)).

(5) That Schedule applies as if—
(a) references to a penalty under section 11 or 12 of that Act were to a penalty under this section, and
(b) the provisions of the Taxes Management Act 1970 having effect in relation to an appeal mentioned in paragraph 3(2) of that Schedule did not include section 50(9) of that Act.]

1.137

AMENDMENT

1. National Insurance Contributions and Statutory Payments Act 2004, s.9(5) (April 6, 2005).

PART VII

[¹INFORMATION

Information held by tax authorities

Supply of information held by tax authorities for fraud prevention and verification

1.138   **122.**—[¹(1) This section applies—
   (a) to information which is held—
      (i) by the Inland Revenue, or
      (ii) by a person providing services to the Inland Revenue, in connection with the provision of those services,
   but is not information to which section 121E above applies, and
   (b) to information which is held—
      (i) by the Commissioners of Customs and Excise, or
      (ii) by a person providing services to the Commissioners of Customs and Excise, in connection with the provision of those services.]
   (2) Information to which this section applies may, with the authority of the Commissioners concerned, be supplied to, or to a person providing services to, the Secretary of State or the Northern Ireland Department—
   (a) for use in the prevention, detection, investigation or prosecution of offences relating to social security; or
   (b) for use in checking the accuracy of information relating to benefits, contributions or national insurance numbers or to any other matter relating to social security and (where appropriate) amending or supplementing such information.
   (3) Information supplied under subsection (2) above shall not be supplied by the recipient to any other person or body unless—
   (a) it could be supplied to that person or body under that subsection;
   (b) it is supplied for the purposes of any civil or criminal proceedings relating to the Contributions and Benefits Act, the Jobseekers Act 1995 or this Act or to any provision of Northern Ireland legislation corresponding to any of them; or
   (c) it is supplied under section 122C below;
   and shall not be so supplied in those circumstances without the authority of the Commissioners concerned.
   (4) But where information supplied under subsection (2) above has been used (in accordance with paragraph (b) of that subsection) in amending or supplementing other information, it is lawful for it to be—
   (a) supplied to any person or body to whom that other information could be supplied; or
   (b) used for any purpose for which that other information could be used.
   (5) This section does not limit the circumstances in which information may be supplied apart from this section.]

AMENDMENTS

1. Social Security Administration (Fraud) Act 1997, s.1 (July 1, 1997).
2. Social Security Contributions (Transfer of Functions, etc.) Act 1999, s.6 and Sch.6, para.2 (April 1, 1999).

(1992 c.5, s.122)

GENERAL NOTE

This and subsequent sections must now be read with CRCA 2005, combining the Commissioners of Inland Revenue with the Commissioners of Customs and Excise to form HRMC. Accordingly, the information flows are now between HMRC as a whole and DWP or other public authorities. These flows are now facilitated electronically by the Generalised Matching Service and similar programmes. These use the National Insurance number and other details to check if, for example, any bank or building society has deducted income tax from interest payable by it to any benefit recipient.

[¹Disclosure of contributions etc. information by Inland Revenue

122AA. —(1) No obligation as to secrecy imposed by statute or otherwise on persons employed in relation to the Inland Revenue shall prevent information held for the purposes of the functions of the Inland Revenue in relation to contributions, statutory sick pay or statutory maternity pay from being disclosed—
  (a) to any of the authorities to which this paragraph applies, or any person authorised to exercise any function of that authority, for the purposes of the functions of that authority, or
  (b) in a case where the disclosure is necessary for the purpose of giving effect to any agreement to which an order under section 179(1) below relates.
(2) The authorities to which subsection(1)(a) above applies are—
  (a) the Health and Safety Executive,
  (b) the Government Actuary's Department,
  (c) the Office for National Statistics, and
  (d) the Occupational Pensions Regulatory Authority.]

AMENDMENT

1. Social Security Contributions (Transfer of Functions, etc.) Act 1999, s.6 and Sch.6, para.3 (April 1, 1999).

Statutory sick pay and other benefits

Disclosure by Secretary of State for purpose of determination of period of entitlement to statutory sick pay

129. Where the Secretary of State considers that it is reasonable for information held by him to be disclosed to an employer, for the purpose of enabling that employer to determine the duration of a period of entitlement under Part XI of the Contributions and Benefits Act in respect of an employee, or whether such a period exists, he may disclose the information to that employer.

Duties of employers—statutory sick pay and claims for other benefits

130.—(1) Regulations may make provision requiring an employer, in a case falling within subsection (3) below to furnish information in connection with the making, by a person who is, or has been, an employee of that employer, of a claim for—
  [¹(a) short-term incapacity benefit;]
  (b) a maternity allowance;
  [¹(c) long-term incapacity benefit;]
  (d) industrial injuries benefit; [³ . . .]

(e) [³. . .].

(2) Regulations under this section shall prescribe—

(a) the kind of information to be furnished in accordance with the regulations;
(b) the person to whom information of the prescribed kind is to be furnished; and
(c) the manner in which, and period within which, it is to be furnished.

(3) The cases are—

(a) where, by virtue of paragraph 2 of Schedule 11 to the Contributions and Benefits Act or of regulations made under paragraph 1 of that Schedule, a period of entitlement does not arise in relation to a period of incapacity for work;
(b) where a period of entitlement has come to an end but the period of incapacity for work which was running immediately before the period of entitlement came to an end continues; and
(c) where a period of entitlement has not come to an end but, on the assumption that—
  (i) the period of incapacity for work in question continues to run for a prescribed period; and
  (ii) there is no material change in circumstances;
 the period of entitlement will have ended on or before the end of the prescribed period.

(4) Regulations [²made with the concurrence of the Inland Revenue]—

(a) may require employers to maintain such records in connection with statutory sick pay as may be prescribed;
(b) may provide for—
  (i) any person claiming to be entitled to statutory sick pay; or
  (ii) any other person who is a party to proceedings arising under Part XI of the Contributions and Benefits Act;
 to furnish to the Secretary of State [² or the Inland Revenue (as the regulations may require)], within a prescribed period, any information required for the determination of any question arising in connection there with; and
(c) may require employers who have made payments of statutory sick pay to furnish to the Secretary of State [² or the Inland Revenue (as the regulations may require)] such documents and information, at such times, as may be prescribed.

[⁴(5) Regulations made with the concurrence of the Inland Revenue may require employers to produce wages sheets and other documents and records to officers of the Inland Revenue, within a prescribed period, for the purpose of enabling them to satisfy themselves that statutory sick pay has been paid, and is being paid, in accordance with regulations under section 5 above, to employees or former employees who are entitled to it.]

AMENDMENTS

1. Social Security (Incapacity for Work) Act 1994, s.11(1) and Sch.1, para.49 (April 6, 1995).
2. Social Security Contributions (Transfer of Functions, etc.) Act 1999, s.6 and Sch.6, para.3 (April 1, 1999).
3. Welfare Reform and Pensions Act 1999, s.88 and Sch.13, Pt IV (April 6, 2001).
4. National Insurance Contributions and Statutory Payments Act 2004, s.9(2) (January 1, 2005).

(1992 c.5, s.131)

Statutory maternity pay and other benefits

Disclosure by Secretary of State for purpose of determination of period of entitlement to statutory maternity pay

131. Where the Secretary of State considers that it is reasonable for information held by him to be disclosed to a person liable to make payments of statutory maternity pay for the purpose of enabling that person to determine—
 (a) whether a maternity pay period exists in relation to a woman who is or has been an employee of his; and
 (b) if it does, the date of its commencement and the weeks in it in respect of which he may be liable to pay statutory maternity pay,
he may disclose the information to that person.

Duties of employers—statutory maternity pay and claims for other benefits

132.—(1) Regulations may make provision requiring an employer in prescribed circumstances to furnish information in connection with the making of a claim by a woman who is or has been his employee for—
 (a) a maternity allowance;
 (b) [¹short-term incapacity benefit;]
 (c) [¹long-term incapacity benefit under section 30A], 40 or 41 of the Contributions and Benefits Act; [³. . .]
 (d) [³. . .].
(2) Regulations under this section shall prescribe—
 (a) the kind of information to be furnished in accordance with the regulations;
 (b) the person to whom information of the prescribed kind is to be furnished; and
 (c) the manner in which, and period within which, it is to be furnished.
(3) Regulations [²made with the concurrence of the Inland Revenue]—
 (a) may require employers to maintain such records in connection with statutory maternity pay as may be prescribed;
 (b) may provide for—
  (i) any woman claiming to be entitled to statutory maternity pay; or
  (ii) any other person who is a party to proceedings arising under Part XII of the Contributions and Benefits Act,
  to furnish to the Secretary of State [²or the Inland Revenue (as the regulations may require)], within a prescribed period, any information required for the determination of any question arising in connection there with; and
 (c) may require persons who have made payments of statutory maternity pay to furnish to the Secretary of State [²or the Inland Revenue (as the regulations may require)] such documents and information, at such time, as may be prescribed.
[⁴(4) Regulations made with the concurrence of the Inland Revenue may require employers to produce wages sheets and other documents and records to officers of the Inland Revenue, within a prescribed period, for the purpose of enabling them to satisfy themselves that statutory maternity pay has been paid, and is being paid, in accordance with regulations under section 5 above, to employees or former employees who are entitled to it.]

1.143

1.144

Social Security Administration Act 1992

AMENDMENTS

1. Social Security (Incapacity for Work) Act 1994, s.11(1) and Sch.1, para.50 (April 6, 1995).
2. Social Security Contributions (Transfer of Functions, etc.) Act 1999, s.6 and Sch.1, para.27 (April 1, 1999).
3. Welfare Reform and Pensions Act 1999, s.88 and Sch.13, Pt IV (April 6, 2001).
4. National Insurance Contributions and Statutory Payments Act 2004, s.9(3) (January 1, 2005).

Social Security Act 1998

(1998 C.14)

1.145 (AS APPLIED AND MODIFIED BY THE TAX CREDITS (APPEALS) REGULATIONS 2002 (SI 2002/2926) AND THE CHILD TRUST FUNDS (NON-TAX APPEALS) REGULATIONS 2005 (SI 2005/990). *Provisions Applying only to Child Trust Fund Appeals are in Italics*)

ARRANGEMENT OF SECTIONS

5. *President of appeal tribunals*
6. *Panel for appointment to appeal tribunals*
7. *Constitution of appeal tribunals*

1.146
12. Appeal to appeal tribunal
13. Redetermination etc. of appeals by tribunal
14. Appeal from tribunal to Commissioner
15. Appeal from a Commissioner on point of law
16. Procedure
17. Finality of decisions
28. Correction of errors and setting aside of decisions
39. Interpretation etc. of Chapter II
79. *Regulations and orders*
80. *Parliamentary control of regulations*
84. *Interpretation: general*
Schedule 1—*Appeal tribunals: supplementary provisions*
Schedule 4—Social Security Commissioners
Schedule 5—Regulations as to procedure: provision which may be made

President of appeal tribunals

1.147 **5.**—*(1) The Lord Chancellor may, after consultation with the Lord Advocate, appoint a President of appeal tribunals.*
(2) A person is qualified to be appointed President if—
(a) he has a 10 year general qualification (construed in accordance with section 71 of the Courts and Legal Services Act 1990); or
(b) he is an advocate or solicitor in Scotland of at least 10 years' standing.
(3) Schedule 1 to this Act shall have effect for supplementing this section.

GENERAL NOTE

1.148 It is not immediately obvious why ss.5 to 7, 79, 80 and 84 and Sch.1 have been applied to child trust fund appeals and not to tax credit appeals (save that s.63(8)(a) of the Tax Credits Act 2002 refers only to Ch.2 of Pt 1 of this Act). It is also not immediately obvious why s.14 and Sch.4 (concerned primarily with the appointment of Commissioners) are applied to both types of appeal. A number of questions arise. If it is necessary to apply the provisions for appointing the President and appeal tribunal panel members to child trust fund cases, what is the effect of not applying them to tax credit appeals? The President, appeal tribunal panel members and Commissioners who were already sitting have not received any new appointments since these provisions were applied to child trust fund cases (and, in the case of Commissioners, tax credit cases). Does that mean they have no jurisdiction to hear these appeals? If not, what was the point in applying the provisions? Are the tax credit procedure regulations all invalid because ss.79 and 80 were not applied for the purposes of tax credit appeals?

By the Transfer of Functions (Lord Advocate and Secretary of State) Order 1999 (SI 1999/678), art.2(1) and Sch., the functions of the Lord Advocate under this section are transferred to the Secretary of State.

Panel for appointment to appeal tribunals

6.—(*1*) *The Lord Chancellor shall constitute a panel of persons to act as members of appeal tribunals.*

(*2*) *Subject to subsection (3) below, the panel shall be composed of such persons as the Lord Chancellor thinks fit to appoint after consultation, in the case of medical practitioners, with the Chief Medical Officer.*

[³(*3A*) *As part of the selection process for the appointment of a medical practitioner as a member of the panel, the Judicial Appointments Commissioner shall consult the Chief Medical Officer.*]

(*3*) *The panel shall include persons possessing such qualifications as may be prescribed by regulations made with the concurrence of the Lord Chancellor.*

(*4*) *The numbers of persons appointed to the panel, and the terms and conditions of their appointments, shall be determined by the Lord Chancellor with the consent of the Secretary of State.*

(*5*) *A person may be removed from the panel by the Lord Chancellor on the ground of incapacity or misbehaviour.*

[³(*5A*) *The appropriate senior judge is the Lord Chief Justice of England and Wales, unless the person to be removed exercises functions wholly or mainly in Scotland, in which case it is the Lord President of the Court of Session.*]

(*6*) *In this section "the Chief Medical Officer" means—*
   (a) *in relation to England, the Chief Medical Officer of the Department of Health;*
   (b) *in relation to Wales, the Chief Medical Officer of the [²National Assembly for Wales]; and*
   (c) *in relation to Scotland, the Chief Medical Officer of the [¹Scottish Administration].*

1.149

AMENDMENTS

1. Scotland Act 1998 (Consequential Modifications) (No.1) Order 1999 (SI 1999/1042), art.5 and Sch.3, Pt I, para.4.
2. National Assembly for Wales (Transfer of Functions) Order 2000 (SI 2000/253), art.7 and Sch.5, para.3 (February 16, 2000).
3. Constitutional Reform Act 2005, Sch.4, paras 271 and 272 (April 3, 2006).

GENERAL NOTE

See the note to s.5.

1.150

Social Security Act 1998

Constitution of appeal tribunals

1.151   **7.**—*(1) Subject to subsection (2) below, an appeal tribunal shall consist of one, two or three members drawn by the President from the panel constituted under section 6 above*

(2) The member, or (as the case may be) at least one member, of an appeal tribunal must—
  (a) have a general qualification (construed in accordance with section 71 of the Courts and Legal Services Act 1990); or
  (b) be an advocate or solicitor in Scotland.

(3) Where an appeal tribunal has more than one member—
  (a) the President shall nominate one of the members as chairman;
  (b) decisions shall be taken by a majority of votes; and
  (c) unless regulations otherwise provide, the chairman shall have any casting vote.

(4) Where it appears to an appeal tribunal that a matter before it involves a question of fact of special difficulty, then, unless regulations otherwise provide, the tribunal may require one or more experts to provide assistance to it in dealing with the question.

(5) In subsection (4) above "expert" means a member of the panel constituted under section 6 above who appears to the appeal tribunal concerned to have knowledge or experience which would be relevant in determining the question of fact of special difficulty.

(6) Regulations shall make provision with respect to—
  (a) the composition of appeal tribunals;
  (b) the procedure to be followed in allocating cases among differently constituted tribunals; and
  (c) the manner in which expert assistance is to be given under subsection (4) above.

(7) Schedule 1 to this Act shall have effect for supplementing this section.

GENERAL NOTE

1.152   See regs 6 and 16 of the Child Trust Funds (Appeals) Regulations 2005.

See also the note to s.5. Does the failure to apply this section to tax credit appeals throw further doubt on the validity of regs 9 and 19 of the Tax Credits (Appeals) (No.2) Regulations 2002?

Appeal to appeal tribunal

1.153   **12.**—[²(1) An appeal which is to an appeal tribunal by virtue of section 63 of the Tax Credits Act 2002, including an application for a direction under section 19(9) of that Act, (a "tax credit appeal") may be brought by—
  (a) a claimant whose claim for a tax credit is the subject of the appeal;
  (b) the person on whom the penalty to which the appeal relates was imposed;
  (c) the person applying for the direction under section 19(9) of that Act; or
  (d) such other person as may be prescribed.]
(2)–(6) [¹. . .]

(7) Regulations may make provision as to the manner in which, and the time within which, appeals are to be brought [², and may in particular extend the time limit for giving notice of appeal specified in section 39(1) of the Tax Credits Act 2002].

(1998 c.14, s.12)

(8) In deciding [² a tax credit appeal] [³ *a child trust fund appeal*], an appeal tribunal—
   (a) [¹. . .]
   (b) shall not take into account any circumstances not obtaining at the time when the decision appealed against was made.
(9) [¹. . .].

MODIFICATIONS

1. Modifications applying to both tax credit appeals and child trust fund appeals by virtue of reg.4 of the Tax Credits (Appeals) Regulations 2002 (SI 2002/2926) and reg.6 of the Child Trust Funds (Non-tax Appeals) Regulations 2005 (SI 2005/191).
2. Modifications applying only to tax credit appeals by virtue of reg.4 of the Tax Credits (Appeals) Regulations 2002 (SI 2002/2926).
3. Modifications applying only to child trust fund appeals by virtue of reg.6 of the Child Trust Funds (Non-tax Appeals) Regulations 2005 (SI 2005/191).

GENERAL NOTE

The unmodified version of this section provides for a right of appeal to an appeal tribunal. This modified version makes only ancillary provision because the rights of appeal are to be found in s.39 of the Tax Credits Act, as modified by s.63 and in ss.21 and 23 of the Child Trust Funds Act 2004, as modified by s.24.

Subsection (8)(a) is not applied to either tax credit appeals or child trust fund appeals. However, it is suggested that s.39(5) of the Tax Credits Act 2002 and s.23(5) of the 2004 Act have much the same effect as subs.(8)(a) would have had.

1.154

Subs.(8)(b)

This prevents a tribunal from taking account of any circumstances not obtaining at the date of the decision against which the appeal has been brought, effectively requiring that new circumstances first be drawn to the attention of HMRC so that they can consider their effect before a tribunal does. The phrase "circumstances not obtaining at the time when the decision appealed against was made" has been held not to prevent a tribunal from considering circumstances that had obtained before that date, even if they had ceased to exist by the time of the decision under appeal (*CIS/2428/1999*). Any other approach would be absurd.

Tribunals are also entitled to have regard to evidence that was not in existence at the date of HMRC's decision, provided it is relevant to circumstances obtaining at or before that date (*R(DLA) 2/01, R(DLA) 2/03*).

1.155

Redetermination etc. of appeals by tribunal

13.—(1) This section applies where an application is made to a person under section 14(10)(a) below for leave to appeal from a decision of an appeal tribunal.

(2) If the person considers that the decision was erroneous in point of law, he may set aside the decision and refer the case either for redetermination by the tribunal or for determination by a differently constituted tribunal.

(3) [². . .]
[¹(4) In [³. . .] section 14 below "the principal parties" means—
   (a) the persons mentioned in subsection (3)(a) and (b) of that section, [². . .]
   (b) [². . .].

1.156

AMENDMENT AND MODIFICATIONS

1. Social Security Contributions (Transfer of Functions, etc.) Act 1999, Sch.7, para.26 (April 1, 1999). Note that subs.(4) is applied to tax credit appeals by virtue

Social Security Act 1998

of reg.5 of the Tax Credits (Appeals) Regulations 2002 (SI 2002/2926) but is omitted for the purposes of child trust fund appeals by virtue of reg.7 of the Child Trust Funds (Non-tax Appeals) Regulations 2005 (SI 2005/191).

2. Modifications applying to both tax credit appeals and child trust fund appeals by virtue of reg.5 of the Tax Credits (Appeals) Regulations 2002 (SI 2002/2926) and reg.7 of the Child Trust Funds (Non-tax Appeals) Regulations 2005 (SI 2005/191).

3. Modification applying only to tax credit appeals by virtue of reg.5 of the Tax Credits (Appeals) Regulations 2002 (SI 2002/2926).

GENERAL NOTE

1.157   By virtue of reg.5 of the Tax Credits (Appeals) Regulations 2002 (SI 2002/2926) and reg.7 of the Child Trust Funds (Non-tax Appeals) Regulations 2005 (SI 2005/191), this section does not apply at all to tax credit penalty appeals under Sch.2 to the Tax Credits Act 2002 or child trust fund penalty appeals under s.21(10) of the Child Trust Funds Act 2004. That is because such penalty appeals are not confined to points of law.

Note that subs.(3) (which requires a legally qualified panel member to set aside a decision where both parties express the view that it is erroneous in point of law) is not applied to any tax credit or child trust fund cases. A legally qualified panel member must be satisfied that a decision is erroneous in point of law before setting it aside. The provision is therefore a useful way of avoiding unnecessary appeals. In practice, all applications for leave to appeal are considered by salaried legally qualified panel members (see reg.27(5) of the Tax Credits (Appeals) (No.2) Regulations 2002 and reg.25(6) of the Child Trust Fund (Appeals) Regulations 2005) who therefore act as a first stage court of appeal from fee-paid panel members. This is quicker than referring cases to the fee-paid legally qualified panel members and the process is speeded up further because HMRC have waived the right to make representations in cases where the legally qualified panel member is minded to set aside a decision in a case where a claimant has applied for leave to appeal. However, it is a breach of the rules of natural justice not to allow a claimant to make representations before setting aside a decision on HMRC's application (*CIS/4533/2001*).

A decision may not be set aside under this section if the legally qualified panel member has no power to grant leave to appeal due to the application being too late or there being no statement of reasons (see the note to reg.27 of the Tax Credits (Appeals) (No.2) Regulations 2002) (*CDLA/1685/2004*). Nor may a decision be set aside under this section once an application for leave to appeal has been determined and leave has been granted (*CF/6923/1999*) but it is less clear whether a refusal of leave to one party prevents the decision being set aside following an application by the other, at any rate if the first applicant has not made an application to a Commissioner.

Appeal from tribunal to Commissioner

1.158   **14.**—(1) Subject to the provisions of this section, an appeal lies to a Commissioner from any decision of an appeal tribunal [².. .] on the ground- that the decision of the tribunal was erroneous in point of law.

(2) [¹.. .].

(3) [¹.. .] An appeal lies under this section at the instance of any of the following—

(a) the [²Board];
(b) the claimant and such other person as may be prescribed;
[³*(b) the appellant in the child trust fund appeal;*]
(c) in any of the cases mentioned in subsection (5) below, a trade union; and
(d) [².. .].
(4) [².. .].

(1998 c.14, s.14)

(5) The following are the cases in which an appeal lies at the instance of a trade union—
  (a) where the claimant is a member of the union at the time of the appeal and was so immediately before the matter in question arose;
  (b) where that matter in any way relates to a deceased person who was a member of the union at the time of his death;
  (c) [². . .].

(6) Subsections [¹. . .], (3) and (5) above, as they apply to a trade union, apply also to any other association which exists to promote the interests and welfare of its members.

(7) If each of the principal parties [³ Board and the appellant] to the appeal expresses the view that the decision appealed against was erroneous in point of law, the Commissioner may set aside the decision and refer the case to a tribunal with directions for its determination.

(8) Where the Commissioner holds that the decision appealed against was erroneous in point of law, he shall set it aside and—
  (a) he shall have power—
    (i) to give the decision which he considers the tribunal should have given, if he can do so without making fresh or further findings of fact; or
    (ii) if he considers it expedient, to make such findings and to give such decision as he considers appropriate in the light of them; and
  (b) in any other case he shall refer the case to a tribunal with directions for its determination.

(9) Subject to any direction of the Commissioner, a reference under subsection (7) or (8)(b) above shall be to a differently constituted tribunal.

(10) No appeal lies under this section without the leave—
  (a) of the person who constituted, or was the chairman of, the tribunal when the decision was given or, in a prescribed case, the leave of such other person as may be prescribed; or
  (b) subject to and in accordance with regulations, of a Commissioner.

(11) Regulations may make provision as to the manner in which, and the time within which, appeals are to be brought and applications made for leave to appeal.

(12) Schedule 4 to this Act shall have effect with respect to the appointment, remuneration and tenure of office of Commissioners and other matters relating to them.

AMENDMENTS AND MODIFICATIONS

1. Social Security Contributions (Transfer of Functions, etc.) Act 1999, Sch.7, para.27 (April 1, 1999).

2. Modifications applying to both tax credit appeals and child trust fund appeals by virtue of reg.6 of the Tax Credits (Appeals) Regulations 2002 (SI 2002/2926) and reg.8 of the Child Trust Funds (Non-tax Appeals) Regulations 2005 (SI 2005/191).

3. Modifications applying only to child trust fund appeals by virtue of reg.8 of the Child Trust Funds (Non-tax Appeals) Regulations 2005 (SI 2005/191). In subs.(7) the added words are in substitution for the words "principal parties".

GENERAL NOTE

By virtue of regs 6 and 7 of the Tax Credits (Appeals) Regulations 2002 (SI 2002/2926) and regs 8 and 9 of the Child Trust Funds (Non-tax Appeals) Regulations 2005 (SI 2005/191), subss.(1) to (10) do not apply at all to tax credit

1.159

Social Security Act 1998

penalty appeals or to child trust fund penalty appeals. The right of appeal to a Commissioner in such cases is conferred by Sch.2 to the Tax Credits Act 2002, as modified by s.63 of that Act and by s.21(10) of the Child Trust Funds Act 2004 as modified by s.24(2) of that Act and is not confined to points of law. Consequently, the words "and applications made for leave to appeal" are omitted from subs.(11) in penalty cases.

By virtue of reg.6 of the Tax Credits (Appeals) Regulations 2002 (SI 2002/2926) and reg.8 of the Child Trust Funds (Non-tax Appeals) Regulations 2005 (SI 2005/191), subss.(3)(c), (5) and (6) apply to tax credit appeals but not to child trust fund appeals.

Social Security Commissioners are judicial office holders of the same seniority as circuit judges. However, their decisions set precedents that are binding on HMRC and tribunals (see the section on *Using this Book* at the beginning of this volume or the note to this section in Volume III). They deal with the majority of appeals on the papers, only holding oral hearings occasionally. They have no power to award costs (*R(FC) 2/90*). Community legal service funding is not generally available for legal representation in England and Wales, although s.6(8)(b) of the Access to Justice Act 1999 enables the Lord Chancellor to authorise the Legal Services Commission to fund representation either in specified circumstances or in an individual case. Grants of funding under these provisions are rare. There has only been one year in which more than five grants have been made for proceedings before Commissioners. On the other hand, legal aid is available in Scotland (Civil Legal Aid (Scotland) Regulations 2002, regs 4(k) and 47). Entitlement to legal aid depends on the applicant's means but any benefit recovered in the proceedings before the Commissioner is not taken into account when calculating the amount of the net liability to the legal aid fund (*ibid.*, reg.33(a)(xi)). A copy of any funding notice issued by the Legal Services Commission or, in Scotland, a copy of a legal aid certificate, must be sent to the Commissioners' office (see reg.6A of the Social Security Commissioners (Procedure) (Tax Credit Appeals) Regulations 2002 and reg.7 of the Social Security Commissioners (Procedure) (Child Trust Funds) Regulations 2005).

Subs. (1)

1.160   Except in penalty appeals, an appeal to a Commissioner lies only on a point of law. This is as opposed to a point of fact and means, in effect, that a Commissioner will not overturn a tribunal's decision unless the tribunal misunderstood the law or there was something wrong with the tribunal's process of reasoning or there was a breach of procedural rules or some other unfairness in the process. In *R(A) 1/72* and *R(IS) 11/99*, Commissioners listed types of errors that would amount to errors of law. More recently, in *CI/1814/2004*, a Tribunal of Commissioners adopted a passage from the judgment of Brooke LJ in *R. (Iran) v Secretary of State for the Home Department* [2005] EWCA Civ 982 and said that that a tribunal errs in law in—

"(i) making perverse or irrational findings on a matter or matters that were material to the outcome ('material matters');
(ii) failing to give reasons or any adequate reasons for findings on material matters;
(iii) failing to take into account and/or resolve conflicts of fact or opinion on material matters;
(iv) giving weight to immaterial matters;
(v) making a material misdirection of law on any material matter;
(vi) committing or permitting a procedural or other irregularity capable of making a material difference to the outcome or the fairness of proceedings"; . . .

"Each of these grounds for detecting any error of law contains the word 'material' (or 'immaterial'). Errors of law of which it can be said that they would have made no difference to the outcome do not matter."

The Tribunal of Commissioners emphasised that perversity or irrationality was very difficult to show. An assessment of disablement is perverse only if it is "so wildly wrong that it can be set aside" (*Murrell v Secretary of State for Social Services* (reported as an appendix to *R(I) 3/84*)), and a finding of fact is perverse if it is based on a misunderstanding that "is plain and incontrovertible and where there is no room for difference about it" (*Braintree District Council v Thompson* [2005] EWCA Civ 178, a housing benefit case in which the Court of Appeal said that a Deputy Commissioner had not been entitled to substitute his view of the facts for the view of the tribunal). It is particularly difficult to show that a decision is irrational or perverse where it required an element of judgment. In *Moyna v Secretary of State for Work and Pensions* [2003] UKHL 44, [2003] 1 W.L.R. 1929 (also reported as *R(DLA) 7/03*). Lord Hoffman, with whom the other members of the House of Lords agreed, said:

> "In any case in which a tribunal has to apply a standard with a greater or lesser degree of imprecision and to take a number of factors into account, there are bound to be cases in which it will be impossible for a reviewing court to say that the tribunal must have erred in deciding the case either way: see *George Mitchell (Chesterhall) Ltd v Finney Lock Seeds Ltd* [1983] 2 A.C. 803, 815–816."

It is necessary to show some flaw in the reasoning.

Although tribunals may be found to have erred in their approach to the evidence before them, Commissioners have often pointed out that tribunals cannot be criticised for not taking account of evidence that was not before them. In *CDLA/7980/1995*, the Commissioner said that—

> "Finality is another important principle. Parties cannot demand a rehearing simply because, at the original hearing, they failed to adduce the right evidence, failed to ask the right questions or failed to advance the right arguments."

However, there is a limited exception to this rule. In *E v Secretary of State for the Home Department* [2004] EWCA Civ 49; [2004] 2 W.L.R. 1351, the Court of Appeal recognised that a decision might be erroneous on point of law where a tribunal had made a mistake of fact that gave rise to unfairness but the decision was not erroneous in point of law on the traditional grounds. At para.(66), they identified four requirements:

> "First, there must have been a mistake as to an existing fact, including a mistake as to the availability of evidence on a particular matter. Secondly, the fact or evidence must have been 'established' [on the appeal on a point of law], in the sense that it was uncontentious or objectively verifiable. Thirdly, the appellant (or his advisors) must not have been responsible for the mistake. Fourthly, the mistake must have played a material (not necessarily decisive) part in the tribunal's reasoning."

For what amounts to a failure to give reasons, or adequate reasons, see the note to reg.21 of the Tax Credits (Appeals) (No.2) Regulations 2002.

Whether a breach of procedural rules, other than the basic rules of natural justice, renders a decision invalid or erroneous in point of law is to be determined by considering whether the legislature intended that to be the effect of such a breach (*R. v Soneji* [2005] UKHL 49; [2006] 1 A.C. 340). Therefore, not every procedural error entitles a party to have a decision set aside on appeal. It largely depends on whether there was any unfairness as a result of the breach.

The basic rules of natural justice are that every party should have a proper opportunity to present his or her case, that there should be no bias and that a decision should be based on the evidence. The rule against bias has been considered in detail in *Locabail (UK) Ltd v Bayfield Properties Ltd* [2000] Q.B. 451. Where a member of a tribunal has any direct personal interest, apart from the most trivial, in the outcome of proceedings, he or she is automatically disqualified from hearing the case, irrespective of his or her knowledge of the interest. However, a party may waive a right to object, provided he or she does so in unequivocal terms, knowing all the material facts. In other cases, the question is whether a reasonable person with knowledge of the relevant circumstances would consider that there was any real danger of bias, in the sense that the tribunal member might unfairly regard with favour or disfavour a party in the proceedings (*Porter v Magill* [2001] UKHL 67; [2002] 2 A.C. 357) and, on appeal, it will be relevant whether the tribunal member knew of the connection with the party because if he or she did not, no favour or disfavour would have been shown. It was stressed in *CS/1753/00*, that the issue was whether there was a likelihood of bias, not whether there was actual bias. Appearances are therefore important and a decision may be set aside if a tribunal member goves the appearance of having fallen asleep (*Stainsby v Datapulse* [2003] EWCA Civ 1951; [2004] I.C.R. 523) but in *Locobail* itself, it was stressed that "the mere fact that a judge, earlier in the same case or in a previous case, had commented adversely on a party or witness, or found the evidence of a party or witness to be unreliable, would not without more found a sustainable objection." In *Lawal v Northern Spirit* [2003] UKHL 35; [2003] I.C.R. 856, the House of Lords held there to have been apparent bias where a party was represented by a barrister who was a part-time judge of the Employment Appeal Tribunal before whom he was appearing. *Lawal* was followed in *Secretary of State for Work and Pensions v Cunningham* [2004] S.L.T. 1007 (also reported as *R(DLA) 7/04*), where a tribunal had relied on a medical report by an examining medical practitioner with whom two members of the tribunal had sat previously and the Court of Session held there had been apparent bias. On the other hand, in *Gillies v Secretary of State for Work and Pensions* [2006] UKHL 2; [2006] 1 W.L.R. 781, it was held by the House of Lords that there was no appearance of bias merely because a member of a tribunal also acted as an examining medical practitioner for the Secretary of State. A long-standing personal friendship with a witness will also give rise to an appearance of bias and a judge was wrong to take into account the inconvenience to the parties in having to adjourn when he refused to recuse himself. "There was either a real possibility of bias, in which case the judge was disqualified by the principle of judicial impartiality, or there was not, in which case there was no valid objection to trial by him." (*AWG Group Ltd v Morrison* [2006] EWCA Civ 6; [2006] 1 W.L.R. 1163 at [20]). Friendship with an advocate will not give rise to an appearance of bias unless the advocate is "a domestic partner of the judge or any other person of either sex in a close personal relationship with the judge" or "a companion or employee of the judge and who lives in the judge's household" (*Guide to Judicial Conduct*, para.7.2.8, which also says that a judge should not try a case in which his or her spouse, children, children-in-law or other close relative living in the judge's household is an advocate).

Subs. (7)

1.161   A setting aside under this subsection should not be cited as authority for any proposition of law (*CI/3596/2001*). This subsection does not apply in penalty cases.

Subs. (8)

1.162   Although an appeal lies only on a point of law, once a Commissioner has found an error of law and has set a decision aside, he or she may substitute a final decision instead of remitting the case to a tribunal, even where that involves findings of fact. A successful appellant cannot insist on a Commissioner referring a case to another tribunal under para.(8)(b) so that the tribunal can consider a factual case entirely different from the one presented to the tribunal whose decision has been set aside if the Commissioner is able, under para.(8)(a)(i) to give the decision the first tribunal should have given on the basis of its findings of fact, especially if the claimant was legally represented before the first tribunal (*CH/2484/2005*, a decision of a Tribunal of Commissioners).

Subs. (10)

1.163   Regulation 27(5) of the Tax Credits (Appeals) (No.2) Regulations 2002 and reg.25(6) of the Child Trust Funds (Appeals) Regulations 2005 are made under this subsection.

Leave to appeal may be granted on grounds other than those raised by the parties (*Krasniqi v Secretary of State for the Home Department* [2006] EWCA Civ 391). Nonetheless, a Commissioner considering an application for leave to appeal is not bound to trawl through the papers looking for grounds that have not been advanced by the applicant (*R.(Anayet Begum) v Social Security Commissioner* [2002] EWHC

(1998 c.14, s.14)

401 (Admin); *Mooney v Secretary of State for Work and Pensions* [2004] S.L.T. 1141 (also reported *sub nom. Mooney v Social Security Commissioner as R(DLA) 5/04*).

If a Commissioner refuses leave to appeal against a tribunal's decision, there is no appeal against the refusal of leave but it may be challenged by way of an application for judicial review (*Bland v Chief Supplementary Benefit Officer* [1983] 1 W.L.R. 262 (also reported as *R(SB) 12/83*)).

Subs. (11)

See reg.27 of the Tax Credits (Appeals) Regulations 2002, regs 6B to 11 of the Social Security Commissioners (Procedure) (Tax Credits Appeals) Regulations 2002, reg.25 of the Child Trust Funds (Appeals) Regulations 2005 and regs 8 to 13 of the Social Security Commissioners (Procedure) (Child Trust Funds) Regulations 2005.

1.164

Appeal from a Commissioner on point of law

15.—(1) Subject to subsections (2) and (3) below, an appeal on a question of law shall lie to the appropriate court from any decision of a Commissioner.

1.165

(2) No appeal under this section shall lie from a decision except—
  (a) with the leave of the Commissioner who gave the decision or, in a prescribed case, with the leave of a Commissioner selected in accordance with regulations; or
  (b) if he refuses leave, with the leave of the appropriate court.

(3) An application for leave under this section in respect of a Commissioner's decision may only be made by—
  (a) a person who, before the proceedings before the Commissioner were begun, was entitled to appeal to the Commissioner from the decision to which the Commissioner's decision relates;
  (b) any other person who was a party to the proceedings in which the first decision mentioned in paragraph (a) above was given;
  (c) any other person who is authorised by regulations to apply for leave;
and regulations may make provision with respect to the manner in which and the time within which applications must be made to a Commissioner for leave under this section and with respect to the procedure for dealing with such applications.

(4) On an application to a Commissioner for leave under this section it shall be the duty of the Commissioner to specify as the appropriate court—
  (a) the Court of Appeal if it appears to him that the relevant place is in England or Wales;
  (b) the Court of Session if it appears to him that the relevant place is in Scotland; and
  (c) the Court of Appeal in Northern Ireland if it appears to him that the relevant place is in Northern Ireland,
except that if it appears to him, having regard to the circumstances of the case and in particular to the convenience of the persons who may be parties to the proposed appeal, that he should specify a different court mentioned in paragraphs (a) to (c) above as the appropriate court, it shall be his duty to specify that court as the appropriate court.

(5) In this section—
  "the appropriate court", except in subsection (4) above, means the court specified in pursuance of that subsection;
  "the relevant place", in relation to an application for leave to appeal from a decision of a Commissioner, means the premises where the person or authority whose decision was the subject of the Commissioner's decision usually exercises his or its functions.

Social Security Act 1998

General Note

1.166 This section is applied to tax credit appeals and child trust fund appeal by reg.8 of the Tax Credits (Appeals) Regulations 2002 (SI 2002/2926) and reg.10 of the Child Trust Funds (Non-tax Appeals) Regulations 2005 (SI 2005/191).

For what amounts to a point of law see the note to s.14(1).

A decision of a Commissioner refusing leave to appeal against a tribunal's decision cannot be challenged by way of an appeal under this section but it may be challenged by way of an application for judicial review (*Bland v Chief Supplementary Benefit Officer* [1983] 1 W.L.R. 262 (also reported as *R(SB) 12/83*)).

The Court of Appeal takes a robust approach to Commissioners' decisions (*Cooke v Secretary of State for Social Security* [2001] EWCA Civ 734 (reported as *R(DLA) 6/01*), so that in practice an applicant for leave to appeal to the Court of Appeal is likely to have to show that the Commissioner was probably wrong, rather than just possibly wrong.

Procedure

1.167 **16.**—(1) Regulations ("procedure regulations") may make any such provision as is specified in Schedule 5 to this Act.

(2) Procedure regulations prescribing the procedure to be followed in cases before a Commissioner shall provide that any hearing shall be in public except in so far as the Commissioner for special reasons otherwise directs.

(3) It is hereby declared—
  (a) that the power to prescribe procedure includes power to make provision as to the representation of one person, at any hearing of a case, by another person whether having professional qualifications or not;
  [¹. . .].
  (b) [¹. . .].
(4) [¹. . .].
(5) [¹. . .].

(6) If it appears to a Commissioner that a matter before him involves a question of fact of special difficulty, he may direct that in dealing with that matter he shall have the assistance of one or more experts.

In this subsection, "expert" means a person appearing to the Commissioner to have knowledge or experience which would be relevant in determining the question of fact of special difficulty.

(7) If it appears to the Chief Commissioner (or, in the case of his inability to act, to such other of the Commissioners as he may have nominated to act for the purpose) that—
  (a) an application for leave under section 14(10)(b) above; or
  (b) an appeal;
falling to be heard by one of the Commissioners involves a question of law of special difficulty, he may direct that the application or appeal be dealt with, not by that Commissioner alone, but by a tribunal consisting of any three or more of the Commissioners.

If the decision of the tribunal is not unanimous, the decision of the majority shall be the decision of the tribunal; and the presiding Commissioner shall have a casting vote if the votes are equally divided.

(8) Where a direction is given under subsection (7)(a) above, section 14(10)(b) above shall have effect as if the reference to a Commissioner were a reference to such a tribunal as is mentioned in subsection (7) above.

(9) Except so far as it may be applied in relation to England and Wales by procedure regulations, Part I of the Arbitration Act 1996 shall not apply to any proceedings under this Chapter.

(1998 c.14, s.16)

MODIFICATION

1. Modifications applying to both tax credit appeals and child trust fund appeals by virtue of reg.9 of the Tax Credits (Appeals) Regulations 2002 (SI 2002/2926) and reg.11 of the Child Trust Funds (Non-tax Appeals) Regulations 2005 (SI 2005/191).

Finality of decisions

17.—[²(1) Subject to the provisions of—
(a) sections 12 to 16 of this Act, and
(b) the Tax Credits Act 2002,
any decision made in accordance with those provisions in respect of an appeal which, by virtue of section 63 of the Tax Credits Act 2002 (or of provisions of this Act applied by regulations made under that section), is to an appeal tribunal or lies to a Commissioner, shall be final.]

[³*(1) Subject to the provisions of—*
(a) sections 12 to 16, and 28 of this Act (as modified by the Child Trust Funds
    (Non-tax Appeals) Regulations 2004), and
(b) sections 21(9) and (10) and 22 to 24 of the Child Trust Funds Act 2004,
any decision made in accordance with those provisions in respect of a child trust fund appeal which, in accordance with section 24 of the Child Trust Funds Act 2004, is to an appeal tribunal or lies to a Commissioner, shall be final.]

(2) If and to the extent that regulations so provide, any finding of fact or other determination embodied in or necessary to such a decision, or on which such a decision is based, shall be conclusive for the purposes of—
(a) further such decisions;
(b) [¹. . .];
(c) [¹. . .].

1.168

MODIFICATIONS

1. Modifications applying to both tax credit appeals and child trust fund appeals by virtue of reg.10 of the Tax Credits (Appeals) Regulations 2002 (SI 2002/2926) and reg.12 of the Child Trust Funds (Non-tax Appeals) Regulations 2005 (SI 2005/191).
2. Modification applying only to tax credit appeals by virtue of reg.10 of the Tax Credits (Appeals) Regulations 2002 (SI 2002/2926).
3. Modification applying only to child trust fund appeals by virtue of reg.12 of the Child Trust Funds (Non-tax Appeals) Regulations 2005 (SI 2005/191).

Correction of errors and setting aside of decisions

28.—(1) Regulations may make provision with respect to—
(a) the correction of accidental errors in any decision or record of a decision made under any relevant enactment; and
(b) the setting aside of any such decision in a case where it appears just to set the decision aside on the ground that—
   (i) a document relating to the proceedings in which the decision was given was not sent to, or was not received at an appropriate time by, a party to the proceedings or a party's representative or was not received at an appropriate time by the body or person who gave the decision; or
   (ii) a party to the proceedings or a party's representative was not present at a hearing related to the proceedings.
(1A) [¹. . .].

1.169

(2) Nothing in subsection (1) above shall be construed as derogating from any power to correct errors or set aside decisions which is exercisable apart from regulations made by virtue of that subsection.

[²(3) In this section "relevant enactment" means—
(a) any of sections 12 to 17 above, and
(b) any enactment contained or referred to in section 19(10), 38 or 39 of, or Schedule 2 to, the Tax Credits Act 2002.]

[³*(3) In this section, "relevant enactment" means—*
(a) any of sections 12 to 17 above (as modified by the Child Trust Funds (Non-tax Appeals) Regulations 2004), and
(b) sections 21(9) and (10) and 22 to 24 of the Child Trust Funds Act 2004.]

MODIFICATIONS

1. Modifications applying to both tax credit appeals and child trust fund appeals by virtue of reg.11 of the Tax Credits (Appeals) Regulations 2002 (SI 2002/2926) and reg.13 of the Child Trust Funds (Non-tax Appeals) Regulations 2005 (SI 2005/191).
2. Modification applying only to tax credit appeals by virtue of reg.11 of the Tax Credits (Appeals) Regulations 2002 (SI 2002/2926).
3. Modification applying only to child trust fund appeals by virtue of reg.13 of the Child Trust Funds (Non-tax Appeals) Regulations 2005 (SI 2005/191).

Supplemental

Interpretation etc. of chapter 2

1.170   **39.**—(1) In this chapter—
"appeal tribunal" means an appeal tribunal constituted under Chapter I of this Part;
[² *"the Board" means the Commissioners of Inland Revenue;*]
[⁴ *"child trust fund appeal" means an appeal under section 22 of the Child Trust Funds Act 2004 which, by virtue of section 24 of that Act, is to an appeal tribunal or lies to a Social Security Commissioner;*]
[³*"claimant" means a person who makes (whether or not jointly with another) a claim for a tax credit in accordance with sections 3 and 4 of the Tax Credits Act 2002, and includes a person entitled to make such a claim on behalf of another person by virtue of regulation 17 or 18 of the Tax Credits (Claims and Notifications) Regulations 2002;*]
"Commissioner" [¹(except in the expression "tax appeal Commissioners)] means the Chief Social Security Commissioner or any other Social Security Commissioner, and includes a tribunal of three or more Commissioners constituted under section 16(7) above;
[². . .].
[². . .].
(2) [². . .].
(3) [². . .].

AMENDMENTS AND MODIFICATIONS

1. Social Security Contributions (Transfer of Functions, etc.) Act 1999, Sch.7, para.35 (April 1, 1999).
2. Modifications applying to both tax credit appeals and child trust fund appeals by virtue of reg.11 of the Tax Credits (Appeals) Regulations 2002 (SI 2002/2926) and reg.13 of the Child Trust Funds (Non-tax Appeals) Regulations 2005 (SI 2005/191).

(1998 c.14, s.39)

3. Modification applying only to tax credit appeals by virtue of reg.11 of the Tax Credits (Appeals) Regulations 2002 (SI 2002/2926).

4. Modification applying only to child trust fund appeals by virtue of reg.13 of the Child Trust Funds (Non-tax Appeals) Regulations 2005 (SI 2005/191).

Regulations and orders

79.—*(1) Subject to [¹subsection (2)] below and paragraph 6 of Schedule 4 to this Act, regulations under this Act shall be made by the Secretary of State*

(2) Regulations with respect to proceedings before the Commissioners (whether for the determination of any matter or for leave to appeal to or from the Commissioners) shall be made by the Lord Chancellor; and where the Lord Chancellor proposes to make regulations under this Act it shall be his duty to consult the Lord Advocate with respect to the proposal.

[¹(2A) . . .]

(3) Powers under this Act to make regulations or orders are exercisable by statutory instrument.

(4) Any power conferred by this Act to make regulations or orders may be exercised—

(a) either in relation to all cases to which the power extends, or in relation to those cases subject to specified exceptions, or in relation to any specified cases or classes of case;

(b) so as to make, as respects the cases in relation to which it is exercised—

(i) the full provision to which the power extends or any less provision (whether by way of exception or otherwise);

(ii) the same provision for all cases in relation to which the power is exercised, or different provision for different cases or different classes of case or different provision as respects the same case or class of case for different purposes of this Act;

(iii) any such provision either unconditionally or subject to any specified condition;

and where such a power is expressed to be exercisable for alternative purposes it may be exercised in relation to the same case for any or all of those purposes.

(5) Powers to make regulations for the purposes of any one provision of this Act are without prejudice to powers to make regulations for the purposes of any other provision.

(6) Without prejudice to any specific provision in this Act, a power conferred by this Act to make regulations includes power to make thereby such incidental, supplementary, consequential or transitional provision as appears to the authority making the regulations to be expedient for the purposes of those regulations.

(7) Without prejudice to any specific provisions in this Act, a power conferred by any provision of this Act to make regulations includes power to provide for a person to exercise a discretion in dealing with any matter.

[¹(8) . . .]

(9) In this section "Commissioner" has the same meaning as in Chapter II of Part I.

MODIFICATION

1. Child Trust Funds (Non-tax Appeals) Regulations 2005 (SI 2005/191), reg.15(2).

GENERAL NOTE

This section is applied to child trust fund appeals only by reg.15 of the Child Trust Funds (Non-tax Appeals) Regulations 2005 (SI 2005/191). See the note to s.5.

Social Security Act 1998

Parliamentary control of regulations

1.173   **80.**—(1) *Subject to the provisions of this section, a statutory instrument containing (whether alone or with other provisions) regulations under—*
  (a) *section 7, 12(2) or 72 above; or*
  (b) *paragraph 12 of Schedule 1, paragraph 9 of Schedule 2 or paragraph 2 of Schedule 5 to this Act,*
shall not be made unless a draft of the instrument has been laid before Parliament and been approved by a resolution of each House of Parliament.

(2) A statutory instrument—
  (a) *which contains (whether alone or with other provisions) regulations made under this Act by the Secretary of State; and*
  (b) *which is not subject to any requirement that a draft of the instrument be laid before and approved by a resolution of each House of Parliament,*
shall be subject to annulment in pursuance of a resolution of either House of Parliament.

(3) A statutory instrument—
  (a) *which contains (whether alone or with other provisions) regulations made under this Act by the Lord Chancellor; and*
  (b) *which is not subject to any requirement that a draft of the instrument be laid before and approved by a resolution of each House of Parliament,*
shall be subject to annulment in pursuance of a resolution of either House of Parliament.

GENERAL NOTE

1.174   This section is applied to child trust fund appeals only by reg.15 of the Child Trust Funds (Non-tax Appeals) Regulations 2005 (SI 2005/191). See the note to s.5.

Interpretation: general

1.175   **84.** *In this Act—*
  "the Administration Act" means the Social Security Administration Act 1992;
  "the Child Support Act" means the Child Support Act 1991;
  "the Contributions and Benefits Act" means the Social Security Contributions and Benefits Act 1992;
  "the Jobseekers Act" means the Jobseekers Act 1995;
  "the Vaccine Damage Payments Act" means the Vaccine Damage Payments Act 1979;
  "prescribe" means prescribe by regulations.

GENERAL NOTE

1.176   This section is applied to child trust fund appeals only by reg.15 of the Child Trust Funds (Non-tax Appeals) Regulations 2005 (SI 2005/191).

SCHEDULE 1

Appeal Tribunals: Supplementary Provisions

[¹ . . .]

Functions of President

1.177   7. The President shall ensure that appropriate steps are taken by an appeal tribunal to secure the confidentiality, in such circumstances as may be prescribed, of any prescribed material or any prescribed classes or categories of material.

[¹ . . .]

Clerks to appeal tribunals

11. The Secretary of State may by regulations provide—
(a) for clerks to be assigned to service appeal tribunals; and
(b) for clerks so assigned to be responsible for summoning members of the panel constituted under section 6 above to serve on such tribunals.

Delegation of certain functions of appeal tribunals

12.—(1) The Secretary of State may by regulations provide—
(a) for [¹ the clerk to the appeal tribunal] to make any determinations which fall to be made by an appeal tribunal and which do not involve the determination of any appeal, application for leave to appeal or reference;
(b) for the procedure to be followed by [¹ the clerk to the appeal tribunal] in making such determinations;
(c) for the manner in which such determinations by [¹ the clerk to the appeal tribunal] may be called in question.
(2) A determination which would have the effect of preventing an appeal, application for leave to appeal or reference being determined by an appeal tribunal is not a determination of the appeal, application or reference for the purposes of sub-paragraph (1) above.
[¹ . . .].

AMENDMENT AND MODIFICATION

1. Child Trust Funds (Non-tax Appeals) Regulations 2005 (SI 2005/191), reg.5(2).

GENERAL NOTE

This schedule is applied to child trust fund appeals by reg.5 of the Child Trust Funds (Non-tax Appeals) Regulations 2005 (SI 2005/191). See the note to s.5.

SCHEDULE 4

SOCIAL SECURITY COMMISSIONERS

Appointment

1.—(1) Her Majesty may from time to time appoint, from among persons who have a 10 year general qualification or advocates or solicitors in Scotland of at least 10 years' standing—
(a) a Chief Social Security Commissioner; and
(b) such number of other Social Security Commissioners as Her Majesty thinks fit.
(2) If the Lord Chancellor considers that, in order to facilitate the disposal of the business of Social Security Commissioners, he should make an appointment in pursuance of this sub-paragraph, he may appoint—
(a) a person who has a 10-year general qualification; or
(b) an advocate or solicitor in Scotland of at least 10 years' standing; or
(c) a member of the bar of Northern Ireland or solicitor of the Supreme Court of Northern Ireland of at least 10 years' standing,
to be a Social Security Commissioner (but to be known as a deputy Commissioner) for such periodor on such occasions as the Lord Chancellor thinks fit.
(3) In this paragraph, "10-year general qualification" shall be construed in accordance with section 71 of the Courts and Legal Services Act 1990.

Remuneration, etc.

2. The Lord Chancellor shall pay to a Commissioner such salary or other remuneration, and such expenses incurred in connection with the work of a Commissioner or any tribunal presided over by a Commissioner, as he may determine.

3.—(1) The Lord Chancellor or, in Scotland, the *Board* may pay to any person who attends any proceedings under section 14 of this Act [², under section 6A of the Pensions Appeal Tribunals Act 1943] [¹or under paragraph 8 of Schedule 7 to the Child Support, Pensions and Social Security Act 2000] such travelling and other allowances as he may determine.
(2) In this paragraph the reference to travelling and other allowances includes a reference to compensation for loss of remunerative time.

Tenure of office

1.183 4.—(1) Commissioners shall vacate their offices on the day on which they attain the age of 70, but subject to section 26(4) to (6) of the Judicial Pensions and Retirement Act 1993 (power to authorise continuance in office up to the age of 75).

(2) Nothing in sub-paragraph (1) above or in section 13 or 32 of the Judicial Pensions Act 1981 (which relate to pensions for Commissioners) shall apply to a person by virtue of his appointment in pursuance of paragraph 1(2) above.

5.—(1) A Commissioner may be removed from office by the Lord Chancellor on the ground of incapacity or misbehaviour.

[³(1A) The Lord Chancellor may remove a person under sub-paragraph (1) only with the concurrence of the appropriate senior judge.

(1B) The appropriate senior judge is the Lord Chief Justice of England and Wales, unless the person exercises functions wholly or mainly in Scotland, in which case it is the Lord President of the Court of Session.]

(2) Nothing in sub-paragraph (1) above applies to a Commissioner appointed before May 23, 1980.

Delegation of functions

1.184 6. The Lord Chancellor may by regulations provide—
  (a) for officers authorised by the Lord Chancellor or, in Scotland, by the *Board* to make any determinations which fall to be made by Commissioners;
  (b) for the procedure to be followed by such officers in making such determinations;
  (c) for the manner in which such determinations by such officers may be called in question.

Certificates

1.185 7. A document bearing a certificate which—
  (a) is signed by a person authorised in that behalf by the *Board*; and
  (b) states that the document, apart from the certificate, is a record of a decision of a Commissioner;
shall be conclusive evidence of the decision; and a certificate purporting to be so signed shall be deemed to be so signed unless the contrary is proved.

Supplemental

1.186 8. Where the Lord Chancellor proposes to exercise a power conferred on him by paragraph 1(2), 5(1) or 6 above, it shall be his duty to consult the Lord Advocate with respect to the proposal.

AMENDMENTS

1. Child Support, Pensions and Social Security Act 2000, s.68 and Sch.7, para.22(3) (July 2, 2001).
2. Armed Forces (Pensions and Compensation Act 2004), s.7(2) (April 6, 2005).
3. Constitutional Reform Act 2005, s.15(1) and Sch.4, para.274 (April 3, 2006).

SCHEDULE 5

REGULATIONS AS TO PROCEDURE: PROVISION WHICH MAY BE MADE

1.187 1. Provision prescribing the procedure to be followed in connection with—
  (a) the making of decisions or determinations by [. . .], an appeal tribunal or a Commissioner; and
  (b) the withdrawal of claims, applications, appeals or references falling to be decided or determined by [. . .], an appeal tribunal or a Commissioner.

2. Provision as to the striking out or reinstatement of proceedings.

3. Provision as to the form which is to be used for any document, the evidence which is to be required and the circumstances in which any official record or certificate is to be sufficient or conclusive evidence.

4. Provision as to the time within which, or the manner in which—
  (a) any evidence is to be produced; or

(1998 c.14, Sch.5)

(b) any application, reference or appeal is to be made, *including provision extending the time limit for giving notice of appeal specified in section 39(1) of the Tax Credits Act 2002.*

5. Provision for summoning persons to attend and give evidence or produce documents and for authorising the administration of oaths to witnesses.

6. Provision with respect to the procedure to be followed on appeals to and in other proceedings before appeal tribunals.

7. Provision for authorising an appeal tribunal consisting of two or more members to proceed with any case, with the consent of the claimant, in the absence of any member.

8. Provision for empowering an appeal tribunal to give directions for the disposal of any purported appeal which the tribunal is satisfied that it does not have jurisdiction to entertain.

9. Provision for the non-disclosure to a person of the particulars of any medical advice or medical evidence given or submitted for the purposes of a determination.

Social Security Contributions (Transfer of Functions, etc.) Act 1999

(1999 c.2)

An Act to transfer from the Secretary of State to the Commissioners of Inland Revenue or the Treasury certain functions relating to national insurance contributions, the National Insurance Fund, statutory sick pay, statutory maternity pay or pension schemes and certain associated functions relating to benefits; to enable functions relating to any of those matters in respect of Northern Ireland to be transferred to the Secretary of State, the Commissioners of Inland Revenue or the Treasury; to make further provision, in connection with the functions transferred, as to the powers of the Commissioners of Inland Revenue, the making of decisions and appeals; to provide that rebates payable in respect of members of money purchase contracted-out pension schemes are to be payable out of the National Insurance Fund; and for connected purposes.

1.188

Arrangement of Sections

Part II

Decisions and Appeals

8. Decisions by officers of Board
9. Regulations with respect to decisions
10. Decisions varying or superseding earlier decisions
11. Appeals against decisions of Board
12. Exercise of right of appeal
13. Regulations with respect to appeals
14. Matters arising as respects decisions
15. *(Omitted)*
16. *(Omitted)*
17. Arrangements for discharge of decision-making functions
18. Amendments relating to decisions and appeals
19. Interpretation of Part II

1.189

Social Security Contributions (Transfer of Functions, etc.) Act 1999

Part III

Miscellaneous and Supplemental

27. Interpretation

Part II

Decisions and Appeals

Decisions by officers of Board

1.190   **8.**—(1) Subject to the provisions of this Part, it shall be for an officer of the Board—
(a) to decide whether for the purposes of Parts I to V of the Social Security Contributions and Benefits Act 1992 a person is or was an earner and, if so, the category of earners in which he is or was to be included;
(b) to decide whether a person is or was employed in employed earner's employment for the purposes of Part V of the Social Security Contributions and Benefits Act 1992 (industrial injuries);
(c) to decide whether a person is or was liable to pay contributions of any particular class and, if so, the amount that he is or was liable to pay,
(d) to decide whether a person is or was entitled to pay contributions of any particular class that he is or was not liable to pay and, if so, the amount that he is or was entitled to pay,
(e) to decide whether contributions of a particular class have been paid in respect of any period,
(f) subject to and in accordance with regulations made for the purposes of this paragraph by the Secretary of State with the concurrence of the Board, to decide any issue arising as to, or in connection with, entitlement to statutory sick pay, [⁴, statutory maternity pay, statutory paternity pay or statutory adoption pay],
(g) to make any other decision that falls to be made [⁴under Parts XI to XIIZB of the Social Security Contributions and Benefits Act 1992 (statutory sick pay, statutory maternity pay, statutory paternity pay and statutory adoption pay)],
[⁴(ga) to make any decision that falls to be made under regulations under section 7 of the Employment Act 2002 (funding of employers' liabilities to make payments of statutory paternity or adoption pay),];
(h) to decide any question as to the issue and content of a notice under subsection (2) of section 121C of the Social Security Administration Act 1992 (liability of directors etc. for company's contributions);
(i) to decide any issue arising under section 27 of the Jobseekers Act 1995 (employment of long-term unemployed: deductions by employers), or under any provision of regulations under that section, as to—
    (i) whether a person is or was an employee or employer of another;
    (ii) whether an employer is or was entitled to make any deduction from his contributions payments in accordance with regulations under section 27 of that Act;

(1999 c.2, s.8)

     (iii) whether a payment falls to be made to an employer in accordance with those regulations;
     (iv) the amount that falls to be so deducted or paid; or
     (v) whether two or more employers are, by virtue of regulations under section 27 of that Act, to be treated as one,
[³(ia) to decide whether to give or withdraw an approval for the purposes of para.3B(1)(b) of Sch.1 to the Social Security Contributions and Benefits Act 1992,];
  (j) [² . . .];
 (k) to decide whether a person is liable to a penalty under—
     (i) paragraph 7A(2) or 7B(2)(h) of Schedule 1 to the Social Security Contributions and Benefits Act 1992; or
     (ii) section 113(1)(a) of the Social Security Administration Act 1992;
 (l) to decide the [² . . .] penalty payable under any of the provisions mentioned in [²paragraph (k)] above; and
(m) to decide such issues relating to contributions, other than the issues specified in paragraphs (a) to (l) above or in paragraphs 16 and 17 of Schedule 3 to the Social Security Act 1998, as may be prescribed by regulations made by the Board.

(2) Subsection (1)(c) and (e) above do not include any decision relating to Class 4 contributions other than a decision falling to be made—
 (a) under subsection (1) of section 17 of the Social Security Contributions and Benefits Act 1992 as to whether by regulations under that subsection a person is or was excepted from liability for Class 4 contributions, or his liability is or was deferred; or
 (b) under regulations made by virtue of subsection (3) or (4) of that section or section 18 of that Act.

(3) Subsection (1)(g) above does not include—
 (a) any decision as to the making of subordinate legislation; or
 (b) any decision as to whether the liability to pay statutory sick pay [⁴, statutory maternity pay, statutory paternity pay or statutory adoption pay] is a liability of the Board rather than the employer.

(4) [¹ . . .].

AMENDMENTS

1. Welfare Reform and Pensions Act 1999, s.88 and Sch.13, Pt VI (April 6, 2000).
2. Child Support, Pensions and Social Security Act 2000, ss.76(6), 85 and Sch.9, Pt VIII (July 28, 2000).
3. Child Support, Pensions and Social Security Act 2000, ss.77(5) (July 28, 2000).
4. Employment Act 2002, ss.9(2) and (3) (December 8, 2002).

DEFINITIONS

"Board"—see s.27.
"contributions"—*ibid.*
"employed earner"—see SSCBA 1992, s.2(1)(a).
"employment"—see SSCBA 1992, s.122.

GENERAL NOTE

This section provides for HMRC to take decisions on a range of specified questions in relation to SMP, SSP, NICs, employment status and related matters. The extensive list of such decisions, set out in subs.(1), covers much of the former jurisdiction of the

1.191

Secretary of State for Social Security under SSAA 1992, s.17(1), with the addition of some further matters. For example, the function of making decisions as to entitlement to SMP or SSP (subs.(1)(f)) was traditionally a function of an adjudication officer (SSAA 1992, s.20(3)) but was then transferred to the Secretary of State (SSA 1998, s.8(1)(d)) before now moving to an officer of the Board (now HMRC). This is one of the areas in which the power to make regulations still rests with the Secretary of State (albeit with the agreement of HMRC), as the policy responsibility for these benefits is retained by the DWP (see General Note to s.2). However, in terms of decision making on matters of entitlement to SSP (and, by analogy, to SMP, SPP and SAP), HMRC has an "exclusive and exhaustive jurisdiction" (per Mr Recorder Luba QC in *Taylor Gordon & Co Ltd v Timmons* ([2004] I.R.L.R. 180, at para.43). Thus an employment tribunal has no jurisdiction under the Employment Rights Act 1996 to entertain an employee's complaint that SSP has not been paid.

For the relevant regulation-making powers, see s.9 and for provision for variation and supersession of decisions made under s.8, see s.10. Appeals against decisions made under s.8 are heard by the General or Special Commissioners, not by appeal tribunals constituted under SSA 1998 (ss.11–13).

Regulations with respect to decisions

1.192   **9.**—(1) Subject to the provisions of this Part and of the Social Security Administration Act 1992, provision may be made by the Board by regulations as to the making by their officer of any decision under or in connection with the Social Security Contributions and Benefits Act 1992, the Social Security Administration Act 1992 or the Jobseekers Act 1995 which falls to be made by such an officer.

(2) Where it appears to an officer of the Board that a matter before him involves a question of fact requiring special expertise, he may direct that in dealing with that matter he shall have the assistance of one or more experts.

(3) In subsection (2) above "expert" means a person appearing to the officer of the Board to have knowledge or experience which would be relevant in determining the question of fact requiring special expertise.

DEFINITIONS

"Board"—see s.27.
"expert"—see subs.(3).

GENERAL NOTE

1.193   Subsection (1), modelled on SSA 1998, s.11, provides for HMRC to make regulations governing procedural matters relating to decisions made by HMRC staff under s.8.

Subsections (2) and (3) enable HMRC to seek specialist advice before making a decision (e.g. as to medical evidence relevant to a claim for SSP). In the first instance SMP or SSP decisions are made by the employer, and only referred for a formal decision where the parties are unable to reach agreement. There are only about 500 referrals each year concerning SMP or SSP; most of these cases concern the linking or employment rules, with perhaps no more than 50 involving a medical issue (*per* Baroness Hollis of Heigham, Parliamentary Under-Secretary of State for Social Security, *Hansard*, H.L. Debs. Vol.596, col.322 (January 14, 1999)).

Decisions varying or superseding earlier decisions

1.194   **10.**—(1) [[1] Subject to subsection (2A) below,] the Board may by regulations make provision—

(1999 c.2, s.10)

(a) for any decision of an officer of the Board under section 8 of this Act (including a decision superseding an earlier decision) to be varied either within the prescribed period or in prescribed cases or circumstances;
(b) for any such decision to be superseded, in prescribed circumstances, by a subsequent decision made by an officer of the Board; and
(c) for any such decision as confirmed or varied by the tax appeal Commissioners on appeal to be superseded, in the event of a material change of circumstances since the decision was made, by a subsequent decision made by an officer of the Board.

(2) The date as from which—
(a) any variation of a decision, or
(b) any decision superseding an earlier decision,

is to take effect shall be determined in accordance with the regulations.

[[1](2A) The decisions in relation to which provision may be made by regulations under this section shall not include decisions falling within section 8(1)(ia) above.]

(3) In this section "prescribed" means prescribed by regulations under this section.

AMENDMENT

1. Child Support, Pensions and Social Security Act 2000, s.77(6) (July 28, 2000).

DEFINITIONS

"Board": s.27.
"prescribed": subs.(3).

GENERAL NOTE

This enabling provision reflects similar powers, governing Secretary of State decisions, contained in SSA 1998, ss.9 (revision) and 10 (supersession).

1.195

Appeals against decisions of Board

11.—(1) This section applies to any decision of an officer of the Board under section 8 of this Act or under regulations made by virtue of section 10(1)(b) or (c) of this Act (whether as originally made or as varied under regulations made by virtue of section 10(1)(a) of this Act).

1.196

(2) In the case of a decision to which this section applies—
(a) if it relates to a person's entitlement to statutory sick pay [[1], statutory maternity pay, statutory paternity pay or statutory adoption pay], the employee and employer concerned shall each have a right to appeal to the tax appeal Commissioners, and
(b) in any other case, the person in respect of whom the decision is made and such other person as may be prescribed shall have a right to appeal to the tax appeal Commissioners.

(3) In subsection (2)(b) above "prescribed" means prescribed by the Board by regulations.

(4) This section has effect subject to section 121D of the Social Security Administration Act 1992 (appeals in relation to personal liability notices).

AMENDMENT

1. Employment Act 2002, s.9(4) (December 8, 2002).

Definitions

"Board"—see s.27.
"prescribed"—see subs.(3)
"the tax appeal Commissioners"—see s.19.

General Note

1.197 This section provides for a right of appeal to an independent tribunal, the tax appeal Commissioners (i.e. the General or Special Commissioners for income tax; see s.19), against any HMRC decision taken under s.8. Both employees and employers have a right of appeal in relation to decisions on SMP and SSP entitlement (subs.(2)(a)). Note also that subs.(2)(b) contains a broader regulation-making power to give interested parties in other decisions a right of appeal. This provision only provides for additional rights of appeal; unlike SSA 1998, s.12(2), there is no power to prescribe in regulations for cases in which there is to be no right of appeal.

Exercise of right of appeal

1.198 **12.**—(1) Any appeal against a decision must be brought by a notice of appeal in writing given within 30 days after the date on which notice of the decision was issued.

(2) The notice of appeal shall be given to the officer of the Board by whom notice of the decision was given.

(3) The notice of appeal shall specify the grounds of appeal, but on the hearing of the appeal the tax appeal Commissioners may allow the appellant to put forward any ground not specified in the notice, and take it into consideration if satisfied that the omission was not wilful or unreasonable.

(4) Subject to [¹paragraph 3B(8) of Schedule 1 to the Social Security Contributions and Benefits Act 1992 (which provides for appeals under that paragraph to be heard by the Special Commissioners), to] section 121D of the Social Security Administration Act 1992 (which provides for an appeal against a decision under that section to be heard by the Special Commissioners) and to regulations under section 46A of the Taxes Management Act 1970 (regulations about jurisdiction), any appeal under this section shall be heard by the General Commissioners, except that the appellant may elect in accordance with section 46(1) of the Taxes Management Act 1970 to bring the appeal before the Special Commissioners instead of the General Commissioners.

(5) Subsections (5A) to (5E) of section 1 of the Taxes Management Act 1970 (which relate to an election to bring proceedings before the Special Commissioners) shall have effect in relation to an election under subsection (4) above as they have effect in relation to an election under subsection (4) of that section.

Amendment

1. Child Support, Pensions and Social Security Act 2000, s.77(7) (July 28, 2000).

Definitions

"Board"—see s.27.
"the General Commissioners"—see s.19.
"the Special Commissioners"—*ibid.*
"the tax appeal Commissioners"—*ibid.*

(1999 c.2, s.12)

GENERAL NOTE

This section, governing rights of appeal, is modelled on the provisions governing tax appeals (Taxes Management Act 1970, s.31) rather than those for social security matters (SSA 1998, s.12).

Subs.(1)
This provision adopts the standard 30-day appeal deadline in s.31(1) of the Taxes Management Act 1970.

Subs.(2)
This requirement mirrors s.31(2) of the Taxes Management Act 1970.

Subs.(3)
This provision is modelled on s.31(5) of the Taxes Management Act 1970 and gives the appellant the opportunity to raise additional grounds before the tribunal to those specified in the notice of appeal.

Subss.(4) and (5)
Subsection (4) follows s.31(4) of the Taxes Management Act 1970 in directing appeals to the lay (and locally-based) General Commissioners unless the appellant elects to go before the Special Commissioners, a national and legally qualified tribunal). Subsection (5) incorporates further provisions of the 1970 Act governing the circumstances in which an appellant's election to go to the Special Commissioners may be withdrawn by agreement with HMRC, or set aside by the General Commissioners.

Regulations with respect to appeals

13.—(1) The Board may, by regulations made with the concurrence of the Lord Chancellor and the Lord Advocate, make provision with respect to appeals to the tax appeal Commissioners under this Part.

(2) Regulations under subsection (1) above may, in particular—
(a) make provision with respect to any of the matters dealt with in the following provisions of the Taxes Management Act 1970—
  (i) section 44 and Schedule 3 (assigning proceedings to General Commissioners);
  (ii) sections 48 to 54 (appeals to the tax appeal Commissioners under the Taxes Acts); and
  (iii) sections 56 and 56A (appeals from their decisions); or
(b) provide for any of those provisions of that Act to apply, with such modifications as may be specified in the regulations, in relation to an appeal to the tax appeal Commissioners under this Part.

(3) In sections 56B and 56C of the Taxes Management Act 1970 (power of Lord Chancellor to make regulations about the practice and procedure to be followed in connection with appeals to the tax appeal Commissioners under the Taxes Acts), any reference to an appeal includes a reference to an appeal to the tax appeal Commissioners under this Part.

(4) Any regulations under section 56B of the Taxes Management Act 1970 which are in force immediately before the commencement of subsection (3) above shall apply in relation to appeals to the tax appeal Commissioners under this Part, subject to any necessary modifications, as they apply in relation to appeals to those Commissioners under the Taxes Acts.

(5) In this section, "the Taxes Acts" has the same meaning as in the Taxes Management Act 1970.

DEFINITIONS

"Board"—see s.27.
"the General Commissioners"—see s.19.
"the tax appeal Commissioners"—*ibid.*
"the Taxes Acts"—see subs.(5).

GENERAL NOTE

1.205　This section enables HMRC to make regulations about the procedures to apply for appeals to the tax appeal Commissioners against decisions under s.8. Such regulations can only be made with the concurrence of the Lord Chancellor and the Lord Advocate, who are responsible for funding the tax appeal Commissioners. In general terms, most of the provisions about appeals in Pt V of the Taxes Management Act 1970 are adopted for the purposes of such appeals. However, given that there are material differences between tax and matters such as SSP and SMP, subs.(2)(b) provides for appropriate modifications to be made to these appellate procedures. This reflects the existing arrangements for appeals to the tax appeal Commissioners in relation to Class 4 NICs, under SSCBA 1992, Sch.2, para.8.

Matters arising as respects decisions

1.206　**14.**—(1) The Board may by regulations make provision as respects matters arising—
　(a) pending any decision of an officer of the Board under section 8 of this Act which relates to—
　　(i) statutory sick pay [1, statutory maternity pay, statutory paternity pay or statutory adoption pay], or
　　(ii) any person's liability for contributions;
　(b) pending the determination by the tax appeal Commissioners of an appeal against any such decision,
　(c) out of the variation, under regulations made under section 10 of this Act or on appeal, of any such decision, or
　(d) out of the making of a decision which, under regulations made under that section, supersedes an earlier decision.
(2) Regulations under this section may, in particular—
　(a) make provision making a person liable to pay contributions pending the determination by the tax appeal Commissioners of an appeal against a decision of an officer of the Board; and
　(b) make provision as to the repayment in prescribed circumstances of contributions paid by virtue of the regulations.
(3) Regulations under this section must be made with the concurrence of the Secretary of State in so far as they relate to statutory sick pay [1, statutory maternity pay, statutory paternity pay or statutory adoption pay].

AMENDMENT

1. Employment Act 2002, s.9(5) (December 8, 2002).

DEFINITIONS

"Board"—see s.27.
"contributions"—*ibid.*

GENERAL NOTE

1.207　This section is modelled on SSA 1998, s.18. It vests HMRC with a parallel regulation-making power to deal with matters arising before a decision is made or an appeal is heard (subss.(1)(a) and (b)), or concerning the consequences of varying or superseding a previous decision (including a variation following an appeal) (subss.(1)(c) and (d)). As such regulations may have implications for benefit rights in relation to SMP and SSP, in those instances the power can only be exercised with the agreement of the Secretary of State for Work and Pensions (subs.(3)).

Arrangements for discharge of decision-making functions

17.—(1) The Secretary of State may make arrangements with the Board for any of his functions under Chapter II of Part I of the Social Security Act 1998 in relation to—
   (a) a decision whether a person was (within the meaning of regulations) precluded from regular employment by responsibilities at home; or
   (b) a decision whether a person is entitled to be credited with earnings or contributions in accordance with regulations made under section 22(5) of the Social Security Contributions and Benefits Act 1992;
to be discharged by the Board or by officers of the Board.

(2) No such arrangements shall affect the responsibility of the Secretary of State or the application of Chapter II of Part I of the Social Security Act 1998 in relation to any decision.

(3) Until the commencement of Chapter II of Part I of the Social Security Act 1998, the references to that chapter in subsections (1) and (2) above shall have effect as references to Part II of the Social Security Administration Act 1992.

1.208

DEFINITION

"Board"—see s.27.

GENERAL NOTE

This section enables decisions on home responsibilities protection or credits to be performed by HMRC as agents for the Secretary of State for Work and Pensions. This arrangement is appropriate as such decisions primarily impact upon entitlement to social security benefits.

1.209

Amendments relating to decisions and appeals

18. Schedule 7 to this Act (which contains amendments relating to decisions and appeals) shall have effect.

1.210

GENERAL NOTE

Schedule 7 provides for the detailed responsibilities of existing legislation relating to decision-making and appeals (Taxes Management Act 1970, SSCBA 1992, SSAA 1992, Pensions Schemes Act 1993, Employment Rights Act 1996 and SSA 1998).

1.211

Interpretation of Part II

19. In this Part—
"the General Commissioners" means the Commissioners for the general purposes of the income tax appointed under section 2 of the Taxes Management Act 1970;
"the Special Commissioners" means the Commissioners for the special purposes of the Income Tax Acts appointed under section 4 of the Taxes Management Act 1970;
"the tax appeal Commissioners" means the General Commissioners or the Special Commissioners.

1.212

Social Security Contributions (Transfer of Functions, etc.) Act 1999

GENERAL NOTE

1.213   This defines the "tax appeal Commissioners" as a generic term covering both the General Commissioners and the Special Commissioners appointed under ss.2 and 4 of the Taxes Management Act 1970 respectively. Curiously, the expression "tax appeal Commissioners" is not actually employed in the Taxes Management Act 1970 itself.

PART III

MISCELLANEOUS AND SUPPLEMENTAL

1.214   **20.–26.** [*Omitted.*]

Interpretation

1.215   **27.** In this Act, unless a contrary intention appears—
"the Board" means the Commissioners of Inland Revenue;
"contributions" means contributions under Part I of the Social Security Contributions and Benefits Act 1992.
28. [*Omitted.*]

GENERAL NOTE

1.216   The provisions in Pt III (with the exception of s.27) fall outside the scope of this volume and so are omitted. Section 20 provides that rebates in respect of money purchase contracted-out pension schemes should be funded from the National Insurance Fund. Sections 21 and 22 deal with the transfer of contracts and property from the former DSS to the Inland Revenue. Section 23 provides for the transfer of functions by Order in Council. Section 24 enables provision to be made for Northern Ireland by Order in Council while s.25 concerns regulation and Order making powers generally; s.26 introduces Schs 8 (savings and transitional provisions), 9 (consequential amendments) and 10 (repeals and revocations). Section 28 governs the short title, commencement and extent of the Act.

Tax Credits Act 2002

(2002 C.21)

ARRANGEMENT OF SECTIONS

PART I

TAX CREDITS

General

1.217   1.   Introductory
2.   Functions of Commissioners

(2002 c.21)

3. Claims
4. Claims: supplementary
5. Period of awards
6. Notifications of changes of circumstances
7. Income test

Child tax credit

8. Entitlement
9. Maximum rate

Working tax credit

10. Entitlement
11. Maximum rate
12. Childcare element

Rate

13. Rate

Decisions

14. Initial decisions
15. Revised decisions after notifications
16. Other revised decisions
17. Final notice
18. Decisions after final notice
19. Power to enquire
20. Decisions on discovery
21. Decisions subject to official error
22. Information, etc. requirements: supplementary
23. Notice of decisions

Payment

24. Payments
25. Payments of working tax credit by employers (*omitted*)
26. Liability of officers for sums paid to employers (*omitted*)
27. Rights of employees
28. Overpayments
29. Recovery of overpayments
30. Underpayments

Penalties

31. Incorrect statements, etc.
32. Failure to comply with requirements
33. Failure by employers to make correct payments (*omitted*)
34. Supplementary

Fraud

35. Offence of fraud
36. Powers in relation to documents

Interest

37. Interest

Appeals

38. Appeals
39. Exercise of right of appeal

Supplementary

40. Annual reports
41. Annual review
42. Persons subject to immigration control
43. Polygamous marriages
44. Crown employment
45. Inalienability
46. Giving of notices by Board
47. Consequential amendments
48. Interpretation

PART II

CHILD BENEFIT AND GUARDIAN'S ALLOWANCE

49.–57. (*Omitted*)

PART III

SUPPLEMENTARY

Information etc.

58. Administrative arrangements
59. Use and disclosure of information

Other supplementary provisions

60. Repeals
61. Commencement
62. Transitional provisions and savings
63. Tax credits appeals etc.: temporary modifications
64. Northern Ireland
65. Regulations, orders and schemes (*omitted*)

66. Parliamentary etc. control of instruments (*omitted*)
67. Interpretation
68. Financial provision (*omitted*)
69. Extent (*omitted*)
70. Short title (*omitted*)

Schedule 1—Rights of employees (*omitted*)
Schedule 2—Penalties: supplementary
Schedule 3—Tax credits: consequential amendments (*omitted*)
Schedule 4—Transfer of functions: consequential amendments (*omitted*)
Schedule 5—Use and disclosure of information (*omitted*)
Schedule 6—Repeals and revocations (*omitted*)

GENERAL NOTE

Scope and scheme of the Act

The Tax Credits Bill 2001 was introduced to the House of Commons as a Treasury measure. It was subject to minimal amendment as it went through its parliamentary proceedings in the House of Commons. The Speaker ruled that it was not a Money Bill (possibly because of Pt II of the Act). It was subject to rigorous challenge in the House of Lords. The criticisms ranged from normal political confrontations about tax and social security measures to a challenge to the fundamental approach, even the title, of the Bill itself. It was at that stage also (after strong protests from the opposition parties and an apology from the minister piloting the Bill through the House) that important government technical and drafting amendments were tabled. The main focus of opposition criticism was on the issue whether tax credits counted as public expenditure or as tax uncollected. In fact, that issue did not feature in the Bill at all as it does not require legislation. The answer (after a disagreement about the right approach, recorded in the note) was published in the Red Book (the Financial Statement) published by the Treasury to accompany the Chancellor 2002 Budget (See *2002 Financial Statement*, Box C2, p.216). It is that tax credits count as public expenditure in so far as they exceed the income tax due from the claimant, and as negative taxation in so far as they do not. Tax credits under the Tax Credits Act 1999 are classified as public expenditure. During Parliamentary debates, it was said that as a ball-park figure, 90 per cent of the amount was public expenditure and 10 per cent tax foregone.

1.218

The Tax Credits Act 2002 ("this Act") repeals and replaces the Tax Credits Act 1999 ("TCA 1999") in its entirety and carries further the reforms started by that Act. But this Act also provides a framework both to extend existing tax credits and for a further round of reform beyond the current scope of tax credits. In doing so, it also takes further the measures introduced by a separate Act, the Social Security Contributions (Transfer of Functions, etc.) Act 1999. That Act transferred certain functions from the then Department of Social Security and its Northern Ireland equivalent to the Treasury and HMRC. This Act transfers further functions by similar measures from what is now the Department for Work and Pensions and its Northern Ireland equivalent, the NI Department for Social Development, to the Treasury and HMRC.

This Act makes provision for the following changes:
(a) replacing several existing forms of support for children by tax and social security provisions with a *child tax credit*;
(b) replacing working families' tax credit, disabled person's tax credit and New Deal 50 plus employment credit with a new, wider *working tax credit*;
(c) replacing the current system for claims, decision making, payment, and appeals relating to tax credits with a new system;
(d) transferring the functions of administering child benefit and guardian's allowance from the DWP to the Treasury and HMRC;
(e) making minor amendments to the rules about entitlement to child benefit;
(f) introducing administrative arrangements to empower co-ordination between the HMRC and those providing social security benefits.

The Act is structured in three Parts. Part I (Tax credits) provides the necessary primary legislative framework to introduce the child tax credit and working tax credit. It also provides a common procedure for those tax credits. Schedules 1–3 to the Act are associated with this Part. Part II (Child benefit and guardian's allowance) makes provision for the transfer of functions concerning child benefit and guardian's allowance to the Treasury and HMRC, and the associated minor amendments to entitlement. Schedule 4 is associated with this Part. Part III (Supplementary) makes additional provision for both other Parts. Schedules 5 and 6 are associated with this Part.

Tax credits

1.219 The introduction of a programme of tax credits has been a major aspect of the approach to reform of the tax and benefit systems by the Treasury since the Labour government took office in 1997. But neither the TCA 1999 nor this Act were opposed in principle on this issue by the other main political parties. The substantive policy and the detail have been criticised, but not the general approach. The main thrust of Pt I of this Act, introducing the child tax credit (CTC) and the working tax credit (WTC), is to extend the tax credits introduced by the TCA 1999 and consolidate those reforms.

Tax credits under the Tax Credits Act 2002

1.220 The introduction of the current reforms was announced by the Chancellor of the Exchequer, Gordon Brown, in his 1999 Budget and confirmed in his 2000 Budget. The detailed shape of the proposals was first announced in an HMRC consultation paper published in July 2001: *New Tax Credits: Supporting families, making work pay and tackling poverty*. This received significant comment from many sources and the HMRC published its *Response* in November 2001.

Child tax credit

1.221 CTC is a means-tested social security benefit for all those responsible for children and qualifying young persons, although it is presented as a tax credit. Government policy for the support of children appears to be motivated by two interacting pressures. The first is that the Government's target is to halve child poverty by 2010 and to abolish it altogether by 2020. The second is the profound demographic shift occurring in Britain, as in the rest of Europe, because of the reduction in the number of children being born, due to a sharp drop in the female fertility rate. The government's response is the CTC, which provides a single tax credit payable to any person who is responsible for one or more children or qualifying young persons (s.8(1)). The Act provides only minimal detail about how CTC works, but the intended figures were published in the 2002 Budget and draft regulations were published before the Bill was given royal assent. Details are set out in the note to ss.8 and 9 below.

Support for children through the tax and social security systems was previously provided in several ways. The first and most important provision was child benefit. The second line of support for children in poorer families was by way of an addition or increase to individual means-tested benefits (or tax credits). Thirdly, and separately from the income-related benefits, contributory and other social security benefits also made provision for dependent children (e.g. the child dependency increases under SSCBA 1992, ss.80 and 85 and the child increase for carer's allowance under SSCBA 1992, s.90). There were further provisions in the Social Security (Dependency) Regulations 1977 (SI 1977/343). Moreover, a few individuals looking after children as their guardians can claim guardian's allowance, under SSCBA 1992, s.77. Finally, and separately again from these sources of assistance for those bringing up children, the Finance Act 2000 introduced the children's tax credit as s.257AA of the ICTA 1988, supported by Sch.13B to that Act. Despite its name, this was not a tax credit, but an income tax reduction. It only overlapped with the social security benefits in so far as the claimants of those benefits were also income tax payers.

(2002 c.21)

This Act sweeps away all mention of SSCBA 1992, ss.80 and 90 (but *not* s.85, which allows for increases for retirement pensioners for an adult caring for children for whom the pensioner is receiving child credit). With them go the relevant regulations. Section 257AA of ICTA 1988 also goes. So also, by regulation, does the overlap between child benefit and CTC. Any overlap with WTC is also avoided by regulation. Further regulations under s.1 were intended to transfer all child elements from all income-related benefits to CTC. That proved far harder than was anticipated. The provisions, intended to be put in place in 2004, have been postponed several times and will not now take effect until 2009 at the earliest. See the general note to s.1.

Working tax credit

WTC is not a social security benefit, although it has its immediate origins in WFTC and DPTC, which were income-related social security benefits. WTC has been repackaged as a tax credit, usually payable by employers through the pay packet, and extended beyond the limits of social security provision to assist all on low pay. It continues the process of integration by absorbing not only the two social security benefits but also New Deal 50 Plus. New Deal 50 Plus was the name given to a variant of the employment credits payable under the Employment and Training Act 1973. As its name suggests, it was a new form of employment assistance brought in to encourage the older claimant back into work. It was not a social security benefit and was never within the scope of the former DSS, being run instead by the former separate Department for Education and Employment and its predecessors.

1.222

WTC is designed as a general provision for all in "qualifying remunerative work", though tantalisingly this Act does not define that central term. Rather, regulations specify that work will qualify (if paid or in the expectation of payment) if it is over 16 hours a week for those with children, those who are disadvantaged by disability, and those over 50. Anyone else over 25 will qualify if working 30 hours a week (Working Tax Credit (Entitlement and Maximum Rate) Regulations 2002 (SI 2002/2005), reg.4). Those under 25 who are not in the specific groups are excluded. The definition is designed to integrate with the national minimum wage to provide a minimum level of take-home pay for all those entitled to claim. HMRC now also has responsibility for enforcement of the national minimum wage.

Despite the integration of benefits and allowances within both WTC and CTC, the two tax credits will operate separately from the point of view of claimants. However, the original intention of paying WTC through the pay packet to the main earner has failed. From April 6, 2006, all WTC payments, like all CTC payments are made directly by HMRC. In principle, WTC (including the childcare credit) goes to the main earner, while CTC goes to the main carer. But in practice they are required to make joint claims and are jointly and severally liable to refund any overpayment. And in addition they are often in practice paid into the same joint bank account. So, although WTC was intended as a true tax credit with CTC as a social security benefit, most claimants fail to see any difference.

Development of the credits

The tax credits system has evolved in a number of ways since its introduction. It is in essence a redistributive system. As it has developed from initial plans to first introduction to a maturing system, its focus has been sharpened on to its main beneficiaries—"mainstream" couples or lone parents who have children at home or school and who are in work and stay in work.

1.223

The most generous real increases in the value of tax credits go to those who can claim the childcare element of WTC. For those with two or more children being looked after, the weekly maximum amount that can be claimed against childcare expenses has risen from 70 per cent of £200 a week to 80 per cent of £300, an annual increase over two years of over £5000. At the same time, the range of those who may be employed as a childcare provider is being increased, so removing whole categories of cases of those who could not receive the credit for practical reasons. The

111

background to this is that the Chancellor has announced (and delivered) a commitment to raise the CTC credits in line with earnings rather than the cost of living. Only one element of CTC has not been altered. The £50,000 floor for the family element has not changed in the opening years, and the level of the credit (£545) has also not been altered, so is slowly declining in real value.

By contrast, the levels of WTC—apart from the childcare element—have been altered by reference to rises in the cost of living, and so are relatively less generous. Nonetheless, the system has confounded one group of critics. Take-up is much heavier than some feared, and the system is coming to be seen as part of the machinery whereby lone parents with younger children really can work.

The administration and delivery of tax credits during introduction was a disaster that does not need retelling. This led to a large number of overpayments—some apparently generated by computers paying out more than they were told, while others arose from a rush to deliver initial payments. Things are running more smoothly now, though in part only because—as several expert agencies have protested—the Revenue (now HMRC) has smoothed the administrative process, and reports suggest that it does not always comply fully with its own rules about making decisions. But the rules themselves assist that smoothness. For example, it is very easy to claim, and to have a claim backdated, as compared with the old rules applied by the then DSS to claims and in particular late claims. Partly, one suspects, because of this, partly because there is a power and commitment to settle disputes rather than fight them, and partly because of a more proactive approach to claimants than was the practice of the old DSS, there have been to date few appeals. However, the Parliamentary Ombudsman reported over 70,000 appeals awaiting settlement or decision in February 2005. Initial cases suggest that the issues that are going forward on appeal are (perhaps predictably) issues such as penalties for failure to declare, and whether an individual should be claiming jointly with a partner—in other words the classic clashes over truth and credibility.

One part of the new system has been delayed. The proposed removal of the child premiums from income support and JSA for transfer to CTC was planned to take place from April 2005. That has now been put back to 2009 at the earliest. This has left in place one of the weaknesses of the transitional structure—its lack of integration with benefits run by the DWP/DSDNI—more exposed than was planned. It can cause trouble particularly where someone loses a job towards the end of the tax year so losing entitlement to both WTC and (for the time being) CTC while finding difficulty gaining DWP replacements.

Commencement

1.224 Section 61 (Commencement) and subsequent sections came into effect on Royal Assent (8 July 2002). Pt I (ss.1–48) is brought into effect under the Tax Credits Act 2002 (Commencement No.1) Order 2002 (SI 2002/1727) made that day. The balance of the Act was brought in by the Tax Credits Act 2002 (Commencement No.2) Order 2003 (SI 2003/392) (Pt II), the Tax Credits Act 2002 (Commencement No.3 and Transitional Provisions and Savings) Order 2003 (SI 2003/938) (the abolition of the child additions and benefits under s.1(3) of the Act) and Tax Credits Act 2002 (Commencement No.4, Transitional Provisions and Savings) Order 2003 (SI 2003/962) (the remainder).

The pattern of introduction of tax credits is as follows:

General:
July 9, 2002   regulation-making powers

For all claimants except those on income support and jobseeker's allowance:
August 1, 2002   making claims and relevant provisions
January 1, 2003   making decisions on claims
April 6, 2003   entitlements to payment of awards and abolition of child additions from all benefits save as below.

For claimants over 60 transferring to or qualifying for state pension credit:
October 1, 2003 making claims and awards.

For other claimants of income support or jobseeker's allowance:
December 31, 2008 phased introduction of CTC to all claimants.

General problems with the 2002 Act

1.225
The first two years of the operation of the Tax Credits Act 2002 cannot, by any stretch of imagination, be called an outstanding success. Overall, it proved far harder to start the system than anticipated. But the Government was proved right on one aspect of the new tax credits. Some claimed that the take-up rates for the credits would be low. This was a longstanding problem with family credit. But the estimated take-up for child tax credit in its first year was 80 per cent, compared to 65 per cent and 57 per cent in the first years of working families' tax credit and family credit respectively. In addition, no less than 480,000 claimants claimed nil credits (i.e. they put in protective claims in 2004-5 but did not receive anything).

General administration of tax credits proved far more complex than planned. Indeed, the government was forced to abandon its intentions of having the credits paid through people's pay packets. This was an aim of government as long ago as 1973 when family income supplement was turned into family credit. It was a firm aim of government in 2002, following the approach of s.6 of the Tax Credits Act 1999. But the 2002 Act contained a more limited measure than the original proposals. Section 25 provides for payment of working tax credit, or prescribed elements, by employers. This was never used to pay the full credit, as the childcare element was paid direct to the family. In 2004 the Chancellor announced that even the partial payment was to cease. With effect from November 7, 2005, no new award of WTC is to be paid through a pay packet. And by April 2006 all payments by employers ceased. From then, payment is made only by HMRC.

The system is also suffering from the consequences of a combination of intended and unintended short-term generosity. The unintended generosity appears to have come from significant overpayments made by error by the computer systems to many thousands of households. These overpayments are errors in many cases where they were in excess of both the amounts claimed and the amounts authorised. Indeed, in the terms of the 2002 Act, they are arguably not "overpayments" at all because they exceeded the amounts awarded under the Act.

The intended generosity comes from the approach taken to administering the credits. The HMRC approach is to accept a claim as it stands, then to investigate it later for accuracy. In the first year of the new scheme, a claimant's income was assumed initially to be that of two years before, whereas the normal rule is to base that assessment on the previous year's income. This was compounded by what several expert observers have reported to be a high error rate in decision making, including serial failure to make a correct decision for many claimants, and serial failures in accepting notifications of changes of circumstances. The combined weight of evidence in the reports of the Parliamentary Ombudsman and the National Association of Citizens Advice Bureaux show serious repeated maladministration and other errors.

Not all overpayments may be the result of official error. Some claimants deliberately refrain from informing HMRC of changes of circumstances that they are not required to report. They then receive a current overpayment to be set off only later by a repayment. It is also reported that HMRC often treat those having to make repayments for previous years more generously than those making repayments for the current year.

Unusually, the fact that tax credits are authorised in two stages means that the statistics of these errors are cruelly accurate. All credits are paid on an award at the start of the in year payment, and are then checked by the entitlement decision at the end of the year. These showed a level of inaccuracy in awards that was itself likely to be very accurate. The total sums paid inaccurately totalled £2.395 billion in 2004–2005. The headline figures appear less than that because a total of overpayments approaching £2 billion were offset by underpayments approaching £0.5 billion. There were about 6.1 million tax creditors in 2004–2005. Of those nearly 500,000 were entitled to, and received, nothing (see above). Another 1 million were benefit claimants who would have been receiving child tax credit but for delays in bringing in that measure. That leaves some 4.5 million creditors subject to these errors. Dividing total errors by that number suggests that the average award was wrong by about £530 in the year.

The full story appears worse. The figures compare entitlement decisions after the year with the award paid by the end of the year. Other information shows that many claimants received regularly changed awards—arriving for many every two months or so according to figures in the reports noted above. But the effect of trying to correct the errors of a previous decision through another decision itself also likely either to be incorrect or to be replaced in a matter of weeks by a third decision has led to payments becoming almost erratic and certainly unpredictable for their recipients. Large overpayments were followed by demands for full repayment. Further, errors spilled over from one tax year to the next as the government decided to recover the overpayments in stages. Complaints systems received large numbers of complaints from claimants experiencing the swings of the system.

Future stability?

1.226 The Government has backed away from three original aspects of the scheme. First, it has ended the requirement that employers pay any part of the tax credits through pay packets. This is also likely to stop further consideration of proposals to extent the tax credit system as a supplement to earnings, for example for housing benefit. Secondly, the Government has postponed the introduction of child tax credits for those who are not working until at least 2007—five years after the intended date of introduction. Both the "welfare to work" aspect of the new tax credits and the "one stop shop" for children's benefits have proved far harder to realise than was anticipated. The arguments in 2001 about whether payment should be to the main earner or the main carer have now proved to be unnecessary. Only one of those options proved possible. Lastly, the Government has drawn back from adjusting the levels of income on which awards are made when confirming entitlement save where there are major changes. The rule providing adjustments for increases over £2,500 is now a rule providing adjustments only for increases over £25,000.

But the underlying aims of the new system are now being achieved. There has been a significant increase in the help for working parents, and in particular in helping families pay for childminders. And a system for dealing with overpayments in an organised way is starting to emerge. It remains to be seen, however, if the system will ever work effectively in delivering timely and predictable help to those bringing up families on low earnings while it is based on an award made without full enquiry followed by a fully retrospective entitlement decision for a whole tax year at a time.

Is credits advice tax advice?

1.227 The hybrid nature of tax credits as part tax, part benefits, part employment subsidies leads to a number of anomalies. One is the question whether advice on tax credits is tax advice. If it is then advisers may need to ensure that they comply with all relevant European and UK regulations about money laundering. This was raised at the Tax Credits Consultative Group Meeting in November 2006. In a note issued after the meeting HMRC advised that, having consulted policy experts at the Treasury (though not, according to the note, lawyers) HMRC does not think that advisers are caught by the rules. In part this is because they do not advertise themselves as offering tax advice. And in part "it seems they give advice on government benefits rather than tax advice". If so, why are they called tax credits?

(2002 c.21, s.1)

PART I

TAX CREDITS

General

Introductory

1.—(1) This Act makes provision for—
(a) a tax credit to be known as child tax credit, and
(b) a tax credit to be known as working tax credit.
(2) In this Act references to a tax credit are to either of those tax credits and references to tax credits are to both of them.
(3) The following (which are superseded by tax credits) are abolished—
(a) children's tax credit under section 257AA of the Income and Corporation Taxes Act 1988 (Chapter 1),
(b) working families' tax credit,
(c) disabled person's tax credit,
(d) the amounts which, in relation to income support and income-based jobseeker's allowance, are prescribed as part of the applicable amount in respect of a child or young person, the family premium, the enhanced disability premium in respect of a child or young person and the disabled child premium,
(e) increases in benefits in respect of children under sections 80 and 90 of the Social Security Contributions and Benefits Act 1992 (Chapter 4) and sections 80 and 90 of the Social Security Contributions and Benefits (Northern Ireland) Act 1992 (Chapter 7), and
(f) the employment credit under the schemes under section 2(2) of the Employment and Training Act 1973 (Chapter 50) and section 1 of the Employment and Training Act (Northern Ireland) 1950 (Chapter 29 (NI)) known as "New Deal 50 Plus".

1.228

DEFINITIONS

"child tax credit"—see s.8.
"tax credit"—see subs.2.
"working tax credit"—see s.10.

GENERAL NOTE

Section 1 is, as its title states, purely an introductory section. Strictly it adds nothing to the enacting provisions of Pt I, but it flags up the two kinds of tax credit payable under the Act and also the benefits repealed (by s.60 and Sch.6). Subsection (1) lists the two tax credits introduced by the Act, but (as with the rest of Pt I) is drafted so that other tax credits could be added to the list in the subsection, and the machinery sections of the Act (which apply to "tax credits" as defined in subs.(2)) would then apply to the new tax credits also. At the date of writing, no specific further tax credits have been suggested. The abolition of the child premiums to income support and JSA were deferred to December 31, 2008.

Indeed, it has proved harder than anticipated to introduce child tax credits for those on income support and jobseeker's allowance. It is understood that there are many cases where one parent of a child is claiming one of these benefits with child

1.229

addition while the other parent is claiming child tax credit for the same child or children. In *CSTC/326/2003* Commissioner Parker considered an argument that the measures taken to postpone the introduction of s.1(3)(d) discriminated against those receiving income support as against those who received the tax credits direct. The appellant's wife received income support. Entitlement to child tax credit was higher than to income support. But under the transitional legislation the appellant could claim CTC only from the date of his claim. No backdating was allowed. The appellant argued that either this was ultra vires the TCA 2002 or it was discriminatory under the European Convention on Human Rights. The Commissioner rejected both arguments. In dealing with somewhat unfocussed arguments about the European Convention on Human Rights, the Commissioner took the view that CTC is a means-tested social security benefit but assumed for the purposes of argument that both Art.8 of, and Art.1, Protocol 1 to, the Convention were engaged. She then considered if there was discrimination within the meaning of Art.14 but found none. Her decision reveals that the process of suspending s.1(3)(d) while benefit claimants are "migrated" to it as being in some confusion. Of the relevant subordinate legislation (in particular SI 2005/773, SI 2005/776 and SI 2005/1106), she comments (at para.16):

> "the last minute nature of the amendment order, the curiosity of two substantially overlapping measures produced on the same day (the transitional provisions order 2005 and the second transitional provisions order), a draft order which was never laid, and the failure to enact a consistent statutory scheme of backdating to prevent double recovery, indicate a history of some haste and confusion by the legislators. There has been a complex web of measures, note always successful, necessitated because the prospects for the completion of intended migration seem ever to recede."

The process of phasing out the child elements in income support and jobseeker's allowance has proved far harder than anticipated and the start has been repeatedly delayed, most recently until the end of 2008. Statistics show that nearly 500,000 claimants, mainly single parents, claim child elements to these benefits. There is an informal view that part of the problem is that there are also thousands of tax credits claims made by the other parents of those children. The transfer process therefore needs to be able to deal with rival claims.

[¹Function of Commissioners

1.230   **2.** The Commissioners for Her Majesty's Revenue and Customs shall be responsible for the payment and management of tax credits.]

AMENDMENT

1. Commissioners for Revenue and Customs Act 2005, Sch.4, para.88 (April 6, 2005).

DEFINITIONS

"tax credits"—see s.1(2).
"the Commissioners for Revenue and Customs"—see CRCA 2005 s.4.

GENERAL NOTE

1.231   This short section replaced its lengthy predecessor as CRCA 2005 came into effect. That Act repealed and replaced the Inland Revenue Regulation Act 1890 to which this section previously referred. All necessary provisions for both the payment of tax credits (and repayment) and management and administration are now either in the CRCA 2005 or this Act. The wording of this section reflects the similar wording in CRCA 2005 applying also to taxes, duties and benefits.

(2002 c.21, s.2)

Claims

3.—(1) Entitlement to a tax credit for the whole or part of a tax year is dependent on the making of a claim for it.

1.232

(2) Where the Board—
- (a) decide under section 14 not to make an award of a tax credit on a claim, or
- (b) decide under section 16 to terminate an award of a tax credit made on a claim,

(subject to any appeal) any entitlement, or subsequent entitlement, to the tax credit for any part of the same tax year is dependent on the making of a new claim.

(3) A claim for a tax credit may be made—
- (a) jointly by the members of a [²couple] both of whom are aged at least sixteen and are in the United Kingdom [(and neither of whom are members of a polygamous unit)]¹; or
- [(aa) jointly by the members of a polygamous unit all of whom are aged at least sixteen and are in the United Kingdom, or]¹;
- (b) by a person who is aged at least sixteen and is in the United Kingdom but is not entitled to make a claim under paragraph (a) (jointly with another).

(4) Entitlement to a tax credit pursuant to a claim ceases—
- (a) in the case of a joint claim, if the persons by whom it was made could no longer jointly make a joint claim; and
- [(aa) in the case of a joint claim under subsection (3)(a), if a member of the [²couple] becomes a member of a polygamous unit, and
- (ab) in the case of a joint claim under subsection (3)(aa), if there is any change in the persons who comprise the polygamous unit, and]¹
- (b) in the case of a single claim, if the person by whom it was made could no longer make a single claim.

(5) [² . . .

(5A) In this Part "couple" means—
- (a) a man and woman who are married to each other and are neither—
  - (i) separated under a court order, nor
  - (ii) separated in circumstances in which the separation is likely to be permanent,
- (b) a man and woman who are not married to each other but are living together as husband and wife,
- (c) two people of the same sex who are civil partners of each other and are neither—
  - (i) separated under a court order, nor
  - (ii) separated in circumstances in which the separation is likely to be permanent, or
- (d) two people of the same sex who are not civil partners of each other but are living together as if they were civil partners.]

(6) [² . . .]

[(6A) In this Part, "polygamous unit" has the meaning given by regulation 2 of the Tax Credits (Polygamous Marriages) Regulations 2003.]¹

(7) Circumstances may be prescribed in which a person is to be treated for the purposes of this Part as being, or as not being, in the United Kingdom.

(8) In this Part—

Tax Credits Act 2002

"joint claim" means a claim under paragraph (a) [or (aa)]¹ of subsection (3), and
"single claim" means a claim under paragraph (b) of that subsection.

AMENDMENTS

1. Modifications for the purposes of application to polygamous units by Tax Credits (Polygamous Marriages) Regulations 2003 (SI 2003/742), reg.4 (April 6, 2003).
2. Civil Partnership Act 2004, s.254 and Sch.24, para.144 (December 5, 2005).

DEFINITIONS

"award"—see s.14(1).
"the Board"—see s.67.
"claim"—see subs.(1), s.4.
"entitlement"—see s.18(1).
"joint claim"—see subs.(8).
"married couple"—see subs.(5).
"prescribed"—see s.67.
"single claim"—see subs.(8).
"tax credit"—see s.1(2).
"tax year"—see s.47.
"unmarried couple"—see subs.(8).

GENERAL NOTE

1.233   This is the first of the sections in the Act that create the necessary compromise for tax credits between the general approach of income tax administration and the general approach of social security administration. Subsection (1) adopts and adapts the requirement from SSAA 1992, s.1(1), that there can be no entitlement to a tax credit without a claim. Subsection (2) reinforces this. Subsections (3) and following set out both the main conditions for making a claim and the requirement that both (or all) those who are partners to a marriage (or equivalent) join in making the claim. Subsection (8) adopts appropriate definitions for joint and single claims. There is also a definition of "claimant" in s.9(8), which would be better placed here in subs.(8).

Determining when a claim is made is important because of the operation of the "three month" rule for a new claim following some changes of circumstances. The ability to make claims by telephone or email in addition to the traditional posted claim means that this may be a matter to be determined on appeal in the light of conflicting evidence from the claimants and HMRC. See *CSIS/48/1992* for the presumption that a document that can be served by post is delivered in ordinary course of post. HMRC treat the rule with a little generosity because it directs staff to assume that for these purposes three months is always 91 days and a single month always has 31 days.

Can the claim be made on an income tax return? It is understood that appeal tribunals have been invited to treat a claim made on an income tax self-assessment return as a sufficient claim for the purposes of this section. Such a claim may meet the mandatory requirements of the Tax Credits (Claims and Notifications) Regulations 2002, reg.5 (see Vol.III). But is it open to an appeal tribunal to decide this, or is it an unappealable decision to be made by HMRC alone (subject to judicial review)? The social security jurisprudence is that the equivalent decisions of the Secretary of State are unappealable. See the note to Social Security (Claims and Payments) Regulations 1987, reg.4 in Vol.III, of this work. It remains to be decided if this approach will also apply to this section and the regulations made under s.4.

Subs. (1)

1.234   The standard claim form is TC600 for new claims. In practice claims can be made electronically or over the telephone. See TC(Claims and Notifications) Regs

2002, reg.5 and *CIS/995/2004* discussed at para.2.276 below. Further, although renewal claims are needed each year, a renewal claim may be treated as being made as the procedure for checking a past claim takes place at the end of that year of claim.

HMRC have accepted that it is appropriate in some cases to make protective claims where a claim will lead to a nil award on the then current information about income, but where a claimant may later in the tax year be entitled to tax credits. In such cases, nil awards will be made. See *Tax Adviser*, June 2003, p.13. HMRC statistics show that in December 2006 there were about 0.8 million claimants with zero awards. This suggests that these claims have become standard practice for many advisers, as the total number of recipients of credit had not risen in the previous two years while the number of zero awards doubled. Another explanation is that 0.6 million lower paid individuals (perhaps self-employed) without children now receive zero awards, and the number of such claimants also doubled in that period. Another reason is that HMRC may revise an award to zero rather than cancel it when a claimant is no longer entitled to receive a positive award.

Subs. (2)

This adopts in part a policy of SSA 1998, s.8, that a claim ceases to have effect when a decision has been made on it. A new claim is required if the Board refuses or ends a tax credit award for a tax year and for any reason the claimant wants that decision revisited. In practice, however, the Board may choose to make a "nil" award, so leaving the matter open to review if circumstances change, rather than a reclaim.

1.235

Subs. (3)

This is the primary provision entitling a claim to be made. It imposes a series of conditions on all claimants:
(a) if a claimant is one of a married or unmarried couple (or of a polygamous unit) then the claim can only be made in the names of both (or all) of them;
(b) the claimant or claimants must be over 16; and
(c) the claimant or claimants (and if more than one, all) must be "in the UK".

The following subsections make provisions for those conditions. But s.42 excludes those subject to immigration control from entitlement except in specified cases. The approach of requiring joint claims is also reinforced by s.4(1)(g), which enables regulations to treat a single claim as a joint claim. This has been extended by regulations under s.43 to cover polygamous units, the policy again being that all the members of a polygamous unit must be linked to the claim.

Following the enactment of the Gender Recognition Act 2004, HMRC have issued guidance that if an individual has gender recognition certificate issues under the Act, then this will or affect the status of the individual as a single or joint claimant: see TCTM 06100. However, there will be a potential interaction with the new definition of "couple" following the enactment of the Civil Partnership Act 2004. See below.

1.236

Subs. (4)

This is designed to stop the claim under subs.(3) continuing if the identity of the claimant(s) changes because an individual gains a partner, a couple breaks up, or a polygamous unit changes membership. But it deals with *entitlement* not *award*, and its inclusion at this point in this section is a little obscure. It links with the provisions on joint claims (or deemed joint claims) to withdraw *entitlement* where joint claimants are no longer *entitled to make* a joint claim, thus stopping both joint claims and claims deemed to be joint. Nonetheless its interaction with ss.17 and 18 and with a continuing *award* is not clear. It appears to suggest that an award can continue without underlying entitlement. However, under the Tax Credits (Claims and Notifications) Regulations 2002 (SI 2002/2014), reg.21, notification must be given whenever a joint claim should become a single claim, or the reverse. In practice, this applies to awards as much as to entitlement.

1.237

Subss. (5A), (6A)

1.238 The original subs.(5) defined "married couple" and subs.(6) defined "unmarried couple". Both definitions have been replaced under the Civil Partnership Act 2004, but the new subsections reflect the former compromise between the income tax definition of a married couple (see ICTA s.282) and the social security definition (*see* Vol.II of this work for SSCBA 1992, s.137).

The application of tax credits to unmarried couples has proved an early source of appeals and procedural problems. The decision by HMRC that two people ought to be claiming jointly as an unmarried couple has predictably led to the same hostile reception as the LTAHAW rules meet in social security cases. Two early decisions of Commissioners suggest that the HMRC approach may at times have been overzealous. In *CTC/3059/2004* a deputy Commissioner decided that an appellant and her husband-to-be were not, on the facts, living together as wife and husband before their marriage although both HMRC and the tribunal had found that they were. (HMRC later supported the appeal to the Commissioner on the basis that the tribunal's findings of fact had gone beyond the evidence). Deputy Commissioner White held:

"12. Though the term "unmarried couple" is defined in the Tax Credits Act 2002, the concept of "living together as husband and wife" is not defined in the legislation. There appears to be no dispute that it is appropriate to use the guidance provided in Commissioners' decisions in relation to other benefits in considering such questions when they arise in relation to tax credits. I agree that the framework established in relation to other benefits is helpful.

13. That framework (*the Commissioner referred to Volume II*) indicates that a number of factors should be considered as a whole in deciding whether, on the balance of probabilities, a man and a woman are living together as husband and wife."

The deputy Commissioner then examined the facts by reference to: where the husband-to-be lived; financial support; sexual relationship; stability of relationship; care of the children of the wife-to-be; and public acknowledgement. He accepted that there were difficulties in using the latter three factors with regard to an engaged couple. But he concluded on the evidence that the engaged couple were not living together.

In *CTC/3864/2004* deputy Commissioner Green held that HMRC and another tribunal had erred on the same question, and again HMRC supported the claimant's appeal. It is to be noted that one ground on which HMRC supported the appeal was that the tribunal failed to provide an explanation why they did not find all the claimant's evidence reliable. The deputy Commissioner agreed, commenting that the tribunal had on one point rejected the claimant's evidence although that was the only evidence before the tribunal on that point. It may be that the HMRC support on this point reflects an HMRC expectation that it might expect to have to meet more exacting standards of evidence as to truth and credibility when appearing before the tax tribunals. More generally, deputy Commissioner Green took the same approach as in *CTC/3059/2004* (although without reference to it) in adopting the decisions of social security commissioners on the question of living together and referring to the guidance formerly in the *Supplementary Benefits Handbook* and in *R(SB) 17/81*.

In *CTC/1629/2005* a deputy Commissioner considered the importance in what has become subs.(5A) of the test of "separated in circumstances in which the separation is likely to be permanent." The context was a claim by a wife whose marriage to her husband was in difficulties. Divorce proceedings had been put on hold after they were started. HMRC decided that the claim she made should have been a joint claim. The tribunal agreed, but that decision was set aside. The deputy Commissioner emphasised the importance in cases such as this of making proper decisions about the credibility of a claimant. In this case the tribunal failed to deal adequately with the claimant's oral evidence and also with correspondence produced by her from others about the status of the marriage. But he does not deal with the question of obtaining evidence from the husband.

In *CTC/2090/2004* Commissioner Bano dealt with some of the consequences of competing claims for child tax credit. He resisted an argument put by HMRC that the appeal tribunal should have summonsed the mother to give evidence before finding for the father on a claim made by him. He also raised issues about the duty on HMRC itself in such a situation. In *CTC/3543/2004* Commissioner Jacobs considered who are the parties to proceedings in cases where there are joint claims. In his view where there is a joint claim both the claimants must be parties to any proceedings against one of them. The Commissioner referred to both SSA 1998 s.14(3)(d) and the Social Security and Child Support (Decisions and Appeals) Regulations 1999, reg.1(2) to decide that if there is an overpayment relating to a joint claim then both the claimants must be parties to the proceedings even if only one has appealed. Conversely it would follow that where a claim should be a joint claim but is not, the non-claimant is not automatically subject to a decision against the claimant.

See the note to s.6 for the effect of the introduction of the potential change of status of couples who become civil partners after December 5, 2005 while one or both of them is receiving tax credits, or who are to be treated as if they are living together as civil partners from that date while one or both is claiming tax credits. Anyone making a new claim after that date must disclose if she or he has a civil partner or is living together with another person as civil partners.

HMRC has issued extensive new guidance to its officials reflecting the above, civil partnerships, recent gender recognition legislation, and the position of same sex couples living together as if in a civil partnership. The focus is on undisclosed partnerships. This is in the Claimant Compliance Manual at paragraphs CCM 1500–15270. CCM 15040 sets out the standard DWP approach but CCM 15045 warns officials about the problems of judging "modern-day relationships"—those where each of the couple keeps her or his own accounts and both look after the children and the housework. CCM 15150 warns officials not to fall for the "3 nights rule" (that two people who only spend 3 nights a week together cannot be a couple). CCM 15120 tells officials not to ask about sexual relationships and to tell appeal tribunals that this is official policy. There is also polite dissent from the views of a Social Security Commissioner about needing strong alternative evidence that a couple are living together in the absence of a sexual relationship. This guidance, of course, is in no way binding on tribunals.

Subs.(7)

This allows jurisdictional limits to be placed on entitlement to tax credit. Again, this breaks away from social security practice (which deals with Great Britain and Northern Ireland separately) to adopt income tax practice. It is supplemented by s.42 (persons subject to immigration control) and regulations made under that section. The main regulations under this subsection are the Tax Credits (Residence) Regulations 2003 (SI 2003/642). These impose a test of "ordinary residence" on most claimants.

Claims: supplementary

4.—(1) Regulations may—
(a) require a claim for a tax credit to be made in a prescribed manner and within a prescribed time,
(b) provide for a claim for a tax credit made in prescribed circumstances to be treated as having been made on a prescribed date earlier or later than that on which it is made,
(c) provide that, in prescribed circumstances, a claim for a tax credit may be made for a period wholly or partly after the date on which it is made,

(d) provide that, in prescribed circumstances, an award on a claim for a tax credit may be made subject to the condition that the requirements for entitlement are satisfied at a prescribed time,

(e) provide for a claim for a tax credit to be made or proceeded with in the name of a person who has died,

(f) provide that, in prescribed circumstances, one person may act for another in making a claim for a tax credit,

(g) provide that, in prescribed circumstances, a claim for a tax credit made by one member of a [2. . .] couple is to be treated as also made by the other member of [2 the couple][1], and

(h) provide that a claim for a tax credit is to be treated as made by a person or persons in such other circumstances as may be prescribed.

(2) The Board may supply to a person who has made a claim for a tax credit (whether or not jointly with another)—

(a) any information relating to the claim, to an award made on the claim or to any change of circumstances relevant to the claim or such an award,

(b) any communication made or received relating to such an award or any such change of circumstances, and

(c) any other information which is relevant to any entitlement to tax credits pursuant to the claim or any such change of circumstances or which appeared to be so relevant at the time the information was supplied.

AMENDMENTS

1. Tax Credits (Polygamous Marriages) Regulations 2003 (SI 2003/742) amends s.4(1)(g) as follows for the purposes of polygamous marriages:
"In section 4(1)(g)—
(a) for "member of a married couple or an unmarried couple" substitute "or more members of a polygamous unit";
(b) for "of the married couple or unmarried couple" substitute "or members".
2. Civil Partnership Act 2004, s.254 and Sch.24, para.145 (December 5, 2005).

DEFINITIONS

"award"—see s.14(1).
"the Board"—see s.67.
"claim"—see s.3(1).
"entitlement"—see s.18(1).
"joint claim"—see s.3(8).
"married couple"—see s.3(5).
"prescribed"—see s.67.
"single claim"—see s.3(8).
"tax credit"—see s.1(2).
"tax year"—see s.47.
"unmarried couple"—see s.3(8).

GENERAL NOTE

1.241 Regulations for the purposes of subs.(1) are made by HMRC by negative procedure: ss.65(2), 66(3). The main regulations made are the Tax Credits (Claims and Notifications) Regulations 2002 (SI 2002/2014). References to "the Board" are now references to the Commissioners for Revenue and Customs: CRCA 2005, s.4.

The most important point relevant to this section is that those Regulations require a claim to be made not later than three months after the date from which it can operate. For a claim to be effective from the beginning of a tax year, it must be made (that is, received by an appropriate office) before July 6 in that year. If made later than that, it will not operate for more than three months before the date on which the claim was actually made. But, unlike backdated claims for social security benefits, the three months backdating is automatic and is not dependent on grounds being shown for a "late claim". Nor is there any discretion to extent the three months' backdating of a claim in any circumstances. See reg.7 of those regulations. The only exception, under reg.8, applies to claimants claiming a disability element of WTC as part of the claim.

Subsection (2) gives HMRC power that it would otherwise not have to inform a claimant of information of which it knows that is relevant to a claim, or to an award or entitlement continuing. This will ensure that either member of a joint claiming couple can be informed of anything that the other member of the couple tells HMRC. This cuts across the privacy as between members of a couple that was respected by HMRC following the introduction of individual self-assessment for income tax.

Period of awards

5.—(1) Where a tax credit is claimed for a tax year by making a claim before the tax year begins, any award of the tax credit on the claim is for the whole of the tax year.

(2) An award on any other claim for a tax credit is for the period beginning with the date on which the claim is made and ending at the end of the tax year in which that date falls.

(3) Subsections (1) and (2) are subject to any decision by the Board under section 16 to terminate an award.

1.242

DEFINITIONS

"award"—see s.14(1).
"the Board"—see s.67.
"claim"—see s.3(1).
"tax credit"—see s.1(2).
"tax year"—see s.47.

GENERAL NOTE

This section applies to both CTC and WTC. It confirms the import of s.3(1), namely that a claim is for one tax year at a time, and provides that any award is for that tax year (or, if made during the year, for what is left of it). This is subject to the power in s.16 to end an award, after which a new claim must be made (s.3(2)). Effect is given to these provisions by the Tax Credits (Claims and Notifications) Regulations 2002 (SI 2002/2014), regs 4–11. Regulations 11 and 12 of those regulations provide a mechanism whereby a reply to a notice relating to one year of claim under s.17 of this Act can be treated as a claim for the following year.

Subsection (2), on its face, prevents retrospective claims, but it must be read with regs 4 and following of the Tax Credits (Claims and Notifications) Regulations 2002. These make provision for the "date on which a claim is made". Under reg.7, the general rule is that a claim is treated as made for the purposes of this subsection up to three months before the date on which the claim is received by an appropriate office, if *entitlement* extends that far back. This, like other issues about *award* and *entitlement*, seems to conflate the making of an award with entitlement (see the note to s.6). It will only be known that a person is entitled once a final decision is made under s.17 of this Act after the end of the year, while the award operates on the basis that the person is probably entitled.

See also Tax Credits Act 2002 (Transitional Provisions) Order 2005 (SI 2005/773), art.6.

1.243

Tax Credits Act 2002

Notifications of changes of circumstances

6.—(1) Regulations may provide that any change of circumstances of a prescribed description which may increase the maximum rate at which a person or persons may be entitled to a tax credit is to do so only if notification of it has been given.

(2) Regulations under subsection (1) may—
   (a) provide for notification of a change of circumstances given in prescribed circumstances to be treated as having been given on a prescribed date earlier or later than that on which it is given,
   (b) provide that, in prescribed circumstances, a notification of a change of circumstances may be given for a period wholly or partly after the date on which it is given, and
   (c) provide that, in prescribed circumstances, an amendment of an award of a tax credit in consequence of a notification of a change of circumstances may be made subject to the condition that the requirements for entitlement to the amended amount of the tax credit are satisfied at a prescribed time.

(3) Regulations may require that, where a person has or persons have claimed a tax credit, notification is to be given if there is a change of circumstances of a prescribed description which may decrease the rate at which he is or they are entitled to the tax credit or mean that he ceases or they cease to be entitled to the tax credit.

(4) Regulations under this section may—
   (a) require a notification to be given in a prescribed manner and within a prescribed time,
   (b) specify the person or persons by whom a notification may be, or is to be, given, and
   (c) provide that, in prescribed circumstances, one person may act for another in giving a notification.

[[1](3A) For the purposes of this section, a change of circumstances shall be treated as having occurred where by virtue of the coming into force of Part 14 of Schedule 24 to the Civil Partnership Act 2004 (amendments of the Tax Credits Act 2002) two people of the same sex are treated as a couple.

(3B) In subsection (3A), "couple" has the meaning given in paragraph 144(3) of Part 14 of Schedule 24 to the Civil Partnership Act 2004.]

AMENDMENT

1. Tax Credits Notification of Changes of Circumstances (Civil Partnership) (Transitional Provisions) Order 2005 (SI 2005/828), art.2 (April 8, 2005).

DEFINITIONS

"award"—see s.14(1).
"claim"—see s.3(1).
"entitlement"—see s.18(1).
"maximum rate"—see ss.9 and 11.
"prescribed"—see s.67.
"tax credit"—see s.1(2).

GENERAL NOTE

The Bill on which this Act was based was tabled in, and passed through, the House of Commons without a clear distinction being drawn between the measures relating to *award* of a tax credit on a claim and the later issue of *entitlement* to that credit. As a result, there is no clear progression in the sections of the Act from claims to award to entitlement. This section might from context appear to be about awards, but subs.(1) is drafted to cover only entitlement issues. The link is provided partly under subs.(2) and partly by s.15, which links changes in awards to the rate at which someone *may be* entitled to a tax credit.

"Change of circumstances" is, of course, a familiar social security concept on which the SSA 1998 relies heavily for powers to change decisions after they are made but where they have continuing effect. There is also a general duty on claimants to report changes of circumstances of relevance to benefit awards. This section allows a similar duty to be imposed on tax credit claimants. The section is purely empowering. Regulations may be made by the Revenue by negative procedure: ss.65(2) and 66(3). The relevant regulations are the Tax Credits (Claims and Notifications) Regulations 2002 (SI 2002/2014), regs 19–29. Those regulations, however, take a substantially different approach to changes of circumstances to those operated for social security benefits.

The nature of a "change of circumstances" and the treatment adopted for making and dealing with changes of circumstance requires some further explanation because of the differences in the ways in which the rules operate compared with those for income support or jobseeker's allowance. The main differences are—

(a) not all changes of circumstances during a year will result in a change of circumstances affecting the award or entitlement;
(b) the duty to notify changes of circumstances is limited in scope and applies only to some changes;
(c) failure to notify when there is a duty to do so may make the person failing to notify liable to penalties and penalty proceedings under ss.31(1) and 32(3).

Relevant changes of circumstances

Because the income test under s.7 is applied to the tax year (or period of award) as a whole, a change in income levels during a year may be irrelevant to award or entitlement levels, and so not constitute a change of circumstances. This will be particularly so towards the end of a tax year. Further, because of the "buffer" built into the income test by s.7(3), any increase of income over the year as a whole of less than £25,000 is irrelevant in any event. Changes in capital are also immaterial, as it is only the (taxable) income from capital that affects the level of award and entitlement. For similar reasons, a change of job (with a gap of under seven days between jobs) will also not affect an award or entitlement unless either it changes the income level significantly over the year as a whole or it decreases the hours worked below 16, or—for WTC only—it increases or decreases the hours above or below 30.

The changes that are relevant are significant income changes, as noted above, and other changes that will stop entitlement or cause its overall level to be changed. This may apply differently to CTC and WTC. But not all those changes must be reported.

1.246

Changes that must be reported

There is no duty to report changes that increase entitlement, even though that may involve someone else's entitlement being reduced. However, it may be in a claimant's own interests to report changes. And in some cases, such as a child reaching 16, HMRC may sometimes assume a change (for example that the claimant no longer has a child in education once he or she is 16 and of school-leaving age) unless told otherwise.

There is also no general duty to report changes of circumstances in cases where the change reduces entitlement to credits. Awards are made for a year at a time, so changes within a year that are likely to be self-cancelling may not result in any change in the overall award. HMRC also checks every award at the end of the year, so can deal with the changes after the year end. When the scheme was introduced those receiving awards were only required to report changes to the makeup of the household, when someone went overseas for a period, and changes in childcare arrangements. That

1.247

Tax Credits Act 2002

duty has been expanded from November 2006 to cover several other circumstances. The duty is imposed by regulation 21 of the Tax Credits (Claims and Notifications) Regulations 2002 (SI 2002/2014) as amended from November 1, 2006 by SI 2006/2689. See para.2.307 below. In addition, the period during which the change must be reported has been reduced from three months to one month.

Changes that may be reported

1.248   Under regs 20 and 25 of the Tax Credits (Claims and Notifications) Regulations 2002, a change of circumstances that may increase an award or entitlement to either WTC or CTC will only do so if notification of the change has been given to HMRC within three months of the date when the change occurred. Later notice will be backdated not more than three months. This time limit is, however, extended under reg.26 for those claiming the disability or severe disability elements of WTC. In all other cases, notification of any change of circumstances that will or may benefit the claimant should be made within the three months' limit to prevent both loss of award and loss of entitlement.

In its publicity, HMRC list as factors where notification is appropriate but not necessary: changes of jobs or job details; a change in the number of children; changes in the arrangements for childcare; changes in the position of young persons over 16 (for example leaving school or starting work and making a separate claim); changes in income; changes in disability circumstances; changes in the receipt of other benefits; and changes of the address of anyone mentioned in a claim.

As with claims, there is no set form required to notify a change of circumstances. It can be done by telephone (to 0845 300 3900 in Britain or 0845 603 2000 in Northern Ireland) or on the internet (at *http://www.hmrc.gov.uk/taxcredits*) or by writing to the Tax Credits offices in Preston and Belfast.

It is understood that some claimants decide not to make a timely statement of a change of circumstances, relying instead on a timely notification at the end of the year under s.17. In effect, this allows the claimant to receive a known current overpayment while accepting there will be a later repayment (or reduction of future tax credits). There is a further advantage to some claimants from this. An in-year change of circumstances can result in an immediate recovery of the whole overpayment. By contrast, an end-of-year overpayment may be recovered by more advantageous (to the claimant) instalments. See the Low Income Tax Reform Group statement of November 9, 2005, arguing that this is both unfair and a discouragement to timely reporting of changes of circumstances. It is not known how many overpayments are deliberately incurred by claimants for a short or medium term advantage. It is also understood that HMRC may telephone claimants before a year end to remind them of the need to report these changes.

Automatic notification?

1.249   Part II of this Act transfers responsibility for child benefit to HMRC. The decision of the House of Lords in *Hinchy v Secretary of State for Work and Pensions* [2005] UKHL 16 confirms the traditional view that a claimant must tell the relevant office about changes of circumstances. It is therefore not enough that, for example, a claimant tells the HMRC Child Benefit Office but not the tax credits office or the local social security office or housing benefit authority of the changed position of one of the claimant's children. However, the growth of public computer-based records and the interlinking of records between departments under the Generalised Matching Service increasingly notifies one department of information known to another. That is no defence under the tax credit scheme to liability to repay any overpaid tax credit. It will be for consideration whether this is relevant to any penalty proceedings under ss.31 or 32. It is understood that HMRC is notified automatically about decisions of the termination of disability living allowance awards.

Failure to report

1.250   Leaving aside fraudulent or other cases of deliberate non-disclosure, if a change of circumstances is not reported when it happens it will be picked up directly or indirectly when the claimant replies to HMRC's final notice issued under s.17. This is because of the declaration necessary under s.17. If it is a relevant change, then the entitlement to WTC and/or CTC will be confirmed at a different rate to that of the award. This will result in an overpayment (see s.28) if the level of award is, as a result, higher than the level of entitlement. It could also result in an underpayment (see s.30), but only to the extent that the notification is regarded as in time for any part of the relevant tax year. In most cases, if the notification is more than three months after the end of the tax year then the right to an increased entitlement will have been lost.

HMRC has announced that it will not seek penalties from a taxpayer who has a nil award following a claim and who then fails to make a mandatory notification of a change of circumstances. See *Tax Adviser*, June 2003, p.13.

Income test

7.—(1) The entitlement of a person or persons of any description to a tax credit is dependent on the relevant income—
  (a) not exceeding the amount determined in the manner prescribed for the purposes of this paragraph in relation to the tax credit and a person or persons of that description (referred to in this Part as the income threshold), or
  (b) exceeding the income threshold by only so much that a determination in accordance with regulations under section 13(2) provides a rate of the tax credit in his or their case.
(2) Subsection (1) does not apply in relation to the entitlement of a person or persons to a tax credit for so long as the person, or either of the persons, is entitled to any social security benefit prescribed for the purposes of this subsection in relation to the tax credit.
(3) In this Part "the relevant income" means—
  (a) if an amount is prescribed for the purposes of this paragraph and the current year income exceeds the previous year income by not more than that amount, the previous year income,
  (b) if an amount is prescribed for the purposes of this paragraph and the current year income exceeds the previous year income by more than that amount, the current year income reduced by that amount,
  (c) if an amount is prescribed for the purposes of this paragraph and the previous year income exceeds the current year income by not more than that amount, the previous year income,
  (d) if an amount is prescribed for the purposes of this paragraph and the previous year income exceeds the current year income by more than that amount, the current year income increased by that amount, and
  (e) otherwise, the current year income.
(4) In this Part "the current year income" means—
  (a) in relation to persons by whom a joint claim for a tax credit is made, the aggregate income of the persons for the tax year to which the claim relates, and
  (b) in relation to a person by whom a single claim for a tax credit is made, the income of the person for that tax year.
(5) In this Part "the previous year income" means—
  (a) in relation to persons by whom a joint claim for a tax credit is made, the aggregate income of the persons for the tax year preceding that to which the claim relates, and
  (b) in relation to a person by whom a single claim for a tax credit is made, the income of the person for that preceding tax year.

1.251

Tax Credits Act 2002

(6) Regulations may provide that, for the purposes of this Part, income of a prescribed description is to be treated as being, or as not being, income for a particular tax year.

(7) In particular, regulations may provide that income of a prescribed description of a person for the tax year immediately before the preceding tax year referred to in subsection (5) is to be treated as being income of that preceding tax year (instead of any actual income of that description of the person for that preceding tax year).

(8) Regulations may for the purposes of this Part make provision—
(a) as to what is, or is not, income, and
(b) as to the calculation of income.

(9) Regulations may provide that, for the purposes of this Part, a person is to be treated—
(a) as having income which he does not in fact have, or
(b) as not having income which he does in fact have.

(10) The Board may estimate the amount of the income of a person, or the aggregate income of persons, for any tax year for the purpose of making, amending or terminating an award of a tax credit; but such an estimate does not affect the rate at which he is, or they are, entitled to the tax credit for that or any other tax year.

AMENDMENTS

1. Subsection (2) is amended as it applies to polygamous units by Tax Credits (Polygamous Marriages) Regulations 2003 (SI 2003/742), reg.6.
2. References to "the Board" are now references to the Commissioners for Revenue and Customs: CRCA 2005, s.4.

DEFINITIONS

"award"—see s.14(1).
"the Board"—see s.67.
"claim"—see s.3(1).
"entitlement"—see s.18(1).
"joint claim"—see s.3(8).
"married couple"—see s.3(5).
"prescribed"—see s.67.
"single claim"—see s.3(8).
"tax credit"—see s.1(2).
"tax year"—see s.47.
"unmarried couple"—see s.3(8).

GENERAL NOTE

1.252 This is a framework and empowering section making provision for the imposition of an income test on all claimants for both CTC and WTC. The relevant regulations are the Tax Credits (Definition of Calculation of Income) Regulations 2002 (SI 2002/2006) and the Tax Credits (Income Thresholds and Determination of Rates) Regulations 2002 (SI 2002/2008). The powers to make regulations are Treasury powers requiring affirmative procedures. The policy behind the Act is to follow WFTC by making the benefit income-related but, unlike WFTC, there is no separate test of capital. Further, the regulations link the income test closely to income tax rules, thus breaking away from the separate social security means tests.

Subs.(1)

1.253 This is worded to refer "a tax credit" so that different amounts may be prescribed for different tax credits. Regulation 3 of the Tax Credits (Income Thresholds and

Determination of Rates) Regulations 2002 sets a threshold for WTC of £5,220, and for CTC of £14,495 with a further higher threshold for the family element only of CTC of £50,000 in reg.8 of those Regulations. See para.2.251.

Although this section defines the amounts of income above which tax credits are reduced by reference to income as "income threshold", HMRC literature, including formal papers, refers to them instead as "taper start points". A Commissioner criticised this change of language, without any accompanying explanation, in CTC 2113 2006. In that case, which concerned the operation of these start points or threshold, the Commissioner criticised the failure of HMRC to explain how its language fitted in with the statutory language. This left a claimant unable to understand the HMRC submissions and the appeal tribunal's decision agreeing with the submission (but using the statutory language also without explanation).

Subs. (2)

This disapplies the income test, so allowing payment of a tax credit without reference to separate means-testing, where the prescribed benefits are in payment. The benefits are prescribed by Tax Credits (Income Thresholds and Determination of Rates) Regulations 2002, reg.4 as covering only some claimants for income support and jobseeker's allowance. In those cases, other regulations operate to stop any claim for CTC (WTC is not applicable) until April 6, 2004 in any event. The regulations stopping claims have, however, been suspended in some cases to December 31, 2006 as the phasing in of CTC for those on income support or JSA has been put back to that date.

1.254

Subs. (3)

This is another part of the Act that has now been put into effect in a substantially different way to that first intended. Paras (c) and (d) have not been put into effect, so only paras (a) (b) and (e) are operational. But from April 6, 2006, the limit prescribed for the purpose of each of those paragraphs was increased from an initial figure of £2,500 to £25,000. The subsection therefore only now applies to the following effect:

(a) and (b): previous year income applies unless current year income is over £25,000 more

(e): current year income applies if there is no previous year income.

In other words, the credits are normally based on the previous year's income. This contrasts with the move of all income tax liability over recent years to a current year basis. As average earnings, and the earnings of most individuals, rise year by year if only to reflect inflation, the result of the current operation of this subsection is to increase the net value of tax credits as compared with income tax by ignoring all but the largest increases in earnings. Further, this will apply only if the increases are earnings. The rule does not apply to capital gains. See further para.2.223.

1.255

Subss. (6)–(9)

See the Tax Credits (Definition and Calculation of Income) Regulations 2002, as amended.

1.256

Subs. (10)

This is a wide power to deal with awards. It allows HMRC to make, change or stop an award during the tax year on the basis of an estimate only. That estimate will be the decision made under ss.14(1), 15(1) or 16(1). Any of these decisions are subject to appeal and, on appeal, it will be for the appeal tribunal to make the estimate (subject to any settlement of the appeal under s.54 of the TMA 1970). See further the note to s.39 below. It is understood that the standard practice of HMRC is to make all initial decisions on the basis of the previous year's income using this power. Where a claim form indicates that the current year's income should be used, HMRC then makes an immediate revision under s.15.

1.257

Tax Credits Act 2002

Child tax credit

Entitlement

1.258   **8.**—(1) The entitlement of the person or persons by whom a claim for child tax credit has been made is dependent on him, or either of them, being responsible for one or more children or qualifying young persons.

(2) Regulations may make provision for the purposes of child tax credit as to the circumstances in which a person is or is not responsible for a child or qualifying young person.

(3) For the purposes of this Part a person is a child if he has not attained the age of sixteen; but regulations may make provision for a person who has attained that age to remain a child for the purposes of this Part after attaining that age for a prescribed period or until a prescribed date.

(4) In this Part "qualifying young person" means a person, other than a child, who—

(a) has not attained such age (greater than 16) as is prescribed, and

(b) satisfies prescribed conditions.

(5) Circumstances may be prescribed in which a person is to be entitled to child tax credit for a prescribed period in respect of a child or qualifying young person who has died.

AMENDMENT

1. Subsection (1) is amended as it applies to polygamous units by Tax Credits (Polygamous Marriages) Regulations 2003 (SI 2003/742), reg.7.

DEFINITIONS

"child"—see subs.(3).
"prescribed"—see s.67.
"qualifying young person"—see subs.(4).

GENERAL NOTE

1.259   This section sets the central tests for claiming child tax credits, namely that there be a child or young person for whom the claimant is, or joint claimants are, responsible. Subsection (1) provides that entitlement to child tax credit is dependent on these tests. It is deliberately parallel to SSCBA 1992, s.141, the section entitling claimants to child benefit for each of the children for whom a claimant is responsible. Subsection (2) makes provision for regulations defining responsibility for a child. This is covered by SSCBA 1992, s.143 and supporting regulations. Subsection (3) defines a child as someone who has not reached the age of 16, but also allows the age to be extended by regulation. Child benefit is payable for all children who have not reached 16 (SSCBA 1992, s.142(1)). Child benefit is also payable for certain children over 16, but for child tax credit purposes they are known as "qualifying young persons". Subsection (4) allows regulations to define that category. The intention is, as with child benefit, to include certain young persons over 16 but not over 19, depending on ongoing education (but not covering students undergoing higher education). The effect confirms a general policy to exclude those over 16 from being "children" for state benefit purposes, but to include them, along with students, in a separate category. This is because those over 16 can claim some benefits in their own right. See further the Child Tax Credit Regulations 2002 (SI 2002/2007).

(2002 c.21, s.8)

Subs. (5)

This is a new rule which makes identical provision as that in s.54 of this Act, ensuring that both child benefit and child tax credit remain payable for a period (set by regulations at eight weeks) after the death of a child or, in the case of child tax credit, qualifying young person.

1.260

Maximum rate

9.—(1) The maximum rate at which a person or persons may be entitled to child tax credit is to be determined in the prescribed manner.

1.261

(2) The prescribed manner of determination must involve the inclusion of—
  (a) an element which is to be included in the case of all persons entitled to child tax credit, and
  (b) an element in respect of each child or qualifying young person for whom the person is, or either of them is or are, responsible.

(3) The element specified in paragraph (a) of subsection (2) is to be known as the family element of child tax credit and that specified in paragraph (b) of that subsection is to be known as the individual element of child tax credit.

(4) The prescribed manner of determination may involve the inclusion of such other elements as may be prescribed.

(5) The prescribed manner of determination—
  (a) may include provision for the amount of the family element of child tax credit to vary according to the age of any of the children or qualifying young persons or according to any such other factors as may be prescribed,
  (b) may include provision for the amount of the individual element of child tax credit to vary according to the age of the child or qualifying young person or according to any such other factors as may be prescribed, and
  (c) must include provision for the amount of the individual element of child tax credit to be increased in the case of a child or qualifying young person who is disabled and to be further increased in the case of a child or qualifying young person who is severely disabled.

(6) A child or qualifying young person is disabled, or severely disabled, for the purposes of this section only if—
  (a) he satisfies prescribed conditions, or
  (b) prescribed conditions exist in relation to him.

(7) If, in accordance with regulations under section 8(2), more than one claimant may be entitled to child tax credit in respect of the same child or qualifying young person, the prescribed manner of determination may include provision for the amount of any element of child tax credit included in the case of any one or more of them to be less than it would be if only one claimant were so entitled.

(8) "Claimant" means—
  (a) in the case of a single claim, the person who makes the claim; and
  (b) in the case of a joint claim, the persons who make the claim.

AMENDMENT

1. Subsection (2) is amended as it applies to polygamous units by Tax Credits (Polygamous Marriages) Regulations 2003 (SI 2003/742), reg.8.

Definitions

"child"—see s.8(3).
"child tax credit"—see s.8.
"claimant"—see subs.(8).
"disabled"—see subs.(6).
"prescribed"—see s.67.
"qualifying young person"—see s.8(4).
"severely disabled"—see subs.(6).

General Note

1.262   This section is again a mixture of defining provisions and empowering provisions. Subsection (1) provides that the way in which entitlement to CTC is to be calculated is to be set out in regulations. The first set of regulations for this purpose are the Child Tax Credit Regulations 2002 (SI 2002/2007). Subsections (2) and (3) provide that in every case an award of CTC must involve both a "family element" for the claimant and an "individual element" for each child or young person. The amount of the individual element must be higher for children or young persons who are disabled, and higher again if they are seriously disabled, but definition of those conditions is left to regulations: subss.(5)(c) and (6). This continues in another form the disabled child premium payable under income support. The other provisions in the section are permissive.

Subs.(7)

1.263   A recurrent problem for child benefit is where more than one person has or claims to have responsibility for a child. Child benefit can only be claimed by one claimant and is indivisible (even between married parents living together). For CTC purposes, this enabling provision seems to imply that a lower amount of CTC can be paid to a claimant where there is more than one claim, thus allowing splitting of entitlement. However, no provision has been made for this in regulations: see Child Tax Credit Regulations 2002 (SI 2002/2007), reg.3.

Section 8 is ambiguous as to whether claims can be made by both parents at the same time if both claim that they are responsible for a child, but this clearly suggests that rival claims can lead to a shared award. The Child Tax Credit Regulations do not make provision for this, but instead follow the approach of child benefit law in providing an award to only one person, with no provision for shared claims. It is not clear how a case is properly handled without discrimination if the tax credit is not shared and joint claimants refuse to indicate that one of them has a prior claim on any basis. It is to be doubted, however, that a solution to the problem by an award to either claimant would provide the basis for a claim by the other that any discrimination was in breach of the European Convention on Human Rights. But it is not obvious that the existing appeal procedures allow a proper determination of such competing claims in a single hearing by a tribunal. If the losing claimant appeals, what right does the successful claimant have to put her or his point of view to the appeal tribunal? There may be a Convention issue here under Art.6. Robust tribunals have been known to solve this dilemma by listing actual or deemed appeals together in cases where the decision(s) under appeal involves a transfer of entitlement from one claimant to another.

Working tax credit

Entitlement

1.264   **10.**—(1) The entitlement of the person or persons by whom a claim for working tax credit has been made is dependent on him, or either of them, being engaged in qualifying remunerative work.

(2) Regulations may for the purposes of this Part make provision—
(a) as to what is, or is not, qualifying remunerative work, and
(b) as to the circumstances in which a person is, or is not, engaged in it.

(3) The circumstances prescribed under subsection (2)(b) may differ by reference to—
(a) the age of the person or either of the persons,
(b) whether the person, or either of the persons, is disabled,
(c) whether the person, or either of the persons, is responsible for one or more children or qualifying young persons, or
(d) any other factors.

(4) Regulations may make provision for the purposes of working tax credit as to the circumstances in which a person is or is not responsible for a child or qualifying young person.

AMENDMENT

1. Subsections (1) and (3) are amended as they apply to polygamous units by Tax Credits (Polygamous Marriages) Regulations 2003 (SI 2003/742), reg.9.

DEFINITIONS

"child"—see s.8(3).
"disabled"—see s.11(7).
"engaged"—see subs.(2).
"qualifying remunerative work"—see subs.(2).
"qualifying young person"—see s.8(4).
"responsible for a child"—see subs.(4).

GENERAL NOTE

This section is the parallel to s.8, laying down the central test for claiming WTC by single or joint claimants, and defining or providing for definition of the key terms.

1.265

Subs.(1)
This makes the central test for WTC "being engaged in qualifying remunerative work". "Remunerative work" is the test used in WFTC and family credit before that (see Family Credit (General) Regulations 1987 (SI 1987/1973, reg.4). It is also used in the regulations defining entitlement to income support and jobseeker's allowance. See the notes to Income Support (General) Regulations 1987, reg.4, and Jobseeker's Allowance Regulations 1996, reg.51, in Vol.II of this work. The test of "work" has been held by Commissioners to be wider than "employment" (*R(FC) 2/90*), although the requirement that it be "remunerative"—defined as work done for payment or in expectation of payment—excludes volunteers (*R(IS) 12/92*).

1.266

Although the test is the same both for tax credits and for income support and JSA, experience has shown that gaps can occur between one award ending and the other starting, particularly where work ends near the end of a tax year for example because of ill health or disablement. HMRC has no powers to assist someone who stops being a credit claimant in these circumstances and is under no duty to forward a claim to the Department for Work and Pensions. Nor can an appeal assist such a claimant.

Subs.(2)
This provides for further definition of what is "qualifying" work, and also when someone is "engaged" in work. This is used to set the number of hours that must be worked in order to count for WTC purposes, but it also allows the start and finish of a period of work to be defined and intermittent work patterns to be subject to regulation.

1.267

Tax Credits Act 2002

See the WTC (Entitlement and Maximum Rate) Regulations 2002 (SI 2002/2005), reg.4.

Subs. (3)

1.268 This permits the qualifying conditions for WTC to be varied between different claimants. Regulation 4 of the Working Tax Credit (Entitlement and Maximum Rate) Regulations 2002 provides that the minimum work level is 16 hours a week for those with children, those over 50, and those suffering disabilities (carrying forward the tests from WFTC, New Deal 50 Plus, and DPTC) but 30 hours a week for other claimants aged 25 or over. No WTC is to be payable to those aged under 25 unless one of the "16-hour" tests applies to them.

Subs. (4)

1.269 This provides that responsibility for a child or qualifying young person may be defined differently for WTC purposes to the definition under s.8 for CTC purposes. This links with s.12, the childcare element of WTC. However, the regulations have not to date adopted any distinction.

Maximum rate

1.270 **11.**—(1) The maximum rate at which a person or persons may be entitled to working tax credit is to be determined in the prescribed manner.

(2) The prescribed manner of determination must involve the inclusion of an element which is to be included in the case of all persons entitled to working tax credit.

(3) The prescribed manner of determination must also involve the inclusion of an element in respect of the person, or either or both of the persons, engaged in qualifying remunerative work—
  (a) having a physical or mental disability which puts him at a disadvantage in getting a job, and
  (b) satisfying such other conditions as may be prescribed.

(4) The element specified in subsection (2) is to be known as the basic element of working tax credit and the element specified in subsection (3) is to be known as the disability element of working tax credit.

(5) The prescribed manner of determination may involve the inclusion of such other elements as may be prescribed.

(6) The other elements may (in particular) include—
  (a) an element in respect of the person, or either of the persons or the two taken together, being engaged in qualifying remunerative work to an extent prescribed for the purposes of this paragraph;
  (b) an element in respect of the persons being the members of [¹ a couple],
  (c) an element in respect of the person not being a member of [¹ a couple] but being responsible for a child or qualifying young person;
  (d) an element in respect of the person, or either or both of the persons, being severely disabled; and
  (e) an element in respect of the person, or either or both of the persons, being over a prescribed age, satisfying prescribed conditions and having been engaged in qualifying remunerative work for not longer than a prescribed period.

(7) A person has a physical or mental disability which puts him at a disadvantage in getting a job, or is severely disabled, for the purposes of this section only if—
  (a) he satisfies prescribed conditions, or
  (b) prescribed conditions exist in relation to him.

(2002 c.21, s.11)

AMENDMENTS

1. For the purposes of applying this section to polygamous units, Tax Credits (Polygamous Marriages) Regulations 2003 (SI 2003/742), reg.10 omits subs.(6)(c) and introduces alternative wording to subss.(3) and (6).
2. Civil Partnership Act 2004, s.254 and Sch.24, para.145 (December 5, 2005).

DEFINITIONS

"child"—see s.8(3).
"married couple"—see s.3(5).
"physical or mental disability"—see subs.(7).
"prescribed"—see s.67.
"qualifying young person"—see s.8(4).
"severely disabled"—see subs.(7).
"unmarried couple"—see s.3(6).

GENERAL NOTE

This parallels s.9 for WTC. Subsection (1) allows the determination of WTC rates to be set by regulations, but subss.(2) and (4) require that anyone entitled to WTC must receive a basic element of credit. There must also be an additional disability element in appropriate cases (carrying forward the policy of DPTC): subss.(3) and (4). Subsection (7) sets the test for the disability element in terms reflecting the terms of award of DPTC and DWA under the previous law (SSCBA 1992, s.129). There may also be a childcare element, but this is provided for in s.12. Subsections (5) and (6) are purely permissive. Effect is given to these provisions by the WTC (Entitlement and Maximum Rate) Regulations 2002 (SI 2002/2005).

1.271

Childcare element

12.—(1) The prescribed manner of determination of the maximum rate at which a person or persons may be entitled to working tax credit may involve the inclusion, in prescribed circumstances, of a childcare element.

1.272

(2) A childcare element is an element in respect of a prescribed proportion of so much of any relevant childcare charges as does not exceed a prescribed amount.

(3) "Childcare charges" are charges of a prescribed description incurred in respect of childcare by the person, or either or both of the persons, by whom a claim for working tax credit is made.

(4) "Childcare", in relation to a person or persons, means care provided—
  (a) for a child of a prescribed description for whom the person is responsible, or for whom either or both of the persons is or are responsible, and
  (b) by a person of a prescribed description.

(5) The descriptions of persons prescribed under subsection (4)(b) may include descriptions of persons approved in accordance with a scheme made by the appropriate national authority under this subsection.

(6) "The appropriate national authority" means—
  (a) in relation to care provided in England, the Secretary of State,
  (b) in relation to care provided in Scotland, the Scottish Ministers,
  (c) in relation to care provided in Wales, the National Assembly for Wales, and
  (d) in relation to care provided in Northern Ireland, the Department of Health, Social Services and Public Safety.

(7) The provision made by a scheme under subsection (5) must involve the giving of approvals, in accordance with criteria determined by or under the scheme, by such of the following as the scheme specifies—
(a) the appropriate national authority making the scheme;
(b) one or more specified persons or bodies or persons or bodies of a specified description, and
(c) persons or bodies accredited under the scheme in accordance with criteria determined by or under it.
(8) A scheme under subsection (5) may authorise—
(a) the making of grants or loans to, and
(b) the charging of reasonable fees by, persons and bodies giving approvals.

AMENDMENT

1. Subsections (3) and (4) are modified, as they apply to polygamous units, by Tax Credits (Polygamous Marriages) Regulations 2003 (SI 2003/742), reg.11.

DEFINITIONS

"appropriate national authority"—see subs.(6).
"child"—see s.8(3).
"childcare"—see subs.(4).
"childcare charges"—see subs.(3).
"maximum rate"—see s.11(1).
"prescribed"—see s.67.
"tax credit"—see s.1(2).

GENERAL NOTE

1.273   The childcare element was introduced to family credit in response to a successful discrimination challenge to the previous law before the European Court of Justice in *Meyers v Adjudication Officer*, Case C-116/94 [1995] All E.R. (EC) 705. Successive governments have made it more generous, and it is now given further prominence by its own section in this Act. However, the section is in form entirely permissive, even if the failure to implement it at all might invite a further challenge to the European Court. Subsections (2)–(4) provide that the element is a credit for a part of the charges incurred by a claimant for "childcare" provided for prescribed children by prescribed persons. Regulation 7 of the Tax Credits (Income Thresholds and Determination of Rates) Regulations 2002 (SI 2002/2008) specifies this proportion to be 70 per cent. This is increased to 80 per cent from April 2006. The important issue here is the identity of those who may provide the childcare. Government policy is that childcare providers should be licensed or supervised. But the way in which that is to be done is a devolved matter for the separate governments of England, Scotland, Wales and Northern Ireland. This reflects the fact that both education and social welfare functions are now functions of the separate national authorities. Subsections (5)–(8) give effect to this. Responsibility for both policy and operation of the childcare registration rules is therefore outside the responsibilities of HMRC and outside the jurisdiction of the appeal tribunals.

National government policy to encourage parents to return to work and to encourage child care arrangements to assist them doing so has not been confined to the child care element of working tax credits, as these benefit only the less well paid. Another major measure is the provision of income and corporation tax relief for child care provision by employers to employees. Sections 318 to 318C of ITEPA (set out below) provide income tax exemption for employees on provision of care for a child by an employer if the relevant conditions are met. There are also associated NI contribution advantages. HMRC publish a useful summary of this as IR118, *Childcare provided by employers*. This raises the question whether it is more advantageous to a parent to receive employer childcare help with the related tax and contribution exemptions, or help independently through the WTC childcare element. The higher paid are more likely to gain from employer provided assistance. There is no easy answer for the lower paid, particularly now that the maximum contribution is 80 per cent of the fees paid up to the raised ceiling, for two or more children, of £300 weekly. Any comparison should be made on the basis that WTC and CTC are both exempt from income tax: ITEPA s.677 below. They also do not count as earnings for NI contributions.

Rate

Rate

13.—(1) Where, in the case of a person or persons entitled to a tax credit, the relevant income does not exceed the income threshold (or his or their entitlement arises by virtue of section 7(2)), the rate at which he is or they are entitled to the tax credit is the maximum rate for his or their case.

(2) Regulations shall make provision as to the manner of determining the rate (if any) at which a person is, or persons are, entitled to a tax credit in any other case.

(3) The manner of determination prescribed under subsection (2)—
(a) may involve the making of adjustments so as to avoid fractional amounts, and
(b) may include provision for securing that, where the rate at which a person or persons would be entitled to a tax credit would be less than a prescribed rate, there is no rate in his or their case.

1.274

DEFINITIONS
"the income threshold"—see s.7(1)(a).
"maximum rate"—see ss.9(1) and 11(1).
"prescribed"—see s.67.
"relevant income"—see s.7(3).
"tax credit"—see s.1(2).

GENERAL NOTE

This short section supplements s.7 in defining the maximum rate of WTC for a claimant, and a minimum level of payment, and provides for regulations to determine these. See the Tax Credits (Income Thresholds and Determination of Rates) Regulations 2002 (SI 2002/2008), which set out a multi-stage formula.

1.275

Decisions

Initial decisions

14.—(1) On a claim for a tax credit the Board must decide—
(a) whether to make an award of the tax credit, and
(b) if so, the rate at which to award it.
(2) Before making their decision the Board may by notice—
(a) require the person, or [either or both][any or all]¹ of the persons, by whom the claim is made to provide any information or evidence which the Board consider they may need for making their decision, or

1.276

(b) require any person of a prescribed description to provide any information or evidence of a prescribed description which the Board consider they may need for that purpose, by the date specified in the notice.

(3) The Board's power to decide the rate at which to award a tax credit includes power to decide to award it at a nil rate.

AMENDMENTS

1. Subsection (2) is modified in its application to polygamous units by Tax Credits (Polygamous Marriages) Regulations 2003 (SI 2003/742), reg.12.
2. References to "the Board" are now references to the Commissioners for Revenue and Customs: CRCA 2005, s.4.
3. The section is disapplied for claimants subject to immigration control. See Tax Credits (Immigration) Regulations 2003 (SI 2003/623) regs 3, 4.

DEFINITIONS

"claim"—see s.3(8).
"the Board"—see s.67.
"tax credit"—see s.1(2).

GENERAL NOTE

1.277 This section imposes a duty on HMRC to decide a claim properly made under s.3 by making an award (or not), but it sets no time limit on that decision. An award is a decision to pay the tax credit. It is not a decision on entitlement. That is made later, under s.18. This explains the section title "initial decisions" (in the first draft of the Bill it was "provisional decisions"). Section 7(10) provides that HMRC may make this decision on the basis of an estimate. A decision under subs.(1) can be appealed (s.38).

This imposes the formal duty to deal with a claim by making or refusing an award. HMRC may use the power to estimate the income of claimants under s.7(10) rather than wait for information from an examination of the claim. Or it may make an award and examine the claim more thoroughly afterwards. A decision to award or refuse under this subsection is subject to appeal: s.38(1). However, HMRC practice is to attempt to deal with any such appeal by a settlement under the terms of s.54 of the Taxes Managements Act 1970. See Code of Practice 23 and the note to s.39 below.

HMRC has now automated most of the process. In *In the Know* for Winter 2004/2005 (a newsletter published periodically for tax credit advisers, and on the HMRC website), it was stated:

> "The days of caseworkers working on a claim from receipt to payment are over. Now, most tax credit claims are captured electronically either on the tax credit computer using rapid data capture techniques or via the Internet. This means that a claim can be automatically checked and processed, the entitlement calculated, a decision notice produced and sent out, and payments made—all without any clerical intervention."

This quotation uses the wrong language. It is not an entitlement decision that is made in this way but an award decision under this section. It also reveals that HMRC do not use the power to enquire under subs.(2) in the usual case. This means that HMRC can use only their powers under s.16 to make an in-year check on a claimant, if the conditions in that section are met. It also clearly states the very different approach taken by HMRC to that of the DWP (and formerly the DSS). There is no "ownership" of a tax credits decision. One team run the computers that make the initial award decisions, then other teams take over to deal with other aspects of the case. There is also no "local office" culture in HMRC tax credit administration. That being so, it would appear to be arguable that the recognition of that aspect of DWP administration by the House of Lords in *Hinchy* would have no application to HMRC.

(2002 c.21, s.14)

Subs.(2)

This empowers HMRC to require further information before making the decision by notice (see s.45 as to the notice). Penalties attach to failure to reply to a notice or to wrong replies (ss.31 and 32). The subsection also permits information to be required from others. This has been applied by the Tax Credits (Claims and Notifications) Regulations 2002 (SI 2002/2014), regs 30–32 to employers and those providing childcare.

1.278

HMRC practice appears not to be using this section and those that follow as drafted. Subsection (2) gives the Revenue powers to seek information "before making their decision". There are separate powers once an award is made. HMRC practice is to examine claims both before and during the award in the same way. In other words, the award is often made and then examined rather than the previous DSS practice of making full enquiries before an award is made and then making retrospective first payments. This is possible for tax credits, as they are based on a full year's claim at a time, in a way that is not possible for most social security benefits, to which individuals have entitlements on a daily or weekly basis. Rather, it follows the approach long used by HMRC under the PAYE system for taxing employment income.

In decision *CIS/995/2004* Commissioner Mesher confirmed the view stated above that the power in this section is available to deal with enquiries only *before* a decision is made. The Commissioner also criticises the standard letter TC602 used by HMRC in connection with these enquiries. It follows that HMRC have no power to impose a penalty under s.32 for failure to answer an enquiry that is purportedly made under this section but not in accordance with its terms. However, the power cited by HMRC in its notices to claimants about both enquiries and examinations cite s.19 powers, not s.14 powers (see WTC/FS1 and WTC/FS2 issued in 2005). But the power under s.19 is available only after a s.18 decision has been taken. If *CIS/995/2004* is correct, it would seem there is no power to impose a penalty for a failure to respond to a check made between the issue of the initial award under this section and the final decision under s.18 save where HMRC can show reasonable grounds for using its s.16 powers. This provides a limit on HMRC checking powers that may not have been intended but nonetheless removes liability to penalties.

Subs.(3)

This allows the award of a nil rate, so awarding a tax credit without payment. This "has the effect of keeping an entitlement going even though no money is in payment or in process. It makes it easier for the claimant and it makes it easier for us" (Baroness Hollis, House of Lords Grand Committee, May 23, 2002, CWH 146). This again reflects the fact that at this stage the decision is an initial decision only. It also means that a claimant with a nil award can ask for a review to deal with a change of circumstances rather than having to make a new claim. This gives a practical solution to a recurring problem under the SSAA 1992 and the SSA 1998 of reviews, revisions and supersessions. The adoption of this practice will, in particular, avoid some of the more awkward aspects of supersession.

1.279

Revised decisions after notifications

15.—(1) Where notification of a change of circumstances increasing the maximum rate at which a person or persons may be entitled to a tax credit is given in accordance with regulations under section 6(1), the Board must decide whether (and, if so, how) to amend the award of the tax credit made to him or them.

1.280

(2) Before making their decision the Board may by notice—
(a) require the person by whom the notification is given to provide any information or evidence which the Board consider they may need for making their decision; or

Tax Credits Act 2002

(b) require any person of a prescribed description to provide any information or evidence of a prescribed description which the Board consider they may need for that purpose,

by the date specified in the notice.

Amendment

1. The section is disapplied for claimants subject to immigration control. See Tax Credits (Immigration) Regulations 2003 (SI 2003/623) regs 3, 4.

Definitions

"the Board"—see s.67.
"maximum rate"—see ss.9(1) and 11(1).
"prescribed"—see s.67.
"tax credit"—see s.1(2).

General Note

1.281
Section 6 makes provision for a claimant to tell HMRC of a change of circumstances that should or may increase the tax credit to be awarded. This section imposes a duty on HMRC to consider if the award made under s.14 should be amended if such a notification is given (subs.(1)). The decision, including a decision not to amend, is appealable (s.38). Subsection (2) gives HMRC the same powers to enquire as s.14(2). The same provisions about notice (s.45) and penalties (ss.31 and 32) apply. Following the comment in s.14, it may be noted that although the heading of the section refers to revision, the text of the section does not. The power in this section is to "amend". That is the term used in the TMA 1970 when either the taxpayer or HMRC changes a tax return (see ss.9ZA and 9ZB of the TMA 1970).

It is understood that the standard practice of HMRC is to make all initial decisions on the basis of the previous year's income using the power in s.7(10). Where a claim form indicates that the current year's income should be used, HMRC then makes an immediate revision under this section. See also the General Note to s.6.

Other revised decisions

1.282
16.—(1) Where, at any time during the period for which an award of a tax credit is made to a person or persons, the Board have reasonable grounds for believing—
   (a) that the rate at which the tax credit has been awarded to him or them for the period differs from the rate at which he is, or they are, entitled to the tax credit for the period; or
   (b) that he has, or they have, ceased to be, or never been, entitled to the tax credit for the period,
the Board may decide to amend or terminate the award.

(2) Where, at any time during the period for which an award of a tax credit is made to a person or persons, the Board believe—
   (a) that the rate at which a tax credit has been awarded to him or them for the period may differ from the rate at which he is, or they are, entitled to it for the period, or
   (b) that he or they may have ceased to be, or never been, entitled to the tax credit for the period,
the Board may give a notice under subsection (3).

(3) A notice under this subsection may—
   (a) require the person, or either or both of the persons, to whom the tax credit was awarded to provide any information or evidence which the

Board consider they may need for considering whether to amend or terminate the award under subsection (1); or
(b) require any person of a prescribed description to provide any information or evidence of a prescribed description which the Board consider they may need for that purpose,

by the date specified in the notice.

AMENDMENTS

1. Subsection (3) is modified as it appplies to polygamous units by Tax Credits (Polygamous Marriages) Regulations 2003 (SI 2003/742), reg.13.
2. The section is disapplied for claimants subject to immigration control. See Tax Credits (Immigration) Regulations 2003 (SI 2003/623) regs 3, 4.

DEFINITIONS

"the Board"—see s.67.
"tax credit"—see s.1(2).

GENERAL NOTE

The procedure laid down in this section gives the Board flexibility to alter a decision at any time because HMRC has "reasonable grounds to believe" that a change is appropriate (subs.(1)). These general terms reflect the flexibility given to the Secretary of State under the SSA 1998, and transferred to the Board by the TCA 1999. But it is clear that, unlike that under the TCA 1999, the procedure is not a mirror of the 1998 Act procedure. As noted in s.15, the drafter has deliberately avoided the revision and supersession language of both the SSAA 1992 and the SSA 1998. Despite the heading of the section, the operative power is to "amend" or "terminate" an award. Both this section and s.15 also avoid introducing the troublesome distinction between revisions and supersessions under the SSA 1998.

Again in contrast to the 1998 procedures, this section provides a power, not a duty. In *CTC/4390/2004* the Commissioner noted that on an appeal against a s.16 decision the tribunal also had a power, not a duty, to act. The express right to appeal a s.16 decision is granted in s.38(1). In such cases it is for the tribunal to decide for itself if there are reasonable grounds to make the decision, and if so it whether a decision is to be made.

The Board has power to give notice if it "believes" that the award of a tax credit may be wrong (subs.(2)). As might be expected, this is wider than the power to amend or terminate. The notice may require information or evidence from claimants and others, as defined in regulations (subs.(3)). Current regulations empower HMRC to seek information from employers and childcare providers (see note to s.14). Penalties attach to the failure to respond or to a false response (ss.31 and 32).

A standard HMRC use of the section is, somewhat obscurely, announced as a footnote to the regular series of official statistics on tax credits. They explain by way of a note to the table of total awards why, every year, there has been a reduction in the total number of awards made for both forms of tax credit in December as compared with the previous April as follows:

"Note: between each April and December families' awards are stopped at (a) 31 August if their only qualifying child falls out of entitlement at that date, or (b) in the autumn if they fail to return their Annual Declaration for the previous year. This introduces some seasonality into the figures."

The "seasonality" for 2006 was a reduction in those receiving CTC, WTC or both by a net figure of 75,000 out of 4.6 million. Most of those were families receiving the family element of CTC only. The number receiving both WTC and CTC increased over the period, as did the number receiving WTC only. The figures also suggest that HMRC usually amends the award to zero rather than terminating it. From 2007 the final date for returning annual declarations is brought forward from August to July.

1.283

This is likely to reduce the seasonality factor. There is also likely to be a reduction now that current year income replaces previous year income only when the increase is over £25,000 between the two.

In *CTC/2576/2004* the Commissioner set aside a decision of a tribunal confirming a decision of HMRC under s.16. The Commissioner also set aside the s.16 decision and referred the matter back to HMRC. HMRC could not produce the actual decision made, and had contradicted itself in letters to the claimant. The tribunal considered this in the same way as a revision or supersession under the SSA 1998. The Commissioner found that the tribunal erred in this approach and should have relied on the TCA 2002 procedures. In addition, HMRC had erred in both its versions of its original decision. The Commissioner commented that "the decision of the Board was not properly articulated in that the intimations of it to the claimant were contradictory". It is not clear from the decision whether s.23 of this Act was also considered, as HMRC conceded that its decisions were in error.

In *CTC/3981/2006* the Commissioner analysed both the s.16 procedure and the effectiveness of appeals against s.16 decisions.

Final notice

1.284   **17.**—(1) Where a tax credit has been awarded for the whole or part of a tax year—
  (a) for awards made on single claims, the Board must give a notice relating to the tax year to the person to whom the tax credit was awarded, and
  (b) for awards made on joint claims, the Board must give such a notice to the persons to whom the tax credit was awarded (with separate copies of the notice for each of them if the Board consider appropriate).
(2) The notice must either—
  (a) require that the person or persons must, by the date specified for the purposes of this subsection, declare that the relevant circumstances were as specified or state any respects in which they were not, or
  (b) inform the person or persons that he or they will be treated as having declared in response to the notice that the relevant circumstances were as specified unless, by that date, he states or they state any respects in which they were not.
(3) "Relevant circumstances" means circumstances (other than income) affecting—
  (a) the entitlement of the person, or joint entitlement of the persons, to the tax credit, or
  (b) the amount of the tax credit to which he was entitled, or they were jointly entitled, for the tax year.
(4) The notice must either—
  (a) require that the person or persons must, by the date specified for the purposes of this subsection, declare that the amount of the current year income or estimated current year income (depending on which is specified) was the amount, or fell within the range, specified or comply with subsection (5), or
  (b) inform the person or persons that he or they will be treated as having declared in response to the notice that the amount of the current year income or estimated current year income (depending on which is specified) was the amount, or fell within the range, specified unless, by that date, he complies or they comply with subsection (5).
(5) To comply with this subsection the person or persons must either—
  (a) state the current year income or his or their estimate of the current year income (making clear which); or

(b) declare that, throughout the period to which the award related, subsection (1) of section 7 did not apply to him or them by virtue of subsection (2) of that section.

(6) The notice may—

(a) require that the person or persons must, by the date specified for the purposes of subsection (4), declare that the amount of the previous year income was the amount, or fell within the range, specified or comply with subsection (7), or

(b) inform the person or persons that he or they will be treated as having declared in response to the notice that the amount of the previous year income was the amount, or fell within the range, specified unless, by that date, he complies or they comply with subsection (7).

(7) To comply with this subsection the person or persons must either—

(a) state the previous year income, or

(b) make the declaration specified in subsection (5)(b).

(8) The notice must inform the person or persons that if he or they—

(a) makes or make a declaration under paragraph (a) of subsection (4), or is or are treated as making a declaration under paragraph (b) of that subsection, in relation to estimated current year income (or the range within which estimated current year income fell); or

(b) states or state under subsection (5)(a) his or their estimate of the current year income;

he or they will be treated as having declared in response to the notice that the amount of the (actual) current year income was as estimated unless, by the date specified for the purposes of this subsection, he states or they state the current year income.

(9) "Specified", in relation to a notice, means specified in the notice.

(10) Regulations may—

(a) provide that, in prescribed circumstances, one person may act for another in response to a notice under this section, and

(b) provide that, in prescribed circumstances, anything done by one member of a [²couple] in response to a notice given under this section is to be treated as also done by the other member of [²the couple].

AMENDMENTS

1. Subsection (10) is modified as it applies to polygamous units by Tax Credits (Polygamous Marriages) Regulations 2003 (SI 2003/742), reg.14.

2. Civil Partnership Act 2004, s.254 and Sch.24, para.145 (December 5, 2005).

3. The section is disapplied for claimants subject to immigration control. See Tax Credits (Immigration) Regulations 2003 (SI 2003/623) regs 3, 4.

DEFINITIONS

"the Board"—see s.67.
"current year income"—see s.7(4).
"joint claims"—see s.3(8).
"married couple"—see s.3(5).
"prescribed"—see s.67.
"previous year income"—see s.7(5).
"relevant circumstances"—see subs.(3).
"specified"—see subs.(9).
"tax credit"—see s.1(2).
"tax year"—see s.47.
"unmarried couple"—see s.3(6).

Tax Credits Act 2002

GENERAL NOTE

1.285
What are now ss.17 and 18 were originally drafted as one clause. It was divided by amendments in the House of Lords into the notice provisions (s.17) and the decision provisions (s.18), to avoid it being overlong. Together the two sections provide the regime for checking the s.14 initial decision on an award before turning it into an entitlement, and then for making the entitlement decision. The underlying pattern is that the award decision must be made in response to a claim. Payment is then made under the award decision for a tax year. At the end of the tax year, HMRC uses the s.17 powers to check whether the claimant is, or remains, entitled to the tax credit awarded, or to some higher or lower rate of tax credit. After checking, a "final decision" is made on entitlement.

The effect of subs.(1) is that all awards of tax credit must be checked. In every case a notice must be sent to a claimant (or joint claimants). Notices must take one of two forms. One is a demand for a declaration that there has been no change of relevant circumstances (subs.(2)(a)). It can also demand details (or an estimate) of the current year's income (subs.(4)(a)). The other is a notice telling people that it will be assumed that there is no change of circumstances unless any changes are reported by a given date (subs.(2)(b)). It can also tell people that it is assumed that their income is of an assumed level or range unless a declaration is made stating otherwise (subs.(4)(b)). The notice may also take either of those approaches about the previous year's income (subs.(6)). Further provisions are laid down in the Tax Credits (Claims and Notifications) Regulations 2002 (SI 2002/2014). The section also states the ways in which people must comply with these notices. Penalties may be imposed on failures to reply and wrong replies (ss.31 and 32).

HMRC calls the notices issued under this section "Annual Declarations". The annual declarations may also constitute claims under s.3. The point may arise as to which years the declaration and claim relate to. In *CTC/1594/2006* the Commissioner accepted HMRC's argument that it was for HMRC to decide this, subject to judicial review rather than appeal, but also suggested it might depend on the wording used.

Decisions after final notice

1.286
18.—(1) After giving a notice under section 17, the Board must decide—
(a) whether the person was entitled, or the persons were jointly entitled, to the tax credit, and
(b) if so, the amount of the tax credit to which he was entitled, or they were jointly entitled, for the tax year.

(2) But, subject to subsection (3), that decision must not be made before a declaration or statement has been made in response to the relevant provisions of the notice.

(3) If a declaration or statement has not been made in response to the relevant provisions of the notice on or before the date specified for the purposes of section 17(4), that decision may be made after that date.

(4) In subsections (2) and (3) "the relevant provisions of the notice" means—
(a) the provision included in the notice by virtue of subsection (2) of section 17,
(b) the provision included in the notice by virtue of subsection (4) of that section, and
(c) any provision included in the notice by virtue of subsection (6) of that section.

(5) Where the Board make a decision under subsection (1) on or before the date referred to in subsection (3), they may revise it if a new declaration or statement is made on or before that date.

(2002 c.21, s.18)

(6) If the person or persons to whom a notice under section 17 is given is or are within paragraph (a) or (b) of subsection (8) of that section, the Board must decide again—
  (a) whether the person was entitled, or the persons were jointly entitled, to the tax credit, and
  (b) if so, the amount of the tax credit to which he was entitled, or they were jointly entitled, for the tax year.

(7) But, subject to subsection (8), that decision must not be made before a statement has been made in response to the provision included in the notice by virtue of subsection (8) of section 17.

(8) If a statement has not been made in response to the provision included in the notice by virtue of that subsection on or before the date specified for the purposes of that subsection, that decision may be made after that date.

(9) Where the Board make a decision under subsection (6) on or before the date referred to in subsection (8), they may revise it if a new statement is made on or before that date.

(10) Before exercising a function imposed or conferred on them by subsection (1), (5), (6) or (9), the Board may by notice require the person, or either or both of the persons, to whom the notice under section 17 was given to provide any further information or evidence which the Board consider they may need for exercising the function by the date specified in the notice.

(11) Subject to sections 19 and 20 and regulations under section 21 (and to any revision under subsection (5) or (9) and any appeal)—
  (a) in a case in which a decision is made under subsection (6) in relation to a person or persons and a tax credit for a tax year, that decision, and
  (b) in any other case, the decision under subsection (1) in relation to a person or persons and a tax credit for a tax year,
is conclusive as to the entitlement of the person, or the joint entitlement of the persons, to the tax credit for the tax year and the amount of the tax credit to which he was entitled, or they were jointly entitled, for the tax year.

AMENDMENTS

1. Subsection (10) is modified as it applies to polygamous units by Tax Credits (Polygamous Marriages) Regulations 2003 (SI 2003/742), reg.15.
2. The section is modified for claimants subject to immigration control. See Tax Credits (Immigration) Regulations 2003 (SI 2003/623) regs 3, 4.

DEFINITIONS

"the Board"—see s.67.
"prescribed"—see s.67.
"relevant provisions of the notice"—see subs.(4).
"tax credit"—see s.1(2).
"tax year"—see s.47.

GENERAL NOTE

HMRC calls these notices "finalised awards". In *CTC/2113/2006* a Commissioner criticised this use of language, and a more general failure to distinguish between awards and entitlements, in HMRC notices and literature in the case papers.

See the note to s.17 for the general scheme of which this is part. Subsection (1) of this section imposes the duty on HMRC to make a decision on entitlement in every case, but only after the s.17 notice procedure has been followed (subs.(2)) or the full time to comply has been allowed (subs.(3)). Subsection (4) links the procedures under this section with the relevant notice provisions in s.17. Subsection (5) allows

1.287

an entitlement decision under subs.(1) to be revised if there is a reply or further reply from a claimant after a decision has been made. The use of "revise" was avoided in earlier sections in favour of "amend" (despite their headings: see ss.15 and 16), but is here applied to changes to a final decision. Such revisions can be of the whole or only part of the decision. The language avoids attaching formalities or threshold conditions to the process. Subsections (6)–(9) repeat the substance of subss.(1)–(5) for claimants who estimated their current year income in their claims or initial responses to the s.17 notice. In either case, HMRC may require further information (subs.(10)). The standard penalty regime applies to subs.(10). Subsection (11) makes a subs.(1) or subs.(6) decision conclusive unless it is revised under subss.(5) or (9), or it is appealed under s.38, or it is altered under any of the powers in ss.19–21. The Claimant Compliance Manual (CCM) (on the CCM, see note to TCA 2002, s.31 below) emphasises that a decision under subs.(6) should be taken by an officer as a "best judgment" decision, not just a guess. "You can use some guess-work but it must be honest guess-work" (at para.10270).

For an analysis of the procedure under s.18, see CTC/2662/2005.

Power to enquire

1.288

19.—(1) The Board may enquire into—
  (a) the entitlement of a person, or the joint entitlement of persons, to a tax credit for a tax year, and
  (b) the amount of the tax credit to which he was entitled, or they were jointly entitled, for the tax year,
if they give notice to the person, or each of the persons, during the period allowed for the initiation of an enquiry.

(2) As part of the enquiry the Board may by notice—
  (a) require the person, or either or both of the persons, to provide any information or evidence which the Board consider they may need for the purposes of the enquiry, or
  (b) require any person of a prescribed description to provide any information or evidence of a prescribed description which the Board consider they may need for those purposes, by the date specified in the notice.

(3) On an enquiry the Board must decide—
  (a) whether the person was entitled, or the persons were jointly entitled, to the tax credit, and
  (b) if so, the amount of the tax credit to which he was entitled, or they were jointly entitled,
for the tax year.

(4) The period allowed for the initiation of an enquiry is the period beginning immediately after the relevant section 18 decision and ending—
  (a) if the person, or either of the persons, to whom the enquiry relates is required by section 8 of the Taxes Management Act 1970 (c.9) to make a return, with the day on which the return becomes final (or, if both of the persons are so required and their returns become final on different days, with the later of those days), or
  (b) in any other case, one year after the beginning of the relevant section 17 date.

(5) "The relevant section 18 decision" means—
  (a) in a case in which a decision must be made under subsection (6) of section 18 in relation to the person or persons and the tax year to which the enquiry relates, that decision; and
  (b) in any other case, the decision under subsection (1) of that section in relation to the person or persons and that tax year.

(6) "The relevant section 17 date" means—
(a) in a case in which a statement may be made by the person or persons in response to provision included by virtue of subsection (8) of section 17 in the notice given to him or them under that section in relation to the tax year, the date specified in the notice for the purposes of that subsection, and
(b) in any other case, the date specified for the purposes of subsection (4) of that section in the notice given to him or them under that section in relation to the tax year.

(7) A return becomes final—
(a) if it is enquired into under section 9A of the Taxes Management Act 1970 (c.9), when the enquiries are completed (within the meaning of section 28A of that Act), or
(b) otherwise, at the end of the period specified in subsection (2) of that section in relation to the return.

(8) An enquiry is completed at the time when the Board give notice to the person or persons of their decision under subsection (3); but if the Board give notice to the persons at different times the enquiry is completed at the later of those times.

(9) The person, or either of the persons, to whom the enquiry relates may at any time before such notice is given apply for a direction that the Board must give such a notice.

(10) Such an application is to be heard and determined in the same way as an appeal against a decision under subsection (3), and the [appeal tribunal] hearing the application must give the direction applied for unless satisfied that the Board have reasonable grounds for not making the decision or giving the notice.

(11) Where the entitlement of a person, or the joint entitlement of persons, to a tax credit for a tax year has been enquired into under this section, it is not to be the subject of a further notice under subsection (1).

(12) Subject to section 20 and regulations under section 21 (and to any appeal), a decision under subsection (3) in relation to a person or persons and a tax credit for a tax year is conclusive as to the entitlement of the person, or the joint entitlement of the persons, to the tax credit for the tax year and the amount of the tax credit to which he was entitled, or they were jointly entitled, for the tax year.

AMENDMENTS

1. Subsections (2), (4) and (9) are modified for polygamous units by Tax Credits (Polygamous Marriages) Regulations 2003 (SI 2003/742), reg.16.
2. Subsection (10) is modified by TCA 2002, s.63(5)(a), the modification being indicated by square brackets.
3. The section is modified for claimants subject to immigration control. See Tax Credits (Immigration) Regulations 2003 (SI 2003/623) regs 3, 4.

DEFINITIONS

"the Board"—see s.67.
"General Commissioners"—see s.47.
"prescribed"—see s.67.
"Special Commissioners"—see s.47.
"the relevant section 17 date"—see subs.(6).

Tax Credits Act 2002

"the relevant section 18 decision"—see subs.(5).
"tax credit"—see s.1(2).

GENERAL NOTE

1.289   This provision gives HMRC a broad general power similar to that in s.9A of the TMA 1970 (power to enquire into self-assessment returns) to enquire into the correctness of a s.18 entitlement decision. An enquiry under this section can be opened at any time after the s.18 decision is made until a year after the final date for replying to a s.17 notice, unless HMRC uses its power to issue a demand for a personal tax return under s.8 of the TMA 1970 on the claimant. A return for a year must be made by January 31 next after the tax year ends (each April) or, if demanded later, three months after it is required. Section 9A (which entitles HMRC to issue a notice of enquiry into a return under s.8) allows about a year (the period is defined precisely) for a HMRC enquiry to follow a personal return.

An individual who is the subject of an enquiry has the same power to apply to a tribunal to stop the enquiry as exists for the equivalent income tax provisions, save that the application goes to the appeal tribunal (see s.63), not a tax tribunal.

The power to look into a decision about entitlement to tax credits is referred to both in this section and in practice as an enquiry. This is to be distinguished from an investigation into a claim for, or award of, a tax credit, which is referred to by HMRC as an examination. The key difference is that an award is provisional, while an enquiry relates to an award that has been or is being finalised to give rise to entitlement. In practice, however, it is likely that any decision to enquire into the entitlement of a claimant for a past year will be accompanied by an examination of any current claim or award and that the enquiry and examination will be conducted and concluded together. An enquiry is to be conducted in accordance with the terms of HMRC Code of Practice 27 *Child Tax Credit and Working Tax Credit, Local Office Enquiries.*

HMRC have issued a short series of factsheets about its powers and practices for claimants: WTC/FS1 on enquiries; WTC/FS2 on examinations; WTC/FS3 on formal requests for information; and WTC/FS4 on meetings with an officer of Revenue and Customs.

HMRC issues detailed statistics of both awards and entitlements, and so provides some insight into the extent to which awards are not turned into entitlements. A comparison of the awards made to the end of the 2004/05 year, as against the entitlements confirmed for that year, show that the total number of claimants entitled to some tax credit (WTC, CTC or both) for the year was 4.28 million. This was a reduction of 364,000 compared with the number of awards (other than zero awards) in effect for the same date. In other words about ⅓ million more awards were made than entitlements were confirmed. All will have created overpayments. However, this is likely to reduce following the changes to the rules about the level of income below which there must be a change of basis from previous year's income to current year's income, to the rules requiring the reporting of changes of circumstances, and shortening the time limits for making annual declarations and reporting changes of circumstances.

Decisions on discovery

1.290   **20.**—(1) Where in consequence of a person's income tax liability being revised the Board have reasonable grounds for believing that a conclusive decision relating to his entitlement to a tax credit for a tax year (whether or not jointly with another person) is not correct, the Board may decide to revise that decision.

(2) A person's income tax liability is revised—
  (a) on the taking effect of an amendment of a return of his under section 9ZA(1) of the Taxes Management Act 1970,

(b) on the issue of a notice of correction under section 9ZB of that Act amending a return of his (provided that he does not give a notice of rejection before the end of the period of thirty days beginning with the date of issue of the notice of correction),
(c) on the amendment of an assessment of his by notice under section 9C of that Act,
(d) on the amendment of a return of his under section 12ABA(3)(a) of that Act,
(e) on the amendment of a return of his under subsection (6)(a) of section 12ABB of that Act after the correction of a partnership return under that section (provided that the amendment does not cease to have effect by reason of the rejection of the correction under subsection (4) of that section),
(f) on the issue of a closure notice under section 28A of that Act making amendments of a return of his;
(g) on the amendment of a return of his under section 28B(4)(a) of that Act,
(h) on the making of an assessment as regards him under section 29(1) of that Act,
(i) on the vacation of the whole or part of an assessment of his under section 32 of that Act,
(j) on giving him relief under section 33 of that Act, or
(k) on the determination (or settlement) of an appeal against the making, amendment or vacation of an assessment or return, or a decision on a claim for relief, under any of the provisions mentioned in paragraphs (c), (f) and (h) to (j).

(3) But no decision may be made under subsection (1)—
(a) unless it is too late to enquire into the person's entitlement under section 19, or
(b) after the period of one year beginning when the person's income tax liability is revised.

(4) Where the Board have reasonable grounds for believing that—
(a) a conclusive decision relating to the entitlement of a person, or the joint entitlement of persons, to a tax credit for a tax year is not correct, and
(b) that is attributable to fraud or neglect on the part of the person, or of either of the persons, or on the part of any person acting for him, or either of them,
the Board may decide to revise that decision.

(5) But no decision may be made under subsection (4)—
(a) unless it is too late to enquire into the entitlement, or joint entitlement, under section 19, or
(b) after the period of five years beginning with the end of the tax year to which the conclusive decision relates.

(6) "Conclusive decision", in relation to the entitlement of a person, or joint entitlement of persons, to a tax credit for a tax year, means—
(a) a decision in relation to it under section 18(1), (5), (6) or (9) or 19(3) or a previous decision under this section, or
(b) a decision under regulations under section 21 relating to a decision within paragraph (a),
including a decision made on an appeal against such a decision.

(7) Subject to any subsequent decision under this section and to regulations under section 21 (and to any appeal), a decision under subsection (1)

or (4) in relation to a person or persons and a tax credit for a tax year is conclusive as to the entitlement of the person, or the joint entitlement of the persons, to the tax credit for the tax year and the amount of the tax credit to which he was entitled, or they were jointly entitled, for the tax year.

AMENDMENT

1. Subsection (4) is modified as it applies to polygamous units by Tax Credits (Polygamous Marriages) Regulations 2003 (SI 2003/742), reg.17.

CROSS-REFERENCES

1.291 TMA 1970:

s.9ZA	Amendment of personal or trustee return by taxpayer
s.9ZB	Correction of personal return by taxpayer
s.9C	Amendment of self-assessment during enquiry to prevent loss of tax
s.12ABA	Amendment of partnership return by taxpayer
s.12ABB	Correction of partnership return by Revenue
s.28A	Completion of enquiry into personal or trustee return
s.28B	Completion of enquiry into partnership return
s.29	Assessment where loss of tax discovered
s.32	Double assessment
s.33	Error or mistake

DEFINITIONS

"conclusive decision"—see subs.(6).
"income tax"—see ICTA 1988, s.1.
"prescribed"—see: s.67.
"tax credit"—see s.1(2).

GENERAL NOTE

1.292 Discovery is the traditional term used for finding out or taking informed guesses about undisclosed income for income tax purposes. The power to make assessments where loss of tax is discovered is in s.29 of the TMA 1970. This section is wider than that, although in part it flows from it. Section 29 allows an officer who discovers unassessed tax or excessive relief to make an assessment of the amount which, in the officer's opinion, ought to be charged to tax, and also imposes other conditions before the power can be used. This section, by contrast, allows action by HMRC in two sets of circumstances.

The first is if HMRC has reasonable grounds for believing an otherwise conclusive decision about tax credit (defined in subs.(6)) is not correct because of a revision of income tax liability (subs.(1)). HMRC may act if one of the TMA 1970 powers listed in subs.(2) has been used for a revision. These include s.29 and also the powers to revisit personal and partnership tax returns and decisions made by settlement or on appeal. Revisions under this power can be made only if it is too late to use s.19. And they cannot be made unless the revision is made within a year of the income tax revision (subs.(3)).

The second power (in subs.(4)) arises where HMRC has reasonable grounds to believe that an otherwise conclusive decision is wrong because of "fraud or neglect". That phrase is not defined in this Act but is the phrase used in similar TMA 1970 provisions (such as s.29). This power cannot be used if the s.19 power is available, and is subject to a time limit of five years from the end of the tax year to which the tax credit relates (subs.(5)). This is the usual time limit for similar actions in the TMA 1970.

A decision made under this section is itself conclusive, subject only to further decisions under this section or on appeal or because of official error (subs.(7)).

Decisions subject to official error

21. Regulations may make provision for a decision under section 14(1), 15(1), 16(1), 18(1), (5), (6) or (9), 19(3) or 20(1) or (4) to be revised in favour of the person or persons to whom it relates if it is incorrect by reason of official error (as defined by the regulations).

GENERAL NOTE

"Official error" is defined by the Tax Credits (Official Error) Regulations 2003 (SI 2003/692). See the note on those regulations. The provision is significantly narrower than the equivalent provision for income tax in s.33 of the TMA 1970 (error or mistake), which applies to any error or mistake.

The large number of claims of official error in the first two years of award of these tax credits has led to a full procedure being evolved to handle the claims. The relevant form for reconsideration of an overpayment is TC846. According to Ministers (see House of Commons Written Answers, December 15, 2004, col. 1087W) 67,000 claimants had submitted the form by the end of November 2004, and overpayments had been cancelled in 1,100 cases.

Information etc. requirements: supplementary

22.—(1) Regulations may make provision as to the manner and form in which—
  (a) information or evidence is to be provided in compliance with a requirement imposed by a notice under section 14(2), 15(2), 16(3), 18(10) or 19(2), or
  (b) a declaration or statement is to be made in response to a notice under section 17.

(2) Regulations may make provision as to the dates which may be specified in a notice under section 14(2), 15(2), 16(3), 17, 18(10) or 19(2).

GENERAL NOTE

These regulation-making powers are necessary because the standard regulations applying to social security decision-making (the Social Security and Child Support (Decisions and Appeals) Regulations 1999 (SI 1999/991)) do not apply and there are no equivalents in the TMA 1970. The regulations made under these powers are the Tax Credits (Claims and Notifications) Regulations 2002 (SI 2002/2014).

Notice of decisions

23.—(1) When a decision is made under section 14(1), 15(1), 16(1), 18(1), (5), (6) or (9), 19(3) or 20(1) or (4) or regulations under section 21, the Board must give notice of the decision to the person, or each of the persons, to whom it relates.

(2) Notice of a decision must state the date on which it is given and include details of any right to appeal against the decision under section 38.

(3) Notice need not be given of a decision made under section 14(1) or 18(1) or (6) on the basis of declarations made or treated as made by the person or persons in response to the notice given to him or them under section 17 if—
  (a) that notice, or
  (b) in the case of a decision under subsection (6) of section 18, that notice or the notice of the decision under subsection (1) of that section,
stated what the decision would be and the date on which it would be made.

DEFINITION

"the Board"—see s.67.

GENERAL NOTE

1.298 This section requires HMRC to adopt the same approach as for social security decisions of giving formal notice of every decision (save in limited cases where notice has already been given). The notice must set out any appeal rights. Section 45 makes provision for the form of a notice. Further details are laid down in the Tax Credits (Claims and Notifications) Regulations 2002 (SI 2002/2014). However, it may be viewed as significant that this provision is in primary legislation, while the equivalent for social security purposes (Social Security and Child Support (Decisions and Appeals) Regulations 1999 (SI 1999/991), reg.28) is made by regulation only. It is suggested therefore that the mandatory terms of subs.(1) (the Board *must* give notice) and subs.(2) (the notice *must* state) are not amenable to the somewhat relaxed approach to formalities applied to the social security equivalent (see the note to reg.28 of those Regulations). In particular, if no notice is given, it is arguable that no effective decision has been made, or alternatively that the decision is not final and the appeal period cannot start running.

Payment

Payments

1.299 **24.**—(1) Where the Board have made an award of a tax credit, the amount of the tax credit awarded must be paid to the person to whom the award is made, subject to subsections (2) and (3).

(2) Where an award of a tax credit is made to the members of [²a couple], payments of the tax credit, or of any element of the tax credit, are to be made to whichever of them is prescribed.

(3) Where an award of a tax credit is made on a claim which was made by one person on behalf of another, payments of the tax credit, or of any element of the tax credit, are to be made to whichever of those persons is prescribed.

(4) Where an award of a tax credit has been made to a person or persons for the whole or part of a tax year, payments may, in prescribed circumstances, continue to be made for any period, after the tax year, within which he is or they are entitled to make a claim for the tax credit for the next tax year.

(5) Payments made under subsection (4) are to be treated for the purposes of this section and the following provisions of this Part as if they were payments of the tax credit for the next tax year.

(6) Subject to section 25, payments of a tax credit must be made by the Board.

(7) Regulations may make provision about the time when and the manner in which a tax credit, or any element of a tax credit, is to be paid by the Board.

(8) If the regulations make provision for payments of a tax credit, or any element of a tax credit, to be made by the Board by way of a credit to a bank account or other account notified to the Board, the regulations may provide that entitlement to the tax credit or element is dependent on an account having been notified to the Board in accordance with the regulations.

(2002 c.21, s.24)

AMENDMENTS

1. Subsection (2) is modified as it applies to polygamous units by Tax Credits (Polygamous Marriages) Regulations 2003 (SI 2003/742), reg.18.
2. Civil Partnership Act 2004, s.254 and Sch.24, para.145 (December 5, 2005).

DEFINITIONS

"claim"—see s.3(8).
"the Board"—see s.67.
"married couple"—see s.3(5).
"prescribed"—see s.67.
"tax credit"—see s.1(2).
"tax year"—see s.47.
"unmarried couple"—see s.3(6).

GENERAL NOTE

From April 2006 HMRC makes all WTC and CTC payments. Payment by employers has been discontinued. Sections 25 (Payment by employers), 26 (liability of officers for sums paid to employers) and 33 (failure by employers to make correct payments) and the related regulations therefore have no current relevance and are not set out in this volume. For the texts see the volume for previous years.

1.300

Rights of employees

27. Schedule 1 (rights of employees not to suffer unfair dismissal or other detriment) has effect.

1.301

DEFINITIONS

"employee"—see s.25(5).

GENERAL NOTE

This section introduces Sch.1. Both this section and the Schedule are based on s.7 of, and Sch.3 to, the TCA 1999. The aim is to provide employees with direct rights to ensure that employers do not discriminate against them because of WTC. The underlying fear is that employers would rather get rid of employees than implement the WTC process. Schedule 1 makes the necessary amendments to the Employment Rights Act (GB) and Order (NI) to give employees a right not to suffer detriment and a right not to be unfairly dismissed because of tax credits. The text of Sch.1 is not included here as it is a matter of employment law.

1.302

Overpayments

28.—(1) Where the amount of a tax credit paid for a tax year to a person or persons exceeds the amount of the tax credit to which he is entitled, or they are jointly entitled, for the tax year (as determined in accordance with the provision made by and by virtue of sections 18 to 21), the Board may decide that the excess, or any part of it, is to be repaid to the Board.

1.303

(2) In this Part such an excess is referred to as an overpayment.
(3) For overpayments made under awards on single claims, the person to whom the tax credit was awarded is liable to repay the amount which the Board decide is to be repaid.
(4) For overpayments made under awards on joint claims, the persons to whom the tax credit was awarded are jointly and severally liable to repay the amount which the Board decide is to be repaid unless the Board decide that each is to repay a specified part of that amount.

153

(5) Where it appears to the Board that there is likely to be an overpayment of a tax credit for a tax year under an award made to a person or persons, the Board may, with a view to reducing or eliminating the overpayment, amend the award or any other award of any tax credit made to the person or persons; but this subsection does not apply once a decision is taken in relation to the person or persons for the tax year under section 18(1).

(6) Where the Board decide under section 16 to terminate an award of a tax credit made to a person or persons on the ground that at no time during the period to which the award related did the person or persons satisfy—

(a) section 8(1) (if the award related to child tax credit), or

(b) section 10(1) (if it related to working tax credit),

the Board may decide that the amount paid under the award, or any part of it, is to be treated for the purposes of this Part (apart from subsection (5)) as an overpayment.

DEFINITIONS

"the Board"—see s.67.
"joint claim"—see s.3(8).
"overpayment"—see subs.(2).
"single claim"—see s.3(8).
"tax credit"—see s.1(2).
"tax year"—see s.47.

GENERAL NOTE

1.304   An overpayment is an excess of a tax credit awarded and paid as against the amount of tax credit to which a claimant is entitled under a final decision about entitlement (subs.(2)). This will usually arise where the final decision on entitlement is for a lesser amount than the amount awarded. It may also arise under a later revision under ss.19 or 20, or when an award was made that should not have been made (subs.(6)). Subsection (1) gives a power to (but does not impose a duty on) HMRC to collect overpayments. The decision of HMRC whether or not to collect an overpayment is not subject to appeal, and is not conditional on the fulfilment of any test by the claimant. This is a different approach from that taken for social security purposes, and by the previous tax credits regime, where it had to be shown in most cases that the claimant had caused the overpayment by a failure to disclose, or a misrepresentation of, a material fact. In addition, the decision on recoverability for social security purposes is subject to appeal.

HMRC published in November 2003 *New Tax Credits—Ensuring compliance*. This notes the high level of overpayments estimated to have been made under the working families' tax credit system. The estimate was that overpayments were an estimated 10–14 per cent of the total of £5.05 billion awarded for 2000–01. The paper sets out HMRC strategy for using the powers in TCA 2002 to combat fraudulent claims and for using the information powers in the Act.

Overpayments proved a generally controversial subject in the first year of operation of the TCA 2002. There was a very considerable level of overpayment in the initial start-up period. The *Financial Statement and Budget Report* for 2004–05, (HM Treasury), Table C8 records an increase in net public expenditure on tax credits between 2002–03 and 2003–04 of £1.4 billion from £3.4 billion to £4.8 billion, with net cost falling back in 2004–05 to £4.1 billion. This was significantly more than the estimate in the Report for 2003–04. The 2004–05 Report comments at para.C67 that this also involves some £0.5 billion "reprofiling of payment schedules" (overpayments recovered outside the original award periods) in these years. On this basis there were many very substantial overpayments made on initial awards. It appears that some of the overpayments arose from computer errors whereby payment was in excess of the level of award. This makes it additionally important to check the level of payments

(2002 c.21, s.28)

received during a year against the level of entitlement for that year. If the award changes from time to time during the year this is not an easy task. HMRC had written off about 150,000 disputed overpayments up to September 30, 2005: *Hansard*, HC Debates, Vol.439, col. 1577W (November 21, 2005). A claimant should notify HMRC of any dispute about an overpayment on form TC846 to be returned to the Overpayments Dispute Team at the Tax Credit Office in Preston (PR1 0SB) or Belfast (BT2 7WF).

See further the commentary on overpayments in the General Note at para.1.286 of the Vol.II of this work. Controversy has been focussed particularly on the decision of HMRC to operate subs.(5) through a computer programme that automatically recovered any overpayment recorded in the computer database. Whether that is a proper exercise of a discretion given in the terms of the subsection may be a matter of debate. However, the Paymaster General announced to the House of Commons Treasury Sub-Committee on October 26, 2005 that with effect from mid-November 2005 this process was being suspended and that overpayments would be processed manually where the overpayment was disputed. See also *Hansard*, HC Debates, Vol.438, col. 268W (October 26, 2005). The government has not, however, agreed that such decisions should be open to appeal. That is still under consideration: *Hansard*, HC Debates, Vol.439, col. 452, Oral Answers to Questions (November 10, 2005).

Recovery of overpayments

29.—(1) Where an amount is liable to be repaid by a person or persons under section 28, the Board must give him, or each of them, a notice specifying the amount.

1.305

(2) The notice must state which of subsections (3) to (5) is to apply in relation to the amount or any specified part of the amount; and a notice may at any time be replaced by another notice containing a different statement.

(3) Where a notice states that this subsection applies in relation to an amount (or part of an amount), it is to be treated for the purposes of Part 6 of the Taxes Management Act 1970 (c.9) (collection and recovery) as if it were tax charged in an assessment and due and payable by the person or persons to whom the notice was given at the end of the period of 30 days beginning with the day on which the notice is given.

(4) Where a notice states that this subsection applies in relation to an amount (or part of an amount), it may, subject to provision made by regulations, be recovered by deduction from payments of any tax credit under an award made for any period to the person, or either or both of the persons, to whom the notice was given.

(5) Where a notice states that this subsection applies in relation to an amount (or part of an amount), [PAYE regulations][1] apply to it as if it were an underpayment of tax for a previous year of assessment by the person or persons to whom the notice was given.

AMENDMENT

1. Words amended by ITEPA 2003, Sch.6, para.266 (April 6, 2003). Subs.(4) is modified by the Tax Credits (Polygamous Marriages) Regulations 2003 (SI 2003/742), reg.12 as it applies to polygamous units.

DEFINITIONS

"the Board"—see s.67.
"overpayment"—see s.28(2).

Tax Credits Act 2002

General Note

1.306 There is no appeal against a decision about either recovery or recoverability under this Act. The decision that can be appealed is the entitlement decision under which the overpayment arises. That decision must be notified to the claimant under s.23, save where one of the exceptions in s.23(3) applies. It may be anticipated that, following equivalent experience in social security cases, some recipients will only object, and attempt to appeal, when they receive notice of an overpayment under this section rather than notice of the decision that gives rise to the overpayment. Whether this can amount to an effective and timely appeal against the entitlement decision will depend on part on how and when the required notices are given, and is for decision under s.39.

This section is the equivalent of s.30 of the TMA 1970. HMRC may give a formal notice to someone whom it has decided has been overpaid tax credit. The notice may activate all or any of three alternative methods of recovering the overpaid tax credit. The first, under subs.(3), is by using ss.60–70A of the TMA 1970. These empower HMRC's collection and recovery powers for unpaid income tax demands. These allow distraint and action in both civil courts and magistrates' courts. Subsection (4) entitles HMRC to collect the overpayment by deducting it from other payments of tax credit: see further Tax Credits (Payments by the Board) Regulations 2002 (SI 2002/2173), reg.12A, inserted by the Tax Credits (Miscellaneous Amendments) Regulations 2004 (SI 2004/762), reg.18. Subsection (5), likely to be used for WTC, empowers the collection by an alteration to the PAYE coding for the claimant (where the tax credit is paid through an employer) in the same way as underpaid past income tax. These powers also apply to interest charged under s.37. HMRC did not have power to use the PAYE system to recover overpayments in 2003–04, and therefore used the power to deduct overpayments from other awards of tax credit, or carried the overpayments forward to 2004–05.

The effect on an ongoing basis of changes in this way will be to increase the amount of income tax, or reduce the amount of tax credit, over the following year, so further severing the immediate practical link that social security benefits usually seek to achieve between the needs of the claimant and the amount received. For example, the award for tax credits in 2003–04 is initially based on the income of 2001–02. If the income for 2003–04 is more than £2,500 higher than that of 2001–02, then there will have been an overpayment of the tax credit for 2003–04, in addition to a probable reduction of tax credits in 2004–05 compared with the previous year. This will be compounded if the overpayment of the previous year is collected by a reduction of the tax credit actually paid in 2004–05. However, the increase in the threshold of income requiring adjustments from £2,500 to £25,000 in 2006 will sharply reduce these adjustments.

HMRC issued a new Code of Practice 26, *What happens if we have paid you too much tax credit?* in December 2003. It was reissued in revised form in 2006. The full text is set out at the end of the volume. This sets out the HMRC procedure in overpayments cases and its policy for dealing with recovery of overpayments in cases that cause hardship. Any dispute about recovery of an overpayment can take place, if at all, in the civil courts.

An additional aspect of the exercise by HMRC of its powers under ss.28 and 29 is the award of what are termed "hardship payments". These are payments made to claimants in excess of current entitlements to tax credits where HMRC accepts that a change in the level of tax credits to the new level of entitlement would cause hardship. This might occur, for example, where recovery of an overpayment towards the end of the tax year removes all entitlement to further payments of tax credits for the rest of that year.

Some doubt has been expressed about whether these hardship payments are within the powers of HMRC under this Act or whether they must be regarded as extra-statutory payments outside the system. It is understood that HMRC takes the view that the administrative approach adopted avoids the complexity that would be caused by what would otherwise have to be a reduction in the reduction of the underlying entitlement to reflect previous overpayments. The approach adopted also has the advantage of greater transparency.

Underpayments

30.—(1) Where it has been determined in accordance with the provision made by and by virtue of sections 18 to 21 that a person was entitled, or persons were jointly entitled, to a tax credit for a tax year and either—
  (a) the amount of the tax credit paid to him or them for that tax year was less than the amount of the tax credit to which it was so determined that he is entitled or they are jointly entitled, or
  (b) no payment of the tax credit was made to him or them for that tax year,

the amount of the difference, or of his entitlement or their joint entitlement, must be paid to him or to whichever of them is prescribed.

(2) Where the claim for the tax credit was made by one person on behalf of another, the payment is to be made to whichever of those persons is prescribed.

DEFINITIONS

"prescribed"—see s.67.
"tax credit"—see s.1(2).
"tax year"—see s.47.

GENERAL NOTE

This provision is the converse of s.28. However, the procedure that triggers it is not a mirror of the provisions giving rise to an overpayment. In particular, see the note to s.6 on notifications of changes of circumstances. If there is an underpayment, this section requires HMRC to make it good. But underpayments, unlike repayments of income tax, or overpayments of tax credit, do not carry interest. Nor does the section impose any time-limit on the payment.

Penalties

Incorrect statements etc.

31.—(1) Where a person fraudulently or negligently—
  (a) makes an incorrect statement or declaration in or in connection with a claim for a tax credit or a notification of a change of circumstances given in accordance with regulations under section 6 or in response to a notice under section 17, or
  (b) gives incorrect information or evidence in response to a requirement imposed on him by virtue of section 14(2), 15(2), 16(3), 18(10) or 19(2) or regulations under section 25,

a penalty not exceeding £3,000 may be imposed on him.

(2) Where a person liable to a penalty under subsection (1) is a person making, or who has made, a claim for a tax credit for a period jointly with another and the penalty is imposed—
  (a) under paragraph (a) of that subsection in respect of the claim, a notification relating to the tax credit claimed or a notice relating to the tax credit awarded on the claim, or
  (b) under paragraph (b) of that subsection in respect of a requirement imposed on him with respect to the tax credit for the period,

a penalty of an amount not exceeding £3,000 may be imposed on the other person unless subsection (3) applies.

Tax Credits Act 2002

(3) This subsection applies if the other person was not, and could not reasonably have been expected to have been, aware that the person liable to the penalty under subsection (1) had fraudulently or negligently made the incorrect statement or declaration or given the incorrect information or evidence.

(4) Where penalties are imposed under subsections (1) and (2) in respect of the same statement, declaration, information or evidence, their aggregate amount must not exceed £3,000.

(5) Where a person acts for another—
  (a) in or in connection with a claim or notification referred to in subsection (1), or
  (b) in response to a notice so referred to,
subsection (1) applies to him (as well as to any person to whom it applies apart from this subsection).

AMENDMENT

1. Subsection (2) is modified as it applies to polygamous units by Tax Credits (Polygamous Marriages) Regulations 2003 (SI 2003/742), reg.20.

DEFINITIONS

"change of circumstances"—see s.6(1).
"claim"—see s.3(8).
"joint claim"—*ibid.*
"tax credit"—see s.1(2).

GENERAL NOTE

1.310   The response in this Act to concern about the potential for fraud in the tax credits system by both claimants and employers is the two-stage decision-making process, backed at each stage by wide information powers and a penalty regime applicable to all those who either fail to provide information or who provide wrong information.

Sections 31–34 and Sch.2 set out a full penalty regime to support the operation of tax credits. It is an enhanced version of the provisions of s.9 of, and Sch.4 to, the TCA 1999, and it draws on the approach in Pt X (Penalties, ss.93–107) in the TMA 1970.

This section deals with the problem where anyone required to make a declaration, statement or notification or to give information or evidence does so "incorrectly" and where the person does so "fraudulently or negligently". It applies both to the person making the declaration, etc., and to anyone acting for that person (subs.(5)), and both could be subject to penalty proceedings in connection with the same matter. This wording echoes the terms of s.98(2) of the TMA 1970, the main penalty-imposing section in that Act. The maximum penalty of £3,000 is also the same as that in s.98 (a figure last adjusted in 1989). It is the same level as in s.9(5) of the TCA 1999. The section also makes provision for the penalty to be imposed on both of two joint claimants in appropriate cases, though subject to a joint maximum of £3,000.

HMRC have published two leaflets of guidance about the exercise of their penalty powers: WTC3, *Tax Credit Penalties, How tax credit examinations are settled*, and WTC4, *Tax Credit penalties, How tax credit enquiries are settled*. They apply to penalties under both this section and s.32. These reflect the differences between examinations (taking place about current claims or awards) and enquiries (taking place when an award is finalised or after entitlement has been established). They are now combined with WTC7, which is set out at the end of this volume. The leaflets set out the procedure for dealing with the imposition of penalties and the basis on which

(2002 c.21, s.31)

HMRC decide at what level a penalty will be set. HMRC's practice follows that applying for similar income tax examinations and enquiries. Discounts to the maximum penalty will be applied to reflect: the extent to which the error was disclosed voluntarily by the claimant; the extent to which the claimant has cooperated with HMRC in the examination or enquiry; the seriousness of the errors or omissions; and whether this is a first or subsequent occasion on which there has been an error or omission. Any decision about a penalty is open to appeal to an appeals tribunal and to a Social Security Commissioner and they are, of course, not bound by these policy statements. However, it is HMRC's practice to seek settlement of a penalty with the individual under s.54 of the Taxes Management Act 1970. It is rare for an income tax penalty appeal not to be settled at some stage.

Fraudulently or negligently

Those sections in the TMA 1970 have been subject to consideration in the courts on a number of occasions, and it is to be expected that the common phraseology of those sections and these (such as "fraudulently or negligently") will receive a similar interpretation. On this basis, the fraud or neglect of an agent will be regarded as the fraud or neglect of the claimant: *Clixby v Pountney* (1968) 44 T.C. 575. It is clearly established in income tax law that the onus of proving fraud or neglect is on HMRC. *Hillenbrand v IRC* (1966) 42 T.C. 617 established that there is no presumption of fraud or neglect because of an omission, although the omission might give a factual basis for a decision on this point. However, if HMRC establish the fraud or neglect, then the burden shifts to the taxpayer to show that any assessment made by HMRC as a result is incorrect. It is also established that HMRC does not have to show the precise nature of discovered income: *Hudson v Humbles* (1965) 42 T.C. 380. That is part of the process of making and appealing an assessment. It is suggested that the same approaches would be appropriate here, save that in addition HMRC and appeal tribunal will be able to take account of evidence gathered for income tax purposes in deciding the outcome of a s.20 review.

Additionally, since the Human Rights Act 1998 came into effect, it is arguable that this section imposes a "criminal" liability under Art.6(3) of the European Convention on Human Rights. (For the text, see Vol.III of this work). Courts have applied the criminal standard to equivalent provisions in income tax and VAT legislation. If Art.6(3) applies then close consideration needs to be given to the burden of proof under this section, the evidence available for establishing or resisting the application of the section and the availability of legal aid.

A penalty under this section bears interest under s.37. It is treated as unpaid tax for the purposes of recovery and collection (Sch.2, para.7). Appeals against penalty decisions are dealt with in Sch.2 (see s.34).

Subsections (2) and (3) deal with a problem that is no longer relevant to income tax, namely the case where one of a couple making a joint claim has failed fully to co-operate with the other, so that the declaration is wrong but one of the joint claimants is not aware that this is so. In such cases responsibility remains joint and several unless one of the claimants can show that the defence in subs.(3) applies. This imposes a double test of both fact and reasonableness.

The conduct of penalty cases

Appeals under s.31 are "criminal" in the sense that Arts 6(2) and (3) of the European Convention on Human Rights apply in addition to Art.6(1). This is clear from the decision of the European Court of Human Rights in *King v United Kingdom (No.2)*, Application 13881/02, of February 17, 2004, [2004] S.T.C. 911. See Vol.3 of this work for the text of the Article and commentary. That approach will be strengthened by the decision of that court in *PM v United Kingdom*, Application 6638/03, of July 19, 2005. In that case a taxpayer was held entitled to invoke the scope of Art.1, Protocol 1 (rights of property) in alleging discrimination about the terms of entitlement to a deduction for maintenance payments under s.347 of the Income and Corporation Taxes Act 1988. As there was no internal remedy for

1.311

1.312

Tax Credits Act 2002

discrimination caused by primary legislation, the European Court awarded damages to the appellant.

The HMRC Claimant Compliance Manual (CCM) refers to s.31 as being a power to punish. But this does not apply to s.32. See the detailed analysis of the equivalent income tax provisions in *Gladders v Prior* [2003] S.T.C. (S.C.D.) 245 (decision of Special Commissioner of Income Tax, not appealed). A notice requiring information does not breach the rule on self-incrimination. See *Sharkey v De Cross* [2005] S.T.C. (S.C.D.) 336 citing *R. v Allen* [2002] A.C. 509 on a similar income tax provision.

There is authority that receipt of a relevant notice is crucial to the activation of the sections, and that the Interpretation Act presumptions do not apply: Macpherson J. in *CEC v Medway Draughting and Technical Service Ltd* [1989] S.T.C. 346 dealing with a similar VAT provision.

The burden of proof rests with HMRC. The degree of proof depends on the seriousness of the allegations: *Rowland v Boyle* [2003] EWHC (Ch) 781 applying the Court of Appeal decision in *Hornal v Neuberger Products Ltd* [1957] 1 Q.B. 247, 273 to a similar provision in income tax legislation. "Fraud or neglect" includes wilful default: *R. v IRC Ex p Knight* [1973] S.T.C. 564.

Tax cases suggest that a tribunal should always give reasons for a penalty decision, even if no formal request is made. See *Brodt v Wells General Commissioners* [1987] S.T.C. 20 where the importance of consistency is stressed. There is an open appeal to the Commissioners.

The level of penalties

1.313　The procedure to be followed by HMRC officers when imposing or applying for tax credits penalties are set out in the *New Tax Credits Claimant Compliance Manual* (abbreviated as CCN). This is available on the HMRC website at *http://www.hmrc.gov.uk/manuals/ccmmanual/Index.htm*. However, some parts of CCM have been withheld from publication under the Freedom of Information Act 2000. See, for example CCM10070 (even the number of that paragraph is withheld, but it is referred to in cross-references not withheld as covering "Penalties: calculation of penalties in incorrect claims"). The main issue withheld in that paragraph is the calculation of the amount of a penalty to be imposed under subs.(4) of this section. CCM 10080 on the calculation of a percentage of an overpaid claim is not withheld, although it makes little sense in the absence of CCM 10070. This is in contrast to the approach adopted by HMRC with regard to penalties under the income tax penalty regime, and in which percentages play a major role. See now the recently published *Code of Practice 9 (2005)* on civil investigation into cases of suspected serious fraud. This specifically details reductions of maximum penalties by the following percentages:

— up to 20 per cent for voluntary disclosure (or 30 per cent for full disclosure with no risk of discovery);

— up to 40 per cent for cooperation with an investigation, including full disclosures of information requested;

— up to 40 per cent for seriousness of errors and omissions.

Withholding information under the 2000 Act does not apply when HMRC must explain to an appeal tribunal how it reaches the level of penalty it has selected. As a result, various parts of the withheld information have come to the attention of individual appeal tribunals. That is not a satisfactory situation.

It would seem that the approach broadly follows the income tax penalty approach save that in the case of tax penalties the maximum amount of the penalty is a set figure and not a percentage of the income tax under-declared. For example, CCM 10080 shows that an officer should look at the percentage of the overclaimed credits as compared with total credits originally claimed. CCM10090 refers to "the relatively small amount of penalties for first offences". CCM 10100 refers to an abatement of a maximum of 50 per cent for full and prompt cooperation with an enquiry

(2002 c.21, s.31)

or examination. These statements, and the examples at CCM10110, all point to the same broad approach as that used for income tax. CCM also emphasises that penalties for second and subsequent incorrect statements are likely to be significantly higher than initial penalties. Officers are required to notify claimants of this when imposing an initial penalty.

That aside, CCM sets out in considerable detail the procedures to be used by individual HMRC officers in the process of imposing or requesting penalties.

CCM 10040 emphasises that the penalty power related to s.17 notifications applies only once although the information applies to two years. However, if there are incorrect s.17 notices at both ends of a year, HMRC may levy two penalties. In addition, there may be separate penalties up to the maximum where there is an incorrect s.17 notification and some other "offence" as the CCM terms it.

Failure to comply with requirements

32.—(1) Where a person fails— 1.314
(a) to provide any information or evidence which he is required to provide by virtue of section 14(2), 15(2), 16(3), 18(10) or 19(2) or regulations under section 25, or
(b) to comply with a requirement imposed on him by a notice under section 17 by virtue of subsection (2)(a), (4)(a) or (6)(a) of that section,
the penalties specified in subsection (2) may be imposed on him.

(2) The penalties are—
(a) a penalty not exceeding £300, and
(b) if the failure continues after a penalty is imposed under paragraph (a), a further penalty or penalties not exceeding £60 for each day on which the failure continues after the day on which the penalty under that paragraph was imposed (but excluding any day for which a penalty under this paragraph has already been imposed).

(3) Where a person fails to give a notification required by regulations under section 6(3), a penalty not exceeding £300 may be imposed on him.

(4) No penalty under subsection (2) may be imposed on a person in respect of a failure after the failure has been remedied.

(5) For the purposes of this section a person is to be taken not to have failed to provide information or evidence, comply with a requirement or give a notification which must be provided, complied with or given by a particular time—
(a) if he provided, complied with or gave it within such further time (if any) as the Board may have allowed,
(b) if he had a reasonable excuse for not providing, complying with or giving it by that time, or
(c) if, after having had such an excuse, he provided, complied with or gave it without unreasonable delay.

(6) Where the members of [1 a couple] both fail as mentioned in subsection (1)(b), the aggregate amount of any penalties under subsection (2) imposed on them in relation to their failures must not exceed the amounts specified in that subsection; and where the members of [1 a couple] both fail as mentioned in subsection (3), the aggregate amount of any penalties imposed on them in relation to their failures must not exceed £300.

AMENDMENT

1. Civil Partnership Act 2004, s.254 and Sch.24, para.145 (December 5, 2005).

DEFINITIONS

"the Board"—see s.67.
"married couple"—see s.3(5).
"unmarried couple"—see s.3(6).

GENERAL NOTE

1.315   See the note to s.31 on the penalty regime as a whole. This section imposes penalties on those who fail to comply with any notices under s.17, who fail to provide information or evidence under any of the powers to require this, or who fail to give notification of a change of circumstances under s.6. It is a parallel to s.9(1) of the TMA 1970, and replaces s.9(3) of the TCA 1999. In common with those Acts, this section imposes a potential penalty on all failures, regardless of the reason for the failure. There is no test of fraud or negligence. The policy of all these measures is to impose a relatively low initial maximum penalty (£300 in all cases), but then to provide a cumulatively daily penalty as a strong deterrent to those who choose to ignore not only the notices and requirements but also the initial penalty. In each case, the maximum daily rate is £60. But the daily rate stops when the failure is remedied.

A penalty under this section bears interest under s.37. It is treated as unpaid tax for the purposes of recovery and collection (Sch.2, para.7). Appeals against penalty decisions are dealt with in Sch.2 (see s.34). By contrast with s.31, this section does not demand proof of fraud or negligence, and may therefore impose a civil penalty rather than a criminal penalty for the purposes of the European Convention on Human Rights.

For details of HMRC's practice in setting and dealing with penalties, see the note to s.31 and HMRC. The full text of WTC7 is set out at the end of the volume. HMRC has announced that it will, on a concessionary basis, not seek penalties from those who fail to comply with the mandatory provisions in this section when the award made to the individual is a nil award.

Subsection (1) lists the powers under which HMRC can demand information within the penalty regime. It is important to note that those powers are not all-embracing but are subject to clear time limits laid down in primary legislation. See further the notes to ss.14 and 19 above.

The CCM (Claimant Compliance Manual—see note to p.160 above) states that:

"Penalties under s.32(1) are not intended to punish a person who will not provide information. The penalties are intended to encourage the person to comply with the notice and if you do not think the penalties will achieve this result you should not normally begin penalty action" (CCM 10230).

The guidance also states that s.32 penalties will not normally be needed for s.14(2) or s.15(2) failures. In-year challenges will normally only be those under s.16 (CCM 10235, 10240). Similarly, CCM discourages s.32 penalties for s.17 notices.

CCM 10300 provides that submissions to appeal tribunals for s.32 penalties must be transferred to and made by a single office of HMRC, the Cross-Cutting Policy (Stockport Technical Unit).

CCM 10170 gives internal guidance on the meaning of "reasonable excuse". The examples of reasonable excuses include notifications lost or delayed in the post because of an unforeseen event, serious illness of the claimant or a close relative, or death of a relative. The examples are somewhat similar to those applying to a social security claim under reg.19 of the Social Security (Claims and Payments) Regulations 1987, on which see Vol.III leaflet WTC7, *Tax Credit Penalties: what happens at the end of a check*. of this work, but a statutory formulation has been avoided. "Too busy" and "did not understand what was required" are said not to be reasonable excuses. CCM 10620 accepts that there is no negligence if a claimant has acted on official guidance, but warns officers to check official telephone logs and any contemporary notes kept by claimants. CCM 10640 accepts that acting on advice of "a legitimate source" such as a CAB or Jobcentre Plus may be a reasonable excuse.

Supplementary

34. Schedule 2 (penalties: supplementary) has effect.

1.316

GENERAL NOTE

This section incorporates Sch.2 into the Act. The Schedule sets out the procedure for determining, appealing and collecting penalties. Paragraph 1 provides for determination of penalties in terms similar to s.100 of the TMA 1970. The appeal procedures in paras 2 and 3 echo those in the TMA 1970. However, they are replaced by the modifications operating for the time being under s.63 of the Act. This routes appeals to appeal tribunals and the Social Security Commissioners rather than to the General Commissioners, Special Commissioners and courts. There were similar provisions in Sch.4 to the TCA 1999.

1.317

Paragraph 5 of the Schedule gives HMRC the same power to mitigate penalties as in s.102 of the TMA 1970. This is in practice how HMRC prefers to deal with penalties. It first indicates what penalty it considers appropriate by reference to its published practice. It then seeks to deal with both the outstanding tax and interest, together with the penalty, by what is known as a contract settlement. In exchange for the taxpayer paying an agreed sum of money, HMRC agrees to waive its rights to any tax, interest and penalties. The outcome is a contract separate from any specific tax provision. This approach was long ago endorsed by the courts: see *Att-Gen v Johnstone* (1926) 10 T.C. 758. Conduct of these "back duty" cases, as they are known, on behalf of taxpayers is regarded as a specific specialist skill by tax experts. The approach of agreeing a monetary settlement may be the practical answer to the issues arising under Art.6(3) of the European Convention on Human Rights as noted under s.31.

Paragraph 6 imposes similar time limits to those in s.103 of that Act.

Fraud

Offence of fraud

35.—(1) A person commits an offence if he is knowingly concerned in any fraudulent activity undertaken with a view to obtaining payments of a tax credit by him or any other person.

1.318

(2) A person who commits an offence under subsection (1) is liable—
(a) on summary conviction, to imprisonment for a term not exceeding six months, or a fine not exceeding the statutory maximum, or both, or
(b) on conviction on indictment, to imprisonment for a term not exceeding seven years, or a fine, or both.

DEFINITION

"tax credit"—see s.1(2).

GENERAL NOTE

Like the penalties provisions, this section reflects the fear of fraud by claimants and others abusing the tax credits system. There is no equivalent of this section in the TCA 1999. The new offence is briefly stated and is clearly intended to have a wide reach. It is not confined to claimants or employers and could be applied, for example, to a childcare provider.

1.319

Powers in relation to documents

36.—(1) Section 20BA of the Taxes Management Act 1970 (c.9) (orders for delivery of documents) applies (with Schedule 1AA and section 20BB) in relation to offences involving fraud in connection with, or in relation to, tax credits as in relation to offences involving serious fraud in connection with, or in relation to, tax.

(2) Section 20C (entry with warrant to obtain documents) of that Act applies (with section 20CC) in relation to offences involving serious fraud in connection with, or in relation to, tax credits as in relation to offences involving serious fraud in connection with, or in relation to, tax (but subject to the modification provided by subsection (3)).

(3) Subsection (1A) of section 20C applies by virtue of subsection (2) as if the references to the proper assessment or collection of tax were to the proper award or payment of a tax credit.

(4) Any regulations under Schedule 1AA to the Taxes Management Act 1970 which are in force immediately before the commencement of subsection (1) apply, subject to any necessary modifications, for the purposes of that Schedule as they apply by virtue of that subsection (until amended or revoked).

DEFINITION

"tax credit"—see s.1(2).

GENERAL NOTE

This applies specific powers available to HMRC for dealing with tax fraud to tax credit fraud. Sections 20BA and 20BB of the TMA 1970 deal with orders for delivery of documents and offences of fraud respectively. Section 20C is a power to enter premises on a warrant, but is available only in cases of serious fraud and can only be obtained from a judicial authority. The statutory instrument currently made under Sch.1AA is the Orders for the Delivery of Documents (Procedure) Regulations 2000 (SI 2000/2875).

Interest

Interest

37.—(1) If an overpayment of a tax credit for a period is attributable to fraud or neglect on the part of the person, or either or both of the persons, to whom the award of the tax credit was made (or a person acting for him, or for either or both of them, in making the claim for the tax credit), the Board may decide that the whole or any part of the overpayment is to carry interest.

(2) Where the Board so decide the overpayment (or part of the overpayment) carries interest at a prescribed rate from the date 30 days after the appropriate date.

(3) "The appropriate date" is—
(a) in the case of an amount treated as an overpayment by virtue of section 28(6), the date of the decision under section 16 to terminate the award; and
(b) in any other case, the date specified for the purposes of subsection (4) of section 17 in the notice given to the person or persons under that section in relation to the tax credit.

(2002 c.21, s.37)

(4) The Board must give notice of a decision under subsection (1) to the person, or each of the persons, to whom it relates; and the notice must state the date on which it is given and include details of the right to appeal against the decision under section 38.

(5) A penalty under any of sections 31 to 33 carries interest at the prescribed rate from the date on which it becomes due and payable; but the Board may in their discretion mitigate any interest or entirely remit any interest which wouldotherwise be carried by a penalty.

(6) Any interest carried under this section by an overpayment or penalty is to be regarded for the purposes of section 29(3) to (5) or paragraph 7 of Schedule 2 as if it were part of the overpayment or penalty.

AMENDMENT

Subsection (1) is modified as it applies to polygamous units by Tax Credits (Polygamous Marriages) Regulations 2003 (SI 2003/742), reg.21.

DEFINITIONS

"the Board"—see s.67.
"prescribed"—*ibid.*
"overpayment"—see s.28.
"tax credit"—see s.1(2).

GENERAL NOTE

Interest has long been imposed on taxpayers who do not make timely payments of income tax. This includes an underpayment (or repayment) of tax reliefs and deductions (see TMA 1970, s.86). By contrast, interest is not imposed on those required to repay an overpayment of social security benefits. Interest was not imposed on overpayments under the TCA 1999, although penalties under s.9 of that Act carried interest (Sch.4, para.8 to that Act).

This section adopts a compromise in imposing interest payments on overpayments caused by fraud or neglect, but not generally. It also imposes again an interest charge on payments of penalties. Interest does not run unless a decision is made to impose it, and that cannot start until either the date on which the award of tax credit was terminated under s.16 or the closing date of a notice issued under s.17.

The "prescribed rate" is set out in the Tax Credits (Interest Rate) Regulations 2003 (SI 2003/123).

1.323

Appeals

Appeals

38.—(1) An appeal may be brought against—
(a) a decision under section 14(1), 15(1), 16(1), 19(3) or 20(1) or (4) or regulations under section 21,
(b) the relevant section 18 decision in relation to a person or persons and a tax credit for a tax year and any revision of that decision under that section,
(c) a determination of a penalty under paragraph 1 of Schedule 2, and
(d) a decision under section 37(1).
(2) "The relevant section 18 decision" means—
(a) in a case in which a decision must be made under subsection (6) of section 18 in relation to the person or persons and the tax credit for the tax year, that decision, and

1.324

Tax Credits Act 2002

(b) in any other case, the decision under subsection (1) of that section in relation to the person or persons and the tax credit for the tax year.

DEFINITIONS

"tax credit"—see s.1(2).
"tax year"—see s.47.

GENERAL NOTE

1.325 This section creates a series of specific rights of appeal. The following decisions or actions of HMRC are subject to the appeal process:

(a) an initial decision to award or refuse tax credits under s.14(1);

(b) a decision whether (and if so, how) to amend a s.14 decision under s.15(1);

(c) a decision amending or terminating a s.14 decision under s.16(1);

(d) a decision on entitlement made under s.18(1) or (6);

(e) a decision after an enquiry under s.19(3);

(f) a decision revising a previous decision on entitlement under s.20(1);

(g) a decision revising a previous decision on entitlement on the grounds of fraud or neglect under s.20(4);

(h) a decision to revise a decision on entitlement because of official error under s.21;

(i) a determination of a penalty under Sch.2 para.1;

(j) a decision to impose interest under s.37(1).

In *CTC/31/2006* the Commissioner rejected as outside his jurisdiction an attempt to appeal a decision of HMRC that a claim was not properly made. The claim had been made on an income tax return, and HMRC had refused to accept it. The Commissioner held that this was not within the terms of s.38. He also held that it could not be read into the section by reference to the European Convention on Human Rights. In the view of the Commissioner judicial review was an adequate means of challenging a decision to refuse a claim that was alleged to be unlawful. *CTC/1594/2006* illustrates the importance of checking for which year or years an appeal is made. This is potentially more of a problem for tax credits than most benefits because of the effect of having an award decision during the same year as the entitlement decision for the previous year. The Commissioner accepted the arguments for HMRC in that case that a claimant could not use an appeal to challenge more than the specific decisions challenged. As Commissioners have observed on more than one occasion, this means that challenges against award decisions may be of limited value. HMRC is no more debarred from altering a tribunal decision about an award at the end of the year than any other award decision. This issue is not always easy to clarify as HMRC uses terminology in its literature that conflates awards and entitlement decisions. See para.1.287.

There were very few appeals heard by appeal tribunals during the first two years of the operation of tax credits under this Act, and none came to the Social Security Commissioners for 18 months. (When asked how many CTC appeals had been made by time and region in February 2005, the Ministerial answer was that "the information requested is not available" (House of Commons Written Answers, col. 1399W). Hopefully, the Council on Tribunals will keep its usual statistics and make good that deficiency. There appear to be a number of reasons for the lack of appeals (and possibly the lack of statistics). Is the question whether something is properly a claim under s.3 appealable? See the note to s.3(1). It is clearly the case that an appeal tribunal can on appeal decide when a claim is made. It is not clear, however, that the tribunal can also decide that something that HMRC do not accept as a claim is in fact a claim. There may be an issue here similar to a decision about the terms of a written contract as against those of an oral contract. The former is a matter of law, but the latter a question of fact on all the evidence.

It is to be emphasised that this section gives the right of appeal, and s.39 as amended by s.63 is concerned only with how the appeal is made. It is often said that the appeal is to HMRC and not an appeal tribunal. That is not correct. The appeal is to the tribunal, while notification of that appeal is to HMRC. The importance of this is that HMRC has no independent right to refuse to pass an appeal on to a tribunal if there is no settlement. However, the tribunal has no jurisdiction to require that an appeal be listed before it. Any such order will be a matter for the Administrative Court on judicial review as in income tax cases.

The absence of appeals undoubtedly reflects the power of the Inland Revenue and now the HMRC to settle cases under s.54 of the TMA 1970. This is a power not possessed by the Department for Work and Pensions or local authorities (or the former Customs and Excise Commissioners). That power is particularly useful in dealing with questions of disputed income and with penalty cases, although it is of limited use in cases such as whether two individuals should be making a joint claim. But on one view HMRC is making too wide a use of that power. In *Tax Credits Agenda for Improvement*, published in September 2004 jointly by the Chartered Institute of Taxation, Citizens Advice, CPAG, The Institute of Chartered Accountants of England and Wales, the Low Income Tax Reform Group, and One Parent Families, the approach of HMRC to settlement was criticised. The bodies jointly asked for:

"adherence to proper procedures when the IR decide to settle an appeal, rather than 'cancelling' the appeal and issuing revised decisions outside the appeal process."

While HMRC have, as noted, a power to settle under s.54 of the TMA it is a process with its own safeguards (see para.1.19 above). Similarly, once an appeal has been made it cannot be "cancelled" otherwise than by a properly reached settlement or as part of the appeal process. Any attempt to interfere with the appeal process outside those protective limits is an interference by one party in the appeal process and as such is likely to be in breach of the "equality of arms" principle laid down by the European Court of Human Rights. That principle demands that all parties have equal access to a court or tribunal as part of the fundamental principle of fair hearings laid down in Art.6 of the European Convention on Human Rights. (See Volume III of this series for that provision and the Human Rights Act 1998 that introduces it into United Kingdom law.)

This section clearly gives separate appeal rights against s.14 decisions as against s.18 decisions. The automated process, followed by checks, that is used for awards (see the notes to s.14) would suggest that the administrative approach adopted by HMRC, while undoubtedly efficient in many cases, may be the reason why the joint protest has arisen.

Separately from these, the appellate authorities can be invoked in two other situations. HMRC cannot itself make a determination of daily penalties under s.32(2) and must instead start proceedings for such penalties before the appellate authorities. This is not technically an appeal (see Sch.2, para.3). An individual subject to an enquiry under s.19 can, under s.19(8), apply to the appellate authorities to direct the enquiry to end. Such an application is to be treated as if it was an appeal (s.19(10)).

[1 Exercise of right of appeal

39.—(1) Notice of an appeal under section 38 against a decision must be given to the Board in the prescribed manner within the period of thirty days after the date on which notice of the decision was given (or, in the case of a decision to which section 23(3) applies, the date of the decision).

(2) Notice of such an appeal must specify the grounds of appeal.

(5) On the hearing of an appeal under section 38 the appeal tribunal may allow the appellant to put forward grounds not specified in the notice, and

1.326

take them into consideration if satisfied that the omission was not wilful or unreasonable.]

AMENDMENT

1. Text of section amended as provided in s.63.

DEFINITIONS

"the Board"—see s.67.
"General Commissioners"—see s.47.
"modifications"—see s.67.
"prescribed"—*ibid.*
"Special Commissioners"—see s.47.

GENERAL NOTE

1.327 The text of the section set out here is that as amended by s.63. The unamended section originally applied to employer appeals, but there is no basis on which these can arise after the abolition of payment by employers after April 6, 2006. The section is the compromise that resulted when the original plan to route all appeals to the General and Special Commissioners proved impossible to implement. Responsibility for the social security tribunals (previously called appeal tribunals), to which the appeals go, was itself transferred from the Department for Work and Pensions to the Department for Constitutional Affairs in April 2006, and will have a common administration within the Tribunals Service. But no further substantive reform of the tax tribunals is planned in the near future, so appeals are likely to continue to be made to the social security tribunals.

Subs. (1)

1.328 This gives a 30-day time-limit on appeals (the usual HMRC time-limit), compared with a normal time-limit of one month from social security decisions to those tribunals. For the prescribed manner of notice of appeal see Tax Credits (Notice of Appeal) Regulations 2002 (SI 2002/3119), reg.2, and for late appeals see reg.5 of those Regulations.

One problem behind this provision is how it deals with appeals about joint claims, and in particular the case where an individual states that he or she is not a joint claimant with another person and that other person has no interest in the appeal proceedings. If the two individuals have both made separate claims (or one has claimed a social security benefit and the other a tax credit) it is open to question whether the ordinary appeal processes would bring the appeals to be heard together, although robust tribunals clearly achieve this.

Subs. (2)

1.328.1 This requires the grounds of appeal to be specified. The equivalent social security requirement is that particulars of the grounds be stated.

The notice of appeal should also indicate clearly which tax year is under appeal. As accepted in *CTC/1594/2006*, an appellant cannot challenge both the entitlement decision for one year and the award decision for the next year unless both those decisions are challenged expressly.

Subs. (5)

1.329 The equivalent provision in the Social Security Act 1998 is s.12(8)(a), which is not applied to tax credit appeals. That rule permits a tribunal not to examine an issue not raised by an appeal, while this appears to be more restrictive. In practice, however, the well-established investigative approach of social security tribunals will lead to much the same in both cases. An omission of important issues by claimants will not often be either wilful or unreasonable, given the complexity of the system.

The inquisitorial role of the tribunal and the burden of proof

It has long been recognised that proceedings before tribunals are inquisitorial rather than adversarial and this has been confirmed by the House of Lords in *Kerr v Department for Social Development* [2004] UKHL 23; [2004] 1 W.L.R. 1372 (also reported as an appendix to *R1/04(SF)*), where some of the consequences of this approach were considered. Baroness Hale of Richmond said:

> "61. Ever since the decision of the Divisional Court in *R. v Medical Appeal Tribunal (North Midland Region), Ex p. Hubble* [1958] 2 Q.B. 228, it has been accepted that the process of benefits adjudication in inquisitorial rather than adversarial. Diplock J. as he then was said this of an industrial injury benefit claim at p.240:
>
>> 'A claim by an insured person to benefit under the Act is not truly analogous to a *lis inter partes*. A claim to benefit is a claim to receive money out of the insurance funds . . . Any such claim investigation to determine whether any, and if so, what amount of benefit is payable out of the fund. In such an investigation, the minister or insurance officer is not a party adverse to the claimant. If analogy be sought in the other branches of the law, it is to be found in an inquest rather than an action.'
>
> 62. What emerges from all this is a co-operative process of investigation in which both the claimant and the department play their part. The department is the one which knows what questions it needs to ask and what information it needs to have in order to determine whether the conditions of entitlement have been met. The claimant is the one who generally speaking can and must supply that information. But where the information is available to the department rather than the claimant, then the department must take the necessary steps to enable it to be traced.
>
> 63. If that sensible approach is taken, it will rarely be necessary to resort to concepts taken from adversarial litigation such as the burden of proof. The first question will be whether each partner in the process has played their part. If there is still ignorance about a relevant matter then generally speaking it should be determined against the one who has not done all that they reasonably could to discover it. As Mr Commissioner Henty put it in *CIS/5321/1998*: 'a claimant must to the best of his or her ability give such information to the AO as he reasonably can, in default of which a contrary inference can always be drawn.' The same should apply to information which the department can reasonably be expected to discover for itself."

In that particular case the claimant had been unable to tell the department whether either his brother or sister, with whom he had lost contact, was in receipt of relevant benefits. The department could have discovered that information had they had the brother's and sister's dates of birth, which the claimant could have given them but for which the department never asked. It was held that the department could not rely on their failure to ask questions which would have led to the right answer to defeat the claim.

Where all relevant questions have been asked and there are still things unknown, it was held in *Kerr* that it has to be decided who should bear the consequences of the collective ignorance. If the ignorance concerns a matter relevant to conditions of entitlement, the claimant has to bear the consequences but if the ignorance concerns an exception to those conditions, the department must bear the consequences. In *Kerr*, the claimant was prima facie entitled to a funeral payment but would not be entitled if his brother or sister was not receiving benefit or had capital. The ignorance as to whether they were receiving benefit or had capital was therefore ignorance concerning an exception to entitlement and the department had to bear the burden and pay the claim. Lord Hope of Craighead set out, at para.[16], the following basic principles to be applied where the information available to a decision-maker falls short of what is needed for a clear decision one way or the other.

"(1) Facts which may reasonably be supposed to be within the claimant's own knowledge are for the claimant to supply at each stage in the inquiry.
(2) But the claimant must be given a reasonable opportunity to supply them. Knowledge as to the information that is needed to deal with his claim lies with the department, not with him.
(3) So it is for the department to ask the relevant questions. The claimant is not to be faulted if the relevant questions to show whether or not the claim is excluded by the Regulations were not asked.
(4) The general rule is that it is for the party who alleges an affirmative to make good his allegation. It is also a general rule that he who desires to take advantage of an exception must bring himself within the provisions of the exception. As Lord Wilberforce observed, exceptions are to be set up by those who rely on them: *Nimmo v Alexander Cowan & Sons Ltd* [1968] A.C. 107, 130."

It is suggested that the tribunal in *Kerr* would not necessarily have been obliged to determine the case in the claimant's favour when the case first came before them. The inquisitorial role of tribunals obliges them to ask questions that the Secretary of State should have asked but has not (*R(IS) 11/99*). It would have been open to the tribunal to ask the claimant whether he knew the dates of birth of his brother and sister and, if the answer was in the affirmative, to give the department the opportunity of investigating the matter further. However, the question whether to adjourn in those circumstances is a matter within the discretion of the tribunal and the department cannot expect always to be given a chance to do something it could perfectly well have done earlier. By the time *Kerr* reached the courts, it was doubtless felt to be a bit late for the department to be making further enquiries.

The effect of the tribunal having an inquisitorial role was also considered by a Tribunal of Commissioners in *R(IS) 17/04*. In 2002, the Secretary of State had superseded awards of benefit from 1988, amounting to some £30,000. The claimant appealed and the Secretary of State made a written submission and produced a considerable amount of evidence. A tribunal chairman directed that a presenting officer attend the hearing to put the Secretary of State's case. In the event, two investigating officers attended as witnesses but there was no presenting officer and a short adjournment established that none would attend. On the basis that the burden of proof lay on the Secretary of State and that the written material was not sufficient in the light of the specific direction that there be a presenting officer, the tribunal allowed the claimant's appeal without putting to her the Secretary of State's case. The Tribunal of Commissioners held the tribunal to have erred. The written material had been sufficient to raise a case for the claimant to answer and the inquisitorial role of the tribunal required the tribunal "to ascertain and determine the true amount of social security benefit to which the claimant was properly entitled", which, once the tribunal had decided not to adjourn, entailed putting the case raised by the Secretary of State's written material to the claimant and enabling her representative to question the witnesses. The Tribunal of Commissioners rejected a submission that a tribunal could not act fairly if it "descended into the arena" and they referred to another decision of a Tribunal of Commissioners, *R(S) 4/82*, where it was said that it was legitimate for a tribunal to put questions, even probing questions, to a claimant to deal with the obvious points that arose on an appeal. However, questions from a tribunal have to be put carefully and phrased neutrally. Plainly it is better that the Secretary of State be represented in highly contentious or complex cases and the Tribunal of Commissioners recorded both the Secretary of State's declared policy "to appear by way of a presenting officer at every tribunal hearing where the tribunal had made a direction requiring a presenting officer to attend" and the Secretary of State's acceptance of a recommendation of the National Audit Office that he should himself identify complex cases where spending money on presenting officers might achieve greater financial savings.

The Tribunal of Commissioners cited with approval *CI/1021/2001*, where it was held that a tribunal is not entitled to rely upon a "failure to discharge the burden of proof as a substitute for a proper enquiry where there is evidence that there is something into which there needs to be an enquiry". A similar approach led a Tribunal of Commissioners in Northern Ireland to hold a tribunal to have erred when, at a "paper hearing", they had incomplete evidence that raised important issues it could not answer and they failed to adjourn in order to give the claimant the opportunity of attending (*R1/02(IB)*). However, it does not follow from *R(IS) 17/04* that decision-making bodies need make no effort to present evidence to a tribunal. In *CTC/ 2090/2004*, the Board of Inland Revenue failed to provide any evidence to a tribunal on the question whether the claimant or his ex-wife had the main responsibility for their daughter. That was important because it determined which of the parents was entitled to child tax credit. Both of the parents had claimed child tax credit and it had been awarded to the claimant's ex-wife. The Board did not ask for an adjournment and did not even send an officer to the hearing. The tribunal heard evidence from the claimant as to which parent had the main responsibility for the child and allowed his appeal. The Board appealed on the ground that its position was neutral and that as child tax credit could not be awarded to both parents, the tribunal's inquisitorial jurisdiction required it to summons the claimant's ex-wife to provide evidence against the claimant in her interest. The Commissioner gave that argument short shrift. Being neutral did not justify inactivity on the Board's part. In the light of *Kerr*, it had been the Board's duty to investigate the cases of both parents properly and avoid inconsistent decisions, which clearly meant enquiring themselves into the question of which parent had the main responsibility. However, the tribunal's decision would not be binding on the claimant's ex-wife and the tribunal had been entitled to assume that the Board was content for the claimant's appeal to be determined without information being obtained from his ex-wife. In other words, the tribunal's inquisitorial duty in respect of the father's claim had been satisfied by obtaining relevant evidence from him.

What, however, is made plain in *R(IS) 17/04* is that the inquisitorial role of the tribunal is not brought into play only for the purpose of assisting a claimant. A tribunal is part of the machinery for determining the true entitlement of a claimant. It follows that a tribunal is at liberty to follow its own view of a case even if that does not coincide with the view of either the claimant or the Secretary of State (*R. v Deputy Industrial Injuries Commissioner, Ex p. Moore* [1965] 1 Q.B. 456 (C.A.) (also reported as an appendix to *R(I) 4/65*).

Evidence
Tribunals are not bound by the common law rules of evidence and so, in *CDLA/2014/2004*, a tribunal erred in refusing to allow a disability consultant to give evidence of his opinion. However, it does not follow that those rules of evidence have no relevance at all. Tribunals have no power to override any privilege of a witness not to give evidence, such as the privilege attaching to solicitor-client communications and the privilege against self-incrimination. Furthermore, the common law rules of evidence may be relevant in the evaluation of evidence because the considerations which have led to the evidence being inadmissible often mean that it has little weight. Thus, there might have been good reasons for treating the disability consultant's evidence with caution, but it was wrong to refuse to consider it at all. Similarly, in *R(IB) 7/05*, the Commissioner held that it was not necessary for the Secretary of State to follow the certification procedure under s.7 of the under the Electronic Communications Act 2000 when there was a challenge to the authenticity of an electronic signature. In *CCS/3749/2003*, it was held that a tribunal should refuse to consider any information about proceedings relating to children of a court sitting in private (because use of the information by a party is potentially a contempt of court) but was entitled to hear evidence about ancillary relief proceedings that had taken in place in private.

Supplementary

Annual reports

1.330   **40.**—(1) The Board must make to the Treasury an annual report about—
(a) [¹ . . .]
(b) the number of awards of child tax credit and of working tax credit,
(c) the number of enquiries conducted under section 19,
(d) the number of penalties imposed under this Part, and
(e) the number of prosecutions and convictions for offences connected with tax credits.

(2) The Treasury must publish each annual report made to it under subsection (1) and lay a copy before each House of Parliament.

AMENDMENTS

1. Commissioners for Revenue and Customs Act 2005, s.50 and Sch.4, para.89 (April 18, 2005).
2. References to "the Board" are now references to the Commissioners for Revenue and Customs: CRCA 2005, s.4.

DEFINITIONS

"the Board"—see s.67.
"child tax credit"—see s.8.
"tax credits"—see s 1(2).
"working tax credit"—see s.10.

GENERAL NOTE

1.331   This section derives from a clause adopted by the House of Lords against the wishes of government, and represents the one major amendment in the Act not moved by the Government itself. The aim is to ensure a specific report that would be put before Parliament each year about both the scale of the tax credits system and the extent of fraud within it. The wording of the section comes from a government amendment moved to replace the Lords clause in the House of Commons. It was recognised that to some extent it duplicates figures already published by HMRC in its more general reports.

Annual review

1.332   **41.**—(1) The Treasury must, in each tax year, review the amounts specified in subsection (2) in order to determine whether they have retained their value in relation to the general level of prices in the United Kingdom as estimated by the Treasury in such manner as it considers appropriate.

(2) The amounts are monetary amounts prescribed—
(a) under subsection (1)(a) of section 7;
(b) for the purposes of any of paragraphs (a) to (d) of subsection (3) of that section;
(c) under section 9;
(d) under section 11, otherwise than by virtue of section 12, or
(e) under subsection (2) of section 13, otherwise than by virtue of subsection (3) of that section.

(3) The Treasury must prepare a report of each review.

(4) The report must include a statement of what each amount would be if it had fully retained its value.

(5) The Treasury must publish the report and lay a copy of it before each House of Parliament.

DEFINITION

"prescribed"—see s.67.

GENERAL NOTE

This provides for the annual uprating review of the monetary amounts used in awarding tax credits.

1.333

Persons subject to immigration control

42.—(1) Regulations may make provision in relation to persons subject to immigration control or in relation to prescribed descriptions of such persons—

(a) for excluding entitlement to, or to a prescribed element of, child tax credit or working tax credit (or both), or

(b) for this Part to apply subject to other prescribed modifications.

(2) "Person subject to immigration control" has the same meaning as in section 115 of the Immigration and Asylum Act 1999 (c.33).

1.334

DEFINITIONS

"child tax credit"—see s.8.
"modifications"—see s.67.
"persons subject to immigration control"—see Immigration and Asylum Act 1999, s.115.
"prescribed"—see s.67.
"working tax credit"—see s.10.

GENERAL NOTE

Although listed in the "supplementary" part of Pt I of the Act, this makes provision for excluding anyone from entitlement to tax credits if he or she is "subject to immigration control", a phrase derived from the Immigration and Asylum Act 1999. The definition covers those who are not nationals of an EEA state and who require leave to enter the United Kingdom or have certain forms of conditional leave. This carries forward the exclusion from WFTC of all such people (s.115(1)(f) of that Act). For the detailed application of this section, see the Tax Credits (Immigration) Regulations 2003 (SI 2003/653).

1.335

Polygamous marriages

43.—(1) Regulations may make provision for this Part to apply in relation to persons who are parties to polygamous marriages subject to prescribed modifications.

(2) A person is a party to a polygamous marriage if—

(a) he is a party to a marriage entered into under a law which permits polygamy, and

(b) either party to the marriage has a spouse additional to the other party.

1.336

DEFINITION

"modifications"—see s.67.

GENERAL NOTE

This is another of the necessary compromises between the general approach to income tax and the general approach to social security. Social security benefits have

1.337

long contained special provisions dealing with polygamous marriages, if only to prevent more than two of the marriage partners benefiting for a particular benefit as a married couple. In contrast, the point is not so significant in the context of income tax as there is now individual assessment. The standard treatment of monogamous marriages is set out in s.3.

Effect is given to this section by the Tax Credits (Polygamous Marriages) Regulations 2003 (SI 2003/742). Where those regulations provide for a modification of the sections of this Act, that is noted in this volume as an amendment to the section.

Crown employment

1.338

44. This Part applies in relation to persons employed by or under the Crown (as in relation to other employees).

DEFINITIONS

"Crown"—see Interpretation Act 1978, Sch.1.
"employed"—see s.25(5).

GENERAL NOTE

1.339

This section avoids any unintended exclusion of civil and other public servants by reason of the Crown Proceedings Act 1947 or otherwise. The Tax Credits (Residence) Regulations 2003 (SI 2003/642) extend this further by applying the Act to Crown Servants working overseas and their partners. The main concern of both this section and those regulations is that Crown servants receive full entitlement to CTC.

Inalienability

1.340

45.—(1) Every assignment of or charge on a tax credit, and every agreement to assign or charge a tax credit, is void; and, on the bankruptcy of a person entitled to a tax credit, the entitlement to the tax credit does not pass to any trustee or other person acting on behalf of his creditors.

(2) In the application of subsection (1) to Scotland—
  (a) the reference to assignment is to assignation ("assign" being construed accordingly), and
  (b) the reference to the bankruptcy of a person is to the sequestration of his estate or the appointment on his estate of a judicial factor under section 41 of the Solicitors (Scotland) Act 1980 (c.46).

DEFINITION

"tax credit"—see s.1(2).

GENERAL NOTE

1.341

This mirrors (and repeats much of the wording of) SSAA 1992, s.187. While informal pledges of both benefit and benefit books occur, that section renders any such arrangement unenforceable in the courts or as against government departments. This section ensures that this also applies to tax credits.

Giving of notices by Board

1.342

46. The Board may give any notice which they are required or permitted to give under this Part in any manner and form which the Board consider appropriate in the circumstances.

DEFINITION

"the Board"—see s.67.

(2002 c.21, s.46)

GENERAL NOTE

No provision is made in this section for regulations or for deemed notice. There is no equivalent of TMA 1970, s.114 (want of form not to invalidate assessments) or 115 (delivery and service of documents) provided for in the Act. However, it is suggested that this does not discharge HMRC from the duty of complying with specific provisions as to content in this Act, in the Tax Credits (Claims and Notifications) Regulations 2002 (SI 2002/2014), or elsewhere. HMRC is also required, by reason of the Art.6 of the European Convention on Human Rights and the Human Rights Act 1998 (see Vol.III in this series), to ensure that proper notice is given of any appeal to the appeal tribunals or the appellant as the case may be.

1.343

Consequential amendments

47. Schedule 3 (consequential amendments) has effect.

1.344

GENERAL NOTE

This section gives effect to Sch.3 (not included in this volume). Section 68(1) ensures that those provisions are co-extensive with the provisions they affect. Most of the provisions are concerned to replace WFTC with WTC and to substitute a reference to CTC in place of references to the various previous child benefits and credits. Paragraph 25 amends s.30C of the SSCBA 1992, and para.30 amends s.42 of that Act. Both deal with transfers between benefit and tax credit.

1.345

Interpretation

48.—[¹(1)] In this Part—
"child" has the meaning given by section 8(3),
[¹"couple" has the meaning given by section 3(5A)],
"the current year income" has the meaning given by section 7(4),
"employee" and "employer" have the meaning given by section 25(5),
"the General Commissioners" means the Commissioners for the general purposes of the income tax appointed under section 2 of the Taxes Management Act 1970 (c.9),
"the income threshold" has the meaning given by section 7(1)(a),
"joint claim" has the meaning given by section 3(8),
[¹ . . .],
"overpayment" has the meaning given by section 28(2) and (6),
"the previous year income" has the meaning given by section 7(5),
"qualifying remunerative work", and being engaged in it, have the meaning given by regulations under section 10(2),
"qualifying young person" has the meaning given by section 8(4),
"the relevant income" has the meaning given by section 7(3),
"responsible", in relation to a child or qualifying young person, has the meaning given by regulations under section 8(2) (for the purposes of child tax credit) or by regulations under section 10(4) (for the purposes of working tax credit),
"single claim" has the meaning given by section 3(8),
"the Special Commissioners" means the Commissioners for the special purposes of the Income Tax Acts appointed under section 4 of the Taxes Management Act 1970 (c.9),
"tax year" means a period beginning with 6th April in one year and ending with 5th April in the next, and
[¹ . . .].

1.346

Tax Credits Act 2002

[¹(2) For the purposes of this Part, two people of the same sex are to be regarded as living together as if they were civil partners if, but only if, they would be regarded as living together as husband and wife were they instead two people of the opposite sex.]

AMENDMENT

1. Civil Partnership Act 2004, ss.254 and 261(4) and Sch.24, para.147 and Sch.30 (December 5, 2005).

GENERAL NOTE

1.347   See also s.67 for further definitions.

PART II

CHILD BENEFIT AND GUARDIAN'S ALLOWANCE

49.–57. (*Omitted*)

PART III

SUPPLEMENTARY

Information etc.

Administrative arrangements

1.348   **58.**—(1) This section applies where regulations under—
(a) section 4 or 6 of this Act,
(b) section 5 of the Social Security Administration Act 1992 (c.5), or
(c) section 5 of the Social Security Administration (Northern Ireland) Act 1992 (c.8),
permit or require a claim or notification relating to a tax credit, child benefit or guardian's allowance to be made or given to a relevant authority.
(2) Where this section applies, regulations may make provision—
(a) for information or evidence relating to tax credits, child benefit or guardian's allowance to be provided to the relevant authority (whether by persons by whom such claims and notifications are or have been made or given, by the Board or by other persons),
(b) for the giving of information or advice by a relevant authority to persons by whom such claims or notifications are or have been made or given, and
(c) for the recording, verification and holding, and the forwarding to the Board or a person providing services to the Board, of claims and notifications received by virtue of the regulations referred to in sub-section (1) and information or evidence received by virtue of paragraph (a).

(2002 c.21, s.58)

(3) "Relevant authority" means—
(a) the Secretary of State,
(b) the Northern Ireland Department, or
(c) a person providing services to the Secretary of State or the Northern Ireland Department.

DEFINITIONS

"child benefit"—see SSCBA 1992, s.141.
"claim"—see s.3(8).
"guardian's allowance"—see SSCBA 1992, s.77.
"relevant authority"—see subs.(3).
"tax credit"—see s.1(2).

GENERAL NOTE

Section 5 of the SSAA 1992 and its Northern Ireland equivalent provide the authority for the Social Security (Claims and Payments) Regulations 1987 (SI 1987/1968) under which regulations for all aspects of claiming benefits are detailed. This section enables claims and notifications for tax credits and child benefit being validly given to both HMRC and the social security authorities, and to anyone acting under contract to the social security authorities. It will, for example, allow claims for child benefit and CTC to be made together to one authority. See also the Tax Credits (Administrative Arrangements) Regulations 2002 (SI 2002/3036).

CRCA 2005 contains a wide general power for HMRC to use for all its statutory purposes all the information that comes into its possession for any purpose. This is subject to limits in Sch.2 of that Act. There are no limits in the Schedule relevant to the management and payment of tax credits.

1.349

Use and disclosure of information

59. Schedule 5 (use and disclosure of information) has effect.

1.350

GENERAL NOTE

This section incorporates Sch.5 into the Act. The Schedule adds further provisions to the statutory authority already available so that tax authorities, social security authorities, other government departments, and local authorities can exchange information. The widest power is the power to give information to anyone for the purposes of the Learning and Skills Act 2000 (para.10). This wide power is linked to a new criminal offence if it is misused (para.10(4)). Paragraph 11 includes disclosures about tax credits in the general offence of disclosing information held by a person in connection with tax, tax credit and social security functions unless the information is disclosed with lawful authority or certain other conditions are met. This replaces the inclusion of tax credits within that section under s.12 of the TCA 1999. Paragraph 9 of the Schedule has given effect by the Tax Credits (Provision of Information) (Functions Relating to Health) Regulations 2003 (SI 2003/731) and the Tax Credits (Provision of Information) (Functions Relating to Health) (No.2) Regulations 2003 (SI 2003/1650) and a series of other short specific provisions.

1.351

Other supplementary provisions

Repeals

60. Schedule 6 (repeals) has effect.

1.352

GENERAL NOTE

1.353 This section incorporates the standard repeals Schedule into the Act. It provides the authority for the abolitions flagged up in s.1(3). It confirms that this Act replaces the whole of the TCA 1999.

Commencement

1.354 **61.** Apart from section 54(1) and (2), the preceding provisions of this Act come into force in accordance with orders made by the Treasury.

GENERAL NOTE

1.355 See end of the introductory General Note to the Act as a whole.

Transitional provisions and savings

1.356 **62.**—(1) The Secretary of State may by order make as respects England and Wales and Scotland, and the Northern Ireland Department may by order make as respects Northern Ireland, any transitional provisions or savings which appear appropriate in connection with the commencement of the abolition of the increases referred to in section 1(3)(e).

(2) Subject to any provision made by virtue of subsection (1), the Treasury may by order make any transitional provisions or savings which appear appropriate in connection with the commencement of any provision of this Act.

GENERAL NOTE

1.357 See the note to the previous section.

Tax credits appeals etc.: temporary modifications

1.358 **63.**—(1) Until such day as the Treasury may by order appoint, Part I of this Act has effect subject to the modifications specified in this section; and an order under this subsection may include any transitional provisions or savings which appear appropriate.

(2) Except in the case of an appeal against an employer penalty, an appeal under section 38 is to an appeal tribunal (rather than to the General Commissioners or Special Commissioners).

(3) The function of giving a direction under section 19(10) is a function of an appeal tribunal (rather than of the General Commissioners or Special Commissioners).

(4) Except in the case of an employer information penalty, proceedings under paragraph 3 of Schedule 2 are by way of information made to an appeal tribunal (rather than to the General Commissioners or Special Commissioners).

(5) So far as is appropriate in consequence of subsections (2) to (4)—
  (a) the references to the General Commissioners or Special Commissioners in sections 19(10) and 39(5) and paragraphs 2 and 3(2) of Schedule 2 are to the appeal tribunal, and
  (b) subsections (3) and (4) of section 39 do not apply.

(6) An appeal under paragraph 2(2) or 4(1) of Schedule 2 from a decision of, or against the determination of a penalty by, an appeal tribunal lies to a Social Security Commissioner (rather than to the High Court or Court of Session).

(2002 c.21, s.63)

(7) So far as is appropriate in consequence of subsection (6), the references in paragraphs 2(2) and 4 of Schedule 2 to the High Court and the Court of Session are to the Social Security Commissioner.

(8) Regulations may apply any provision contained in—
 (a) Chapter 2 of Part I of the Social Security Act 1998 (c.14) (social security appeals: Great Britain),
 (b) Chapter 2 of Part II of the Social Security (Northern Ireland) Order 1998 (SI 1998/1506 (N.I. 10)) (social security appeals: Northern Ireland), or
 (c) section 54 of the Taxes Management Act 1970 (c.9) (settling of appeals by agreement),

in relation to appeals which, by virtue of this section, are to an appeal tribunal or lie to a Social Security Commissioner, but subject to such modifications as are prescribed.

(9) Except in the case of appeals against employer penalties, subsections (6) and (7) of section 39 do not apply.

(10) "Appeal tribunal" means an appeal tribunal constituted—
 (a) in Great Britain, under Chapter 1 of Part I of the Social Security Act 1998, or
 (b) in Northern Ireland, under Chapter 1 of Part II of the Social Security (Northern Ireland) Order 1998.

(11) "Employer penalty" means—
 (a) a penalty under section 31 or 32 relating to a requirement imposed by virtue of regulations under section 25, or
 (b) a penalty under section 33.

(12) "Employer information penalty" means a penalty under section 32(2)(a) relating to a requirement imposed by virtue of regulations under section 25.

(13) "Social Security Commissioner" means—
 (a) in Great Britain, the Chief Social Security Commissioner or any other Social Security Commissioner appointed under the Social Security Act 1998 (c.14) or a tribunal of three or more Commissioners constituted under section 16(7) of that Act, and
 (b) in Northern Ireland, the Chief Social Security Commissioner or any other Social Security Commissioner appointed under the Social Security Administration (Northern Ireland) Act 1992 (c.8) or a tribunal of two or more Commissioners constituted under Article 16(7) of the Social Security (Northern Ireland) Order 1998 (SI 1998/1506 (N.I. 10)).

DEFINITIONS

"appeal tribunal"—see subs.(10).
"employer information penalty"—see subs.(12).
"employer penalty"—see subs.(11).
"General Commissioners"—see s.47.
"modifications"—see s.67.
"Social Security Commissioner"—see subs.(13).
"Special Commissioners"—see s.47.

GENERAL NOTE

Subs.1

This section modifies provisions of this Act, and enables regulations to be made, so that proceedings that would otherwise be determined by tax commissioners

1.359

(i.e. the General Commissioners or the Special Commissioners) with a right of appeal against the tax commissioners' determinations are instead determined by appeal tribunals constituted under the Social Security Act 1998 with a right of appeal to a Social Security Commissioner, except in the case of proceedings to which employers are a party. The modifications are described in the heading of the section as being temporary but no date has been set for them to cease to apply. See further the general note to s.38 for this important transitional provision. However, following the decision to put s.25 into abeyance (see note to p.163 above), the reservation of appeals to the General and Special Commissioners in subss.63(2), (4), (9), (11), and (12) is deprived of practical content with effect from April 1, 2006, since when all payments of credit are made direct by HMRC.

Subss. (2)–(5)

1.360   Appeal tribunals are to determine appeals against decisions of Her Majesty's Revenue and Customs, applications under s.19(9) and penalty proceedings under para.3 of Sch.3. Exceptions are made for proceedings concerned with the imposition of penalties on employers.

Subss. (6) and (7)

1.361   Provision is made for the right of appeal to the High Court or Court of Session against decisions of tax commissioners in penalty proceedings to become a right of appeal to a Social Security Commissioner against a decision of an appeal tribunal. Regulations under subs.(8) make provision for appeals to Social Security Commissioners against other decisions of appeal tribunals in tax credit cases.

Subs. (8)

1.362   See the Tax Credits (Appeals) Regulations 2002 under which the provisions relating to appeals in the Social Security Act 1998 and s.54 of the Taxes Management Act 1970 are applied, with modifications, to tax credit appeals in the light of subss.(2)–(7). Note that this subsection permits regulations to be made only in relation of "appeals". The modification of s.12 of the Social Security Act 1998 by reg.4(2) of the 2002 Regulations assumes that an application under s.19(9) is an appeal within the terms of this section and within the term "tax credits appeal" as defined in reg.2 of the Regulations. That may be justifiable by reference to s.19(10). It is less clear that information penalty proceedings under para.3 of Sch.3 come within the term "appeals" but it would be unfortunate if they did not. In any event, s.12 of the 1998 Act appears to be applied to appeals properly so called and to applications under s.19(9) but not to proceedings brought under para.3 of Sch.3 to this Act. Section 13 of the 1998 Act is not applied to penalty proceedings under Sch.2 of this Act at all and s.14 of the 1998 Act is applied in a different way for penalty proceedings than for other proceedings. In particular, leave to appeal to a Social Security Commissioner is not required in penalty proceedings and an appeal lies on a point of law only to the extent that para.4(1)(b) of Sch.4 to this Act so provides. Sections 15, 16, 17, 28 and 39 of the 1998 Act are applied to all tax credit appeals.

Northern Ireland

1.363   **64.**—(1) The Northern Ireland Act 1998 (c.47) has effect subject to the amendments in subsections (2) and (3).

(2) In Schedule 2 (excepted matters), after paragraph 10 insert—

"**10A.** Tax credits under Part 1 of the Tax Credits Act 2002.
10B. Childbenefit and guardian's allowance."

(3) In section 87 (consultation and co-ordination on social security matters), after subsection (6) insert—

"(6A) But this section does not apply to the legislation referred to in subsection (6) to the extent that it relates to child benefit or guardian's allowance."

(4) For the purposes of that Act, a provision of—
(a) an Act of the Northern Ireland Assembly; or
(b) a Bill for such an Act,

which amends or repeals any of the provisions of the Employment Rights (Northern Ireland) Order 1996 (SI 1996/1919 (N.I. 16)) dealt with in Schedule 1 shall not be treated as dealing with tax credits if the Act or Bill deals with employment rights conferred otherwise than by that Schedule in the same way.

DEFINITION

"tax credits"—see s.1(2).

GENERAL NOTE

The provisions on Northern Ireland are necessary because of the transfer of the administration of child benefit and guardian's allowance from the Northern Ireland authorities to the Home Civil Service. The amendments also confirm the effect of s.16 of the Tax Credits Act 1999 in reserving tax credits as excepted matters.

Regulations, orders and schemes

65.—(1) Any power to make regulations under sections 3, 7 to 13, 42 and 43, and any power to make regulations under this Act prescribing a rate of interest, is exercisable by the Treasury.

(2) Any other power to make regulations under this Act is exercisable by the Board.

(3) Subject to subsection (4), any power to make regulations, orders or schemes under this Act is exercisable by statutory instrument.

(4) The power—
(a) of the Department of Health, Social Services and Public Safety to make schemes under section 12(5), and
(b) of the Northern Ireland Department to make orders under section 62(1),

is exercisable by statutory rule for the purposes of the Statutory Rules (Northern Ireland) Order 1979 (S.I. 1979/1573 (N.I. 12)).

(5) Regulations may not be made under section 25 or 26 in relation to appeals in Scotland without the consent of the Scottish Ministers.

(6) Regulations may not be made under section 39(6) or 63(8) without the consent of the Lord Chancellor and the Scottish Ministers.

(7) Any power to make regulations under this Act may be exercised—
(a) in relation to all cases to which it extends, to all those cases with prescribed exceptions or to prescribed cases or classes of case,
(b) so as to make as respects the cases in relation to which it is exercised the full provision to which it extends or any less provision (whether by way of exception or otherwise),
(c) so as to make the same provision for all cases in relation to which it is exercised or different provision for different cases or classes of case or different provision as respects the same case or class of case for different purposes,

(d) so as to make provision unconditionally or subject to any prescribed condition,
(e) so as to provide for a person to exercise a discretion in dealing with any matter.

(8) Any regulations made under a power under this Act to prescribe a rate of interest may—

(a) either themselves specify a rate of interest or make provision for any such rate to be determined by reference to such rate or the average of such rates as may be referred to in the regulations,
(b) provide for rates to be reduced below, or increased above, what they otherwise would be by specified amounts or by reference to specified formulae,
(c) provide for rates arrived at by reference to averages to be rounded up or down,
(d) provide for circumstances in which alteration of a rate of interest is or is not to take place, and
(e) provide that alterations of rates are to have effect for periods beginning on or after a day determined in accordance with the regulations in relation to interest running from before that day as well as from or from after that day.

(9) Any power to make regulations or a scheme under this Act includes power to make any incidental, supplementary, consequential or transitional provision which appears appropriate for the purposes of, or in connection with, the regulations or scheme.

DEFINITIONS

"the Board"—see s.67, but note that the functions of the Board have been transferred to Her Majesty's Revenue and Customs by the Commissioners for Revenue and Customs Act 2005.
"prescribe"—see s.67.

Parliamentary etc. control of instruments

1.366   66.—(1) No regulations to which this subsection applies may be made unless a draft of the instrument containing them (whether or not together with other provisions) has been laid before, and approved by a resolution of, each House of Parliament.

(2) Subsection (1) applies to—
(a) regulations prescribing monetary amounts that are required to be reviewed under section 41,
(b) regulations made by virtue of subsection (2) of section 12 prescribing the amount in excess of which charges are not taken into account for the purposes of that subsection, and
(c) the first regulations made under sections 7(8) and (9), 9, 11, 12 and 13(2).

(3) A statutory instrument containing—
(a) regulations under this Act,
(b) a scheme made by the Secretary of State under section 12(5), or
(c) an Order in Council under section 52(7),

is (unless a draft of the instrument has been laid before, and approved by a resolution of, each House of Parliament) subject to annulment in pursuance of a resolution of either House of Parliament.

(2002 c.21, s.66)

(4) A statutory instrument containing a scheme made by the Scottish Ministers under section 12(5) is subject to annulment in pursuance of a resolution of the Scottish Parliament.

(5) A statutory rule containing a scheme made by the Department of Health, Social Services and Public Safety under section 12(5) is subject to negative resolution within the meaning of section 41(6) of the Interpretation Act (Northern Ireland) 1954 (c. 33 (N.I.)).

Interpretation

67. In this Act—
"the Board" means the Commissioners of Inland Revenue,
"modifications" includes alterations, additions and omissions, and "modifies" is to be construed accordingly,
"the Northern Ireland Department" means the Department for Social Development in Northern Ireland,
"prescribed" means prescribed by regulations, and
"tax credit" and "tax credits" have the meanings given by section 1(2).

GENERAL NOTE

For references to "the Board" see now s.2 above and CRCA 2005, s.1.

68.–70. *Omitted.*

Sch.1. *Omitted.*

SCHEDULE 2

PENALTIES: SUPPLEMENTARY

Determination of penalties by Board

1.—(1) The Board may make a determination—
(a) imposing a penalty under section 31, 32(2)(b) or (3) or 33; and
(b) setting it at such amount as, in their opinion, is appropriate.

(2) The Board must give notice of a determination of a penalty under this paragraph to the person on whom the penalty is imposed.

(3) The notice must state the date on which it is given and give details of the right to appeal against the determination under section 38.

(4) After the notice of a determination under this paragraph has been given the determination must not be altered except on appeal.

(5) A penalty determined under this paragraph becomes payable at the end of the period of 30 days beginning with the date on which the notice of determination is given.

2.—(1) On an appeal to them under section 38 against the determination of a penalty under para.1, the [¹appeal tribunal] may—
(a) if it appears that no penalty has been incurred, set the determination aside,
(b) if the amount determined appears to be appropriate, confirm the determination,
(c) if the amount determined appears to be excessive, reduce it to such other amount (including nil) as they consider appropriate, or
(d) if the amount determined appears to be insufficient, increase it to such amount not exceeding the permitted maximum as they consider appropriate.

(2) An appeal from a decision of the [¹appeal tribunal] under sub-paragraph (1) lies, at the instance of the person on whom the penalty was imposed, to [¹a Social Security Commissioner] and on such an appeal the [¹Commissioner] has a similar jurisdiction to that conferred on the [¹appeal tribunal] by sub-paragraph (1).

Penalty proceedings before Commissioners

3.—(1) The Board may commence proceedings for a penalty under section 32(2)(a).

(2) Proceedings under this paragraph are by way of information in writing, made to the [¹appeal tribunal], and upon summons issued by them to the defendant (or defender) to appear before them at a time and place stated in the summons; and they must hear and decide each case in a summary way.

4.—(1) An appeal against the determination of a penalty in proceedings under paragraph 3 lies [¹a Social Security Commissioner]—
- (a) by any party on a question of law, and
- (b) by the defendant (or, in Scotland, the defender) against the amount of the penalty.

(2) On any such appeal the [¹Commissioner] may—
- (a) if it appears that no penalty has been incurred, set the determination aside,
- (b) if the amount determined appears to be appropriate, confirm the determination,
- (c) if the amount determined appears to be excessive, reduce it to such other amount (including nil) as the [¹Commissioner] considers appropriate, or
- (d) if the amount determined appears to be insufficient, increase it to such amount not exceeding the permitted maximum as the [¹Commissioner] considers appropriate.

Mitigation of penalties

1.371   5. The Board may in their discretion mitigate any penalty under this Part or stay or compound any proceedings for any such penalty and may also, after judgment, further mitigate or entirely remit any such penalty.

Time limits for penalties

1.372   6.—(1) In the case of a penalty under s.31 relating to a tax credit for a person or persons for the whole or part of a tax year (other than a penalty to which sub-paragraph (3) applies), the Board may determine the penalty at any time before the latest of—
- (a) the end of the period of one year beginning with the expiry of the period for initiating an enquiry under section 19 into the entitlement of the person, or the joint entitlement of the persons, for the tax year,
- (b) if such an enquiry is made, the end of the period of one year beginning with the day on which the enquiry is completed, and
- (c) if a decision relating to the entitlement of the person, or the joint entitlement of the persons, for the tax year is made under section 20(1) or (4), the end of the period of one year beginning with the day on which the decision is made.

(2) In the case of a penalty under section 32 relating to a tax credit for a person or persons for the whole or part of a tax year (other than a penalty to which sub-paragraph (3) applies), the Board may determine the penalty, or commence proceedings for it, at any time before—
- (a) if an enquiry into the entitlement of the person, or the joint entitlement of the persons, for the tax year is made under section 19, the end of the period of one year beginning with the day on which the enquiry is completed, and
- (b) otherwise, the end of the period of one year beginning with the expiry of the period for initiating such an enquiry.

(3) In the case of—
- (a) a penalty under section 31 or 32 relating to a requirement imposed by virtue of regulations under section 25; or
- (b) a penalty under section 33,

the Board may determine the penalty, or commence proceedings for it, at any time before the end of the period of six years after the date on which the penalty was incurred or began to be incurred.

Recovery of penalties

1.373   7.—(1) A penalty payable under this Part is to be treated for the purposes of Part VI of the Taxes Management Act 1970 (c.9) (collection and recovery) as if it were tax charged in an assessment and due and payable.

(2) Regulations under section 203(2)(a) of the Income and Corporation Taxes Act 1988 (c.1) (PAYE) apply to a penalty payable under this Part as if it were an underpayment of tax for a previous year of assessment.

MODIFICATION

1. This Schedule is set out above as modified by ss.63(5) and (7).

DEFINITIONS

"appeal tribunal"—s.63(10).
"the Board"—s.57 but note that the functions of the Board have been transferred to HMRC by CRCA 2005.
"Social Security Commissioner"—s.63(13).
"tax credit"—by virtue of s.67, see s.1(2).
"tax year"—s.47.

GENERAL NOTE

This Schedule is set out as modified by s.63, which has the effect that, except in cases involving employer penalties or employer information penalties (neither of which can arise since payment by employers was abolished from April 6, 2006), the jurisdiction of the General Commissioners and Special Commissioners is exercised by appeal tribunals and the jurisdiction of the High Court and the Court of Session as the Court of Exchequer in Scotland is exercised by Social Security Commissioners. See the Social Security Act 1998, the Tax Credits (Notice of Appeal) Regulations 2002, the Tax Credits (Appeals) (No.2) Regulations 2002 and the Social Security Commissioners (Procedure) (Tax credits Appeals) Regulations 2002 for procedural provisions. For more general information, see the note to s.39.

Para.2

Initial penalty determinations are by HMRC under para.1 except where the penalty is an initial penalty for failing to provide information to be imposed under s.32(2)(a). Section 38 provides a right of appeal against determinations under para.1 and s.39 provides for its exercise. Section 63(2) provides that an appeal is to an appeal tribunal constituted under the Social Security Act 1998, except in the case of an employer penalty. Paragraph 2 makes provision for the powers of the tribunal and, as modified by ss.63(6) and (7) for an appeal to a Commissioner who "has a similar jurisdiction to that conferred [on the appeal tribunal]". In other words, the appeal is not confined to points of law. Section 14 of the Social Security Act 1998 is applied by reg.6 of the Tax Credits (Appeals) Regulations 2002 to appeals under this paragraph in such a way that leave to appeal is also not required.

Paras 3 and 4

Paragraph 3 provides for HMRC to bring proceedings before a tribunal for an initial information penalty under s.32(2)(a). See para.6(2) for the time limit for bringing such proceedings. Paragraph 4 provides a right of appeal to a Commissioner. It is similar to that provided in para.2 but see the note to s.63(8).

Para.5

Section 54 of the Taxes Management Act 1970 would enable an appeal to a tribunal under para.2 to be compromised but this provision also allows proceedings under para.3 to be abandoned and for an appeal to a Commissioner to be compromised. Note that HMRC may reduce a penalty imposed by a tribunal but may not increase it. There is no provision for an appeal by HMRC against the amount of any reduction in a penalty.

Sch.3–Sch.6. *Omitted.*

Employment Act 2002

Employment Act 2002

(2002 c.22)

Arrangement of Sections

Part I

Statutory Leave and Pay

Chapter 1

Paternity and Adoption

Rights to leave and pay

1.378
1. Paternity leave [*omitted*]
2. Statutory paternity pay [*omitted*]★
3. Adoption leave [*omitted*]
4. Statutory adoption pay [*omitted*]★

Administration and enforcement: pay

5. [*repealed*]
6. Financial arrangements [*omitted*]
7. Funding of employers' liabilities
8. Regulations about payment
9. Decisions and appeals [*omitted*]
10. Powers to require information
11. Penalties: failures to comply
12. Penalties: fraud, etc.
13. Supply of information held by the Board
14. Supply of information held by the Secretary of State
15. Use of information by the Board
16. Interpretation

Chapter 2

Maternity

17. Rights during and after maternity leave [*omitted*]
18. Maternity pay period [*omitted*]★
19. Rate of statutory maternity pay [*omitted*]★
20. Entitlement to statutory maternity pay [*omitted*]★
21. Funding of employers' liabilities: statutory maternity pay [*omitted*]★

(2002 c.22)

Part II

Tribunal Reform

22–28. [*Omitted*]

Part III

Dispute Resolution, etc.

29–40. [*Omitted*]

Part IV

Miscellaneous and General

41–55. [*Omitted*]

Schedule 1—Penalties: procedure and appeals
Schedules 2–8 [*Omitted*]

*These sections make amendments to SSCBA 1992 which are incorporated in the text of that legislation elsewhere in this volume.

General Note

On the background to the Employment Act 2002, see the General Note to SSCBA 2002, Pt 12ZA. **1.379**

Part I

Statutory Leave and Pay

Chapter 1

Paternity and Adoption

Administration and enforcement: pay

Financial arrangements

6. [*Omitted.*]

General Note

This section amends SSAA 1992 and SSCBA 1992 to ensure that SPP and SAP are treated in the same was as SPP and SMP in terms of their administration. **1.380**

Funding of employers' liabilities

7.—(1) The Secretary of State shall by regulations make provision for the payment by employers of statutory paternity pay and statutory adoption pay to be funded by the Board to such extent as the regulations may specify.

(2) Regulations under subsection (1) shall—
(a) make provision for a person who has made a payment of statutory paternity pay or statutory adoption pay to be entitled, except in such circumstances as the regulations may provide, to recover an amount equal to the sum of—
   (i) the aggregate of such of those payments as qualify for small employers' relief; and
   (ii) an amount equal to 92 per cent of the aggregate of such of those payments as do not so qualify; and
(b) include provision for a person who has made a payment of statutory paternity pay or statutory adoption pay qualifying for small employers' relief to be entitled, except in such circumstances as the regulations may provide, to recover an additional amount equal to the amount to which the person would have been entitled under section 167(2)(b) of the Social Security Contributions and Benefits Act 1992 (corresponding provision for statutory maternity pay) had the payment been a payment of statutory maternity pay.

(3) For the purposes of subsection (2), a payment of statutory paternity pay or statutory adoption pay qualifies for small employers' relief if it would have so qualified were it a payment of statutory maternity pay, treating the period for which the payment is made, in the case of statutory paternity pay, or the payee's adoption pay period, in the case of statutory adoption pay, as the maternity pay period.

(4) Regulations under subsection (1) may, in particular—
(a) make provision for funding in advance as well as in arrear;
(b) make provision for funding, or the recovery of amounts due under provision made by virtue of subsection (2)(b), by means of deductions from such amounts for which employers are accountable to the Board as the regulations may provide, or otherwise;
(c) make provision for the recovery by the Board of any sums overpaid to employers under the regulations.

(5) Where in accordance with any provision of regulations under subsection (1) an amount has been deducted from an employer's contributions payments, the amount so deducted shall (except in such cases as the Secretary of State may by regulations provide) be treated for the purposes of any provision made by or under any enactment in relation to primary or secondary Class 1 contributions—
(a) as having been paid (on such date as may be determined in accordance with the regulations), and
(b) as having been received by the Board, towards discharging the employer's liability in respect of such contributions.

(6) Regulations under this section must be made with the concurrence of the Board.

(7) In this section, "contributions payments", in relation to an employer, means any payments which the employer is required, by or under any enactment, to make in discharge of any liability in respect of primary or secondary Class 1 contributions.

(2002 c.22, s.7)

Definitions

"the Board"—see s.16.
"contributions payments"—see subs.(7).
"employer"—see *ibid.*

General Note

See further the SPP and SAP (Administration) Regs 2002, especially regs 3–8.   1.382

Regulations about payment

8.—(1) The Secretary of State may make regulations with respect to the payment by employers of statutory paternity pay and statutory adoption pay.   1.383
(2) Regulations under subsection (1) may, in particular, include provision—
 (a) about the records to be kept by employers in relation to payments of statutory paternity pay and statutory adoption pay, including the length of time for which they are to be retained;
 (b) for the production of wages sheets and other documents and records to officers of the Board for the purpose of enabling them to satisfy themselves that statutory paternity pay and statutory adoption pay have been paid and are being paid, in accordance with the regulations, to employees who are entitled to them;
 (c) for requiring employers to provide information to employees (in their itemised pay statements or otherwise);
 (d) for requiring employers to make returns to the Board containing such particulars with respect to payments of statutory paternity pay and statutory adoption pay as the regulations may provide.
(3) Regulations under subsection (1) must be made with the concurrence of the Board.

Definitions

"the Board"—see s.16.
"employer"—see *ibid.*

General Note

See further the SPP and SAP (Administration) Regs 2002, regs 9 and 10.   1.384

Decisions and appeals

9. [*Omitted.*]

General Note

This section amends ss.8, 11 and 14 of the Social Security Contributions (Transfer of Functions, etc.) Act 1999; the relevant amendments are incorporated elsewhere in this volume.   1.385

Powers to require information

10.—(1) The Secretary of State may by regulations make provision enabling an officer of the Board authorised by the Board for the purposes of this section to require persons of a description specified in the regulations to provide, or produce for inspection, within such period as the   1.386

regulations may require, such information or documents as the officer may reasonably require for the purpose of ascertaining whether statutory paternity pay or statutory adoption pay is or was payable to or in respect of any person.

(2) The descriptions of person which may be specified by regulations under subsection (1) include, in particular—
  (a) any person claiming to be entitled to statutory paternity pay or statutory adoption pay,
  (b) any person who is, or has been, the spouse or partner of such a person as is mentioned in paragraph (a),
  (c) any person who is, or has been, an employer of such a person as is mentioned in paragraph (a),
  (d) any person carrying on an agency or other business for the introduction or supply to persons requiring them of persons available to do work or to perform services, and
  (e) any person who is a servant or agent of any such person as is specified in paragraphs (a) to (d).

(3) Regulations under subsection (1) must be made with the concurrence of the Board.

DEFINITIONS

"the Board"—see s.16.
"employer"—see *ibid*.

GENERAL NOTE

1.387 See further the SPP and SAP (Administration) Regs 2002, especially regs 11–14.

Penalties: failures to comply

1.388 **11.**—(1) Where a person—
  (a) fails to produce any document or record, provide any information or make any return, in accordance with regulations under section 8, or
  (b) fails to provide any information or document in accordance with regulations under section 10,
he shall be liable to the penalties mentioned in subsection (2) below (subject to subsection (4)).

(2) The penalties are—
  (a) a penalty not exceeding £300, and
  (b) if the failure continues after a penalty is imposed under paragraph (a), a further penalty or penalties not exceeding £60 for each day on which the failure continues after the day on which the penalty under that paragraph was imposed (but excluding any day for which a penalty under this paragraph has already been imposed).

(3) Where a person fails to keep records in accordance with regulations under section 8, he shall be liable to a penalty not exceeding £3,000.

(4) Subject to subsection (5), no penalty shall be imposed under subsection (2) or (3) at any time after the failure concerned has been remedied.

(5) Subsection (4) does not apply to the imposition of a penalty under subsection (2)(a) in respect of a failure within subsection (1)(a).

(6) Where, in the case of any employee, an employer refuses or repeatedly fails to make payments of statutory paternity pay or statutory adoption pay

in accordance with any regulations under section 8, the employer shall be liable to a penalty not exceeding £3,000.

(7) Section 118(2) of the Taxes Management Act 1970 (c.9) (extra time for compliance, etc.) shall apply for the purposes of subsections (1), (3) and (6) as it applies for the purposes of that Act.

(8) Schedule 1 to this Act (penalties: procedure and appeals) has effect in relation to penalties under this section.

DEFINITIONS

"the Board"—see s.16.
"employer"—see *ibid.*

GENERAL NOTE

This provision, imposing penalties on employers who fail to comply with the requirements of the SPP and SAP schemes, is modelled on the equivalent provision for tax credits: TCA 2002, s.32.

1.389

Penalties: fraud etc.

12.—(1) Where a person fraudulently or negligently—
(a) makes any incorrect statement or declaration in connection with establishing entitlement to statutory paternity pay, or
(b) provides any incorrect information or document of a kind mentioned in regulations under section 10(1) so far as relating to statutory paternity pay,

he shall be liable to a penalty not exceeding £300.

(2) Where a person fraudulently or negligently—
(a) makes any incorrect statement or declaration in connection with establishing entitlement to statutory adoption pay, or
(b) provides any incorrect information or document of a kind mentioned in regulations under section 10(1) so far as relating to statutory adoption pay,

he shall be liable to a penalty not exceeding £3,000.

(3) Where an employer fraudulently or negligently makes incorrect payments of statutory paternity pay, he shall be liable to a penalty not exceeding £300.

(4) Where an employer fraudulently or negligently makes incorrect payments of statutory adoption pay, he shall be liable to a penalty not exceeding £3,000.

(5) Where an employer fraudulently or negligently—
(a) produces any incorrect document or record, provides any incorrect information or makes any incorrect return, of a kind mentioned in regulations under section 8; or
(b) receives incorrect payments in pursuance of regulations under section 7;

he shall be liable to a penalty not exceeding £3,000 or, if the offence relates only to statutory paternity pay, £300.

(6) Schedule 1 (penalties: procedure and appeals) has effect in relation to penalties under this section.

1.390

DEFINITIONS

"the Board"—see s.16.
"employer"—see *ibid.*

General Note

1.391   This provision, imposing penalties on employers who act fraudulently in connection with the SPP and SAP schemes, is modelled on the equivalent provision for tax credits: TCA 2002, s.31.

Supply of information held by the Board

1.392   **13.**—(1) This section applies to information which is held for the purposes of functions relating to statutory paternity pay or statutory adoption pay—
   (a) by the Board, or
   (b) by a person providing services to the Board, in connection with the provision of those services.
(2) Information to which this section applies may be supplied—
   (a) to the Secretary of State or the Department; or
   (b) to a person providing services to the Secretary of State or the Department;
for use for the purposes of functions relating to social security, child support or war pensions.

Definitions

"the Board"—see s.16.
"the Department"—see *ibid.*

Supply of information held by the Secretary of State

1.393   **14.**—(1) This section applies to information which is held for the purposes of functions relating to statutory paternity pay or statutory adoption pay—
   (a) by the Secretary of State or the Department, or
   (b) by a person providing services to the Secretary of State or the Department, in connection with the provision of those services.
(2) Information to which this section applies may be supplied—
   (a) to the Board, or
   (b) to a person providing services to the Board,
for use for the purposes of functions relating to statutory paternity pay or statutory adoption pay.

Definitions

"the Board"—see s.16.
"the Department"—see *ibid.*

Use of information by the Board

1.394   **15.**—(1) Information which is held—
   (a) by the Board, or
   (b) by a person providing services to the Board, in connection with the provision of those services,
for the purposes of any functions specified in any paragraph of subsection (2) below may be used for the purposes of, or for any purposes connected with, the exercise of any functions specified in any other paragraph of that subsection, and may be supplied to any person providing services to the Board for those purposes.
(2) The functions referred to in subsection (1) above are—
   (a) the functions of the Board in relation to statutory paternity pay;

(b) their functions in relation to statutory adoption pay, and
(c) their functions in relation to tax, contributions, statutory sick pay, statutory maternity pay or tax credits, or functions under Part III of the Pension Schemes Act 1993 (c.48) (certification of pension scheme, etc.) or Part III of the Pension Schemes (Northern Ireland) Act 1993 (c.49) (corresponding provisions for Northern Ireland).

(3) In subsection (2)(c) above, "contributions" means contributions under Part I of the Social Security Contributions and Benefits Act 1992 (c.4) or Part I of the Social Security Contributions and Benefits (Northern Ireland) Act 1992 (c.7).

DEFINITION

"the Board"—see s.16.

Interpretation

16. In sections 5 to 15—
"the Board" means the Commissioners of Inland Revenue;
"the Department" means the Department for Social Development or the Department for Employment and Learning;
"employer" and "employee" have the same meanings as in Parts 12ZA and 12ZB of the Social Security Contributions and Benefits Act 1992.

CHAPTER 2

MATERNITY

17.–21. [*Omitted.*]

GENERAL NOTE

Section 17 amends the provisions governing the right to maternity leave under the Employment Rights Act 1996. Sections 18–20 amend ss.164 and 165 of the SSCBA 1992, and substitutes a new s.166 of that Act, while s.21 substitutes a new s.167 of the same Act. These amendments are incorporated elsewhere in this volume.

SCHEDULE 1

PENALTIES: PROCEDURE AND APPEALS

Determination of penalties by officer of Board

1.—(1) Subject to sub-paragraph (2) and except where proceedings have been instituted under paragraph 5, an officer of the Board authorised by the Board for the purposes of this paragraph may make a determination—
(a) imposing a penalty under section 11 or 12, and
(b) setting it at such amount as, in his opinion, is correct or appropriate.

(2) Sub-paragraph (1) does not apply to the imposition of such a penalty as is mentioned in section 11(2)(a).

(3) Notice of a determination of a penalty under this paragraph shall be served on the person liable to the penalty and shall state the date on which it is issued and the time within which an appeal against the determination may be made.

(4) After the notice of a determination under this paragraph has been served the determination shall not be altered except in accordance with this paragraph or on appeal.

Employment Act 2002

(5) If it is discovered by an officer of the Board authorised by the Board for the purposes of this paragraph that the amount of a penalty determined under this paragraph is or has become insufficient, the officer may make a determination in a further amount so that the penalty is set at the amount which, in his opinion, is correct or appropriate.

Provisions supplementary to paragraph 1

1.398 2.—(1) A penalty determined under paragraph 1 above shall be due and payable at the end of the period of thirty days beginning with the date of the issue of the notice of determination.

(2) Part 6 of the Taxes Management Act 1970 (c.9) shall apply in relation to a penalty determined under para.1 as if it were tax charged in an assessment and due and payable.

Appeals against penalty determinations

1.399 3.—(1) An appeal may be brought against the determination of a penalty under paragraph 1.

(2) The provisions of the Taxes Management Act 1970 relating to appeals, except section 50(6) to (8), shall have effect in relation to an appeal against such a determination as they have effect in relation to an appeal against an assessment to tax.

(3) On an appeal by virtue of sub-paragraph (2) against the determination of a penalty under paragraph 1, the General or Special Commissioners may—
   (a) if it appears to them that no penalty has been incurred, set the determination aside,
   (b) if the amount determined appears to them to be appropriate, confirm the determination,
   (c) if the amount determined appears to them to be excessive, reduce it to such other amount (including nil) as they consider appropriate,
   (d) if the amount determined appears to them to be insufficient, increase it to such amount not exceeding the permitted maximum as they consider appropriate.

(4) An appeal from a decision of the Commissioners against the amount of a penalty which has been determined under paragraph 1 or this paragraph shall lie, at the instance of the person liable to the penalty—
   (a) to the High Court, or
   (b) in Scotland, to the Court of Session as the Court of Exchequer in Scotland, and on that appeal the court shall have the like jurisdiction as is conferred on the Commissioners by virtue of this paragraph.

Penalty proceedings before Commissioners

1.400 4.—(1) An officer of the Board authorised by the Board for the purposes of this paragraph may commence proceedings for any penalty to which sub-paragraph (1) of paragraph 1 does not apply by virtue of sub-paragraph (2) of that paragraph.

(2) Proceedings under this paragraph shall be by way of information in writing, made to the General or Special Commissioners, and upon summons issued by them to the defendant (or, in Scotland, the defender) to appear before them at a time and place stated in the summons; and they shall hear and decide each case in a summary way.

(3) Part 6 of the Taxes Management Act 1970 (c.9) shall apply in relation to a penalty determined in proceedings under this paragraph as if it were tax charged in an assessment and due and payable.

(4) An appeal against the determination of a penalty in proceedings under this paragraph shall lie to the High Court or, in Scotland, to the Court of Session as the Court of Exchequer in Scotland—
   (a) by any party on a question of law; and
   (b) by the defendant (or, in Scotland, the defender) against the amount of the penalty.

(5) On any such appeal the court may—
   (a) if it appears that no penalty has been incurred, set the determination aside;
   (b) if the amount determined appears to be appropriate, confirm the determination;
   (c) if the amount determined appears to be excessive, reduce it to such other amount (including nil) as the court considers appropriate;
   (d) if the amount determined appears to be insufficient, increase it to such amount not exceeding the permitted maximum as the court considers appropriate.

Penalty proceedings before court

1.401 5.—(1) Where in the opinion of the Board the liability of any person for a penalty under section 11 or 12 arises by reason of the fraud of that or any other person, proceedings for the penalty may be instituted before the High Court or, in Scotland, the Court of Session as the Court of Exchequer in Scotland.

(2002 c.22, Sch.1)

(2) Subject to sub-paragraph (3), proceedings under this paragraph shall be instituted—
  (a) in England and Wales, in the name of the Attorney General; and
  (b) in Scotland, in the name of the Advocate General for Scotland.

(3) Sub-paragraph (2) shall not prevent proceedings under this paragraph being instituted in England and Wales under the Crown Proceedings Act 1947 (c.44) by and in the name of the Board as an authorised department for the purposes of that Act.

(4) Any proceedings under this paragraph instituted in England and Wales shall be deemed to be civil proceedings by the Crown within the meaning of Part II of the Crown Proceedings Act 1947.

(5) If in proceedings under this paragraph the court does not find that fraud is proved but considers that the person concerned is nevertheless liable to a penalty, the court may determine a penalty notwithstanding that, but for the opinion of the Board as to fraud, the penalty would not have been a matter for the court.

Mitigation of penalties

6. The Board may in their discretion mitigate any penalty under section 11 or 12, or stay or compound any proceedings for a penalty, and may also, after judgment, further mitigate or entirely remit the penalty.

Time-limits for penalties

7. A penalty under section 11 or 12 may be determined by an officer of the Board, or proceedings for the penalty may be commenced before the Commissioners or the court, at any time within six years after the date on which the penalty was incurred or began to be incurred.

Interest on penalties

8.—(1) After paragraph (p) of section 178(2) of the Finance Act 1989 (c.26) (setting rates of interest) there shall be inserted—

"(q) paragraph 8 of Schedule 1 to the Employment Act 2002."

(2) A penalty under section 11 or 12 shall carry interest at the rate applicable under section 178 of the Finance Act 1989 from the date on which it becomes due and payable until payment.

Interpretation

9. In this Schedule—
"the Board" means the Commissioners of Inland Revenue;
"General Commissioners" and "Special Commissioners" have the same meanings as in the Taxes Management Act 1970 (c.9).

1.402

1.403

1.404

1.405

Income Tax (Earnings and Pensions) Act 2003

(2003 c.1)

ARRANGEMENT OF SELECTED SECTIONS

PART 1

OVERVIEW

1. Overview of contents of this Act
2. Abbreviations and general index in Schedule 1

1.406

Income Tax (Earnings and Pensions) Act 2003

PART 2

EMPLOYMENT INCOME: CHARGE TO TAX

CHAPTER 1

INTRODUCTION

3. Structure of employment income Parts
4. "Employment" for the purposes of the employment income Parts
5. Application to offices and officeholders

CHAPTER 2

TAX ON EMPLOYMENT INCOME

6. Nature of charge to tax on employment income
7. Meaning of "employment income", "general earnings" and "specific employment income"
8. Meaning of "exempt income"

CHAPTER 3

OPERATION OF TAX CHARGE

9. Amount of employment income charged to tax
10. Meaning of "taxable earnings" and "taxable specific income"
11. Calculation of "net taxable earnings"
12. Calculation of "net taxable specific income"
13. Person liable for tax

CHAPTER 7

APPLICATION OF PROVISIONS TO AGENCY WORKERS

Agency workers

44. Treatment of workers supplied by agencies

(2003 c.1)

Part 3

Employment Income: Earnings and Benefits, etc. Treated as Earnings

Chapter 1

Earnings

62. Earnings

Chapter 2

Taxable Benefits: The Benefits Code

The benefits code

63. The benefits code
64. Relationship between earnings and benefits code
65. Dispensations relating to benefits within provisions not applicable to lower-paid employment

General definitions for benefits code

66. Meaning of "employment" and related expressions

Chapter 3

Taxable Benefits: Expenses Payments

70. Sums in respect of expenses
71. Meaning of paid or put at disposal by reason of the employment
72. Sums in respect of expenses treated as earnings

Chapter 4

Taxable Benefits: Vouchers and Credit-tokens

Cash vouchers: introduction

73. Cash vouchers to which this chapter applies
74. Provision for, or receipt by, member of employee's family

Income Tax (Earnings and Pensions) Act 2003

Meaning of "cash voucher"

75. Meaning of "cash voucher"
76. Sickness benefits-related voucher

Benefit of cash voucher treated as earnings

81. Benefit of cash voucher treated as earnings

Non-cash vouchers: introduction

82. Non-cash vouchers to which this chapter applies

Meaning of "non-cash voucher"

84. Meaning of "non-cash voucher"

Benefit of non-cash voucher treated as earnings

87. Benefit of non-cash voucher treated as earnings

Credit-tokens: introduction

90. Credit-tokens to which this chapter applies

Meaning of "credit-token"

92. Meaning of "credit-token"

Benefit of credit-token treated as earnings

94. Benefit of credit-token treated as earnings

General supplementary provisions

95. Disregard for money, goods or services obtained

Chapter 10

Taxable Benefits: Residual Liability to Charge

Introduction

201. Employment-related benefits
202. Excluded benefits

(2003 c.1)

Cash equivalent of benefit treated as earnings

203. Cash equivalent of benefit treated as earnings

Determination of the cost of the benefit

204. Cost of the benefit: basic rule
210. Exemption of minor benefits

CHAPTER 11

TAXABLE BENEFITS: EXCLUSION OF LOWER-PAID EMPLOYMENTS FROM PARTS OF BENEFIT CODE

Introduction

216. Provisions not applicable to lower-paid employments

What is lower-paid employment?

217. Meaning of "lower-paid employment"
218. Calculation of earnings rate for a tax year
219. Extra amounts to be added in connection with a car

PART 4

EMPLOYMENT INCOME: EXEMPTIONS

CHAPTER 11

MISCELLANEOUS EXEMPTIONS

318. Childcare: exemption for employer-provided care
318A. Childcare: exemption for other care
318B. Childcare: meaning of "care", "child" and "parental responsibility"
318C. Childcare: meaning of "qualifying child care"

Income Tax (Earnings and Pensions) Act 2003

PART 5

EMPLOYMENT INCOME: DEDUCTIONS ALLOWED FROM EARNINGS

CHAPTER 1

DEDUCTIONS ALLOWED FROM EARNINGS: GENERAL RULES

Introduction

327. Deductions from earnings: general

General rules

328. The income from which deductions may be made
329. Deductions from earnings not to exceed earnings
330. Prevention of double deductions
331. Order for making deductions
332. Meaning of "the deductibility provisions"

CHAPTER 2

DEDUCTIONS FOR EMPLOYEE'S EXPENSES

Introduction

333. Scope of this chapter: expenses paid by the employee
334. Effect of reimbursement, etc.

General rule for deduction of employee's expenses

336. Deductions for expenses: the general rule

Travel expenses

337. Travel in performance of duties
338. Travel for necessary attendance
339. Meaning of "workplace" and "permanent workplace"

PART 9

PENSION INCOME

CHAPTER 1

INTRODUCTION

565. Structure of Part 9

(2003 c.1)

Chapter 2

Tax on Pension Income

566. Nature of charge to tax on pension income and relevant definitions
567. Amount charged to tax
568. Person liable for tax

Chapter 3

United Kingdom Social Security Pensions

569. United Kingdom pensions
570. "Pension": interpretation
571. Taxable pension income
572. Person liable for tax

Chapter 5

United Kingdom Social Security Pensions

577. United Kingdom social security pensions
578. Taxable pension income
579. Person liable for tax

Chapter 16

Exemption for Certain Lump Sums

637. Exemption for lump sums provided under certain pension schemes etc.

Part 10

Social Security Income

Chapter 1

Introduction

655. Structure of Part 10

Chapter 2

Tax on Social Security Income

656. Nature of charge to tax on social security income

201

Income Tax (Earnings and Pensions) Act 2003

657. Meaning of "social security income", "taxable benefits", etc.
658. Amount charged to tax
659. Person liable for tax

Chapter 3

Taxable UK Social Security Benefits

660. Taxable benefits: UK benefits—Table A
661. Taxable social security income
662. Person liable for tax

Chapter 4

Taxable UK Social Security Benefits: Exemptions

Incapacity benefit

663. Long-term incapacity benefit: previous entitlement to invalidity benefit
664. Short-term incapacity benefit not payable at the higher rate

Income support

665. Exempt unless payable to member of couple involved in trade dispute
666. Child maintenance bonus
667. Amounts in excess of taxable maximum
668. Taxable maximum
669. Interpretation

Jobseeker's allowance

670. Child maintenance bonus
671. Amounts in excess of taxable maximum
672. Taxable maximum: general
673. Taxable maximum: income-based jobseeker's allowance
674. Taxable maximum: contribution-based jobseeker's allowance
675. Interpretation

Increases in respect of children

676. Increases in respect of children

Chapter 5

UK Social Security Benefits Wholly Exempt from Income Tax

677. UK social security benefits wholly exempt from tax: Table B

(2003 c.1)

Chapter 6

Taxable Foreign Benefits

678. Taxable benefits: foreign benefits
679. Taxable social security income
680. Person liable for tax

Part 13

Supplementary Provisions

Interpretation

720. [*repealed*]
721. Other definitions

Introduction and General Note

This Act (destined to be known as ITEPA or ITEPA 2003) is the second of the major income tax Acts produced by the Tax Law Rewrite Project, and the first that repeals and replaces a major part of the Income and Corporation Taxes Act 1988 (ICTA). (The first was the Capital Allowances Act 2001.) It took effect from and including the start of the 2003–04 income tax year, April 6, 2003, the same day that the TCA 2002 came fully into effect. It is of considerable importance to tax credits because it entirely rewrites the income tax rules dealing with earnings from employments and offices, pension income, and social security income. The time-hallowed "Schedule E" and its charge to tax on "offices and employments on emoluments therefrom" has at last been relegated to history and a codified set of provisions taxing employment income, pension income and social security income put in its place. The approach of TCA 2002 is to rely on income tax rules for the calculation of income for tax credits purposes. The provisions of ITEPA are therefore the rules that will apply to the great majority of claimants for tax credits.

1.407

ITEPA is of considerable length and detail, running to 725 sections and 8 Schedules on enactment. (And that is despite a decision in principle to minimise the use of schedules in Rewrite Bills.) Besides consolidating the existing statute law from the ICTA 1988 and its many amendments, and incorporating provisions previously in schedules and regulations into the main part of the Act, ITEPA also includes in codified form relevant decisions of the courts. It also turns into legislative form some of the extra statutory concessions and Revenue practices by which the previous legislation was operated. It also removes redundant legislation, corrects inconsistencies, and makes other minor changes to the previous law. Some policy changes were also made in other legislation before ITEPA was enacted, and these were then incorporated into ITEPA. It is therefore more than simply a consolidation of the law, and is better viewed as a code. It has been drafted in the form of a code, and therefore includes signposting provisions and a far stronger internal structure than the previous legislation.

ITEPA also uses, where possible, plain English. Its language is therefore updated from the "old" language of "Sch.E" and "emoluments".

The Tax Credits (Definition and Calculation of Income) Regulations 2002, as amended to take into account ITEPA, refer to a considerable number of provisions of ITEPA. This selection of sections from ITEPA includes the more important of those sections, together with the sections that set out the internal signposting of ITEPA and its definitions. It is not a complete reproduction of all ITEPA sections, as some of the anti-avoidance provisions that are applied to tax credits are highly technical and, in practice, sometimes quite controversial in application, while others will, it is anticipated, rarely be directly relevant to tax credits claims. In particular, the following parts are entirely omitted:

Part 4: Employment income: Exemptions
Part 6: Employment Income: Income which is not earnings or share-related
Part 7: Employment income: Share-related income and exemptions
Part 8: Former employees: Deductions for liabilities
Part 9: Pay As You Earn
Schs 2–8

Part 2, Chapter 8 of ITEPA (ss.48–61) deal with the so-called IR35 provisions, namely the provisions under which income of a "pocket book" company could be treated as the employment income of the individual who owned the company so that income was not diverted so as to be excluded from income tax. It was understood that these sections would apply to tax credits and they were therefore included in the 2003–04 edition of this volume. However, amendments to the Working Tax Credit (Entitlement and Maximum Rate) Regulations 2002 were made by the Tax Credits (Miscellaneous Amendments No.2) Regulations 2003 (SI 2003/2815) to clarify the intended policy that these provisions do not apply to tax credits. They are therefore no longer of relevance to this volume.

Part 7 of ITEPA was repealed completely and replaced by new provisions by the Finance Act 2003, s.140 and Sch.22 with effect from April 15, 2003. The original Pt 7 was outside the scope of tax credits income calculations. The new Pt 7 is not, by reason of amendment of the Tax Credits (Definition and Calculation of Income) Regulations 2002 (SI 2002/2006), reg.4. See the note to that regulation. The text of the new Pt 7 is not reproduced in this volume.

But particular attention has been paid to sections making special provision for those who are sick or disabled, and to the taxation of state pensions and social security benefits.

Interpreting and applying ITEPA

1.408 While from a technical viewpoint ITEPA is a consolidation measure, it varies in several ways from the consolidation performed by the ICTA 1988, part of which it repeals and replaces. There are a series of both policy and technical changes in ITEPA, compared with the sections of ICTA 1988 that it replaces. But ITEPA, as noted above, is also used to incorporate both practices and case law. The ITEPA Bill was accompanied by the usual tables of origins and destinations. But it also provides two other aids to those interpreting and applying it. Schedule 1 includes a full index of defined terms used in ITEPA, including terms it derives from ICTA 1988 and other income tax legislation. Reference should be made to Sch.1 Pt 2 for any phrase that needs interpretation. The ITEPA Bill was publishedfully in draft before submission to Parliament. The draft Bill was accompanied by a commentary. The draft Bill was then amended before publication as a Parliamentary Bill, accompanied by three volumes of explanatory notes. Volumes I and II contain extensive notes on clauses. Much of Vol.II comprises Annex 1. This is a detailed explanation of 183 changes made by the Bill to the previous law. Volume III consists of Annex 2. These are 72 separate notes on technical points in clauses. Finally, Annex 3 lists former extra statutory concessions now enacted for the first time.

There is another significant change to the way the ITEPA Bill was handled compared with not only ICTA 1988 but most Public Acts. It was not debated in substance in Parliament. Instead, it was considered by a Joint Committee of the Houses. The Joint Committee recommended the Bill to both Houses with a few further (minimal, and technical) changes. With those changes only, the Bill received royal assent. In effect, the debating process of Parliament was bypassed in favour of the much wider consultation conducted as part of the Tax Law Rewrite Project. But that also means that the interpretative techniques described as ascertaining the "intention of Parliament" cannot be applied in the form of *Pepper v Hart* arguments. Rather, in so far as there is any change with the previous law, the intention is in the notes presented with the Bill. And, in addition, the reports of the Tax Law Rewrite Project give a definitive, if technically non-authoritative, account of what the previous legislation is understood to mean.

The result should be an Act in which there is far less room for genuine doubt or dispute about what the words mean, if full regard is had to the pedigree of the Act. Bearing that pedigree in mind, no attempt is made in this volume to do more than indicate these sources.

ITEPA and the Commissioners for Revenue and Customs Act 2005

The merger of the Inland Revenue and HM Customs and Excise, and the creation of the new joint HMRC (the new Commissioners and its officers under the new title "officer of Revenue and Customs"), requires textual amendment to most sections in ITEPA. The approach taken by the Rewrite team was to replace previous references—in many forms to "the Commissioners", "the Board", or "an inspector" or "an officer" with either "the Board" (if the function was unlikely to be delegated) or "an officer of the Board" in all other cases. CRCA 2005 adopts a different approach not entirely consistent with this. This is of limited importance in ITEPA. But, for example, the reference to the Board of Inland Revenue in s.343 should now be read as a reference to "the Commissioners", but probably "the Inland Revenue" in s.344 should now be "an officer of Revenue and Customs"—although that is not clear. This lack of clarity is emphasised by the repeal of the definition of those terms as part of the repeal of the definitions in s.720 (which formerly defined "the Inland Revenue" as meaning any officer of the Board. The old text—save for s.720—has not been amended by CRCA 2005 expressly and has been left in this edition.

1.409

Part 1

Overview

Overview of contents of this Act

1.—(1) This Act imposes charges to income tax on—
(a) employment income (see Parts 2 to 7),
(b) pension income (see Part 9), and
(c) social security income (see Part 10).
(2) *Repealed*
(3) This Act also—
(a) confers certain reliefs in respect of liabilities of former employees (see Part 8);
(b) provides for the assessment, collection and recovery of income tax in respect of employment, pension or social security income that is PAYE income (see Part 2); and
(c) allows deductions to be made from such income in respect of payroll giving (see Part 12).

1.410

Abbreviations and general index in Schedule 1

2.—(1) Schedule 1 (abbreviations and defined expressions) applies for the purposes of this Act.

1.411

(2) In Schedule 1—
(a) Part 1 gives the meaning of the abbreviated references to Acts and instruments used in this Act; and
(b) Part 2 lists the places where expressions used in this Act are defined or otherwise explained.
(3) *Omitted.*

PART 2

EMPLOYMENT INCOME: CHARGE TO TAX

CHAPTER 1

INTRODUCTION

Structure of employment income Parts

1.412   **3.**—(1) The structure of the employment income Parts is as follows—This Part imposes the charge to tax on employment income, and sets out—
(a) how the amount charged to tax for a tax year is to be calculated; and
(b) who is liable for the tax charged;
Part 3 sets out what are earnings and provides for amounts to be treated as earnings;
Part 4 deals with exemptions from the charge to tax under this Part (and, in some cases, from other charges to tax);
Part 5 deals with deductions from taxable earnings;
Part 6 deals with employment income other than earnings or share-related income; and
Part 7 deals with share-related income and exemptions.
(2) In this Act "the employment income Parts" means this Part and Parts 3 to 7.

GENERAL NOTE

1.413   Part 4 (Employment income: Exemptions)—ss.227–326—is entirely omitted from this work. It comprises a codified list of all exemptions from the charge to income tax otherwise imposed by ITEPA on various earnings and benefits, under the following chapter heads: mileage allowances and passenger payments; transport travel and subsistence; education and training; recreational benefits; non-cash vouchers and credit-tokens; removal benefits and expenses; special kinds of employee; pension provision; termination of employment; and miscellaneous. The general rule of income tax law is that it is for a claimant to claim for, and show that he or she is entitled to, the benefit of an exemption.
    Part 6 is also entirely omitted. It comprises ss.386–416, and deals with payments to, and benefits from, non-approved pension schemes, and payments on termination of employment.
    Part 7 is also entirely omitted. It is a lengthy part—ss.417–564 and Schs 2–5. They deal with the detail of the various kinds of tax charge on, and exemption of, share-related income including all forms of benefits obtained by shares or interests in shares.

"Employment" for the purposes of the employment income Parts

4.—(1) In the employment income Parts "employment" includes in particular—
(a) any employment under a contract of service,
(b) any employment under a contract of apprenticeship, and
(c) any employment in the service of the Crown.

(2) In those Parts, "employed", "employee" and "employer" have corresponding meanings.

1.414

General Note

There are no general income tax (or, more generally, tax) rules defining whether an individual is an employee or self-employed, or whether a relationship is an employment relationship. That is a matter to be decided by general law. There is considerable case law on the subject, some of it deriving from income tax and some from social security cases. Under the Social Security Contributions (Transfer of Functions) Act 1999, s.8, decisions about the same question for the purposes of the Social Security Contributions and Benefits Act 1992 were transferred to the Inland Revenue and, on appeal, to the tax appeal tribunals. There is, however, no equivalent provision in the TCA 2002. It would seem, therefore, that appeals about Revenue decisions about employment for tax credit purposes go to appeal tribunals, not tax appeal tribunals.

1.415

Application to offices and office-holders

5.—(1) The provisions of the employment income Parts that are expressed to apply to employments apply equally to offices, unless otherwise indicated.
(2) In those provisions as they apply to an office—
(a) references to being employed are to being the holder of the office;
(b) "employee" means the office-holder;
(c) "employer" means the person under whom the office-holder holds office.
(3) In the employment income Parts "office" includes in particular any position which has an existence independent of the person who holds it and may be filled by successive holders.

1.416

Chapter 2

Tax on Employment Income

Nature of charge to tax on employment income

6.—(1) The charge to tax on employment income under this Part is a charge to tax on—
(a) general earnings; and
(b) specific employment income.
The meaning of "employment income", "general earnings" and "specific employment income" is given in section 7.
(2) The amount of general earnings or specific employment income which is chargedto tax in a particular tax year is set out in section 9.

1.417

(3) The rules in Chapters 4 and 5 of this Part, which are concerned with—
(a) the residence and domicile of an employee in a tax year; and
(b) the tax year in which amounts are received or remitted to the United Kingdom;
apply for the purposes of the charge to tax on general earnings but not that on specific employment income.

(4) The person who is liable for any tax charged on employment income is set out in section 13.

(5) Employment income is not charged to tax under this Part if it is within the charge to tax under Case I of Schedule D by virtue of section 314(1) of ICTA (divers and diving supervisors).

Meaning of "employment income", "general earnings" and "specific employment income"

1.418   **7.**—(1) This section gives the meaning for the purposes of the Tax Acts of "employment income", "general earnings" and "specific employment income".

(2) "Employment income" means—
(a) earnings within Chapter 1 of Part 3;
(b) any amount treated as earnings (see subsection (5)); or
(c) any amount which counts as employment income (see subsection (6)).

(3) "General earnings" means—
(a) earnings within Chapter 1 of Part 3; or
(b) any amount treated as earnings (see subsection (5));
excluding in each case any exempt income.

(4) "Specific employment income" means any amount which counts as employment income (see subsection (6)), excluding any exempt income.

(5) Subsection (2)(b) or (3)(b) refers to any amount treated as earnings under—
(a) Chapters 7 and 8 of this Part (application of provisions to agency workers and workers under arrangements made by intermediaries),
(b) Chapters 2 to 11 of Part 3 (the benefits code),
(c) Chapters 12 of Part 3 (payments treated as earnings), or
(d) section 262 of CAA 2001 (balancing charges to be given effect by treating them as earnings).

(6) Subsection (2)(c) or (4) refers to any amount which counts as employment income by virtue of—
(a) Part 6 (income which is not earnings or share-related),
(b) Part 7 (share-related income and exemptions), or
(c) any other enactment.

Meaning of "exempt income"

1.419   **8.** For the purposes of the employment income Parts, an amount of employment income within paragraph (a), (b) or (c) of section 7(2) is "exempt income" if, as a result of any exemption in Part 4 or elsewhere, no liability to income tax arises in respect of it as such an amount.

(2003 c. 1, s. 9)

Chapter 3

Operation of Tax Charge

Amount of employment income charged to tax

9.—(1) The amount of employment income which is charged to tax under this Part for a particular tax year is as follows.

(2) In the case of general earnings, the amount charged is the net taxable earnings from an employment in the year.

(3) That amount is calculated under section 11 by reference to any taxable earnings from the employment in the year (see section 10(2)).

(4) In the case of specific employment income, the amount charged is the net taxable specific income from an employment for the year.

(5) That amount is calculated under section 12 by reference to any taxable specific income from the employment for the year (see section 10(3)).

(6) Accordingly, no amount of employment income is charged to tax under this Part for a particular tax year unless—
  (a) in the case of general earnings, they are taxable earnings from an employment in that year; or
  (b) in the case of specific employment income, it is taxable specific income from an employment for that year.

1.420

Meaning of "taxable earnings" and "taxable specific income"

10.—(1) This section explains what is meant by "taxable earnings" and "taxable specific income" in the employment income Parts.

(2) "Taxable earnings" from an employment in a tax year are to be determined in accordance with—
  (a) Chapter 4 of this Part (rules applying to employees resident, ordinarily resident and domiciled in the UK); or
  (b) Chapter 5 of this Part (rules applying to employees resident, ordinarily resident or domiciled outside the UK).

(3) "Taxable specific income" from an employment for a tax year means the full amount of any specific employment income which, by virtue of Part 6 or 7 or any other enactment, counts as employment income for that year in respect of the employment.

1.421

Calculation of "net taxable earnings"

11.—(1) For the purposes of this Part, the "net taxable earnings" from an employment in a tax year are given by the formula—

$$TE - DE,$$

where—
TE means the total amount of any taxable earnings from the employment in the tax year; and
DE means the total amount of any deductions allowed from those earnings under provisions listed in sections 327(3) to (5) (deductions from earnings: general).

1.422

209

(2) If the amount calculated under subsection (1) is negative, the net taxable earnings from the employment in the year are to be taken to be nil instead.

(3) Relief may be available under section 380(1) of ICTA (set-off against general income)—

(a) where TE is negative; or
(b) in certain exceptional cases where the amount calculated under subsection (1) is negative.

(4) If a person has more than one employment in a tax year, the calculation under subsection (1) must be carried out in relation to each of the employments.

Calculation of "net taxable specific income"

1.423   **12.**—(1) For the purposes of this Part the "net taxable specific income" from an employment for a tax year is given by the formula—

$$TSI - DSI,$$

where—

TSI means the amount of any taxable specific income from the employment for the tax year; and

DSI means the total amount of any deductions allowed from that income under provisions of the Tax Acts not included in the lists in section 327(3) and (4) (deductions from earnings: general).

(2) If the amount calculated under subsection (1) is negative, the net taxable specific income from the employment for the year is to be taken to be nil instead.

(3) If a person has more than one kind of specific employment income from an employment for a tax year, the calculation under subsection (1) must be carried out in relation to each of those kinds of specific employment income; and in such a case the "net taxable specific income" from the employment for that year is the total of all the amounts so calculated.

Person liable for tax

1.424   **13.**—(1) The person liable for any tax on employment income under this Part is the taxable person mentioned in subsection (2) or (3). This is subject to subsection (4).

(2) If the tax is on general earnings, "the taxable person" is the person to whose employment the earnings relate.

(3) If the tax is on specific employment income, "the taxable person" is the person in relation to whom the income is, by virtue of Part 6 or 7 or any other enactment, to count as employment income.

(4) If the tax is on general earnings received, or remitted to the United Kingdom, after the death of the person to whose employment the earnings relate, the person's personal representatives are liable for the tax.

(5) In that event the tax is accordingly to be assessed on the personal representatives and is a debt due from and payable out of the estate.

(2003 c.1, s.44)

CHAPTER 7

APPLICATION OF PROVISIONS TO AGENCY WORKERS

Agency workers

Treatment of workers supplied by agencies

44.—(1) This section applies if—
(a) an individual ("the worker") personally provides, or is under an obligation personally to provide, services (which are not excluded services) to another person ("the client");
(b) the services are supplied by or through a third person ("the agency") under the terms of an agency contract;
(c) the worker is subject to (or to the right of) supervision, direction or control as to the manner in which the services are provided; and
(d) remuneration receivable under or in consequence of the agency contract does not constitute employment income of the worker apart from this chapter.
(2) If this section applies—
(a) the services which the worker provides, or is obliged to provide, to the client under the agency contract are to be treated for income tax purposes as duties of an employment held by the worker with the agency; and
(b) all remuneration receivable under or in consequence of the agency contract (including remuneration which the client pays or provides in relation to the services) is to be treated for income tax purposes as earnings from that employment.

PART 3

EMPLOYMENT INCOME: EARNINGS AND BENEFITS, ETC. TREATED AS EARNINGS

CHAPTER 1

EARNINGS

Earnings

62.—(1) This section explains what is meant by "earnings" in the employment income Parts.
(2) In those Parts, "earnings", in relation to an employment, means—
(a) any salary, wages or fee;
(b) any gratuity or other profit or incidental benefit of any kind obtained by the employee if it is money or money's worth; or
(c) anything else that constitutes an emolument of the employment.

(3) For the purposes of subsection (2), "money's worth" means something that is—
(a) of direct monetary value to the employee; or
(b) capable of being converted into money or something of direct monetary value to the employee.

(4) Subsection (1) does not affect the operation of statutory provisions that provide for amounts to be treated as earnings (and see section 721(7)).

CHAPTER 2

TAXABLE BENEFITS: THE BENEFITS CODE

The benefits code

The benefits code

1.427 **63.**—(1) In the employment income Parts "the benefits code" means—
this chapter,
Chapter 3 (expenses payments),
Chapter 4 (vouchers and credit-tokens),
Chapter 5 (living accommodation),
Chapter 6 (cars, vans and related benefits),
Chapter 7 (loans),
[. . .]¹
Chapter 10 (residual liability to charge), and
Chapter 11 (exclusion of lower-paid employments from parts of benefits code).

(2) If an employment is an excluded employment, the general effect of section 216(1) (provisions not applicable to lower-paidemployments) is that only the following chapters apply to the employment—
this chapter,
Chapter 4 (vouchers and credit-tokens),
Chapter 5 (living accommodation), and
Chapter 11 (exclusion of lower-paidemployments from parts of benefits code).

(3) Section 216(5) and (6) explain and restrict the effect of section 216(1).

(4) In the benefits code, "excluded employment" means an employment to which the exclusion in section 216(1) applies.

AMENDMENT

1. Words repealed by FA 2003. Sch.43.

Relationship between earnings and benefits code

1.428 **64.**—(1) This section applies if, apart from this section, the same benefit would give rise to two amounts ("A" and "B")—
(a) A being an amount of earnings as defined in Chapter 1 of this Part; and
(b) B being an amount to be treated as earnings under the benefits code.
(2) In such a case—
(a) A constitutes earnings as defined in Chapter 1 of this Part; and

(b) the amount (if any) by which B exceeds A is to be treated as earnings under the benefits code.

(3) This section does not apply in connection with living accommodation to which Chapter 5 of this Part applies.

(4) In that case section 109 applies to determine the relationship between that chapter and Chapter 1 of this Part.

(5) [. . .]¹.

(6) [. . .]¹.

AMENDMENT

1. Subss.(5) and (6) repealed by FA 2003, Sch.43.

Dispensations relating to benefits within provisions not applicable to lower-paid employment

65.—(1) This section applies for the purposes of the listed provisions where a person ("P") supplies the Inland Revenue with a statement of the cases and circumstances in which—
(a) payments of a particular character are made to or for any employees; or
(b) benefits or facilities of a particular kind are provided for any employees,
whether they are employees of P or some other person.

(2) The "listed provisions" are the provisions listed in section 216(4) (provisions of the benefits code which do not apply to lower-paid employments).

(3) If the Inland Revenue are satisfied that no additional tax is payable by virtue of the listed provisions by reference to the payments, benefits or facilities mentioned in the statement, they must give P a dispensation under this section.

(4) A "dispensation" is a notice stating that the Inland Revenue agree that no additional tax is payable by virtue of the listed provisions by reference to the payments, benefits or facilities mentioned in the statement supplied by P.

(5) If a dispensation is given under this section, nothing in the listed provisions applies to the payments, or the provision of the benefits or facilities, covered by the dispensation or otherwise has the effect of imposing any additional liability to tax in respect of them.

(6) If in their opinion there is reason to do so, the Inland Revenue may revoke a dispensation by giving a further notice to P.

(7) That notice may revoke the dispensation from—
(a) the date when the dispensation was given; or
(b) a later date specified in the notice.

(8) If the notice revokes the dispensation from the date when the dispensation was given—
(a) any liability to tax that would have arisen if the dispensation had never been given is to be treated as having arisen; and
(b) P and the employees in question must make all the returns which they would have had to make if the dispensation had never been given.

(9) If the notice revokes the dispensation from a later date—
(a) any liability to tax that would have arisen if the dispensation had ceased to have effect on that date is to be treated as having arisen; and
(b) P and the employees in question must make all the returns which they would have had to make if the dispensation had ceased to have effect on that date.

General definitions for benefits code

Meaning of "employment" and related expressions

1.430   **66.**—(1) In the benefits code—
   (a) "employment" means a taxable employment under Part 2; and
   (b) "employed", "employee" and "employer" have corresponding meanings.
   (2) Where a chapter of the benefits code applies in relation to an employee—
   (a) references in that chapter to "the employment" are to the employment of that employee; and
   (b) references in that chapter to "the employer" are to the employer in respect of that employment.
   (3) For the purposes of the benefits code an employment is a "taxable employment under Part 2" in a tax year if the earnings from the employment for that year are (or would be if there were any) general earnings to which the charging provisions of Chapter 4 or 5 of Part 2 apply.
   (4) In subsection (3)—
   (a) the reference to an employment includes employment as a director of a company; and
   (b) "earnings" means earnings as defined in Chapter of this Part.

CHAPTER 3

TAXABLE BENEFITS: EXPENSES PAYMENTS

Sums in respect of expenses

1.431   **70.**—(1) This chapter applies to a sum paid to an employee in a tax year if the sum—
   (a) is paid to the employee in respect of expenses; and
   (b) is so paid by reason of the employment.
   (2) This chapter applies to a sum paid away by an employee in a tax year if the sum—
   (a) was put at the employee's disposal in respect of expenses;
   (b) was so put by reason of the employment; and
   (c) is paid away by the employee in respect of expenses.
   (3) For the purposes of this chapter it does not matter whether the employment is held at the time when the sum is paid or paidaway so long as it is held at some point in the tax year in which the sum is paid or paidaway.
   (4) References in this chapter to an employee accordingly include a prospective or former employee.
   (5) This chapter does not apply to the extent that the sum constitutes earnings from the employment by virtue of any other provision.

Meaning of paid or put at disposal by reason of the employment

1.432   **71.**—(1) If an employer pays a sum in respect of expenses to an employee it is to be treated as paid by reason of the employment unless—

(a) the employer is an individual, and
(b) the payment is made in the normal course of the employer's domestic, family or personal relationships.

(2) If an employer puts a sum at an employee's disposal in respect of expenses it is to be treated as put at the employee's disposal by reason of the employment unless—
(a) the employer is an individual, and
(b) the sum is put at the employee's disposal in the normal course of the employer's domestic, family or personal relationships.

Sums in respect of expenses treated as earnings

72.—(1) If this chapter applies to a sum, the sum is to be treated as earnings from the employment for the tax year in which it is paid or paidaway.

(2) Subsection (1) does not prevent the making of a deduction allowed under any of the provisions listed in subsection (3).

(3) The provisions are—
section 336 (deductions for expenses: the general rule);
section 337 (travel in performance of duties);
section 338 (travel for necessary attendance);
section 340 (travel between group employments);
section 341 (travel at start or finish of overseas employment);
section 342 (travel between employments where duties performed abroad);
section 343 (deduction for professional membership fees);
section 344 (deduction for annual subscriptions);
section 346 (deduction for employee liabilities);
section 353 (deductions from earnings charged on remittance).

1.433

CHAPTER 4

TAXABLE BENEFITS: VOUCHERS AND CREDIT-TOKENS

Cash vouchers: introduction

Cash vouchers to which this chapter applies

73.—(1) This chapter applies to a cash voucher provided for an employee by reason of the employment which is received by the employee.

(2) A cash voucher provided for an employee by the employer is to be regarded as provided by reason of the employment unless—
(a) the employer is an individual; and
(b) the provision is made in the normal course of the employer's domestic, family or personal relationships.

(3) A cash voucher provided for an employee and appropriated to the employee—
(a) by attaching it to a card held for the employee; or
(b) in any other way;
is to be treated for the purposes of this chapter as having been received by the employee at the time when it is appropriated.

1.434

Provision for, or receipt by, member of employee's family

1.435 **74.**—For the purposes of this chapter any reference to a cash voucher being provided for or received by an employee includes a reference to it being provided for or received by a member of the employee's family.

Meaning of "cash voucher"

Meaning of "cash voucher"

1.436 **75.**—(1) In this chapter "cash voucher" means a voucher, stamp or similar document capable of being exchanged for a sum of money which is—
(a) greater than;
(b) equal to; or
(c) not substantially less than,
the expense incurred by the person at whose cost the voucher, stamp or similar document is provided.

(2) For the purposes of subsection (1) it does not matter whether the document—
(a) is also capable of being exchanged for goods or services;
(b) is capable of being exchanged singly or together with other vouchers, stamps, or documents;
(c) is capable of being exchanged immediately or only after a time.

(3) Subsection (1) is subject to section 76 (sickness benefits-related voucher).

Sickness benefits-related voucher

1.437 **76.**—(1) This section applies where—
(a) the expense incurred by the person at whose cost a voucher, stamp or similar document is provided ("the provision expense") includes costs to that person of providing sickness benefits ("sickness benefits costs"),
(b) the voucher, stamp or document would be a cash voucher (apart from this section) but for the fact that the sum of money for which it is capable of being exchanged ("the exchange sum") is substantially less than the provision expense, and
(c) the whole or part of the difference between the exchange sum and the provision expense represents the sickness benefits costs.

(2) The voucher, stamp or document is a cash voucher within the meaning of this chapter if—

$$E = \frac{PE}{D}$$

or

$$E \text{ is not substantially less than } \frac{PE}{D},$$

where—
E is the exchange sum;
PE is the provision expense; and

(2003 c.1, s.76)

D is the amount of the difference between E and PE which represents the sickness benefits costs.

(3) In this section "sickness benefits" mean benefits in connection with sickness, personal injury or death.

Benefit of cash voucher treated as earnings

Benefit of cash voucher treated as earnings

81.—(1) The cash equivalent of the benefit of a cash voucher to which this chapter applies is to be treated as earnings from the employment for the tax year in which the voucher is received by the employee.

(2) The cash equivalent is the sum of money for which the voucher is capable of being exchanged.

1.438

Non-cash vouchers: introduction

Non-cash vouchers to which this chapter applies

82.—(1) This chapter applies to a non-cash voucher provided for an employee by reason of the employment which is received by the employee.

(2) A non-cash voucher provided for an employee by the employer is to be regarded as provided by reason of the employment unless—
  (a) the employer is an individual; and
  (b) the provision is made in the normal course of the employer's domestic, family or personal relationships.

(3) A non-cash voucher provided for an employee and appropriated to the employee—
  (a) by attaching it to a card held for the employee; or
  (b) in any other way,
is to be treated for the purposes of this chapter as having been received by the employee at the time when it is appropriated.

1.439

Meaning of "non-cash voucher"

Meaning of "non-cash voucher"

84.—(1) In this chapter "non-cash voucher" means—
  (a) a voucher, stamp or similar document or token which is capable of being exchanged for money, goods or services;
  [[1](ab) a childcare voucher]
  (b) a transport voucher, or
  (c) a cheque voucher,
but does not include a cash voucher.

(2) For the purposes of subsection (1)(a) it does not matter whether the document or token is capable of being exchanged—
  (a) singly or together with other vouchers, stamps, documents or tokens;
  (b) immediately or only after a time.

1.440

[¹(2A) In this chapter "childcare voucher" means a voucher, stamp or similar document or token intended to enable a person to obtain the provision of case for a child (whether or not in exchange for it).]

(3) In this chapter "transport voucher" means a ticket, pass or other document or token intended to enable a person to obtain passenger transport services (whether or not in exchange for it).

(4) In this chapter "cheque voucher" means a cheque—
  (a) provided for an employee; and
  (b) intended for use by the employee wholly or mainly for payment for—
    (i) particular goods or services; or
    (ii) goods or services of one or more particular classes;
and, in relation to a cheque voucher, references to a voucher being exchanged for goods or services are to be read accordingly.

AMENDMENT

1. Finance Act 2004, Sch.13, para.2 (April 6, 2005).

Benefit of non-cash voucher treated as earnings

Benefit of non-cash voucher treated as earnings

1.441
87.—(1) The cash equivalent of the benefit of a non-cash voucher to which this chapter applies is to be treated as earnings from the employment for the tax year in which the voucher is received by the employee.

(2) The cash equivalent is the difference between—
  (a) the cost of provision; and
  (b) any part of that cost made good by the employee to the person incurring it.

(3) In this chapter the "cost of provision" means, in relation to a non-cash voucher, the expense incurred in or in connection with the provision of—
  (a) the voucher, and
  (b) the money, goods or services for which it is capable of being exchanged,
by the person at whose cost they are provided.

[¹(3A) In the case of a childcare voucher, the reference in subsection (3)(b) to the services for which the voucher is capable of being exchanged is to the provision of care for a child which may be obtained by using it.]

(4) In the case of a transport voucher, the reference in subsection (3)(b) to the services for which the voucher is capable of being exchanged is to the passenger transport services which may be obtained by using it.

(5) If a person incurs expense in or in connection with the provision of non-cash vouchers for two or more employees as members of a group or class, the expense incurred in respect of one of them is to be such part of that expense as is just and reasonable.

(6) This section is subject to section 89 (reduction for meal vouchers).

AMENDMENT

1. Finance Act 2004, Sch.13, para.2 (April 6, 2005).

(2003 c.1, s.90)

Credit-tokens: introduction

Credit-tokens to which this chapter applies

90.—(1) This chapter applies to a credit-token provided for an employee by reason of the employment which is used by the employee to obtain money, goods or services.

(2) A credit-token provided for an employee by the employer is to be regarded as provided by reason of the employment unless—
  (a) the employer is an individual; and
  (b) the provision is made in the normal course of the employer's domestic, family or personal relationships.

1.442

Meaning of "credit-token"

Meaning of "credit-token"

92.—(1) In this chapter "credit-token" means a credit card, debit card or other card, a token, a document or other object given to a person by another person ("X") who undertakes—
  (a) on the production of it, to supply money, goods or services on credit; or
  (b) if a third party ("Y") supplies money, goods or services on its production, to pay Y for what is supplied.

(2) A card, token, document or other object can be a credit-token even if—
  (a) some other action is required in addition to its production in order for the money, goods or services to be supplied;
  (b) X in paying Y may take a discount or commission.

(3) For the purposes of this section—
  (a) the use of an object given by X to operate a machine provided by X is to be treated as its production to X, and
  (b) the use of an object given by X to operate a machine provided by Y is to be treated as its production to Y.

(4) A "credit-token" does not include a cash voucher or a non-cash voucher.

1.443

Benefit of credit-token treated as earnings

Benefit of credit-token treated as earnings

94.—(1) On each occasion on which a credit-token to which this chapter applies is used by the employee in a tax year to obtain money, goods or services, the cash equivalent of the benefit of the token is to be treated as earnings from the employment for that year.

(2) The cash equivalent is the difference between—
  (a) the cost of provision; and
  (b) any part of that cost made good by the employee to the person incurring it.

1.444

219

(3) In this section the "cost of provision" means the expense incurred—
(a) in or in connection with the provision of the money, goods or services obtained on the occasion in question; and
(b) by the person at whose cost they are provided.
(4) If a person incurs expense in or in connection with the provision of credit-tokens for two or more employees as members of a group or class, the expense incurred in respect of one of them is to be such part of that expense as is just and reasonable.

General supplementary provisions

Disregard for money, goods or services obtained

95.—(1) This section applies if the cash equivalent of the benefit of a cash voucher, a non-cash voucher or a credit-token—
(a) is to be treated as earnings from an employee's employment under this chapter; or
(b) would be so treated but for a dispensation given under section 96.
(2) Money, goods or services obtained—
(a) by the employee or another person in exchange for the cash voucher or non-cash voucher; or
(b) by the employee or a member of the employee's family by use of the credit-token,
are to be disregarded for the purposes of the Income Tax Acts.
(3) But the goods or services are not to be disregarded for the purposes of applying sections 362 and 363 (deductions where non-cash voucher or credit-token provided).
[[1](3A) In the case of a childcare voucher, the reference in subsection (2)(a) to the services obtained in exchange for the voucher is to the provision of care for a child which may be obtained by using it.]
(4) In the case of a transport voucher, the reference in subsection (2)(a) to the services obtained in exchange for the voucher is to the passenger transport services obtained by using it.

AMENDMENT

1. Finance Act 2004, Sch.13, para.2 (April 6, 2005).

CHAPTER 10

TAXABLE BENEFITS: RESIDUAL LIABILITY TO CHARGE

Introduction

Employment-related benefits

201.—(1) This chapter applies to employment-related benefits.

(2) In this chapter—

"benefit" means a benefit or facility of any kind;

"employment-related benefit" means a benefit, other than an excluded benefit, which is provided in a tax year—
- (a) for an employee; or
- (b) for a member of an employee's family or household;

by reason of the employment.

For the definition of "excluded benefit" see section 202.

(3) A benefit provided by an employer is to be regarded as provided by reason of the employment unless—
- (a) the employer is an individual; and
- (b) the provision is made in the normal course of the employer's domestic, family or personal relationships.

(4) For the purposes of this chapter it does not matter whether the employment is held at the time when the benefit is provided so long as it is held at some point in the tax year in which the benefit is provided.

(5) References in this chapter to an employee accordingly include a prospective or former employee.

Excluded benefits

202.—(1) A benefit is an "excluded benefit" for the purposes of this chapter if—
- (a) any of Chapters 3 to 9 of the benefits code applies to the benefit;
- (b) any of those chapters would apply to the benefit but for an exception; or
- (c) the benefit consists in the right to receive, or the prospect of receiving, sums treated as earnings under section 221 (payments where employee absent because of sickness or disability).

(2) In this section, "exception", in relation to the application of a chapter of the benefits code to a benefit, means any enactment in the chapter which provides that the chapter does not apply to the benefit. But for this purpose section 86 (transport vouchers under pre-26th March 1982 arrangements) is not an exception.

1.447

Cash equivalent of benefit treated as earnings

Cash equivalent of benefit treated as earnings

203.—(1) The cash equivalent of an employment-related benefit is to be treated as earnings from the employment for the tax year in which it is provided.

1.448

(2) The cash equivalent of an employment-related benefit is the cost of the benefit less any part of that cost made good by the employee to the persons providing the benefit.

(3) The cost of an employment-related benefit is determined in accordance with section 204 unless—
- (a) section 205 provides that the cost is to be determined in accordance with that section; or
- (b) section 206 provides that the cost is to be determined in accordance with that section.

Income Tax (Earnings and Pensions) Act 2003

Determination of the cost of the benefit

Cost of the benefit: basic rule

1.449   **204.** The cost of an employment-related benefit is the expense incurred in or in connection with provision of the benefit (including a proper proportion of any expense relating partly to provision of the benefit and partly to other matters).

Exemption of minor benefits

1.450   **210.**—(1) The Treasury may make provision by regulations for exempting from the application of this Chapter such minor benefits as may be specified by regulation.

(2) An exemption conferred by such regulations is conditional on the benefit being made available to the employer's employees generally on similar terms.

GENERAL NOTE

1.451   For regulations made under this section see the Income Tax (Exemption of Minor Benefits) Regulations 2002 (SI 2002/205) as amended by the Income Tax (Exemption of Minor Benefits)(Amendment) Regulations 2003 (SI 2003/1434). These regulations are not included in this volume. They remove taxation from minor benefits, such as free meals, provided by employers that would otherwise be liable to taxation.

CHAPTER 11

TAXABLE BENEFITS: EXCLUSION OF LOWER-PAID EMPLOYMENT FROM PARTS OF BENEFITS CODE

Introduction

Provisions not applicable to lower-paid employments

1.452   **216.**—(1) The chapters of the benefits code listed in subsection (4) do not apply to an employment in relation to a tax year if—
   (a) it is lower-paid employment in relation to that year (see section 217); and
   (b) condition A or B is met.

(2) Condition A is that the employee is not employed as a director of a company.

(3) Condition B is that the employee is employed as a director of a company but has no material interest in the company and either—
   (a) the employment is as a full-time working director; or
   (b) the company is non-profit-making or is established for charitable purposes only.

"Non-profit-making" means that the company does not carry on a trade and its functions do not consist wholly or mainly in the holding of investments or other property.

(4) The chapters referred to in subsection (1) are—
Chapter 3 (taxable benefits: expenses payments);
Chapter 6 (taxable benefits: cars, vans and related benefits);
Chapter 7 (taxable benefits: loans);
[. . .]¹
Chapter 10 (taxable benefits: residual liability to charge).
(5) Subsection (1)—
(a) means that in any of those chapters a reference to an employee does not include an employee whose employment is within the exclusion in that subsection, if the context is such that the reference is to an employee in relation to whom the chapter applies; but
(b) does not restrict the meaning of references to employees in other contexts.
(6) Subsection (1) has effect subject to—
section 188(2) (discharge of loan: where employment becomes lower-paid);
[. . .]¹, and
section 220 (employment in two or more related employments).

AMENDMENT

1. Words repealed by FA 2003, Sch.43.

What is lower-paid employment?

Meaning of "lower-paid employment"

217.—(1) For the purposes of this chapter an employment is "lower-paid employment" in relation to a tax year if the earnings rate for the employment for the year (calculated under section 218) is less than £8,500.

(2) Subsection (1) is subject to section 220 (employment in two or more related employments).

1.453

Calculation of earnings rate for a tax year

218.—(1) For any tax year the earnings rate for an employment is to be calculated as follows—

1.454

Step 1

Find the total of the following amounts—
(a) the total amount of the earnings from the employment for the year within Chapter 1 of this Part;
(b) the total of any amounts that are treated as earnings from the employment for the year under the benefits code (see subsections (2) and (3));
(c) the total of any amounts that are treated as earnings from the employment for the year under Chapter 12 of this Part (payments treated as earnings); and
(d) in the case of an employment within section 56(2) (deemed employment of worker by intermediary), the amount of the deemed employment payment for the year (see section 54), excluding any exempt income.

Step 2

Add to that total any extra amount required to be added for the year by section 219 (extra amounts to be added in connection with a car).

Step 3

Subtract the total amount of any authorised deductions (see subsection (4)) from the result of step 2.

Step 4

The earnings rate for the employment for the year is given by the formula—

$$\frac{Y}{R \times E}$$

where—
R is the result of step 3;
Y is the number of days in the year; and
E is the number of days in the year when the employment is held.

(2) Section 216(1) (provisions not applicable to lower-paid employment) is to be disregarded for the purpose of determining any amount under step 1.

(3) If the benefit of living accommodation is to be taken into account under step 1, the cash equivalent is to be calculated in accordance with section 105 (even if the cost of providing the accommodation exceeds £75,000).

(4) For the purposes of step 3, "authorised deduction" means any deduction that would (assuming it was an amount of taxable earnings) be allowed from any amount within step 1 under—

section 346 (employee liabilities);
section 352 (agency fees paid by entertainers);
section 355 (corresponding payments by non-domiciled employees with foreign employers);
section 368 (fixed sum deductions from earnings payable out of public revenue);
section 370 (travel costs and expenses where duties performed abroad: employee's travel);
section 371 (travel costs and expenses where duties performed abroad: visiting spouse's [1, civil partner's] or child's travel);
section 373 (non-domiciled employee's travel costs and expenses where duties performed in United Kingdom);
section 374 (non-domiciled employee's spouse's [1, civil partner's] or child's travel costs and expenses where duties performed in United Kingdom);
section 376 (foreign accommodation and subsistence costs and expenses (overseas employments));
section 377 (costs and expenses in respect of personal security assets and services);
section 713 (payroll giving to charities); section 592(7) of ICTA (contributions to exempt approved schemes); section 594 of ICTA (contributions to exempt statutory schemes); or section 262 of CAA 2001 (capital allowances to be given effect by treating them as deductions).

AMENDMENT

1. Tax and Civil Partnership Regulations 2005 (SI 2005/3229), reg.142 (December 5, 2005).

(2003 c.1, s.219)

Extra amounts to be added in connection with a car

219.—(1) The provisions of this section apply for the purposes of section 218(1) in the case of a tax year in which a car is made available as mentioned in section 114(1) (cars, vans and related benefits) by reason of the employment.

(2) Subsection (3) applies if in the tax year—
(a) an alternative to the benefit of the car is offered; and
(b) the amount that would be earnings within Chapter 1 of this Part if the benefit of the car were to be determined by reference to the alternative offered exceeds the benefit code earnings (see subsection (4)).

(3) The amount of the excess is an extra amount to be added under step 2 in section 218(1).

(4) For the purposes of subsection (2) "the benefit code earnings" is the total for the year of—
(a) the cash equivalent of the benefit of the car (calculated in accordance with Chapter 6 of this Part); and
(b) the cash equivalent (calculated in accordance with that chapter) of the benefit of any fuel provided for the car by reason of the employment.

(5) Subsection (6) applies if in the tax year there would be an amount of general earnings consisting of—
(a) earnings within Chapter 1 of this Part; or
(b) an amount treated as earnings from the employment under c.3 (expenses payments) or Chapter 4 (vouchers and credit-tokens) of this Part, if section 239 or 269 (exemptions in respect of payments or benefits connected with taxable cars, etc.) did not apply to the discharge of a liability, or to a payment or benefit, in connection with the car.

(6) The amount of general earnings mentioned in subsection (5) is an extra amount to be added under step 2 in section 218(1).

(7) Section 216(1) (provisions not applicable to lower-paid employment) is to be disregarded for the purpose of determining any amount under this section.

1.455

PART 4

EMPLOYMENT INCOME: EXEMPTIONS

CHAPTER 11

MISCELLANEOUS EXEMPTIONS

[Childcare: exemption for employer-provided care

318.—(1) No liability to income tax arises [1 . . .] in respect of the provision for an employee of care for a child if conditions A to D are met. For the meaning of "care" and "child", see section 318B.

(2) If those conditions are met only as respects part of the provision, no such liability arises in respect of that part.

1.456

(3) Condition A is that the child—
(a) is a child or stepchild of the employee and is maintained (wholly or partly) at the employee's expense,
(b) is resident with the employee, or
(c) is a person in respect of whom the employee has parental responsibility.

For the meaning of "parental responsibility", see section 318B.

(4) Condition B is that—
(a) the premises on which the care is provided are not used wholly or mainly as a private dwelling, and
(b) any applicable registration requirement is met.

(5) The registration requirements are—
(a) in England and Wales, that under Part 10A of the Children Act 1989;
(b) in Scotland, that under Part 1 or 2 of the Regulation of Care (Scotland) Act 2001;
(c) in Northern Ireland, that under Part XI of the Children (Northern Ireland) Order 1995.

(6) Condition C is that—
(a) the premises on which the care is provided are made available by the scheme employer alone, or
(b) the partnership requirements are met.

In this section "scheme employer" means the employer operating the scheme under which the care is provided (who need not be the employer of the employee).

(7) The partnership requirements are—
(a) that the care is provided under arrangements made by persons who include the scheme employer,
(b) that the premises on which it is provided are made available by one or more of those persons, and
(c) that under the arrangements the scheme employer is wholly or partly responsible for financing and managing the provision of the care.

(8) Condition D is that the care is provided under a scheme that is open—
(a) to the scheme employer's employees generally, or
(b) generally to those of the scheme employer's employees at a particular location,

and that the employee to whom it is provided is either an employee of the scheme employer or is an employee working at the same location as employees of the scheme employer to whom the scheme is open.

AMENDMENT

1. FA 2005, s.16(5) (April 6, 2005).

GENERAL NOTE

1.457   This and the following sections are inserted into ITEPA by Finance Act 2004, s.78 and Sch.13 from April 6, 2005. They are set out here as they are seen by some as alternatives to the provision of childcare in return for payment by an individual using the childcare element of WTC.

Section 318C was amended from April 6, 2007 for England by the Income Tax (Qualifying Child Care) Regulations 2007 (SI 2007/849). The formal introduction to the regulations makes clear that these changes were made in coordination with changes to the equivalent regulations for the childcare element of tax credits.

(2003 c.1, s.318A)

Childcare: limited exemption for other care

318A.—(1) If conditions A to C are met in relation to the provision for an employee of care for a [¹ child—
  (a) no liability to income tax arises under section 62 (general definition of earnings), and
  (b) liability] to income tax by virtue of Chapter 10 of Part 3 (taxable benefits: residual liability to charge) arises only in respect of so much of the cash equivalent of the benefit as exceeds the exempt amount.
For the meaning of "care" and "child", see section 318B.
  (2) If those conditions are met only as respects part of the provision, subsection (1) applies in respect of that part.
  (3) Condition A is that the child—
  (a) is a child or stepchild of the employee and is maintained (wholly or partly) at the employee's expense, or
  (b) is resident with the employee and is a person in respect of whom the employee has parental responsibility.
For the meaning of "parental responsibility", see section 318B.
  (4) Condition B is that the care is qualifying child care.
For the meaning of "qualifying child care", see section 318C.
  (5) Condition C is that the care is provided under a scheme that is open—
  (a) to the employer's employees generally, or
  (b) generally to those at a particular location.
  (6) For the purposes of this section the "exempt amount", in any tax year, is [²£55] for each qualifying week in that year.
  (7) A "qualifying week" means a tax week in which care is provided for a child in circumstances in which conditions A to C are met. "tax week" means one of the successive periods in a tax year beginning with the first day of that year and every seventh day after that (so that the last day of a tax year or, in the case of a tax year ending in a leap year, the last two days is treated as a separate week).
  (8) An employee is only entitled to one exempt amount even if care is provided for more than one child. It does not matter that another person may also be entitled to an exempt amount in respect of the same child.
  (9) An employee is not entitled to an exempt amount under this section and under section 270A (limited exemption for childcare vouchers) in respect of the same tax week.

1.458

AMENDMENTS

  1. FA 2005, s.16(6) (April 6, 2005).
  2. Income Tax (Exempt Amounts for Childcare Vouchers and for Employer Contracted Childcare) Order 2006 (SI 2006/882), art.2 (April 6, 2006).

Childcare: meaning of "care", "child" and "parental responsibility"

318B.—(1) For the purposes of sections 318 and 318A (exemptions for employer-provided or employer-contracted childcare) "care" means any form of care or supervised activity that is not provided in the course of the child's compulsory education.
  (2) For the purposes of those sections a person is a "child" until the last day of the week in which falls the 1st September following the child's fifteenth birthday (or sixteenth birthday if the child is disabled).

1.459

(3) For the purposes of subsection (2) a child is disabled if—
(a) a disability living allowance is payable in respect of him, has ceased to be payable solely because he is a patient,
(b) he—
  (i) is registered as blind in a register compiled by a local authority under section 29 of the National Assistance Act 1948 (welfare services),
  (ii) has been certified as blind in Scotland and in consequence is registered as blind in a register maintained by or on behalf of a local authority in Scotland, or
  (iii) has been certified as blind in Northern Ireland and in consequence is registered as blind in a register maintained by or on behalf of a Health and Social Services Board, or
(c) he ceased to be so registered as blind within the previous 28 weeks.

(4) In subsection (3)(a) "patient" means a person (other than a person who is serving a sentence imposed by a court in a prison or custody institution or, in Scotland, a young offenders' institution) who is regarded as receiving free in-patient treatment within the meaning of the Social Security (Hospital In-Patients) Regulations 1975 or the Social Security (Hospital In-Patients) Regulations (Northern Ireland) 1975.

(5) For the purposes of sections 318 and 318A "parental responsibility" means all the rights, duties, powers, and authority which by law a parent of a child has in relation to the child and the child's property.

(6) In this section and section 318C "local authority" means—
(a) in relation to England, the council of a county or district, a metropolitan district, a London Borough, the Common Council of the City of London or the Council of the Isles of Scilly;
(b) in relation to Wales, the council of a county or county borough;
(c) in relation to Scotland, a council constituted under section 2 of the Local Government etc. (Scotland) Act 1994.

Childcare: meaning of "qualifying child care"

318C.—(1) For the purposes of section 318A "qualifying child care" means registered or approved care within any of subsections (2) to (6) below that is not excluded by subsection (7) below.

(2) Care provided for a child in England is registered or approved care if it is provided—
(a) by a person registered under Part 10A of the Children Act 1989,
(b) by a school or establishment that does not need to be registered under that Part to provide the care because of an exemption under paragraph 1 or 2 of Schedule 9A to that Act,
(c) in the case of care provided for a child out of school hours [4. . .], by a school on school premises or by a local authority, [4. . .]
(d) by a child care provider approved by an organisation accredited under the Tax Credit (New Category of Child Care Provider) Regulations 1999,
(e) [3. . .], [4. . .]
[1(ea) by a child care provider approved in accordance with the Tax Credits (Approval of Child Care Providers) Scheme 2005, [4. . .]]
[4(eb) by a child care provider registered under the Childcare (Voluntary Registration) Regulations 2007, or]

(2003 c.1, s.318C)

(f) by a domiciliary care worker under the Domiciliary Care Agencies Regulations 2002.

(3) Care provided for a child in Wales is registered or approved care if it is provided—

(a) by a person registered under Part 10A of the Children Act 1989,

(b) by a school or establishment that does not need to be registered under that Part to provide the care because of an exemption under paragraph 1 or 2 of Schedule 9A to that Act,

(c) in the case of care provided for a child out of school hours [4. . .], by a school on school premises or by a local authority, [4. . .]

(d) by a child care provider approved by an organisation accredited under the Tax Credit (New Category of Child Care Provider) Regulations 1999, [1[4 ...]

(e) by a domiciliary care worker under the Domiciliary Care Agencies (Wales) Regulations 2004] [4. . .]

[4(f) by a child care provider approved under the Tax Credits (Approval of Child Care Providers) (Wales) Scheme 2007.]

(4) Care provided for a child in Scotland is registered or approved care if it is provided—

(a) by a person in circumstances where the care service provided by him—
  (i) consists of child minding or of day care of children within the meaning of section 2 of the Regulation of Care (Scotland) Act 2001, and
  (ii) is registered under Part 1 of that Act, or

(b) by a local authority in circumstances where the care service provided by the local authority—
  (i) consists of child minding or of day care of children within the meaning of section 2 of the Regulation of Care (Scotland) 2001, and
  (ii) is registered under Part 2 of that Act.

(5) Care provided for a child in Northern Ireland is registered approved care if it is provided—

(a) by a person registered under Part XI of the Children (Northern Ireland) Order 1995, or

(b) by an institution or establishment that does not need to be registered under that Part to provide the care because of an exemption under Article 121 of that Order, or

(c) in the case of care provided for a child out of school hours [4. . .], by a school on school premises or by an education and library board or an HSS trust.

(6) Care provided for a child outside the United Kingdom is registered or approved child care if it is provided by a child care provider approved by an organisation accredited under the Tax Credit (New Category of Child Care Provider) Regulations 2002.

(7) Child care is excluded from section 318A—

(a) if it is provided by the partner of the employee in question, [4. . .]

(b) if it is provided by a relative of the child wholly or mainly in the child's home or (if different) the home of a person having parental responsibility for the child, [1, or

(c) in the case of care falling within subsection (2)(ea) [4or (3)(f)] if—
  (i) it is provided wholly or mainly in the home of a relative of the child, and

(ii) the provider usually provides care there solely in respect of one or more children to whom the provider is a relative.]

(8) In subsection (7)—

"partner" means one of a [² couple (within the meaning given by section 137(1) of Social Security Contributions and Benefits Act 1992 or section 133(1) of SSCB(NI)A 1992)]; and

"relative" means parent, grandparent, aunt, uncle, brother or sister, whether by blood, half blood or marriage [²or civil partnership].]

[¹(9) In subsection (7)(c), "relative in relation to a child, also includes—
(a) a local authority foster parent in relation to the child,
(b) a foster parent with whom the child has been placed by a voluntary organisation,
(c) a person who fosters the child privately (within the meaning of section 66 of the Children Act 1989, or
(d) a step-parent of the child.]

AMENDMENTS

1. Section 318C Income Tax (Earnings and Pensions) Act 2003 (Amendment) Regulations 2005 (SI 2005/770), regs 1(1), 3(b) and 4–6 (April 6, 2005).
2. Tax and Civil Partnership Regulations 2005 (SI 2005/3229), reg.144 (December 5, 2005).
3. Section 318C Income Tax (Earnings and Pensions) Act 2003 (Amendment) Regulations 2005 (SI 2005/770), regs 1(2) and 3(a) (January 1, 2006).
4. Income Tax (Qualifying Child Care) Regulations 2007 (SI 2007/849), reg.2 (April 6, 2007).

PART 5

EMPLOYMENT INCOME: DEDUCTIONS ALLOWED FROM EARNINGS

CHAPTER 1

DEDUCTIONS ALLOWED FROM EARNINGS: GENERAL RULES

Introduction

Deductions from earnings: general

327.—(1) This Part provides for deductions that are allowed from the taxable earnings from an employment in a tax year in calculating the net taxable earnings from the employment in the tax year for the purposes of Part II (see section 11(1)).

(2) In this Part, unless otherwise indicated by the context—
(a) references to the earnings from which deductions are allowed are references to the taxable earnings mentioned in subsection (1); and
(b) references to the tax year are references to the tax year mentioned there.

(3) The deductions for which this Part provides are those allowed under—

Chapter 2 (deductions for employee's expenses);
Chapter 3 (deductions from benefits code earnings);
Chapter 4 (fixed allowances for employee's expenses);
Chapter 5 (deductions for earnings representing benefits or reimbursed expenses); and
Chapter 6 (deductions from seafarers' earnings).

(4) Further provision about deductions from earnings is made in—

section 232 (giving effect to mileage allowance relief);

section 619 of ICTA (contributions under retirement annuity contracts); and

section 262 of CAA 2001 (capital allowances to be given effect by treating them as deductions from earnings).

(5) Further provision about deductions from income including earnings is made in—

Part 12 (payroll giving);

section 592(7) of ICTA (contributions to exempt approved schemes); and

section 594(1) of ICTA (contributions to exempt statutory schemes).

General rules

The income from which deductions may be made

328.—(1) The general rule is that deductions under this Part are allowed— 1.462
(a) from any earnings from the employment in question; and
(b) not from earnings from any other employment. This is subject to subsections (2) to (4).

(2) Deductions under section 351 (expenses of ministers of religion) are allowed from earnings from any employment as a minister of a religious denomination.

(3) Deductions under section 368 (fixed sum deductions from earnings payable out of public revenue) are allowed only from earnings payable out of the public revenue.

(4) Deductions limited to specified earnings (see subsection (5)) are allowed—
(a) only from earnings from the employment that are taxable earnings under certain of the charging provisions of Chapters 4 and 5 of Part 2; and
(b) not from other earnings from it.

(5) "Deductions limited to specified earnings" are deductions under—

sections 336 to 342 (deductions from earnings charged on receipt: see sections 335(2) and 354);

section 353 (deductions from earnings charged on remittance);

sections 370 to 374 (travel deductions from earnings charged on receipt), and Chapter 6 of this Part (deductions from seafarers' earnings: see section 378(1)(a)).

Deductions from earnings not to exceed earnings

329.—(1) The amount of a deduction allowed under this Part may not exceed the earnings from which it is deductible. 1.463

If two or more deductions allowed under this Part are deductible from the same earnings, the amounts deductible may not in aggregate exceed those earnings.

(3) If deductions allowed otherwise than under this Part fall to be allowed from the same earnings as amounts deductible under this Part, the amounts deductible under this Part may not exceed the earnings remaining after the other deductions.

(4) Subsections (1) and (2) do not apply to a deduction under section 351 (expenses of ministers of religion), and subsection (3) applies as if such a deduction were allowed otherwise than under this Part.

(5) This section is to be disregarded for the purposes of the deductibility provisions (see section 332).

(6) See also section 380 of ICTA (which provides that where a loss in an employment is sustained, relief may be given against other income).

Prevention of double deductions

1.464   330.—(1) A deduction from earnings under this Part is not allowed more than once in respect of the same costs or expenses.

(2) If apart from this subsection—
   (a) a deduction would be allowed under Chapter 4 of this Part (fixed allowances for employee's expenses) for a sum fixed by reference to any kind of expenses; and
   (b) the employee would be entitled under another provision to a deduction for an amount paid in respect of the same kind of expenses;
only one of those deductions is allowed.

Order for making deductions

1.465   331.—(1) This Part needs to be read with section 835(3) and (4) of ICTA (general rule that deductions are to be allowed in the order resulting in the greatest reduction of liability to income tax).

In the case of deductions under this Part, the general rule in that section is subject to—
   (a) section 23(3) (which requires certain deductions to be made in order to establish "chargeable overseas earnings"); and
   (b) section 381 (which requires deductions under other provisions to be taken into account before deductions under Chapter 6 of this Part (seafarers)).

Meaning of "the deductibility provisions"

1.466   332. For the purposes of this Part, "the deductibility provisions" means the following provisions (which refer to amounts or expenses that would be deductible if they were incurred and paid by an employee)—
   the definition of "business travel" in section 171(1) (definitions for Chapter 6 of Part 3),
   section 179(6) (exception for certain advances for necessary expenses),
   the definition of "business travel" in section 236(1) (definitions for Chapter 2 of Part 4),
   section 240(1)(c) and (5) (exemption of incidental overnight expenses and benefits),
   section 252(3) (exception from exemption of work-related training provision for non-deductible travel expenses),

section 257(3) (exception from exemption for individual learning account training provision for non-deductible travel expenses),
section 305(5) (offshore oil and gas workers: mainland transfers),
section 310(6)(b) (counselling and other outplacement services),
section 311(5)(b) (retraining courses),
section 361(b) (scope of Chapter 3 of this Part: cost of benefits deductible as if paid by employee),
section 362(1)(c) and (2)(b) (deductions where non-cash voucher provided),
section 363(1)(b) and (2)(b) (deductions where credit-token provided),
section 364(1)(b) and (2) (deductions where living accommodation provided),
section 365(1)(b) and (2) (deductions where employment-related benefit provided).

CHAPTER 2

DEDUCTIONS FOR EMPLOYEE'S EXPENSES

Introduction

Scope of this chapter: expenses paid by the employee

333.—(1) A deduction from a person's earnings for an amount is allowed under the following provisions of this chapter only if the amount— 1.467
  (a) is paid by the person; or
  (b) is paid on the person's behalf by someone else and is included in the earnings.
(2) In the following provisions of this chapter, in relation to a deduction from a person's earnings, references to the person paying an amount include references to the amount being paid on the person's behalf by someone else if or to the extent that the amount is included in the earnings.
(3) Subsection (1)(b) does not apply to the deductions under—
  (a) section 351(2) and (3) (expenses of ministers of religion); and
  (b) section 355 (deductions for corresponding payments by non-domiciled employees with foreign employers),
and subsection (2) does not apply in the case of those deductions.
(4) Chapter 3 of this Part provides for deductions where—
  (a) a person's earnings include an amount treated as earnings under Chapter 4, 5 or 10 of Part 3 (taxable benefits: vouchers, etc., living accommodation and residual liability to charge); and
  (b) an amount in respect of the benefit in question would be deductible under this chapter if the person had incurred and paid it.

Effect of reimbursement, etc.

334.—(1) For the purposes of this chapter, a person may be regarded as paying an amount despite— 1.468
  (a) its reimbursement; or
  (b) any other payment from another person in respect of the amount.

233

(2) But where a reimbursement or such other payment is made in respect of an amount, a deduction for the amount is allowed under the following provisions of this chapter only if or to the extent that—
  (a) the reimbursement; or
  (b) so much of the other payment as relates to the amount; is included in the person's earnings.
(3) *Omitted.*

General rule for deduction of employee's expenses

Deductions for expenses: the general rule

1.469 **336.**—(1) The general rule is that a deduction from earnings is allowed-for an amount if—
  (a) the employee is obliged to incur and pay it as holder of the employment; and
  (b) the amount is incurred wholly, exclusively and necessarily in the performance of the duties of the employment.
(2) The following provisions of this chapter contain additional rules allowing deductions for particular kinds of expenses and rules preventing particular kinds of deductions.
(3) No deduction is allowed under this section for an amount that is deductible under sections 337 to 342 (travel expenses).

Travel expenses

Travel in performance of duties

1.470 **337.**—(1) A deduction from earnings is allowed for travel expenses if—
  (a) the employee is obliged to incur and pay them as holder of the employment; and
  (b) the expenses are necessarily incurred on travelling in the performance of the duties of the employment.
(2) This section needs to be read with section 359 (disallowance of travel expenses: mileage allowances and reliefs).

Travel for necessary attendance

1.471 **338.**—(1) A deduction from earnings is allowed for travel expenses if—
  (a) the employee is obliged to incur and pay them as holder of the employment; and
  (b) the expenses are attributable to the employee's necessary attendance at any place in the performance of the duties of the employment.
(2) Subsection (1) does not apply to the expenses of ordinary commuting or travel between any two places that is for practical purposes substantially ordinary commuting.
(3) In this section, "ordinary commuting" means travel between—

(a) the employee's home and a permanent workplace; or
(b) a place that is not a workplace and a permanent workplace.

(4) Subsection (1) does not apply to the expenses of private travel or travel between any two places that is for practical purposes substantially private travel.

(5) In subsection (4), "private travel" means travel between—
(a) the employee's home and a place that is not a workplace; or
(b) two places neither of which is a workplace.

(6) This section needs to be read with section 359 (disallowance of travel expenses: mileage allowances and reliefs).

Meaning of "workplace" and "permanent workplace"

339.—(1) In this Part, "workplace", in relation to an employment, means a place at which the employee's attendance is necessary in the performance of the duties of the employment.

(2) In this Part "permanent workplace", in relation to an employment, means a place which—
(a) the employee regularly attends in the performance of the duties of the employment; and
(b) is not a temporary workplace.
This is subject to subsections (4) and (8).

(3) In subsection (2), "temporary workplace", in relation to an employment, means a place which the employee attends in the performance of the duties of the employment—
(a) for the purpose of performing a task of limited duration; or
(b) for some other temporary purpose.
This is subject to subsections (4) and (5).

(4) A place which the employee regularly attends in the performance of the duties of the employment is treated as a permanent workplace and not a temporary workplace if—
(a) it forms the base from which those duties are performed; or
(b) the tasks to be carried out in the performance of those duties are allocated there.

(5) A place is not regarded as a temporary workplace if the employee's attendance is—
(a) in the course of a period of continuous work at that place—
   (i) lasting more than 24 months, or
   (ii) comprising all or almost all of the period for which the employee is likely to hold the employment; or
(b) at a time when it is reasonable to assume that it will be in the course of such a period.

(6) For the purposes of subsection (5), a period is a period of continuous work at a place if over the period the duties of the employment are performed to a significant extent at the place.

(7) An actual or contemplated modification of the place at which duties are performed is to be disregarded for the purposes of subsections (5) and (6) if it does not, or would not, have any substantial effect on the employee's journey, or expenses of travelling, to and from the place where they are performed.

(8) An employee is treated as having a permanent workplace consisting of an area if—

(a) the duties of the employment are defined by reference to an area (whether or not they also require attendance at places outside it);
(b) in the performance of those duties the employee attends different places within the area;
(c) none of the places the employee attends in the performance of those duties is a permanent workplace; and
(d) the area would be a permanent workplace if subsections (2), (3), (5), (6) and (7) referred to the area where they refer to a place.

PART 9

PENSION INCOME

CHAPTER 1

INTRODUCTION

Structure of Part 9

1.473   **565.** The structure of this Part is as follows—
Chapter 2—
(a) imposes the charge to tax on pension income; and
(b) provides for deductions to be made from the amount of income chargeable;
Chapters 3 to 15 set out the types of income which are charged to tax under this Part and, for each type of income, identify—
(a) the amount of income chargeable to tax for a tax year; and
(b) the person liable to pay any tax charged;
[¹ Chapter 15A makes provision about exemptions and charges in relation to lump sums under registered pension schemes; Chapters 17 and 18 deal with other] exemptions from the charge to tax (whether under this Part or any other provision).

AMENDMENT

1. FA 2004, Sch.31, para.2 (April 6, 2006).

GENERAL NOTE

1.474   In the ICTA, most forms of pension income were taxed in the same way as emoluments under Schedule E. One of the main changes undertaken as part of the Tax Law Rewrite Project was to extract all the various provisions relating to the taxation of pensions of employees and office holders (both in the United Kingdom and overseas) and put them together in a single code. That code now forms Pt 9 of ITEPA 2003. It contains all the primary legislation from the ICTA 1988 and successive Finance Acts on the taxation of state pensions (including social security pensions), occupational pensions payable to officeholders and employees, and personal pensions. It recognises the division between earnings and pensions, but prevails over the separate provisions in Pt 10, dealing with social security income. It includes provisions in separate chapters dealing with foreign pension income.

The Tax Credits (Definition and Calculation of Income) Regulations 2002 rely on that code for defining pension income for the purposes of the tax credits income test.

(2003 c.1, s.565)

This selection of sections sets out the key provisions from that code. Foreign pensions, are not, however, included as pension income for tax credits purposes, so no reference is made to those chapters of Pt 9 of ITEPA. Foreign pensions should therefore be considered as foreign income, not pension income, for tax credits purposes. The Finance Act 2004, Pt 4 and associated Schedules, completely replaced the taxation rules applying to pensions and pension funds (though not the taxation of ordinary social security pension income) with a fundamentally new regime. As part of that, much of Pt 9 of this Act was repealed and replaced. But the new provisions are beyond the scope of this volume and are omitted, and only the general rules and social security pension rules are included.

Chapter 2

Tax on Pension Income

Nature of charge to tax on pension income and relevant definitions

566.—(1) The charge to tax on pension income under this Part is a charge to tax on that income excluding any exempt income.   1.475

(2) "Pension income" means the pensions, annuities and income of other types to which the provisions listed in subsection (4) apply.

This definition applies for the purposes of the Tax Acts.

(3) "Exempt income" means pension income on which no liability to income tax arises as a result of any provision of Chapters 16 to 18 of this Part.

This definition applies for the purposes of this Part.

(4) These are the provisions referred to in subsection (2)—

Provision	*Income*	*Chapter (of this Part)*
Section 569	United Kingdom pensions	Chapter 3
Section 573	Foreign pensions	Chapter 4
Section 577	United Kingdom social security pensions	Chapter 5
[¹ Section 579A	Pensions under registered pension schemes]	Chapter 5A
[¹ . . .]		
[¹ . . .]		
[¹ . . .]		
[¹ . . .]		
[¹ . . .]		
[¹ . . .]		
Section 609	Annuities for the benefit of dependants	Chapter 10
Section 610	Annuities under sponsored superannuation schemes	Chapter 10
Section 611	Annuities in recognition of another's services	Chapter 10
Section 615	Certain overseas government pensions paid in the United Kingdom	Chapter 11

Income Tax (Earnings and Pensions) Act 2003

Provision	Income	Chapter (of this Part)
Section 619 [¹ . . .]	The House of Commons Members' Fund	Chapter 12
Section 629	Pre-1973 pensions paid under OPA 1973	Chapter 14
Section 633	Voluntary annual payments	Chapter 15
[¹ Section 636B	Pensions treated as arising from payment of trivial commutation lump sums and winding-up lump sums under registered pension schemes]	Chapter 15A
[¹ Section 636C	Pensions treated as arising from payment of trivial commutation lump sum death benefits and winding-up lump sum death benefits under registered pension schemes]	Chapter 15A

AMENDMENT

1. FA 2004, Sch.31 para.3 (April 6, 2006).

Amount charged to tax

1.476   **567.**—(1) The amount of pension income which is charged to tax under this Part for a particular tax year is as follows.

(2) In relation to each pension, annuity or other item of pension income, the amount charged to tax is the "net taxable pension income" for the tax year.

(3) The net taxable pension income for a pension, annuity or other item of pension income for a tax year is given by the formula—

$$\frac{TPI}{DPI}$$

where—
TPI means the amount of taxable pension income for that pension, annuity or item of pension income for that year (see subsection (4)); and
DPI means the total amount of any deductions allowed from the pension, annuity or item of pension income (see subsection (5)).

(4) For the purposes of this Act—
(a) the amount of taxable pension income for a pension, annuity or other item of pension income for a tax year is determined in accordance with Chapters 13 to [¹15A] of this Part (which contain provisions relating to this amount for each type of pension income); and
(b) in determining the amount of taxable pension income for a pension, annuity or other item of pension income, any exempt income is to be excluded.

(5) The deductions allowed from a pension, annuity or other item of pension income are those under—
section 617 (10% deduction from an overseas government pension to which section 615 applies);
Part 22 (payroll giving).

238

AMENDMENT

1. FA 2004, Sch.31 para.4 (April 6, 2006).

Person liable for tax

568. For the provision identifying which person is liable for any tax charged under this Part on a pension, annuity or other item of pension income, see Chapters 3 to 15.

CHAPTER 3

UNITED KINGDOM PENSIONS: GENERAL RULES

United Kingdom pensions

569.—(1) This section applies to any pension paid by or on behalf of a person who is in the United Kingdom.
(2) But this section does not apply to a pension if any provision of Chapters 5 to 14 of this Part applies to it.
(3) For pensions paid by or on behalf of a person who is outside the United Kingdom, see Chapter 4 of this Part.

GENERAL NOTE

Most UK pensions will be caught under the new Chapter 5A, ss.579A–D, taxing pensions under registered pension schemes on the same basis as ss.571 and 572 below, subject to the exceptions for some lump sums and other payments detailed in the FA 2004 provisions. The detailed new provisions are omitted as they will be of limited importance to most tax credit claimants.

"Pension": interpretation

570. In this chapter, "pension" includes a pension which is paid voluntarily or is capable of being discontinued.

Taxable pension income

571. If section 569 applies, the taxable pension income for a tax year is the full amount of the pension accruing in that year, irrespective of when any amount is actually paid.

Person liable for tax

572. If section 569 applies, the person liable for any tax charged under this Part is the person receiving or entitled to the pension.

CHAPTER 5

UNITED KINGDOM SOCIAL SECURITY PENSIONS

United Kingdom social security pensions

577.—(1) This section applies to—
 the state pension;
 graduated retirement benefit;

industrial death benefit;
widowed mother's allowance;
widowed parent's allowance; and
widow's pension.

[1 (1A) But this section does not apply to any social security pension lump sum (within the meaning of section 7 of F(No.2)A 2005).]

(2) In this section—
"state pension" means any pension payable under—
 (a) section 44, 48A, 48B, 48BB, 51 or 78 of SSCBA 1992; or
 (b) section 44, 48, 48B, 48BB, 51 or 78 of SSCB(NI)A 1992;
"graduated retirement benefit" means any benefit payable under—
 (a) section 36 or 37 of the National Insurance Act 1965 (Chapter 51); or
 (b) section 35 or 36 of the National Insurance Act (Northern Ireland) 1966 (Chapter 6 (NI));
"industrial death benefit" means any benefit payable under—
 (a) section 94 of, and Part 6 of Schedule 7 to SSCBA 1992; or
 (b) section 94 of, and Part 6 of Schedule 7 to SSCB(NI)A 1992;
"widowed mother's allowance" means any allowance payable under—
 (a) section 37 of SSCBA 1992; or
 (b) section 37 of SSCB(NI)A 1992;
"widowed parent's allowance" means any allowance payable under—
 (a) section 39A of SSCBA 1992; or
 (b) section 39A of SSCB(NI)A 1992;
"widow's pension" means any pension payable under—
 (a) section 38 of SSCBA 1992; or
 (b) section 38 of SSCB(NI)A 1992.

(3) In subsection (2), in paragraph (b) of the definition of state pension, the reference to section 48 of SSCB(NI)A 1992 is a reference to the section 48 inserted by paragraph 3(1) of Schedule 2 to the Pensions (Northern Ireland) Order 1995 (SI 1995/3213 (NI 22)).

(4) Chapter 17 of this Part provides a partial exemption for a pension to which this section applies in respect of any part of the pension which is attributable to an increase in respect of a child (see section 645).

AMENDMENT

1. F(2)A 2005, s.10(2) (July 20, 2005).

GENERAL NOTE

1.484 This section lists forms of state pension to be brought within the charge to tax in s.578. The exclusion of social security lump sums is because separate provision is made to tax those sums in ss.7 and 8 of F(No.2)A 2005. Lump sums are treated as income for income tax purposes but are given special treatment to prevent the recipients losing their age-related personal allowances. They are also to be taxed regardless of the residence or domicile of the recipients. Section 8 sets the date on which the tax charge is to apply. It is usually in the tax year in which the right to the pension starts.

Taxable pension income

1.485 **578.** If section 577 applies, the taxable pension income for a tax year is the full amount of the pension, benefit or allowance accruing in that year, irrespective of when any amount is actually paid.

Person liable for tax

579. If section 577 applies, the person liable for any tax charged under this Part is the person receiving or entitled to the pension, benefit or allowance.

1.486

PART 10

SOCIAL SECURITY INCOME

CHAPTER 1

INTRODUCTION

Structure of Part 10

655.—(1) The structure of this Part is as follows—
Chapter 2—
  (a) imposes the charge to tax on social security income; and
  (b) provides for deductions to be made from the amount of income chargeable;
Chapter 3 sets out the United Kingdom social security benefits which are charged to tax under this Part and identifies—
  (a) the amount of income chargeable to tax for a tax year; and
  (b) the person liable to pay any tax charged;
Chapters 4 and 5 deal with exemptions from the charge to tax on United Kingdom social security benefits (whether under this Part or any other provision);
Chapters 6 and 7 make provisions about foreign benefits.
(2) For other provisions about the taxation of social security benefits see—
section 151 of FA 1996 (power for the Treasury to make orders about the taxation of benefits payable under Government pilot schemes);
section 84 of FA 2000 (exemption of payments under New Deal 50plus);
section 85 of FA 2000 (exemption of payments under Employment Zones programme).
(3) For the charge to tax on social security pensions see Part 9.

1.487

GENERAL NOTE

"Social security income" is another head of charge created from the Tax Law Rewrite Project. Previously, all forms of social security income were fitted, sometimes somewhat uncomfortably, in Schedule E. Part 10 of ITEPA is now used to codify the charge to income tax on all forms of social security benefit and allowance other than pensions. As this section records, Pt 9 deals with pensions. The opportunity has also been taken to set out the various provisions in a systematic way, and dealing with both United Kingdom and other benefits.

Because of the general importance of these provisions for social security purposes, the Part has been included more extensively than other Parts of ITEPA for social security purposes, and not restricted to those relevant only for tax credits purposes.

Subsection (1) is a signposting provision.

Subsection (2) lists the three sections (not included in this volume) under which limited exemptions from income tax may be made for social security benefits. The

1.488

power under s.151 of FA 1996 is used to exempt payments made to claimants under pilot schemes. For current exemptions under this provision, see: the Taxation of Benefits under Government Pilot Schemes (Return to Work Credit and Employment Retention and Advancements Schemes) Order 2003 (SI 2003/2339) (not reproduced in this volume), in effect from October 1, 2003; and the Taxation of Benefits under government Pilot Schemes (Working Neighbourhoods Pilot and In Work Credit) Order 2004 (SI 2004/575), in effect from April 6, 2004. Both orders fully exempt payments under those schemes form income tax. The reference to s.84 of FA 2000 is superseded from the start of working tax credit as New Deal payments have now been incorporated into the credit.

Subsection (3) is a signpost to s.577 (United Kingdom social security pensions).

CHAPTER 2

TAX ON SOCIAL SECURITY INCOME

Nature of charge to tax on social security income

1.489   **656.**—(1) The charge to tax on social security income is a charge to tax on that income excluding any exempt income.

(2) "Exempt income" is social security income on which no liability to income tax arises as a result of any provision of Chapters 4, 5 or 7 of this Part.

This definition applies for the purposes of this Part.

DEFINITIONS

"social security income"—see s.657(2).
"tax"—see ICTA, s.832(3).

GENERAL NOTE

1.490   This section is extremely important because it emphasises that the exemption provisions in the Part override the charges to tax. In practice, very few forms of UK social security income are chargeable to tax under this Part. Remember that pensions are chargeable under Pt 9. In most cases statutory sick pay and the other statutory payments are chargeable to tax under Pt 2. Any such payments that are not caught by Pt 3 are caught by a "safety net" provision in this Part.

Provisions in this part exempt child benefit, guardian's allowance and child tax credit and so exclude all child-related benefit. Other provisions exempt all disablement related benefits payable to the disabled or incapacitated individual.

Tax credits under the TCA 2002 are themselves exempted from tax under this Part. So are the local government benefits of housing benefit and council tax benefit. Benefits received from the national health service, in kind or in cash, are not income for any income tax purpose, and are not affected by this Part. Welfare benefits in kind, such as welfare foods and publicly provided accommodation, are not within the definition of "social security income" in s.657 and so are excluded from the charge to tax under this Part. They do not fall to be charged under any other part of ITEPA 2003.

This leaves income tax payable only on some parts of some payments of income support, jobseeker's allowance and incapacity benefit, and also on bereavement allowance (in practice linked with pension entitlements but not a form of pension income) and carer's allowance (formerly known as invalid care allowance).

The equivalent approach is adopted for foreign social security payments.

(2003 c.1, s.657)

Meaning of "social security income", "taxable benefits", etc.

657.—(1) This section defines—
"social security income" for the purposes of the Tax Acts; and
"taxable benefits", "Table A" and "Table B" for the purposes of this Part.
(2) "Social security income" means—
(a) the United Kingdom social security benefits listed in Table A;
(b) the United Kingdom social security benefits listed in Table B;
(c) the foreign benefits to which section 678 applies; and
(d) the foreign benefits to which section 681(2) applies.
(3) "Taxable benefits" means—
(a) the United Kingdom social security benefits listed in Table A; and
(b) the foreign benefits to which section 678 applies.
(4) Subsections (2) and (3) are subject to section 660(2).
(5) "Table A" means Table A in section 660.
(6) "Table B" means Table B in section 677.

GENERAL NOTE

This section defines the term "social security income" used in s.656, which is the charging section. Unless a form of income is within the scope of the definition in subs.(2), it is not liable to income tax under this Part. Nor will it be liable to income tax under any other general provision in the Taxes Act. However, the interpretation of the scope of this section must take into account the very wide provisions dealing with benefits provided by employers in Pt 2, which in practice covers some forms of payments that are in principle social security payments (such as statutory maternity pay). Further, anything that is a "pension" is taxable under Pt 9 and is removed from this Part by s.655(3).

Amount charged to tax

658.—(1) The amount of social security income which is charged to tax under this Part for a particular tax year is as follows.
(2) In relation to a taxable benefit, the amount charged to tax is the net taxable social security income for the tax year.
(3) The net taxable social security income for a taxable benefit for a tax year is given by the formula—
$$TSSI - PGD$$
where—
TSSI means the amount of taxable social security income for that benefit for that year (see subsections (4) to (7)); and
PGD means the amount of the deduction (if any) allowed from the benefit under Part 12 (payroll giving).
(4) In relation to bereavement allowance, carer's allowance, incapacity benefit and income support (which are listed in Table A), the amount of taxable social security income is determined in accordance with section 661.
(5) In relation to any other benefit listed in Table A, the amount of taxable social security income is the amount of the benefit that falls to be charged to tax.
(6) In relation to foreign benefits to which section 678 applies, the amount of taxable social security income is determined in accordance with section 679.
(7) In determining for the purposes of this Act the amount of taxable social security income, any exempt income is to be excluded.

DEFINITIONS

"exempt income"—see s.656(2).
"social security income"—see s.657(2).
"tax year"—see s.721(1).
"taxable benefit"—see s.657(3).

Person liable for tax

1.494   659. The person liable for any tax charged under this Part is identified in—
(a) section 662 (United Kingdom benefits); or
(b) section 680 (foreign benefits).

CHAPTER 3

TAXABLE UNITED KINGDOM SOCIAL SECURITY BENEFITS

Taxable benefits: United Kingdom benefits—Table A

1.495   660. (1) This is Table A:

1.496   TABLE A

                        TAXABLE UK BENEFITS

Social security benefit	Payable under	
Bereavement allowance	SSCBA 1992	Section 39B
	SSCB(NI)A 1992	Section 39B
Carer's allowance	SSCBA 1992	Section 70
	SSCB(NI)A 1992	Section 70
Incapacity benefit	SSCBA 1992	Section 30A(1) or (5), 40 or 41
	SSCB(NI)A 1992	Section 30A(1) or (5), 40 or 41
Income support	SSCBA 1992	Section 123
	SSCB(NI)A 1992	Section 124
Jobseeker's allowance	JSA 1995	Section 1
	JS(NI)O 1995	Article 3
Statutory adoption pay	SSCBA 1992	Section 171ZL
	Any provision made for Northern Ireland which corresponds to section 171ZL of SSCBA 1992	
Statutory maternity pay	SSCBA 1992	Section 164
	SSCB(NI)A 1992	Section 160
Statutory paternity pay	SSCBA 1992	Section 171ZA or 171ZB

(2003 c.1, s.660)

Social security benefit	Payable under	
	Any provision made for Northern Ireland which corresponds to section 171ZA or section 171ZB of SSCBA 1992	
Statutory sick pay	SSCBA 1992	Section 151
	SSCB(NI)A 1992	Section 147.

(2) A benefit listed below is not "social security income" or a "taxable benefit" if it is charged to tax under another Part of this Act—
statutory adoption pay;
statutory maternity pay;
statutory paternity pay;
statutory sick pay.

DEFINITIONS

"social security income"—see s.657(2).
"taxable benefit"—see s.657(3).

GENERAL NOTE

For the full forms of the abbreviations in Table A see Sch.1, Pt 1 to the Act. Subsection (2) provides that a charge to tax under Pt 2 of the Act takes priority over this Part, but the section ensures that all statutory payments are taxable.

1.497

Taxable social security income

661.—(1) This section applies in relation to each of the following taxable benefits listed in Table A—
bereavement allowance;
carer's allowance;
incapacity benefit; and
income support.
(2) The amount of taxable social security income for a taxable benefit for a tax year is the full amount of the benefit accruing in the tax year irrespective of when any amount is actually paid.

1.498

DEFINITIONS

"tax year"—see s.721(1).
"taxable benefit"—see s.675(3).

GENERAL NOTE

This is a new rule under ITEPA introduced to replace both inconsistent previous legislation and a lack of legislation, the rules apparently varying from one benefit to another for no good reason. "Accrued" is standard income tax language not normally used for social security purposes. In social security terms, as the section makes clear, it means payable not paid.

1.499

Person liable for tax

662.—The person liable for any tax charged under this Part on a taxable benefit listed in Table A is the person receiving or entitled to the benefit.

1.500

GENERAL NOTE

1.501 "Received or entitled" is familiar income tax language applied to social security income by ITEPA in place of a lack of any clear previous rule. As the wording indicates it covers both the person for whom the benefit is payable and the person who actually receives it. The wording will make joint claimants for jobseeker's allowance both liable for any income tax on the allowance. It is, however, not clear how this is applied to appointees appointed to receive income support for a claimant.

CHAPTER 4

TAXABLE UK SOCIAL SECURITY BENEFITS: EXEMPTIONS

Incapacity benefit

Long-term incapacity benefit: previous entitlement to invalidity benefit

1.502 **663.**—(1) No liability to income tax arises on long-term incapacity benefit if—
  (a) a person is entitled to the benefit for a day of incapacity for work which falls in a period of incapacity for work which is treated for the purposes of that benefit as having begun before April 13, 1995; and
  (b) the part of that period which is treated as having fallen before that date includes a day for which that person was entitled to invalidity benefit.

(2) In this section—
"invalidity benefit" means invalidity benefit under—
  (a) Part 2 of SSCBA 1992; or
  (b) Part 2 of SSCB(NI)A 1992;
"long-term incapacity benefit" means incapacity benefit payable under—
  (a) section 30A(5), 40 or 41 of SSCBA 1992; or
  (b) section 30A(5), 40 or 41 of SSCB(NI)A 1992.

Short-term incapacity benefit not payable at the higher rate

1.503 **664.**—(1) No liability to income tax arises on short-term incapacity benefit unless it is payable at the higher rate.

(2) In this section—
  (a) "short-term incapacity benefit" means incapacity benefit payable under—
    (i) section 30A(1) of SSCBA 1992; or
    (ii) section 30A(1) of SSCB(NI)A 1992;
  (b) the reference to short-term incapacity benefit payable at the higher rate is to be construed in accordance with—
    (i) section 30B of SSCBA 1992; or
    (ii) section 30B of SSCB(NI)A 1992.

Income support

Exempt unless payable to member of couple involved in trade dispute

665.—(1) No liability to income tax arises on income support unless—
(a) the income support is payable to one member of [¹a couple] ("the claimant"); and
(b) section 126 of SSCBA 1992 or section 125 of SSCB(NI)A 1992 (trade disputes) applies to the claimant but not to the other member of the couple.

(2) In this section, [¹couple has] the same meaning as in section 137(1) of SSCBA 1992 or section 133(1) of SSCB(NI)A 1992.

AMENDMENT

1. Tax and Civil Partnership Regulations 2005 (SI 2005/3229), reg.163 (December 5, 2005).

Child maintenance bonus

666. No liability to income tax arises on a part of income support which is attributable to a child maintenance bonus (within the meaning of section 10 of CSA 1995 or Article 4 of CS(NI)O 1995).

Amounts in excess of taxable maximum

667.—(1) If the amount of income support paid to a person ("the claimant") for a week or a part of a week exceeds the claimant's taxable maximum for that period, no liability to income tax arises on the excess.

(2) The claimant's taxable maximum for a period is determined under section 668.

Taxable maximum

668.—(1) A claimant's taxable maximum for a week is determined under this subsection if the applicable amount for the purpose of calculating the income support consists only of an amount in respect of the relevant couple.

The taxable maximum is equal to one half of the applicable amount.

(2) A claimant's taxable maximum for a week is determined under this subsection if the applicable amount includes amounts that are not in respect of the relevant couple.

The taxable maximum is equal to one half of the amount which is included in the applicable amount in respect of the relevant couple.

(3) A claimant's taxable maximum for a part of a week is determined as follows—

Step 1

Assume that the income support is paid to the claimant for the whole of, rather than part of, the week.

Step 2

Determine under subsection (1) or (2) what the claimant's taxable maximum for that week would be on that assumption.

Step 3

Determine the claimant's taxable maximum for the part of the week using this formula—

$$\frac{N}{7} \times TMW$$

where—
N is the number of days in the part of the week for which the claimant is actually paid the income support; and
TMW is the taxable maximum for the whole week determined under step 2.

Interpretations

1.508   **669.**—(1) In section 668, except in relation to Northern Ireland—
"applicable amount" means the amount prescribed in relation to income support in regulations made under section 135 of SSCBA 1992;
[¹ "couple" has the same meaning as in section 137(1) of Social Security Contributions and Benefits Act 1992;]
(2) In section 668, in relation to Northern Ireland—
"applicable amount" means the amount prescribed in relation to income support in regulations made under section 131 of SSCB(NI)A 1992;
[¹ "couple" has the same meaning as in section 133(1) of Social Security Contributions and Benefits (Northern Ireland) Act 1992;]
(3) In section 668, "relevant couple", in relation to a claimant, means the [¹ . . .] couple of which the claimant is a member.

AMENDMENT

1. Tax and Civil Partnership Regulations 2005 (SI 2005/3229), reg.164 (December 5, 2005).

GENERAL NOTE

1.509   This section applies the definition of "couple" adopted for social security purposes following the replacement by the Civil Partnership Act 2004 of all references to "married couples" and "unmarried couples" for the purposes of ITEPA. The effect is to impose the social security meaning of "couple" on the income tax treatment of social security income, and not the income tax definition.

Jobseeker's allowance

Child maintenance bonus

1.510   **670.** No liability to income tax arises on a part of a jobseeker's allowance which is attributable to a child maintenance bonus (within the meaning of section 10 of CSA 1995 or Article 4 of CS(NI)O 1995).

(2003 c.1, s.671)

Amounts in excess of taxable maximum

671.—(1) If the amount of jobseeker's allowance paid to a person ("the claimant") for a week or a part of a week exceeds the claimant's taxable maximum for that period, no liability to income tax arises on the excess.

(2) The claimant's taxable maximum for a period is determined under sections 672 to 674.

Taxable maximum: general

672.—(1) A claimant's taxable maximum for a week is determined—
  (a) under section 673, if the claimant is paid an income-based jobseeker's allowance for that week; or
  (b) under section 674, if the claimant is paid a contribution-based jobseeker's allowance for that week.

(2) A claimant's taxable maximum for a part of a week is determined as follows—

Step 1

Assume that the jobseeker's allowance is paid to the claimant for the whole of, rather than part of, the week.

Step 2

Determine under section 673 or 674 what the claimant's taxable maximum for that week would be on that assumption.

Step 3

Determine the claimant's taxable maximum for the part of the week using this formula—

$$\frac{N}{7} \times TMW$$

where—
  N is the number of days in the part of the week for which the claimant is actually paid the jobseeker's allowance; and
  TMW is the taxable maximum for the whole week determined under step 2.

Taxable maximum: income-based jobseeker's allowance

673.—(1) A claimant's taxable maximum for a week is determined under this section if—
  (a) the claimant is paid an income-based jobseeker's allowance for that week, or
  (b) the claimant is assumed under section 672(2) to be paid an income-based jobseeker's allowance for that week.

(2) If the claimant is not a member of a [1 . . .] couple, the claimant's taxable maximum for the week is equal to the age-related amount which would be applicable to the claimant if a contribution based jobseeker's allowance were payable to the claimant for that week.

(3) If the claimant is a member of a [1 . . .] couple, the claimant's taxable maximum for the week is equal to the portion of the applicable amount which is included in the jobseeker's allowance in respect of the couple for that week.

(4) But if—

249

(a) the claimant is a member of a [¹ . . .] couple; and
(b) the other member of that couple is prevented by section 14 of JSA 1995 or Article 16 of JS(NI)O 1995 (trade disputes) from being entitled to a jobseeker's allowance;

the claimant's taxable maximum for that week is equal to half the portion of the applicable amount which is included in the jobseeker's allowance in respect of the couple for that week.

AMENDMENT

1. Tax and Civil Partnership Regulations 2005 (SI 2005/3229), reg.165 (December 5, 2005).

Taxable maximum: contribution-based jobseeker's allowance

1.514   **674.**—(1) A claimant's taxable maximum for a week is determined under this section if—
(a) the claimant is paid a contribution-based jobseeker's allowance for that week; or
(b) the claimant is assumed under section 672(2) to be paid a contribution-based jobseeker's allowance for that week.

(2) If the claimant is not a member of a [¹ . . .] couple, the claimant's taxable maximum for the week is equal to the age-related amount which is applicable to the claimant for that week.

(3) If the claimant is a member of a [¹ . . .] couple, the claimant's taxable maximum for the week is equal to the portion of the applicable amount which would be included in the jobseeker's allowance in respect of the couple if an income-based jobseeker's allowance were payable to the claimant for that week.

AMENDMENT

1. Tax and Civil Partnership Regulations 2005 (SI 2005/3229), reg.166 (December 5, 2005).

Interpretation

1.515   **675.**—(1) In sections 671 to 674, except in relation to Northern Ireland—
"age-related amount" and "applicable amount" mean the amounts determined as such in accordance with regulations made under section 4 of JSA 1995;
"contribution-based jobseeker's allowance" and "income-based jobseeker's allowance" have the same meaning as in section 1(4) of JSA 1995;
"married couple" and "unmarried couple" have the same meaning as in section 35(1) of JSA 1995.

(2) In sections 671 to 674, in relation to Northern Ireland—
"age-related amount" and "applicable amount" mean the amounts determined as such in accordance with regulations made under Article 6 of JS(NI)O 1995;
"contribution-based jobseeker's allowance" and "income-based jobseeker's allowance" have the same meaning as in Article 3(4) of JS(NI)O 1995;
[¹"couple" has the same meaning as in s.351(1) of JSA 1995.]

AMENDMENT

1. Tax and Civil Partnership Regulations 2005 (SI 2005/3229), reg.167 (December 5, 2005).

(2003 c.1, s.676)

Increases in respect of children

Increases in respect of children

676. No liability to income tax arises on a part of a taxable benefit listed in Table A which is attributable to an increase in respect of a child.

GENERAL NOTE

This is superseded from 2003–04 for incapacity benefit and carer's allowance, by the introduction of child tax credit, which is exempt from tax.

CHAPTER 5

UK SOCIAL SECURITY BENEFITS WHOLLY EXEMPT FROM INCOME TAX

UK social security benefits wholly exempt from tax: Table B

677.—(1) No liability to income tax arises on the United Kingdom social security benefits listed in Table B.

TABLE B—PART I

BENEFITS PAYABLE UNDER PRIMARY LEGISLATION

Social security benefit	Payable under
Attendance allowance	SSCBA 1992, s.64
	SSCB(NI)A 1992, s.64
Back to work bonus	JSA 1995, s.26
	JS(NI)O 1995, Article 28
Bereavement payment	SSCBA 1992, s.36
	SSCB(NI)A 1992, s.36
Child benefit	SSCBA 1992, s.141
	SSCB(NI)A 1992, s.137
Child's special allowance	SSCBA 1992, s.56
	SSCB(NI)A 1992, s.56
Child tax credit	TCA 2002, Part 1
Council tax benefit	SSCBA 1992, s.131
Disability living allowance	SSCBA 1992, s.71
	SSCB(NI)A 1992, s.71
Guardian's allowance	SSCBA 1992, s.77
	SSCB(NI)A 1992, s.77
Housing benefit	SSCBA 1992, s.130
	SCB(NI)A 1992, s.129
Industrial injuries benefit (apart from industrial death benefit)	SSCBA 1992, s.94
	SSCB(NI)A 1992, s.94

Social security benefit	Payable under
Pensioner's Christmas bonus	SSCBA 1992, s.148
	SSCB(NI)A 1992, s.144
Payments out of the social fund	SSCBA 1992, s.138
	SSCB(NI)A 1992, s.134
Severe disablement allowance	SSCBA 1992, s.68
	SSCB(NI)A 1992, s.68
State maternity allowance	SSCBA 1992, s.35
	SSCB(NI)A 1992, s.35
State pension credit	SPCA 2002, s.1
	SPCA(NI) 2002, s.1
Working tax credit	TCA 2002, Part 1

TABLE B—PART 2

1.520 BENEFITS PAYABLE UNDER REGULATIONS

Social security benefit	Payable under regulations made under
Payments to reduce under-occupation by housing benefit claimants	WRPA 1999, s.79
	WRP(NI)O 1999, Article 70

(2) Industrial death benefit is charged to tax under Part 9 (see section 577).

(3) In this section "industrial death benefit" means any benefit payable under—
  (a) section 94 of, and Part 6 of Schedule 7 to, SSCBA 1992; or
  (b) section 94 of, and Part 6 of Schedule 7 to, SSCB(NI)A 1992.

CHAPTER 6

TAXABLE FOREIGN BENEFITS

Taxable benefits: foreign benefits

1.521 **678.**—(1) This section applies to any benefit which is payable under the law of a country or territory outside the United Kingdom if—
  (a) it is substantially similar in character to a benefit listed in Table A, and
  (b) it is payable to a person resident in the United Kingdom.

(2) But this section does not apply to a benefit which is charged to tax under Pt 9 (pension income).

GENERAL NOTE

1.522 This is a new statutory provision in ITEPA. Until its enactment, the Inland Revenue refrained from taxing foreign social security benefits on the basis of an extra-statutory concession. The only real problem area is the divide between social security income, exempt under this provision, and pension income, taxed under Pt 9.

Taxable social security income

679.—(1) If section 678 applies, the taxable social security income for a taxable benefit for a tax year is the amount on which tax would be chargeable if the benefit were chargeable to tax under Case V of Schedule D (see in particular the provisions of ICTA listed in subsection (2)).

(2) Those provisions of ICTA are—
(a) sections 65 and 68 (calculation of the amount of the income on which tax is to be charged in the tax year);
(b) section 584 (relief for unremittable overseas income);
(c) section 585 (relief on delayed remittances).

Person liable for tax

680.—The person liable for any tax charged under this Part on a benefit to which section 678 applies is the person receiving or entitled to the benefit.

PART 13

SUPPLEMENTARY PROVISIONS

Interpretation

Other definitions

721.—(1) In this Act—
"cash voucher" has the same meaning as in Chapter 4 of Part 3 (see section 75);
"credit-token" has the same meaning as in Chapter 4 of Part 3 (see section 92);
"foreign employer" means—
(a) in the case of an employee resident in the United Kingdom, an individual, partnership or body of persons resident outside the United Kingdom and not resident in the United Kingdom or the Republic of Ireland, and
(b) in the case of an employee not resident in the United Kingdom, an individual, partnership or body of persons resident outside and not resident in the United Kingdom;
"non-cash voucher" has the same meaning as in Chapter 4 of Part 3 (see section 84);
"the normal self-assessment filing date", in relation to a tax year, means the 31st January following the tax year;
"personal representatives", in relation to a person who has died, means—

(a) in the United Kingdom, persons responsible for administering the estate of the deceased; and
(b) in a country or territory outside the United Kingdom, those persons having functions under its law equivalent to those of administering the estate of the deceased;

"tax year" means, in relation to income tax, a year for which any Act provides for income tax to be charged; and

"the tax year 2003–04" means the tax year beginning on 6th April, 2003 (and any corresponding expression in which two years are similarly mentioned is to be read in the same way).

(2) In the application of this Act to Scotland, "assignment" means an assignation.

(3) Any reference in this Act to being domiciled in the United Kingdom is to be read as a reference to being domiciled in any part of the United Kingdom.

(4) For the purposes of this Act the following are members of a person's family—
(a) the person's spouse [¹or civil partner],
(b) the person's children and their spouses [¹or civil partners],
(c) the person's parents, and
(d) the person's dependants.

(5) For the purposes of this Act the following are members of a person's family or household—
(a) members of the person's family,
(b) the person's domestic staff, and
(c) the person's guests.

(6) The following provisions (which relate to the legal equality of illegitimate children) are to be disregarded in interpreting references in this Act to a child or children—
(a) section 1 of the Family Law Reform Act 1987 (Chapter 42),
(b) the paragraph inserted in Schedule 1 to the Interpretation Act 1978 (Chapter 30) by paragraph 73 of Schedule 2 to the 1987 Act,
(c) section 1(2) of the Law Reform (Parent and Child) (Scotland) Act 1986 (Chapter 9),
(d) Article 155 of the Children (Northern Ireland) Order 1995 (SI 1995 No.755 (NI 2)).

(7) In the employment income Parts any reference to earnings which is not limited by the context—
(a) to earnings within Chapter 1 of Part 3, or
(b) to any other particular description of earnings; includes a reference to any amount treated as earnings by any of the provisions mentioned in section 7(5) (meaning of "employment income" etc.).

AMENDMENT

1. Tax and Civil Partnership Regulations 2005 (SI 2005/3229), reg.168 (December 5, 2005).

GENERAL NOTE

See further for definitions ITA 2007, Sch.4 of which (not included in this work) includes an index of terms defined for the Income Tax Acts.

(2004 c.6)

Child Trust Funds Act 2004

(2004 c.6)

ARRANGEMENT OF SECTIONS

Introductory

1. Child trust funds
2. Eligible children
3. Requirements to be satisfied
4. Inalienability

Opening and transfers

5. Opening by responsible person or child
6. Opening by Inland Revenue
7. Transfers

Contributions and subscriptions

8. Initial contribution by Inland Revenue
9. Supplementary contribution by Inland Revenue
10. Further contributions by Inland Revenue
11. Recouping Inland Revenue contributions
12. Subscription limits

Tax

13. Relief from income tax and capital gains tax
14. Insurance companies and friendly societies

Information etc.

15. Information from account providers etc.
16. Information about children in care of authority
17. Use of information
18. Disclosure of information

Payments after death

19. Payments after death of child

Penalties

20. Penalties
21. Decisions, appeals, mitigation and recovery

Appeals

22. Rights of appeal
23. Exercise of rights of appeal
24. Temporary modifications

Supplementary

25. Northern Ireland
26. Money
27. Commencement
28. Regulations and orders
29. Interpretation
30. Extent
31. Short title

An Act to make provision about child trust funds and for connected purposes.

INTRODUCTION AND GENERAL NOTE

1.528   The basic scheme of the Child Trust Fund Act 2004 is that all children in the United Kingdom born after August 31, 2002 will have a "child trust fund account", which will in effect be a universal savings policy. Building societies and other financial institutions will have to seek HMRC approval to be an "account provider" under this Act. It is a condition of approval that account providers offer equity-based stakeholder accounts (although cash accounts may also be offered). The Treasury will provide an initial endowment of £250 for each child at the point when the account is opened, or £500 in the case of children in low income families or those who are being looked after by a local authority. The Government's intention is to make a further endowment (of an amount as yet unspecified) when every child reaches the age of seven. Parents, relatives and family friends will be able to make further contributions to the child trust fund account at any time. The minimum such investment is £10 (unless the account provider permits smaller deposits) and the maximum annual aggregate contribution by family and friends is £1,200. Subject to some very narrow exceptions, no withdrawals will be permitted until the child is 18, so that the child reaches adulthood with a "nest-egg" which can then be re-invested, spent on education or setting up in business, etc. The cost of the scheme is estimated to be in the order of £4 billion over 18 years.

The Government has set out four objectives for child trust fund accounts. These are "to help people understand the benefits of saving and investing; to encourage parents and children to develop the savings habit; to ensure that all children have a financial asset at the start of their adult life; and to build on financial education and help people make better financial choices throughout their lives" (Lord McIntosh of Haringey, Parliamentary Under-Secretary of State, *Hansard* HL Debates Vol.658, col.351, February 26, 2004). The Child Trust Fund Act may thus be seen as an example of the Government's commitment to the principles of "asset-based welfare" and "progressive universalism". It will, of course, take some time to assess whether the scheme fulfils its goals.

The idea of child trust funds emerged through the work of the Institute of Public Policy Research (IPPR) in 2000 and was canvassed by the Treasury in its consultation paper *Savings and Assets for All*, The Modernisation of Britain's Tax and benefit System, Number 8 (April 2001). The proposal also appeared in the Labour Party's 2001 general election manifesto. The Government set out its proposals more fully in the Treasury papers *Delivering Saving and Assets* (November 2001) and especially in *Detailed proposals for the Child Trust Fund* (October 2003). The House of Commons

(2004 c.6)

Treasury Committee has issued a report supporting the initiative, although making some further recommendations: *Child Trusts Funds* (Second Report of Session 2003–04, HC 86), and see further *Government Response to the Committee's Second Report on Child Trust Funds* (HC 86) (First Special Report of Session 2003–04, HC 387). In the 2003 Budget the Chancellor of the Exchequer announced the Government's intention that the scheme should commence operations in April 2005 (but confirming that it would also apply to all children born after August 31, 2002). For a full analysis of the scheme, see N. Wikeley, "Child Trust Funds—asset-based welfare or a recipe for increased inequality?" (2004) 11 *Journal of Social Security Law* 189.

Section 1 of the Act explains what is meant by a child trust fund, whilst s.2 defines the crucial qualifying category of "eligible children". The nature and management of child trust fund accounts is governed by s.3. Funds in such accounts are inalienable (s.4). The expectation is that accounts will be opened by a "responsible person", typically a parent, or by the child (in the case of a child aged 16 or over, who, for example, has just arrived in the country); see s.5, which makes the award of child benefit the trigger for entitlement to a child trust fund account. The fallback position is that HMRC will open an account (s.6) for any child lacking a child trust fund. Accounts may be transferred to another financial institution (s.7). The initial and supplementary Treasury contributions to be made at the opening of the account are governed by ss.8 and 9. All children receive the initial contribution under s.8 (children being looked after by local authorities receive a higher rate) and children in low income families qualify for the supplementary contribution under s.9. Section 10 makes provision for further Treasury contributions to be made at some late date (or dates). Where Treasury contributions have been credited in error, they can be recovered by virtue of s.11. Section 12 deals with contributions by parents and others to child trust fund accounts. The tax position is covered by ss.13 and 14 while ss.15–18 make provision for the disclosure and exchange of information relating to accounts. Section 19 makes special provision for the situation where a payment is due after a child beneficiary has died. Sections 20 and 21 concern penalties and ss.22–24 set out appeal rights. The remaining sections of the Act are supplementary in nature (ss.25–31). The first regulations under the Act are the Child Trust Funds Regulations 2004 (SI 2004/1450).

Commencement and extent

The supplementary provisions in this Act (ss.25–31) came into force on Royal Assent (May 13, 2004): see s.27. Various procedural provisions came into force on January 1, 2005: Child Trust Funds Act 2004 (Commencement No.1) Order 2004 (SI 2004/2422, C.103). The remainder of the Act was brought into force by the Child Trust Funds Act 2004 (Commencement No.2) Order 200 (SI 2004/3369, C.158). The Child Trust Funds Regulations 2004 (SI 2004/1450) came into force for various purposes on January 1, 2005 and for remaining purposes on "the appointed day", namely April 6, 2005. The Act extends to the whole of the United Kingdom (see further ss.25 and 30).

1.529

Introductory

Child trust funds

1.—(1) This Act makes provision about child trust funds and related matters.

(2) In this Act "child trust fund" means an account which—
(a) is held by a child who is or has been an eligible child (see section 2),
(b) satisfies the requirements imposed by and by virtue of this Act (see section 3), and

1.530

(c) has been opened in accordance with this Act (see sections 5 and 6).

(3) The matters dealt with by and under this Act are to be under the care and management of the Inland Revenue.

DEFINITIONS

"child": s.29.
"child trust fund": subs.(2) and s.29.
"eligible child": ss.2 and 29.
"Inland Revenue": s.29.

GENERAL NOTE

1.531　This is a genuinely introductory section.

Subs.(1)
1.532　This provision is no more illuminating than the long title to the Act.

Subs.(2)
1.533　This is more helpful than subs.(1) in that it stipulates the three defining characteristics of a child trust fund—that it be held by an "eligible child" (see s.2), that it meet the statutory requirements (see s.3) and that it has been opened in the appropriate manner (either by a "responsible person" (typically a parent) under s.5 or by HMRC under s.6).

Subs.(3)
1.534　This reflects a standard principle of revenue law (see e.g. Taxes Management Act 1970, s.1(1)), namely that such matters are "under the care and management of the Inland Revenue". The only difference is one of nomenclature in the reference to "the Inland Revenue", rather than the more usual statutory formula of "the Board". This principle enables the Revenue to apply the law with a degree of administrative flexibility in appropriate cases. For example, in the context of taxation, this is the basis upon which the Revenue has traditionally promulgated extra-statutory concessions and reached settlements in disputes with taxpayers.

Eligible children

1.535　**2.**—(1) For the purposes of this Act a child is an "eligible child" if the child was born after 31st August 2002 and either—
  (a) a person is entitled to child benefit in respect of the child, or
  (b) entitlement to child benefit in respect of the child is excluded by the provisions specified in subsection (2)(a) or (b) (children in care of authority),
but subject as follows.

(2) The provisions referred to in subsection (1)(b) are—
  (a) paragraph 1(c) of Schedule 9 to the Social Security Contributions and Benefits Act 1992 (c. 4) and regulations made under it, and
  (b) paragraph 1(1)(f) of Schedule 9 to the Social Security Contributions and Benefits (Northern Ireland) Act 1992 (c. 7) and regulations made under it.

(3) Where entitlement to child benefit in respect of a child is excluded because of a directly applicable Community provision or an international agreement, subsection (1) applies as if that exclusion did not apply.

(4) Where a person is entitled to child benefit in respect of a child only because of a directly applicable Community provision or an international agreement, subsection (1) applies as if the person were not so entitled.

(2004 c.6, s.2)

(5) A child who—
(a) does not have the right of abode in the United Kingdom within the meaning given by section 2 of the Immigration Act 1971 (c.77),
(b) is not a qualified person, or a family member of a qualified person, within the meaning of the Immigration (European Economic Area) Regulations 2000 (SI 2000/2326), and
(c) is not settled in the United Kingdom within the meaning given by section 33(2A) of the Immigration Act 1971,

is not an eligible child.

(6) A person is not to be regarded for the purposes of subsection (1)(a) as entitled to child benefit in respect of a child (otherwise than by virtue of subsection (3)) unless it has been decided in accordance with—
(a) Chapter 2 of Part 1 of the Social Security Act 1998 (c.14), or
(b) Chapter 2 of Part 2 of the Social Security (Northern Ireland) Order 1998 (SI 1998/1506 (N.I. 10)),

that the person is so entitled (and that decision has not been overturned).

(7) Regulations may amend subsection (1) by substituting for the reference to 31st August 2002 a reference to an earlier date.

DEFINITIONS

"child": s.29.
"eligible child": subs.(1) and s.29.

GENERAL NOTE

This section defines the concept of an "eligible child", the first of the three fundamental features of a child trust fund. The basic definition is to be found in subs.(1), as expanded by subs.(2) to deal with the special case of children being looked after by a local authority. Cases that have an international dimension are covered by subss.(3)–(5). Subsection (6) acts as a definition provision for subs.(1). Subsection (7) provides the potential for the scope of the child trust fund scheme to be expanded to include children born before the cut-off date for eligibility for a child trust fund.

1.536

Subs.(1)
This is the core definition of who is an "eligible child". There are two basic rules. First, the child must have been born *after* August 31, 2002. This date was chosen to align entitlement with the school year (at least in England and Wales), so that all pupils in any given school year (after that date) would be equally entitled. There will, however, be cases involving siblings born either side of the eligibility date: for the position of children who were born *before* September 1, 2002, see further the annotation to subs.(7) below. Secondly, *either* someone must be entitled to child benefit for that child (subs.(1)(a); see further subs.(6)) *or* that person's entitlement is excluded because the child is being looked after by a local authority (subss.(1)(b) and (2)). Thus in general terms, and subject to that special case, entitlement to child benefit is employed as a gateway to eligibility for a child trust fund. Subsections (3)–(5) make special provision for cases with an international dimension.

1.537

Subs.(2)
The case of a child being looked after by a local authority is the only situation in which the rule requiring that a person be entitled to child benefit in respect of the child is waived. It must follow that in the other situations set out in SSCBA 1992, Sch.9 in which there is no entitlement to child benefit, there is also no entitlement to a child trust fund. These situations include children in detention (but

1.538

259

see s.10(4)) and married children. These exclusions, and particularly the latter, may eventually affect a handful of children who are recent immigrants to the country.

Subs. (3)

1.539
There will be some children who live in the United Kingdom but in respect of whom child benefit is not payable because of EU law or an international agreement. This provision ensures that such children remain eligible for a child trust fund, notwithstanding that there is no child benefit entitlement. In practice this will apply most commonly to some children who live in Northern Ireland but whose parent works in the Republic of Ireland. In such circumstances, under the EU rules governing the benefit entitlement of migrant workers in Reg.1408/71, child benefit is payable by the benefit authorities in the Republic. As a result of subs.(3) such children are eligible for a child trust fund account.

Subs. (4)

1.540
This deals with the converse position to that in subs.(3). In some cases there is entitlement to child benefit in the United Kingdom solely because of provisions in EU law or under an international agreement. This would apply where a citizen and resident of the Republic of Ireland (or any other EU country) works in the United Kingdom but his or her child lives in the Republic (or other Member State). Again, EU Reg.1408/71 provides that child benefit is payable by the UK authorities. This subsection provides, in effect, that children in this type of case will not be eligible for a child trust fund, unless and until they come to live in the United Kingdom. This will affect fewer than 500 children, according to official estimates. The Government's view is that "there is no case for the UK Government to pay endowments to encourage saving for and by children whose ties are not within the UK" (Ruth Kelly, Financial Secretary to the Treasury, Standing Committee A, col.37, January 6, 2004). This exclusion will not affect the special position of the children of Crown servants, such as army personnel, who are entitled to child benefit when stationed overseas by virtue of a provision in purely domestic law (Child Benefit (General) Regulations 2003 (SI 2003/493), reg.30).

However, it is by no means certain that the exclusion of EU workers (and their children) who reside outside but work in the United Kingdom from eligibility for child trust funds will necessarily survive legal scrutiny. There are a number of different avenues that might be used to challenge the validity of this provision under EU law. First, Art.7(2) of EU Reg.1612/68 requires migrant workers to "enjoy the same social and tax advantages as national workers". Of course, one of the fundamental purposes of the child trust fund scheme is to benefit the child, rather than the worker. Indeed, case law demonstrates that the social or tax advantage must be of some direct or indirect benefit to the worker, and not just to a family member (*Centre Public d'Aide Sociale de Courcelles v Lebon*, Case 316/85 [1987] E.C.R. 2811). But a broad view of the child trust fund scheme might meet this requirement. See also *Reina v Landeskredit Bank Baden-Württemberg* Case 65/81 [1982] E.C.R. 33, in which it was held that an interest-free childbirth loan granted only to German nationals was a social advantage within Art.7(2), and so could not be denied to an Italian couple. Although one of the fundamental objectives of the child trust fund scheme is to benefit *children* by providing them with a valuable asset on attaining their majority, it does not require too much imagination to see that the scheme might be construed as being of indirect benefit to the parent-worker. Yet the other purposes of the 2004 Act are framed in terms of domestic policy imperatives, such as encouraging savings, which have no obvious linkage with the free movement of labour. Moreover, the ECJ jurisprudence on Art.7(2) has typically concerned the migrant worker who goes both to work and *live* in another Member State, and not merely to work there; the problem identified in this note is strictly more to do with 'frontier workers' than 'migrant workers'. On that basis, therefore, it may be that s.2(4) is not inconsistent with Art.7(2) of Reg.1612/68.

(2004 c.6, s.2)

Even if this is the case, it does not necessarily follow that s.2(4) is EU-compliant. A second or parallel type of challenge might be made on the basis that the child trust fund scheme confers a "family benefit" within the scope of Reg.1408/71, so bringing into play Ch.7 of that Regulation. Given the linkage between entitlement to child benefit and eligibility for a child trust fund payment, this point is at least arguable. Finally, there remains the broader argument that this provision in the 2004 Act is in breach of Art.12 of the Treaty itself, which prohibits "within the scope of the application" of the Treaty "any discrimination on grounds of nationality". Section 2(4) makes no express reference to parents' nationality, but may be viewed as indirectly discriminatory in that its operation in practice is more likely to affect (for example) Irish nationals than British nationals. In recent years the ECJ has demonstrated greater willingness to invoke Art.12 for the benefit of citizens of other Member States (see e.g. *Martínez Sala* [1998] E.C.R. I-2691 and Case C-184/99 *Grzelcyk* [2001] E.C.R. I-6193; Case C-209/03 *R. (Bidar) v Ealing London Borough Council* [2005] 2 W.L.R. 1078; and see further R.C.A. White, 'Residence, Benefit Entitlement and Community Law' [2005] 12 *Journal of Social Security Law* 10).

Subs.(5)
A child who lacks a proper immigration status cannot be an "eligible child". This covers children who, under the Immigration Act 1971, have no right of abode or are not settled in the United Kingdom. However, subs.(5)(c) may give rise to problems in the context of citizenship of the Union: see further the Advocate General's Opinion of November 11, 2004 in Case C-209/03 *Bidar*. Children who have no entitlement to reside in the United Kingdom under EEA law are likewise excluded from access to the child trust fund scheme.

1.541

Subs.(6)
This provides that a person is not entitled to child benefit until a decision has been taken to that effect (and has not been overturned) in accordance with the SSA Act 1998 (or its Northern Ireland equivalent). Thus HMRC decision to award child benefit acts as the trigger for eligibility for a child trust fund account.

1.542

Subs.(7)
For the purposes of this Act a child is only an "eligible child" if born after August 31, 2002 (subs.(1)). This provision allows the Government to use secondary legislation to substitute an earlier date for the purpose of this definition, thus bringing older children into the scope of eligibility for a child trust fund account. Any such regulations will be subject to the affirmative procedure (see ss.28(5) and (6)(a)). There are obvious arguments in favour of such an extension in the scheme's remit, not least the fact that under the present arrangements older siblings are potentially disadvantaged, and parents and other relatives may naturally wish to make equal financial provision for children in the same family, irrespective of the accident of their date of birth. This problem will be particularly acute in the case of twins, and doubtless there are some, where one twin was born in the last minutes of August 31, 2002 and the younger twin arrived after the stroke of midnight. The House of Commons Treasury Committee recommended that consideration be given to extending the scope of the children to include older children, but without government endowments (*Second Report*, Session 2003–04, HC 86, para.34). The Government has not, to date, demonstrated any significant enthusiasm for extending the remit of the scheme even in this limited way, noting the potential burden on providers.

1.543

Requirements to be satisfied

3.—(1) A child trust fund may be held only with a person (referred to in this Act as an "account provider") who has been approved by the Inland Revenue in accordance with regulations.

1.544

(2) An account is not a child trust fund unless it is an account of one of the descriptions prescribed by regulations.

(3) The provision which may be made by regulations under subsection (1) includes making approval of an account provider dependent on the person undertaking to provide accounts of such of the descriptions for which provision is made by regulations under subsection (2) as is prescribed by the regulations.

(4) The terms of a child trust fund must—
(a) secure that it is held in the name of a child,
(b) secure that the child is beneficially entitled to the investments under it,
(c) secure that all income and gains arising on investments under it constitute investments under it,
(d) prevent withdrawals from it except as permitted by regulations, and
(e) provide that instructions may be given to the account provider with respect to its management only by the person who has the authority to manage it.

(5) Regulations may impose other requirements which must be satisfied in relation to child trust funds.

(6) The person who has the authority to manage a child trust fund held by a child—
(a) if the child is 16 or over, is the child, and
(b) if the child is under 16, is the person who has that authority by virtue of subsection (7) (but subject to subsection (10)).

(7) If there is one person who is a responsible person in relation to the child, that person has that authority; and if there is more than one person who is such a person, which of them has that authority is to be determined in accordance with regulations.

(8) For the purposes of this Act a person is a responsible person in relation to a child under 16 if the person has parental responsibility in relation to the child and is not—
(a) a local authority or, in Northern Ireland, an authority within the meaning of the Children (Northern Ireland) Order 1995 (S.I. 1995/755 (N.I. 2)), or
(b) a person under 16.

(9) "Parental responsibility" means—
(a) parental responsibility within the meaning of the Children Act 1989 (c.41) or the Children (Northern Ireland) Order 1995, or
(b) parental responsibilities within the meaning of the Children (Scotland) Act 1995 (c.36).

(10) Regulations may provide that, in circumstances prescribed by the regulations, the person who has the authority to manage a child trust fund held by a child under 16 is to be the Official Solicitor (in England and Wales or Northern Ireland) or the Accountant of Court (in Scotland).

(11) A person who has the authority to manage a child trust fund by virtue of subsection (10) is entitled to give any instructions to the account provider with respect to its management which appear to the person who has that authority to be for the benefit of the child.

(12) Where a contract is entered into by or on behalf of a child who is 16 or over in connection with a child trust fund—
(a) held by the child, or

(2004 c.6, s.3)

(b) held by another child in relation to whom the child has parental responsibility,

the contract has effect as if the child had been 18 or over when it was entered into.

DEFINITIONS

"account provider": subs.(1) and s.29.
"child": s.29.
"child trust fund": *ibid.*
"Inland Revenue": *ibid.*
"parental responsibility": subs.(9).
"responsible person": subs.(8).

GENERAL NOTE

This section sets out various administrative and procedural requirements which must be satisfied in order for a child trust fund account to come into existence. Only authorised financial institutions may offer child trust fund accounts (subs.(1)) and such accounts must meet a number of criteria (subss.(2)–(5)). This section also defines who has the authority to manage the child's account. This will usually be a person with parental responsibility or, in the case of a child aged at least 16, the child him or herself (subss.(6)–(12)). 1.545

Subs.(1)

Financial institutions, known as "account providers" in this Act, must be approved by HMRC before they can offer child trust fund accounts. The details of the approval process, which are set out in regulations, are modelled on those that apply to Individual Savings Accounts (ISAs) (see Child Trust Funds Regulations 2004, regs 14–17 and 19–20). Institutions denied approval have a right of appeal (see s.22(1)). 1.546

Subs.(2)

Approval operates at two levels. First, the account provider itself must be approved by HMRC under subs.(1). Secondly, by virtue of this subsection, only certain types of accounts may qualify as child trust fund accounts. In order to qualify an account must meet the criteria which are set out in regulations and are based on the arrangements governing ISAs (see Child Trust Funds Regulations 2004, reg.8). 1.547

Subs.(3)

This provision means that the regulations governing the approval of financial institutions may require account providers to provide particular types of account as a condition of such approval. The general rule is that, in order to be authorised as an account provider for the purposes of the child trust fund scheme, institutions must offer stakeholder accounts to the general public (see Child Trust Funds Regulations 2004, reg.14(2)(b)(i)). The characteristics of a stakeholder account are defined in the Schedule to the Regulations. The policy justification for this requirement is that it will enable beneficiaries to gain from the potentially higher returns from equities as a long-term investment. Further, the risk of a fall in the value of equities is reduced by the requirement to spread the investment over a number of companies (*ibid.*, para.2(2)(c)) and to transfer the investment to other assets (e.g. cash or gilts) as the maturity date nears. 1.548

Subs.(4)

This provision sets out the core requirements which must be met in order for an account to qualify for the purposes of the child trust fund scheme. For further details, see Child Trust Funds Regulations 2004, reg.8. 1.549

Child Trust Funds Act 2004

The general rule is that no withdrawals are permitted from a child trust fund account before the child attains 18 (subs.(4)(d)). The Government's argument is that this restriction is essential if such accounts are to achieve their long-term goals. The only exceptions to this principle in the regulations as originally drafted related to withdrawals on closure in the event of the child's death and to deductions for management charges due (Child Trust Funds Regulations 2004, reg.18; there is a cap of 1.5 per cent on administration fees: *ibid.*, Sch., para.3(2)). However, following sustained pressure in Parliament, the Government conceded that a further exception should be made in the case of children suffering from a terminal illness. See now Child Trust Funds Regulations 2004, reg.18A. In contrast to the tight restrictions on withdrawals before the age of 18, there are no controls whatsoever on how young adults apply their child trust fund account holdings on reaching that age.

Subs.(5)

1.550   For further details, see Child Trust Funds Regulations 2004, reg.8.

Subs.(6)

1.551   The effect of this provision, taken together with the definitions and qualifications in the following subsections, is that the child trust fund account is managed by the child, if he or she is 16 or over, and otherwise by the person with parental responsibility in respect of that child. This provision was inserted as a government amendment to the original Bill, which had given 16 and 17 year olds in Scotland the right to manage their accounts, but not their peers south of the border (reflecting the special rules in Scots law relating to the age of majority). Following debate, the Government accepted that it was difficult to sustain this distinction in the context of the child trust fund, and so brought forward this provision to ensure that all 16 and 17 year olds in the United Kingdom have the right to manage their child trust fund account. Such individuals are deemed to have full contractual authority to manage their accounts by virtue of subs.(12). They will not be able to withdraw funds until they reach the age of 18 (see subs.(4)(d)).

Subss.(7)–(9)

1.552   In the case of children under the age of 16, the "responsible person" is designated as the individual with the authority to manage the child trust fund account (subs.(7)). The basic rule is that the "responsible person" in respect of a child under 16 is the person with parental responsibility for that child under the Children Act 1989 (or the relevant legislation for other parts of the United Kingdom: see subs.(9)). There are two exceptions to this rule (subs.(8))—first, a local authority (which may have parental responsibility by virtue of a care order) cannot be a "responsible person"; secondly, a young parent under the age of 16 cannot assume that role. It follows, for example, that the child trust fund accounts of both a 15-year-old mother and her baby will have to be managed by a third party.

It is common, of course, for two individuals to share parental responsibility for a child, as in the case of a married couple (Children Act 1989, s.2(1)). In such cases voucher will be sent to the holder of the child benefit award (see s.5 and Child Trust Funds Regulations 2004, reg.3(2)). Moreover, there can be only one person with authority to manage the child trust fund account, known as the "registered contact" (*ibid.*, reg.8(1)(d)). Typically this will be a "single responsible person", i.e. a person with parental responsibility (see further *ibid.*, reg.13).

Subs.(10)

1.553   This was another government amendment to the original Bill. It is designed to deal with the problem created by the lack of a "responsible person" for some children in local authority care. A local authority cannot be a responsible person (subs.(8)(a)). In the case of most children being looked after by a local authority, this will not matter, as the child's parent will retain parental responsibility and so be a responsible person. However, there will be a minority of cases in which no individual person holds parental responsibility (e.g. some orphans in care). The Government has announced that the Official Solicitor (in England, Wales and Northern Ireland) or the Accountant of Court (in Scotland) will undertake the function of managing the accounts of children in care for whom there is no one with parental responsibility. See now Child Trust Funds Regulations 2004, reg.33A.

Inalienability

4.—(1) Any assignment of, or agreement to assign, investments under a child trust fund, and any charge on or agreement to charge any such investments, is void.

(2) On the bankruptcy of a child by whom a child trust fund is held, the entitlement to investments under it does not pass to any trustee or other person acting on behalf of the child's creditors.

(3) "Assignment" includes assignation; and "assign" is to be construed accordingly.

(4) "Charge on or agreement to charge" includes a right in security over or an agreement to create a right in security over.

(5) "Bankruptcy", in relation to a child, includes the sequestration of the child's estate.

1.554

DEFINITIONS

"assign": subs.(3).
"assignment": *ibid.*
"bankruptcy": subs.(5)
"charge on or agreement to charge": subs.(4).
"child trust fund": s.29.

GENERAL NOTE

The principle of the inalienability of social security benefits is enshrined in SSAA 1992, s.187 (see also Tax Credits Act 2002, s.45). This section provides, in similar fashion, for the inalienability of investments held under a child trust fund. The parallel provision in SSAA 1992, s.187 was applied (in the Scottish context) in *Mulvey v Secretary of State for Social Security*, 1997 S.C. (HL) 105, where the House of Lords held that the bankrupt's right to income support could not be owed to the permanent trustee (the Scottish equivalent of a trustee in bankruptcy). However, the House of Lords held that deductions could lawfully be made from income support to pay a social fund debt incurred prior to sequestration.

1.555

Opening and transfers

Opening by responsible person or child

5.—(1) In the case of each child who is first an eligible child by virtue of section 2(1)(a) the Inland Revenue must issue, in a manner prescribed by regulations, a voucher in such form as is so prescribed.

(2) The voucher must be issued to the person who is entitled to child benefit in respect of the child (or, in the case of a child who is such an eligible child because of section 2(3), to a responsible person).

1.556

Child Trust Funds Act 2004

(3) An application may be made—
(a) if the child is 16 or over, by the child, or
(b) otherwise, by a responsible person,
to open for the child with an account provider a child trust fund of any description provided by the account provider.
(4) The application is to be made—
(a) within such period beginning with the day on which the voucher is issued as is prescribed by regulations, and
(b) in accordance with regulations.
(5) When the application has been made the account provider must—
(a) open, in accordance with regulations, a child trust fund of that description for the child, and
(b) inform the Inland Revenue in accordance with regulations.

DEFINITIONS

"account provider": s.29.
"child": *ibid.*
"child trust fund": *ibid.*
"eligible child": s.2(1) and s.29.
"Inland Revenue": s.29.
"responsible person": ss.3(8) and 29.

GENERAL NOTE

1.557 This section sets out the framework within which child trust fund accounts are to be opened, typically by the "responsible person" (as defined by s.3(8)) and in exceptional cases by the child (assuming he or she is 16 or over). The default position is that an account must be opened by HMRC (see further s.6).

Subs.(1)
This places a duty on HMRC to issue a voucher in respect of any eligible child (within the normal definition in s.2(1)(a)). The issue of the voucher will be triggered by the award of child benefit (which, as a result of the Tax Credits Act 2002, is now administered by HMRC rather than the Department for Work and Pensions). See further Child Trust Funds Regulations 2004, reg.3.

Subs.(2)
1.558 The voucher must be issued to the individual who is entitled to child benefit. The voucher is in the amount of the initial Treasury contribution to be paid to all eligible children (£250). It should be noted that the process of issuing vouchers is designed to be an automatic process—there is no requirement in the legislation for the parent or other responsible person to make an independent claim for a child trust fund account voucher. In the special cross-border situation where the child lives in the United Kingdom but the parent works in another EU Member State (e.g. the Republic of Ireland) there will be no child benefit recipient in this jurisdiction (see annotation to s.2(3)). Accordingly in such cases the voucher must be issued to a responsible person for that child.

Subs.(3)
1.559 This enables the "responsible person" to apply to open a child trust fund account with an approved account provider (see further subs.(4)). As originally drafted, the Bill would have required the responsible person physically to present the voucher to the account provider. As a result of a government amendment, the details of this procedure are now left to regulations. The Child Trust Funds Regulations 2004 still envisage a physical transfer of the voucher (reg.5(1), condition 1), but may in the

future make provision for an entirely on-line application process. The "responsible person" is not, as such, under a statutory duty to make such an application. If he or she fails to do so, the default position is that ultimately HMRC will step in (see further s.6). In exceptional cases a child aged 16 or 17 may make an application to open a child trust fund account in his or her own name. The most likely circumstance in which this will arise is in the future where a child (born after August 31, 2002) moves to the United Kingdom at the age of 16 having never previously had an entitlement to a child trust fund account.

Subs. (4)
The application procedure is set out in regulations (see Child Trust Funds Regulations 2004, regs 5 and 13). The responsible person can select both the account provider and the type of account for the child trust fund. The voucher issued by HMRC will be valid for one year from the date of issue (*ibid.*, reg.3(2)), so applicants have a year in which to make the application. If they fail to do so, HMRC's default duty under s.6 arises.

1.560

Subs. (5)
Once a valid application has been made, an account provider is required to open a child trust fund account for the child in question and to inform the Revenue that it has done so. The Child Trust Funds Regulations 2004 require institutions to make both fortnightly and annual returns of such information to the Revenue (regs 30 and 32).

1.561

Opening by Inland Revenue

6.—(1) In the case of each child to whom this section applies, the Inland Revenue must apply to open for the child with an account provider selected in accordance with regulations a child trust fund of a description so selected.

1.562

(2) The application is to be made in accordance with regulations.
(3) The account provider must—
(a) open, in accordance with regulations, a child trust fund of that description for the child, and
(b) inform the Inland Revenue in accordance with regulations.
(4) This section applies—
(a) to a child in respect of whom a voucher is issued under section 5(1) but in whose case subsection (5) is satisfied, and
(b) to a child who is first an eligible child by virtue of section 2(1)(b).
(5) This subsection is satisfied in the case of a child if—
(a) the period prescribed under section 5(4) expires without a child trust fund having been opened for the child, or
(b) the child is under 16 and it appears to the Inland Revenue that there is no-one who is a responsible person in relation to the child.
(6) No liability is to arise in respect of the selection of an account provider, or a description of child trust fund, in accordance with regulations under this section.

DEFINITIONS
"account provider": s.29.
"child": *ibid.*
"child trust fund": *ibid.*
"eligible child": s.2(1) and s.29.
"Inland Revenue": s.29.
"responsible person": ss.3(8) and 29.

GENERAL NOTE

1.563
Normally a child's parent (or other adult who is the child benefit recipient), as a "responsible person", will make an application for a child trust fund account in accordance with s.5. There will inevitably be cases where no such application is made. This section therefore performs a 'mop-up' function, placing the onus on HMRC to ensure that accounts are opened for such children who would otherwise miss out. HMRC's obligation under subs.(1) to open a child trust fund account arises in two types of case. The first is where either, following an award of child benefit, a voucher has been issued to the "responsible person" but no application has been made to open a child trust fund account for that child within the required period (12 months) or there appears to be no "responsible person" for that child (subss.(4)(a) and (5)). The second is where the child is being looked after by a local authority and so there is no individual entitled to child benefit (subs.(4)(b)).

Subs.(1)

1.564
In cases to which this section applies (see subss.(4) and (5) and the General Note), HMRC *must* take the initiative and apply to open a child trust fund account for the child in question. The details of the procedure to be adopted are set out in the Child Trust Funds Regulations 2004, reg.6. Account providers are not required to offer these default HMRC-allocated accounts under this arrangement. However, *if* institutions do agree to offer such accounts, they must then accept any HMRC application to open such an account (see subs.(3) and Child Trust Funds Regulations 2004, reg.6(2)). HMRC will maintain a list of account providers willing to offer such accounts, and select account holders in rotation to ensure parity of treatment (*ibid.*, reg.6(3)). If account holders offer more than one type of stakeholder account, the account will likewise be chosen in rotation (*ibid.*, reg.6(4)). The legislation expressly exempts HMRC from any liability in respect of such decisions (subs.(6)). In these cases HMRC's role is furthermore limited to *opening* the account; it will have no role in *managing* the account in such a case. It will always be open to parents to transfer the account to another provider (s.7).

Subs.(2)

1.565
See further Child Trust Funds Regulations 2004, reg.6.

Subs.(3)

1.566
This is in parallel terms to the obligation imposed on account providers by s.5(5).

Subss.(4) and (5)

1.567
See the General Note to this section.

Subs.(6)

1.568
See the annotation to subs.(1).

Transfers

1.569
7. Regulations may make provision about the circumstances in which—
(a) a child trust fund which is an account of one of the descriptions prescribed by regulations may become an account of another of those descriptions, and
(b) a child trust fund held with one account provider may be transferred to another.

DEFINITIONS

"account provider": s.29.
"child trust fund": *ibid.*

General Note

This allows regulations to be made which permit the responsible person to change the type of child trust fund account (e.g. from a cash to a stakeholder account) and to move from one provider to another. The procedural rules for transfers are similar to those relating to transfers of ISA accounts, but require transfers to be free of charge (save for share dealing costs); see further Child Trust Funds Regulations 2004, reg.21.

Contributions and subscriptions

Initial contribution by Inland Revenue

8.—(1) The Inland Revenue must pay to an account provider such amount as is prescribed by regulations if the account provider has—
   (a) informed the Inland Revenue under section 5(5) or 6(3) that a child trust fund has been opened, and
   (b) made a claim to the Inland Revenue in accordance with regulations.

(2) On receipt of the payment the account provider must credit the child trust fund with the amount of the payment.

Definitions

"account provider": s.29.
"child trust fund": *ibid.*
"Inland Revenue": *ibid.*

General Note

This section explains how the initial Treasury contribution of £250 stated on the voucher issued to the child benefit recipient is actually converted, albeit indirectly, into cash (the voucher itself cannot be exchanged for money: see Child Trust Funds Regulations 2004, reg.3(1)). Once a child trust fund account has been opened, either in the normal way (s.5) or through the process of HMRC allocation (s.6), the account provider is required to notify HMRC. Account providers then make a claim to HMRC (these are to be made on a fortnightly basis—see Child Trust Funds Regulations 2004, reg.30. HMRC must in turn pay the account holder "such amount as is prescribed by regulations" by way of an initial contribution (subs.(1)), which the account holder must credit to the relevant account (subs.(2)). Children born into the poorest families may also qualify for a "supplementary contribution" under s.9. There is, moreover, the prospect of a further Treasury contribution for all eligible children when they reach the age of seven (see s.10).

The regulations describe the "initial" and "supplementary" contributions as "Government contributions" (Child Trust Funds Regulations 2004, reg.7). The basic rule for children born on or after the appointed day (April 6, 2005) is that the initial contribution will be £250, or £500 for those in local authority care (*ibid.*, reg.7(4)). Slightly higher amounts have been prescribed for those born on or after September 1, 2002 (the first date on which a child could qualify as an eligible child under s.2(1)) but before the appointed day. These higher amounts are designed to reflect the fact that these children have not had the benefit of interest on their investments to date. The rates are £277 for children born after August 31, 2002 but before the end of the 2002/03 tax year, £268 for those born in the 2003/04 tax year, and £256 for those born between April 6, 2004 and the appointed day (*ibid.*, reg.7(2)). For children in care, the equivalent figures are £553, £536 and £512.

Child Trust Funds Act 2004

Supplementary contribution by Inland Revenue

1.573   **9.**—(1) If this section applies to a child the Inland Revenue must inform the account provider with whom a child trust fund is held by the child that this section applies to the child.

(2) If the account provider makes a claim to the Inland Revenue in accordance with regulations, the Inland Revenue must pay to the account provider such amount as is prescribed by regulations.

(3) On receipt of the payment the account provider must credit the child trust fund with the amount of the payment.

(4) This section applies to a child if—
(a) a child trust fund is held by the child,
(b) the child was first an eligible child by virtue of section 2(1)(a), and
(c) the condition in subsection (5) is satisfied in relation to the child.

(5) That condition is that it has been determined in accordance with the provision made by and by virtue of sections 18 to 21 of the Tax Credits Act 2002 (c. 21)—
  (a) that a person was, or persons were, entitled to child tax credit in respect of the child for the child benefit commencement date, and
  (b) that either the relevant income of the person or persons for the tax year in which that date fell does not exceed the income threshold or the person, or either of the persons, was entitled to a relevant social security benefit for that date,
and that determination has not been overturned.

(6) In subsection (5)(b)—
"the income threshold" has the meaning given by section 7(1)(a) of the Tax Credits Act 2002,
"the relevant income", in relation to a person or persons and a tax year, has the meaning given by section 7(3) of that Act in relation to a claim by the person or persons for a tax credit for the tax year,
"relevant social security benefit" means any social security benefit prescribed for the purposes of section 7(2) of that Act, and
"tax year" means a period beginning with 6th April in one year and ending with 5th April in the next.

(7) If the child benefit commencement date is earlier than 6th April 2005, this section applies in relation to the child even if the condition in subsection (5) is not satisfied in relation to the child provided that the condition in subsection (8) is so satisfied.

(8) That condition is that—
  (a) income support, or income-based jobseeker's allowance, was paid for the child benefit commencement date to a person whose applicable amount included an amount in respect of the child, or
  (b) working families' tax credit, or disabled person's tax credit, was paid for that date to a person whose appropriate maximum working families' tax credit, or appropriate maximum disabled person's tax credit, included a credit in respect of the child.

(9) If the child benefit commencement date is earlier than 6th April 2003, subsection (5) has effect as if—
  (a) the reference in paragraph (a) to the child benefit commencement date were to any date in the tax year beginning with 6th April 2003,

(b) the reference in paragraph (b) to the tax year in which the child benefit commencement date fell were to the tax year beginning with 6th April 2003, and
(c) the reference in paragraph (b) to being entitled to a relevant social security benefit for the child benefit commencement date were to being so entitled for any date in that tax year for which the person was, or the persons were, entitled to child tax credit in respect of the child.

(10) "Child benefit commencement date", in relation to a child, means—
(a) the first day for which child benefit was paid in respect of the child (otherwise than because of a directly applicable Community provision or an international agreement), or
(b) in the case of a child to whom section 2(3) applies or section 2(5) has applied, such day as is prescribed by regulations.

DEFINITIONS

"account provider": s.29.
"child": *ibid*.
"child benefit commencement date": subs.(10).
"child trust fund": s.29.
"eligible child": ss.2(1) and 29.
"income threshold": subs.(6)
"Inland Revenue": s.29.
"relevant income": subs.(6).
"relevant social security benefit": *ibid*.
"tax year": *ibid*.

GENERAL NOTE

In addition to the initial contribution under s.8, children born into families on low incomes will be eligible for a "supplementary contribution" to boost their child trust fund account investment at the outset. This section sets out the rules governing the award of the supplementary contribution. Subss.(1)–(3) specify the procedure to be followed. Subsection (4) spells out the criteria for receipt of the supplementary condition. Children being looked after in local authority care will *not* qualify for this extra amount (see subs.(4)(b)), but they will in any event qualify for an equivalent amount under s.8 by virtue of their status. The means-test is explained in subs.(5), with various terms defined by subss.(6) and (10). Subsections (7)–(9) deal with various awkward transitional cases.

Subs.(1)

There is no need for parents on low incomes to claim the supplementary contribution; indeed, there is no facility for them to do so. Instead, the legislation requires HMRC to inform the account provider if a child is eligible for the supplementary contribution. HMRC will have this information as it is responsible for administering child tax credit under the Tax Credits Act 2002, which acts as the trigger for entitlement to the extra Treasury contribution (see subss.(4)(c) and (5)).

Subss.(2) and (3)

Having been informed that the child in question is eligible for the supplementary contribution, the account provider may then make a claim for that extra amount (subs.(2); see Child Trust Funds Regulations 2004, reg.30(6)(b)). This section then requires HMRC to pay the account provider the appropriate amount by way of a supplementary contribution. In the case of children born after the appointed day,

1.574

1.575

1.576

this is a further £250 (*ibid.*, reg.7(7)), making £500 in total. The amounts are increased for those born on or after September 1, 2002 but before the appointed day (*ibid.*, reg.7(6)). The account provider must then credit the extra amount to the child's account (subs.(3)). Subsequent regulations amending the amount of the supplementary contribution under subs.(2) will be subject to the affirmative procedure (see ss.28(5) and (6)(b)).

Subs.(4)

1.577 This sets out the criteria for the award of the supplementary contribution. The child must have a child trust fund account, have qualified on the basis of an award of child benefit and meet the child tax credit means-test set out in subs.(5). The second of these requirements has the effect of excluding children who initially qualified for an account because they were in care (see s.2(1)(b)), as they will, in any event, receive the higher initial contribution (see annotation to s.8).

Subs.(5)

1.578 This provision sets out the means-test which determines whether a child is eligible to receive the supplementary as well as the initial Treasury contribution. Two separate conditions must each be satisfied. In the case of both these requirements, the determination of entitlement must have been a final one in accordance with ss.18–21 of the Tax Credits Act 2002 and must not have been overturned.

The first condition is that someone was entitled to child tax credit for the child in question at the date when child benefit was first paid (known as the "child benefit commencement date": see subs.(10)). The second requirement is that *either* their income does not exceed the child tax credit income threshold for the tax year in issue *or* that person is entitled to a "relevant social security benefit". The statutory authority for the child tax credit income threshold is Tax Credits Act 2002, s.7(1)(a) (see subs.(6)). The annual amount of this threshold is prescribed in regulations, and for the 2005/06 tax year is £13,910 (Tax Credits (Income Threshold and Determination of Rates) Regulations 2002 (SI 2002/2008), reg.3(3), as amended by Tax Credits Up-rating Regulations 2005 (SI 2005/681), reg.4). The expression "relevant social security benefit" is defined by reference to Tax Credits Act 2002, s.7(2)) (see subs.(6)), and so includes only income support, income-based jobseeker's allowance and pension credit (Tax Credits (Income Threshold and Determination of Rates) Regulations 2002 (SI 2002/2008), reg.4, as amended by Tax Credits (Miscellaneous Amendments No.2) Regulations 2003 (SI 2003/2815), reg.18).

These tests require some modification so that they operate in the desired fashion for eligible children born in the transitional period between August 31, 2002 and April 6, 2005. There are two sets of special transitional rules contained in subss.(7)–(9).

Subss.(7) and (8)

1.579 The first transitional problem relates to the phasing in of child tax credit for families in receipt of income support or income-based jobseeker's allowance. Child tax credit, payable under the Tax Credits Act 2002, came into force on April 6, 2003, at least so far as new claimants and those claiming working tax credit (the successor to working families' tax credit) were concerned. Originally it was anticipated that families already in receipt of income support or income-based jobseeker's allowance would move over to child tax credit a year later on April 6, 2004. In fact, only new claimants of these benefits have received child tax credit from that date. The revised plan was that the process of 'migration' for existing benefits cases would then start in October 2004, with a view to such transfers being completed by the end of the 2004/05 tax year. (In the meantime all such families have received the cash equivalent of child tax credit through their existing benefits). Some families have therefore not meet the strict terms of subs.(5) because, although they were getting income support or income-based jobseeker's allowance at the material time, they were not yet, as a result of this phasing process, receiving child tax credit. Subsections (7) and (8) deal with this by disapplying the means-test based on entitlement to child tax credit in subs.(5). Instead, they provide alternatively that it is sufficient that a child born before April 6, 2005 was in a household which received one of the means-tested benefits or tax credits listed in subs.(8) in respect of that child.

As matters have transpired, this process of migration has been further delayed and had not been commenced, let alone completed, by the end of the 2004/05 tax year. The current plan is to have this process completed by December 31, 2008: see Tax Credits Act 2002 (Commencement No.4, Transitional Provisions and Savings) Order 2003 (SI 2003/962 (c. 51)) as amended.

Subs.(9)

This deals with a separate transitional problem relating to children born between September 1, 2002 and April 5, 2003. The first condition in the means-test (subs.(5)(a)) is that a person was entitled to child tax credit in respect of the child when child benefit was first paid. However, child tax credit did not come into operation until April 6, 2003, and so subs.(5)(a) cannot be satisfied if child benefit was payable *before* that date. There are also knock-on problems in terms of complying with subs.(5)(b) in such cases. This sub-section resolves these problems by deeming the child benefit commencement date (and hence the entitlement to child tax credit) as having been in the 2003/04 tax year.

1.580

Further contributions by Inland Revenue

10.—(1) Regulations may make provision for the making by the Inland Revenue in the circumstances mentioned in subsection (2) of payments to account providers of child trust funds held by—

(a) eligible children, or

(b) any description of eligible children,

of amounts prescribed by, or determined in accordance with, regulations.

(2) The circumstances referred to in subsection (1) are—

(a) the children attaining such age as may be prescribed by the regulations, or

(b) such other circumstances as may be so prescribed.

(3) The regulations must include provision—

(a) for making account providers aware that such amounts are payable,

(b) about the claiming of such payments by account providers, and

(c) about the crediting of child trust funds by account providers with the amount of such payments.

(4) For the purposes of this section, a child is to be treated as being an eligible child if entitlement to child benefit in respect of the child is excluded by—

(a) paragraph 1(a) of Schedule 9 to the Social Security Contributions and Benefits Act 1992 (c. 4) (children in custody), or

(b) paragraph 1(1)(a) to (d) of Schedule 9 to the Social Security Contributions and Benefits (Northern Ireland) Act 1992 (c. 7) (corresponding provision for Northern Ireland).

1.581

DEFINITIONS

"account provider": s.29.
"child": *ibid*.
"child trust fund": *ibid*.
"eligible child": ss.2(1) and 29.
"Inland Revenue": s.29.

GENERAL NOTE

1.582 This is an enabling measure, allowing regulations to be made which may provide for a further Treasury contribution to be credited to the child's account at a later date. Any regulations made under subs.(1) or (2) will be subject to the affirmative procedure (see s.28(5) and (6)(a)).

Subss. (1) and (2)

1.583 The powers enshrined in the section are expressed in broad terms—thus regulations may provide that further contributions are made to all eligible children, or just to a subset of them (subs.(1)). The trigger for a further contribution may be when the child attains a particular age, as set out in regulations, or some other factor (subs.(2)). At present these details are not contained in the Child Trust Funds Regulations 2004 but will be announced at a later date. The Government's stated intention is that there will be one further contribution which will be payable to all eligible children at the age of seven (rather than three payments at ages 5, 11 and 16, as suggested in *Savings and Assets for All*). It follows that the first such payments will not become due until 2009. In its 2004 Pre-Budget Report the Government announced a consultation process on the appropriate levels for such further contributions. The consultation paper suggested that there be a further universal payment of £250 at age seven, with an extra £250 for children in low-income families (Treasury Press Notice 5, December 2, 2004). A further consultation was initiated by the 2005 Budget, with a view to seeing whether there is support for a further contribution to children of secondary school age and, if so, at what age and in what amounts. In both consultations the Government has invited views on the appropriate ratio of progressivity (currently 1:2, i.e. £250 universal and £500 means-tested). The rationale for further contributions is that they will enable additional endowment funds to be targeted on those most in need. It will also help to keep the accounts 'live' by reminding both children and their parents of the existence and growth of such funds. Note also that account providers will have to issue annual account statements (Child Trust Funds Regulations 2004, reg.10).

Subs. (3)

1.584 As well as specifying matters such as the amount of the further contribution and the age at which it becomes payable, the regulations which are to be made nearer the time must also address the various procedural matters referred to in this sub-section.

Subs. (4)

1.585 A child will remain an eligible child for these purposes even if there is no child benefit entitlement at the date when the further contribution becomes payable because he or she is detained in custody. Clearly children aged seven are not going to be in custody. However, a future government might decide to make further Treasury contributions to children at the age of 12 or over, when this could become an issue. The Government's view, as a matter of principle, was that it was not justifiable "to disadvantage such children on the grounds that they were in custody on a particular birthday". Such an exclusion from the further contribution might also result in anomalies depending on the length of time the child was in custody and when their birthday fell.

Recouping Inland Revenue contributions

1.586 **11.**—(1) Regulations may make provision requiring that, in circumstances prescribed by the regulations, a person of a description so prescribed is to account to the Inland Revenue for amounts credited to a child trust fund in respect of Inland Revenue contributions (together with any income and gains arising in consequence of the crediting of those amounts).

(2004 c.6, s.11)

(2) "Inland Revenue contributions" means payments made by the Inland Revenue which were required to be made under or by virtue of sections 8 to 10 or which the Inland Revenue considered were required to be so made.

DEFINITIONS

"child trust fund": s.29.
"Inland Revenue": *ibid.*
"Inland Revenue contributions": subs.(2).

GENERAL NOTE

In some cases payments will be made under ss.8, 9 or 10 which should not have been so credited; in social security parlance these would be described as overpayments. This section allows the Treasury to make regulations governing the recovery of such payments, e.g. where more than one account has been opened or where the child in question was never an eligible child within s.2. The intention is that recovery will be possible from the account provider, the child, the registered contact (typically the parent) and anyone into whose hands the funds have come.

1.587

Subscription limits

12.—(1) No subscription may be made to a child trust fund otherwise than by way of a monetary payment.

(2) Regulations may prescribe the maximum amount that may be subscribed to a child trust fund in each year (otherwise than by way of credits made under or by virtue of this Act or income or gains arising on investments under the child trust fund).

(3) "Year", in relation to a child trust fund held by a child, means—
(a) the period beginning with the day on which the child trust fund is opened and ending immediately before the child's next birthday, and
(b) each succeeding period of twelve months.

1.588

DEFINITIONS

"child trust fund": s.29.
"year": subs.(3).

GENERAL NOTE

Whereas ss.8–11 are all concerned with Treasury contributions to a child trust fund account, this section deals with contributions to such accounts by others, for example a child's family and friends. Such non-governmental contributions may only be in money terms (subs.(1)), and so shares cannot be transferred to a child trust fund account. There will also be an annual aggregate limit on such non-governmental contributions, prescribed by regulations made under subs.(2). This cap is to be £1,200 a year at the outset (Child Trust Fund Regulations 2004, reg.9(2); there is no facility to carry over any unused allowance to a following year (*ibid.*, reg.9(3)). A year, in this context, means each year from the date of the individual child's birthday (subs.(3)), not each calendar year or each tax year. The minimum contribution on any one transaction is £10, unless the account provider permits a smaller amount (Child Trust Fund Regulations 2004, Sch., para.2(4)).

There is no provision in the Act for automatic indexation of the annual aggregate limit; the Government intends to treat the cap in the same way as the ISA limit, so any uprating will be announced in the Budget or simply through regulations.

1.589

Tax

Relief from income tax and capital gains tax

1.590   **13.**—(1) Regulations may make provision for and in connection with giving relief from—
(a) income tax, and
(b) capital gains tax,
in respect of investments under child trust funds.
  (2) The regulations may, in particular, include—
(a) provision for securing that losses are disregarded for the purposes of capital gains tax where they accrue on the disposal of investments under child trust funds, and
(b) provision dealing with anything which, apart from the regulations, would have been regarded for those purposes as an indistinguishable part of the same asset.
  (3) The regulations may specify how tax relief is to be claimed by persons entitled to it or by account providers on their behalf.
  (4) The regulations may include provision requiring that, in circumstances prescribed by the regulations, the person prescribed by the regulations is to account to the Inland Revenue for—
(a) tax from which relief has been given under the regulations, and
(b) income or gains arising in consequence of the giving of relief under the regulations,
or for an amount determined in accordance with the regulations in respect of such tax.
  (5) Provision made by virtue of this section may disapply, or modify the effect of, any enactment relating to income tax or capital gains tax.

DEFINITIONS

"account provider": s.29.
"child trust fund": *ibid.*
"Inland Revenue": *ibid.*

GENERAL NOTE

1.591   This section is concerned with the tax treatment of investments held in child trust funds. It allows regulations to make provision for relief in respect of income tax and capital gains tax (subs.(1)), and how such tax relief should be claimed (subs.(3)). Such regulations may effectively ring-fence child trust fund investments from any other investments held by the child concerned; this will mean that any capital losses arising on the disposal of child trust fund investments will not be deductible from any capital gains outside the child trust fund (subs.(2)(a)). Regulations will also provide for the separate identification of disposals of shares within and outside a child trust fund (subs.(2)(b)). Regulations may provide for the repayment of tax relief that is given in circumstances where it should not have been (subs.(4)). Subsection (5) is a general power that enables regulations to modify income tax and capital gains tax legislation for child trust fund accounts (see generally Child Trust Funds Regulations 2004, Pt 3 and especially regs 24 and 36).

Insurance companies and friendly societies

1.592   **14.**—(1) Subsections (1) and (5) to (9) of section 333B of the Income and Corporation Taxes Act 1988 (c. 1) (involvement of insurance companies and friendly societies with ISAs) have effect in relation to insurance companies and friendly societies as if child trust fund business were [¹ plan business] (within the meaning of section 333B).

(2) "Child trust fund business", in relation to an insurance company or friendly society, means business of the insurance company or friendly society that is attributable to child trust funds.

AMENDMENT

1. Income Tax (Trading and Other Income) Act 2005, s.882 and Sch.1, para.628 (April 6, 2005).

DEFINITIONS

"child trust fund": s.29.
"child trust fund business": subs.(2).

GENERAL NOTE

This section enables the income and gains made on investments held in child trust fund accounts provided in the form of life insurance policies to be free from corporation tax. This will not prevent the profits made by insurance companies and friendly societies on such business from being taxed. See further Child Trust Funds (Insurance Companies) Regulations 2004 (SI 2004/2680).

1.593

Information etc.

Information from account providers etc.

15.—(1) Regulations may require, or authorise officers of the Inland Revenue to require, any relevant person—
   (a) to make documents available for inspection on behalf of the Inland Revenue, or
   (b) to provide to the Inland Revenue any information,
relating to, or to investments which are or have been held under, a child trust fund.
   (2) The following are relevant persons—
   (a) anyone who is or has been the account provider in relation to the child trust fund,
   (b) the person by whom the child trust fund is or was held,
   (c) the person (if any) to whom a voucher was issued under section 5(1) in respect of the child by whom the child trust fund is or was held,
   (d) the person who applied to open the child trust fund (unless it was opened by the Inland Revenue),
   (e) anyone who has given instructions with respect to the management of the child trust fund, and
   (f) anyone entitled to child benefit in respect of the child.
   (3) The regulations may include provision requiring documents to be made available or information to be provided—
   (a) in the manner and form, and
   (b) by the time and at the place,
prescribed by or under the regulations.

1.594

DEFINITIONS

"account provider": s.29.
"child": *ibid.*

277

"child trust fund": *ibid.*
"Inland Revenue": *ibid.*
"relevant person": subs.(2).

GENERAL NOTE

1.595 This section enables the Treasury to make regulations requiring account providers and other "relevant persons" (as defined by subs.(2)) to supply information or make documents available for inspection (and subject to requirements stipulated under subs.(3)). The Child Trust Funds Regulations 2004 require account holders to supply HMRC with both fortnightly and annual returns (regs 30 and 32). The fortnightly returns will both act as a claim for payment of the government contributions and enable HMRC to identify children for whom accounts have not been opened.

Information about children in care of authority

1.596 **16.**—(1) Regulations may require, or authorise officers of the Inland Revenue to require, an authority—
   (a) to make documents available for inspection on behalf of the Inland Revenue, or
   (b) to provide to the Inland Revenue any information,
which the Inland Revenue may require for the discharge of any function relating to child trust funds and which is information to which subsection (2) applies.

(2) This subsection applies to information relating to a child who falls or has fallen within—
   (a) paragraph 1(c) of Schedule 9 to the Social Security Contributions and Benefits Act 1992 (c. 4), or
   (b) paragraph 1(1)(f) of Schedule 9 to the Social Security Contributions and Benefits (Northern Ireland) Act 1992 (c. 7),
by reason of being, or having been, in the care of the authority in circumstances prescribed by regulations under that provision.

(3) The regulations may include provision requiring documents to be made available or information to be provided—
   (a) in the manner and form, and
   (b) by the time and at the place,
prescribed by or under the regulations.

DEFINITIONS

"child": s.29.
"child trust fund": *ibid.*
"Inland Revenue": *ibid.*

GENERAL NOTE

1.597 The normal rule is that a child is an "eligible child" if child benefit is payable in respect of him or her (s.2(1)(a)). Receipt of child benefit thus acts as a passport to entitlement to the child trust fund. HMRC is also responsible for administering child benefit and accordingly has access to all the relevant information in such cases. However, child benefit cannot be claimed for children in local authority care, for whom special provision has to be made to make them "eligible children" (ss.2(1)(b) and 2(2)). As these children will not appear in the records of current child benefit payments, HMRC will have to obtain the necessary information direct from local authorities. This section accordingly enables the Treasury to make regulations requiring local authorities to provide the information necessary to arrange for a child trust fund account to be opened or for further contributions to be made. Local authorities are required to make monthly returns (Child Trust Funds Regulations 2004, reg.33).

Use of information

17.—(1) Information held for the purposes of any function relating to child trust funds—
(a) by the Inland Revenue, or
(b) by a person providing services to the Inland Revenue, in connection with the provision of those services,
may be used, or supplied to any person providing services to the Inland Revenue, for the purposes of, or for any purposes connected with, the exercise of any such function.

(2) Information held for the purposes of any function relating to child trust funds—
(a) by the Inland Revenue, or
(b) by a person providing services to the Inland Revenue, in connection with the provision of those services,
may be used, or supplied to any person providing services to the Inland Revenue, for the purposes of, or for any purposes connected with, the exercise of any other function of the Inland Revenue.

(3) Information held for the purposes of any function other than those relating to child trust funds—
(a) by the Inland Revenue, or
(b) by a person providing services to the Inland Revenue, in connection with the provision of those services,
may be used, or supplied to any person providing services to the Inland Revenue, for the purposes of, or for any purposes connected with, the exercise of any function of the Inland Revenue relating to child trust funds.

(4) Information held by the Secretary of State or the Department for Social Development in Northern Ireland, or any person providing services to the Secretary of State or that Department, may be supplied to—
(a) the Inland Revenue, or
(b) a person providing services to the Inland Revenue, in connection with the provision of those services,
for use for the purposes of, or for any purposes connected with, the exercise of any function of the Inland Revenue relating to child trust funds.

1.598

DEFINITIONS

"child trust fund": s.29.
"Inland Revenue": *ibid.*

GENERAL NOTE

This section allows information relating to child trust funds to be shared both within government and between government departments and their contractors (typically their IT providers). Subsection (1) allows information relating to child trust funds to be used for purposes relating to such funds. Subsection (2), on the other hand, enables such information to be used for other (non-child trust fund) purposes by HMRC (e.g. official evaluations of savings policies). Subsection (3) permits information held by HMRC in connection with other purposes to be used for child trust fund purposes. This allows HMRC to access information about a person's child tax

1.599

credit status in order to determine eligibility for the supplementary contribution (see s.9(5)). Finally, subs.(4) allows other government departments to provide information to HMRC (or its contractors) for reasons connected with child trust funds. In particular, this will enable HMRC to obtain information from the Department for Work and Pensions about a person's benefit status. This will be relevant to determining entitlement to the supplementary condition in respect of children born on or after September 1, 2002 but before child tax credit became payable to the household in question.

Disclosure of information

1.600   **18.** [*Section omitted.*]

GENERAL NOTE

This section amends the Finance Act 1989, s.182 and so brings the child trust fund scheme within the existing statutory provisions which deal with the confidentiality of personal information held by HMRC, and the exceptions to that principle.

Payments after death

Payments after death of child

1.601   **19.**—(1) Where a relevant child dies, the Inland Revenue may make a payment to the personal representatives of the child if any one or more of the conditions specified in subsection (3) is satisfied.

(2) "Relevant child" means a child who is or has been an eligible child (or would have been had this Act come into force on the date referred to in section 2(1)).

(3) The conditions are—
  (a) that either no payment had been made under section 8 by the Inland Revenue or, if one had, the amount of the payment had not been credited to the child trust fund held by the child,
  (b) that section 9 applied to the child (or would have had this Act come into force on the date referred to in section 2(1)) but either no payment had been made under that section by the Inland Revenue or, if one had, the amount of the payment had not been credited to the child trust fund held by the child, and
  (c) that the Inland Revenue was required by regulations under section 10 to make a payment in respect of the child but either the payment had not been made or, if it had, the amount of the payment had not been credited to the child trust fund held by the child.

(4) The amount of the payment is to be equal to the amount of the payment or payments which had not been made or credited.

DEFINITIONS

"child": s.29.
"child trust fund": *ibid.*
"eligible child": *ibid.*
"Inland Revenue": *ibid.*
"relevant child": subs.(2).

(2004 c.6, s.19)

General Note

This section gives HMRC the power to make child trust fund payments in respect of children born after August 31, 2002 but who have died before such payments have been credited to an account. Any one (or more) of three requirements must be satisfied. These are (1) that no initial contribution has been paid under s.8 (or it has not been credited to the account); (2) that the child was entitled to a supplementary contribution under s.9 but this had not been paid or credited to the account; or (3) that a further contribution was due under s.10 but again had not been paid or credited (subs.(3)). The amount payable is a sum equal to the amount of the outstanding payment(s) (subs.(4)) and is payable to the child's personal representatives (subs.(1)). Note that there is no absolute right to such a payment; HMRC *may* make such a payment. The element of discretion has been inserted to allow HMRC to refuse to make payments in cases where the child has been unlawfully killed by the parent. The personal representatives have a right of appeal in the event of a dispute about payment (s.22(5)).

1.602

Penalties

Penalties

20.—(1) A penalty of £300 may be imposed on any person who fraudulently—
(a) applies to open a child trust fund,
(b) makes a withdrawal from a child trust fund otherwise than as permitted by regulations under section 3(4)(d), or
(c) secures the opening of a child trust fund by the Inland Revenue.
(2) A penalty not exceeding £3,000 may be imposed on—
(a) an account provider who fraudulently or negligently makes an incorrect statement or declaration in connection with a claim under section 8 or 9 or regulations under section 10 or 13, and
(b) any person who fraudulently or negligently provides incorrect information in response to a requirement imposed by or under regulations under section 15.
(3) Penalties may be imposed on—
(a) an account provider who fails to make a claim under section 8 or 9 or regulations under section 10 by the time required by regulations under the section concerned, and
(b) any person who fails to make a document available, or provide information, in accordance with regulations under section 15.
(4) The penalties which may be imposed under subsection (3) are—
(a) a penalty not exceeding £300, and
(b) if the failure continues after a penalty under paragraph (a) is imposed, a further penalty or penalties not exceeding £60 for each day on which the failure continues after the day on which the penalty under that paragraph was imposed (but excluding any day for which a penalty under this paragraph has already been imposed).
(5) No penalty under subsection (3) may be imposed on a person in respect of a failure after the failure has been remedied.
(6) For the purposes of subsection (3) a person is to be taken not to have failed to make a claim, make available a document or provide information which must be made, made available or provided by a particular time—

1.603

(a) if the person made it, made it available or provided it within such further time (if any) as the Inland Revenue may have allowed,
(b) if the person had a reasonable excuse for not making it, making it available or providing it by that time, or
(c) if, after having had such an excuse, the person made it, made it available or provided it without unreasonable delay.

(7) A penalty may be imposed on an account provider in respect of—
(a) the provision by the account provider, as a child trust fund, of an account which does not meet the condition in subsection (8),
(b) a failure by the account provider to comply with section 8(2) or 9(3) or with a requirement imposed on the account provider by regulations under section 5(5), 6(3), 7 or 10(3), or
(c) a breach of section 12(1), or regulations under section 12(2), in relation to a child trust fund held with the account provider.

(8) An account meets the condition referred to in subsection (7)(a) if—
(a) it is of one of the descriptions prescribed by regulations under section 3(2),
(b) section 3(4) is complied with in relation to it, and
(c) the requirements imposed by regulations under section 3(5) are satisfied in relation to it.

(9) The penalty which may be imposed under subsection (7) on the account provider is a penalty not exceeding—
(a) £300, or
(b) £1 in respect of each account affected by the matter, or any of the matters, in respect of which the penalty is imposed,
whichever is greater.

DEFINITIONS

"account provider": s.29.
"child trust fund": *ibid.*
"Inland Revenue": *ibid.*

GENERAL NOTE

1.604   This section makes provision for penalties to be imposed in connection with child trust fund applications and related matters. Individuals who fraudulently apply to open or secure the opening of an account, or make an account withdrawal, are subject to a penalty of £300 (subs.(1)). Account providers and others who make fraudulent or negligent statements or declarations are liable to a penalty not exceeding £3,000 (subs.(2)). Account providers and others are also liable to a £300 penalty (and £60 per day thereafter for continued non-compliance) for failing to make claims in respect of reimbursements or for failing to provide information or produce documentation (subss.(3) and (4); see further subss.(5) and (6)). Subsections (7)–(9) make further provision for penalties to be imposed on account providers in respect of non-compliance with various statutory requirements.

Any penalties under this section are imposed by HMRC (s.21(1)), subject to the various procedural requirements in s.21. There is a right of appeal against any decision to impose a penalty, or its amount (s.22(6)).

Decisions, appeals, mitigation and recovery

1.605   **21.**—(1) It is for the Inland Revenue to impose a penalty under section 20.
(2) If the Inland Revenue decide to impose such a penalty the decision must (subject to the permitted maximum) set it at such amount as, in their opinion, is appropriate.

(2004 c.6, s.21)

(3) A decision to impose such a penalty may not be made after the end of the period of six years beginning with the date on which the penalty was incurred or began to be incurred.

(4) The Inland Revenue must give notice of such a decision to the person on whom the penalty is imposed.

(5) The notice must state the date on which it is given and give details of the right to appeal against the decision under section 22.

(6) After the notice has been given, the decision must not be altered except on appeal.

(7) But the Inland Revenue may, in their discretion, mitigate any penalty under section 20.

(8) A penalty under section 20 becomes payable at the end of the period of 30 days beginning with the date on which notice of the decision is given.

(9) On an appeal under section 22 against a decision under this section, the [¹appeal tribunal] may—
   (a) if it appears that no penalty has been incurred, set the decision aside,
   (b) if the amount set appears to be appropriate, confirm the decision,
   (c) if the amount set appears to be excessive, reduce it to such other amount (including nil) as they consider appropriate, or
   (d) if the amount set appears to be insufficient, increase it to such amount not exceeding the permitted maximum as they consider appropriate.

(10) An appeal from a decision of the [¹appeal tribunal] under subsection (9) lies, at the instance of the person on whom the penalty was imposed, to [¹a Social security Commissioner] and on such an appeal the [¹Commissioner] has a similar jurisdiction to that conferred on the [¹appeal tribunal] by that subsection.

(11) A penalty is to be treated for the purposes of Part 6 of the Taxes Management Act 1970 (c. 9) (collection and recovery) as if it were tax charged in an assessment and due and payable.

MODIFICATION

1. This section is set out above as modified by s.24(2).

DEFINITIONS

"appeal tribunal"—s.24(6).
"the Inland Revenue"—s.29 but note that the functions of the Inland Revenue have been transferred to HMRC by CRCA 2005.
"Social Security Commissioner"—s.24(7).

GENERAL NOTE

This section is set out as modified by s.24, which has the effect that, until further notice, the jurisdiction of the General Commissioners and Special Commissioners is exercised by appeal tribunals and the jurisdiction of the High Court and the Court of Session as the Court of Exchequer in Scotland is exercised by Social Security Commissioners.

1.606

Subs.(9)
Note that an appeal tribunal may increase a penalty. See s.23 and also reg.3 of the Child Trust Funds (Non-tax Appeals) Regulations 2005 for what is required in a notice of appeal and s.12 of the Social Security Act 1998 and the Child Trust Funds (Appeals) Regulations 2005 for other procedural provisions. Also, see generally the note to s.39 of the Tax Credits Acts 2002.

1.607

Subs.(10)

1.608 The person on whom the penalty has been imposed may appeal from the decision of an appeal tribunal to a Social Security Commissioner. He or she does not require leave to appeal and the appeal is not confined to points of law. HMRC have no right of appeal to a Social Security Commissioner. See s.14 of the Social Security Act 1998 and the Social Security Commissioners (Procedure) (Child Trust Funds) Regulations 2005 for procedural provisions.

Appeals

Rights of appeal

1.609 **22.**—(1) A person may appeal against—
(a) a decision by the Inland Revenue not to approve the person as an account provider, or
(b) a decision by the Inland Revenue to withdraw the person's approval as an account provider.

(2) A person who is a relevant person in relation to a child may appeal against a decision by the Inland Revenue—
(a) not to issue a voucher under section 5 in relation to the child,
(b) not to open a child trust fund for the child under section 6,
(c) not to make a payment under section 8 or 9 in respect of the child, or
(d) not to make a payment under regulations under section 10 in respect of the child.

(3) "Relevant person", in relation to a child, means—
(a) the person (if any) entitled to child benefit in respect of the child,
(b) anyone who applied to open a child trust fund for the child, and
(c) anyone who has, at any time, given instructions with respect to the management of the child trust fund held by the child.

(4) A person who is required by the Inland Revenue to account for an amount under regulations under section 11 or 13 may appeal against the decision to impose the requirement.

(5) The personal representatives of a child who has died may appeal against a decision by the Inland Revenue not to make a payment to them under section 19.

(6) A person on whom a penalty under section 20 is imposed may appeal against the decision to impose the penalty or its amount.

DEFINITIONS

"account provider": s.29.
"child": *ibid.*
"child trust fund": *ibid.*
"Inland Revenue": *ibid.*
"relevant person": subs.(3).

GENERAL NOTE

1.610 This section sets out the categories of person who can appeal against a decision relating to the child trust fund. In so far as there are any appeals, most appeals will presumably be brought by individuals and will concern the entitlement to child trust fund payments in individual cases (subs.(2)). However, companies who are refused permission by HMRC to act as account providers also have a right of appeal (subs.(1)). Subsections (4)–(6) ensure that various other persons have a right of appeal as appropriate. In particular, subs.(6) provides that any person on whom a

(2004 c.6, s.22)

penalty is imposed has a right of appeal against both the decision to levy the penalty and also the amount. The tribunal's powers on hearing appeals under this section are set out in s.21(9). In the short to medium term, child trust fund appeals will be heard by appeal tribunals and, on further appeal, by the Social Security Commissioners (s.24, temporarily modifying s.23: see General Note to s.21).

Exercise of rights of appeal

23.—(1) Notice of an appeal under section 22 against a decision must be given to the Inland Revenue in the manner prescribed by regulations within the period of thirty days after the date on which notice of the decision was given.

(2) Notice of such an appeal must specify the grounds of appeal.

(3) [¹. . .]

(4) [¹. . .]

(5) On the hearing of an appeal under section 22 the [¹appeal tribunal] may allow the appellant to put forward grounds not specified in the notice, and take them into consideration if satisfied that the omission was not wilful or unreasonable.

(6) [¹. . .]

(7) [¹. . .]

MODIFCATION

1. This section is set out above as modified by s.24(3).

DEFINITIONS

"appeal tribunal"—s.24(6).
"the Inland Revenue"—s.29 but note that the functions of the Inland Revenue have been transferred to HMRC by CRCA 2005.

GENERAL NOTE

Subs.(1)
See reg.3 of the Child Trust Funds (Non-tax Appeals) Regulations 2005 for the prescribed manner for giving notice of appeal.

Subs.(3)
This section provides for appeals to be brought before the General Commissioners and Special Commissioners but s.24(3) provides for their jurisdiction to be exercised, until further notice, by appeal tribunals from whom there is a right of appeal to a Social Security Commissioner on a point of law under s.14 of the Social Security Act 1998 (see s.24(5)).

Subs.(5)
This is in different terms from s.12(8)(a) of the Social Security Act 1998 (which does not apply to child trust fund appeals but provides that, in social security cases, a tribunal "need not consider any issue that is not raised by the appeal"). The tribunal is positively barred from taking account of grounds wilfully or unreasonably omitted from the notice of appeal in a child trust fund appeal. However, the tribunal is not discouraged from dealing with other matters not raised by the appellant. It is suggested that, in general, the approach required under this provision is much the same as that required under s.12(8)(a) of the 1998 Act because appellants very often cannot reasonably be expected to raise in a notice of appeal matters that are in fact significant.

Temporary modifications

24.—(1) Until such day as may be appointed by order—

1.611

1.612

1.613

1.614

1.615

1.616

(a) section 21 has effect subject to subsection (2),
(b) section 23 has effect subject to subsection (3), and
(c) section 182(2ZB) of the Finance Act 1989 (c. 26) has effect subject to subsection (4).

(2) The references to—
(a) the General Commissioners or Special Commissioners in subsection (9) of section 21, and
(b) the Commissioners in subsection (10) of that section,

are to the appeal tribunal; and an appeal from a decision of the appeal tribunal under subsection (9) of that section lies to a Social Security Commissioner rather than the High Court or the Court of Session (so that the reference to the court in subsection (10) of that section is to the Social Security Commissioner).

(3) An appeal under section 22 is to an appeal tribunal (rather than to the General Commissioners or Special Commissioners) so that—
(a) subsections (3), (4), (6) and (7) of section 23 do not apply, and
(b) the reference to the Commissioners in subsection (5) of that section is to the appeal tribunal.

(4) The reference to the General Commissioners or the Special Commissioners in section 182(2ZB) of the Finance Act 1989 is to an appeal tribunal.

(5) Regulations may apply any provision contained in—
(a) the Social Security Act 1998 (c. 14) (social security appeals: Great Britain),
(b) the Social Security (Northern Ireland) Order 1998 (S.I. 1998/1506 (N.I. 10)) (social security appeals: Northern Ireland), or
(c) section 54 of the Taxes Management Act 1970 (settling of appeals by agreement),

in relation to appeals which by virtue of this section are to an appeal tribunal, or lie to a Social Security Commissioner, but subject to such modifications as are prescribed by the regulations.

(6) "Appeal tribunal" means an appeal tribunal constituted—
(a) in Great Britain, under Chapter 1 of Part 1 of the Social Security Act 1998, or
(b) in Northern Ireland, under Chapter 1 of Part 2 of the Social Security (Northern Ireland) Order 1998.

(7) "Social Security Commissioner" means—
(a) in Great Britain, the Chief Social Security Commissioner or any other Social Security Commissioner appointed under the Social Security Act 1998 or a tribunal of three or more Commissioners constituted under section 16(7) of that Act, and
(b) in Northern Ireland, the Chief Social Security Commissioner or any other Social Security Commissioner appointed under the Social Security Administration (Northern Ireland) Act 1992 (c. 8) or a tribunal of two or more Commissioners constituted under Article 16(7) of the Social Security (Northern Ireland) Order 1998 (S.I. 1998/1506 (N.I. 10)).

DEFINITIONS

"appeal tribunal": subs.(6).
"General Commissioners": s.29.
"Social Security Commissioner": subs.(7).
"Special Commissioners": s.29.

(2004 c.6, s.24)

GENERAL NOTE

Although s.23 provides for appeals to be routed through the tax appeals machinery, this section provides that, for the time being at least, any appeals relating to child trust fund matters will be heard by appeal tribunals constituted under the SSA 1998, with a right of further appeal to the Social Security Commissioner. This applies to appeals against penalty decisions under s.21 (subs.(2)) and other child trust fund decisions under s.22 (subs.(3)). See the Child Trust Funds (Appeals) Regulations 2005 and the Social Security Commissioners (Procedure) (Child Trust Funds) Regulations 2005 for procedural provisions. The same type of "temporary modification" has applied to tax credit appeals since their introduction in April 2003 and shows no immediate sign of coming to an end (see Tax Credits Act 2002, s.63).

1.617

Supplementary

Northern Ireland

25. In Schedule 2 to the Northern Ireland Act 1998 (c. 47) (excepted matters), after paragraph 9 insert—
"9A Child Trust Funds."

1.618

GENERAL NOTE

The child trust fund scheme is added to the Schedule of excepted matters in the Northern Ireland Act 1998, so ensuring that the Fund is governed by legislation common to the whole of the United Kingdom (see also s.30).

26.	[*Omitted.*]	1.619
27.	[*Omitted.*]	1.620
28.	[*Omitted.*]	1.621
29.	[*Omitted.*]	1.622
30.	[*Omitted.*]	1.623
31.	[*Omitted.*]	1.624

Income Tax (Trading and Other Income) Act 2005

(2005 C.5)

CONTENTS

PART 1

OVERVIEW

1.	Overview of Act	1.625
2.	Overview of priority rules	

Income Tax (Trading and Other Income) Act 2005

PART 2

TRADING INCOME

CHAPTER 1

INTRODUCTION

3. Overview of Part 2
4. Provisions which must be given priority over Part 2

CHAPTER 2

INCOME TAXED AS TRADE PROFITS

Charge to tax on trade profits

5. Charge to tax on trade profits
6. Territorial scope of charge to tax
7. Income charged
8. Person liable

Trades and trade profits

9. Farming and market gardening

Starting and ceasing to trade

17. Effect of becoming or ceasing to be a UK resident

Rent-a-room and foster-care relief

23. Rent-a-room and foster-care relief

CHAPTER 3

TRADE PROFITS: BASIC RULES

24. Professions and vocations
25. Generally accepted accounting practice
26. Losses calculated on same basis as profits
27. Receipts and expenses

28. Items treated under CAA 2001 as receipts and expenses
29. Interest
31. Relationship between rules prohibiting and allowing deductions

CHAPTER 4

TRADE PROFITS: RULES RESTRICTING DEDUCTIONS

Introduction

32. Professions and vocations

Capital expenditure

33. Capital expenditure

Wholly and exclusively and losses rules

34. Expenses not wholly and exclusively for trade and unconnected

Bad and doubtful debts

35. Bad and doubtful debts

Unpaid remuneration

36. Unpaid remuneration

Business entertainment and gifts

45. Business entertainment and gifts: general rule

Social security contributions

53. Social security contributions

CHAPTER 6

TRADE PROFITS: RECEIPTS

Introduction

95. Professions and vocations

Income Tax (Trading and Other Income) Act 2005

Capital receipts

96. Capital receipts

Debts released

97. Debts incurred and later released

CHAPTER 15

BASIS PERIODS

INTRODUCTION

196. Professions and vocations
197. Meaning of "accounting date"
198. General rule

PART 3

PROPERTY INCOME

CHAPTER 1

INTRODUCTION

260. Overview of Part 3
261. Provisions which must be given priority over Part 3
262. Priority between Chapters within Part 3

CHAPTER 2

PROPERTY BUSINESSES

Introduction

263. Introduction

Basic meaning of UK and overseas property business

264. UK property business
265. Overseas property business

(2005 c.5)

Generating income from land

266. Meaning of "generating income from land"

CHAPTER 3

PROFITS OF PROPERTY BUSINESSES: BASIC RULES

Charge to tax on profits of a property business

268. Charge to tax on profits of a property business
269. Territorial scope of charge to tax
270. Income charged
271. Person liable

Calculation of profits

272. Profits of a property business: application of trading income rules

PART 4

SAVINGS AND INVESTMENT INCOME

CHAPTER 1

INTRODUCTION

365. Overview of Part 4
366. Provisions which must be given priority over Part 4
367. Priority between Chapters within Part 4
368. Territorial scope of Part 4 charges

CHAPTER 2

INTEREST

Charge to tax on interest

369. Charge to tax on interest
370. Income charged
371. Person liable

Other income taxed as interest

372. Building society dividends

CHAPTER 3

DIVIDENDS ETC. FROM UK RESIDENT COMPANIES ETC.

Introduction

382. Contents of Chapter

Charge to tax on dividends and other distributions

383. Charge to tax on dividends and other distributions
384. Income charged
385. Person liable

CHAPTER 4

DIVIDENDS FROM NON-UK RESIDENT COMPANIES

Charge to tax on dividends from non-UK resident companies

402. Charge to tax on dividends from non-UK resident companies
403. Income charged
404. Person liable

CHAPTER 7

PURCHASED LIFE ANNUITY PAYMENTS

422. Charge to tax on purchased life annuity payments
423. Meaning of "purchased life annuity"
424. Income charged
425. Person liable

Part 5

Miscellaneous Income

Chapter 1

Introduction

574. Overview of Part 5
575. Provisions which must be given priority over Part 5
576. Priority between Chapters within Part 5

Chapter 5

Settlements: Amounts Treated as Income of Settlor

Charge to tax under Chapter 5

619. Charge to tax under Chapter 5
620. Meaning of "settlement" and "settlor"

Income charged and person liable

621. Income charged
622. Person liable

Chapter 8

Income not Otherwise Charged

687. Charge to tax on income not otherwise charged
688. Income charged
689. Person liable

Part 6

Exempt Income

Chapter 1

Introduction

690. Overview of Part 6

Income Tax (Trading and Other Income) Act 2005

Chapter 2

National Savings Income

691.	National Savings Bank ordinary account interest [*omitted*]
692.	Income from savings certificates [*omitted*]

Chapter 8

Other Annual Payments

Certain annual payments by individuals

730.	Foreign maintenance payments

Periodical payments of personal injury damages etc.

731.	Periodical payments of personal injury damages
732.	Compensation awards
733.	Persons entitled to exemptions for personal injury payments etc.
734.	Payments from trusts for injured persons

Health and employment insurance payments

735.	Health and employment insurance payments
736.	Health and employment risks and benefits

Payments to adopters

744.	Payments to adopters: England and Wales

Chapter 9

Other Income

751.	Interest on damages for personal injury
753.	Interest on repayment of student loan
776.	Scholarship income
780.	Disabled person's vehicle maintenance grant

Chapter 10

General

783.	General disregard of exempt income for income tax purposes

(2005 c.5)

PART 7

INCOME CHARGED UNDER THIS ACT: RENT-A-ROOM AND FOSTER-CARE RELIEF

CHAPTER 1

RENT-A-ROOM RELIEF

Introduction

784. Overview of Chapter 1
785. Person who qualifies for relief

Basic definitions

786. Meaning of "rent-a-room receipts"
787. Meaning of "residence"
788. Meaning of "total rent-a-room amount"

Individual's limit

789. The individuals limit

CHAPTER 2

FOSTER-CARE RELIEF

Introduction

803. Overview of Chapter 2
804. Person who qualifies for relief

Basic definitions

805. Meaning of "foster-care receipts"
806. Meaning of providing foster care
807. Calculation of "total foster-care receipts" [*omitted*]

PART 10

GENERAL PROVISIONS

CHAPTER 1

INTRODUCTION

864. Overview of Part 10

Income Tax (Trading and Other Income) Act 2005

CHAPTER 2

GENERAL CALCULATON RULES ETC.

868.   Social security contributions: non-trades etc.

INTRODUCTION AND GENERAL NOTE

1.626   ITTOIA is the third of the series of Acts produced under the Tax Law Rewrite Project. It came into effect on April 6, 2005. Together with ITEPA it has rewritten all the main charging provisions of income tax as they apply to individuals, partnerships and trusts. Provisions applying to companies have not been rewritten, but they are not relevant to tax credits.

ITTOIA completes the abolition of all the former income tax schedules as its provisions replace the old Sch.A (taxation of income from land in the United Kingdom) and Sch.D, Cases I to VI (trading and professional income, investment income, and foreign source income). Following the approach adopted in ITEPA it also merges provisions about the taxation of UK-source income with the taxation of foreign source income. The relevance here is that assessment of income for tax credits purposes includes worldwide income. With effect from the tax year 2006–07 no reference therefore need be made to the old law for tax credits purposes.

The pattern adopted by ITTOIA is as follows. The charges to tax under the various Schedules and other separate charging sections have been converted into charges on different classes of income, and the rules relating to each kind of income are set out in separate Parts of the Act. These are then followed by general exemptions and other provisions. Each part has "signposts" in it, including an initial overview and provisions dealing with priorities between charging provisions.

The most important difference between kinds or classes of income is the one that lies between ITEPA and ITTOIA: is an individual employed or self-employed? ITTOIA operates if ITEPA does not, but the decision whether someone is employed or not in that narrower sense is left outside both Acts and for the ordinary law—and in the social security context is usually to be determined under the provisions of s.8 of the Social Security (Transfer of Functions) Act 1999.

The new charges to tax, exemptions and reliefs are:

Part 2 Trading income (including professions and vocations)

Part 3 Property income (including both UK and foreign land)

Part 4 Savings and investment income (including interest and dividends)

Part 5 Miscellaneous income (the "sweeper")

Part 6 Exempt income

Part 7 Rent-a-room and foster care reliefs

Trading income replaces the old Sch.D Cases I and II and part of Case VI. Property income replaces the old Sch.A and part of Sch.D Case V. Savings and investment income replaces the old Sch.D Case III and Case IV, part of Case V and part of Case VI. It also replaces Sch.F. (It also includes the former Sch.C, which was repealed and replaced by provisions included in Sch.D some years ago). As the former Sch.B was repealed many years ago, this completes the repeal for income tax (and therefore tax credits) purposes of all the old 1803 income tax schedules.

A consistent pattern within each part is to place the most important provisions at the start of the Part. For example, in the savings and investment income part the charge on interest comes first, then dividends, with less commonly used provisions following in decreasing order of importance. The Act also seeks to put all the important measures in the main text of the Act, rather than in schedules. This explains the need for a lengthy Pt 7, dealing with the important but inevitably detailed provisions that exempt small incomes from income tax if drawn from renting rooms in the individual's only or main residence or from foster care payments (or both).

The sections selected for inclusion
The sections set out in this work are selected for two reasons: first, they are the main sections of the Act and the ones to which reference is most likely to be made, directly or indirectly, in straightforward tax credits cases involving either the self-employed or forms of savings and investment income. Second, sections are included where they deal expressly with social security income or the kinds of income received in particular by those with disabilities. Provisions providing exemption from two specific kinds of income widely received by those with entitlement to tax credits are also included: tax relief under the rent-a-room scheme exempting income where a resident owner lets part of his or her house to a lodger; and the exemption of income paid to foster parents under foster-care relief.

The law is as applied for 2007–08 after any amendments in the Finance Acts. No history of amendments is set out. However, the full history of the original ITTOIA provisions (to which as yet little amendment has been made) are in the full explanatory notes to ITTOIA issued by the Tax Law Rewrite Project.

Part 1

Overview

Overview of Act

1.—(1) This Act imposes charges to income tax under—
(a) Part 2 (trading income),
(b) Part 3 (property income),
(c) Part 4 (savings and investment income), and
(d) Part 5 (certain miscellaneous income).
(2) *Repealed.*
(3) Exemptions from those charges are dealt with in Part 6 (exempt income) but any Part 6 exemptions which are most obviously relevant to particular types of income are also mentioned in the provisions about those types of income.
(4) What is or is not mentioned in those provisions does not limit the effect of Part 6.
(5) This Act also contains—
(a) provision about rent-a-room relief and foster-care relief (see Part 7),
(b) special rules for foreign income (see Part 8),
(c) special rules for partnerships (see Part 9), and
(d) certain calculation rules and general provisions (see Part 10).
(6) For abbreviations and defined expressions used in this Act, see 885 and Sch.4.

Overview of priority rules

2.—(1) This Act contains some rules establishing an order of priority in respect of certain amounts which would otherwise—

(a) fall within a charge to income tax under two or more Chapters or Parts of this Act, or
(b) fall within a charge to income tax under a Chapter or Part of this Act and ITEPA 2003.

(2) See, in particular—
section 4 (provisions which must be given priority over Part 2),
section 261 (provisions which must be given priority over Part 3),
section 262 (priority between Chapters within Part 3),
section 366 (provisions which must be given priority over Part 4),
section 367 (priority between Chapters within Part 4),
section 575 (provisions which must be given priority over Part 5), and
section 576 (priority between Chapters within Part 5).

(3) But the rules in those sections need to be read with other rules law (whether in this Act or otherwise) about the scope of particular provisions or the order of priority to be given to them.

(4) Section 171(2) of FA 1993 (profits of Lloyd's underwriters charged only under Chapter 2 of Part 2 of this Act) is one example of another rule of law.

PART 2

TRADING INCOME

CHAPTER 1

Overview of Part 2

1.630

3.—(1) This Part imposes charges to income tax under—
(a) Chapter 2 (the profits of a trade, profession or vocation which meet the territorial conditions mentioned in section 6),
(b) Chapter 17 (amounts treated as adjustment income under section 228), and
(c) Chapter 18 (post-cessation receipts that are chargeable under this Part).

(2) Part 6 deals with exemptions from the charges under this Part.

(3) See, in particular, the exemptions under sections 777 (VAT repayment supplements) and 778 (incentives to use electronic communications).

(4) The charges under this Part apply to non-UK residents as well as UK residents but this is subject to sections 6(2) and (3) and 243(3) and (4) (charges on non-UK residents only on UK income).

(5) The rest of this Part contains rules relevant to the charges to tax under this Part.

(6) This section needs to be read with the relevant priority rules (see sections 2 and 4).

GENERAL NOTE

1.631

Part 2 rewrites (and to some extent also codifies) the previous provisions in Sch.D Case I (income from trade wholly or partly in the UK) and Case II (income from professions and vocations) and aspects of Case IV (other income) previously in ICTA 1988 and subsequent Finance Acts. But the definition of "trade" remains in ICTA 1988 s.832. The charges under this Part on non-UK residents are not covered in this work.

(2005 c.5, s.4)

Provisions which must be given priority over Part 2

4.—(1) Any receipt or other credit item, so far as it falls within—   1.632
  (a) Chapter 2 of this Part (receipts of trade, profession or vocation), and
  (b) Chapter 3 of Part 3 so far as it relates to a UK property business,
is dealt with under Part 3.
  (2) Any receipt or other credit item, so far as it falls within—
  (a) this Part, and
  (b) Part 2, 9 or 10 of ITEPA 2003 (employment income, pension income or social security income),
is dealt with under the relevant Part of ITEPA 2003.

CHAPTER 2

INCOME TAXED AS TRADE PROFITS

Charge to tax on trade profits

Charge to tax on trade profits

5. Income tax is charged on the profits of a trade, profession or vocation.   1.633

Territorial scope of charge to tax

6.—(1) Profits of a trade arising to a UK resident are chargeable to tax under this Chapter wherever the trade is carried on.   1.634
  (2) Profits of a trade arising to a non-UK resident are chargeable to tax under this Chapter only if they arise—
  (a) from a trade carried on wholly in the United Kingdom, or
  (b) in the case of a trade carried on partly in the United Kingdom and partly elsewhere, from the part of the trade carried on in the United Kingdom.
  (3) This section applies to professions and vocations as it applies to trades.

Income charged

7.—(1) Tax is charged under this Chapter on the full amount of the profits of the tax year.   1.635
  (2) For this purpose the profits of a tax year are the profits of the basis period for the tax year.
  (3) For the rules identifying the basis period for a tax year, see Chapter 15.
  (4) This section is subject to Part 8 (foreign income: special rules).
  (5) And, for the purposes of section 830 (meaning of "relevant foreign income"), the profits of a trade, profession or vocation arise from a source outside the United Kingdom only if the trade, profession or vocation is carried on wholly outside the United Kingdom.

Person liable

8. The person liable for any tax charged under this Chapter is the person receiving or entitled to the profits.   1.636

Trades and trade profits

Farming and market gardening

1.637　9.—(1) Farming or market gardening in the United Kingdom is treated for income tax purposes as the carrying on of a trade or part of a trade (whether or not the land is managed on a commercial basis and with a view to the realisation of profits).

(2) All farming in the United Kingdom carried on by a person, other than farming carried on as part of another trade, is treated for income tax purposes as one trade.

(3) In the case of farming carried on by a firm, this rule is explained by section 859(1).

Starting and ceasing to trade

Effect of becoming or ceasing to be a UK resident

1.638　17.—(1) This section applies if—
(a) an individual carries on a trade wholly or partly outside the United Kingdom otherwise than in partnership, and
(b) the individual becomes or ceases to be UK resident.

(2) The individual is treated for income tax purposes—
(a) as permanently ceasing to carry on the trade at the time of the change of residence, and
(b) so far as the individual continues to carry on the trade, as starting to carry on a new trade immediately afterwards.

(3) But subsection (2) does not prevent a loss made before the change of residence from being deducted under section 831 of ITA 2007 against profits arising after the change.

(4) This section applies to professions and vocations as it applies to trades.

(5) In the case of a trade carried on by a firm, see sections 852(6) (7) and 854(5).

Rent-a-room and foster-care relief

Rent-a-room and foster-care relief

1.639　23.—(1) The rules for calculating the profits of a trade carried on by an individual are subject to Chapter 1 of Part 7 (rent-a-room relief).

(2) That Chapter provides relief on income from the use of furnished accommodation in the individual's only or main residence (see, in particular, sections 792 and 796).

(3) The rules for calculating the profits of a trade, profession or vocation carried on by an individual are subject to Chapter 2 of Part 7 (foster-care relief).

(4) That Chapter provides relief on income from the provision by the individual of foster care (see, in particular, sections 813, 816, 822 and 823).

(2005 c.5, s.24)

CHAPTER 3

TRADE PROFITS: BASIC RULES

Professions and vocations

24. Apart from section 30 (animals kept for trade purposes), the provisions of this Chapter apply to professions and vocations as they apply to trades.

1.640

Generally accepted accounting practice

25.—(1) The profits of a trade must be calculated in accordance with generally accepted accounting practice, subject to any adjustment required or authorised by law in calculating profits for income tax purposes.
  (2) This does not—
  (a) require a person to comply with the requirements of the Companies Act 1985 (c. 6) or the Companies (Northern Ireland) Order 1986 (S.I. 1986/1032 (N.I. 6)) except as to the basis of calculation, or
  (b) impose any requirements as to audit or disclosure.
  (3) This section is subject to section 160 (barristers and advocates in early years of practice).
  (4) This section does not affect provisions of the Income Tax Acts relating to the calculation of the profits of Lloyd's underwriters.

1.641

Losses calculated on same basis as profits

26.—(1) The same rules apply for income tax purposes in calculating losses of a trade as apply in calculating profits.
  (2) This is subject to any express provision to the contrary.

1.642

Receipts and expenses

27.—(1) In the Income Tax Acts, in the context of the calculation of the profits of a trade, references to receipts and expenses are to any items brought into account as credits or debits in calculating the profits.
  (2) There is no implication that an amount has been actually received or paid.
  (3) This section is subject to any express provision to the contrary.

1.643

Items treated under CAA 2001 as receipts and expenses

28. The rules for calculating the profits of a trade need to be read with—
  (a) the provisions of CAA 2001 which treat charges as receipts of a trade, and
  (b) the provisions of CAA 2001 which treat allowances as expenses of a trade.

1.644

Interest

29. For the purpose of calculating the profits of a trade, interest is an item of a revenue nature, whatever the nature of the loan.

1.645

Relationship between rules prohibiting and allowing deductions

31.—(1) Any relevant permissive rule in this Part—
  (a) has priority over any relevant prohibitive rule in this Part, but

1.646

301

(b) is subject to sections 48 (car or motor cycle hire) and 55 (crime-related payments).

(2) In this section "any relevant permissive rule in this Part" means any provision of—

(a) Chapter 5 (apart from sections 60 to 67),
(b) Chapter 11, or
(c) Chapter 13,

which allows a deduction in calculating the profits of a trade.

(3) In this section "any relevant prohibitive rule in this Part", in relation to any deduction, means any provision of this Part (apart from sections 48 and 55) which might otherwise be read as—

(a) prohibiting the deduction, or
(b) restricting the amount of the deduction.

CHAPTER 4

TRADE PROFITS: RULES RESTRICTING DEDUCTIONS

Introduction

Professions and vocations

1.647   32. The provisions of this Chapter apply to professions and vocations as they apply to trades.

Capital expenditure

Capital expenditure

1.648   33. In calculating the profits of a trade, no deduction is allowed for items of a capital nature.

Wholly and exclusively and losses rules

Expenses not wholly and exclusively for trade and unconnected losses

1.649   34.—(1) In calculating the profits of a trade, no deduction is allowed for—
(a) expenses not incurred wholly and exclusively for the purposes of the trade, or
(b) losses not connected with or arising out of the trade.

(2) If an expense is incurred for more than one purpose, this section does not prohibit a deduction for any identifiable part or identifiable proportion of the expense which is incurred wholly and exclusively for the purposes of the trade.

Bad and doubtful debts

Bad and doubtful debts

1.650   35.—(1) In calculating the profits of a trade, no deduction is allowed for a debt owed to the person carrying on the trade, except so far as—

(a) the debt is bad,
(b) the debt is estimated to be bad, or
(c) the debt is released wholly and exclusively for the purposes of the trade as part of a statutory insolvency arrangement.

(2) If the debtor is bankrupt or insolvent, the whole of the debt is estimated to be bad for the purposes of subsection (1)(b), except so far as any amount may reasonably be expected to be received on the debt.

Unpaid remuneration

Unpaid remuneration

36.—(1) This section applies if, in calculating the profits of a trade of a period of account—

1.651

(a) an amount is charged in the accounts for the period in respect of employees' remuneration, and
(b) a deduction for the remuneration would otherwise be allowable for the period.

(2) No deduction is allowed for the remuneration for the period of account unless it is paid before the end of the period of 9 months immediately following the end of the period of account.

(3) If the remuneration is paid after the end of that 9 month period, deduction for it is allowed for the period of account in which it is paid.

Business entertainment and gifts

Business entertainment and gifts: general rule

45.—(1) The general rule is that no deduction is allowed in calculating the profits of a trade for expenses incurred in providing entertainment or gifts in connection with the trade.

1.652

(2) A deduction for expenses which are incurred—
(a) in paying sums to or on behalf of an employee of the person carrying on the trade ("the trader"), or
(b) in putting sums at the disposal of an employee of the trader,
is prohibited by the general rule if (and only if) the sums are paid, or put at the employee's disposal, exclusively for meeting expenses incurred or to be incurred by the employee in providing the entertainment or gift.

(3) The general rule is subject to exceptions—
for entertainment (see section 46), and
for gifts (see section 47).

(4) For the purposes of this section and those two sections—
(a) "employee", in relation to a company, includes a director of the company and a person engaged in the management of the company,
(b) "entertainment" includes hospitality of any kind, and
(c) the expenses incurred in providing entertainment or a gift include expenses incurred in providing anything incidental to the provision of entertainment or a gift.

Social security contributions

Social security contributions

1.653　**53.**—(1) In calculating the profits of a trade, no deduction is allowed for any contribution paid by any person under—
(a) Part 1 of the Social Security Contributions and Benefits Act 1992 (c. 4), or
(b) Part 1 of the Social Security Contributions and Benefits (Northern Ireland) Act 1992 (c. 7).
(2) But this prohibition does not apply to an employer's contribution.
(3) For this purpose "an employer's contribution" means—
(a) a secondary Class 1 contribution,
(b) a Class 1A contribution, or
(c) a Class 1B contribution,
within the meaning of Part 1 of the Social Security Contributions and Benefits Act 1992 or of the Social Security Contributions and Benefits (Northern Ireland) Act 1992.

CHAPTER 6

TRADE PROFITS: RECEIPTS

Introduction

Professions and vocations

1.654　**95.** Apart from section 105 (industrial development grants), the provisions of this Chapter apply to professions and vocations as they apply to trades.

Capital receipts

Capital receipts

1.655　**96.**—(1) Items of a capital nature must not be brought into account as receipts in calculating the profits of a trade.
(2) But this does not apply to items which, as a result of any provision of this Part, are brought into account as receipts in calculating the profits of the trade.

Debts released

Debts incurred and later released

1.656　**97.**—(1) This section applies if—
(a) in calculating the profits of a trade, a deduction is allowed for the expense giving rise to a debt owed by the person carrying on the trade,

(b) all or part of the debt is released, and
(c) the release is not part of a statutory insolvency arrangement.
(2) The amount released—
(a) is brought into account as a receipt in calculating the profits of the trade, and
(b) is treated as arising on the date of the release.

Chapter 15

Basis Periods

Introduction

Professions and vocations

196. The provisions of this Chapter apply to professions and vocations as they apply to trades.

1.657

Accounting date

Meaning of "accounting date"

197.—(1) In this Chapter "accounting date", in relation to a tax year, means—
(a) the date in the tax year to which accounts are drawn up, or
(b) if there are two or more such dates, the latest of them.
(2) This is subject to—
(a) section 211(2) (middle date treated as accounting date), and
(b) section 214(3) (date treated as accounting date if date changed in tax year in which there is no accounting date).

1.658

The normal rules

General rule

198.—(1) The general rule is that the basis period for a tax year is the period of 12 months ending with the accounting date in that tax year.
(2) This applies unless a different basis period is given by one of the following sections—
    section 199 (first tax year),
    section 200 (second tax year),
    section 201 (tax year in which there is no accounting date),
    section 202 (final tax year),
    section 209 or 210 (first accounting date shortly before end of tax year),
    section 212 (tax year in which middle date treated as accounting date),

1.659

section 215 (change of accounting date in third tax year), and section 216 (change of accounting date in later tax year).

PART 3

PROPERTY INCOME

CHAPTER 1

INTRODUCTION

Overview of Part 3

1.660   260.—(1) This Part imposes charges to income tax under—
(a) Chapter 3 (the profits of a UK property business or an overseas property business),
(b) Chapter 7 (amounts treated as adjustment income under section 330),
(c) Chapter 8 (rent receivable in connection with a UK section 12(4) concern),
(d) Chapter 9 (rent receivable for UK electric-line wayleaves),
(e) Chapter 10 (post-cessation receipts arising from a UK property business), and
(f) Chapter 11 (overseas property income of a person to whom the remittance basis applies).
(2) Part 6 deals with exemptions from the charges under this Part.
(3) See, in particular, the exemptions under sections 769 (housing grants), 777 (VAT repayment supplements) and 778 (incentives to use electronic communications).
(4) The charges under Chapters 3, 7, 8, 9 and 10 apply to non-UK residents as well as UK residents but this is subject to section 269 (charges on non-UK residents only on UK source income).
(5) This section needs to be read with the relevant priority rules (see sections 2 and 261).

GENERAL NOTE

1.661   Part 3 brings together and rewrites the income tax rules formerly in Sch.A (applying to income from UK land) and Sch.D Case V (applying to income from overseas land) formerly in ICTA 1988 as amended. The way in which income from land has been taxed has varied over the years. The most recent approach, adopted here, is to align the income of landlords and others receiving income from the exploitation of land closely to the taxation of income from trade, and therefore to the rules now set out in Pt 2.

Provisions which must be given priority over Part 3

1.662   261. Any receipt or other credit item, so far as it falls within—
(a) Chapter 3 of this Part so far as it relates to an overseas property business or Chapter 8 or 9 of this Part (rent receivable in connection with a UK section 12(4) concern or for UK electric-line wayleaves), and
(b) Chapter 2 of Part 2 (receipts of a trade, profession or vocation),
is dealt with under Part 2.

(2005 c.5, s.262)

Priority between Chapters within Part 3

262.—(1) Any receipt, so far as it falls within—   1.663
  (a) Chapter 3 so far as it relates to a UK property business, and
  (b) Chapter 8 (rent receivable in connection with a UK section 12(4) concern),
is dealt with under Chapter 8.

(2) Any receipt, so far as it falls within—
  (a) Chapter 3 so far as it relates to a UK property business, and
  (b) Chapter 9 (rent receivable for UK electric-line wayleaves),
is dealt with under Chapter 9.

(3) Any receipt, so far as it falls within Chapter 8 (rent receivable in connection with a UK section 12(4) concern) and Chapter 9 (rent receivable for UK electric-line wayleaves), is dealt with under Chapter 9.

CHAPTER 2

PROPERTY BUSINESSES

Introduction

Introduction

263.—(1) This Chapter explains for the purposes of this Act what is   1.664
meant by—
  (a) a person's UK property business (see section 264), and
  (b) a person's overseas property business (see section 265).
(2) Both those sections need to be read with—
  (a) section 266 (which explains what is meant by generating income from land), and
  (b) section 267 (which provides that certain activities do not count as activities for generating income from land).
(3) In the case of the property business of a firm, the basic rules in sections 264 and 265 are explained in section 859(2) and (3).
(4) References in this Act to an overseas property business are to an overseas property business so far as any profits of the business are chargeable to tax under Chapter 3 (as to which see, in particular, section 269).
(5) Accordingly, nothing in Chapter 4 or 5 is to be read as treating an amount as a receipt of an overseas property business if the profits concerned would not be chargeable to tax under Chapter 3.
(6) In this Act "property business" means a UK property business or an overseas property business.

Basic meaning of UK and overseas property business

UK property business

264. A person's UK property business consists of—   1.665

307

(a) every business which the person carries on for generating income from land in the United Kingdom, and
(b) every transaction which the person enters into for that purpose otherwise than in the course of such a business.

Overseas property business

1.666   **265.** A person's overseas property business consists of—
(a) every business which the person carries on for generating income from land outside the United Kingdom, and
(b) every transaction which the person enters into for that purpose otherwise than in the course of such a business.

Generating income from land

Meaning of "generating income from land"

1.667   **266.**—(1) In this Chapter "generating income from land" means exploiting an estate, interest or right in or over land as a source of rents or other receipts.
(2) "Rents" includes payments by a tenant for work to maintain or repair leased premises which the lease does not require the tenant to carry out.
(3) "Other receipts" includes—
(a) payments in respect of a licence to occupy or otherwise use land,
(b) payments in respect of the exercise of any other right over land, and
(c) rentcharges and other annual payments reserved in respect of, or charged on or issuing out of, land.
(4) For the purposes of this section a right to use a caravan or houseboat at only one location is treated as a right deriving from an estate or interest in land.

CHAPTER 3

PROFITS OF PROPERTY BUSINESSES: BASIC RULES

Charge to tax on profits of a property business

Charge to tax on profits of a property business

1.668   **268.** Income tax is charged on the profits of a property business.

Territorial scope of charge to tax

1.669   **269.**—(1) Profits of a UK property business are chargeable to tax under this Chapter whether the business is carried on by a UK resident or a non-UK resident.
(2) Profits of an overseas property business are chargeable to tax under this Chapter only if the business is carried on by a UK resident.
(3) But, in the case of an overseas property business carried on by a UK resident to whom the remittance basis applies, the only profits of the business chargeable to tax under this Chapter are those in respect of land in the Republic of Ireland.

(2005 c.5, s.269)

(4) For a UK resident to whom the remittance basis applies, see also Chapter 11 (charge to tax on overseas property income other than income arising in Republic of Ireland).

Income charged

270.—(1) Tax is charged under this Chapter on the full amount of the profits arising in the tax year.
(2) Subsection (1) is subject to Part 8 (foreign income: special rules).

1.670

Person liable

271. The person liable for any tax charged under this Chapter is the person receiving or entitled to the profits.

1.671

Calculation of profits

Profits of a property business: application of trading income rules

272.—(1) The profits of a property business are calculated in the same way as the profits of a trade.
(2) *Omitted.*
(3) *Omitted.*

1.672

PART 4

SAVINGS AND INVESTMENT INCOME

CHAPTER 1

INTRODUCTION

Overview of Part 4

365.—(1) This Part imposes charges to income tax under—
(a) Chapter 2 (interest),
(b) Chapter 3 (dividends etc. from UK resident companies etc.),
(c) Chapter 4 (dividends from non-UK resident companies),
(d) Chapter 5 (stock dividends from UK resident companies),
(e) Chapter 6 (release of loan to participator in close company),
(f) Chapter 7 (purchased life annuity payments),
(g) Chapter 8 (profits from deeply discounted securities),
(h) Chapter 9 (gains from contracts for life insurance etc.),
(i) Chapter 10 (distributions from unauthorised unit trusts),
(j) Chapter 11 (transactions in deposits),
(k) Chapter 12 (disposals of futures and options involving guaranteed returns), and

1.673

(l) Chapter 13 (sales of foreign dividend coupons).

(2) Part 6 deals with exemptions from the charges under this Part.

(3) See, in particular, any exemptions mentioned in the particular Chapters.

(4) The charges under this Part apply to non-UK residents as well as UK residents but this is subject to section 368(2) (charges on non-UK residents only on UK source income).

(5) This section needs to be read with the relevant priority rules (see sections 2 and 366).

General Note

1.674 Part 4 brings together a number of separate charges to income tax on what used to be termed unearned income: interest and similar income from the former Sch.D Cases III (UK source) and IV (foreign securities) and V (foreign possessions), with dividends from the former Sch.F (distributions from UK companies) and again Sch.D Case V (dividends from foreign companies), and other payments such as annuities and income gains from life assurance policies and other forms of investment. Originally to be called investment income, it was given a wider flavour by adding "savings" to the heading. But it is not all-encompassing because other forms of unearned income are included in Pt 5. In practice, wide use is made of tax-exempt forms of saving and investment. The details of the exemptions are in Pt 6 of the Act, which—along with pension savings under Pt 9 of ITEPA and the treatment of capital gains under the separate regime under the Taxation of Chargeable Gains Act 1992—mean that many people pay only limited income tax on their savings income. Most of these exemptions also apply for tax credits. Tax credits also take no account of capital gains. As a result, claimants can protect their savings from tax credits as well as income tax.

Provisions which must be given priority over Part 4

1.675 **366.**—(1) Any income, so far as it falls within—
(a) any Chapter of this Part, and
(b) Chapter 2 of Part 2 (receipts of a trade, profession or vocation),
is dealt with under Part 2.

(2) Any income, so far as it falls within—
(a) any Chapter of this Part, and
(b) Chapter 3 of Part 3 so far as the Chapter relates to a UK property business,
is dealt with under Part 3.

(3) Any income, so far as it falls within—
(a) any Chapter of this Part other than Chapter 3 or 6, and
(b) Part 2, 9 or 10 of ITEPA 2003 (employment income, pension income or social security income),
is dealt with under the relevant Part of ITEPA 2003.

(4) Nothing in this section prevents amounts both—
(a) being counted as income for the purposes of Chapter 9 of this Part (gains from contracts for life insurance etc.), and
(b) being taken into account in calculating income, or counting as income, for the purposes of other Parts of this Act,
but see section 527 (reduction for sums taken into account otherwise than under Chapter 9).

Priority between Chapters within Part 4

1.676 **367.**—(1) Any income, so far as it falls within Chapter 2 (interest) and Chapter 8 (profits from deeply securities), is dealt with under Chapter 8.

(2) Any income, so far as it falls within Chapter 3 (dividends etc. UK resident companies etc.) and another Chapter, is dealt with under Chapter 3 (but this is subject to subsection (3)).

(3) Any income, so far as it falls within—
(a) Chapter 2 (interest) as a result of section 372 (building society dividends) or 379 (industrial and provident society payments), and
(b) Chapter 3,

is dealt with under Chapter 2.

Territorial scope of Part 4 charges

368.—(1) Income arising to a UK resident is chargeable to tax under this Part whether or not it is from a source in the United Kingdom.

(2) Income arising to a non-UK resident is chargeable to tax under this Part only if it is from a source in the United Kingdom.

(3) References in this section to income which is from a source in the United Kingdom include, in the case of any income which does not have a source, references to income which has a comparable connection to the United Kingdom.

(4) This section is subject to any express or implied provision to the contrary in this Part (or elsewhere in the Income Tax Acts).

CHAPTER 2

INTEREST

Charge to tax on interest

Charge to tax on interest

369.—(1) Income tax is charged on interest.

(2) The following sections extend what is treated as interest for certain purposes—
section 372 (building society dividends),
section 373 (open-ended investment company interest distributions),
section 376 (authorised unit trust interest distributions),
section 379 (industrial and provident society payments),
section 380 (funding bonds), and
section 381 (discounts).

(3) For exemptions, see in particular—
(a) Chapter 2 of Part 6 (national savings income),
(b) Chapter 3 of Part 6 (income from individual investment plans),
(c) Chapter 4 of Part 6 (SAYE interest),
(d) Chapter 6 of Part 6 (income from FOTRA securities),
(e) sections 749 to 756 (interest arising from repayment supplements, reserve certificates, damages for personal injury, employees' share schemes, repayments of student loans, the redemption of funding bonds and interest on certain foreign currency securities), and

(f) sections 757 to 767 (interest and royalty payments).

(4) Subsection (1) is also subject to Chapter 3 of Part 12 of ITA 2007 (exemptions for interest on securities to which Chapter 2 of that Part applies).

Income charged

1.679   **370.**—(1) Tax is charged under this Chapter on the full amount of the interest arising in the tax year.

(2) Subsection (1) is subject to Part 8 (foreign income: special rules).

Person liable

1.680   **371.** The person liable for any tax charged under this Chapter is the person receiving or entitled to the interest.

Other income taxed as interest

Building society dividends

1.681   **372.**—(1) Any dividend paid by a building society is treated as interest for the purposes of this Act.

(2) In this section "dividend" includes any distribution (whether or not described as a dividend).

CHAPTER 3

DIVIDENDS ETC. FROM UK RESIDENT COMPANIES ETC.

Introduction

Contents of Chapter

1.682   **382.**—(1) This Chapter—
(a) imposes a charge to income tax on dividends and other distributions of UK resident companies (see section 383),
(b) treats dividends as paid in some circumstances (see sections 386 to 391), and
(c) makes special provision where the charge is in respect of shares awarded under an approved share incentive plan (see sections 392 to 396).

(2) This Chapter also makes provision about tax credits, tax being treated as paid and reliefs available in respect of certain distributions which applies whether or not the distributions are otherwise dealt with under this Chapter (see sections 397 to 401).

(3) For exemptions from the charge under this Chapter, see in particular—

(2005 c.5, s.382)

Chapter 3 of Part 6 (income from individual investment plans),
Chapter 5 of that Part (venture capital trust dividends),
section 770 (amounts applied by SIP trustees acquiring dividend shares or retained for reinvestment), and
section 498 of ITEPA 2003 (no charge on shares ceasing to be subject to SIP in certain circumstances).

(4) In this Chapter "dividends" does not include income treated as arising under section 410 (stock dividends).

Charge to tax on dividends and other distributions

Charge to tax on dividends and other distributions

383.—(1) Income tax is charged on dividends and other distributions of a UK resident company. 1.683

(2) For income tax purposes such dividends and other distributions are to be treated as income.

(3) For the purposes of subsection (2), it does not matter that those dividends and other distributions are capital apart from that subsection.

Income charged

384.—(1) Tax is charged under this Chapter on the amount or value of the dividends paid and other distributions made in the tax year. 1.684

(2) Subsection (1) is subject to—
section 393(2) and (3) (later charge where cash dividends retained in SIPs are paid over), and
section 394(3) (distribution when dividend shares cease to be subject to SIP).

(3) See also section 398 (under which the amount or value of the dividends or other distributions is treated as increased if any person is entitled to a tax credit in respect of them).

Person liable

385.—(1) The person liable for any tax charged under this Chapter is— 1.685
(a) the person to whom the distribution is made or is treated as made (see Part 6 of ICTA and sections 386(3) and 389(3)), or
(b) the person receiving or entitled to the distribution.

(2) Subsection (1) is subject to—
section 393(4) (later charge where cash dividends retained in SIPs are paid over), and
section 394(4) (distribution when dividend shares cease to be subject to SIP).

CHAPTER 4

DIVIDENDS FROM NON-UK RESIDENT COMPANIES

Charge to tax on dividends from non-UK resident companies

Charge to tax on dividends from non-UK resident companies

1.686   **402.**—(1) Income tax is charged on dividends of a non-UK resident company.

(2) For exemptions, see in particular section 770 (amounts applied by SIP trustees acquiring dividend shares or retained for reinvestment).

(3) Subsection (1) is also subject to section 498 of ITEPA 2003 (no charge on shares ceasing to be subject to SIP in certain circumstances).

(4) In this Chapter "dividends" does not include dividends of a capital nature.

Income charged

1.687   **403.**—(1) Tax is charged under this Chapter on the full amount of the dividends arising in the tax year.

(2) Subsection (1) is subject to—

section 406(2) and (3) (later charge where cash dividends retained in SIPs are paid over),

section 407(3) (dividend payment when dividend shares cease to be subject to SIP), and

Part 8 (foreign income: special rules).

Person liable

1.688   **404.**—(1) The person liable for any tax charged under this Chapter is the person receiving or entitled to the dividends.

(2) Subsection (1) is subject to—

section 406(4) (later charge where cash dividends retained in SIPs are paid over), and

section 407(4) (dividend payment when dividend shares cease to be subject to SIP).

CHAPTER 7

PURCHASED LIFE ANNUITY PAYMENTS

Charge to tax on purchased life annuity payments

1.689   **422.**—(1) Income tax is charged on annuity payments made under a purchased life annuity.

(2) For exemptions, see in particular—
 (a) section 717 (exemption for part of purchased life annuity payments),
 (b) section 725 (annual payments under immediate needs annuities),

(c) section 731 (periodical payments of personal injury damages), and
(d) section 732 (compensation awards).

Meaning of "purchased life annuity"

423.—(1) In this Chapter "purchased life annuity" means an annuity—
(a) granted for consideration in money or money's worth in the ordinary course of a business of granting annuities on human life, and
(b) payable for a term ending at a time ascertainable only by reference to the end of a human life.

(2) For this purpose it does not matter that the annuity may in some circumstances end before or after the life.

1.690

Income charged

424.—(1) Tax is charged under this Chapter on the full amount of the annuity payments arising in the tax year.

(2) Subsection (1) is subject to Part 8 (foreign income: special rules).

1.691

Person liable

425. The person liable for any tax charged under this Chapter is the person receiving or entitled to the annuity payments.

1.692

PART 5

MISCELLANEOUS INCOME

CHAPTER 1

INTRODUCTION

Overview of Part 5

574.—(1) This Part imposes charges to income tax under—
(a) Chapter 2 (receipts from intellectual property),
(b) Chapter 3 (films and sound recordings: non-trade businesses),
(c) Chapter 4 (certain telecommunication rights: non-trading income),
(d) Chapter 5 (settlements: amounts treated as income of settlor),
(e) Chapter 6 (beneficiaries' income from estates in administration),
(f) Chapter 7 (annual payments not otherwise charged), and
(g) Chapter 8 (income not otherwise charged).

(2) Part 6 deals with exemptions from the charges under this Part.

(3) See, in particular, any exemptions mentioned in the Chapters of this Part.

(4) The charges under this Part apply to non-UK residents as well as UK residents but this is subject to section 577(2) (charges on non-UK residents only on UK source income).

1.693

(5) This section needs to be read with the relevant priority rules (see sections 2, 575 and 576).

Provisions which must be given priority over Part 5

1.694   575.—(1) Any income, so far as it falls within—
   (a) any Chapter of this Part, and
   (b) Chapter 2 of Part 2 (receipts of a trade, profession or vocation),
is dealt with under Part 2.
   (2) Any income, so far as it falls within—
   (a) any Chapter of this Part, and
   (b) Chapter 3 of Part 3 so far as the Chapter relates to a UK property business,
is dealt with under Part 3.
   (3) Any income, so far as it falls within—
   (a) any Chapter of this Part, and
   (b) Chapter 2 or 3 of Part 4 (interest and dividends etc. from UK resident companies etc.),
is dealt with under the relevant Chapter of Part 4.
   (4) Any income, so far as it falls within—
   (a) any Chapter of this Part, and
   (b) Part 2, 9 or 10 of ITEPA 2003 (employment income, pension income or social security income),
is dealt with under the relevant Part of ITEPA 2003.

Priority between Chapters within Part 5

1.695   576. Any income, so far as it falls within Chapter 2 (receipts from intellectual property) and Chapter 3 (films and sound recordings: non-trade businesses), is dealt with under Chapter 3.

CHAPTER 5

SETTLEMENTS: AMOUNTS TREATED AS INCOME OF SETTLOR

Charge to tax under Chapter 5

Charge to tax under Chapter 5

1.696   619.—(1) Income tax is charged on—
   (a) income which is treated as income of a settlor as a result of section 624 (income where settlor retains an interest),
   (b) income which is treated as income of a settlor as a result of section 629 (income paid to unmarried minor children of settlor),
   (c) capital sums which are treated as income of a settlor as a result of section 633 (capital sums paid to settlor by trustees of settlement), and
   (d) capital sums which are treated as income of a settlor as a result of section 641 (capital sums paid to settlor by body connected with settlement).

(2005 c.5, s.619)

(2) The charge on the settlor under subsection (1)(a) or (b) above operates on distribution income by treating the income as if it were income to which Chapter 2 of Part 2 of ITA 2007 (rates at which income tax is charged) applies as a result of subsection (2)(b) that section (income chargeable under Chapter 3, 5 or 6 of Part 4: etc. from UK resident companies etc. and release of loan to participator in close company).

(3) In subsection (2) "distribution income" means income which represents income received by the trustees of the settlement, or any other person to whom it is payable, which is—
  (a) income chargeable under Chapter 3 of Part 4 (dividends etc. from UK resident companies etc.),
  (b) income chargeable under Chapter 4 of Part 4 (dividends from non-UK resident companies),
  (c) income chargeable under Chapter 5 of Part 4 (stock dividends from UK resident companies),
  (d) income chargeable under Chapter 6 of Part 4 (release of loan to participator in close company), or
  (e) a relevant foreign distribution chargeable under Chapter 8 of this Part (income not otherwise charged).

(4) In subsection (3) "relevant foreign distribution" means any distribution of a non-UK resident company which—
  (a) is not chargeable under Chapter 4 of Part 4, but
  (b) would be chargeable under Chapter 3 of that Part if the company were UK resident.

GENERAL NOTE

The provisions in this chapter are complex but important as they include very wide anti-avoidance provisions that can affect income earners at all levels. They are all applied to the calculation of income for tax credit purposes, and therefore now have a double effect on many middle range income earners who seek to use trusts to cut their incomes. Sections 624–628 contain provisions designed to stop tax avoidance by putting money into a form of trust where the settlor has an interest in the trust, unless it is a trust between spouses or partners, or it is to a charity. Section 629 is a very widely drawn provision that has the effect of transferring back to a settlor any income given by the settlor to an unmarried minor child of the settlor (for example, by putting money in a building society account in the name of the child, or buying National Savings Certificates in the child's name). But see now the tax provisions designed to assist child trust funds, which allow all these provisions to be sidestepped to a limited extent if a child trust fund is used.

1.697

Meaning of "settlement" and "settlor"

620.—(1) In this Chapter—

"settlement" includes any disposition, trust, covenant, agreement, or transfer of assets (except that it does not include a charitable loan arrangement), and

"settlor", in relation to a settlement, means any person by whom the settlement was made.

(2) A person is treated for the purposes of this Chapter as having made a settlement if the person has made or entered into the settlement directly or indirectly.

(3) A person is, in particular, treated as having made a settlement if the person—

1.698

(a) has provided funds directly or indirectly for the purpose of the settlement,
(b) has undertaken to provide funds directly or indirectly for the purpose of the settlement, or
(c) has made a reciprocal arrangement with another person for the other person to make or enter into the settlement.

(4) This Chapter applies to settlements wherever made.

(5) In this section—

"charitable loan arrangement" means any arrangement so far as it consists of a loan of money made by an individual to a charity either—
(a) for no consideration, or
(b) for a consideration which consists only of interest, and

"charity" includes—
(a) trustees of the National Heritage Memorial Fund
(b) Historical Buildings and Monuments Commission for England
(c) National Endowment for Science, Technology and the Arts.

Income charged and person liable

Income charged

1.699 **621.** Tax is charged under this Chapter on all income and capital sums to which section 619(1) applies.

Person liable

1.700 **622.** The person liable for any tax charged under this Chapter is the settlor.

CHAPTER 8

INCOME NOT OTHERWISE CHARGED

Charge to tax on income not otherwise charged

1.701 **687.**—(1) Income tax is charged under this Chapter on income from any source that is not charged to income tax under or as a result of any other provision of this Act or any other Act.

(2) Subsection (1) does not apply to annual payments.

(3) Subsection (1) does not apply to income that would be charged to income tax under or as a result of another provision but for an exemption.

(4) The definition of "income" in section 878(1) does not apply for the purposes of this section.

(5) For exemptions from the charge under this Chapter, see in particular—
section 768 (commercial occupation of woodlands), and
section 779 (gains on commodity and financial futures).

Income charged

1.702 **688.**—(1) Tax is charged under this Chapter on the full amount of the income arising in the tax year.

(2) Subsection (1) is subject to—
(a) Chapter 1 of Part 7 (which provides relief on income from the use of furnished accommodation in an individual's only or main residence: see, in particular, sections 794 and 798),
(b) Chapter 2 of that Part (which provides relief on income from the provision by an individual of foster care: see, in particular, sections 814 and 817), and
(c) Part 8 (foreign income: special rules).

Person liable

689. The person liable for any tax charged under this Chapter is the person receiving or entitled to the income.

1.703

PART 6

EXEMPT INCOME

CHAPTER 1

INTRODUCTION

Overview of Part 6

690.—(1) This Part provides for certain exemptions from charges to income tax under this Act.

1.704

(2) The exemptions are dealt with in—
(a) Chapter 2 (national savings income),
(b) Chapter 3 (income from individual investment plans),
(c) Chapter 4 (SAYE interest),
(d) Chapter 5 (venture capital trust dividends),
(e) Chapter 6 (income from FOTRA securities),
(f) Chapter 7 (purchased life annuity payments),
(g) Chapter 8 (other annual payments), and
(h) Chapter 9 (other income).

(3) Chapter 10 explains that, in general, the effect of the exemptions is that the exempt amounts are ignored for other income tax purposes.

(4) Other exemptions, such as exemptions relating to particular categories of persons, may also be relevant to the charges to income tax under this Act.

(5) And the exemptions dealt with in this Part may themselves be relevant to charges to income tax outside this Act.

Income Tax (Trading and Other Income) Act 2005

Chapter 8

Other Annual Payments

Certain annual payments by individuals

Foreign maintenance payments

1.705   **730.**—(1) No liability to income tax arises under Part 5 in respect of an annual payment if—
(a) it is a maintenance payment,
(b) it arises outside the United Kingdom, and
(c) had it arisen in the United Kingdom it would be exempt from income tax under section 727 (certain annual payments by individuals).

(2) In subsection (1) "maintenance payment" means a periodical payment which meets conditions A and B.

(3) Condition A is that the payment is made under a court order or a written or oral agreement.

(4) Condition B is that the payment is made by a person—
(a) as one of the parties to a marriage [1 or civil partnership] to, or for the benefit of, and for the maintenance of, the other party,
(b) to any person under 21 for that person's own benefit, maintenance or education, or
(c) to any person for the benefit, maintenance or education of a person under 21.

(5) In subsection (4) "marriage" includes a marriage that has been dissolved or annulled [1, and "civil partnership" includes a civil partnership that has been dissolved or annulled].

(6) Subsection (1) also applies to a payment made by an individual's personal representatives if—
(a) the individual would have been liable to make it, and
(b) that subsection would have applied if the individual had made it.

Amendment

1. Tax and Civil Partnership Regulations 2005 (SI 2005/3229), reg.197 (December 5, 2005).

Periodical payments of personal injury damages etc.

Periodical payments of personal injury damages

1.706   **731.**—(1) No liability to income tax arises for the persons specified in section 733 in respect of periodical payments to which subsection (2) or annuity payments to which subsection (3) applies.

(2) This subsection applies to periodical payments made pursuant to—
(a) an order of the court, so far as it is made in reliance on section 2 of the Damages Act 1996 (c. 48) (periodical payments) (including an order as varied),

(b) an order of a court outside the United Kingdom which is similar to an order made in reliance on that section (including an order as varied),
(c) an agreement, so far as it settles a claim or action for damages in respect of personal injury (including an agreement as varied),
(d) an agreement, so far as it relates to making payments on account of damages that may be awarded in such a claim or action (including an agreement as varied), or
(e) a Motor Insurers' Bureau undertaking in relation to a claim or action in respect of personal injury (including an undertaking as varied).

(3) This subsection applies to annuity payments made under an annuity purchased or provided—
(a) by the person by whom payments to which subsection (2) applies would otherwise fall to be made, and
(b) in accordance with such an order, agreement or undertaking as is mentioned in subsection (2) or a varying order, agreement or undertaking.

(4) In this section "damages in respect of personal injury" includes in respect of a person's death from personal injury.

(5) In this section "personal injury" includes disease and impairment of physical or mental condition.

(6) In this section "a Motor Insurers' Bureau undertaking" means an undertaking given by—
(a) the Motor Insurers' Bureau (being the company of that name incorporated on 14th June 1946 under the Companies Act 1929 (c. 23)), or
(b) an Article 75 insurer under the Bureau's Articles of Association.

Compensation awards

732.—(1) No liability to income tax arises for the persons specified in section 733 in respect of annuity payments if they are made under an annuity purchased or provided under an award of compensation made under the Criminal Injuries Compensation Scheme.

(2) The Treasury may by order provide for sections 731, 733 and 734 to apply, with such modifications as they consider necessary, to periodical payments by way of compensation for personal injury for which provision is made under a scheme or arrangement other than the Criminal Injuries Compensation Scheme.

(3) In this section—
"the Criminal Injuries Compensation Scheme" means—
(a) the schemes established by arrangements made under the Criminal Injuries Compensation Act 1995 (c. 53),
(b) arrangements made by the Secretary of State for compensation for criminal injuries in operation before the commencement of those schemes, or
(c) the scheme established under the Criminal Injuries (Northern Ireland) Order 2002 (S.I. 2002/796) (N.I.1), and
"personal injury" includes disease and impairment of physical or mental condition.

Persons entitled to exemptions for personal injury payments etc.

733. The persons entitled to the exemptions given by sections 731(1) and 732(1) for payments are—

(a) the person entitled to the damages under the order, agreement, or to the compensation under the award in question ("A"),
(b) a person who receives the payment in question on behalf of A, and
(c) a trustee who receives the payment in question on trust for the benefit of A under a trust under which A is, while alive, the only person who may benefit.

Payments from trusts for injured persons

734.—(1) No liability to income tax arises for the persons specified in subsection (2) in respect of sums paid under a lifetime trust—
(a) to the person ("A") who is entitled to—
   (i) a payment under an order, agreement or undertaking within section 731(2) or an annuity purchased or provided as mentioned in section 731(3), or
   (ii) compensation under an award within section 732(1), or
(b) for the benefit of A.
(2) The persons are—
(a) A, and
(b) if subsection (1)(b) applies, a person who receives the sum on behalf of A.
(3) For the purposes of subsection (1), sums are paid under a lifetime trust if they are paid—
(a) by the trustees of a trust under which A is, while alive, the only person who may benefit, and
(b) out of payments within section 731(2) or (3) or 732(1) which are received by them on trust for A.

Health and employment insurance payments

Health and employment insurance payments

735.—(1) No liability to income tax arises under this Act in respect of an annual payment under an insurance policy if—
(a) the payment is a benefit provided under so much of the policy as insures against a health or employment risk (see section 736),
(b) no part of any premiums under the policy has been deductible in calculating the income of the insured for income tax purposes, and
(c) the conditions in sections 737 and 738 and, so far as applicable, in sections 739 and 740 are met in relation to the policy.
(2) Subsection (1)(b) is subject to section 743.
(3) For the meaning of "the insured", see sections 742 and 743(2).

Health and employment risks and benefits

736.—(1) For the purposes of sections 735 and 737 to 743, a policy insures against a health risk if it insures against the insured becoming, or becoming in any specified way, subject—
(a) to any physical or mental illness, disability, infirmity or defect, or
(b) to any deterioration in a condition resulting from any such illness, disability, infirmity or defect.

(2005 c.5, s.736)

(2) For the purposes of sections 735 and 737 to 743, a policy insures against an employment risk if it insures against circumstances arising as a result of which the insured ceases—
(a) to be employed or hold office, or
(b) to carry on any trade, profession or vocation.

(3) For the purposes of section 735, this section and sections 737 to 743, references to insurance against a risk include insurance providing for benefits payable otherwise than by way of indemnity if the circumstances insured against occur.

Payments to adopters

Payments to adopters: England and Wales

744. No liability to income tax arises in respect of the following payments—   1.712
  (a) any payment or reward falling within section 57(3) of the Adoption Act 1976 (c. 36) (payments authorised by the court) which is made to a person who has adopted or intends to adopt a child,
  (b) payments under section 57(3A)(a) of that Act (payments by adoption agencies of legal or medical expenses of persons seeking to adopt),
  (c) payments of allowances under regulations under section 57A of that Act (permitted allowances to persons who have adopted or intend to adopt children),
  (d) payments of financial support made in the course of providing adoption support services within the meaning of the Adoption and Children Act 2002 (c. 38) (see section 2(6) and (7) of that Act), and
  (e) payments made under regulations under paragraph 3(1) of Schedule 4 to that Act (transitional and transitory provisions: adoption support services).

CHAPTER 9

OTHER INCOME

Interest on damages for personal injury

751.—(1) No liability to income tax arises in respect of interest on damages for personal injury or death if—   1.713
  (a) it is included in a sum awarded by a court,
  (b) it does not relate to the period between the making and satisfaction of the award, and
  (c) in the case of an award by a court in a country outside the United Kingdom, it is exempt from any charge to tax in that place.

(2) No liability to income tax arises in respect of interest if—
  (a) it is included in a payment in satisfaction of a cause of action (including a payment into court), and
  (b) it would fall within subsection (1) if it were included in a sum awarded by a court in respect of a cause of action.

(3) In subsection (1)—
"damages" in Scotland includes solatium, and
"personal injury" includes disease and impairment of physical or mental condition.

Interest on repayment of student loan

1.714   753.—(1) No liability to income tax arises in respect of interest if—
(a) it is paid to a person to whom a student loan has been made, and
(b) it relates to an amount repaid to the person after being recovered from the person in respect of the loan.
(2) In this section "student loan" means a loan made under—
section 22 of the Teaching and Higher Education Act 1998 (c. 30),
section 73(f) of the Education (Scotland) Act 1980 (c. 44), or
Article 3 of the Education (Student Support) (Northern Ireland) Order 1998 (S.I. 1998/1760 (N.I. 14)).

Scholarship income

1.715   776.—(1) No liability to income tax arises in respect of income from a scholarship held by an individual in full-time education at a university, college, school or other educational establishment.
(2) This exemption is subject to section 215 of ITEPA 2003 (under which only the scholarship holder is entitled to the exemption if the scholarship is provided by reason of another person's employment).
(3) In this section "scholarship" includes a bursary, exhibition or other similar educational endowment.

Disabled person's vehicle maintenance grant

1.716   780.—(1) No liability to income tax arises in respect of a disabled person's vehicle maintenance grant.
(2) For this purpose a "disabled person's vehicle maintenance grant" means a grant to any person owning a vehicle that is made under—
(a) paragraph 2 of Schedule 2 to the National Health Service Act 1977 (c. 49),
(b) section 46(3) of the National Health Service (Scotland) Act 1978 (c. 29), or
(c) Article 30 of the Health and Personal Social Services (Northern Ireland) Order 1972 (S.I. 1972/1265 (N.I. 14)), and Training Act (Northern Ireland) 1950 (c. 29 (N.I.)).

CHAPTER 10

GENERAL

General disregard of exempt income for income tax purposes

1.717   783.—(1) Amounts of income which are exempt from income tax as a result of this Part (whether because the type of income concerned is exempt from every charge to income tax or because it is exempt from every charge that is relevant to those particular amounts) are accordingly to be ignored for all other income tax purposes.

(2005 c.5, s.783)

(2) An exception to this is that interest on deposits in ordinary accounts with the National Savings Bank which is exempt under this Part from every charge to income tax is not to be ignored for the purpose of providing information.

(3) This express exception to subsection (1) is without prejudice to the existence of any other implied or express exception to that subsection (whether in connection with the provision of information or otherwise).

PART 7

INCOME CHARGED UNDER THIS ACT: RENT-A-ROOM AND FOSTER-CARE RELIEF

CHAPTER 1

RENT-A-ROOM RELIEF

Introduction

Overview of Chapter 1

784.—(1) This Chapter provides relief on income from the use of furnished accommodation in an individual's only or main residence. The relief is referred to in this Chapter as "rent-a-room relief".   1.718

(2) The form of relief depends on whether the individual's total rent-a-room amount exceeds the individual's limit (see sections 788 to 790).

(3) If it does not, the income is not charged to income tax unless the individual elects otherwise (see sections 791 to 794).

(4) If it does, the individual may elect for alternative methods of calculating the income (see sections 795 to 798).

Person who qualifies for relief

785.—(1) An individual qualifies for rent-a-room relief for a tax year if the individual—   1.719
  (a) has rent-a-room receipts for the tax year (see section 786), and
  (b) does not derive any taxable income other than rent-a-room receipts from a relevant trade, letting or agreement.

(2) "Taxable income" means receipts or other income in respect of which the individual is liable to income tax for the tax year.

(3) A relevant trade, letting or agreement is one from which the individual derives rent-a-room receipts for the tax year.

Basic definitions

Meaning of "rent-a-room receipts"

786.—(1) For the purposes of this Chapter an individual has rent-a-room receipts for a tax year if—   1.720

(a) the receipts are in respect of the use of furnished accommodation in a residence in the United Kingdom or in respect of goods or services supplied in connection with that use,
(b) they accrue to the individual during the income period for those receipts (see subsections (3) and (4)),
(c) for some or all of that period the residence is the individual's only or main residence, and
(d) the receipts would otherwise be brought into account in calculating the profits of a trade or UK property business or chargeable to income tax under Chapter 8 of Part 5 (income not otherwise charged).

(2) Meals, cleaning and laundry are examples of goods or services supplied in connection with the use of furnished accommodation in a residence.

(3) If the receipts would otherwise be brought into account in calculating the profits of a trade, the income period is the basis period for the tax year (see Chapter 15 of Part 2).

(4) Otherwise the income period is the period which—
(a) begins at the beginning of the tax year or, if later, the beginning of the letting in respect of which the receipts arise, and
(b) ends at the end of the tax year or, if earlier, the end of that letting.

Meaning of "residence"

1.721   787.—(1) In this Chapter "residence" means—
(a) a building, or part of a building, occupied or intended to be occupied as a separate residence, or
(b) a caravan or houseboat.

(2) If a building, or part of a building, designed for permanent use as a single residence is temporarily divided into two or more separate residences, it is still treated as a single residence.

Meaning of "total rent-a-room amount"

1.722   788.—(1) For the purposes of this Chapter an individual's "total rent-a-room amount" for a tax year is the total of—
(a) the individual's rent-a-room receipts for the tax year, and
(b) any relevant balancing charges for the tax year (see section 802).

(2) In calculating the total rent-a-room amount, no deduction is allowed for expenses or any other matter.

Individual's limit

The individual's limit

1.723   789.—(1) For the purposes of this Chapter an individual's limit for a tax year depends on whether the individual meets the exclusive receipts condition for the tax year (see section 790).

(2) If the individual does, the individual's limit for the tax year is the basic amount for the tax year.

(3) If the individual does not, the individual's limit for the tax year is half that amount.

(4) The basic amount for a tax year is £4250.

(2005 c.5, s.789)

(5) The Treasury may by order amend the sum for the time being specified in subsection (4).

Chapter 2

Foster-care Relief

Introduction

Overview of Chapter 2

803.—(1) This Chapter provides relief on income from the provision by an individual of foster care.

The relief is referred to in this Chapter as "foster-care relief".

(2) The form of relief depends on whether the individual's total foster-care receipts exceed the individual's limit (see sections 807 to 811).

(3) If they do not, the income is not charged to income tax (see sections 812 to 814).

(4) If they do, the individual may elect for an alternative method of calculating the income (see sections 815 to 819).

(5) If the foster-care receipts are the receipts of a trade, special rules apply—
  (a) if the period of account of the trade does not end on 5th April (see sections 820 to 823), and
  (b) in relation to capital allowances (see sections 824 to 827).

(6) The provisions of this Chapter which are expressed to apply in relation to trades also apply in relation to professions and vocations.

1.724

Person who qualifies for relief

804.—(1) An individual qualifies for foster-care relief for a tax year if the individual—
  (a) has foster-care receipts for the tax year (see section 805), and
  (b) does not derive any taxable income other than foster-care receipts from a relevant trade or arrangement.

(2) "Taxable income" means receipts or other income in respect of which the individual is liable to income tax for the tax year.

(3) A relevant trade or arrangement is one from which the individual derives foster-care receipts for the tax year.

1.725

Basic definitions

Meaning of "foster-care receipts"

805.—(1) For the purposes of this Chapter an individual has foster-care receipts for a tax year if—
  (a) the receipts are in respect of the provision of foster care,
  (b) they accrue to the individual during the income period for those receipts (see subsections (2) and (3)), and

1.726

(c) the receipts would otherwise be brought into account in calculating the profits of a trade or chargeable to income tax under Chapter 8 of Part 5 (income not otherwise charged).

(2) If the receipts would otherwise be brought into account in calculating the profits of a trade, the income period is the basis period for the tax year (see Chapter 15 of Part 2).

(3) Otherwise the income period is the tax year.

Meaning of providing foster care

806.—(1) For the purposes of this Chapter foster care is provided if an individual—
(a) provides accommodation and maintenance for a child, and
(b) does so as a foster carer.

(2) An individual is a foster carer if the child is placed with the individual under any of the following enactments, unless the individual is excluded by subsection (5).

(3) The enactments are—
(a) section 23(2)(a) or 59(1)(a) of the Children Act 1989 (c. 41) (provision of accommodation for children by local authorities or voluntary organisations),
(b) regulations under section 5 of the Social Work (Scotland) Act 1968 (c. 49),
(c) section 70 of the Children (Scotland) Act 1995 (c. 36), and
(d) Article 27(2)(a) or 75(1)(a) of the Children (Northern Ireland) 1995 (S.I. 1995/755 (N.I. 2)) (provision of accommodation for children by authorities or voluntary organisations).

(4) An individual is also a foster carer if—
(a) the individual is approved as a foster carer by a local authority or a voluntary organisation in accordance with regulations under section 5 of the Social Work (Scotland) Act 1968 (c. 49), and
(b) the child in respect of whom the accommodation is provided is being "looked after" by a local authority within the meaning of section 17(6) of the Children (Scotland) Act 1995 (c. 36), unless the individual is excluded by subsection (5).

(5) The following are excluded individuals—
(a) a parent of the child,
(b) an individual who is not a parent of the child but who has parental responsibility (or, in Scotland, parental responsibilities) in relation to the child,
(c) if the child is in care and there was a residence order in force with respect to the child immediately before the care order was made, an individual in whose favour the residence order was made, and
(d) (in Scotland) if the child is in care and there was a residence order or contact order in force with respect to the child immediately before the child was placed in care, an individual in whose favour the residence order or contact order was made.

(2005 c.5, s.864)

Part 10

General Provisions

Chapter 1

Introduction

Overview of Part 10

864. This Part— 1.728
(a) contains general rules which are of wider application than to a particular Part of this Act including certain calculation rules (see Chapter 2), and
(b) deals with supplementary matters including general definitions (see Chapter 3).

Social security contributions

Social security contributions: non-trades etc.

868.—(1) This section applies for the purpose of calculating profits or other income charged to income tax. 1.729
(2) For this purpose "profits or other income" does not include—
(a) the profits of a trade, profession, or vocation,
(b) the profits of a property business, or
(c) employment income,
but see subsection (6).
(3) No deduction is allowed for any contribution paid by any person under—
(a) Part 1 of the Social Security Contributions and Benefits Act 1992 (c.4), or
(b) Part 1 of the Social Security Contributions and Benefits (Northern Ireland) Act 1992 (c.7).
(4) But this prohibition does not apply to an employer's contribution.
(5) For this purpose "an employer's contribution" means—
(a) a secondary Class 1 contribution,
(b) a Class 1A contribution, or
(c) a Class 1B contribution,
within the meaning of Part 1 of the Social Security Contributions and Benefits Act 1992 (c.4) or of the Social Security Contributions and Benefits (Northern Ireland) Act 1992 (c.7).
(6) Provision corresponding to that made by this section is made by—
(a) section 53 (in relation to trades, professions and vocations),
(b) section 272 (in relation to property businesses), and
(c) section 360A of ITEPA 2003 (in relation to employment income).

Commissioners for Revenue and Customs Act 2005

Commissioners for Revenue and Customs Act 2005

(2005 c.11)

ARRANGEMENT OF SECTIONS

Commissioners and officers

1.730
1. The Commissioners
2. Officers of Revenue and Customs
3. Declaration of confidentiality
4. Her Majesty's Revenue and Customs

Functions

5. Commissioners' initial functions
7. Former Inland Revenue matters
9. Ancillary powers

Exercise of functions

12. Commissioners' arrangements
13. Exercise of Commissioners' functions by officers

Information

17. Use of information
18. Confidentiality
23. Freedom of information

Offences

31. Obstruction
32. Assault
33. Power of arrest

General

50. Consequential amendments, &c.

Schedule 1 Former Inland Revenue Matters

INTRODUCTION AND GENERAL NOTE

1.731   This Act provides the necessary statutory machinery to bring about a major restructuring of the policy formation and administration of all United Kingdom taxes and of the tax credits, benefits and other matters formerly administered by the Commissioners (or Board) of Inland Revenue and the Commissioners of HM Customs and Excise. Although this may seem a major reform in the British context as it abolishes the oldest British government department, it is perhaps a catching-up exercise with others. The United Kingdom is the last of the European Union states to bring together the collection of its direct and indirect taxes. The process was not simply a merger. The central policy teams of both the Inland Revenue and Customs and Excise were transferred to the Treasury, uniting the previously divided fiscal policy teams. Law enforcement has also been transferred elsewhere. The Act creates a separate Revenue and Customs Prosecution Office (under provisions not set out in this book), while some enforcement officers were transferred to the new Serious Crimes agency.

The opportunity was also taken to start the process of rationalising the powers of the previous two Departments, reflecting a process of integration that started some time before the formal merger took place in April 2005. The Inland Revenue Regulation Act 1890, set out in previous editions of this volume, has been repealed in entirety as have other administrative provisions dealing with the two Departments. Like its predecessors, the new Department, formally known as Her Majesty's Revenue and Customs (or HMRC), is headed by a body of Commissioners and not Ministers of the Crown. But for legal purposes the Commissioners for Revenue and Customs (as they are known) together are deemed to be a Minister of the Crown. As part of the merger, the hallowed (if not revered) status of Her Majesty's Inspector of Taxes has gone, as have other separate roles for individual officers of the two Departments. Instead, they now become "officers of Revenue and Customs"—though we doubt that the old practice of using initials (HMIT) will be used for the new name! One result is that the past custom of having the names of individual inspectors of tax on the names of court and tribunal cases has ended. All new tax, duty, tax credit and benefit cases will be taken in the name of HM Revenue and Customs.

The Act provides the relevant authority for HMRC to take over all existing responsibilities from the previous Boards and officers and for all necessary changes to be read into Acts of Parliament and subordinate legislation. We have adopted those revisions in this volume. References to "the Board" (meaning the Board of Inland Revenue) are therefore replaced by references to "the Commissioners", and references to "an officer of the Board" or similar by references to "an officer of Revenue and Customs". This will have the incidental effect of standardising widely variant language in past Acts. Further, wide powers of delegation are contained in this Act. In practice powers will be given to "the Commissioners" or "an officer of Revenue and Customs". But the former has authority to delegate almost all its functions to officers. An example of this delegation being standard practice is the delegation under the Tax Credits Act 2002. This Act replaces s.2 of that Act and, in effect, reads this Act into the administrative provisions relevant to that Act.

The Act was intended to come into effect on April 1, 2005, the beginning of the financial and tax year. The start was delayed a few days by the process leading up to the general election in May, but in effect HMRC may be regarded as being established with effect from the beginning of the 2005 tax year.

Commissioners and officers

The Commissioners

1.—(1) Her Majesty may by Letters Patent appoint Commissioners for Her Majesty's Revenue and Customs.

(2) The Welsh title of the Commissioners shall be Comisynwyr Cyllid a Thollau Ei Mawrhydi.

(3) A Commissioner—
(a) may resign by notice in writing to the Treasury, and
(b) otherwise, shall hold office in accordance with the terms and conditions of his appointment (which may include provision for dismissal).

(4) In exercising their functions, the Commissioners act on behalf of the Crown.

(5) Service as a Commissioner is service in the civil service of the State.

1.732

Officers of Revenue and Customs

1.733　**2.**—(1) The Commissioners may appoint staff, to be known as officers of Revenue and Customs.

(2) A person shall hold and vacate office as an officer of Revenue and Customs in accordance with the terms of his appointment (which may include provision for dismissal).

(3) An officer of Revenue and Customs shall comply with directions of the Commissioners (whether he is exercising a function conferred on officers of Revenue and Customs or exercising a function on behalf of the Commissioners).

(4) Anything (including anything in relation to legal proceedings) by or in relation to one officer of Revenue and Customs may be continued by or in relation to another.

(5) Appointments under subsection (1) may be made only with the approval of the Minister for the Civil Service as to terms and conditions of service.

(6) Service in the employment of the Commissioners is service in the civil service of the State.

(7) In Schedule 1 to the Interpretation Act 1978 (c. 30) (defined expressions) at the appropriate place insert—

"'Officer of Revenue and Customs' has the meaning given by section 2(1) of the Commissioners for Revenue and Customs Act 2005."

Declaration of confidentiality

1.734　**3.**—(1) Each person who is appointed under this Act as a Commissioner or officer of Revenue and Customs shall make a declaration acknowledging his obligation of confidentiality under section 18.

(2) A declaration under subsection (1) shall be made—
 (a) as soon as is reasonably practicable following the person's appointment, and
 (b) in such form, and before such a person, as the Commissioners may direct.

(3) For the purposes of this section, the renewal of a fixed term appointment shall not be treated as an appointment.

"Her Majesty's Revenue and Customs"

1.735　**4.**—(1) The Commissioners and the officers of Revenue and Customs may together be referred to as Her Majesty's Revenue and Customs.

(2) The Welsh title of the Commissioners and the officers of Revenue and Customs together shall be Cyllid a Thollau Ei Mawrhydi.

(3) In Schedule 1 to the Interpretation Act 1978 (defined expressions) at the appropriate place insert—

"'Her Majesty's Revenue and Customs' has the meaning given by section 4 of the Commissioners for Revenue and Customs Act 2005."

Functions

Commissioners' initial functions

1.736　**5.**—(1) The Commissioners shall be responsible for—

(a) the collection and management of revenue for which the Commissioners of Inland Revenue were responsible before the commencement of this section,
(b) the collection and management of revenue for which the Commissioners of Customs and Excise were responsible before the commencement of this section, and
(c) the payment and management of tax credits for which the Commissioners of Inland Revenue were responsible before the commencement of this section.

(2) The Commissioners shall also have all the other functions which before the commencement of this section vested in—
(a) the Commissioners of Inland Revenue (or in a Commissioner), or
(b) the Commissioners of Customs and Excise (or in a Commissioner).

(3) This section is subject to section 35.

(4) In this Act "revenue" includes taxes, duties and national insurance contributions.

Former Inland Revenue matters

7.—(1) This section applies to the matters listed in Schedule 1.

(2) A function conferred by an enactment (in whatever terms) on any of the persons specified in subsection (3) shall by virtue of this subsection vest in an officer of Revenue and Customs—
(a) if or in so far as it relates to a matter to which this section applies, and
(b) in so far as the officer is exercising a function (whether or not by virtue of paragraph (a)) which relates to a matter to which this section applies.

(3) Those persons are—
(a) an officer of the Commissioners of Inland Revenue,
(b) an officer of the Board of Inland Revenue,
(c) an officer of inland revenue,
(d) a collector of Inland Revenue,
(e) an inspector of taxes,
(f) a collector of taxes,
(g) a person authorised to act as an inspector of taxes or collector of taxes for specific purposes,
(h) an officer having powers in relation to tax,
(i) a revenue official,
(j) a person employed in relation to Inland Revenue (or "the Inland Revenue"), and
(k) an Inland Revenue official.

(4) In so far as an officer of Revenue and Customs is exercising a function which relates to a matter to which this section applies, section 6(1) shall not apply.

(5) This section is subject to section 35.

Ancillary powers

9.—(1) The Commissioners may do anything which they think—
(a) necessary or expedient in connection with the exercise of their functions, or
(b) incidental or conducive to the exercise of their functions.

(2) This section is subject to section 35.

Commissioners for Revenue and Customs Act 2005

Commissioners' arrangements

1.739
12.—(1) The Commissioners shall make arrangements for—
(a) the conduct of their proceedings, and
(b) the conduct of the proceedings of any committee established by them.
(2) Arrangements under subsection (1) may, in particular—
(a) make provision for a quorum at meetings;
(b) provide that a function of the Commissioners—
  (i) may be exercised by two Commissioners, or
  (ii) may be exercised by a specified number of Commissioners (greater than two).
(3) A decision to make arrangements under subsection (1) must be taken with the agreement of more than half of the Commissioners holding office at the time.

Exercise of Commissioners' functions by officers

1.740
13.—(1) An officer of Revenue and Customs may exercise any function of the Commissioners.
(2) But subsection (1)—
(a) does not apply to the functions specified in subsection (3), and
(b) is subject to directions under section 2(3) and arrangements under section 12.
(3) The non-delegable functions mentioned in subsection (2)(a) are—
(a) making, by statutory instrument, regulations, rules or an order,
(b) approving an application for a warrant to search premises under section 20 C of the Taxes Management Act 1970 (c. 9),
(c) approving an application for a warrant to enter premises under Part 7 of Schedule 13 to the Finance Act 2003 (c. 14), and
(d) giving instructions for the disclosure of information under section 20(1)(a), except that an officer of Revenue and Customs may give an instruction under section 20(1)(a) authorising disclosure of specified information relating to—
  (i) one or more specified persons,
  (ii) one or more specified transactions, or
  (iii) specified goods.

Information

Use of information

1.741
17.—(1) Information acquired by the Revenue and Customs in connection with a function may be used by them in connection with any other function.
(2) Subsection (1) is subject to any provision which restricts or prohibits the use of information and which is contained in—
(a) this Act,
(b) any other enactment, or
(c) an international or other agreement to which the United Kingdom or Her Majesty's Government is party.

(2005 c.11, s.17)

(3) In subsection (1) "the Revenue and Customs" means—
(a) the Commissioners,
(b) an officer of Revenue and Customs,
(c) a person acting on behalf of the Commissioners or an officer of Revenue and Customs,
(d) a committee established by the Commissioners,
(e) a member of a committee established by the Commissioners,
(f) the Commissioners of Inland Revenue (or any committee or staff of theirs or anyone acting on their behalf),
(g) the Commissioners of Customs and Excise (or any committee or staff of theirs or anyone acting on their behalf), and
(h) a person specified in section 6(2) or 7(3).
(4) In subsection (1) "function" means a function of any of the persons listed in subsection (3).
(5) In subsection (2) the reference to an enactment does not include—
(a) an Act of the Scottish Parliament or an instrument made under such an Act, or
(b) an Act of the Northern Ireland Assembly or an instrument made under such an Act.
(6) Part 2 of Schedule 2 (which makes provision about the supply and other use of information in specified circumstances) shall have effect.

Confidentiality

18.—(1) Revenue and Customs officials may not disclose information which is held by the Revenue and Customs in connection with a function of the Revenue and Customs. 1.742
(2) But subsection (1) does not apply to a disclosure—
(a) which—
(i) is made for the purposes of a function of the Revenue and Customs, and
(ii) does not contravene any restriction imposed by the Commissioners,
(b) which is made in accordance with section 20 or 21,
(c) which is made for the purposes of civil proceedings (whether or not within the United Kingdom) relating to a matter in respect of which the Revenue and Customs have functions,
(d) which is made for the purposes of a criminal investigation or criminal proceedings (whether or not within the United Kingdom) relating to a matter in respect of which the Revenue and Customs have functions,
(e) which is made in pursuance of an order of a court,
(f) which is made to Her Majesty's Inspectors of Constabulary, the Scottish inspectors or the Northern Ireland inspectors for the purpose of an inspection by virtue of section 27,
(g) which is made to the Independent Police Complaints Commission, or a person acting on its behalf, for the purpose of the exercise of a function by virtue of section 28, or
(h) which is made with the consent of each person to whom the information relates.
(3) Subsection (1) is subject to any other enactment permitting disclosure.

(4) In this section—
(a) a reference to Revenue and Customs officials is a reference to any person who is or was—
   (i) a Commissioner,
   (ii) an officer of Revenue and Customs,
   (iii) a person acting on behalf of the Commissioners or an officer of Revenue and Customs, or
   (iv) a member of a committee established by the Commissioners,
(b) a reference to the Revenue and Customs has the same meaning as in section 17,
(c) a reference to a function of the Revenue and Customs is a reference to a function of—
   (i) the Commissioners, or
   (ii) an officer of Revenue and Customs,
(d) a reference to the Scottish inspectors or the Northern Ireland inspectors has the same meaning as in section 27, and
(e) a reference to an enactment does not include—
   (i) an Act of the Scottish Parliament or an instrument made under such an Act, or
   (ii) an Act of the Northern Ireland Assembly or an instrument made under such an Act.

Freedom of information

1.743   23.—(1) Revenue and customs information relating to a person, the disclosure of which is prohibited by section 18(1), is exempt information by virtue of section 44(1)(a) of the Freedom of Information Act 2000 (c. 36) (prohibitions on disclosure) if its disclosure—
(a) would specify the identity of the person to whom the information relates, or
(b) would enable the identity of such a person to be deduced.
(2) Except as specified in subsection (1), information the disclosure of which is prohibited by section 18(1) is not exempt information for the purposes of section 44(1)(a) of the Freedom of Information Act 2000.
(3) In subsection (1) "revenue and customs information relating to a person" has the same meaning as in section 19.

Obstruction

1.744   31.—(1) A person commits an offence if without reasonable excuse he obstructs—
(a) an officer of Revenue and Customs,
(b) a person acting on behalf of the Commissioners or an officer of Revenue and Customs, or
(c) a person assisting an officer of Revenue and Customs.
(2) A person guilty of an offence under this section shall be liable on summary conviction to—
(a) imprisonment for a period not exceeding 51 weeks,
(b) a fine not exceeding level 3 on the standard scale, or
(c) both.
(3) In the application of this section to Scotland or Northern Ireland the reference in subsection (2)(a) to 51 weeks shall be taken as a reference to six months.

(2005 c.11, s.32)

Assault

32.—(1) A person commits an offence if he assaults an officer of Revenue and Customs.

(2) A person guilty of an offence under this section shall be liable on summary conviction to—
 (a) imprisonment for a period not exceeding 51 weeks,
 (b) a fine not exceeding level 5 on the standard scale, or
 (c) both.

(3) In the application of this section to Scotland or Northern Ireland the reference in subsection (2)(a) to 51 weeks shall be taken as a reference to six months.

Power of arrest

33.—(1) An authorised officer of Revenue and Customs may arrest a person without warrant if the officer reasonably suspects that the person—
 (a) has committed an offence under section 30, 31 or 32,
 (b) is committing an offence under any of those sections, or
 (c) is about to commit an offence under any of those sections.

(2) In subsection (1) "authorised" means authorised by the Commissioners.

(3) Authorisation for the purposes of this section may be specific or general.

(4) In Scotland or Northern Ireland, a constable may arrest a person without warrant if the constable reasonably suspects that the person—
 (a) has committed an offence under this Act,
 (b) is committing an offence under this Act, or
 (c) is about to commit an offence under this Act.

General

Consequential amendments, &c.

50.—(1) In so far as is appropriate in consequence of section 5 a reference in an enactment, instrument or other document to the Commissioners of Customs and Excise, to customs and excise or to the Commissioners of Inland Revenue (however expressed) shall be taken as a reference to the Commissioners for Her Majesty's Revenue and Customs.

(2) In so far as is appropriate in consequence of sections 6 and 7 a reference in an enactment, instrument or other document to any of the persons specified in section 6(2) or 7(3) (however expressed) shall be taken as a reference to an officer of Revenue and Customs.

SCHEDULE 1

Former Inland Revenue Matters

1 Capital gains tax.
2 Charities.

3 Child benefit.
4 Child tax credit.
5 Child trust funds.
6 Corporation tax (and amounts assessable or chargeable as if they were corporation tax).
7 Guardian's allowance.
8 Income tax.
9 Inheritance tax.
10 The issue of bank notes.
11 National insurance contributions.
12 The National Insurance Fund.
13 The national minimum wage.
14 Oil and gas royalties.
15 Payment of or in lieu of rates.
16 Payment in lieu of tax reliefs, in so far as the Commissioners of Inland Revenue were responsible before the commencement of section 5.
17 Pension schemes.
18 Petroleum revenue tax.
19 Rating lists.
20 Recovery of taxes due in other member States, in relation to matters corresponding to those for which the Commissioners of Inland Revenue were responsible before the commencement of section 5.
21 Stamp duty.
22 Stamp duty land tax.
23 Stamp duty reserve tax.
24 Statutory adoption pay.
25 Statutory maternity pay.
26 Statutory paternity pay.
27 Statutory sick pay.
28 Student loans.
29 Valuation lists in relation to council tax.
30 Valuation of property.
31 Working tax credit.

Income Tax Act 2007

(2007 C.3)

ARRANGEMENT OF SELECTED SECTIONS

PART 1

OVERVIEW

1.749
1. Overview of Income Tax Acts
2. Overview of Act

(2007 c.3)

PART 2

BASIC PROVISIONS

CHAPTER 1

CHARGES TO INCOME TAX

3. Overview of charges to income tax
4. Income tax an annual tax

PART 14

INCOME TAX LIABILITY: MISCELLANEOUS RULES

CHAPTER 2

RESIDENCE

829. Residence of individuals temporarily abroad
830. Residence of individuals working abroad
831. Foreign income of individuals in the United Kingdom for a temporary purpose
832. Employment income of individuals in the United Kingdom for a temporary purpose

CHAPTER 3

JOINTLY HELD PROPERTY

836. Jointly held property
837. Jointly held property: declarations of unequal beneficial interests

PART 16

INCOME TAX ACT DEFINITIONS ETC

CHAPTER 1

DEFINITIONS

988. Overview of Chapter
989. The definitions
992. Meaning of "company"

Income Tax Act 2007

CHAPTER 2

OTHER INCOME TAX ACTS PROVISIONS

1011. References to married persons, or civil partners, living together

(SCHEDULES OMITTED)

INTRODUCTION AND GENERAL NOTE

1.750   This Act came into effect on April 6, 2007. It is the fourth of the Acts produced as part of the Tax Law Rewrite Project. It brings to a close the complete rewrite of all primary legislation dealing with income tax save only for the areas (not relevant to this work) listed in s.1 below. As s.1 signposts, it is to be read with ITEPA and ITTOIA. Save as mentioned in that section, all the parts of the Income and Corporation Taxes Act 1988 that referred to income tax have now been repealed and replaced. The extracts from that Act previously in this volume have therefore been deleted. Only a few sections from this Act are relevant to this work, but section 2 is included to show the full and extensive contents of the Act. As with the other Tax Law Rewrite Acts, an extensive explanatory note (running for this Act to three volumes) was published with the Act. Anyone wishing to consider any reference to the Act further should look at that note as a starting point.

PART 1

OVERVIEW

Overview of Income Tax Acts

1.751   **1.**—(1) The following Acts make provision about income tax—
(a) ITEPA 2003 (which is about charges to tax on employment income, pension income and social security income),
(b) ITTOIA 2005 (which is about charges to tax on trading income, property income, savings and investment income and some other miscellaneous income), and
(c) this Act (which contains the other main provisions about income tax).
(2) There are also provisions about income tax elsewhere: see in particular—
(a) Part 18 of ICTA (double taxation relief),
(b) CAA 2001 (allowances for capital expenditure), and
(c) Part 4 of FA 2004 (pension schemes etc).
(3) Schedule 1 to the Interpretation Act 1978 (c.30) defines "the Income Tax Acts" (as all enactments relating to income tax).

Overview of Act

1.752   **2.**— (1) This Act has 17 Parts.

(2007 c.3, s.1)

(2) Part 2 contains basic provisions about income tax including-
(a) provision about the annual nature of income tax (Chapter 1),
(b) the rates at which income tax is charged (Chapter 2), and
(c) the calculation of income tax liability (Chapter 3).
(3) Part 3 is about taxpayers' personal reliefs including—
(a) personal allowances (Chapter 2),
(b) blind persons' allowances (Chapter 2), and
(c) tax reductions for married couples and civil partners (Chapter 3).
(4) Part 4 is about loss relief including relief for—
(a) trade losses (Chapters 2 and 3),
(b) losses from property businesses (Chapter 4),
(c) losses in an employment or office (Chapter 5),
(d) losses on disposal of shares (Chapter 6), and
(e) losses from miscellaneous transactions (Chapter 7).
(5) Part 5 is about relief under the enterprise investment scheme.
(6) Part 6 is about—
(a) relief for investment in venture capital trusts, and
(b) other matters relating to venture capital trusts.
(7) Part 7 is about community investment tax relief.
(8) Part 8 is about a variety of reliefs including relief for—
(a) interest payments (Chapter 1),
(b) gifts to charity including gift aid (Chapters 2 and 3),
(c) annual payments and patent royalties (Chapter 4), and
(d) maintenance payments (Chapter 5).
(9) Part 9 contains special rules about settlements and trustees including—
(a) general provision about settlements and trustees (Chapter 2),
(b) special income tax rates for trusts (Chapters 3, 4, 5 and 6),
(c) rules about trustees' expenses (Chapters 4 and 8),
(d) rules about trustees' discretionary payments (Chapter 7),
(e) rules about unauthorised unit trusts (Chapter 9), and
(f) rules about heritage maintenance settlements (Chapter 10).
(10) Part 10 contains special rules about charitable trusts etc.
(11) Part 11 is about manufactured payments and repos.
(12) Part 12 is about accrued income profits.
(13) Part 13 is about tax avoidance in relation to—
(a) transactions in securities (Chapter 1),
(b) transfers of assets abroad (Chapter 2),
(c) transactions in land (Chapter 3),
(d) sales of occupation income (Chapter 4), and
(e) trade losses (Chapter 5).
(14) Part 14 deals with some miscellaneous rules about income tax liability, including—
(a) limits on liability to income tax for non-UK residents (Chapter 1),
(b) special rules about residence (Chapter 2), and
(c) rules about jointly held property (Chapter 3).
(15) Part 15 is about the deduction of income tax at source.
(16) Part 16 contains definitions which apply for the purposes of the Income Tax Acts and other general provisions which apply for the purposes of those Acts.
(17) Part 17—
(a) contains provisions to be used in interpreting this Act,
(b) introduces Schedule 1 (minor and consequential amendments),

(c) introduces Schedule 2 (transitional provisions and savings),
(d) introduces Schedule 3 (repeals and revocations, including of spent enactments),
(e) introduces Schedule 4 (index of defined expressions that apply for the purposes of this Act),
(f) confers powers on the Treasury to make orders, and
(g) makes provision about the coming into force of this Act.

PART 2

BASIC PROVISIONS

CHAPTER 1

CHARGES TO INCOME TAX

Overview of charges to income tax

1.753   **3.**—(1) Income tax is charged under—
(a) Part 2 of ITEPA 2003 (employment income),
(b) Part 9 of ITEPA 2003 (pension income),
(c) Part 10 of ITEPA 2003 (social security income),
(d) Part 2 of ITTOIA 2005 (trading income),
(e) Part 3 of ITTOIA 2005 (property income),
(f) Part 4 of ITTOIA 2005 (savings and investment income), and
(g) Part 5 of ITTOIA 2005 (miscellaneous income).
(2) Income tax is also charged under other provisions, including—
(a) Chapter 5 of Part 4 of FA 2004 (registered pension schemes: tax charges),
(b) section 7 of F(No.2)A 2005 (social security pension lump sums),
(c) Part 10 of this Act (special rules about charitable trusts etc),
(d) Chapter 2 of Part 12 of this Act (accrued income profits), and
(e) Part 13 of this Act (tax avoidance).

Income tax an annual tax

1.754   **4.**—(1) Income tax is charged for a year only if an Act so provides.
(2) A year for which income tax is charged is called a "tax year".
(3) A tax year begins on 6 April and ends on the following 5 April.
(4) "The tax year 2007–08" means the tax year beginning on 6 April 2007 (and any corresponding expression in which two years are similarly mentioned is to be read in the same way).
(5) Every assessment to income tax must be made for a tax year.
(6) Subsection (5) is subject to Chapter 15 of Part 15 (by virtue of which an assessment may relate to a return period).

GENERAL NOTE

1.755   The Rewrite Acts retain the long-standing approach of providing framework legislation for income tax. It is the relevant section in each year's Finance Act that actually imposes the tax for the year. That section triggers s.4 and thence the charging sections in s.3 and in ITEPA and ITTOIA. The list of charging sections here may be compared with the similar—but not identical—list of chapters to the Tax Credits (Definition and Calculation of Income) Regulations 2002 below.

Part 14

Income Tax Liability: Miscellaneous Rules

Chapter 2

Residence

Residence of individuals temporarily abroad

829.—(1) This section applies if—
(a) an individual has left the United Kingdom for the purpose only of occasional residence abroad, and
(b) at the time of leaving the individual was both UK resident and ordinarily UK resident.

(2) Treat the individual as UK resident for the purpose of determining the individual's liability for income tax for any tax year during the whole or a part of which the individual remains outside the United Kingdom for the purpose only of occasional residence abroad.

General Note

This section and those that follow rewrite the former ss.334–336 of ICTA. They set out the only legislative meanings given to "resident" for income tax purposes. The detailed view of how HMRC assesses residence and ordinary residence in the light of these provisions and the relevant case law is set out in HMRC booklet IR20.

Residence of individuals working abroad

830.—(1) This section applies for income tax purposes if an individual works full-time in one or both of—
(a) a foreign trade, and
(b) a foreign employment.

(2) In determining whether the individual is UK resident ignore any living accommodation available in the United Kingdom for the individual's use.

(3) A trade is foreign if no part of it is carried on in the United Kingdom.

(4) An employment is foreign if all of its duties are performed outside the United Kingdom.

(5) An employment is also foreign if in the tax year in question—
(a) the duties of the employment are in substance performed outside the United Kingdom, and
(b) the only duties of the employment performed in the United Kingdom are duties which are merely incidental to the duties of the employment performed outside the United Kingdom in the year.

(6) In this section—
"employment" includes an office, and
"trade" includes profession and vocation.

Foreign income of individuals in the United Kingdom for temporary purpose

831.—(1) Subsection (2) applies in relation to an individual if—
  (a) the individual is in the United Kingdom for some temporary purpose only and with no view to establishing the individual's residence in the United Kingdom, and
  (b) in the tax year in question the individual has not actually resided in the United Kingdom at one or several times for a total period equal to 183 days (or more).

In determining whether an individual is within paragraph (a) ignore any living accommodation available in the United Kingdom for the individual's use.

(2) Apply the following rules in determining the individual's liability for income tax.

Rule 1

In relation to pension or social security income arising from a source outside the United Kingdom, treat the individual as non-UK resident for the purposes of the following—
  (a) Chapter 4 of Part 9 of ITEPA 2003 (tax on foreign pensions),
  (b) Chapter 5A of that Part (tax on pensions under registered pension schemes) but only if the income is an annuity under a registered pension scheme within paragraph 1(1)(f) of Schedule 36 to FA 2004,
  (c) Chapter 10 of that Part (tax on employment-related annuities),
  (d) Chapter 15 of that Part (tax on voluntary annual payments),
  (e) section 647 of ITEPA 2003 (meaning of "foreign residence condition") but only in its application for the purposes of section 651 of that Act (which provides an exemption for tax under Chapter 14 of Part 9 of that Act), and
  (f) Chapter 6 of Part 10 of ITEPA 2003 (taxable foreign benefits).

See sections 566 and 657 of ITEPA 2003 for the definitions of "pension income" and "social security income".

Rule 2

In relation to income arising from a source outside the United Kingdom, treat the individual as non-UK resident for the purposes of any charge under a provision mentioned in section 830(2) of ITTOIA 2005 (which contains a list of provisions under which relevant foreign income is charged).

In this rule "income" does not include income chargeable as a result of section 844 of ITTOIA 2005 (unremittable income: income charged on withdrawal of relief after source ceases).

(3) Paragraph (e) of Rule 1 in subsection (2) applies only if—
  (a) the individual makes a claim as mentioned in section 647(3)(a) of ITEPA 2003, and
  (b) the Commissioners are satisfied that subsection (2) of this section applies in relation to the individual.

(4) Subsection (5) applies in relation to an individual if subsection (2) would have applied in relation to the individual but for subsection (1)(b).

(5) Apply the rules set out in subsection (2) in determining the individual's liability for income tax.

But—
(a) instead of treating the individual as non-UK resident in relation to the income and for the purposes mentioned in those rules, treat the individual as UK resident, and
(b) ignore subsection (3).

Employment income of individuals in the United Kingdom for temporary purpose

832.—(1) Subsection (2) applies in relation to an individual if—
(a) the individual is in the United Kingdom for some temporary purpose only and with no intention of establishing the individual's residence in the United Kingdom, and
(b) during the tax year in question the individual spends (in total) less than 183 days in the United Kingdom.

In determining whether an individual is within paragraph (a) ignore any living accommodation available in the United Kingdom for the individual's use.

(2) Treat the individual as non-UK resident for the purposes of Chapters 4 and 5 of Part 2 of ITEPA 2003 (which set out rules for determining taxable earnings from employment).

(3) Subsection (4) applies in relation to an individual if subsection (2) would have applied in relation to the individual but for subsection (1)(b).

(4) Treat the individual as UK resident for the purposes of the provisions mentioned in subsection (2).

CHAPTER 3

JOINTLY HELD PROPERTY

Jointly held property

836.—(1) This section applies if income arises from property held in the names of individuals—
(a) who are married to, or are civil partners of, each other, and
(b) who live together.

(2) The individuals are treated for income tax purposes as beneficially entitled to the income in equal shares.

(3) But this treatment does not apply in relation to any income within any of the following exceptions.

Exception A
Income to which neither of the individuals is beneficially entitled.
Exception B
Income in relation to which a declaration by the individuals under section 837 has effect (unequal beneficial interests).
Exception C
Income to which Part 9 of ITTOIA 2005 applies (partnerships).
Exception D
Income arising from a UK property business which consists of, or so far as it includes, the commercial letting of furnished holiday accommodation (within the meaning of Chapter 6 of Part 3 of ITTOIA 2005).

Exception E

Income consisting of a distribution arising from property consisting of—
- (a) shares in or securities of a close company to which one of the individuals is beneficially entitled to the exclusion of the other, or
- (b) such shares or securities to which the individuals are beneficially entitled in equal or unequal shares.

"Shares" and "securities" have the same meaning as in section 254 of ICTA.

Exception F

Income to which one of the individuals is beneficially entitled so far as it is treated as a result of any other provision of the Income Tax Acts as—
- (a) the income of the other individual, or
- (b) the income of a third party.

GENERAL NOTE

1.762 This section and the machinery section that follows should be read with s.1011 below. It sets out the general rule that couples living together are assumed to own any property, and therefore to receive any income from that property, in equal shares. Section 837 allows the couple to alter that position. However, that will make little difference to tax credits claims as entitlement is assessed on the total incomes of both members of the couple. Note that this rule does not apply to unmarried or unregistered couples, but again that does not affect tax credit entitlement. It does however affect income tax liability where the two members of the couple are liable to income tax at different rates at the margin.

Jointly held property: declarations of unequal beneficial interests

1.763 **837.**—(1) The individuals may make a joint declaration under this section if—
- (a) one of them is beneficially entitled to the income to the exclusion of the other, or
- (b) they are beneficially entitled to the income in unequal shares, and their beneficial interests in the income correspond to their beneficial interests in the property from which it arises.

(2) The declaration must state the beneficial interests of the individuals in—
- (a) the income to which the declaration relates, and
- (b) the property from which that income arises.

(3) The declaration has effect only if notice of it is given to an officer of Revenue and Customs—
- (a) in such form and manner as the Commissioners for Her Majesty's Revenue and Customs may prescribe, and
- (b) within the period of 60 days beginning with the date of the declaration.

(4) The declaration has effect in relation to income arising on or after the date of the declaration.

(5) The declaration continues to have effect until such time (if any) as there is a change in the beneficial interests of the individuals in either—
- (a) the income to which the declaration relates, or
- (b) the property from which that income arises.

(2007 c. 3, s. 988)

Part 16

Income Tax Acts Definitions Etc

Chapter 1

Definitions

Overview of Chapter

988.—(1) This Chapter contains definitions which apply for the purposes of the Income Tax Acts, except where, in those Acts, the context otherwise requires.

(2) To find a definition go first to section 989, which sets out some of the definitions in full.

(3) If a definition is not set out in full in section 989, the section indicates where it is set out in full.

(4) In some cases it is stated that a definition does not apply for the purposes of specified provisions of the Income Tax Acts (see, for example, sections 990(2), 992(3) and 1007(4)).

(5) And in some cases it is stated that a definition has effect only for the purposes of specific provisions of the Income Tax Acts (see, for example, sections 991, 993, 995 and 1006).

1.764

The definitions

989.—The following definitions apply for the purposes of the Income Tax Acts—

"Act" has the meaning given by section 990,

. . .

"bank" is to be read in accordance with section 991,

. . .

"body of persons" means any body politic, corporate or collegiate and any company, fraternity, fellowship or society of persons whether corporate or not corporate,

. . .

"capital allowance" means any allowance under CAA 2001,

"the Capital Allowances Act" means CAA 2001,

"chargeable gain" has the same meaning as in TCGA 1992,

"chargeable period" means an accounting period of a company or a tax year,

"charity" means a body of persons or trust established for charitable purposes only,

. . .

"company" has the meaning given by section 992,

. . .

"dividend income" has the meaning given by section 19

. . .

"farming" has the meaning given by section 996,

"for accounting purposes" has the meaning given by section 997(4),

. . .

1.765

347

"generally accepted accounting practice" has the meaning given by section 997(1) and (3),

"grossing up" is to be read in accordance with section 998,

. . .

"international accounting standards" has the meaning given by section 997(5),

. . .

"non-UK resident" means not resident in the United Kingdom (and references to a non-UK resident or a non-UK resident person are to a person who is not resident there),

"normal self-assessment filing date", in relation to a tax year, means the 31 January following the tax year,

"notice" means notice in writing or in a form authorised (in relation to the case in question) by directions under section 118 of FA 1998,

. . .

"overseas property business" has the meaning given by Chapter 2 of Part 3 of ITTOIA 2005,

"period of account"—
(a) in relation to a person, means any period for which the person draws up accounts, and
(b) in relation to a trade, profession, vocation or other business, means any period for which the accounts of the business are drawn up,

. . .

"personal representatives" in relation to a person who has died, means—
(a) in the United Kingdom, persons responsible for administering the estate of the deceased, and
(b) in a territory outside the United Kingdom, those persons having functions under its law equivalent to those of administering the estate of the deceased,

"profits or gains" does not include chargeable gains,

. . .

"relevant foreign income" has the meaning given by section 830(1) to (3) of ITTOIA 2005 but also includes, for any purpose mentioned in any provision listed in section 830(4) of that Act, income treated as relevant foreign income for that purpose by that provision,

"research and development" is to be read in accordance with section 1006,

"retail prices index" means—
(a) the general index of retail prices (for all items) published by the Office for National Statistics, or
(b) if that index is not published for a relevant month, any substituted index or index figures published by that Office,

. . .

"Schedule A business" means any business the profits of which are chargeable to corporation tax under Schedule A, including the business in the course of which any transaction is (as a result of paragraph 1(2) of that Schedule) to be treated as entered into,

. . .

"settled property" (together with references to property comprised in a settlement) is to be read in accordance with section 466,

"settlor" is to be read in accordance with sections 467 to 473,

. . .

(2007 c.3, s.989)

"stepchild", in relation to a civil partner, is to be read in accordance with section 246 of the Civil Partnership Act 2004 (c.33),

. . .

"tax" is to be read in accordance with section 832(3) of ICTA,
"tax credit" means a tax credit under section 397(1) of ITTOIA 2005,
"tax year" has the meaning given by section 4(2),
"the tax year 2007–08" (and any corresponding expression in which two years are similarly mentioned) has the meaning given by section 4(4),
"total income" has the meaning given by section 23 (see Step 1 in that section and also section 31),
"trade" includes any venture in the nature of trade,

. . .

"UK generally accepted accounting practice" has the meaning given by section 997(2),
"UK property business" has the meaning given by Chapter 2 of Part 3 of ITTOIA 2005,
"UK resident" means resident in the United Kingdom (and references to a UK resident or a UK resident person are to a person who is resident there),

. . .

"year of assessment" means a tax year, and
"the year 1988–1989" means the tax year 1988–1989 (and any corresponding expression in which two years are similarly mentioned is to be read in the same way).

Meaning of "company"

992.—(1) In the Income Tax Acts "company" means any body corporate or unincorporated association, but does not include a partnership, a local authority or a local authority association.

(2) Subsection (1) needs to be with read with section 468 of ICTA (authorised unit trusts).

. . .

References to married persons, or civil partners, living together

1011.—Individuals who are married to, or are civil partners of, each other are treated for the purposes of the Income Tax Acts as living together unless—
 (a) they are separated under an order of a court of competent jurisdiction,
 (b) they are separated by deed of separation, or
 (c) they are in fact separated in circumstances in which the separation is likely to be permanent.

PART II

TAX CREDITS

Tax Credits Act 2002 (Commencement No.3 and Transitional Provisions and Savings) Order 2003

(SI 2003/938)

The Treasury, in relation to articles 1 and 2, in exercise of the powers conferred upon them by section 61 of the Tax Credits Act 2002 and the Secretary of State for Work and Pensions, in relation to articles 1 and 3 to 5 in exercise of the powers conferred on him by s.62(1) of that Act and of all other powers enabling each of them in that behalf, hereby make the following Order:

ARRANGEMENT OF ARTICLES

1. Citation and interpretation.
2. Appointed day.
3. Saving provision.
4. Transitional application of sections 37 and 39A of the Contributions and Benefits Act.
5. Transitional application of section 154 of the Administration Act.

Schedule—Repeals specified in Schedule 6 to the 2002 Act which are commenced by this order.

Citation and interpretation

1.—(1) This Order may be cited as the Tax Credits Act 2002 (Commencement No.3 and Transitional Provisions and Savings) Order 2003.

(2) In this Order—
"the 2002 Act" means the Tax Credits Act 2002; the Administration Act" means the Social Security Administration Act 1992;
"the Contributions and Benefits Act" means the Social Security Contributions and Benefits Act 1992.

Appointed day

2. The day appointed for the coming into force of—
(a) section 1(3)(e) of the 2002 Act (abolition of increases in benefits in respect of children under sections 80 and 90 of the Contributions and Benefits Act);
(b) section 60 of, and Schedule 6, to, the 2002 Act, in so far as they repeal the provisions specified in the Schedule to this Order, is 6th April 2003.

Saving provision

3.—(1) Notwithstanding the coming into force of the specified provisions, the Contributions and Benefits Act and the Administration Act shall, in cases to which paragraph (2) applies, subject to paragraph (3), continue to have effect from the commencement date as if those provisions had not come into force.

(2) This paragraph applies where a person—
(a) is entitled to a relevant increase on the day before the commencement date; or
(b) claims a relevant increase on or after the commencement date and it is subsequently determined that he is entitled to a relevant increase in respect of a period which includes the day before the commencement date.

(3) The provisions saved by paragraph (1) shall continue to have effect until—
(a) subject to sub-paragraph (c), where a relevant increase ceases to be payable to a person to whom paragraph (2) applies for a period greater than 58 days beginning with the day on which it was last payable, on the day 59 days after the day on which it was last payable; or
(b) in any other case, subject to sub-paragraph (c), on the date on which entitlement to a relevant increase ceases;
(c) where regulation 6(19) or (23) of the Social Security (Claims and Payments) Regulations 1987 applies to a further claim for a relevant increase, on the date on which entitlement to that relevant increase ceases.

(4) In this article—
"the commencement date" means 6th April 2003;
"a relevant increase" means an increase under section 80 or 90 of the Contributions and Benefits Act;
"the specified provisions" means the provisions of the 2002 Act which are brought into force by article 2.

Transitional application of sections 37 and 39A of the Contributions and Benefits Act

4. For the purposes of the continuing application of sections 37 (widowed mother's allowance) and 39A (widowed parent's allowance) of the Contributions and Benefits Act in cases to which article 3(2) applies, those sections shall apply as if the amendments specified in paragraphs 26 and 28 of Schedule 3 to the 2002 Act had not come into force.

Transitional application of section 154 of the Administration Act

5. For the purposes of the continuing application of section 154(2)(c) of the Administration Act in cases to which article 3(2) applies, that section shall apply as if it had not been repealed in Schedule 6 to the 2002 Act and the reference to child benefit in that section shall be treated as including a reference to child tax credit under section 8 of the 2002 Act.

(SI 2003/938, Sch.)

Article 2 SCHEDULE

Repeals Specified in Schedule 6 to the 2002 Act Which are Commenced by this Order

Act	Provision
Contributions and Benefits Act	In section 20(1), the words "(with increase for child dependants)" (in each place) and in paragraph (f)(i), the words "and child". In section 30B(3), the word "80,". In section 56(1), the words "(and in particular to those of section 81 below)". Section 60(6). In sections 61(1) and (2), the words "on account of a child or an adult". In section 63(c) and (f)(i), the words "and child". In section 77(1), the words following paragraph (b). In section 78(4)(d), the word "80". Sections 80 and 81. In section 89(1), the words "section 80 and" and in the heading the words "child or". In section 90, the words "child or". In section 91(1)(b), the words "for an adult dependant". In Schedule 4, in Part IV, in column (1), the entries relating to widowed mother's allowance, widowed parent's allowance and child's special allowance and col.(2). In Schedule 5, in paragraph 2(5)(b) the word "80".
Administration Act	In section 3(3), the words "(together with any increase under section 80(5) of the Contributions and Benefits Act)". Section 150(1)(f).

Tax Credits Act 2002 (Commencement No.4, Transitional Provisions and Savings) Order 2003

(SI 2003/962 (c.51)) (as amended)

The Treasury, in exercise of the powers conferred upon them by sections 61 and 62(2) of the Tax Credits Act 2002, hereby make the following Order:

Arrangement of Articles

1. Citation and interpretation.
2. Commencement of provisions of the Act.
3. Savings.
4. Savings.
5. Transitional provisions.

Schedule 1—Provisions of Sch.6 to the Act coming into force on 6th April 2003
Schedule 2—Provisions of Sch.6 to the Act coming into force on 8th April 2003

Tax Credits Act 2002 (Commencement No.4) Order 2003

Citation and interpretation

2.9 1.—(1) This Order may be cited as the Tax Credits Act 2002 (Commencement No.4, Transitional Provisions and Savings) Order 2003.
(2) In this Order—
"the Act" means the Tax Credits Act 2002;
"the 1999 Act" means the Tax Credits Act 1999; and
"the superseded tax credits" means working families' tax credit and disabled person's tax credit.

Commencement of provisions of the Act

2.10 2.—(1) [. . .]
(2) [. . .]
(3) [. . .]
(4) [. . .]
(5) Section 1(3)(d) of the Act (child premia in respect of income support and income-based jobseeker's allowance) shall come into force on [¹31st December 2008].

AMENDMENT

1. Tax Credits Act 2002 (Commencement and Transitional Provisions) Order 2006 (SI 2006/3369 (C.124)), art.2 (December 14, 2006).

GENERAL NOTE

2.11 Section 1(3)(d) is the only major part of the 2002 Act not yet in force. Its introduction has been postponed by a series of provisions, and the latest postponement puts off the start of the phased introduction until 2009. For a discussion of the problems leading to this postponement see para.1.229 above.

Tax Credits Act 2002 (Transitional Provisions) Order 2005

(SI 2005/773) (AS AMENDED)

The Treasury in exercise of the powers conferred upon them by section 62(2) of the Tax Credits Act 2002 make the following Order:

Citation and interpretation

2.12 1. This Order may be cited as the Tax Credits Act 2002 (Transitional Provisions) Order 2005.
2.13 2. In this Order—
"the Board" means the Commissioners of Inland Revenue;
"benefit week" has the meaning given in regulation 2(1) of the Income Support Regulations in relation to the child premia in respect of income support and regulation 1(3) of the Jobseeker's Allowance Regulations in relation to the child premia in respect of income based jobseeker's allowance;
"the child premia in respect of income support or income based jobseeker's allowance" means the amounts referred to in section 1(3)(d) of the Tax Credits Act 2002;
"polygamous unit" has the meaning given in the Tax Credits (Polygamous Marriages) Regulations 2003.

(SI 2005/773, s.2) (as amended)

Claims and entitlement

3.—(1) A claim for a child tax credit is treated as made by the person specified in article 4 ("the specified person") on the date specified in article 5 ("the specified date") for the period specified in article 6.

(2) If the specified person is a member of a married couple or an unmarried couple or a polygamous unit, the specified person and the other member of the couple or member or members of polygamous unit are treated as making a joint claim.

(3) The specified person is treated as being responsible for the child or children or qualifying young person or persons to whom his entitlement to the child premia in respect of income support or income based jobseeker's allowance relates.

Specified person

4.—(1) For the purposes of article 3 a specified person is a person who—
(a) until the specified date was receiving the child premia in respect of income support or income support jobseeker's allowance, and
(b) has not made a claim for a child tax credit.
This is subject to paragraph (2).

(2) A person claiming income support in accordance with regulation 6(2) of the Income Support (General) Regulations 1987 or regulation 6(2) of the Income Support (General) Regulations (Northern Ireland) 1987 (lone parent returning to work) is not a specified person.

Specified date

5. For the purposes of this Order the specified date is the day following the date notified to an officer of the Board—
(a) by the Department for Work and Pensions if the specified person is claiming in Great Britain, or
(b) by the Department for Social Development if the specified person is claiming in Northern Ireland,
as the proposed final day of the last benefit week for which the child premia in respect of income support or income based jobseeker's allowance is to be paid to the specified person.

Period of award

6. Notwithstanding section 5(2) of the Tax Credits Act 2002, an award on a claim under article 3 is for the period beginning with the later of—
(a) the specified date, and
(b) the date on which the Board notify the Department for Work and Pensions or the Department for Social Development, as appropriate, of an award of child tax credit, and
ending at the end of the tax year in which that date falls.

Transitional provision

7. Notwithstanding regulation 7 of the Tax Credits (Claims and Notifications) Regulations 2002, a person shall not be entitled to a tax credit in respect of any day prior to the day on which he makes a claim for it ("the earlier day") if—

(a) the earlier day falls before [¹31st December 2008], and on the earlier day the claimant is entitled, or in the case of a joint claim, either of the claimants is entitled, to the child premia in respect of income support or income based jobseeker's allowance.

AMENDMENT

1. Tax Credits Act 2002 (Commencement and Transitional Provisions) Order 2006 (SI 2006/3369 (C.124)), art.4 (December 14, 2006).

Working Tax Credit (Entitlement and Maximum Rate) Regulations 2002

(SI 2002/2005) (AS AMENDED)

Whereas a draft of this instrument, which prescribes the amount in excess of which, by virtue of subsection (2) of section 12 of the Tax Credits Act 2002, charges are not to be taken into account for the purposes of that subsection, and which also contains the first regulations made under sections 11 and 12 of that Act, has been laid before, and approved by resolution of, each House of Parliament:

Now, therefore, the Treasury, in exercise of the powers conferred upon them by sections 10, 11, 12, 65(1) and (7) and 67 of the Tax Credits Act 2002, hereby make the following Regulations:

REGULATIONS

PART 1

GENERAL

1. Citation, commencement and effect.
2. Interpretation.
3. Other elements of working tax credit.

PART II

CONDITIONS OF ENTITLEMENT

BASIC ELEMENT

4. Entitlement to basic element of working tax credit: qualifying remunerative work.
5. Time off in connection with childbirth and adoption.
5A. Time off in connection with childbirth and placement for adoption: further provisions.

(SI 2002/2005) (as amended)

6.	Periods of illness or incapacity for work.
7.	Term-time and other seasonal workers.
7A.	Strike periods.
7B.	Persons suspended from work.
7C.	Pay in lieu of notice.
7D.	Ceasing to undertake work or working for less than 16 hours per week.
8.	Gaps between jobs.

Disability element

9.	Disability element and workers who are to be treated as at a disadvantage in getting a job.
9A.	Initial claims.
9B.	Training for work, etc.

30-hour element

10.	30-hour element.

Second-adult element

11.	Second-adult element.

Lone-parent element

12.	Lone-parent element.

Childcare element

13.	Entitlement to childcare element of working tax credit.
14.	Entitlement to childcare element of working tax credit.
15.	Calculation of relevant childcare charges.
16.	Change of circumstances.

Severe disability element

17.	Severe disability element.

50 Plus element

18.	50 Plus element.

Working Tax Credit (Entitlement and Maximum Rate) Regulations 2002

Death of a child or qualifying young person for whom the claimant is responsible

19. Entitlement after death of a child or qualifying young person for whom the claimant is responsible.

PART III

MAXIMUM RATE

20. Maximum rates of elements of working tax credit.

Schedule 1—Disability which puts a person at a disadvantage in getting a job.
Schedule 2—Maximum rates of the elements of a working tax credit.

PART I

GENERAL

Citation, commencement and effect

2.20   **1.** These Regulations may be cited as the Working Tax Credit (Entitlement and Maximum Rate) Regulations 2002 and shall come into force—
   (a) for the purpose of enabling claims to be made, on 1st August 2002;
   (b) for the purpose of enabling decisions on claims to be made, on 1st January 2003; and
   (c) for all other purposes, on April 6, 2003;
and shall have effect for the tax year beginning on 6th April 2003 and subsequent tax years.

DEFINITIONS
   "claim"—see TCA 2002, s.3(8).
   "tax year"—see TCA 2002, s.47.

GENERAL NOTE

2.21   These regulations give substance to ss.10 (entitlement) and 11 (maximum rate) of the TCA 2002. These are the only sections in the Act that apply specifically to the award and entitlement to working tax credit. Most of the provisions in those sections are enabling only. These are the regulations giving substance to working tax credit.

Interpretation

2.22   **2.**—(1) In these Regulations, except where the context otherwise requires—
   "the Act" means the Tax Credits Act 2002, and a reference without more to a numbered section is a reference to the section of the Act bearing that number;
   "the Board" means the Commissioners of Inland Revenue;
   "the Contributions and Benefits Act" means the Social Security Contributions and Benefits Act 1992;

(SI 2002/2005, reg. 2) (as amended)

"child" has the same meaning as it has in the Child Tax Credit Regulations 2002;

"claim" means a claim for working tax credit and "joint claim" and "single claim" have the meanings respectively assigned in [¹section 3(8)];

"claimant" means the person making a claim and, in the case of a joint claim, means either of the claimants;

[³"couple" has the meaning given by section 3(5A) of the Act;]

"the determination of the maximum rate" means the determination of the maximum rate of working tax credit;

[¹"employed", except in the expression "self-employed" means employed under a contract of service or apprenticeship where the earnings under the contract are chargeable to income tax as employment income under Parts II–VII of the Income Tax (Earnings and Pensions) Act 2003 [² otherwise than by reason of Chapter 8 of Part 2 of that Act (deemed employment in respect of arrangements made by intermediaries)];]

[⁴"employment zone" means an area within Great Britain—
(a) subject to a designation for the purposes of the Employment Zones Regulations 2003 by the Secretary of State, or
[⁵(b) listed in the Schedule to the Employment Zones (Allocation to Contractors) Pilot Regulations 2006],
pursuant to section 60 of the Welfare Reform and Pensions Act 1999.]

"employment zone programme" means a programme which is—
(a) established for one or more employment zones; and
(b) designed to assist claimants for a jobseeker's allowance to obtain sustainable employment;

[¹"initial claim" shall be construed in accordance with regulation 9A;]

"local authority" means—
(a) in relation to England, the council of a county or district, a metropolitan district, a London Borough, the Common Council of the City of London or the Council of the Isles of Scilly;
(b) in relation to Wales, the council of a county or county borough; or;
(c) in relation to Scotland, a council constituted under section 2 of the Local Government, etc. (Scotland) Act 1994;

[¹"partner" means a member of a [³. . .] couple making a joint claim;]

"patient" means a person (other than a person who is serving a sentence, imposed by a court, in a prison or youth custody institution or, in Scotland, a young offenders' institution) who is regarded as receiving free in-patient treatment within the meaning of the Social Security (Hospital In-Patients) Regulations 1975;

"period of award" shall be construed in accordance with [¹section 5];

"qualifying young person" means a person who satisfies regulation 5 of the Child Tax Credit Regulations 2002;

"relevant childcare charges" has the meaning given by regulation 14;

[¹. . .]

"self-employed" means engaged in the carrying on of a trade profession or vocation;

"sports award" means an award made by one of the Sports Councils named in section 23(2) of the National Lottery etc. Act 1993 out of sums allocated to it for distribution under that section;

"surrogate child" means a child in respect of whom an order has been made under section 30 of the Human Fertilisation and Embryology Act 1990;

[¹. . .]

"training allowance" means an allowance (whether by way of periodical grants or otherwise) payable—
  (a) out of public funds by a Government department or by or on behalf of the Secretary of State, Scottish Enterprise or Highlands and Islands Enterprise or the Department for Employment and Learning ("the relevant paying authority");
  (b) to a person in respect of his maintenance or in respect of a member of his family; and
  (c) for the period, or part of the period, during which he is following a course of training or instruction—
    (i) provided by, or in pursuance of arrangements made with, the relevant paying authority; or
    (ii) approved by the relevant paying authority in relation to him, but does not include an allowance, paid by a Government department, Northern Ireland department or the Scottish Executive to or in respect of a person by reason of the fact that he is training as a teacher, or is following a course of full-time education, other than under arrangements made under section 2 of the Employment and Training Act 1973, section 2 or 3 of the Disabled Persons (Employment) Act (Northern Ireland) 1945, or section 1(1) of the Employment and Training Act (Northern Ireland) 1950;
[[1]"training for work" shall be construed in accordance with regulation 9B;]
"week" means a period of seven days beginning with midnight between Saturday and Sunday.

(2) For the purposes of these Regulations a person is responsible for a child or qualifying young person if he is treated as being responsible for that child or qualifying young person in accordance with the rules contained in regulation 3 of the Child Tax Credit Regulations 2002.

(3) A reference in these Regulations to an enactment applying to Great Britain but not to Northern Ireland shall, unless the context otherwise requires, include a reference to the corresponding enactment applying in Northern Ireland.

[[1](4) In these Regulations as they apply to an office a reference to being employed includes a reference to being the holder of an office.]

AMENDMENTS

1. Working Tax Credit (Entitlement and Maximum Rate) (Amendment) Regulations 2003 (SI 2003/701), reg.3 (April 6, 2003).
2. Tax Credits (Miscellaneous Amendments No.2) Regulations 2003 (SI 2003/2815), reg.13 (November 26, 2003).
3. Civil Partnership Act 2004 (Tax Credits, etc.) (Consequential Amendments) Order 2005 (SI 2005/2919), art.2(2) (December 5, 2005).
4. Tax Credits (Miscellaneous Amendments) Regulations 2006 (SI 2006/766), reg.20(2) (April 6, 2006).
5. Tax Credits (Miscellaneous Amendments) Regulations 2007 (SI 2007/824), reg.3 (April 6, 2007).

DEFINITIONS

See also TCA 2002, s.47. For definitions of terms used in income tax legislation see ITEPA 2003, Sch.1, and the index of definitions in ITA 2007, Sch.4 (not included in this work).

(SI 2002/2005, reg.3) (as amended)

Other elements of working tax credit

3.—(1) For the purposes of determining the maximum rate of working tax credit, in addition to the basic element and the disability element, the following elements are prescribed—
(a) a 30 hour element;
(b) a second adult element;
(c) a lone parent element;
(d) a childcare element;
(e) a severe disability element; and
(f) a 50 Plus element.

(2) It is a condition of entitlement to the other elements of working tax credit that the person making the claim for working tax credit is entitled to the basic element.

(3) If the claim for working tax credit is a joint claim, and both members of the couple satisfy the conditions of entitlement for—
(a) the disability element;
(b) the severe disability element; or
(c) the 50 Plus element,
the award must include two such elements.

DEFINITIONS

"basic element"—see TCA 2002, s.11(4).
"claim"—see reg.2.
"joint claim"—see reg.2.

GENERAL NOTE

Section 11(2) of the TCA 2002 requires that all awards of working tax credit must contain a common element (known as the basic element—see s.11(4)). Section 11(3) requires that there be an element related to those with disabilities putting them at a disadvantage in getting a job. The list of other elements in s.11(6) is, however, permissive only. This regulation sets out the other elements to which claimants may for the time being be entitled as part of their working tax credit award, save one: the childcare element is not included because it is dealt with separately under s.12 of the TCA 2002.

The structure adopted is to require all claimants to show that they are entitled to the basic element in accordance with reg.4. Unless a claimant establishes that entitlement, he or she does not qualify for working tax credit at all. Once entitlement to the basic element is shown, a claimant may claim any or all of the other elements—subject, of course, to showing additional separate entitlement to each of them.

PART II

CONDITIONS OF ENTITLEMENT

Basic element

Entitlement to basic element of working tax credit: qualifying remunerative work

4.—(1) Subject to the qualification in paragraph (2), a person shall be treated as engaged in qualifying remunerative work if, and only if, he satisfies all of the following conditions.

First condition

2.26   The person—
(a) is working at the date of the claim; or
(b) has an offer of work which he has accepted at the date of the claim and the work is expected to commence within 7 days of the making of the claim.

In relation to a case falling within sub-paragraph (b) of this condition, references in the second third and fourth conditions below to work which the person undertakes are to be construed as references to the work which the person will undertake when it commences.

In such a case the person is only to be treated as being in qualifying remunerative work when he begins the work referred to in that subparagraph.

Second condition

2.27   The person—
[1(a) is aged at least 16 and—
   (i) undertakes work for not less than 16 hours per week,
   (ii) either he or his partner is responsible for a child or qualifying young person, or he has a physical or mental disability which puts him at a disadvantage in getting a job and satisfies regulation 9(1)(c),]
(b) satisfies the conditions in regulation 18, or
(c) is aged at least 25 and undertakes not less than 30 hours work per week in any other case.

Third condition

2.28   The work which the person undertakes is expected to continue for at least 4 weeks after the making of the claim or, in a case falling within sub-paragraph (b) of the first condition, after the work starts.

Fourth condition

2.29   The work is done for payment or in expectation of payment. Paragraphs (3) and (4) provide the method of determining the number of hours of qualifying remunerative work that a person undertakes.

Regulations 5 to 8 apply in relation to periods of absence from work connected with childbirth or adoption, sickness, seasonal absence from work in relation to which there is a recognised yearly cycle of employment and those who have a gap between periods of work.

Regulation 9 prescribes the conditions which must be satisfied by, or exist in relation to, a person so that he is to be treated as having a physical or mental disability which puts him at a disadvantage in getting a job.

(2) A person who would otherwise satisfy the conditions in paragraph (1) shall not be regarded as engaged in qualifying remunerative work to the extent that he is—
(a) engaged by a charitable or voluntary organisation, or is a volunteer, if the only payment received by him or due to be paid to him is a payment by way of expenses which falls to be disregarded under item 1 in Table 7 in regulation 19 of the Tax Credits (Definition and Calculation of Income) Regulations 2002;

(SI 2002/2005, reg. 4) (as amended)

(b) engaged in caring for a person who is not a member of his household but is temporarily residing with him if the only payment made to him for providing that care is disregarded income by virtue of item 3 or 4 in Table 8 in regulation 19 of the Tax Credits (Definition and Calculation of Income) Regulations 2002;
(c) engaged on a scheme for which a training allowance is being paid;
(d) participating in the Intensive Activity Period specified in regulation 75(1)(a)(iv) of the Jobseeker's Allowance Regulations 1996 or the Preparation for Employment Programme specified in regulation 75(1)(a)(v) of the Jobseeker's Allowance Regulations (Northern Ireland) 1996;
(e) engaged in an activity in respect of which—
   (i) a sports award has been made, or is to be made, to him, and
   (ii) no other payment is made, or is expected to be made, to him; or
(f) participating in an employment zone programme, that is to say a programme established for one or more areas designated pursuant to section 60 of the Welfare Reform and Pensions Act 1999, and subject to the [³ Employment Zones 2003 and the Employment Zones (Allocation to Contractors) Pilot Regulations 2005] if he receives no payments under that programme other than—
   (i) discretionary payments disregarded in the calculation of a claimant's income under item 6(b) in [¹Table 6] in regulation 19 of the Tax Credits (Definition and Calculation of Income) Regulations 2002; or
   (ii) training premiums.
[⁴(g) a person who—
   (i) is serving a custodial sentence or has been remanded in custody awaiting trial or sentence, and
   (ii) is engaged in work (whether inside or outside a prison) while he is serving the sentence or remanded in custody.]
[² This is subject to the following qualification.
(2A) Neither sub-paragraph (c) nor sub-paragraph (d) of paragraph (2) applies if—
   (a) in a case falling within sub-paragraph (c), the training allowance, or
   (b) in a case falling within sub-paragraph (d), any payment made by the Secretary of State, or, in Northern Ireland, by the Department for Social Development, in connection with the Intensive Activity Period,
is chargeable to income tax as the profits of a trade, profession or vocation.]
(3) The number of hours for which a person undertakes qualifying remunerative work is—
   (a) in the case of an apprentice, employee or officeholder, the number of hours of such work which he normally performs—
      (i) under the contract of service or of apprenticeship under which he is employed, or
      (ii) in the office in which he is employed;
   (b) in the case of an agency worker, the number of hours in respect of which remuneration is normally paid to him by an employment agency with whom he has a contract of employment; or
   (c) in the case of a person who is self-employed, the number of hours he normally performs for payment or in expectation of payment.
This is subject to the following qualification.

Working Tax Credit (Entitlement and Maximum Rate) Regulations 2002

(4) In reckoning the number of hours of qualifying remunerative work which a person normally undertakes—
(a) any period of customary or paid holiday; and
(b) any time allowed for meals or refreshment, unless the person is, or expects to be paid earnings in respect of that time, shall be disregarded.

[¹(5) In reckoning the number of hours of qualifying remunerative work which a person normally undertakes, any time allowed for visits to a hospital, clinic or other establishment for the purpose only of treating or monitoring the person's disability shall be included; but only if the person is, or expects to be, paid in respect of that time.]

AMENDMENTS

1. Working Tax Credit (Entitlement and Maximum Rate) (Amendment) Regulations 2003 (SI 2003/701), reg.4 (April 6, 2003).
2. Tax Credits (Miscellaneous Amendments) Regulations 2004 (SI 2004/762), reg.5 (April 6, 2004).
3. Tax Credits (Miscellaneous Amendments) Regulations 2006 (SI 2006/766), reg.20(3) (April 6, 2006).
4. Tax Credits (Miscellaneous Amendments) Regulations 2007 (SI 2007/824), reg.4 (April 6, 2007).

DEFINITIONS

"agency worker"—see ITEPA 2003, s.44.
"child"—see reg.2.
"claim"—see reg.2.
"employed"—see reg.2.
"Employment Zone programme"—see reg.2.
"office-holder"—see ITEPA 2003, s.5.
"partner"—see reg.2.
"qualifying young person"—see reg.2.
"responsible for a child"—see TCA 2002, s.48.
"self-employed"—see reg.2.
"sports award"—see reg.2.
"training allowance"—see reg.2.
"week"—see reg.2.

GENERAL NOTE

2.30 The structure of this key regulation is somewhat misleading. It suggests that there are four conditions for qualifying for entitlement to the basic element of working tax credit. This somewhat disguises the fact that there are four different and alternative bases for claiming working tax credit, all of which are wrapped up together in the "second condition", while the other three conditions are common to all groups of claimant.

First condition

2.31 Section 10(1) requires that all claimants for working tax credit must be in "qualifying remunerative work". This condition defines the scope of being "in" work. A claimant cannot receive working tax credit until he or she has started work (or, in the case of joint claimants or members of a polygamous unit, one of them has started work), or the work is to start within seven days.

Second condition

2.32 As noted above, this creates four alternative conditions, or routes to entitlement:
Route 1 is for a claimant working 16 or more hours a week and who, or whose partner, is responsible for a child or qualifying young person. This replaces the adult

element of WFTC. The requirement of responsibility for a child or qualifying young person is the same test as for child tax credit purposes, and the regulations adopt the relevant definitions from the Child Tax Credit Regulations. In practical terms, they are the same tests as those for claiming child benefit for a child. The 16-hour test and the reference to remunerative work reflect the similar test in reg.5 of the Income Support (General) Regulations 1987 (SI 1987/1967).

Route 2 is for a disabled claimant suffering prejudice in the job market. It replaces the former disabled person's tax credit. The full conditions for this route are in reg.9. It again uses the 16-hour test.

Route 3 is for those over 50 who would, before these tax credits were introduced, have been entitled to a grant from the "New Deal 50 Plus" scheme of the former Department for Education and Employment. The conditions are set out in reg.18.

Route 4 is the safety net basis of claim for anyone over 25 who is working full time (defined as 30 hours a week) but receiving only minimal earnings. The assumption behind working tax credit is that all employees are receiving the national minimum wage (and it is the task of HMRC to enforce the national minimum wage legislation). But this will not take a claimant who is working substantially less than the national maximum working week of 48 hours above the income threshold for working tax credit. And there will be many self-employed (for example, subsistence farmers) who will meet the 30-hour work test but also have an income below the working tax credit threshold. This route, like Route 3 to the working tax credit, is not a social security benefit of any kind. It is a subsidy to the low paid without reference to any social circumstances, and its effect is, as noted, to link with the national minimum wage to provide a national minimum take-home pay for all workers, whether employed or self-employed, over 25.

Third condition

This imposes a minimum level of continuity before working tax credit can be claimed. For WFTC the equivalent test was that the work was likely to continue for five weeks. It is separate from, but presumably to be read with, the 16 and 30-hour requirements of the second condition. In other words, it would seem that it has in cases of doubt to be shown that the work will be at a level of 16 or 30 hours a week for those four weeks. That will be a question of fact in all cases. The self-employed may have to show that they are, in that sense, "ordinarily self employed", which is the test for payment of Class 2 NI contributions. In the modern context of flexible employment and allegedly zero-hours contracts, close attention may have to be paid not only to the terms of agreement between the two parties to the work relationship but also to whether there is "an irreducible minimum of obligation on each side to create a contract of service": Stephenson L.J. in *Nethermere (St Neots) Ltd v Gardiner* [1984] I.C.R. 612, CA. If there is, the question is then whether on the facts it is shown that it will (or, at the end of the year, did) last for four weeks at the required level. But there is a possible practical problem of timing for a claimant in this sort of work because of the interaction of this requirement with the terms of the first condition—requiring that the work start within seven days of the offer of work— and the backdating rule that prevents a claim being made more than three months after entitlement starts.

2.33

Fourth condition

This echoes the well known test from the previous family credit reg.4 of the former Family Credit (General) Regulations 1987 (SI 1987/1973) and from income support (reg.5 of the Income Support (General) Regulations 1987 (SI 1987/1967)). The test is that the work is done either for payment or in the expectation of it. There is considerable case law from the Courts and Commissioners on whether work is, in this sense, remunerative. It is to be expected that the same test will apply to tax credits also. For the question whether work is remunerative, see in particular *R(IS) 22/95* and the decision of the Court of Appeal in *Chief Adjudication Officer v Ellis* (reported

2.34

as the appendix to that decision). In *R(FIS) 1/86* it was established that the remuneration did not come from the work. That may cause other problems for tax credits, as it may not be clear whether money received in this way from work is "employment income". However, the courts have found, for example, that tips paid to a taxi driver are earnings from the driver's employment even though paid by third parties: see *Shilton v Wilmshurst* [1991] S.T.C. 88, HL. But, as with WFTC, the question whether the work is remunerative, and the question of the level of earnings from the work, are for separate determination.

Para. (2)

2.35 This paragraph lists seven specific activities that are excepted from "work" for working tax credit purposes. The addition of condition (g) in 2007 avoids claims that arose in individual cases from prisoners working in the community on day release.

The number of hours worked

2.36 Paragraphs (3)–(5), together with regs 5–8, help define the number of hours worked by a claimant or partner. Subject to the specific provisions, it is essentially a question of fact to be determined over the claim period which will (unlike for the previous benefits replaced by working tax credit) normally be a full year. The practical approach of *R(FC) 1/92* was to look at the hours actually worked, rather than the contractual requirements. The wording of this form of the rule would suggest that this is the proper approach to be taken.

Paragraph (3) provides the starting point for deciding the number of hours, but each category of work is tested against what is "normal". The main previous test was by reference to the hours worked in the week of claim, or either of the two previous weeks, or the following week, or the week next following any current holiday. Anyone meeting those tests was then assumed to be "normally" employed at the relevant level. This makes it clearer that the issue is one of fact, and is for most claimants a significant simplification of the rules. Paragraph (4) repeats the previous disregard of paid holidays and unpaid breaks, and para.(5) extends this to allow the inclusion of paid medical visits.

In *CTC/2103/2006*, a deputy Commissioner decided that it was not correct to calculate the number of hours worked in a fluctuating situation by averaging hours across a month from a monthly pay slip. There was also no requirement in the legislation that 16 hours be worked every week. There was no set, or hard and fast, rule for deciding the number of hours worked. It is a question of fact in each case. However, it is one that causes repeated problems in administering tax credits. For this reason claimants are now required to notify HMRC within one month if their work hours change so that they stop working for 30, or 16, hours a week, as the case may be. See para.2.307 below. It will not always be easy to establish when that duty arises in cases of uncertainty such as that in *CTC/2103/2006*. But reg.7D below will provide a one-month period that deals with most cases.

[¹ Time off in connection with [²childbirth] and adoption

2.37 5.—(1) This regulation applies for any period during which a person—
  (a) is paid maternity allowance,
  (b) is paid statutory maternity pay,
  (c) is absent from work during an ordinary maternity leave period under section 71 of the Employment Rights Act 1996 or Article 103 of the Employment Rights (Northern Ireland) Order 1996;
  [³(ca) is absent from work during the first 13 weeks of an additional maternity leave period under section 73 of the Employment Rights Act 1996 or article 105 of the Employment Rights (Northern Ireland) Order 1996,]
  (d) is paid statutory paternity pay,

(SI 2002/2005, reg.5) (as amended)

- (e) is absent from work during a paternity leave period under s.80A of the Employment Rights Act 1996 or Article 112A of the Employment Rights (Northern Ireland) Order 1996,
- (f) is paid statutory adoption pay, [³. . .]
- (g) is absent from work during an ordinary adoption leave period under section 75A of the Employment Rights Act 1996 or Article 107A of the Employment Rights (Northern Ireland) Order 1996. [³,or
- (ga) is absent from work during the first 13 weeks of an additional adoption leave period under section 75B of the Employment Rights Act 1996 or article 107B of the Employment Rights (Northern Ireland) Order 1996.]

(2) For the purposes of the conditions in regulation 4(1), the person is treated as being engaged in qualifying remunerative work during the period. This is subject to paragraph (3).

(3) The person must have been engaged in qualifying remunerative work immediately before the beginning of the period.

(4) A person who is self-employed is treated as engaged in qualifying remunerative work for the requisite number of hours during any period for which paragraph (1) would have applied in his case but for the fact that the work he performed in the week immediately before the period began, although done for payment or in the expectation of payment, was not performed under a contract of service or apprenticeship.]

AMENDMENTS

1. Working Tax Credit (Entitlement and Maximum Rate) (Amendment) Regulations 2003 (SI 2003/701), reg.5 (April 6, 2003).

2. Tax Credits (Miscellaneous Amendments) Regulations 2004 (SI 2004/762), reg.6 (April 6, 2004).

3. Tax Credits (Miscellaneous Amendments) Regulations 2007 (SI 2007/824), reg.5 (April 6, 2007).

DEFINITIONS

"qualifying remunerative employment"—see reg.4.
"self-employed"—see reg.2.
"week"—see reg.2.

GENERAL NOTE

This regulation was rewritten to take account of the extended rights of mothers and fathers, including adoptive parents, to parental leave as from 2003. It is designed to stop an award of working tax credit being terminated by such leave. See also reg.5A.

2.38

[¹ Time off in connection with childbirth and placement for adoption: further provisions

5A.—(1) This regulation applies to a person for any period—
- (a) which falls within a period to which regulation 5 applies; and
- (b) which follows the birth or the placement for adoption of the child in connection with whose birth or placement entitlement to the allowance, pay or leave mentioned in regulation 5(1) arises.

(2) A person who was undertaking qualifying remunerative work for at least 16 hours per week, immediately before the beginning of a period to

2.39

which regulation 5 applies, shall be treated as satisfying the requirements of regulation 4(1) during the period mentioned in paragraph (1) above.

(3) Paragraph (4) of regulation 5 applies for the purpose of this regulation as it applies for the purpose of that regulation.]

AMENDMENT

1. Tax Credits (Miscellaneous Amendments) Regulations 2004 (SI 2004/762), reg.7 (April 6, 2004).

GENERAL NOTE

2.40 This regulation reduces the number of hours, for which a person must have been engaged in qualifying remunerative work immediately before beginning a period of statutory leave in connection with the birth or placement for adoption of a child, in order to qualify for tax credit for so much of that period as follows the birth or placement for adoption of the relevant child.

[¹Periods of illness or incapacity for work

2.41 **6.**—(1) This regulation applies for any period during which a person—
(a) is paid statutory sick pay;
(b) is paid short-term incapacity benefit at the lower rate under sections 30A–30E of the Contributions and Benefits Act;
(c) is paid income support on the grounds of incapacity for work under paragraphs 7 and 14 of Schedule 1B to the Income Support (General) Regulations 1987, or
(d) receives national insurance credits on the grounds of incapacity for work under reg.8B of the Social Security (Credits) Regulations 1975.

(2) For the purposes of the conditions in regulation 4(1), the person is treated as being engaged in qualifying remunerative work during the period. This is subject to paragraphs (3) and (4).

(3) The person must have been engaged in qualifying remunerative work immediately before the beginning of the period.

(4) If the person is paid income support as specified in paragraph (1)(c) or receives national insurance credits as specified in paragraph (1)(d) he is treated as being engaged in qualifying remunerative work for a period of 28 weeks only, beginning with the day on which he is first paid income support or receives national insurance credits (as the case may be).

(5) A person who is self-employed is treated as engaged in qualifying remunerative work for the requisite number of hours during any period for which paragraph (1) would have applied in his case but for the fact that the work he performed in the week immediately before the period began, although done for payment or in the expectation of payment, was not performed under a contract of service or apprenticeship.]

AMENDMENT

1. Working Tax Credit (Entitlement and Maximum Rate) (Amendment) Regulations 2003 (SI 2003/701), reg.6 (April 6, 2003).

DEFINITIONS

"incapacity for work"—see Social Security Contributions and Benefits Act 1992, s.171A.
"qualifying remunerative employment"—see reg.4.

(SI 2002/2005, reg.6) (as amended)

"self-employed"—see reg.2.
"week"—see reg.2.

GENERAL NOTE

This paragraph allows continuity of a claim for working tax credit into a period of sickness or disability, provided that one of the four alternative forms of benefit is received for the period. Paragraph 7 of Sch.1B to the Income Support (General) Regulations 1987 (SI 1987/1967) deal with those treated as incapable of work under the SSCBA 1992 and those entitled to statutory sick pay. Paragraph 14 deals with pregnant women who are incapable of work by reason of the pregnancy or are within 11 weeks before the expected date of confinement or seven weeks after the pregnancy ends. There is a 28-week limit on the overlap between working tax credit and either income support or contribution credits.

2.42

Term time and other seasonal workers

7.—(1) For the purposes of the conditions in regulation 4(1), paragraph (2) applies if a person—
  (a) works at a school, other educational establishment or other place of employment;
  (b) there is a recognisable cycle to his employment there; and
  (c) the length of that recognisable cycle is one year and includes periods of school holidays or similar vacations during which he does not work.

(2) If this paragraph applies, the periods mentioned in paragraph (1)(c) are disregarded in determining whether the conditions in regulation 4(1) are satisfied.

2.43

GENERAL NOTE

This carries forward to working tax credit the provisions of reg.4(4) of the Family Credit (General) Regulations 1987 (SI 1997/1973) dealing with cyclical and "term-time only" employments. But it puts the effect of those employments on a claimant's entitlement in an entirely new context. This is because the question of hours worked and sums earned are now entirely divorced from each other. To claim working tax credit the claimant must establish normal work of 16 hours a week. But that no longer carries with it an assumption of normal earnings during that assumed work. The income test is by reference to actual earnings over the entire year. As a consequence, this rule will operate to the advantage of those such as supply teachers, school learning support assistants and seasonal staff. They will continue to get their working tax credit throughout the year if the conditions of this regulation are met, while their earnings will be established without reference to assumed earnings during assumed hours of work. For example, someone working 20 hours a week for 40 weeks a year at, say, £125 a week, will meet the hours test for every week of the year if the conditions of this regulation are met, but will earn from that source only £5,000 so will be below the minimum figure of earnings for claiming working tax credit in full. This means also a continuing entitlement to claim childcare charges when appropriate. In addition, because child tax credit is now separated from working tax credit and will be separated from all other benefits, there will be no adverse effect on any child tax credit entitlement from fluctuating work patterns.

2.44

[¹Strike periods

7A.—(1) This regulation applies for any period during which a person is on strike.

2.45

(2) For the purposes of the conditions in regulation 4(1), the person is treated as being engaged in qualifying remunerative work during the period. This is subject to paragraph (3).
(3) The person—
(a) must have been engaged in qualifying remunerative work immediately before the beginning of the period, and
(b) must not be on strike for longer than a period of 10 consecutive days on which he should have been working.]

AMENDMENT

1. Working Tax Credit (Entitlement and Maximum Rate) (Amendment) Regulations 2003 (SI 2003/701), reg.7 (April 6, 2003).

DEFINITION

"qualifying remunerative employment"—see reg.4.

GENERAL NOTE

2.46 This rule is a relaxation from the strict set of rules preventing workers benefiting during a strike. The effect of this regulation is to stop a break in entitlement occurring for a strike of 10 consecutive days or less.

[¹**Persons suspended from work**

2.47 **7B.**—(1) This regulation applies for any period during which a person is suspended from work while complaints or allegations against him are investigated.
(2) For the purposes of the conditions in regulation 4(1), the person is treated as being engaged in qualifying remunerative work during the period. This is subject to paragraph (3).
(3) The person must have been engaged in qualifying remunerative work immediately before the beginning of the period.]

AMENDMENT

1. Working Tax Credit (Entitlement and Maximum Rate) (Amendment) Regulations 2003 (SI 2003/701), reg.7 (April 6, 2003).

DEFINITIONS

"qualifying remunerative employment"—see reg.4.

GENERAL NOTE

2.48 This deals with a practical problem similar in part to that behind reg.7A. However, in the case of someone is suspended from work, for example while a complaint is investigated, the period of suspension will often not be known.

[¹**Pay in lieu of notice**

2.49 **7C.**—(1) This regulation applies if a person stops work and receives pay in lieu of notice.
(2) For the purposes of the conditions in regulation 4(1), the person shall not be treated as being engaged in qualifying remunerative work during the period for which he receives the pay.]
[² (3) This regulation is subject to regulation 7D.]

(SI 2002/2005, reg. 7C) (as amended)

AMENDMENTS

1. Working Tax Credit (Entitlement and Maximum Rate) (Amendment) Regulations 2003 (SI 2003/701), reg.7 (April 6, 2003).
2. Working Tax Credit (Entitlement and Maximum Rate) (Amendment) Regulations 2007 (SI 2007/968), reg.2 (April 6, 2007).

DEFINITION

"qualifying remunerative employment"—see reg.4.

GENERAL NOTE

This deals in a pragmatic way with the problem caused when someone stops work before a period of notice has ended, but who receives pay in lieu of notice (often abbreviated to PILON). This regulation excludes the claimant from entitlement to working tax credit. But a problem may arise if the employee does not find other work during that period (and he or she may be prevented from doing so). The provisions about calculating earnings from employment for jobseeker's allowance purposes allow sums to be spread over the period for which they are paid, unless they are excluded from earnings for that purpose, and so may exclude entitlement to JSA. See regs 94 and 98 of the Jobseeker's Allowance Regulations 1996 (SI 1996/207) and the notes to them in Vol.II of this work. So the individual may be excluded from both working tax credit and jobseeker's allowance.

2.50

[¹Ceasing to undertake work or working for less than 16 hours per week

7D.—(1) This regulation applies for the four-week period immediately after—
  (a) a person who has been undertaking qualifying remunerative work for not less than 16 hours per week ceases to work or starts to work less than 16 hours per week, or
  (b) a person who has been undertaking qualifying remunerative work for not less than 30 hours per week ceases to work or starts to work less than 16 hours per week.

(2) For the purposes of the conditions in regulation 4(1), the person is treated as being engaged in qualifying remunerative work during that period.
This is subject to paragraph (3).

(3) The person must have been engaged in qualifying remunerative work immediately before the beginning of that period.]

2.51

GENERAL NOTE

This regulation provides for a four week run-on of WTC to those claimants whose hours fall below 16 hours a week. Where entitled, claimants will be eligible to claim income support or JSA whilst in receipt of WTC for the four week period (although the WTC will be treated as income for assessing entitlement to those benefits). The purpose of this rule is to reduce overpayments of tax credits and to ease the transition from tax credits to benefits. It is consistent with the shift from April 2007 of a mandatory reporting requirement on tax credits claimants to inform HMRC within a month of ceasing work.

2.52

Gaps between jobs

8. For the purposes of the conditions in regulation 4(1), a person shall be treated as being engaged in qualifying remunerative work for the requisite number of hours if he has been so engaged within the past seven days.

2.53

Working Tax Credit (Entitlement and Maximum Rate) Regulations 2002

DEFINITION

"qualifying remunerative employment"—see reg.4.

GENERAL NOTE

2.54 Regulation 4 allows someone to make a claim for working tax credit if he or she has an offer of a job starting within seven days of the claim (see the first condition in reg.4). However, if there is a gap of not more than that period between jobs, this regulation allows the gap to be bridged so as to avoid the need to make a new claim. This is also consistent with the provisions of the Tax Credits (Claims and Notifications) Regulations 2002 (SI 2002/2014), reg.10, allowing claims for working tax credit seven days in advance.

Disability element

[¹Disability element and workers who are to be treated as at a disadvantage in getting a job

2.55 **9.**—(1) The determination of the maximum rate must include the disability element if the claimant, or, in the case of a joint claim, one of the claimants—
  (a) undertakes qualifying remunerative work for at least 16 hours per week;
  (b) has any of the disabilities listed in Part I of Schedule 1, or in the case of an initial claim, satisfies the conditions in Part II of Schedule 1; and
  (c) is a person who satisfies any of Cases A to G on a day for which the maximum rate is determined in accordance with these Regulations.

(2) Case A is where the person has been in receipt of the higher rate of short-term incapacity benefit, long-term incapacity benefit or severe disablement allowance for at least one day in the preceding 182 days.

(3) Case B is where, for at least one day in the preceding 182 days, the person has been a person [² for whom at least one of the following benefits has been payable and for whom the applicable amount] included a higher pensioner or disability premium [²in respect of him] determined—
  (a) in the case of income support, in accordance with [² paragraphs 10(1)(b) or (2)(b) or 11, and where applicable 12,] of Part III of Schedule 2 to the Income Support (General) Regulations 1987;
  (b) in the case of income-based jobseeker's allowance, in accordance with [²paragraphs 12(1)(a), or (b)(ii), or (c), or 13, and where applicable 14 of Part 3 of] Schedule 1 to the Jobseeker's Allowance Regulations 1996;
  (c) in the case of housing benefit, in accordance with [² [³paragraphs 11(1)(b) or 11(2)(b) or 12, and where applicable, 13 of Part 3 Schedule 3 of the Housing Benefit Regulations 2006];
  (d) in the case of Council Tax Benefit, in accordance with [² [³paragraphs 11(1)(b) or 11(2)(b) or 12, and where applicable, 13 of Part 3 of Schedule 1 of the Council Tax Benefit Regulations 2006].

For the purposes of this Case "the applicable amount" has the meaning given by section 135 of the Contributions and Benefits Act.

(4) Case C is where the person is a person to whom at least one of the following is payable—
  (a) a disability living allowance;

(SI 2002/2005, reg.9) (as amended)

(b) an attendance allowance;
(c) a mobility supplement or a constant attendance allowance which is paid, in either case, in conjunction with a war pension or industrial injuries disablement benefit.

(5) Case D is where the person has an invalid carriage or other vehicle provided under—
(a) section 5(2)(a) of, and Schedule 2 to, the National Health Service Act 1977,
(b) section 46 of the National Health Service (Scotland) Act 1978; or
(c) Article 30(1) of the Health and Personal Social Services (Northern Ireland) Order 1972.

(6) Case E is where the person—
(a) has received, on account of his incapacity for work, statutory sick pay, occupational sick pay, short-term incapacity benefit payable at the lower rate or income support, for a period of 140 qualifying days, or has been credited with Class 1 or Class 2 contributions under the Contributions and Benefits Act for a period of 20 weeks on account of incapacity for work, and where the last of those days or weeks (as the case may be) fell within the preceding 56 days;
(b) has a disability which is likely to last for at least six months, or for the rest of his life if his death is expected within that time; and
(c) has gross earnings which are less than they were before the disability began by at least the greater of 20 per cent and £15 per week.

For the purpose of this Case "qualifying days" are days which form part of a single period of incapacity for work within the meaning of Part XI of the Contributions and Benefits Act.

(7) Case F is where the person—
(a) has undertaken training for work for at least one day in the preceding 56 days; and
(b) has received the higher rate of short-term incapacity benefit, long-term incapacity benefit or severe disablement allowance within 56 days before the first day of that period of training for work.
Regulation 9B explains the meaning of "training for work" and of a period of training for work.

(8) Case G is where the person was entitled, [2 for at least one day in the preceding 56 days], to the disability element of working tax credit or to disabled person's tax credit by virtue of his having satisfied the requirements of Case A, B, E or F at some earlier time.

For the purposes of this Case a person is treated as having an entitlement to the disability element of working tax credit if that element is taken into account in determining the rate at which the person is entitled to a tax credit.

(9) For the purposes of the Act, a person who satisfies paragraph (1)(b) is to be treated as having a physical or mental disability which puts him at a disadvantage in getting a job.]

AMENDMENTS

1. Working Tax Credit (Entitlement and Maximum Rate) (Amendment) Regulations 2003 (SI 2003/701), reg.8 (April 6, 2003).
2. Tax Credits (Miscellaneous Amendments No.2) Regulations 2003 (SI 2003/2815), reg.14 (November 26, 2003).
3. Housing Benefit and Council Tax Benefit (Consequential Provisions) Regulations 2006 (SI 2006/217), reg.22(2) (March 6, 2006).

DEFINITIONS
"claim"—see reg.2.
"initial claim"—see reg.9A.
"joint claim"—see reg.2.
"qualifying remunerative employment"—see reg.4.
"training for work"—see reg.9B.
"week"—see reg.2.

GENERAL NOTE

2.56 This complex regulation in effect replaces the whole of the Disability Work Allowance (General) Regulations 1991 (SI 1991/2887), so its complexity has to be viewed as a considerable simplification! It provides the conditions for a claim to working tax credit by Route 2, and replaces DPTC. It imposes three separate sets of conditions, all of which must be met to meet the second condition in reg.4 of these Regulations. The first of the three conditions is the requirement that the claimant work 16 or more hours a week in qualifying remunerative work. This restates one of the requirements of the second condition, but with the specific addition of the reference to "qualifying remunerative" work. The other two conditions may be termed the "disability conditions".

In *CTC/643/2005* a Commissioner decided that entitlement under reg.9(1) arises only during the period when a claimant is also entitled under one of the cases A to G. This follows from the reference in reg.9(1)(c) to the claimant satisfying any of Cases A to G "on a day for which the maximum rate is determined . . .". A claimant could not claim the disability element throughout a year unless he or she met the requirements of one of the cases throughout the year.

In *CSTC/76/2006* the Commissioner considered how the conditions are to be applied to joint claimants. She confirmed the view of HMRC that all the disablement conditions are to be met by the same individual and that individual must also undertake work for at least 16 hours a week. She rejected an attempt to argue a claim under this regulation where one of the joint claimants worked to the required extent and the other was disabled. This reflects the origin of this provision in the former disabled person's tax credit and disability working allowance. It is also consistent with the entitlement of a working partner to claim carer's allowance if caring for a disabled partner to the required level.

First disability condition

2.57 To come within this condition, the claimant must have one or more of the disabilities listed in Pt 1 of Sch.1 to these Regulations (see below). These have been brought forward from the conditions of entitlement to DPTC and disability working allowance. Paragraph (5) emphasises that a person meeting this condition is to be treated as being put at a disadvantage by reason of the disability.

Second disability condition

2.58 To come within this condition, the claimant must meet the conditions of one or more of seven separate "cases" labelled Case A to Case G. Briefly these link with other benefits or activities as follows:

Case A: entitlement to long-term incapacity benefit or the higher rate of short-term incapacity benefit, or severe disablement allowance;

Case B: entitlement to a higher pensioner or disability premium of income support, income-based jobseeker's allowance, housing benefit and/or council tax benefit;

Case C: entitlement to disability living allowance, attendance allowance, mobility supplement or constant attendance allowance;

Case D: membership of the Motability scheme;

(SI 2002/2005, reg.9) (as amended)

Case E: entitlement to occupational or statutory sick pay, short-term incapacity benefit, income support or "disability credits"; a continuing disability; and earnings that have reduced since the disability started by 20 per cent or £15 a week;

Case F: training for work linked with payment of the benefits in Case A;

Case G: immediate previous entitlement to the disability element of WTC or DPTC under Cases A, B, E or F.

There are special rules that apply to initial claims, noted under reg.9A below.

[¹Initial claims

9A.—(1) In regulation 9(1)(b) an "initial claim" means a claim which—
(a) is made for the disability element of working tax credit, and
(b) relates to a person who has not had an entitlement to that element or to disabled person's tax credit during the two years immediately preceding the making of the claim.

(2) In paragraph (1) any reference to the making of a claim includes the giving of notification, in accordance with regulation 20 of the Tax Credits (Claims and Notifications) Regulations 2002, of a change of circumstances falling within that regulation.

(3) For the purposes of paragraph (1)(b), a person is treated as having an entitlement to the disability element of working tax credit if, by virtue of the person being a person who satisfies regulation 9, that element is taken into account in determining the rate at which the person is entitled to a tax credit.]

AMENDMENT

1. Working Tax Credit (Entitlement and Maximum Rate) (Amendment) Regulations 2003 (SI 2003/701), reg.8 (April 6, 2003).

DEFINITIONS

"claim"—see reg.2.
"claimant"—see reg.2.
"disability element"—see reg.9.

GENERAL NOTE

This regulation makes clear that an "initial claim" for the purposes of reg.9 is a first claim involving disability, or a notification that may involve the addition of a disability element to an award already made on other grounds. This clarifies the scope of reg.9(1), which extends the test of disability under the second disability condition for a first claim. An initial claim will have an extended relevance for working tax credit as compared with its predecessors as the claim will, in normal course of events, last for the balance of the tax year from the effective date of claim.

[¹Training for work, etc.

9B.—(1) In [²regulation 9], "training for work" means training for work received—
(a) in pursuance of arrangements made under—
  (i) section 2(1) of the Employment and Training Act 1973,
  (ii) section 2(3) of the Enterprise and New Towns (Scotland) Act 1990, or
  (iii) section 1(1) of the Employment and Training Act 1950, or

Working Tax Credit (Entitlement and Maximum Rate) Regulations 2002

(b) on a course whose primary purpose is the teaching of occupational or vocational skills, and which the person attends for 16 hours or more a week.

(2) For the purposes of regulation 9(7), a period of training for work means a series of consecutive days of training for work, there being disregarded any day specified in paragraph (3).

(3) Those days are any day on which the claimant was—
 (a) on holiday;
 (b) attending court as a justice of the peace, a party to any proceedings, a witness or a juror;
 (c) suffering from some disease or bodily or mental disablement as a result of which he was unable to attend training for work, or his attendance would have put at risk the health of other persons;
 (d) unable to participate in training for work because—
  (i) he was looking after a child because the person who usually looked after that child was unable to do so;
  (ii) he was looking after a member of his family who was ill;
  (iii) he was required to deal with some domestic emergency; or
  (iv) he was arranging or attending the funeral of his partner or a relative; or
 (e) authorised by the training provider to be absent from training for work.

(4) For the purposes of paragraph (3)(d)(iv) "relative" means close relative, grandparent, grandchild, uncle, aunt, nephew or niece; and in this paragraph "close relative" means parent, parent-in-law, son, son-in-law, daughter, daughter-in-law, step-parent, step-son, step-daughter, brother, sister, or the spouse of any of the preceding persons or, if that person is one of an unmarried couple, the other member of that couple.]

AMENDMENTS

1. Working Tax Credit (Entitlement and Maximum Rate) (Amendment) Regulations 2003 (SI 2003/701), reg.8 (April 6, 2003).
2. Tax Credits (Miscellaneous Amendments) Regulations 2004 (SI 2004/762), reg.8 (April 6, 2004).

DEFINITIONS

"claim"—see reg.2.
"claimant"—see reg.2.
"week"—see reg.2.

GENERAL NOTE

2.62   This definition is necessary to clarify the scope of Case F in reg.9(7).

30 hour element

30 hour element

2.63   **10.**—(1) The determination of the maximum rate must include a 30 hour element if the claimant, or in the case of a joint claim, at least one of the claimants, is engaged in qualifying remunerative work for at least 30 hours per week.

(2) The determination of the maximum rate must also include the 30-hour element if—
 (a) the claim is a joint claim,

(SI 2002/2005, reg.10) (as amended)

(b) at least one of the claimants is responsible for one or more children or qualifying young people,
(c) the aggregate number of hours for which the couple engage in qualifying remunerative work is at least 30 hours per week, and
(d) at least one member of the couple engages in qualifying remunerative work for at least 16 hours per week.

[¹(3) For the purposes of determining whether the condition in paragraph (2)(c) is met, the words "for not less than 16 hours per week" in paragraph (a) of the second condition in regulation 4(1) are omitted.]

AMENDMENT

1. Working Tax Credit (Entitlement and Maximum Rate) (Amendment) Regulations 2003 (SI 2003/701), reg.9 (April 6, 2003).

DEFINITION

"child"—see reg.2.
"claim"—see reg.2.
"claimant"—see reg.2.
"couple"—see reg.2.
"joint claim"—see TCA 2002, s.3.
"qualifying remunerative work"—see reg.4.
"qualifying young person"—see reg.2.
"responsible"—see TCA 2002, s.48.
"week"—see reg.2.

GENERAL NOTE

An additional element of £705 a year is payable if the claimant or couple work 30 hours a week. Paragraphs (1) and (2) together ensure that the total of 30 hours can be worked by either of the couple or by both together if one or both of them are responsible for a child or qualifying young person. Paragraph (3) deals with a drafting problem in applying the second condition in reg.4 for establishing that a claimant is engaged in qualifying remunerative work to both members of a couple jointly working 30 hours a week but where only one is working over 16 hours.

2.64

Second adult element

[¹**Second adult element**

11.—(1) The determination of the maximum rate must include the second adult element if the claim is a joint claim.

2.65

This is subject to the following provisions of this regulation.

(2) The determination of the maximum rate shall not include the second adult element if—
(a) one of the claimants is aged 50 or over;
(b) the 50 plus element is payable, and
(c) neither of the claimants is engaged in qualifying remunerative work for at least 30 hours per week.

(3) But subsection (2) does not apply if at least one of the claimants—
(a) is responsible for a child or a qualifying young person, or
(b) satisfies regulation 9(1).

(4) The determination of the maximum rate shall also not include the second adult element if—

(a) neither claimant has responsibility for a child or qualifying young person; and
(b) one claimant is serving a custodial sentence of more than twelve months.]

AMENDMENT

1. Working Tax Credit (Entitlement and Maximum Rate) (Amendment) Regulations 2003 (SI 2003/701), reg.10 (April 6, 2003).

DEFINITIONS

"50 Plus element"—see reg.18.
"child"—see reg.2.
"claimant"—see reg.2.
"joint claim"—see reg.2.
"qualifying remunerative work"—see reg.4.
"qualifying young person"—see reg.2.
"responsible"—see TCA 2002, s.48.
"week"—see reg.2.

GENERAL NOTE

2.66 The value of the second adult element is a little below that of the basic element. The effect of para.2 is that it limits entitlements of those within it where they work less than 30 hours a week. The effect is that both this element and the increased 30-hour element for those over 50 can be claimed only if one of the claimants works over 30 hours a week.

Lone parent element

Lone parent element

2.67 **12.** The determination of the maximum rate must include the lone parent element if—
(a) the claim is a single claim; and
(b) the claimant is responsible for [¹a child or qualifying young person].

AMENDMENT

1. Working Tax Credit (Entitlement and Maximum Rate) (Amendment) Regulations 2003 (SI 2003/701), reg.11 (April 6, 2003).

DEFINITION

"child"—see reg.2.
"claim"—see reg.2.
"qualifying young person"—see reg.2.
"responsible"—see TCA 2002, s.48.

GENERAL NOTE

2.68 The value of the lone parent element is the same as that of the second adult element.

(SI 2002/2005, reg.13) (as amended)

Childcare element

Entitlement to childcare element of working tax credit

13.—(1) The determination of the maximum rate must include a childcare element where that person, or in the case of a joint claim at least one of those persons, is incurring relevant childcare charges and—
  (a) is a person, not being a member of a [³. . .] couple, engaged in [¹qualifying remunerative work];
[¹(b) is a member or are members of a [³. . .] couple where both are engaged in qualifying remunerative work; or
  (c) is a member or are members of a [³. . .] couple where one is engaged in qualifying remunerative work and the other—
      (i) is incapacitated;
      (ii) is an in-patient in hospital; or
      (iii) is in prison (whether serving a custodial sentence or remanded in custody awaiting trial or sentence).]
(2) For the purposes of paragraph (1), a person is not treated as incurring relevant childcare charges where the average weekly charge calculated in accordance with regulation 15 is nil or where an agreement within regulation 15(4) has not yet commenced.
[¹(3) [². . .]
(4) For the purposes of para.(1)(c)(i), the other member of a couple is incapacitated in any of the circumstances specified in paragraphs (5) to (8).]
(5) The circumstances specified in this paragraph are where either council tax benefit or housing benefit is payable under Part VII of the Contributions and Benefits Act to the other member or his partner and the applicable amount of the person entitled to the benefit includes—
  (a) a disability premium; or
  (b) a higher pensioner premium by virtue of the satisfaction of—
      (i) in the case of housing benefit, [⁴ paragraph 11(2)(b) of Schedule 1 to the Counsil Tax Benefit Regulations 2006];
      (ii) in the case of housing benefit, [⁴ paragraph 11(2)(b) of Schedule 3 to the Housing Benefit Regulations 2006],
    on account of the other member's incapacity or [⁴ regulation 18(1)(c) of the Council Tax Benefit Regulations 2006] (treatment of childcare charges) or, as the case may be, [⁴ regulation 28(1)(c) of the Housing Benefit Regulations 2006] (treatment of childcare charges) applies in that person's case;
(6) The circumstances specified in this paragraph are where there is payable in respect of him one or more of the following pensions or allowances—
  (a) short-term incapacity benefit [¹payable at the higher rate] under section 30A of the Contributions and Benefits Act;
  (b) long-term incapacity benefit under section 40 or 41 of the Contributions and Benefits Act;
  (c) attendance allowance under section 64 of that Act;
  (d) severe disablement allowance under section 68 of that Act;
  (e) disability living allowance under section 71 of that Act;
  (f) increase of disablement pension under section 104 of that Act;
  (g) a pension increase under a war pension scheme or an industrial injuries scheme which is analogous to an allowance or increase of disablement pension under sub-paragraph (b), (d) or (e) above.

2.69

Working Tax Credit (Entitlement and Maximum Rate) Regulations 2002

(7) The circumstances specified in this paragraph are where a pension or allowance to which sub-paragraph [¹(c)], (d), (e) or (f) of paragraph (6) refers, was payable on account of his incapacity but has ceased to be payable only in consequence of his becoming a patient.

(8) The circumstances specified in this paragraph are where he has an invalid carriage or other vehicle provided to him under section 5(2)(a) of and Schedule 2 to the National Health Service Act 1977, section 46 of the National Health Service (Scotland) Act 1978; or Article 30(1) of the Health and Personal Social Services (Northern Ireland) Order 1972.

AMENDMENTS

1. Working Tax Credit (Entitlement and Maximum Rate) (Amendment) Regulations 2003 (SI 2003/701), reg.12 (April 6, 2003).
2. Tax Credits (Miscellaneous Amendments) Regulations 2004 (SI 2004/762), reg.9 (April 6, 2004).
3. Civil Partnership Act 2004 (Tax Credits, etc.) (Consequential Amendments) Order 2005 (SI 2005/2919), art.2(3) (December 5, 2005).
4. Housing Benefit and Council Tax Benefit (Consequential Provisions) Regulations 2006 (SI 2006/217), reg.22(3) (March 6, 2006).

DEFINITIONS

"child"—see reg.2.
"childcare"—see reg.14.
"couple"—see TCA 2002, s.3.
"claimant"—see reg.2.
"joint claim"—see reg.2.
"partner"—see reg.2.
"patient"—see reg.2.
"qualifying remunerative work"—see reg.4.
"relevant childcare charges"—see reg.14.

GENERAL NOTE

2.70　Specific provision is made for the childcare element in TCA 2002, s.12. The element may be claimed by those entitled to working tax credit and incurring relevant childcare charges for a child for whom a claimant is responsible in three circumstances:
   (a) a lone parent working 16 hours a week;
   (b) a couple both of whom are working 16 hours a week; or
   (c) a couple, one of whom is working 16 hours a week and the other of whom is incapacitated, in hospital or in prison.

Incapacitated

2.71　The test of incapacity is set out in paras (4)–(8). Each of these tests refers to entitlement to a form of benefit to which only the disabled or incapacitated are entitled. This follows the policy of the tax credits legislation in relying on the determination by others of disability or incapacity in most cases. Paragraph (5) is by reference to housing benefit and council tax benefit, paras (6) and (7) by reference to benefits awarded by the Department for Work and Pensions, and para.(8) by reference to the Motability scheme.

Entitlement to childcare element of working tax credit

2.72　**14.**—(1) [¹Subject to paragraph (1A),] for the purposes of section 12 of the Act charges incurred for childcare are charges paid by the person, or in the case of a joint claim, by either or both of the persons, for childcare provided for any child for whom the person, or at least one of the persons,

(SI 2002/2005, reg.14) (as amended)

is responsible [³ within the meaning of regulation 3 of the Child Tax Credit Regulations 2002].

In these Regulations, such charges are called "relevant childcare charges".

[¹(1A) Childcare charges do not include charges in respect of care provided by [⁶—
  (a) a relative of the child, wholly or mainly in the child's home, or
  (b) a provider mentioned in regulation 14(2)(e)(ia), in circumstances where the care is excluded from being qualifying child care by Article 5(2)(c) of the Tax Credits (Approval of Child Care Providers) Scheme 2005.]
[⁹(c) a provider mentioned in regulation 14(2)(c), in circumstances where the care is excluded from being qualifying chid care by article 4(2)(c) of the Tax Credits (Approval of Home Child Care Providers) Scheme (Northern Ireland) 2006.]
[¹⁰ (d) a provider mentioned in regulation 14(2)(f)(ii), in circumstances where the care is excluded from being qualifying child care by Article 5(3)(d) of the Tax Credits (Approval of Child Care Providers) (Wales) Scheme 2007.]
(1B) For the purposes of this regulation—
  (a) "relative" means parent, grandparent, aunt, uncle, brother or sister whether by blood, half blood, marriage [⁷, civil patnership] or affinity;
  (b) "the child's home" means the home of the person, or in the case of a joint claim of either or both of the persons, responsible for the child.]
(2) "Child care" means care provided for a child—
  (a) in England and Wales—
    (i) by persons registered under Part XA of the Children Act 1989;
    (ii) in schools or establishments which are exempted from registration under Part XA of the Children Act 1989 by virtue of paragraph 1 or 2 of Schedule 9A to that Act;
    (iii) in respect of any period [³on or before] [². . . the last day he is treated as a child for the purposes of this regulation,] where the care is provided out of school hours, by a school on school premises or by a local authority; [³. . .]
    (iv) by a childcare provider approved by an accredited organisation within the meaning given by regulation 4 of the Tax Credit (New Category of Child Care Provider) Regulations 1999; [³or]
    [⁴(v) by a foster parent under the Fostering Services Regulations 2002 or the Fostering Services (Wales) Regulations 2003 in relation to a child other than one whom he is fostering;]
  (b) in Scotland—
    (i) by a person in circumstances where the care service provided by him consists of child minding or of day care of children within the meaning of section 2 of the Regulation of Care (Scotland) Act 2001 and is registered under Part I of that Act; [³. . .]
    [⁹(ia) by a child care agency where the service consists of or includes supplying, or introducing to persons who use the service, child carers within the meaning of sections 2(7) and (8) of the Regulation of Care (Scotland) Act 2001;]
    (ii) by a local authority in circumstances where the care service provided by the local authority consists of child minding or of day care of children within the meaning of section 2 of the Regulation

Working Tax Credit (Entitlement and Maximum Rate) Regulations 2002

    of Care (Scotland) Act 2001 and is registered under Part II of that Act; [³or]
   [⁴(iii) by a foster carer under the Fostering of Children (Scotland) Regulations 1996 in relation to a child other than one whom he is fostering;]
  (c) in Northern Ireland—
    (i) by persons registered under Part XI of the Children (Northern Ireland) Order 1995; [³. . .]
   (ii) by institutions and establishments exempt from registration under that Part by virtue of Article 121 of that Order; or
   [⁴(iii) in respect of any period ending on or before the day on which he ceases to be a child for the purposes of this regulation, where the care is provided out of school hours by a school on school premises or by an Education and Library Board or a Health and Social Services Trust; or
   (iv) by a foster parent under the Foster Placement (Children) Regulations (Northern Ireland) 1996 in relation to a child other than one whom he is fostering; or]
   [⁹(v) by a child care provider approved in accordance with the Tax Credits (approval of Home Child Care Providers) Scheme (Northern Ireland) 2006.]
  (d) [¹anywhere outside the United Kingdom]—
    (i) by a childcare provider approved by an accredited organisation within the meaning given by regulation 4 of the Tax Credit (New Category of Child Care Provider) Regulations 2002; or
   (ii) [¹. . .]
[¹(e) in England—
    (i) [⁶. . .]
   [⁶(ia) by a child care provider approved in accordance with the Tax Credits (Approval of Child Care Providers) Scheme 2005; [¹⁰. . .]
  [¹⁰(ib) by a child care provider registered under the Childcare (Voluntary Registration) Regulations 2007; or]
   (ii) by a domiciliary care worker under the Domiciliary Care Agencies Regulations 2002.]
[⁵(f) in Wales
    (i) by a domiciliary care worker under the Domiciliary Care Agencies (Wales) Regulations 2004;] [¹⁰or
   (ii) by a child care provider approved under the Tax Credits (Approval of Child Care Providers) (Wales) Scheme 2007.]

(3) For the purposes of this regulation a person is a child until the last day of the week in which falls 1st September following that child's 15th birthday (or 16th birthday if the child is disabled).

(4) For the purposes of paragraph (3), a child is disabled where—
(a) a disability living allowance is payable in respect of that child, or has ceased to be payable solely because he is a patient;
(b) the child is registered as blind in a register compiled by a local authority under section 29 of the National Assistance Act 1948 (welfare services) or, in Scotland, has been certified as blind and in consequence is registered as blind in a register maintained by or on behalf of a local authority in Scotland, or, in Northern Ireland has been certified as blind and in consequence is registered as blind in a register maintained by or on behalf of a Health and Social Services Board; or

(SI 2002/2005, reg.14) (as amended)

(c) the child ceased to be registered as blind in such a register within the 28 weeks immediately preceding the date of claim.

(5) Charges paid in respect of the child's compulsory education or charges paid by a person to a partner or by a partner to the person in respect of any child for whom either or any of them is responsible are not relevant childcare charges.

(6) Where regulation 15(4) (agreement for the provision of future childcare) applies—

(a) the words "charges paid" in paragraph (1) include charges which will be incurred; and
(b) the words "childcare provided" in paragraph (1) include care which will be provided.

(7) [³. . .]

(8) Relevant childcare charges are calculated on a weekly basis in accordance with regulation 15.

AMENDMENTS

1. Working Tax Credit (Entitlement and Maximum Rate) (Amendment) Regulations 2003 (SI 2003/701), reg.13 (April 6, 2003).
2. Tax Credits (Miscellaneous Amendments No.2) Regulations 2003 (SI 2003/2815), reg.15 (November 26, 2003).
3. Tax Credits (Miscellaneous Amendments) Regulations 2004 (SI 2004/762), reg.10 (April 6, 2004).
4. Working Tax Credit (Entitlement and Maximum Rate) (Amendment) Regulations 2004 (SI 2004/1276), reg.2 (June 1, 2004).
5. Tax Credits (Miscellaneous Amendments No.3) Regulations 2004 (SI 2004/2663), reg.3 (November 3, 2004).
6. Working Tax Credit (Entitlement and Maximum Rate) (Amendment) Regulations 2005 (SI 2005/769), reg.4(b) (April 6, 2005).
7. Civil Partnership Act 2004 (Tax Credits, etc.) (Consequential Amendments) Order 2005 (SI 2005/2919), art.2(4) (December 5, 2005).
8. Working Tax Credit (Entitlement and Maximum Rate) (Amendment) Regulations 2005 (SI 2005/769), reg.4(a) (January 1, 2006).
9. Tax Credits (Miscellaneous Amendments) Regulations 2006 (SI 2006/766), reg.20(4) (April 6, 2006).
10. Tax Credits (Miscellaneous Amendments) Regulations 2007 (SI 2007/824), reg.6 (April 6, 2007).

DEFINITIONS

"child"—see reg.2.
"claim"—see reg.2.
"partner"—see reg.2.
"patient"—see reg.2.

GENERAL NOTE

The main content of this regulation is the definition of the main phrases on which reg.13 relies. "Child" receives a slightly limited definition compared with the standard approach for child tax credit and working tax credit, as para.(3) puts an upper limit on the relevant age of a child. The provision does not apply at all to those over 16, who are known as "qualifying young persons" for working tax credit and child tax credit purposes. There is an upwards extension of the age limit for disabled children in paras (3) and (4). This is by reference to payment of any level of disability living allowance or by blindness. There is also a limit applying to the youngest children. Paragraph (7) links with reg.13(3) to exclude a claim by someone on

2.73

maternity, paternity or adoption leave by reference only to the child in respect of whom the leave is granted.

"Child care" is given an extensive definition. This is necessary because responsibility for childcare legislation is part of the devolved responsibilities of the Scottish and Northern Irish parliaments and the Welsh assembly. In addition, the definition has been extended to childcare outside the United Kingdom. This links with the provisions in the Tax Credits (Residence) Regulations 2003 (SI 2003/642) under which Crown servants outside the United Kingdom, and their partners, are regarded as being in the United Kingdom for tax credits purposes. Accordingly, staff provided with approved childcare facilities by, for example, defence establishments, can qualify for the childcare element of working tax credit. Any dispute about whether someone is providing "childcare" is for the authorities responsible for that particular set of registration rules.

"Relevant childcare charges" is defined by reference to charges for "childcare", with the important exception in para.(1A) of childcare provided by a (registered) relative in the child's home. It can, however, be provided in the carer's home even though the carer is, say, a grandparent. The condition ensures that both the carer, and the carer's premises, are open to inspection. Paragraph (5) excludes charges for education as against care, and payments made by one of a married or unmarried couple to the other (although the one to whom the payments are made may not be responsible for the child).

Calculation of relevant childcare charges

2.74   **15.**—(1) Relevant childcare charges are calculated by aggregating the average weekly charge paid for childcare for each child in respect of whom charges are incurred [¹and rounding up the total to the nearest whole pound]. This is subject to [¹paragraphs (1A) and (2)].

[¹(1A) In any case in which the charges in respect of childcare are paid weekly, the average weekly charge for the purposes of paragraph (1) is established—
  (a) where the charges are for a fixed weekly amount, by aggregating the average weekly charge paid for childcare for each child in respect of whom charges are incurred in the most recent four complete weeks; or
  (b) where the charges are for variable weekly amounts, by aggregating the charges for the previous 52 weeks and dividing the total by 52.]

(2) In any case in which the charges in respect of childcare are paid monthly, the average weekly charge for the purposes of paragraph (1) is established—
  (a) where the charges are for a fixed monthly amount, by multiplying that amount by 12 and dividing the product by 52; or
  (b) where the charges are for variable monthly amounts, by aggregating the charges for the previous 12 months and dividing the total by 52.

(3) In a case where there is insufficient information for establishing the average weekly charge paid for childcare in accordance with paragraphs (1) and (2), an officer of the Board shall estimate the charge—
  (a) in accordance with information provided by the person or persons incurring the charges; and
  (b) by any method which in the officer's opinion is reasonable.

(4) If a person—
  (a) has entered into an agreement for the provision of childcare; and
  (b) will incur under that agreement relevant childcare charges in respect of childcare during the period of the award, the average weekly charge for childcare is based upon a written estimate of the future weekly charges provided by that person.

(SI 2002/2005, reg.15) (as amended)

AMENDMENT

1. Working Tax Credit (Entitlement and Maximum Rate) (Amendment) Regulations 2003 (SI 2003/701), reg.14 (April 6, 2003).

DEFINITIONS

"child"—see reg.14(3).
"childcare"—see reg.14(2).
"relevant childcare charges"—see reg.14(1).

GENERAL NOTE

This regulation sets out the methods to be used in calculating the amount of childcare charges on which the childcare element is to be based. The regulation was amended just before it came into effect because the previous form of the regulation was accepted as being seriously flawed. This is because it had attempted to use weekly payment rules from the previous approach used for WFTC for the new system of annual calculation and award. This created potential unfairness as between those who pay monthly for their childcare on an annualised basis and those who pay weekly on an actual basis. While the monthly payers usually have a steady pattern of payments, the weekly payers often pay more during school terms than during school holidays.

The rules deal with monthly payments by either using the fixed monthly charge, or the average of the last 12 monthly charges, to determine the weekly figure. Varying weekly charges are calculated by reference to the last 52 weeks, while fixed weekly charges are calculated by reference to the last four weeks. Presumably, however, regard must be had to more than four past weeks in applying this rule to avoid the problem of assessing the charges for the wrong four weeks.

There are two important provisos to these rules. The first is that HMRC may rely on estimates based on "any method . . . which is reasonable". This should allow a solution to the problem of increases in the charges that should be reflected in increases in the childcare element. The second proviso, in para.(4), allows an estimate of the future charges to be taken into account provided that the claimant has entered into a written agreement for the provision of childcare.

Change of circumstances

16.—(1) There is a relevant change in circumstances if—
(a) [1. . .]
(b) [1during the period of an award, the weekly relevant childcare charges, rounded up to the nearest whole pound]—
  (i) exceed the average weekly charge calculated in accordance with regulation 15 by £10 a week or more;
  (ii) are less than the average weekly charge calculated in accordance with regulation 15 by £10 a week or more; or
  (iii) are nil.
If there is a relevant change in circumstances, the amount of the childcare element of working tax credit shall be recalculated with effect from the specified date.

[1(2) For the purposes of paragraph (1), the weekly relevant childcare charge—
(a) where the childcare charges are for a fixed weekly amount, is the aggregate of the weekly charge paid for childcare for each child in respect of whom charges are incurred in each of the four consecutive weeks in which the change occurred; or
(b) where the childcare charges are for variable weekly amounts, is established by aggregating the anticipated weekly charge paid for childcare

Working Tax Credit (Entitlement and Maximum Rate) Regulations 2002

for each child in respect of whom charges will be incurred for the following 52 weeks and dividing the total by 52.]

(3) If in any case the charges in respect of childcare are paid monthly, the weekly relevant childcare charge for the purposes of paragraph (1) is established—

(a) where the charges are for a fixed monthly amount, by multiplying that amount by 12 and dividing the product by 52; or

(b) where the charges are for variable monthly amounts, by aggregating the [¹anticipated] charges for the [¹next] 12 months and dividing the total by 52.

(4) In a case where there is insufficient information for establishing the weekly relevant childcare charge paid for childcare in accordance with paragraphs (2) and (3), an officer of the Board shall estimate the charge—

(a) in accordance with information provided by the person or persons incurring the charges; and

(b) by any method which in the officer's opinion is reasonable.

(5) For the purpose of paragraph (1) the specified date is—

(a) where the childcare charges are increased, the later of—
 (i) the first day of the week in which the change occurred, and
 (ii) the first day of the week in which falls the day which is three months prior to the date notification of the change is given,

(b) where the childcare charges are decreased, the first day of the week following

the four consecutive weeks in which the change occurred.

AMENDMENT

1. Working Tax Credit (Entitlement and Maximum Rate) (Amendment) Regulations 2003 (SI 2003/701), reg.15 (April 6, 2003).

DEFINITIONS

"award"—see TCA 2002, s.14.
"change of circumstances"—see TCA 2002, s.6.

GENERAL NOTE

2.77 This regulation brings into play the mechanisms for amending or terminating an award of working tax credit. Section 6(3) of the TCA 2002 makes provision for regulations to impose a duty on a claimant to report a change of circumstances that may decrease the rate of entitlement to a tax credit. Regulation 21 of the Tax Credits (Claims and Notifications) Regulations 2002 (SI 2002/2014) imposes the requirement that notification of a change of circumstances as defined in this regulation must be given within one month of the change occurring. Regulations 22–24 of those Regulations set out how and by whom this is to be done.

Failure to notify may make the claimant liable to a penalty of £300 under s.32(3) of the TCA 2002.

Severe disability element

Severe disability element

2.78 **17.**—(1) The determination of the maximum rate must include the severe disability element if the claimant, or, in the case of a joint claim, one of the claimants satisfies paragraph (2).

(2) A person satisfies this paragraph if a disability living allowance, attributable to the care component payable at the highest rate prescribed under section 72(3) of the Contributions and Benefits Act or an attendance allowance at the higher rate prescribed under section 65(3) of that Act—
  (a) is payable in respect of him; or
  (b) would be so payable but for a suspension of benefit by virtue of regulations under section 113(2) of the Contributions and Benefits Act (suspension during hospitalisation), or an abatement as a consequence of hospitalisation.

DEFINITIONS
"claimant"—see reg.2.
"joint claim"—see reg.2.

GENERAL NOTE

This is separate from the disability element provided for in reg.9. It adds a further £980 to the entitlement of the claimant or claimants. But it is restricted to the case where the disabled individual is receiving the highest rate of the care component of disability living allowance (or the attendance allowance equivalent), which means that both day and night attention or supervision are needed.

There is no express provision dealing with interaction with the disability element. *CST/76/2006* makes it clear that the language of reg.9 requires that, in the case of a joint claim, the person who is disabled must also be the same person who is working 16 hours a week: see para.2.56. But this regulation does not repeat that language. Nor is this element dependent on the receipt of the disability element under reg.9. The mandatory language of reg.17 suggests that all joint claimants are entitled to the severe disability element if either of them meets the general conditions to claim WTC and either is in receipt of the highest rate of the care component of disability living allowance (or the higher rate of attendance allowance). It would follow that this element may be claimed by claimants following any of the four Routes noted at para.2.32 and not merely Route 2.

2.79

50 Plus element

50 Plus element

18.—(1) The determination of the maximum rate must include the 50 plus element if—
  (a) in the case of a single claim, the claimant satisfies paragraph(3); or
  (b) in the case of a joint claim, at least one of the claimants satisfies that paragraph.
This is subject to the qualification in paragraph (2).
  (2) The 50 plus element shall not be payable in respect of a claimant—
  (a) for a continuous period of longer than 12 months; or
  (b) for periods amounting in aggregate to more than 12 months if the gap between any consecutive pair of those periods is not more than 26 weeks.
  (3) A claimant satisfies this paragraph if—
  [¹(a) he is aged at least 50; and
  (b) he starts qualifying remunerative work; and]
  (c) he undertakes qualifying remunerative work for at least 16 hours per week; and

2.80

(d) he satisfies the condition in paragraphs (4), (6), (7), (8) or (9).
(4) The condition is that—
(a) for a period of at least six months immediately before his starting [¹qualifying remunerative] work as mentioned in paragraph (3)(b); or
(b) for consecutive periods, amounting in the aggregate to at least six months, the last of which ends immediately before his starting [¹qualifying remunerative] work as mentioned in paragraph (3)(b), paragraph (5) is satisfied.

[²(4A) For the purposes of paragraph (4)(b) "consecutive periods" are periods, any pair of which is separated by a gap of not more than 12 weeks.]

(5) This paragraph is satisfied while the claimant is receiving—
(a) income support;
(b) a jobseeker's allowance;
(c) incapacity benefit;
(d) severe disablement allowance; [². . .]
(e) both a state retirement pension and [²state pension credit within the meaning of the State Pension Credit Act 2002; or]

[²(f) a training allowance paid by the Secretary of State under section 2(1) of the Employment and Training Act 1973 to a person in his capacity as a participant in either of the schemes provided by, or under arrangements made with, the Secretary of State and known as "Work-Based Learning for Adults" and "Training for Work".]

(6) The condition is that for at least six months immediately prior to his starting [¹qualifying remunerative] work—
(a) another person was receiving—
　(i) the payment mentioned in sub-paragraphs (a) to (d) of paragraph (5); or
　(ii) both the payments mentioned in paragraph (5)(e); and
(b) an increase in respect of the claimant, as a dependant of the other person—
　(i) in a case falling within sub-paragraph (a)(i) was payable with that payment; or
　(ii) in a case falling within sub-paragraph (a)(ii) was payable with that pension.

(7) The condition is that for at least six months immediately prior to his starting [¹qualifying remunerative] work as mentioned in paragraph (3)(b) he satisfied the conditions entitling him to be credited with contributions or earnings in accordance with the Social Security (Credits) Regulations 1975.

(8) The condition is that—
(a) the condition in paragraph (4)(a), (6) or (7) would have been satisfied if the reference to six months were omitted;
(b) immediately prior to the period during which that condition, as modified by sub-paragraph (a), is satisfied there is a period during which the condition in paragraph (9) is satisfied; and
(c) the total of the periods during which—
　(i) the condition in paragraph (4)(a), (6) or (7), as modified by sub-para.(a), is satisfied; and
　(ii) the condition in para.(9) is satisfied, equals or exceeds six months.

(9) The condition is that the claimant, or, in the case of a joint claim, one of the claimants, is receiving—

(SI 2002/2005, reg.18) (as amended)

(a) [¹carer's] allowance;
(b) bereavement allowance; or
(c) widowed parent's allowance.

DEFINITIONS

"claimant"—see reg.2.
"joint claim"—see reg.2.
"qualifying remunerative work"—see reg.4.

AMENDMENTS

1. Tax Credits (Miscellaneous Amendments No.2) Regulations 2003 (SI 2003/2815), reg.16 (November 26, 2003).
2. Tax Credits (Miscellaneous Amendments) Regulations 2004 (SI 2004/762), reg.11 (April 6, 2004).

GENERAL NOTE

Unlike all the other elements of working tax credit, this is limited in time. It is payable only for a maximum of 12 months in total (though not necessarily in one period): para.(2). This is one of the routes to working tax credit that does not involve a social security element. It is instead the replacement of the former "New Deal 50 Plus" payable by the former Department for Employment under employment legislation. Its aim is to give an encouragement for those over 50 and on benefit to get back to work. The regulation lays down two sets of requirements for the element to be paid: first, the claimant must now have qualifying remunerative work for 16 hours a week, and secondly, he or she must have been claiming benefits or incapacity credits before the work, or someone else was claiming benefits for him or her, for a period of at least six months. Part of the period of six months may be counted, under paras (8) and (9), by reference to the award of invalid care allowance (now carer's allowance) or an award to a widow or widower.

2.81

Death of a child or qualifying young person for whom the claimant is responsible

Entitlement after death of a child or qualifying young person for whom the claimant is responsible

19.—(1) Paragraph (2) applies if—
(a) the death occurs of a child or qualifying young person;
(b) working tax credit is payable to a person who was, or to a couple at least one of whom was, immediately before the death responsible for that child or qualifying young person;
(c) the prescribed conditions for an element of working tax credit were satisfied because the claimant, or at least one of the claimants, was responsible for that child or qualifying person, but would not have been satisfied but for that responsibility; and
(d) the prescribed conditions would have continued to be satisfied but for the death.

(2) If this paragraph applies, working tax credit shall continue to be payable, as if the child or qualifying young person had not died, for the period for which child tax credit continues to be payable in accordance with regulation 6 of the Child Tax Credit Regulations 2002.

2.82

DEFINITIONS

"child"—see reg.2.
"qualifying young person"—see reg.2.

GENERAL NOTE

2.83   Section 55 of the TCA 2002 provides an extension of the payment of child benefit for a period of eight weeks after the death of a child for whom the benefit is paid. Section 5(5) makes similar provision for child tax credit, and effect is given to this by reg.6 of the Child Tax Credit Regulations 2002 (SI 2002/2007). This regulation matches those extensions for working tax credit also, s.10(3)(d) of the TCA 2002 providing authority for this.

Claimants are required, from November 2006, to report the death of a child or qualifying young person for whom they are receiving additional credit within one month of the death. See para.2.307.

PART III

MAXIMUM RATE

Maximum rates of elements of Working Tax Credit

2.84   **20.**—(1) The maximum annual rate of working tax credit (excluding the childcare element) payable to a single claimant or to a couple making a joint claim is the sum of whichever of the following elements are applicable—
(a) the basic element specified in column.(2) of the table in Schedule 2 at paragraph 1;
(b) in respect of a claimant who satisfies regulation 9(1), the disability element specified in column (2) of the table in Schedule 2 at paragraph 2;
(c) the 30-hour element specified in column (2) of the table in Schedule 2 at paragraph 3 in respect of—
  (i) a single claimant who works for not less than 30 hours per week;
  (ii) a couple either or both of whom work for not less than 30 hours per week; or
  (iii) a couple, at least one of whom is responsible for a child or a qualifying young person and at least one of whom works for 16 hours per week if their hours of work when aggregated amount to at least 30 hours per week;
(d) the second-adult element specified in column (2) of the table in Schedule 2 at paragraph 4 where regulation 11 so provides;
(e) the lone-parent element specified in column (2) of the table in Schedule 2 at paragraph 5 where regulation 12 applies;
(f) the severe disability element specified in column (2) of the table in Schedule 2 at paragraph 6—
  (i) in respect of a single claimant who satisfies regulation 17; or
  (ii) in respect of a member of a couple making a joint claim who satisfies regulation 17; and
(g) the 50 Plus element in respect of a person who satisfies regulation 18(2) at whichever of the rates specified in column 2 of the Table in Schedule 2 at paragraph 7 applies in his case.

(SI 2002/2005, reg.20) (as amended)

(2) The maximum rate of the childcare element of a working tax credit is [³80] per cent of the maxima specified in paragraph (3).

(3) The maxima are—

(a) [²£175] per week, where the [¹claimant or, in the case of a joint claim, at least one of the claimants, is responsible for] only one child in respect of whom relevant childcare charges are paid; and

(b) [²£300] per week where the [¹claimant or, in the case of a joint claim, at least one of the claimants, is responsible for] more than one child in respect of whom relevant childcare charges are paid.

AMENDMENTS

1. Working Tax Credit (Entitlement and Maximum Rate) (Amendment) Regulations 2003 (SI 2003/701), reg.16 (April 6, 2003).
2. Tax Credits Up-rating Regulations 2005 (SI 2005/681), reg.3(1) (April 6, 2005).
3. Tax Credits Up-rating Regulations 2006 (SI 2006/963), reg.3(1) (April 6, 2006).

DEFINITIONS

"claimant"—see reg.2.
"joint claim"—see reg.2.

GENERAL NOTE

This regulation emphasises that the entitlement of a claimant or claimants to working tax credit is made up of each of the elements to which there is entitlement. It is "the sum of whichever of the . . . elements are applicable". However, as noted above, there must be entitlement under reg.4. to the basic element in all cases. Paragraph (1) provides the necessary drafting provision to tie each of the other elements (save for the childcare element), the conditions for which have been defined above, into the rate of award and entitlement to working tax credit to the claimant or claimants under s.11 of the TCA 2002.

2.85

Paragraphs (2) and (3) then provide the effective rate of the childcare element. They set the maximum weekly childcare element at £300 for care for two or more children, and £175 for care for a single child.

The current figures for the maximum rates of all elements other than the childcare element are in Sch.2.

The varying levels of working tax credit by reference to these differing elements and the different routes by which, under reg.4, claims can be made for working tax credit can be illustrated by some short examples. The examples show the maximum entitlement to working tax credit in each case. They do not take into account the income or benefit entitlements of the claimant(s).

Route 1: Lone-parent with three children, working 32 hours a week, and incurring childcare costs of £350 a week.

Her entitlement is:

Basic element	£1,730
30-hour element	£705
Lone parent element	£1,700
Childcare element	£12,480 (limited to 80 per cent of £300 a week)
Maximum entitlement	£16,615

In addition, the lone parent will be entitled to child benefit, and child tax credit for herself and the three children.

Route 2: Couple with no children, one of whom is working for 16 hours a week despite also being entitled to disability living allowance, and the other of whom is working for over 30 hours a week.

Working Tax Credit (Entitlement and Maximum Rate) Regulations 2002

Basic element	£1,730
30-hour element	£705
Second adult element	£1,700
Disability element	£2,310
Maximum entitlement	£6,445

Under this Route, the person receiving the disability living allowance (or otherwise disabled) must be working for 16 hours a week: reg.9(1)(a).

Route 3: Couple, both over 70. One has just started work for 20 hours a week. The couple are receiving their state retirement pension and state pension credit. They have no serious disabilities.

Basic element	£1,730
50 plus element	£1,185 *(lower rate)*
Maximum entitlement	£2,915

There is no entitlement to the second adult element in this case: reg.11(2).

Route 4: Unmarried couple. He is 26 and working 32 hours a week. She is 18, expecting their child soon, and is not and has not been working.
Their entitlement is:

Basic entitlement	£1,730
30-hour element	£705
Second adult element	£1,700
Maximum entitlement	£4,135

The couple will be entitled to child benefit, child tax credit (including the additional element for the first year) and perhaps also working tax credit with the childcare element, maternity benefits and statutory paternity pay when the child is born.

SCHEDULE 1   Regulation 9(1)

DISABILITY WHICH PUTS A PERSON AT A DISADVANTAGE IN GETTING A JOB

PART I

2.86
1. When standing he cannot keep his balance unless he continually holds onto something.
2. Using any crutches, walking frame, walking stick, prosthesis or similar walking aid which he habitually uses, he cannot walk a continuous distance of 100 metres along level ground without stopping or without suffering severe pain.
3. He can use neither of his hands behind his back as in the process of putting on a jacket or of tucking a shirt into trousers.
4. He can extend neither of his arms in front of him so as to shake hands with another person without difficulty.
5. He can put neither of his hands up to his head without difficulty so as to put on a hat.
6. Due to lack of manual dexterity he cannot, with one hand, pick up a coin which is not more than 2½ centimetres in diameter.
7. He is not able to use his hands or arms to pick up a full jug of 1 litre capacity and pour from it into a cup, without difficulty.
8. He can turn neither of his hands sideways through 180 degrees.
9. He—
   (a) is registered as blind or registered as partially sighted in a register compiled by a local authority under section 24(9)(g) of the National Assistance Act 1948;
   (b) has been certified as blind or as partially sighted and, in consequence, registered as blind or partially sighted in a register maintained by or on behalf of a council constituted under the Local Government (Scotland) Act 1994; or

(SI 2002/2005, Sch.1) (as amended)

(c) has been certified as blind and in consequence is registered as blind in a register maintained by or on behalf of a Health and Social Services Board in Northern Ireland.

10. He cannot see to read 16 point print at a distance greater than 20 centimetres, if appropriate, wearing the glasses he normally uses.

11. He cannot hear a telephone ring when he is in the same room as the telephone, if appropriate, using a hearing aid he normally uses.

12. In a quiet room he has difficulty in hearing what someone talking in a loud voice at a distance of 2 metres says, if appropriate, using a hearing aid he normally uses.

13. People who know him well have difficulty in understanding what he says.

14. When a person he knows well speaks to him, he has difficulty in understanding what that person says.

15. At least once a year during waking hours he is in a coma or has a fit in which he loses consciousness.

16. He has a mental illness for which he receives regular treatment under the supervision of a medically qualified person.

17. Due to mental disability he is often confused or forgetful.

18. He cannot do the simplest addition and subtraction.

19. Due to mental disability he strikes people or damages property or is unable to form normal social relationships.

20. He cannot normally sustain an 8-hour working day or a 5-day working week due to a medical condition or intermittent or continuous severe pain.

PART II

21. As a result of an illness or accident he is undergoing a period of habilitation or rehabilitation.

2.87

GENERAL NOTE

Under reg.9 of these Regulations, a person is treated as having a disability which puts him or her at a disadvantage in getting a job only if one of the paragraphs of this Schedule applies to him or her. If a paragraph does apply, reg.9 deems the claimant to be at a disadvantage in getting a job, whether or not the disability actually has that effect. See the notes to regs 9 and 9A for the application of these tests to initial and repeat claims.

2.88

The Schedule requires the exercise of a considerable amount of judgement. For instance, the words "without difficulty" frequently appear. The difficulty need not be severe and plainly a person may have difficulty with an action without necessarily suffering pain when performing it. Slowness may well be sufficient.

Attention is drawn to the final condition in para.20 before detailed comment is made on the specific disabilities. This is the overarching condition that a person cannot sustain a full working day or a full working week due either to a medical condition (of any nature, physical or mental) or intermittent or continuous severe pain. *R(S) 11/51* emphasised that this has to be determined by what a claimant can reasonably be expected to do with regard to his or her age, education, training and other personal factors. It is suggested that this should be the starting point for consideration of the application of this Schedule, with reference being made to the specific disabilities in that context.

Para.2

Note that this test is not the same as the test prescribed in reg.12(1)(a)(ii) of the Social Security (Disability Living Allowance) Regulations 1991 (SI 1991/2890) in respect of the mobility component of disability living allowance. Not only is the distance of 100 metres prescribed, but the question is whether that distance can be walked "without stopping" or without "severe pain" (rather than "severe discomfort"). It should also be noted that only artificial aids which are habitually used are to be taken into account, so there is no need to consider whether an aid which is not used might be suitable. In *R(M) 2/89*, the Commissioner held that a person walks only when putting one foot in front of the other, so that a person who has to swing

2.89

Working Tax Credit (Entitlement and Maximum Rate) Regulations 2002

through crutches, rather than using them to help him or her move both legs separately, cannot walk.

Para. 6

2.90 Two-and-a-half centimetres (1 inch) is the diameter of a 50 pence coin. Since their reduction in size, other coins, apart from the £2 coin, are smaller. Note that the claimant satisfies the test (and so may qualify for benefit) if he or she can pick up a large coin in one hand but not the other. In *CDWA 3123/1997* the claimant had no thumb on his left hand and the terminal joint of his right thumb was missing. He maintained that he was only able to pick up a coin of 2.5 centimetres in diameter by pushing it across a surface and catching it in his hand. The Commissioner holds that the tests in Sch.1 were to be performed in the normal way and not by employing some unusual or awkward manoeuvre. The normal way of picking up coins with one hand was to use the pinch grip between the thumb and fingers. An ability to pick up with the fingers alone was irrelevant because that ability did not demonstrate the presence or absence of the pinch grip. The Commissioner also confirmed that para.6 would be satisfied if the claimant could not pick up a coin of the prescribed size with one hand even if he could with the other.

Para. 7

2.91 This is a test of both steadiness and strength, using both hands or arms at once if necessary. The Commissioner in *CDWA 3123/1997* confirmed that the position was different under para.7 (as compared with para.6) since, here, the question was whether the claimant could perform the pouring task using both hands and arms together. An inability to do so with either hand alone is immaterial if he or she can manage the task with both hands. But any realistic difficulty, however slight, in carrying out that task would satisfy the test in para.7. Arguably, an ability to pick up and pour with one hand alone, where the claimant has no use of the other arm at all, would mean that the claimant would not qualify under this paragraph, although that question did not arise in that case.

Para. 8

2.92 Presumably, this is a test of wrist movements and is intended to be performed with the elbows kept still.

Para. 10

2.93 ## 16 point print is 4 mm high. It is this size.

Paras 12–14

2.94 If hearing or understanding is possible, but only with difficulty (perhaps after repetition), the claimant still qualifies. The precise relationship between paras 12 and 14 is unclear. Difficulty in understanding may arise for reasons other than loss of hearing and, indeed, a person without hearing may be able to understand through lip-reading. Can a person who can hear a loud voice, but not an ordinary conversational voice, at a distance of 2 metres qualify under para.14 if he or she cannot lip-read? In principle, the answer would seem to be "yes". That would not mean that para.12 had no effect because the person would only be able to qualify under para.14 if he or she was further disadvantaged by an inability to make use of other methods of comprehending speech.

Para. 16

2.95 Medication taken on prescription will be enough, provided that it is regular. Mental illness is not defined, but, if a person is receiving treatment there is likely to be a diagnosis of an illness and if it is an illness of the mind it will be mental illness.

Para. 17

2.96 Mental disability is not defined and neither is the extent of confusion or forgetfulness required. On one view, any confusion or forgetfulness suggests some disability

(SI 2002/2005, Sch.1) (as amended)

of the mind and the question is whether the degree of confusion or forgetfulness is sufficient to warrant the view that the legislator intended such a claimant to qualify (see the approach of the Court Appeal in *W v L* [1974] Q.B. 711). On the other hand, in *R(A) 2/92*, a Commissioner considered that a specific diagnosis was required and that suggests that the first question is whether there is such a diagnosis. Only after that has been answered does one go on to consider whether there is any resulting confusion or forgetfulness.

Para.19
See the note to para.17. The approach taken in *R(A) 2/92* would create real difficulties here given the view expressed there that "personality disorder" can be distinguished from "mental disability".

2.97

Para.21
This applies only on an initial claim.

2.98

SCHEDULE 2   **Regulation 20(1)**

MAXIMUM RATES OF THE ELEMENTS OF A WORKING TAX CREDIT

[¹*Relevant element of Working Tax Credit*	*Maximum annual rate*
1. Basic element	£1,730
2. Disability element	£2,310
3. 30-hour element	£705
4. Second adult element	£1,700
5. Lone parent element	£1,700
6. Severe disability element	£980
7. 50 plus element— (a) in the case of a person who normally undertakes qualifying remunerative work for at least 16 hours, but less than 30 hours, per week; and (b) in the case of a person who normally undertakes qualifying remunerative work for at least 30 hours per week	£1,185 £1,770]

2.99

AMENDMENT

1. Tax Credits Up-rating Regulations 2007 (SI 2007/828), reg.3 and Sch. (April 6, 2006).

Tax Credits (Definition and Calculation of Income) Regulations 2002

(SI 2002/2006) (AS AMENDED)

Whereas a draft of this instrument, which contains the first regulations made under section 7(8) and (9) of the Tax Credits Act 2002, has been laid before, and approved by resolution of, each House of Parliament:

Tax Credits (Definition and Calculation of Income) Regulations 2002

Now, therefore, the Treasury, in exercise of the powers conferred upon them by sections 7(8) and (9), 65(1), (7) and (9) and 67 of the Tax Credits Act 2002, hereby make the following Regulations:

PART I

General provisions

2.100 1.   Citation, commencement and effect.
       2.   Interpretation.

PART II

INCOME FOR THE PURPOSES OF TAX CREDITS

General

3.   Calculation of income of claimant.

CHAPTER 2

Employment income

4.   Employment income.

CHAPTER 3

Pension income

5.   Pension income.

CHAPTER 4

Trading income

6.   Trading income.

(SI 2002/2006) (as amended)

CHAPTER 5

Social security income

7. Social security income.

CHAPTER 6

Student income

8. Student income.
9. Payments of income in connection with students to be disregarded for the purposes of regulation 3.

CHAPTER 7

Investment income

10. Investment income.

CHAPTER 8

Property income

11. Property income.

CHAPTER 9

Foreign income

12. Foreign income.

CHAPTER 10

Notional income

Tax Credits (Definition and Calculation of Income) Regulations 2002

13. Introduction.
14. Claimants treated for any purpose as having income by virtue of the Income Tax Acts.
15. Claimants depriving themselves of income in order to secure entitlement.
16. Claimants to whom income becomes available upon the making of a claim.
17. Claimants providing services to other persons for less than full earnings.

CHAPTER 11

Miscellaneous income

18. Miscellaneous income.

PART III

Sums disregarded in the calculation of income

General disregards in the calculation of income

19. General disregards in the calculation of income.

INTRODUCTION AND GENERAL NOTE

2.101 Section 7 of TCA 2002 provides that entitlement to a tax credit is subject to an income test. These regulations provide the detail of that test. They do so by adopting, with some important modifications, the rules for deciding on the income of an individual in the rewritten income tax legislation adopted over the last few years by Parliament from the draft bills produced by the Tax Law Rewrite Project. The Acts produced by the Rewrite Project have modernised the language and presentation of income tax law, and parallel changes in annual Finance Acts have also rationalised parts of it. This has made it easier to abandon the previous approach of having a different set of defining rules of income for benefit purposes and to adopt the income tax rules into the benefit system.

The rewritten income tax law

2.102 With effect from April 6, 2007 all the former primary legislation dating back to the 1840s under which income tax was imposed and collected has been repealed and replaced by the new rewritten legislation. This is contained in three major Acts, the Income Tax (Earnings and Pensions) Act 2003, the Income Tax (Trading and Other Income) Act 2005 and the Income Tax Act 2007. In practice these contain all the income rules necessary for any tax credits calculation save for the rules about capital allowances in the Capital Allowances Act 2000, another rewrite measure.

A fundamental change in approach

2.103 The income test used for tax credits is fundamentally different to that used for the income-related benefits such as income support, jobseeker's allowance and housing benefit. The main differences are as follows:

(SI 2002/2006) (as amended)

(1) *There is no capital rule.* There has never been a wealth tax in the United Kingdom, save for that, in effect, imposed on those claiming means-tested benefits. The approach is to tax income from capital as (and if) it arises. This is the approach now adopted for tax credits.

(2) *Capital gains are irrelevant.* Income tax is supplemented for individuals by a separate capital gains tax, e.g. on the capital gain made on selling an asset. Capital gains are also ignored for tax credits purposes.

(3) *There are no rules deeming income from capital held.* The rules treating capital as income, and attributing tariff income to capital, have been abolished and not replaced.

(4) *There is no all-inclusive definition of income.* The previous approach was to base the calculation of non-earned income on "gross income and any capital treated as income". The income tax based approach is to calculate income from each named source and to then aggregate the totals to establish the relevant income. If income arises from a source that is not one of the named sources, it is excluded from the calculation.

(5) *Claimants may choose forms of income that avoid the calculation.* The rules generally follow the approach of income tax in looking at actual income from capital, if any. They no longer follow the approach of the rules for the income-related benefits (perhaps more correctly the income and capital related benefits) of assuming income from capital at set rates while ignoring actual income from capital. They also leave any capital gains out of account. However, there remain some important anti-avoidance provisions based on the former family credit rules that take some account of capital and notional income. See regs 13–17 below.

Differences between tax credits income calculations and income tax assessments

The approach taken in the new rules is to abandon almost all of the previous rules and to use instead those that can be found in the current income tax legislation. This allows HMRC to base its tax credits calculations on its income tax assessments or, in most cases, on the self-assessments of those individuals to income tax or the assessment and collection of income tax from employees by employers and agencies through the PAYE (Pay As You Earn) system. There are, however, some important differences from income tax assessments and these should also be noted:

2.104

(1) *Couples are assessed jointly, not separately.* The income tax system was transferred from a system in which married couples were assessed on their joint incomes in the name of the husband to a system of separate assessment of each partner in 1990. One reason for this was the growing concern about discrimination against couples who were married, and assessed jointly, as against those who were unmarried and separately assessed. The new rules require both married and unmarried couples to make joint applications for working tax credit and child tax credit. This is the first time that HMRC has been concerned to calculate the joint income of unmarried couples, and it will bring sharply into focus the need to look carefully at when two individuals are required to make a joint claim. The starting point in any calculation of income for tax credits purposes is therefore to establish who the claimant is or claimants are. If two people become a couple, or a couple breaks up, then that fact must be reported to HMRC and a new claim made.

(2) *The income tax personal allowances do not apply to tax credits.* Instead, claimants are entitled to the appropriate "elements". One important effect of this, combined with the first point, is that the widespread practice of transferring income from the working partner of a couple to the non-working partner, so as to claim the maximum value from personal allowances and to minimise

Tax Credits (Definition and Calculation of Income) Regulations 2002

higher-rate tax, and so to reduce income tax, will not work to reduce income for tax credits purposes.

(3) *The taxable forms of income are not identical to those used for income tax.* They are similar, but include some additional items, including rules dealing with income foregone and income of which a person has deprived himself or herself.

(4) *Claimants are taxed on worldwide income.* This is linked to (3). Tax credits may only be claimed by those who are ordinarily resident in the United Kingdom, but they are subject to the obligation to declare their full incomes, regardless of any reliefs by way of double taxation or exemption that they might receive under the Income Tax Acts or double taxation agreements.

(5) *Claimants are usually assessed on last year's income.* The income tax rules now use the current year's income for almost all income tax assessments. Since 2007, calculations of income for tax credits purposes will, with rare exceptions, be based on the income of the previous year. Note will only be taken of the income of the current year if there was no income in the previous year, or the current year's income exceeds that of the previous year by at least £25,000.

(6) *The thresholds for income tax and each tax credit are different.* There is now a single personal allowance for income tax and NI contributions for all those under 65, with a higher figure for those over 65. But there are separate thresholds for working tax credit and child tax credit, and these are not linked to income tax.

(7) *Deductions and exclusions are not identical.* Nor are specific inclusions, so the assessment of income from employment for income tax purposes will not be identical, and nor will the total income.

The drafting techniques used in these Regulations are also those of the Rewrite Project, for example in the use of signposting provisions and the use of the "command" tense of verbs in taking the user step by step through a calculation. Following this approach, reg.3 lays down in clear terms how income is to be calculated. But it is, in practice, the fifth of five questions that need to be answered to establish the relevant income of a claimant or claimants.

The questions to be decided:

2.105
(1) Who is claiming?

(2) IS or JSA . . . or SPC?

(3) Which tax year?

(4) Are there any income changes during the tax year?

(5) What income?

The questions are as follows:

(1) Who is claiming?

2.106
Is the claim a single claim, a joint claim or a claim by a polygamous unit? The income of each claimant must be calculated.

(2) IS, JSA, SPC?

2.107
Automatic entitlement to child tax credit has yet to be introduced for those on income support and jobseeker's allowance, although it now exists for those of pensionable age receiving state pension credit instead. The 16 hour rule effectively prevents those on these benefits claiming working tax credit as well.

(3) Which tax year?

2.108
As noted above, in most cases the relevant income for tax credits is the income of the previous year not the current year income used for most income tax purposes.

(SI 2002/2006) (as amended)

But attention must be paid to current income where there is a sharp increase in income between one year and the next. (This does not apply to capital gains, so will most often catch employees, as sums received from employment are seldom regarded as capital).

(4) Are there any changes during the year?
The award of tax credit under ss.5 and 14 of the Act are by reference initially to the income of the previous year. But there may be relevant changes of circumstances that lead to a revision of the award if there is a notified change of circumstances under reg.6. The decision on entitlement is made only after the end of the tax year under s.19.

2.109

(5) What kinds of income?
This is determined by the current regulations.

2.110

CROSS-REFERENCES

The notes to each paragraph set out in full the Parts, Chapters and section titles to all Chapters and Sections of the Taxes Act, ITEPA and Finance Acts referred to in these regulations. The regulations include cross references to a considerable number of income tax provisions, only some of which will be of more than occasional importance to tax credits assessments. In addition, as explained below, major parts of both Acts are of no relevance to tax credits. The volume contains a selection of the more important provisions from both Acts, and the cross references supplement that by noting the full title of each Chapter and section referred to in these Regulations.

2.111

PART I

General provisions

Citation, commencement and effect

1. These Regulations may be cited as the Tax Credits (Definition and Calculation of Income) Regulations 2002 and shall come into force—
    (a) for the purpose of enabling claims to be made, on 1st August 2002;
    (b) for the purpose of enabling awards to be made, on 1st January 2003; and
    (c) for all other purposes, on 6th April 2003;
and shall have effect for the tax year beginning on 6th April 2003 and subsequent tax years.

2.112

DEFINITIONS

"award"—see TCA 2002, s.5.
"claim"—see TCA 2002, s.3.
"tax year"—see reg.2.

Interpretation

2.—(1) In these Regulations, unless the context otherwise requires—
"the Act" means the Tax Credits Act 2002;
"the Contributions and Benefits Act" means the Social Security Contributions and Benefits Act 1992; [³. . .]
"the Employment Act" means the Employment and Training Act 1973 [³; and

2.113

"the Northern Ireland Contributions and Benefits Act" means the Social Security Contributions and Benefits (Northern Ireland) Act 1992.]

(2) In these Regulations except where the context otherwise requires—

"the 1992 Fund" means moneys made available from time to time by the Secretary of State for Social Security for the benefit of persons eligible for payment in accordance with the provisions of a scheme established by him on 24th April 1992 as respects England and Wales and Northern Ireland and on 10th April 1992 as respects Scotland;

[6"the Board" means the Commissioners for Her Majesty's Revenue and Customs";]

"child" has the meaning given in the Child Tax Credit Regulations 2002;

"claim" means a claim for child tax credit or working tax credit and "joint claim" and "single claim" shall be construed in accordance with [2section 3(8)] of the Act and "claimant" shall be construed accordingly;

[4"couple" has the meaning given by section 3(5A) of the Act;]

[1"earnings" shall be construed in accordance with section 62 of the ITEPA;]

"the Eileen Trust" means the charitable trust of that name established on 29th March 1993 out of funds provided by the Secretary of State for Social Security for the benefit of persons eligible in accordance with its provisions;

[1. . .];

[5"employment zone" means an area within Great Britain—
  (i) subject to a designation for the purposes of the Employment Zones Regulations 2003 by the Secretary of State, or
[7(ii) listed in the Schedule to the Employment Zones (Allocation to Contractors) Pilot Regulations 2006,]
  pursuant to section 60 of the Welfare Reform and Pensions Act 1999;]

"employment zone programme" means a programme which is—
  (a) established for one or more employment zones; and
  (b) designed to assist claimants for a Jobseeker's Allowance to obtain sustainable employment;

"family" means—
  (a) in the case of a joint claim, the [4. . .] couple by whom the claim is made and any child or qualifying young person for whom at least one of them is responsible, in accordance with regulation 3 of the Child Tax Credit Regulations 2002; and
  (b) in the case of a single claim, the claimant and any child or qualifying young person for whom he is responsible in accordance with regulation 3 of the Child Tax Credit Regulations 2002;

"the Independent Living Fund" means the charitable trust of that name established out of funds provided by the Secretary of State for Social Services for the purpose of providing financial assistance to those persons incapacitated by or otherwise suffering from very severe disablement who are in need of such assistance to enable them to live independently;

"the Independent Living Funds" means the Independent Living Fund, the Independent Living (Extension) Fund and the Independent Living (1993) Fund;

(SI 2002/2006, reg.2) (as amended)

"the Independent Living (Extension) Fund" means the trust of that name established on 25th February 1993 by the Secretary of State for Social Security and Robin Glover Wendt and John Fletcher Shepherd;

"the Independent Living (1993) Fund" means the trust of that name established on 25th February 1993 by the Secretary of State for Social Security and Robin Glover Wendt and John Fletcher Shepherd;

[¹"ITEPA" means the Income Tax (Earnings and Pensions) Act 2003;]

[⁶"ITTOIA" means the Income Tax (Trading and Other Income) Act 2005;]

"the Macfarlane (Special Payments) Trust" means the trust of that name established on 29th January 1990 partly out of funds provided by the Secretary of State for Health for the benefit of certain persons suffering from haemophilia;

"the Macfarlane (Special Payments) (No.2) Trust" means the trust of that name established on 3rd May 1991 partly out of funds provided by the Secretary of State for Health for the benefit of certain persons suffering from haemophilia and other beneficiaries;

"the Macfarlane Trust" means the charitable trust established partly out of funds provided by the Secretary of State for Health to the Haemophilia Society for the relief of poverty or distress among those suffering from haemophilia;

"the Macfarlane Trusts" means the Macfarlane Trust, the Macfarlane (Special Payments) Trust and the Macfarlane (Special Payments) (No.2) Trust;

"pensionable age" has the meaning given by the rules in paragraph 1 of Schedule 4 to the Pensions Act 1995;

"pension fund holder", in relation to a [⁵registered pension scheme], means the trustees, managers or scheme administrators of the scheme [⁵. . .];

"qualifying young person" has the meaning given in the Child Tax Credit Regulations 2002;

[⁵"registered pension scheme" has the meaning given by section 150(2) of the Finance Act 2004;]

[⁵. . .]
[⁵. . .]
[⁶. . .];
[¹. . .];

"the Service Pensions Order" means the Naval, Military and Air Forces, etc. (Disablement and Death) Service Pensions Order 1983;

"tax year" means a period beginning with the 6th April in one year and ending with 5th April in the next;

"the Taxes Act" means the Income and Corporation Taxes Act 1988;

"voluntary organisation" means a body, other than a public or local authority, the activities of which are carried on otherwise than for profit;

"war pension" has the meaning given in section 25(4) of the Social Security Act 1989.

(3) For the purposes of these Regulations, whether a person is responsible for a child or a qualifying young person is determined in accordance with regulaton 3 of the Child Tax Credit Regulations 2002.

(4) In these Regulations—
(a) a reference to a claimant's partner is a reference to a claimant's spouse [⁴or civil partner] or a person with whom the claimant lives as a spouse [⁴or civil partner]; and

Tax Credits (Definition and Calculation of Income) Regulations 2002

(b) a reference to a claimant's former partner is a reference to a claimant's former spouse [⁴or civil partner] or a person with whom the claimant has lived as a spouse [⁴or civil partner]; and
(c) a reference in these Regulations to an Extra Statutory Concession is a reference to that Concession as published by the Inland Revenue on 1st July 2002.

AMENDMENTS

1. Tax Credits (Definition and Calculation of Income) (Amendment) Regulations 2003 (SI 2003 No.732), reg.4 (April 6, 2003).
2. Tax Credits (Miscellaneous Amendments No.2) Regulations 2003 (SI 2003/2815), reg.3 (November 26, 2003).
3. Tax Credits (Miscellaneous Amendments) Regulations 2004 (SI 2004/762), reg.13 (April 6, 2004).
4. Civil Partnership Act 2004 (Tax Credits, etc.) (Consequential Amendments) Order 2005 (SI 2005/2919), art.3(2) (December 5, 2005).
5. Taxation of Pension Schemes (Consequential Amendments) Order 2006 (SI 2006/745), art.26(2) (April 6, 2006).
6. Tax Credits (Miscellaneous Amendments) Regulations 2006 (SI 2006/766), reg.7 (April 6, 2006).
7. Tax Credits (Miscellaneous Amendments) Regulations 2007 (SI 2007/824), reg.8 (April 6, 2007).

GENERAL NOTE

2.114 See also the definitions in TCA 2002, ss.48 and 65 (above) and ITA 2007 Sch.4 (not included in this work).

PART II

INCOME FOR THE PURPOSES OF TAX CREDITS

CHAPTER 1

General

Calculation of income of claimant

2.115 **3.**—(1) The manner in which income of a claimant, or, in the case of a joint claim, the aggregate income of the claimants, is to be calculated for a tax year for the purposes of Part I of the Act is as follows.

Step 1

2.116 Calculate and then add together—
(a) the pension income (as defined in regulation 5(1));
(b) the investment income (as defined in regulation 10);
(c) the property income (as defined in regulation 11);
(d) the foreign income (as defined in regulation 12); and
(e) the notional income (as defined in regulation 13),
of the claimant, or, in the case of a joint claim, of the claimants.
If the result of this step is £300 or less, it is treated as nil.

(SI 2002/2006, reg. 3) (as amended)

If the result of this step is more than £300, only the excess is taken into account in the following steps.

Step 2

Calculate and then add together—
- (a) the employment income (as defined in regulation 4);
- (b) the social security income (as defined in regulation 7);
- (c) the student income (as defined in regulation 8); and
- (d) the miscellaneous income (as defined in regulation 18), of the claimant, or in the case of a joint claim, of the claimants.

Step 3

Add together the results of steps 1 and 2.

Step 4

Calculate the trading income (as defined in regulation 6) of the claimant, or in the case of a joint claim, of the claimants.

Add the result of this step to that produced by step 3 [¹ . . .] in the year.

If there has been a trading loss in the year, [¹ subtract] the amount of that loss from the result of step 3.

[⁴A loss shall not be available for tax credit purposes, unless the trade was being carried on upon a commercial basis and with a view to the realisation of profits in the trade or, where the carrying on of the trade formed part of a larger undertaking, in the undertaking as a whole.]

[²Any trading loss in the year not set off as a result of the calculations in Steps One to Four above due to an insufficiency of income may be carried forward and set off against trading income (if any) of the same trade, profession or vocation in subsequent years (taking earlier years first) for the purposes of calculation of income under this regulation.]

(2) Subject to the qualifications in the following paragraphs of this regulation, and the provisions of Part III, the result of step 4 in paragraph (1) is the income of the claimant, or, in the case of a joint claim, of the claimants, for the purposes of the Act.

(3) Income which—
- (a) arises in a territory outside the United Kingdom; and
- (b) is, for the time being, unremittable for the purposes of [⁴Chapter 4 of Part 8 of ITTOIA],

is disregarded in calculating the income of the claimant or, in the case of a joint claim, of the claimants.

(4) Paragraph (5) applies in the case of a claimant who is [¹, for income tax purposes]
- (a) resident [¹and domiciled but not ordinarily resident] in the United Kingdom; [². . .]
- (b) resident and ordinarily resident but not domiciled in the United Kingdom [²or]
- [²(c) resident but neither ordinarily resident nor domiciled in the United Kingdom.]

(5) In the case of a person to whom this paragraph applies—
- [¹(a) any income arising outside the United Kingdom is to be taken into account, subject to any specific provision of these Regulations, regardless of the domicile or residence of the claimant; and]

Tax Credits (Definition and Calculation of Income) Regulations 2002

(b) references to a sum being [¹taken into account] are to be construed as including a sum which would be taxable if he were resident, ordinarily resident and domiciled in the United Kingdom.

[¹(5A) Any income is to be taken into account, subject to any specific provision of these Regulations, notwithstanding the provision of any Order in Council under section 788 of the Taxes Act (double taxation agreements).]

(6) In the case of a claimant who would be chargeable to income tax but for some special exemption or immunity from income tax, income shall be calculated on the basis of the amounts which would be so chargeable but for that exemption or immunity.

[¹(6A) Income paid to a claimant in a currency other than sterling shall be converted into sterling at the average of the exchange rates applicable for the conversion of that currency into sterling in the period of 12 months [⁵ending on 31st March] in the tax year in which the income arises.]

(7) In calculating income under this Part there shall be deducted [¹. . .]—
  (a) [¹the amount of] any banking charge or commission payable in converting to sterling a payment of income which is made in a currency other than sterling;
  (b) [¹the grossed up amount of] any qualifying donation (within the meaning of section 25 of the Finance Act 1990 (donations to charity by individuals)), made by the claimant or, in the case of a joint claim, by either or both of the claimants; [². . .] [⁴. . .]
[³(c) the amount of any contribution made by the claimant, or in the case of a joint claim, by either or both of the claimants to a registered pension scheme together with the amount of any tax relief due on those contributions.]
[³. . .]
[²(8) If—
  (a) a claimant has sustained a loss in relation to a [⁴ UK property business] or an overseas property business; and
  (b) the relief to which he is entitled in accordance with section 379A(2) and (3) of the Taxes Act exceeds the amount of his property income or foreign income for tax credits purposes, for the year in question;
the amount of his total income for tax credit purposes, computed in accordance with the preceding provisions of this regulation, shall be reduced by the amount of the excess.

[⁴In this paragraph "UK property business" and "overseas property business" have the same meaning as the have in the Taxes Act.]

AMENDMENTS

1. Tax Credits (Definition and Calculation of Income) (Amendment) Regulations 2003 (SI 2003/732), reg.5 (April 6, 2003).
2. Tax Credits (Miscellaneous Amendments No.2) Regulations 2003 (SI 2003/2815), reg.4 (November 26, 2003).
3. Taxation of Pension Schemes (Consequential Amendments) Order 2006 (SI 2006/745), art.26(3) (April 6, 2006).
4. Tax Credits (Miscellaneous Amendments) Regulations 2006 (SI 2006/766), reg.8 (April 6, 2006).
5. Tax Credits (Miscellaneous Amendments) Regulations 2007 (SI 2007/824), reg.9 (April 6, 2007).

(SI 2002/2006, reg.3) (as amended)

General Note

Regulation 3(1) and (2) state that there are four steps to calculating the aggregate income of a claimant or joint claimants for a tax year, but it is suggested that this would be better presented as five steps. The four steps are:
(1) Add the totals of income from sources subject to the £300 discount and deduct that discount.
(2) Add the totals from all other sources, apart from trading income.
(3) Add the totals of (1) and (2).
(4) Add to, or subtract from, the total from (3) the net income (or net loss) from trading income.

The "fifth step" is then to deduct from that sum the various general deductions, exclusions, exemptions and disregards in these regulations. These are set out in reg.3(3) (unremittable income), reg.3(7) (other general deductions), reg.9 (exempt scholarship income) and the Tables 6, 7 and 8 in reg.19 (general disregards).

Paragraph (7) is part of the "fifth step", along with para.(3). It provides for two important deductions commonly made against income for income tax purposes. The first is to allow the deduction from income for tax credits purposes of any sums given to charities within the terms of the FA 1990, s.25. That is the provision authorising the tax deduction for "gift aid" payments for all non-refundable gifts of money to charities made otherwise than by covenant, the charity being treated as receiving the sum under deduction of tax at the basic rate. The other allows deductions from total income for contributions to registered pension schemes under the FA 2004 and related provisions.

Paragraphs (3) to (6) are a motley of provisions dealing with foreign elements. The combined effect of paras (4), (5), and (5A) include all foreign income in the income to be used to calculate tax credits notwithstanding that for income tax purposes the income is excluded from a charge to income tax in the United Kingdom either because of the domicile of the taxpayer or because of a double tax agreement. It seems that para.(6) has, in part, the same aim, but it is not clear how it can override the tax exemptions applicable to diplomats and consuls under general international law and, in the United Kingdom, the Diplomatic Privileges Act 1964 and the Consular Relations Act 1968.

2.120

Chapter 2

Employment income

Employment income

4.—(1) In these Regulations, "employment income" means—
(a) any [¹earnings] from an office or employment received in the tax year;
(b) so much of any payment made to a claimant in that year in respect of expenses as is chargeable to income tax [¹by virtue of section 62 or section 72 of ITEPA];
(c) [¹the cash equivalent of] any non-cash voucher received by the claimant in that year and chargeable to income tax under [¹section 87 of ITEPA];
(d) [¹the cash equivalent of] any credit-token received by the claimant in that year and chargeable to income tax under [¹section 94 of ITEPA];
(e) [¹the cash equivalent of] any cash voucher received by the claimant in that year and chargeable to income tax under [¹section 81 of ITEPA];

2.121

[¹(f) any amount chargeable to tax under Chapter 3 of Part VI of ITEPA;]
(g) so much of a payment of statutory sick pay, received by the claimant during the year, as is subject to income tax [¹by virtue of section 660 of ITEPA;]
(h) the amount (if any) by which a payment of [¹statutory maternity pay, statutory paternity pay or statutory adoption pay] exceeds £100 per week;
(i) any amount charged to income tax for that year [¹under section 120 or section 149 of ITEPA;]
[¹(j) any sum to which section 225 of ITEPA applies;]
(k) any amount paid in that year by way of strike pay to the claimant as a member of a trade union;
[²(l) any amount charged to income tax for that year under Part 7 of ITEPA.]
[⁶(m) any amount paid to a person serving a custodial sentence or remanded in custody awaiting trial or sentence, for work done while serving the sentence or remanded in custody.]

For the purposes of this paragraph, references to the receipt of a payment of any description are references to its receipt by or on behalf of the claimant, or in the case of a joint claim of either of the claimants, in any part of the world.

This paragraph is subject to the following qualifications.

(2) Employment income does not include pension income.

[³(2A) [⁵. . .]

(2B) [⁵. . .]

[²(3) This paragraph applies if (apart from section 64 of ITEPA) the same benefit would give rise to two amounts ("A" and "B")—
(a) "A" being an amount of earnings from a claimant's employment as defined in section 62 of ITEPA, and
(b) "B" being an amount to be treated as earnings under any provision of Chapter 10 of Part 3 of ITEPA.

In such a case, the amount to be taken into account in computing the claimant's employment income is the greater of A and B, and the lesser amount shall be disregarded.]

(4) In calculating employment income, the payments and benefits listed in Table 1 shall be disregarded.

Table 1. Payments [¹and benefits] disregarded in the calculation of employment income

2.122

1. Any payment in respect of qualifying removal expenses, or the provision of any qualifying removal benefit, within the meaning of [¹Chapter 7 of Part IV of ITEPA].

[¹2A. The payment or reimbursement of expenses incurred in the provision of transport to a disabled employee (as defined in section 246(4) of ITEPA) by his employer, if no liability to income tax arises in respect of that payment or reimbursement (as the case may be) by virtue of section 246 of ITEPA.

2B. The provision to a disabled employee (as defined in section 246(4) of ITEPA) by his employer of a car, the provision of fuel for the car, or the reimbursement of expenses incurred in connection with the car, if no liability to income tax arises in respect of that provision or reimbursement (as the case may be) by virtue of section 247 of ITEPA.

2C. The payment or reimbursement of expenses incurred on transport, if no liability to income tax arises in respect of that payment or reimbursement (as the case may be) by virtue of section 248 of ITEPA.]

3. Travel facilities provided for the claimant as a member of the naval, military or air forces of the Crown for the purpose of going on, or returning from, leave.

[⁶**3A.** The payment by the Secretary of State for Defence of an operational allowance to a member of Her Majesty's forces in respect of service in an operational area specified by the Secretary of State for Defence.]

4. Payment or reimbursement of expenses in connection with the provision for, or use by, the claimant as a person holding an office or employment of a car-parking space at or near his place of work.

5. Any benefit or non-cash voucher provided to the claimant, or to any member of his family or household, [¹in respect of which no liability to income tax arises by virtue of Chapter 5 of Part IV of ITEPA.]

6. Any payment of incidental overnight expenses [¹in respect of which no liability to income tax arises by virtue of section 240 of ITEPA.]

[¹**7.** Food, drink and mess allowances for the armed forces and training allowances payable to members of the reserve forces in respect of which no liability to income tax arises by virtue of section 297 or 298 of ITEPA.]

8. The value of meal vouchers issued to the claimant as an employee [¹if section 89 of ITEPA applies to the vouchers.]

9. Any cash payment received by the claimant as a miner in lieu of free coal, or the provision of the coal itself, [¹in respect of which no liability to income tax arises by virtue of section 306 of ITEPA.]

10. An award made to the claimant as a director or employee by way of a testimonial to mark long service [¹if, or to the extent that, no liability to income tax arises in respect of it by virtue of section 323 of ITEPA.]

11. Payment of a daily subsistence allowance [¹in respect of which no liability to income tax arises by virtue of section 304 of ITEPA.].

[¹**11A.** The payment or reimbursement of reasonable expenses incurred by an employee who has a permanent workplace at an offshore installation, on transfer transport, related accommodation and subsistence or local transport, if no liability to income tax arises in respect of that payment or reimbursement (as the case may be) by virtue of section 305 of ITEPA.

For the purposes of this item, expressions which are defined in section 305 of ITEPA have the same meaning here as they do there.

11B. Payment of an allowance to a person in employment under the Crown in respect of which no liability to income tax arises by virtue of section 299 of ITEPA.

11C. The payment or reimbursement to an employee of any sum in connection with work-related training, or individual learning account training (as respectively defined in sections 251 and 256 of ITEPA) if no liability to income tax arises in respect of that payment or reimbursement (as the case may be) by virtue of any provision of Chapter 4 of Part IV of ITEPA.

11D. The provision for an employee of a non-cash voucher or a credit-token, to the extent that liability to income tax does not arise in respect of that voucher or credit-token (as the case may be), under Chapter 4 of [²Part 3 of ITEPA, by virtue of any provision of Chapter 6 of Part 4 of ITEPA.]

11E. The provision for an employee of free or subsidised meal vouchers or tokens (within the meaning of section 317(5) of ITEPA), if no liability to income tax arises in respect of that provision by virtue of section 317 of ITEPA.]

[⁶ **11F.** The provision of one mobile telephone for an employee in respect of which no liability to income tax arises by virtue of section 319 of ITEPA.]

12. An award made to the claimant under a Staff Suggestion Scheme, if the conditions specified in [¹sections 321 and 322 of ITEPA [³are satisfied].]

13. Travelling and subsistence allowances paid to or on behalf of the claimant by his employer [¹in respect of which no liability to income tax arises by virtue of section 245 of ITEPA.]

14. Any gift consisting of goods, or a voucher or token to obtain goods, [¹in respect of which no liability to income tax arises by virtue of section 270 or 324 of ITEPA.]

[¹**14A.** Any payment or reimbursement of expenses incurred in connection with an employment-related asset transfer (as defined in section 326(2) of ITEPA), if no liability to income tax arises in respect of that payment or reimbursement (as the case may be) by virtue of section 326 of ITEPA.

14B. Any payment of expenses incurred by an employee in connection with a taxable car if no liability to income tax arises in respect of the payment by virtue of section 239(2) of ITEPA.]

[²**14C.** The discharge of any liability of an employee in connection with a taxable car if no liability to income tax arises by virtue of section 239(1) of ITEPA.

14D. A benefit connected with a taxable car if no liability to income tax arises by virtue of section 239(4) of ITEPA.]

15. A cash voucher, non-cash voucher or credit-token to the extent that it is used by the recipient for the provision of childcare, the costs of which if borne by the recipient would be relevant childcare charges within the meaning of regulation 14 of the Working Tax Credit (Entitlement and Maximum Rate) Regulations 2002.

[³**16.** A payment made by the Department for Work and Pensions under section 2 of the Employment Act—
  (a) by way of In-Work Credit, Job Grant or Return to Work Credit, or
  (b) under the Employment Retention and Advancement Scheme or the Working Neighbourhoods Pilot.]

[⁵**16A.** A payment made by the Department for Employment and Learning in Northern Ireland under section 1 of the Employment and Training Act (Northern Ireland) 1950 by way of Return to Work Credit.]

[²**17.** The payment or reimbursement of reasonable additional household expenses incurred by an employee who works from home, within the meaning of section 316A of ITEPA.

18. The payment or reimbursement of retraining course expenses within the meaning of the section 311 of ITEPA.]

[⁴**19.** Provision of computer equipment in respect of which no liability to income tax arises by virtue of section 320 of ITEPA.]

(SI 2002/2006, reg.4) (as amended)

(5) From the amount of employment income, calculated in accordance with the preceding provisions of this regulation, there shall be deducted the amount of any deduction permitted in calculating [¹calculating earnings by virtue of any provision of sections [²231 to 232,] 336–344, or s.346, 347, 351, 352, 362, 363, 367, 368, 370, 371, 373, 374, 376, 377 or 713 of ITEPA].

AMENDMENTS

1. Tax Credits (Definition and Calculation of Income) (Amendment) Regulations 2003 (SI 2003/732), reg.6 (April 6, 2003).
2. Tax Credits (Miscellaneous Amendments No.2) Regulations 2003 (SI 2003/2815), reg.5 (November 26, 2003).
3. Tax Credits (Miscellaneous Amendments) Regulations 2004 (SI 2004/762), reg.14 (April 6, 2004).
4. Tax Credits (Miscellaneous Amendments No.3) Regulations 2004 (SI 2004/2663) reg.2 (November 3, 2004).
5. Tax Credits (Miscellaneous Amendments) Regulations 2006 (SI 2006/766), reg.9 (April 6, 2006).
6. Tax Credits (Miscellaneous Amendments) Regulations 2007 (SI 2007/824), reg.10 (April 6, 2007).

CROSS-REFERENCES

The regulation adopts for tax credits purposes the following chapters and sections of ITEPA, all relating to employment income:
Pt 3: Employment income: Earnings and benefits etc treated as earnings
    s.62   Earnings
Pt 3, Ch.4 Taxable benefit: vouchers and credit-tokens
    s.72   Sums in respect of expenses treated as earnings
    s.81   Benefit of cash voucher treated as earnings
    s.87   Benefit of non-cash voucher treated as earnings
    s.89   Reduction for meal vouchers
    s.94   Benefit of credit-token treated as earnings
Pt 3, Ch.6 Taxable benefits: cars, vans and related vehicles
    s.120   Benefit of car treated as earnings
    s.149   Benefit of car fuel treated as earnings
Pt 3, Ch.10 Taxable benefits: residual liability to charge
    s.201   Employment-related benefits
    s.211   Special rules for scholarships: introduction
Pt 3, Ch.11 Taxable benefits: exclusion of lower-paid employments
Pt 3, Ch.12 Payments treated as earnings
    s.225   Payments for restrictive covenants
Pt 4: Employment income: exemptions
    s.239   Payments and benefits connected with taxable cars and vans and exempt heavy goods vehicles
    s.240   Incidental overnight expenses and benefits
    s.245   Travelling and subsistence during public transport strikes
    s.246   Transport between work and home for disabled employees
    s.247   Provision of cars for disabled employees
    s.248   Transport home: late-night working and failure of car-sharing arrangements
Pt 4, Ch.4 Exemptions: education and training
    s.251   Meaning of "work-related training"
    s.256   Meaning of "individual learning account training"
Pt 4, Ch.5 Exemptions; recreational benefits
Pt 4, Ch.6 Exemptions: non-cash vouchers and credit-tokens
    s.270   Exemptions of small gifts of vouchers and tokens from third parties

Tax Credits (Definition and Calculation of Income) Regulations 2002

Pt 4, Ch.7 Exemptions: removal benefits and expenses
- s.297 Armed forces' food, drink and mess allowances
- s.298 Reserve and auxiliary forces' training allowances
- s.299 Crown employees' foreign service allowances
- s.304 Experts seconded to the European Commission
- s.305 Offshore oil and gas workers: mainland transfers
- s.306 Miners, etc.: coal and allowances in lieu of coal
- s.317 Subsidised meals
- s.321 Suggestion awards
- s.322 Suggestion awards: "the permitted maximum"
- s.323 Long service awards
- s.324 Small gifts from third parties
- s.326 Expenses incidental to transfer of a kind not normally met by transferor

Pt 5: Employment income: deductions allowed from earnings
- s.336 Deductions for expenses: the general rule
- s.337 Travel in performance of duties
- s.338 Travel for necessary attendance
- s.339 Meaning of "workplace" and "permanent workplace"
- s.340 Travel between group employments
- s.341 Travel at start and finish of overseas employment
- s.342 Travel between employments where duties performed abroad
- s.343 Deduction for professional membership fees
- s.344 Deduction for annual subscriptions
- s.346 Deduction for employee liabilities
- s.347 Payments made after leaving employment
- s.351 Expenses of ministers of religion
- s.352 Limited deduction for agency fees paid by entertainers
- s.362 Deductions where non-cash voucher provided
- s.363 Deductions where credit-token provided
- s.367 Fixed sum deductions for repairing and maintaining work equipment
- s.368 Fixed sum deductions from earnings payable out of public revenue
- s.370 Travel costs and expenses where duties performed abroad: employee's travel
- s.371 Travel costs and expenses where duties performed abroad: visiting spouse's or child's travel
- s.373 non-domiciled employee's travel costs and expenses where duties performed in United Kingdom
- s.374 Non-domiciled employee's spouse's or child's travel costs and expenses where duties performed in United Kingdom
- s.376 Foreign accommodation and subsistence costs and expenses (overseas employments)
- s.377 Costs and expenses in respect of personal security assets and sevices

Pt 6, Ch.3 Payments and benefits on termination of employment
- s.660 Taxable benefits; United Kingdom benefits: Table A

Pt 12: Payroll giving
- s.713 Donations to charity: payroll deduction scheme

GENERAL NOTE

2.123 This regulation defines "employment income" for the purposes of reg.3. Although the result may be obvious in most cases, four questions have to be asked to set the context of a tax credits calculation of employment income when regard is had to a particular source of income:

What income is relevant?
What exemptions and deductions apply?

Whose income is it?
When is the income brought into calculation?
These are discussed in turn. The same pattern is followed in the notes on other regulations.

What income is relevant? The scope of ITEPA and regulation 4

2.124 In marginal cases it is always necessary to ask both if an income-generating activity is employment, self-employment or something else, and what earnings come from any employment, as against any other source.

Employment and self-employment

2.125 The common context of a dispute about whether an activity is or is not an employment is the contention by the individual concerned that he or she is self-employed. This issue is discussed in the general note to reg.6 below. "Office" used to be a separate provision in the old Sch.E, reflecting the antiquity of the phraseology used. ITEPA, s.5 now relegates the status of office-holders (rightly in terms of relative importance) to a secondary status in the legislation. It also codifies the common law definition of "office". For all tax credits purposes, as for all ITEPA purposes, "employee" is to be read as including office holders, and "being employed" includes holding an office. "Office" is now defined (in words adopted from the income tax case of *GWR v Bater* [1920] 3 K.B. 266) as including "any position which has an existence independent of the person who holds it and may be filled by successive holders". For a discussion of that in the context of the borderline between holding an office and being self-employed see *Edwards v Clinch* [1982] A.C. 845.

Employment income

2.126 ITEPA deals with the income taxation of employment income in Pts 1–8 of the Act. For the structure of those Parts, see s.3 of ITEPA, and for the main charge to tax, see s.6. As can be seen from the list of cross-references, the policy and drafting approaches taken for the purposes of calculating employment income for tax credits purposes are to select from the provisions of those parts (ss.1–564), rather than simply to adopt the whole code, or those parts of the code felt appropriate. TCTM04101 directs HMRC officers to "Note that, although based on income tax law, not all of the additional rules for income chargeable to tax under Sch.E have been included in the tax credit employment income rules", and "not all of the general exemptions and reliefs from inclusion as income chargeable under Sch.E have been included . . .". This will also apply to ITEPA. The only major part of the code omitted as a whole is Pt 7 (Employment income: share-related income and exemptions—ss.417–554), although Pt 8 (relating to former employees) is also excluded. Elsewhere, close attention has to be paid to those charges and exemptions that are included (as listed in the cross-reference list derived from reg.3) and those that are excluded.

So, for example, while most sections in Pt 3 (Employment Income: earnings and benefits etc treated as earnings) are adopted, Ch.5 (taxable benefits: living accommodation) is not, nor is Ch.7 (taxable benefits: loans). Similarly, while most of the sections in Pt 4 (Employment income: exemptions) are allowed also as exemptions for tax credits purposes, again the approach has been to select those that are applied and those that are not. The same is true of Pt 5 (Employment income: deductions allowed from earnings). This reflects in part an assessment of the provisions that are not relevant (e.g. Pt 4, Ch.10 (exemptions on termination of employment)) are excluded as not relevant either to working tax credit or to child tax credit, but that does not always appear to explain the omission. For example, the exemption for subsidised meals in s.317 is applied, but not the exemption for care for children in s.318.

The resulting picture is one of some complexity, because one cannot simply adopt the income tax assessment of all employees for tax credits without looking through at least some of them to see on which sections of ITEPA the charge to tax is based or the exemption or deduction is claimed. In any case, other than the most straightforward, it may therefore be necessary to look at the breakdown of any charge to tax not based simply on earnings and the usual expenses and deductions. That also means that the approach of adopting a figure from the P45 or P60 supplied to an employee at the end of an employment or the end of a tax year may not be enough in those cases. While this might sound an over-exact approach to the calculation of income, it has to be borne in mind that the effective value of any charge or exemption for tax credit purposes is, at the margin, 37 per cent of the amount charged or claimed. So, a failure to allow a deduction for a £150 expense (which, if deductible at the basic rate of income tax, will have in effect cost the employee not £150 but £117) will "cost" the employee £55 in lost tax credits, or nearly half the actual cost to the employee of the amount for which the deduction is claimed.

To follow that point with a relevant example, it would seem from the exclusion of s.317 that a claimant for WTC may claim for childcare charges if paid by the employee, but is liable to have the value of the advantage of employer-provided childcare taken into account as income for tax credits purposes although, of course, the employee will not be paying for, and therefore not able to claim for, that provision. However, this depends how the employer provides the advantage. If the employer provides childcare through the mechanism of providing the employee with a cash voucher, non-cash voucher or credit-token, the exclusion from calculation of that value by Table 1, Item 15, is broader than the income tax exclusion. As the working tax credit childcare element is not itself taxable to income tax (Taxes Act, s.617A), the justification for this mismatch is not clear.

Differences between income tax assessments and tax credit calculations of employment income

2.127 The only full way of noting the differences between total net (i.e. after deductions) employment income for income tax purposes and for tax credits purposes is by precise reference to individual provisions in ITEPA. This must cover the ITEPA sections included in, and excluded from, reg.4 together with those provisions that are included in reg.4 but not by reference to specific provisions in ITEPA. Cross-references from reg.4 are not assisted by the reenactment of the employment income provisions since the regulation was drafted, as the previous drafting order of the regulation has been lost. As ITEPA is an immediately contemporary codification of employment income taxation, no reference for 2003–04 need be made to any other provision. In future years, it may be assumed that changes will, where appropriate, be made in parallel.

The full list of sections of ITEPA included by cross reference is set out above, and from that the obvious gaps can be identified. There are no differences with regard to cash earnings or equivalent (see ss.62 and 72 of ITEPA). But only some parts of the Pt 3 provisions on taxable benefits apply. Chapter 3 (expense payments), Ch.4 (vouchers and credit-tokens), Ch.6 (cars, vans and related benefits) and Ch.10 (residual liability) apply, but no part of Ch.5 (living accommodation), Ch.7 (loans), Ch.8 (notional loans in respect of acquisition of shares), or Ch.9 (disposals of shares for more than market value) apply. And of the six specific payments treated as earnings by ch.12, only one (restrictive covenants under s.225) is expressly brought into the calculation.

Two kinds of income only are mentioned in reg.4 that are not related directly to specific provisions in ITEPA. Regulation 4(1)(h) requires inclusion of only the excess of statutory maternity pay over £100. For income tax purposes the sum is fully taxable. Regulation 4(1)(k) requires the inclusion of strike pay, whether or not that is otherwise taxable under this or any other head of income. These both reflect social security rules rather than income tax rules.

What exemptions and deductions apply?

2.128 The exclusions from para.(4) are far harder to summarise. Part 4 deals with exemptions. Chapter 1 deals with general exemptions rules. Of the specific rules,

(SI 2002/2006, reg. 4) (as amended)

Ch.2 (mileage allowances and passenger payments) is not within the scope of tax credits, and nor are many of the specific exemptions related to transport, travel and subsistence in Ch.3. Of ss.237–248 in that Chapter, only ss.239, 240 and 245–8 are permitted exclusions for tax credits calculations. Chapter 4 (education and training) exemptions are allowed, as are Ch.5 (recreational benefits) and Ch.7 (removal expenses). But the exemptions in Ch.8 (special kinds of employees) and Ch.11 (miscellaneous exemptions) are included on a selected basis only. In part, this selection excludes exemptions related to foreign elements, and to living accommodation (the benefit of which is excluded from the calculation of income), and so reflects the broader policy of the definition of relevant income. But there is no substitute in this Part of the Act for a detailed comparison of individual provisions.

There are only three exemptions mentioned in reg.4 without express reference to ITEPA provisions. In the Table, Item 3 (forces' leave) is defined broadly rather than in terms of s.296 of ITEPA, which is to the same effect. Item 4 (parking) is also broader than the equivalent s.237. Likewise, Item 15 (cash vouchers, etc.) is broader than ss.266–267.

By comparison, the deductions rules incorporated in para.(5) by section number follow closely the equivalent rules in Pt 5 of ITEPA, with only minor omissions. The differences are restricted largely to foreign issues or irrelevant categories of deduction, such as those related to (non-included) living accommodation.

TCTM confirms the HMRC view that most of the provisions in this regulation "mirror" or "are identical with" the equivalent ITEPA provisions. The guidance is to apply the same considerations for tax credits calculations in those cases as for income tax on employment income (and there are specific cross-references to the Inspectors Manual on Sch.E—to become employment income). It may in general be thought that the tax credits appeal authorities and tax appeal authorities would also strive to a common approach, as it may be predicted that that is the approach that superior courts would take if asked to consider the same rules in the different contexts.

In practice, HMRC relies on the information given by claimants to decide on any exemptions or deductions. If a claimant does not claim any expenses, then they will not usually be considered. And it will usually be too late to ask for them to be taken into account on an appeal, as the three month rule applies to these changes as it does to all other aspects of a claim. See *CTC/2113/2006*.

Whose income is it?

This is rarely in issue in a tax credits context. One of the few practical problems arises where income is shared between husband and wife, but the joint claimant rules render that irrelevant here. The identity of the income tax payer, applying here also, is set out in ITEPA, s.13. The taxable person, and therefore the person whose income it is for tax credits purposes, is the person to whose employment the earnings relate. 2.129

When is the income brought into calculation?

The employment income to be calculated for tax credits is the income "received by the claimant . . . in" or "paid to" the claimant in the tax year in question: para.(1). That tax year will either be the current year or the previous year, as determined under s.7(3) of the TCA 2002. The income for a tax year is therefore the income, in that sense, of the year. This is consistent with the general income tax rules for assessment on a current year basis. ITEPA, s.19 provides for taxation to be based on the "net taxable earnings from an employment in the year". It is calculated when received, not when earned. That is a question of fact. This may be important for bonuses and other non-regular payments. In practice, that is also how the PAYE system operates. 2.130

Tax Credits (Definition and Calculation of Income) Regulations 2002

CHAPTER 3

Pension income

Pension income

2.131   **5.**—[¹(1) In these Regulations, except where the context otherwise require, "pension income" means—
   (a) any pension to which section 577 or 629 of ITEPA applies;
   (b) any pension to which section 569 of ITEPA applies;
   (c) any voluntary annual payment to which section 633 of ITEPA applies;
   [²(d) any pension, annuity or income withdrawal to which section 579A of ITEPA applies;
   (e) any unauthorised member payments to which section 208(2)(a) or (b) of the Finance Act 2004 applies;]
   (f) any periodical payment to which section 619 of ITEPA applies;
   [². . .]
   [². . .]
   [². . .]
   [². . .]
   [²(k) any annuity paid under a retirement annuity contract to which Chapter 9 of Part 9 of ITEPA applies;]
   (l) any annuity to which section 609, 610 or 611 of ITEPA applies; and
   (m) any payment to which section 623 of ITEPA applies.]
   [³(n) any social security lump sum to which section 7 of the Finance Act 2005 applies; and
   (o) any lump sum to which section 636B or 636C of ITEPA applies.]
   (2) In calculating the amount of a person's pension income there shall be disregarded any [¹payment or benefit mentioned] in Column 1 of Table 2 to the extent specified in the corresponding entry in Column 2.

Table 2. [¹Pensions, other payments and benefits] disregarded in the calculation of pension income

2.132

1. Payment	2. Extent of disregard
1. A wounds pension or disability pension to which [¹section 641 of ITEPA] applies.	So much of the payment as is disregarded by virtue of [¹section 641 of ITEPA].
2. An annuity or additional pension payable to a holder of the Victoria Cross, George Cross or any other decoration mentioned in [¹section 638 of ITEPA].	The whole of the annuity or additional pension and, if both are payable, the whole of both such annuity and additional pension.
3. A pension or allowance to which [¹section 639 of ITEPA] applies.	[¹The amount of the pension or allowance.]
4. A pension or allowance by reason of payment of which a	[¹The amount treated as falling within section 639 of ITEPA by

(SI 2002/2006, reg.5) (as amended)

1. Payment	2. Extent of disregard
pension or allowance specified in [¹section 639 of ITEPA] is withheld or abated.	virtue of section 640(2) of that Act.]
5. In the case of a claimant in receipt of a pension under the Service Pensions Order, any increase in the rate of that pension in respect of a dependant who is not a member of the claimant's family.	The amount of the increase.
6. A mobility supplement, or a payment in respect of attendance, paid in conjunction with a war pension.	The amount of the supplement or payment.
7. Any supplementary pension under Article 29(1A) of the Service Pensions Order.	The amount of the supplementary pension.
8. A pension awarded at the supplementary rate under article 27(3) of the Personal Injuries (Civilians) Scheme 1983.	The amount for the time being specified in paragraph 1(c) of Schedule 4 to the Scheme.
9. A pension awarded on retirement through disability caused by injury on duty or by a work-related illness.	[¹The exempt amount of the pension calculated in accordance with section 644(3) of ITEPA.]
[¹10. A lump sum on which no liability to income tax arises by virtue of [² section 636A of ITEPA].	The amount of the lump sum.
11. Coal or smokeless fuel provided as mentioned in section 646(1) of ITEPA, or an allowance in lieu of such provision.	The amount on which no liability to income tax arises by virtue of that section.]

[¹(3) From the amount of pension income, calculated in accordance with the preceding provisions of this regulation, there shall be deducted any amount deductible for income tax purposes in computing pension income (as defined in ITEPA) under section 713 of that Act.]

AMENDMENTS

1. Tax Credits (Definition and Calculation of Income) (Amendment) Regulations 2003 (SI 2003/732), reg.7 (April 6, 2003).
2. Taxation of Pension Schemes (Consequential Amendments) Order 2006 (SI 2006/745), art.26(4) (April 6, 2006).
3. Tax Credits (Miscellaneous Amendments) Regulations 2006 (SI 2006/766), reg.10 (April 6, 2006).

GENERAL NOTE

This regulation defines "pension income" for the purposes of reg.3. "Pension income" is a new concept evolved by the Tax Law Rewrite Project and launched in

ITEPA. Previously, taxation of pensions has mainly been as if pensions were emoluments, and therefore subject to Sch.E, with other rules bringing certain kinds of pension into various cases of Sch.D. The pension income provisions in ITEPA bring together most of the various charges to tax on different kinds of pensions, including some pensions payable to the former self-employed, and also pensions payable without reference to work of any kind. It also includes social security provisions by way of pension.

What income is relevant?

2.134　ITEPA Pt 9 rewrote the whole of the relevant provisions of the then income tax legislation dealing with income tax on pensions. However, no sooner had it been rewritten than much of it was rewritten again—by the Finance Act 2004. The provisions of FA 2004 came into effect on April 6, 2006. The amended Pt 9 applies to all pension income (including social security pensions from the UK and abroad, voluntary pensions, and pensions payable for ill-health retirements). The aim behind reg.5 is to include all pensions as income under this regulation for tax credits purposes.

What exemptions and deductions apply?

2.135　Again, the pattern is to adopt all relevant provisions in ITEPA, Pt 9. Of the three chapters dealing with exemptions, Ch.16 (exemption for certain lump sums) applies fully. Ch.17 (exemptions: any taxpayer) applies in large part. The sections not applied relate for the most part to foreign pensions, and are dealt with under the foreign income provision in reg.12. This also applies to Ch.18 (exemptions: non-United Kingdom resident taxpayers). The only other section not applied is ITEPA, s.645 (social security pensions: increases for children), which does not apply by reason of the repeal of those provisions and their replacement by child tax credit by TCA 2002 (save for the oversight of the rare payments under s.85 of the SSCBA 1992 not being repealed by the Act).

Whose income is it?

2.136　ITEPA, s.572 provides that the person liable for any tax charged is the person receiving or entitled to the pension. This is therefore the operative rule for inclusion of pension income for the calculation of tax credits income. It is the alternative to deal with those who are not entitled to a pension being received (as with voluntary pensions), but will rarely present problems. There is no significance for tax credits purposes in most cases about pensions to couples. If it is significant then, of course, entitlement is a question of law and receipt a question of fact.

When is the income brought into the calculation?

2.137　This also follows from s.572. As a result, pension income is to be included when entitlement arises. If there is no entitlement, as with voluntary pensions, then it is when the pension is received. That should follow the income tax treatment.

CHAPTER 4

Trading income

Trading income

2.138　**6.** The claimant's trading income is—
　　(a) the amount of his taxable profits for the tax year from—
　　　　(i) any trade carried on in the United Kingdom or elsewhere;
　　　　(ii) any profession or vocation the income from which does not fall under any other provisions of these Regulations; or

(b) if the claimant is a partner in the trade, profession or vocation, his taxable profit for the year arising from his share of the partnership's trading or professional income.

[¹ Here "taxable profits" has the same meaning as it has in Part 2 of ITTOIA but disregarding Chapter 16 of that Part (averaging profits of farmers and creative artists.]

AMENDMENT

1. Tax Credits (Miscellaneous Amendments) Regulations 2006 (SI 2006/766), reg.11 (April 6, 2006).

GENERAL NOTE

This regulation defines "trading income" for the purposes of reg.3. It does so, since 2006, by reference to the newly codified rules for taxing trading income set out in ITTOIA 2005. This now includes all income from trades, professions and vocations and some related forms of income. It covers income both sourced in the United Kingdom and sourced abroad.

Employment and self-employment

The critical distinction in the case of many of those with smaller incomes who claim to be traders or self-employed is whether that is a true description in both law and fact of the individual's status. This is directly relevant for the calculation of tax credits because it must be decided if regs 4 or 6 applies. Following from that decision are subsidiary questions about the exemptions and deductions that must be calculated in finding the net income; the question of which period of income is to be taken into account; and the provision in Step 4 of reg.3 allowing trading losses to be deducted from other income. The rules assume that there cannot be a net loss by way of employment income, and do not allow for it. But this is an important overall change in the tax credit rules because previously no income losses were allowed.

The status of employee or self-employed is important for several reasons besides the current context:

Income tax: employment income or trading income?
NI contributions: Class 1 or Class 2 contributions?
VAT: is the person carrying on registerable activities?
Benefits: is the individual entitled to benefits available only to employees?

In addition, there are other issues that arise from the employment status, such as the minimum wage, holiday entitlements, and employer liability, that are again to be decided separately.

Drawing a line between employment and self-employment has always been difficult. It is also wide open to abuse, for example to reduce NI contributions but to increase benefit entitlement. This has led to people claiming to be an employee for some purposes and self-employed for others, and to different government agencies in the past adopting different answers to an individual's status in different contexts.

One result has been a series of initiatives to concentrate the decision-making on this issue so as to avoid inconsistent official decisions. Another is a series of legislative initiatives to define more clearly where the borderline is and to deal with abusive situations.

As a result of various initiatives, HMRC are now the effective deciders, subject to appeal, of employment status. The Social Security (Transfer of Functions, etc.) Act 1999 transferred NI contribution administration to the Inland Revenue. In addition, s.8 of that Act transferred to the Inland Revenue the decision whether someone is employed or self-employed for most social security benefit purposes. Appeals from a HMRC decision under s.8, about contributions, and about income tax liability, all go to the tax appeal commissioners. In the case of the s.8 decisions, most of these were previously dealt with on appeal by social security appeal tribunals, so this was a transfer of appeal jurisdiction. HMRC has also inherited responsibility for the national minimum wage legislation.

There are several provisions that now provide that someone is, or is to be treated as, an employee rather than self-employed. Two of these deserve emphasis. The first is the category of workers who in practical terms are somewhere between the two main groups—agency workers. ITEPA, Pt 1, Ch.7 deals with agency workers. Section 44 provides that in most such cases the worker is regarded as the employee of the agency even if that is not the formal status adopted. The second concerns Ch.8 of that Part, which codifies the controversial "IR35" rules for what are sometimes known as "pocket book companies". These rules provide that in stated situations an individual who is under an obligation to provide services to a third party via an intermediary in circumstances where the worker is not paid as an employee by the intermediary can be treated as being an employee of the intermediary with a deemed employment income from that intermediary. This is used, for example, where someone works for a genuine third party, but where the contractual relationship with the third party is, typically, through a company of which the individual is the only shareholder. The company then pays the individual in some indirect way—benefits, loans, dividends—which the individual claims (if asked) to be either not income at all or not employment income.

What income is relevant? What exemptions and deductions apply?

2.141 "Trade" is defined in the Taxes Act, s.832 as "every trade, manufacture, adventure or concern in the nature of trade". There is considerable case law on this meaning, of which reference might be made in the marginal case to the decisions of the House of Lords in *Ransom v Higgs* [1974] 1 W.L.R. 1594 and *Ensign Tankers v Stokes* [1992] 1 A.C. 655. In *Ransom*, the House of Lords made clear the wide factual scope of "trade", in the light of the extending definition. The fact, for example, that no particular name could be given to the activity did not stop it being a trading activity if it was an economic or commercial activity aimed at generating profit (even if it did not do so). The converse of this is that activities that appear to be commercial but are not aimed at making a profit may be regarded in some cases as tax avoidance manoeuvres and not as trading (*Ensign Tankers*). Reference in marginal cases is usually made to the so-called "badges of trade". The badges were first identified by the Royal Commission on the Taxation of Income in 1952 as:
  (a) the subject-matter of the sale or realisation;
  (b) the length of the period of ownership of assets realised;
  (c) the frequency or number of similar transactions by that person;
  (d) whether there was supplementary work on or in connection with the assets realised or the realisation;
  (e) the reasons for the realisation of the assets;
  (f) motive.

Two other points should be emphasised. First, there is a need to distinguish activities generating capital from those generating income. For the calculation of tax credits income, all activities generating capital should be ignored. (This introduces into the tax credits context a much fought-over income tax borderline removed in part for income tax purposes by the introduction of capital gains tax.) Secondly, and seemingly by contrast to the first, a "one off" activity generating profit may be a trading activity. The statutory definition indicates that a single activity may be caught as an "adventure" or a "concern in the nature of trade". From these follow a third point: a payment is either a trading payment or it is capital. There is no middle ground. If a receipt is not a trading receipt, it cannot be brought into charge to income tax (and it is therefore suggested to tax credits either) under other income charging provisions. See *Jones v Leeming* [1930] A.C. 415.

As reg.6 reflects, the charge to income tax on the self-employed is based on the accounts of the business. Increasingly, both the legislative provision for, and the HMRC practice relating to, the taxation of commercial activity is accounts-based. The concern in calculating income for tax credits is therefore with the claimant's business accounts for any trade.

In practice, in the simplest cases, the accounts will be "three-liners". HMRC will accept these for income tax purposes and presumably also for tax credits purposes. The three lines are:

(SI 2002/2006, reg. 6) (as amended)

(a) income;
(b) deductions (including capital allowances if any);
(c) net income.

It is assumed that the net income is the difference between the other two! Three-line accounts in this form are accepted where the gross income (turnover) of the trading activity is less than £15,000 a year. If turnover is over that limit, then full accounts itemising income and expenditure will need to be provided, or at least the individual will have to provide all the details required in the standard self-employment pages to the self-assessment form for income tax. In the more complex cases, there should be two sets of accounts: the ordinary working accounts produced for the business (be it company, partnership or individual) and the tax computations or adjustments necessary to change the accounts from the approach adopted for the business to the approach necessary for income tax purposes. For example, the standard item "depreciation" on capital assets held for the business must be removed and replaced by a claim for any specific capital allowances to which the taxpayer is entitled. A second and further set of such computations may be necessary for tax credits purposes—or at least points may need following up. It is common for a business run by a husband to make a payment to an otherwise-non-earning wife. That is a deduction for trading purposes, but must be added back in for the joint claim they should be making for tax credits purposes as earnings of the wife. The business may be paying rent for the accommodation to the owners of the premises used. If that is the jointly owned (or owned in common) home of the joint claimants, again the rental income needs to go back into the tax credits calculation as property income.

Whose income is it?

It is the income of the individual or partner running the business. The tax credits rules are silent as to partners' shares, so it will be the same share of the trading income as for income tax. That is based on the proposition that for English law purposes (but not Scottish law) a partnership is not a separate entity, so the trading income of the partnership is directly the trading income of the partners, divided as they decide or, by default, under the general rules of the Partnership Act 1890.

2.142

When is the income to be brought into the calculation?

The standard rule for income tax, and therefore tax credits, is that the tax payable in any one tax year (April 6 to April 5) is the income of that year. But for ongoing trades the tax is charged instead on the income of the "basis period" for that year. The basis period for a year is defined as the 12 months immediately following the basis period of the previous year. This is designed to prevent gaps occurring between tax years. In practice, this will be the 12 months accounts period for the business ending in that tax year. Many businesses end their accounting years on April 30. This creates the maximum convenient (for the business) gap between the accounts year and the tax year. Where a business using this practice ends its accounts, for example, on April 30, 2005, that will be the basis period for the tax year 2005–2006.

2.143

There are special rules for the opening and closing years of a business, and anti-avoidance rules where a business changes its accounting year.

CHAPTER 5

Social security income

Social security income

7.—(1) The claimant's social security income is the total amount payable—

2.144

Tax Credits (Definition and Calculation of Income) Regulations 2002

    (a) under any provision of the Social Security Act 1988, the Contributions and Benefits Act or the Jobseekers Act 1995 or under section 69 of the Child Support, Pensions and Social Security Act 2000;
    (b) [¹. . .];
    (c) by the Secretary of State in respect of the non-payment of a payment which ought to have been made under a provision mentioned in sub-paragraph (a); and
    (d) by way of an ex-gratia payment made by the Secretary of State, or in Northern Ireland by the Department for Social Development, in connection with a benefit, pension or allowance under the Contributions and Benefits Act.

This is subject to the following provisions of this regulation.

(2) Pensions under the Contributions and Benefits Act which are pension income by virtue of regulation 5(1)(a) are not social security income.

(3) In calculating the claimant's social security income the payments in Table 3 shall be disregarded.

Table 3. Payments under, or in connection with, the Act, the Social Security Act 1988, the Contributions and Benefits Act or the Jobseekers Act 1995 disregarded in calculation of social security income

2.145

1. An attendance allowance under section 64 of the Contributions and Benefits Act.
2. A back to work bonus under section 26 of the Jobseekers Act 1995.
3. A bereavement payment under section 36 of the Contributions and Benefits Act.
4. Child benefit under Part II of the Act.
5. A Christmas bonus under section 148 of the Contributions and Benefits Act.
6. Council tax benefit under section 131 of the Contributions and Benefits Act.
7. A disability living allowance under section 71 of the Contributions and Benefits Act.
8. Disabled person's tax credit under section 129 of the Contributions and Benefits Act.
9. Any discretionary housing payment pursuant to regulation 2(1) of the Discretionary Financial Assistance Regulations 2001.
10. An ex-gratia payment by the Secretary of State or, in Northern Ireland, the Department for Social Development, to a person over pensionable age by way of supplement to incapacity benefit.
11. A guardian's allowance under section 77 of the Contributions and Benefits Act.

(SI 2002/2006, reg. 7) (as amended)

12. Housing benefit under section 130 of the Contributions and Benefits Act.
13. Income support under section 124 of the Contributions and Benefits Act, unless it is chargeable to tax under [¹section 665 of ITEPA.].
14. Incapacity benefit which is— (a) short term incapacity benefit payable at the lower rate; or (b) payable to a person who had received invalidity benefit before 13th April 1995 if the period of incapacity for work is treated, by virtue of regulation 2 of the Social Security (Incapacity Benefit) (Transitional) Regulations 1995 (days to be treated as days of incapacity for work) as having begun before that date.
15. Industrial injuries benefit [¹(except industrial death benefit)] under section 94 of the Contributions and Benefits Act.
16. A contribution-based jobseeker's allowance under the Jobseekers Act 1995, to the extent that it exceeds the maximum contained in [¹section 674 of ITEPA.].
17. An income-based jobseeker's allowance under the Jobseekers Act 1995.
18. A maternity allowance under section 35 of the Contributions and Benefits Act.
19. A severe disablement allowance under section 68 or 69 of the Contributions and Benefits Act
20. A social fund payment under Part VIII of the Contributions and Benefits Act.
[¹**20A.** Statutory adoption pay under Part XIIZB of the Contributions and Benefits Act.
21A. Statutory paternity pay under Part XIIZA of the Contributions and Benefits Act.]
21. Statutory maternity pay under Part XII of the Contributions and Benefits Act.
22. Statutory sick pay under Part IX of the Contributions and Benefits Act.
23. Working families' tax credit under section 128 of the Contributions and Benefits Act.
24. A payment by way of compensation for the non-payment of, or in respect of loss of entitlement (whether wholly or partly) of, income support, jobseeker's allowance, [²or housing benefit].
25. A payment in lieu of milk tokens or the supply of vitamins under the Welfare Food Regulations 1996.

Tax Credits (Definition and Calculation of Income) Regulations 2002

(4) If an increase in respect of a child dependant is payable with an allowance, benefit, pension or other payment ("the main payment") listed in Table 3, the increase shall also be wholly disregarded in calculating the income of the recipient of the main payment.

(5) [¹...]

[¹(5A) From the amount of social security income, calculated in accordance with the preceding provisions of this regulation, there shall be deducted any amount deductible for income tax purposes in computing social security income (as defined in ITEPA) under section 713 of ITEPA.]

(6) A reference in this regulation to an enactment applying only in Great Britain includes a reference to a corresponding enactment applying in Northern Ireland.

AMENDMENTS

1. Tax Credits (Definition and Calculation of Income) (Amendment) Regulations 2003 (SI 2003/732), reg.8 (April 6, 2003).
2. Tax Credits (Miscellaneous Amendments No.2) Regulations 2003 (SI 2003/2815), reg.6 (November 26, 2003).

CROSS-REFERENCE

ITEPA, s.713   Donations to charity: payroll giving scheme

GENERAL NOTE

2.146   This regulation defines "social security income" for the purposes of reg.3. "Social security income" is another creation of the Tax Law Rewrite Project. Like pension income, it forms a separate code in Pt X of ITEPA (ss.655–681). But, unlike the employment income and pensions income regulations, this regulation adopts the approach of parallel legislation to Pt X of ITEPA rather than adopting ITEPA provisions themselves. Nonetheless, the relevant ITEPA provisions are included in this volume both for cross-reference and for more general reference in handling social security benefits.

Part 10 of ITEPA is in the following pattern. Chapter 1 sets out the structure of the Part. Chapter 2 deals with general points on tax on social security income, including a definition of the terms used. Chapter 3 lists the taxable United Kingdom social security benefits. This is in the form of Table A to s.660. Chapter 4 lists exemptions from the ch.3 charge to specific benefits. Chapter 5 lists benefits wholly exempt from tax, in the form of Table B to s.677. Chapter 6 lists taxable foreign benefits, and ch.7 lists exemptions from the benefits brought in under ch.6. Of those chapters, chs 6 and 7 are irrelevant to the head of the tax credits income calculation as it is limited to United Kingdom benefits only.

What income is relevant?

2.147   As just noted, reg.7 is expressly limited to benefits to which a claimant is entitled under United Kingdom legislation only. Foreign social security benefits are to be included under foreign income. There are two other limitations on social security income. The first, deriving from a parallel with ITEPA, is that state retirement benefits are treated as pension income not as social security income. The second, not deriving from that source, is the treatment of the statutory payments (sick, maternity, adoption, paternal) as employment income. ITEPA treats these as social security income (although this is a default rule—if they are taxed as employment income then they are excluded here: ITEPA s.660(2)).

With those exclusions, the other benefits that are taxable under Table A in ITEPA, and also relevant for calculating tax credit income, are:
    Widowed mother's/parent's allowance
    Carer's allowance

(SI 2002/2006, reg. 7) (as amended)

Incapacity benefit (some)
Income support (some)
Jobseeker's allowance (some)

In each case there are provisions about how much of the income is taxed. In practice, much of that tax is collected under the PAYE scheme.

What exclusions and deductions apply?

The list in Table 3 parallels the list in Table B to s.677 of ITEPA (payments wholly exempt), along with the provisions, in particular, for jobseeker's allowance and incapacity benefit, save for the statutory payments (noted above) and the treatment of present and past tax credits. CTC and WTC are not taxable. The list is very extensive, and it leaves relevant to tax credits only the short list of benefits noted in the previous paragraph. 2.148

There is no specific provision in the regulations dealing with overpayments of benefit. In practice, this may not be a major problem because of the limited extent to which account is taken of benefits. But the position might arise where, say, a widowed parent's allowance was overpaid (perhaps because of the living together rule) so that income previously paid was required to be repaid. For income tax purposes, late account can be taken of this for up to five years after the event. For tax credits purposes, the reduction in income for the relevant period will be relevant only in so far as there can be a recalculation of the income for tax credits, and there is a timely claim made. As the main time-limit is three months, there will only be a limited extent to which such adjustments can be requested, even with the benefit of a rapid notification of the change of circumstances. The two benefits administered by HMRC, child benefit and guardian's allowance, are exempt in any event.

Social security beneficiaries may also set charitable giving against their income.

Whose income is it?

The regulation is silent on this point, which therefore falls to be decided by reference to the social security rules. ITEPA, s.662 imposes the income tax on the person receiving or entitled to the benefit, so covering appointees as well as claimants. 2.149

When is the income brought into the calculation?

The calculation is based on the amount actually received in the year, regardless of the period for which it is received. 2.150

CHAPTER 6

Student income

[¹Student Income

8. "Student income" means, in relation to a student— 2.151
[²(a) in England, any adult dependant's grant payable—
    [³(i) under regulation 41 of the Education (Student Support) Regulations 2006 in relation to an academic year which begins on or after 1st September 2006 but before 1st September 2007; or
    (ii) under regulation 43 of the Education (Student Support) Regulations 2007 in relation to an academic year which begins on or after 1st September 2007;]
(b) in Scotland, any dependant's grant payable under regulation 4(1)(c) of the Students' Allowances (Scotland) Regulations 1999; [². . .]
(c) in Northern Ireland, any grant which corresponds to income treated as student income in England and Wales by virtue of paragraph (a);]
[² and

Tax Credits (Definition and Calculation of Income) Regulations 2002

(d) in Wales, any adult dependant's grant payable—
(i) under regulation 17 of the Education (Student Support) Regulations 2005 in relation to an academic year which begins on or after 1st September 2005 but before 1st September 2006; or
(ii) under regulation 22 of the Assembly Learning Grants and Loans (Higher Education) (Wales) Regulations 206 in relation to an academic year which begins on or after 1st September 2006.]

AMENDMENTS

1. Tax Credits (Miscellaneous Amendments No.2) Regulations 2003 (SI 2003/2815), reg.7 (November 26, 2003).
2. Tax Credits (Miscellaneous Amendments) Regulations 2006 (SI 2006/766), reg.12 (April 6, 2006).
3. Tax Credits (Miscellaneous Amendments) Regulations 2007 (SI 2007/824), reg.11 (April 6, 2007).

GENERAL NOTE

2.152   This regulation defines "student income" for the purposes of reg.3. "Student income" is not a head of taxation under the Taxes Act or under the scheme used by the Tax Law Rewrite Project. Instead, this is taken from social security law. It must be read with the exemptions in regs 9 and 19, and the general principles of income tax.

The effect of the narrow point in reg.8 with the various exemptions is to exclude most forms of income that students receive (other than earnings).

The award of student grants is now a devolved function, and differing rules now apply in the four countries of the UK. Only parts of the various forms of grant are included as student income, and most students' grants will be excluded. The equivalent income tax rules (in s.776 of ITTOIA) exempt most forms of scholarship income, subject to anti-avoidance provisions, on the principle that such income is a gift or grant, not taxable income. Interest on the reimbursement of student loan income is also exempt (s.753 of ITTOIA). (HMRC monitor this as it is the authority responsible for collecting repayments of student grants through earnings.) Reg.9 applies these provisions to tax credit calculations.

Two other sources of student "income", in the widest sense, are or may be exempt from inclusion under general principles: loans and gifts. The extent to which this is so illustrates the difference between the means-tested benefits approach to assessing a claimant's income, and the rules for calculating tax credits income.

The question of the status of loans was discussed by the Court of Appeal at some length in *Morrell v Secretary of State for Work and Pensions* [2003] EWCA Civ 526. A claimant for income support had been receiving regular monthly sums from her mother by way of loan. Some of the money was paid by the mother to the claimant's landlord. The question was whether the sums were income for the purposes of income support. The Court of Appeal followed the recent decision of that Court in *Leeves v Chief Adjudication Officer* [1999] 1 E.L.R. 90. In that case the question was whether a student grant was to be treated as income for income support purposes. Potter L.J. adopted the submission for the claimant that "income" should be given its ordinary and natural meaning, and that money accruing in respect of which there was an obligation of immediate and equivalent repayment was not income. On the facts, the student grant for maintenance was income but immediately repayable debts were not. The grant was income until the demand for repayment was made, when it ceased to be income.

But a further question arises for tax credits purposes. The payments must not only have the quality of income, but must fall under one of the kinds of income being taken into account. The definition of "student income" in reg.8 does not cover these loans, nor gifts, even if they are recurring. The question is whether such loans or gifts are income within any of the other kinds of income in the regulations. We shall return to that at para.2.207.

(SI 2002/2006, reg.8) (as amended)

Further sources of income linked to education and training are exempt under the specific provisions listed in Table 6 of reg.19—items 4, 5, 6 and 7 are all relevant.

[¹Payments of income in connection with students to be disregarded for the purposes of regulation 3

9. Income which is exempt from income tax by virtue of section 753 or 776 of ITTOIA (which deal respectively with interest on the repayment of student loans and scholarship income) is disregarded in calculating a claimant's income under regulation 3.]

2.153

AMENDMENT

1. Tax Credits (Miscellaneous Amendments) Regulations 2006 (SI 2006/766), reg.13 (April 6, 2006).

GENERAL NOTE

This regulation is an exempting regulation only. See note to reg.8.

2.154

CHAPTER 7

Investment income

Investment income

10.—(1) In these Regulations, "investment income" means the gross amount of—
(a) any interest of money whether yearly or otherwise, or any annuity or other annual payment, whether such payment is payable within or out of the United Kingdom, either as a charge on any property of the person paying it by virtue of any deed or will or otherwise, or as a reservation out of it, or as a personal debt or obligation by virtue of any contract, or whether the payment is received and payable half-yearly or at any shorter or longer periods, but not including property income;
(b) any discounts on securities;
(c) any income from securities payable out of the public revenues of the United Kingdom or Northern Ireland;
(d) dividends and other distributions of a company resident in the United Kingdom and any tax credit associated with that payment; and
(e) any amount treated as forming part of the individual's income for the year for income tax purposes by virtue of [³Chapter 9 of Part 4 of ITTOIA disregarding section 535 (top slicing relief)].
This is subject to the following qualification.
(2) In calculating investment income, there shall be disregarded—
(a) any amount listed in column 1 of Table 4 to the extent shown in the corresponding entry in column 2;
(b) any amount listed in column 1 of Table 5 during the period shown in the corresponding entry in column 2;
(c) any income arising from savings certificates, and interest on tax reserve certificates, exempted from tax by [³section 692, 693 or 750 of ITTOIA] (savings certificates and tax reserve certificates);

2.155

Tax Credits (Definition and Calculation of Income) Regulations 2002

(d) the first £70 in any tax year of interest on deposits with National Savings and Investments, exempted from income tax by [³section 691 of ITTOIA (National Savings Bank ordinary account interest)];

(e) any payment to a claimant which does not form part of his income for the purposes of income tax by virtue of [³section 727 of ITTOIA (certain annual payments by individuals).]

Table 4. Payments disregarded in the calculation of investment income

2.156

1. Description of income to be disregarded	2. Extent of disregard
1. Any interest, dividends, distributions, profits or gains in respect of investments under— (a) a Personal Equity Plan; or (b) an Individual Savings Account; in respect of which the claimant is entitled to relief from income tax under [³Chapter 3 of Part 6 of ITTOIA] or which is taxed only in accordance with regulation 23 of the Individual Savings Account Regulations 1998.	The whole amount, unless it is interest under a personal equity plan to which regulation 17A(2) of the Personal Equity Plan Regulations 1989 applies. Interest to which that paragraph applies is disregarded only to the extent that it does not exceed the annual limit of £180 mentioned in that regulation.
2. [³. . .]	[³. . .]
[³**3.** Any interest payable under a certified SAYE savings arrangement for the purposes of Chapter 4 of Part 6 of ITTOIA.]	The whole amount.
4. Any winnings from betting, including pool betting, or lotteries or games with prizes.	The whole amount.
5. Any interest on a payment of £10,000 made by the Secretary of State to a person who was held prisoner by the Japanese during the Second World War or to the spouse of such a person, if the payment is held in a distinct account and no payment (other than interest) has been added to the account.	The whole amount of the interest.

(SI 2002/2006, reg.10) (as amended)

1. Description of income to be disregarded	2. Extent of disregard
6. Any interest on a payment made to the claimant by, or on behalf, of a government of country outside the United Kingdom, either from its own resources or with contributions from any other organisation, by way of compensation for a victim of National Socialism if the payment is held in a distinct account and no payment (other than interest) has been added to the account. Here a reference to a victim of National Socialism is a reference to a person who was required to work as a slave or a forced labourer for National Socialists or their sympathisers during the Second World War, or suffered property loss, or suffered injury or is the parent of a child who died, at the hands of National Socialists or their sympathisers during the Second World War.	The whole amount of the interest.
7. Any monies paid to the claimant by a bank or building society as compensation in respect of an unclaimed account held by a Holocaust victim and which vested in the Custodian of Enemy Property under section 7 of the Trading with the Enemy Act 1939 and treated as exempt from income tax by [4section 756A of ITTOIA]	The amount [4of interest exempted from income tax under section 756A of ITTOIA.]

8. Any interest, or payment [3. . .], which is disregarded for income tax purposes by virtue of—
    [3(a) section 751 of ITTOIA (interest on damages for personal injury),or]
    (b) [3section 731 of ITTOIA (periodical
	The amount so disregarded.

431

Tax Credits (Definition and Calculation of Income) Regulations 2002

1. Description of income to be disregarded	2. Extent of disregard
payments of personal injury damages)] (personal injury damages in the form of periodical payments).	
[¹9]. Annuity payments under an award of compensation made under the Criminal Injuries Compensation Scheme (within the meaning of [³section 732(3) of ITTOIA].	The amount of any payment which is treated as not being income of the claimant or his partner by virtue of [³section 731 of ITTOIA.]
[¹10]. A payment under a life annuity.	The amount of interest eligible for relief under section 353 of the Taxes Act by virtue of section 365 of that Act.
[¹11]. Any interest, or payment in respect of interest, which is compensation to a person who is under the age of 18 years for the death of one or both of his parents.	The whole of the interest or payment.
12. A purchased life annuity to which [³Chapter 7 of Part 4 of ITTOIA] applies.	[³The amount exempted under section 717 of ITTOIA as calculated under section 719 of that Act.]
[³ 13. Any payments which are exempt from Income tax by virtue of— (a) section 725 of ITTOIA (annual payments under immediate needs annuities), or (b) section 735 of ITTOIA (health and employment insurance payments).]	The whole amount.

(SI 2002/2006, reg.10) (as amended)

Table 5. Payments in connection with very severe disablement, Creutzfeldt–Jakob disease and haemophilia

1. Description of income to be disregarded	2. Applicable period
1. A trust payment made to— (a) a diagnosed person; (b) the diagnosed person's partner; or (c) the person who was his partner at the date of his death.	The period beginning on the date on which the trust payment is made and ending with the death of the person to whom the payment is made.
2. A trust payment made to a parent of a deceased diagnosed person, or a person acting in the place of his parent.	The period beginning on the date on which the trust payment is made and ending two years after that date.
3. The amount of any payment out of the estate of a person to whom a trust payment has been made, which is made to the person who was the diagnosed person's partner at the date of his death.	The period beginning on the date on which the payment is made and ending on the date on which that person dies.
4. The amount of any payment out of the estate of a person to whom a trust payment has been made, which is made to a parent of a deceased diagnosed person, or a person acting in the place of his parent.	The period beginning on the date on which the payment is made and ending two years after that date.

(3) The amounts disregarded under Items 3 and 4 in Table 5 shall not exceed the total amount of any trust payments made to the person to whom the trust payment had been made.

(4) In this regulation, "diagnosed person" means—
(a) a person who has been diagnosed as suffering from, or who after his death has been diagnosed has having suffered from, variant Creutzfeldt–Jakob disease;
(b) a person who is suffering or has suffered from haemophilia; or
(c) a person in respect of whom a payment has been made from the 1992 Fund, the Eileen Trust or the Independent Living Funds; and a reference to a person being a member of the diagnosed person's household at the date of the diagnosed person's death includes a person who would have been a member of his household but for the diagnosed person being in residential accommodation, a residential care home or a nursing home on that date.

(5) In this regulation—

"relevant trust" means—
(a) a trust established out of funds provided by the Secretary of State in respect of persons who suffered, or who are suffering, from variant Creutzfeldt–Jakob disease for the benefit of persons eligible for payments in accordance with its provisions;
(b) the Macfarlane Trusts; or
(c) the 1992 Fund, the Eileen Trust or the Independent Living Funds.

"residential accommodation", "residential care home" and "nursing home" have the meanings given by regulation 2(1) of the Income Support (General) Regulations 1987; and

"trust payment" means a payment under a relevant trust.

AMENDMENTS

1. Tax Credits (Definition and Calculation of Income) (Amendment) Regulations 2003 (SI 2003/732), reg.9 (April 6, 2003).
2. Tax Credits (Miscellaneous Amendments No.2) Regulations 2003 (SI 2003/2815), reg.8 (November 26, 2003).
3. Tax Credits (Miscellaneous Amendments) Regulations 2006 (SI 2006/766), reg.14 (April 6, 2006).
4. Tax Credits (Miscellaneous Amendments) Regulations 2007 (SI 2007/824), reg.12 (April 6, 2007).

GENERAL NOTE

2.158 This regulation was drafted ahead of, and anticipated, the relevant provisions of ITTOIA. But there were some changes to the Rewrite Bill after this regulation was brought into force, including the retitling of the relevant part of ITTOIA to cover "Savings and investment income". That accurately reflects the scope of this regulation. It completely reshapes the relevant provisions in the previous income tax legislation and, more than any other part of the Rewrite Acts, should be considered in the new form and not as a continuation of old history.

The relevant provisions in ITTOIA are in Pt 4, which has the following structure:

Chapter 1	Introduction
Chapter 2	Interest
Chapter 3	Dividends from UK resident companies
Chapter 4	Dividends from non-UK resident companies
Chapter 5	Stock dividends from UK resident companies
Chapter 6	Release of loan to participator in close company
Chapter 7	Purchased life annuity payments
Chapter 8	Profits from deeply discounted securities
Chapter 9	Gains from contracts for life assurance
Chapter 10	Distributions from unauthorised unit trusts
Chapter 11	Transactions in deposits
Chapter 12	Disposals of futures and options involving guaranteed Returns
Chapter 13	Sales of foreign dividend coupons.

Most of these chapters contain provisions designed to prevent avoidance, in particular by turning income into capital by one means or another. But by bringing them all together the overall picture is now far clearer than it was before ITTOIA in that the full pattern of the scope of the income tax charges on forms of income from savings and investments can be seen from this list.

But reg.10 retains, at least for the time being, much of the flavour of the previous law, its wording still coming from the former s.18 of the Income and Corporation Taxes Act 1988.

(SI 2002/2006, reg.10) (as amended)

Income from savings and investments is included in the calculation of income for tax credits purposes no account is taken of capital when someone claims a tax credit under the 2002 Act. In practice, however, some of the most popular forms of savings are shielded from an income tax charge, and assessment to tax credits, by the very important disregards listed out in Table 4. Interest and dividends received from saving held within an ISA (individual savings account) are protected not only from income tax but also tax credits assessment by item 1. Interest and bonuses paid under SAYE schemes (save as you earn) are protected by item 3. But interest on ordinary deposits with banks or building societies is taxable (subject to deduction of income tax at source).

Because reg.10 follows the former law, and not the present income tax law, express provision has been made to remove winnings from betting and lotteries. This is not an exemption but rather a limitation set by case law on the previous legislation. [Winnings were excluded to stop losses being claimed.]

CHAPTER 8

Property income

Property income

11.—(1) In these Regulations, "property income" means the annual taxable profits arising from a business carried on for the exploitation, as a source of rents or other receipts, of any estate, interest or rights in or over land in the United Kingdom.

Expressions which are used in this paragraph which are defined in [² Part 3 of ITTOIA] for the purposes of [² that Part] bear the same meaning here as they bear in [² that Part].

This paragraph is subject to the following [¹qualifications].

[² (2) In calculating property income there shall be disregarded any profits—
  (a) treated as nil by section 791 to 794 of ITTOIA (full rent-a-room relief); or
  (b) excluded from profits by section 795 to 798 of ITTOIA (alternative calculation of profits if amount exceeds limit).]

[¹(3) [² Where a property business (as defined in Part 3 of ITTOIA] makes a loss to which the relief provisions of section 379A of the Taxes Act apply, then such relief as may arise under subsection (1) of that section shall be applied in calculating property income for the purposes of this regulation.]

2.159

AMENDMENTS

1. Tax Credits (Miscellaneous Amendments No.2) Regulations 2003 (SI 2003/2815), reg.9 (November 26, 2003).
2. Tax Credits (Miscellaneous Amendments) Regulations 2006 (SI 2006/766), reg.15 (April 6, 2006).

GENERAL NOTE

This regulation reflects Pt 3 of ITTOIA under the same heading. However, the label is perhaps the least helpful of the new titles created by the Tax Law Rewrite Project. Part 3 and this regulation are limited to real property, and do not apply to any other kind of property. But it was thought better to avoid referring to income from land because the drafters wished to use popular terms and avoid legal complications.

2.160

Tax Credits (Definition and Calculation of Income) Regulations 2002

The rules in Pt 3 remove another distinction in the former income tax law. Because taxation of income from land is usually sourced-based—that is, taxed where the land it—different rules used to apply to income from land in the UK and income received in the UK from land elsewhere. That distinction has now largely been removed in ITTOIA. But it has not been removed for tax credits purposes. Following the pattern of the old law, income from foreign land is foreign income within reg.12. In income tax practice, double taxation agreements normally reserve the taxation of income from land to the state where the land is, exempting it—or providing relief—elsewhere. But that does not apply for tax credits purposes. So someone who has, say, an apartment in Spain which is let for part of the year may not pay any UK income tax on the rent, but should have it taken into account for tax credits purposes under reg.12 alongside any income from UK land brought within reg.11.

CHAPTER 9

Foreign income

2.161
12.—(1) In these Regulations, "foreign income" means income arising, in the year in question, from [³a source outside the United Kingdom or from foreign holdings] which are not—
  (a) employment income;
  (b) trading income; or
  (c) investment income falling within regulation 10(1)(e).
This is subject to the following provisions of this regulation.
  [³(2) The reference in paragraph (1) to "foreign holdings" shall be construed in accordance with section 571 of ITTOIA.]
  (3) In calculating the claimant's foreign income there shall be disregarded—
  (a) any payment by way of an annuity or pension payable under any special provision for victims of National Socialist persecution which is made by the law of the Federal Republic of Germany, or any part of it, or of Austria;
  [⁴(aa) any monies paid by a bank or building society which are exempted from income tax under section 756A of ITTOIA (interest on certain deposits of victims of National-Socialist persecution).]
  [³(b) the amount authorised to be deducted by the relevant provision if the claimant's foreign income comprises or includes a pension to which the following provisions of ITEPA apply—
    (i) sections 567(5) and 617 (deduction allowed for taxable pension income);
    (ii) section 575(2) (taxable pension income: foreign pensions);
    (iii) section 613(3) (taxable pension income: foreign annuities); and
    (iv) section 635(3) (taxable pension income: foreign voluntary annual payments); and]
  (c) any amount which would be disregarded for the purposes of income tax by virtue of—
    (i) Extra Statutory Concession A10 (lumps sums paid by overseas pension schemes);
    (ii) [¹s.681 of ITEPA];
    (iii) [³section 751(1)(c) of ITTOIA] (interest on damages for personal injuries awarded by a foreign court); or

436

(SI 2002/2006, reg.12) (as amended)

    (iv) Extra Statutory Concession A44 (education allowances payable to public officials of overseas territories); [³or

    (v) section 730 of ITTOIA (foreign maintenance payments)].

[²(4) Where an overseas property business ;[³(within the meaning of Part 3 of ITTOIA)] makes a loss to which the relief provisions of section 379A of the Taxes Act apply, by virtue of section 379B of that Act, then such relief as may arise under section 379A(1) shall be applied in calculating foreign income for the purposes of this regulation.]

AMENDMENTS

1. Tax Credits (Definition and Calculation of Income) (Amendment) Regulations 2003 (SI 2003/732), reg.10 (April 6, 2003).
2. Tax Credits (Miscellaneous Amendments No.2) Regulations 2003 (SI 2003/2815), reg.10 (November 26, 2003).
3. Tax Credits (Miscellaneous Amendments) Regulations 2006 (SI 2006/766), reg.16 (April 6, 2006).
4. Tax Credits (Miscellaneous Amendments) Regulations 2007 (SI 2007/824), reg.13 (April 6, 2007).

GENERAL NOTE

The provisions in reg.3 above ensure that all forms of the foreign income of a tax credits claimant are potentially relevant to the calculation of income for tax credits purposes even if they would be exempt from income tax in the United Kingdom. "Foreign income" is not a specific head of charge for income tax purposes. And in practice most problems are dealt with not under the United Kingdom legislation but under the terms of the relevant double tax agreements. That approach and those agreements do not apply for tax credits purposes, so there is need to make express provision instead.

This regulation, as amended from 2006, provides for all foreign income charged to income tax to be relevant for tax credits save for specific exemptions. It also provides for the priorities between competing charges that arise, for example, where income is both foreign income and employment income, to prevent a double charge. The combination of exemptions and rules giving priority to other heads of assessment result in this head of charge still being of limited importance. But note that this provision will apply to some kinds of foreign pension and foreign savings or investment income.

"Foreign holdings" is defined in s.571 of ITTOIA as meaning shares and other securities outside the UK that are issued by a government or public authority of another country or by or on behalf of a body of persons not resident in the UK.

2.162

CHAPTER 10

Notional Income

Introduction

13. In these Regulations, "notional income" means income which, by virtue of regulations 14 to 17 a claimant is treated as having, but which he does not in fact have.

2.163

GENERAL NOTE

This regulation emphasises that the provisions of regs 14–17 are not parallels to income tax in the ordinary sense, in that the income is not in fact income of the

2.164

Tax Credits (Definition and Calculation of Income) Regulations 2002

claimant (or any of the joint claimants). It may, as the notes to the following regulations show, be the income of someone else.

This, and the regulations that follow, are a good example of the much clearer drafting style now adopted by HMRC as compared with the former concentrated style of regulations. In particular, regs 15–17 between them cover only part of what used to be reg.26 of the Family Credit (General) Regulations 1987 (SI 1987/1973). The pattern adopted is to include as income, in reg.14, sums treated as income by reference to selected anti-avoidance provisions. Regulations 15–17 then continue the treatment as income of other sums that were so treated under the Family Credit (General) Regulations 1987.

Claimants treated for any purpose as having income by virtue of the Income Tax Acts

2.165 **14.**—(1) If an amount is treated for any purpose as the claimant's income under any provision mentioned in paragraph (2), he is to be treated as having that amount of income.

(2) The provisions mentioned in paragraph (1) are—
(a) the following provisions of the Taxes Act—
[¹. . .];
   (ix) section 714 (transfers of securities: treatment of deemed sums and reliefs) or 716 (transfer of unrealised interest);
   (x) section 730 (transfer of income arising from securities);
   (xi) section 730A (treatment of price differential on sale and repurchase of securities;
   (xii) section 739 (prevention of avoidance of income tax);
   (xiii) section 740 (liability of non-transferors);
   (xiv) section 761 (charge to income tax of offshore income gain); and
   (xv) section 776 (transactions in land: taxation of chargeable gains); and
[¹(b) the following provisions of ITTOIA—
   (i) sections 277 to 283 (amounts treated as receipts: leases);
   (ii) Chapter 5 of Part 4 (stock dividends from UK resident companies);
   (iii) Chapter 6 of Part 4 (release of loan to participator in close company);
   (iv) section 427 (charge to tax on profits from deeply discounted securities);
   (v) Chapter 11 of Part 4 (transactions in securities);
   (vi) sections 624 to 628 (income treated as income of settlor: retained interests);
   (vii) sections 629 to 632 (income treated as income of settlor: unmarried children);
   (viii) section 633 (capital sums paid to settlor by trustees of settlement);
   (ix) section 641 (capital sums paid to settlor by body connected with settlement);
   (x) section 652 (estate income: absolute interests in residue); and
   (xi) sections 654 to 655 (estate income: interests in residue);
(c) section 84 and Schedule 15 to the Finance Act 2004 (charge to income tax by reference to enjoyment of property previously owned).]

438

(SI 2002/2006, reg.14) (as amended)

AMENDMENT

1. Tax Credits (Miscellaneous Amendments) Regulations 2006 (SI 2006/766), reg.17 (April 6, 2006).

GENERAL NOTE

This regulation has been rewritten substantially with effect from the 2006–07 income tax year, but its contents remains broadly the same. It collects together a series of important income tax anti-avoidance provisions and includes them together as providing "notional income" for step 1 of the calculation of income for tax credits purposes under reg.3(1).

Note that this regulation is worded so that the assessment for tax credit purposes depends on self-assessment or an assessment for income tax purposes. A claimant who is treated as having an amount of any of these kinds of income for income tax purposes is treated as having that amount of income for the purposes of this regulation. It may therefore be assumed, it is suggested, that the issue will not arise for tax credits purposes unless it has already been identified for income tax purposes.

The regulation collects together both well-known and less well-known anti-avoidance provisions. The newest, in para.(2)(c), attracted considerable attention when enacted. It is the provision that deems someone who has given her or his property away (usually for inheritance tax purposes) but who continues to have a right to reside in the property to be in receipt of income and so liable to income tax on (broadly) the rent that could have been received from the property. That also applies for a tax credit assessment.

2.166

Claimants depriving themselves of income in order to secure entitlement

15. If a claimant has deprived himself of income for the purpose of securing entitlement to, or increasing the amount of, a tax credit, he is treated as having that income.

2.167

GENERAL NOTE

This is equivalent to Income Support (General) Regulations 1987 (SI 1987/1967), reg.42(1), and the note on that in Vol.II in this series should be consulted. Note, however, that this provision is defined by reference to deprivation for the purposes of securing or increasing entitlement to tax credits (and not, for example, income support). TCTM04920 gives the example of someone who transfers entitlement to an occupational pension to someone else by deed of gift. Without reference to authority, it emphasises that securing or increasing entitlement to tax credit may not be a claimant's main motive but it must be a significant one. That is a question of fact.

2.168

Claimants to whom income becomes available upon the making of a claim

16.—(1) If income would become available to a claimant upon the making of an application for that income, he is treated as having that income.
This is subject to the following qualification.
(2) Paragraph (1) does not apply in relation to income—
(a) under a trust derived from a payment made in consequence of a personal injury;
(b) under a personal pension scheme or retirement annuity contract;
(c) consisting in a sum to which Item 8 of Table 4 in regulation 10 refers (compensation for personal injuries which is administered by the Court); or

2.169

Tax Credits (Definition and Calculation of Income) Regulations 2002

(d) consisting in a rehabilitation allowance made under section 2 of the Employment Act.

[¹(3) Paragraph (1) also does not apply to income by way of—
 (a) a Category A or Category B retirement pension,
 (b) a graduated retirement benefit, or
 (c) a shared additional pension,
payment of which has been deferred.

Here—

"Category A retirement pension" means a pension to which a person is entitled by virtue of section 44 of the Contributions and Benefits Act or the Northern Ireland Contributions and Benefits Act;

"Category B retirement pension" means a pension to which a person is entitled by virtue of any of sections 48A to 48C of the Contributions and Benefits Act or sections 48A to 48C of the Northern Ireland Contributions and Benefits Act;

"graduated retirement benefit" means a pension payable under –
 (a) sections 36 and 37 of the National Insurance Act 1965; or
 (b) sections 35 and 36 of the National Insurance Act (Northern Ireland) 1966; and

"shared additional pension" means a pension to which a person is entitled by virtue of section 55A of the Contributions and Benefits Act or section 55A of the Northern Ireland Contributions and Benefits Act.]

AMENDMENT

1. Tax Credits (Miscellaneous Amendments) Regulations 2004 (SI 2004/762), reg.15 (April 6, 2004).

DEFINITIONS

"Category A retirement pension"—see para.(3).
"Category B retirement pension"—see *ibid*.
"graduated retirement benefit"—see *ibid*.
"shared additional pension"—see *ibid*.

GENERAL NOTE

2.170   See the note to the similar provision in Income Support (General) Regulations 1987 (SI 1987/1967), reg.42(2)–(4). The precise operative scope of this provision is not clear. For income support, sums not received may not count as earnings or other income. But most of the charges to income tax, as noted above, are on those "receiving or entitled to". So entitlement is enough to bring the sums in both for income tax purposes and tax credit purposes, even if they are not received. This regulation could, however, extend that to cover sums to which entitlement had not arisen, for example because no demand had been made for the sum under a contractual entitlement operative on such demand.

Claimants providing services to other persons for less than full earnings

2.171   **17.**—(1) If a claimant provides a service for another person and—
 (a) the other person makes no payment of earnings or pays less than those paid for a comparable employment (including self-employment) in the area; and
 (b) the Board are satisfied that the means of the other person are sufficient for him to pay for, or to pay more for, the service,

(SI 2002/2006, reg.17) (as amended)

the claimant is to be treated as having such an amount of employment income, or in the case of a service provided in the course of a trade or business, such an amount of trading income as is reasonable for the employment of the claimant to provide the service.

This is subject to the following qualification.

(2) Paragraph (1) does not apply where—
(a) the claimant is a volunteer or is engaged to provide the service by a charitable or voluntary organisation and the Board are satisfied that it is reasonable for the claimant to provide the service free of charge; or
(b) the service is provided in connection with the claimant's participation in an employment or training programme—
 (i) in Great Britain in accordance with regulation 19(1)(q) of the Jobseeker's Allowance Regulations 1996 other than where it is provided in connection with the claimant's participation in the Intensive Activity period specified in regulation 75(1)(a)(iv) of those Regulations; or
 (ii) in Northern Ireland in accordance with regulation 19(1)(p) of the Jobseeker's Allowance Regulations (Northern Ireland) 1996 other than where it is provided in connection with the claimant's participation in the Preparation for Employment Programme specified in regulation 75(1)(a)(v) of those Regulations.

GENERAL NOTE

See the note in Vol.II in this series to the similar (though differently drafted) provision in Income Support (General) Regulations 1987 (SI 1987/1967), reg.42(6).

2.172

CHAPTER 11

Miscellaneous income

Miscellaneous income

18. In these Regulations, "miscellaneous income" means income which does not fall within any other provision of these Regulations and which is subject to income tax under [¹ Part 5 of ITTOIA].

2.173

AMENDMENT

1. Tax Credits (Miscellaneous Amendments) Regulations 2006 (SI 2006/766), reg.18 (April 6, 2006).

GENERAL NOTE

Part 5 of ITTOIA contains the "sweeper" provisions to bring within liability to income tax any forms of income that fall outside the specific charges to income tax. If, therefore, something can properly be regarded as employment income, trading income, savings and investment income, pension income, social security income or some other more specific form of income, then this provision does not apply. But it is not a "catch-all", and there is no global definition of "income" in United Kingdom income tax legislation.

Part 5 applies to "annual profits or gains" not otherwise charged to tax. It does not catch gifts or loans, nor does it catch single "one-off" payments unless they are

2.174

Tax Credits (Definition and Calculation of Income) Regulations 2002

of a trading or business nature. Nor does it catch receipts of capital sums, which in tax terms fall to be taxed under the Taxation of Chargeable Gains Act 2001, if at all. See the note to reg.6.

PART III

Sums disregarded in the calculation of income

General disregards in the calculation of income

2.175   **19.**—(1) For the purposes of regulation 3—
(a) the sums specified in Table 6 are disregarded in the calculation of income;
(b) the sums specified in column 1 of Table 7 are disregarded in the calculation of income if the condition in the corresponding entry in column 2 of that Table is satisfied; and
(c) the sums specified in column 1 of Table 8 are disregarded in the calculation of income to the extent specified in the corresponding entry in column 2 of that Table.
(2) In this regulation—
"the JSA Regulations" means the Jobseeker's Allowance Regulations 1996; and
"the JSA (NI) Regulations" means the Jobseeker's Allowance (Northern Ireland) Regulations 1996.

Table 6. Sums disregarded in the calculation of income

2.176

1. Any payment of an employment credit under a scheme under section 2(2) of the Employment Act known as "New Deal 50 Plus" or the corresponding scheme under section 1 of the Employment and Training Act (Northern Ireland) 1950.
2. Any payment made— (a) under section 15 of the Disabled Persons (Employment Act) 1944 or section 15 of the Disabled Persons (Employment) Act (Northern Ireland) 1945; or (b) in accordance with arrangements made under section 2 of the Employment Act or section 1 of the Employment and Training Act (Northern Ireland) 1950 to assist disabled persons to obtain or retain employment despite their disability.
3. Any mandatory top-up payment made pursuant to— (a) section 2 of the Employment Act [³ or section 1 of the Employment and Training Act (Northern Ireland) 1950] in respect of the claimant's participation in— (i) an employment programme specified in regulation 75(1)(a)(ii)(bb) of the JSA Regulations or regulation 75(1)(a)(ii) of the JSA (NI) Regulations (Voluntary Sector Option of the New Deal);

(SI 2002/2006, reg.19) (as amended)

        (ii) an employment programme specified in regulation 75(1)(a)(ii)(cc) of the JSA Regulations (Environmental Task Force Option of the New Deal) or regulation 75(1)(a)(iii) of the JSA (NI) Regulations; or
        (iii) the Intensive Activity Period of the New Deal Pilots for 25 Plus specified in regulation 75(1)(a)(iv) of the JSA Regulations or, in Northern Ireland, the Preparation for Employment Programme specified in regulation 75(1)(a)(v) of the JSA (NI) Regulations; or
  (b) a written arrangement entered into between—
        (i) the Secretary of State and the person who has arranged for the claimant's participation in the Intensive Activity Period of the New Deal for 25 Plus and which is made in respect of his participation in that Period; or
        (ii) the Department for Employment and Learning and the person who has arranged for the claimant's participation in the Preparation for Employment Programme and which is made in respect of the claimant's participation in the Programme.
[³This item applies only to the extent that the payment is not taxable as a profit of a trade, profession or vocation.]

---

4. Any discretionary payment pursuant to section 2 of the Employment Act, or, in Northern Ireland, section 1(1) of the Employment and Training Act (Northern Ireland) 1950 to meet, or help to meet, special needs in respect of the claimant's participation in the Full-Time Education and Training Option of the New Deal as specified in regulation 75(1)(b)(ii) of the JSA Regulations or of the JSA (NI) Regulations.

---

5. Any—
  (a) education maintenance allowance in accordance with regulations made under section 518 of the Education Act 1996 (payment of school expenses; grant of scholarships, etc.); or
  (b) payment (not within sub-paragraph (a)) in respect of a course of study attended by a child or qualifying young person payable—
        (i) in accordance with regulations made under section 518 of the Education (Scotland) Act 1980 (power to assist persons to take advantage of educational facilities) or section 12(2)(c) of the Further and Higher Education (Scotland) Act 1992 (provision of financial assistance to students); or
        (ii) by virtue of regulations made in Article 50, 51 or 55(1) of the Education and Libraries (Northern Ireland) Order 1986 (provisions to assist persons to take advantage of educational facilities).

---

6. Any payment made by an employment zone contractor payable in respect of the claimant's participation in the employment zone programme by way of—
  (a) a training premium;
  (b) a discretionary payment, being a fee, grant, loan or otherwise; or
  (c) any arrears of subsistence allowance paid as a lump sum.

---

7. [³. . .]

Tax Credits (Definition and Calculation of Income) Regulations 2002

8. An amount of income equal to any qualifying maintenance payment within section 347B of the Taxes Act.
[²**9.** Any payment by way of foster care receipts to the extent that those receipts qualify for relief under [⁴ Chapter 2 of Part 7 to ITTOIA].]
10. Any payment of maintenance, whether under a court order or not, which is made or due to be made by— (a) the claimant's former partner, or the claimant's partner's former partner; or (b) the parent of a child or qualifying young person where that child or qualifying young person is a member of the claimant's household except where that parent is the claimant or the claimant's partner.
11. Any payment in respect of a child or qualifying young person who is a member of the claimant's household made— [²(a) to adopters which is exempt from income tax by virtue of [⁴ sections 744 to 746 of ITTOIA];] (b) by a local authority in pursuance of paragraph 15(1) of Schedule 1 to the Children Act 1989 (local authority contribution to child's maintenance); [³(bb) by a local authority by way of special guardianship support services pursuant to regulations under section 14F(1)(b) of the Children Act 1989; or] (c) by an authority, as defined in Article 2 of the Children (Northern Ireland) Order 1995, in pursuance of Article 15 of, and paragraph 17 of Schedule 1 to, that Order (contribution by an authority to child's maintenance).
12. Any payment in respect of travelling expenses— (a) in relation to England and Wales, under regulation 3, 5 or 8 of the National Health Service (Travelling Expenses and Remission of Charges) Regulations 1988; (b) in relation to Scotland, under regulation 3, 5 or 8 of the National Health Service (Travelling Expenses and Remission of Charges) (Scotland) Regulations 1988; (c) in relation to Northern Ireland under regulation 3, 5 or 8 of the Travelling Expenses and Remission of Charges Regulations (Northern Ireland) 1989; or (d) made by the Secretary of State for Health, the Scottish Ministers, the Secretary of State for Wales, or the Department of Health, Personal Social Services and Public Safety and which is analogous to a payment specified in paragraph (a), (b) or (c).
13. Any payment made by the Secretary of State or the Scottish Ministers under a scheme established to assist relatives and other persons to visit persons in custody.
[²**14.** Any payment under the Community Care (Direct Payments) Act 1996, section 57 of the Health and Social Care Act 2001, section 12B of the Social Work (Scotland) Act 1968, Article 15A of the Health and Personal Social Services (Direct Payments) (Northern Ireland) Order

(SI 2002/2006, reg.19) (as amended)

1996 or section 8 of the Carers and Direct Payments Act (Northern Ireland) 2002.]
[¹**14A.** Any payment made under the "Supporting People" programme— (a) in England and Wales, under section 93 of the Local Government Act 2000; (b) in Scotland, under section 91 of the Housing (Scotland) Act 2001; or (c) in Northern Ireland, under Article 4 of the Housing Support Services (Northern Ireland) Order 2002.]
15. [¹Any payment or a voucher] provided under section 95 or 98 of the Immigration and Asylum Act 1999 for any former asylum-seeker or his dependants.
16. Any payment of a provident benefit by a trade union. Here— "provident benefit" has the meaning given in section 467(2) of the Taxes Act; and "trade union" has the meaning given in section 467(4) of the Taxes Act.

Table 7. Sums disregarded in calculating income if conditions are satisfied

1. Description of payment	*2. [³Conditions] that must be satisfied*
1. Any payment in respect of any expenses incurred by a claimant who is engaged by a charitable or voluntary organisation or is a volunteer.	The claimant does not receive remuneration or profit from the engagement and is not treated as possessing any employment income under regulation 17 in respect of that engagement.
2. A payment by way of— (a) travelling expenses reimbursed to the claimant; (b) a living away from home allowance under section 2(2)(d) of the Employment Act, section 2(4)(c) of the Enterprise and New Towns (Scotland) Act 1990 or section 1 of the Employment and Training Act (Northern Ireland) 1950; (c) training grant; or	The claimant— (a) participates in arrangements for training made under— (i) section 2 of the Employment Act; (ii) section 2 of the Enterprise and New Towns (Scotland) Act 1990; or (iii) section 1 of the Employment and Training Act (Northern Ireland) 1950; or

2.177

Tax Credits (Definition and Calculation of Income) Regulations 2002

1. Description of payment	*2. [³ Conditions] that must be satisfied*
(d) childcare expenses reimbursed to the claimant in respect of his participation in— (i) a New Deal option; (ii) the Intensive Activity Period of the New Deal Pilots for 25 Plus; or (iii) the Preparation for Employment Programme.	(b) attends a course at an employment rehabilitation centre established under section 2 of the Employment Act. [³The payment is not taxable as a profit of a trade, profession or vocation.]

Table 8. Sums partly disregarded in the calculation of income

2.178

Type of payment to be disregarded	*Limit on, or exception to, the extent of disregard*
1. Any discretionary payment made pursuant to section 2 of the Employment Act, or, in Northern Ireland, section 1(1) of the Employment and Training Act (Northern Ireland) 1950 to meet, or help meet, the claimant's special needs in undertaking a qualifying course within the meaning of regulation 17A(7) of the JSA Regulations or regulation 17A(7) of the JSA (NI) Regulations.	A payment is not within this item to the extent that it relates to travel expenses incurred as a result of the claimant's attendance on the course if an amount in respect of those expenses has already been disregarded pursuant to regulation 8.
2. Any payment made in respect of a career development loan paid pursuant to section 2 of the Employment Act.	A payment is not within this item to the extent that the loan has been applied for or paid in respect of living expenses for the period of education and training supported by the loan.
3. Any payment made to the claimant or his partner in respect of a person who is not normally a member of the claimant's household but is temporarily in his care, by— (a) a health authority; (b) a local authority;	A payment is only to be disregarded by virtue of this item if [¹(a)] any profits[⁴. . .] arising from the payment mentioned in col.1 are treated as nil by [⁴ section 791 to 794 of ITTOIA (full rent-a-room relief)]; or

446

(SI 2002/2006, reg.19) (as amended)

Type of payment to be disregarded	Limit on, or exception to, the extent of disregard
(c) a voluntary organisation; (d) that person pursuant to section 26(3A) of the National Assistance Act 1948; (e) a primary care trust established under section 16A of the National Health Service Act 1977.	[¹(b) excluded from profits [⁴by section 795 to 798 of ITTOIA (alternative calculation of profits if amount exceeds limit).]
4. Any payment made in Northern Ireland to the claimant or his partner in respect of a person who is not normally a member of the claimant's household but is temporarily in his care— (a) pursuant to Article 36(7) of the Health and Personal Social Services (Northern Ireland) Order 1972 by an authority; a voluntary organisation; or the person concerned; or (b) by a training school within the meaning of section 137 of the Children and Young Persons Act (Northern Ireland) 1968. In this item "an authority" has the meaning given by Article 2 of the Children (Northern Ireland) Order 1995.	A payment is only to be disregarded by virtue of this item if— [¹(a)] any profits [⁴. . .] arising from the payment mentioned in column 1 are treated as nil by [⁴ section 791 to 794 of ITTOIA (full rent-a-room relief)]; or [¹(b) excluded from profits [⁴by section 795 to 798 of ITTOIA (alternative calculation of profits if amount exceeds limit).]
5. Any payment under an insurance policy taken out to insure against the risk of being unable to maintain the repayments— (a) on a loan which is secured on the dwelling house which the claimant occupies as his home; or	A payment is only to be disregarded by virtue of this item to the extent that it is used to— (a) maintain the repayments referred to in col.(1); and (b) meet any amount due by way of premiums on—

447

Tax Credits (Definition and Calculation of Income) Regulations 2002

Type of payment to be disregarded	Limit on, or exception to, the extent of disregard
(b) under a regulated agreement or under a hire-purchase agreement or a conditional sale agreement. For the purposes of paragraph (b)— "regulated agreement" has the meaning given in the Consumer Credit Act 1974; and "hire-purchase agreement" and "conditional sale agreement" have the meanings given in Part 3 of the Hire-Purchase Act 1964.	(i) that policy; or (ii) in a case to which paragraph (a) of this item applies, an insurance policy taken out to insure against loss or damage to any building or part of a building which is occupied by the claimant as his home and which is required as a condition of the loan referred to in column (1).
[¹6]. Any payment in respect of the claimant's attendance at court as a juror or witness.	This item applies only to the extent that the payment is not compensation for loss of earnings or for the loss of payment of social security income.
[¹7]. Any payment of a sports award except to the extent that it has been made in respect of living expenses.	For the purposes of this item "living expenses" does not include— (a) the cost of vitamins, minerals or other special dietary supplements intended to enhance the performance of the claimant in the sport in respect of which the award was made; or (b) accommodation costs incurred as a consequence of living away from home whilst training for, or competing in, the sport in respect of which the award was made.

(SI 2002/2006, reg.19) (as amended)

AMENDMENTS

1. Tax Credits (Definition and Calculation of Income) (Amendment) Regulations 2003 (SI 2003/732), reg.11 (April 6, 2003).
2. Tax Credits (Miscellaneous Amendments No.2) Regulations 2003 (SI 2003/2815), reg.11 (November 26, 2003).
3. Tax Credits (Miscellaneous Amendments) Regulations 2004 (SI 2004/762), reg.16 (April 6, 2004).
4. Tax Credits (Miscellaneous Amendments) Regulations 2006 (SI 2006/766), reg.19 (April 6, 2006).

CROSS-REFERENCES

| Taxes Act, s.347B | Qualifying maintenance payments |
| F(2)A 1992, Sch.10 | Furnished Accommodation |

GENERAL NOTE

This regulation adds to the exemptions and exceptions in regs 3 and 9 that apply generally to income. Exceptions, exemptions and deductions that are specific to one or more kinds of income, but not all kinds of income, are detailed under the specific regulations.

2.179

Table 6
This sets out the sums to be disregarded in total. For fuller notes, see the equivalent provisions to the similar items in Income Support (General) Regulations 1987 (SI 1987/1967), Sch.9 (in Vol.II in this series). Several of the provisions are wider than the equivalent provision in the Income Support (General) Regulations 1987 because these provisions also apply to Northern Ireland, while the Income Support (General) Regulations 1987 apply to Great Britain only.

2.180

Paragraph 1—see Sch.9, para.63.
Paragraph 2—see Sch.9, para.51.
Paragraph 3—see Sch.9, para.62.
Paragraph 4—see Sch.9, para.13.
Paragraph 5—see Sch.9, para.11.
Paragraph 6—see Sch.9, para.72.
Paragraph 7—this is redefined to cover post-training sums.
Para.8—this excludes all sums within the scope of Taxes Act, s.347B (certain periodic payments made by one party to a marriage or former marriage to the other party for the maintenance of the other party or their children under a court order or agreement).
Paragraph 9—see Sch.9, para.26.
Paragraph 10—this widens out the scope of para.8.
Paragraph 11—see Sch.9, para.25.
Paragraph 12—see Sch.9, para.48.
Paragraph 13—see Sch.9, para.50.
Paragraph 14—see Sch.9, para.58.
Paragraph 14A—this is a new provision.
Paragraph 15—this is specifically focussed on former asylum-seekers or dependants.
Paragraph 16—s.467 of the Taxes Act provides exemption from tax to trade unions that provide provident benefits to their members not exceeding £4,000 as a capital sum or £825 a year as an annuity during sickness, incapacity or old age, or after an accident, theft or death. The excludes the annuities from counting as income of claimants.

Tax Credits (Definition and Calculation of Income) Regulations 2002

However, there are some differences between the tax credit provisions and the income support provisions listed. For example, the disregard in para.11 in Table 6 omits to mention local authority payments in Scotland under ss.34(6) or 50 of the Children Act 1975, whereas these payments are included in the equivalent income support rule: see Income Support (General) Regulations 1987 (SI 1987/1967), Sch.9, para.25(1)(b)). This would suggest that such payments in Scotland are disregarded for income support purposes but not for tax credits assessments. Note that, so far as England and Wales is concerned, the Children Act 1975 was repealed by the Children Act 1989, but this did not extend to Scotland: Children Act 1989, s.108(11).

Table 7

2.181 For item 1 see also the Income Support (General) Regulations 1987 (SI 1987/1967), Sch.9 para.2. For Item 2, see Sch.9, para.13.

Table 8

2.182 The final table lists those disregards that apply to part only of a payment. Item 1 is to the same effect as Income Support (General) Regulations 1987 (SI 1987/1967), Sch.9, para.65. Item 2 is based on Sch.9, para.59. Item 3 is similar to Sch.9, para.27, but excepts from it any payments that are or would be protected from income tax under the rent-a-room provisions (see reg.11). Item 4 is the equivalent provision for Northern Ireland. Item 5 parallels Sch.9, paras 29 and 30ZA. Item 6 is the same as Sch.9, para.43. Item 7 is based on Sch.9, para.69.

Child Tax Credit Regulations 2002

(SI 2002/2007) (AS AMENDED)

Whereas a draft of this instrument, which contains the first regulations made under section 9 of the Tax Credits Act 2002 has been laid before, and approved by resolution of, each House of Parliament:

Now, therefore, the Treasury, in exercise of the powers conferred on them by sections 8, 9, 65 and 67 of the Tax Credits Act 2002, hereby make the following Regulations:

ARRANGEMENT OF REGULATIONS

2.183
1. Citation, commencement and effect.
2. Interpretation.
3. Circumstances in which a person is or is not responsible for a child or qualifying young person.
4. Period for which a person who attains the age of 16 remains a child.
5. Maximum age and prescribed conditions for a qualifying young person.
6. Entitlement to child tax credit after death of child or qualifying young person.
7. Determination of the maximum rate at which a person or persons may be entitled to child tax credit.
8. Prescribed conditions for a disabled or severely disabled child or qualifying young person.

(SI 2002/2007, reg. 1) (as amended)

Citation, commencement and effect

1. These Regulations may be cited as the Child Tax Credit Regulations 2002 and shall come into force—
- (a) for the purpose of enabling claims to be made, on 1st August 2002;
- (b) for the purpose of enabling awards to be made, on 1st January 2003; and
- (c) for all other purposes on 6th April 2003; and shall have effect for the tax year beginning on 6th April 2003 and subsequent tax years.

Interpretation

2.—(1) In these Regulations, unless the context otherwise requires—
"the Act" means the Tax Credits Act 2002;
"advanced education" means full-time education for the purposes of—
- (a) a course in preparation for a degree, a diploma of higher education, a higher national diploma, a higher national diploma or higher national certificate of Edexcel or the Scottish Qualifications Authority, or a teaching qualification; or
- (b) any other course which is of a standard above ordinary national diploma, a national diploma or national certificate of Edexcel [². . .], a general certificate of education (advanced level), [²or Scottish national qualifications at higher or advanced higher level];

[⁴"approved training" has the meaning given by regulation 1(3) of the Child Benefit (General) Regulations 2006;]
[¹"the Board" means the Commissioners [⁴for Her Majesty's Revenue and Customs];]
"the Careers Service" means—
- (a) in England and Wales, a person with whom the Secretary of State or the National Assembly of Wales has made arrangements under s.10(1) of the Employment Act, and a local education authority to whom the Secretary of State or the National Assembly of Wales has given a direction under section 10(2) of that Act;
- (b) in Scotland, a person with whom the Scottish Ministers have made arrangements under section 10(1) of the Employment Act and any education authority to which a direction has been given by the Scottish Ministers under section 10(2) of that Act; and
- (c) [¹. . .];

"child" means a person who has not attained the age of sixteen or who falls within the terms of regulation 4;
"claimant" has the meaning in section 9(8) of the Act, except in regulation 7, where that expression and "joint claimants" have the meanings given in regulation 7(1);
"the Connexions Service" means a person of any description with whom the Secretary of State has made an arrangement under section 114(2)(a) of the Learning and Skills Act 2000 and section 10(1) of the Employment Act, and any person to whom he has given a direction under section 114(2)(b) of the former Act and section 10(2) of the latter Act;
"the Contributions and Benefits Act" means the Social Security Contributions and Benefits Act 1992;
[³"couple" has the meaning given by section 3(5A) of the Act];
"custodial sentence"—
- (a) in England and Wales, has the meaning in section 76 of the Powers of Criminal Courts (Sentencing) Act 2000;

2.184

2.185

(b) in Scotland, means detention under a sentence imposed by a court under section 44, 205, 207 or 208 of the Criminal Procedure (Scotland) Act 1995; and
(c) in Northern Ireland, means a custodial sentence under the Criminal Justice (Children) (Northern Ireland) Order 1998;

"disability living allowance" means a disability living allowance under section 71 of the Contributions and Benefits Act;

"the Employment Act" means the Employment and Training Act 1973;

"the family element of child tax credit" and "the individual element of child tax credit" shall be construed in accordance with section 9(3) of the Act;

"joint claim" and "single claim" shall be construed in accordance with section 3(8) of the Act;

"looked after by a local authority" has the meaning in section 22 of the Children Act 1989, section 17(6) of the Children (Scotland) Act 1995 or (in Northern Ireland) Article 25 of the Children (Northern Ireland) Order 1995 (with the modification that for the reference to a local authority there is substituted a reference to an authority within the meaning in Article 2 of that Order);

the "main responsibility test" has the meaning given in rule 2.2. of regulation 3;

the "normally living with test" has the meaning given in rule 1.1. of regulation 3;

"Part I" means Part I of the Act;

"patient" means a person (other than a person who is serving a custodial sentence) who is regarded as receiving free in-patient treatment within the meaning of the Social Security (Hospital In-patients) Regulations 1975, or the Social Security (Hospital In-patients) Regulations (Northern Ireland) 1975;

"placing for adoption" means placing for adoption in accordance with the Adoption Agencies Regulations 1983, the Adoption Agencies (Scotland) Regulations 1984 or the Adoption Agencies Regulations (Northern Ireland) 1989;

"qualifying young person" means a person, other than a child, who—
(a) has not attained the age of [4twenty]; and
(b) satisfies the conditions in regulation 5(3) and (4);

"recognised educational establishment" means an establishment recognised by the Secretary of State, the Scottish Ministers or the Department for Employment and Learning, as the case may be, as being, or as comparable to, a university, college or school;

"remunerative work" means work which is—
(a) done for payment or in expectation of payment;
(b) undertaken for not less than 24 hours a week, calculated in accordance with regulation 4(3) of the Working Tax Credit (Entitlement and Maximum Rate) Regulations 2002; and
(c) not excluded from the meaning of engagement in remunerative work by regulation 4(2) of those Regulations;

and other expressions have the same meanings as defined in the Act.

(2) In the application of these Regulations to Northern Ireland, a reference to a provision of an enactment which applies only to Great Britain or England and Wales, shall be construed, so far as necessary, as including a reference to the corresponding enactment applying to Northern Ireland.

(SI 2002/2007, reg.2) (as amended)

AMENDMENTS

1. Child Tax Credit (Amendment) Regulations 2003 (SI 2003/738), reg.3 (April 6, 2003).
2. Tax Credits (Miscellaneous Amendments No.2) Regulations 2003 (SI 2003/2815), reg.17 (November 26, 2003).
3. Civil Partnership Act 2004 (Tax Credits, etc.) (Consequential Amendments) Order 2005 (SI 2005/2919), art.4(2) (December 5, 2005).
4. Child Tax Credit (Amendment) Regulations 2006 (SI 2006/222), reg.3 (April 6, 2006).

2.186

Circumstances in which a person is or is not responsible for a child or qualifying young person

3.—(1) For the purposes of child tax credit the circumstances in which a person is or is not responsible for a child or qualifying young person shall be determined in accordance with the following Rules.

2.187

Rule 1

1.1. A person shall be treated as responsible for a child or qualifying young person who is normally living with him (the "normally living with test").
1.2. This Rule is subject to rules 2 to 4.

2.188

Rule 2 (Competing claims)

2.1. This Rule applies where—
(a) a child or qualifying young person normally lives with two or more persons in—
  (i) different households; or
  (ii) the same household, where those persons are not limited to the members of a [2 . . .] couple; or
  (iii) a combination of (i) and (ii); and
(b) two or more of those persons make separate claims (that is, not a single joint claim made by a [2 . . .] couple) for child tax credit in respect of the child or qualifying young person.
2.2. The child or qualifying young person shall be treated as the responsibility of—
(a) only one of those persons making such claims; and
(b) whichever of them has (comparing between them) the main responsibility for him (the "main responsibility test");
subject to rules 3 and 4.

2.189

Rule 3

3.1. The persons mentioned in rule 2.2. (other than the child or qualifying young person) may jointly elect as to which of them satisfies the main responsibility test for the child or qualifying young person, and in default of agreement the Board may determine that question on the information available to them at the time of their determination.

2.190

Rule 4

4.1. A child or qualifying young person shall be treated as not being the responsibility of any person during any period in which any of the following Cases applies.

2.191

453

Case A	The child or qualifying young person is provided with, or placed in, accommodation under Part III of the Children Act 1989, Part II of the Children (Scotland) Act 1995 or Part IV of the Children (Northern Ireland) Order 1995, and the cost of that child's or qualifying young person's accommodation or maintenance is borne wholly or partly— (i) out of local authority funds under section 23 of the Children Act 1989 or section 26 of the Children (Scotland) Act 1995; (ii) in Northern Ireland, by an authority, within the meaning in Article 2, and under Article 27, of that Order; or (iii) out of other public funds. This Case shall not apply in the circumstances prescribed in regulation 3 of the Child Benefit (General) Regulations 1976, or regulation 3 of the Child Benefit (General) Regulations (Northern Ireland) 1979.
Case B	The child or qualifying young person— (i) is being looked after by a local authority; and (ii) has been placed for adoption by that authority in the home of a person proposing to adopt him, and a local authority is making a payment in respect of the child's or qualifying young person's accommodation or maintenance, or both, under section 23 of the Children Act 1989, section 26 of the Children (Scotland) Act 1995 or Article 27 of the Children (Northern Ireland) Order 1995. This Case applies in Northern Ireland with the modification that for references to a local authority there are substituted references to an authority (within the meaning in Article 2 of that Order).
Case C	A custodial sentence— (a) for life; (b) without limit of time; (c) of detention during Her Majesty's pleasure; (d) in Northern Ireland, of detention during the pleasure of the Secretary of State; or (e) for a term or period of more than four months, has been passed on the child or qualifying young person.
Case D	The child (having attained the age of sixteen or qualifying young person claims and is awarded child tax credit in his or her own right, in respect of a child for whom he or she is responsible, for that period.
[¹Case E	The child (having attained the age of sixteen) or the qualifying young person, claims incapacity benefit in

	his or her own right and that benefit is paid to or in respect of him or her for that period.
	This Case does not apply at any time ("the later time") during a period of incapacity for work which began before 6th April 2004 in the case of a person in respect of whom, at a time—
	    (a) during that period of incapacity, and
	    (b) before that date,
	both incapacity benefit and child tax credit were payable, if child tax credit has been payable in respect of him or her continuously since 5th April 2004 until that later time. For the purposes of this Case "period of incapacity" shall be construed in accordance with section 30C of the 1992 Act (incapacity benefit: days and periods of incapacity for work) but disregarding subsections (5) and (5A) of that section.]

[³Case F	The child (having attained the age of sixteen) or the qualifying young person claims and receives working tax credit in his or her own right (whether alone or on a joint claim).
	This Case does not apply in the case of a child or qualifying young person, for whom another ("the recipient"), had made a claim for child tax credit before, and was entitled to receive child tax credit immediately before, the making of these Regulations, until—
	    (a) the child or qualifying young person ceases to receive relevant education or approved training (in each case within the meaning of regulation 1(3) of the Child Benefit (General) Regulations 2006),
	    (b) the recipient ceases to receive child tax credit for any other reason, or
	    (c) 24th August 2006,
	whichever occurs first.]

(2) Where—
(a) a claimant is treated as responsible for a child or qualifying young person by virtue of the preceding Rules, and
(b) the child or qualifying young person has a child of his or her own, normally living with him or her,
the claimant shall also be treated as responsible for, and as having made a claim for child tax credit in respect of, the child of the child or qualifying young person (but without prejudice to the facts as to which of them is mainly responsible for that child).

AMENDMENTS

1. Tax Credits (Miscellaneous Amendments) Regulations 2004 (SI 2004/762), reg.2 (April 6, 2004).

2. Civil Partnership Act 2004 (Tax Credits, etc.) (Consequential Amendments) Order 2005 (SI 2005/2919), art.4(3) (December 5, 2005).

3. Child Tax Credit (Amendment No. 2) Regulations 2006 (SI 2006/1163), reg.2 (May 24, 2006).

DEFINITIONS

"child"—see reg.2(1).
"claimant"—see *ibid*.
"custodial sentence"—see *ibid*.
"joint claim"—see *ibid*.
"looked after by a local authority"—see *ibid*.
"main responsibility test"—see *ibid*.
"normally living with test"—see *ibid*.
"placing for adoption"—see *ibid*.
"qualifying young person"—see *ibid*.

GENERAL NOTE

2.192 Section 8(1) of the TCA 2002 provides that entitlement to child tax credit is dependent upon the claimant (and/or his or her partner in the case of a joint claim) "being responsible for one or more children or qualifying young persons". The 2002 Act then provides that this expression may be defined further by regulations (s.8(2)). This regulation accordingly sets out a number of rules for determining whether a person is or is not responsible for a child or young person. The starting point is in r.1, namely that as a general rule, a person is responsible for a child or young person normally living with him or her. This presumption is then subject to r.2, which deals with competing claims, as well as r.3 (election by the parties or determination by HMRC in default of such agreement) and r.4 (special cases, principally involving children or young persons being accommodated at public expense and so not to be the subject of a child tax credit award).

2.193 *Para.(1)*

2.194 *Rule 1:* The presumption is that a person is responsible for a child or qualifying young person "who is normally living with him" (r.1, para.1.1). This "normally living with test" has been inherited from WFTC (and, before that, family credit: see Family Credit (General) Regulations 1987 (SI 1987/1973, reg.7(1)). The "normally living with test" was new to family credit, although the phrase "living with" the claimant was (and still is) used in the child benefit legislation (SSCBA 1992, s.143 and see, in particular *R(F) 2/79* and *R(F) 2/81*).

In the context of family credit (and later WFTC), *CFC 1537/1995* decided that a child "normally lives with" a person for the purposes of reg.7(1) if he or she spent more time with that person than anyone else. This was the construction that made sense of reg.7(2) of the 1987 Regulations, which made provision for cases where a child either spent equal amounts of time in different households or there was doubt as to which household a child was living in. But reg.7(2) only applied in cases of real doubt; if there was simply a factual dispute this was not enough to bring it into play. Where reg.7(2) applied, there was then a series of tests. The first was receipt of child benefit, the rules for which include methods of establishing priorities between claimants. If no one was receiving child benefit then if only one person had claimed child benefit, that person had priority. If there had been no claims (or more than one claim), the final test was who had "primary responsibility".

2.195 *Rule 2:* Rule 2, which applies to competing claims for child tax credit, adopts a slightly different approach to the old reg.7(2). Accordingly, it does not necessarily follow that *CFC 1537/1995* applies in precisely the same way. Rule 2 applies where two or more people (not being a couple) make child tax credit claims and the relevant child or qualifying young person "normally lives with two or more persons" *either* in different households *or* in the same household (other than in the case of a couple with a child in the same household) *or* in an arrangement that is a combination of these two first possibilities (r.2, para.2.1). Thus, r.2 only comes into play when the child or young person may, as a matter of fact, already be regarded as "normally" (but separately) living with at least two persons. For example, a child might spend weekdays living with one parent and weekends with the other parent in a different household. Although the child will spend more time living with the weekday parent, it is perfectly proper to say that he or she *also* normally lives with the weekend parent, at least for part of the week. This being so, the definition of "normally living with" applied in *CFC 1537/1995* (i.e. spending more time with one person than anyone else) cannot apply for the purposes of the meaning of "normally lives" in r.2, para.2.1, as that is specifically designed to deal with the situation where a child or young person by definition "normally" lives in more than one place. However, where r.2 does so apply, the general rule is that, as between the competing claimants, the child or young person is treated as the responsibility of the person with "main responsibility" for him or her (r.2, para.2.2). Thus, although *CFC 1537/1995* should be applied with care in this context, ultimately it may be a distinction without a difference.

As we have seen, the former reg.7(2) of the 1987 Regulations resolved problematic cases by reference first to the person in receipt of child benefit and then, in the absence of a child benefit claim, to the person with "primary responsibility" for the child or young person. Rule 2 makes no reference to the child benefit position. Instead, cases of shared care—as these will inevitably be—are to be determined by reference to who has "main responsibility" for the child or young person. This is presumably likely to be determined on a time basis, and so the weekdays parent in the example above is likely to be regarded as the one with such responsibility. As with the former reg.7(2), "responsibility" has no special meaning in the legislation and so must be determined according to the ordinary everyday meaning of the word. It would not seem that there is any material difference between "primary responsibility" (reg.7) and "main responsibility" (r.2). It would also appear that under r.2, as under the former reg.7, responsibility or the normality of living may be judged on an overall basis over a period. This is different from the income support provision, where the test of responsibility still has to be applied week by week (*CIS 49/1991* and *Whelan v Chief Adjudication Officer, The Independent*, November 14, 1994).

It will be evident from the analysis above that there is, under these Rules, no provision for the division of child tax credit between competing parents. The Rules are premised on establishing which claimant (or which couple of joint claimants) is entitled to child tax credit for a given child or young person, not on apportioning child tax credit entitlement between separated individual claimants (e.g. 5/7 to the weekdays parent and 2/7 to the weekend parent). Although the practical and administrative difficulties with such an arrangement are obvious, it did appear from the primary legislation that this might be a possibility (see, e.g. TCA 2002, ss.8(2) and 9(7)). There remains, therefore, the prospect of human rights challenges in this area, as with social security benefits which have elements related to a child or children's presence in a particular household for part-weeks in cases of shared care: see the General Note to Income Support (General) Regulations 1987 (SI 1987/1967), reg.15, in Vol.II in this series).

The attribution of responsibility for a child or young person to a particular person under r.2 is itself subject to rs 3 and 4.

Rule 3: Where there are competing claims under r.2, the parties may by agreement notify HMRC as to which of them satisfies the main responsibility test for the child or young person in question. If the adults in question fail to agree, HMRC may determine that question on the information then available.

2.196

2.197　　*Rule 4:* Rule 4 sets out a number of specific circumstances (or Cases) in which a child or young person is not to be treated as the responsibility of a tax credit claimant, even though any of rs 1–3 above might otherwise apply. Cases A–C all deal with situations in which a child or young person is being accommodated at public expense in one way or another and so payment of child tax credit is inappropriate. These are similar to the exclusions under the child benefit scheme. Case D covers the special case of a child (aged at least 16) or young person who has herself been awarded child tax credit in respect of her own child (see also para.(2) where child tax credit has not been awarded in such circumstances to the young parent).

2.198　　*Case A:* This exclusion covers children or young persons who are provided with or placed in accommodation under Pt III of the Children Act 1989 or associated legislation. The exception in reg.3 of the Child Benefit (General) Regulations 1976 (now Child Benefit (General) Regulations 2003 (SI 2003/493), reg.2) deals with children or young persons who are provided with residential accommodation on account of their disability.

2.199　　*Case B:* This exclusion applies where (i) a child or young person is being looked after by a local authority (in the sense that term is used under the Children Act 1989); (ii) he or she has been placed for adoption, and (iii) a fostering allowance is in payment.

2.200　　*Case C:* CTC will continue to be paid unless the child or young person has been sentenced to detention for a period of four months or longer. This is more generous than the equivalent rules for income support and income-based jobseeker's allowance, under which benefit for the child or young person ceases immediately he or she is taken into custody (Income Support (General) Regulations 1987 (SI 1987/1967), reg.16(5)(f) and (6); see also reg.15(3) regarding home leave). It is also more generous than the former WFTC and DPTC rules, under which there was no entitlement to the elements of those tax credits relating to children where a custodial sentence had been passed (Family Credit (General) Regulations 1987 (SI 1987/1973), reg.8(2)(e)). The justifications for the change given by ministers are the extra costs associated with contact and the need to enable families to maintain contact with the child or young person for whom they are responsible, and to assist with that person's re-integration in the community. It is difficult to see how these arguments do not apply equally forcefully in the context of income support and income-based jobseeker's allowance.

2.201　　*Case D:* See also para.(2) below.

2.202　　*Case E:* The effect of this provision is that a person is not to be treated as responsible for a child or a qualifying young person in respect of whom incapacity benefit is payable. There is transitional protection during a period of incapacity which began before April 6, 2004 for cases where both incapacity benefit and child tax credit were in payment in respect of the child or qualifying young person before that date.

2.203　　*Case F:* This exclusion means that a person is not to be treated as responsible for a child or qualifying young person who is receiving WTC in his or her own right, whether alone or as part of a joint claim, with a spouse or partner. It also provides for a period of transitional protection for some CTC recipients.

2.204　　*Paragraph (2):* This deals with the special case where a person (the claimant) is found to be responsible for a child or young person under rs 1–4 above (and so the exception in Case D of r.4 does not apply) and that child or young person herself has a child. In such circumstances, the claimant is treated as responsible for child tax credit purposes for both his or her child (or young person) and that child's own child.

(SI 2002/2007, reg.4) (as amended)

Period for which a person who attains the age of 16 remains a child

4. A person who attains the age of sixteen remains a child for the purposes of Part I from the date on which he attained that age until immediately before 1st September which next follows that date.

2.205

DEFINITIONS

"child"—see reg.2(1).
"Pt I"—see *ibid.*

GENERAL NOTE

Section 8(3) of the TCA 2002 defines a child as a person who "has not attained the age of sixteen", but the same provision enables regulations to be made allowing a person to remain a "child" for tax credit purposes "for a prescribed period or until a prescribed date". This regulation provides that a child remains a child for both child tax credit and working tax credit purposes until September 1 following his or her 16th birthday.

2.206

Maximum age and prescribed conditions for a qualifying young person

5.—(1) For the purposes of Part I, a person ceases to be a qualifying young person (unless disqualified earlier under the following paragraphs) on the date on which he attains the age of [^{4}twenty].

2.207

(2) A person who is not a child, but has not attained the age of [^{4}twenty] years, is a qualifying young person for any period during which the following conditions are satisfied with regard to him [^{1}(and once a person falls within the terms of paragraph (3)(b), he shall be treated as having satisfied the first condition from the [^{5}relevant leaving date] mentioned in that paragraph)].

(3) The first condition is that he is [^{4}. . .]—
(a) receiving full-time education, not being—
  (i) advanced education, or
  (ii) education received by that person by virtue of his employment or of any office held by him; [^{4}. . .]
[^{4}(ab) undertaking approved training which is not provided to him by virtue of his employment or any office held by him; or]
(b) under the age of eighteen years and—
  [^{2}[^{4}(i) he ceased to receive full-time education or to undertake approved training (the date of that event being referred to as "the relevant leaving date");]
  (ii) within three months of the [^{4}relevant leaving date], he has notified the Board (in the manner prescribed by regulation 22 of the Tax Credits (Claims and Notifications) Regulations 2002) that he is registered for work or training with the Careers Service, the Connexions Service or the Department for Employment and Learning; and
  (iii) not more than 20 weeks has elapsed since the [^{4}relevant leaving date.]
[^{4}(3A) A person who has attained the age of nineteen years satisfies paragraph (3)(a) or (ab) only where the course of education or training began before he attained that age.]

(4) The second condition is that the period in question is not (and does not include)—

(a) a week in which he (having ceased to receive full-time education [⁴or approved training]) becomes engaged in remunerative work; [⁴or]
(b) [⁴. . .]
(c) a period in respect of which that person receives income support or income-based jobseeker's allowance within the meaning of section 1(4) of the Jobseekers Act 1995.

(5) For the purposes of paragraphs (3) and (4) full-time education is education received by a person attending a course of education—
(a) at a recognised educational establishment, or
(b) if the education is recognised by the Secretary of State, the Scottish Ministers [³, the Board] or the Department for Employment and Learning, elsewhere;

where in pursuit of that course, the time spent receiving instruction or tuition, undertaking supervised study, examination or practical work or taking part in any exercise, experiment or project for which provision is made in the curriculum of the course, exceeds or exceeds on average 12 hours a week in normal term-time, and shall include normal gaps between the ending of one course and the commencement of another, where the person is enrolled on and commences the latter course.

(6) In calculating the time spent in pursuit of the course, no account shall be taken of time occupied by meal breaks or spent on unsupervised study.

[⁴(7) In determining whether a person is undertaking a course of fulltime education or approved training, there shall be disregarded any interruption—
(a) for a period of up to 6 months, whether beginning before or after the person concerned attains age 16, to the extent that it is reasonable in the opinion of the Board to do so; and
(b) for any period due to illness or disability of the mind or body of the person concerned provided that it is reasonable in the opinion of the Board to do so.]

AMENDMENTS

1. Child Tax Credit (Amendment) Regulations 2003 (SI 2003/738), reg.4 (April 6, 2003).
2. Child Tax Credit (Amendment) Regulations 2003 (SI 2003/738), reg.5 (April 6, 2003).
3. Child Tax Credit (Amendment) Regulations 2003 (SI 2003/738), reg.6 (April 6, 2003).
4. Child Tax Credit (Amendment) Regulations 2006 (SI 2006/222), reg.4 (April 6, 2006).
5. Tax Credits (Miscellaneous Amendments) Regulations 2006 (SI 2006/766), reg.3 (April 6, 2006).

DEFINITIONS

"advanced education"—see reg.2(1).
"Careers Service"—see *ibid*.
"Connexions Service"—see *ibid*.
"child"—see *ibid*.
"full-time education"—see para.(5).
"Pt I"—see reg.2(1).
"qualifying young person"—see *ibid*.
"recognised educational establishment"—see *ibid*.
"relevant training programme"—see *ibid*.
"remunerative work"—see *ibid*.

(SI 2002/2007, reg.5) (as amended)

GENERAL NOTE

Section 8(4) of the TCA 2002 enables regulations to be made prescribing conditions to be met by a person in order to count as a "qualifying young person" (CTC being payable in respect of children and qualifying young persons (TCA 2002, s.8(1)). This regulation provides that the maximum age for a "qualifying young person" is the date on which he or she reaches the age of 19 (para.(1)). It also spells out the conditions which must be met by a person who is no longer a child (on which note the extended meaning of "child" in reg.4) in order to rank as a "qualifying young person" (paras (2)–(6)). Two conditions must be satisfied in this regard (they are cumulative and not alternative). First, the young person must *either* be receiving full-time education, as defined by para.(3)(a) (and see also paras (5) and (6)) *or* be aged under 18, have ceased to receive full-time education, be registered for work or training with one of the relevant official agencies, and have met the latter two criteria for no more than 20 consecutive weeks (para.(3)(b)). Secondly, the period in question must not be or include a week in which the young person becomes engaged in remunerative work (having ceased full-time education), or a period in which he or she received a training allowance under a training programme or received income support or income-based jobseeker's allowance (para.(4)).

These conditions are modelled on those that apply to child benefit, on which see SSCBA 1992, s.142 (and the commentary in Vol.I of this series). The definition of full-time education likewise is in identical terms to the relevant provision for child benefit purposes (Child Benefit (General) Regulations 2003 (SI 2003/493), reg.5.

2.208

Entitlement to child tax credit after death of child or qualifying young person

6. If—

(a) a child or qualifying young person dies; and
(b) a person is (or would, if a claim had been made, have been) entitled to child tax credit in respect of the child or qualifying young person immediately before the death,

that person shall be entitled to child tax credit in respect of the child or qualifying young person for the period of eight weeks immediately following the death or, in the case of a qualifying young person, until the date on which he or she would have attained the age of [¹twenty] if earlier.

2.209

AMENDMENT

1. Child Tax Credit (Amendment) Regulations 2006 (SI 2006/222), reg.5 (April 6, 2006).

DEFINITIONS

"child"—see reg.2(1).
"qualifying young person"—see *ibid*.

GENERAL NOTE

Section 8(5) of the TCA 2002 enables regulations to be made allowing entitlement to child tax credit to continue for a prescribed period notwithstanding the death of the relevant child or qualifying young person. This regulation makes provision for the continued payment of child tax credit for a further eight weeks in such a situation. The same concession has been made in relation to child benefit (SSCBA 1992, s.145A, inserted by TCA 2002, s.55).

2.210

Determination of the maximum rate at which a person or persons may be entitled to child tax credit

2.211

7.—(1) In the following paragraphs—
(a) in the case of a single claim (but not a joint claim), the person making the claim is referred to as the "claimant"; and
(b) in the case of a joint claim, the members of the [¹. . .] couple making the claim are referred to as the "joint claimants".

(2) The maximum rate at which a claimant or joint claimants may be entitled to child tax credit shall be the aggregate of—
(a) the family element of child tax credit; and
(b) an individual element of child tax credit, in respect of each child or qualifying young person for whom—
  (i) the claimant; or
  (ii) either or both of the joint claimants;
as the case may be, is or are responsible.

(3) The family element of child tax credit—
(a) in a case where any of the children referred to in paragraph (2)(b) above is under the age of one year, is £1,090; and
(b) in any other case, is £545.

(4) The individual element of child tax credit for any child or qualifying young person referred to in paragraph (2)(b) above—
(a) where the child is disabled, is [²£4,285];
(b) where the child is severely disabled, is [²£5,265];
(c) in the case of any other child, is [²£1,845];
(d) where the qualifying young person is disabled, is [²£4,285];
(e) where the qualifying young person is severely disabled, is [²£5,265]; and
(f) in the case of any other qualifying young person, is [²£1,845].

AMENDMENTS

1. Civil Partnership Act 2004 (Tax Credits, etc.) (Consequential Amendments) Order 2005 (SI 2005/2919), art.4(4) (December 5, 2005).
2. Tax Credits Up-rating Regulations 2007 (SI 2007/828), reg.2 (April 6, 2007).

DEFINITIONS

"child"—see reg.2(1).
"claimant"—see *ibid.* and para.(1)(a).
"the family element of child tax credit"—see reg.2(1).
"the individual element of child tax credit"—see *ibid.*
"joint claim"—see *ibid.*
"qualifying young person"—see *ibid.*
"single claim"—see *ibid.*

GENERAL NOTE

2.212

Section 9 of the TCA 2002 makes provision for the maximum rate of child tax credit. This regulation provides the detail on how this rate is to be arrived at (para.(2)). It also sets out the actual annual rates for the component elements (paras (3) and (4)). Claimants who are entitled to income support or income-based jobseeker's allowance are automatically entitled to the maximum child tax credit applicable in their circumstances (TCA 2002, s.7(2) and Tax Credits (Income Thresholds and Determination of Rates) Regulations 2002 (SI 2002/ 2008), reg.4). The entitlement of other claimants is dependent upon the operation of the thresholds and

(SI 2002/2007, reg.7) (as amended)

withdrawal rates specified in the Income Thresholds and Determination of Rates Regulations.

Prescribed conditions for a disabled or severely disabled child or qualifying young person

8.—(1) For the purposes of section 9 of the Act a child or qualifying young person—
  (a) is disabled if he satisfies the requirements of paragraph (2); and
  (b) is severely disabled if he satisfies the requirements of paragraph (3).
(2) A person satisfies the requirements of this paragraph if—
  (a) disability living allowance is payable in respect of him, or has ceased to be so payable solely because he is a patient; or
  (b) he is—
    (i) registered as blind in a register compiled by a local authority under section 29 of the National Assistance Act 1948 (welfare services);
    (ii) in Scotland, has been certified as blind in a register maintained by or on behalf of a local government area (as defined in the Local Government etc. (Scotland) Act 1994), or
    (iii) in Northern Ireland, has been certified as blind and in consequence is registered as blind in a register maintained by or on behalf of a Health and Social Services Board; or
  (c) he ceased to be so registered or certified as blind within the 28 weeks immediately preceding the date of claim.
(3) A person satisfies the requirements of this paragraph if the care component of disability living allowance—
  (a) is payable in respect of him; or
  (b) would be so payable but for either a suspension of benefit in accordance with regulations under section 113(2) of the Contributions and Benefits Act or an abatement as a consequence of hospitalisation,
at the highest rate prescribed under section 72(3) of that Act.

2.213

DEFINITIONS
  "the Act"—see reg.2(1).
  "child"—see *ibid*.
  "the Contributions and Benefits Act"—see *ibid*.
  "disability living allowance"—see *ibid*.
  "patient"—see *ibid*.
  "qualifying young person"—see *ibid*.

GENERAL NOTE

Sections 9(5)(d) and (6) of the TCA 2002 make provision for a disabled child element and a severely disabled child element to be component parts of child tax credit. This regulation defines those terms. Thus, a child or qualifying young person is disabled if disability living allowance (DLA) is payable for them (or has ceased to be payable but only because he or she is now a patient) or if he or she is a registered blind person (or has ceased to be so registered in the immediately preceding 28 weeks) (para.(2)). A child or qualifying young person is severely disabled if they are entitled to the highest rate of the DLA care component (i.e. they satisfy both the "day" and "night" conditions in terms of their need for personal care or supervision): para.(3). The rates for these elements are set out in regs 8(4)(a) and (b).

2.214

Tax Credits (Income Thresholds and Determination of Rates) Regulations 2002

(SI 2002/2008) (AS AMENDED)

Whereas a draft of this instrument, which contains the first regulations made under section 13(2) of the Tax Credits Act 2002, has been laid before, and approved by resolution of, each House of Parliament:

Now, therefore, the Treasury, in exercise of the powers conferred upon them by sections 8(1) to (3), 13(2) and (3), 65(1) and (7) and 67 of the Tax Credits Act 2002, hereby make the following Regulations:

Made by the Treasury under ss.8(1)–(3), 13(2) and (3), 65(1) and (7) and 67 of the Tax Credits Act 2002.

1. Citation, commencement and effect.
2. Interpretation.
3. Manner in which amounts to be determined for the purposes of section 7(1)(a) of the Act.
4. Social security benefits prescribed for the purposes of section 7(2) of the Act.
5. Amounts prescribed for the purposes of section 7(3)(a) and (b) of the Act.
6. Manner of determining the rate at which a person is, or persons are, entitled to a tax credit.
7. Determination of rate of working tax credit.
8. Determination of rate of child tax credit.
9. Cases in which there is no rate of tax credit.

Citation, commencement and effect

1.—(1) These Regulations may be cited as the Tax Credits (Income Thresholds and Determination of Rates) Regulations 2002 and shall come into force—

(a) for the purpose of enabling claims to be made, on August 1, 2002;
(b) for the purpose of enabling decisions on claims to be made, on 1st January 2003; and
(c) for all other purposes, on 6th April 2003.

(2) These Regulations shall have effect for the tax year beginning with 6th April 2003 and subsequent tax years.

DEFINITIONS

"claim"—see TCA 2002, s.3.
"decision on claim"—see TCA 2002, s.14.
"tax year"—see reg.2.

Interpretation

2. In these Regulations—
"the Act" means the Tax Credits Act 2002;
"the income threshold" has the meaning given by section 7(1)(a) of the Act;
"period of award" shall be construed in accordance with section 5 of the Act;

(SI 2002/2008, reg.2) (as amended)

"the relevant income" has the meaning given by section 7(3) of the Act;
"tax year" means a period beginning with 6th April in one year and ending with 5th April in the next.

Manner in which amounts to be determined for the purposes of section 7(1)(a) of the Act

3.—(1) This regulation prescribes the manner in which amounts are to be determined for the purposes of section 7(1)(a) of the Act.

(2) In the case of a person or persons entitled to working tax credit, the amount in relation to that tax credit is [¹£5,220].

(3) In the case of a person or persons entitled to child tax credit, the amount in relation to that tax credit is [²£14,495].

AMENDMENTS

1. Tax Credits Up-rating Regulations 2005 (SI 2005/681), reg.4 (April 6, 2005).
2. Tax Credit Up-rating Regulations 2007 (SI 2007/828), reg.4(1) (April 6, 2007).

DEFINITION

"the Act"—see reg.2.

GENERAL NOTE

This regulation makes the necessary provision to give full operative effect to s.7(1) of the Act (income test).

HMRC does not use the term "income threshold". Instead it describes it in its literature as "taper start point". However, as the Commissioner noted in *CTC/2113/2006*, a failure to explain that this is how HMRC refers to the income thresholds can cause confusion.

Subsection (1)

Section 7(1) of TCA 2002 imposes an income test on all claimants for tax credits, the test being whether the relevant income of the claimant (or claimants) for the tax year exceeds "the amount" for that tax credit. If the relevant income does exceed the amount, then it must be calculated by how much it does so. This applies to all claimants apart from those within s.7(2) and reg.4 below. In other words, "the amount" is the income threshold for claiming that tax credit. Only those with no incomes or incomes below the threshold can claim the full tax credit for the year. The section allows, and this regulation provides, different thresholds for different tax credits.

The thresholds are reconsidered annually, and have been set at:

Year	CTC (£ pa)	WTC (£ pa)
2003–04	13,230	5,060
2004–05	13,480	5,060
2005–06	13,910	5,220
2006–07	14,155	5,220
2007–08	14,495	5,220
2008–09	*not yet set*	*6,420*

The existence of separate thresholds means that in many cases separate calculations have to be made under s.7(1) about entitlement to each tax credit. The current thresholds have the effect that many more people are entitled to the child tax credit

Tax Credits (Income Thresholds and Determination of Rates) Regulations 2002

than to the working tax credit. Regulations 7 and 8 of these Regulations make provision for dealing with this.

Social security benefits prescribed for the purposes of section 7(2) of the Act

2.221   4. The following are social security benefits prescribed for the purposes of section 7(2) of the Act in relation to child tax credit and working tax credit—
(a) income support under Part VII of the Social Security Contributions and Benefit Act 1992 other than income support to which a person is entitled only by virtue of regulation 6(2) and (3) of the Income Support (General) Regulations 1987;
(b) income support under Part VII of the Social Security Contributions and Benefit (Northern Ireland) Act 1992 other than income support to which a person is entitled only by virtue of regulation 6(2) and (3) of the Income Support (General) Regulations (Northern Ireland) 1987;
(c) an income-based jobseeker's allowance within the meaning of the Jobseekers Act 1995 or the Jobseekers (Northern Ireland) Order 1995.
[1(d) state pension credit within the meaning of the State Pension Credit Act 2002 or the State Pension Credit Act (Northern Ireland) 2002.]

DEFINITION

"the Act"—see reg.2.

AMENDMENT

1. Tax Credits (Miscellaneous Amendments No.2) Regulations 2003 (SI 2003/2815), reg.18 (November 26, 2003).

GENERAL NOTE

2.222   Section 7(2) of the TCA 2002 provides that those entitled to any of the social security benefits prescribed for the purposes of that subsection are not to be subject to the income test in s.7(1). This does not apply to exclude the claimant from any other requirements for an award.

Three benefits only have been prescribed by this regulation. They are:
(a) income support payable to any claimant. The exception applies to anyone who is a lone parent treated by regs 6(2) or (3) of the Income Support (General) Regulations 1987 (and its Northern Ireland equivalent) as being entitled to income support for the first 14 days of a period of remunerative work because he or she was a lone parent who was, for at least 26 weeks before the work started, receiving income support or income-based jobseeker's allowance;
(b) income-based jobseeker's allowance;
(c) state pension credit.

Amounts prescribed for the purposes of section 7(3)(a) and (b) of the Act

2.223   5. The amount prescribed for the purposes of section 7(3)(a) and (b) of the Act is [1£25,000].

AMENDMENT

1. Tax Credit Up-rating Regulations 2006 (SI 2006/963), reg.4(2) (April 6, 2006).

(SI 2002/2008, reg.5) (as amended)

DEFINITIONS

"the Act"—see reg.2.

GENERAL NOTE

Setting the figures for s.7(3)(a) and (b) at £25,000, together with a failure to set any figures for s.7(3)(c) and (d) has completely altered the way s.7(3) works as compared with the original intention of the Act.

The original model provided a nuanced basis for awarding CTC and WTC by reference to the higher of the incomes of the claimants for the year of award and the previous year. With the figures in s.7(3) either not set, or set at £25,000, the effect of the section is that almost all claimants for both CTC and WTC receive their awards in one year by reference only to their income in the previous year. Only if the claimant receives a sharp increase in income (and capital gains do not count) will current year income be used to reduce that award. The reduction will apply for the whole year even if the income is received only at the end of the year.

The other effect of this alteration is to make tax credits significantly more generous to most claimants, in part by reducing sharply the number of overpayments caused by pay rises.

2.224

Manner of determining the rate at which a person is, or persons are, entitled to a tax credit

6. Regulations 7, 8 and 9 make provision as to the manner of determining the rate (if any) at which a person is, or persons are, entitled to a tax credit in any case where—
  (a) the relevant income exceeds the income threshold; and
  (b) his or their entitlement does not arise by virtue of section 7(2) of the Act.

2.225

DEFINITIONS

"entitlement"—see TCA 2002, ss.8 and 10.
"income threshold"—see reg.2.
"relevant income"—see reg.2.
"the Act"—see reg.2.

GENERAL NOTE

This is, on its face, purely a signposting regulation. It serves to remind the reader of the exception from the income test in s.7 of the TCA 2002, and also to tie in the £26 rule in reg.9 with the two main regulations: reg.7 dealing with working tax credit, and reg.8 dealing with child tax credit. As will be seen from those regulations, that order is intentional as entitlement to working tax credit, if any, must be calculated before entitlement to child tax credit.

There is, however, a drafting mismatch between the wording of this regulation and the approach of regs 7 and 8, which appears to deflect its intention. Regulation 6 states that the other regulations make provision for determining the rate of *entitlement* to tax credits. By contrast, regs 7 and 8 talk about periods of *award*. "Period of award" is defined in reg.2 of these Regulations by reference to s.5 of the TCA 2002 (entitled "periods of award"). And regs 7 and 8 of these Regulations refer to the elements of the credits to which a claimant "may be entitled" (regs 7(2)(a) and 8(2)).

The purpose of s.5 of TCA 2002 is to determine the period for which an award of tax credit is made. Awards are made under s.14 of the Act, and are made in advance of, or at the start of, the year of claim, using s.7(10) of the Act to estimate the income. At that point, the "period of award" can in most cases only be the whole tax year, or the balance of that year from the effective starting date of the

2.226

467

Tax Credits (Income Thresholds and Determination of Rates) Regulations 2002

award. Awards must ignore uncertain future changes as they are not then known. Regulations 7 and 8 set out in considerable detail how to deal with part-years. But, save for the case of claims made only part-way through a year, the "relevant period" for an award will always be the whole year, and the complexities of regs 7 and 8 are not needed.

The full calculations under regs 7 and 8 of these Regulations cannot be made until the end of the tax year, when the task of HMRC is to make entitlement decisions under s.18 of the Act. So why refer to periods of award rather than periods of entitlement? It would appear that this mismatch between *award* and *entitlement* is a leftover of the changes made to the Tax Credits Bill during its passage through Parliament (as discussed in the notes to those sections). It is suggested that, to make practical sense of this regulation, the definition of "period of award" as applied to both regs 7 and 8 has to take in periods of entitlement as well.

Determination of rate of working tax credit

2.227　**7.**—(1) In relation to a person or persons entitled to working tax credit, the rate shall be determined by finding the rate for each relevant period and, where necessary, adding together those rates.

(2) "Relevant period" means any part of the period of award throughout which—
　(a) the elements of working tax credit (other than the childcare element) to which the person or persons may be entitled, remain the same; and
　(b) there is no relevant change of circumstances for the purposes of the childcare element of working tax credit, within the meaning of reg.16(1) of the Working Tax Credit (Entitlement and Maximum Rate) Regulations 2002 (change of circumstances for the purposes of childcare element).

(3) The rate for each relevant period shall be found in accordance with the following steps—

Step 1—Finding the daily maximum rate for each element other than the childcare element

2.228　For each element of the tax credit (other than the childcare element) to be included in the case of the person or persons entitled to the tax credit, find the daily maximum rate using the following formula:

$$\frac{MR}{N1}$$

where:
　"MR" is the maximum rate in relation to that element for the tax year to which the claim for the tax credit relates;
　"N1" is the number of days in that tax year.

Step 2—Finding the maximum rate for the relevant period for each element other than the childcare element

2.229　For each element of the tax credit to be so included, find the amount produced by multiplying the daily maximum rate (found under Step 1 and rounded up to the nearest penny) by the number of days in the relevant period.

468

(SI 2002/2008, reg. 7) (as amended)

Step 3—finding the income for the relevant period

Find the income for the relevant period by using the following formula: 2.230

$$\frac{I}{N1} \times N2$$

where:
"I" is the relevant income for the tax year to which the claim for the tax credit relates;
"N1" is the number of days in that tax year;
"N2" is the number of days in the relevant period.

Step 4—Finding the threshold for the relevant period

Find the threshold for the relevant period using the following formula: 2.231

$$\frac{[^1 £5,220]}{N1} \times N2$$

where:
"N1" is the number of days in that tax year;
"N2" is the number of days in the relevant period.

Step 5—Finding the amount of the reduction

Find the amount which is 37 per cent of the amount by which the income for the relevant period (found under Step 3 and rounded down to the nearest penny) exceeds the threshold for the relevant period (found under Step 4 and rounded up to the nearest penny). 2.232

Step 6—Reducing the elements of the tax credit (other than any childcare element)

If the amount found under Step 5 (rounded down to the nearest penny) is less than or equal to the total of the amounts found under Step 2 for the elements of the tax credit, deduct the amount found under Step 5 (rounded down to the nearest penny) from the total of those amounts found under Step 2. 2.233

Step 7—Finding the actual weekly childcare costs for the relevant period

Find the relevant childcare charges for the relevant period in accordance with reg.15 of the Working Tax Credit (Entitlement and Maximum Rate) Regulations 2002. 2.234

Step 8—Finding the actual childcare costs for the relevant period

Multiply the result of Step 7 by $\frac{52}{N1} \times N2$ 2.235

Here, N1 and N2 have the same meanings as in Step 3.
The result of this step is the amount of actual childcare costs for the relevant period.

Step 9—Finding the prescribed maximum childcare costs for the relevant period

Divide whichever of the maxima in reg.20(3) of the Working Tax Credit (Entitlement and Maximum Rate) Regulations 2002 is applicable by seven, 2.236

Tax Credits (Income Thresholds and Determination of Rates) Regulations 2002

round the result up to the nearest penny and multiply the resulting figure by the number of days in the relevant period.

The result of this is the prescribed maximum childcare costs for the relevant period.

Step 10—Finding the childcare element for the period

2.237 Take the lesser of the results of Steps 8 and 9.

Multiply that figure by [²80] per cent and round the result up to the nearest penny.

The result of this step is the maximum rate of the childcare element for the relevant period.

Step 11—Reducing the elements of the tax credit (including any childcare element)

2.238 If the amount found under Step 5 (rounded down to the nearest penny) exceeds the total of the amounts found under Step 2 for the elements of the tax credit—
  (a) deduct the excess from the amount found under Step 10 for any childcare element; and
  (b) reduce the total of the amounts found under Step 2 for the other elements of the tax credit to nil.

Step 12—Finding the rate for the relevant period

2.239 Add together—
  (a) the total of the amounts found under Step 2 for the elements of the tax credit (other than any childcare element) after reduction in accordance with Step 6 or Step 11; and
  (b) the amount found under Step 10 for any childcare element after any reduction in accordance with Step 11.

This is the rate for the relevant period.

(4) "Child care element" has the meaning given by section 12(2) of the Act.

AMENDMENTS

1. Tax Credits Up-rating Regulations 2005 (SI 2005/681), reg.4(3) (April 6, 2005).
2. Tax Credit Up-rating Regulations 2006 (SI 2006/963), reg.4(2) (April 6, 2006).

DEFINITIONS

"childcare element"—see TCA 2002, s.12.
"period of award"—see reg.2.
"rate"—see TCA 2002, s.13.

GENERAL NOTE

2.240 See the general note to reg.6 above. The effect of this regulation and reg.8— both together and separately—is to limit the amount of tax credit that a claimant can have to the relevant daily (or in the case of childcare element of working tax credit only, weekly) amount of the credit, if circumstances of a claimant change during a tax year. This approach is, as a result, less generous than the personal allowances for income tax, including children's tax credit. For example, the main personal allowance of an individual is the same amount for that individual throughout the year as

(SI 2002/2008, reg.7) (as amended)

is, for example, a bereaved person's allowance or a blind person's allowance. By contrast, the basis of calculation imposed by this regulation and reg.8 is that the elements of both working tax credit and child tax credit are payable only for the precise periods of the year for which the claimant can meet the requirement for that credit and element. For example, the family element of child tax credit increases from £545 to £1,090 for a family with a child under one in it. But under reg.8 that only increases the total child tax credit from the day when the child is born. Parents will only receive the full £1,090 in the relevant year if the child is actually born on April 6. Equally, however, the additional child tax credit continues to be payable up to the day before the child's first birthday in the following year (subject to the income test and save for marginal cases).

Paras (1) and (2)
As noted above, "period of award" must be read as including also "period of entitlement" to make sense of this regulation. Likewise, the reference to "may be entitled" in para.(2) should include "is entitled". 2.241

Para. (3)
This paragraph is written in the "step-by-step" style, using the command tense of relevant verbs, that has been adopted as part of the Tax Law Rewrite approach to tax regulations. It is also written so that the rules in the paragraph can be operated in full by a computer. 2.242

Relevant periods of a full year
In most cases, as noted above, the complexities of this rule can be sidestepped because the question of an award of, or entitlement to, a tax credit can be judged by the full tax year. If the decision relates to a full year, then the steps can be telescoped as follows: 2.243

Step 1 with Step 2: Identify the annual amount of each element of working tax credit to which the claimant is entitled, apart from the childcare element, for that tax year. 2.244

Step 3: Identify the relevant income for the tax year (current year income or previous year income). 2.245

Step 4 with Step 5 and Step 6: If the income from Step 3 exceeds the annual amount from Steps 1 and 2, reduce the amount from Steps 1 and 2 by 37 per cent of that excess. The result is the excess income for the tax year. 2.246

Step 7 with Step 8: Find the relevant childcare charges for the tax year. 2.247

Step 9 with Step 10: The childcare element is, from 2006, 80 per cent of either £15,600 (for two or more children) or £9,100 (for one child), or, if less, 80 per cent of the total childcare charges for the tax year. 2.248

Steps 11 and 12: If there is excess income for the tax year from Steps 4–6, reduce the annual amount from Steps 1 and 2 by the amount of that excess, if necessary to nil. If the excess is greater than that amount, next reduce the amount from Steps 9 and 10 by the amount by which that excess income exceeds the annual amount from Steps 1 and 2. If the excess income is greater than both amounts, then the amount of working tax credit for the tax year is nil. 2.249

Note from this that the childcare element of working tax credit is to be calculated on a weekly, not daily, basis in the event of any problem, and also is to be left in payment after the other elements have stopped being payable under these rules.

Tax Credits (Income Thresholds and Determination of Rates) Regulations 2002

Relevant periods of less than a year

2.250   These periods arise only where there is a change of circumstances during a year that brings a relevant period to an end and/or starts a new one. Until 2006 this could cause problems where this happened in circumstances where claimants were not under a duty to report changes. The extension of the duty to report under reg.21 of the Tax Credits (Claims and Notifications) Regulations 2002, together with the reduction of the period in which the changes must be reported to one month, and the extension of award or entitlement by reg.7D of the Working Tax Credit (Entitlement and Maximum Rate) Regulations 2002 for 4 weeks after someone ceases work or works for less than 16 hours a week, have removed many of these problems.

Determination of rate of child tax credit

2.251   **8.**—(1) In relation to a person or persons entitled to child tax credit, the rate shall be determined by finding the rate for each relevant period and, where necessary, adding together those rates.
(2) "Relevant period" means—
(a) in the case of a person or persons entitled to child tax credit only, any part of the period of award throughout which the maximum rate at which he or they may be entitled to the tax credit remains the same;
(b) in the case of a person or persons entitled to both child tax credit and working tax credit, any part of the period of award throughout which the maximum rate of child tax credit to which he or they may be entitled remains the same and both sub-paras (a) and (b) of reg.7(2) are met.
(3) The rate for each relevant period shall be found in accordance with the following steps—

Step 1—Finding the daily maximum rate for each element

2.252   For each element of the tax credit to be included in the case of the person or persons entitled to the tax credit, find the daily maximum rate using the following formula:

$$\frac{MR}{NI}$$

where:
"MR" is the maximum rate in relation to that element for the tax year to which the claim for the tax credit relates;
"NI" is the number of days in that tax year.

Step 2—Finding the maximum rate for the relevant period for each element

2.253   For each element of the tax credit to be so included, find the amount produced by multiplying the maximum rate (found under Step 1 and rounded up to the nearest penny) by the number of days in the relevant period.

Step 3—Finding income for the relevant period

2.254   Find the income for the relevant period by using the following formula:

$$\frac{I}{NI} \times N2$$

(SI 2002/2008, reg. 8) (as amended)

where:
"I" is the relevant income for the tax year to which the claim for the tax credit relates;
"NI" is the number of days in that tax year;
"N2" is the number of days in the relevant period.

Step 4—Finding the threshold for the relevant period

Find the amount produced by the following formula:

$$\frac{[^1\pounds14{,}495]}{NI} \times N2$$

where:
"NI" is the number of days in that tax year;
"N2" is the number of days in the relevant period.

The threshold for the relevant period is—
- (a) in the case of a person or persons entitled to child tax credit only, that amount;
- (b) in the case of a person or persons entitled to both child tax credit and working tax credit—
  - (i) that amount; or
  - (ii) if greater, the lowest amount of income for the relevant period (found under Step 3) which, disregarding reg.9, would result in a determination in accordance with reg.7 providing for no rate of working tax credit in his or their case for that period.

Step 5—Finding the amount of the reduction of the elements of the tax credit (other than the family element)

Find the amount (if any) which is 37 per cent of the amount by which the income for the relevant period (found under Step 3 and rounded down to the nearest penny) exceeds the threshold for the relevant period (found under Step 4 and rounded up to the nearest penny).

Step 6—Reducing the elements of the tax credit (other than the family element)

If the amount found under Step 5 (rounded down to the nearest penny) is less than the total of the amounts found under Step 2 for the elements of the tax credit (other than the family element), deduct the amount found under Step 5 (rounded down to the nearest penny) from the total of those amounts.

Step 7—Reducing the elements of the tax credit (other than the family element) to nil

If the amount found under Step 5 (rounded down to the nearest penny) is equal to or exceeds the total of the amounts found under Step 2 for the elements of the tax credit (other than the family element), reduce the total of those amounts to nil.

Step 8—Finding the amount of the reduction of the family element

Find the amount (if any) which is 6.67 per cent of the amount by which the income for the relevant period (found under Step 3 and rounded down to the nearest penny) exceeds—

Tax Credits (Income Thresholds and Determination of Rates) Regulations 2002

(a) in any case where the total of the amounts found under Step 2 for the elements of the tax credit (other than the family element) would be reduced in accordance with Step 7 to nil if the relevant income were £50,000 or less, "X";
(b) in any other case, "Y";

where:

"X" is the amount found in accordance with Step 9 and rounded up to the nearest penny;

"Y" is the lowest amount of income for the relevant period (found under Step 3 and rounded up to the nearest penny) which would result in the total of the amounts of the elements of the tax credit (other than the family element) being reduced to nil in accordance with Step 7.

Step 9—Finding "X" for the purposes of Step 8

2.260   Find "X" using the following formula:

$$\frac{£50,000}{N1} \times N2$$

where:

"N1" is the number of days in that tax year;
"N2" is the number of days in the relevant period.

Step 10—Reducing the family element

2.261   Deduct any amount found under Step 8 (rounded down to the nearest penny) from the amount found under Step 2 for the family element.

Step 11—Finding the rate for the relevant period

2.262   Add together—
(a) the total of the amounts found under Step 2 for the elements of the tax credit (other than the family element) after any reduction in accordance with Step 6 or Step 7; and
(b) the amount found under Step 2 for the family element after any reduction in accordance with Step 10.

This is the rate for the relevant period.

(4) "The family element" means the family element of child tax credit within the meaning given by section 9(3) of the Act.

AMENDMENT

1. Tax Credits Up-rating Regulations 2007 (SI 2007/828), reg.4(2) (April 6, 2007).

DEFINITIONS

"period of award"—see reg.2.
"the Act"—see reg.2.

GENERAL NOTE

2.263   See the general note to reg.6 above and the opening note to reg.7.

Paras (1) and (2)

2.264   The same comments apply as those to paras (1) and (2) of reg.7.

Para. (3)
This appears to be the equivalent for child tax credit of reg.7, but it has two additional elements. First, the effect of the steps is to remove an award of or entitlement to working tax credit before that of child tax credit. This may be important where one of a couple is receiving one of the credits while the other is receiving the other tax credit. The effect is to take the credit from the earner (and the duty to pay from the employer) before it is taken from the carer.

Secondly, the family element of child tax credit is removed only when a second, higher income threshold of £50,000 is exceeded. Further, the family element (currently £545 a year, increased to £1,090 if any of the children are less than a year old: Child Tax Credit Regulations 2002 (SI 2002/2007), reg.7(3)) is reduced only by 6.67 per cent of the excess of relevant income over £50,000. As the cut-off point for payment of child tax credit is £26 (reg.9 below), this makes the top relevant income to receive any tax credit about £66,000, but only where there is a child aged under one.

Relevant periods of a full year
In parallel with reg.7, reg.8 is straightforward as applied to a period of award of a full year. Steps 1–6 require that the annual amount of all elements (including the family element) be found, that the income for the year also be found, and that the excess of the income over the £14,495 threshold, if any, be calculated. The maximum amount of child tax credit is found by reducing the annual amount of all elements *excluding* the family element by 37 per cent of the excess of the income over the threshold.

Relevant periods of less than a year
The changes noted in para.2.250 for the equivalent rule for WTC apply equally to CTC and have also removed most of the potential problems for this provision also.

Cases in which there is no rate of tax credit

9.—(1) In the case of a person or persons entitled to working tax credit only or child tax credit only, where the rate at which the person or persons would be entitled to the tax credit (as determined in accordance with reg.7 or 8) would be less than £26, there is no rate in his or their case.

(2) In the case of a person or persons entitled to both working tax credit and child tax credit, where the total of the rates at which the person or persons would be entitled to the tax credits (as determined in accordance with regulations 7 and 8) would be less than £26, there are no rates in his or their case.

GENERAL NOTE

This cut-off provision is authorised by s.13(3)(b) of the Act.

Tax Credits (Claims and Notifications) Regulations 2002

(SI 2002/2014) (AS AMENDED)

The Commissioners of Inland Revenue, in exercise of the powers conferred upon them by ss.4(1), 6, 14(2), 15(2), 16(3), 17(10), 19(2), 22(1)(b) and (2), 65(1), (2) and (7) and 67 of the Tax Credits Act 2002, hereby make the following Regulations:

Tax Credits (Claims and Notifications) Regulations 2002

ARRANGEMENT OF REGULATIONS

PART I

GENERAL

1. Citation, commencement and effect.
2. Interpretation.
3. Use of electronic communications to make claims or to give notices or notifications.

PART II

CLAIMS

4. Interpretation of this Part.
5. Manner in which claims to be made.
6. Amended claims.
7. Time-limit for claims (if otherwise entitled to tax credit up to three months earlier).
8. Date of claims—disability element of working tax credit.
9. Advance claims before the year begins.
10. Advance claims—working tax credit.
11. Circumstances in which claims to be treated as made—notices containing provision under section 17(2)(a), (4)(a) or (6)(a) of the Act.
12. Circumstances in which claims to be treated as made—notices containing provision under section 17(2)(b), (4)(b) and (6)(b) of the Act.
13. Circumstances in which claims made by one member of a couple to be treated as also made by the other member of the couple.
14. Circumstances in which awards to be conditional and claims treated as made—decisions under section 14(1) of the Act made before 6th April 2003.
15. Persons who die after making a claim.
16. Persons who die before making joint claims.
17. Circumstances where one person may act for another in making a claim—receivers, etc.
18. Circumstances where one person may act for another in making a claim—other appointed persons.

PART III

NOTIFICATIONS OF CHANGES OF CIRCUMSTANCES

19. Interpretation of this Part.
20. Increases of maximum rate of entitlement to a tax credit as a result of changes of circumstances to be dependent on notification.
21. Requirement to notify changes of circumstances which may decrease the rate at which a person or persons is or are entitled to tax credit or mean that entitlement ceases.
22. Manner in which notifications to be given.

23. Person by whom notification may be, or is to be, given.
24. Amended notifications.
25. Date of notification—cases where change of circumstances which may increase the maximum rate.
26. Date of notification—disability element and severe disability element for working tax credit.
26A. Date of notification—disability element and severe disability element for child tax credit.
27. Advance notification.
28. Circumstances where one person may act for another in giving a notification—receivers, etc.
29. Circumstances where one person may act for another in giving a notification—other appointed persons.
29A. Form in which evidence of birth or adoption to be provided.

PART IV

NOTICES TO PROVIDE INFORMATION OR EVIDENCE

30. Employers.
31. Persons by whom childcare is provided.
32. Dates to be specified in notices under section 14(2), 15(2), 16(3), 18(10) or 19(2) of the Act.

PART V

FINAL DECISIONS

33. Dates to be specified in notices under section 17 of the Act.
34. Manner in which declaration or statement in response to a notice under section 17 of the Act to be made.
35. Circumstances where one person may act for another in response to a notice under section 17 of the Act—receivers, etc.
36. Circumstances where one person may act for another in response to a notice under section 17 of the Act.

PART I

GENERAL

Citation, commencement and effect

1.—(1) These Regulations may be cited as the Tax Credits (Claims and Notifications) Regulations 2002 and shall come into force on 12th August 2002.

Tax Credits (Claims and Notifications) Regulations 2002

(2) These Regulations have effect in relation to claims for a tax credit for periods of award beginning on or after 6th April 2003.

Interpretation

2.272   **2.** In these Regulations—
"the Act" means the Tax Credits Act 2002;
"appropriate office" means an office of—
   (a) the Board,
   (b) the Department for Work and Pensions, or
   (c) the Department for Social Development in Northern Ireland;
"the Board" means the Commissioners of Inland Revenue;
[2"couple" has the meaning given by section 3(5A) of the Act;]
"disability element" shall be construed in accordance with section 11(4) of the Act;
"joint claim" has the meaning given by section 3(8) of the Act;
[2. . .]
[1"relevant authority" means—
   (a) the Board;
   (b) the Secretary of State or the Department for Social Development in Northern Ireland; or
   (c) a person providing services to the Board, the Secretary of State or that Department in connection with tax credits;]
"severe disability element" has the meaning in regulation 17 of the Working Tax Credit Regulations;
"single claim" has the meaning given by section 3(8) of the Act;
"tax year" means a period beginning on 6th April in one year and ending with 5th April in the next;
[2. . .]
"the Working Tax Credit Regulations" means the Working Tax Credit (Entitlement and Maximum Rate) Regulations 2002.

AMENDMENTS

1. Tax Credits (Claims and Notifications and Payments by the Board) (Amendment) Regulations 2003 (SI 2003/723), reg.3(1) (April 6, 2003).
2. Civil Partnership Act 2004 (Tax Credits, etc.) (Consequential Amendments) Order 2005 (SI 2005/2919), art.4(2) (December 5, 2005).

Use of electronic communications to make claims or to give notices or notifications

2.273   **3.**—(1) In these Regulations "writing" includes writing produced by electronic communications that are approved by directions issued by or on behalf of the Board.

(2) If a claim which is required by these Regulations to be made to [1a relevant authority at an appropriate office] is made in writing produced by electronic communications, it shall be treated for the purposes of these Regulations as having been made to, and received by, [1a relevant authority at an appropriate office] on the date on which it is recorded on an official computer system.

(3) If a notice or notification which is required by these Regulations to be given to [1a relevant authority at an appropriate office] is given in writing produced by electronic communications, it shall be treated for the purposes of these Regulations as having been given to, and received by, [1a relevant

(SI 2002/2014, reg.3) (as amended)

authority at an appropriate office] on the date on which it is recorded on an official computer system.

(4) In this regulation—
(a) "electronic communications" has the meaning given by section 132(10) of the Finance Act 1999;
(b) "official computer system" means a computer system maintained by or on behalf of the Board to—
   (i) send or receive information, or
   (ii) process or store information.

AMENDMENT

1. Tax Credits (Claims and Notifications and Payments by the Board) (Amendment) Regulations 2003 (SI 2003/723), reg.3(2) (April 6, 2003).

DEFINITIONS

"appropriate office"—see reg.2.
"the Board"—see *ibid*.
"electronic communications"—see para.(4)(a).
"official computer system"—see para.(4)(b).
"relevant authority"—see reg.2.
"writing"—see para.(1).

GENERAL NOTE

See further the decision of Mr Commissioner Mesher in *CIS/995/2004*, discussed in the annotations to reg.4 below and Tax Credits Act 2002, s.14(2) above.

This regulation enables use of the internet and an official website for claims. The HMRC website claim facility was closed down after severe problems with fraud. The House of Commons Public Accounts Committee has since disclosed that the website was established outside recommended security procedures. It remains closed at the time of writing.

2.274

PART II

CLAIMS

Interpretation of this Part

4. In this Part (and Part III) "the relevant date", in relation to a claim for a tax credit, means—
(a) in cases where regulation 6 applies, the date on which the claim would be treated as being made by that regulation disregarding regulations 7 and 8;
(b) in cases where sub-paragraph (b) of regulation 11(3) applies, the date on which the claim would be treated as being made by that sub-paragraph disregarding regulations 7 and 8;
(c) in any other case, the date on which the claim is received by [¹ a relevant authority at an appropriate office].

2.275

AMENDMENT

1. Tax Credits (Claims and Notifications and Payments by the Board) (Amendment) Regulations 2003 (SI 2003/723), reg.3(2) (April 6, 2003).

Tax Credits (Claims and Notifications) Regulations 2002

DEFINITIONS

"appropriate office"—see reg.2.
"relevant authority"—see *ibid*.
"the relevant date"—see reg.4.

GENERAL NOTE

2.276   The general rule is that the "relevant date" (or date of claim in social security terms) is the date on which the claim for tax credits is received by "a relevant authority at an appropriate office" (para.(c)). On the basis of the definition of these latter terms in reg.2, this will normally, but not always, be an HMRC office. For the date of receipt of electronic communications, e.g. online claims for tax credits, see reg.3. There are two modifications to the general rule in para.(c). First, amended claims are treated as made on the date on which the amended claim is received (see para.(a) and reg.6(3)). Secondly, where a claimant responds to a final notice under TCA 2002, s.17 within the specified time, the date of claim is the previous April 6 (reg.11(3)(a)). If the claimant's declaration is submitted beyond that time limit, then the date of claim is the latest date on which such declaration is received (see para.(b) and reg.11(3)(b)). Note that there are special rules governing the effective date of claim by refugees who have made a successful application for asylum and who subsequently make a retrospective claim for tax credits (see Tax Credits (Immigration) Regulations 2003 (SI 2003/653), regs 3 and 4).

Mr Commissioner Mesher's decision in *CIS/995/2004* deals with the complex interaction between tax credits and income support and what constitutes a claim for the former. Early in 2003 the claimant in *CIS/995/2004* claimed income support. On January 10, 2003, he also completed an online application form for child tax credit (CTC) and transmitted it to the Inland Revenue. In March 2003 the claimant received a TC602 letter from the Inland Revenue notifying him of his family's CTC entitlement for the 2003/04 tax year and asking him to sign and return the accompanying declaration. Having made further enquiries, the claimant discovered that he would be better off retaining entitlement to income support. He accordingly did not sign and return the TC602 declaration. However, the Revenue started making CTC payments in April 2003 and notified the DWP of this fact. This led the Secretary of State to decide that the claimant was no longer entitled to income support as his income exceeded his applicable amount.

The claimant appealed to a tribunal which disallowed his appeal, holding that reg.7 of the Social Security (Working Tax Credit and Child Tax Credit) Consequential Amendments Regulations 2003 (SI 2003/455) required the DWP to treat the claimant's income as including an amount equivalent to his CTC entitlement. Although finding error in the tribunal's reasoning in other respects, the Commissioner held that the tribunal had come to the only conclusion open to it as a matter of law and on the evidence before it. In particular, the Commissioner rejected the claimant's argument that he had only made a preliminary application for CTC which could not be completed until he had signed and returned the TC602 declaration. On the contrary, the online completion and transmission of the application form, notwithstanding the absence of any written confirmation at the time or later, amounted to a claim. Mr Commissioner Mesher thus held that the claimant had made a valid claim on January 10, 2003, whether in an approved electronic format (and so under regs 3 and 5(2)(a)—a point which did not have to be resolved) or alternatively under the wide power in reg.5(2)(b). A valid award of CTC had then followed. The Commissioner expressly left open the question whether an appeal tribunal or Commissioner has jurisdiction to go behind the Board's determination that a claim had been made.

The informality with which HMRC will accept renewals claims was emphasised in a public letter to the Institute of Chartered Accountants in England and Wales published on October 1, 2004. Speaking of renewal claims, the Deputy Chairman of the then Inland Revenue said:

"Claimants simply have to confirm or correct the information we hold about their circumstances and report their income for the year just finished. For those not in a position to provide actual income figures at the time they reply, an estimate will be accepted. The information necessary to renew can be accepted by telephone or through our e-portal or by filling in a short paper form."

He added: "I should also make clear, in answer to a concern you raise, that renewals information is logged on receipt, even if it has not yet been processed, to make sure the payments continue."

Manner in which claims to be made

5.—(1) This regulation prescribes the manner in which a claim for a tax credit is to be made.

(2) A claim must be made to [¹a relevant authority at an appropriate office]—
  (a) in writing on a form approved or authorised by the Board for the purpose of the claim; or
  (b) in such other manner as the Board may accept as sufficient in the circumstances of any particular case.

(3) A claim must contain the information requested on the form (or such of that information as the Board may accept as sufficient in the circumstances of the particular case).

(4) In particular, a claim must include in respect of every person by whom the claim is made—
  (a) a statement of the person's national insurance number and information or evidence establishing that that number has been allocated to the person; or
  (b) information or evidence enabling the national insurance number that has been allocated to the person to be ascertained; or
  (c) an application for a national insurance number to be allocated to the person which is accompanied by information or evidence enabling such a number to be so allocated.

This paragraph is subject to paragraph (6).

(5) "National insurance number" means the national insurance number allocated within the meaning of regulation 9 of the Social Security (Crediting and Treatment of Contributions, and National Insurance Numbers) Regulations 2001.

(6) Paragraph (4) does not apply if the Board are satisfied that the person or persons by whom the claim was made had a reasonable excuse for making a claim which did not comply with the requirements of that paragraph.

(7) At any time after a claim has been made but before the Board have given notice of their decision under section 14(1) of the Act in relation to the claim, the person or persons by whom the claim was made may amend the claim by giving notice orally or in writing to [¹a relevant authority at an appropriate office].

AMENDMENT

1. Tax Credits (Claims and Notifications and Payments by the Board) (Amendment) Regulations 2003 (SI 2003/723), reg.3(2) (April 6, 2003).

DEFINITIONS

"the Act"—see reg.2.
"appropriate office"—see *ibid*.

Tax Credits (Claims and Notifications) Regulations 2002

"the Board"—see *ibid*.
"National insurance number"—see para.(5).
"relevant authority"—see reg.2.
"writing"—see reg.3(1).

GENERAL NOTE

Para. (2)

2.278   This rule is similar to, but not identical to, the standard social security provision in reg.4(1) of the Social Security (Claims and Payments) Regulations 1987 (SI 1987/1968). The fundamental difference is that it is not possible to make an oral claim for a social security benefit under reg.4(1) of the 1987 Regulations. This appears to be possible in the case of tax credits as the requirement that the claim be in writing appears only in para.(a), which will cover the great majority of cases, and not in the residual category envisaged by para.(b).

Paras (4)–(6)

2.279   The requirement to provide a national insurance number (or the information or evidence specified) mirrors the requirement for social security benefits set out in SSAA 1992, s.1(1B). Note however HMRC discretion not to apply this requirement if satisfied that the claimant had a reasonable excuse for making a claim which failed to comply with it (para.(6)). There is no equivalent discretion to disapply the requirement in the social security scheme.

Para. (7)

2.280   This provision is similar to the social security rule in reg.5(1) of the Social Security (Claims and Payments) Regulations 1987 (SI 1987/1968). However, a tax credits claim can be amended by giving oral notice, whereas the social security rule requires written notice. See further reg.6 on the determination of the date of claim for amended claims for tax credits.

Amended claims

2.281   **6.**—(1) In the circumstances prescribed by paragraph (2) a claim for a tax credit which has been amended shall be treated as having been made as amended and, subject to regulations 7 and 8, as having been made on the date prescribed by paragraph (3).

(2) The circumstances prescribed by this paragraph are where a person has amended or persons have amended the claim in accordance with reg.5(7).

(3) The date prescribed by this paragraph is the date on which the claim being amended was received by [¹ a relevant authority at an appropriate office].

AMENDMENT

1. Tax Credits (Claims and Notifications and Payments by the Board) (Amendment) Regulations 2003 (SI 2003/723), reg.3(2) (April 6, 2003).

DEFINITIONS

"appropriate office"—see reg.2.
"relevant authority"—see *ibid*.

Time-limit for claims (if otherwise entitled to tax credit up to three months earlier)

2.282   **7.**—(1) In the circumstances prescribed by paragraph (2), a claim for a tax credit received by [¹ a relevant authority at an appropriate office] shall be treated as having been made on the date prescribed by paragraph (3).

(SI 2002/2014, reg.7) (as amended)

(2) The circumstances prescribed by this paragraph are those where the person or persons by whom the claim is made would (if a claim had been made) have been entitled to the tax credit either—
  (a) on the date falling three months before the relevant date (or on 6th April 2003, if later); or
  (b) at any later time in the period beginning on the date in subparagraph (a) and ending on the relevant date.

(3) The date prescribed by this paragraph is the earliest date falling within the terms of paragraph (2)(a) or (b) when the person or the persons by whom the claim is made would (if a claim had been made) have become entitled to the tax credit.

AMENDMENT

1. Tax Credits (Claims and Notifications and Payments by the Board) (Amendment) Regulations 2003 (SI 2003/723), reg.3(2) (April 6, 2003).

DEFINITIONS

"appropriate office"—see reg.2.
"relevant authority"—see *ibid*.

GENERAL NOTE

The standard rule is that tax credits claims can be backdated only three months. This has given rise to a number of appeals, but there are no exceptions or discretions in the rule save for that in reg.8. Regulation 25 imposes a similar time limit on notifying changes of circumstances that may increase awards. This contrasts with the relevant income tax rule that allows corrections to be made (for example because no claim has been made for an allowance or no deduction for an expense) for up to six years after the relevant time. It also contrasts with the powers for HMRC to amend tax credits awards and entitlements to deal with overpayments.

Once a claim has been made, there may be an amendment to deal with corrections when the annual declaration is made ahead of the entitlement decision.

It is therefore better to make a claim if there may be entitlement rather than waiting to see. This has led to the widespread practice, accepted by HMRC, of protective claims, and also to the practice of HMRC reducing awards to nil rather than terminating them during the year where circumstances change. Statistics show that at any one time in recent years there are about ½ million nil or protective claims in the system.

2.283

Date of claims—disability element of working tax credit

8.—(1) In the circumstances prescribed by paragraph (2) the claim referred to in sub-paragraph (f) of that paragraph shall be treated as having been made on the date prescribed by paragraph (3).

(2) The circumstances prescribed by this paragraph are where—
  (a) a claim for working tax credit including the disability element ("the original claim") was made by a person or persons;
  (b) on the original claim, the decision of the Board under section 14(1) of the Act was not to make an award of the tax credit;
  (c) the reason for that decision was that the person or any of the persons did not satisfy [¹paragraph (1)(c) of regulation 9] of the Working Tax Credit Regulations;
  (d) at the relevant date in relation to the original claim, the person or any of the persons had made a claim for any of the benefits referred to in that paragraph that had not been determined;

2.284

483

(e) after that date, the claim for the benefit was determined in favour of the person by whom it was made; and

(f) a further claim for working tax credit including the disability element is made by the person or persons, within 3 months of the date that the claim for the benefit was determined.

(3) The date prescribed by this paragraph is—

(a) the first date in respect of which the benefit claimed was payable; or

(b) if later, the date on which the original claim was made (or treated as made under regulation 7).

AMENDMENT

1. Tax Credits (Claims and Notifications) (Amendment) Regulations 2003 (SI 2003/3240), reg.3 (January 1, 2004).

DEFINITIONS

"the Act"—see reg.2.
"the Board"—see *ibid*.
"disability element"—see *ibid*.
"the original claim"—see para.(2)(a).
"the relevant date"—see reg.4.
"the Working Tax Credit Regulations"—see reg.2.

GENERAL NOTE

2.285 This makes special provision for the date of a claim for working tax credit including the disability element of that tax credit. It covers the situation where a claim for working tax credit on this basis is disallowed because the claimant is not entitled to a qualifying benefit, although a claim for that benefit is pending and is subsequently allowed, and a further claim for working tax credit is made within three months of the determination of the claim for the qualifying benefit (para.(2)). In such a case, the date of claim is either the first date in respect of which the qualifying benefit was payable or, if later, the date on which the original working tax credit claim was made (para.(3)).

Advance claims before the year begins

2.286 **9.**—(1) In the circumstances prescribed by paragraph (2) a claim for a tax credit may be made for a period after the relevant date.

(2) The circumstances prescribed by this paragraph are where a tax credit is claimed for a tax year by making a claim before the tax year begins.

(3) This regulation shall cease to have effect in relation to the tax year beginning on 6th April 2004 and subsequent tax years.

DEFINITIONS

"the relevant date"—see reg.4.
"tax year"—see reg.2.

GENERAL NOTE

2.287 This regulation provides, at least at the outset of the tax credits scheme, for claims for such credits to be made before the beginning of the tax year to which they relate (see also reg.14). There is further provision in reg.10 for advance claims for working tax credit where a person is about to start work.

(SI 2002/2014, reg.10) (as amended)

Advance claims—working tax credit

10.—(1) In the circumstances prescribed by paragraph (2) a claim for a tax credit may be made for a period after the relevant date.
(2) The circumstances prescribed by this paragraph are where—
(a) the tax credit in question is working tax credit; and
(b) the case falls within sub-paragraph (b) of the First Condition in regulation 4(1) of the Working Tax Credit Regulations (person who has accepted an offer of work which is expected to commence within seven days).
(3) In the circumstances prescribed by paragraph (2)—
(a) an award on a claim for tax credit may be made subject to the condition that the requirements for entitlement are satisfied no later than the date prescribed by paragraph (4); and
(b) if those requirements are satisfied no later than that date, the claim shall be treated as being made on the date on which they are satisfied.
(4) The date prescribed by this paragraph is the date falling 7 days after the relevant date.

DEFINITIONS

"the relevant date"—see reg.4.
"the Working Tax Credit Regulations"—see reg.2.

GENERAL NOTE

This rule allows for working tax credit claims to be made up to seven days in advance where a person has accepted an offer of employment and is expected to commence within that week.

Circumstances in which claims to be treated as made—notices containing provision under section 17(2)(a), (4)(a) or (6)(a) of the Act

11.—(1) In the circumstances prescribed by paragraph (2), a claim for a tax credit is to be treated as made.
(2) The circumstances prescribed by this paragraph are where (in the case where there has been a previous single claim) a person has or (in the case where there has been a previous joint claim) both persons have made a declaration in response to provision included in a notice under section 17 of the Act by virtue of—
(a) subsection (2)(a) of that section;
(b) subsection (4)(a) of that section;
(c) subsection (6)(a) of that section; or
(d) any combination of those subsections.
The declaration made shall (subject to regulation 5(3)) be treated as a claim for tax credit by that person or persons for the tax year following that to which the notice relates.
(3) The claim shall be treated as made—
[²(a) in a case where the declaration is made by [³31st July] next following the end of the tax year to which the claim relates, on 6th April preceding that date;
(aa) in a case where the declaration, not having been made by the date mentioned in sub-paragraph (a), is made before 31st January next following the end of the tax year to which the claim relates, and, in

Tax Credits (Claims and Notifications) Regulations 2002

the opinion of the Board, the claimant had good cause for not making the declaration as mentioned in that sub-paragraph, on 6th April preceding the date on which the declaration is made;]
(b) in any other case, on the latest date on which the declaration is received by [¹ a relevant authority at an appropriate office] (subject to the application of regulation 7).

[²(4) Paragraph (3) does not apply—
(a) in the case where there has been a previous single claim (to which the notice referred to in paragraph (2) relates) if the person by whom it was made could no longer make a single claim; or
(b) in the case where there has been a previous joint claim (to which the notice referred to in paragraph (2) relates) if the persons by whom it was made could no longer make a joint claim.]

AMENDMENTS

1. Tax Credits (Claims and Notifications and Payments by the Board) (Amendment) Regulations 2003 (SI 2003/723), reg.3(2) (April 6, 2003).
2. Tax Credits (Miscellaneous Amendments) Regulations 2004 (SI 2004/762), reg.3(2) (April 6, 2004).
3. Tax Credits (Miscellaneous Amendments) Regulations 2007 (SI 2007/824), reg.14(2) (April 6, 2007).

DEFINITIONS

"the Act"—see reg.2.
"appropriate office"—see *ibid*.
"the Board"—see *ibid*.
"joint claim"—see *ibid*.
"relevant authority"—see *ibid*.
"single claim"—see *ibid*.
"tax year"—see *ibid*.

GENERAL NOTE

2.291   This allows the claimant's (or claimants') declaration in response to a HMRC final notice under various provisions of the TCA 2002, s.17, to be treated as a claim for tax credits. This effectively eases the process of making renewal claims for subsequent tax years. This assumes that the claimant(s) provide the necessary information as requested on the official form (para.(2) and reg.5(3)). The date of claim is the preceding April 6, i.e. the start of the tax year, assuming the declaration is returned within the designated time (para.(3)).
There are further deeming rules under reg.12 in relation to s.17 final notices.

Circumstances in which claims to be treated as made—notices containing provision under section 17(2)(b), (4)(b) and (6)(b) of the Act

2.292   **12.**—(1) In either of the circumstances prescribed by paragraphs (2) and (4) a claim for a tax credit is to be treated as made.
(2) The circumstances prescribed by this paragraph are where a person is or persons are treated as having made a declaration in response to provision included in a notice under section 17 of the Act by virtue of—
(a) subsection (2)(b) of that section; and
(b) subsection (4)(b) of that section,
   or a combination of those subsections and subsection (6)(b) of that section.

(SI 2002/2014, reg.12) (as amended)

(3) The declaration referred to in paragraph (2) shall (subject to regulation 5(3)) be treated as a claim by that person or persons for tax credit for the tax year following that to which the notice relates.

(4) The circumstances prescribed by this paragraph are where a person or any of the persons has—
   (a) made a statement under paragraph (b) of subsection (2) of section 17 of the Act in response to such a notice by the date specified for the purposes of that subsection; or
   (b) made a statement under paragraph (b) of subsection (4) of that section in response to such a notice by the date specified for the purposes of that subsection,

or a combination of any of those subsections and subsection (6)(b) of that section.

(5) The notice referred to in paragraph (4), together with (and as corrected by) the statement or statements there referred to, shall (subject to regulation 5(3)) be treated as a claim for tax credit by that person or persons for the tax year following that to which the notice relates.

(6) The claim shall be treated as made on 6th April preceding the dates specified in the notice for the purposes of subsection (2) or (4) of section 17 of the Act.

(7) Paragraph (5) shall not apply—
   (a) in the case where there has been a previous single claim (to which the notice relates), the person by whom it was made could no longer make a single claim; or
   (b) in the case where there has been a previous joint claim (to which the notice relates), the persons by whom it was made could no longer jointly make a joint claim.

DEFINITIONS

"the Act"—see reg.2.
"joint claim"—see *ibid*.
"single claim"—see *ibid*.
"tax year"—see *ibid*.

GENERAL NOTE

Regulation 11 makes provision for the claimant's declaration in response to an HMRC final notice to be treated as a claim for tax credits for the following tax year. This regulation makes similar provision for those cases in which the claimant is sent a final notice informing them that they will be treated as having declared that their circumstances as are specified in the notice. On the position of couples, see further reg.13.

2.293

Circumstances in which claims made by one member of a couple to be treated as also made by the other member of the couple

13.—(1) In the circumstances prescribed by paragraph (2) a claim for a tax credit made by one member of a [¹. . .] couple is to be treated as also made by the other member of the [¹. . .] couple.

2.294

(2) The circumstances prescribed by this paragraph are those where one member of a [¹. . .] couple is treated by regulation 12 as having made a claim for a tax credit in response to a notice under section 17 of the Act given to both members of the couple.

AMENDMENT

1. Civil Partnership Act 2004 (Tax Credits, etc.) (Consequential Amendments) Order 2005 (SI 2005/2919), art.5(3) (December 5, 2005).

DEFINITIONS

"the Act"—see reg.2.
"married couple"—see *ibid*.
"unmarried couple"—see *ibid*.

GENERAL NOTE

2.295   This reflects the general rule in TCA 2002, s.3(3) that couples must make a claim for tax credits jointly. This is important also as both claimants are jointly and severally liable for any overpayment.

Circumstances in which awards to be conditional and claims treated as made—decisions under section 14(1) of the Act made before 6th April 2003

2.296   **14.**—*(transitional only – spent)*

Persons who die after making a claim

2.297   **15.**—(1) This regulation applies where any person who has made a claim for a tax credit dies—
(a) before the Board have made a decision in relation to that claim under section 14(1) of the Act;
(b) having given a notification of a change of circumstances increasing the maximum rate at which a person or persons may be entitled to the tax credit, before the Board have made a decision whether (and, if so, how) to amend the award of tax credit made to him or them; or
(c) where the tax credit has been awarded for the whole or part of a tax year, after the end of that tax year but before the Board have made a decision in relation to the award under section 18(1), (5), (6) or (9) of the Act.

(2) In the case of a single claim, the personal representatives of the person who has died may proceed with the claim in the name of that person.

(3) In the case of a joint claim where only one of the persons by whom the claim was made has died, the other person with whom the claim was made may proceed with the claim in the name of the person who has died as well as in his own name.

(4) In the case of a joint claim where both the persons by whom the claim was made have died, the personal representatives of the last of them to die may proceed with the claim in the name of both persons who have died.

(5) For the purposes of paragraph (4), where persons have died in circumstances rendering it uncertain which of them survived the other—
(a) their deaths shall be presumed to have occurred in order of seniority; and
(b) the younger shall be treated as having survived the elder.

DEFINITIONS

"the Act"—see reg.2.
"the Board"—see *ibid*.

(SI 2002/2014, reg.15) (as amended)

"joint claim"—see *ibid.*
"single claim"—see *ibid.*
"tax year"—see *ibid.*

GENERAL NOTE

This regulation makes provision as to how a claim is to proceed after the person or persons die after making it. In short, the personal representatives of the deceased person(s) may proceed with the claim (paras (2) and (4)), although in the case of a couple where only one partner has died the survivor may proceed with the claim in both their names (para.(3); see further reg.16). Paragraph (5) reflects the property law rule on contemporaneous deaths to be found in Law of Property Act 1925, s.184.

2.298

Persons who die before making joint claims

16.—(1) This regulation applies where one member of a [1. . .] couple dies and the other member of the [1. . .] couple wishes to make a joint claim for a tax credit.

2.299

(2) The member who wishes to make the claim may make and proceed with the claim in the name of the member who has died as well as in his own name.

(3) Any claim made in accordance with this regulation shall be for a tax credit for a period ending with—
  (a) the date of the death of the member of the [1. . .] couple who has died; or
  (b) if earlier, 5th April in the tax year to which the claim relates.

AMENDMENT

1. Civil Partnership Act 2004 (Tax Credits, etc.) (Consequential Amendments) Order 2005 (SI 2005/2919), art.5(4) (December 5, 2005).

DEFINITIONS

"joint claim"—see reg.2.
"married couple"—see *ibid.*
"unmarried couple"—see *ibid.*

GENERAL NOTE

See note to reg.15.

2.300

Circumstances where one person may act for another in making a claim—receivers, etc.

17.—(1) In the circumstances prescribed by paragraph (2), any receiver or other person mentioned in sub-paragraph (b) of that paragraph may act for the person mentioned in sub-paragraph (a) of that paragraph in making a claim for a tax credit.

2.301

(2) The circumstances prescribed by this paragraph are where—
  (a) a person is, or is alleged to be, entitled to a tax credit but is unable for the time being to make a claim for a tax credit; and
  (b) there are any of the following—
    (i) a receiver appointed by the Court of Protection with power to make a claim for a tax credit on behalf of the person;
    (ii) in Scotland, a tutor, curator or other guardian acting or appointed in terms of law who is administering the estate of the person; and

(iii) in Northern Ireland, a controller appointed by the High Court, with power to make a claim for a tax credit on behalf of the person.

Circumstances where one person may act for another in making a claim—other appointed persons

2.302 18.—(1) In the circumstances prescribed by paragraph (2), any person mentioned in sub-paragraph (b) of that paragraph may act for the person mentioned in sub-paragraph (a) of that paragraph in making a claim for a tax credit.

(2) The circumstances prescribed by this paragraph are where—
(a) a person is, or is alleged to be, entitled to a tax credit but is unable for the time being to make a claim for a tax credit; and
(b) in relation to that person, there is a person appointed under—
  (i) regulation 33(1) of the Social Security (Claims and Payments) Regulations 1987;
  (ii) regulation 33(1) of the Social Security (Claims and Payments) Regulations (Northern Ireland) 1987; or
  (iii) paragraph (3).

(3) Where there is no person mentioned in regulation 17(2)(b) in relation to the person who is unable to act, the Board may appoint under this paragraph a person who—
(a) has applied in writing to the Board to be appointed to act on behalf of the person who is unable to act; and
(b) if a natural person, is aged 18 years or more.

(4) An appointment under paragraph (3) shall end if—
(a) the Board terminate it;
(b) the person appointed has resigned from the appointment having given one month's notice in writing to the Board of his resignation; or
(c) the Board are notified that a receiver or other person mentioned in regulation 17(2)(b) has been appointed in relation to the person who is unable to make a claim.

DEFINITIONS

"the Board"—see reg.2.
"writing"—see reg.3(1).

GENERAL NOTE

2.303 HMRC operate this provision by use of form TC 689. This has caused some controversy, for example about the period for which the authority given by the form remains valid. The form and related practices are under review.

PART III

NOTIFICATIONS OF CHANGES OF CIRCUMSTANCES

Interpretation of this Part

2.304 19. In this Part "the notification date", in relation to a notification, means—
(a) the date on which the notification is given to [¹a relevant authority at an appropriate office]; or

(SI 2002/2014, reg.19) (as amended)

(b) in cases where regulation 24 applies, the date on which the notification would be treated by that regulation as being given disregarding regulations 25 and 26.

AMENDMENT

1. Tax Credits (Claims and Notifications and Payments by the Board) (Amendment) Regulations 2003 (SI 2003 No.723), reg.3(2) (April 6, 2003).

DEFINITIONS

"appropriate office"—see reg.2.
"relevant authority"—see *ibid.*

Increases of maximum rate of entitlement to a tax credit as a result of changes of circumstances to be dependent on notification

20.—(1) Any change of circumstances of a description prescribed by para.(2) which may increase the maximum rate at which a person or persons may be entitled to tax credit is to do so only if notification of it has been given in accordance with this Part.

(2) The description of changes of circumstances prescribed by this paragraph are changes of circumstances other than those in consequence of which the Board have given notice of a decision under section 16(1) of the Act in accordance with section 23 of the Act.

2.305

DEFINITIONS

"the Act"—see reg.2.
"the Board"—see *ibid.*

GENERAL NOTE

The effect of this provision is that increases in the maximum rate of entitlement to a tax credit, as a result of some relevant change of circumstances, are dependent upon notification. The normal rule is that changes which have the effect of increasing entitlement are backdated for a maximum of three months from the date of notification (reg.25).

2.306

Requirement to notify changes of circumstances which may decrease the rate at which a person or persons is or are entitled to tax credit or mean that entitlement ceases

21.—(1) [¹Subject to paragraph (1A),] where a person has or persons have claimed a tax credit, notification is to be given within the time prescribed by paragraph (3) if there is a change of circumstances of the description prescribed by paragraph (2) which may decrease the rate at which he is or they are entitled to the tax credit or mean that he ceases or they cease to be entitled to the tax credit.

[¹(1A) Paragraph (1) does not apply where advance notification has been given under regulation [² 27(2), (2A) or (3)].]

(2) The changes of circumstances described by this paragraph are those where—
   (a) entitlement to the tax credit ceases by virtue of section 3(4), or regulations made under section 3(7), of the Act;
   (b) there is a change in the relevant child care charges which falls within regulation 16(1)(b) (omitting paragraph (i)) of the Working Tax Credit Regulations;

2.307

(c) a person ceases to undertake work for at least 16 hours per week for the purposes of—
  (i) the Second Condition in regulation 4(1) (read with regulations 4(3) to (5) and 5 to 8), or
  (ii) regulation 13(1),
of the Working Tax Credit Regulations;
(d) a person ceases to undertake work for at least 30 hours per week for the purposes of the Second Condition in regulation 4(1) of the Working Tax Credit Regulations (read with regulations 4(3) to (5) and 5 to 8), except in a case where he still falls within the terms of paragraph (a) or (b) of that Condition;
(e) a person ceases to undertake, or engage in, qualifying remunerative work for at least 16 hours per week for the purposes of—
  (i) regulation 9(1)(a) (disability element),
  (ii) regulation 10(2)(d) (30 hour element), or
  (iii) regulation 18(3)(c) (50 plus element),
of the Working Tax Credit Regulations;
(f) a person ceases to engage in qualifying remunerative work for at least 30 hours per week, for the purposes of—
  (i) regulation 10(1) (30 hour element), or
  (ii) regulation 11(2)(c) (second adult element), in a case where the other claimant mentioned in that provision is not so engaged for at least 30 hours per week,
of the Working Tax Credit Regulations;
(g) a couple cease to engage in qualifying remunerative work for at least 30 hours per week, for the purposes of regulation 10(2)(c) (30 hour element) of the Working Tax Credit Regulations;
(h) a person ceases to be treated as responsible for a child or qualifying young person, for the purposes of child tax credit or of the Working Tax Credit Regulations;
  (i) in a case where a person has given advance notification under regulation 27(2B) that a child is expected to become a qualifying young person, the child does not become a qualifying young person for the purposes of Part 1 of the Act;
(j) a person ceases to be a qualifying young person for the purposes of Part 1 of the Act, other than by attaining the age of twenty; or
(k) a child or qualifying young person dies.]

(3) The time prescribed by this paragraph is the period of [³ one] months beginning on the date on which the change of circumstances occurs or [²(except in the case of paragraph (2)(j))], if later, the period of [³one] months beginning on [² the date on which the person first becomes aware of the change in circumstances].

AMENDMENTS

1. Tax Credits (Claims and Notifications and Payments by the Board) (Amendment) Regulations 2003 (SI 2003/723), reg.4 (April 6, 2003).
2. Tax Credits (Claims and Notifications) (Amendment) Regulations 2006 (SI 2006/2689), regs 4 and 5 (November 1, 2006).
3. Tax Credits (Claims and Notifications) (Amendment) Regulations 2006 (SI 2006/2689), reg.6 (April 6, 2007).

(SI 2002/2014, reg.21) (as amended)

DEFINITIONS

"the Act"—see reg.2.
"Working Tax Credit Regulations"—see *ibid*.

GENERAL NOTE

2.308

The amendments to this regulation in 2006 significantly harden the previously relaxed regime about reporting changes that may terminate or decrease an award of credits. First, many more changes of circumstances must now be reported. Second, the time limit for reporting is reduced from three months to one month. The duty to notify is imposed by s.6(3) of TCA 2002 read with this regulation. Failure to comply with s.6(3) may incur a penalty not exceeding £300: s.32(3) of the Act. Fraudulently or negligently making an incorrect statement under that section can incur a penalty of up to £3,000: s.31(1)(a) of the Act. HMRC literature draws attention to these penalties.

In broad terms (and as stated by HMRC in the literature) the changes of circumstances that must now be reported within a month are:

For both tax credits:
- Getting married or becoming a civil partner
- Living together with someone else as husband and wife or civil partners
- Stopping living together with a spouse or civil partner or other partner
- Leaving the UK for more than 8 weeks
- Death of child or young person for whom claimant is responsible
- Child leaves home to live with someone else

For CTC:
- Child does not become or stops being qualifying young person when 16 (eg leaves college or training) or until 20
- Young person starts to claim benefits or credits personally
- Child or young person stops being entitled to support from claimant

For WTC:
- Claimant or partner stops working for 16 hours a week
- Claimant or partner stops working for 30 hours a week
- Claimant or partner stops paying for childcare or bill goes down by £10 a week
- Being on strike for over 10 days

The duty to report under this regulation also covers any other circumstance in which entitlement to or an award of tax credits should end under s.3(4) or (7) of TCA 2002. This includes changes in a polygamous relationship, ceasing to be entitled by reason of ceasing to be a resident of the UK, or adverse changes in immigration status. It does not include changes in disablement as for instance where disability living allowance stops being paid. This may be because HMRC is informed of this automatically by DWP. There is also no general duty to report changes of income if hours of work are not affected.

Manner in which notifications to be given

22.—(1) This regulation prescribes the manner in which a notification is to be given.

2.309

(2) A notification must be given to [¹a relevant authority at an appropriate office].

(3) A notification may be given orally or in writing.

(4) At any time after a notification has been given but before the Board have made a decision under section 15(1) or 16(1) of the Act in consequence of the notification, the person or persons by whom the notification was given may amend the notification by giving notice orally or in writing to [¹a relevant authority at an appropriate office].

Tax Credits (Claims and Notifications) Regulations 2002

AMENDMENT

1. Tax Credits (Claims and Notifications and Payments by the Board) (Amendment) Regulations 2003 (SI 2003 No.723), reg.3(2) (April 6, 2003).

DEFINITIONS

"the Act"—see reg.2.
"appropriate office"—see *ibid*.
"the Board"—see *ibid*.
"relevant authority"—see *ibid*.
"writing"—reg.3(1).

GENERAL NOTE

2.310   Problems of proof may emerge from the combination of reg.22(2) and (3) when linked in particular to penalty cases under s.32(3). Adequate notification to an "appropriate office" of a "relevant authority" would appear, from reg.2, to include notification given at a Jobcentre Plus office. This can give rise to disputes where an individual maintains that he or she has informed the local social security office and regards that as notification also to HMRC, particularly if the local office does not keep records in the same way as HMRC best practice. It is not clear whether local housing benefit services are regarded as persons providing services to the Secretary of State under the current regime by which investigations for housing benefit also include other benefits. There is a duty on such authorities to pass on information received. See Tax Credits (Administrative Arrangements) Regulations 2002, regs 3, 5.

Person by whom notification may be, or is to be, given

2.311   **23.**—(1) In the case of a single claim, notification is to be given by the person by whom the claim for a tax credit was made.

(2) In the case of a joint claim, notification may be given by either member of the [1. . .] couple by whom the claim for a tax credit was made.

AMENDMENT

1. Civil Partnership Act 2004 (Tax Credits, etc.) (Consequential Amendments) Order 2005 (SI 2005/2919), art.5(5) (December 5, 2005).

DEFINITIONS

"joint claim"—see reg.2.
"married couple"—see *ibid*.
"single claim"—see *ibid*.
"unmarried couple"—see *ibid*.

Amended notifications

2.312   **24.**—(1) In the circumstances prescribed by paragraph (2) a notification which has been amended shall be treated as having been given as amended and, subject to regulations [²25, 26 and 26A], as having been given on the date prescribed by paragraph(3).

(2) The circumstances prescribed by this paragraph are where the person or persons by whom the notification is given amends or amend the notification in accordance with regulation 22(4).

(3) The date prescribed by this paragraph is the date on which the notification being amended was given to [¹a relevant authority at an appropriate office].

(SI 2002/2014, reg.24) (as amended)

AMENDMENTS

1. Tax Credits (Claims and Notifications and Payments by the Board) (Amendment) Regulations 2003 (SI 2003 No.723), reg.3(2) (April 6, 2003).
2. Tax Credits (Miscellaneous Amendments) Regulations 2004 (SI 2004/762), reg.3(3) (April 6, 2004).

DEFINITIONS

"appropriate office"—see reg.2.
"relevant authority"—see *ibid*.

Date of notification—cases where change of circumstances which may increase the maximum rate

25.—(1) Where a notification of a change of circumstances which may increase the maximum rate at which a person or persons may be entitled to tax credit is given in the circumstances prescribed by paragraph (2), that notification is to be treated as having been given on the date specified by paragraph (3).

(2) The circumstances prescribed by this paragraph are where notification is given to [¹a relevant authority at an appropriate office] of a change of circumstances which has occurred other than in the circumstances prescribed by regulation 26(2).

(3) The date specified by this paragraph is—
(a) the date falling three months before the notification date; or
(b) if later, the date of the change of circumstances.

2.313

AMENDMENT

1. Tax Credits (Claims and Notifications and Payments by the Board) (Amendment) Regulations 2003 (SI 2003/723), reg.3(2) (April 6, 2003).

DEFINITIONS

"appropriate office"—see reg.2.
"the notification date"—see reg.19.
"relevant authority"—see reg.2.

GENERAL NOTE

Where a change in circumstances leads to an increase in the claimant's entitlement to tax credits, the change can be backdated for up to three months before the date of notification. The requirement for notification itself in such circumstances is contained in reg.20. See also notes on reg.7 (time limit for claims).

2.314

Date of notification—disability element and severe disability element for working tax credit

26.—(1) In the circumstances prescribed by either paragraph (2) or (3), the notification of a change of circumstances referred to in subparagraph (f) of either of those paragraphs is to be treated as having been given on the date specified by paragraph (4).

(2) The circumstances prescribed by this paragraph are where—
(a) a claim for working tax credit including the disability element, the severe disability element, or both those elements ("the original claim") was made by a person or persons;

2.315

Tax Credits (Claims and Notifications) Regulations 2002

 (b) on the original claim, the decision of the Board under section 14(1) of the Act was not to award the [¹credit], or to award it without one or both of those elements;
 (c) the reason for that decision was that the person or any of the persons was not entitled to the element because he did not satisfy [¹regulation 9(1)(c)], or regulation 17(2), as the case may be, of the Working Tax Credit Regulations;
 (d) at the relevant date in relation to the original claim, the person or any of the persons had made a claim for any of the benefits referred to in those regulations that had not been determined;
 (e) after that date, the claim for the benefit was determined in favour of the person by whom it was made; and
 (f) notification is given of the change of circumstances which results in the person or any of the persons becoming entitled to that element or those elements, as the case may be, within three months of the date that the claim for the benefit was determined.
(3) The circumstances prescribed by this paragraph are where—
 (a) a notification was given of a change of circumstances which might result in the person or any of the persons by whom the claim was made becoming entitled to the disability element or the severe disability element of working tax credit ("the original notification");
 (b) on the notification, the decision of the Board under section 15(1) of the Act was not to amend the award of the tax credit made to him or them;
 (c) the reason for that decision was that the person or any of the persons was not entitled to the element because he did not satisfy [¹regulation 9(1)(c)], or regulation 17(2), as the case may be, of the Working Tax Credit Regulations;
 (d) at the notification date in relation to the original notification, the person or either of the persons had made a claim that had not been determined for any of the benefits referred to in those Regulations;
 (e) after that date, the claim for the benefit was determined in favour of the person by whom it was made; and
 (f) a further notification of the change of circumstances is given by the person or any of the persons, within three months of the date that the claim for benefit was determined.
(4) The date prescribed by this paragraph is—
 (a) the first date in respect of which the benefit claimed is payable; or
 (b) if later, the date on which—
  (i) in the circumstances prescribed by paragraph (2), the original claim was made (or treated as made under regulation 7); or
  (ii) in the circumstances prescribed by paragraph (3), the original notification was given (or treated as given under regulation 25).

AMENDMENT

1. Tax Credits (Claims and Notifications) (Amendment) Regulations 2003 (SI 2003/3240), reg.4 (January 1, 2004).

DEFINITIONS

"the Act"—see reg.2.
"the Board"—see *ibid.*
"disability element"—see *ibid.*
"the notification date"—see reg.19.

(SI 2002/2014, reg.26) (as amended)

"the original claim"—see para (2)(a).
"the original notification"—see para.(3)(a).
"relevant date"—see reg.4.
"severe disability element"—see reg.2.
"Working Tax Credit Regulations"—see *ibid*.

GENERAL NOTE

The effect of this regulation is that a claim for the disability or severe disability element of working tax credit, based on a claim made for a disability or incapacity benefit, may be backdated to the first date in respect which that benefit is payable, if the award of that benefit is notified to HMRC within three months of its having been made.

In *CTC/1594/2006* the Commissioner emphasised that the extension of time under this regulation and reg.26A applies only when a claim for disability living allowance had been made at the time of the tax credits claim. Claims for disability living allowance are not retrospective and cannot be backdated.

2.316

[¹Date of notification—disability element and severe disability element for child tax credit

26A.—(1) In the circumstances prescribed by either paragraph (2) or (3), the notification of a change of circumstances referred to in sub-paragraph (f) of either of those paragraphs is to be treated as having been given on the date specified by paragraph (4).

(2) The circumstances prescribed by this paragraph are where—
(a) a claim for child tax credit including the disability element, the severe disability element or both those elements ("the original claim") was made by a person or persons in respect of a child;
(b) on the original claim the decision of the Board under section 14(1) of the Act was not to award the credit, or to award it without one or both of those elements;
(c) the reason for that decision was that the person or the persons were not entitled to the element because the child did not satisfy regulation 8(2) or (3), as the case may be, of the Child Tax Credit Regulations 2002;
(d) at the relevant date in relation to the original claim, the person or any of the persons had made a claim for a disability living allowance in respect of that child ("the other claim") and the other claim had not been determined;
(e) after that date, the other claim was determined in favour of the person by whom it was made; and
(f) notice is given of the change of circumstances which results in the person or any of the persons becoming entitled to that element or those elements, as the case may be, within three months of the date that the other claim was determined.

(3) The circumstances prescribed by this paragraph are where—
(a) a notification was given of a change of circumstances which might result in the person or any of the persons by whom the claim was made becoming entitled to the disability element or the severe disability element of child tax credit ("the original notification");
(b) on the notification, the decision of the Board under section 15(1) of the Act was not to amend the award of the tax credit made to him or them;

2.317

Tax Credits (Claims and Notifications) Regulations 2002

(c) the reason for that decision was that the person or any of the persons was not entitled to the element because regulation 8(2) or (3), as the case may be, of the Child Tax Credit Regulations 2002 was not satisfied in respect of the child in relation to whom the claim was made;

(d) at the notification date in relation to the original notification, the person or either of the persons had made, in respect of the child, a claim that had not been determined for a disability living allowance ("the other claim");

(e) after that date, the other claim was determined in favour of the person by whom it was made; and

(f) a further notification of the change of circumstances is given by the person or any of the persons, within three months of the date that the other claim was determined.

(4) The date prescribed by this paragraph is—

(a) the first date in respect of which the disability living allowance is payable; or

(b) if later, the date on which—

(i) in the circumstances prescribed by paragraph (2), the original claim was made (or treated as made under regulation 7); or

(ii) in the circumstances prescribed by paragraph (3), the original notification was given (or treated as given under regulation 25).]

AMENDMENT

1. Tax Credits (Miscellaneous Amendments) Regulations 2004 (SI 2004/762), reg.3(4) (April 6, 2004).

DEFINITIONS

"the Act"—see reg.2.
"the Board"—see *ibid*.
"the disability element"—see *ibid*.
"the notification date"—see reg.19.
"the original claim"—see para.(2)(a).
"the original notification"—see para.(3)(a).
"the other claim"—see paras (2)(d) and (3)(d).
"the severe disability element"—see reg.2.

GENERAL NOTE

2.318 The effect of this regulation is that a claim for the disability or severe disability element of child tax credit, based on a claim made in respect of the child for disability living allowance, may be backdated to the first date in respect which that allowance is payable, providing the award is notified to HMRC within three months of its having been made.

Advance notification

2.319 **27.**—(1) In [¹any] of the circumstances prescribed by paragraphs (2) [¹, 2A] and (3) a notification of a change of circumstances may be given for a period after the date on which it is given.

(2) The circumstances prescribed by this paragraph are those prescribed by regulation 10(2) (working tax credit: person who has accepted an offer of work expected to commence within seven days), the reference to "the claim" being read as a reference to the notification.

(SI 2002/2014, reg.27) (as amended)

[¹(2A) The circumstances prescribed by this paragraph are where either regulation 15(4) (agreement for the provision of future childcare) or regulation 16(1) (relevant change in circumstances) of the Working Tax Credit Regulations applies.]

(3) The circumstances prescribed by this paragraph are where a tax credit has been claimed for the tax year beginning on 6th April 2003 by making a claim before that tax year begins, and the notification relates to that tax year and is given before that date.

(4) In the circumstances prescribed by paragraph (2), an amendment of an award of a tax credit in consequence of a notification of a change of circumstances may be made subject to the condition that the requirements for entitlement to the amended amount of the tax credit are satisfied at the time prescribed by paragraph (5).

(5) The time prescribed by this paragraph is the latest date which—
(a) is not more than seven days after the date on which the notification is given; and
(b) falls within the period of award in which the notification is given.

[¹(5A) In the circumstances prescribed by paragraph (2A), an amendment of an award of tax credit in consequence of a notification of a change of circumstances may be made subject to the condition that the requirements for entitlement to the amended amount of the tax credit are satisfied at the time prescribed by paragraph (5B).

(5B) The time prescribed by this paragraph is the first day of the week—
(a) in which the agreement within regulation 15(4) of the Working Tax Credit Regulations commences or the relevant change of circumstances occurs; and
(b) which is not more than seven days after the date on which notification is given and falls within the period of award in which the notification is given.

(5C) For the purposes of paragraph (5B), "week" means a period of 7 days beginning with midnight between Saturday and Sunday.]

(6) "Period of award" shall be construed in accordance with section 5 of the Act.

AMENDMENT

1. Tax Credits (Claims and Notifications and Payments by the Board) (Amendment) Regulations 2003 (SI 2003/723), reg.5 (April 6, 2003).

DEFINITIONS

"the Act"—see reg.2.
"the claim"—see para.(2).
"period of award"—see para.(6).
"tax year"—see reg.2.
"week"—see para.(5C).

Circumstances where one person may act for another in giving a notification—receivers etc.

28.—(1) In the circumstances prescribed by paragraph (2) any receiver or other person mentioned in sub-paragraph (b) of that paragraph may act for the person mentioned in sub-paragraph (a) of that paragraph in giving a notification.

Tax Credits (Claims and Notifications) Regulations 2002

(2) The circumstances prescribed by this paragraph are where—
(a) a person is unable for the time being to give a notification; and
(b) there are any of the following—
  (i) a receiver appointed by the Court of Protection with power to proceed with a claim for a tax credit on behalf of the person;
  (ii) in Scotland, a tutor, curator or other guardian acting or appointed in terms of law who is administering the estate of the person; and
  (iii) in Northern Ireland, a controller appointed by the High Court, with power to proceed with a claim for a tax credit on behalf of the person.

GENERAL NOTE

2.321 See also reg.35 in respect of receivers, etc. acting in response to final notices under TCA 2002, s.17.

Circumstances where one person may act for another in giving a notification—other appointed persons

2.322 **29.**—(1) In the circumstances prescribed by paragraph (2) any person mentioned in sub-paragraph (b) of that paragraph may act for the person mentioned in sub-paragraph (a) of that paragraph in giving a notification.
(2) The circumstances prescribed by this paragraph are where—
(a) a person is unable for the time being to give a notification; and
(b) in relation to that person, there is a person appointed under—
  (i) regulation 33(1) of the Social Security (Claims and Payments) Regulations 1987;
  (ii) regulation 33(1) of the Social Security (Claims and Payments) Regulations (Northern Ireland) 1987; or
  (iii) regulation 18(3);
and the provisions of regulation 18(3) shall apply to notifications and (under regulation 36) responses to notices under section 17 of the Act, as they apply to claims.

DEFINITION

"the Act"—see reg.2.

GENERAL NOTE

2.323 See also reg.36 in respect of appointees acting in response to final notices under TCA 2002, s.17.

[¹Form in which evidence of birth or adoption to be provided

2.324 **29A.** If the Board require the person, or either or both of the persons, by whom a claim is made to provide a certificate of a child's birth or adoption, the certificate so produced must be either an original certificate or a copy authenticated in such manner as would render it admissible in proceedings in any court in the jurisdiction in which the copy was made.]

AMENDMENT

1. Tax Credits (Miscellaneous Amendments No.2) Regulations 2004 (SI 2004/1241), reg.4 (May 1, 2004).

(SI 2002/2014, reg.30) (as amended)

Part IV

Notices to Provide Information or Evidence

Employers

30.—(1) For the purposes of sections 14(2)(b), 15(2)(b), 16(3)(b) and 19(2)(b) of the Act the persons specified in paragraph (2) are prescribed, and, in relation to those persons, the information or evidence specified in paragraph (4) is prescribed.

(2) The persons specified in this paragraph are—
(a) any person named by a person or either of the persons by whom a claim for a tax credit is made as his employer or the employer of either of them; and
(b) any person whom the Board have reasonable grounds for believing to be an employer of a person or either of the persons by whom such a claim is made.

(3) "Employer" has the meaning given by section 25(5) of the Act.

(4) The information or evidence specified in this paragraph is information or evidence, including any documents or certificates, which relates to—
(a) the claim for the tax credit in question;
(b) the award of the tax credit in question; or
(c) any question arising out of, or under, that claim or award.

Definitions

"the Act"—see reg.2.
"the Board"—see *ibid*.
"employer"—see para.(3).

Persons by whom childcare is provided

31.—(1) For the purposes of sections 14(2)(b), 15(2)(b), 16(3)(b) and 19(2)(b) of the Act the persons specified in paragraph (2) are prescribed, and, in relation to those persons, the information or evidence specified in paragraph (3) is prescribed.

(2) The persons specified in this paragraph are—
(a) any person named by a person or persons by whom a claim for the childcare element of working tax credit is made as being, in relation to him or either of them, a person by whom childcare is provided; and
(b) any person whom the Board have reasonable grounds for believing to be, in relation to a person or persons by whom such a claim is made, a person by whom childcare is provided.

(3) The information or evidence specified in this paragraph is information or evidence, including any documents or certificates, which relates to—
(a) the claim for the tax credit in question;
(b) the award of the tax credit in question; or
(c) any question arising out of, or under, that claim or award.

(4) "Child care" has the meaning given by regulation 14(2) of the Working Tax Credit Regulations.

DEFINITIONS

"the Act"—see reg.2.
"the Board"—see *ibid*.
"childcare"—see para.(4).

Dates to be specified in notices under section 14(2), 15(2), 16(3), 18(10) or 19(2) of the Act

2.327 **32.** In a notice under section 14(2), 15(2), 16(3), 18(10) or 19(2) of the Act, the date which may be specified shall not be less than 30 days after the date of the notice.

DEFINITION

"the Act"—see reg.2.

PART V

FINAL DECISION

[¹Dates to be specified in notices under section 17 of the Act

2.328 **33.** In a notice under section 17 of the Act—
(a) the date which may be specified for the purposes of subsection (2) or subsection (4) shall be not later than [²31st July] following the end of the tax year to which the notice relates, or 30 days after the date on which the notice is given, if later; and
(b) the date which may be specified for the purposes of subsection (8) shall be not later than 31st January following the end of the tax year to which the notice relates, or 30 days after the date on which the notice is given, if later.]

AMENDMENTS

1. Tax Credits (Miscellaneous Amendments) Regulations 2004 (SI 2004/762), reg.3(5) (April 6, 2004).
2. Tax Credits (Miscellaneous Amendments) Regulations 2007 (SI 2007/824), reg.14(3) (April 6, 2007).

DEFINITIONS

"the Act"—see reg.2.
"tax year"—see *ibid*.

[¹Manner in which declaration or statement in response to a notice under section 17 of the Act to be made

2.329 **34.**—(1) This regulation prescribes the manner in which a declaration or statement in response to a notice under section 17 of the Act must be made.
(2) A declaration or statement must be made—
(a) in writing in a form approved by the Board for that purpose;
(b) orally to an officer of the Board; or
(c) in such other manner as the Board may accept as sufficient in the circumstances of any particular case.

(SI 2002/2014, reg.34) (as amended)

(3) In a case falling within paragraph (2)(b) one of two joint claimants may act for both of them in response to a notice under section 17 if, at the time the declaration or statement is made, a joint claim could be made by both of them.]

AMENDMENT

1. Tax Credits (Miscellaneous Amendments) Regulations 2004 (SI 2004/762), reg.3(5) (April 6, 2004).

DEFINITIONS

"the Act"—see reg.2.
"the Board"—see *ibid*.
"joint claim"—see *ibid*.

Circumstances where one person may act for another in response to a notice under section 17 of the Act—receivers, etc.

35.—(1) In the circumstances prescribed by paragraph (2) any receiver or other person mentioned in sub-paragraph (b) of that paragraph may act for the person mentioned in sub-paragraph (a) of that paragraph in response to a notice under section 17 of the Act.

(2) The circumstances prescribed by this paragraph are where—
(a) a person is unable for the time being to act in response to a notice under section 17 of the Act; and
(b) there are any of the following—
  (i) a receiver appointed by the Court of Protection with power to proceed with a claim for a tax credit on behalf of the person;
  (ii) in Scotland, a tutor, curator or other guardian acting or appointed in terms of law who is administering the estate of the person; and
  (iii) in Northern Ireland, a controller appointed by the High Court, with power to proceed with a claim for a tax credit and proceed with the claim on behalf of the person.

2.330

DEFINITION

"the Act"—see reg.2.

Circumstances where one person may act for another in response to a notice under section 17 of the Act

36.—(1) In the circumstances prescribed by paragraph (2) any person mentioned in sub-paragraph (b) of that paragraph may act for the person mentioned in sub-paragraph (a) of that paragraph in response to a notice under section 17 of the Act.

(2) The circumstances prescribed by this paragraph are where—
(a) a person is unable for the time being to act in response to a notice under section 17 of the Act; and
(b) in relation to that person, there is a person appointed under—
  (i) regulation 33(1) of the Social Security (Claims and Payments) Regulations 1987;
  (ii) regulation 33(1) of the Social Security (Claims and Payments) Regulations (Northern Ireland) 1987; or
  (iii) regulation 18(3).

2.331

DEFINITION

"the Act"—see reg.2.

Tax Credits [¹(Payment by the Commissioners)] Regulations 2002

(SI 2002/2173) (AS AMENDED)

2.332 The Commissioners of Inland Revenue, in exercise of the powers conferred upon them by sections 24(2), (3), (4), (7) and (8), 65(1), (2) and (7) and 67 of the Tax Credits Act 2002, hereby make the following Regulations:

1. Citation, commencement and effect.
2. Interpretation.
3. Child tax credit and childcare element—member of a couple prescribed for the purposes of s.24(2) of the Act.
4. Working tax credit (excluding any childcare element)—member of a couple prescribed for the purposes of s.24(2) of the Act.
5. Member of a couple prescribed for the purposes of s.24(2) of the Act where one of the members of the couple has died.
6. Person prescribed for the purposes of s.24(3) of the Act where an award of a tax credit is made on a claim which is made by one person on behalf of another.
7. Prescribed circumstances for the purposes of s.24(4) of the Act.
8. Time of payment by way of a credit to a bank account or other account.
9. Time of payment other than by way of a credit to a bank account or other account, etc.
10. Single payment of small sums of tax credit.
11. Postponement of payment.
12. Amounts of payments.
12A. Recovery of overpayments of tax credits from other payments of tax credit.
13. Manner of payment.
14. Entitlement to tax credit or element dependent on a bank account or other account having been notified to the Board.

AMENDMENT

1. Tax Credit (Payment by Employers, etc.) (Amendment) Regulations 2005 (SI 2005/2200) reg.7(2) (August 29, 2005).

GENERAL NOTE

2.333 The original policy intention of making employers responsible for payments of WTC (other than the child care element) has now been abandoned. Since April 2006 HMRC has assumed responsibility for making all payments of both CTC and WTC. Accordingly the Working Tax Credit (Payment by Employers) Regulations 2002 (SI 2002/2172) have now been revoked: see Tax Credit (Payment by Employers, etc.) (Amendment) Regulations 2005 (SI 2005/2200), reg.9.

Citation, commencement and effect

2.334 **1.**—(1) These Regulations may be cited as the Tax Credits (Payments by [²the Commissioners]) Regulations 2002 and shall come into force on 6th April 2003.

(2) These Regulations have effect in relation to payments of a tax credit, or any element of a tax credit, which must be made [¹. . .] in relation to the tax year beginning with 6th April 2003 and subsequent tax years.

[¹(3) Regulations 8 to 14 have effect only in relation to such payments as must be made by the Board.]

AMENDMENTS

1. Tax Credits (Claims and Notifications and Payments by the Board) (Amendment) Regulations 2003 (SI 2003/723), reg.7 (April 6, 2003).
2. Tax Credit (Payment by Employers, etc.) (Amendment) Regulations 2005 (SI 2005/2200), reg.7(2) (August 29, 2005).

Interpretation

2. In these Regulations—
"the Act" means the Tax Credits Act 2002;
[¹"the Commissioners" means Commissioners for Her Majesty's Revenue and Customs (see section 1 of the Commissioners for Revenue and Customs Act 2005);]
[²"couple" has the meaning given by section 3(5A) of the Act;]
"employee" and "employer" have the meaning given by section 25(5) of the Act;
[². . .];
"period of award" shall be construed in accordance with section 5 of the Act;
"the relevant tax year" means the whole or part of the tax year for which an award of a tax credit has been made to a person or persons (referred to in section 24(4) of the Act);
"tax year" means a period beginning with 6th April in one year and ending with 5th April in the next;
[² . . .].

AMENDMENTS

1. Tax Credit (Payment by Employers, etc.) (Amendment) Regulations 2005 (SI 2005/2200), reg.7(3) (August 29, 2005).
2. Civil Partnership Act 2004 (Tax Credits, etc.) (Consequential Amendments) Order 2005 (SI 2005/2919), art.6(2) (December 5, 2005).

Child tax credit and childcare element—member of a couple prescribed for the purposes of section 24(2) of the Act

3.—(1) This regulation has effect in relation to payments of—
(a) child tax credit; and
(b) any childcare element of working tax credit.
(2) Subject to regulation 5, the member of a [⁴couple] prescribed by paragraph (3) is prescribed for the purposes of section 24(2) of the Act.
(3) The member of a [⁴couple] [²prescribed by this paragraph is—
(a) where the [⁴couple] are for the time being resident at the same address—
  (i) the member who is identified by both members of the [⁴couple] as the main carer;
  (ii) in default of a member being so identified, the member who appears to [³ the Commissioner] to be the main carer; and
(b) where—
  (i) the members of the [⁴couple] are for the time being resident at different addresses, or

Tax Credits [¹(Payment by the Commissioners)] Regulations 2002

(ii) one member of the [⁴couple] is temporarily absent from the address at which they live together,

the member who appears to [³ the Commissioner] to be the main carer.

Here "main carer" means the member of the [⁴couple] who is the main carer for the children and qualifying young persons for whom either or both of the members is or are responsible.]

(4) "Children" means persons who have not attained the age of 16 or who fall within the terms of regulation 4 of the Child Tax Credit Regulations 2002.

(5) "Qualifying young persons" means persons, other than children, who—
  (a) have not attained the age of nineteen; and
  (b) satisfy the conditions in regulation 5(3) and (4) of the Child Tax Credit Regulations 2002.

(6) Where payments are being made to the member of a [⁴couple] prescribed by virtue of paragraph (3) and the members of the [⁴couple] jointly give notice to [³ the Commissioners] that, as a result of a change of circumstances, the payments should be made to the other member as the main carer, the other member shall [², except where the notice appears to [³the Commissioners] to be unreasonable,] be treated as prescribed by virtue of paragraph (3).

[¹(7) For the purposes of this regulation, a person is responsible for a child or qualifying young person if he is treated as being responsible for that child or qualifying young person in accordance with the rules contained in regulation 3 of the Child Tax Credit Regulations 2002.]

AMENDMENTS

1. Tax Credits (Claims and Notifications and Payments by the Board) (Amendment) Regulations 2003 (SI 2003/723), reg.8 (April 6, 2003).
2. Tax Credits (Miscellaneous Amendments No.2) Regulations 2004 (SI 2004/1241), reg.5 (May 1, 2004).
3. Tax Credit (Payment by Employers, etc.) (Amendment) Regulations 2005 (SI 2005/2200), reg.7(4) (August 29, 2005).
4. Civil Partnership Act 2004 (Tax Credits, etc.) (Consequential Amendments) Order 2005 (SI 2005/2919), art.6(3) (December 5, 2005).

DEFINITIONS

"the Act"—see reg.2.
"children"—see para.(4).
"married couple"—see reg.2.
"qualifying young persons"—see para.(5).
"unmarried couple"—see reg.2.

GENERAL NOTE

2.337 Section 24(2) of the TCA 2002 permits payments of tax credits, or elements within tax credits, in the case of a joint claim to whichever member of a married or unmarried couple is prescribed. This regulation deals with the payment of child tax credit and any childcare element of working tax credit by HMRC. It provides that such tax credits are payable by HMRC to the partner identified by the couple as the main carer of the children concerned or, in default, the partner identified as such by HMRC (para.(3)). The couple can ask HMRC to change the method of payment to the other partner as the main carer (para.(6)).

(SI 2002/2173, reg.4) (as amended)

Working tax credit (excluding any childcare element)—member of a couple prescribed for the purposes of section 24(2) of the Act

4.—(1) This regulation has effect in relation to payments of working tax credit other than payments of any childcare element.

(2) Subject to regulation 5, the member of a [²couple] prescribed by para.(3) is prescribed for the purposes of section 24(2) of the Act.

(3) The member of a [²couple] prescribed by this paragraph is—
(a) if only one member of the [²couple] is engaged in remunerative work, that member;
(b) if both members of the [²couple] are engaged in remunerative work—
 (i) the member elected jointly by them; or
 (ii) in default of any election, such of them as appears to the Board to be appropriate.

(4) Where payments are being made to the member of [²couple] prescribed by virtue of paragraph (3)(b) and the members of the [²couple] jointly give notice to [¹the Commissioners] that, as a result of a change of circumstances, they wish payments to be made to the other member, the other member shall be treated as prescribed by virtue of paragraph (3)(b).

(5) For the purposes of paragraph (3), a member of a [²couple] is engaged in remunerative work if—
(a) he is engaged in qualifying remunerative work; or
(b) he works not less than 16 hours per week and the other member of the [²couple] is engaged in qualifying remunerative work.

(6) "Qualifying remunerative work", and being engaged in it, have the meaning given by regulation 4 of the Working Tax Credit (Entitlement and Maximum Rate) Regulations 2002.

2.338

AMENDMENTS

1. Tax Credit (Payment by Employers, etc.) (Amendment) Regulations 2005 (SI 2005/2200), reg.7(4) (August 29, 2005).
2. Civil Partnership Act 2004 (Tax Credits, etc.) (Consequential Amendments) Order 2005 (SI 2005/2919), art.6(3) (December 5, 2005).

DEFINITIONS

"the Act"—see reg.2.
"married couple"—see *ibid*.
"qualifying remunerative work"—see para.(6).
"unmarried couple"—see reg.2.

GENERAL NOTE

This deals with payment of working tax credit (excluding any childcare element, on which see reg.3) by HMRC. In the case of a couple, such working tax credit should be paid by HMRC to the member of the couple who is in remunerative work for working tax credit purposes (see paras (5) and (6)) or, if they both are, to the partner nominated jointly by the couple or, in default, as HMRC sees appropriate (para.(3)). As with reg.3, the couple have the option of changing their election (para.(4)).

2.339

Member of a couple prescribed for the purposes of section 24(2) of the Act where one of the members of the couple has died

5.—(1) This regulation applies where one of the members of a [¹couple] has died.

2.340

(2) The member of the [¹couple] prescribed by paragraph (3) is prescribed for the purposes of section 24(2) of the Act.

(3) The member of the [¹couple] prescribed by this paragraph is the member who survives.

(4) For the purposes of this regulation, where persons have died in circumstances rendering it uncertain which of them survived the other—
   (a) their deaths shall be presumed to have occurred in order of seniority; and
   (b) the younger shall be treated as having survived the elder.

AMENDMENT

1. Civil Partnership Act 2004 (Tax Credits, etc.) (Consequential Amendments) Order 2005 (SI 2005/2919), art.6(3) (December 5, 2005).

DEFINITIONS

"the Act"—see reg.2.
"married couple"—see *ibid*.
"unmarried couple"—see reg.2.

GENERAL NOTE

2.341   This regulation is self-explanatory. Paragraph (4) follows the general property law rule on survivorship laid down by s.184 of the Law of Property Act 1925.

Person prescribed for the purposes of section 24(3) of the Act where an award of a tax credit is made on a claim which is made by one person on behalf of another

2.342   **6.** For the purposes of section 24(3) of the Act, the person prescribed is—
   (a) the person by whom the claim on behalf of another was made; or
   (b) if at any time [¹the Commissioners] do not consider it appropriate for payments of the tax credit to be made to that person, the person on behalf of whom the claim was made.

AMENDMENT

1. Tax Credit (Payment by Employers, etc.) (Amendment) Regulations 2005 (SI 2005/2200), reg.7(4) (August 29, 2005).

DEFINITION

"the Act"—see reg.2.

GENERAL NOTE

2.343   See also regs 17, 18, 28 and 29 of the Tax Credits (Claims and Notifications) Regulations 2002 (SI 2002/2014).

Prescribed circumstances for the purposes of section 24(4) of the Act

2.344   **7.**—(1) Either of the circumstances prescribed by paragraphs (2) and (3) are prescribed circumstances for the purposes of section 24(4) of the Act.

(2) The circumstances prescribed by this paragraph are where—
   (a) a claim for a tax credit for the next tax year has been made or treated as made by the person or persons by the date specified for the purposes of subsection (4) of section 17 of the Act in the notice given to him or them under that section in relation to the relevant tax year; and

(SI 2002/2173, reg.7) (as amended)

(b) [¹the Commissioners] have not made a decision under section 14(1) of the Act in relation to that claim.
(3) The circumstances prescribed by this paragraph are where—
(a) a claim for a tax credit for the next tax year has not been made or treated as made by the person or persons; and
(b) [¹the Commissioners] have not made a decision under section 18(1) of the Act in relation to the person and persons for the relevant tax year.

AMENDMENT

1. Tax Credit (Payment by Employers, etc.) (Amendment) Regulations 2005 (SI 2005/2200), reg.7(4) (August 29, 2005).

DEFINITIONS

"the Act"—see reg.2.
"the relevant tax year"—see *ibid.*
"tax year"—see *ibid.*

GENERAL NOTE

Section 24(4) of the TCA 2002 enables payments of tax credits to continue to be paid in a following tax year in the absence of a claim and award in certain circumstances. This regulation thus allows payments to continue to be made, without interruption, at the start of each tax year while claims are being renewed in two types of circumstances. The first is where a renewal claim has been made or treated as made but has yet to be determined by HMRC (para.(2)). The second is a step further back, where no such renewal claim has been made but HMRC similarly has yet to make its final decision on the previous year (para.(3)).

2.345

Time of payment by way of a credit to a bank account or other account

8.—(1) [³. . .] This regulation applies where the tax credit or element is to be paid by way of a credit to a bank account or other account notified to [²the Commissioners].
(2) [¹Subject to paragraph (2A),] the tax credit or element shall be paid—
(a) each week; or
(b) every four weeks,
in accordance with any election given by the person to whom payment is to be made.
[¹(2A) If a person makes elections under paragraph (2) for child tax credit and any childcare element of working tax credit to be paid at differing intervals, the elections shall have no effect and [²the Commissioners] pay the child tax credit and any childcare element together either each week or every four weeks as appears to them to be appropriate.]
(3) [³ . . .]
(4) This regulation is subject to regulations 10 and 11.

2.346

AMENDMENTS

1. Tax Credits (Claims and Notifications and Payments by the Board) (Amendment) Regulations 2003 (SI 2003/723), reg.9 (April 6, 2003).
2. Tax Credit (Payment by Employers, etc.) (Amendment) Regulations 2005 (SI 2005/2200), reg.7(4) (August 29, 2005).
3. Tax Credit (Payment by Employers, etc.) (Amendment) Regulations 2005 (SI 2005/2200), reg.9(2) (April 1, 2006).

Tax Credits [¹(Payment by the Commissioners)] Regulations 2002

GENERAL NOTE

2.347 Employees paid tax credits by HMRC direct to their bank accounts have the option of having such payments paid weekly or four-weekly (para.(2)). However, it is not possible to have child tax credit and the childcare element of working tax credit paid at different intervals (para.(2A)). The intervals for payment via methods other than direct to a bank account are left to the discretion of HMRC (see reg.9). However, payment via bank accounts is clearly intended to be the standard method for HMRC to pay tax credits (see regs 13 and 14).

Time of payment other than by way of a credit to a bank account or other account, etc.

2.348 **9.**—(1) This regulation applies where—
(a) the tax credit or element is to be paid other than by way of a credit to a bank account or other account notified to [¹the Commissioners]; or
(b) [² . . .].
(2) The tax credit or element shall be paid at such times as appear to [¹the Commissioners] to be appropriate.

AMENDMENTS

1. Tax Credit (Payment by Employers, etc.) (Amendment) Regulations 2005 (SI 2005/2200), reg.7(4) (August 29, 2005).
2. Tax Credit (Payment by Employers, etc.) (Amendment) Regulations 2005 (SI 2005/2200), reg.9(2) (April 1, 2006).

[¹Single payment of small sums of tax credit

2.349 **10.** The tax credit or element may be paid by way of a single payment, and at such time, and in such manner, as appear to [²the Commissioners] to be appropriate, in any of the following cases—
(a) where [²the Commissioners] are paying only child tax credit to a person and the weekly rate at which it is payable is less than £2;
(b) where [²the Commissioners] are paying both any childcare element (but no other element) of working tax credit and child tax credit to a person and the total weekly rate at which they are payable is less than £2;
(c) where [²the Commissioners] are paying only working tax credit (apart from any childcare element) to a person and the weekly rate at which it is payable (excluding any such childcare element) is less than £2;
(d) where [²the Commissioners] are paying both working tax credit (including elements other than, or in addition to, any childcare element) and child tax credit to a person who has elected under regulation 8(2) to have them paid at the same intervals and the total weekly rate at which they are payable is less than £2;
(e) where [²the Commissioners] are paying both working tax credit (apart from any childcare element) and child tax credit to a person who has elected under regulation 8(2) to have them paid at differing intervals and—
  (i) the total weekly rate at which any such childcare element and the child tax credit are payable is less than £2; or
  (ii) the weekly rate at which the working tax credit is payable (excluding any such childcare element) is less than £2.]

(SI 2002/2173, reg.10) (as amended)

AMENDMENTS

1. Tax Credits (Claims and Notifications and Payments by the Board) (Amendment) Regulations 2003 (SI 2003/723), reg.10 (April 6, 2003).
2. Tax Credit (Payment by Employers, etc.) (Amendment) Regulations 2005 (SI 2005/2200), reg.7(4) (August 29, 2005).

GENERAL NOTE

The original version of this regulation, which was substituted by the version above before it came into force, was just one sentence long: so much for simplicity. The basic principle, however, remains the same: if tax credits are payable at an aggregate level of less than £2 a week, then HMRC will pay them in such manner as it deems appropriate (typically by way of a lump sum).

2.350

Postponement of payment

11.—(1) [¹The Commissioners] may postpone payment of the tax credit or element in any of the circumstances specified in paragraphs (2) and (3).

2.351

(2) The circumstances specified in this paragraph are where there is a pending determination of an appeal against a decision of an appeal tribunal, a Social Security Commissioner or a court relating to—
   (a) the case in question; or
   (b) another case where it appears to [¹the Commissioners] that, if the appeal were to be determined in a particular way, an issue would arise as to whether the award in the case in question should be amended or terminated under section 16(1) of the Act.

(3) The circumstances specified in this paragraph are where confirmation is pending of—
   (a) the details of a bank account or other account by way of a credit to which payment is to be made; or
   (b) the address of the person to whom payment is to be made, where it appears to [¹the Commissioners] that such details or address as were previously notified to them are incorrect.

(4) For the purposes of paragraph (2), the circumstances where a determination of an appeal is pending include circumstances where a decision of an appeal tribunal, a Social Security Commissioner or a court has been made and [¹the Commissioners]—
   (a) are awaiting receipt of the decision;
   (b) in the case of a decision by an appeal tribunal, are considering whether to apply for a statement of reasons or have applied for, and are awaiting receipt of, a statement of reasons; or
   (c) have received the decision or statement of reasons and are considering—
       (i) whether to apply for permission to appeal; or
       (ii) where permission is not needed or has been given, whether to appeal.

(5) "Appeal tribunal" has the meaning given by section 63(10) of the Act.
(6) "Social Security Commissioner" has the meaning given by section 63(13) of the Act.

AMENDMENT

1. Tax Credit (Payment by Employers, etc.) (Amendment) Regulations 2005 (SI 2005/2200), reg.7(4) (August 29, 2005).

DEFINITIONS

"the Act"—see reg.2.
"Appeal tribunal"—see para.(5).
"Social Security Commissioner"—see para.(6).

GENERAL NOTE

2.352 This regulation sets out the two types of circumstances in which a payment of tax credits by HMRC may be postponed. The first is the straightforward situation where HMRC believes that either the bank details or recipient's address previously notified to them is incorrect (para.(3)). The second is where there is an appeal pending in relation either to the particular case or to another case in which the outcome might lead to the amendment or termination of the award in the instant case (para.(2)). This is, therefore, the tax credits equivalent of the anti-test case rule. (But note, however, that it is limited to the postponement of payment, and does not make provision for limiting the effect of test cases in terms of backdating entitlement to tax credits.) The "pending determination" must be one against a decision of an appeal tribunal, Social Security Commissioner or court (para.(2)). The notion of "pending" is defined by para.(4). There are no explicit time limits stated within this regulation on HMRC's consideration of whether or not to lodge an appeal, but there are, of course, fairly tight time constraints on the exercise of such a right in the first place.

Amounts of payments

2.353 **12.**—(1) The tax credit or element shall be paid in accordance with the most recent decision by [¹the Commissioners] under section 14(1), 15(1) or 16(1) of the Act.

(2) Where the tax credit or element is to be paid other than by way of a single payment, it shall be paid so far as possible in such amounts as will result in the person to whom payment is to be made receiving regular payments of similar amounts over the entire period of award.

(3) Where an award of tax credit is amended, the total amount paid prior to the award being amended [²may] be taken into account by [¹the Commissioners] in determining the amount of any further payments for the remainder of the period of award.

(4) Where payments under section 24(4) of the Act are to be made, the rate at which the person or persons were entitled to the tax credit for the relevant tax year shall be taken into account by [¹the Commissioners] in determining the amounts of those payments.

AMENDMENTS

1. Tax Credit (Payment by Employers, etc.) (Amendment) Regulations 2005 (SI 2005/2200), reg.7(4) (August 29, 2005).
2. Tax Credits (Miscellaneous Amendments) Regulations 2007 (SI 2007/824), reg.15 (April 6, 2007).

DEFINITION

"the Act"—see reg.2.

GENERAL NOTE

2.354 This regulation provides for the amount of tax credits payable to be determined by HMRC's most recent relevant decision (para.(1)). Such payments should, so far as possible, be apportioned equally over regular payment intervals (para.(2)). The original formulation of para.(2) was mandatory in requiring HMRC to take prior payments into account in arriving at the appropriate amount due for payment

(SI 2002/2173, reg.12) (as amended)

following an amended award. Paragraph (2) now gives HMRC more flexibility in deciding the amount of any further tax credits where an award of tax credits is amended. Since April 2007, HMRC have been able to exercise a discretion in such cases. So, where claimants report a fall in income during the year, their tax credit payments will be adjusted for the rest of the year but will not include a one-off payment for the earlier part of the year. Their final award will be determined at the end of the year when their actual income is known, and any underpayment will be made good at that stage. Amounts of tax credits for subsequent years can be based on a preceding year's tax credit entitlement (para.(4); see further reg.7).

[¹Recovery of overpayments of tax credit from other payments of tax credit

12A.—(1) This regulation applies where notice is given to a person or persons under subsection (4) of section 29 of the Act (deduction of overpayments from payments of tax credit).

(2) The maximum rate at which an overpayment may be recovered from payments of tax credit is—
  (a) where the only amount of tax credit to which the person is, or, in the case of a joint claim, the persons are, entitled, is the family element of child tax credit, 100% of that tax credit;
  (b) where the total amount of tax credit to which the person is, or, in the case of a joint claim, the persons are, entitled is not subject to reduction—
      (i) by virtue of section 7(2) of the Act; or
      (ii) because their income for the relevant year does not exceed the relevant income threshold prescribed in his or their case in regulation 3 of the Tax Credits (Income Thresholds and Determination of Rates) Regulations 2002;
      10% of that tax credit; and
  (c) in any other case, 25% of the tax credit to which the person is, or in the case of a joint claim, the persons are, entitled.

(3) In paragraph (2) a reference to the amount to which a person is, or persons are, entitled is a reference to the amount to which they would be entitled but for the operation of that paragraph.]

2.355

AMENDMENT

1. Tax Credits (Miscellaneous Amendments) Regulations 2004 (SI 2004/762), reg.18 (April 6, 2004).

DEFINITION

"the Act"—see reg.2.

Manner of payment

13.—(1) Subject to paragraph (2), the tax credit or element shall be paid by way of a credit to a bank account or other account notified to [²the Commissioners] by the person to whom payment is to be made.

(2) Where [¹it does not appear to [²the Commissioners] to be appropriate] for the tax credit or element to be paid by way of a credit to a bank account or other account notified to [²the Commissioners] by the person to whom payment is to be made, the tax credit or element may be paid in such manner as appears to [²the Commissioners] to be appropriate.

2.356

513

(3) Subject to regulation 14, if no bank account or other account has been notified to [²the Commissioners], the tax credit or element shall be paid in such manner as appears to [²the Commissioners] to be appropriate.

AMENDMENTS

1. Tax Credits (Claims and Notifications and Payments by the Board) (Amendment) Regulations 2003 (SI 2003/723), reg.11 (April 6, 2003).
2. Tax Credit (Payment by Employers, etc.) (Amendment) Regulations 2005 (SI 2005/2200), reg.7(4) (August 29, 2005).

GENERAL NOTE

2.357 This regulation establishes the presumption in favour of payment by HMRC of tax credits to be direct to recipients' bank accounts.

Entitlement to tax credit or element dependent on a bank account or other account having been notified to the Board

2.358 **14.**—(1) Subject to paragraphs (2) and (3), if by the end of the relevant period no bank account or other account has been notified to [²the Commissioners] by the person to whom payment of a tax credit or element is to be made, that person shall cease to be entitled to the tax credit or element for the remainder of the period of the award until a bank account or other account is notified to [²the Commissioners].

(2) Where a person who has ceased to be entitled to a tax credit or an element by virtue of paragraph (1) subsequently notifies to [²the Commissioners] a bank account or other account, paragraph (1)—
  (a) shall not have effect for the period of three months prior to the date on which [²the Commissioners] receive the notification; and
  (b) shall cease to have effect for the remainder of the period of award.

(3) Where there are exceptional circumstances which are expected to result in a person not being able to obtain a bank account or other account throughout the period of award, paragraph (1) shall not have effect in relation to that person's entitlement to a tax credit or element for the period of award.

(4) "The relevant period" means whichever of the following periods ends latest—
  (a) the period of eight weeks beginning on the date on which [²the Commissioners] [¹give] notice in writing for the purposes of this regulation to the person to whom payment is to be made of the requirement that a bank account or other account be notified to them;
  (b) in cases where, within the period mentioned in sub-paragraph (a), the person to whom payment is to be made—
    (i) requests from [²the Commissioners] authority to open an account for which such authority is required; and
    (ii) provides sufficient information from which [²the Commissioners] can give that authority,
   the period of three weeks beginning on the date on which [²the Commissioners] [¹give] that authority;
  (c) in cases where the person to whom payment is to be made has a reasonable excuse—
    (i) for not being able to take all necessary steps to obtain a bank account or other account within whichever of the periods set out in sub-paragraph (a) or (b) ends latest; or

(SI 2002/2173, reg.14) (as amended)

  (ii) for not being able to notify to [²the Commissioners] the bank account or other account within that period,

the period ending with the date by which the account can reasonably be expected to be notified to [²the Commissioners].

(5) "Writing" includes writing produced by electronic communications that are approved by [²the Commissioners].

AMENDMENTS

1. Tax Credits (Claims and Notifications and Payments by the Board) (Amendment) Regulations 2003 (SI 2003/723), reg.12 (April 6, 2003).
2. Tax Credit (Payment by Employers, etc.) (Amendment) Regulations 2005 (SI 2005/2200), reg.7(4) (August 29, 2005).

DEFINITIONS

"the relevant period"—see para.(4).
"writing"—see para.(5).

GENERAL NOTE

This regulation further demonstrates that entitlement to a tax credit is to be dependent on a bank account or other account having been notified to HMRC.

2.359

Tax Credits (Administrative Arrangements) Regulations 2002

(SI 2003/3036)

The Commissioners of Inland Revenue, in exercise of the powers conferred upon them by ss.58 and 65(1), (2), (7) and (9) of the Tax Credits Act 2002, hereby make the following Regulations:

ARRANGEMENT OF ARTICLES

1. Citation and commencement.
2. Interpretation.
3. Provision of information or evidence to relevant authorities.
4. Giving of information or advice by relevant authorities.
5. Recording, verification and holding, and forwarding, of claims, etc. received by relevant authorities.

2.360

GENERAL NOTE

Section 58 of the TCA 2002 provides for regulations to make provision as to the administrative arrangements to apply between a relevant authority (i.e. the Secretary of State, the equivalent Northern Ireland Department or a person providing services to either of these authorities: TCA 2002, s.58(3)) and HMRC, who have the care and management of tax credits (see TCA 2002, s.2). Section 58 applies where regulations under TCA 2002, s.4 or 6 permit or require a claim or notification relating to a tax credit to be made or given to such a relevant authority. These Regulations have therefore been made under s.58 in order to provide for administrative arrangements in relation to claims and notifications made or given to a relevant authority in accordance with the Tax Credits (Claims and Notifications) Regulations 2002 (SI 2002/2014). Regulation 5 of those Regulations requires claims to be made to "an appropriate office", which means an office of the Board, the DWP or its Northern Ireland equivalent (reg.2).

2.361

Tax Credits (Administrative Arrangements) Regulations 2002

Citation and commencement

1. These Regulations may be cited as the Tax Credits (Administrative Arrangements) Regulations 2002 and shall come into force on 1st January 2003.

Interpretation

2. In these Regulations—
"the Board" means the Commissioners of Inland Revenue;
"the principal Regulations" means the Tax Credits (Claims and Notifications) Regulations 2002;
"relevant authority" means—
(a) the Secretary of State;
(b) the Department for Social Development in Northern Ireland; or
(c) a person providing services to the Secretary of State or that Department.

Provision of information or evidence to relevant authorities

3.—(1) Information or evidence relating to tax credits which is held—
(a) by the Board; or
(b) by a person providing services to the Board, in connection with the provision of those services,
may be provided to a relevant authority for the purposes of, or for any purposes connected with, the exercise of that relevant authority's functions under the principal Regulations.

(2) Information or evidence relating to tax credits may be provided to a relevant authority by persons other than the Board (whether or not persons by whom claims or notifications relating to tax credits are or have been made or given).

DEFINITIONS

"the Board" —see reg.2.
"the principal Regulations"—see *ibid*.
"relevant authority"—see *ibid*.

Giving of information or advice by relevant authorities

4. A relevant authority to which a claim or notification is or has been made or given by a person in accordance with the principal Regulations may give information or advice relating to tax credits to that person.

DEFINITIONS

"the principal Regulations"—see reg.2.
"relevant authority"—see *ibid*.

Recording, verification and holding, and forwarding, of claims etc. received by relevant authorities

5.—(1) A relevant authority may record and hold claims and notifications received by virtue of the principal Regulations and information or evidence received by virtue of regulation 3(2).

(SI 2003/3036, reg. 5)

(2) Subject to paragraphs (3) and (4), a relevant authority must forward to the Board or a person providing services to the Board such a claim or notification, or such information or evidence, as soon as reasonably practicable after being satisfied that it is complete.

(3) Before forwarding a claim in accordance with paragraph (2), a relevant authority must verify—
  (a) that any national insurance number provided in respect of the person by whom the claim is made exists and has been allocated to that person;
  (b) that the matters verified in accordance with sub-paragraph (a) accord with—
    (i) its own records; or
    (ii) in the case of a person providing services to the Secretary of State or the Department for Social Development in Northern Ireland, records held by the Secretary of State or that Department; and
  (c) whether the details of any relevant claim for benefit that have been provided are consistent with those held by it.

(4) If a relevant authority cannot locate any national insurance number in respect of a person by whom such a claim is made, it must forward to the Board or a person providing services to the Board the claim (notwithstanding that it is not complete).

(5) "National insurance number" means the national insurance number allocated within the meaning of—
  (a) regulation 9 of the Social Security (Crediting and Treatment of Contributions, and National Insurance Numbers) Regulations 2001; or
  (b) regulation 9 of the Social Security (Crediting and Treatment of Contributions, and National Insurance Numbers) Regulations (Northern Ireland) 2001.

(6) "Claim for benefit" means a claim for—
  (a) a benefit in relation to which—
    (i) the Secretary of State has functions under the Social Security Contributions and Benefits Act 1992; or
    (ii) the Department for Social Development in Northern Ireland has functions under the Social Security Contributions and Benefits (Northern Ireland) Act 1992; or
  (b) a jobseeker's allowance under—
    (i) the Jobseekers Act 1995; or
    (ii) the Jobseekers (Northern Ireland) Order 1995.

DEFINITIONS

"the Board"—see reg.2.
"the principal Regulations"—see *ibid*.
"relevant authority"—see *ibid*.

The Tax Credits (Notice of Appeal) Regulations 2002

The Tax Credits (Notice of Appeal) Regulations 2002

(SI 2002/3119)

Made	17th December 2002
Laid before Parliament	17th December 2002
Coming into force	7th January 2003

The Commissioners of Inland Revenue, in exercise of the powers conferred upon them by sections 39(1), 65(2) and 67 of the Tax Credits Act 2002, hereby make the following Regulations:

Citation and commencement

2.367   1. These Regulations may be cited as the Tax Credits (Notice of Appeal) Regulations 2002 and shall come into force on 7th January 2003.

Prescribed manner of notice of appeal

2.368   2.—(1) The prescribed manner of giving notice of appeal to the Board under section 39(1) of the Tax Credits Act 2002 is as follows.

(2) The notice must—
 (a) be given in writing,
 (b) contain sufficient information to identify the appellant and the decision against which the appeal is being made, and
 (c) be signed by or on behalf of the appellant.

(3) In paragraph (2)(a) "writing" includes writing produced by electronic communications if those electronic communications are approved by the Board.

(4) In paragraph (2)(c) "signed", where the notice is in writing produced by electronic communications, means authenticated in such manner as may be approved by the Board.

(5) In this regulation "the Board" means the Commissioners of Inland Revenue.

DEFINITIONS

 "the Board"—see para.(5).
 "signed"—see para.(4).
 "writing"—see para.(3).

GENERAL NOTE

2.369   A typed name can amount to a signature when it has been adopted by the person concerned through his or her signing another document or taking some other active step in an appeal (*R(DLA) 2/98*). In *CIB/460/2003*, the claimant's mother, who had not been appointed to act on behalf of the claimant, signed the appeal. No-one had objected and the claimant himself had signed the form issued by the clerk asking him, among other things, whether he wanted to withdraw the appeal. He had said "no". The Commissioner rejected a submission made on behalf of the Secretary of State to the effect that the appeal was not valid.
 See para.(4) for signatures on electronic documents.

(SI 2002/3196) (as amended)

The Tax Credits (Appeals) (No.2) Regulations 2002

(SI 2002/3196) (AS AMENDED)

Made   *18th December 2002*
Coming into force   *1st January 2003*

ARRANGEMENT OF REGULATIONS

PART I

General

1. Citation, commencement, duration and interpretation   2.370
2. Service of notices or documents

PART II

General Appeal Matters

3. Other persons with a right of appeal or a right to make an application for a direction
4. Time within which an appeal is to be brought
5. Late appeals
6. Making of an application for an extension of time
7. Making an application for a direction
8. Death of a party to an appeal or an application for a direction

PART III

Appeal Tribunals for Tax Credits

CHAPTER 1

Appeal Tribunals

9. Composition of appeal tribunals
10. Assignment of clerks to appeal tribunals: function of clerks

CHAPTER 2

Procedure in Connection with Determination of Appeals, Applications for Directions and Penalty Proceedings

11. Consideration and determination of appeals, applications for a direction and penalty proceedings
12. Choice of hearing
13. Withdrawal of application for a direction or penalty proceedings

14. Non-disclosure of medical advice or evidence
15. Summoning of witnesses and administration of oaths

CHAPTER 3

Striking Out Appeals and Applications For A Direction

16. Cases which may be struck out
17. Reinstatement of struck out cases

CHAPTER 4

Oral Hearings

18. Procedure at oral hearings
19. Manner of providing expert assistance
20. Postponement and adjournment

CHAPTER 5

Decisions of Appeal Tribunals and Related Matters

21. Decisions of appeal tribunals
22. Late applications for a statement of reasons of tribunal decision
23. Record of tribunal proceedings
24. Correction of accidental errors
25. Setting aside decisions on certain grounds
26. Provisions common to regulations 24 and 25
27. Application for leave to appeal to a Commissioner from a decision of an appeal tribunal

Whereas a draft of this instrument was laid before Parliament in accordance with section 80(1) of the Social Security Act 1998 and approved by a resolution of each House of Parliament.

Now, therefore, the Secretary of State for Work and Pensions, in exercise of the powers conferred upon him by sections 7(6), 12(2) and (7), 14(10) and (11), 16(1), 28(1), 39(1), 79(1) and (3) to (7) and 84 of, and paragraphs 11 and 12 of Schedule 1 and Schedule 5 to the Social Security Act 1998 and all other powers enabling him in that behalf, after consultation with the Council on Tribunals in accordance with section 8 of the Tribunals and Inquiries Act 1992, hereby makes the following Regulations:

PART I

GENERAL

Citation, commencement, duration and interpretation

2.371   **1.**—(1) These Regulations may be cited as the Tax Credits (Appeals) (No.2) Regulations 2002 and shall come into force on 1st January 2003.

(2) These Regulations shall cease to have effect on such day as is appointed by order made under section 63(1) of the Tax Credits Act 2002 (tax credits appeals etc.: temporary modifications).

(SI 2002/3196, reg.1) (as amended)

(3) In these Regulations, unless the context otherwise requires—
"the Act" means the Social Security Act 1998;
"the 2002 Act" means the Tax Credits Act 2002;
"the Appeals Regulations" means the Tax Credits (Appeals) Regulations 2002;
"the Decisions and Appeals Regulations" means the Social Security and Child Support (Decisions and Appeals) Regulations 1999;
"the Working Tax Credit Regulations" means the Working Tax Credit (Entitlement and Maximum Rate) Regulations 2002;
"appeal" means an appeal under section 38 of the 2002 Act;
"an application for a direction" means an application for a direction to close down an enquiry made under section 19(9) of the 2002 Act;
"a case" means, for the purposes of Chapter 3 of Part 3, an appeal or an application for a direction;
"clerk to the appeal tribunal" means a clerk assigned to the appeal tribunal in accordance with regulation 10;
[1"couple" means—
  (a) a man and woman who are married to each other and are members of the same household;
  (b) a man and woman who are not married to each other but are living together as husband and wife;
  (c) two people of the same sex who are civil partners of each other and are members of the same household; or
  (d) two people of the same sex who are not civil partners of each other but are living together as if they were civil partners,
and for the purposes of paragraph (d), two people of the same sex are to be regarded as living together as if they were civil partners if, but only if, they would be regarded as living together as husband and wife were they instead two people of the opposite sex;]
"court" means the High Court, the Court of Appeal, the Court of Session, the High Court or Court of Appeal in Northern Ireland, the House of Lords or the Court of Justice of the European Community;
"the date of notification" means—
  (a) the date of the notice of a decision of the Board given under section 23(2) of the 2002 Act; or
  (b) the date that notification of a decision of the Board, other than notice of a decision given under section 23(2) of the 2002 Act, is treated as having been given or sent in accordance with regulation 2(b);
"decision" means, for the purposes of Chapter 5 of Part 3,—
  (a) the decision of an appeal tribunal on an appeal;
  (b) a direction under section 19(10) of the 2002 Act given in response to an application for a direction, or the refusal to make such a direction; and
  (c) a penalty determination made in penalty proceedings;
"financially qualified panel member" means a panel member who satisfies the requirements of paragraph 4 of Schedule 3 to the Decisions and Appeals Regulations;
"joint claim" means a claim made under section 3(3)(a) of the 2002 Act and any reference in these Regulations to "joint claimant" shall be construed accordingly;

"legally qualified panel member" means a panel member who satisfies the requirements of paragraph 1 of Schedule 3 to the Decisions and Appeals Regulations;

"medically qualified panel member" means a panel member who satisfies the requirements of paragraph 2 of Schedule 3 to the Decisions and Appeals Regulations;

"panel" means the panel constituted under section 6 of the Act;

"panel member" means a person appointed to the panel;

"panel member with a disability qualification" means a panel member who satisfies the requirements of paragraph 5 of Schedule 3 to the Decisions and Appeals Regulations;

"partner" means, [1. . .], the other member of [1a] couple;

"party to the proceedings" means the Board and any other person—
- (a) who is an appellant in an appeal brought against a decision or determination set out in section 38 of the 2002 Act;
- (b) who is an applicant for a direction to close down an enquiry under section 19(9) of the 2002 Act;
- (c) who is a defendant (or defender) in penalty proceedings brought under paragraph 3 of Schedule 2 to the 2002 Act;
- (d) who is a person with a right of appeal or a right to make an application for a direction under regulation 3;

"penalty determination" means a decision made in accordance with paragraph 3 of Schedule 2 to the 2002 Act;

"penalty proceedings" means proceedings under paragraph 3 of Schedule 2 to the 2002 Act;

"President" means the President of appeal tribunals appointed under section 5 of the Act;

"single claim" means a claim made under section 3(3)(b) of the 2002 Act;

"tax credit" means child tax credit or working tax credit, construing those terms in accordance with section 1(1) and (2) of the 2002 Act, and any reference in these Regulations to "child tax credit" or "working tax credit" shall be construed accordingly.

AMENDMENT

1. Civil Partnership (Pensions, Social Security and Child Support) (Consequential, etc. Provisions) Order 2005 (SI 2005/2877), para.36(2) of Sch.3 (December 5, 2005).

GENERAL NOTE

"party to the proceedings"

In *CTC/2612/2005*, the Commissioner pointed out that where only one member of a couple who should have been joint claimants had appealed, the other was not a party to the proceedings, which was unfair as she was potentially liable to repay an overpayment. The real problem was that it was unclear whether the Inland Revenue had issued a decision addressed to both of them. If they had, it is suggested that an appeal by one of member of the couple could have been treated as an appeal by both of them unless it was clear that only one of them wished to appeal (see *R(A) 2/06*).

A more complex problem arose in *CTC/4390/2004*, where two separated parents each claimed child tax credit. It was pointed out that the legislation made no provision for them to be parties to a single appeal even though a decision could be binding only on the parties to it (see *CTC/2090/2004*). However, by the time the case reached the Commissioner, there were appeals by both parents (because the award to one parent had been terminated when the other parent won his appeal before the tribunal) and, with the agreement of the parties, the Commissioner, when allowing an appeal against the tribunal's decision, directed that the appeal be reheard at the same time as the other parent's appeal against the termination of her award.

Service of notices or documents

2.—Where, by any provision of these Regulations—
(a) any notice or other document is required to be given or sent to the clerk to the appeal tribunal or to the Board, that notice or document shall be treated as having been so given or sent on the day that it is received by the clerk to the appeal tribunal or by the Board, and
(b) any notice or other document is required to be given or sent to any person other than the clerk to the appeal tribunal or the Board, that notice or document shall, if sent to that person's last known address, be treated as having been given or sent on the day that it was posted.

DEFINITIONS

"the Board"—see s.39(1) of the Social Security Act 1998 as modified by reg.12 of the Tax Credits (Appeals) Regulations 2002.
"clerk to the appeal tribunal"—see reg.1(3).

GENERAL NOTE

A fax is received for the purposes of reg.2(a) when it is successfully transmitted to, and received by, a fax machine, irrespective of when it is actually collected from the fax machine (*R(DLA) 3/05*). Furthermore, the faxed request for a statement of reasons in that case was received by the clerk to the appeal tribunal when received at the tribunal venue, even though the clerk did not visit that venue until some days later. The Commissioner said that it would have been different if the venue had been a casual venue, such as local authority premises. Here, it was a dedicated venue and the fax number had been given to representatives precisely to enable them to communicate with the clerk. There was nothing in any document issued with the decision notice to indicate that the request for a statement of reasons had to be addressed to a different place.

The "last known address" to which documents must be sent for para.(b) to apply need not be the person's last known *residence* because the concepts are different. Moreover, the sender must consider the address to be reliable and, if he does not, should take reasonable steps to see whether a more reliable one exists (*CCS/2288/2005*). This approach exists to aid the innocent claimant and not the one who has failed to take reasonable steps to keep HMRC or the clerk to the tribunal aware of his whereabouts. Generally they are entitled to rely on a claimant to inform them of any move.

Deemed receipt of a document cannot cure a breach of the rules of natural justice so that, if a tribunal does not receive medical evidence submitted by the claimant in support of an application for a postponement, the decision of the tribunal can be set aside as being erroneous in point of law (*CG/2973/2004*). Decisions can also be set aside under reg.25 where documents go astray. That does not preclude an appeal, although an application for setting aside under reg.25 remains the more appropriate procedure (*CIB/303/1999*, declining to follow *R(SB) 55/83* but agreeing with *R(SB) 19/83*).

A provision similar to reg.2(b) relating to immigration appeals was held to be invalid in *R. v Secretary of State for the Home Department, ex parte Saleem* [2001] 1 W.L.R. 443, but there are sufficient remedies in these Regulations for the injustice that reg.2(b) might otherwise cause and Commissioners have distinguished *ex parte Saleem* and held the equivalent provision relating to social security and child support appeals to be valid (*CCS/6302/1999* and *CIB/303/1999*).

Part II

General Appeal Matters

Other persons with a right of appeal or a right to make an application for a direction

3.—For the purposes of section 12(2) of the Act (as applied and modified by the Appeals Regulations), where—
  (a) a person has made a claim for a tax credit but is unable for the time being to make an appeal against a decision in respect of that tax credit; or
  (b) a person is the person in respect of whom an enquiry has been initiated under section 19(1) of the 2002 Act, but is unable for the time being to make an application for a direction,
the following other persons have a right of appeal to an appeal tribunal or a right to make an application for a direction—
    (i) a receiver appointed by the Court of Protection with power to make a claim for a tax credit on behalf of the person;
    (ii) in Scotland, a [¹judicial factor, or guardian acting or appointed under the Adults with incapacity (Scotland) Act 2000 who has power to claim, or as the case may be, receive a tax credit on his behalf] who is administering the estate of the person;
    (iii) a person appointed under regulation 33(1) of the Social Security (Claims and Payments) Regulations 1987 (persons unable to act);
    (iv) where there is no person mentioned in sub-paragraph (iii) in relation to the person who is unable to act, a person who has applied in writing to the Board to be appointed to act on behalf of the person who is unable to act and, if a natural person, is aged 18 years or more and who has been so appointed by the Board for the purposes of this subparagraph.

Amendment

1. Social Security, Child Support and Tax Credits (Miscellaneous Amendments) Regulations 2005 (SI 2005/337), reg.4(2) (March 18, 2005).

Definitions

  "the Act"—see reg.1(3).
  "the Appeals Regulations"—*ibid*.
  "appeal"—*ibid*.
  "an application for a direction"—*ibid*.
  "the Board"—see s.39(1) of the Social Security Act 1998 as modified by reg.12 of the Tax Credits (Appeals) Regulations 2002.
  "tax credit"—reg.1(3).

General Note

Section 12(2) of the Social Security Act 1998, mentioned in the opening words of this regulation, has actually been "modified" out of existence because it and subs.(1) have been replaced by a single subsection. This regulation is made under the substituted s.12(1)(d).

It is arguable that this regulation is at least partly unnecessary as those mentioned in it could submit appeals on the basis of their general authority to act on behalf of

(SI 2002/3196, reg.3) (as amended)

the real appellant. Certainly it has not been thought necessary to make similar provision in respect of appeals to Commissioners.

Time within which an appeal is to be brought

4.—(1) Where a dispute arises as to whether an appeal was brought within the time limit specified in section 39(1) of the 2002 Act, the dispute shall be referred to, and be determined by, a legally qualified panel member.

(2) The time limit specified in section 39(1) of the 2002 Act may be extended in accordance with regulation 5.

DEFINITIONS

"the 2002 Act"—see reg.1(3).
"appeal"—*ibid.*
"legally qualified panel member"—see reg.1(3).

GENERAL NOTE

The time limit specified in s.39(1) of the Tax Credits Act 2002 is the 30 days usual in tax cases rather than the month usual in social security cases.

Late appeals

5.—(1) The time within which an appeal must be brought may be extended where the conditions specified in paragraphs (2) to (8) are satisfied, but no appeal shall in any event be brought more than one year after the expiration of the last day for appealing under section 39(1) of the 2002 Act.

(2) An application for an extension of time under this regulation shall be made in accordance with regulation 6 and shall be determined by a legally qualified panel member, except that where the Board consider that the conditions in paragraphs (4)(b) to (8) are satisfied, the Board may grant the application.

(3) An application under this regulation shall contain particulars of the grounds on which the extension of time is sought, including details of any relevant special circumstances for the purposes of paragraph (4).

(4) An application for an extension of time shall not be granted unless—
   (a) the panel member is satisfied that, if the application is granted, there are reasonable prospects that the appeal will be successful; or
   (b) the panel member is, or the Board are, satisfied that it is in the interests of justice for the application to be granted.

(5) For the purposes of paragraph (4) it is not in the interests of justice to grant an application unless the panel member is, or the Board are, as the case may be, satisfied that—
   (a) the special circumstances specified in paragraph (6) are relevant to the application; or
   (b) some other special circumstances exist which are wholly exceptional and relevant to the application,
and as a result of those special circumstances, it was not practicable for the appeal to be made within the time limit specified in section 39(1) of the 2002 Act.

(6) For the purposes of paragraph (5)(a), the special circumstances are that—

(a) the applicant or a partner or dependant of the applicant has died or suffered serious illness;
(b) the applicant is not resident in the United Kingdom; or
(c) normal postal services were disrupted.

(7) In determining whether it is in the interests of justice to grant the application, regard shall be had to the principle that the greater the amount of time that has elapsed between the expiration of the time within which the appeal is to be brought under section 39(1) of the 2002 Act and the making of the application for an extension of time, the more compelling should be the special circumstances on which the application is based.

(8) In determining whether it is in the interests of justice to grant an application, no account shall be taken of the following—
(a) that the applicant or any person acting for him was unaware of or misunderstood the law applicable to his case (including ignorance or misunderstanding of the time limit imposed by section 39(1) of the 2002 Act); or
(b) that a Commissioner or a court has taken a different view of the law from that previously understood and applied.

(9) An application under this regulation for an extension of time which has been refused may not be renewed.

(10) The panel member who determines an application under this regulation shall record a summary of his decision in such written form as has been approved by the President.

(11) As soon as practicable after the decision is made a copy of the decision shall be sent or given to every party to the proceedings.

DEFINITIONS

"the 2002 Act"—see reg.1(3).
"appeal"—*ibid.*
"the Board"—see s.39(1) of the Social Security Act 1998 as modified by reg.12 of the Tax Credits (Appeals) Regulations 2002.
"court"—reg.1(3).
"legally qualified panel member"—*ibid.*
"panel member"—*ibid.*
"partner"—*ibid.*
"President"—*ibid.*

GENERAL NOTE

Para. (1)

2.380 The absolute time limit prohibiting the bringing of appeals more than a year late is not incompatible with the European Convention on Human Rights (*Denson v Secretary of State for Work and Pensions* [2004] EWCA Civ 462 (also reported as *R(CS) 4/04*). Nonetheless, it can work injustice, particularly in a case where an unrepresented claimant has been challenging the wrong decision and nobody tells him or her until it is too late which decision it is that must be challenged if he or she is to succeed in obtaining the benefit sought.

In *R(TC) 1/05*, there was no evidence that anyone had considered whether there were grounds for admitting a late appeal. There was also a suggestion that notice of the original decision had not been sent to the claimant so that the appeal was not late at all. The Commissioner considered that the tribunal's brief reasons suggested that if the chairman had considered whether to extend the time for appealing, he would have refused. However, the Commissioner held the decision was invalid because, if the appeal had been late and there was no extension of time, the tribunal had had no jurisdiction to hear the appeal. The claimant was entitled to have the question of an extension of time properly considered. Had the chairman clearly refused an extension of time, the Commissioner said that it appeared that he would have had no jurisdiction to consider an appeal against that refusal, notwithstanding that there appeared to be no clear finding that notice of the decision under appeal had ever been issued. However, it is suggested that, if the tribunal had declined jurisdiction on the ground that time had not been extended, the refusal to accept jurisdiction would have been appealable and a failure to record a finding as to whether notice of the original decision had been issued might have led to the appeal being allowed. In an ordinary case, of course, the question of extending time is considered by a legally qualified panel member before the case is listed for hearing by a tribunal and, in some cases, a tribunal cannot be composed only of a legally qualified panel member.

It has been held that, because a decision of a legally qualified panel member must be treated as a decision of a tribunal, an appeal lies against a refusal to extend the time for appealing (*CIS/1363/2005 and others*). However, any challenge by HMRC to a grant of an extension of time for appealing must wait until the appeal is determined and presumably will be made only if the appeal is allowed. At the time of going to press, the decision of the Court of Appeal on the application for leave to appeal by the Secretary of State for Work and Pensions with regard to *CIS/1363/2005 and others* is awaited.

Para. (2)
HMRC may decide that a late appeal should be admitted under para.(4)(b) (but not under para.(4)(a)). Presumably it is not expected that an appeal tribunal will then object, because it is not clear what it could do if it did object. Presumably it is also not expected that HMRC will use this power where it is the applicant. It may be arguable that the decision of the panel member is a decision of an appeal tribunal for the purpose of permitting an appeal to be brought against it under s.14 of the Social Security Act 1998.

Para. (4)
Whereas under para.(2) HMRC can consider whether the conditions in paras (4)(b) to (8) are satisfied, only a legally qualified panel member can consider whether the condition in para.(4)(a) is satisfied. Sub-para.(a) bestows a fairly broad discretion on a legally qualified panel member to grant an extension of time and makes it unnecessary for him or her to consider the narrow conditions of paras (4)(b) to (8) in a meritorious case.

Para. (8)(a)
If a claimant is ignorant of the time limit for appealing because HMRC failed to provide the information required by s.23(2) of the Tax Credits Act 2002, it is arguable that time for appealing has not started to run. If this is correct, it is unnecessary for the would-be appellant to apply for an extension of time (which might be difficult in the light of para.8(a)) and instead he or she should apply for a ruling under reg.4(1).

Para. (8)(b)
Understood by whom? Presumably not the applicant because the view must also be different from that previously applied. But is it the understanding of HMRC as a whole that matters or of a particular officer or of the legally qualified panel member considering the application? Whatever the answer, it is not easy to see what sub-para.(b) adds to sub-para.(a).

Making of an application for an extension of time

6.—An application for an extension of time for making an appeal to an appeal tribunal shall be made in writing to the Board and shall—
  (a) include sufficient information to determine—
    (i) the identity of the appellant;
    (ii) the subject of the application in respect of which an extension of time is sought; and

The Tax Credits (Appeals) (No.2) Regulations 2002

  (iii) the grounds on which an extension of time is sought; and
(b) be signed by or on behalf of the appellant.

DEFINITIONS

"appeal"—see reg.1(3).
"appeal tribunal"—see s.39(1) of the Social Security Act 1998.
"the Board"—see s.39(1) of the Social Security Act 1998 as modified by reg.12 of the Tax Credits (Appeals) Regulations 2002.

GENERAL NOTE

2.386 See the note to reg.2 of the Tax Credits (Notice of Appeal) Regulations 2002 for what amounts to a signature, but note that there is no equivalent in these Regulations to reg.2(4) of those Regulations dealing with electronic documents.

Making an application for a direction

2.387 **7.**—An application for a direction to be made by an appeal tribunal shall—
(a) be made in writing to the Board;
(b) contain sufficient information for the Board to determine the identity of the applicant; and
(c) be signed by or on behalf of the applicant.

DEFINITIONS

"an application for a direction"—see reg.1(3).
"appeal tribunal"—see s.39(1) of the Social Security Act 1998.
"the Board"—see s.39(1) of the Social Security Act 1998 as modified by reg.12 of the Tax Credits (Appeals) Regulations 2002.

GENERAL NOTE

2.388 See the note to reg.2 of the Tax Credits (Notice of Appeal) Regulations 2002 for what amounts to a signature, but note that there is no equivalent in these Regulations to reg.2(4) of those Regulations dealing with electronic documents.

Death of a party to an appeal or an application for a direction

2.389 **8.**—(1) In any proceedings relating to an appeal or an application for a direction, on the death of a party to those proceedings (other than the Board) the following persons may proceed with the appeal or application for a direction in the place of such deceased party—
(a) where the proceedings are in relation to a single claim, the personal representatives of the person who has died;
(b) where the proceedings are in relation to a joint claim, where only one of the persons by whom the claim was made has died, the other person with whom the claim was made;
(c) where the proceedings are in relation to a joint claim where both the persons by whom the claim was made have died, the personal representatives of the last of them to die;
(d) for the purposes of paragraph (c), where persons have died in circumstances rendering it uncertain which of them survived the other—
   (i) their deaths shall be presumed to have occurred in order of seniority; and
   (ii) the younger shall be treated as having survived the elder.

(SI 2002/3196, reg. 8) (as amended)

(2) Where there is no person mentioned in paragraphs (1)(a) to (1)(c) to proceed with the appeal or application for a direction, the Board may appoint such person as they think fit to proceed with that appeal or that application in the place of such deceased party referred to in paragraph (1).

(3) A grant of probate, confirmation or letters of administration to the estate of the deceased party, whenever taken out, shall have no effect on an appointment made under paragraph (2).

(4) Where a person appointed under paragraph (2) has, prior to the date of such appointment, taken any action in relation to the appeal or application for a direction on behalf of the deceased party, the effective date of appointment by the Board shall be the day immediately prior to the first day on which such action was taken.

DEFINITIONS

"appeal"—see reg.1(3).
"an application for a direction"—*ibid.*
"the Board"—see s.39(1) of the Social Security Act 1998 as modified by reg.12 of the Tax Credits (Appeals) Regulations 2002.
"joint claimant"—reg.1(3).
"party to the proceedings"—*ibid.*
"single claimant"—*ibid.*

PART III

APPEAL TRIBUNALS FOR TAX CREDITS

CHAPTER 1

APPEAL TRIBUNALS

Composition of appeal tribunals

9.—(1) Subject to the following provisions of this regulation, an appeal tribunal, for the purposes of these Regulations, shall consist of a legally qualified panel member.

(2) Subject to paragraphs (3), (4) and (6), an appeal tribunal shall consist of a legally qualified panel member, a medically qualified panel member and a panel member with a disability qualification where the issue, or one of the issues, raised on the appeal is—
  (a) whether or not there is an entitlement, under regulation 9 of the Working Tax Credit Regulations, to have the disability element of working tax credit included in the maximum rate;
  (b) whether a member of [1 a couple] is incapacitated for the purposes of regulation 13(1)(b)(ii) of the Working Tax Credit Regulations;
  (c) whether a child is disabled for the purposes of regulation 14(3) of the Working Tax Credit Regulations;

2.390

(d) whether there is an entitlement under regulation 17 of the Working Tax Credit Regulations to have the severe disability element of working tax credit included in the maximum rate;
(e) whether the conditions set out in regulation 8 of the Child Tax Credit Regulations 2002 for a disabled or severely disabled child or qualifying young person are satisfied.

(3) Subject to paragraph (4), an appeal tribunal shall consist of a legally qualified panel member and a financially qualified panel member where the appeal, application for a direction or penalty proceedings may require consideration by members of the appeal tribunal of issues which are, in the opinion of the President, difficult and which relate to—
(a) profit and loss accounts, revenue accounts or balance sheets relating to any enterprise;
(b) an income and expenditure account in the case of an enterprise not trading for profit; or
(c) the accounts of any trust fund.

(4) Where the composition of an appeal tribunal would fall to be prescribed under both paragraphs (2) and (3), it shall consist of a legally qualified panel member, a medically qualified panel member and a panel member with a disability qualification.

(5) Where the composition of an appeal tribunal is prescribed under paragraph (1) or (3), the President may determine that the appeal tribunal shall include such an additional member drawn from the panel constituted under section 6 of the Act as he considers appropriate for the purposes of providing further experience for that additional panel member or for assisting the President in the monitoring of standards of decision making by panel members.

(6) A person shall not act as a medically qualified panel member of an appeal tribunal in any appeal if he has at any time advised or prepared a report upon any person whose medical condition is relevant to the issue in the appeal, or has at any time regularly attended such a person.

AMENDMENT

1. Civil Partnership (Pensions, Social Security and Child Support) (Consequential, etc. Provisions) Order 2005 (SI 2005/2877), para.36(3) of Sch.3 (December 5, 2005).

DEFINITIONS

"the Act"—see reg.1(3).
"the Working Tax Credit Regulations"—*ibid.*
"appeal"—*ibid.*
"appeal tribunal"—see s.39(1) of the Social Security Act 1998.
"an application for a direction"—see reg.1(3).
"the Board"—see s.39(1) of the Social Security Act 1998 as modified by reg.12 of the Tax Credits (Appeals) Regulations 2002.
"court"—reg.1(3).
"financially qualified panel member"—*ibid.*
"legally qualified panel member"—*ibid.*
"medically qualified panel member"—*ibid.*
"panel"—*ibid.*
"panel member"—*ibid.*
"panel member with a disability qualification"—*ibid.*
"partner"—*ibid.*

(SI 2002/3196, reg.9) (as amended)

"President"—*ibid.*
"tax credit"—*ibid.*

GENERAL NOTE

The general rule established by para.(1) is that a tribunal consists of a single lawyer. However, para.(2) provides for tribunals consisting of a lawyer, a doctor and another member with experience of disability and para.(3) provides for tribunals consisting of a lawyer ad an accountant. Oddly, para.(4) provides that, where the conditions of both paras (2) and (3) are satisfied, the constitution of the tribunal is the same as that under para.(2). The equivalent provision relating to social security cases provides for a tribunal consisting of a lawyer, a doctor and an accountant, which seems more logical (see reg.36(4) of the Social Security and Child Support (Decisions and Appeals) Regulations 1999 (SI 1999/991).

It is not inappropriate for a doctor who prepares reports for HMRC to sit as a medically qualified panel member (*Gillies v Secretary of State for Work and Pensions* [2006] UKHL 2; [2006] 1 W.L.R. 781 (also reported as *R(DLA) 5/06*), but it may be inappropriate for a chairman or other panel member to sit on a tribunal considering a report compiled by a doctor or accountant with whom they have sat on previous occasions (*Secretary of State for Work and Pensions v Cunningham* 2004 S.L.T. 1007 (also reported as *R(DLA) 7/04*). Lawyers, generally, are not entitled to appear before tribunals on which they sit, for similar reasons. In practice, therefore, chairmen and members do not sit in the areas where they practise. It is open to a claimant to ask a member of a tribunal to stand down if he or she fears that there will be bias, whether conscious or unconscious, but that will usually mean that there will have to be an adjournment, particularly if the request is made on the day of the hearing. A claimant may waive the right to object to the apparent lack of independence of a member of the tribunal, but the waiver must be voluntary, informed and unequivocal (*Millar v Dickson* [2001] UKPC D4; [2002] 1 W.L.R. 1615). See further the note on the right to a fair hearing in the annotation to s.14(1) of the 1998 Act.

In *CIB/2620/2000*, it was said that there might be some "exceptional cases where the absence of a tribunal member of the same sex as the claimant may inhibit the presentation or understanding of the claimant's case to such an extent that there will be a breach of the requirements of natural justice and of Article 6 of the European Convention on Human Rights if the tribunal is not reconstituted." However, no point had been taken before the tribunal as to the absence of a woman member and, although the case was concerned with a female medical condition, the tribunal was not required to investigate the effect of the condition on the claimant because it was not in dispute. Accordingly, there was no lack of fairness in that particular case.

2.391

Assignment of clerks to appeal tribunals: function of clerks

10. The Secretary of State shall assign a clerk to service each appeal tribunal and the clerk so assigned shall be responsible for summoning members of the panel constituted under section 6 of the Act to serve on the tribunal.

2.392

DEFINITIONS

"the Act"—see reg.1(3).
"appeal tribunal"—see s.39(1) of the Social Security Act 1998.
"panel"—see reg.1(3).

Chapter 2

Procedure in Connection with Determination of Appeals, Applications for Directions and Penalty Proceedings

Consideration and determination of appeals, applications for a direction and penalty proceedings

2.393 **11.**—(1) The procedure in connection with the consideration and determination of an appeal, an application for a direction or penalty proceedings shall, subject to the following provisions of these Regulations, be such as a legally qualified panel member shall determine.

(2) A legally qualified panel member may give directions requiring a party to the proceedings to comply with any provision of these Regulations and may at any stage of the proceedings, either of his own motion or on a written application made to the clerk to the appeal tribunal by any party to the proceedings, give such directions as he may consider necessary or desirable for the just, effective and efficient conduct of the proceedings and may direct any party to the proceedings to provide such particulars or to produce such documents as may be reasonably required.

(3) Where a clerk to the appeal tribunal is authorised to take steps in relation to the procedure of the tribunal he may give directions requiring any party to the proceedings to comply with any provision of these Regulations.

DEFINITIONS

"appeal"—see reg.1(3).
"an application for a direction"—see reg.1(3).
"clerk to the appeal tribunal"—*ibid*.
"legally qualified panel member"—*ibid*.
"party to the proceedings"—*ibid*.
"penalty proceedings"—*ibid*.

GENERAL NOTE

2.394 The wide power conferred by para.(2) to issue directions must be exercised judicially. Thus, a legally qualified panel member is not generally entitled to subvert the decision of a tribunal to adjourn for a medical report by directing that the case be relisted without the report. On the other hand, if the case is relisted and no point is taken about the absence of the report, the Commissioner may decide that the final decision is not erroneous in point of law (*CSDLA/866/2002*).

Where a claimant has failed to produce evidence within the time allowed in a direction but produces it at a hearing before a tribunal, the tribunal may be entitled to refuse to admit the evidence. However, it must act proportionately, having regard to the purposes for which the time limit was placed in the direction and the prejudice caused by the failure to comply with it (*CIB/4253/2004*). Where the evidence can easily be absorbed at the hearing by the tribunal and any other party, it is unlikely to be appropriate to refuse to admit it. A failure to comply at all with a direction to produce evidence does not always justify the drawing of an adverse inference, although it may well do so (*CCS/3757/2004*). If an appellant is given due warning, an appeal may be struck out under reg.16(1)(b) for failure to comply with a direction.

(SI 2002/3196, reg.12) (as amended)

[¹Choice of hearing

12.—(1) Where an appeal or an application for a direction is made to an appeal tribunal the appellant or applicant and any other party to the proceedings shall notify the clerk to the appeal tribunal, on a form approved by the Secretary of State, whether he wishes to have an oral hearing or whether he is content for the appeal or application to proceed without an oral hearing.

(2) The form shall include a statement informing the appellant or applicant that, if he does not notify the clerk to the appeal tribunal as required by paragraph (1) within the period specified in paragraph (3), the appeal or, as the case may be, the application may be struck out in accordance with regulation 16(1).

(3) Notification in accordance with paragraph (1)—
(a) if given by the appellant, the applicant or any party to the proceedings other than the Board, must be given or sent to the clerk to the appeal tribunal within 14 days of the date on which the form is issued to him; or
(b) if given by the Board, must be given or sent to the clerk to the appeal tribunal within 14 days of the date on which the form is issued to the appellant or applicant,

or within such longer period as the clerk may direct.

(4) Where an oral hearing is requested in accordance with paragraphs (1) and (3) the appeal tribunal shall hold an oral hearing unless the case is struck out under regulation 16(1).]

(5) The chairman, or in the case of an appeal tribunal which has only one member, that member, may of his own motion direct an oral hearing of the appeal or application for a direction be held if he is satisfied that such a hearing is necessary to enable the appeal tribunal to reach a decision.

2.395

AMENDMENT

1. Social Security, Child Support, and Tax Credits (Decisions and Appeals) Amendment Regulations 2004 (SI 2004/3368), reg.6(2) (December 21, 2004).

DEFINITIONS

"appeal"—see reg.1(3).
"appeal tribunal"—see s.39(1) of the Social Security Act 1998.
"an application for a direction"—see reg.1(3).
"the Board"—see s.39(1) of the Social Security Act 1998 as modified by reg.12 of the Tax Credits (Appeals) Regulations 2002. The term must, however, now be read as meaning Her Majesty's Revenue and Customs (see the Commissioners for Revenue and Customs Act 2005).
"clerk to the appeal tribunal"—*ibid.*
"party to the proceedings"—*ibid.*

GENERAL NOTE

The form on which a person may opt for an oral hearing may be issued either by HMRC, when the papers for the appeal are sent out to both the appellant and the clerk, or by the clerk to the tribunal. A clerk cannot rely on an indication in the appellant's letter of appeal that a hearing is not wanted (*R3/04(IB)*). If an appellant does not return the form, the appeal is liable to be struck out under reg.16(1)(c).

2.396

If a tribunal is wholly unable to do justice at a paper hearing, it ought to adjourn and direct an oral hearing but, otherwise, a tribunal is generally entitled to take the view that a person who has rejected the option of an oral hearing having had notice of the issues has had an adequate opportunity to put his case and has lost the chance of strengthening it by giving oral evidence (*CDLA/1347/1999*). However, in *CIS/4248/2001*, it was held that an oral hearing should have been directed in a case where an apparently unrepresented claimant had opted for a paper hearing of an appeal against a decision that benefit amounting to some £10,000 had been overpaid and was recoverable from her. She had put forward a case that was tenable if she was believed. In *R1/02(IB)*, a Tribunal of Commissioners in Northern Ireland set aside a decision of a tribunal which did not adjourn in the face of incomplete evidence raising questions it could not answer.

Withdrawal of application for a direction or penalty proceedings

2.397   **13.**—(1) An application for a direction may be withdrawn by the applicant, or penalty proceedings may be withdrawn by the Board, at any time before that application is, or those proceedings are, determined, either—

(a) at an oral hearing; or
(b) by giving notice in writing of withdrawal to the clerk to the appeal tribunal.

(2) If an application for a direction is, or penalty proceedings are, withdrawn in accordance with paragraph (1)(a), the clerk to the appeal tribunal shall send a notice in writing to any party to the proceedings who is not present when the application for a direction is, or penalty proceedings are, withdrawn, informing him that the application for a direction has, or the penalty proceedings have, been withdrawn.

(3) If an application for a direction is, or penalty proceedings are, withdrawn in accordance with paragraph (1)(b), the clerk to the appeal tribunal shall send a notice in writing to every party to the proceedings informing them that the application for a direction has, or penalty proceedings have, been withdrawn.

DEFINITIONS

"an application for a direction"—see reg.1(3).
"the Board"—see s.39(1) of the Social Security Act 1998 as modified by reg.12 of the Tax Credits (Appeals) Regulations 2002.
"clerk to the appeal tribunal"—reg.1(3).
"party to the proceedings"—*ibid*.
"penalty proceedings"—*ibid*.

GENERAL NOTE

2.398   Once an appeal has been withdrawn, an appeal tribunal has no jurisdiction to consider it, even if the other parties to the proceedings give their consent (*Rydqvist v Secretary of State for Work and Pensions* [2002] EWCA Civ 947; [2002] 1 W.L.R. 3343). However, it is open to the would-be appellant to submit a new appeal and it is possible that consent by HMRC apparently given to consider a withdrawn appeal might in some circumstances be construed as acceptance of a late appeal under reg.5(2). The equivalent of reg.5(2) for social security cases was not in force at the time the issue arose in *Rydqvist*.

Non-disclosure of medical advice or evidence

2.399   **14.**—(1) Where, in connection with an appeal, an application for a direction or penalty proceedings, there is medical advice or medical evidence relating to a person which has not been disclosed to him and in the opinion of a legally qualified panel member, the disclosure to that person of that advice or evidence would be harmful to his health, such advice or evidence shall not be required to be disclosed to that person.

(2) Advice or evidence such as is mentioned in paragraph (1)—
(a) shall not be disclosed to any person acting for or representing the person to whom it relates;
(b) shall not be disclosed to a joint claimant of the person to whom it relates or any person acting for or representing that joint claimant;
(c) in a case where a claim for a tax credit is made by reference to the disability of a person other than the claimant or joint claimant and the advice or evidence relates to that other person, shall not be disclosed to the claimant, joint claimant or any person acting for or representing the claimant or joint claimant,

unless a legally qualified panel member is satisfied that it is in the interests of the person to whom the advice or evidence relates to do so.

(3) A tribunal shall not be precluded from taking into account for the purposes of the determination advice or evidence which has not been disclosed to a person under the provisions of paragraph (1) or (2).

DEFINITIONS

"appeal"—see reg.1(3).
"an application for a direction"—*ibid*.
"claimant"—see s.39(1) of the Social Security Act 1998 as modified by reg.12 of the Tax Credits (Appeals) Regulations 2002.
"joint claimant"—reg.1(3).
"legally qualified panel member"—*ibid*.
"penalty proceedings"—*ibid*.
"tax credit"—*ibid*.

GENERAL NOTE

In *R(A) 4/89*, the Attendance Allowance Board withheld from a claimant "additional information" supplied by a doctor who in effect said that when he arrived outside the claimant's house the claimant was sitting with his back to a window but when he went in the claimant was lying on a couch claiming to be unable to respond to the doctor's questions. The doctor was therefore implying that the claimant was a fraud. The Commissioner held that this was not "medical evidence", but was factual evidence, and that, in any event, the power to withhold evidence that was prejudicial, rather than helpful, to a claimant should be exercised with caution. He held the Board to have erred in law because it was common fairness to let a claimant be aware of an allegation that he was a fraud. It is difficult to see how evidence of the sort considered in that case could possibly be harmful to the claimant" health. A doctor's wish to avoid embarrassment is not a ground for withholding evidence.

In *CDLA/1347/1999*, the Commissioner suggested that, if a tribunal is minded to reveal evidence that has been withheld on medical advice, it might be prudent to give the medical advisor the opportunity of justifying his advice before revealing the evidence. He also agreed with a suggestion that, if reasons for a decision were being given, withheld evidence should be referred to in a supplementary statement of reasons given to the other parties (and the claimant's representative if the evidence has been revealed to him or her) but not given to the claimant. That would have the effect that, in the event of an appeal, the Commissioner would know how the evidence had been approached.

2.400

Provisions such as this one are used much less often now that medical practice is generally to give people full information about serious conditions from which they are suffering. They have not had to be considered by Commissioners or the courts since the Human Rights Act 1998 came into force. However, properly applied, this regulation requires the balancing of the risk of real harm to a claimant against the risk of unfairness in the proceedings and it is suggested that there is unlikely to be a breach of the European Convention on Human Rights provided that the exercise is properly carried out. That is particularly so if the claimant has a representative to whom disclosure can be made (*R. (Roberts) v Parole Board* [2005] UKHL 45).

Summoning of witnesses and administration of oaths

15.—(1) A chairman, or in the case of an appeal tribunal which has only one member, that member, may by summons, or in Scotland, by citation, require any person in Great Britain to attend as a witness at a hearing of an appeal, an application for a direction or penalty proceedings, at such time and place as shall be specified in the summons or citation and, subject to paragraph (2), at the hearing to answer any question or produce any documents in his custody or under his control which relate to any matter in question in that appeal, application or those proceedings but—

(a) no person shall be required to attend in obedience to such summons or citation unless he has been given at least 14 days' notice of the hearing or, if less than 14 days' notice is given, he has informed the tribunal that the notice given is sufficient; and

(b) no person shall be required to attend and give evidence or to produce any document in obedience to such summons or citation unless the necessary expenses of attendance are paid or tendered to him.

(2) No person shall be compelled to give any evidence or produce any document or other material that he could not be compelled to give or produce on a trial of an action in a court of law in that part of Great Britain where the hearing takes place.

(3) In exercising the powers conferred by this regulation, the chairman, or in the case of an appeal tribunal which has only one member, that member, shall take into account the need to protect any matter that relates to intimate personal or financial circumstances, is commercially sensitive, consists of information communicated or obtained in confidence or concerns national security.

(4) Every summons or citation issued under this regulation shall contain a statement to the effect that the person in question may apply in writing to a chairman to vary or set aside the summons or citation.

(5) A chairman, or in the case of an appeal tribunal which has only one member, that member, may require any witness, including a witness summoned under the powers conferred by this regulation, to give evidence on oath or affirmation and for that purpose there may be administered an oath or affirmation in due form.

DEFINITIONS

"appeal"—see reg.1(3).
"appeal tribunal"—see s.39(1) of the Social Security Act 1998.
"an application for a direction"—reg.1(3).
"penalty proceedings"—*ibid.*

(SI 2002/3196, reg.15) (as amended)

GENERAL NOTE

The power to issue a summons appears not to be backed by any power to enforce it. CPR r.34.4 enables the High Court to issue an enforceable summons in aid of a tribunal but only if the tribunal has no power to issue a summons itself. In the light of this regulation, it is doubtful that a summons can be issued by the High Court to assist a tribunal hearing a tax credit appeal.

2.402

CHAPTER 3

STRIKING OUT APPEALS AND APPLICATIONS FOR A DIRECTION

Cases which may be struck out

16.—(1) Subject to paragraphs (2) and (3), a case may be struck out by the clerk to the appeal tribunal—
  (a) for want of prosecution including an appeal not made within the time specified in section 39(1) of the 2002 Act and in these Regulations; [1 . . .]
  (b) [1 . . .] for failure of the appellant or applicant to comply with a direction given under these Regulations where the appellant or applicant has been notified that failure to comply with the direction could result in the case being struck out [1; or]
[1(c) for failure of the appellant or applicant to notify the clerk to the appeal tribunal, in accordance with regulation 12, whether he wishes to have an oral hearing of his case.]
(2) Where the clerk to the appeal tribunal determines to strike out the case, he shall notify the appellant or applicant that his case has been struck out and of the procedure for reinstatement of the case as specified in regulation 17.
(3) The clerk to the appeal tribunal may refer any matter for determination under this regulation to a legally qualified panel member for decision by the panel member rather than the clerk to the appeal tribunal.

2.403

AMENDMENT

1. Social Security, Child Support, and Tax Credits (Decisions and Appeals) Amendment Regulations 2004 (SI 2004/3368), reg.6(3) (December 21, 2004).

DEFINITIONS

  "the 2002 Act"—see reg.1(3).
  "appeal"—*ibid.*
  "a case"—*ibid.*
  "clerk to the appeal tribunal"—*ibid.*
  "legally qualified panel member"—*ibid.*
  "panel member"—*ibid.*

GENERAL NOTE

It has been held that, because a decision of a legally qualified panel member must be treated as a decision of a tribunal, an appeal lies to a Commissioner against the striking out of an appeal or a refusal to reinstate a struck out appeal (*CIS/1363/2005 and others*), although leave will seldom be granted because procedural or other

2.404

irregularities in the proceedings before the legally qualified panel member will seldom be material. It follows that reasons for striking out an appeal or not reinstating it must be given, but it is suggested that they can be given in the decision notice because any proper reason for summarily striking out an appeal should be capable of being expressed in a sentence or two.

Any challenge by HMRC to a refusal to strike out an appeal or to a reinstatement of an appeal must wait until the appeal is determined, because such a decision does not end the proceedings before the tribunal, and such a challenge will presumably be made only if the appeal is allowed by the tribunal.

At the time of going to press, the decision of the Court of Appeal on the application for leave to appeal by the Secretary of State for Work and Pensions with regard to *CIS/1363/2005 and others* is awaited.

Reinstatement of struck out cases

2.405

17.—(1) The clerk to the appeal tribunal may reinstate a case which has been struck out in accordance with regulation [¹16(1)(c)] where—
  (a) the appellant or applicant has made representations to him or, as the case may be, further representations in support of his case with reasons why he considers that his case should not have been struck out;
  (b) the representations are made in writing within one month of the order to strike out the case being issued; and
  (c) the clerk is satisfied in the light of those representations that there are reasonable grounds for reinstating the case,
but if the clerk is not satisfied that there are reasonable grounds for reinstatement a legally qualified panel member shall consider whether the case should be reinstated in accordance with paragraph (2).

(2) A legally qualified panel member may reinstate a case which has been struck out in accordance with regulation 16 where—
  (a) the appellant or applicant has made representations or, as the case may be, further representations in support of his case with reasons why he considers that his case should not have been struck out, to the clerk to the appeal tribunal, in writing within one month of the order to strike out the case being issued, and the panel member is satisfied in the light of those representations that there are reasonable grounds for reinstating the case;
  (b) the panel member is satisfied that the case is not a case which may be struck out under regulation 16; or
  (c) the panel member is satisfied that notwithstanding that the case is one which may be struck out under regulation 16, it is not in the interests of justice for the case to be struck out.

AMENDMENT

1. Social Security, Child Support, and Tax Credits (Decisions and Appeals) Amendment Regulations 2004 (SI 2004/3368), reg.6(4) (December 21, 2004).

DEFINITIONS

"a case"—see reg.1(3).
"clerk to the appeal tribunal"—*ibid*.
"legally qualified panel member"—*ibid*.
"panel member"—*ibid*.

(SI 2002/3196, reg.18) (as amended)

CHAPTER 4

ORAL HEARINGS

Procedure at oral hearings

18.—(1) Subject to the following provisions of this Part, the procedure for an oral hearing shall be such as the chairman, or in the case of an appeal tribunal which has only one member, such as that member, shall determine.

(2) Except where paragraph (4) applies, not less than 14 days' notice (beginning with the day on which notice is given and ending on the day before the hearing of the appeal or application for a direction, is to take place) of the time and place of any oral hearing of an appeal or an application for a direction shall be given to every party to the proceedings.

(3) If such notice has not been given to a person to whom it should have been given under the provisions of paragraph (2) the hearing may proceed only with the consent of that person.

(4) Any party to the proceedings may waive his right under paragraph (2) to receive not less than 14 days' notice of the time and place of any oral hearing by giving notice to the clerk to the appeal tribunal.

(5) If a party to the proceedings to whom notice has been given under paragraph (2) fails to appear at the hearing the chairman, or in the case of an appeal tribunal which has only one member, that member, may, having regard to all the circumstances including any explanation offered for the absence—
  (a) proceed with the hearing notwithstanding his absence; or
  (b) give such directions with a view to the determination of the appeal or application for a direction as he may think proper.

(6) If a party to the proceedings has waived his right to be given notice under paragraph (2) the chairman, or in the case of an appeal tribunal which has only one member, that member, may proceed with the hearing notwithstanding his absence.

(7) An oral hearing of an appeal, application for a direction or penalty proceedings shall be in public except where the chairman, or in the case of an appeal tribunal which has only one member, that member, is satisfied that it is necessary to hold the hearing, or part of the hearing, in private—
  (a) in the interests of national security, morals, public order or children;
  (b) for the protection of private or family life of one or more parties to the proceedings; or
  (c) in special circumstances, because publicity would prejudice the interests of justice.

(8) At an oral hearing—
(a) any party to the proceedings shall be entitled to be present and be heard; and
(b) the following persons may be present by means of a live television link—
   (i) a party to the proceedings or his representative or both; or
   (ii) where an appeal tribunal consists of more than one member, a tribunal member other than the chairman,
   provided that the person who constitutes or is the chairman of the tribunal gives permission [¹ . . .].

2.406

(9) A person who has the right to be heard at a hearing may be accompanied and may be represented by another person whether having professional qualifications or not and, for the purposes of the proceedings at the hearing, any such representative shall have all the rights and powers to which the person whom he represents is entitled.

(10) The following persons shall also be entitled to be present at an oral hearing (whether or not it is otherwise in private) but shall take no part in the proceedings—
(a) the President;
(b) any person undergoing training as a chairman or member of an appeal tribunal or as a clerk to an appeal tribunal;
(c) any person acting on behalf of the President in the training or supervision of panel members or in the monitoring of standards of decision-making by panel members;
(d) with the leave of the chairman, or in the case of an appeal tribunal which has only one member, with the leave of that member, any other person; and
(e) a member of the Council on Tribunals or of the Scottish Committee of the Council on Tribunals.

(11) Nothing in paragraph (10) affects the rights of—
(a) any person mentioned in sub-paragraphs (a) and (b) of that paragraph where he is sitting as a member of a tribunal or acting as its clerk; or
(b) the clerk to the tribunal,

and nothing in this regulation prevents the presence at an oral hearing of any witness or of any person whom the chairman, or in the case of an appeal tribunal which has only one member, that member, permits to be present in order to assist the appeal tribunal or the clerk.

(12) Any person entitled to be heard at an oral hearing may address the tribunal, may give evidence, may call witnesses and may put questions directly to any other person called as a witness.

(13) For the purpose of arriving at its decision an appeal tribunal shall, and for the purpose of discussing any question of procedure may, notwithstanding anything contained in these Regulations, order all persons not being members of the tribunal, other than the person acting as clerk to the appeal tribunal, to withdraw from the hearing except that—
(a) a member of the Council on Tribunals or of the Scottish Committee of the Council on Tribunals, the President or any other person mentioned in paragraph (10)(c); and
(b) with the leave of the chairman, or in the case of an appeal tribunal which has only one member, with the leave of that member, any person mentioned in paragraph (10)(b) or (d),

may remain present at any such sitting.

(14) In this regulation "live television link" means a live television link or other facilities which allow a person who is not physically present at an oral hearing to see and hear proceedings and be seen and heard by those physically present.

AMENDMENT

1. Social Security, Child Support and Tax Credits (Miscellaneous Amendments) Regulations 2005 (SI 2005/337), reg.4(3) (March 18, 2005).

(SI 2002/3196, reg.18) (as amended)

DEFINITIONS

"appeal"—see reg.1(3).
"appeal tribunal"—see s.39(1) of the Social Security Act 1998.
"an application for a direction"—see reg.1(3).
"clerk to the appeal tribunal"—*ibid.*
"live television link"—see para.(14).
"party to the proceedings"—see reg.1(3).
"penalty proceedings"—*ibid.*
"President"—*ibid.*

GENERAL NOTE

Para. (1)

The legally qualified panel member has considerable latitude in deciding how a hearing will be conducted but it must be fair. If the rules of natural justice (which effectively guarantee a fair hearing) are broken, the decision of the tribunal is liable to be set aside on appeal on the ground that it is erroneous in point of law. See further the annotation to s.14(1) of the Social Security Act 1998.

A tribunal is entitled to take account of all that it sees and hears at a hearing but if it sees something that appears important, fairness generally requires that the party concerned should be given an opportunity of commenting on what the tribunal has seen. In *CDLA/145/2006*, the Commissioner cautioned tribunals against giving too much weight to observations of a claimant's apparent well-being that might be unrepresentative and so be unreliable as evidence of his health generally. Giving a claimant an opportunity to comment enables the claimant to put the observation into a broader context. However, the Commissioner also pointed out that, where an observation merely confirms a conclusion that the tribunal would have reached anyway, a failure to invite the claimant to comment on it will not render the decision erroneous in point of law although, unless a chairman makes clear what significance a recorded observation had in the tribunal's reasoning when he or she is writing the statement of reasons, it is likely to be assumed that it must have had an effect on the decision. The Commissioner also said that a chairman did not have to ask precise questions amounting to a cross-examination of the claimant but could ask an open question that gave a claimant the opportunity to comment. He said—

". . . the chairman did not point out to the claimant the significance of the observations that the tribunal had made. But the claimant must have realised this. He had presented his claim on the basis of pain and exhaustion and the observations were clearly directly relevant to that."

What is important is whether, taking the hearing as a whole, the claimant has an adequate opportunity to address the issues raised by any significant observations.

A tribunal should satisfy itself that an interpreter appointed by the tribunal to assist a party or witness adequately meets the needs of the person (*CDLA/2748/2002*).

Para. (5)

In *Cooke v Glenrose Fish Company* [2004] I.C.R. 1188, the Employment Appeal Tribunal suggested that an employment tribunal should always at least consider telephoning an appellant who has failed to appear before proceeding in his absence and should ordinarily do so where there was an indication that the appellant had been intending to appear at the hearing because, for instance, solicitors were on the record. An oversight can then be rectified. However, the Employment Appeal Tribunal also held that employment tribunals were entitled to take a robust approach and generally to proceed to hear cases where there was an unexplained absence, because any injustice could be put right on review. The provision in these regulations equivalent to a review would be reg.25(1)(b), which permits the setting aside of a decision where a party or his representative was not present at a hearing. The Appeal

2.407

2.408

Tribunal remarked that "it would appear to be a necessary concomitant of the more stringent attitude encouraged by [the President] that there be the less stringent attitude on a review if a party who has not attended comes forward with a genuine and full explanation and shows that the original hearing was not one from which he deliberately absented himself".

Where a claimant sent a message to a representative to say she would not be attending a hearing and wished the tribunal to proceed in her absence and the representative made no application for an adjournment, a Commissioner declined to hold the tribunal to have erred in not adjourning (*CSIB/404/2005*). However, he set the tribunal's decision aside for failure to deal adequately with questions concerning the claimant's mental health, even though it was difficult to see how the tribunal could have allowed the claimant's appeal on the evidence before it. That may suggest that, where the claimant's presence is really required to establish the facts and the non-attendance might have been attributable, at least in part, to the claimant's mental health, a tribunal really should consider whether an adjournment would be in the interests of justice, just as they would if the claimant had not asked for a hearing (see the annotation to reg.39). Of course, a tribunal is entitled to take into account the fact that the claimant has asked for a hearing and then failed to attend it in considering whether justice requires an adjournment and whether attendance in the future is likely.

Para. (7)

2.409   In *CIB/2751/2002 and CS/3202/2002*, the Commissioner considered how the duty to hold a hearing in public affects domiciliary hearings and he suggested that it might be necessary to hold the hearing near the claimant's home rather than in it. However, it is suggested that, if it is necessary to hold a hearing in a claimant's home, it will generally be necessary to hold the hearing in private in order to protect his or her private or family life.

Para. (9)

2.410   A person has a right to be represented by any person (subject to their proper behaviour). Thus a chairman erred in refusing to hear submissions form a person he described as a "McKenzie friend" and it was an error of law for him to insist that the claimant specify at the beginning of the hearing whether the person accompanying her was going to act as a representative in the conventional sense (*CIS/1753/2000*). Representatives may also be witnesses insofar as they can give evidence from their own knowledge (*CDLA/2462/2003*).

Para. (12)

2.411   In *R(DLA) 3/06*, a Tribunal of Commissioners allowed an appeal against a tribunal who had drawn an adverse inference against a 12-year old claimant, alleged to have learning difficulties and hearing problems, because her foster parent and appointee had failed to arrange for her to give evidence to the tribunal despite a summons. The Commissioners gave general guidance about the calling of child witnesses, suggesting that a tribunal should be slow to require a child to give evidence against his or her wishes and the wishes of responsible adults.

Manner of providing expert assistance

2.412   **19.**—(1) Where an appeal tribunal requires one or more experts to provide assistance to it in dealing with a question of fact of special difficulty under section 7(4) of the Act, such an expert shall, if the chairman, or in the case of an appeal tribunal which has only one member, that member, so requests, attend at the hearing and give evidence.

(2) If the chairman or in the case of an appeal tribunal which has only one member, that member, considers it appropriate, the expert shall enquire into and provide a written report on the question to be dealt with in accordance with paragraph (1).

(3) A copy of any written report received from an expert in accordance with paragraph (2) shall be supplied to every party to the proceedings.

DEFINITIONS

"appeal tribunal"—see s.39(1) of the Social Security Act 1998.
"party to the proceedings"—see reg.1(3).

GENERAL NOTE

The expert may assist the tribunal as a witness, which implies that the parties may cross-examine him or her. There is no provision for an expert to sit as an assessor.

2.413

Postponement and adjournment

20.—(1) Where a person to whom—
   (a) notice of an oral hearing is given; or
   (b) in the case of penalty proceedings, a summons has been issued under paragraph 3(2) of Schedule 2 to the 2002 Act,
wishes to request a postponement of that hearing he shall do so in writing to the clerk to the appeal tribunal stating his reasons for the request, and the clerk to the appeal tribunal may grant or refuse the request as he thinks fit or may pass the request to a legally qualified panel member who may grant or refuse the request as he thinks fit.

(2) Where the clerk to the appeal tribunal or the panel member, as the case may be, refuses a request to postpone the hearing he shall—
   (a) notify in writing the person making the request of the refusal; and
   (b) place before the appeal tribunal at the hearing both the request for the postponement and notification of its refusal.

(3) A panel member or the clerk to the appeal tribunal may of his own motion at any time before the beginning of the hearing postpone the hearing.

(4) An oral hearing may be adjourned by the appeal tribunal at any time on the application of any party to the proceedings or of its own motion.

2.414

DEFINITIONS

"appeal tribunal"—see s.39(1) of the Social Security Act 1998.
"clerk to the appeal tribunal"—*ibid.*
"legally qualified panel member"—*ibid.*
"panel member"—*ibid.*
"party to the proceedings"—*ibid.*
"penalty proceedings"—*ibid.*

GENERAL NOTE

The distinction between a postponement and an adjournment is that the former occurs before a hearing and the latter occurs once the hearing has begun, although an application for an adjournment may be made right at the beginning of a hearing. The effect of para.(2) is that a tribunal may consider adjourning if a postponement has been refused and the party does not appear. However, in *CDLA/3680/1997*, the Commissioner said that a person who has been refused a postponement or has not received a reply to a request for a postponement should "take all possible steps to appear, or to have someone appear on his or her behalf, before the tribunal in order to assist the tribunal in considering whether there should be an adjournment".

Para.(4) applies only to oral hearings. There is no express power to adjourn paper hearings but such a power is to be implied (*CDLA/1552/1998* and see also the note to reg.12).

2.415

The power to postpone or adjourn proceedings must not be used arbitrarily or capriciously and, in particular, must not be used in order to defeat the general purpose of the legislation, but otherwise there is a complete discretion so long as it is exercised judicially. Thus, in *CIS/2292/2000*, a tribunal erred in rejecting an application for an adjournment made by the representative of a claimant in prison, in circumstances where the claimant's oral evidence had an important part to play. Applications for adjournments because a representative is unavailable have to be considered properly. While a person has no absolute right to representation, he or she does have an absolute right to be treated fairly and that might require having regard to a desire to be represented by a particular person (*R. v Social Security Commissioner, Ex p. Bibi* (unreported, May 23, 2000)). The inquisitorial function of a tribunal is not a complete substitute for representation, particularly in cases that are not straightforward (*CIB/1009/2004, CIB/2058/2004*).

A tribunal may itself need to offer an adjournment where a medically qualified member of the tribunal raises a new objection to the claimant's case and the claimant might wish to seek his or her own medical advice on the point (*Evans v Secretary of State for Social Security* (reported as *R(I) 5/94*), *Butterfield v Secretary of State for Defence* [2002] EWHC 2247 (Admin)).

A legally qualified panel member should not subvert a decision to adjourn for a medical report by immediately directing that the case be relisted without the report (*CSDLA/866/2002*).

At a hearing following an adjournment, a tribunal may be constituted by one or members who sat on the earlier tribunal and one or more who did not, provided no evidence was taken before the adjournment. If evidence was taken before the adjournment, the tribunal should generally be entirely the same or entirely differently constituted and, in the latter case, must have a complete rehearing, although they are entitled to accept a record of the evidence of a witness who gave evidence at the first hearing provided the rules of natural justice are not infringed (*R(U) 3/88*).

A decision to adjourn is appealable only if it disposes of the substantive issues before the tribunal and either makes the outcome inevitable or prevents a final decision from being made (*CDLA/557/2001*). Otherwise, the parties must wait until the final decision is made and appeal against that decision. A refusal to adjourn is not itself appealable (*Carpenter v Secretary of State for Work and Pensions* [2003] EWCA Civ 33 (reported as *R(IB) 6/03*) but an unfair refusal to adjourn may make the final decision of the tribunal erroneous in point of law so that an appeal may be brought against that final decision (*R. v Medical Appeal Tribunal (Midland Region), Ex p. Carrarini* [1966] 1 W.L.R. 883 (also reported as an appendix to *R(I) 13/65*).

CHAPTER 5

DECISIONS OF APPEAL TRIBUNALS AND RELATED MATTERS

Decisions of appeal tribunals

21.—(1) Every decision of an appeal tribunal shall be recorded in summary by the chairman, or in the case of an appeal tribunal which has only one member, by that member and shall be referred to as a decision notice.

(2) The decision notice specified in paragraph (1) shall be in such written form as shall have been approved by the President and shall be signed by the chairman, or in the case of an appeal tribunal which has only one member, by that member.

(3) As soon as may be practicable after an appeal or an application for a direction has, or penalty proceedings have, been decided by an appeal

(SI 2002/3196, reg.21) (as amended)

tribunal, a copy of the decision notice [¹ . . .] shall be sent or given to every party to the proceedings who shall also be informed of—
  (a) his right under paragraph (4); and
  (b) the conditions governing appeals to a Commissioner.
  (4) [¹Subject to paragraph (4A),] a party to the proceedings may apply in writing to the clerk to the appeal tribunal for a statement of the reasons for the tribunal's decision within one month of the sending or giving of the decision notice to every party to the proceedings or within such longer period as may be allowed in accordance with regulation 22.
  [¹(4A) Where—
  (a) the decision notice is corrected in accordance with regulation 24; or
  (b) an application under regulation 25 for the decision to be set aside is refused for reasons other than a refusal to extend the time for making the application,
the period specified in paragraph (4) shall run from the date on which notice of the correction or the refusal of the application for setting aside is sent to the applicant.]
  (5) Following the application made under paragraph (4), the chairman, or in the case of an appeal tribunal which has only one member, that member, shall record a statement of the reasons and a copy of that statement shall be given or sent to every party to the proceedings as soon as may be practicable.
  (6) If the decision is not unanimous, the decision notice specified in paragraph (1) shall record that one of the members dissented and the statement of reasons referred to in paragraph (5) shall include the reasons given by the dissenting member for dissenting.

AMENDMENT

1. Social Security, Child Support and Tax Credits (Miscellaneous Amendments) Regulations 2005 (SI 2005/337), reg.4(4) (March 18, 2005).

DEFINITIONS

  "appeal"—see reg.1(3).
  "appeal tribunal"—see s.39(1) of the Social Security Act 1998.
  "an application for a direction"—see reg.1(3).
  "Commissioner"—see s.39(1) of the Social Security Act 1998.
  "clerk to the appeal tribunal"—see reg.1(3).
  "decision"—*ibid*.
  "decision notice"—see para.(1).
  "party to the proceedings"—see reg.1(3).
  "penalty proceedings"—*ibid*.
  "President"—*ibid*.

GENERAL NOTE

Para.(1)
  Where the Secretary of State's decision is defective in form but the tribunal agrees with its substance, it is not necessary for the tribunal to reformulate the Secretary of State's decision in the tribunal's decision notice unless the decision as expressed by the Secretary of State is wrong in some *material* respect or there is likely to be some practical benefit to the claimant or to the adjudication process in future in reformulating the decision (*CIB/4751/02* at para.82). On the other hand, attempting to reformulate the decision may serve to focus the tribunal's mind on the correct issues and so it may have a value. Where a statement of reasons is requested under para.(4), the

2.417

statement should explain what the decision under appeal should have been even if the decision notice does not.

Para.(2)

2.418　There is no obligation to give reasons in a decision notice and so any reasons that are given cannot be criticised for inadequacy. In *CIB/4497/98*, it was held that the remedy for any inadequacy in the reasons given on a decision notice was to apply for a full statement of reasons under what is now para.(4). However, a bad reason given in a decision notice can render a decision erroneous in point of law (*R(IS) 11/99*). A decision will also be held to be erroneous in point of law if a reason given in a decision notice is inconsistent with a statement of reasons given under para.(4) (*CCR/3396/2000, CIS/2345/2001*).

Para.(4)

2.419　A refusal to adjourn is not a "decision" for which a statement of reasons may be requested under this paragraph, although an unexplained refusal to adjourn may make a final decision erroneous in point of law unless an explanation that is not perverse may be inferred from the circumstances (*Carpenter v Secretary of State for Work and Pensions* [2003] EWCA Civ 33 (reported as *R(IB) 6/03*)).

Para.(5)

2.420　There is no express provision for the giving of a statement of reasons in the absence of a request but there is no reason in principle why the chairman should not do so. It is also suggested that, although a party has no right to a decision if no application is made within a month or such further time as may be allowed under reg.22, a chairman remains able to issue a statement if satisfied that it is right to do so. A chairman's power to write a statement of reasons survives the termination of his or her appointment to the panel. The statement must at least be adopted by the chairman (or possibly another member) of the tribunal who heard the appeal. Therefore a statement written by a regional chairman in the erroneous belief that it could not be written by the chairman who heard the appeal because her appointment had come to an end, was not valid (*CIS/2132/98*). It is usually an error of law to fail to issue a statement of reasons when a request is made within the prescribed time and there are occasions when an application for leave to appeal should be treated as such a request (*R(IS) 11/99*). An application for leave to appeal received within the time allowed for asking for a statement of reasons is, in practice, treated as a request for such a statement. In *CDLA/5793/97*, it had been held that such a request was implied "whenever the claimant's application for leave to appeal raises an issue that is not fully explained in the summary grounds issued as part of a decision notice or by the other documents in the case". However, although they commended the practice of treating an application for leave received within one month of the issue of a decision notice as an application for a statement of reasons, a Tribunal of Commissioners in Northern Ireland has emphasised in *R3/02(IB)* that there is no rule of law requiring a legally qualified panel member to do so. In both *R(IS) 11/99* and *R3/02(IB)*, it is stated that there are occasions when a error of law can be demonstrated without there being a statement of reasons and that a Commissioner can determine an appeal in those circumstances, although it is obviously not possible to challenge a tribunal's decision on the grounds of inadequacy of reasoning in circumstances where there is no written statement of reasons. Furthermore, a tribunal's decision will not be erroneous in law for breach of the duty imposed by this paragraph if the decision notice issued under para.(1) in fact contains all that would be required in a full statement of reasons (*R(IS) 11/99*), or if the two documents read together provide an adequate statement between them (*CIS/2345/2001*). The practice of some chairman of stating that the summary reasons on a decision notice amount to a full statement of reasons has been frowned upon, on the basis that such summary reasons are more likely to contain errors than fuller statements produced in response to a request. In *CSDLA/551/99*, the

(SI 2002/3196, reg.21) (as amended)

Commissioner went as far as to say it was of no effect and that a separate statement was required in all cases, but that is not the conventional view and is inconsistent with what was said in *R(IS) 11/99*. Unlike its predecessors, this paragraph includes no express duty to record the tribunal's findings but that makes no practical difference because it is necessary to record a tribunal's findings on any matters in dispute as part of the explanation for its decision. (*R(I) 4/02* and also *R2/01(IB)*, a decision of a Tribunal of Commissioners in Northern Ireland). Indeed, it has been said in *Evans v Secretary of State for Social Security* (reported as *R(I) 5/94*) that there are occasions when a record of a tribunal's findings provides a complete explanation for the decision.

In *CH/2553/2005*, the clerk did not receive the request for a statement of reasons and the applicant failed to chase up the request until the absolute time-limit for applying for an extension of time under reg.54 had expired. It was held that the chairman was under no *duty* to issue a statement of reasons. It was also held that a chairman has the *power* to issue a statement of reasons without a request but that, if he or she does so after the time within which a request may be made, the statement is not treated as one and so does not start time running for the purposes of the time-limit for applying for leave to appeal. The Commissioner declined to say whether, and in what circumstances, such a statement of reasons could be challenged for inadequacy.

In *CDLA/1807/03*, the tribunal chairman produced two statements of reasons for the tribunal's decision, the second because he had forgotten he had already written a statement. The reasons differed. The Commissioner commented that the reasons should be a statement of the *tribunal's* reasons and not the chairman's later rationalisation of the conclusion reached by the tribunal and that at least one of the statements plainly did not accurately reflect the tribunal's reasons. He set aside the tribunal's decision. Inexplicable inconsistency between the decision notice and the statement of reasons led to an appeal being allowed in *CCR/3396/00*.

The inadequacy of tribunals' reasons is probably the most common ground upon which tribunals' decisions are set aside by Commissioners. The standard of reasoning required in tax credits cases is no different from that required in other areas of law. In the context of planning, Lord Brown of Eaton-under-Heywood summarised the effect of case law in *South Bucks District Council v Porter (No.2)* [2004] UKHL 33 [2004] 1 W.L.R. 1953 at [36]:

"The reasons for a decision must be intelligible and they must be adequate. They must enable the reader to understand why the matter was decided as it was and what conclusions were reached on the 'principal important controversial issues', disclosing how any issue of law or fact was resolved. Reasons can be briefly stated, the degree of particularity required depending entirely on the nature of the issues falling for decision. The reasoning must not give rise to a substantial doubt as to whether the decision-maker erred in law, for example by misunderstanding some relevant policy or some other important matter or by failing to reach a rational decision on relevant grounds. But such adverse inference will not readily be drawn. The reasons need refer only to the main issues in the dispute, not to every material consideration. They should enable disappointed developers to assess their prospects of obtaining some alternative development permission, or, as the case may be, their unsuccessful opponents to understand how the policy or approach underlying the grant of permission may impact upon future such applications. Decision letters [which contain statements of reasons] must be read in a straightforward manner, recognising that they are addressed to parties well aware of the issues involved and the arguments advanced. A reasons challenge will only succeed if the party aggrieved can satisfy the court that he has genuinely been substantially prejudiced by the failure to provide an adequately reasoned decision."

(The reference to policy is a reference to planning policies that must be taken into account in such cases. There is probably no equivalent policy in tax credits and so that reference should be disregarded.)

One of the great difficulties, of course, is judging where to draw the line between what need be mentioned and what need not. In *R. (Asha Foundation) v Millennium Commission* [2003] EWCA Civ 88, the Court of Appeal considered the approach Sedley J had taken in *R. v Higher Education Funding Council Ex p. Institute of Dental Surgery* [1994] 1 W.L.R. 242 to the question of whether there was a duty to give any reasons at all and held that, where there is a duty to give reasons, the same approach should be taken to the question whether reasons were adequate. Sedley J's approach required the balancing of a number of considerations, which might vary from case to case. He said:

"The giving of reasons may among other things concentrate the decision-maker's mind on the right questions; demonstrate to the recipient that this is so; show that the issues have been conscientiously addressed and how the result has been reached or alternatively alert the recipient to a justiciable flaw in the process.

On the other side of the argument, it may place an undue burden on decision-makers; demand an appearance of unanimity where there is diversity; call for the articulation of sometimes inexpressible value judgments; and offer an invitation to the captious to comb the reasons for previously unsuspected grounds of challenge."

The Court of Appeal said in *Flannery v Halifax Estate Agencies Ltd* [2000] 1 W.L.R. 377 that, where there is expert evidence and analysis advanced by both parties, a statement of reasons must "enter into the issues" in order to explain why the unsuccessful party's evidence has failed to prevail. However, in *English v Emery Reimbold & Strick Ltd* [2002] EWCA Civ 605, the Court of Appeal sought to discourage the "cottage industry" of applications inspired by *Flannery* and followed *Eagil Trust Co Ltd v Pigott-Brown* [1985] 3 All E.R. 119, 122 in which Griffiths L.J. had stressed that there was no duty on a judge in giving his reasons to deal with every argument presented to him. The Court also said that, while a judge will often need to refer to a piece of evidence or to a submission which he has accepted or rejected, provided the reference is clear, it may be unnecessary to detail, or even summarise, the evidence or submission in question.

"The essential requirement is that the terms of the judgment should enable the parties and any appellate tribunal readily to analyse the reasoning that was essential to the Judge's decision."

A similar need to deal with the major issues in a case but not necessarily to refer to every piece of evidence emerges from the social security cases. In *R(A) 1/72*, the Chief Commissioner, considering an appeal from a delegated medical practitioner acting on behalf of the Attendance Allowance Board, said:—

"The obligation to give reasons for the decision in [a case involving a conflict of evidence] imports a requirement to do more than only to state the conclusion, and for the determining authority to state that on the evidence the authority is not satisfied that the statutory conditions are met, does no more than this. It affords no guide to the selective process by which the evidence has been accepted, rejected, weighed or considered, or the reasons for any of these things. It is not, of course, obligatory thus to deal with every piece of evidence or to over elaborate, but in an administrative quasi-judicial decision the minimum requirement must at least be that the claimant, looking at the decision should be able to discern on the face of it the reasons why the evidence has failed to satisfy the authority. For the purpose of the regulation which requires the reasons for the review decision to be set out, a decision based, and only based, on a conclusion that the total effect of the evidence fails to satisfy, without reasons given for reaching that conclusion, will in many cases be no adequate decision at all."

However, in *CDLA/5419/99*, it was pointed out that the fact that a claimant is unsuccessful does not always imply rejection of the evidence produced by the claimant. In that case, the claimant's doctor said that the claimant required attention but he did not specify how much. The tribunal accepted that the claimant required some attention but not sufficient to qualify for disability living allowance. The Commissioner said that the doctor's evidence had therefore not supported the element of the claimant's case upon which she failed and that, in the circumstances of the case, there had been no duty to refer to the doctor's evidence at all. A similar point has been made by a Tribunal of Commissioners in Northern Ireland (*R2/04(DLA)*) and by the Court of Appeal in Northern Ireland (*Quinn v Department for Social Development* [2004] NICA 22). In the former case, however, the Commissioners added that, "where it is evident that the claimant attaches great significance to a letter or report, it may be prudent for a tribunal to say, briefly, that it has read the document but derived no assistance from it". It may also be helpful to say why no assistance was derived from the document if the relevance or value of the evidence is likely to be controversial. Similarly, in *R(M) 1/96*, the Commissioner held that the fact of a previous award does not raise any presumption in the claimant's favour or result in the need for consistency having to be treated as a separate issue on a renewal claim, but, nonetheless, the requirement for a tribunal to give reasons for its decision means that it is usually necessary for it to explain why it is not renewing a previous award, unless that is obvious from its findings. Often it *is* obvious so that, for instance, in *Quinn*, the Court accepted that, in the circumstances of that particular case, there had been no need for the tribunal to refer to a medical report obtained for the purpose of determining the previous claim. It is not necessarily an error of law to fail to comply with the best practice suggested in *R2/04(DLA)*.

It is acknowledged in *Baron v Secretary of State for Social Services* (reported as an appendix to *R(M) 6/86*) that there are limits to the extent to which a tribunal can be expected to give reasons for decisions on matters of judgment, such as the distance a claimant could walk without having to stop or the extent of breathlessness and pain which caused him to stop. Similarly, in *R3/01(IB)*, a Tribunal of Commissioners in Northern Ireland has held that there is no universal obligation on an appeal tribunal to explain an assessment of credibility. It will usually be sufficient to say that a witness is not believed or is exaggerating. It is the decision that has to be explained. A tribunal is not obliged to give reasons for its reasons. There may be situations when a further explanation will be required but the only standard is that the reasons should explain the decision. In *CCS/1626/2002*, the Commissioner said the a person could hardly complain about the adequacy of findings of fact or reasoning lying behind an estimate of income when the need to make an estimate was due to that person's failure to provide better evidence.

In *Baron*, it was held that:

"The overriding test must always be: is the tribunal providing both parties with the materials which will enable them to know that the tribunal has made no error of law in reaching its findings of fact?"

However, in *R(I) 3/03*, a Tribunal of Commissioners criticised the Secretary of State for Work and Pensions for supporting, by reference to an occasional infelicitous word in a statement of reasons, an unrealistic argument advanced by a claimant to the effect that a tribunal had overlooked a basic proposition of law. They said that there are some propositions of law, such as the nature of the civil burden and standard of proof, that are of such fundamental importance in the work of tribunals that it is almost inconceivable that tribunals will have overlooked them and that it should therefore be assumed that they have understood them unless there is something to show otherwise in the substance of what a tribunal has decided.

The European Court of Human Rights has taken much the same approach to the duty to give reasons as the United Kingdom's courts. In *Hirvisari v Finland* 2001, it was said:

"Although Article 6(1) obliges courts to give reasons for their decisions, it cannot be understood as requiring a detailed answer to every argument. Thus, in dismissing an appeal, an appellate court may, in principle, simply endorse the reasons for the lower court's decision . . . A lower court or authority in turn must give such reasons as to enable the parties to make effective use of any existing rights of appeal."

In *R(IS) 5/04*, it was held that a delay in providing reasons did not necessarily render a decision erroneous in point of law. The Commissioner said that a delay in providing reasons may itself amount to a breach of Art.6 of the European Convention on Human Rights (although, if the tribunal's decision was not flawed in any other respect, the remedy for such a breach would presumably be an award of damages by a court) and she also held that a delay may be relevant because it may indicate that the reasons are unreliable. However, in the particular case before her, where the statement of reasons had been requested on July 1, 2002 and was not sent to the parties until October 29, 2002, the Commissioner found there to have been no error of law. The Court of Appeal has since taken the same approach in relation to delays in the promulgation of decisions by employment tribunals. Delay may give rise to the state's liability to pay compensation to the victim of the delay but, where an appeal against the tribunal's decision lies only on a point of law, it is not enough to claim that the decision is "unsafe" because of the delay. However, there may be exceptional cases in which unreasonable delay in promulgating a decision can properly be treated as a serious procedural error or material irregularity giving rise to a question of law if there is a real risk that, due to the delayed decision, the party complaining was deprived of the substance of his right to a fair trial under Art.6 of the Convention. It is necessary to consider whether the delay has caused the tribunal to reach a wrong finding or to overlook or forget evidence (*Bangs v Connex South Eastern Ltd* [2005] EWCA Civ 14, in which it was held that there had been no error of law despite the fact that the tribunal's decision was not promulgated until a year after the hearing ended.) Effectively, delay is merely a factor to be borne in mind when assessing the adequacy of a statement of reasons.

In *Barke v Seetec Business Technology Centre Ltd* [2005] EWCA Civ 578, the Court of Appeal approved the practice in the employment appeal tribunal of sifting appeals and inviting employment tribunals to supplement their reasons when the reasons appear to be inadequate. This is done to save the costs of an appeal and of a rehearing where the reasons can adequately be supplemented, although it was recognised in *Barke* that it will not always be appropriate if, for example "the inadequacy of reasoning is on its face so fundamental that there is a real risk that supplementary reasons will be reconstructions of proper reasons, rather than the unexplained actual reasons for the decision". It was also said that the employment appeal tribunal "should always be alive to the danger that an employment tribunal might tailor its response to a request for explanations or further reasons (usually subconsciously rather than deliberately) so as to put the decision in the best possible light". In *CA/4297/2004*, the Commissioner distinguished *Barke* and held that a salaried chairman considering an application for leave to appeal to a Commissioner had been wrong to ask the fee-paid chairman of the tribunal to supplement his statement of reasons for the tribunal's decision and that the fee-paid chairman had had no power to do so. The Commissioner pointed out that appeals to Commissioners are usually dealt with speedily without oral hearings and that the cost and length of rehearings before tribunals are relatively modest. That is quite apart from the danger referred to by the Commissioner of a fee-paid chairman being led into introducing reasoning on issues that were not in fact considered by the whole tribunal. Since then, the Court of Appeal has declined to apply *Barke* on an appeal from the Asylum and Immigration Tribunal, stressing that the procedural rules of that tribunal were different from those governing employment tribunals (*Hatungimana v Secretary of State for the Home Department* [2006] EWCA Civ 231). This lends support to the stance taken in *CA/4297/2004*. There were clearly practical arguments against the course taken by the salaried chairman in the case before the Commissioner because some substantial delay was caused due to the claimant having to be given the opportunity to comment on the supplemented statement.

(SI 2002/3196, reg. 21) (as amended)

However, it is arguable that the Commissioner went too far in suggesting that reasons can never be supplemented when an application is made for leave to appeal. What might, perhaps, have been permissible would have been for the salaried chairman to have referred the application to the fee-paid chairman for determination, with an indication that he might feel able to answer the grounds of appeal. That would have caused some delay but not as much as was actually causes in that case. A modest expansion of reasons when leave to appeal is being refused (or granted) has been regarded as acceptable in some cases (e.g., *R(M) 2/78*). It would be for the Commissioner to consider whether the supplementary reasons were reliable against the background of the case.

Para. (6)
A decision will be set aside by a Commissioner if there has been a failure to include reasons for dissent (*CDLA/572/2001*).

Late applications for a statement of reasons of tribunal decision

22.—(1) The time for making an application for the statement of reasons for a tribunal's decision may be extended where the conditions specified in paragraphs (2) to (8) are satisfied, but, subject to [¹regulation 21(4A)], no application shall in any event be brought more than three months after the date of the sending or giving of the notice of the decision of the appeal tribunal.

(2) An application for an extension of time under this regulation shall be made in writing and shall be determined by a legally qualified panel member.

(3) An application under this regulation shall contain particulars of the grounds on which the extension of time is sought, including details of any relevant special circumstances for the purposes of paragraph (4).

(4) The application for an extension of time shall not be granted unless the panel member is satisfied that it is in the interests of justice for the application to be granted.

(5) For the purposes of paragraph (4) it is not in the interests of justice to grant the application unless the panel member is satisfied that—
  (a) the special circumstances specified in paragraph (6) are relevant to the application; or
  (b) some other special circumstances are relevant to the application,
and as a result of those special circumstances it was not practicable for the application to be made within the time limit specified in regulation 21(4).

(6) For the purposes of paragraph (5)(a), the special circumstances are that—
  (a) the applicant or a partner or dependant of the applicant has died or suffered serious illness;
  (b) the applicant is not resident in the United Kingdom; or
  (c) normal postal services were disrupted.

(7) In determining whether it is in the interests of justice to grant the application, the panel member shall have regard to the principle that the greater the amount of time that has elapsed between the expiration of the time within which the application for a copy of the statement of reasons for a tribunal's decision is to be made and the making of the application for an extension of time, the more compelling should be the special circumstances on which the application is based.

(8) In determining whether it is in the interests of justice to grant the application, no account shall be taken of the following—

(a) that the person making the application or any person acting for him was unaware of, or misunderstood, the law applicable to his case (including ignorance or misunderstanding of the time limits imposed by these Regulations); or

(b) that a Commissioner or a court has taken a different view of the law from that previously understood and applied.

(9) An application under this regulation for an extension of time which has been refused may not be renewed.

(10) The panel member who determines an application under this regulation shall record a summary of his determination in such written form as has been approved by the President.

(11) As soon as practicable after the determination is made, notice of the determination shall be sent or given to every party to the proceedings.

(12) Any person who under paragraph (11) receives notice of the determination may, within one month of the determination being sent to him, apply in writing for a copy of the reasons for that determination and a copy shall be supplied to him.

(13) [¹ . . .]

AMENDMENT

1. Social Security, Child Support and Tax Credits (Miscellaneous Amendments) Regulations 2005 (SI 2005/337), reg.4(5) (March 18, 2005).

DEFINITIONS

"appeal tribunal"—see s.39(1) of the Social Security Act 1998.
"Commissioner"—*ibid.*
"court"—see reg.1(3).
"decision"—*ibid.*
"legally qualified panel member"—*ibid.*
"panel member"—*ibid.*
"partner"—*ibid.*
"party to the proceedings"—*ibid.*
"President"—*ibid.*

GENERAL NOTE

The terms of this regulation are similar to the terms of reg.5 but there is no equivalent to reg.5(4)(a) and so the only flexibility is that permitted by the phrase "wholly exceptional" in para.(5)(b).

Record of tribunal proceedings

23.—(1) A record of the proceedings at an oral hearing, which is sufficient to indicate the evidence taken, shall be made by the chairman, or in the case of an appeal tribunal which has only one member, by that member, in such medium as he may direct.

[¹(2) The clerk to the appeal tribunal shall preserve—
(a) the record of proceedings;
(b) the decision notice; and
(c) any statement of the reasons for the tribunal's decision,
for the period specified in paragraph (3).

(3) That period is six months from the date of—
(a) the decision made by the appeal tribunal;
(b) any statement of reasons for the tribunal's decision;

(SI 2002/3196, reg.23) (as amended)

    (c) any correction of the decision in accordance with regulation 24;
    (d) any refusal to set aside the decision in accordance with regulation 25; or
    (e) any determination of an application under regulation 27 for leave to appeal against the decision,

or until the date on which those documents are sent to the office of the Social Security and Child Support Commissioners in connection with an appeal against the decision or an application to a Commissioner for leave to appeal, if that occurs within the six months.

(4) Any party to the proceedings may within the time specified in paragraph (3) apply in writing for a copy of the record of proceedings and a copy shall be supplied to him.]

AMENDMENT

1. Social Security, Child Support and Tax Credits (Miscellaneous Amendments) Regulations 2005 (SI 2005/337), reg.4(6) (March 18, 2005).

DEFINITIONS

    "appeal tribunal"—see s.39(1) of the Social Security Act 1998.
    "clerk to the appeal tribunal"—see reg.1(3).
    "decision"—*ibid.*
    "decision notice"—see reg.21(1).
    "party to the proceedings"—see reg.1(3).

GENERAL NOTE

Para. (1)

    The opening words of the regulation show that the "record of proceedings" is a note of the evidence and submissions received at the hearing. This is often taken to refer to the oral evidence and submissions but it probably extends to at least a record of what written evidence was before the tribunal which may in turn imply a duty on someone to keep a copy of that evidence. In practice, the Tribunals Service keeps the whole file for six months from the last action on the file, which complies with the duty however the regulation is construed.   2.424.1

    Where an appeal is based on what happened at the hearing, a Commissioner will be slow to go behind a full record of proceedings (*CS/343/1994*) but will admit evidence if it is necessary to do so where a full and particularised allegation is made that the conduct of the hearing led to a breach of the rules of natural justice (*R(M) 1/89*).

Paras (2) and (3)

    It was suggested, *obiter*, in *CSIB/439/2004*, that keeping the documents for only six months might breach the right to a fair hearing guaranteed by Art.6 of the European Convention on Human Rights, given that appeals can be brought after that period has ended. However, all parties should have had the decision notice and any statement of reasons and would have had at least six months in which to ask for a record of proceedings and, if a party has destroyed his own copies of documents or has failed to ask for a record of proceedings, it is not clear that he should be able to complain that the tribunal has also destroyed its copy of the documents. The effect of the six-month period is that it remains necessary for an applicant to provide the documents necessary to support a very late application for leave to appeal or a very late appeal.   2.424.2

Para. (4)

    A failure to comply with the duty to provide a copy of the record of proceedings will not always render a tribunal's decision erroneous in point of law but it will do so if, in a particular case, it is necessary to have regard to the evidence given at the hearing or to any contention put forward at the hearing in order to decide whether some other ground of appeal is made out and the lack of a record makes the task   2.425

impossible (*CDLA/1389/1997*). The duty is not complied with if the record of proceedings is incomprehensible (*CIB/3013/1997*). It may be thought that the obvious course of action where a record is simply illegible is to ask the chairman to provide a legible version if that is still practical.

Correction of accidental errors

24.—(1) The clerk to the appeal tribunal or a legally qualified panel member may at any time correct accidental errors in [¹the notice of any decision] of an appeal tribunal made under the 2002 Act.

[¹(2) A correction made to a decision notice shall be deemed to be part of the decision notice and written notice of the correction shall be given as soon as practicable to every party to the proceedings.]

AMENDMENT

1. Social Security, Child Support and Tax Credits (Miscellaneous Amendments) Regulations 2005 (SI 2005/337), reg.4(7) (March 18, 2005).

DEFINITIONS

"the 2002 Act"—see reg.1(3).
"appeal tribunal"—see s.39(1) of the Social Security Act 1998.
"clerk to the appeal tribunal"—see reg.1(3).
"decision"—*ibid.*
"decision notice"—see reg.21(1).
"legally qualified panel member"—see reg.1(3).
"party to the proceedings"—*ibid.*

GENERAL NOTE

Regulation 24 allows correction only of accidental errors in the decision notice, "such as a typing mistake or misspelling of a name or an omission about which both sides if asked, would agree" (*CI/3887/1999*). Such a correction extends the time for applying for a statement of reasons (see reg.21(4A)). If notice of the correction is not given as it should be under para.(2), the time for applying for a statement of reasons is left in abeyance (*CI/3887/1999*). The amendments have made clear that this regulation does not permit corrections to the statement of reasons, which may be permissible under an implied power to correct minor slips but will not affect time limits.

A decision is only effective when it is sent out (*R(I) 14/74*). Until then, it may be altered informally. Even if an oral "decision" has been given, the case may be recalled by the tribunal before it is sent out, if it appears to it that it has made a serious mistake (*CI/141/1987*, applying *Re Harrison's Share* [1955] Ch. 260). Generally, it would then be necessary to have a rehearing.

Setting aside decisions on certain grounds

25.—(1) On an application made by a party to the proceedings, a decision of an appeal tribunal made under the 2002 Act, may be set aside by a legally qualified panel member in a case where it appears just to set the decision aside on the ground that—
  (a) a document relating to the proceedings in which the decision was made was not sent to, or was not received at an appropriate time by, a party to the proceedings or the party's representative or was not received at an appropriate time by the person who made the decision;
  (b) a party to the proceedings in which the decision was made or the party's representative was not present at a hearing relating to the proceedings.

(SI 2002/3196, reg.25) (as amended)

(2) In determining whether it is just to set aside a decision on the ground set out in paragraph (1)(b), the panel member shall determine whether the party making the application gave notice that he wished to have an oral hearing, and if that party did not give such notice the decision shall not be set aside unless that member is satisfied that the interests of justice manifestly so require.

(3) An application under this regulation shall—
 (a) be made within one month of the date on which—
  (i) a copy of the decision notice is sent or given to the parties to the proceedings in accordance with regulation 21(3); or
  (ii) the statement of the reasons for the decision is given or sent in accordance with regulation 21(5),
  whichever is the later;
 (b) be in writing and signed by a party to the proceedings or, where the party has provided written authority to a representative to act on his behalf, that representative;
 (c) contain particulars of the grounds on which it is made; and
 (d) be sent to the clerk to the appeal tribunal.

(4) Where an application to set aside a decision is entertained under paragraph (1), every party to the proceedings shall be sent a copy of the application and shall be afforded a reasonable opportunity of making representations on it before the application is determined.

[[1](4A) Where a legally qualified panel member refuses to set aside a decision he may treat the application to set aside the decision as an application under regulation 21(4) for a statement of the reasons for the tribunal's decision, subject to the time limits set out in regulation 21(4) and (4A).]

(5) Notice in writing of a determination on an application to set aside a decision shall be sent or given to every party to the proceedings as soon as may be practicable and the notice shall contain a statement giving the reasons for the determination.

(6) The time within which an application under this regulation must be made may be extended by a period not exceeding one year where the conditions specified in paragraphs (7) to (11) are satisfied.

(7) An application for an extension of time shall be made in accordance with paragraph (3)(b) to (d), shall include details of any relevant special circumstances for the purposes of paragraph (9) and shall be determined by a legally qualified panel member.

(8) An application for an extension of time shall not be granted unless the panel member is satisfied that—
 (a) if the application is granted there are reasonable prospects that the application to set aside will be successful; and
 (b) it is in the interests of justice for the application for an extension of time to be granted.

(9) For the purposes of paragraph (8) it is not in the interests of justice to grant an application for an extension of time unless the panel member is satisfied that—
 (a) the special circumstances specified in paragraph (10) are relevant to the application; or
 (b) some other special circumstances exist which are wholly exceptional and relevant to that application,
and as a result of those special circumstances, it was not practicable for the application to set aside to be made within the time limit specified in paragraph (3)(a).

(10) For the purposes of paragraph (9)(a), the special circumstances are that—
  (a) the applicant or a partner or dependant of the applicant has died or suffered serious illness;
  (b) the applicant is not resident in the United Kingdom; or
  (c) normal postal services were disrupted.

(11) In determining whether it is in the interests of justice to grant an application for an extension of time, the panel member shall have regard to the principle that the greater the amount of time that has elapsed between the expiry of the time within which the application to set aside is to be made and the making of the application for an extension of time, the more compelling should be the special circumstances on which the application for an extension is based.

(12) An application under this regulation for an extension of time which has been refused may not be renewed.

AMENDMENT

1. Social Security, Child Support and Tax Credits (Miscellaneous Amendments) Regulations 2005 (SI 2005/337), reg.4(8) (March 18, 2005).

DEFINITIONS

"the 2002 Act"—see reg.1(3).
"appeal tribunal"—see s.39(1) of the Social Security Act 1998.
"clerk to the appeal tribunal"—see reg.1(3).
"decision"—*ibid.*
"decision notice"—see reg.21(1).
"legally qualified panel member"—see reg.1(3).
"panel member"—*ibid.*
"partner"—*ibid.*
"party to the proceedings"—*ibid.*

GENERAL NOTE

2.429   *Para. (1)*
The scope of this power to set aside a decision is limited to cases where documents have gone astray or parties have not attended hearings. Section 28(2) of the Social Security Act 1998 appears to contemplate a more general implied power to set aside decisions where justice demands it, but such a power for tribunals to set aside their decisions has been held not to exist by the High Court (*Secretary of State for Defence v President of the Pensions Appeal Tribunals (England and Wales)* [2004] EWHC 141 (Admin)) and has been doubted by the Court of Appeal (*Akewushola v Secretary of State for the Home Department* [2000] 1 W.L.R. 2295). This may not matter a great deal in this jurisdiction because, if there is an application for leave to appeal in a case other than a penalty case, a decision may be set aside under s.13(2) of the 1998 Act provided the legally qualified panel member is satisfied that the decision is erroneous in point of law. Most real injustices are errors of law. Indeed, most cases where this regulation could be applied could also result in successful appeals. In *R(SB) 19/93*, it was said that it was preferable for an application to be made under a forerunner of this regulation rather than for an appeal to be brought. However, a failure to make such an application, or a failure on the part of a legally qualified chairman to set aside a decision under this regulation, do not prevent an appeal being brought (*CIB/303/1999, CG/2973/2004*). That is why it is unnecessary to have a separate right of appeal against decisions under this regulation (see reg.26(2)).

Tribunals are entitled to take a robust approach to the non-appearance of parties and to proceed to hear cases in their absence, but a necessary concomitant of such

(SI 2002/3196, reg.25) (as amended)

a robust approach must be a greater preparedness to set aside decisions under sub-para.(b) (*Cooke v Glenrose Fish Company* [2004] I.C.R. 1188).

It is specifically provided that, even where the conditions of sub-paras (a) or (b) are satisfied, a decision need be set aside only if it is "just". This is consistent with the European Convention on Human Rights. Under the Convention, a person who did not receive notice of a hearing is not entitled as of right to have the decision set aside, unless he has a real prospect of success on a rehearing (*Akram v Adam* [2004] EWCA Civ 1601; [2005] 1 W.L.R. 2762).

Para. (12)
Where renewal of an application is forbidden, it will usually be possible to apply for leave to appeal and ask for the decision to be set aside under s.13 of the Social Security Act 1998 instead.

2.430

Provisions common to regulations 24 and 25

26.—(1) [¹ . . .]

2.431

(2) There shall be no appeal against a correction made under regulation 24 or a refusal to make such a correction or against a determination made under regulation 25.

(3) Nothing in this Chapter shall be construed as derogating from any power to correct errors or set aside decisions which is exercisable apart from these Regulations.

AMENDMENT

1. Social Security, Child Support and Tax Credits (Miscellaneous Amendments) Regulations 2005 (SI 2005/337), reg.4(9) (March 18, 2005).

DEFINITIONS

"appeal tribunal"—see s.39(1) of the Social Security Act 1998.
"Commissioner"—*ibid.*
"decision"—see reg.1(3).

[¹Service of decision notice by electronic mail

26A. For the purposes of the time limits in regulations 21 to 25, a properly addressed copy of a decision notice sent by electronic mail is effective from the date it is sent.]

2.432–2.433

AMENDMENT

1. Social Security, Child Support and Tax Credits (Miscellaneous Amendments) Regulations 2005 (SI 2005/337), reg.4(10) (March 18, 2005).

Application for leave to appeal to a Commissioner from a decision of an appeal tribunal

27.—(1) Subject to section 14 of the Act (as applied and modified by the Appeals Regulations) [¹and paragraph (1A)], an application for leave to appeal to a Commissioner from a decision on an appeal under section 12 or 13 of the Act (as applied and modified by the Appeals Regulations) shall—
   (a) be sent to the clerk to the appeal tribunal within the period of one month of the date of the applicant being sent a written statement of the reasons for the decision against which leave to appeal is sought; and

2.434

(b) [³be in writing and signed by the applicant or, where he has given written authority to a representative to make the application on his behalf, by that representative;
(c) contain particulars of the grounds on which the applicant intends to rely;
(d) contain sufficient particulars of the decision of the appeal tribunal to enable the decision to be identified; and
(e) if the application is made late, contain the grounds for seeking late acceptance.

(1A) Where after the written statement of the reasons for the decision has been sent to the parties to the proceedings—
(a) the decision notice is corrected in accordance with regulation 24; or
(b) an application under regulation 25 for the decision to be set aside is refused for reasons other than a refusal to extend the time for making the application,

the period specified in paragraph (1)(a) shall run from the date on which notice of the correction or the refusal of the application for setting aside is sent to the applicant.].

(2) Where an application for leave to appeal to a Commissioner is made by the Board, the clerk to an appeal tribunal shall, as soon as may be practicable, send a copy of the application to every other party to the proceedings.

(3) A person determining an application for leave to appeal to a Commissioner shall record his determination in writing and send a copy to every party to the proceedings.

(4) Where there has been a failure to apply for leave to appeal within the period of time specified in paragraph (1)(a) but an application is made within one year of the last date for making an application within that period, a legally qualified panel member may, if for special reasons he thinks fit, accept and proceed to consider and determine the application.

(5) Where an application for leave to appeal against a decision of an appeal tribunal is made—
(a) if the person who constituted, or was the chairman of, the appeal tribunal when the decision was given was a fee-paid legally qualified panel member, the application may be determined by a salaried legally qualified panel member; or
(b) if it is impracticable, or would be likely to cause undue delay, for the application to be determined by whoever constituted, or was the chairman of, the appeal tribunal when the decision was given, the application may be determined by another legally qualified panel member.

AMENDMENT

1. Social Security, Child Support and Tax Credits (Miscellaneous Amendments) Regulations 2005 (SI 2005/337), reg.4(11) (March 18, 2005).

DEFINITIONS

"the Act"—see reg.1(3).
"the Appeals Regulations"—*ibid*.
"appeal tribunal"—see s.39(1) of the Social Security Act 1998.
"the Board"—see s.39(1) of the Social Security Act 1998 as modified by reg.12 of the Tax Credits (Appeals) Regulations 2002.

(SI 2002/3196, reg.27) (as amended)

"Commissioner"—see s.39(1) of the Social Security Act 1998.
"clerk to the appeal tribunal"—see reg.1(3).
"decision"—*ibid*.
"decision notice"—see reg.21(1).
"legally qualified panel member"—see reg.1(3).
"party to the proceedings"—*ibid*.

GENERAL NOTE

Para. (1)
Leave to appeal is not required on penalty appeals brought under Sch.2 to the Tax Credits Act 2002, as modified by s.63.

No provision is made for an application for leave to appeal to be made when there is no statement of reasons. In practice, if an application for leave is made before a statement of reasons is issued, it will be treated first as an application for such a statement. If it too late and no statement is issued, a legally qualified panel member must reject the application (because the time for applying to a chairman for leave to appeal cannot start to run until a statement of reasons is issued) but an application may then be made to a Commissioner who may accept it (*CSDLA/536/1999*), provided the applicant can demonstrate an arguable point of law despite the lack of a statement of reasons (*R(IS) 11/99*).

An application for leave to appeal may be made by fax (*CDLA/4895/2001*).

Para. (4)
There is a broad discretion to extend the time for appealing where that is necessary to enable justice to be done. The approach of the Court of Appeal in *R. v Secretary of State for the Home Department, Ex p. Mehta* [1975] 1 W.L.R. 1087 was followed in *R(M) 1/87* and it was held that it was wrong to consider only whether there were special reasons for the delay in applying for leave to appeal. In *CCS/2064/1999*, it was suggested that relevant factors included the strength of the grounds of appeal, the amount of money involved, whether the decision affected current entitlement, whether there was an adequate alternative remedy, the difficulties that the lapse of time might create for making further findings of fact and the way in which the parties had conducted the case, including their respective contributions to delay. The amount of delay may also be relevant but, in *CSDLA/71/1999*, the Commissioner made it plain that "special reasons" for admitting a late application for leave to appeal would not necessarily be found merely because the application was made only two or three days late, even if the applicant had an arguable case on the merits. In that case, the applicant was not helped by the fact that the original explanation for the delay advanced by his representative turned out not to be true. The Commissioner refused leave to appeal.

Para. (5)
Applications for leave to appeal are almost invariably determined by salaried tribunal chairmen. This is more efficient insofar as speed is concerned, but there are times when a fee-paid chairman who heard an appeal would be better able to answer a ground of appeal when giving reasons for granting or refusing leave to appeal or would be better able to consider setting aside a decision instead of granting leave to appeal.

2.435

2.436

2.437

The Social Security Commissioners (Procedure etc.) Regulations 2002

The Social Security Commissioners (Procedure) (Tax Credits Appeals) Regulations 2002

(SI 2002/3237) (AS AMENDED)

Made   18th December 2002
Laid before Parliament   28th November 2002
Coming into force   1st January 2003

ARRANGEMENT OF REGULATIONS

PART I

2.438
1. Citation, commencement and duration
2. Interpretation
3. General powers of a Commissioner
4. Transfer of proceedings between Commissioners
5. Delegation of functions to authorised officers
6. Manner of and time for service of notices, etc.
6A. Funding of legal services

PART II

APPLICATIONS FOR LEAVE TO APPEAL AND APPEALS

6B. Application of this Part
7. Application to a Commissioner for leave to appeal
8. Notice of application to a Commissioner for leave to appeal
9. Determination of application
10. Notice of appeal
11. Time limit for appealing
12. Acknowledgement of a notice of appeal and notification to each respondent

PART III

PROCEDURE

13. Representation
14. Respondent's written observations
15. Written observations in reply
16. Directions
17. Non-disclosure of medical evidence
18. Requests for hearings
19. Hearings
20. Summoning of witnesses
21. Withdrawal of applications for leave to appeal and for appeals
22. Irregularities

(SI 2002/3237) (as amended)

Part IV

Decisions

23. Determinations and decisions of a Commissioner
24. Correction of accidental errors in decisions
25. Setting aside decisions on certain grounds
26. Provisions common to regulations 24 and 25

Part V

Applications for Leave to Appeal to the Appellate Court

27. Application to a Commissioner for leave to appeal to the Appellate Court

The Lord Chancellor, in exercise of the powers conferred upon him by sections 79(2) and 84 of the Social Security Act 1998, and by sections 14, 15, 16, 28 and 39 of, and Schedules 4 and 5 to, the Social Security Act 1998 as applied and modified by the Tax Credits (Appeals) Regulations 2002, after consultation in accordance with section 79(2) of the Social Security Act 1998 and paragraph 8 of Schedule 4 to that Act and with the Council on Tribunals in accordance with section 8 of the Tribunals and Inquiries Act 1992, makes the following Regulations, a draft of which has, in accordance with section 80(1) of the Social Security Act 1998 been laid before and approved by resolution of each House of Parliament:

Part I

General Provisions

Citation, commencement and duration

1.—(1) These Regulations may be cited as the Social Security Commissioners (Procedure) (Tax Credits Appeals) Regulations 2002 and shall come into force on 1st January 2003.

(2) These Regulations shall cease to have effect on such day as is appointed by order made under section 63(1) of the Tax Credits Act 2002 (tax credit appeals etc.: temporary modifications).

2.439

Interpretation

2. In these Regulations, unless the context otherwise requires—
 "the 1998 Act" means the Social Security Act 1998, as applied and modified by the Tax Credits (Appeals) Regulations 2002;
 "the 2002 Act" means the Tax Credits Act 2002;
 "appeal" means an appeal which by virtue of section 63 of the 2002 Act is from an appeal tribunal to a Social Security Commissioner;
 "appeal tribunal" means an appeal tribunal constituted under Chapter 1 of Part 1 of the 1998 Act;

2.440

"authorised officer" means an officer authorised by the Lord Chancellor, or in Scotland by the Secretary of State, in accordance with paragraph 6 of Schedule 4 to the 1998 Act;
"chairman" means—
  (i) the person who was the chairman or the sole member of the appeal tribunal which gave the decision against which leave to appeal is being sought; or
  (ii) any other person authorised to deal with applications for leave to appeal to a Commissioner against that decision under section 14 of the 1998 Act;
[1"funding notice" means the notice or letter from the Legal Services Commission confirming that legal services are to be funded;
"joint claimant" means a person making a claim under section 3(3)(a) of the 2002 Act;
[1"legal aid certificate" means the certificate issued by the Scottish Legal Aid Board confirming that legal services are to be funded;]
"legally qualified" means being a solicitor or barrister, or in Scotland, a solicitor or advocate;
[1"Legal Services Commission" means the Legal Services Commission established under section 1 of the Access to Justice Act 1999;
"live television link" means a television link or other audio and video facilities which allow a person who is not physically present at an oral hearing to see and hear proceedings and be seen and heard by all others who are present (whether physically present or otherwise);]
"month" means a calendar month;
"office" means an Office of the Social Security Commissioners;
"party" means a party to the proceedings;
"penalty proceedings" means proceedings taken under Schedule 2 of the 2002 Act;
"proceedings" means any proceedings before a Commissioner, whether by way of an application for leave to appeal to, or from, a Commissioner, or by way of an appeal, or otherwise;
"respondent" means—
  (i) any person or organisation other than the applicant or appellant who is one of the principal parties as defined in section 13 of the 1998 Act;
  (ii) any other person taking part in the proceedings in accordance with section 14 of the 1998 Act or at the direction or with the leave of the Commissioner;
[1"Scottish Legal Aid Board" means the Scottish Legal Aid Board established under section 1 of the Legal Aid (Scotland) Act 1986;]
"summons", in relation to Scotland, corresponds to "citation" and regulation 20 shall be construed accordingly;
"tax credit" means a child tax credit or a working tax credit, construing those terms in accordance with section 1(1) and (2) of the 2002 Act.

AMENDMENT

1. Social Security and Child Support Commissioners (Procedure) (Amendment) Regulations 2005 (SI 2005/207), reg.4(3) (February 28, 2005).

(SI 2002/3237, reg.2) (as amended)

DEFINITION

"Commissioner"—see s.39(1) of the Social Security Act 1998.

General powers of a Commissioner

3.—(1) Subject to the provisions of these Regulations, a Commissioner may adopt any procedure in relation to proceedings before him.

(2) A Commissioner may—
(a) extend or abridge any time limit under these Regulations (including, subject to regulations 7(3) and 11(2), granting an extension where the time limit has expired);
(b) expedite, postpone or adjourn any proceedings.

(3) Subject to paragraph (4), a Commissioner may, on or without the application of a party, strike out any proceedings for want of prosecution or abuse of process.

(4) Before making an order under paragraph (3), the Commissioner shall send notice to the party against whom it is proposed that it should be made giving him an opportunity to make representations why it should not be made.

(5) A Commissioner may, on application by the party concerned, give leave to reinstate any proceedings which have been struck out in accordance with paragraph (3) and, on giving leave, he may give directions as to the conduct of the proceedings.

(6) Nothing in these Regulations shall affect any power which is exercisable apart from these Regulations.

DEFINITIONS

"Commissioner"—see s.39(1) of the Social Security Act 1998.
"party"—see reg.2.
"proceedings"—see reg.2.

Transfer of proceedings between Commissioners

4. If it becomes impractical or inexpedient for a Commissioner to continue to deal with proceedings which are or have been before him, any other Commissioner may rehear or deal with those proceedings and any related matters.

DEFINITIONS

"Commissioner"—see s.39(1) of the Social Security Act 1998.
"proceedings"—see reg.2.

Delegation of functions to authorised officers

5.—(1) The following functions of the Commissioners may be exercised by legally qualified authorised officers, to be known as legal officers to the Commissioners—
(a) giving directions under regulations 6 and 16;
(b) determining requests for or directing hearings under regulation 18;
(c) summoning witnesses, and setting aside a summons made by a legal officer, under regulation 20;

(d) postponing a hearing under regulation 3;
(e) giving leave to withdraw or reinstate applications or appeals under regulation 21;
(f) waiving irregularities under regulation 22 in connection with any matter being dealt with by a legal officer;
(g) extending or abridging time, directing expedition, giving notices, striking out and reinstating proceedings under regulation 3.

(2) Any party may, within 14 days of being sent notice of the direction or order of a legal officer, make a written request to a Commissioner asking him to reconsider the matter and confirm or replace the direction or order with his own, but, unless ordered by a Commissioner, a request shall not stop proceedings under the direction or order.

DEFINITIONS

"appeal"—see reg.2.
"authorised officer"—*ibid*.
"Commissioner"—see s.39(1) of the Social Security Act 1998.
"party"—see reg.2.
"proceedings"—*ibid*.
"summons"—*ibid*.

Manner of and time for service of notices, etc.

6.—(1) A notice to or document for any party shall be deemed duly served if it is—
(a) delivered to him personally; or
(b) properly addressed and sent to him by prepaid post at the address last notified by him for this purpose, or to his ordinary address; or
[¹(ba) subject to paragraph (1A), sent by email; or]
(c) served in any other manner a Commissioner may direct.

[¹(1A) A document may be served by email on any party if the recipient has informed the person sending the email in writing—
(a) that he is willing to accept service by email;
(b) of the email address to which the documents should be sent; and
(c) if the recipient wishes to so specify, the electronic format in which documents must be sent.]

(2) A notice to or other document for a Commissioner shall be [¹—
(a) delivered to the office in person;
(b) sent to the office by prepaid post;
(c) sent to the office by fax; or
(d) where the office has given written permission in advance, sent to the office by email].

(3) For the purposes of any time limit, a properly addressed notice or other document sent by prepaid post, fax or email is effective from the date it is sent.

AMENDMENT

1. Social Security and Child Support Commissioners (Procedure) (Amendment) Regulations 2005 (SI 2005/207), reg.4(4) (February 28, 2005).

DEFINITIONS

"Commissioner"—see s.39(1) of the Social Security Act 1998.
"office"—see reg.2.
"party"—*ibid*.

(SI 2002/3237, reg.6A) (as amended)

[¹Funding of legal services

6A. If a party is granted funding of legal services at any time, he shall—
(a) where funding is granted by the Legal Services Commission, send a copy of the funding notice to the office;
(b) where funding is granted by the Scottish Legal Aid Board, send a copy of the legal aid certificate to the office; and
(c) notify every other party that funding has been granted.]

AMENDMENT

1. Social Security and Child Support Commissioners (Procedure) (Amendment) Regulations 2005 (SI 2005/207), reg.4(5) (February 28, 2005).

DEFINITIONS

"funding notice"—see reg.2.
"legal aid certificate"—*ibid*.
"Legal Services Commission"—*ibid*.
"office"—*ibid*.
"party"—*ibid*.
"Scottish Legal Aid Board"—*ibid*.

GENERAL NOTE

In his *Practice Memorandum No.5*, the Chief Commissioner states that, where the Commissioners' office receives a copy of a funding notice or legal aid certificate, it will send a copy to all the other parties in the case and, therefore, sending a copy of a funding notice or legal aid certificate to the office will be regarded as adequate notification to the other parties.

PART II

APPLICATIONS FOR LEAVE TO APPEAL AND APPEALS

[¹Application of this Part

6B. In this Part—
(a) regulations 7, 8 and 9 apply to appeals other than an appeal against a determination in penalty proceedings;
(b) regulations 10, 11 and 12 apply to all appeals.]

AMENDMENT

1. Social Security and Child Support Commissioners (Procedure) (Amendment) Regulations 2005 (SI 2005/207), reg.4(6) (February 28, 2005).

DEFINITIONS

"appeal"—see reg.2.
"penalty proceedings"—*ibid*.

Application to a Commissioner for leave to appeal

7.—(1) An application to a Commissioner for leave to appeal against the decision of an appeal tribunal may be made only where the applicant has sought to obtain leave from the chairman and leave has been refused or the application has been rejected.

(2) Subject to paragraph (3) an application to a Commissioner shall be made within one month of notice of the refusal or rejection being sent to the applicant by the appeal tribunal.

(3) A Commissioner may for special reasons accept a late application or an application where the applicant failed to seek leave from the chairman within the specified time, but did so on or before the final date.

(4) In paragraph (3) the final date means the end of a period of 13 months from the date on which the decision of the appeal tribunal or, if later, any separate statement of the reasons for it, was sent to the applicant by the appeal tribunal.

DEFINITIONS

"appeal tribunal"—see reg.2.
"chairman"—*ibid*.
"Commissioner"—see s.39(1) of the Social Security Act 1998.
"final date"—see para.(4).
"month"—see reg.2.

GENERAL NOTE

Para. (1)

2.449 An application is "rejected" by a tribunal chairman where the chairman has no jurisdiction to accept it because, for instance, the applicant has not obtained a statement of reasons or has applied for leave to appeal more than a year after the time specified (*CSDLA/536/1999, CS/1952/2001*). By virtue of para.(3), a Commissioner will have jurisdiction to consider an application in the former case but not the latter. By virtue of reg.27, a Commissioner is entitled to waive the requirement first to apply to a tribunal chairman and is likely to do so in a case where the tribunal chairman would be bound to reject an application. It is arguable that an application is also "rejected", rather than "refused", in a case where it is made late and the chairman could extend the time but refuses to do so.

Para. (2)

2.450 The date the application is made is the date it is sent (see reg.8(3)). Time may be extended under para.(3), but the mere fact that an application is only one or two days late will not necessarily guarantee an extension (*CSDLA/71/1999*).

Para. (3)

2.451 For the meaning of "special reasons", see the note to reg.27 of the Tax Credits (Appeals) (No.2) Regulations 2002. If a late application to a chairman is accepted for consideration but leave to appeal is refused, it is unnecessary for a Commissioner to consider whether there are "special reasons" if the application to the Commissioner is made within the month allowed by para.(2) (*CIB/4791/2001*).

Para. (4)

2.452 The "final date" is the day *after* the last day allowed by reg.27(4) of the Tax Credits (Appeals) (No.2) Regulations 2002 for an application to a tribunal chairman (*CIB/4791/2001*). It has been held that, where there is no statement of reasons, the 13 months runs from the date the applicant was given or sent the decision notice (*CIS/1952/2001*), but it is arguable that the true position is that there is no statutory time limit in such a case but that, for the sake of consistency, a Commissioner should nonetheless refuse to find "special reasons" for accepting an application brought more than 13 months after a decision notice is issued.

(SI 2002/3237, reg.8) (as amended)

Notice of application to a Commissioner for leave to appeal

8.—(1) An application to a Commissioner for leave to appeal shall be made by notice in writing, and shall contain—
(a) the name and address of the applicant;
(b) the grounds on which the applicant intends to rely;
(c) if the application is made late, the grounds for seeking late acceptance; and
(d) an address for sending notices and other documents to the applicant.
(2) The notice in paragraph (1) shall have with it copies of—
(a) the decision against which leave to appeal is sought;
(b) if separate, the written statement of the appeal tribunal's reasons for it; and
(c) the notice of refusal or rejection sent to the applicant by the appeal tribunal.
(3) Where an application for leave to appeal is made by the Board, they shall send each respondent a copy of the notice of application and any documents sent with it when they are sent to the Commissioner.

2.453

DEFINITIONS

"appeal tribunal"—see reg.2.
"the Board"—see s.39(1) of the Social Security Act 1998 as modified by reg.12 of the Tax Credits (Appeals) Regulations 2002.
"Commissioner"—see s.39(1) of the Social Security Act 1998.
"respondent"—see reg.2.

GENERAL NOTE

Para.(1)
An application must contain the grounds. Thus, in *CSDLA/1207/2000* where the claimant's representative faxed a letter without grounds and also posted a letter with the grounds, the fax was not a valid application but the letter was.

2.454

Para.(2)
A failure to send a copy of the tribunal's statement of reasons with the application, as required by para.(2)(b), is an irregularity. Such an irregularity may be waived under reg.27. If an applicant has no statement of reasons because he or she failed to apply for one within the prescribed time, the tribunal's decision cannot be challenged on the ground of inadequacy reasons (*R(IS) 11/99*) and, if that is the only ground of appeal, the Commissioner is unlikely to waive an irregularity arising from a breach of para.(2)(b) (*CSDLA/300/2000*).

2.455

Determination of application

9.—(1) The office shall send written notice to the applicant and each respondent of the determination of an application for leave to appeal to a Commissioner.
(2) Subject to a direction by a Commissioner, where a Commissioner grants leave to appeal under regulation 7—
(a) notice of appeal shall be deemed to have been sent on the date when notice of the determination is sent to the applicant; and
(b) the notice of application shall be deemed to be a notice of appeal sent under regulation 10.
(3) If a Commissioner grants an application for leave to appeal he may, with the consent of the applicant and each respondent, treat and determine the application as an appeal.

2.456

The Social Security Commissioners (Procedure etc.) Regulations 2002

Definitions

"appeal"—see reg.2.
"Commissioner"—see s.39(1) of the Social Security Act 1998.
"office"—see reg.2.
"respondent"—*ibid.*

Notice of appeal

2.457 **10.**—(1) Subject to regulation 9(2), an appeal shall be made by notice in writing and shall contain—
(a) the name and address of the appellant;
(b) [¹where applicable,] the date on which the appellant was notified that leave to appeal had been granted;
(c) the grounds on which the appellant intends to rely;
(d) if the appeal is made late, the grounds for seeking late acceptance; and
(e) an address for sending notices and other documents to the appellant.
(2) The notice in paragraph (1) shall have with it copies of—
(a) the notice informing the appellant that leave to appeal has been granted;
(b) the decision against which leave to appeal has been granted; and
(c) if separate, the written statement of the appeal tribunal's reasons for it.

Amendment

1. Social Security and Child Support Commissioners (Procedure) (Amendment) Regulations 2005 (SI 2005/207), reg.4(7) (February 28, 2005).

Definitions

"appeal"—see reg.2.
"appeal tribunal"—*ibid.*

General Note

2.458 As reg.9(2) is invariably applied when a Commissioner grants leave, this regulation applies only where a chairman grants leave or on an appeal against a determination in penalty proceedings (when leave to appeal is not required). Note that a copy of a tribunal's statement of reasons is required even in a penalty case, despite the fact that an appeal in such a case is not restricted to points of law and that reg.11(1) is drafted without reference to the obtaining of a statement of reasons.

Time limit for appealing [¹ . . .]

2.459 **11.**—(1) In the case of an appeal against a determination in penalty proceedings, the notice of appeal shall not be valid unless it is sent to a Commissioner within one month of the decision of the appeal tribunal being sent to the applicant.
(2) For all other appeals, a notice of appeal shall not be valid unless it is sent to a Commissioner within one month of the date on which the appellant was sent written notice that leave to appeal had been granted.
(3) A Commissioner may for special reasons accept late notice of appeal.]

Amendment

1. Social Security and Child Support Commissioners (Procedure) (Amendment) Regulations 2005 (SI 2005/207), regs 4(8) and (9) (February 28, 2005).

(SI 2002/3237, reg.11) (as amended)

DEFINITIONS

"appeal"—see reg.2.
"appeal tribunal"—*ibid*.
"Commissioner"—see s.39(1) of the Social Security Act 1998.
"month"—see reg.2.
"penalty proceedings"—*ibid*.

GENERAL NOTE

Para. (1)

In his *Practice Memorandum No.6*, the Chief Social Security Commissioner states that, where, either on the tribunal's own initiative or following a request made within the time allowed by regs 21(4) and 22 of the Tax Credits (Appeals) (No.2) Regulations 2002, a statement of reasons for a tribunal's decision is sent to the appellant separately from the decision notice, the statement of reasons will be treated as "the decision of the appeal tribunal" for the purposes of the time limit for appealing in penalty proceedings.

2.460

Para. (2)

In practice, this paragraph applies only when a tribunal chairman has granted leave to appeal, because a person granted leave to appeal by a Commissioner is almost invariably deemed to have appealed under reg.9(2).

2.461

Acknowledgement of a notice of appeal and notification to each respondent

12. The office shall send—
(a) to the appellant, an acknowledgement of the receipt of the notice of appeal;
(b) to each respondent, a copy of the notice of appeal.

2.462

DEFINITIONS

"appeal"—see reg.2.
"office"—*ibid*.
"respondent"—*ibid*.

GENERAL NOTE

In practice, whenever there is an appeal from a decision of a tribunal, the Office of the Social Security and Child Support Commissioners obtains the tribunal file from the clerk to the tribunal and a complete bundle of papers is made up from the file and copied to each party.

2.463

PART III

PROCEDURE

Representation

13. A party may conduct his case himself (with assistance from any person if he wishes) or be represented by any person whom he may appoint for the purpose.

2.464

DEFINITION

"party"—see reg.2.

The Social Security Commissioners (Procedure etc.) Regulations 2002

General Note

2.465 Representatives other than solicitors, barristers and advocates are expected to provide written authority to act, signed by the party. In *CSDLA/2/2001*, two different representatives, each purporting to be acting on behalf of the same claimant, lodged separate applications for leave to appeal. The Commissioner said that a representative should obtain a fresh mandate from a claimant before sending an application for leave to appeal to a Commissioner, rather than relying on a mandate obtained before a tribunal hearing. Furthermore, the representative ought to discuss the case with the claimant and obtain specific instructions to apply for leave to appeal.

See also the note to reg.18(9) of the Tax Credits (Appeals) (No.2) Regulations 2002.

Respondent's written observations

2.466 **14.**—(1) A respondent may submit to a Commissioner written observations on an appeal within one month of being sent written notice of it.

(2) Written observations shall include—
(a) the respondent's name and address and address for sending documents;
(b) a statement as to whether or not he opposes the appeal; and
(c) the grounds upon which the respondent proposes to rely.

(3) The office shall send a copy of any written observations from a respondent to every other party.

(4) Where there is more than one respondent, the order of and time for written observations shall be as directed by a Commissioner under regulation 16.

Definitions

"appeal"—see reg.2.
"Commissioner"—see s.39(1) of the Social Security Act 1998.
"month"—see reg.2.
"office"—*ibid*.
"party"—*ibid*.
"respondent"—*ibid*.

General Note

2.467 See the note to reg.15.

Written observations in reply

2.468 **15.**—(1) Any party may submit to a Commissioner written observations in reply within one month of being sent written observations under regulation 14.

(2) The office shall send a copy of any written observations in reply to every other party.

(3) Where—
(a) written observations have been received under regulation 14; and
(b) each of the principal parties expresses the view that the decision appealed against was erroneous in point of law;
a Commissioner may make an order under section 14(7) of the 1998 Act setting aside the decision and may dispense with the procedure in paragraphs (1) and (2).

Definitions

"the 1998 Act"—see reg.2.

"Commissioner"—see s.39(1) of the Social Security Act 1998.
"month"—see reg.2.
"office"—*ibid*.
"party"—*ibid*.
"principal parties"—see s.13(4) of the Social Security Act 1998 as modified by reg.5 of the Tax Credits (Appeals) Regulations 2002.

GENERAL NOTE

Regulations 14 and 15 make provision for sequential observations. However, where a Commissioner considering an application for leave to appeal or giving case management directions on an appeal identifies what appears to be an obvious ground for allowing an appeal, the parties may be directed under reg.16 to indicate simultaneously whether they have any objection to the tribunal's decision being set aside on that ground. If no objection is received, the Commissioner determines the appeal when the responses are received or the time for responding has expired. This shortens the time taken to determine uncontentious appeals. If an objection of substance is received, the Commissioner obtains further observations in response.

Directions

16.—(1) Subject to paragraph (2), where a Commissioner considers that an application or appeal made to him gives insufficient particulars to enable the question at issue to be determined, he may direct the party making the application or appeal, or any respondent, to furnish any further particulars which may be reasonably required.

(2) No person shall be compelled to give any evidence or produce any document or other material that he could not be compelled to give or produce on a trial of an action in a court of law in that part of Great Britain where the hearing takes place.

(3) A Commissioner may, before determining the application or appeal, direct the appeal tribunal to submit a statement of such facts or other matters as he considers necessary for the proper determination of that application or appeal.

(4) At any stage of the proceedings, a Commissioner may, on or without an application, give any directions as he may consider necessary or desirable for the efficient despatch of the proceedings.

(5) Without prejudice to regulations 14 and 15, or to paragraph (4), and subject to paragraph (2), a Commissioner may direct any party before him, to make any written observations as may seem to him necessary to enable the question at issue to be determined.

(6) An application under paragraph (4) shall be made in writing to a Commissioner and shall set out the direction which the applicant seeks.

(7) Unless a Commissioner shall otherwise determine, the office shall send a copy of an application under paragraph (4) to every other party.

DEFINITIONS

"appeal"—see reg.2.
"appeal tribunal"—see reg.2.
"Commissioner"—see s.39(1) of the Social Security Act 1998.
"office"—see reg.2.
"party"—*ibid*.
"proceedings"—*ibid*.
"respondent"—*ibid*.

General Note

Para. (2)

2.471 A Commissioner will often obtain statements from the tribunal when an appeal is based on allegations about the conduct of a hearing before the tribunal, provided the allegation is sufficiently particularised to merit investigation at all (*R(M) 1/89*). However, statements will not be obtained if the allegation is adequately supported by other evidence, unless fairness to the members of the tribunal requires then to be afforded an opportunity to comment in a case where the allegation amounts to one of personal misconduct (*CDLA/5574/2002*).

A statement obtained under para.(2) cannot amount to a statement of reasons within the terms of reg.21(4) of the Tax Credits (Appeals) (No.2) Regulations 2002 and para.(2) should not be used for a "fishing expedition" where the applicant or appellant has not obtained a statement of reasons and cannot demonstrate a prima facie case that the tribunal has erred in law (*R3/02(IB)*, a decision of a Tribunal of Commissioners in Northern Ireland).

Para. (3)

2.472 Case management directions are usually issued when leave to appeal is granted by a Commissioner or upon receipt of an appeal where a chairman has granted leave or leave is not required. Such directions often shorten the procedure required by regs 14 and 15 (see the note to reg.15). However, case management directions may be issued at any stage of the proceedings. They commonly require submissions to be made on specific issues or for specific written or documentary evidence to be produced. For the power to issue a summons requiring attendance in person, see reg.20.

Non-disclosure of medical evidence

2.473 **17.**—(1) Where, in any proceedings, there is before a Commissioner medical evidence relating to a person which has not been disclosed to that person and in the opinion of the Commissioner the disclosure to that person of that evidence would be harmful to his health, such evidence shall not be disclosed to that person.

(2) Evidence such as is mentioned in paragraph (1)—

(a) shall not be disclosed to any person acting for or representing the person to whom it relates;

(b) shall not be disclosed to a joint claimant of the person to whom it relates or any person acting for or representing that joint claimant;

(c) in a case where a claim for a tax credit is made by reference to the disability of a person other than the claimant or joint claimant and the evidence relates to that other person, shall not be disclosed to the claimant, joint claimant or any person acting for or representing the claimant or joint claimant;

unless the Commissioner considers that it is in the interests of the person to whom the evidence relates to disclose it.

(3) Non-disclosure under paragraphs (1) or (2) does not preclude the Commissioner from taking the evidence concerned into account for the purpose of the proceedings.

Definitions

"claimant"—see s.39(1) of the Social Security Act 1998 as modified by reg.12 of the Tax Credits (Appeals) Regulations 2002.
"Commissioner"—see s.39(1) of the Social Security Act 1998.
"joint claimant"—see reg.2.

(SI 2002/3237, reg.17) (as amended)

"proceedings"—*ibid.*
"tax credit"—*ibid.*

GENERAL NOTE

See the note to reg.14 of the Tax Credits (Appeals) (No.2) Regulations 2002. 2.474

Requests for hearings

18.—(1) Subject to paragraphs (2), (3), (4) and (5), a Commissioner may determine any proceedings without a hearing. 2.475

(2) In appeals against a determination in penalty proceedings, where a request for a hearing is made by the party on whom the penalty has been imposed, a Commissioner shall grant the request.

(3) Where a request for a hearing is made by any party other than as provided by paragraph (2), a Commissioner shall grant the request unless he is satisfied that the proceedings can properly be determined without a hearing.

(4) Where a Commissioner refuses a request for a hearing, he shall send written notice to the person making the request, either before or at the same time as making his determination or decision.

(5) A Commissioner may, without an application and at any stage, direct a hearing.

DEFINITIONS

"Commissioner"—see s.39(1) of the Social Security Act 1998.
"party"—see reg.2.
"penalty proceedings"—*ibid.*
"proceedings"—*ibid.*

GENERAL NOTE

In penalty proceedings, the party on whom the penalty was imposed may insist on there being an oral hearing. In other cases, there is no requirement to hold an oral hearing even when one is requested. That is consistent with the European Convention on Human Rights, which does not require a second-tier tribunal to hold an oral hearing where there has been an opportunity to have an oral hearing before the first-tier tribunal (*Hoppe v Germany* [2003] F.L.R. 384). Similarly, at common law a case can be determined without an oral hearing unless that would be unfair because, for instance, oral evidence is required or the case is complex (*R. (Thompson) v Law Society* [2004] EWCA Civ 167; [2004] 1 W.L.R. 2522). It is suggested that, under para.(2), a Commissioner may properly refuse a request for an oral hearing where oral evidence would be irrelevant and there is no reason to suppose that oral argument could make any difference to the outcome. 2.476

There is even less of a duty to hold an oral hearing where none has been requested. In particular, a Commissioner is not required to direct an oral hearing just because he or she is minded to reject an appeal that has been supported by the respondent (*Miller v Secretary of State for Work and Pensions* 2002 G.W.D 25–861 (Court of Session, unreported, July 12, 2002).

Hearings

19.—(1) This regulation applies to any hearing of an application or appeal to which these Regulations apply. 2.477

(2) Subject to paragraph (3), the office shall give reasonable notice of the time and place of any hearing before a Commissioner.

(3) Unless all the parties concerned agree to a hearing at shorter notice, the period of notice specified under paragraph (2) shall be at least 14 days before the date of the hearing.

(4) If any party to whom notice of a hearing has been sent fails to appear at the hearing, the Commissioner may proceed with the case in that party's absence, or may give directions with a view to the determination of the case.

(5) Any hearing before a Commissioner shall be in public, unless the Commissioner for special reasons directs otherwise

(6) Where a Commissioner holds a hearing the following persons or organisations shall be entitled to be present and be heard—
   (a) the person or organisation making the application or appeal;
   (b) the claimant;
   (c) the Board;
   (d) a trade union, employers' association or other association which would have had a right of appeal under the 1998 Act;
   (e) a person acting for another in making a claim for a tax credit, or acting for another in making an application for a direction under section 19(9) of the 2002 Act;
   (f) a person acting for another in giving notification of a change of circumstances;
   (g) a person acting for another in response to a notice given under section 17 of the 2002 Act; and
   (h) with the leave of the Commissioner, any other person.

[1(6A) Subject to the direction of a Commissioner—
   (a) any person or organisation entitled to be present and be heard at a hearing; and
   (b) any representatives of such a person or organisation, may be present by means of a live television link.

(6B) Any provision in these Regulations which refers to a party or representative being present is satisfied if the party or representative is present by means of a live television link.]

(7) Any person entitled to be heard at a hearing may address the Commissioner and—
   (a) in the case of an appeal against a determination in penalty proceedings, the party on whom the penalty has been imposed may give evidence, call witnesses and put questions directly to any other person called as a witness;
   (b) in all other cases, a person entitled to be heard may with the leave of the Commissioner, give evidence, call witnesses and put questions directly to any other person called as a witness.

(8) Nothing in these Regulations shall prevent a member of the Council on Tribunals or of the Scottish Committee of the Council in his capacity as such from being present at a hearing before a Commissioner which is not held in public.

AMENDMENT

1. Social Security and Child Support Commissioners (Procedure) (Amendment) Regulations 2005 (SI 2005/207), reg.4(10) (February 28, 2005).

DEFINITIONS

"the 1998 Act"—see reg.2.
"the 2002 Act"—*ibid*.
"appeal"—*ibid*.

(SI 2002/3237, reg.19) (as amended)

"the Board"—see s.39(1) of the Social Security Act 1998 as modified by reg.12 of the Tax Credits (Appeals) Regulations 2002.
"claimant"—*ibid*.
"Commissioner"—see s.39(1) of the Social Security Act 1998.
"office"—*ibid*.
"party"—*ibid*.
"penalty proceedings"—*ibid*.
"tax credit"—*ibid*.

Summoning of witnesses

20.—(1) Subject to paragraph (2), a Commissioner may summon any person to attend a hearing as a witness, at such time and place as may be specified in the summons, to answer any questions or produce any documents in his custody or under his control which relate to any matter in question in the proceedings.

(2) A person shall not be required to attend in obedience to a summons under paragraph (1) unless he has been given at least 14 days' notice before the date of the hearing or, if less than 14 days, has informed the Commissioner that he accepts such notice as he has been given.

(3) Upon the application of a person summoned under this regulation, a Commissioner may set the summons aside.

(4) A Commissioner may require any witness to give evidence on oath and for this purpose an oath may be administered in due form.

DEFINITIONS

"Commissioner"—see s.39(1) of the Social Security Act 1998.
"proceedings"—see reg.2.
"summons"—*ibid*.

GENERAL NOTE

See the note to reg.15 of the Tax Credits (Appeals) (No.2) Regulations 2002.

2.478

2.479

Withdrawal of applications for leave to appeal and appeals

21.—(1) At any time before it is determined, an applicant may withdraw an application to a Commissioner for leave to appeal against a decision of an appeal tribunal by giving written notice to a Commissioner.

(2) At any time before the decision is made, the appellant may withdraw his appeal with the leave of a Commissioner.

(3) A Commissioner may, on application by the party concerned, give leave to reinstate any application or appeal which has been withdrawn in accordance with paragraphs (1) and (2) and, on giving leave, he may make directions as to the conduct of the proceedings.

DEFINITIONS

"appeal"—see reg.2.
"appeal tribunal"—*ibid*.
"Commissioner"—see s.39(1) of the Social Security Act 1998.
"party"—see reg.2.
"proceedings"—*ibid*.

GENERAL NOTE

Note that a Commissioner's approval is not required if an application for leave to appeal is to be withdrawn, whether it is an application for leave to appeal to a

2.480

2.481

The Social Security Commissioners (Procedure etc.) Regulations 2002

Commissioner or an application for leave to appeal to the Court of Appeal or Court of Session (see reg.27(4)).

Irregularities

2.482   **22.** Any irregularity resulting from failure to comply with the requirements of these Regulations shall not by itself invalidate any proceedings, and the Commissioner, before reaching his decision, may waive the irregularity or take steps to remedy it.

DEFINITIONS

"Commissioner"—see s.39(1) of the Social Security Act 1998.
"proceedings"—see reg.2.

PART IV

DECISIONS

Determinations and decisions of a Commissioner

2.483   **23.**—(1) The determination of a Commissioner on an application for leave to appeal shall be in writing and signed by him.

(2) The decision of a Commissioner on an appeal shall be in writing and signed by him and, unless it was a decision made with the consent of the parties or an order setting aside a tribunal's decision under section 14(7) of the 1998 Act, he shall include the reasons.

(3) The office shall send a copy of the determination or decision and any reasons to each party.

(4) Without prejudice to paragraphs (2) and (3), a Commissioner may announce his determination or decision at the end of a hearing.

DEFINITIONS

"the 1998 Act"—see reg.2.
"appeal"—*ibid.*
"Commissioner"—see s.39(1) of the Social Security Act 1998.
"office"—see reg.2.
"party"—*ibid.*

GENERAL NOTE

2.484   A decision given by consent without reasons, as permitted by para.(2), has effect in the particular proceedings in which it is made but is not binding authority in any other case. Therefore, it is wrong to rely upon directions given in such a decision when making a written submission to a Commissioner (*CSDLA/101/2000*).

Correction of accidental errors in decisions

2.485   **24.**—(1) Subject to regulations 4 and 26, the Commissioner who gave the decision may at any time correct accidental errors in any decision or record of a decision.

(2) A correction made to, or to the record of, a decision shall become part of the decision or record, and the office shall send a written notice of the correction to any party to whom notice of the decision has been sent.

(SI 2002/3237, reg.24) (as amended)

DEFINITIONS

"Commissioner"—see s.39(1) of the Social Security Act 1998.
"decision"—see reg.26(1).
"office"—see reg.2.
"party"—*ibid*.

GENERAL NOTE

See the note to reg.24 of the Tax Credits (Appeals) (No.2) Regulations 2002.

2.486

Setting aside decisions on certain grounds

25.—(1) Subject to regulations 4 and 26, on an application made by any party, the Commissioner who gave the decision in proceedings may set it aside where it appears just to do so on the ground that—

(a) a document relating to the proceedings was not sent to, or was not received at an appropriate time by, a party or his representative or was not received at an appropriate time by the Commissioner; or

(b) a party or his representative was not present at a hearing before the Commissioner.

(2) An application under this regulation shall be made in writing to a Commissioner within one month from the date on which the office gave written notice of the decision to the party making the application.

(3) Unless the Commissioner considers that it is unnecessary for the proper determination of an application made under paragraph (1), the office shall send a copy of it to each respondent, who shall be given a reasonable opportunity to make representations on it.

(4) The office shall send each party written notice of a determination of an application to set aside a decision and the reasons for it.

2.487

DEFINITIONS

"Commissioner"—see s.39(1) of the Social Security Act 1998.
"decision"—see reg.26(1).
"month"—see reg.2.
"office"—*ibid*.
"party"—*ibid*.
"proceedings"—*ibid*.
"respondent"—*ibid*.

GENERAL NOTE

See the note to reg.25(1) of the Tax Credits (Appeals) (No.2) Regulations 2002. Note that an unsuccessful application for a decision to be set aside does not prejudice the possibility of an appeal, provided the application was not late (see reg.27(2)(b) below).

2.488

Provisions common to regulations 24 and 25

26.—(1) In regulations 24 and 25, the word "decision" shall include determinations of applications for leave to appeal, orders setting aside tribunal decisions under section 14(7) of the 1998 Act and decisions on appeals.

(2) There shall be no appeal against a correction or a refusal to correct under regulation 24 or a determination given under regulation 25.

2.489

577

The Social Security Commissioners (Procedure etc.) Regulations 2002

Definitions

"the 1998 Act"—see reg.2.
"appeal"—*ibid.*

Part V

Applications for Leave to Appeal to the Appellate Court

Application to a Commissioner for leave to appeal to the Appellate Court

27.—(1) Subject to paragraph (2), an application to a Commissioner under section 15 of the 1998 Act for leave to appeal against a decision of a Commissioner shall be made in writing, stating the grounds of the application, within three months from the date on which the applicant was sent written notice of the decision.

[¹(2) Where—
(a) any decision or record of a decision is corrected under regulation 24; or
(b) an application for a decision to be set aside under regulation 25 is refused for reasons other than that the application was made outside the period specified in regulation 25(2),
the period specified in paragraph (1) shall run from the date on which written notice of the correction or refusal of the application to set aside is sent to the applicant.]

(3) A person who under regulation 18 of the Tax Credits (Claims and Notifications) Regulations 2002 may act for another in making a claim for a tax credit is authorised for the purposes of section 15 of the 1998 Act to apply for leave to appeal against the decision of a Commissioner.

(4) Regulations 21(1) and 21(3) shall apply to an application to a Commissioner for leave to appeal from a Commissioner's decision as they apply to the proceedings in that regulation.

Amendment

1. Social Security and Child Support Commissioners (Procedure) (Amendment) Regulations 2005 (SI 2005/207), reg.4(11) (February 28, 2005).

Definitions

"the 1998 Act"—see reg.2.
"Commissioner"—see s.39(1) of the Social Security Act 1998.
"month"—see reg.2.
"proceedings"—*ibid.*
"tax credit"—*ibid.*

General Note

The three-month time limit may be extended by the Commissioner under reg.3(2)(a) but, if the Commissioner refuses to do so, the court cannot extend the time (*White v Chief Adjudication Officer* [1986] 2 All E.R. 905 (also reported as an appendix to *R(S) 8/85*)). It would be necessary to challenge the Commissioner's refusal by way of an application for judicial review. For the criteria for granting leave to appeal and the procedure for renewing an application to the court, see the note to s.15 of the Social Security Act 1998.

(SI 2003/123) (as amended)

Tax Credits (Interest Rate) Regulations 2003

(SI 2003/123)

The Treasury, in exercise of the powers conferred upon them by ss.37(2) and (5), 65(1) and (8) and 67 of the Tax Credits Act 2002, hereby make the following Regulations:

ARRANGEMENT OF ARTICLES

1. Citation and commencement.
2. Interpretation.
3. Interest on overpayments of tax credit and penalties.
4. Prescribed rate of interest.

2.492

Citation and commencement

1. These Regulations may be cited as the Tax Credits (Interest Rate) Regulations 2003 and shall come into force on 18th February 2003.

2.493

GENERAL NOTE

The tax credits regime does not adopt quite the same approach to interest on overpayments as HMRC does for late payments of income tax. Whereas interest on late payments of income tax has long been a feature of revenue law, s.37 of the TCA 2002 adopts a compromise approach to tax credits. Thus, interest is charged on overpayments caused by fraud or neglect, but not otherwise. These regulations specify the rate of interest to be applied on such overpayments, and also on any penalty under ss.31–33 (penalties for incorrect statements, failure to comply with requirements, etc.).

2.494

Interpretation

2.—(1) In these Regulations—
"the Board" means the Commissioners of Inland Revenue;
"established rate" means—
  (a) on the coming into force of these Regulations, 6.5 per cent per annum;
  (b) in relation to any date after the first reference date after the coming into force of these Regulations, the reference rate found on the immediately preceding reference date;
"operative date" means the sixth day of each month;
"reference date" means the day of each month which is the 12 working day before the sixth day of the following month;
"tax credit" means child tax credit or, as the case may be, working tax credit, provision for which is made by the Tax Credits Act 2002;
"working day" means any day other than a non-business day within the meaning of section 92 of the Bills of Exchange Act 1882.
(2) For the purposes of regulation 4(2) the reference rate found on a reference date is the percentage per annum found by averaging the base lending rates at close of business on that date of—
  (a) Bank of Scotland;
  (b) Barclays Bank plc;

2.495

(c) Lloyds Bank plc;
(d) HSBC Bank plc;
(e) National Westminster Bank plc;
(f) The Royal Bank of Scotland plc,

and, if the result is not a whole number, rounding the result to the nearest such number, with any result midway between two whole numbers rounded down.

DEFINITION

"reference rate"—see reg.4(2).

Interest on overpayments of tax credit and penalties

3.—(1) Where the Board decide in accordance with section 37(1) of the Tax Credits Act 2002 that the whole or part of an overpayment of a tax credit which is attributable to fraud or neglect is to carry interest, the rate of interest for the purposes of section 37(2) of that Act is that prescribed by regulation 4.

(2) The rate of interest for the purposes of section 37(5) of the Tax Credits Act 2002 (interest on a penalty under any of sections 31–33 of that Act) is that prescribed by regulation 4.

DEFINITION

"the Board"—see reg.2(1).

Prescribed rate of interest

4.—(1) The rate of interest which is prescribed is, subject to paragraph (2), 6.5 per cent per annum.

(2) Where, on a reference date after the coming into force of these Regulations, the reference rate found on that date ("RR") differs from the established rate, the rate of interest which is prescribed shall, on and after the next operative date, be the percentage per annum found by applying the formula:

$$RR + 2.5.$$

DEFINITION

"established rate"—see reg.2(1).

Tax Credits (Immigration) Regulations 2003

(SI 2003/653)

The Treasury, in exercise of the powers conferred upon them by sections 42 and 65(1), (3), (7) and (9) of the Tax Credits Act 2002, hereby make the following Regulations:

ARRANGEMENT OF ARTICLES

1. Citation and commencement
2. Interpretation

(SI 2003/653) (as amended)

3. Exclusion of persons subject to immigration control from entitlement to tax credits
4. Modifications of Part 1 of the Act for refugees whose asylum claims have been accepted
5. Transitional relief—claimants moving from income support and incomebased Jobseeker's Allowance to child tax credit

Citation and commencement

1. These Regulations may be cited as the Tax Credits (Immigration) Regulations 2003 and shall come into force on 6th April 2003.

Interpretation

2. In these Regulations—
"the Act" means the Tax Credits Act 2002;
"the Child Tax Credit Regulations" means the Child Tax Credit Regulations 2002;
[¹"couple" has the meaning given by section 3(5A) of the Act;]
"immigration rules" has the meaning given by section 33 of the Immigration Act 1971;
"joint claim" has the meaning given by section 3(8) of the Act;
"limited leave" has the meaning given by section 33 of the Immigration Act 1971;
[¹. . .]
"person subject to immigration control" has the meaning in section 115(9) of the Immigration and Asylum Act 1999;
"refugee" means a person who has been recorded by the Secretary of State as a refugee within the definition in Article 1 of the Convention relating to the Status of Refugees done at Geneva on 28th July 1951 as extended by Article 1(2) of the Protocol relating to the Status of Refugees done at New York on 31st January 1967;
"tax credit" refers to either child tax credit or working tax credit and references to tax credits are to both of them;
"the Working Tax Credit Regulations" means the Working Tax Credit (Entitlement and Maximum Rate) Regulations 2002.

AMENDMENT

1. Civil Partnership Act 2004 (Tax Credits, etc.) (Consequential Amendments) Order 2005 (SI 2005/2919), art.7(2) (December 5, 2005).

Exclusion of persons subject to immigration control from entitlement to tax credits

3.—(1) No person is entitled to child tax credit or working tax credit while he is a person subject to immigration control, except in the following Cases, and subject to paragraphs (2) to (9).

Case 1

He is a person who—
(a) has been given leave to enter, or remain in, the United Kingdom by the Secretary of State upon the undertaking of another person or persons, pursuant to the immigration rules, to be responsible for his maintenance and accommodation; and

(b) has been resident in the United Kingdom for a period of at least five years commencing on or after the date of his entry into the United Kingdom, or the date on which the undertaking was given in respect of him, whichever is the later.

Case 2

2.503   He is a person who—
(a) falls within the terms of paragraph (a) of Case 1; and
(b) has been resident in the United Kingdom for less than the five years mentioned in para.(b) of Case 1,
but the person giving the undertaking has died or, where the undertaking was given by more than one person, they have all died.

Case 3

2.504   He is a person who satisfies the following conditions—
(a) he has limited leave to enter or remain in the United Kingdom;
(b) that leave was subject to a condition that he does not have recourse to public funds, during that period of limited leave;
(c) he has, during so much as has elapsed of that period of limited leave (including that period as extended), supported himself without recourse to public funds, other than any such recourse by reason of the previous satisfaction of these conditions;
(d) he is temporarily without funds during that period of leave because remittances to him from abroad have been disrupted;
(e) there is a reasonable expectation that his supply of funds will be resumed; and
(f) the period (or aggregate of periods) for which this Case applies does not exceed 42 days during any single period of limited leave (including any extension to that period).

Case 4

2.505   Where the claim is for working tax credit, he is—
(a) a national of a state which has ratified the European Convention on Social and Medical Assistance (done in Paris on 11th December 1953) or of a state which has ratified the Council of Europe Social Charter (signed in Turin on 18th October 1961); and
(b) lawfully present in the United Kingdom.
The Case so described also applies where—
(a) the claim is for child tax credit;
(b) the award of child tax credit would be made on or after 6th April 2004; and
(c) immediately before the award is made (and as part of the transition of claimants entitled to elements of income support and income-based Jobseeker's Allowance, to child tax credit) the person is, or will on the making of a claim be, entitled to any of the amounts in relation to income support or income-based Jobseeker's Allowance which are described in section 1(3)(d) of the Act.

Case 5

2.506   Where the claim is for child tax credit, he is—
(a) a person who is lawfully working in the United Kingdom; and

(SI 2003/653, reg. 3) (as amended)

    (b) a national of a State with which the Community has concluded an Agreement under Article 310 of the Treaty of Amsterdam amending the Treaty on European Union, the Treaties establishing the European Communities and certain related Acts providing, in the field of social security, for the equal treatment of workers who are nationals of the signatory State and their families.

(2) Where one member of a [¹ . . .] couple is a person subject to immigration control, and the other member is not or is within any of Cases 1 to 5 or regulation 5—
    (a) the calculation of the amount of tax credit under the Act, the Child Tax Credit Regulations and the Working Tax Credit Regulations (including any second adult element or other element in respect of, or determined by reference to, that person);
    (b) the method of making (or proceeding with) a joint claim by the couple; and
    (c) the method of payment of the tax credit,
shall, subject to paragraph (3), be determined in the same way as if that person were not subject to such control.

(3) Where the other member is within Case 4 or 5 or regulation 5, para. (2) shall only apply to the tax credit to which he (in accordance with those provisions) is entitled.

(4) Where a person has submitted a claim for asylum as a refugee and in consequence is a person subject to immigration control, in the first instance he is not entitled to tax credits, subject to paragraphs (5) to (9).

(5) If that person—
    (a) is notified that he has been recorded by the Secretary of State as a refugee; and
    (b) claims tax credit within three months of receiving that notification,
paragraphs (6) to (9) and regulation 4 shall apply to him.

(6) He shall be treated as having claimed tax credits—
    (a) on the date when he submitted his claim for asylum; and
    (b) on every 6th April (if any) intervening between the date in sub-paragraph (a) and the date of the claim referred to in paragraph (5)(b),
rather than on the date on which he makes the claim referred to in paragraph (5)(b).

(7) Regulations 7 and 8 of the Tax Credits (Claims and Notifications) Regulations 2002 shall not apply to claims treated as made by virtue of paragraph (6).

(8) He shall have his claims for tax credits determined as if he had been recorded as a refugee on the date when he submitted his claim for asylum.

(9) The amount of support provided under—
    (a) section 95 or 98 of the Immigration and Asylum Act 1999;
    (b) regulations made under Schedule 9 to that Act, by the Secretary of State in respect of essential living needs of the claimant and his dependants (if any); or
    (c) regulations made under paragraph 3 of Schedule 8 to that Act,
(after allowing for any deduction for that amount under regulation 21ZB(3) of the Income Support (General) Regulations 1987) shall be deducted from any award of tax credits due to the claimant by virtue of paragraphs (6) and (8).

AMENDMENT

1. Civil Partnership Act 2004 (Tax Credits, etc.) (Consequential Amendments) Order 2005 (SI 2005/2919), art.7(3) (December 5, 2005).

DEFINITIONS

"the Act"—see reg.2.
"the Child Tax Credit Regulations"—see *ibid*.
"immigration rules"—see *ibid*.
"joint claim"—see *ibid*.
"limited leave"—see *ibid*.
"married couple"—see *ibid*.
"person subject to immigration control"—see *ibid*.
"refugee"—see *ibid*.
"tax credit"—see *ibid*.
"unmarried couple"—see *ibid*.
"the Working Tax Credit Regulations"—see *ibid*.

GENERAL NOTE

2.507 These regulations are made under s.42(1) of the Tax Credits Act 2002, which enables regulations to make provision for the exclusion of "persons subject to immigration control" from entitlement to child tax credit or working tax credit (or both). For these purposes, a "person subject to immigration control" has the same meaning as in s.115 of the Immigration and Asylum Act 1999. Section 115(9) of the 1999 Act is the starting point for this definition, and defines a "person subject to immigration control" as a person who *either* requires leave to enter or remain in the United Kingdom but does not have it *or* has such leave but this is (i) subject to a condition that he does not have recourse to public funds, or (ii) as a result of a maintenance undertaking, or (iii) through the continuation of leave pending certain appeals. For detailed commentary on this definition, see the annotations to reg.21(3) of the Income Support (General) Regulations 1987 (SI 1987/1967) in Vol.II in this series. It should be noted that a person who is a national of an EEA state (i.e. a national of an EU Member State or of Iceland, Liechtenstein or Norway) can *never* be a person subject to immigration control for the purposes of social security or tax credits.

The structure of reg.3 itself falls into three parts. Paragraph (1) sets out the general rule, along with certain exceptions. The position of couples, where one partner is a person subject to immigration control but the other is not, is dealt with in paras (2) and (3). Paragraphs (4)–(9) are concerned with the particular status of asylum seekers. These rules can never apply to British citizens. An individual who becomes a British citizen by naturalisation ceases to be subject to any immigration control on becoming a British citizen.

Para. (1)

2.508 The general rule is that a person subject to immigration control is not entitled to either child tax credit or working tax credit (para.(1)). This general rule is then subject to the five exceptions listed in Cases 1–5. These Cases have been adapted from the exceptions to the general rule precluding persons subject to immigration control from being entitled to the various means-tested benefits, as set out in the Schedule to the Social Security (Immigration and Asylum) Consequential Amendments Regulations 2000 (SI 2000/636: see Vol.II in this series). Thus, Case 1 in para.(1) mirrors para.3 in Pt I of the Schedule to the 2000 Regulations; Case 2 follows para.2 of Pt I of the Schedule and Case 3 is similar to para.1 in Pt I of the Schedule (but includes a 42-day limit in sub-para.(f)). These first three Cases operate as exceptions to the preclusionary rule for both child tax credit and working tax credit. The exception in Case 4 is in the same terms as para.4 in Pt I of the Schedule to the 2000 Regulations and applies to all working tax credit claims. It also applies to child tax credit claims in respect of awards made on or after April 6, 2004 where, immediately before the award the claimant was (or would have been) entitled to a child allowance or family or disabled child premium as part of an award of income support or income-based jobseeker's allowance. The exception in Case 5 is adapted from para.2 of Pt II of the Schedule to the 2000 Regulations, which deals with exceptions from the preclusionary rule in respect of certain noncontributory benefits.

There is also a special rule, applying to child tax credit only, which provides transitional relief for claimants moving from income support or income-based jobseeker's allowance to child tax credit (see reg.5).

Paras (2) and (3)
Paragraph (2) provides that where only one member of a married or unmarried couple is a person subject to immigration control, and the other is not, entitlement to tax credits is determined in the same way as if neither of them were so subject. The same applies where the other member is either within one of the excepted cases in para.(1) or covered by the transitional provisions in reg.5 below. Note also the qualification in para.(3).

2.509

Paras (4)–(9)
These provisions enable backdated claims to tax credits to be made where an asylum claim has been accepted. A claimant who has submitted a claim for asylum is a person subject to immigration control and so in the first instance is not entitled to tax credits (para.(4)). However, if such an application is accepted, the claimant may claim tax credits retrospectively (para.(5)). Any such retrospective claim must be made within three months of the notification from the IND (para.(5)(a)). This contrasts favourably with the 28 days allowed for retrospective claims for income support in similar situations (Income Support (General) Regulations 1987 (SI 1987/1967), reg.21ZB). In the event of a successful application for asylum, the claim for tax credits is treated as having been made on the date of the submission of the claim for asylum, not the post-acceptance date of the actual claim for tax credits (para.(6)(a)). The claim is also regarded as having been renewed on every intervening April 6, demonstrating an awareness of the delays which are well known in the system for determining asylum applications (para.(6)(b)). Accordingly, the normal time-limits in regs 7 and 8 of the Tax Credits (Claims and Notifications) Regulations 2002 (SI 2002/2014) for claiming tax credits are disapplied (para.(7)) and the claim treated as if the applicant had been recorded as a refugee on the date when the asylum application was actually made (para.(8)). Any arrears of tax credits which are due, following the application of these provisions, are then subject to an offset in recognition of any sums provided by way of asylum support under various statutory provisions (para.(9)).

2.510

Note that, by virtue of reg.4, the provisions of Pt I of the TCA 2002 apply to the determination of claims for tax credits made by refugees whose asylum claims have been accepted, subject to the omission of ss.14–17 and various modifications to ss.18 and 19 of the 2002 Act.

Modifications of Part I of the Act for refugees whose asylum claims have been accepted

4.—(1) For the purposes of claims falling within paragraph (2), Part I of the Act shall apply subject to the modifications set out in paras (3)–(5).

2.511

(2) A claim falls within this paragraph if it is a claim for tax credits which a person is treated as having made by virtue of regulation 3(6), other than a claim which he is treated as having made in the tax year in which he made his claim under regulation 3(5).

(3) Omit sections 14 to 17 (initial decisions, revised decisions and final notices).

(4) In section 18 (decisions after final notices)—

(a) in subsection (1) for "After giving a notice under section 17" substitute "In relation to each claim for a tax credit made by a person or persons for the whole or part of a tax year";
(b) omit subsections (2) to (9);
(c) for subsection (10) substitute—
"(10) Before making their decision the Board may by notice—
(a) require the person, or either or both of the persons, by whom the claim is made to provide any information or evidence which the Board consider they may need for making their decision; or
(b) require any person of a prescribed description to provide any information or evidence of a prescribed description which the Board consider they may need for that purpose,
by the date specified in the notice.";
(d) in subsection (11) omit—
(i) "any revision under subsection (5) or (9) and";
(ii) paragraph (a);
(iii) in paragraph (b), "in any other case,".
(5) In section 19 (enquiries)—
(a) in subsection (4), for paragraphs (a) and (b) substitute
"one year after that decision or, if—
(a) the person, or either of the persons, to whom the enquiry relates is required by section 8 of the Taxes Management Act 1970 to make a return; and
(b) the return becomes final on a day more than one year after that decision,
with that day (or, if both of the persons are so required and their returns become final on different days, with the later of those days).;"
(b) in subsection (5) omit paragraph (a) and, in paragraph (b) "in any other case,";
(c) omit subsection (6).

DEFINITIONS

"the Act"—see reg.2.
"tax credit"—see *ibid*.

GENERAL NOTE

2.512 See note to reg.3.

Transitional relief—claimants moving from income support and income-based jobseeker's allowance to child tax credit

2.513 5. In relation to child tax credit, a person is not treated for the purposes of these Regulations as subject to immigration control where—
(a) the award of child tax credit would be made on or after 6th April 2004;
(b) immediately before the award of child tax credit is made, he is, or will on the making of a claim be, entitled to any of the amounts in relation to income support or income-based jobseeker's allowance which are described in section 1(3)(d) of the Act; and
(c) he is a person who, immediately before the award of child tax credit is made—
(i) was receiving or entitled to income support by virtue of regulation 12(1) of the Social Security (Persons From Abroad) Miscellaneous Amendments Regulations 1996, and his claim

(SI 2003/653, reg.5) (as amended)

for asylum has not been recorded by the Secretary of State as having been decided (other than on appeal) or abandoned; or
(ii) was receiving or entitled to income support or income-based jobseeker's allowance by virtue of regulation 12(3) of the Social Security (Immigration and Asylum) Consequential Amendments Regulations 2000, and his claim for asylum has not been so recorded as having been decided (other than on appeal) or abandoned.

DEFINITIONS

"the Act"—see reg.2.
"person subject to immigration control"—see *ibid*.

GENERAL NOTE

This provides for transitional relief (on or after April 6, 2004) for claimants moving over from the specified elements of income support or income-based jobseeker's allowance to child tax credit.

Tax Credits (Residence) Regulations 2003

(SI 2003/654) (AS AMENDED)

The Treasury, in exercise of the powers conferred upon them by sections 3(7) and 65(1), (7) and (9) of the Tax Credits Act 2002, hereby make the following Regulations:

REGULATIONS

1. Citation and commencement
2. Interpretation
3. Circumstances in which a person is treated as not being in the United Kingdom
4. Persons temporarily absent from the United Kingdom
5. Crown servants posted overseas
6. Partners of Crown servants posted overseas
7. Transitional provision—income support and income-based Jobseeker's Allowance

Citation and commencement

1.—These Regulations may be cited as the Tax Credits (Residence) Regulations 2003 and shall come into force on 6th April 2003.

Interpretation

2.—(1) In these Regulations—
"the Act" means the Tax Credits Act 2002;
"child" has the same meaning as it has in the Child Tax Credit Regulations 2002;
[1"couple" has the meaning given by section 3(5A) of the Act];
"Crown servant posted overseas" has the meaning given in regulation 5(2);
"partner" means where a person is a member of a [1 . . .] couple, the other member of that couple;
"qualifying young person" has the meaning given in regulation 2, read with reg.5, of the Child Tax Credit Regulations 2002;

587

"relative" means brother, sister, ancestor or lineal descendant.

(2) In these Regulations, a person is responsible for a child or qualifying young person if he is treated as being responsible for that child or qualifying young person in accordance with the rules contained in regulation 3 of the Child Tax Credit Regulations 2002.

AMENDMENT

1. Civil Partnership Act 2004 (Tax Credits, etc.) (Consequential Amendments) Order 2005 (SI 2005/2919), art.8(2) (December 5, 2005).

GENERAL NOTE

2.518   This regulation follows the pattern of all tax credit provisions in adopting the definitions of "child" and "qualifying young person" from the Child Tax Credit Regulations 2002 (SI 2002/2007).

Circumstances in which a person is treated as not being in the United Kingdom

2.519   **3.**—(1) A person shall be treated as not being in the United Kingdom for the purposes of Part I of the Act if he is not ordinarily resident in the United Kingdom.

(2) Paragraph (1) does not apply to a Crown servant posted overseas or his partner.

(3) A person who is in the United Kingdom as a result of his deportation, expulsion or other removal by compulsion of law from another country to the United Kingdom shall be treated as being ordinarily resident in the United Kingdom.

(4) For the purposes of working tax credit, a person shall be treated as being ordinarily resident if he is exercising in the United Kingdom his rights as a worker pursuant to Council Regulation (EEC) 1612/68 [2as amended by Council Directive No.2004/38/EC] or Commission Regulation (EEC) 1251/70 or he is a person with a right to reside in the United Kingdom pursuant to [2Council Directive No.2004/38/EC].

[1(5) A person shall be treated as not being in the United Kingdom for the purposes of Part 1 of the Act where he—
  (a) makes a claim for child tax credit (other than being treated as making a claim under regulation 11 or 12 of the Tax Credits (Claims and Notifications) Regulations 2002 or otherwise), on or after 1st May 2004; and
  (b) does not have a right to reside in the United Kingdom.]

AMENDMENTS

1. Tax Credits (Residence) (Amendment) Regulations 2004 (SI 2004/1243), reg.3 (May 1, 2004).
2. Tax Credits (Miscellaneous Amendments) Regulations 2006 (SI 2006/766), reg.4 (April 6, 2006).

DEFINITIONS

"Crown servant posted overseas"—see reg.2.
"partner"—see reg.2.

GENERAL NOTE

2.520   Section 3(3) of the TCA 2002 makes it a requirement for entitlement to tax credits that the claimant is "in the United Kingdom". This regulation, authorised by s.3(7),

imposes the income test of "ordinary residence" as an additional requirement for entitlement. Read together with the section, the regulations require that a claimant must show:
(a) ordinary residence in the United Kingdom, and
(b) presence in the United Kingdom or, if he or she is not present in the United Kingdom, that the absence is temporary.

The approach taken here is consistent with the general jurisdictional approach to income tax in the United Kingdom. In common with some other parts of the common law world, income tax is residence-based, rather than nationality-based (as in the United States) or source-based (as in other parts of Europe). Income tax uses two main tests: residence and ordinary residence. The Tax Credits (Definition and Calculation of Income) Regulations 2002 (SI 2002/2006), reg.3 removes the significance of both those tests for the purposes of defining the relevant income of a claimant. These Regulations impose the test at another level. Those Regulations also disapply the definitions of "residence" in the various United Kingdom double tax agreements (which, for income tax purposes, override the national legislation).

Ordinary residence

"Ordinary residence" was used as the test for WFTC (Family Credit (General) Regulations 1987 (SI 1987/1973), reg.3) where the test was worded as a requirement that the claimant be both present and ordinarily resident. In *R(M) 1/85*, the Commissioner followed *Shah* (below) for those purposes as defining the term. The new form of words appears to avoid the problem with the previous wording commented on in Vol.II of the 2002 edition of this work. One change, however, is that the test is now applied to the whole of the United Kingdom, as Northern Ireland no longer has a separate system for these purposes.

2.521

"Ordinary residence" is a question of fact, not law. For the only relevant provisions in income tax law, see the ITA 2007, ss.829–832. It is separate from the other test used for income tax, "residence". "Residence" is determined for income tax purposes by reference to each tax year. "Ordinary residence" is based on a longer view, though perhaps not so long a view as "habitual residence". It is clear from both case law and practice that a claimant can have two ordinary residences at the same time for income tax purposes, and that the status of ordinary residence can be acquired on arrival in the United Kingdom if the claimant arrives with the intention of staying. That may be compared with the approach often taken for social security purposes to "habitual residence". For the leading authorities on the approach to be taken to the test see *Levene v IRC* [1928] A.C. 217; *IRC v Lysaght* [1928] A.C. 234; and *Shah v Barnet LBC* [1983] 2 A.C. 309, HL.

HMRC has a code of practice, published as booklet IR20, which defines how HMRC treat disputed issues of ordinary residence. HMRC treat the question as partly one of intention and partly one of actual presence. The working practice is to treat someone as resident in the United Kingdom if he or she is present for more than 183 days in total in any one year (whenever that year starts), and to treat someone as ordinarily resident if present for more than an average of 91 days in each of four consecutive years. A new arrival who has a job lasting more than three years here and/or who buys a house here is likely to be treated as ordinarily resident on arrival, and the reverse will be true of those leaving. IR20 should be treated with some caution as it applies to tax credits. Commentators have taken the view on a number of occasions that the HMRC view is one that supports HMRC's own approach to the definitions, rather than necessarily takes a neutral view on the issues. Secondly, and linked with this, the HMRC code in IR20 is designed to include people who would probably prefer to be excluded from the charge to United Kingdom income tax. Will the same approach be applied where HMRC might wish to exclude the claimant, while the claimant's interest will be to be included? In other words, will HMRC apply its allegedly expansive view of its jurisdiction under IR20 in the same way when paying out tax credits as when collecting in tax? HMRC have now published a guidance leaflet that broadly follows the income tax approach: *Child and*

Working Tax Credits and Child Benefit: residence rules—Guidance for intermediaries. It is on the HMRC website at *http://www.hmrc. gov.uk/taxcredits/residence-rules.htm*. The same approach is followed in the official manuals to HMRC staff.

In practice, problems will usually arise in the following situations:

2.522 *(1) When someone who has been ordinarily resident in the United Kingdom goes overseas:* the usual issue here will be that the claimant is no longer as a matter of fact "in" the United Kingdom to claim child tax credit for any children. Subject to the temporary absence rule in reg.4, and the rules for Crown servants in regs 5 and 6, the claimant will cease to qualify for tax credits. However, if the person (or one of two joint claimants leaving together) returns often enough to remain "present", then it will be a question of fact whether the claimant is ordinarily resident despite the overseas link. Where one of two joint claimants goes overseas and the other does not, the claim should become a single claim.

2.523 *(2) When someone arrives in the United Kingdom:* the first practical requirement for working tax credit purposes is that the claimant has a job. If he or she has come to the United Kingdom to work and that work is likely to last at least 3 years, then current Revenue practice is to treat the person as ordinarily resident here on arrival. The position of the worker whose work here may not last that period but who has rights under EU law as a worker is protected by reg.3(4). It is suggested that if the person is accepted as ordinarily resident under either rule for working tax credit purposes then he or she should also be accepted as able to claim child tax credit as well. There will also be a practical argument in other cases that if the claimant is treated as liable to United Kingdom income tax, then he or she will expect United Kingdom tax credits. However, the liability to income tax may arise on residence alone before the individual becomes ordinarily resident in the United Kingdom.

2.524 *(3) When someone has strong links with the United Kingdom and another state:* there may be ordinary residence in both states. This will be a question of fact. Unlike regs 5 and 6 below, this regulation does not deal expressly with partners making joint claims. The position is clear from s.3 of the Act. A couple must make a joint claim if both are "in" the United Kingdom. If one of the couple is not present or ordinarily resident here, then only the other partner can make the claim. But this will have the effect of excluding the non-resident partner's income from the income calculation. It may therefore be in the interests of some claimants for child tax credit to claim, say, that the mother is present and ordinarily resident, but that the father is not. This is not now a concern for income tax purposes as all married couples are assessed to income tax separately.

The Treasury published a consultative document with the 2003 Budget about the tests of residence, ordinary residence and domicile, entitled: *Reviewing the residence and domicile rules as they affect the taxation of individuals: a background paper*. It is available on the HM Treasury website. It contains a valuable summary of current practice and the problems it generates.

Para. (2)

2.525 Paragraph (2) relates to regs 5 and 6 below. Paragraph (3) deals with the problem that some of these individuals might not otherwise be regarded as ordinarily resident and so would be deprived of claims to either working tax credit or child tax credit. But see also the Tax Credits (Immigration) Regulations 2003 (SI 2003/653). Paragraph (4), which relates to working tax credit only, makes the necessary exception to protect the rights of movement of workers and others under EU law. See Vol.III of this work. It is not entirely clear why this is limited to working tax credit, as child tax credit would appear to be a social security family benefit for EU law purposes and therefore something to which someone with EU rights might also lay claim. Perhaps the aim is to ensure that in order to claim child tax credit in these situations the individual must first claim, or be entitled to claim, working tax credit. But that may exclude higher earners who are outside the income rules for working tax credit but not for child tax credit.

Para. (5)

It was intended to make this provision lapse on May 1, 2006 (see SI 2004/1243, reg.1), but the lapsing provision was itself revoked by SI 2006/766, reg.4, so continuing this paragraph in force without a time limit.

The paragraph therefore now introduces for all claims after May 1, 2004 the requirement that a claimant has a "right to reside" before making any child tax credit claim. It does not apply to working tax credit claims. It therefore does not apply to in-work benefits. It applies, in particular, to those who have moved to the United Kingdom from the new member states of the European Union ("A8 and A2" citizens), and their families, if they are not economically active.

"Right to reside" has superseded the previous test of "habitual residence" for social security benefits generally. See the Social Security (Habitual Residence) (Amendment) Regulations 2004 (SI 2004/1232), discussed in Volume II of this work. The term is not defined by legislation. It does not apply to British citizens. Nor does it apply to any citizen of the European Economic Area legally working or self-employed in the United Kingdom or third country citizens with indefinite leave to remain in the United Kingdom. But it applies to any European Economic Area citizen who is economically inactive.

The test, including its application to child tax credit, was considered in a series of decisions taken by a Tribunal of Commissioners as decisions *CIS/3573/2005, CPC/2920/2005, CIS/2559/2005* and *CIS/2680/2005*. The Tribunal decided that the test of "right to reside" is a general test applying to all potentially within its scope. Further, the test is not met by reference to the other tests of lawful residence or actual habitual residence. Rather, it reflects the provisions of EU Council Directive 90/364 that Member States:

> "shall grant the right of residence to nationals of member states who do not enjoy this right under other provisions of Community Law . . . provided they . . . have sufficient resources to avoid becoming a burden on the social assistance system of the host member state during the period of their residence."

The Court of Appeal has dismissed an appeal against the decision of the Tribunal of Commissioners in *Abdirahman v Secrtary of State for Work and Pensions* [2007] EWCA Civ 657; see further the commentary in Vol II.

In *Zalewska v Department for Social Development*, delivered May 9, 2007, the Court of Appeal in Northern Ireland upheld a decision of a Northern Ireland Social Security Commissioner that the use of the derogation from European Union law under which the test of "right to reside" was adopted was itself compatible with European Union law. It also affirmed the decision of the Commissioner that, notwithstanding that the appellant in that case, who was Polish, was a worker, the Commissioner was correct in law in holding that the law permitted refusal of income support to the appellant in the circumstances of the case. The Commissioner's decision is *C6/05-06(IS)*.

HMRC guidance about the operation of the "right to reside" rule is included in its detailed *Child and Working Tax Credits and Child Benefit: residence rules guidance for intermediaries*. See *http://www.hmrc.gov.uk/taxcredits/residence-rules.htm*. Following the approach of the Tribunal of Commissioners, this states that groups subject to the "right to reside" must have "sufficient resources not to become a burden on the social assistance system of the UK". This may be expected to exclude those claiming or seeking to claim income support, jobseeker's allowance, or housing benefit. But it is suggested that it cannot exclude all claimants from elsewhere in the European Economic Area for child tax credit, given that the income text for child tax credit is such that it is payable to all but the highest earning parents responsible for children.

Persons temporarily absent from the United Kingdom

4.—(1) A person who is ordinarily resident in the United Kingdom and is temporarily absent from the United Kingdom shall be treated as being in the United Kingdom during the first—

(a) 8 weeks of any period of absence; or
(b) 12 weeks of any period of absence where that period of absence, or any extension to that period of absence, is in connection with—
  (i) the treatment of his illness or physical or mental disability;
  (ii) the treatment of his partner's illness or physical or mental disability;
  (iii) the death of a person who, immediately prior to the date of death, was his partner;
  (iv) the death, or the treatment of the illness or physical or mental disability, of a child or qualifying young person for whom either he or his partner is, or both of them are, responsible; or
  (v) the death, or the treatment of the illness or physical or mental disability, of his or his partner's relative.

(2) A person is temporarily absent from the United Kingdom if at the beginning of the period of absence his absence is unlikely to exceed 52 weeks.

DEFINITIONS

"ordinarily resident"—see reg.3.
"partner"—see reg.2.

GENERAL NOTE

2.528   This regulation deals with the practical application of the requirement that a claimant be "in" the United Kingdom as well as ordinarily resident here. It adopts the approach long used in social security law of ignoring temporary absence. See, for comparison, Income Support (General) Regulations 1987 (SI 1987/1967), reg.4. The current rule appears reasonably generous as it ignores the first eight weeks of "any" period of absence. Presumably, a claimant could make a visit back to the United Kingdom before the end of eight (or 12) weeks to re-establish presence before starting a second period of absence, and so on. On the facts, this would also avoid the 52-week rule in para.(2). On the wording, it would seem that the 52-week rule reapplies at the beginning of each period of absence.

See reg.6 below for a modification of this regulation as it applies to the partners of Crown servants employed overseas. One problem with these provisions in practice is that they allow an individual to be treated as remaining in the United Kingdom, but they do not allow the individual to be treated as continuing to work here. One result is that although the main elements of tax credits remain payable, an individual going overseas for a short period can retain WTC but lose the childcare credit.

Crown servants posted overseas

2.529   **5.**—(1) A Crown servant posted overseas shall be treated as being in the United Kingdom.

(2) A Crown servant posted overseas is a person performing overseas the duties of any office or employment under the Crown in right of the United Kingdom—
(a) who is, or was, immediately prior to his posting or his first of consecutive postings, ordinarily resident in the United Kingdom; or
(b) who, immediately prior to his posting or his first of consecutive postings, was in the United Kingdom in connection with that posting.

GENERAL NOTE

2.530   This regulation and reg.6 protect the position of British public servants and their partners (and therefore also their children) when working outside the United

(SI 2003/654, reg.5) (as amended)

Kingdom. Section 44 of the TCA 2002 removes any doubt about the application of the tax credits scheme to Crown employees.

Partners of Crown servants posted overseas

6.—(1) The partner of a Crown servant posted overseas who is accompanying the Crown servant posted overseas shall be treated as being in the United Kingdom when he is either—
  (a) in the country where the Crown servant is posted; or
  (b) absent from that country in accordance with regulation 4 as modified by paragraphs (3) and (4).

(2) Regulation 4 applies to the partner of a Crown servant posted overseas with the modifications set out in paragraphs (3) and (4).

(3) Omit the words "ordinarily resident in the United Kingdom and is".

(4) In relation to a partner who is accompanying the Crown servant posted overseas the references to "United Kingdom" in the phrase "temporarily absent from the United Kingdom", in both places where it occurs, shall be construed as references to the country where the Crown servant is posted.

DEFINITIONS

"Crown servant posted overseas"—see reg.5.
"partner"—see reg.2.

Transitional provision—income support and income-based jobseeker's allowance

7.—A person is exempt from the requirement to be ordinarily resident in the United Kingdom (which is set out in regulation 3(1)) in respect of child tax credit on and for three years after the date on which the award of child tax credit is made where—
  (a) the award of child tax credit would be made on or after 6th April 2004;
  (b) immediately before the award of child tax credit is made, he is, or will be on the making of a claim, entitled to any of the amounts in relation to income support and income-based jobseeker's allowance which are described in section 1(3)(d) of the Act; and
  (c) he is a person to which one or more of the following provisions applies—
    (i) paragraph (b) or (c) in the definition of "person from abroad" in regulation 21(3) of the Income Support (General) Regulations 1987;
    (ii) paragraph (b) or (c) in the definition of "person from abroad" in regulation 85(4) of the Jobseeker's Allowance Regulations 1996;
    (iii) paragraph (b) or (c) in the definition of "person from abroad" in regulation 21(3) of the Income Support (General) (Northern Ireland) Regulations 1987;
    (iv) paragraph (b) or (c) in the definition of "person from abroad" in regulation 85(4) of the Jobseeker's Allowance Regulations (Northern Ireland)1996.

GENERAL NOTE

This is a narrow three-year transitional provision for child tax credit only. It takes effect from or after April 6, 2004—the date when CTC was planned to replace the child additions to income support and jobseeker's allowance. It is limited to:

(a) claimants receiving either income support or income-based jobseeker's allowance including child additions immediately before the rule comes into effect; but only if
(b) they are claiming those benefits as refugees or following a grant of exceptional leave to enter or remain in the United Kingdom under the Immigration Acts.

It should be read with the Tax Credits (Immigration) Regulations 2003 (SI 2003/653).

Tax Credits (Official Error) Regulations 2003

(SI 2003/692)

The Commissioners of Inland Revenue, in exercise of the powers conferred upon them by sections 21 and 65(2), (3), (7) and (9) of the Tax Credits Act 2002 hereby make the following Regulations:

ARRANGEMENT OF REGULATIONS

2.534
1. Citation and commencement
2. Interpretation
3. (*Untitled*)

Citation and commencement

2.535
1. These Regulations may be cited as the Tax Credits (Official Error) Regulations 2003 and shall come into force on 6th April 2003.

Interpretation

2.536
2.—(1) In these Regulations—
"the Board" means the Commissioners of Inland Revenue;
"official error" means an error relating to a tax credit made by—
(a) an officer of the Board;
(b) an officer of the Department for Work and Pensions;
(c) an officer of the Department for Social Development in Northern Ireland; or
(d) a person providing services to the Board or to an authority mentioned in paragraph (b) or (c) of this definition, in connection with a tax credit or credits,
to which the claimant, or any of the claimants, or any person acting for him, or any of them, did not materially contribute, excluding any error of law which is shown to have been an error by virtue of a subsequent decision by a "Social Security Commissioner or by a court;"
"Social Security Commissioner" has the meaning given by section 63(13);
"tax year" means a period beginning with 6th April in one year and ending with April 5 in the next.
(2) In these Regulations, references to a section are to that section of the Tax Credits Act 2002.

(SI 2003/692) (as amended)

GENERAL NOTE

2.537
The double inverted commas at the end of the very last line of the definition of "official error" are a typographical error in the HMSO version of these regulations. The lack of a heading to reg.3 is also unfortunate.

2.538
3.—(1) A decision under section 14(1), 15(1), 16(1), 18(1), (5), (6) or (9), 19(3) or 20(1) or (4) may be revised in favour of the person or persons to whom it relates if it is incorrect by reason of official error, subject to the following paragraphs.

(2) In revising a decision, the officer or person in question need not consider any issue that is not raised by the application for revision by the claimant or claimants or, as the case may be, did not cause him to act on his own initiative.

(3) A decision mentioned in paragraph (1) may be revised at any time not later than five years after the end of the tax year to which the decision relates.

DEFINITIONS

"official error"—see reg.2(1).
"tax year"—see *ibid.*

GENERAL NOTE

2.539
These regulations, made under s.21 of the TCA 2002, provide for decisions under the various specified sections of the Act (see reg.3(1)) to be revised in favour of the claimant(s) if they are incorrect because of "official error". The definition of "official error" in reg.2(1) is identical in all material respects to that which applies in the social security scheme under the Social Security and Child Support (Decisions and Appeals) Regulations 1999 (SI 1999/991) (see reg.1(3) and the commentary in Vol.III of this series). However, whereas a social security decision may be revised on the basis of official error and arrears of benefit paid back to the date of the original claim (SSA 1998, s.9(3) and reg.3(5)(a) of the 1999 Regulations), a claim for tax credits is subject to a time limit of five years after the end of the tax year to which the decision relates (reg.3(3)).

Tax Credits (Provision of Information) (Functions Relating to Health) Regulations 2003

(SI 2003/731) (AS AMENDED)

The Commissioners of Inland Revenue, in exercise of the powers conferred upon them by sections 65(2) and 67 of, and paragraph 9(2) of Schedule 5 to, the Tax Credits Act 2002, hereby make the following Regulations:

ARRANGEMENT OF REGULATIONS

2.540
1. Citation and commencement
2. Interpretation
3. Prescribed functions relating to health

Tax Credits (Provision of Information etc.) Regulations 2003

Citation and commencement

2.541　1. These Regulations may be cited as the Tax Credits (Provision of Information) (Functions Relating to Health) Regulations 2003 and shall come into force on 6th April 2003.

General Note

2.542　Section 59 of and Sch.5 to the TCA 2002 make provision for the use and disclosure of information relating to claims by and between HMRC and government departments. These regulations prescribe functions for the purposes of para.9 of Sch.5 to the 2002 Act, which enables information relating to tax credits, child benefit or guardian's allowance to be provided by HMRC to the Department of Health, the National Assembly for Wales, the Scottish Ministers, or the Department of Health, Social Services and Public Safety in Northern Ireland for the purposes of such functions relating to health as may be prescribed. These functions are set out in reg.3. Information may also be provided to persons providing services to, or exercising functions on behalf of, those Departments or persons.

These regulations are supplemented by the Tax Credits (Provision of Information) (Functions Relating to Health) (No.2) Regulations 2003 (SI 2003/1650).

Interpretation

2.543　2. In these Regulations—
"child tax credit" shall be construed in accordance with section 8 of the Tax Credits Act 2002;
[[1]"couple" has the meaning given by section 3(5A) of the Act;]
"disability element" means the disability element of working tax credit as specified in section 11(3) of the Tax Credits Act 2002;
"family" means—
　(a) in the case of a joint claim for a tax credit under the Tax Credits Act 2002, the [[1]. . .] couple by whom the claim is made and any child or qualifying young person for whom at least one of them is responsible, in accordance with regulation 3 of the Child Tax Credit Regulations 2002;
　(b) in the case of a single claim for a tax credit under the Tax Credits Act 2002, the claimant and any child or qualifying young person for whom he is responsible in accordance with regulation 3 of the Child Tax Credit Regulations 2002;
"qualifying family" means a family—
　(a) that has a relevant income of £14,200 or less; and
　(b) one member of which is receiving—
　　(i) working tax credit and child tax credit; or
　　(ii) working tax credit which includes a disability element; or
　　(iii) child tax credit, not being eligible for working tax credit;
"qualifying young person" has the meaning given by regulation 2(1), read with regulation 5(3) and (4), of the Child Tax Credit Regulations 2002;
"relevant income" has the same meaning as in section 7(3) of the Tax Credits Act 2002;
"working tax credit" shall be construed in accordance with section 10 of the Tax Credits Act 2002.

Amendment

1. Civil Partnership Act 2004 (Tax Credits, etc.) (Consequential Amendments) Order 2005 (SI 2005/2919), art.9(2) (December 5, 2005).

(SI 2003/731, reg.3) (as amended)

Prescribed functions relating to health

3. The following functions are prescribed for the purposes of paragraph 9 of Schedule 5 to the Tax Credits Act 2002 (provision of information by the Board of Inland Revenue for health purposes)—

(a) the issue by or on behalf of the Secretary of State, the National Assembly for Wales, the Scottish Ministers or the Department of Health, Social Services, and Public Safety in Northern Ireland of a certificate confirming that the family is a qualifying family;

(b) verification by or on behalf of the Secretary of State, the National Assembly for Wales, the Scottish Ministers or that Department at any time that a family is a qualifying family at that time;

(c) the issue on behalf of the Secretary of State or that Department of milk tokens and free vitamins to persons entitled to receive free of charge milk (including dried milk) or vitamins in accordance with the Welfare Food Regulations 1996 or the Welfare Food Regulations (Northern Ireland) 1988;

(d) the making on behalf of the Secretary of State or that Department of payments to such persons in accordance with those Regulations;

(e) the giving on behalf of the Secretary of State or that Department of information relating to milk tokens and related health matters to such persons in accordance with those Regulations.

2.544

DEFINITIONS

"family"—see reg.2.
"qualifying family"—see *ibid*.

The Tax Credits (Polygamous Marriages) Regulations 2003

(SI 2003/742) (AS AMENDED)

The Treasury, in exercise of the powers conferred upon them by sections 3(7), 7(8) and (9), 8, 10 to 12, 42, 43 and 65(1), (3), (7) and (9) of the Tax Credits Act 2002, and the Commissioners of Inland Revenue, in exercise of the powers conferred on them by sections 4(1), 6, 24 and 65(2), (3), (7) and (9) of that Act, and of all other powers enabling them in that behalf, hereby make the following Regulations:

ARRANGEMENT OF REGULATIONS

1. Citation, commencement and effect
2. Interpretation
3.–21. Modifications to Pt I of the Act for members of polygamous units
22–25. Amendments to the Child Tax Credit Regulations 2002
26–34. Amendments to the Working Tax Credit (Entitlement and Maximum Rate) Regulations 2002
35–47. Amendments to the Tax Credits (Definition and Calculation of Income) Regulations 2002
39–47A. Amendments to the Tax Credits (Claims and Notifications) Regulations 2002
48–50. Amendments to the Tax Credits (Payment by the Board) Regulations 2002
51–52. Amendments to the Tax Credits (Residence) Regulations 2003
53–56. Amendments to the Tax Credits (Immigration) Regulations 2003

2.545

The Tax Credits (Polygamous Marriages) Regulations 2003

INTRODUCTION AND GENERAL NOTE

2.546 These regulations provide alternative language to that of single claims and joint claims, and the associated definitions for single and joint claims, in cases where the claimant is a party to a polygamous marriage. Part I of the TCA 2002 and all relevant regulations are altered to give consistent effect to the policy that all the members of a polygamous marriage, or "unit" as it is called, must jointly claim for and be responsible for any tax credits payable to any of them. This is a different approach from that usually taken for social security benefits purposes, under which polygamous marriages are usually ignored for benefit purposes unless they are in fact monogamous. See the Social Security and Family Allowances (Polygamous Marriages) Regulations 1975 (SI 1975/561) in Vol.I of this work.

Section 43(1) of the TCA 2002 empowers regulations to apply Pt I of that Act to persons who are parties to a polygamous marriage. "Party to a polygamous marriage" is defined by s.43(2) to include any marriage entered into under a law which permits polygamy and under which any party to the marriage has more than one spouse, that is, more than one husband or wife. The drafters have chosen to adopt different language in these Regulations and the amendments made by these Regulations to the TCA 2002 and other regulations. Instead of "polygamous marriage", the term used throughout is "polygamous unit". The significance of this is discussed in reg.2 below.

The remaining regulations give effect to those modifications as necessary within the other regulations implementing the TCA 2002. Any necessary commentary is added to the relevant amended regulation.

Citation, commencement and effect

2.547 **1.**—(1) These Regulations may be cited as the Tax Credits (Polygamous Marriages) Regulations 2003 and shall come into force on 6th April 2003, immediately after the coming into force of the Child Tax Credit (Amendment) Regulations 2003.

(2) Regulations 22 to 56 only have effect in relation to members of polygamous units (and in the case of regulations 35 to 38, former members of such units).

Interpretation

2.548 **2.**—In these Regulations—
"the Act" means the Tax Credits Act 2002;
"polygamous couple" means a man and a woman who are married under a law which permits polygamy where—
  (a) they are not separated under a court order or in circumstances in which the separation is likely to be permanent; and
  (b) either of them has an additional spouse;
"polygamous unit" means—
  (a) a polygamous couple; and
  (b) any person who is married to either member of the polygamous couple and who is not separated from that member under a court order or in circumstances in which the separation is likely to be permanent.

GENERAL NOTE

2.549 Section 43(2) of the TCA 2002 provides that a person is a party to a polygamous marriage if:
  (a) he or she is a party to a marriage entered into under a law which permits polygamy; and
  (b) he or she has a spouse additional to any other party to the marriage.

(SI 2003/742, reg.2) (as amended)

The effect of this definition is to limit the scope of the operation of the modifications made under these Regulations to take account also of the definition of "married couple" in s.3(5) of the TCA 2002.

Modifications to Part I of the Act for members of polygamous units

3.—Regulations 4 to 21 prescribe modifications to Part I of the Act so far as it applies to members of polygamous units.

4. In section 3—
(a) in subsection (3)(a) after "United Kingdom", insert "(and neither of whom are members of a polygamous unit)";
(b) after subsection (3)(a) insert—
"(aa) jointly by the members of a polygamous unit all of whom are aged at least 16 and are in the United Kingdom, or";
(c) in subsection (3)(b) after "paragraphs (a)", insert "or (aa)";
(d) after subsection (4)(a), insert—
"(aa) in the case of a joint claim under subsection (3)(a), if a member of the married or unmarried couple becomes a member of a polygamous unit; and
(ab) in the case of a joint claim under subsection (3)(aa), if there is any change in the persons who comprise the polygamous unit, and";
(e) after subsection (6), insert—
"(6A) In this Part 'polygamous unit' has the meaning given by regulation 2 of the Tax Credits (Polygamous Marriages) Regulations 2003.";
(f) in subsection (8), in the definition of "joint claim", after "para.(a)" insert "or para.(aa)".

5. In section 4(1)(g)—
(a) for "member of a married couple or an unmarried couple", substitute "or more members of a polygamous unit";
(b) for "of the married couple or unmarried couple", substitute "or members".

6. In section 7(2), for "either" substitute "any";

7. In section 8(1), for "either or both" substitute "any or all".

8. In section 9(2)(b), for "either or both" substitute "any or all".

9. In section 10—
(a) in subsection (1), for "either or both" substitute "any or all";
(b) in subsection (3), for "either" wherever it appears substitute "any".

10. In section 11—
(a) in subsection (3), for "either or both" substitute "any or all";
(b) in subsection (6)(a), for "either of the persons or the two" substitute "any of the persons or all";
(c) in subsection (6)(b), for "married couple or unmarried couple" substitute "polygamous unit";
(d) omit subsection (6)(c);
(e) in both subsection (6)(d) and (e), for "either or both" substitute "any or all".

11. In both section 12(3) and (4)(a), for "either or both" substitute "any or all".

12. In section 14(2)(a), for "either or both" substitute "any or all".

13. In section 16(3)(a), for "either or both" substitute "any or all".

14. In section 17(10)(b)—

(a) for "member of a married couple or an unmarried couple", substitute "or more members of a polygamous unit";
(b) for "married couple or unmarried couple", substitute "or members".
15. In section 18(10), for "either or both" substitute "any or all".
16. In section 19—
(a) in subsection (2)(a), for "either or both" substitute "any or all";
(b) in subsection (4)(a), for "either" substitute "any" and for "both" substitute "more than one";
(c) in subsection (9), for "either" substitute "any".
17. In section 20(4)(b), for "either" (wherever it appears) substitute "any".
18. In section 24(2)—
(a) for "married couple or an unmarried couple", substitute "polygamous unit";
(b) for "whichever of them" substitute "one or more of those persons as".
19. In section 29(4), for "either or both" substitute "any or all".
20. In section 31(2)—
(a) after "another" insert "or others";
(b) for "unless subsection (3) applies" substitute "or each of them unless subsection (3) applies to the person in question".
21. In section 37(1), for "either or both" (in each place they appear) substitute "any or all".

Amendments to the Child Tax Credit Regulations 2002

2.551   22.—Amend the Child Tax Credit Regulations 2002 (for members of polygamous units only) as follows.
23. In regulation 2(1)—
(a) for the definition of "joint claim", substitute the following definition—
"'joint claim' means a claim under section 3(3)(aa) of the Act, as inserted by regulation 4(b) of the Tax Credits (Polygamous Marriages) Regulations 2003;";
(b) insert at the appropriate place the following definition—"'polygamous unit' has the meaning in the Tax Credits (Polygamous Marriages) Regulations 2003;".
24. In regulation 3(1), in rule 2.1., for "married couple or unmarried couple" in each place it appears substitute "polygamous unit".
25. In regulation 7—
(a) in paragraph (1)(b), for "married couple or unmarried couple" substitute "polygamous unit";
(b) in paragraph (2)(b)(ii), for "either or both" substitute "any or all".

Amendments to the Working Tax Credit (Entitlement and Maximum Rate) Regulations 2002

2.552   26. Amend the Working Tax Credit (Entitlement and Maximum Rate) Regulations 2002 (for members of polygamous units only) as follows.
27. In regulation 2(1)—
(a) for the definition of "joint claim", substitute the following definition—" 'joint claim' means a claim under section 3(3)(aa) of the Act (as inserted by regulation 4(b) of the Tax Credits (Polygamous Marriages) Regulations 2003);";
(b) insert at the appropriate place the following definition—" 'polygamous unit' has the meaning in the Tax Credits (Polygamous Marriages) Regulations 2003;".

(SI 2003/742, reg.28) (as amended)

28. In regulation 3(3)—
(a) for "both members of the couple satisfy", substitute "more than one member of the polygamous unit satisfies"; and
(b) for "two such elements", substitute "one such element for each of them that satisfies those conditions".

29. In regulation 4(1), in paragraph (a)(ii) of the Second Condition, for "his partner" substitute "any other member of the polygamous unit".

30. In regulation 10(2)—
(a) in sub-paragraph (c), for "couple" substitute "members of the polygamous unit";
(b) in sub-paragraph (d), for "couple" substitute "unit".

31. In regulation 11—
(a) in paragraph (1), after "element" insert "(and an additional such element for each member of the polygamous unit exceeding two in number)";
(b) in paragraph (2)(c), for "neither of the claimants" substitute "no claimant";
(c) in paragraph (4), in the words preceding sub-paragraph (a), after "adult element" insert "for any claimant";
(d) in paragraph (4)(a), for "neither claimant" substitute "none of the claimants"; and
(e) in paragraph (4)(b), for "one claimant" substitute "the claimant in question".

32. In regulation 13—
(a) omit paragraph (1)(a);
(b) in paragraph (1)(b), for "married or unmarried couple where both" substitute "polygamous unit where at least two of them";
(c) in paragraph (1)(c), for the words preceding paragraph (i) substitute "is a member or are members of a polygamous unit where at least one member is engaged in qualifying remunerative work and at least one other".
(d) in paragraph (4), for "the other member of a couple" substitute "another member of the polygamous unit";
(e) in paragraph (5), for "the other member or his partner" substitute "him or another member of the polygamous unit".

33. In regulation 14—
(a) in paragraph (1), for "either or both" substitute "any or all";
(b) in paragraph (1B), for "either or both" substitute "any or all";
(c) in paragraph (5), for "a partner or by a partner" substitute "another member of the same polygamous unit or".

34. In regulation 20—
(a) in paragraph (1), for "single claimant or to a couple" substitute "polygamous unit";
(b) omit paragraph (1)(c)(i);
(c) in paragraph (1)(c)(ii), for "a couple either or both" substitute "the members of a polygamous unit, any or all of whom";
(d) in paragraph (1)(c)(iii), for "a couple" substitute "the members of a polygamous unit";
(e) omit paragraph (1)(e);
(f) omit paragraph (1)(f)(i);
(g) in paragraph (1)(f)(ii), for "couple" substitute "polygamous unit".

Amendments to the Tax Credits (Definition and Calculation of Income) Regulations 2002

2.553   **35.** Amend the Tax Credits (Definition and Calculation of Income) Regulations 2002 (for members or former members of polygamous units only) as follows.

36. In regulation 2 (interpretation)—
(a) in paragraph (2), in the definition of "family" for "married or unmarried couple" substitute "members of the polygamous unit";
(b) in paragraph (2), insert at the appropriate places the following definitions—
"'joint claim' means a claim under section 3(3)(aa) of the Act, as inserted by regulation 4(b) of the Tax Credits (Polygamous Marriages) Regulations 2003; "polygamous unit" has the meaning in the Tax Credits (Polygamous Marriages) Regulations 2003;";
(c) in paragraph (4)(a), for the words from "a claimant's spouse" to the end substitute "another member of the same polygamous unit";
(d) in paragraph (4)(b), for the words from "claimant's former spouse" to the end substitute "person who was formerly a member with the claimant of the same polygamous unit".

37. In regulation 3(7), (calculation of income of claimant)—
(a) in sub-paragraph (b), for "either or both" substitute "any or all";
(b) in sub-paragraph (c), for "either or both" substitute "any or all".

38. In regulation 4(1) (employment income), in the words succeeding sub-para.(k), for "either" substitute "any".

Amendments to the Tax Credits (Claims and Notifications) Regulations 2002

2.554   **39.** Amend the Tax Credits (Claims and Notifications) Regulations 2002 (for members of polygamous units only) as follows.

40. In regulation 2 (interpretation)—
(a) for the definition of "joint claim" substitute the following definition—
" 'joint claim', means a claim under section 3(3)(aa) of the Act, as inserted by regulation 4(b) of the Tax Credits (Polygamous Marriages) Regulations 2003;";
(b) insert at the appropriate place the following definition—
"'polygamous unit' has the meaning in the Tax Credits (Polygamous Marriages) Regulations 2003;".

41. In regulation 11(2), for "both" substitute "all of the".

42. In regulation 13—
(a) in paragraph (1), for the words from "one member" to the end substitute "one or more members of a polygamous unit is to be treated as also made by the other member or members of that unit";
(b) in paragraph (2)—
(i) for "member of a married couple or an unmarried couple", substitute "or more members of a polygamous unit";
(ii) for "both members of the couple", substitute "all the members of the unit".

43. In regulation 15—
(a) in paragraph (3) for the words from "only one" to the end, substitute "one or more members of a polygamous unit die, the other member or members of the unit may proceed with the claim in the name or

(SI 2003/742, reg.43) (as amended)

names of the person or persons who have died, as well as in their own name or names";
(b) in paragraph (4), for "both" (in each place it appears) substitute "all of".

44. In regulation 16—
(a) in paragraph (1), for the words from "member of a" to the end, substitute "or more members of a polygamous unit die and the other member or members of the unit wish to make a joint claim for a tax credit";
(b) for paragraph (2), substitute—
"(2) The survivor or survivors may make and proceed with the claim in the name of the member or members who have died as well as in his or their own names.;"
(c) in paragraph (3)(a)—
   (i) for "married couple or unmarried couple", substitute "polygamous unit";
   (ii) add at the end "(or the earliest such date if more than one)".

45. In regulation 23(2), for "either member of the married couple or unmarried couple" substitute "any member of the polygamous unit".

46. In regulation 30(2), for "either" (in each place it appears) substitute "any".

47. In regulation 31(2)(a), for "either" substitute "any".

[¹**47A.** In regulation 34(3)—
(a) for "one of two joint claimants" substitute "any member of a polygamous unit"; and
(b) for "both" (in each place where it occurs) substitute "all".]

Amendments to the Tax Credits (Payment by the Board) Regulations 2002

48. Amend the Tax Credits (Payments by the Board) Regulations 2002 (for members of polygamous units only) as follows.

49. In regulation 2 (interpretation)—
(a) omit the definitions of "married couple" and "unmarried couple";
(b) insert at the appropriate place the following definition—
" 'polygamous unit' has the meaning in the Tax Credits (Polygamous Marriages) Regulations 2003;".

50. In regulation 3—
(a) in the heading, for "couple" substitute "polygamous unit";
(b) for paragraphs (2) to (6) substitute—
"(2) There shall be established, for each particular child or qualifying young person for whom any or all of the members of the polygamous unit is or are responsible—
(a) the member of that unit who is (for the time being) identified by all the members of the unit as the main carer for that child or qualifying young person; or
(b) in default of such a member, the member of that unit who appears to the Board to be the main carer for that child or qualifying young person.
(3) The individual element of child tax credit for any child or qualifying young person shall be paid to the main carer of that child or qualifying young person.

2.555

(4) The family element of child tax credit for any polygamous unit shall be divided (pro rata) by the number of children and qualifying young persons for whom any or all of the members of that unit is or are responsible, and the proportion so attributable to each such child or qualifying young person shall be paid to the main carer of that child or qualifying young person.

(5) Any childcare element of working tax credit shall be divided (pro rata) by the number of children referred to in paragraph (2) in respect of whom relevant childcare charges are paid, and the proportion so attributable to each such child shall be paid to the main carer of that child.

(6) In this regulation—
"child" has the meaning given by the Child Tax Credit Regulations 2002;
"qualifying young person" has the meaning given by those Regulations; and
"relevant childcare charges" has the meaning given by regulation 14(1) of the Working Tax Credit (Entitlement and Maximum Rate) Regulations 2002."

Amendments to the Tax Credits (Residence) Regulations 2003

51. Amend the Tax Credits (Residence) Regulations 2003 (for members of polygamous units only) as follows.

52. In regulation 2 (Interpretation)—
(a) in the definition of "partner", for the words from "married" to the end, substitute "polygamous unit, any other member of that unit";
(b) insert at the appropriate place the following definition—" 'polygamous unit' has the meaning in the Tax Credits (Polygamous Marriages) Regulations 2003;".

Amendments to the Tax Credits (Immigration) Regulations 2003

53. Amend the Tax Credits (Immigration) Regulations 2003 (for members of polygamous units only) as follows.

54. In regulation 2 (Interpretation)—
(a) for the definition of "joint claim", substitute the following definition—
"joint claim" means a claim under section 3(3)(aa) of the Act, as inserted by regulation 4(b) of the "Tax Credits (Polygamous Marriages) Regulations 2003";
(b) insert at the appropriate place the following definition—
"polygamous unit" has the meaning in the "Tax Credits (Polygamous Marriages) Regulations 2003;".

55. In regulation 3(2)—
(a) for the words from "married couple" to "and the other", substitute "polygamous unit is a person subject to immigration control and any other";
(b) in sub-paragraph (b), for "couple" substitute "unit".

56. In regulation 4(1) (modifications to the Tax Credits Act 2002), add at the end "(which, in the case of a claim by the members of a polygamous unit, are subject to the modifications made by regulations 4 to 21 of the Tax Credits (Polygamous Marriages) Regulations 2003)".

AMENDMENT

1. Tax Credits (Miscellaneous Amendments) Regulations 2004 (SI 2004/762), reg.19 (April 6, 2004).

(SI 2003/1650) (as amended)

Tax Credits (Provision of Information) (Functions Relating to Health) (No.2) Regulations 2003

(SI 2003/1650)

The Commissioners of Inland Revenue, in exercise of the powers conferred upon them by sections 65(2) and 67 of, and paragraph 9 of Schedule 5 to the Tax Credits Act 2002 hereby make the following Regulations:

ARRANGEMENT OF REGULATIONS

1. Citation, commencement and extent
2. Prescribed functions relating to health

2.558

GENERAL NOTE

These regulations supplement the Tax Credits (Provision of Information) (Functions Relating to Health) Regulations 2003 (SI 2003/731).

2.559

Citation, commencement and extent

1.—(1) These Regulations may be cited as the Tax Credits (Provision of Information) (Functions Relating to Health) (No.2) Regulations 2003 and shall come into force on 17th July 2003.

(2) These Regulations do not extend to Northern Ireland.

2.560

Prescribed functions relating to health

2.—(1) The function specified in paragraph (2) is prescribed for the purposes of paragraph 9 of Schedule 5 to the Tax Credits Act 2002 (provision of information by the Board of Inland Revenue for health purposes).

(2) The function specified in this paragraph is the conduct, by a person providing services to the Secretary of State and the Scottish Ministers, of a survey of the mental health of persons in Great Britain who are under the age of 17 on 1st September 2003.

(3) Nothing in these Regulations limits the operation of the Tax Credits (Provision of Information Relating to Health) Regulations 2003.

2.561

Tax Credits (Provision of Information) (Function Relating to Employment and Training) Regulations 2003

(SI 2003/2041)

The Commissioners of Inland Revenue, in exercise of the powers conferred upon them by sections 65(2) and 67 of, and paragraph 5(2) of Schedule 5 to, the Tax Credits Act 2002, hereby make the following Regulations:

Tax Credits (Provision of Information etc.) Regulations 2003

ARRANGEMENT OF REGULATIONS

2.562
1. Citation, commencement and extent
2. Prescribed function relating to employment and training

GENERAL NOTE

2.563
These regulations, made under para.5 of Sch.5 to the Tax Credits Act 2002, enable information relating to tax credits, child benefit or guardian's allowance to be provided by HMRC to the Secretary of State for the purposes of the operation of the Employment Retention and Advancement Scheme established under s.2 of the Employment and Training Act 1973.

Citation, commencement and extent

2.564
1.—(1) These Regulations may be cited as the Tax Credits (Provision of Information) (Function Relating to Employment and Training) Regulations 2003 and shall come into force on 29th August 2003.

(2) These Regulations do not extend to Northern Ireland.

Prescribed function relating to employment and training

2.565
2.—(1) The function specified in paragraph (2) is prescribed for the purposes of paragraph 5 of Schedule 5 to the Tax Credits Act 2002 (provision of information by the Board of Inland Revenue for employment and training purposes).

(2) The function specified in this paragraph is the operation of the Employment Retention and Advancement Scheme, that is to say the scheme for assisting persons to improve their job retention or career advancement, established by the Secretary of State under section 2 of the Employment and Training Act 1973.

Tax Credits Act 2002 (Child Tax Credit) (Transitional Provisions) Order 2003

(SI 2003/2170)

The Treasury, in exercise of the powers conferred upon them by section 62(2) of the Tax Credits Act 2002, make the following Order:

ARRANGEMENT OF ARTICLES

2.566
1. Citation and commencement
2. Transitional provision

GENERAL NOTE

2.567
Section 1(3)(d) of the Tax Credits Act 2002 provides for the abolition of various component elements of the applicable amount for the purposes of income support

(SI 2003/2170)

and income-based jobseeker's allowance (namely the child allowances, family premium, disabled child premium and enhanced disability premium for a child or young person). This Order makes transitional provision in connection with the introduction of child tax credit, but only for pensioners formerly in receipt of the minimum income guarantee in income support. The Order thus applies to persons who were in receipt of income support, were aged not less than 60 and were responsible for a child, throughout the period beginning on August 22, 2003 and ending on September 28, 2003 (Art2(1)). In such a case a person is deemed to have made a claim for child tax credit (a) on August 22, 2003 for the purpose of enabling a decision to be made by HMRC on the claim and (b) on the first day of the first benefit week beginning on or after September 29, 2003 for all other purposes, e.g. as regards payment (Art.2(2)). This Order is thus associated with the introduction of state pension credit as from October 2003.

Citation and commencement

1. This Order may be cited as the Tax Credits Act 2002 (Child Tax Credit) (Transitional Provisions) Order 2003 and shall come into force on 22nd August 2003.

Transitional provision

2.—(1) This article applies in the case of a person who throughout the period beginning on 22nd August 2003 and ending on 28th September 2003 is—
  (a) in receipt of income support;
  (b) aged not less than 60; and
  (c) responsible for a child (within the meaning of regulation 3 of the Child Tax Credit Regulations 2002).

(2) Where this article applies to a person, he shall be treated as having made a claim for child tax credit in respect of the child for whom he is responsible as mentioned in paragraph (1)(c) of this article—
  (a) on 22nd August 2003 for the purposes of enabling the Board to make an initial decision on the claim; and
  (b) on the first day of the first benefit week in relation to income support beginning on or after 29th September 2003 for all other purposes.

(3) In paragraph (2) "benefit week" has the same meaning—
  (a) in relation to a person in Great Britain, as it bears in regulation 2(1) of the Income Support (General) Regulations 1987; and
  (b) in relation to a person in Northern Ireland, as it bears in regulation 2(1) of the Income Support (General) Regulations (Northern Ireland) 1987.

Tax Credits (Provision of Information) (Evaluation and Statistical Studies) Regulations 2003

(SI 2003/3308)

The Commissioners of Inland Revenue, in exercise of the powers conferred upon them by sections 65(2) and 67 of, and paragraph 4(2) of Schedule 5 to, the Tax Credits Act 2002 make the following Regulations:

Tax Credits (Provision of Information etc.) Regulations 2003

Citation, commencement and extent

2.570   **1.**—(1) These Regulations may be cited as the Tax Credits (Provision of Information) (Evaluation and Statistical Studies) Regulations 2003 and shall come into force on 9th January 2004.

(2) These Regulations do not extend to Northern Ireland.

Purposes for which information may be provided

2.571   **2.** The purposes of conducting evaluation and statistical studies in relation to—
  (a) the education of children and young people under the age of 17; and
  (b) the provision and use of child care,
are prescribed under paragraph 4 of Schedule 5 to the Tax Credits Act 2002 (provision of information by the Board of Inland Revenue for evaluation and statistical studies).

Here "child care" means any care provided for a child whether or not of a description prescribed for any purpose under the Act.

Tax Credits (Provision of Information) (Evaluation and Statistical Studies) (Northern Ireland) Regulations 2004

(SI 2004/1414)

The Commissioners of Inland Revenue, in exercise of the powers conferred upon them by sections 65(2) and 67 of, and paragraph 4(2) of Schedule 5 to, the Tax Credits Act 2002 make the following Regulations:

Citation, commencement and extent

2.572   **1.** These Regulations may be cited as the Tax Credits (Provision of Information) (Evaluation and Statistical Studies) (Northern Ireland) Regulations 2004, shall come into force on 14th June 2004 and extend only to Northern Ireland.

Purposes for which information may be provided

2.573   **2.** The purposes of conducting evaluation and statistical studies about community relations, education and employment of persons in Northern Ireland under the age of 18, are prescribed under paragraph 4 of Schedule 5 to the Tax Credits Act 2002 (provision of information by the Board of Inland Revenue for evaluation and statistical studies).

Tax Credits (Provision of Information) (Functions Relating to Health) (Scotland) Regulations 2004

(SI 2004/1895 (S.6))

The Commissioners of Inland Revenue, in exercise of the powers conferred upon them by sections 65(2) and 67 of, and paragraph 9 of Schedule 5 to, the Tax Credits Act 2002, make the following Regulations:

(SI 2004/1895 (S.6), reg.1)

Citation, commencement and extent

1. These Regulations may be cited as the Tax Credits (Provision of Information) (Functions Relating to Health) (Scotland) Regulations 2004, shall come into force on 11th August 2004 and extend only to Scotland.

Purpose for which information may be provided

2.—(1) The purpose of conducting surveys of the health of children and young people under the age of 17 and their families, by the Scottish Ministers or persons providing services to them, or exercising functions on behalf of them, is prescribed under paragraph 9 of Schedule 5 to the Tax Credits Act 2002 (provision of information by the Board of Inland Revenue for health purposes).

(2) Nothing in these Regulations affects the operation of the Tax Credits (Provision of Information) (Functions Relating to Health) Regulations 2003 or the Tax Credits (Provision of Information) (Functions Relating to Health) (No.2) Regulations 2003.

Tax Credits (Provision of Information) (Function Relating to Employment and Training) Regulations 2005

(SI 2005/66)

The Commissioners of Inland Revenue, in exercise of the powers conferred upon them by sections 65(2) and 67 of, and paragraph 5(2) of Schedule 5 to, the Tax Credits Act 2002, make the following Regulations:

Citation and commencement

1. These Regulations may be cited as the Tax Credits (Provision of Information) (Function Relating to Employment and Training) Regulations 2005 and shall come into force on 8th February 2005.

Prescribed function relating to employment and training

2.—(1) The function specified in paragraph (2) is prescribed for the purposes of paragraph 5 of Schedule 5 to the Tax Credits Act 2002 (provision of information by the Board of Inland Revenue for employment and training purposes).

(2) The function specified in this paragraph is evaluation of, and research in relation to, the employment and training programmes administered—
  (a) in Great Britain, by the Department for Work and Pensions; or
  (b) in Northern Ireland, the Department for Employment and Learning.

Tax Credits (Approval of Child Care Providers) Scheme 2005

(SI 2005/93)

The Secretary of State for Education and Skills, being the appropriate national authority under section 12(6) of the Tax Credits Act 2002 and in exercise of the powers

Tax Credits (Approval of Child Care Providers) Scheme 2005

conferred on the Secretary of State by sections 12(5), (7) and (8) and 65(9) of that Act, and after consultation with the Council of Tribunals in accordance with section 8(1) of the Tribunals and Inquiries Act 1992, hereby makes the following Scheme:

Citation, commencement and application

2.578   **1.**—(1) This Scheme shall be known as the Tax Credits (Approval of Child Care Providers) Scheme 2005 and shall come into force on 6th April 2005.
(2) This Scheme applies in relation to England.

Definitions

2.579   **2.** In this Scheme—
"the 1989 Act" means the Children Act 1989;
"approval body" means the body referred to in article 3;
"approval criteria" has the meaning given to it in article 7;
"child" has the meaning attributed to it by the Child Tax Credit Regulations 2002;
"domestic premises" means any premises which are wholly or mainly used as a private dwelling and "premises" includes any area and any vehicle;
"parent" includes a person who—
  (a) has parental responsibility for a child;
  (b) is a local authority foster parent in relation to a child;
  (c) is a foster parent with whom a child has been placed by voluntary organisation; or
  (d) fosters a child privately;
"parental responsibility" and "fosters a child privately" have the meanings attributed to those respective expressions by sections 3 and 66 of the 1989 Act;
"qualifying child care" has the meaning ascribed to it in article 5;
"relative" in relation to a child means a grand-parent, brother, sister, uncle or aunt (whether of the full blood or half blood or by affinity) or a step-parent;
"relevant first-aid certificate" means a certificate in respect of a course of first-aid training—
  (a) which is suitable to the care of babies and children;
  (b) which includes training in the following areas: dealing with emergencies; resuscitation; shock; choking; anaphylactic shock; and
  (c) which has been undertaken by the applicant not more than three years before the date upon which the application for approval is made;
"the Tribunal" means the Tribunal established by section 9 of the Protection of Children Act 1999;
"the Tribunal Regulations" means the Protection of Children and Vulnerable Adults and Care Standards Tribunal Regulations 2002.

Specified body

2.580   **3.** The body specified for the purpose of giving approvals under this Scheme is Nestor Primecare Services Limited.

Requirements of the Scheme

2.581   **4.** For the purposes of regulations made under section 12 of the Tax Credits Act 2002, a person shall be a child care provider approved in accordance with this Scheme only—

(SI 2005/93, reg. 4)

(a) if he is for the time being approved by the approval body; and
(b) in respect of the provision by him of qualifying child care.

DEFINITIONS

"approval body"—see art.2.
"qualifying child care"—see *ibid.*

Qualifying Child Care

5.—(1) Qualifying child care means care for a child provided by an individual on domestic premises for reward but does not include care referred to in paragraph (2).

(2) Qualifying child care does not include—
(a) childminding which is subject to registration pursuant to Part 10A of the 1989 Act;
(b) child care provided wholly or mainly in the child's own home in respect of a child to whom the provider is a parent or relative; or
(c) child care provided wholly or mainly in the home of a relative of the child where such care is usually provided solely in respect of one or more child to whom the provider is a parent or relative.

2.582

DEFINITIONS

"the 1989 Act"—see art.2.
"child"—see *ibid.*
"domestic premises"—see *ibid.*
"parent"—see *ibid.*
"relative"—see *ibid.*

Approved person

6.—(1) A person shall be given approval as a child care provider under this Scheme if the approval body is satisfied that the approval criteria are met in relation to that person.

(2) A person who has been given approval under paragraph (1) shall cease to be so approved if that approval is withdrawn by the approval body.

(3) The approval body may withdraw an approval if satisfied that the approval criteria are no longer met in relation to that person.

2.583

DEFINITIONS

"approval body"—see art.2.
"approval criteria"—see *ibid.*

Approval criteria

7. In relation to an application for approval as a child care provider the approval criteria are—
(a) that the applicant is 18 years of age or over;
(b) that the applicant—
  (i) has obtained one of the qualifications from time to time specified in a list maintained by the Department for Education and Skills for the purpose of this article; or
  (ii) has attended a basic course of training in the care of children being one specified in a list maintained by the Department for Education and Skills for the purpose of this article;

2.584

Tax Credits (Approval of Child Care Providers) Scheme 2005

(c) that the applicant has obtained a relevant first-aid certificate; and
(d) that the applicant is not considered unsuitable to work with or have unsupervised access to children.

DEFINITIONS

"approval criteria"—see art.2.
"child"—see *ibid*.
"relevant first-aid certificate"—see *ibid*.

Approval system

2.585   **8.**—(1) The approval body shall operate a system for the determination of applications for approval made to it under this Scheme and shall make adequate arrangements to publicise the details of that system.

(2) Without prejudice to the generality of paragraph (1), the approval system referred to in that paragraph shall in particular—
  (a) provide for a procedure by which an applicant may apply for approval;
  (b) set out requirements relating to the provision by an applicant of documentary or other evidence necessary to demonstrate that the approval criteria are met;
  (c) provide for a procedure whereby approvals may be withdrawn;
  (d) provide for the applicant to be given notice in writing in respect of a determination to grant, refuse or withdraw an approval;
  (e) provide for a procedure whereby it may be ascertained whether an individual is for the time being approved under the Scheme; and
  (f) provide for the keeping of appropriate records relating to applications for approvals and to the grant, refusal or withdrawal of such approvals.

(3) The approval body shall maintain a record of those persons to whom an approval is granted for the time being under this Scheme.

(4) The records referred to in paragraphs (2) and (3) may be kept by means of a computer.

DEFINITIONS

"approval body"—see art.2.
"approval criteria"—see *ibid*.

Provision of information by approval body

2.586   **9.** The approval body shall supply to the Commissioners of Inland Revenue such information as they may require for the discharge of any of their functions relating to working tax credit and which is information relating to the approval, or the refusal or withdrawal of approval, of persons under this Scheme.

DEFINITION

"approval body"—see art.2.

Period of approval

2.587   **10.**—(1) An approval given under this Scheme shall state the period of its validity which shall not exceed a period of 12 months.

(2) Nothing in this article shall prejudice the application of article 6(2).

(SI 2005/93, reg.11)

Appeals

11.—(1) Where the approval body refuses an application for the grant of an approval or withdraws an approval previously granted, an appeal shall lie to the Tribunal against that decision.

(2) The provisions of the Tribunal Regulations shall apply to an appeal under paragraph (1) as they apply to an appeal under section 79M of the 1989 Act and as if those provisions were set out in this Scheme, but with the modifications referred to in paragraph (3).

(3) Schedule 2 to the Tribunal Regulations shall apply as if—
(a) any reference to an appeal under the 1989 Act were a reference to an appeal under article 11(1) of this Scheme;
(b) any reference to any registration were a reference to an approval given under this Scheme;
(c) any reference to the cancellation of registration were a reference to the withdrawal of an approval under this Scheme;
(d) any reference to the registration body or the respondent were a reference to the approval body; and
(e) paragraph 3(3)(c) of that Schedule were modified as specified in paragraph (4) of this article and any reference to the said paragraph 3 were a reference to that paragraph as so modified.

(4) The said paragraph 3(3)(c) shall apply as if—
(a) the decision referred to in sub-paragraph (ii) of that paragraph were to the decision to refuse to grant or to withdraw an approval under this Scheme; and
(b) sub-paragraph (iii) of that paragraph did not apply.

(5) On an appeal, the Tribunal may—
(a) confirm the refusal to grant the approval or the withdrawal of the approval;
(b) direct that the said refusal or withdrawal shall not have, or shall cease to have, effect; or
(c) direct the approval body to reconsider any decision which is the subject of the appeal.

2.588

DEFINITIONS

"the 1989 Act"—see art.2.
"approval body"—see *ibid.*
"the Tribunal"—see *ibid.*
"the Tribunal Regulations"—see *ibid.*

Fees

12. The approval body may charge any person seeking approval under this Scheme such reasonable fee as it shall, subject to the approval of the Secretary of State, determine.

2.589

DEFINITION

"approval body"—see art.2.

Revocation and saving

13.—(1) Subject to paragraph (2), the Tax Credit (Approval of Home Child Care Providers) Scheme 2003 (hereinafter referred to as "the 2003 Scheme") is hereby revoked.

2.590

(2) The provisions of the 2003 Scheme shall continue to have effect to the extent necessary to give full effect to paragraph (3).

(3) Any approval granted to any child care provider under the 2003 Scheme and which is in force on 6th April 2005 shall continue to have effect in respect of that provider under that Scheme until whichever is the earliest of—
- (a) the date on which the approval is withdrawn or suspended in accordance with the 2003 Scheme;
- (b) the date on which the child care provider concerned is given an approval by the approval body pursuant to article 6 of this Scheme; or
- (c) 31st December 2005.

DEFINITION

"approval body"—see art.2.

PART III

STATUTORY SICK PAY

Statutory Sick Pay (General) Regulations 1982

(SI 1982/894) (AS AMENDED)

The Secretary of State for Social Services, in exercise of the powers conferred upon him by sections 1(3) and (4), 3(5) and (7), 4(2), 5(5), 6(1), 8(1) to (3), 17(4), 18(1), 20 and 26(1) and (3) to (5) of, paragraph 1 of Schedule 1 to, and paragraphs 2(3) and 3(2) of Schedule 2 to, the Social Security and Housing Benefits Act 1982(a) and of all other powers enabling him in that behalf, hereby makes the following regulations.

ARRANGEMENT OF REGULATIONS

1. Citation, commencement and interpretation
2. Persons deemed incapable of work
2A. Linking periods of incapacity for work
3. Period of entitlement ending or not arising
3A. Maximum entitlement to Statutory Sick Pay in a period of entitlement
4. Contract of service ended for the purpose of avoiding liability for statutory sick pay
5. Qualifying days
6. Calculation of entitlement limit
7. Time and manner of notification of incapacity for work
8. Manner in which statutory sick pay may not be paid
9. Time limits for paying statutory sick pay
9A. Liability of the Secretary of State for payments of statutory sick pay
9B. Insolvency of employer
9C. Payments by the Secretary of State
10. Persons unable to act
11. Rounding to avoid fractional amounts
12. Days not to be treated as, or as parts of, periods of interruption of employment
13. Records to be maintained by employers
13A. Production of employer's records
14. Provision of information in connection with determination of questions
15. Provision of information by employers to employees
15A. Statements relating to the payment of statutory sick pay
16. Meaning of "employee"
17. Meaning of "earnings"
18. Payments to be treated or not to be treated as contractual remuneration
19. Normal weekly earnings
20. Treatment of one or more employers as one
21. Treatment of more than one contract of service as one
21A. Election to be treated as different employers not to apply to recovery of statutory sick pay
22. [*repealed*]

Citation, commencement and interpretation

1.—(1) These regulations may be cited as the Statutory Sick Pay (General) Regulations 1982, and shall come into operation on 6th April 1983.

(2) In these regulations—

"the Act" means the Social Security and Housing Benefits Act 1982;

[¹"the Contributions and Benefits Act" means the Social Security Contributions and Benefits Act 1992;]

[²"income tax month" means the period beginning on the 6th day of any calendar month and ending on the 5th day of the following calendar month;]

(3) Unless the context otherwise requires, any reference—

(a) in these regulations to a numbered section or Schedule is a reference to the section or Schedule, as the case may be, of or to the Act bearing that number;

(b) in these regulations to a numbered regulation is a reference to the regulation bearing that number in these regulations; and

(c) in any of these regulations to a numbered paragraph is a reference to the paragraph bearing that number in that regulation.

AMENDMENTS

1. Social Security (Miscellaneous Provisions) Amendment (No.2) Regulations 1992 (SI 1992/2595), reg.14 (November 16, 1992).

2. Social Security Contributions, Statutory Maternity Pay and Statutory Sick Pay (Miscellaneous Amendments) Regulations 1996 (SI 1996/777), reg.2(2) (April 6, 1996).

GENERAL NOTE

The relevant provisions in Pt I of the Social Security and Housing Benefits Act 1982 have now been replaced by Pt XII of the SSCBA 1992.

Persons deemed incapable of work

2.—(1) A person who is not incapable of work of which he can reasonably be expected to do under a particular contract of service may be deemed to be incapable of work of such a kind by reason of some specific disease or bodily or mental disablement for any day on which either—

(a) (i) he is under medical care in respect of a disease or disablement as aforesaid,

(ii) it is stated by a registered medical practitioner that for precautionary or convalescent reasons consequential on such disease or disablement he should abstain from work, or from work of such a kind; and

(iii) he does not work under that contract of service; or

[¹(b) he is—

(i) excluded or abstains from work, or from work of such a kind, pursuant to a request or notice in writing lawfully made under an enactment; or

(ii) otherwise prevented from working pursuant to an enactment,

by reason of his being a carrier, or having been in contact with a case, of a relevant disease.]

(2) A person who at the commencement of any day is, or thereafter on that day becomes, incapable of work of such a kind by reason of some specific disease or bodily or mental disablement, and

(a) on that day, under that contract of service, does no work, or no work except during a shift which ends on that day having begun on the previous day; and

(SI 1982/894, reg.2) (as amended)

   (b) does no work under that contract of service during a shift which begins on that day and ends on the next,

shall be deemed to be incapable of work of such a kind by reason of that disease or bodily or mental disablement throughout that day.

[¹(3) For the purposes of paragraph (1)(b)—

"enactment" includes an enactment comprised in, or in an instrument made under—

(a) an Act; or

(b) an Act of the Scottish Parliament; and

"relevant disease" means—

(a) in England and Wales, any disease, food poisoning, infection, infectious disease or notifiable disease—
   (i) to which section 20(1) of the Public Health (Control of Disease) Act 1984 (stopping of work to prevent spread of disease) applies; or
   (ii) to which—
      (aa) regulation 3 (public health enactments applied to certain diseases) of, and Schedule 1 to,
      (bb) regulation 9(1) (provisions for preventing the spread of typhus and relapsing fever) of, and Schedule 3 to, or
      (cc) regulation 9(2) (provisions for preventing the spread of food poisoning and food borne infections) of, and Schedule 4 to,
     the Public Health (Infectious Diseases) Regulations 1988 applies; or
   (iii) to which regulations 8 and 9 (examination, etc. of persons on aircraft and powers in respect of persons leaving aircraft) of the Public Health (Aircraft) Regulations 1979 applies; or
   (iv) to which regulations 9 and 10 (examination, etc. of persons on ships and powers in respect of certain persons on ships) of the Public Health (Ships) Regulations 1979 applies; and

(b) in Scotland, any food poisoning or infectious disease—
   (i) to which section 71(1) of the Health Services and Public Health Act 1968 (compensation for stopping employment to prevent spread of disease in Scotland) applies;
   (ii) to which—
      (aa) regulations 8 and 9 (examination, etc. of persons on aircraft and powers in respect of persons leaving aircraft) of the Public Health (Aircraft)(Scotland) Regulations 1971; or
      (bb) regulations 9 and 10 (examination, etc. of persons on ships and powers in respect of certain persons on ships) of the Public Health (Ships)(Scotland) Regulations 1971,
   applies.]

AMENDMENT

1. Statutory Sick Pay (General) Amendment Regulations 2006 (SI 2006/799), reg.2 (April 10, 2006).

DEFINITION

"contract of service"—see SSCBA 1992, s.163(1).

General Note

Para. (1)

3.5   Regulation 2 of the SSP (General) Regulations is in virtually identical terms to the former regs 3(1) and (2) of the old Unemployment, Sickness and Invalidity Benefit Regulations 1983 (SI 1983/1598), which covered deemed sickness for the purposes of sickness benefit (see the 1994 volume of *Bonner*, p.687). The relevant case law in that context revolved around the vexed question of whether the regulation covers a pregnant claimant who is herself fit for work but is recommended to refrain from work because of the danger of contracting a disease which would threaten the life of the foetus she is carrying. Earlier cases have involved school teachers who are pregnant when there is an outbreak of Rubella in the school.

There are two reported decisions under the old law which are worthy of note. In *R(S) 24/54* it was held that a precautionary absence from work was not within sub-para.(a) of the regulation because she was not under medical care in respect of the disease during a period in which she had been advised to refrain from work simply to avoid contact with the disease. That decision was rejected by the Commissioner in *R(S) 1/72* where the facts were identical, except that the claimant was awaiting the outcome of tests to determine whether she was immune to Rubella and could therefore return to work. In fact, the results of those tests were not available for about five weeks owing in part to a postal strike. The Commissioner found that during the whole of that time she was under medical care in respect of the disease and was, therefore, deemed to be incapable of work and entitled to benefit. Fortunately for her, the results showed that she was immune and she was able to return to work. No question arose as to whether she would have continued to qualify for benefit if she had not been immune and had been advised to remain off work. But, the line of the Commissioner's reasoning in that case and his rejection of *R(S) 24/54* rather than any attempt to distinguish it suggest that he may well have held that the claimant would remain under medical care until the danger from the infection was past.

In *R(S) 4/93* the claimant was an assistant in a veterinary practice, who was potentially in danger of infection by toxoplasmosis from handling cats. She was given certificates advising her to refrain from work over a period of about six weeks. Her claim for statutory sick pay was refused by her employer and she applied to an AO for a decision on her entitlement to statutory sick pay. The Commissioner adopted the reasoning in both of the earlier cases. Thus she found that the claimant was entitled to benefit for a period of five days while awaiting the outcome of tests, which were negative, but not entitled for a further period of five weeks for which a claim had been made. The Commissioner did not specifically address the point that there had been a change in wording to the regulation since the earlier cases. The regulation now specifically refers to absence which is recommended for "precautionary" reasons. But, given that such reasons must be "consequential on such disease", meaning one for which she is "under medical care", it is probable that the new words add nothing to the interpretation.

It is, on the face of it, a rather fine distinction to hold, as in *R(S) 4/93*, that the claimant is under medical care while awaiting the outcome of the tests but not under medical care once they are known. Nor is it in point to observe, as does the Commissioner in *R(S) 24/54*, that the claimant is not unfit for work, only unable to work in the particular place she was employed, because the whole point of this regulation is for a claimant to be *deemed* unfit even though she may be fit. No doubt some justice is done for a claimant whose contribution record qualifies her for contribution-based jobseeker's allowance (presumably she is not to be disqualified for voluntary leaving), but where the claimant does not have such an entitlement the loss of statutory sick pay will be hard felt.

A claimant with a contribution record could also now potentially qualify for incapacity benefit because the regulations for that benefit specifically provide for a pregnant woman who has to refrain from work because of a danger to herself or her unborn child (see Incapacity for Work (General) Regulations 1995 (SI 1995/311), reg.14—see Vol.I in this series).

(SI 1982/894, reg.2) (as amended)

The amendments made in 2006, substituting a new subs.(1)(b) and inserting a new (3), do not change the original policy intention, but merely update these provisions to reflect modern public health legislation.

[¹Linking periods of incapacity for work

2A. In subsection (3) of section 2 of the 1982 Act (linking periods of incapacity for work), 8 weeks shall be substituted for 2 weeks.]

AMENDMENT

1. Statutory Sick Pay (General) Amendment Regulations 1986 (SI 1986/477), reg.2 (April 6, 1986).

GENERAL NOTE

Section 2 of the 1982 Act, along with the other original provisions relating to statutory sick pay, was repealed by the Social Security (Consequential Provisions) Act 1992, s.3 and Sch.1. The eight-week linking rule is now to be found in SSCBA 1992, s.152(3).

Period of entitlement ending or not arising

3.—(1) In a case where an employee is detained in legal custody or sentenced to a term of imprisonment (except where the sentence is suspended) on a day which in relation to him falls within a period of entitlement, that period shall end with that day.

(2) A period of entitlement shall not arise in relation to a period of incapacity for work if the employee in question is in legal custody or sentenced to or undergoing a term of imprisonment (except where the sentence is suspended).

[⁴(2A) A period of entitlement in respect of an employee who was entitled to incapacity benefit, maternity allowance or severe disablement allowance shall not arise in relation to any day within a period of incapacity for work beginning with the first day on which paragraph 2(d) of Schedule 11 to the Contributions and Benefits Act ceases to have effect where the employee in question is a person to whom regulation 13A of the Social Security (Incapacity for Work) (General) Regulations 1995 (welfare to work beneficiary) applies.]

[⁶(2B) Paragraph (2A) shall not apply, in the case of an employee who was entitled to incapacity benefit, where paragraph 2(d)(i) of Schedule 11 to the Contributions and Benefits Act ceases to have effect by virtue of paragraph 5A of that Schedule.]

[¹(3) A period of entitlement as between an employee and his employer shall end after 3 years if it has not otherwise ended in accordance with [³section 153(2) of the Contributions and Benefits Act] or with regulations (other than this paragraph) made under [³section 153(6) of the Contributions and Benefits Act].]

[²[³(4) Where a period of entitlement is current as between an employee and her employer and the employee—
  (a) is pregnant or has been confined; and
  (b) is incapable of work wholly or partly because of pregnancy or confinement on any day which falls on or after the beginning of the [⁵4th week] before the expected week of confinement; and
  (c) is not by virtue of that pregnancy or confinement entitled to statutory maternity pay under Part XII of the Contributions and Benefits Act or to maternity allowance under section 35 of that Act;

Statutory Sick Pay (General) Regulations 1982

the period of entitlement shall end on that day or, if earlier, on the day she was confined.]

[³(5) Where an employee—
(a) is pregnant or has been confined; and
(b) is incapable of work wholly or partly because of pregnancy or confinement on any day which falls on or after the beginning of the [⁵4th week] before the expected week of confinement; and
(c) is not by virtue of that pregnancy or confinement entitled to statutory maternity pay under Part XII of the Contributions and Benefits Act or to maternity allowance under section 35 of that Act;
a period of entitlement as between her and her employer shall not arise in relation to a period of incapacity for work where the first day in that period falls within 18 weeks of the beginning of the week containing the day referred to at (b) above or, if earlier, of the week in which she was confined.]

(6) In paragraphs (4) and (5), "confinement" and "confined" have the same, meanings as in [³section 171 of the Contributions and Benefits Act].]

AMENDMENTS

1. Statutory Sick Pay (General) Amendment Regulations 1986 (SI 1986/477), reg.3 (April 6, 1986).
2. Statutory Sick Pay (General) Amendment (No.2) Regulations 1987 (SI 1987/868), reg.2 (June 7, 1987).
3. Social Security Maternity Benefits and Statutory Sick Pay (Amendment) Regulations 1994 (SI 1994/1367), reg.9 (June 11, 1994).
4. Social Security (Welfare to Work) Regulations 1998 (SI 1998/2231), reg.6 (October 5, 1998).
5. Social Security, Statutory Maternity Pay and Statutory Sick Pay (Miscellaneous Amendments) Regulations 2002 (SI 2002/2690), reg.13 (November 24, 2002).
6. Employment Equality (Age) (Consequential Amendments) Regulations 2007 (SI 2007/825), reg.5(2) (April 6, 2007).

DEFINITIONS

"confined"—see para.(6).
"confinement"—see *ibid*.
"employee"—see SSCBA 1992, s.163(1) and reg.16.
"employer"—see SSCBA 1992, s.163(1).
"period of entitlement"—see *ibid*.
"period of incapacity for work"—see *ibid*.
"week"—see *ibid*.

[¹Maximum entitlement to statutory sick pay in a period of entitlement

3A.—(1) For the purpose of determining whether an employee's maximum entitlement to statutory sick pay has been reached in a period of entitlement as between him and an employer of his, days falling within a previous period of entitlement as between the employee and any person who is or has in the past been an employer of his are, subject to paragraph (3), to be counted in the circumstances specified in paragraph (2).

(2) The circumstances specified for the purpose of paragraph (1) are—
(a) the period of entitlement as between the employee and his employer arose not more than 8 weeks after the last day in respect of which a person who is or has in the past been an employer of his was liable to make to him a payment of statutory sick pay; and either

(b) the employee has provided his employer with a statement issued in accordance with regulation 15A by a previous employer of his—
  (i) on or before the seventh day after the first qualifying day in the period of entitlement; or
  (ii) within such longer period as the employer may require, so however that where an employee shows good cause for delay in providing the statement, he may provide it later than the time specified in heads (i) and (ii) above but not later than the ninety-first day after the first qualifying day in the period of entitlement; or
(c) the employer has himself issued such a statement to the employee.

(3) Where an employee provides his employer with more than one statement or the employer himself issued more than one statement such as is referred to in paragraph (2), the employer shall have regard to one only of those statements and if the number of weeks specified in the statements is not the same he shall have regard to the statement which specifies the greatest number of weeks.

(4) For the purposes of paragraph (2)(b), a statement enclosed in an envelope which is properly addressed and sent by prepaid post shall be deemed to have been provided on the day which it was posted.

(5) The employer shall return the statement to the employee where—
(a) a period of entitlement does not arise as between the employee and his employer; or
(b) the employee leaves his employment with the employer within eight weeks of its commencement, and the employer is not himself required to provide the employee with a statement in accordance with regulation 15A,

and in such cases regulation 13(2) shall not apply to him.]

AMENDMENT

1. Statutory Sick Pay (General) Amendment Regulations 1986 (SI 1986/477), reg.4 (April 6, 1986).

DEFINITIONS

"employee"—see SSCBA 1992, s.163(1) and reg.16.
"employer"—see SSCBA 1992, s.163(1).
"period of entitlement"—see *ibid*.
"qualifying day"—see *ibid*.

Contract of service ended for the purpose of avoiding liability for statutory sick pay

4.—(1) The provisions of this regulation apply in any case where an employer's contract of service with an employee is brought to an end by the employer solely or mainly for the purpose of avoiding liability for statutory sick pay.

(2) Where a period of entitlement is current on the day on which the contract is brought to an end, the employer shall be liable to pay statutory sick pay to the employee until the occurrence of an event which, if the contract would have caused the period of entitlement to come to an end under section 3(2)(a), (b) or (d) or regulation 3(1) [¹of these regulations or

Statutory Sick Pay (General) Regulations 1982

regulation 10(2) of the Statutory Sick Pay (Mariners, Airmen and Persons Abroad) Regulations 1982], or (if earlier) until the date on which the contract would have expired.

AMENDMENT

1. Statutory Sick Pay (Mariners, Airmen and Persons Abroad) Regulations 1982 (SI 1982/1349), reg.10(3) (April 6, 1983).

DEFINITIONS

"contract of service"—see SSCBA 1992, s.163(1).
"employee"—see *ibid.* and reg.16.
"employer"—see SSCBA 1992, s.163(1).
"period of entitlement"—see *ibid.*

Qualifying days

3.11 **5.**—(1) In this regulation, "week" means a period of 7 consecutive days, beginning with Sunday.

(2) Where an employee and an employer of his have not agreed which day or days in any week are or were qualifying days [¹or where in any day or days are or were such as are referred to in paragraph (3)], the qualifying day or days in that week shall be—
  (a) the day or days on which it is agreed between the employer and employee that the employee is or was required to work (if not incapable) for that employer or, if it is so agreed that there is or was no such day;
  (b) the Wednesday, or, if there is no such agreement between and employee as mentioned in sub-paragraph (a);
  (c) every day, except that or those (if any) on which it is agreed between the employer and the employee that none of that employer's employees are or were required to work (any agreement that all day such days being ignored).

[¹(3) No effect shall be given to any agreement between an employer to treat as qualifying days—
  (a) any day where the day is identified, whether expressly or reference to that or another day being a day of incapacity relation to the employee's contract of service with an employer;
  (b) any day identified, whether expressly or otherwise, by period of entitlement or to a period of incapacity for work.]

AMENDMENT

1. Statutory Sick Pay (General) Amendment Regulations 1985 (SI 1985/126), reg.2 (March 5, 1985).

DEFINITIONS

"contract of service"—see SSCBA 1992, s.163(1).
"employee"—see *ibid.* and reg.16.
"employer"—see SSCBA 1992, s.163(1).
"period of entitlement"—see *ibid.*
"period of incapacity for work"—see *ibid.*
"qualifying day"—see *ibid.*
"week"—see *ibid.*

(SI 1982/894, reg.5) (as amended)

General Note

This prescribes the manner in which qualifying days are to be determined in the absence of any effective agreement between employer on which days are to rank as such (see also SSCBA 1992, s.154). *R(SSP) 1/85* decides that "required to work" in sub-paras (a) and (c) means obliged to work under one's terms of employment, and does not embrace the situation in which the employee was merely asked to work. Thus, there the employee's normal practice of working voluntary overtime on Saturdays could not turn Saturday into a qualifying day where the contract of service merely provided for 39 hours' work on Mon–Fri. That decision (at para.10) explains how what is now SSCBA 1992, s.154 and this paragraph interrelate to set out a series of alternatives, to be applied in turn as necessary, to determine qualifying days in any particular case.

Para. (3)
This renders ineffective any agreement which, expressly or otherwise, identifies qualifying days by reference to it or another day being one of incapacity, or by reference to a period of entitlement or period of incapacity for work.

3.12

3.13

Calculation of entitlement limit

6.—(1) Where an employee's entitlement to statutory sick pay is calculated by reference to different weekly rates in the same period of entitlement [2. . .], the entitlement limit shall be calculated in the manner described in paragraphs (2) and (3), or, as the case may be, (4) and (5); and where a number referred to in paragraph (2)(b) or (d) or (4)(a)(ii) or (d)(ii) is not a whole number [1of thousandths, it shall be rounded up to the next thousandth].

(2) For the purpose of determining whether an employee has reached his maximum entitlement to statutory sick pay in respect of a period of entitlement there shall be calculated—
   (a) the amount of statutory sick pay to which the employee became entitled during the part of the period of entitlement before the change in the weekly rate;
   (b) the number by which the weekly rate (before the change) must be multiplied in order to produce the amount mentioned in subparagraph (a);
   (c) the amount of statutory sick pay to which the employee has so far become entitled during the part of the period of entitlement after the change in the weekly rate; and
   (d) the number by which the weekly rate (after the change) must be multiplied in order to produce the amount mentioned in subparagraph (c);
   (e) the sum of the amounts mentioned in sub-paragraphs (a) and (c); and
   (f) the sum of the number mentioned in sub-paragraphs (b) and (d).

(3) When the sum mentioned in paragraph (2)(f) reaches [2 28], the sum mentioned in paragraph (2)(e) reaches the entitlement limit.
   (4) [2. . .]
   (5) [2. . .]

3.14

Amendments

1. Statutory Sick Pay (General) Amendment Regulations 1984 (SI 1984/385), reg.2(a) (April 16, 1984).
2. Statutory Sick Pay (General) Amendment Regulations 1986 (SI 1986/477), reg.9 (April 6, 1986).

Statutory Sick Pay (General) Regulations 1982

DEFINITIONS

"employee"—see SSCBA 1992, s.163(1) and reg.16.
"period of entitlement"—see SSCBA 1992, s.163(1).

Time and manner of notification of incapacity for work

3.15

7.—(1) Subject to paragraph (2), notice of any day of incapacity for work shall be given by or on behalf of an employee to his employer—
   (a) in a case where the employer has decided on a time limit (not being one which requires the notice to be given earlier than [1. . .] the first qualifying day in the period of incapacity for work which includes that day of incapacity for work [1or by a specified time during that qualifying day]) and taken reasonable steps to make it known to the employee, within that time limit; and
   (b) in any other case, on or before the seventh day after that day of incapacity for work.

(2) Notice of any day of incapacity for work may be given [2one month] later than as provided by paragraph (1) where there is good cause for giving it later [2, or if in the particular circumstances that is not practicable, as soon as it is reasonably practicable thereafter] so however that it shall in any event be given on or before the 91st day after that day.

(3) A notice contained in a letter which is properly addressed and sent by prepaid post shall be deemed to have been given on the day on which it was posted.

(4) Notice of any day of incapacity for work shall be given by or on behalf of an employee to his employer—
   (a) in a case where the employer has decided on a manner in which it is to be given (not being a manner which imposes a requirement such as is specified in paragraph (5)) and taken reasonable steps to make it known to the employee, in that manner; and
   (b) in any other case, in any manner, so however that unless otherwise agreed between the employer and employee it shall be given in writing.

(5) The requirements mentioned in paragraph (4)(a) are that notice shall be given—
   (a) personally;
   (b) in the form of medical evidence;
   (c) more than once in every 7 days during a period of entitlement;
   (d) on a document supplied by the employer; or
   (e) on a printed form.

AMENDMENTS

1. Statutory Sick Pay (General) Amendment Regulations 1984 (SI 1984/385), reg.2(b) (April 16, 1984).
2. Social Security Contributions, Statutory Maternity Pay and Statutory Sick Pay (Miscellaneous Amendments) Regulations 1996 (SI 1996/777), reg.2(3) (April 6, 1996).

DEFINITIONS

"employee"—see SSCBA 1992, s.163(1) and reg.16.
"employer"—see SSCBA 1992, s.163(1).
"period of entitlement"—see *ibid*.

(SI 1982/894, reg. 7) (as amended)

"period of incapacity for work"—see *ibid*.
"qualifying day"—see *ibid*.

Manner in which statutory sick pay may not be paid

8. Statutory sick pay may not be paid in kind or by way of the provision of board or lodging or of services or other facilities.

Time limits for paying statutory sick pay

9.—(1) In this regulation, "payday" means a day on which it has been agreed, or it is the normal practice, between an employer and an employee of his, that payments by way of remuneration are to be made, or, where there is no such agreement or normal practice, the last day of a calendar month.

(2) In any case where—
(a) a decision has been made by an insurance officer, local tribunal or Commissioner in proceedings under Part I that an employee is entitled to an amount of statutory sick pay; and
(b) the time for bringing an appeal against the decision has expired and either—
 (i) no such appeal has been brought; or
 (ii) such an appeal has been brought and has been finally disposed of, that amount of statutory sick pay is to be paid within the time specified in paragraph (3).

(3) Subject to paragraphs (4) and (5), the employer is required to pay the amount not later than the first pay day after—
(a) where an appeal has been brought, the day on which the employer receives notification that it has been finally disposed of;
(b) where leave to appeal has been refused and there remains no further opportunity to apply for leave, the day on which the employer receives notification of the refusal; and
(c) in any other case, the day on which the time for bringing an appeal expires.

(4) Subject to paragraph (5), where it is impracticable, in view of the employer's methods of accounting for and paying remuneration, for the requirement of payment referred to in paragraph (3) to be met by the pay day referred to in that paragraph, it shall be met not later than the next following pay day.

(5) Where the employer would not have remunerated the employee for his work on the day of incapacity for work in question (if it had not been a day of incapacity for work) as early as the pay day specified in paragraph (3) or (if it applies) paragraph (4), the requirement of payment shall be met on the first day on which the employee would have been remunerated for his work on that day.

DEFINITIONS

"employee"—see SSCBA 1992, s.163(1) and reg.16.
"employer"—see SSCBA 1992, s.163(1).

[¹Liability of the Secretary of State for payments of statutory sick pay

9A.—(1) Notwithstanding the provisions of section 1 of the Act and subject to paragraph (4), where—

Statutory Sick Pay (General) Regulations 1982

    (a) an adjudicating authority has determined that an employer is liable to
    (b) the time for appealing against the determination has expired; and
    (c) no appeal against the determination has been lodged or leave to appeal against the determination is required and has been refused,
then for any day of incapacity for work in respect of which it was determined the employer was liable to make those payments, and for any further days of incapacity for work which fall within the same spell of incapacity for work and in respect of which the employer was liable to make payments of statutory sick pay to that employee, the liability to make payments of statutory sick pay in respect of those days shall, to the extent that payment has not been made by the employer, be that of the Secretary of State and not the employer.

(2) For the purposes of this regulation a spell of incapacity for work consists of consecutive days of incapacity for work with no day of the week disregarded.

(3) In paragraph (1) above "adjudicating authority" means, as the case may be, the Chief or other adjudication officer, a Social Security Appeal Tribunal or the Chief or any other Social Security Commissioner.

(4) This regulation shall not apply to any liability of an employer to make a payment of statutory sick pay where the day of incapacity for work in respect of which the liability arose falls within a period of entitlement which commenced before 6th April 1987.]

AMENDMENT

1. Statutory Sick Pay (General) Amendment Regulations 1987 (SI 1987/ 372), reg.2 (April 6, 1987).

DEFINITIONS

    "employee"—see SSCBA 1992, s.163(1) and reg.16.
    "employer"—see SSCBA 1992, s.163(1).
    "period of entitlement"—see *ibid.*
    "week"—see *ibid.*

GENERAL NOTE

3.19   This regulation, together with regs 9B and 9C, prescribe the circumstances in which the liability to pay statutory sick pay is to be that of the Board of the Inland Revenue (now HMRC) and not the employer. (Although the regulation still refers to the Secretary of State, those functions were transferred—along with those under regs 9B and 9C—to the Board by s.1(2) of and Sch.2 to the Social Security Contributions (Transfer of Functions, etc.) Act 1999.) The relevant circumstances are where it is determined that statutory sick pay is payable but the employer neither pays the amount due nor appeals against the decision (reg.9A) and where the employer was insolvent at the time (reg.9B). Provision is also made (reg.9C) requiring HMRC to make the payments for which they are liable at weekly intervals.

[¹**Insolvency of employer**

3.20   **9B.**—(1) Notwithstanding the provisions of section 1 of the Act and subject to paragraph (3), any liability arising under Part I of the Act to make a payment of statutory sick pay in respect of a day of incapacity for work in relation to an employee's contract of service with his employer shall be that of the Secretary of State and not that of the employer where the employer is insolvent on that day.

(SI 1982/894, reg.9B) (as amended)

(2) For the purposes of paragraph (1) an employer shall be taken to be insolvent if, and only if—
  (a) in England and Wales—
    (i) he has been adjudged bankrupt or has made a composition or arrangement with his creditors;
    (ii) he had died and his estate falls to be administered in accordance with an order under section 421 of the Insolvency Act 1986; or
    (iii) where an employer is a company, a winding-up order [². . .] is made or a resolution for voluntary winding-up is passed with respect to it [²or it enters administration], or a receiver or manager of its undertaking is duly appointed, or possession is taken by or on behalf of the holders of any debentures secured by a floating charge, or any property of the company comprised in or subject to the charge or a voluntary arrangement proposed for the purposes of Part 1 of the Insolvency Act 1986 is approved under that Part;
  (b) in Scotland—
    (i) an award of sequestration is made on his estate or he executes a trust deed for his creditors or enters into a composition contract;
    (ii) he has died and a judicial factor appointed under section 11A of the Judicial Factors (Scotland) Act 1889 is required by that section to divide his insolvent estate among his creditors; or
    (iii) where the employer is a company, a winding-up order [². . .] is made or a resolution for voluntary winding-up is passed with respect to it [²or it enters administration] or a receiver of its undertaking is duly appointed or a voluntary arrangement proposed for the purposes of Part 1 of the Insolvency Act 1986 is approved under that Part.
shall not apply where the employer became insolvent before 6th April 1987.]

AMENDMENTS

1. Statutory Sick Pay (General) Amendment Regulations 1987 (SI 1987/ 372), reg.2 (April 6, 1987).
2. Enterprise Act 2002 (Insolvency) Order 2003 (SI 2003/2096), art.5 and Sch.2, para.42 (September 15, 2003).

DEFINITIONS

  "contract of service"—see SSCBA 1992, s.163(1).
  "employee"—see *ibid.* and reg.16.
  "employer"—see SSCBA 1992, s.163(1).

[¹Payments by the Secretary of State

9C. Where the Secretary of State becomes liable in accordance with regulation 9A or 9B to make payments of statutory sick pay to a person, the first payment shall be made as soon as reasonably practicable after he becomes so liable, and payments thereafter shall be made at weekly intervals, by means of an instrument of payment [², instrument for benefit payment] or by such other means as appears to the Secretary of State to be appropriate in the circumstances of the particular case.]

3.21

Statutory Sick Pay (General) Regulations 1982

AMENDMENTS

1. Statutory Sick Pay (General) Amendment Regulations 1987 (SI 1987/372), reg.2 (April 6, 1987).
2. Social Security (Claims and Payments etc.) Amendment Regulations 1996 (SI 1996/672), reg.3 (April 4, 1996).

Persons unable to act

3.22   **10.**—(1) Where in the case of any employer—
 (a) statutory sick pay is payable to him or he is alleged to be entitled to it;
 (b) he is unable for the time being to act, and either—
  (i) no receiver has been appointed by the Court of Protection with power to receive statutory sick pay on his behalf; or
  (ii) in Scotland, his estate is not being administered by any tutor, curator or other guardian acting or appointed in terms of law,
the Secretary of State may, upon written application to him by a person who, if a natural person, is over the age of 18, appoint that person to exercise, on behalf of the employee, any right to which he may be entitled under Part I and to deal on his behalf with any sums payable to him.

(2) Where the Secretary of State has made an appointment under paragraph (1)—
 (a) he may at any time in his absolute discretion revoke it;
 (b) the person appointed may resign his office after having given one month's notice in writing to the Secretary of State of his intention to do so; and
 (c) the appointment shall terminate when the Secretary of State is notified that a receiver or other person to whom paragraph (1)(c) applies has been appointed.

(3) Anything required by Part I to be done by or to any employee who is unable to act may be done by or to the person appointed under this regulation to act on his behalf, and the receipt of the person so appointed shall be a good discharge to the employee's employer for any sum paid.

DEFINITIONS

"employee"—see SSCBA 1992, s.163(1) and reg.16.
"employer"—see SSCBA 1992, s.163(1).

GENERAL NOTE

3.23   The Secretary of State's functions under this regulation were transferred to the Board of the Inland Revenue (now HMRC) by s.1(2) of and Sch.2 to the Social Security Contributions (Transfer of Functions, etc.) Act 1999.

Rounding to avoid fractional amounts

3.24   **11.** Where any payment of statutory sick pay is made and the statutory sick pay due for the period for which the payment purports to be made includes a fraction of a penny, the payment shall be rounded up to the next whole number of pence.

(SI 1982/894, reg.12) (as amended)

Days not to be treated as, or as parts of, periods of interruption of employment

12. In a case to which paragraph 3 of Schedule 2 applies, the day of incapacity for work mentioned in sub-paragraph (1)(b) of that paragraph shall not be, or form part of, a period of interruption of employment where it is a day which, by virtue of section 17(1) or (2) of the Social Security Act 1975 or any regulations made thereunder, is not to be treated as a day of incapacity for work.

Records to be maintained by employers

13.—[¹(1)] Every employer shall maintain for 3 years after the end of each tax year a record, in relation to each employee of his, of—
  (a) any day in that tax year which was one of 4 or more consecutive days on which, according to information supplied by or on behalf of the employee, the employee was incapable by reason of some specific disease or bodily or mental disablement of doing work which he could reasonably be expected to do under any contract of service between him and the employer, whether or not he would normally have been expected to work on that day; [²and
  (b) any payment of statutory sick pay made in respect of any day recorded under sub-paragraph (a).]
[³(1A) For the purposes of paragraph (1)(b) only, the employer is not to be regarded as having made a payment of statutory sick pay where, in respect of any day recorded under paragraph (1)(a), the employee is entitled to receive, and does in fact receive, a payment or payments by way of contractual remuneration from his employer which, in aggregate, equal or exceed the amount of statutory sick pay payable in respect of that day.]
  (2) [².. .]
  (3) [².. .]
  (4) [².. .]
  (5) [².. .]

AMENDMENTS

1. Statutory Sick Pay (General) Amendment Regulations 1986 (SI 1986/477), reg.5 (April 6, 1986).
2. Social Security Contributions, Statutory Maternity Pay and Statutory Sick Pay (Miscellaneous Amendments) Regulations 1996 (SI 1996/777), reg.2(4) (April 6, 1996).
3. Statutory Sick Pay (General) Amendment Regulations 1996 (SI 1996/3042), reg.52 (April 6, 1997).

DEFINITIONS

"contract of service"—see SSCBA 1992, s.163(1).
"employee"—see *ibid.* and reg.16.
"employer"—see SSCBA 1992, s.163(1).

[¹Production of employer's records

13A.—(1) An authorised officer of the Commissioners of Inland Revenue may by notice require an employer to produce to him at the place of keeping such records as are in the employer's possession or power and as (in the officer's reasonable opinion) contain, or may contain, information relevant to satisfy him that statutory sick pay has been paid and is being paid in accordance with these regulations to employees or former employees who are entitled to it.

(2) A notice referred to in paragraph (1) shall be in writing and the employer shall produce the records referred to in that paragraph within 30 days after the date of such a notice.

(3) The production of records in pursuance of this regulation shall be without prejudice to any lien which a third party may have in respect of those records.

(4) References in this regulation to "records" means—
  (a) any wage sheet or deductions working sheet; or
  (b) any other document which relates to the calculation or payment of statutory sick pay to his employees or former employees,
whether kept in written form, electronically, or otherwise.

(5) In paragraph (1), "place of keeping" means such place in Great Britain that an employer and an authorised officer may agree upon, or, in the absence of such agreement—
  (a) any place in Great Britain where records referred to in paragraph (1) are normally kept; or
  (b) if there is no such place, the employer's principal place of business in Great Britain.]

AMENDMENT

1. Statutory Maternity Pay (General) and Statutory Sick Pay (General) (Amendment) Regulations 2005 (SI 2005/989), reg.3(2) (April 6, 2005).

DEFINITIONS

"records"—see reg.13A(4).
"place of keeping"—see reg.13A(5).

Provision of information in connection with determination of questions

14. Any person claiming to be entitled to statutory sick pay, or any other person who is a party to proceedings arising under Part I, shall, if he receives notification from the Secretary of State that any information is required from him for the determination of any question arising in connection therewith, furnish that information to the Secretary of State within 10 days of receiving that notification.

GENERAL NOTE

The Secretary of State's functions under this regulation were transferred to the Board of the Inland Revenue (now HMRC) by s.1(2) of and Sch.2 to the Social Security Contributions (Transfer of Functions, etc.) Act 1999.

Provision of information by employers to employees

15.—(1) [³Subject to paragraph (1A),] in a case which falls within paragraph (a), (b) or (c) of section 18(3) (provision of information by employers in connection with the making of claims for [²short term incapacity] and other benefits), the employer shall furnish to his employee, in writing on a form approved by the Secretary of State for the purpose [³, or in a form in

(SI 1982/894, reg. 15) (as amended)

which it can be processed by equipment operating automatically in response to instructions given for that purpose], the information specified in paragraphs (2), (3) or (4) below, respectively within the time specified in the appropriate one of those paragraphs.

[³(1A) For the purposes of paragraph (1), where, in the particular circumstances of a case, it is not practicable for the employer to furnish the information within the specified time mentioned in paragraph (2), (3), (4)(b)(ii) or (5), he shall, not later than the first pay day within the meaning of regulation 9(1) immediately following the relevant specified time, furnish the information to his employee.]

(2) In a case which falls within paragraph (a) (no period of entitlement arising in relation to a period of incapacity for work) of section 18(3)—
- (a) the information mentioned in paragraph (1) is a statement of all the reasons why, under the provisions of paragraph 1 of Schedule 1 and regulations made thereunder, a period of entitlement does not arise; and
- (b) it shall be furnished not more than 7 days after the day on which the employee's employer is notified by or on behalf of the employee of the incapacity for work on the fourth day of the period of incapacity for work.

(3) In a case which falls within paragraph (b) (period of entitlement ending but period of incapacity for work continuing) of section 18(3)—
[¹(a) the information mentioned in paragraph (1) above is a statement informing the employee of—
  - (i) the reason why the period of entitlement ended;
  - (ii) the date of the first day in the period of entitlement or where the employer has taken into account days falling within a previous period of entitlement as between the employee and a person who is or was an employer of his, the date of the first day in that previous period of entitlement;
  - (iii) the date of the last day in respect of which the employer is or was liable to make a payment of statutory sick pay to him;
  - (iv) the number of qualifying days falling within the last week (beginning with Sunday) in the period of entitlement in which the employer is or was liable to make to him a payment of statutory sick pay; and either
  - (v) where the period of entitlement ends otherwise than by virtue of section 3(2)(b) of the Act, the number of weeks (a week being 7 days beginning with Sunday) and days in respect of which the employer was liable to make a payment of statutory sick pay to him in that period of entitlement; or
  - (vi) where the period of entitlement ends otherwise than by virtue of section 3(2)(b) of the Act and where the employee provided the employer with a statement issued to him in accordance with regulation 15A by a person who is or was an employer of his, the number of weeks (a week being 7 days beginning with Sunday) and days in respect of which he and the previous employer were together liable to make a payment of statutory sick pay to him; and
- (b) the statement shall be furnished not more than 7 days after the day on which the period of entitlement ended, or, if earlier, on the day on which it is already required to be furnished under paragraph (4).]

(4) In a case which falls within paragraph (c) (period of entitlement expected to end before period of incapacity for work ends, on certain assumptions) of section 18(3)—
[¹(a) the information mentioned in paragraph (1) above is a statement informing the employee of—
  (i) the reason why the period of entitlement is expected to end;
  (ii) the date of the first day in the period of entitlement or where the employer has taken into account days of incapacity for work in a previous of entitlement as between the employee and person who is or was an employer of his, the date of the first day in that previous period of entitlement;
  (iii) the date of the last day in respect of which the employer is or was expected to be liable to make a payment of statutory sick pay to him;
  (iv) the number of qualifying days falling within the last week (beginning with Sunday) in the period of entitlement in which the employer is or was expected to be liable to make to him a payment of statutory sick pay; and either
  (v) where the period of entitlement is expected to end otherwise than by virtue of section 3(2)(b) of the Act, the number of weeks (a week being 7 days beginning with Sunday) and days in respect of which the employer will have been liable to make a payment of statutory sick pay to him in that period of entitlement; or
  (vi) where the period of entitlement is expected to end otherwise than by virtue of section 3(2)(b) of the Act and where the employee provided the employer with a statement issued to him in accordance with regulation 15A by a person who is or was an employer of his, the number of weeks (a week being 7 days beginning with Sunday) and days in respect of which he and the previous employer were
(b) the statement shall be furnished—
  (i) in a case where the period of entitlement is expected to end in accordance with section 3(2)(b) of the Act (maximum entitled to statutory sick pay), on or before the 42nd day before the period of entitlement is expected to end; or
  (ii) in any other case, on or before the seventh day before the period of entitlement is expected to end
[³. . .].]

(5) For the purposes of section 18(3)(c)(i) (period for which the period of incapacity for work is to be assumed to continue to run) the prescribed period shall be 14 days.

AMENDMENTS

1. Statutory Sick Pay (General) Amendment Regulations 1986 (SI 1986/477), reg.6 (April 6, 1986).
2. Social Security (Incapacity Benefit) (Consequential and Transitional Amendments and Savings) Regulations 1995 (SI 1995/829), reg.15 (April 13, 1995).
3. Social Security Contributions, Statutory Maternity Pay and Statutory Sick Pay (Miscellaneous Amendments) Regulations 1996 (SI 1996/777), reg.2(5) (April 6, 1996).

(SI 1982/894, reg.15) (as amended)

DEFINITIONS

"employee"—see SSCBA 1992, s.163(1) and reg.16.
"employer"—see SSCBA 1992, s.163(1).
"period of entitlement"—see *ibid.*
"period of incapacity for work"—see *ibid.*
"prescribed"—see *ibid.*
"qualifying day"—see *ibid.*
"week"—see *ibid.*

GENERAL NOTE

The references to ss.3(2)(b) and 18(3) of the 1982 Act should now be read as referring to SSCBA 1992, s.153(2)(b) and SSAA 1992, s.130(3), respectively.

3.31

[¹**Statements relating to the payment of statutory sick pay**

15A.—(1) Subject to the provisions of this regulation, where—
(a) an employee is about to leave his employment with his employer, or has been employed by him in the past;
(b) the period of entitlement as between the employee and that employer will come or has come to an end within the period of 8 weeks ending with the day on which the employee's contract of service with the employer concerned expires or is brought to an end; and
[²(c) the employer is or was liable to make a payment of statutory sick pay to the employee in respect of any week within that period, and for this purpose a week includes any days rounded up to a week in accordance with paragraph (4)], [³and
(d) the employee requests one or more statements in relation to the payment of statutory sick pay,]
the employer shall provide the employee with [³one or more statements] in writing containing the information specified in paragraph (2) within 7 days of the [³employee making the request under sub-paragraph (d), or where it is not practicable, not later than his first pay day within the meaning of regulation 9(1) which would have fallen within the next income tax month immediately following that request.]
(2) The information mentioned in paragraph (1) is—
(a) the date of the first day of the period of entitlement;
(b) the number of weeks (a week being 7 days beginning with Sunday) [². . .] in respect of which the employer was liable to make a payment of statutory sick pay to the employee in that period of entitlement;
(c) the date of the last day in respect of which the employer was liable to make to the employee a payment of statutory sick pay;
(d) the date the statement was made by the employer; and
(e) the full name, address and, if there is one, telephone number of the employer making the statement.
(3) For the purposes of paragraph (2)(a) and (b) above, the period of entitlement includes any previous period of entitlement relevant for the purposes of regulation 3A (maximum entitlement to statutory sick pay in a period of entitlement).
(4) For the purposes of this regulation, where the total number of days in the period of entitlement in respect of which the employer is or was liable to make the employee a payment in respect of statutory sick pay amounts in aggregate to less than a complete week or number of weeks, then the number

3.32

Statutory Sick Pay (General) Regulations 1982

of weeks shall be determined by disregarding the remainder where it is 3 days or less and if it is not by rounding them up to a week.

(5) Where a question arises under Part I of the 1982 Act as to or in connection with entitlement to statutory sick pay, a written statement or, as the case may be, a revised written statement containing the information specified in paragraph (2) shall be provided by the employer to the employee within 7 days of the question being determined.

(6) A question is determined for the purpose of paragraph (5) when the time for appealing from a decision of an adjudication officer, a local tribunal or a Commissioner, as the case may be, has expired or leave to appeal has been refused.

(7) [³. . .]

(8) An employer may, at the request of a person who is or was employed by him, provide a second copy of the statement if he is satisfied that the person making the request has a need for it.]

AMENDMENTS

1. Statutory Sick Pay (General) Amendment Regulations 1986 (SI 1986/477), reg.7 (April 6, 1986).
2. Statutory Sick Pay (General) Amendment (No.2) Regulations 1987 (SI 1987/868), reg.3 (June 7, 1987).
3. Social Security Contributions, Statutory Maternity Pay and Statutory Sick Pay (Miscellaneous Amendments) Regulations 1996 (SI 1996/777), reg.2(6) (April 6, 1996).

DEFINITIONS

"contract of service"—see SSCBA 1992, s.163(1).
"employee"—see SSCBA 1992, s.163(1) and reg.16.
"employer"—see SSCBA 1992, s.163(1).
"period of entitlement"—see *ibid*.
"week"—see *ibid*.

Meaning of "employee"

3.33   **16.**—(1) [²Subject to paragraph (1ZA),] in a case where, and in so far as, a person [². . .] is treated as an employed earner by virtue of the Social Security (Categorisation of Earners) Regulations 1978, he shall be treated as an employee for the purposes of Part I and in a case where, and in so far as, such a person is treated otherwise than as an employed earner by virtue of those regulations, he shall not be treated as an employee for the purposes of Part I.

[³(1ZA) Paragraph (1) shall have effect in relation to a person who—
  (a) is under the age of 16; and
  (b) would or, as the case may be, would not have been treated as an employed earner by virtue of the Social Security (Categorisation of Earners) Regulations 1978 had he been over that age,
as it has effect in relation to a person who is or, as the case may be, is not so treated.]

[¹(1A) Any person who is in employed earner's employment within the meaning of the Act under a contract of apprenticeship shall be treated as an employee for the purposes of Part I.]

(2) A person who is in employed earner's employment within the meaning of the Act but whose employer—

(SI 1982/894, reg.16) (as amended)

    (a) does not fulfil the conditions prescribed in regulation 119(1)(b) of the Social Security (Contributions) Regulations 1979 as to residence or presence in Great Britain, or
    (b) is a person who, by reason of any international treaty to which the United Kingdom is a party or of any international convention binding the United Kingdom—
        (i) is exempt from the provisions of the Act, or
        (ii) is a person against whom the provisions of that Act are not enforceable,
shall not be treated as an employee for the purposes of Part I.

AMENDMENTS

1. Statutory Sick Pay (Compensation of Employers) and Miscellaneous Provisions Regulations 1983 (SI 1983/376), reg.5(2) (April 6, 1983).
2. Employment Equality (Age) Regulations 2006 (SI 2006/1031), reg.49(1) and Sch.8, Pt 2, para.50 (October 1, 2006).
3. Employment Equality (Age) (Consequential Amendments) Regulations 2007 (SI 2007/825), reg.5(3) (April 6, 2007).

DEFINITIONS

"employee"—see SSCBA 1992, s.163(1) and reg.16.
"employer"—see SSCBA 1992, s.163(1).
"prescribed"—see *ibid.*

Meaning of "earnings"

17.—(1) [^{3}...]   3.34
[^{4}(2) For the purposes of section 163(2) of the Contributions and Benefits Act, the expression "earnings" refers to gross earnings and includes any remuneration or profit derived from a person's employment except any payment or amount which is—
    (a) excluded [^{8}or disregarded in the calculation of a person's earnings under regulation 25, 27 or 123 of, or Schedule 3 to, the Social Security (Contributions) Regulations 2001] [^{7}(or would have been so excluded had he not been under the age of 16)];
    (b) a chargeable emolument under section 10A of the Social Security Contributions and Benefits Act 1992, except where, in consequence of such a chargeable emolument being excluded from earnings, a person would not be entitled to statutory sick pay [^{7}(or where such a payment or amount would have been so excluded and in consequence he would not have been entitled to statutory sick pay had he not been under the age of 16)].]
[^{1}(2A) [^{3}...]]
(3) For the purposes of [^{5}section 163(2) of the Contributions and Benefits Act] the expression "earnings" includes also—
[^{8}(za) any amount retrospectively treated as earnings by regulations made by virtue of section 4B(2) of the Contributions and Benefits Act;]
    (a) any sum payable by way of maternity pay or payable by the Secretary of State in pursuance of section 40 of the Employment Protection (Consolidation) Act 1978 in respect of maternity pay;
    (b) any sum which is payable by the Secretary of State by virtue of section 122(3)(a) of that Act in respect of arrears of pay and which by virtue

of section 42(1) of that Act is to go towards discharging a liability to pay maternity pay;

(c) any sum payable in respect of arrears of pay in pursuance of an order for reinstatement or re-engagement under that Act;

(d) any sum payable by way of pay in pursuance of an order under that Act for the continuation of a contract of employment;

(e) any sum payable by way of remuneration in pursuance of a protective award under the Employment Protection Act 1975;

(f) any sum payable to any employee under the Temporary Short time Working Compensation Scheme administered under powers conferred by the Employment Subsidies Act 1978;

(g) any sum paid in satisfaction of any entitlement to statutory sick pay;

[²(h) any sum payable by way of statutory maternity pay under Part V of the Social Security Act 1986, including sums payable in accordance with regulations made under section 46(8)(b) of that Act.]

[⁶(i) any sum payable by way of statutory paternity pay, including any sums payable in accordance with regulations made under section 171ZD(3) of the Contributions and Benefits Act;

(j) any sum payable by way of statutory adoption pay, including any sums payable in accordance with regulations made under section 171ZM(3) of the Contributions and Benefits Act.]

(4) [³. . .]

(5) [³. . .]

AMENDMENTS

1. Statutory Sick Pay (Compensation of Employers) and Miscellaneous Provisions Regulations 1983 (SI 1983/376), reg.5(3) (April 6, 1983).

2. Statutory Sick Pay (General) Amendment (No.2) Regulations 1987 (SI 1987/868), reg.4 (June 7, 1987).

3. Social Security (Miscellaneous Provisions) Amendment (No.2) Regulations 1992 (SI 1992/2595), reg.15 (November 16, 1992).

4. Social Security Contributions, Statutory Maternity Pay and Statutory Sick Pay (Miscellaneous Amendments) Regulations 1999 (SI 1999/567), reg.13 (April 6, 1999).

5. Social Security, Statutory Maternity Pay and Statutory Sick Pay (Miscellaneous Amendments) Regulations 2002 (SI 2002/2690), reg.14(a) (November 24, 2002).

6. Social Security, Statutory Maternity Pay and Statutory Sick Pay (Miscellaneous Amendments) Regulations 2002 (SI 2002/2690), reg.14(b) (April 6, 2003).

7. Employment Equality (Age) Regulations 2006 (SI 2006/1031), reg.49(1) and Sch.8, Pt 2, para.51 (October 1, 2006).

8. Social Security, Occupational Pension Schemes and Statutory Payments (Consequential Provisions) Regulations 2007 (SI 2007/1154), reg.5(2) and (3) (April 6, 2007).

DEFINITION

"employee"—see SSCBA 1992, s.163(1) and reg.16.

Payments to be treated or not to be treated as contractual remuneration

18. For the purposes of paragraph 2(1) and (2) of Schedule 2 to the Act, those things which are included within the expression "earnings" by regulation (except paragraph (3)(g) thereof) shall be, and those things which are excluded from that expression by that regulation shall not be, treated as contractual remuneration.

(SI 1982/894, reg.19) (as amended)

Normal weekly earnings

19.—(1) For the purposes of section 26, an employee's normal weekly earnings shall be determined in accordance with the provisions of this regulation.

(2) In this regulation—

"the critical date" means the first day of the period of entitlement in relation to which a person's normal weekly earnings fall to be determined, or, in a case to which paragraph 2(c) of Schedule 1 applies, the relevant date within the meaning of Schedule 1;

"normal pay day" means a day on which the terms of an employee's contract of service require him to be paid, or the practice in his employment is for him to be paid, if any payment is due to him; and

"day of payment" means a day on which the employee was paid.

(3) Subject to paragraph (4), the relevant period (referred to in section 26(2)) is the period between—

(a) the last normal pay day to fall before the critical date; and
(b) the last normal pay day to fall at least 8 weeks earlier than the normal pay day mentioned in sub-paragraph (a), including the normal pay day mentioned in sub-paragraph (a) but excluding that first mentioned in sub-paragraph (b).

(4) In a case where an employee has no identifiable normal pay day, paragraph (3) shall have effect as if the words "day of payment" were substituted for the words "normal pay day" in each place where they occur.

(5) In a case where an employee has normal pay days at intervals of, or approximating to one or more calendar months (including intervals of or approximating to a year) his normal weekly earnings shall be calculated by dividing his earnings in the relevant period by the number of calendar months in that period (or, if it is not a whole number, the nearest whole number), multiplying the result by 12 and dividing by 52.

(6) In a case to which paragraph (5) does not apply and the relevant period is not an exact number of weeks, the employee's normal weekly earnings shall be calculated by dividing his earnings in the relevant period by the number of days in the relevant period and multiplying the result by 7.

(7) In a case where the normal pay day mentioned in sub-paragraph (a) of paragraph (3) exists but that first mentioned in sub-paragraph (b) of that paragraph does not yet exist, the employee's normal weekly earnings shall be calculated as if the period for which all the earnings under his contract of service received by him before the critical date represented payment were the relevant period.

(8) In a case where neither of the normal pay days mentioned in paragraph (3) yet exists, the employee's normal weekly earnings shall be the remuneration to which he is entitled, in accordance with the terms of his contract of service for, as the case may be—

(a) a week's work; or
(b) a number of calendar month's work, divided by that number of months multiplied by 12 and divided by 52.

3.36

DEFINITIONS

"contract of service"—see SSCBA 1992, s.163(1).
"employee"—see SSCBA 1992, s.163(1) and reg.16.
"period of entitlement"—see *ibid*.

General Note

3.37 For some of the difficulties in applying this regulation, see *R(SSP)1/89*. There, the relevant period for a school dinner lady extended from the end of one term until the last pay day before her period of incapacity began. This was 11 weeks, but as the relevant period began the day after the last pay day at the end of term it could not include the lump-sum payment that was made as a retainer throughout the vacation. Without that sum her average weekly earnings did not qualify her for statutory sick pay.

Treatment of one or more employers as one

3.38 **20.**—(1) In a case where the earnings paid to an employee in respect of 2 more employments are aggregated and treated as a single payment of earnings under regulation 12(1) of the Social Security (Contributions) Regulations 1979, the employers of the employee in respect of those employments shall be treated as one for all purposes of Part I.

(2) Where 2 or more employers are treated as one under the provisions of paragraph (1), liability for the statutory sick pay payable by them to the employee shall be apportioned between them in such proportions as they may agree or, in default of agreement, in the proportions which the employee's earnings from each employment bear to the amount of the aggregated earnings.

(3) [¹Subject to paragraphs (4) and (5)] where a contract of service ("the current contract") was preceded by a contract of service entered into between the same employer and employee ("the previous contract"), and the interval between the date on which the previous contract ceased to have effect and that on which the current contract came into force was not more than 8 weeks, then, for the purposes of establishing the employee's maximum entitlement within the meaning of section 5 (limitation on entitlement to statutory sick pay in any one period of entitlement or tax year), the provisions of Part I shall not have effect as if the employer were a different employer in relation to each of those contracts of service.

[¹(4) Where a contract of service ("the current contract") was preceded by two or more contracts of service entered into between the same employer and employee ("the previous contracts") and the previous contracts—
  (a) existed concurrently for at least part of their length; and
  (b) the intervals between the dates on which each of the previous contracts ceased to have effect and that on which the current contract came into force was not more than 8 weeks,
then, for the purposes of establishing the employee's maximum entitlement within the meaning of section 5 the provisions of Part I shall not have effect as if the employer were a different employer in relation to the current contract and whichever of the previous contracts was the contract by virtue of which the employer had become liable to pay the greatest proportion of statutory sick pay in respect of any tax year or period of entitlement.

(5) If, in any case to which paragraph (4) applies, the same proportion of the employer's liability for statutory sick pay becomes due under each of the previous contracts, then, for the purpose of establishing the employee's maximum entitlement within the meaning of section 5, the provisions of Part I shall have effect in relation to only one of the previous contracts.]

Amendment

1. Statutory Sick Pay (Compensation of Employers) and Miscellaneous Provisions Regulations 1983 (SI 1983/376), reg.5(4) (April 6, 1983).

(SI 1982/894, reg.20) (as amended)

DEFINITIONS

"contract of service"—see SSCBA 1992, s.163(1).
"employee"—see SSCBA 1992, s.163(1) and reg.16.
"employer"—see SSCBA 1992, s.163(1).
"period of entitlement"—see *ibid*.

GENERAL NOTE

Specific provision is made in Statutory Sick Pay (National Health Service Employees) Regulations 1991 (SI 1991/589) in the case of NHS workers with divided contracts.

3.39

Treatment of more than one contract of service as one

21. Where 2 or more contracts of service exist concurrently between one employer and one employee, they shall be treated as one for all purposes of Part I except where, by virtue of regulation 11 of the Social Security (Contributions) Regulations 1979, the earnings from those contracts of service are not aggregated for the purposes of earnings-related contributions.

3.40

DEFINITIONS

"contract of service"—see SSCBA 1992, s.163(1).
"employee"—see SSCBA 1992, s.163(1) and reg.16.
"employer"—see SSCBA 1992, s.163(1).

[¹Election to be treated as different employers not to apply to recovery of statutory sick pay

21A.—(1) Paragraph (2) below applies for the purposes of section 159A of the Contributions and Benefits Act (power to provide for recovery by employers of sums paid by way of statutory sick pay) and of any order made under that section.

(2) Where an employer has made 2 or more elections under regulation 3 of the Income Tax (Employments) Regulations 1993 to be treated as a different employer in respect of each of the groups of employees specified in the election, the different employers covered by each of those elections shall be treated as one employer.]

3.41

AMENDMENT

1. Statutory Sick Pay Percentage Threshold Order 1995 (Consequential) Regulations 1995 (SI 1995/513), reg.3 (April 6, 1995).

DEFINITIONS

"employee"—see SSCBA 1992, s.163(1) and reg.16.
"employer"—see SSCBA 1992, s.163(1).

[¹Offences

22. [². . .]

3.42

AMENDMENTS

1. Statutory Maternity Pay (General) and Statutory Sick Pay (General) (Amendment) Regulations 2001 (SI 2001/206), reg.2 (February 23, 2001).
2. Statutory Maternity Pay (General) and Statutory Sick Pay (General) (Amendment) Regulations 2005 (SI 2005/989), reg.3(3) (immediately before April 6, 2005).

GENERAL NOTE

3.43   The repeal of this provision was consequential upon the bringing into force of the National Insurance Contributions and Statutory Payments Act 2004.

Statutory Sick Pay (Mariners, Airmen and Persons Abroad) Regulations 1982

(SI 1982/1349) (AS AMENDED)

The Secretary of State for Social Services, in exercise of the powers conferred upon him by sections 3(5) and (7), 22(1) and 26(1) of and paragraph 1 of Schedule 1 to the Social Security and Housing Benefits Act 1982(a) and of all other powers enabling him in that behalf, hereby makes the following regulations.

ARRANGEMENT OF REGULATIONS

3.44
1. Citation, commencement and interpretation
2. Mariners—interpretation
3. Airmen—interpretation
4. Continental shelf—interpretation
5. Persons in other member States—meaning of "employee"
5A. Persons absent from Great Britain—meaning of "employee"
6. Mariners—meaning of "employee"
7. Airmen—meaning of "employee"
8. Continental shelf—meaning of "employee"
9. Meaning of "employee"—general
10. Persons abroad—general
11. (*repealed*)
12. (*repealed*)
13. (*repealed*)
14. Time for compliance with requirements of Part I and regulations

Citation, commencement and interpretation

3.45   **1.**—(1) These regulations may be cited as the Statutory Sick Pay (Mariners, Airmen and Persons Abroad) Regulations 1982, and shall come into operation on 6th April 1983.

(2) In these Regulations—

"the Act" means the Social Security and Housing Benefits Act 1982;

"Part I" means Part I of the Act;

[1"the Contributions and Benefits Act," means the Social Security Contributions and Benefits Act 1992;

"the Contributions Regulations" means the Social Security (Contributions) Regulations 1979;]

"the General Regulations" means the Statutory Sick Pay (General) Regulations 1982;

and other expressions, unless the context otherwise requires, have the same meanings as in Part I.

(3) Unless the context otherwise requires, any reference—

(a) in these regulations to a numbered regulation is a reference to the regulation bearing that number in these regulations; and
(b) in any of these regulations to a numbered paragraph is a reference to the paragraph bearing that number in that regulation.

AMENDMENT

1. Social Security Contributions, Statutory Maternity Pay and Statutory Sick Pay (Miscellaneous Amendments) Regulations 1996 (SI 1996/777), reg.3(2) (April 6, 1996).

GENERAL NOTE

These Regulations make special provision for statutory sick pay under what is now Pt XI of the SSCBA 1992 as it affects mariners, airmen, persons abroad and persons employed in operations on the Continental Shelf. Under s.163(1) of the SSCBA 1992, a person is not, as a rule, an "employee", and therefore not qualified to receive statutory sick pay, unless he or she is employed in Great Britain. Regulations 5–8 prescribe exceptions to this rule, so that certain persons who are employed in other Member States but who are subject to the legislation of the United Kingdom, certain mariners and airmen, and certain persons employed on the Continental Shelf, are "employees", though employed outside Great Britain; and so that certain limited classes of mariners and airmen are not "employees" though employed in Great Britain. Further general provision on the meaning of "employee" is made by reg.9, while reg.10 makes general provision regarding persons from abroad. Regulations 11–13, which provided for exceptions to reg.10, were repealed in 1996.

3.46

Some of the requirements of the Act and regulations made under it impose time-limits. Regulation 14 relaxes those requirements in their application to persons who are outside the United Kingdom and for that reason cannot comply with them.

It should be noted that these regulations have never been fully updated to include appropriate references to SSCBA 1992. Accordingly, all references to Pt I of the Social Security and Housing Benefits Act 1982 in these regulations should be read as references to Pt XI of SSCBA 1992.

Mariners—interpretation

2. In regulations 6 and 11, the expressions "British ship," "foreign-going ship" "managing owner," "mariner," "owner" and "radio officer" have the same meanings as in Case C of Part VIII of the Social Security (Contributions) Regulations 1979, and the expressions "ship" and "ship or vessel," except in regulation 6(2), include hovercraft.

3.47

GENERAL NOTE

The provisions relating to Case C of Pt VIII of the Social Security (Contributions) Regulations 1979 have been re-enacted in Case C of Pt IX of the Social Security Contributions Regulations 2001 (SI 2001/1004).

3.48

Airmen—interpretation

3. In regulations 7 and 12—
"airman" means a person who is, or has been, employed under a contract of service either as a pilot, commander, navigator or other member of the crew of any aircraft, or in any other capacity on board any aircraft where—
(a) the employment in that other capacity is for the purposes of the aircraft or its crew or of any passengers or cargo or mails carried thereby; and

3.49

(b) the contract is entered into in the United Kingdom with a view to its performance (in whole or in part) while the aircraft is in flight, but does not include a person in so far as his employment is as a serving member of the forces;

"British aircraft" means any aircraft belonging to Her Majesty and any aircraft registered in the United Kingdom of which the owner (or managing owner if there is more than one owner) resides or has his principal place of business in Great Britain, and references to the owner of an aircraft shall, in relation to an aircraft which has been hired, be taken as referring to the person for the time being entitled as hirer to possession and control of the aircraft by virtue of the hiring or any subordinate hiring.

DEFINITION

"contract of service"—see SSCBA 1992, s.163(1).

Continental shelf—interpretation

4. In this regulation and regulations 8 and 13—

"designated area" means any area which may from time to time be designated by Order in Council under the Continental Shelf Act 1964 as an area within which the rights of the United Kingdom with respect to the sea-bed and subsoil and their natural resources may be exercised;

"prescribed area" means an area over which Norway or any member State (other than the United Kingdom) exercises sovereign rights for the purpose of exploring the seabed and subsoil and exploiting their natural resources, being an area outside the territorial seas of Norway or that member State [¹or any other area which is from time to time specified under section 22(5) of the Oil and Gas (Enterprise) Act 1982];

"prescribed employment" means employment in a designated area or prescribed area in connection with [¹any activity mentioned in section 23(2) of the Oil and Gas (Enterprise) Act 1982 in any designated area or in any prescribed area.]

AMENDMENT

1. Social Security and Statutory Sick Pay (Oil and Gas (Enterprise) Act 1982) (Consequential) Regulations 1982 (SI 1982/1738), reg.5 (April 6, 1983).

DEFINITION

"prescribed"—see SSCBA 1992, s.163(1).

Persons in other member States—meaning of "employee"

5. Subject to regulations 6(2), 7(2) and 9, a person who is—
(a) gainfully employed in a member State other than the United Kingdom in such circumstances that if his employment were in Great Britain he would be an employee for the purposes of Part I or a person treated as such an employee under regulation 16 of the General Regulations; and
(b) subject to the legislation of the United Kingdom under Council Regulation (EEC) No. 1408/71;

notwithstanding that he is not employed in Great Britain, shall be treated as an employee for the purposes of Part I.

(SI 1982/1349, reg.5) (as amended)

DEFINITIONS

"Pt I"—see reg.1(2).
"the General Regulations"—*ibid*.

[¹Persons absent from Great Britain—meaning of "employee"

5A. Subject to regulations 5, 6(2) and 9, where a person, while absent from Great Britain for any purpose, is gainfully employed by an employer who is liable to pay in respect of him secondary Class 1 contributions under section 6 of the Contributions and Benefits Act 1992 or regulation 120 of the Contributions Regulations, he shall be treated as an employee for the purposes of Part XI of the Contributions and Benefits Act.]

AMENDMENT

1. Social Security Contributions, Statutory Maternity Pay and Statutory Sick Pay (Miscellaneous Amendments) Regulations 1996 (SI 1996/777), reg.3(3) (April 6, 1996).

DEFINITIONS

"employer"—see SSCBA 1992, s.163(1).
"the Contributions and Benefits Act"—see reg.1(2).
"the Contributions Regulations"—*ibid*.

GENERAL NOTE

The Social Security Contributions Regulations 2001 (SI 2001/1004) have now revoked and superseded the Social Security Contributions Regulations 1979 (SI 1979/591). Regulation 146 of the 2001 Regulations is the parallel provision to reg.120 of the 1979 Regulations.

Mariners—meaning of "employee"

6.—(1) Subject to regulation 9, where a mariner—
(a) is employed as such and—
  (i) the employment is on board a British ship; or
  (ii) the employment is on board a ship and the contract in respect of the employment is entered into the United Kingdom with a view to its performance (in whole or in part) while the ship or vessel is on her voyage; and
  (iii) in a case to which head (ii) applies, the person by whom the mariner's earnings are paid, or, in the case of employment as a master or member of the crew of a ship or vessel, either that person or the owner of the ship or vessel (or the managing owner if there is more than one owner) has a place of business in Great Britain; or
(b) is employed as a master, member of the crew or radio officer on board any ship or vessel, not being a mariner to whom the last preceding subparagraph applies; and
  (i) in the case of the employment being as a radio officer, if the contract under which the employment is performed is entered into in the United Kingdom, the employer or the person paying the radio officer his earnings for that employment has a place of business in Great Britain, or,

Statutory Sick Pay (Mariners, etc.) Regulations 1982

      (ii) in the case of the employment being as a master, member of the crew or radio officer, if the contract is not entered into in the United Kingdom, the employer or the person paying the earnings has his principal place of business in Great Britain,

then, unless he is a mariner to whom paragraph (2) applies, he shall, notwithstanding that he may not be employed in Great Britain, be treated as an employee for the purposes of Part I.

  (2) A mariner who—

    (a) is in employment (including any period of leave, other than leave for the purpose of study, accruing from the employment) as a master or member of the crew of a ship, where—

      (i) the employment is on a foreign-going ship; or

      (ii) the employment is partly on a foreign-going ship and partly otherwise than on such a ship, and it is a requirement of the contract of service which relates to that employment that any payment of earnings in respect of that employment is to be made during the employment on the foreign-going ship; or

    (b) has been in such employment as is mentioned in sub-paragraph (a), where—

      (i) not more than thirteen weeks have elapsed since he was last in such employment;

      (ii) he continues to be employed by the employer by whom he was employed when he was last in such employment; and

      (iii) he is not employed (by that employer or any other) on terms which are inconsistent with his being able to resume such employment as is mentioned in sub-paragraph (a) after not more than thirteen weeks have elapsed since he was last in such employment;

shall, notwithstanding that he may be employed in Great Britain, not be treated as an employee for the purposes of Part I.

DEFINITIONS

  "British ship"—see reg.2.
  "contract of service"—see SSCBA 1992, s.163(1).
  "employer"—*ibid*.
  "foreign-going ship"—see reg.2.
  "managing owner"—*ibid*.
  "mariner"—*ibid*.
  "owner"—*ibid*.
  "Pt I"—see reg.1(2).
  "radio officer"—see reg.2.
  "ship"—*ibid*.
  "ship or vessel"—*ibid*.
  "week"—see SSCBA 1992, s.163(1).

Airmen—meaning of "employee"

3.55   **7.**—(1) Subject to regulation 9 and the following provisions of this regulation, where an airman is employed as such on board any aircraft, and the employer of that airman or the person paying the airman his earnings in respect of the employment (whether or not the person making the payment is acting as agent for the employer) or the person under whose directions the terms of the airman's employment and the amount of the earnings to be paid in respect thereof are determined has—

(SI 1982/1349, reg.7) (as amended)

    (a) in the case of the aircraft being a British aircraft, a place of business in Great Britain; or
    (b) in any other case, his principal place of business in Great Britain, then, notwithstanding that he may not be employed in Great Britain, he shall be treated as an employee for the purposes of Part I.
  (2) Subject to the provisions of paragraph (3), an airman shall not be treated as an employee for those purposes if he is not domiciled, and has no place of residence, in Great Britain.
  (3) The provisions of paragraph (2) shall have effect subject to any Order in Council giving effect to any reciprocal agreement made under section 143 of the Social Security Act 1975 (reciprocity with other countries).

DEFINITIONS

    "airman"—see reg.3.
    "British aircraft"—*ibid.*
    "employee"—see SSCBA 1992, s.163(1).
    "employer"—*ibid.*
    "Pt I"—see reg.1(2).

GENERAL NOTE

Para. (3)
  Section 143 of the Social Security Act 1975 has now been replaced in similar terms by s.179 of the SSAA 1992.

3.56

Continental shelf—meaning of "employee"

  8. Subject to regulation 9, a person in prescribed employment, not-withstanding that he may not be employed in Great Britain, shall be treated as an employee for the purposes of Part I.

3.57

DEFINITIONS

    "employee"—see SSCBA 1992, s.163(1).
    "Part I"—see reg.1(2).
    "prescribed employment"—see reg.4.
    "prescribed"—see SSCBA 1992, s.163(1).

Meaning of "employee"—general

  9. No person who, by virtue of regulation 16 of the General Regulations, would not be treated as an employee for the purposes of Part I if his employment were in Great Britain, shall be treated as an employee by virtue of any of regulations 5–8.

3.58

DEFINITIONS

    "employee"—see SSCBA 1992, s.163(1).
    "Part I"—see reg.1(2).
    "the General Regulations"—*ibid.*

[1Persons abroad—general

  10. In a case where a mariner, an airman or a continental shelf employee, respectively, within the meaning of regulation 6(1), 7 or 8, or a person who, is an employee or, is treated as an employee under regulation 5 or 5A, is incapable of work during a period of entitlement to statutory sick pay while

3.59

Statutory Sick Pay (Mariners, etc.) Regulations 1982

absent from Great Britain, his entitlement to statutory sick pay shall cease only if he fails to satisfy the conditions of entitlement under Part XI of the Contributions and Benefits Act notwithstanding that his employer ceases, during the period of entitlement, to be liable to pay, in respect of him, secondary Class 1 contributions under section 6 of the Contributions and Benefits Act or regulation 120 of the Contributions Regulations.]

AMENDMENT

1. Social Security Contributions, Statutory Maternity Pay and Statutory Sick Pay (Miscellaneous Amendments) Regulations 1996 (SI 1996/777), reg.3(4) (April 6, 1996).

DEFINITIONS

"employee"—see SSCBA 1992, s.163(1).
"employer"—*ibid.*
"period of entitlement"—*ibid.*
"the Contributions and Benefits Act"—see reg.1(2).
"the Contributions Regulations"—*ibid.*

GENERAL NOTE

3.60   See note to reg.5A.

Mariners—exception to regulation 10

3.61   **11.** [¹. . .]

AMENDMENT

1. Social Security Contributions, Statutory Maternity Pay and Statutory Sick Pay (Miscellaneous Amendments) Regulations 1996 (SI 1996/777), reg.3(5) (April 6, 1996).

Airmen—exception to regulation 10

3.62   **12.** [¹. . .]

AMENDMENT

1. Social Security Contributions, Statutory Maternity Pay and Statutory Sick Pay (Miscellaneous Amendments) Regulations 1996 (SI 1996/777), reg.3(6) (April 6, 1996).

Continental shelf—exception to regulation 10

3.63   **13.** [¹. . .]

AMENDMENT

1. Social Security Contributions, Statutory Maternity Pay and Statutory Sick Pay (Miscellaneous Amendments) Regulations 1996 (SI 1996/777), reg.3(7) (April 6, 1996).

Time for compliance with requirements of Part I and regulations

3.64   **14.** Where—
   (a) an employee is outside the United Kingdom;
   (b) Part I or regulations made there under require any act to be done forthwith or on the happening of a certain event or within a specified time; and

(c) because the employee is outside the United Kingdom he or his employer cannot comply with the requirement;

the employee or the employer, as the case may be, shall be deemed to have complied with it if he performs the act as soon as reasonably practicable.

DEFINITIONS

"employee"—see SSCBA 1992, s.163(1).
"employer"—*ibid*.
"Pt I"—see reg.1(2).

Statutory Sick Pay (Medical Evidence) Regulations 1985

(SI 1985/1604) (AS AMENDED)

The Secretary of State for Social Services, in exercise of the powers conferred upon him by section 17(2A) of the Social Security and Housing Benefits Act 1982, and of all other powers enabling him in that behalf, by this instrument, which contains only provisions consequential upon section 20 of the Social Security Act 1985 and regulations made under the aforesaid section 17(2A), makes the following regulations:

ARRANGEMENT OF ARTICLES

1. Citation, commencement and interpretation
2. Medical information

SCHEDULE 1—Part I—Rules
             Part II—Form of Doctor's Statement
             Part III—Notes
SCHEDULE 1A—Part I—Rules
              Part II—Form of Special Statement

Citation, commencement and interpretation

1.—(1) These regulations may be cited as the Statutory Sick Pay (Medical Evidence) Regulations 1985 and shall come into operation on 6th April 1986.

(2) In these regulations, unless the context otherwise requires

"the 1982 Act" means the Social Security and Housing Benefits Act 1982;

"signature" means, in relation to a statement given in accordance with these regulations, the name by which the person giving that statement is usually known (any name other than the surname being either in full or otherwise indicated) written by that person in his own handwriting; and "signed" shall be construed accordingly.

(3) [[1]. . .]

AMENDMENT

1. Social Security (Miscellaneous Provisions) Amendment Regulations 1992 (SI 1992/247), reg.6(2) (March 9, 1992).

Statutory Sick Pay (Medical Evidence) Regulations 1985

General Note

3.67   These Regulations and the rules in Sch.1 prescribe the form of the statement to be issued by a doctor advising an employee that he or she should refrain from work (or need not refrain from work) for a period up to six months, or longer in certain circumstances. Regulation 2(2) provides that medical information cannot be required in respect of an employee's first seven days in any spell of incapacity for work.

Medical information

3.68   **2.**—[¹(1) Medical information required under section 17(2) of the 1982 Act relating to incapacity for work shall be provided either—
  (a) in the form of a statement given by a doctor in accordance with the rules set out in Part I of Schedule 1 to these Regulations on the form set out in Part II of that Schedule; or
  (b) where the doctor—
    (i) has not given a statement under sub-paragraph (a) of this paragraph since the patient was examined and wishes to give such a statement but more than one day has passed since the examination; or
    (ii) advises that the patient should refrain from work on the basis of a written report from another doctor, set out in Part I of Schedule 1A to these Regulations on the form set out in Part II of that Schedule; or
  (c) by such other means as may be sufficient in the circumstances of any particular case.]
(2) An employee shall not be required under section 17(2) of the 1982 Act to provide medical information in respect of the first 7 days in any spell of incapacity for work; and for this purpose "spell of incapacity" means a continuous period of incapacity for work which is immediately preceded by a day on which the claimant either worked or was not incapable of work.

Amendment

1. Social Security (Miscellaneous Provisions) Amendment Regulations 1992 (SI 1992/247), reg.6(3) (March 9, 1992).

SCHEDULE [¹]   Regulation 1(3)

Part I

Rules

3.69   1. In these rules, unless the context otherwise requires

  "patient" means the person in respect of whom a statement is given in accordance with these rules;
  "doctor" means a registered medical practitioner not being the patient;
  "2 weeks" means any period of 14 consecutive days.

  2. The doctor's statement shall be in the form set out in Part II of this Schedule.
  [² 3 Where the patient—
    (a) is on the list of a person providing primary medical services under the National Health Service Act 1977 or the National Health Service (Scotland) Act 1978 and is being attended by a doctor performing such services; or

(SI 1985/1604, Sch.1) (as amended)

 (b) is on the list of a doctor, or list held jointly by two or more doctors performing personal medical services in connection with a pilot scheme under the National Health Service (Primary Care) Act 1997 and is being attended by such a doctor,

the doctor's statement shall be on the form provided by the Secretary of State for the purpose and shall be signed by the attending doctor.]

 4. In any other case, the doctor's statement shall be on a form provided by the Secretary of State for the purpose and shall be signed by the doctor attending the patient.

 5. Every doctor's statement shall be completed in ink or other indelible substance and shall contain the following particulars:—

 (a) the patient's name;
 (b) the date of the examination on which the doctor's statement is based;
 (c) the diagnosis of the patient's disorder in respect of which the doctor is advising the patient to refrain from work or, as the case may be, which has caused the patient's absence from work;
 (d) the date on which the doctor's statement is given;
 (e) the address of the doctor,

and shall bear, opposite the words "Doctor's signature", the signature of the doctor making the statement written after there have been entered the patient's name and the doctor's diagnosis.

 6. Subject to rules 7 and 8 below, the diagnosis of the disorder in respect of which the doctor is advising the patient to refrain from work or, as the case may be, which has caused the patient's absence from work shall be specified as precisely as the doctor's knowledge of the patient's condition at the time of the examination permits.

 7. The diagnosis may be specified less precisely where, in the doctor's opinion, a disclosure of the precise disorder would be prejudicial to the patient's well-being, or to the patient's position with his employer.

 8. In the case of an initial examination by a doctor in respect of a disorder stated by the patient to have caused incapacity for work, where—

 (a) there are no clinical signs of that disorder, and
 (b) in the doctor's opinion, the patient need not refrain from work,

instead of specifying a diagnosis "unspecified" may be entered.

 9. A doctor's statement must be given on a date not later than one day after the date of the examination on which it is based, and no further doctor's statement based on the same examination shall be furnished other than a doctor's statement by way of replacement of an original which has been lost or mislaid, in which case it shall be clearly marked "duplicate".

 10. Where, in the doctor's opinion, the patient will become fit to resume work on a day not later than 2 weeks after the date of the examination on which the doctor's statement is based, the doctor's statement shall specify that day.

 11. Subject to rules 12 and 13 below, the doctor's statement shall specify the minimum period during which, in the doctor's opinion, the patient should, by reason of his disorder, refrain from work.

 12. The period specified shall begin on the date of the examination on which the doctor's statement is based and shall not exceed 6 months unless the patient has, on the advice of a doctor, refrained from work for at least 6 months immediately preceding that date.

 13. Where—

 (a) the patient has, on the advice of a doctor, refrained from work for at least 6 months immediately preceding the date of the examination on which the doctor's statement is based; and
 (b) in the doctor's opinion, it will be necessary for the patient to refrain from work for the foreseeable future,

instead of specifying a period, the doctor may, having regard to the circumstances of the particular case, enter, after the word "until", the words "further notice".

 14. The Notes set out in Part III of this Schedule shall accompany the form of doctor's statement provided by the Secretary of State.

Statutory Sick Pay (Medical Evidence) Regulations 1985

PART II

FORM OF DOCTOR'S STATEMENT

DOCTOR'S STATEMENT

3.70 In confidence to

Mr/Mrs/Miss
....

I examined you today/yesterday and advised you that:
(a) you need not refrain from work   *(b)* you should refrain from work

for ....

OR until

Diagnosis of your disorder
causing absence from work ....

Doctor's remarks

Doctor's signature   Date of signing

PART III

NOTES

3.71 The following notes shall accompany the form of doctor's statement provided by the Secretary of State:
On the doctor's statement:
(1) After the words "you should refrain from work for", the period entered must not exceed 6 months unless the patient has, on the advice of a doctor, already refrained from work for a continuous period of 6 months.
(2) After the words "you should refrain from work until"—
  (a) if the patient is being given a date when he can return to work, the date entered should not be more than 2 weeks after the date of the examination;
  (b) if the patient has already been incapable of work for at least 6 months and recovery of capacity for work in the foreseeable future is not expected, "further notice" may be entered.

AMENDMENTS

1. Social Security (Miscellaneous Provisions) Amendment Regulations 1992 (SI 1992/247), reg.6(4) (March 9, 1992).

(SI 1985/1604, Sch.1) (as amended)

2. General Medical Services and Personal Medical Services Transitional and Consequential Provisions Order 2004 (SI 2004/865), art.119 and Sch.1, para.3 (April 1, 2004).

GENERAL NOTE

Paragraph 3 of Pt I to this Schedule is phrased in a slightly different form so far as Wales is concerned: see General Medical Services Transitional and Consequential Provisions (Wales) (No.2) Order 2004 (SI 2004/1016 (W.113), art.95 and Sch.1, para.3.

3.72

SCHEDULE 1A [¹**Regulation 2(1)**

PART I

RULES

1. In these rules, unless the context otherwise requires—

3.73

"patient" means the person in respect of whom a statement is given in accordance with these rules;
"doctor" means a registered medical practitioner not being the patient;
"special statement" means the form prescribed in Part II of this Schedule.

2. Where a doctor advises a patient to refrain from work on the basis of a written report which he has received from another doctor or where a doctor has not issued a statement since the claimant was examined and he wishes to issue a statement more than a day after the examination he shall use the special statement.

3. The special statement shall be completed in the manner described in paragraph 5 of Part I to Schedule 1.

4. Subject to rules 5 and 6 below, the diagnosis of the patient's disorder in respect of which the doctor is advising the patient to refrain from work or as the case may be, which has caused the patient's absence from work shall be specified as precisely as the doctor's knowledge of the patient's condition permits.

5. The diagnosis may be specified less precisely where in the doctor's opinion, a disclosure of the precise disorder would be prejudicial to the patient's well being, or to the patient's position with his employer.

6. In a case of a disorder stated by the patient to have caused incapacity for work, where—
   (a) no clinical signs have been found of that disorder; and
   (b) in the doctor's opinion, the patient need not refrain from work, "unspecified" may be entered.

7. Part B of the special statement must only be given on a date not later than one month after the date of the written report on which the special statement is based and that part shall only be used where the patient is being advised to refrain from work for a specified period of not more than one month.

Statutory Sick Pay (Medical Evidence) Regulations 1985

[¹PART II

FORM OF SPECIAL STATEMENT

3.74

FOR SOCIAL SECURITY AND
STATUTORY SICK PAY
PURPOSES ONLY

Special Statement
by the Doctor

In confidence to

Mr/Mrs/Miss/Ms ....

(A) I examined you on the

(B) I have not examined you but, on the basis of a recent written report from—

following dates ....

Doctor .... (Name if known)

....

of

....

and advised you that you should refrain from work

....

From .... To ....

.... (Address)

Diagnosis of your disorder
causing absence from work

I have advised you that you should refrain
From work for/until

....

....

Doctor's remarks

Doctor's
signature

Date of signing

The special circumstances in which this form may be used are described in the handbook "Medical Evidence for Social Security and Statutory Sick Pay Purposes".

AMENDMENT

1. Social Security (Miscellaneous Provisions) Amendment Regulations 1992 (SI 1992/247), reg.6(5) and Sch.2 (March 9, 1992).

(SI 1991/589) (as amended)

Statutory Sick Pay (National Health Service Employees) Regulations 1991

(SI 1991/589) (AS AMENDED)

The Secretary of State for Social Security in exercise of the powers conferred by sections 26(1) and (5A), 45(1) and 47 of the Social Security and Housing Benefits Act 1982 and of all other powers enabling him in that behalf, by this instrument, which contains only regulations consequential upon paragraph 16 of Schedule 6 to the Social Security Act 1990, hereby makes the following Regulations:

ARRANGEMENT OF REGULATIONS

1. Citation, commencement and interpretation
2. Treatment of more than one contract of employment as one contract
3. Notification of election
4. Provision of information by employees
5. Treatment of two or more employers as one
6. Time for which an election is to have effect

Citation, commencement and interpretation

1.—(1) These Regulations may be cited as the Statutory Sick Pay (National Health Service Employees) Regulations 1991 and shall come into force on 1st April 1991.

(2) In these Regulations, a "health authority" [²shall in relation to Wales have the same meaning it has in section 8] of the National Health Service Act 1977, and in relation to Scotland mean the health board within the meaning of section 2 of the National Health Service (Scotland) Act 1978.

[¹(3) In these Regulations, "Primary Care Trust" means a Primary Care Trust established under section 16A of the National Health Service Act 1977.]

[²(4) In these Regulations, "Strategic Health Authority" means a Strategic Health Authority established under section 8 of the National Health Service Act 1977.]

[³(5) In these Regulations, a reference to "NHS trust" shall be construed to include a reference to an NHS foundation trust within the meaning of section 1(1) of the Health and Social Care (Community Health and Standards) Act 2003 where the application for authorisation to become an NHS foundation trust was made by an NHS trust.]

AMENDMENTS

1. Health Act 1999 (Supplementary, Consequential etc. Provisions) (No.2) Order 2000 (SI 2000/694), art.3 and Sch., para.2(2) (April 1, 2000).
2. National Health Service Reform and Health Care Professions Act 2002 (Supplementary, Consequential etc. Provisions) Regulations 2002 (SI 2002/2469), reg.4 and Sch.1, Pt 2, para.50 (October 1, 2002).
3. Health and Social Care (Community Health and Standards) Act 2003 (Supplementary and Consequential Provision) (NHS Foundation Trusts) Order 2004 (SI 2004/696), art.3(17) and Sch.17 (April 1, 2004).

Statutory Sick Pay (National Health Service Employees) Regulations 1991

Treatment of more than one contract of employment as one contract

3.77   **2.** Where, in consequence of the establishment of one or more National Health Service Trusts under Part I of the National Health Service and Community Care Act 1990 or the National Health Service (Scotland) Act 1978, a person's contract of employment is treated by a scheme under that Part or Act as divided so as to constitute two or more contracts, [¹or where an order under paragraph 23(1) of Schedule 5A to the National Health Service Act 1977 provides that a woman's contract of employment is so divided,] he may elect for all those contracts to be treated as one contract for the purposes of Part I of the Social Security and Housing Benefits Act 1982.

AMENDMENT

1. Health Act 1999 (Supplementary, Consequential etc. Provisions) (No.2) Order 2000 (SI 2000/694), art.3 and Sch., para.2(3) (April 1, 2000).

Notification of election

3.78   **3.** A person who makes an election under regulation 2 above shall give written notification of that election to each of his employers under the two or more contracts of service mentioned in that regulation, before the end of the fourth day of incapacity for work in the period of incapacity for work in relation to a contract of service with the employer with whom this day first occurs.

Provision of information by employees

3.79   **4.** A person who makes an election under regulation 2 above shall, as soon as is reasonably practicable after giving notice of that election, provide each of his employers under the two or more contracts of service mentioned in that regulation with the following information—
   (a) the name and address of each of his employers; and
   (b) the date his employment with each of those employers commenced; and
   (c) details of his earnings during the relevant period and for this purpose "earnings" and "relevant period" have the same meanings as they have for the purposes of section 26(2) of the Social Security and Housing Benefits Act 1982.

Treatment of two or more employers as one

3.80   **5.** The employer to be regarded for the purposes of statutory sick pay as the employee's employer under the one contract where 2 or more contacts of service are treated as one in accordance with regulation 2 above, shall be—
   [¹(a) in the case of a person whose contract of employment is treated by a scheme under Part I of the National Health Service and Community Care Act 1990 or the National Health Service (Scotland) Act 1978 as divided—
       (i) the Health Authority or Primary Care Trust from which the employee was transferred, in a case where any one of the employee's contracts of service is with that Health Authority or Primary Care Trust; or

(SI 1991/589, reg.5) (as amended)

    (ii) the first NHS trust to which a contract of service was transferred in a case where none of the employee's contracts of service are with the Health Authority or Primary Care Trust from which he was transferred;

or

(b) in the case of a person whose contract of employment is divided as provided by an order under paragraph 23(1) of Schedule 5A to the National Health Service Act 1977—
    (i) the [²Strategic Health Authority], NHS trust or Primary Care Trust from which the employee was transferred, in a case where any one of the employee's contracts of service is with that body; or
    (ii) the first Primary Care Trust to which a contract of service was transferred in a case where none of the employee's contracts of service are with the body from which he was transferred.]

AMENDMENTS

1. Health Act 1999 (Supplementary, Consequential etc. Provisions) (No.2) Order 2000 (SI 2000/694), art.3 and Sch., para.2(4) (April 1, 2000).
2. National Health Service Reform and Health Care Professions Act 2002 (Supplementary, Consequential etc. Provisions) Regulations 2002 (SI 2002/2469), reg.6 and Sch.3 (October 1, 2002).

Time for which an election is to have effect

6. An election made under regulation 2 shall lapse at the end of the period of incapacity for work in relation to the contract of service with the employer mentioned in regulation 5.

3.81

Statutory Sick Pay Percentage Threshold Order 1995

(SI 1995/512)

Whereas a draft of the following Order was laid before Parliament in accordance with the provisions of section 3(3) of the Statutory Sick Pay Act 1994 and approved by resolution of each House of Parliament:

3.82

Now, therefore, the Secretary of State for Social Security, in exercise of the powers conferred by sections 159A and 175(3) and (4) of the Social Security Contributions and Benefits Act 1992 and of all other powers enabling him in that behalf, hereby makes the following Order:

Art.1. Citation, commencement and interpretation
Art.2. Right of employer to recover statutory sick pay
Art.3. Recovery by deduction from contributions payments
Art.4. Recovery from the Secretary of State
Art.5. Repeals and revocations
Art.6. Consequential amendments [*omitted*]

Citation, commencement and interpretation

1.—(1) This Order may be cited as the Statutory Sick Pay Percentage Threshold Order 1995 and shall come into force on 6th April 1995.

3.83

(2) In this Order, unless the context otherwise requires, "income tax month" means the period beginning on the 6th day of any calendar month and ending on the 5th day of the following calendar month.

(3) A reference in this Order to a payment of statutory sick pay shall not include any such payment made in respect of a day of incapacity for work before the coming into force of this Order.

(4) Unless the context otherwise requires, any reference in this Order to a numbered article is a reference to the article bearing that number in this Order and any reference in an article to a numbered paragraph is a reference to the paragraph of that article bearing that number.

General Note

3.84 This Order makes provision for employers to recover payments of statutory sick pay where such payments amount to more than 13 per cent of their liability for Class 1 contributions payments in any income tax month. Consequently, this facility only arises where there is widespread sickness absence in a workplace. Article 2 sets out how the amount an employer may recover is to be determined. Article 3 provides for the amount determined under art.2 to be recovered by deduction from Class 1 National Insurance contributions payments. Article 4 provides for repayment by or on behalf of HMRC to employers where the amount they are entitled to deduct exceeds their contributions payments. Article 5 repeals and revokes the former enactments which provided for recovery of statutory sick pay by small employers. Article 6 (not included here) makes amendments to various enactments which are consequential on the repeals and revocations in art.5.

Right of employer to recover statutory sick pay

3.85 **2.**—(1) Subject to paragraph (2) an employer is entitled to recover in accordance with articles 3 and 4 the amount, if any, by which the payments of statutory sick pay made by him in any income tax month exceed 13 per cent. of the amount of his liability for contributions payments in respect of that income tax month.

(2) For the purposes of calculating the amount an employer is entitled to recover under paragraph (1), there shall be excluded any payment of statutory sick pay which was not made—
  (a) in the income tax month in which he received notice, in accordance with regulation 7 of the Statutory Sick Pay (General) Regulations 1982, of the day or days of incapacity for work to which the payment related;
  (b) in a case where it would have been impracticable to make the payment in that income tax month in view of the employer's methods of accounting for and paying remuneration, in the following income tax month; or
  (c) in a case where a decision had been made by an adjudication officer, social security appeal tribunal or Commissioner that the employee was entitled to that payment, within the time-limits set out in regulation 9 of those Regulations.

Definition

"income tax month"—see art.1(2).

Recovery by deduction from contributions payments

3.86 **3.**—(1) An employer may recover an amount determined in accordance with article 2 in respect of any income tax month by making one or more deductions from his contributions payments for that or any following income

tax month within 6 years from the end of the tax year in which he became entitled to recover that amount, except where and insofar as—
  (a) that amount has been repaid to him by or on behalf of the Secretary of State under article 4; or
  (b) he has made a request in writing under article 4 that that amount be repaid to him, and he has not received notification by or on behalf of the Secretary of State that the request is refused.

(2) A deduction from contributions payments made in accordance with paragraph (1) shall be disregarded for the purposes of determining whether an employer has discharged any liability of his in respect of Class 1 contributions.

DEFINITION

"income tax month"—see art.1(2).

Recovery from the Secretary of State

4.—(1) If the amount which an employer is or would otherwise be entitled to deduct under article 3 exceeds the amount of his contributions payments in respect of earnings paid in an income tax month, and the Secretary of State is satisfied that that is so, then provided that the employer has requested him in writing to do so, there shall be repaid to the employer by or on behalf of the Secretary of State such amount as the employer was unable to deduct.

(2) If an employer is not liable for any contributions payments in an income tax month but would otherwise be entitled to deduct an amount under article 3, and the Secretary of State is satisfied that that is so, then provided the employer has in writing requested him to do so, that amount shall be repaid to the employer by or on behalf of the Secretary of State.

DEFINITION

"income tax month"—see art.1(2).

GENERAL NOTE

The Secretary of State's functions under this article were transferred to the Board of the Inland Revenue (now HMRC) by s.1(2) of, and Sch.2 to, the Social Security Contributions (Transfer of Functions, etc.) Act 1999.

Repeals and revocations

5. Subject to the savings made by regulations under section 159A(4) of the Social Security Contributions and Benefits Act 1992—
  (a) sections 158 and 159 of the Social Security Contributions and Benefits Act 1992 shall be repealed; and
  (b) the Statutory Sick Pay (Compensation of Employers) and Miscellaneous Provisions Regulations 1983 and the Statutory Sick Pay (Small Employers' Relief) Regulations 1991 shall be revoked.

Consequential amendments

6. [*omitted.*]

Statutory Sick Pay and Statutory Maternity Pay (Decisions) Regulations 1999

(SI 1999/776)

The Secretary of State for Social Security, in exercise of powers conferred by section 20(3) of the Social Security Administration Act 1992, sections 8(1)(f) and 25(3) of the Social Security Contributions (Transfer of Functions, etc.) Act 1999 and of all other powers enabling him in that behalf, with the concurrence of the Commissioners of Inland Revenue, hereby makes the following Regulations:

ARRANGEMENT OF REGULATIONS

3.91
1. Citation, commencement and interpretation
2. Application for the determination of any issue arising as to, or in connection with, entitlement to statutory sick pay or statutory maternity pay
3. Applications in connection with statutory sick pay or statutory maternity pay
4. Revocation of regulation 20 of the Social Security (Adjudication) Regulations 1995

Citation, commencement and interpretation

3.92
1.—(1) These Regulations may be cited as the Statutory Sick Pay and Statutory Maternity Pay (Decisions) Regulations 1999 and shall come into force on 1st April 1999.

(2) In these Regulations—
(a) "the Contributions and Benefits Act" means the Social Security Contributions and Benefits Act 1992;
(b) "employee" and "employer" have, in relation to—
   (i) statutory sick pay, the meanings given by section 163(1) of the Contributions and Benefits Act;
   (ii) statutory maternity pay, the meanings given by section 171(1) of the Contributions and Benefits Act.

Application for the determination of any issue arising as to, or in connection with, entitlement to statutory sick pay or statutory maternity pay

3.93
2.—(1) An application for the determination of any issue arising as to, or in connection with, entitlement to statutory sick pay or statutory maternity pay may be submitted to an officer of the Board by—
(a) the Secretary of State; or
(b) the employee concerned.

(2) Such an issue shall be decided by an officer of the Board only on the basis of such an application or on his own initiative.

DEFINITION

"employee"—see reg.1(2).

(SI 1999/776, s.3)

Applications in connection with statutory sick pay or statutory maternity pay

3.—(1) An application for the determination of any issue referred to in regulation 2 above shall be made only in writing, in a form approved for the purpose by the Board, or in such other manner, being in writing, as an officer of the Board may accept as sufficient in the circumstances.

(2) Where such an application is made by an employee, it shall—
(a) be delivered or sent to an office of the Board within 6 months of the earliest day in respect of which entitlement to statutory sick pay or statutory maternity pay is in issue;
(b) state the period in respect of which entitlement to statutory sick pay or statutory maternity pay is in issue; and
(c) state the grounds (if any) on which the applicant's employer has denied liability for statutory sick pay or statutory maternity pay in respect of the period specified in the application.

DEFINITION

"employer"—see reg.1(2).

Revocation of regulation 20 of the Social Security (Adjudication) Regulations 1995

4. Regulation 20 of the Social Security (Adjudication) Regulations 1995 is hereby revoked.

3.94

3.95

PART IV

STATUTORY MATERNITY PAY

Statutory Maternity Pay (General) Regulations 1986

(SI 1986/1960) (AS AMENDED)

The Secretary of State for Social Services, in exercise of the powers conferred by sections 46(4), (7) and (8), 47(1), (3), (6) and (7), 48(3) and (6), 50(1), (2), (4) and (5), 51(1)(g), (k), (n) and (r) and (4), 54(1), 83(1) and 84(1) of, and paragraphs 6, 8 and 12(3) of Schedule 4 to, the Social Security Act 1986(a), and of all other powers enabling him in that behalf, by this instrument, which contains only regulations made under the sections of the Social Security Act 1986 specified above and provisions consequential upon those sections and before the end of a period of 12 months from the commencement of those sections, makes the following regulations:

ARRANGEMENT OF REGULATIONS

PART I

INTRODUCTION

1. Citation, commencement and interpretation 4.1

PART II

ENTITLEMENT

2. Maternity pay period
3. Contract of service ended for the purpose of avoiding liability for statutory maternity pay
4. Modification of entitlement provisions
5. Treatment of more than one contract of service as one
6. Prescribed rate of statutory maternity pay
7. Liability of Secretary of State to pay statutory maternity pay
8. Work after confinement
9. No liability to pay statutory maternity pay
9A. Working for not more than 10 days in the Maternity Pay Period
10. Death of woman

PART III

CONTINUOUS EMPLOYMENT AND NORMAL WORKING HOURS

11. Continuous employment
12. Continuous employment and unfair dismissal
13. Continuous employment and stoppages of work
14. Change of employer

15. Reinstatement after service with the armed forces
16. Normal working weeks
16A. Meaning of "week"

Part IV

General Provisions

17. Meaning of "employee"
18. Treatment of two or more employers as one
19. Payments to be treated as contractual remuneration
20. Meaning of "earnings"
21. Normal weekly earnings
21A. *(repealed)*
21B. Effect of maternity allowance on statutory maternity pay

Part V

Administration

22. Evidence of expected week of confinement
23. Notice of absence from work
24. Notification of employment after confinement
25. Provision of information in connection with determination of questions
25A. Provision of information relating to claims for certain other benefits
26. Records to be maintained by employers
26A. Production of employer's records

Part VI

Payment

27. Payment of statutory maternity pay
28. Rounding to avoid fractional amounts
29. Time when statutory maternity pay is to be paid
30. Payments by the Secretary of State
31. Persons unable to act

Part VII

Offences

32. *(repealed)*

(SI 1986/1960, reg.1) (as amended)

Part I

Introduction

Citation, commencement and interpretation

1.—(1) These regulations may be cited as the Statutory Maternity Pay (General) Regulations 1986 and shall come into operation in the case of regulations 1, 22 and 23 on 15th March, 1987, and in the case of the remainder of the regulations on 6th April, 1987.

(2) In these regulations, unless the context otherwise requires—
"the 1975 Act" means the Social Security Act 1975;
"the 1978 Act" means the Employment Protection (Consolidation) Act 1978;
"the 1986 Act" means the Social Security Act 1986.
[1"the Contributions and Benefits Act" means the Social Security Contributions and Benefits Act 1992.]
[2"statutory maternity leave" means ordinary maternity leave and any additional maternity leave under, respectively, sections 71 and 73 of the Employment Rights Act 1996.]

(3) Unless the context otherwise requires, any references in these regulations to—
(a) a numbered regulation is a reference to the regulation bearing that number in these regulations and any reference in a regulation to a numbered paragraph is a reference to the paragraph of that regulation bearing that number;
(b) any provision made by or contained in an enactment or instrument shall be construed as a reference to that provision as amended or extended by any enactment or instrument and as including a reference to any provision which it re-enacts or replaces, or which may reenact or replace it, with or without modifications.

Amendments

1. Social Security (Miscellaneous Provisions) Amendment (No.2) Regulations 1992 (SI 1992/2595), reg.12 (November 16, 1992).
2. Statutory Maternity Pay (General) (Amendment) Regulations 2005 (SI 2005/729), reg.2 (April 6, 2005).

General Note

The text of these Regulations pre-dates SSCBA 1992 and was not amended at the time of the SSCBA 1992 to reflect the provisions in the 1992 Act. The Regulations remain in force, of course, by virtue of s.17(2)(b) of the Interpretation Act 1978. As a result, regulations which survive unamended from the original text refer to the SSA 1975 and SSA 1986, whilst post-1992 amendments refer to the parallel provisions in SSCBA 1992. References to the 1975 Act should therefore be read as referring to SSCBA 1992, and those to Pt V of the SSA 1986 as referring to Pt XII of the SSCBA 1992.

Statutory Maternity Pay (General) Regulations 1986

Part II

Entitlement

The Maternity Pay Period

4.4 [¹ **2.** —(1) Subject to paragraphs (3) to (5), where—
(a) a woman gives notice to her employer of the date from which she expects his liability to pay her statutory maternity pay to begin; and
(b) in conformity with that notice ceases to work for him in a week which is later than the 12th week before the expected week of confinement,
the first day of the maternity pay period shall be the day on which she expects his liability to pay her statutory maternity pay to begin in conformity with that notice provided that day is not later than the day immediately following the day on which she is confined.
(2) The maternity pay period shall be a period of 39 consecutive weeks.
(3) In a case where a woman is confined—
(a) before the 11th week before the expected week of confinement; or
(b) after the 12th week before the expected week of confinement and the confinement occurs on a day which precedes that mentioned in a notice given to her employer as being the day on which she expects his liability to pay her statutory maternity pay to begin,
section 165 of the Contributions and Benefits Act shall have effect so that the first day of the maternity pay period shall be the day following the day on which she is so confined.
(4) In a case where a woman is absent from work wholly or partly because of pregnancy or confinement on any day—
(a) which falls on or after the beginning of the 4th week before the expected week of confinement; but
(b) not later than the day immediately following the day on which she is confined,
the first day of the maternity pay period shall be the day following the day on which she is so absent.
(5) In a case where a woman leaves her employment—
(a) at any time falling after the beginning of the 11th week before the expected week of confinement and before the start of the maternity pay period, but
(b) not later than the day on which she is confined,
the first day of the maternity pay period shall be the day following the day on which she leaves her employment.]

Amendment

1. Statutory Maternity Pay, Social Security (Maternity Allowance) and Social Security (Overlapping Benefits) (Amendment) Regulations 2006 (SI 2006/2379), reg.3(2) (October 1, 2006).

General Note

4.5 This regulation was substantially recast with a new version substituted with effect from October 1, 2006 which applies in relation to women whose expected week of

(SI 1986/1960, reg.2) (as amended)

confinement falls on or after April 1, 2007. The new version of the regulation was prompted by the enactment of the Work and Families Act 2006, which improved the SMP scheme. There are two main differences between the current and previous versions of the regulation.

First, SMP is now payable for 39 weeks as opposed to the 26 weeks that applied before October 1, 2006 (para.(2)); note that before November 24, 2002, the previous maximum period had been 18 weeks.

Secondly, before October 1, 2006 the maternity pay period for SMP purposes started from the week following the week that the woman ceased work in accordance with the requisite notice given to her employer. In practice this meant the Sunday following the day she stopped work in accordance with the notice. The new rule enables the maternity pay period to start on any day of the week as specified by the woman in her notice to the employer. This allows the start of the maternity pay period to match the start of the woman's maternity leave. Accordingly the general rule for determining the start of the maternity pay period is set out in para.(1). There are then a number of further special cases detailed in paras(3)–(5). Paragraph (3) covers those situations where the woman gives birth early. Paragraph (4) makes special provision to deal with the situation where the woman stops working because of a pregnancy-related absence in the four weeks before the expected week of confinement. Finally, para.(5) covers women who leave their employment after the start of the 11th week before the expected week of confinement, but before the maternity pay period commences and not later than day of actual confinement.

Contract of service ended for the purpose of avoiding liability for statutory maternity pay

3.—(1) A former employer shall be liable to make payments of statutory maternity pay to any woman who was employed by him for a continuous period of at least eight weeks and whose contract of service with him was brought to an end by the former employer solely or mainly for the purpose of avoiding liability for statutory maternity pay.

(2) In order to determine the amount payable by the former employer—
(a) the woman shall be deemed for the purposes of Part V of the 1986 Act to have been employed by him from the date her employment with him ended until the end of the week immediately preceding the 14th week before the expected week of confinement on the same terms and conditions of employment as those subsisting immediately before her employment ended; and
(b) her normal weekly earnings for the period of 8 weeks immediately preceding the 14th week before the expected week of confinement shall for those purposes be calculated by reference to her normal weekly earnings for the period of 8 weeks ending with the last day in respect of which she was paid under her former contract of service.

4.6

GENERAL NOTE

This regulation, made under SSCBA 1992, s.164(8), sets out the principles governing entitlement to statutory maternity pay where an employer dismisses a woman with a view to avoiding liability to pay statutory maternity pay. In order for this provision to apply, the woman must have been continuously employed for at least eight weeks (para.(1)). Such action will also constitute an automatically unfair dismissal under Employment Rights Act 1999, s.99 and an act of sex discrimination.

4.7

Statutory Maternity Pay (General) Regulations 1986

Modification of entitlement provisions

4.—(1) [¹. . .]

(2) In relation to a woman in employed earner's employment who was confined before the 14th week before the expected week of confinement [¹section 164(2)(a) and (b) of the Contributions and Benefits Act] shall have effect as if for the conditions there set out, there were substituted the conditions that—
  (a) she would but for her confinement have been in employed earner's employment with an employer for a continuous period of at least 26 weeks ending with the week immediately preceding the 14th week before the expected week of confinement; and
  (b) her normal weekly earnings for the period of 8 weeks ending with the week immediately preceding the week of her confinement are not less than the lower earnings limit in force [¹under section 5(1)(a) of the Contributions and Benefits Act] immediately before the commencement of the week of her confinement.

[¹(3) In relation to a woman to whom paragraph (2) applies, section 166 of the Contributions and Benefits Act shall be modified so that subsection (2) has effect as if the reference to the period of 8 weeks immediately preceding the 14th week before the expected week of confinement was a reference to the period of 8 weeks immediately preceding the week in which her confinement occurred.]

AMENDMENT

1. Social Security Maternity Benefits and Statutory Sick Pay (Amendment) Regulations 1994 (SI 1994/1367), reg.3 (June 11, 1994).

GENERAL NOTE

Para. (2)

If the baby is born either before or in the qualifying week, statutory maternity pay is still payable so long as the woman would have been employed for 26 weeks by the end of the qualifying week, on the assumption that the baby had not in fact been born early.

Treatment of more than one contract of service as one

5. Where 2 or more contracts of service exist concurrently between one employer and one employee, they shall be treated as one for the purposes of Part V of the 1986 Act, except where, by virtue of regulation 11 of the Social Security (Contributions) Regulations 1979 the earnings from those contracts of service are not aggregated for the purposes of earnings-related contributions.

[¹Prescribed rate of statutory maternity pay

6. The rate of statutory maternity pay prescribed under section 166(1)(b) of the Contributions and Benefits Act is a weekly rate of [²£112.75.]

AMENDMENTS

1. Social Security, Statutory Maternity Pay and Statutory Sick Pay (Miscellaneous Amendments) Regulations 2002 (SI 2002/2690), reg.3 (April 6, 2003).
2. Social Security Benefits Up-rating Order 2007 (SI 2007/88), art.10 (April 1, 2007).

(SI 1986/1960, reg. 7) (as amended)

Liability of Secretary of State to pay Statutory Maternity Pay

7.—(1) Where—
(a) an adjudicating authority has determined that an employer is liable to make payments of statutory maternity pay to a woman; and
(b) the time for appealing against that determination has expired; and
(c) no appeal against the determination has been lodged or leave to appeal against the determination is required and has been refused, then for any week in respect of which the employer was liable to make payments of statutory maternity pay but did not do so, and for any subsequent weeks in the maternity pay period the liability to make those payments shall, notwithstanding section 46(3) of the 1986 Act, be that of the Secretary of State and not the employer.

(2) In paragraph (1) adjudicating authority means, as the case may be, the Chief or any other adjudication officer, a Social Security Appeal Tribunal or the Chief or any other Social Security Commissioner.

(3) Liability to make payments of statutory maternity pay shall, notwithstanding section 46(3) of the 1986 Act, be a liability of the Secretary of State and not the employer as from the week in which the employer first becomes insolvent until the end of the maternity pay period.

(4) For the purposes of paragraph (3) an employer shall be taken to be insolvent if, and only if—
(a) in England and Wales—
  (i) he has been adjudged bankrupt or has made a composition or arrangement with his creditors;
  (ii) he has died and his estate falls to be administered in accordance with an order under section 421 of the Insolvency Act 1986; or
  (iii) where an employer is a company, a winding-up order [1. . .] is made or a resolution for voluntary winding-up is passed with respect to it [1or it enter administration], or a receiver or manager of its undertaking is duly appointed, or possession is taken by or on behalf of the holders of any debentures secured by a floating charge, of any property of the company comprised in or subject to the charge or a voluntary arrangement proposed for the purposes of Part 1 of the Insolvency Act 1986 is approved under that Part;
(b) in Scotland—
  (i) an award of sequestration is made on his estate or he executes a trust deed for his creditors or enters into a composition contract;
  (ii) he has died and a judicial factor appointed under section 1A of the Judicial Factors (Scotland) Act 1889 is required by that section to divide his insolvent estate among his creditors; or
  (iii) where the employer is a company, a winding-up order [1. . .] is made or a resolution for voluntary winding-up is passed with respect to it [1or it enter administration] or a receiver of its undertaking is duly appointed or a voluntary arrangement proposed for the purposes of Part 1 of the Insolvency Act 1986 is approved under that Part.

AMENDMENT

1. Enterprise Act 2002 (Insolvency) Order 2003 (SI 2003/2096), art.5 and Sch.2, para.44 (September 15, 2003).

GENERAL NOTE

4.13   The functions under this regulation were transferred from the Secretary of State for Social Security to the Board of the Inland Revenue (now HMRC) under s.1(2) of and Sch.2 to the Social Security (Transfer of Functions, etc.) Act 1999. References in this regulation to SSA 1986, s.46(3) should now be read as referring to SSCBA 1992, s.164(3).

Work after. confinement

4.14   **8.**—(1) Where in the week immediately preceding the 14th week before the expected week of confinement a woman had two or more employers but one or more of them were not liable to make payments to her of statutory maternity pay ("non-liable employer"), section 47(6) of the 1986 Act shall not apply in respect of any week after the week of confinement but within the maternity pay period in which she works only for a non-liable employer.

(2) Where after her confinement a woman—
(a) works for an employer who is not liable to pay her statutory maternity pay and is not a non-liable employer, but
(b) before the end of her maternity pay period ceases to work for that employer, the person who before she commenced work was liable to make payments of statutory maternity pay to her shall, notwithstanding section 46 of the 1986 Act, not be liable to make such payments to her for any weeks in the maternity pay period after she ceases work.

GENERAL NOTE

4.15   References in this regulation to SSA 1986, ss.46 and 47(6) should now be read as referring to SSCBA 1992, ss.164 and 165(6).

No liability to pay statutory maternity pay

4.16   **9.** Notwithstanding the provisions of section 46(1) of the 1986 Act, no liability to make payments of statutory maternity pay to a woman shall arise in respect of a week within the maternity pay period for any part of which she is detained in legal custody or sentenced to a term of imprisonment (except where the sentence is suspended), or of any subsequent week within that period.

GENERAL NOTE

4.17   The reference in this regulation to SSA 1986, s.46(1) should now be read as referring to SSCBA 1992, s.164(1).

[¹ Working for not more than 10 days in the Maternity Pay Period

4.18   **9A.** In a case where a woman does any work under a contract of service with her employer on any day, but for not more than 10 days (whether consecutive or not), during her maternity pay period, statutory maternity pay shall continue to be payable to the employee by the employer.]

AMENDMENT

1. Statutory Maternity Pay, Social Security (Maternity Allowance) and Social Security (Overlapping Benefits) (Amendment) Regulations 2006 (SI 2006/2379), reg.3(3) (October 1, 2006).

(SI 1986/1960, reg.9A) (as amended)

General Note

This provision applies in relation to women whose expected week of confinement falls on or after April 1, 2007. It enables a woman to work for up to 10 days under her contract during the statutory maternity pay period for the employer paying her SMP and still retain her SMP for that week—previously a week's SMP was lost for any week in which such work was undertaken.

Death of woman

10. An employer shall not be liable to make payments of statutory maternity pay in respect of a woman for any week within the maternity pay period which falls after the week in which she dies.

Part III

Continuous Employment and Normal Working Hours

Continuous employment

11.—(1) Subject to the following provisions of this regulation, where in any week a woman is, for the whole part of the week,—
 (a) incapable of work in consequence of sickness or injury; or
 (b) absent from work on account of a temporary cessation of work; or
 (c) absent from work in circumstances such that, by arrangement or custom, she is regarded as continuing in the employment of her employer for all or any purpose; or
 (d) absent from work wholly or partly because of pregnancy or confinement, [²or
 (e) absent from work in consequence of taking paternity leave, adoption leave or parental leave under Part 8 of the Employment Rights Act 1996,]
and returns to work for her employer after the incapacity for or absence from work, that week shall be treated for the purposes of Part V of the 1986 Act as part of a continuous period of employment with that employer, notwithstanding that no contract of service exists with that employer in respect of that week.

(2) Incapacity for work which lasts for more than 26 consecutive weeks shall not count for the purposes of paragraph (1)(a).

(3) Paragraph (1)(d) shall only apply to a woman who—
 (a) has a contract of service with the same employer both before and after her confinement but not during any period of absence from work due to her confinement and the period between those contracts does not exceed 26 weeks; or
 (b) returns to work in accordance with section 45(1) of the 1978 Act or in pursuance of an offer made in circumstances described in section 56A(2) of that Act after a period of absence from work wholly or partly occasioned by pregnancy or confinement.

[¹(3A) Where a woman who is pregnant—
 (a) is an employee in an employed earner's employment in which the custom is for the employer—

(i) to offer work for a fixed period of not more than 26 consecutive weeks;
(ii) to offer work for such period on 2 or more occasions in a year for periods which do not overlap; and
(iii) to offer the work available to those persons who had worked for him during the last or a recent such period, but
(b) is absent from work—
(i) wholly or partly because of the pregnancy or her confinement; or
(ii) because of incapacity arising from some specific disease or bodily or mental disablement,
then in her case paragraph (1) shall apply as if the words "and returns to work for an employer after the incapacity for or absence from work" were omitted and paragraph (4) shall not apply.]

(4) Where a woman is employed under a contract of service for part only of the week immediately preceding the 14th week before the expected week of confinement, the whole of that week shall count in computing any period of continuous employment for the purposes of Part V of the 1986 Act.

AMENDMENTS

1. Statutory Maternity Pay (General) Amendment Regulations 1990 (SI 1990/622), reg.2 (April 6, 1990).
2. Social Security, Statutory Maternity Pay and Statutory Sick Pay (Miscellaneous Amendments) Regulations 2002 (SI 2002/2690), reg.4 (April 6, 2003).

DEFINITIONS

"the 1978 Act"—see reg.1(2).
"the 1986 Act"—*ibid*.

Continuous employment and unfair dismissal

12.—(1) This regulation applies to a woman in relation to whose dismissal an action is commenced which consists—
(a) of the presentation by her of a complaint under section 67(1) of the 1978 Act; or
(b) of her making a claim in accordance with a dismissals procedure agreement designated by an order under section 65 of that Act; or
(c) of any action taken by a conciliation officer under section 134(3) of that Act; [¹or
(d) of a decision arising out of the use of a statutory dispute resolution procedure contained in Schedule 2 to the Employment Act 2002 in a case where, in accordance with the Employment Act 2002 (Dispute Resolution) Regulations 2004, such a procedure applies.]

(2) If in consequence of an action of the kind specified in paragraph (1) a woman is reinstated or re-engaged by her employer or by a successor or associated employer of that employer the continuity of her employment shall be preserved for the purposes of Part V of the 1986 Act and any week which falls within the interval beginning with the effective date of termination and ending with the date of reinstatement or re-engagement, as the case may be, shall count in the computation of her period of continuous employment.

(3) In this regulation—
"successor" and "dismissals procedure agreement" have the same meanings as in section 30(3) and (4) of the Trade Union and Labour Relations Act 1974; and

(SI 1986/1960, reg.12) (as amended)

"associated employer" shall be construed in accordance with section 153(4) of the 1978 Act.

AMENDMENT

1. Statutory Maternity Pay (General) and the Statutory Paternity Pay and Statutory Adoption Pay (General) (Amendment) Regulations 2005 (SI 2005/358), reg.3 (April 6, 2005).

DEFINITIONS

"the 1978 Act"—see reg.1(2).
"associated employer"—see para.(3).
"dismissals procedure agreement"—*ibid.*
"successor"—*ibid.*

Continuous employment and stoppages of work

13.—(1) Where for any week or part of a week a woman does no work because there is, within the meaning of section 19 of the 1975 Act a stoppage of work due to a trade dispute at her place of employment the continuity of her employment shall, subject to paragraph (2), be treated as continuing throughout the stoppage but, subject to paragraph (3), no such week shall count in the computation of her period of employment.

(2) Subject to paragraph (3), where during the stoppage of work a woman is dismissed from her employment, the continuity of her employment shall not be treated in accordance with paragraph (1) as continuing beyond the commencement of the day she stopped work.

(3) The provisions of paragraph (1) to the extent that they provide that a week in which a stoppage of work occurred shall not count in the computation of a period of employment, and paragraph (2) shall not apply to a woman who proves that at no time did she have a direct interest in the trade dispute in question.

GENERAL NOTE

The reference in this regulation to SSA 1975, s.19 should now be read as referring to SSCBA 1992, s.27.

Change of employer

14. A woman's employment shall, notwithstanding the change of employer, be treated as continuous employment with the second employer where—
   (a) the employer's trade or business or an undertaking (whether or not it is an undertaking established by or under an Act of Parliament) is transferred from one person to another;
   (b) by or under an Act of Parliament, whether public or local and whenever passed, a contract of employment between any body corporate and the woman is modified and some other body corporate is substituted as her employer;
   (c) on the death of her employer, the woman is taken into the employment of the personal representatives or trustees of the deceased;
   (d) the woman is employed by partners, personal representatives or trustees and there is a change in the partners, or, as the case may be, personal representatives or trustees;

(e) the woman is taken into the employment of an employer who is, at the time she entered his employment, an associated employer of her previous employer, and for this purpose "associated employer" shall be construed in accordance with section 153(4) of the 1978 Act;

(f) on the termination of her employment with an employer she is taken into the employment of another employer and [¹those employers are the governors of a school maintained by a local education authority and that authority].

AMENDMENT

1. Statutory Maternity Pay (General) Amendment Regulations 1990 (SI 1990/622), reg.3 (April 6, 1990).

DEFINITION

"the 1978 Act"—see reg.1(2).

Reinstatement after service with the armed forces, etc.

15. If a woman who is entitled to apply to her former employer under the Reserve Forces (Safeguard of Employment) Act 1985 enters the employment of that employer not later than the 6 month period mentioned in section 1(4)(b) of that Act, her previous period of employment with that employer (or if there was more than one such period, the last of those periods) and the period of employment beginning in the said period of 6 months shall be treated as continuous.

Normal working weeks

16.—(1) For the purposes of section 48(5) of the 1986 Act, a woman's contract of service shall be treated as not normally involving or having involved employment for less than 16 hours weekly where she is normally employed for 16 hours or more weekly.

(2) Where a woman's relations with her employer were governed for a continuous period of at least 2 years by a contract of service which normally involved employment for not less than 16 hours weekly and this period was followed by a further period, ending with the week immediately preceding the 14th week before the expected week of confinement, in which her relations with that employer were governed by a contract of service which normally involved employment for less than 16 hours, but not less than 8 hours weekly, then her contract of service shall be treated for the purpose of section 48(5) of the 1986 Act as not normally involving or having involved employment for less than 16 hours weekly.

(3) Where a woman's relations with her employer are or were governed for a continuous period of at least 2 years by a contract of service which involved—
  (a) for not more than 26 weeks in that period, employment for 8 hours or more but less than 16 hours weekly; and
  (b) for the whole of the remainder of that period employment for not less than 16 hours weekly, the contract of service shall be treated for the purposes of section 48(5) of the 1986 Act as not normally involving or having involved employment for less than 16 hours weekly.

(SI 1986/1960, reg.16) (as amended)

General Note

The references in this regulation to SSA 1986, s.48(5) should now be read as referring to SSCBA 1992, s.166(5).

[¹Meaning of "week"

16A. Where a woman has been in employed earner's employment with the same employer in each of 26 consecutive weeks (but no more than 26 weeks) ending with the week immediately preceding the 14th week before the expected week of confinement then for the purpose of determining whether that employment amounts to a continuous period of at least 26 weeks, the first of those 26 weeks shall be a period commencing on the first day of her employment with the employer and ending at midnight on the first Saturday thereafter or on that day where her first day is a Saturday.]

Amendment

1. Statutory Maternity Pay (General) Amendment Regulations 1990 (SI 1990/622), reg.4 (April 6, 1990).

Part IV

General Provisions

Meaning of "employee"

17.—(1) [¹Subject to paragraph (1A),] in a case where, and in so far as, a woman [¹. . .] is treated as an employed earner by virtue of the Social Security (Categorisation of Earners) Regulations 1978 she shall be treated as an employee for the purposes of Part V of the 1986 Act and in a case where, and in so far as, such a woman is treated otherwise than as an employed earner by virtue of those regulations, she shall not be treated as an employee for the purposes of Part V.

[²(1A) Paragraph (1) shall have effect in relation to a woman who—
  (a) is under the age of 16; and
  (b) would or, as the case may be, would not have been treated as an employed earner by virtue of the Social Security (Categorisation of Earners) Regulations 1978 had she been over that age,
as it has effect in relation to a woman who is, or, as the case may be, is not so treated.]

(2) Any woman who is in employed earner's employment within the meaning of the 1975 Act under a contract of apprenticeship shall be treated as the employee for the purposes of Part V.

(3) A woman who is in employed earner's employment within the meaning of the 1975 Act but whose employer—
  (a) does not fulfil the conditions prescribed in regulation 119(1)(b) of the Social Security (Contributions) Regulations 1979 as to residence or presence in Great Britain, or
  (b) is a woman who, by reason of any international treaty to which the United Kingdom is a party of any international convention binding the United Kingdom—

(i) is exempt from the provisions of the 1975 Act, or
(ii) is a woman against whom the provisions of that Act are not enforceable, shall not be treated as an employee for the purposes of Part V of the 1986 Act.

AMENDMENTS

1. Employment Equality (Age) Regulations 2006 (SI 2006/1031), reg.49(1) and Sch.8, Part 2, para.53 (October 1, 2006).
2. Employment Equality (Age) (Consequential Amendments) Regulations 2007 (SI 2007/825), reg.6 (April 6, 2007).

Treatment of two or more employers as one

4.31 18.—(1) In a case where the earnings paid to a woman in respect of 2 or more employments are aggregated and treated as a single payment of earnings under regulation 12(1) of the Social Security (Contributions) Regulations 1979, the employers of the woman in respect of those employments shall be treated as one for all purposes of Part V of the 1986 Act.

(2) Where two or more employers are treated as one under the provisions of paragraph (1), liability for statutory maternity pay payable by them to a woman shall be apportioned between them in such proportions as they may agree or, in default of agreement, in the proportions which the woman's earnings from each employment bear to the amount of the aggregated earnings.

GENERAL NOTE

4.32 Specific provision is also made in the Statutory Maternity Pay (National Health Service Employees) Regulations 1991 (SI 1991/590) for NHS workers with divided contracts.

Payments to be treated as contractual remuneration

4.33 19. For the purposes of paragraph 12(1) and (2) of Schedule 4 to the 1986 Act, the payments which are to be treated as contractual remuneration are sums payable under the contract of service—
  (a) by way of remuneration;
  (b) for incapacity for work due to sickness or injury; and
  (c) by reason of pregnancy or confinement.

DEFINITION

"the 1986 Act"—see reg.1(2).

Meaning of "earnings"

4.34 20.—(1) [¹. . .]
[²(2) For the purposes of section 171(4) of the Contributions and Benefits Act, the expression "earnings" refers to gross earnings and includes any remuneration or profit derived from a woman's employment except any payment or amount which is—
  (a) excluded [⁶or disregarded in the calculation of a person's earnings under regulation 25, 27 or 123 of, or Schedule 3 to, the Social Security (Contributions) Regulations 2001] (payments to be disregarded and payments to directors to be disregarded respectively)

(SI 1986/1960, reg.20) (as amended)

[⁵(or would have been so excluded had she not been under the age of 16)];
(b) a chargeable emolument under section 10A of the Social Security Contributions and Benefits Act 1992, except where, in consequence of such a chargeable emolument being excluded from earnings, a woman would not be entitled to statutory maternity pay. [⁵(or where such a payment or amount would have been so excluded and in consequence she would not have been entitled to statutory maternity pay had she not been under the age of 16)]]

(3) [¹. . .]

(4) For the purposes of section [³section 171(4) of the Contributions and Benefits Act] the expression "earnings" includes also—

[⁶(za) any amount retrospectively treated as earnings by regulations made by virtue of section 4B(2) of the Contributions and Benefits Act;]
(a) any sum payable in respect of arrears of pay in pursuance of an order for reinstatement or re-engagement under the 1978 Act;
(b) any sum payable by way of pay in pursuance of an order under the 1978 Act for the continuation of a contract of employment;
(c) any sum payable by way of remuneration in pursuance of a protective award under the Employment Protection Act 1975;
(d) any sum payable by way of statutory sick pay, including sums payable in accordance with regulations made under section 1(5) of the Social Security and Housing Benefits Act 1982.
[⁴(e) any sum payable by way of statutory maternity pay, including sums payable in accordance with regulations made under section 164(9)(b) of the Contributions and Benefits Act;
(f) any sum payable by way of statutory paternity pay, including sums payable in accordance with regulations made under section 171ZD(3) of the Contributions and Benefits Act;
(g) any sum payable by way of statutory adoption pay, including sums payable in accordance with regulations made under section 171ZM(3) of the Contributions and Benefits Act.]

(5) [¹. . .]
(6) [¹. . .]

AMENDMENTS

1. Social Security (Miscellaneous Provisions) Amendment (No.2) Regulations 1992 (SI 1992/2595), reg.13 (November 16, 1992).
2. Social Security Contributions, Statutory Maternity Pay and Statutory Sick Pay (Miscellaneous Amendments) Regulations 1999 (SI 1999/567), reg.12 (April 6, 1999).
3. Social Security, Statutory Maternity Pay and Statutory Sick Pay (Miscellaneous Amendments) Regulations 2002 (SI 2002/2690), reg.5(a) (November 24, 2002).
4. Social Security, Statutory Maternity Pay and Statutory Sick Pay (Miscellaneous Amendments) Regulations 2002 (SI 2002/2690), reg.5(b) (April 6, 2003).
5. Employment Equality (Age) Regulations 2006 (SI 2006/1031), reg.49(1) and Sch.8, Pt 2, para.53 (October 1, 2006, and in relation to any case where the expected week of confinement begins on or after January 14, 2007).
6. Social Security, Occupational Pension Schemes and Statutory Payments (Consequential Provisions) Regulations 2007 (SI 2007/1154), reg.4(2) and (3) (April 6, 2007).

Statutory Maternity Pay (General) Regulations 1986

Normal weekly earnings

4.35
21.—(1) For the purposes of [¹Part XII of the Contributions and Benefits Act], a woman's normal weekly earnings shall be calculated in accordance with the following provisions of this regulation.

(2) In this regulation—

"the appropriate date" means the first day of the 14th week before the expected week of confinement, or the first day in the week in which the woman is confined, whichever is the earlier. [¹. . .]

"normal pay day" means a day on which the terms of a woman's contract of service require her to be paid, or the practice in her employment is for her to be paid, if any payment is due to her; and "day of payment" means a day on which the woman was paid.

(3) Subject to paragraph (4), the relevant period for the purposes of [¹section 171(4) of the Contributions and Benefits Act] is the period between—

(a) the last normal pay day to fall before the appropriate date; and
(b) the last normal pay day to fall at least eight weeks earlier than the normal pay day mentioned in sub-paragraph (a), including the normal pay day mentioned in sub-paragraph (a) but excluding that first mentioned in sub-paragraph (b).

(4) In a case where a woman has no identifiable normal pay day, paragraph (3) shall have eVect as if the words "day of payment" were substituted for the words "normal pay day" in each place where they occur.

(5) In a case where a woman has normal pay days at intervals of or approximating to one or more calendar months (including intervals of or approximating to a year) her normal weekly earnings shall be calculated by dividing her earnings in the relevant period by the number of calendar months in that period (or, if it is not a whole number, the nearest whole number), multiplying the result by 12 and dividing by 52.

(6) In a case to which paragraph (5) does not apply and the relevant period is not an exact number of weeks, the woman's normal weekly earnings shall be calculated by dividing her earnings in the relevant period by the number of days in the relevant period and multiplying the result by 7.

[³(7) In any case where—

(a) a woman is awarded a pay increase (or would have been awarded such an increase had she not then been absent on statutory maternity leave); and
(b) that pay increase applies to the whole or any part of the period between the beginning of the relevant period and the end of her period of statutory maternity leave,

her normal weekly earnings shall be calculated as if such an increase applied in each week of the relevant period.]

AMENDMENTS

1. Social Security Maternity Benefits and Statutory Sick Pay (Amendment) Regulations 1994 (SI 1994/1367), reg.5 (June 11, 1994).
2. Statutory Maternity Pay (General) Amendment Regulations 1996 (SI 1996/1335), reg.2 (June 12, 1996).
3. Statutory Maternity Pay (General) (Amendment) Regulations 2005 (SI 2005/729), reg.3 (April 6, 2005).

(SI 1986/1960, reg.21) (as amended)

GENERAL NOTE

The new reg.21(7) is designed to give effect to the ECJ judgment in *Alabaster v Woolwich PLC and the Secretary of State for Social Security* (C-147/02), [2004] I.R.L.R. 486). It ensures that employers must recalculate a woman's entitlement (or potential entitlement) to statutory maternity pay to reflect any pay rise that the woman would have received, but for her maternity leave, and which is effective at any time between the start of the period used to calculate her entitlement and the end of her maternity leave. For the Court of Appeal judgment following the decision of the ECJ, see *Alabaster v Barclays Bank Plc and the Secretary of State for Social Security* [2005] EWCA Civ 508; [2005] ICR 1246.

4.36

[¹Effect of statutory maternity pay on [²incapacity benefit]

21A. [³. . .]

4.37

AMENDMENTS

1. Statutory Maternity Pay (General) Amendment Regulations 1988 (SI 1988/532), reg.3 (April 6, 1988).
2. Social Security (Incapacity Benefit) (Consequential and Transitional Amendments and Savings) Regulations 1995 (SI 1995/829), reg.18 (April 13, 1995).
3. Social Security, Statutory Maternity Pay and Statutory Sick Pay (Miscellaneous Amendments) Regulations 2002 (SI 2002/2690), reg.6 (November 24, 2002).

[¹Effect of maternity allowance on statutory maternity pay

21B. Where a woman, in any week which falls within the maternity pay period, is—
  (a) in receipt of maternity allowance pursuant to the provisions of sections 35 and 35A of the Contributions and Benefits Act; and
  (b) entitled to receive statutory maternity pay in consequence of [²—
    (i) receiving a pay increase referred to in regulation 21(7), or
    (ii) being treated as having been paid retrospective earnings under regulation 20(4)(za),]
the employer shall not be liable to make payments of statutory maternity pay in respect of such a week unless, and to the extent by which, the rate of statutory maternity pay exceeds the rate of maternity allowance received by her in that week.]

4.38

AMENDMENTS

1. Statutory Maternity Pay (General) (Amendment) Regulations 2005 (SI 2005/729), reg.4 (April 6, 2005).
2. Social Security, Occupational Pension Schemes and Statutory Payments (Consequential Provisions) Regulations 2007 (SI 2007/1154), reg.4(4) (April 6, 2007).

PART V

ADMINISTRATION

Evidence of expected week of confinement

4.39   **22.**—(1) A woman shall in accordance with the following provisions of this regulation, provide the person who is liable to pay her statutory maternity pay with evidence as to—
   (a) the week in which the expected date of confinement occurs, and
   (b) where her entitlement to statutory maternity pay depends upon the fact of her confinement, the week in which she was confined.
   (2) For the purpose of paragraph (1)(b) a certificate of birth shall be sufficient evidence that the woman was confined in the week in which the birth occurred.
   (3) The evidence shall be submitted to the person who will be liable to make payments of statutory maternity pay not later than the end of the third week of the maternity pay period so however that where the woman has good cause the evidence may be submitted later than that date but not later than the end of the 13th week of the maternity pay period.
   (4) For the purposes of paragraph (3) evidence contained in an envelope which is properly addressed and sent by prepaid post shall be deemed to have been submitted on the day on which it was posted.

Notice of absence from work

4.40   **23.**—(1) Where a woman is confined before the beginning of the 14th week before the expected week of confinement, she shall be entitled to payments of statutory maternity pay only if—
   (a) she gives notice to the person who will be liable to pay it [²of the date on which she was confined], and
   (b) that notice is given within [²28 days] of the date she was confined or if in the particular circumstances that is not practicable, as soon as is reasonably practicable thereafter; and
   (c) where the person so requests, the notice in writing.
   (2) Where a woman is confined before the date stated in a notice provided in accordance with [¹section 164(4) of the Contributions and Benefits Act] as being the date her absence from work is due to begin, she shall be entitled to payments of statutory maternity pay only if—
   (a) she gives a further notice to the person who will be liable to pay it specifying the date she was confined and the date her absence from work [². . .] began, and
   (b) that further notice is given within [²28 days] of the date she was confined or if in the particular circumstances that is not practicable, as soon as is reasonably practicable thereafter; and
   (c) where the person so requests, the notice is in writing.
   (3) For the purposes of this regulation, a notice contained in an envelope which is properly addressed and sent by prepaid post shall be deemed to be given on the date on which it is posted.
   [¹[²(4) Subject to paragraph (5), section 164(4) of the Contributions and Benefits Act (statutory maternity pay entitlement and liability to pay) shall

(SI 1986/1960, reg.23) (as amended)

not have effect in the case of a woman who leaves her employment with the person who will be liable to pay her statutory maternity pay after the beginning of the week immediately preceding the 14th week before the expected week of confinement.]

(5) A woman who is exempted from section 164(4) of the Contributions and Benefits Act by paragraph (4) but who is confined before the 11th week before the expected week of confinement shall only be entitled to statutory maternity pay if she gives the person who will be liable to pay it notice specifying the date she was confined.]

AMENDMENTS

1. Social Security Maternity Benefits and Statutory Sick Pay (Amendment) Regulations 1994 (SI 1994/1367), reg.6 (June 11, 1994).
2. Social Security, Statutory Maternity Pay and Statutory Sick Pay (Miscellaneous Amendments) Regulations 2002 (SI 2002/2690), reg.7 (November 24, 2002).

Notification of employment after confinement

24. A woman who after the date of confinement but within the maternity pay period commences work in employed earner's employment with a person who is not liable to make payments of statutory maternity pay to her and is not a non-liable employer for the purposes of regulation 8(1), shall within seven days of the day she commenced work inform any person who is so liable of the date she commenced work.

Provision of information in connection with determination of questions

25. Any woman claiming to be entitled to statutory maternity pay, or any other person who is a party to proceedings arising under the 1986 Act relating to statutory maternity pay, shall, if she receives notification from the Secretary of State that any information is required from her for the determination of any question arising in connection therewith, furnish that information to the Secretary of State within 10 days of receiving that notification.

DEFINITION

"the 1986 Act"—see reg.1(2).

GENERAL NOTE

The functions under this regulation were transferred from the Secretary of State for Social Security to the Board of the Inland Revenue (now HMRC) under s.1(2) of and Sch.2 to the Social Security (Transfer of Functions, etc.) Act 1999.

[¹Provision of information relating to claims for certain other benefits

25A.—(1) Where an employer who has been given notice in accordance with [³section 164(4)(a) or (9)(ea) of the Contributions and Benefits Act] or regulation 23 by a woman who is or has been an employee—
   (a) decides that he has no liability to make payments of statutory maternity pay to her; or
   (b) has made one or more payments of statutory maternity pay to her but decides, before the end of the maternity pay period and for a reason

Statutory Maternity Pay (General) Regulations 1986

specified in paragraph (3), that he has no liability to make further payments to her,
then, in connection with the making of a claim by the woman for a maternity allowance or incapacity benefit, he shall furnish her with the information specified in the following provisions of this regulation.

(2) Where the employer decides he has no liability to make payments of statutory maternity pay to the woman, he shall furnish her with details of the decision and the reasons for it.

(3) Where the employer decides he has no liability to make further payments of statutory maternity pay to the woman because [³. . .] she has within the maternity pay period been detained in legal custody or sentenced to a term of imprisonment which was not suspended, [³. . .], he shall furnish her with—
  (a) details of his decision and the reasons for it; and
  (b) details of the last week in respect of which a liability to pay statutory maternity pay arose and the total number of weeks within the maternity pay period in which such a liability arose.

(4) The employer shall—
  (a) return to the woman any maternity certificate provided by her in support of the notice referred to in paragraph (1); and
  (b) comply with any requirements imposed by the preceding provisions of this regulation—
    (i) in a case to which paragraph (2) applies, within 7 days of the decision being made, or, if earlier, within [³ 28 days] of the day the woman gave notice of her intended absence or of her confinement if that had occurred; or
    (ii) in a case to which paragraph (3) refers, within 7 days of being notified of the woman's detention or sentence [³. . .].

(5) In this regulation, 'incapacity benefit' means [²incapacity benefit] or a severe disablement allowance.]

AMENDMENTS

1. Statutory Maternity Pay (General) Amendment Regulations 1990 (SI 1990/622), reg.7 (April 6, 1990).
2. Social Security (Incapacity Benefit) (Consequential and Transitional Amendments and Savings) Regulations 1995 (SI 1995/829), reg.18 (April 13, 1995).
3. Social Security, Statutory Maternity Pay and Statutory Sick Pay (Miscellaneous Amendments) Regulations 2002 (SI 2002/2690), reg.8 (November 24, 2002).

Records to be maintained by employers

26.—(1) Every employer shall maintain for 3 years after the end of the tax year in which the maternity pay period ends a record in relation to any woman who is or was an employee of his of—
  (a) the date of the first day of absence from work wholly or partly because of pregnancy or confinement as notified by her and, if different, the date of the first day when such absence commenced;
  (b) the weeks in that tax year in which statutory maternity pay was paid and the amount paid in each week; and
  (c) any week in that tax year which was within her maternity pay period but for which no payment of statutory maternity pay was made to her and the reasons no payment was made.

(SI 1986/1960, reg.26) (as amended)

(2) Except where he was not liable to make a payment of statutory maternity pay and subject to paragraphs (3) and (4), every employer shall retain for 3 years after the end of the tax year in which the maternity pay period ends any medical certificate or other evidence relating to the expected week of confinement, or as the case may be, the confinement which was provided to him by a woman who is or was an employee of his.

(3) Where an employer returns a medical certificate to an employee of his for the purpose of enabling her to make a claim for benefit under the 1975 Act, it shall be sufficient for the purposes of paragraph (2) if he retains a copy of that certificate.

(4) An employer shall not retain any certificate of birth provided to him as evidence of confinement by a woman who is or was an employee of his but shall retain a record of the date of birth.

DEFINITION

"the 1975 Act"—see reg.1(2).

[¹Production of employer's records

26A.—(1) An authorised officer of the Commissioners of Inland Revenue may by notice require an employer to produce to him at the place of keeping such records as are in the employer's possession or power and as (in the officer's reasonable opinion) contain, or may contain, information relevant to satisfy him that statutory maternity pay has been paid and is being paid in accordance with these regulations to employees or former employees who are entitled to it.

(2) A notice referred to in paragraph (1) shall be in writing and the employer shall produce the records referred to in that paragraph within 30 days after the date of such a notice.

(3) The production of records in pursuance of this regulation shall be without prejudice to any lien which a third party may have in respect of those records.

(4) References in this regulation to "records" means—
   (a) any wage sheet or deductions working sheet; or
   (b) any other document which relates to the calculation or payment of statutory maternity pay to his employees or former employees,
whether kept in written form, electronically, or otherwise.

(5) In paragraph (1), "place of keeping" means such place in Great Britain that an employer and an authorised officer may agree upon, or, in the absence of such agreement—
   (a) any place in Great Britain where records referred to in paragraph (1) are normally kept; or
   (b) if there is no such place, the employer's principal place of business in Great Britain.]

AMENDMENT

1. Statutory Maternity Pay (General) and Statutory Sick Pay (General) (Amendment) Regulations 2005 (SI 2005/989), reg.2(2) (April 6, 2005).

PART VI

PAYMENT

Payment of statutory maternity pay

4.47   27. Payment of statutory maternity pay may be made in a like manner to payments of remuneration but shall not include payments in kind or by way of the provision of board or lodgings or of services or other facilities.

Rounding to avoid fractional amounts

4.48   [¹28. Where any payment of statutory maternity pay is paid for any week or part of a week and the amount due includes a fraction of a penny, the payment shall be rounded up to the next whole number of pence.]

AMENDMENT

1. Statutory Maternity Pay, Social Security (Maternity Allowance) and Social Security (Overlapping Benefits) (Amendment) Regulations 2006 (SI 2006/2379), reg.3(4) (October 1, 2006, and in relation to women whose expected week of confinement falls on or after April 1, 2007).

Time when statutory maternity pay is to be paid

4.49   29.—(1) In this regulation, "payday" means a day on which it has been agreed, or it is the normal practice between an employer or former employer and a woman who is or was an employee of his, that payments by way of remuneration are to be made, or, where there is no such agreement or normal practice, the last day of a calendar month.
  (2) In any case where—
  (a) a decision has been made by an adjudication officer, appeal tribunal or Commissioner in proceedings under [Social Security Administration Act 1992] as a result of which a woman is entitled to an amount of statutory maternity pay; and
  (b) the time for bringing an appeal against the decision has expired and either—
    (i) no such appeal has been brought; or
    (ii) such an appeal has been brought and has been finally disposed of that amount of statutory maternity pay shall be paid within the time specified in paragraph (3).
  (3) Subject to paragraphs (4) and (5), the employer or former employer shall pay the amount not later than the first pay day after—
  (a) where an appeal has been brought, the day on which the employer or former employer receives notification that it has been finally disposed of,
  (b) where leave to appeal has been refused and there remains no further opportunity to apply for leave, the day on which the employer or former employer receives notification of the refusal; and
  (c) in any other case, the day on which the time for bringing an appeal expires.
  (4) Subject to paragraph (5), where it is impracticable, in view of the employer's or former employer's methods of accounting for and paying

(SI 1986/1960, reg. 29) (as amended)

remuneration, for the requirement of payment referred to in paragraph (3) to be met by the pay day referred to in that paragraph, it shall be met not later than the next following pay day.

(5) Where the employer or former employer would not have remunerated the woman for her work in the week in question as early as the pay day specified in paragraph (3) or (if it applies) paragraph (4), the requirement of payment shall be met on the first day on which the woman would have been remunerated for her work in that week.

Payments by the Secretary of State

30. Where the Secretary of State becomes liable in accordance with regulation 7 to make payments of statutory maternity pay to a woman, the first payment shall be made as soon as reasonably practicable after he becomes so liable, and payments thereafter shall be made at weekly intervals, by means of an instrument of payment or by such other means as appears to the Secretary of State to be appropriate in the circumstances of any particular case.

GENERAL NOTE

The functions under this regulation were transferred from the Secretary of State for Social Security to the Board of the Inland Revenue (now HMRC) under s.1(2) of and Sch.2 to the Social Security (Transfer of Functions, etc.) Act 1999.

Persons unable to act

31.—(1) Where in the case of any woman—
(a) statutory maternity pay is payable to her or she is alleged to be entitled to it;
(b) she is unable for the time being to act;
(c) either—
  (i) no receiver has been appointed by the Court of Protection with power to receive statutory maternity pay on her behalf, or
  (ii) in Scotland, her estate is not being administrated by any tutor, curator or other guardian acting or appointed in terms of law,
the Secretary of State may, upon written application to him by a person who, if a natural person, is over the age of 18, appoint that person to exercise, on behalf of the woman any right to which she may be entitled under Part V of the 1986 Act and to deal on her behalf with any sums payable to her.

(2) Where the Secretary of State has made an appointment under paragraph (1)—
(a) he may at any time in his absolute discretion revoke it;
(b) the person appointed may resign his office after having given one month's notice in writing to the Secretary of State of his intention to do so; and
(c) the appointment shall terminate when the Secretary of State is notified that a receiver or other person to whom paragraph (1)(c) applies has been appointed.

(3) Anything required by Part V of the 1986 Act to be done by or to any woman who is unable to act may be done by or to the person appointed under this regulation to act on her behalf, and the receipt of the person so appointed shall be a good discharge to the woman's employer or former employer for any sum paid.

Statutory Maternity Pay (General) Regulations 1986

GENERAL NOTE

4.53 The functions under this regulation were transferred from the Secretary of State for Social Security to the Board of the Inland Revenue (now HMRC) under s.1(2) of and Sch.2 to the Social Security (Transfer of Functions, etc.) Act 1999.

PART VII

OFFENCES

[¹Offences

4.54 **32.** [². . .]

AMENDMENTS

1. Statutory Maternity Pay (General) and Statutory Sick Pay (General) (Amendment) Regulations 2001.
2. Statutory Maternity Pay (General) and Statutory Sick Pay (General) (Amendment) Regulations 2005 (SI 2005/989), reg.2(3) (immediately before April 6, 2005).

GENERAL NOTE

4.55 The penalty for such an offence is set out in s.113(3) of the SSAA 1992.

Statutory Maternity Pay (Medical Evidence) Regulations 1987

(SI 1987/235) (as amended)

4.56 The Secretary of State for Social Services, in exercise of the powers conferred by sections 49 and 84(1) of and paragraph 6 of Schedule 4 to the Social Security Act 1986, and of all other powers enabling him in that behalf, by this instrument, which is made before the end of the period of 12 months from the commencement of the enactments contained in the 1986 Act under which it is made, makes the following regulations:

ARRANGEMENT OF REGULATIONS

1. Citation, commencement and interpretation
2. Evidence of pregnancy and confinement

SCHEDULE—Part I—Rules
     Part II—Form of certificate

Citation, commencement and interpretation

4.57 **1.**—(1) These regulations may be cited as the Statutory Maternity Pay (Medical Evidence) Regulations 1987 and shall come into force on 15th March 1987.

(SI 1987/235, reg.1) (as amended)

(2) In these regulations, unless the context otherwise requires—

"the Act" means the Social Security Act 1986;

[¹"registered midwife" means a midwife who is registered as a midwife with the Nursing and Midwifery Council under the Nursing and Midwifery Order 2001;]

"doctor" means a registered medical practitioner;

"signature" means, in relation to any statement or certificate given in accordance with these regulations, the name by which the person giving that statement or certificate, as the case may be, is usually known (any name other than the surname being either in full or otherwise indicated) written by that person in his own handwriting; and "signed" shall be construed accordingly.

[²"Primary Care Trust" means a Primary Care Trust established under section 16A of the National Health Service Act 1977.]

AMENDMENTS

1. Nursing and Midwifery Order 2001 (Consequential Amendments) Order 2002 (SI 2002/881), art.2 and Sch., para.2 (April 17, 2002).

2. National Health Service Reform and Health Care Professions Act 2002 (Supplementary, Consequential etc. Provisions) Regulations 2002 (SI 2002/2469), reg.11 and Sch.8 (October 1, 2002).

Evidence of pregnancy and confinement

2. The evidence as to pregnancy and the expected date of confinement which a woman is required to provide to a person who is liable to pay her statutory maternity pay shall be furnished in the form of a maternity certificate given by a doctor or by a registered midwife, not earlier than the beginning of the [¹20th week] before the expected week of confinement, in accordance with the rules set out in Part I of the Schedule to these regulations—

(a) in the appropriate form as set out in Part II of that Schedule; or
(b) in a form substantially to the like effect with such variations as the circumstances may require.

4.58

AMENDMENT

1. Social Security (Medical Evidence) and Statutory Maternity Pay (Medical Evidence) (Amendment) Regulations 2001 (SI 2001/2931), reg.3(2) (September 28, 2001).

DEFINITIONS

"doctor"—see reg.1(2).
"registered midwife"—see *ibid.*

SCHEDULE   **Regulation 2**

PART I

RULES

1. In these rules any reference to a woman is a reference to the woman in respect of whom a maternity certificate is given in accordance with these rules.

4.59

Statutory Maternity Pay (Medical Evidence) Regulations 1987

2. A maternity certificate shall be given by a doctor or registered midwife attending the woman and shall not be given by the woman herself.

3. The maternity certificate shall be on a form provided by the Secretary of State for the purpose and the wording shall be that set out in the appropriate part of the form specified in Part II of this Schedule.

4. Every maternity certificate shall be completed in ink or other indelible substance and shall contain the following particulars—
  (a) the woman's name;
  (b) the week in which the woman is expected to be confined or, if the maternity certificate is given after confinement, the date of that confinement and the date the confinement was expected to take place [1. . .];
  (c) the date of the examination on which the maternity certificate is based;
  (d) the date on which the maternity certificate is signed; and
  [4(e) the address of the doctor or where the maternity certificate is signed by a registered midwife the personal identification number given to her on her registration in [6. . .] the register maintained by the Nursing and Midwifery Council [6("NMC") under article 5 of] the Nursing and Midwifery Order 2001 and the expiry date of that registration,]

and shall bear opposite the word "Signature", the signature of the person giving the maternity certificate written after there has been entered on the maternity certificate the woman's name and the expected date or, as the case may be, the date of the confinement.

5. After a maternity certificate has been given, no further maternity certificate based on the same examination shall be furnished other than a maternity certificate by way of replacement of an original which has been lost or mislaid, in which case it shall be clearly marked "duplicate".

(SI 1987/235, Sch.) (as amended)

[² PART II

FORM OF CERTIFICATE

MATERNITY CERTIFICATE 4.60

Please fill in this form in ink

Name of patient

Fill in this part if you are giving the certificate before the confinement.

Do not fill this in more [³than 20 weeks] before the week the baby is expected.

I certify that I examined you on the date given below. In my opinion you can expect to have your baby in the week that includes

.... / .... / ....

Week means period of 7 days starting on a Sunday and ending on a Saturday. Fill in this part if you are giving the certificate after the confinement.

I certify that I attended you in connection with the birth which took place on .... / .... / .... when you were delivered of a child [ ] children.

In my opinion your baby was expected in the week that includes ..../ .... / ....

Date of examination ..... / ..... / ......

Date of signing .... / .... / ....

Signature

Registered midwives

Please give your [⁶NMC] Personal Identification Number and the expiry date of your registration with the [⁶NMC].

Doctors

Please stamp your name and address here if the form has not been stamped by the [⁵"Primary Care Trust or Local Health Board in whose medical performers list you are included (or, in Scotland, by the Health Board in whose primary medical services performers list you are included)].

AMENDMENTS

1. Social Security (Miscellaneous Provisions) Amendment Regulations 1991 (SI 1991/2284) reg.23 (November 1, 1991).
2. Social Security (Miscellaneous Provisions) Amendment Regulations 1991 (SI 1991/2284) reg.24 (November 1, 1991).

Statutory Maternity Pay (Medical Evidence) Regulations 1987

3. Social Security (Medical Evidence) and Statutory Maternity Pay (Medical Evidence) (Amendment) Regulations 2001 (SI 2001/2931), reg.3(3) (September 28, 2001).

4. Nursing and Midwifery Order 2001 (Consequential Amendments) Order 2002 (SI 2002/881), art.2 and Sch., para.3 (April 17, 2002).

5. General Medical Services and Personal Medical Services Transitional and Consequential Provisions Order 2004 (SI 2004/865), art.119 and Sch.1, para.5 (April 1, 2004).

6. Health Act 1999 (Consequential Amendments) (Nursing and Midwifery) Order 2004 (SI 2004/1771), art.3 and Sch., para.51 (August 1, 2004).

DEFINITIONS

"doctor"—see reg.1(2).
"registered midwife"—see *ibid*.
"signature"—see *ibid*.
"signed"—see *ibid*.

Statutory Maternity Pay (Persons Abroad and Mariners) Regulations 1987

(SI 1987/418) (AS AMENDED)

The Secretary of State for Social Services, in exercise of the powers conferred upon him by sections 80 and 84(1) of the Social Security Act 1986 and of all other powers enabling him in that behalf, by this instrument, which is made before the end of the period of 12 months from the commencement of the enactments under which it is made, makes the following Regulations:

ARRANGEMENT OF REGULATIONS

4.61

1. Citation, commencement and interpretation
2. Persons in other member States—meaning of "employee"
2A. Persons absent from Great Britain—meaning of "employee"
3. Meaning of "employee"—general
4. (*repealed*)
5. Women who worked in the European Community
6. Time for compliance with Part V of the 1986 Act and Regulations
7. Mariners
8. Continental shelf
9. (*repealed*)

Citation, commencement and interpretation

4.62   1.—(1) These Regulations may be cited as the Statutory Maternity Pay (Persons Abroad and Mariners) Regulations 1987 and shall come into force on 6th April 1987.

(2) In these Regulations, the "1986 Act" means the Social Security Act 1986;
[¹"the Contributions and Benefits Act" means the Social Security Contributions and Benefits Act 1992, "the Contributions Regulations" means the Social Security (Contributions) Regulations 1979"], and the

(SI 1987/418, reg.1) (as amended)

"General Regulations" means the Statutory Maternity Pay (General) Regulations 1986.

(3) Unless the context otherwise requires, any reference in these Regulations to a numbered regulation is a reference to the regulation bearing that number in these Regulations and any reference in a regulation to a numbered paragraph is a reference to the paragraph of that regulation bearing that number.

AMENDMENT

1. Social Security Contributions, Statutory Maternity Pay and Statutory Sick Pay (Miscellaneous Amendments) Regulations 1996 (SI 1996/777), reg.4(2) (April 6, 1996).

GENERAL NOTE

These Regulations were made under the authority of what is now SSCBA 1992, s.170 and make special provision for statutory maternity pay as regards persons who are abroad or who are mariners. See also SMP (General) Regulations 1986 (SI 1986/1960), reg.17(3).

Persons in other member States—meaning of "employee"

2. Subject to regulation 3, a woman who is—
   (a) gainfully employed in a member State other than the United Kingdom in such circumstances that if her employment were in Great Britain she would be an employee for the purposes of Part V of the 1986 Act or a woman treated as such an employee under regulation 17 of the General Regulations; and
   (b) subject to the legislation of the United Kingdom under Council Regulation (EEC) No. 1408/71; notwithstanding that she is not employed in Great Britain, shall be treated as an employee for the purposes of Part V of the 1986 Act.

DEFINITIONS

"the 1986 Act"—see reg.1(2).
"the General Regulations"—see *ibid*.

[¹Persons absent from Great Britain—meaning of "employee"

2A. Subject to regulations 2, 3 and 7(3), where a woman, while absent from Great Britain for any purpose, is gainfully employed by an employer who is liable to pay in respect of her secondary Class 1 contributions under section 6 of the Contributions and Benefits Act or regulation 120 of the Contributions Regulations, she shall be treated as an employee for the purposes of Part XII of the Contributions and Benefits Act.]

AMENDMENT

1. Social Security Contributions, Statutory Maternity Pay and Statutory Sick Pay (Miscellaneous Amendments) Regulations 1996 (SI 1996/777), reg.4(3) (April 6, 1996).

DEFINITIONS

"the Contributions and Benefits Act"—see reg.1(2).
"the Contributions Regulations"—see *ibid*.

Statutory Maternity Pay (Persons Abroad and Mariners) Regulations 1987

Meaning of "employee"—general

3. No woman who, by virtue of regulation 17 of the General Regulations, would be treated as not being an employee for the purposes of Part V of the 1986 Act if her employment were in Great Britain, shall be treated as an employee by virtue of these Regulations.

DEFINITIONS

"the 1986 Act"—see reg.1(2).
"the General Regulations"—see *ibid*.

Women outside the European Community

4. [¹. . .]

AMENDMENT

1. Social Security Contributions, Statutory Maternity Pay and Statutory Sick Pay (Miscellaneous Amendments) Regulations 1996 (SI 1996/777), reg.4(4) (April 6, 1996).

Women who worked in the European Community

5.—(1) A woman who is an employee or treated as an employee under regulation 2 and who—
   (a) in the week immediately preceding the 14th week before the expected week of confinement was in employed earner's employment with an employer in Great Britain, and
   (b) had in any week within the period of [¹26 weeks] immediately preceding that week been employed by the same employer in another member State,
shall be treated for the purposes of sections 46(2) and 48 of the 1986 Act as having been employed in employed earner's employment in those weeks in which she was so employed in the other member State.
   (2) [¹. . .]

AMENDMENT

1. Social Security Contributions, Statutory Maternity Pay and Statutory Sick Pay (Miscellaneous Amendments) Regulations 1996 (SI 1996/777), reg.4(5) (April 6, 1996).

DEFINITION

"the 1986 Act"—see reg.1(2).

Time for compliance with Part V of the 1986 Act and Regulations

6. Where—
   (a) a woman is outside the United Kingdom;
   (b) Part V of the 1986 Act or Regulations made under that Act or under Part III of the Social Security Act 1975 require any act to be done forthwith or on the happening of a certain event or within a specified time; and
   (c) because the woman is outside the United Kingdom she or her employer cannot comply with the requirement;

(SI 1987/418, reg.6) (as amended)

the woman or the employer, as the case may be, shall be deemed to have complied with it if the act is performed as soon as reasonably practicable.

DEFINITION

"the 1986 Act"—see reg.1(2).

Mariners

7.—(1) In this regulation, "foreign-going ship", "home-trade ship" and "mariner" have the same meanings as in Case C of Part VIII of the Social Security (Contributions) Regulations 1979 and the expressions "ship" and "ship or vessel", except in paragraph (3), include hovercraft.

(2) Subject to regulation 3, a mariner engaged in employment on board a home-trade ship with an employer who has a place of business within the United Kingdom shall be treated as an employee for the purposes of Part V of the 1986 Act, notwithstanding that she may not be employed in Great Britain.

(3) A mariner who is engaged in employment—
(a) on a foreign-going ship; or
(b) on a home-trade ship with an employer who does not have a place of business within the United Kingdom, shall not be treated as an employee for the purposes of Part V of the 1986 Act, notwithstanding that she may have been employed in Great Britain.

4.70

DEFINITIONS

"foreign-going ship"—see para.(1).
"home-trade ship"—see *ibid*.
"mariner"—see *ibid*.
"ship"—see *ibid*.
"ship or vessel"—see *ibid*.

Continental shelf

8.—(1) In this regulation—
"designated area" means any area which may from time to time be designated by Order in Council under the Continental Shelf Act 1964 as an area within which the rights of the United Kingdom with respect to the seabed and subsoil and their natural resources may be exercised;
"prescribed area" means an area over which Norway or any member State (other than the United Kingdom) exercises sovereign rights for the purpose of exploring the seabed and subsoil and exploiting their natural resources, being an area outside the territorial seas of Norway or that member State or any other area which is from time to time specified under section 22(5) of the Oil and Gas (Enterprise) Act 1982;
"prescribed employment" means employment in a designated area or prescribed area in connection with any activity mentioned in section 23(2) of the Oil and Gas (Enterprise) Act 1982 in any designated area or in any prescribed area.

(2) Subject to regulation 3, a woman in prescribed employment shall be treated as an employee for the purposes of Part V of the 1986 Act notwithstanding that she may not be employed in Great Britain.

4.71

Statutory Maternity Pay (Persons Abroad and Mariners) Regulations 1987

DEFINITIONS

"the 1986 Act"—see reg.1(2).
"designated area"—see para.(2).
"prescribed area"—see *ibid*.
"prescribed employment"—see *ibid*.

Persons Abroad—maternity pay period not commencing or ending

4.72   **9.** [¹. . .]

AMENDMENT

1. Social Security Contributions, Statutory Maternity Pay and Statutory Sick Pay (Miscellaneous Amendments) Regulations 1996 (SI 1996/777), reg.4(6) (April 6, 1996).

Statutory Maternity Pay (National Health Service Employees) Regulations 1991

(SI 1991/590)

4.73   The Secretary of State for Social Security, in exercise of the powers conferred by sections 49, 50(2A), 84(1) of, and paragraph 6 of Schedule 4 to the Social Security Act 1986 and of all other powers enabling him in that behalf, by this instrument, which contains only Regulations consequential upon paragraph 22 of Schedule 6 to the Social Security Act 1990, makes the following Regulations:

ARRANGEMENT OF REGULATIONS

1. Citation, commencement and interpretation
2. Treatment of more than one contract of employment as one contract
3. Notification of election
4. Provision of information
5. Treatment of two or more employers as one
6. Time for which an election is to have effect

Citation, commencement and interpretation

4.74   **1.**—(1) These Regulations may be cited as the Statutory, Maternity Pay (National Health Service Employees) Regulations 1991 and shall come into force on 1st April 1991.

(2) In these Regulations, a "health authority" [²shall in relation to Wales have the same meaning it has in section 8] of the National Health Service Act 1977, and in relation to Scotland mean the health board within the meaning of section 2 of the National Health Service (Scotland) Act 1978.

[¹(3) In these Regulations, "Primary Care Trust" means a Primary Care Trust established under section 16A of the National Health Service Act 1977.]

(SI 1991/590, reg. 1)

[²(4) In these Regulations, "Strategic Health Authority" means a Strategic Health Authority established under section 8 of the National Health Service Act 1977.]

[³(5) In these Regulations, a reference to "NHS trust" shall be construed to include a reference to an NHS foundation trust within the meaning of section 1(1) of the Health and Social Care (Community Health and Standards) Act 2003 where the application for authorisation to become an NHS foundation trust was made by an NHS trust.]

AMENDMENTS

1. Health Act 1999 (Supplementary, Consequential etc. Provisions) (No.2) Order 2000 (SI 2000/694), art.3 and Sch., para.3(2) (April 1, 2000).
2. National Health Service Reform and Health Care Professions Act 2002 (Supplementary, Consequential etc. Provisions) Regulations 2002 (SI 2002/2469), reg.4 and Sch.1, Pt 2, para.51 (October 1, 2002).
3. Health and Social Care (Community Health and Standards) Act 2003 (Supplementary and Consequential Provision) (NHS Foundation Trusts) Order 2004 (SI 2004/696), art.3(17) and Sch.17 (April 1, 2004).

Treatment of more than one contract of employment as one contract

2. Where, in consequence of the establishment of one or more National Health Service Trusts under Part I of the National Health Service and Community Care Act 1990, or the National Health Service (Scotland) Act 1978, a woman's contract of employment is treated by a scheme under that Part or Act as divided so as to constitute two or more contracts, [¹or where an order under paragraph 23(1) of Schedule 5A to the National Health Service Act 1977 provides that a woman's contract of employment is so divided,] she may elect for all those contracts to be treated as one contract for the purposes of Part V of the Social Security Act 1986.

4.75

AMENDMENT

1. Health Act 1999 (Supplementary, Consequential etc. Provisions) (No.2) Order 2000 (SI 2000/694), art.3 and Sch., para.3(3) (April 1, 2000).

Notification of election

3. A woman who makes an election under regulation 2 above shall give written notification of that election to each of her employers under the two or more contracts of service mentioned in that regulation at least [¹28 days] before the first day she is going to be absent from work with any of her employers, wholly or partly because of pregnancy, or if in the particular circumstances that is not practicable, as soon as is reasonably practicable.

4.76

AMENDMENT

1. Social Security, Statutory Maternity Pay and Statutory Sick Pay (Miscellaneous Amendments) Regulations 2002 (SI 23002/2690), reg.11 (November 24, 2002).

Provision of information

4. A woman who makes an election under regulation 2 above shall, within [¹28 days] of giving notice of that election or if in the particular circumstances that is not practicable, as soon as is reasonably practicable thereafter,

4.77

Statutory Maternity Pay (National Health Service Employees) Regulations 1991

provide each of her employers under the two or more contracts of service mentioned under that regulation with the following information—
  (a) the name and address of each of those employers; and
  (b) the date her employment with each of those employers commenced; and
  (c) details of her earnings during the relevant period from each employer and for this purpose the expressions "earnings" and "relevant period" have the same meanings as they have for the purposes of section 50(3) of the Social Security Act 1986.

AMENDMENT

1. Social Security, Statutory Maternity Pay and Statutory Sick Pay (Miscellaneous Amendments) Regulations 2002 (SI 2002/2690), reg.12 (November 24, 2002).

Treatment of two or more employers as one

4.78 5. The employer to be regarded for the purposes of statutory maternity pay as the employer under the one contract where 2 or more contracts of service are treated as one in accordance with regulation 2 above shall be—
  [1(a) in the case of a woman whose contract of employment is treated by a scheme under Part I of the National Health Service and Community Care Act 1990 or the National Health Service (Scotland) Act 1978 as divided—
    (i) the Health Authority or Primary Care Trust from which the woman was transferred, in a case where any one of the contracts of service is with that Health Authority or Primary Care Trust; or
    (ii) the first NHS trust to which a contract of service was transferred in a case where none of the contracts of service are with the Health Authority or Primary Care Trust from which she was transferred;
  or
  (b) in the case of a woman whose contract of employment is divided as provided by an order under paragraph 23(1) of Schedule 5A to the National Health Service Act 1977—
    (i) the [2Strategic Health Authority], NHS trust or Primary Care Trust from which the woman was transferred, in a case where any one of the contracts of service is with that body; or
    (ii) the first Primary Care Trust to which a contract of service was transferred in a case where none of the contracts of service are with the body from which she was transferred.]

AMENDMENTS

1. Health Act 1999 (Supplementary, Consequential etc. Provisions) (No.2) Order 2000 (SI 2000/694), art.3 and Sch., para.3(4) (April 1, 2000).
2. National Health Service Reform and Health Care Professions Act 2002 (Supplementary, Consequential etc. Provisions) Regulations 2002 (SI 2002/2469), reg.6 and Sch.3 (October 1, 2002).

Time for which an election is to have effect

4.79 6. An election made under regulation 2 shall lapse at the end of the maternity pay period.

(SI 1994/1882) (as amended)

Statutory Maternity Pay (Compensation of Employers) and Miscellaneous Amendment Regulations 1994

(SI 1994/1882) (AS AMENDED)

The Secretary of State for Social Security, in exercise of powers conferred on him by sections 35(3), 167(1), (1A), (1B) and (4), 171(1) and 175(1) to (4) of the Social Security Contributions and Benefits Act 1992 and of all other powers enabling him in that behalf after agreement by the Social Security Advisory Committee that proposals in respect of regulation 9 should not be referred to it, hereby makes the following Regulations:

ARRANGEMENT OF REGULATIONS

1. Citation, commencement and interpretation
2. Meaning of "small employer"
3. Determination of the amount of additional payment to which a small employer shall be entitled
4. Right of employers to prescribed amount
5. Application for advance funding from the Board
6. Deductions from payments to the Board
6A. Payments to employers by the Board
7. Date when certain contributions are to be treated as paid
7A. Overpayments
8. Revocation
9. *Omitted*

4.80

Citation, commencement and interpretation

1.—(1) These Regulations may be cited as the Statutory Maternity Pay (Compensation of Employers) and Miscellaneous Amendment Regulations 1994 and regulations 2–7 shall have effect in relation to payments of statutory maternity pay due on or after 4th September 1994.

(2) This regulation and regulation 9 shall come into force on July 31, 1994.

(3) Regulations 2 to 8 shall come into force on 4th September 1994.

(4) In these Regulations—

[¹"the Board" means the Commissioners of Inland Revenue;]

"the Contributions and Benefits Act" means the Social Security Contributions and Benefits Act 1992;

"the Maternity Allowance Regulations" means the Social Security (Maternity Allowance) Regulations 1987;

[¹. . .];

[¹"contributions payments" has the same meaning as in section 167(8) of the Contributions and Benefits Act;]

[¹"the Contributions Regulations" means the Social Security (Contributions) Regulations 2001;]

"employer" shall include a person who was previously an employer of a woman to whom a payment of statutory maternity pay was made, whether or not that person remains her employer at the date any

4.81

deduction from contributions payments is made by him in accordance with regulation 5 or, as the case may be, any payment is received by him in accordance with regulation 6;

[¹"the Employment Act" means the Employment Act 2002;]

"income tax month" means the period beginning on the 6th day of any calendar month and ending on the 5th day of the following calendar month; [¹. . .];

[¹"income tax quarter" means, in any tax year, the period beginning on 6th April and ending on 5th July the period beginning on 6th July and ending on 5th October the period beginning on 6th October and ending on 5th January or the period beginning on 6th January and ending on 5th April;]

"qualifying day" means the first day in the week immediately preceding the 14th week before the expected week of confinement in which a woman who is or has been an employee first satisfies the conditions of entitlement to statutory maternity pay for which a deduction from a contributions payment is made by her employer in respect of a payment of statutory maternity pay made by him;

"qualifying tax year" means the tax year preceding the tax year in which the qualifying day in question falls.

[¹"statutory adoption pay" means any payment under section 171ZL of the Contributions and Benefits Act;

"statutory paternity pay" means any payment under section 171ZA or 171ZB of the Contributions and Benefits Act;

"tax year" means the period of 12 months beginning on 6th April in any year;

"writing" includes writing delivered by means of electronic communications approved by directions issued by the Board pursuant to regulations made under section 132 of the Finance Act 1999;]

[¹(5) Any reference in these Regulations to the employees of any employer includes, where the context permits, a reference to his former employees.]

(6) [¹. . .].

AMENDMENT

1. Statutory Maternity Pay (Compensation of Employers) Amendment Regulations 2003 (SI 2003/672), reg.2 (April 6, 2003).

GENERAL NOTE

4.82   These Regulations make provision for employers to be reimbursed for the cost of paying statutory maternity pay. The basic rule is that employers can recover 92 per cent of the total gross statutory maternity pay payments they make in any tax month (reg.4(a)). This is done by deducting such costs from tax payments, National Insurance contributions and other sums due to HMRC (reg.6). In certain circumstances employers may apply for advance funding from HMRC in order to meet their statutory maternity pay liabilities (reg.5; but see reg.7A regarding overpayments of such sums). Small employers—currently defined as those whose total National Insurance contributions do not exceed £45,000 in the previous tax year (reg.2(1))—are entitled to 100 per cent of the cost of their statutory maternity pay payments (reg.4(b)) together with a further 4.5 per cent of the total statutory maternity pay paid (reg.3). This additional amount is intended to compensate small employers for the cost of employers' National Insurance contributions on statutory maternity pay.

(SI 1994/1882, reg.1) (as amended)

Regulation 9 of these Regulations contained a miscellaneous amendment to reg.3(4) of the Social Security (Maternity Allowance) Regulations 1987 (SI 1987/416), which has itself subsequently been revoked, and so is not included in this volume (see Vol.I).

Meaning of "small employer"

2.—(1) Subject to the following provisions of this regulation, a small employer is an employer whose contributions payments for the qualifying tax year do not exceed [¹£45,000].

(2) For the purposes of this regulation, the amount of an employer's contributions payments shall be determined without regard to any deductions that may be made from them under any enactment or instrument.

(3) Where in the qualifying tax year an employer has made contributions payments in one or more, but less than 12, of the income tax months, the amount of his contributions payments for that tax year shall be estimated by adding together all of those payments, dividing the total amount by the number of those months in which he has made those payments and multiplying the resulting figure by 12.

(4) Where in the qualifying tax year an employer has made no contributions payments, but does have such payments in one or more income tax months which fall both—

(a) in the tax year in which the qualifying day falls; and
(b) before the qualifying day or, where there is more than one such day in that tax year, before the first of those days,

then the amount of his contributions payments for the qualifying tax year shall be estimated in accordance with paragraph (3) but as if the amount of the contributions payments falling in those months had fallen instead in the corresponding tax months in the qualifying tax year.

AMENDMENT

1. Statutory Maternity Pay (Compensation of Employers) Amendment Regulations 2004 (SI 2004/698), reg.2 (April 6, 2004).

DEFINITIONS

"contributions payments"—see reg.1(4).
"employer"—see *ibid.*
"qualifying day"—see *ibid.*
"qualifying tax year"—see *ibid.*

Determination of the amount of additional payment to which a small employer shall be entitled

3. In respect of any payment of statutory maternity pay [¹made in the tax year commencing [²6th April 2002], or in any subsequent tax year,] a small employer shall be [³entitled to recover an additional amount] being an amount equal to [²4.5 per cent.] of such payment, that percentage being the total amount of secondary Class 1 contributions estimated by the Secretary of State as to be paid in respect of statutory maternity pay by all employers in that year, expressed as a percentage of the total amount of statutory maternity pay estimated by him to be paid by all employers in that year.

701

Statutory Maternity Pay and Miscellaneous Amendment Regulations 1994

AMENDMENTS

1. Statutory Maternity Pay (Compensation of Employers) Amendment Regulations 1995 (SI 1995/566), reg.2 (April 6, 1995).
2. Statutory Maternity Pay (Compensation of Employers) Amendment Regulations 2002 (SI 2002/225), reg.2 (April 6, 2002).
3. Statutory Maternity Pay (Compensation of Employers) Amendment Regulations 2003 (SI 2003/672), reg.3 (April 6, 2003).

DEFINITIONS

"employer"—see reg.1(4).
"payment of statutory maternity pay"—see *ibid*.
"small employer"—see reg.2(1).

[¹Right of employers to prescribed amount

4.85
4. An employer who has made, or is liable to make, any payment of statutory maternity pay shall be entitled to recover—
(a) an amount equal to 92 per cent of such payment; or
(b) if he is a small employer—
  (i) an amount equal to such payment; and
  (ii) an additional amount under regulation 3, in accordance with the provisions of these Regulations.]

AMENDMENT

1. Statutory Maternity Pay (Compensation of Employers) Amendment Regulations 2003 (SI 2003/672), reg.4 (April 6, 2003).

DEFINITIONS

"employer"—see reg.1(4).
"payment of statutory maternity pay"—see *ibid*.
"small employer"—see reg.2(1).

[¹Application for advance funding from the Board

4.86
5.—(1) If an employer is entitled to recover an amount determined in accordance with regulation 4 in respect of statutory maternity pay which he is required to pay to an employee or employees in any income tax month or income tax quarter and the amount exceeds the aggregate of—
(a) the total amount of tax which the employer is required to pay to the collector of taxes in respect of deductions from the emoluments of his employees in accordance with the Income Tax (Employments) Regulations 1993 for that income tax month or income tax quarter;
(b) the total amount of deductions made by the employer from the emoluments of his employees for that income tax month or income tax quarter in accordance with regulations made under section 22(5) of the Teaching and Higher Education Act 1998 or section 73B of the Education (Scotland) Act 1980 or in accordance with Article 3(5) of the Education (Student Support) (Northern Ireland) Order 1988;
(c) the total amount of contributions payments which the employer is required to pay to the collector of taxes in respect of the emoluments of his employees (whether by means of deduction or otherwise) in accordance with the Contributions Regulations for that income tax month or income tax quarter;

(SI 1994/1882, reg. 5) (as amended)

    (d) the total amount of payments which the employer is required to pay to the collector of taxes in respect of deductions made on account of tax from payments to sub-contractors in accordance with section 559 of the Income and Corporation Taxes Act 1988 for that income tax month or income tax quarter; and

    (e) the statutory paternity pay, statutory adoption pay and statutory maternity pay which the employer is required to pay to his employees in that income tax month or income tax quarter,

the employer may apply to the Board in accordance with paragraph (2) for funds ("advance funding") to pay that excess (or so much of it as remains outstanding) to the employee or employees.

(2) Where—

    (a) the conditions in paragraph (1) are satisfied; or

    (b) the employer considers that the conditions in paragraph (1) will be satisfied on the date of any subsequent payment of emoluments to one or more employees who are entitled to a payment of statutory maternity pay,

the employer may apply to the Board for advance funding on a form approved for that purpose by the Board.

(3) An application by an employer under paragraph (2) shall be for an amount not exceeding the amount of statutory maternity pay which the employer is entitled to recover in accordance with regulation 4 and which he is required to pay to an employee or employees for the income tax month or income tax quarter to which the payment of emoluments relates.]

AMENDMENT

1. Statutory Maternity Pay (Compensation of Employers) Amendment Regulations 2003 (SI 2003/672), reg.4 (April 6, 2003).

DEFINITIONS

    "advance funding"—see para.(1).
    "the Board"—see reg.1(4).
    "the Contributions Regulations"—see *ibid.*
    "contributions payments"—see *ibid.*
    "employer"—see *ibid.*
    "income tax month"—see *ibid.*
    "income tax quarter"—see *ibid.*
    "statutory adoption pay"—see *ibid.*
    "statutory paternity pay"—see *ibid.*

[¹Deductions from payments to the Board

6. An employer who is entitled to recover an amount under regulation 4 may do so by making one or more deductions from the aggregate of the amounts specified in sub-paragraphs (a) to (e) of regulation 5(1), except where and insofar as—

    (a) those amounts relate to earnings paid before the beginning of the income tax month or income tax quarter in which the payment of statutory maternity pay was made;

    (b) those amounts are paid by him later than six years after the tax year in which the payment of statutory maternity pay was made;

    (c) the employer has received advance funding from the Board in accordance with an application under regulation 5; or

4.87

(d) the employer has made a request in writing under regulation 5 that the amount which he is entitled to recover under regulation 4 be paid to him and he has not received notification by the Board that such request is refused.]

AMENDMENT

1. Statutory Maternity Pay (Compensation of Employers) Amendment Regulations 2003 (SI 2003/672), reg.4 (April 6, 2003).

DEFINITIONS

"advance funding"—reg.5(1).
"the Board"—see reg.1(4).
"employer"—see *ibid*.
"income tax month"—see *ibid*.
"income tax quarter"—see *ibid*.
"writing"—see *ibid*.

[¹Payments to employers by the Board

4.88   **6A.** If, in an income tax month or an income tax quarter—
(a) the total amount that the employer is entitled to deduct under regulation 6 is less than the amount which the employer is entitled to recover under regulation 4;
(b) the Board is satisfied that this is so; and
(c) the employer has so requested in writing, the Board shall pay to the employer the sum that the employer is unable to deduct under regulation 6.]

AMENDMENT

1. Statutory Maternity Pay (Compensation of Employers) Amendment Regulations 2003 (SI 2003/672), reg.4 (April 6, 2003).

DEFINITIONS

"the Board"—see reg.1(4).
"income tax month"—see *ibid*.
"income tax quarter"—see *ibid*.
"writing"—see *ibid*.

Date when certain contributions are to be treated as paid

4.89   **7.** Where an employer has made a deduction from a contributions payment under [¹regulation 6], the date on which it is to be treated as having been paid for the purposes of [¹section 167(6)] of the Contributions and Benefits Act (amount deducted to be treated as paid and received towards discharging liability in respect of Class 1 contributions) is—
(a) in a case where the deduction did not extinguish the contributions payment, the date on which the remainder of the contributions payment or, as the case may be, the first date on which any part of the remainder of the contributions payment was paid; and
(b) in a case where the deduction extinguished the contributions payment, the 14th day after the end of the income tax month during which there were paid the earnings in respect of which the contributions payment was payable.

(SI 1994/1882, reg. 7) (as amended)

AMENDMENT

1. Statutory Maternity Pay (Compensation of Employers) Amendment Regulations 2003 (SI 2003/672), reg.5 (April 6, 2003).

DEFINITIONS

"the Contributions and Benefits Act"—see reg.1(4).
"contributions payments"—see *ibid.*
"employer"—see *ibid.*
"income tax month"—see *ibid.*

[¹Overpayments

7A.—(1) Where advance funding has been provided to an employer in accordance with an application under regulation 5, the Board may recover any part of it not used to pay statutory maternity pay ("the overpayment").

(2) An officer of the Board shall decide to the best of his judgement the amount of the overpayment and shall give notice in writing of his decision to the employer.

(3) A decision under paragraph (2) may be in respect of funding provided in accordance with regulation 5 for one or more income tax months or income tax quarters in a tax year—
   (a) in respect of one or more classes of employees specified in a decision notice (where a notice does not name any individual employee); or
   (b) in respect of one or more individual employees named in a decision notice.

(4) Subject to paragraphs (5), (6) or (7), Part 6 of the Taxes Management Act 1970 (collection and recovery) shall apply with any necessary modifications to a decision under this regulation as if the amount specified were an assessment and as if the amount set out in the notice were income tax charged on the employer.

(5) Where a decision under paragraph (2) relates to more than one employee, proceedings may be brought to recover the amount overpaid without distinguishing the sum to be repaid in respect of each employee and without specifying the employee in question.

(6) A decision to recover an amount made in accordance with this regulation shall give rise to one cause of action or matter of complaint for the purpose of proceedings under sections 65, 66 or 67 of the Taxes Management Act 1970.

(7) Nothing in paragraph (5) shall prevent separate proceedings being brought for the recovery of any amount which the employer is liable to repay in respect of each employee to whom the decision relates.]

DEFINITIONS

"the Board"—see reg.1(4).
"the overpayment"—see para.(1).
"advance funding"—see reg.5(1).
"employee"—see reg.1(5).
"employer"—see reg.1(4).
"income tax month"—see *ibid.*
"income tax quarter"—see *ibid.*
"tax year"—see *ibid.*
"writing"—see *ibid.*

Revocation

4.91   8. The Statutory Maternity Pay (Compensation of Employers) Regulations 1987 are hereby revoked.

Statutory Maternity Pay (General) (Modification and Amendment) Regulations 2000

(SI 2000/2883)

The Secretary of State for Social Security, in exercise of the powers conferred on him by sections 164(4), (9)(e) and (10), 165(1) and (3), 171(1) and 175(1) to (4) of the Social Security Contributions and Benefits Act 1992 and of all other powers enabling him in that behalf, after agreement by the Social Security Advisory Committee that proposals to make these Regulations should not be referred to it, hereby makes the following Regulations:

ARRANGEMENT OF REGULATIONS

4.92
1. Citation, commencement and interpretation
2. Modification of s.164(2)(a) of the Contributions and Benefits Act
3. Amendment of the Statutory Maternity Pay Regulations
4. Transitional provision

Citation, commencement and interpretation

4.93   1.—(1) These Regulations may be cited as the Statutory Maternity Pay (General) (Modification and Amendment) Regulations 2000 and shall come into force on 17th November 2000.
(2) In these Regulations—
"the Contributions and Benefits Act" means the Social Security Contributions and Benefits Act 1992;
"the Statutory Maternity Pay Regulations" means the Statutory Maternity Pay (General) Regulations 1986.

Modification of s.164(2)(a) of the Contributions and Benefits Act

4.94   2. Subject to regulation 4, in relation to a woman who is dismissed, or whose employment is otherwise terminated without her consent, after the beginning of the week immediately preceding the 14th week before the expected week of confinement, section 164(2)(a) of the Contributions and Benefits Act (conditions of entitlement to statutory maternity pay) shall be modified and have effect so that the words, "wholly or partly because of pregnancy or confinement" shall not apply.

DEFINITION

"Contributions and Benefits Act"—see reg.1(2).

GENERAL NOTE

4.95   In order to qualify for statutory maternity pay, the general rule under SSCBA 1992, s.164(2)(a) is that the claimant must have been continuously employed in an

(SI 2000/2883, reg.2) (as amended)

employed earner's employment for 26 weeks up to the 15th week before the expected week of confinement but has then ceased to work for the employer "wholly or partly because of pregnancy or confinement". This latter requirement caused problems for women who were dismissed for some other reason (e.g. redundancy). These Regulations were therefore enacted in 2000 (but with effect from 4th March 2001: reg.4) so as to extend the right to statutory maternity pay to all women, unless they left their job voluntarily.

Amendment of the Statutory Maternity Pay Regulations

3. . . .   4.96

GENERAL NOTE

The amendments made by reg.3 have been incorporated into the text of the Statutory Maternity Pay (General) Regulations 1986 (SI 1986/1960) in this volume.   4.97

Transitional provision

4. In relation to a woman whose expected week of confinement begins before 4th March 2001, the Contributions and Benefits Act and the Statutory Maternity Pay Regulations shall have effect as if these Regulations were not in force.   4.98

DEFINITIONS

"Contributions and Benefits Act"—see reg.1(2).
"Statutory Maternity Pay Regulations"—see *ibid*.

PART V

STATUTORY PATERNITY PAY AND STATUTORY ADOPTION PAY

Statutory Paternity Pay and Statutory Adoption Pay (Weekly Rates) Regulations 2002

(SI 2002/2818) (AS AMENDED)

Whereas a draft of the following Regulations was laid before Parliament in accordance with section 176(1)(a) of the Social Security Contributions and Benefits Act 1992 and approved by a resolution of each House of Parliament:

Now, therefore, the Secretary of State, in exercise of the powers conferred on her by sections 171ZE(1) and 171ZN(1) of the Social Security Contributions and Benefits Act 1992 and section 5(1)(l) of the Social Security Administration Act 1992, by this instrument, which contains only provision made by virtue of sections 2, 4 and 53 of and paragraphs 8 and 11 of Schedule 7 to the Employment Act 2002 and is made before the end of the period of 6 months from the coming into force of those enactments, hereby makes the following Regulations—

ARRANGEMENT OF REGULATIONS

1. Citation and commencement.
2. Weekly rate of payment of statutory paternity pay.
3. Weekly rate of payment of statutory adoption pay.
4. Rounding of fractional amounts.

Citation and commencement

1.—These Regulations may be cited as the Statutory Paternity Pay and Statutory Adoption Pay (Weekly Rates) Regulations and shall come into force on 8th December 2002.

GENERAL NOTE

These Regulations specify the weekly rate of statutory paternity pay and statutory adoption pay. In the current year, statutory paternity pay is the lower of £112.75 per week or 90 per cent of the employee's normal weekly earnings where the paternity pay period starts after that date (reg.2). Statutory adoption pay is set at the lower of £112.75 per week or 90 per cent of the employee's normal weekly earnings (reg.3). Fractional amounts are rounded in accordance with reg.4.

[1Weekly rate of payment of statutory paternity pay

2. The weekly rate of payment of statutory paternity pay shall be the smaller of the following two amounts—
  (a) [2£112.75];
  (b) 90 per cent. of the normal weekly earnings of the person claiming statutory paternity pay, determined in accordance with regulations 39 and 40 of the Statutory Paternity Pay and Statutory Adoption Pay (General) Regulations 2002.]

Statutory Paternity Pay and Statutory Adoption Pay Regulations 2002

AMENDMENTS

1. Statutory Paternity Pay and Statutory Adoption Pay (Weekly Rates) (Amendment) Regulations 2004 (SI 2004/925), reg.2 (April 4, 2004).
2. Social Security Benefits Up-rating Order 2007 (SI 2007/88), art.11(a) (April 1, 2007).

Weekly rate of payment of statutory adoption pay

5.5 **3.** The weekly rate of payment of statutory adoption pay shall be the smaller of the following two amounts—
(a) [¹£112.75];
(b) 90 per cent of the normal weekly earnings of the person claiming statutory adoption pay, determined in accordance with regulations 39 and 40 of the Statutory Paternity Pay and Statutory Adoption Pay (General) Regulations 2002.

AMENDMENT

1. Social Security Benefits Up-rating Order 2007 (SI 2007/88), art.11(b) (April 1, 2007).

Rounding of fractional amounts

5.6 [¹**4.** Where any payment of—
(a) statutory paternity pay is made on the basis of a calculation at—
   (i) the weekly rate specified in regulation 2(b); or
   (ii) the daily rate of one-seventh of the weekly rate specified in regulation 2(a) or (b); or
(b) statutory adoption pay is made on the basis of a calculation at—
   (i) the weekly rate specified in regulation 3(b); or
   (ii) the daily rate of one-seventh of the weekly rate specified in regulation 3(a) or (b),
and that amount includes a fraction of a penny, the payment shall be rounded up to the next whole number of pence.]

AMENDMENT

1. Statutory Paternity Pay and Statutory Adoption Pay (General) and the Statutory Paternity Pay and Statutory Adoption Pay (Weekly Rates) (Amendment) Regulations 2006 (SI 2006/2236), reg.4 (October 1, 2006).

GENERAL NOTE

5.7 The amended version of reg.4 applies in relation to an entitlement to SPP (birth) in respect of children whose expected week of birth begins on or after April 1, 2007 and to SPP (adoption) and SAP in respect of children expected to be placed for adoption, where the placement is expected to occur on or after April 1, 2007 (see reg.2 of SI 2006/2236).

(SI 2002/2819) (as amended)

Statutory Paternity Pay and Statutory Adoption Pay (National Health Service Employees) Regulations 2002

(SI 2002/2819) (AS AMENDED)

The Secretary of State, in exercise of the powers conferred on her by virtue of sections 171ZJ(9) and (10) and 171ZS(9) and (10) of the Social Security Contributions and Benefits Act 1992 and with the concurrence of the Commissioners of Inland Revenue by this instrument, which contains only provision made by virtue of sections 2 and 4 of the Employment Act 2002 and is made before the end of the period of 6 months from the coming into force of those enactments hereby makes the following Regulations—

ARRANGEMENT OF SECTIONS

1. Citation, commencement and interpretation.
2. Treatment of more than one contract of employment as one contract.
3. Notification of election.
4. Provision of information.
5. Treatment of two or more employers as one.
6. Time for which an election is to have effect.

Citation, commencement and interpretation

1.—(1) These Regulations may be cited as the Statutory Paternity Pay and Statutory Adoption Pay (National Health Service Employees) Regulations 2002 and shall come into force on 8th December 2002.

(2) In these Regulations—

"the Act" means the Social Security Contributions and Benefits Act 1992;

"the 1977 Act" means the National Health Service Act 1977;

"the 1978 Act" means the National Health Service (Scotland) Act 1978;

"the 1990 Act" means the National Health Service and Community Care Act 1990;

"the 2002 Act" means the National Health Service Reform and Health Care Professions Act 2002;

"Health Authority" means, in relation to Wales, a Health Authority established under section 8 of the 1977 Act and in relation to Scotland means a Health Board established under section 2 of the 1978 Act;

[[1]"NHS trust" shall be construed to include a reference to an NHS foundation trust within the meaning of section 1(1) of the Health and Social Care (Community Health and Standards) Act 2003 where the application for authorisation to become an NHS foundation trust was made by an NHS trust.]

"Primary Care Trust" means a Primary Care Trust established under section 16A of the 1977 Act;

"statutory adoption pay period" means the period prescribed under section 171ZN(2) of the Act as the period in respect of which statutory adoption pay is payable to a person;

"statutory paternity pay period" means the period determined in accordance with section 171ZE(2) of the Act as the period in respect of which statutory paternity pay is payable to a person;

713

"Strategic Health Authority" means a Strategic Health Authority established under section 8 of the 1977 Act.

AMENDMENT

1. Health and Social Care (Community Health and Standards) Act 2003 (Supplementary and Consequential Provision) (NHS Foundation Trusts) Order 2004 (SI 2004/696), art.3(1) and Sch.1, para.42 (April 1, 2004).

GENERAL NOTE

These Regulations, made under the authority of SSCBA 1992, ss.171ZJ(9) and (10) and 171ZS(9) and (10), make special provision for those NHS workers who are employed under two or more separate contracts of employment with different NHS Trusts. The regulations enable them to elect to have such contracts treated as one contract for the purposes of entitlement to statutory paternity pay and statutory adoption pay.

Treatment of more than one contract of employment as one contract

2. Where, in consequence of the establishment of one or more National Health Service Trusts under section 5 of the 1990 Act or section 12A of the 1978 Act, a person's contract of employment is treated by a scheme under section 6 of the 1990 Act or section 12B of the 1978 Act as divided so as to constitute two or more contracts, or where an order under paragraph 23(1) of Schedule 5A to the 1977 Act provides that a person's contract is so divided, he may elect for all those contracts to be treated as one contract for the purposes of Parts 12ZA and 12ZB of the Act.

DEFINITIONS

"the Act"—see reg.1(2).
"the 1977 Act"—see *ibid*.
"the 1978 Act"—see *ibid*.
"the 1990 Act"—see *ibid*.

Notification of election

3. A person who makes an election under regulation 2 above shall give written notification of that election to each of his employers under the two or more contracts of employment mentioned in that regulation at least 28 days before the beginning of the statutory paternity pay period or adoption pay period or, if in the particular circumstances that is not practicable, as soon as is reasonably practicable.

DEFINITIONS

"statutory adoption pay period"—see reg.1(2).
"statutory paternity pay period"—see *ibid*.

Provision of information

4. A person who makes an election under regulation 2 above shall, within 28 days of giving notification of that election or, if in the particular circumstances that is not practicable, as soon as is reasonably practicable thereafter, provide each of his employers under the two or more contracts of employment mentioned in that regulation with the following information—
    (a) the name and address of each of those employers;

(SI 2002/2819, reg.4) (as amended)

(b) the date his employment with each of those employers commenced; and
(c) details of his normal weekly earnings during the relevant period from each employer, and for this purpose the expressions "normal weekly earnings" and "relevant period" have the same meanings as they have for the purposes of Parts 12ZA and 12ZB of the Act.

DEFINITIONS

"normal weekly earnings"—para.(c) and SSCBA 1992, ss.171ZJ(6) and 171ZS(6) and Statutory Paternity Pay and Statutory Adoption Pay (General) Regulations 2002 (SI 2002/2822), reg.40.
"relevant period"—para.(c) and SSCBA 1992, ss.171ZJ(7) and 171ZS(7) and Statutory Paternity Pay and Statutory Adoption Pay (General) Regulations 2002 (SI 2002/2822), reg.40(3).

Treatment of two or more employers as one

5. The employer to be regarded for the purposes of statutory paternity pay or statutory adoption pay as the employer under the one contract where two or more contracts are treated as one in accordance with regulation 2 above shall be— 5.14

(a) in the case of a person whose contract of employment is treated by a scheme under section 6 of the 1990 Act or section 12B of the 1978 Act as divided—
  (i) the Health Authority or Primary Care Trust from which the person was transferred in a case where any one of the contracts of employment is with that Health Authority or Primary Care Trust; or
  (ii) the first NHS trust to which a contract of employment was transferred in a case where none of the contracts of employment is with the Health Authority or Primary Care Trust; or
(b) in the case of a person whose contract of employment is divided as provided by an order under paragraph 23(1) of Schedule 5A to the 1977 Act—
  (i) the Strategic Health Authority, NHS trust or Primary Care Trust from which the person was transferred, in a case where any one of the contracts of employment is with that body; or
  (ii) the first Primary Care Trust to which a contract of employment was transferred in a case where none of the contracts of employment is with the body from which he was transferred.

DEFINITIONS

"the 1977 Act"—see reg.1(2).
"the 1978 Act"—see *ibid.*
"Health Authority"—see *ibid.*
"Primary Care Trust"—see *ibid.*
"Strategic Health Authority"—see *ibid.*

Time for which an election is to have eVect

6. An election made under regulation 2 shall lapse at the end of the statutory paternity pay period or, as the case may be, the adoption pay period. 5.15

715

DEFINITIONS

"statutory adoption pay period"—see reg.1(2).
"statutory paternity pay period"—see *ibid*.

Statutory Paternity Pay and Statutory Adoption Pay (Administration) Regulations 2002

(SI 2002/2820)

The Secretary of State, in exercise of the powers conferred on her by sections 7(1), (2)(a) and (b), (4)(a), (b) and (c) and (5), 8(1) and (2)(a), (b) and (c), 10(1) and (2) and 51(1) of the Employment Act 2002 and sections 8(1)(f) and (ga) and 25 of the Social Security Contributions (Transfer of Functions, etc.) Act 1999 and with the concurrence of the Commissioners of Inland Revenue, hereby makes the following Regulations—

ARRANGEMENT OF SECTIONS

1. Citation and commencement.
2. Interpretation.
3. Funding of employers' liabilities to make payments of statutory paternity or statutory adoption pay.
4. Application for funding from the Board.
5. Deductions from payments to the Board.
6. Payments to employers by the Board.
7. Date when certain contributions are to be treated as paid.
8. Overpayments.
9. Records to be maintained by employers.
10. Inspection of employers' records.
11. Provision of information relating to entitlement to statutory paternity pay or statutory adoption pay.
12. Application for the determination of any issue arising as to, or in connection with, entitlement to statutory paternity pay or statutory adoption pay.
13. Applications in connection with statutory paternity pay or statutory adoption pay.
14. Provision of information.

Citation and commencement

1. These Regulations may be cited as the Statutory Paternity Pay and Statutory Adoption Pay (Administration) Regulations 2002 and shall come into force on 8th December 2002.

GENERAL NOTE

These Regulations provide for employers to be reimbursed for the cost of making payments of statutory paternity pay and statutory adoption pay. They are therefore modelled in part on the Statutory Maternity Pay (Compensation of Employers) and Miscellaneous Amendment Regulations 1994 (SI 1994/1882). As with the regulations governing statutory maternity pay, they provide for employers to claim back 92 per cent of the total costs of their statutory paternity pay and statutory adoption pay payments, or 100 per cent in the case of small employers, with a small additional

(SI 2002/2820, reg.1) (as amended)

element in the latter instance (reg.3). Employers receive such monies by making deductions from income tax, National Insurance contributions and other payments that would otherwise be due to HMRC (reg.4). There is provision for HMRC to make a direct payment to an employer where such deductions would otherwise be insufficient (reg.6). HMRC also has the power to recover overpayments from employers (reg.8).

These Regulations also require employers to maintain relevant records (reg.9) and to permit HMRC officers to inspect such records (reg.10). Furthermore, employers who decide that they have no liability to pay statutory paternity pay or statutory adoption pay to an employee or ex-employee must give any such person details of that decision and the reasons for it (reg.11). Any question relating to entitlement to statutory paternity pay or statutory adoption pay may be submitted by the employee concerned to HMRC for decision (regs 12 and 13). HMRC has information-gathering powers as set out in reg.14.

Regulations 2 and 11 of these regulations are amended for the purposes of adoptions from overseas by the Statutory Paternity Pay (Adoption) and Statutory Adoption Pay (Adoptions from Overseas) (Administration) Regulations 2003 (SI 2003/1192).

Interpretation

2.—(1) In these Regulations—

"adopter", in relation to a child, means a person with whom the child is matched for adoption;

"adoption leave" means leave under section 75A of the Employment Rights Act 1996;

"adoption pay period" means the period prescribed under section 171ZN(2) of the Contributions and Benefits Act as the period in respect of which statutory adoption pay is payable to a person;

"the Board" means the Commissioners of Inland Revenue;

"the Contributions and Benefits Act" means the Social Security Contributions and Benefits Act 1992;

"contributions payments" has the same meaning as in section 7 of the Employment Act;

"the Contributions Regulations" means the Social Security (Contributions) Regulations 2001;

"the Employment Act" means the Employment Act 2002;

"income tax month" means the period beginning on the 6th day of any calendar month and ending on the 5th day of the following calendar month;

"income tax quarter" means the period beginning on the 6th day of April and ending on the 5th day of July, the period beginning on the 6th day of July and ending on the 5th day of October, the period beginning on the 6th day of October and ending on the 5th day of January or the period beginning on the sixth day of January and ending on the 5th day of April;

"paternity leave" means leave under section 80A or section 80B of the Employment Rights Act 1996;

"paternity pay period" means the period determined in accordance with section 171ZE(2) of the Contributions and Benefits Act as the period in respect of which statutory paternity pay is payable to a person;

"statutory adoption pay" means any payment under section 171ZL of the Contributions and Benefits Act;

"statutory paternity pay" means any payment under section 171ZA or section 171ZB of the Contributions and Benefits Act;

"tax year" means the 12 months beginning with 6th April in any year;

5.19

"writing" includes writing delivered by means of electronic communications approved by directions issued by the Board pursuant to regulations under section 132 of the Finance Act 1999;

(2) Any reference in these Regulations to the employees of an employer includes former employees of his.

Funding of employers' liabilities to make payments of statutory paternity or statutory adoption pay

3.—(1) An employer who has made any payment of statutory paternity pay or statutory adoption pay shall be entitled—
   (a) to an amount equal to 92 per cent of such payment; or
   (b) if the payment qualifies for small employer's relief by virtue of section 7(3) of the Employment Act—
      (i) to an amount equal to such payment; and
      (ii) to an additional payment equal to the amount to which the employer would have been entitled under section 167(2)(b) of the Contributions and Benefits Act had the payment been a payment of statutory maternity pay.

(2) The employer shall be entitled in either case (a) or case (b) to apply for advance funding in respect of such payment in accordance with regulation 4, or to deduct it in accordance with regulation 5 from amounts otherwise payable by him.

DEFINITIONS

"Contributions and Benefits Act"—see reg.2(1).
"Employment Act"—see *ibid*.
"statutory adoption pay"—see *ibid*.
"statutory paternity pay"—see *ibid*.

Application for funding from the Board

4.—(1) If an employer is entitled to a payment determined in accordance with regulation 3 in respect of statutory paternity pay or statutory adoption pay which he is required to pay to an employee or employees for an income tax month or income tax quarter, and the payment exceeds the aggregate of—
   (a) the total amount of tax which the employer is required to pay to the collector of taxes in respect of the deductions from the emoluments of his employees in accordance with the Income Tax (Employments) Regulations 1993 for the same income tax month or income tax quarter;
   (b) the total amount of the deductions made by the employer from the emoluments of his employees for the same income tax month or income tax quarter in accordance with regulations under section 22(5) of the Teaching and Higher Education Act 1998 or section 73B of the Education (Scotland) Act 1980 or in accordance with article 3(5) of the Education (Student Support) (Northern Ireland) Order 1998;
   (c) the total amount of contributions payments which the employer is required to pay to the collector of taxes in respect of the emoluments of his employees (whether by means of deduction or otherwise) in

(SI 2002/2820, reg. 4) (as amended)

accordance with the Contributions Regulations for the same income tax month or income tax quarter; and
(d) the total amount of payments which the employer is required to pay to the collector of taxes in respect of the deductions made on account of tax from payments to sub-contractors in accordance with section 559 of the Income and Corporation Taxes Act 1988 for the same income tax month or income tax quarter,

the employer may apply to the Board in accordance with paragraph (2) for funds to pay the statutory paternity pay or statutory adoption pay (or so much of it as remains outstanding) to the employee or employees.

(2) Where—
(a) the condition in paragraph (1) is satisfied; or
(b) the employer considers that the condition in paragraph (1) will be satisfied on the date of any subsequent payment of emoluments to one or more employees who are entitled to payment of statutory paternity pay or statutory adoption pay,

the employer may apply to the Board for funding in a form approved for that purpose by the Board.

(3) An application by an employer under paragraph (2) shall be for an amount up to, but not exceeding, the amount of the payment to which the employer is entitled in accordance with regulation 3 in respect of statutory paternity pay and statutory adoption pay which he is required to pay to an employee or employees for the income tax month or income tax quarter to which the payment of emoluments relates.

DEFINITIONS

"the Board"—see reg.2(1).
"contributions payments"—see *ibid*.
"the Contributions Regulations"—see *ibid*.
"income tax month"—see *ibid*.
"income tax quarter"—see *ibid*.
"statutory adoption pay"—see *ibid*.
"statutory paternity pay"—see *ibid*.

Deductions from payments to the Board

5. An employer who is entitled to a payment determined in accordance with regulation 3 may recover such payment by making one or more deductions from the aggregate of the amounts specified in subparagraphs (a) to (d) of regulation 4(1) except where and in so far as—
   (a) those amounts relate to earnings paid before the beginning of the income tax month or income tax quarter in which the payment of statutory paternity pay or statutory adoption pay was made;
   (b) those amounts are paid by him later than six years after the end of the tax year in which the payment of statutory paternity pay or statutory adoption pay was made;
   (c) the employer has received payment from the Board under regulation 4; or
   (d) the employer has made a request in writing under regulation 4 that the payment to which he is entitled in accordance with regulation 3 be paid to him and he has not received notification by the Board that the request is refused.

5.22

Statutory Paternity Pay and Statutory Adoption Pay Regulations 2002

DEFINITIONS

"the Board"—see reg.2(1).
"income tax month"—see *ibid*.
"income tax quarter"—see *ibid*.
"statutory adoption pay"—see *ibid*.
"statutory paternity pay"—see *ibid*.
"tax year"—see *ibid*.
"writing"—see *ibid*.

Payments to employers by the Board

6. If the total amount which an employer is or would otherwise be entitled to deduct under regulation 5 is less than the payment to which the employer is entitled in accordance with regulation 3 in an income tax month or income tax quarter, and the Board are satisfied that this is so, then provided that the employer has in writing requested them to do so, the Board shall pay the employer such amount as the employer was unable to deduct.

DEFINITIONS

"the Board"—see reg.2(1).
"income tax month"—see *ibid*.
"income tax quarter"—see *ibid*.
"writing"—see *ibid*.

Date when certain contributions are to be treated as paid

7. Where an employer has made a deduction from a contributions payment under regulation 5, the date on which it is to be treated as having been paid for the purposes of section 7(5) of the Employment Act (when amount deducted from contributions payment to be treated as paid and received by the Board) is—
   (a) in a case where the deduction did not extinguish the contributions payment, the date on which the remainder of the contributions payment or, as the case may be, the first date on which any part of the remainder of the contributions payment was paid; and
   (b) in a case where the deduction extinguished the contributions payment, the 14th day after the end of the income tax month or income tax quarter during which there were paid the earnings in respect of which the contributions payment was payable.

DEFINITIONS

"the Board"—see reg.2(1).
"contributions payments"—see *ibid*.
"Employment Act"—see *ibid*.
"income tax month"—see *ibid*.
"income tax quarter"—see *ibid*.

Overpayments

8.—(1) This regulation applies where funds have been provided to the employer pursuant to regulation 4 in respect of one or more employees and it appears to an officer of the Board that the employer has not used the whole or part of those funds to pay statutory paternity pay or statutory adoption pay.

(SI 2002/2820, reg. 8) (as amended)

(2) An officer of the Board shall decide to the best of his judgement the amount of funds provided pursuant to regulation 4 and not used to pay statutory paternity pay or statutory adoption pay and shall serve notice in writing of his decision on the employer.

(3) A decision under this regulation may cover funds provided pursuant to regulation 4—
   (a) for any one income tax month or income tax quarter, or more than one income tax month or income tax quarter, in a tax year; and
   (b) in respect of a class or classes of employees specified in the decision notice (without naming the individual employees), or in respect of one or more employees named in the decision notice.

(4) Subject to the following provisions of this regulation, Part 6 of the Taxes Management Act 1970 (collection and recovery) shall apply with any necessary modifications to a decision under this regulation as if it were an assessment and as if the amount of funds determined were income tax charged on the employer.

(5) Where an amount of funds determined under this regulation relates to more than one employee, proceedings may be brought for the recovery of that amount without distinguishing the amounts making up that sum which the employer is liable to repay in respect of each employee and without specifying the employee in question, and the amount determined under this regulation shall be one cause of action or one matter of complaint for the purposes of proceedings under sections 65, 66 or 67 of the Taxes Management Act 1970.

(6) Nothing in paragraph (5) prevents the bringing of separate proceedings for the recovery of any amount which the employer is liable to repay in respect of each employee.

DEFINITIONS
   "the Board"—see reg.2(1).
   "income tax month"—see *ibid*.
   "income tax quarter"—see *ibid*.
   "statutory adoption pay"—see *ibid*.
   "statutory paternity pay"—see *ibid*.
   "tax year"—see *ibid*.
   "writing"—see *ibid*.

Records to be maintained by employers

9. Every employer shall maintain for three years after the end of a tax year in which he made payments of statutory paternity pay or statutory adoption pay to any employee of his a record of—
   (a) if the employee's paternity pay period or adoption pay period began in that year—
       (i) the date on which that period began; and
       (ii) the evidence of entitlement to statutory paternity pay or statutory adoption pay provided by the employee pursuant to regulations made under section 171ZC(3)(c) or section 171ZL(8)(c) of the Contributions and Benefits Act;
   (b) the weeks in that tax year in which statutory paternity pay or statutory adoption pay was paid to the employee and the amount paid in each week; and

(c) any week in that tax year which was within the employee's paternity pay period or adoption pay period but for which no payment of statutory paternity pay or statutory adoption pay was made to him and the reason no payment was made.

DEFINITIONS

"adoption pay period"—see reg.2(1).
"the Contributions and Benefits Act"—see *ibid*.
"paternity pay period"—see *ibid*.
"statutory adoption pay"—see *ibid*.
"statutory paternity pay"—see *ibid*.
"tax year"—see *ibid*.

Inspection of employers' records

10.—(1) Every employer, whenever called upon to do so by any authorised officer of the Board, shall produce the documents and records specified in paragraph (2) to that officer for inspection, at such time as that officer may reasonably require, at the prescribed place.

(2) The documents and records specified in this paragraph are—
(a) all wages sheets, deductions working sheets, records kept in accordance with regulation 9 and other documents and records whatsoever relating to the calculation or payment of statutory paternity pay or statutory adoption pay to his employees in respect of the years specified by such officer; or
(b) such of those wages sheets, deductions working sheets, or other documents and records as may be specified by the authorised officer.

(3) The "prescribed place" mentioned in paragraph (1) means—
(a) such place in Great Britain as the employer and the authorised officer may agree upon; or
(b) in default of such agreement, the place in Great Britain at which the documents and records referred to in paragraph (2)(a) are normally kept; or
(c) in default of such agreement and if there is no such place as is referred to in sub-paragraph (b) above, the employer's principal place of business in Great Britain.

(4) The authorised officer may—
(a) take copies of, or make extracts from, any document or record produced to him for inspection in accordance with paragraph (1);
(b) remove any document or record so produced if it appears to him to be necessary to do so, at a reasonable time and for a reasonable period.

(5) Where any document or record is removed in accordance with paragraph (4)(b), the authorised officer shall provide—
(a) a receipt for the document or record so removed; and
(b) a copy of the document or record, free of charge, within seven days, to the person by whom it was produced or caused to be produced where the document or record is reasonably required for the proper conduct of a business.

(6) Where a lien is claimed on a document produced in accordance with paragraph (1), the removal of the document under paragraph (4)(b) shall not be regarded as breaking the lien.

(SI 2002/2820, reg.10) (as amended)

(7) Where records are maintained by computer, the person required to make them available for inspection shall provide the authorised officer with all facilities necessary for obtaining information from them.

DEFINITIONS

"the Board"—see reg.2(1).
"prescribed place"—see para.(3).
"statutory adoption pay"—see reg.2(1).
"statutory paternity pay"—see *ibid*.

Provision of information relating to entitlement to statutory paternity pay or statutory adoption pay

11.—(1) Where an employer who has been given evidence of entitlement to statutory paternity pay or statutory adoption pay pursuant to regulations made under section 171ZC(3)(c) or section 171ZL(8)(c) of the Contributions and Benefits Act by a person who is or has been an employee decides that he has no liability to make payments of statutory paternity pay or statutory adoption pay to the employee, the employer shall furnish the employee with details of the decision and the reasons for it.

(2) Where an employer who has been given such evidence of entitlement to statutory adoption pay has made one or more payments of statutory adoption pay to the employee but decides, before the end of the adoption pay period, that he has no liability to make further payments to the employee because he has been detained in legal custody or sentenced to a term of imprisonment which was not suspended, the employer shall furnish the employee with—
(a) details of his decision and the reasons for it; and
(b) details of the last week in respect of which a liability to pay statutory adoption pay arose and the total number of weeks within the adoption pay period in which such a liability arose.

(3) The employer shall—
(a) return to the employee any evidence provided by him as referred to in paragraph (1) or (2); and
(b) comply with the requirements imposed by paragraph (1) within 28 days of—
  (i) in the case of entitlement to statutory paternity pay under section 171ZA(1) of the Contributions and Benefits Act, the day the employee gave notice of his intended absence or the end of the fifteenth week before the expected week of birth, whichever is the later; or
  (ii) in the case of entitlement to statutory paternity pay under section 171ZB(1) or of statutory adoption pay under section 171ZL(1) of the Contributions and Benefits Act, the end of the seven-day period that starts on the date on which the adopter is notified of having been matched with the child;
(c) comply with the requirements imposed by paragraph (2) within seven days of being notified of the employee's detention or sentence.

(4) For the purposes of paragraph (3)(b)(ii), an adopter is notified of having been matched with a child on the date on which he receives notification, under regulation 11(2) of the Adoption Agencies Regulations 1983 or regulation 12(3) of the Adoption Agencies (Scotland) Regulations 1996 that an adoption agency has decided that he would be a suitable adoptive parent for the child.

DEFINITIONS

"adopter"—see reg.2(1).
"adoption pay period"—see *ibid*.
"the Contributions and Benefits Act"—see *ibid*.
"statutory adoption pay"—see *ibid*.
"statutory paternity pay"—see *ibid*.

GENERAL NOTE

5.29   This regulation is modified for the purposes of adoptions from overseas by the Statutory Paternity Pay (Adoption) and Statutory Adoption Pay (Adoptions from Overseas) (Administration) Regulations 2003 (SI 2003/1192).

Application for the determination of any issue arising as to, or in connection with, entitlement to statutory paternity pay or statutory adoption pay

5.30   **12.**—(1) An application for the determination of any issue arising as to, or in connection with, entitlement to statutory paternity pay or statutory adoption pay may be submitted to an officer of the Board by the employee concerned.

(2) Such an issue shall be decided by an officer of the Board only on the basis of such an application or on his own initiative.

DEFINITIONS

"the Board"—see reg.2(1).
"statutory adoption pay"—see *ibid*.
"statutory paternity pay"—see *ibid*.

Applications in connection with statutory paternity pay or statutory adoption pay

5.31   **13.**—(1) An application for the determination of any issue referred to in regulation 12 shall be made in a form approved for the purpose by the Board.

(2) Where such an application is made by an employee, it shall—
(a) be made to an officer of the Board within six months of the earliest day in respect of which entitlement to statutory paternity pay or statutory adoption pay is in issue;
(b) state the period in respect of which entitlement to statutory paternity pay or statutory adoption pay is in issue; and
(c) state the grounds (if any) on which the applicant's employer had denied liability for statutory paternity pay or statutory adoption pay in respect of the period specified in the application.

DEFINITIONS

"the Board"—see reg.2(1).
"statutory adoption pay"—see *ibid*.
"statutory paternity pay"—see *ibid*.

Provision of information

5.32   **14.**—(1) Any person specified in paragraph (2) shall, where information or documents are reasonably required from him to ascertain whether statutory paternity pay or statutory adoption pay is or was payable, furnish that information or those documents within 30 days of receiving a notification from an officer of the Board requesting such information or documents.

(2) The requirement to provide such information or documents applies to—
  (a) any person claiming to be entitled to statutory paternity pay or statutory adoption pay;
  (b) any person who is, or has been, the spouse [1, the civil partner] or partner of such a person as is specified in paragraph (a);
  (c) any person who is, or has been, an employer of such a person as is specified in paragraph (a);
  (d) any person carrying on an agency or other business for the introduction or supply to persons requiring them of persons available to do work or to perform services; and
  (e) any person who is a servant or agent of any such person as is specified in paragraphs (a) to (d).

DEFINITIONS

"the Board"—see reg.2(1).
"statutory adoption pay"—see *ibid*.
"statutory paternity pay"—see *ibid*.

AMENDMENT

1. Civil Partnership Act 2004 (Amendments to Subordinate Legislation) Order 2005 (SI 2005/2114), art.2(17) and Sch.17, para.2 (December 5, 2005).

Statutory Paternity Pay and Statutory Adoption Pay (Persons Abroad and Mariners) Regulations 2002

(SI 2002/2821)

The Secretary of State, in exercise of the powers conferred upon her by virtue of sections 171ZI, 171ZJ(1), 171ZR and 171ZS(1) of the Social Security Contributions and Benefits Act 1992 and with the concurrence of the Treasury, by this instrument, which contains only provision made by virtue of sections 2 and 4 of the Employment Act 2002 and is made before the end of the period of 6 months from the coming into force of those enactments, hereby makes the following Regulations:

ARRANGEMENT OF REGULATIONS

1. Citation, commencement and interpretation.
2. Restriction on scope.
3. Treatment of persons in other EEA States as employees.
4. Treatment of certain persons absent from Great Britain as employees.
5. Entitlement to statutory paternity pay where person has worked in an EEA State.

5.33

6. Entitlement to statutory adoption pay where person has worked in an EEA State.
7. Time for compliance with Parts XIIZA and XIIZB of the Act or regulations made under them.
8. Mariners.
9. Continental Shelf.

Citation, commencement and interpretation

1.—(1) These Regulations may be cited as the Statutory Paternity Pay and Statutory Adoption Pay (Persons Abroad and Mariners) Regulations 2002 and shall come into force on 8th December 2002.

(2) In these Regulations—

"the Act" means the Social Security Contributions and Benefits Act 1992;
"adopter", in relation to a child, has the same meaning as it has in the General Regulations;
"the Contributions Regulations" means the Social Security Contributions Regulations 2001;
"EEA" means European Economic Area;
"EEA Agreement" means the Agreement on the European Economic Area signed at Oporto on 2nd May 1992 as adjusted by Protocol signed at Brussels on 17th March 1993;
"EEA State" means a State which is a contracting party to the EEA Agreement;
"the General Regulations" means the Statutory Paternity Pay and Statutory Adoption Pay (General) Regulations 2002;
"statutory paternity pay (birth)" and "statutory paternity pay (adoption)" have the same meaning as they have in the General Regulations;
"week" means a period of 7 days beginning with Sunday.

(3) For the purposes of these Regulations, a person is notified of having been matched with a child for the purposes of adoption on the date on which he receives notification, under regulation 11(2) of the Adoption Agencies Regulations 1983 or regulation 12(3) of the Adoption Agencies (Scotland) Regulations 1996, that an adoption agency has decided that the person would be a suitable adoptive parent for the child, either individually or jointly with another person.

GENERAL NOTE

These Regulations modify Pts XIIZA and XIIZB of the SSCBA 1992, which govern statutory paternity pay and statutory adoption pay respectively, in relation to persons abroad, those who work as mariners and persons who work on the Continental Shelf. They are modified in relation to adoptions from overseas by the Statutory Paternity Pay (Adoption) and Statutory Adoption Pay (Adoptions from Overseas) (Persons Abroad and Mariners) Regulations 2003 (SI 2003/1193).

Restriction on scope

2. A person who would not be treated under regulation 32 of the General Regulations as an employee for the purposes of Parts 12ZA (statutory paternity pay) and 12ZB (statutory adoption pay) of the Act if his employment were in Great Britain shall not be treated as an employee under these Regulations.

(SI 2002/2821, reg.2)

DEFINITIONS

"the Act"—see reg.1(2).
"the General Regulations"—see *ibid*.

Treatment of persons in other EEA States as employees

3. A person who is—
(a) gainfully employed in an EEA State other than the United Kingdom in such circumstances that, if his employment were in Great Britain, he would be an employee for the purposes of Parts 12ZA and 12ZB of the Act, or a person treated as such an employee under regulation 32 of the General Regulations; and
(b) subject to the legislation of the United Kingdom under Council Regulation (EEC) No.1408/71,
notwithstanding that he is not employed in Great Britain, shall be treated as an employee for the purposes of Parts 12ZA and 12ZB of the Act.

DEFINITIONS

"the Act"—see reg.1(2).
"EEA"—see *ibid*.
"EEA State"—see *ibid*.
"the General Regulations"—see *ibid*.

Treatment of certain persons absent from Great Britain as employees

4. Subject to regulation 8(3), where a person, while absent from Great Britain for any purpose, is gainfully employed by an employer who is liable to pay secondary Class 1 contributions in respect of his employment under section 6 of the Act or regulation 146 of the Contributions Regulations, he shall be treated as an employee for the purposes of Parts 12ZA and 12ZB of the Act.

DEFINITIONS

"the Act"—see reg.1(2).
"the Contributions Regulations"—see *ibid*.

Entitlement to statutory paternity pay where person has worked in an EEA State

5.—(1) A person who is an employee or treated as an employee under regulation 3 and who—
(a) in the week immediately preceding the 14th week before the expected week of the child's birth was in employed earner's employment with an employer in Great Britain; and
(b) had in any week within the period of 26 weeks immediately preceding that week been employed by the same employer in another EEA State,
shall be treated for the purposes of section 171ZA of the Act (entitlement to statutory paternity pay (birth)) as having been employed in employed earner's employment in those weeks in which he was so employed in the other EEA State.

(2) A person who is an employee or treated as an employee under regulation 3 and who—

Statutory Paternity Pay and Statutory Adoption Pay Regulations 2002

(a) in the week in which the adopter is notified of being matched with the child for purposes of adoption was in employed earner's employment with an employer in Great Britain; and
(b) had in any week within the period of 26 weeks immediately preceding that week been employed by the same employer in another EEA State,

shall be treated for the purposes of section 171ZB of the Act (entitlement to statutory paternity pay (adoption)) as having been employed in employed earner's employment in those weeks in which he was so employed in the other EEA State.

DEFINITIONS

"the Act"—see reg.1(2).
"adopter"—see *ibid*.
"EEA"—see *ibid*.
"EEA State"—see *ibid*.
"statutory paternity pay (adoption)"—see *ibid*.
"statutory paternity pay (birth)"—see *ibid*.
"week"—see *ibid*.

Entitlement to statutory adoption pay where person has worked in an EEA State

5.40   **6.** A person who is an employee or treated as an employee under regulation 3 and who—
(a) in the week in which he is notified that he has been matched with the child for the purposes of adoption was in employed earner's employment with an employer in Great Britain; and
(b) had in any week within the period of 26 weeks immediately preceding that week been employed by the same employer in another EEA State,

shall be treated for the purposes of section 171ZL of the Act (entitlement to statutory adoption pay) as having been employed in employed earner's employment in those weeks in which he was so employed in the other EEA State.

DEFINITIONS

"the Act"—see reg.1(2).
"EEA"—see *ibid*.
"EEA State"—see *ibid*.
"week"—see *ibid*.

Time for compliance with Parts 12ZA and 12ZB of the Act or regulations made under them

5.41   **7.** Where—
(a) a person is outside the United Kingdom;
(b) Parts 12ZA or 12ZB of the Act or regulations made under them require any act to be done forthwith or on the happening of a certain event or within a specified time; and
(c) because the person is outside the United Kingdom he or his employer cannot comply with the requirement,

(SI 2002/2821, reg. 7)

the person or the employer, as the case may be, shall be deemed to have complied with it if the act is performed as soon as reasonably practicable.

DEFINITION

"the Act"—see reg.1(2).

Mariners

8.—(1) In this regulation, "foreign-going ship", "home-trade ship" and "mariner" have the same meanings as in Case C of Part 9 of the Contributions Regulations (mariners) and the expressions "ship" and "ship or vessel", except in paragraph (3), include hovercraft.

(2) A mariner engaged in employment on board a home-trade ship with an employer who has a place of business within the United Kingdom shall be treated as an employee for the purposes of Parts 12ZA and 12ZB of the Act, notwithstanding that he may not be employed in Great Britain.

(3) A mariner who is engaged in employment—
(a) on a foreign-going ship; or
(b) on a home-trade ship with an employer who does not have a place of business within the United Kingdom,

shall not be treated as an employee for the purposes of Parts 12ZA and 12ZB of the Act, notwithstanding that he may have been employed in Great Britain.

5.42

DEFINITIONS

"the Act"—see reg.1(2).
"the Contributions Regulations"—see *ibid*.
"foreign-going ship"—see para.(1).
"home-trade ship"—see *ibid*.
"mariner"—see *ibid*.
"ship"—see *ibid*.
"ship or vessel"—see *ibid*.

Continental shelf

9.—(1) In this regulation—
"designated area" means any area which may from time to time be designated by Order in Council under section 1(7) of the Continental Shelf Act 1964 as an area within which the rights of the United Kingdom with respect to the seabed and subsoil and their natural resources may be exercised;
"prescribed employment" means any employment (whether under a contract of service or not) in a designated area in connection with continental shelf operations, as defined in section 120(2) of the Act.

(2) A person in prescribed employment shall be treated as an employee for the purposes of Parts 12ZA and 12ZB of the Act notwithstanding that he may not be employed in Great Britain.

5.43

DEFINITIONS

"the Act"—see reg.1(2).
"designated area"—see para.(1).
"prescribed employment"—see *ibid*.

Statutory Paternity Pay and Statutory Adoption Pay (General) Regulations 2002

(SI 2002/2822) (AS AMENDED)

The Secretary of State, in exercise of the powers conferred on her by sections 171ZA(2)(a), 171ZB(2)(a), 171ZC(3)(a), (c), (d), (f) and (g), 171ZD(2) and (3), 171ZE(2)(a), (b)(i), (3), (7) and (8), 171ZG(3), 171ZJ(1), (3), (4), (7) and (8), 171ZL(8)(b) to (d), (f) and (g), 171ZM(2) and (3), 171ZN(2), (5) and (6), 171ZP(6), 171ZS(1), (3), (4), (7) and (8), and 175(4) of the Social Security Contributions and Benefits Act 1992 and section 5(1)(g), (i) and (p) of the Social Security Administration Act 1992 and with the concurrence of the Commissioners of Inland Revenue in so far as such concurrence is required, by this instrument, which contains only provision made by virtue of sections 2, 4 and 53 of and paragraphs 8 and 11 of Schedule 7 to the Employment Act 2002 and is made before the end of the period of 6 months from the coming into force of those enactments, hereby makes the following Regulations—

ARRANGEMENT OF REGULATIONS

PART 1

Introduction

1. Citation and commencement.
2. Interpretation.
3. Application.

PART 2

Statutory paternity pay (birth)

4. Conditions of entitlement to statutory paternity pay (birth): relationship with newborn child and child's mother.
5. Modification of entitlement conditions: early birth.
6. Period of payment of statutory paternity pay (birth).
7. Additional notice requirements for statutory paternity pay (birth).
8. Qualifying period for statutory paternity pay (birth).
9. Evidence of entitlement to statutory paternity pay (birth).
10. Entitlement to statutory paternity pay (birth) where there is more than one employer.

PART 3

Statutory paternity pay (adoption)

11. Conditions of entitlement to statutory paternity pay (adoption): relationship with child and with person with whom the child is placed for adoption.

(SI 2002/2822) (as amended)

12. Period of payment of statutory paternity pay (adoption).
13. Additional notice requirements for statutory paternity pay (adoption).
14. Qualifying period for statutory paternity pay (adoption).
15. Evidence of entitlement to statutory paternity pay (adoption).
16. Entitlement to statutory paternity pay (adoption) where there is more than one employer.

PART 4

Statutory paternity pay: provisions applicable to both statutory paternity pay (birth) and statutory paternity pay (adoption)

17. Work during a statutory paternity pay period.
18. Cases where there is no liability to pay statutory paternity pay.
19. Statutory paternity pay and contractual remuneration.
20. Avoidance of liability for statutory paternity pay.

PART 5

Statutory adoption pay

21. Adoption pay period.
22. Adoption pay period in cases where adoption is disrupted.
23. Additional notice requirements for statutory adoption pay.
24. Evidence of entitlement to statutory adoption pay.
25. Entitlement to statutory adoption pay where there is more than one employer.
26. Work during an adoption pay period.
27. Cases where there is no liability to pay statutory adoption pay.
27A. Working for not more than 10 days during an adoption pay period.
28. Statutory adoption pay and contractual remuneration.
29. Termination of employment before start of adoption pay period.
30. Avoidance of liability for statutory adoption pay.

PART 6

Statutory paternity pay and statutory adoption pay: provisions applicable to both statutory paternity pay and statutory adoption pay

31. Introductory.
32. Treatment of persons as employees.
33. Continuous employment.
34. Continuous employment and unfair dismissal.
35. Continuous employment and stoppages of work.
36. Change of employer.
37. Reinstatement after service with the armed forces, etc.
38. Treatment of one or more employers or two or more contracts of service as one.
39. Meaning of "earnings".
40. Normal weekly earnings.
41. Payment of statutory paternity pay and statutory adoption pay.
42. Time when statutory paternity pay and statutory adoption pay are to be paid.

Statutory Paternity Pay and Statutory Adoption Pay Regulations 2002

43. Liability of the Board to pay statutory paternity pay or statutory adoption pay.
44. Liability of the Board to pay statutory adoption pay in cases of legal custody or imprisonment.
45. Payments by the Board.
46. Persons unable to act.
47. Service of notices by post.

PART 1

INTRODUCTION

Citation and commencement

5.45   1. These Regulations may be cited as the Statutory Paternity Pay and Statutory Adoption Pay (General) Regulations 2002 and shall come into force on 8th December 2002.

Interpretation

5.46   2.—(1) In these Regulations—
"the Act" means the Social Security Contributions and Benefits Act 1992;
"adopter", in relation to a child, means a person who has been matched with the child for adoption;
"adoption agency" has the meaning given, in relation to England and Wales, by section 1(4) of the Adoption Act 1976 and in relation to Scotland, by section 1(4) of the Adoption (Scotland) Act 1978;
"the Board" means the Commissioners of Inland Revenue;
"the Contributions Regulations" means the Social Security (Contributions) Regulations 2001;
"expected week", in relation to the birth of a child, means the week, beginning with midnight between Saturday and Sunday, in which it is expected that the child will be born;
"statutory paternity pay (adoption)" means statutory paternity pay payable in accordance with the provisions of Part 12ZA of the Act where the conditions specified in section 171ZB(2) of the Act are satisfied;
"statutory paternity pay (birth)" means statutory paternity pay payable in accordance with the provisions of Part 12ZA of the Act where the conditions specified in section 171ZA(2) of the Act are satisfied.
(2) For the purposes of these Regulations—
(a) a person is matched with a child for adoption when an adoption agency decides that that person would be a suitable adoptive parent for the child, either individually or jointly with another person; and
(b) a person is notified of having been matched with a child on the date on which he receives notification of the agency's decision, under regulation 11(2) of the Adoption Agencies Regulations 1983 or regulation 12(3) of the Adoption Agencies (Scotland) Regulations 1996.

Application

5.47   3.(1) Subject to the provisions of Part 12ZA of the Act (statutory paternity pay) and of these Regulations, there is entitlement to—

(SI 2002/2822, reg. 3) (as amended)

(a) statutory paternity pay (birth) in respect of children—
   (i) born on or after 6th April 2003; or
   (ii) whose expected week of birth begins on or after that date;
(b) statutory paternity pay (adoption) in respect of children—
   (i) matched with a person who is notified of having been matched on or after 6th April 2003; or
   (ii) placed for adoption on or after that date.

(2) Subject to the provisions of Part 12ZB of the Act (statutory adoption pay) and of these Regulations, there is entitlement to statutory adoption pay in respect of children—
(a) matched with a person who is notified of having been matched on or after 6th April 2003; or
(b) placed for adoption on or after that date.

DEFINITIONS

"the Act"—see reg.2(1).
"expected week"—see *ibid*.
"statutory paternity pay (adoption)"—see *ibid*.
"statutory paternity pay (birth)"—see *ibid*.

PART 2

STATUTORY PATERNITY PAY (BIRTH)

Conditions of entitlement to statutory paternity pay (birth): relationship with newborn child and child's mother

4. The conditions prescribed under section 171ZA(2)(a) of the Act are those prescribed in regulation 4(2)(b) and (c) of the Paternity and Adoption Leave Regulations 2002.

5.48

DEFINITION

"the Act"—see reg.2(1).

GENERAL NOTE

See the annotation to SSCBA 1992, s.171ZA.

5.49

Modification of entitlement conditions: early birth

5. Where a person does not meet the conditions specified in section 171ZA(2)(b) to (d) of the Act because the child's birth occurred earlier than the 14th week before the expected week of the birth, it shall have effect as if, for the conditions there set out, there were substituted the conditions that—
(a) the person would, but for the date on which the birth occurred, have been in employed earner's employment with an employer for a continuous period of at least 26 weeks ending with the week immediately preceding the 14th week before the expected week of the child's birth;
(b) his normal weekly earnings for the period of 8 weeks ending with the week immediately preceding the week in which the child is born are

5.50

not less than the lower earnings limit in force under section 5(1)(a) of the Act immediately before the commencement of the week in which the child is born.

DEFINITIONS

"the Act"—see reg.2(1).
"expected week"—see *ibid*.

Period of payment of statutory paternity pay (birth)

5.51

6.—(1) Subject to paragraph (2) and regulation 8, a person entitled to statutory paternity pay (birth) may choose the statutory paternity pay period to begin on—
  (a) the date on which the child is born or, where he is at work on that day, the following day;
  (b) the date falling such number of days after the date on which the child is born as the person may specify;
  (c) a predetermined date, specified by the person, which is later than the first day of the expected week of the child's birth.

(2) In a case where statutory paternity pay (birth) is payable in respect of a child whose expected week of birth begins before 6th April 2003, the statutory paternity pay period shall begin on a predetermined date, specified by the person entitled to such pay in a notice under section 171ZC(1) of the Act, which is at least 28 days after the date on which that notice was given, unless the person liable to pay statutory paternity pay (birth) agrees to the period beginning earlier.

(3) A person may choose for statutory paternity pay (birth) to be paid in respect of a period of a week.

(4) A choice made in accordance with paragraph (1) or (2) is not irrevocable, but where a person subsequently makes a different choice in relation to the beginning of the statutory pay period, section 171ZC(1) of the Act shall apply to it.

DEFINITIONS

"the Act"—see reg.2(1).
"expected week"—see *ibid*.
"statutory paternity pay (birth)"—see *ibid*.

Additional notice requirements for statutory paternity pay (birth)

5.52

7.—(1) Where the choice made by a person in accordance with paragraph (1) of regulation 6 and notified in accordance with section 171ZC(1) of the Act is that mentioned in sub-paragraph (a) or (b) of that paragraph, the person shall give further notice to the person liable to pay him statutory paternity pay, as soon as is reasonably practicable after the child's birth, of the date the child was born.

(2) Where the choice made by a person in accordance with paragraph (1) of regulation 6 and notified in accordance with section 171ZC(1) of the Act is that specified in sub-paragraph (c) of that paragraph, and the date of the child's birth is later than the date so specified, the person shall, if he wishes to claim statutory paternity pay (birth), give notice to the person liable to pay it, as soon as is reasonably practicable, that the period in respect of

which statutory paternity pay is to be paid shall begin on a date different from that originally chosen by him.

(3) That date may be any date chosen in accordance with paragraph (1) of regulation 6.

DEFINITIONS

"the Act"—see reg.2(1).
"statutory paternity pay (birth)"—see *ibid*.

Qualifying period for statutory paternity pay (birth)

8. The qualifying period for the purposes of section 171ZE(2) of the Act (period within which the statutory paternity pay period must occur) is a period which begins on the date of the child's birth and ends—
(a) except in the case referred to in paragraph (b), 56 days after that date;
(b) in a case where the child is born before the first day of the expected week of its birth, 56 days after that day.

DEFINITIONS

"the Act"—see reg.2(1).
"expected week"—see *ibid*.

Evidence of entitlement to statutory paternity pay (birth)

9.—(1) A person shall provide evidence of his entitlement to statutory paternity pay (birth) by providing in writing to the person who will be liable to pay him statutory paternity pay (birth)—
(a) the information specified in paragraph (2);
(b) a declaration that he meets the conditions prescribed under section 171ZA(2)(a) of the Act and that it is not the case that statutory paternity pay (birth) is not payable to him by virtue of the provisions of section 171ZE(4) of the Act.

(2) The information referred to in paragraph (1)(a) is as follows—
(a) the name of the person claiming statutory paternity pay (birth);
(b) the expected week of the child's birth and, where the birth has already occurred, the date of birth;
(c) the date from which it is expected that the liability to pay statutory paternity pay (birth) will begin;
(d) whether the period chosen in respect of which statutory paternity pay (birth) is to be payable is a week.

(3) The information and declaration referred to in paragraph (1) shall be provided at least 28 days before the date mentioned in sub-paragraph (c) of paragraph (2) or, if that is not reasonably practicable, as soon as is reasonably practicable thereafter.

(4) Where the person who will be liable to pay statutory paternity pay (birth) so requests, the person entitled to it shall inform him of the date of the child's birth within 28 days, or as soon as is reasonably practicable thereafter.

DEFINITIONS

"the Act"—see reg.2(1).
"expected week"—see *ibid*.
"statutory paternity pay (birth)"—see *ibid*.

General Note

5.55 The evidence of entitlement to statutory paternity pay (birth) is essentially a form of self-certification by the father or prospective father. This contrasts with the requirement to produce a medical certificate for statutory maternity pay purposes. The justification for the self-certification approach here is that it "balances the need for a light-touch procedure with the desire employers have expressed for some form of evidence to justify their payment of Statutory Paternity Pay" (*Government's Response on Simplification of Maternity leave, Paternity Leave and Adoption Leave* (DTI, 2001), para.41).

Entitlement to statutory paternity pay (birth) where there is more than one employer

5.56 **10.** Statutory paternity pay (birth) shall be payable to a person in respect of a statutory pay week during any part of which he works only for an employer—
(a) who is not liable to pay him statutory paternity pay (birth); and
(b) for whom he has worked in the week immediately preceding the 14th week before the expected week of the child's birth.

Definitions

"expected week"—see *ibid*.
"statutory paternity pay (birth)"—see *ibid*.

Part 3

Statutory Paternity Pay (Adoption)

Conditions of entitlement to statutory paternity pay (adoption): relationship with child and with person with whom the child is placed for adoption

5.57 **11.**—(1) The conditions prescribed under section 171ZB(2)(a) of the Act are that a person—
(a) is married to [2, the civil partner] or the partner of a child's adopter (or in a case where there are two adopters, married to [2, the civil partner] or the partner of the other adopter); and
(b) has, or expects to have, the main responsibility (apart from the responsibility of the child's adopter, or in a case where there two adopters, together with the other adopter) for the upbringing of the child.

(2) For the purposes of paragraph (1), "partner" means a person (whether of a different sex or the same sex) who lives with the adopter and the child in an enduring family relationship but is not a relative of the adopter of a kind specified in paragraph [1(2A)].

[1(2A) The relatives of the adopter referred to in paragraph (2) are the adopter's parent, grandparent, sister, brother, aunt or uncle.]

(3) References to relationships in paragraph [1(2A)]—
(a) are to relationships of the full blood or half blood, or, in the case of an adopted person, such of those relationships as would exist but for the adoption; and

(SI 2002/2822, reg.11) (as amended)

(b) include the relationship of a child with his adoptive, or former adoptive parents but do not include any other adoptive relationships.

AMENDMENTS

1. Statutory Paternity Pay and Statutory Adoption Pay (Amendment) Regulations 2004 (SI 2004/488), reg.2 (April 6, 2004).
2. Civil Partnership Act 2004 (Amendments to Subordinate Legislation) Order 2005 (SI 2005/2114), art.2(17) and Sch.17, para.3 (December 5, 2005).

DEFINITIONS

"the Act"—see reg.2(1).
"adopter"—see *ibid*.
"partner"—see para.(2).

GENERAL NOTE

This regulation sets out the prescribed conditions for the purposes of SSCBA 1992, s.171ZB(2)(a), i.e. for the payment of statutory paternity pay in the case of adoption. The claimant must either be the adoptive parent's spouse or partner and expect to have the main responsibility (other than the adopter) for the child's upbringing. The definition of "partner" in para.(2) is innovative, in that it recognises that partners may be in a heterosexual or same sex relationship. The only qualifications are that the partner lives with the adopter and the child in "an enduring family relationship" and is not a relative of the adopter as defined in paras (2A) and (3). Guidance on the notion of "an enduring family relationship" in the context of a same-sex relationship might be sought in the decisions in *Fitzpatrick v Sterling Housing Association* [2001] A.C. 27 and *Ghaidan v Godin-Mendoza* [2004] UKHL 30; [2004] 3 W.L.R. 113. This explicit statutory recognition in English law of parity of treatment for heterosexual and same-sex couples pre-dated the Civil Partnership Act 2004.

5.58

Period of payment of statutory paternity pay (adoption)

12.—(1) Subject to paragraph (2) and regulation 14, a person entitled to statutory paternity pay (adoption) may choose the statutory paternity pay period to begin on—
  (a) the date on which the child is placed with the adopter or, where the person is at work on that day, the following day;
  (b) the date falling such number of days after the date on which the child is placed with the adopter as the person may specify;
  (c) a predetermined date, specified by the person, which is later than the date on which the child is expected to be placed with the adopter.

(2) In a case where statutory paternity pay (adoption) is payable in respect of a child matched with an adopter who is notified of having been matched before 6th April 2003, the statutory paternity pay period shall begin on a predetermined date, specified by the person entitled to such pay in a notice under section 171ZC(1) of the Act, which is at least 28 days after the date on which that notice was given, unless the person liable to pay statutory paternity pay (birth) agrees to the period beginning earlier.

(3) A person may choose for statutory paternity pay (adoption) to be paid in respect of a period of a week.

(4) A choice made in accordance with paragraph (1) is not irrevocable, but where a person subsequently makes a different choice in relation to the

5.59

beginning of the statutory paternity pay period, section 171ZC(1) of the Act shall apply to it.

DEFINITIONS

"the Act"—see reg.2(1).
"adopter"—see *ibid*.
"statutory paternity pay (adoption)"—see *ibid*.
"statutory paternity pay (birth)"—see *ibid*.

Additional notice requirements for statutory paternity pay (adoption)

5.60   **13.**—(1) Where the choice made by a person in accordance with paragraph (1) of regulation 12 and notified in accordance with section 171ZC(1) of the Act is that mentioned in sub-paragraph (a) or (b) of that paragraph, the person shall give further notice to the person liable to pay him statutory paternity pay as soon as is reasonably practicable of the date on which the placement occurred.

(2) Where the choice made by a person in accordance with paragraph (1) of regulation 12 and notified in accordance with section 171ZC(1) of the Act is that mentioned in sub-paragraph (c) of that paragraph, or a date is specified under paragraph (2) of that regulation, and the child is placed for adoption later than the date so specified, the person shall, if he wishes to claim statutory paternity pay (adoption), give notice to the person liable to pay it, as soon as is reasonably practicable, that the period in respect of which statutory paternity pay is to be paid shall begin on a date different from that originally chosen by him.

(3) That date may be any date chosen in accordance with paragraph (1) of regulation 12.

DEFINITIONS

"the Act"—see reg.2(1).
"statutory paternity pay (adoption)"—see *ibid*.

Qualifying period for statutory paternity pay (adoption)

5.61   **14.** The qualifying period for the purposes of section 171ZE(2) of the Act (period within which the statutory pay period must occur) is a period of 56 days beginning with the date of the child's placement for adoption.

DEFINITION

"the Act"—see reg.2(1).

Evidence of entitlement for statutory paternity pay (adoption)

5.62   **15.**—(1) A person shall provide evidence of his entitlement to statutory paternity pay (adoption) by providing in writing to the person who will be liable to pay him statutory paternity pay (adoption)—
  (a) the information specified in paragraph (2);
  (b) a declaration that he meets the conditions prescribed under section 171ZB(2)(a) of the Act and that it is not the case that statutory paternity pay (adoption) is not payable to him by virtue of the provisions of section 171ZE(4) of the Act;

(c) a declaration that he has elected to receive statutory paternity pay (adoption), and not statutory adoption pay under Part 12ZB of the Act.

(2) The information referred to in paragraph (1) is as follows—
(a) the name of the person claiming statutory paternity pay (adoption);
(b) the date on which the child is expected to be placed for adoption or, where the child has already been placed for adoption, the date of placement of the child;
(c) the date from which it is expected that the liability to pay statutory paternity pay (adoption) will begin;
(d) whether the period chosen in respect of which statutory paternity pay (adoption) is to be payable is a week;
(e) the date the adopter was notified he had been matched with the child for the purposes of adoption.

(3) The information and declarations referred to in paragraph (1) shall be provided to the person liable to pay statutory paternity pay at least 28 days before the date mentioned in sub-paragraph (c) of paragraph (2) or, if that is not reasonably practicable, as soon as is reasonably practicable thereafter.

(4) Where the person who will be liable to pay statutory paternity pay (adoption) so requests, the person entitled to it shall inform him of the date of the child's placement within 28 days, or as soon as is reasonably practicable thereafter.

DEFINITIONS

"the Act"—see reg.2(1).
"statutory paternity pay (adoption)"—see *ibid*.

Entitlement to statutory paternity pay (adoption) where there is more than one employer

16. Statutory paternity pay (adoption) shall be payable to a person in respect of a statutory pay week during any part of which he works only for an employer—
(a) who is not liable to pay him statutory paternity pay (adoption); and
(b) for whom he has worked in the week in which the adopter is notified of being matched with the child.

5.63

DEFINITIONS

"adopter"—see *ibid*.
"statutory paternity pay (adoption)"—see *ibid*.

PART 4

STATUTORY PATERNITY PAY: PROVISIONS APPLICABLE TO BOTH STATUTORY PATERNITY PAY (BIRTH) AND STATUTORY PATERNITY PAY (ADOPTION)

Work during a statutory paternity pay period

17.—(1) Where, in a case where statutory paternity pay is being paid to a person who works during the statutory paternity pay period for an

5.64

employer who is not liable to pay him statutory paternity pay and who does not fall within paragraph (b) of regulation 10 or, as the case may be, paragraph (b) of regulation 16, there shall be no liability to pay statutory paternity pay in respect of any remaining part of the statutory paternity pay period.

(2) In a case falling within paragraph (1), the person shall notify the person liable to pay statutory paternity pay within seven days of the first day during which he works during the statutory pay period.

(3) The notification mentioned in paragraph (2) shall be in writing, if the person who has been liable to pay statutory paternity pay so requests.

Cases where there is no liability to pay statutory paternity pay

5.65 **18.** There shall be no liability to pay statutory paternity pay in respect of any week—
  (a) during any part of which the person entitled to it is entitled to statutory sick pay under Part 11 of the Act;
  (b) following that in which the person claiming it has died; or
  (c) during any part of which the person entitled to it is detained in legal custody or sentenced to a term of imprisonment (except where the sentence is suspended), or which is a subsequent week within the same statutory paternity pay period.

DEFINITION

"the Act"—see reg.2(1).

Statutory paternity pay and contractual remuneration

5.66 **19.** For the purposes of section 171ZG(1) and (2) of the Act, the payments which are to be treated as contractual remuneration are sums payable under a contract of service—
  (a) by way of remuneration;
  (b) for incapacity for work due to sickness or injury;
  (c) by reason of the birth or adoption of a child.

DEFINITION

"the Act"—see reg.2(1).

Avoidance of liability for statutory paternity pay

5.67 **20.**—(1) A former employer shall be liable to make payments of statutory paternity pay to a former employee in any case where the employee had been employed for a continuous period of at least 8 weeks and his contract of service was brought to an end by the former employer solely, or mainly, for the purpose of avoiding liability for statutory paternity pay.

(2) In a case falling within paragraph (1)—
  (a) the employee shall be treated as if he had been employed for a continuous period ending with the child's birth or, as the case may be, the placement of the child for adoption;
  (b) his normal weekly earnings shall be calculated by reference to his normal weekly earnings for the period of 8 weeks ending with the last day in respect of which he was paid under his former contract of service.

(SI 2002/2822, reg.21) (as amended)

PART 5

Statutory adoption pay

Adoption pay period

21.—(1) Subject to paragraph (2), a person entitled to statutory adoption pay may choose the adoption pay period to begin—
  (a) on the date on which the child is placed with him for adoption or, where he is at work on that day, on the following day;
  (b) subject to paragraph (2), on a predetermined date, specified by him, which is no more than 14 days before the date on which the child is expected to be placed with him and no later than that date.

(2) In a case where statutory adoption pay is payable in respect of a child matched with an adopter who is notified of having been matched before 6th April 2003, the statutory adoption pay period shall begin on a predetermined date which is—
  (a) on or after 6th April 2003; and
  (b) no more than 14 days before the date on which the child is expected to be placed with the adopter.

(3) Subject to paragraph (4), where the choice made is that mentioned in sub-paragraph (b) of paragraph (1) or in a case where paragraph (2) applies, the adoption pay period shall, unless the employer agrees to the adoption pay period beginning earlier, begin no earlier than 28 days after notice under section 171ZL(6) of the Act has been given.

(4) Where the beginning of the adoption pay period determined in accordance with paragraph (3) is later than the date of placement, it shall be the date of placement.

(5) Subject to regulation 22, the duration of any adoption pay period shall be a continuous period of [¹39] weeks.

(6) A choice made under paragraph (1), or a date specified under paragraph (2), is not irrevocable, but where a person subsequently makes a different choice, section 171ZL(6) of the Act shall apply to it.

AMENDMENT

1. Statutory Paternity Pay and Statutory Adoption Pay (General) and the Statutory Paternity Pay and Statutory Adoption Pay (Weekly Rates) (Amendment) Regulations 2006 (SI 2006/2236), reg.4 (October 1, 2006).

DEFINITIONS

  "the Act"—see reg.2(1).
  "adopter"—see *ibid.*

Adoption pay period in cases where adoption is disrupted

22.—(1) Where—
  (a) after a child has been placed for adoption—
    (i) the child dies;
    (ii) the child is returned to the adoption agency under section 30(3) of the Adoption Act 1976 or section 30(3) of the Adoption (Scotland) Act 1978; or

(b) the adoption pay period has begun prior to the date the child has been placed for adoption, but the placement does not take place, the adoption pay period shall terminate in accordance with the provisions of paragraph (2).

(2) The adoption pay period shall, in a case falling within paragraph (1), terminate 8 weeks after the end of the week specified in paragraph (3).

(3) The week referred to in paragraph (2) is—
(a) in a case falling within paragraph (1)(a)(i), the week during which the child dies;
(b) in a case falling within paragraph (1)(a)(ii), the week during which the child is returned;
(c) in a case falling within paragraph (1)(b), the week during which the person with whom the child was to be placed for adoption is notified that the placement will not be made.

(4) For the purposes of paragraph (3), "week" means a period of 7 days beginning with Sunday.

DEFINITION

"week"—see para.(4).

Additional notice requirements for statutory adoption pay

23.—(1) Where a person gives notice under section 171ZL(6) of the Act he shall at the same time give notice of the date on which the child is expected to be placed for adoption.

(2) Where the choice made in accordance with paragraph (1) of regulation 21 and notified in accordance with section 171ZL(6) of the Act is that mentioned in sub-paragraph (a) of that paragraph, the person shall give further notice to the person liable to pay him statutory adoption pay as soon as is reasonably practicable of the date the child is placed for adoption.

DEFINITION

"the Act"—see reg.2(1).

Evidence of entitlement to statutory adoption pay

24.—(1) A person shall provide evidence of his entitlement to statutory adoption pay by providing to the person who will be liable to pay it—
(a) the information specified in paragraph (2), in the form of one or more documents provided to him by an adoption agency, containing that information;
(b) a declaration that he has elected to receive statutory adoption pay, and not statutory paternity pay (adoption) under Part 12ZA of the Act.

(2) The information referred to in paragraph (1) is—
(a) the name and address of the adoption agency and of the person claiming payment of statutory adoption pay;
(b) the date on which the child is expected to be placed for adoption or, where the child has already been placed for adoption, the date of placement; and
(c) the date on which the person claiming payment of statutory adoption pay was informed by the adoption agency that the child would be placed for adoption with him.

(SI 2002/2822, reg.24) (as amended)

(3) The information and declaration referred to in paragraph (1) shall be provided to the person liable to pay statutory adoption pay at least 28 days before the date chosen as the beginning of the adoption pay period in accordance with paragraph (1) of regulation 21, or, if that is not reasonably practicable, as soon as is reasonably practicable thereafter.

DEFINITIONS

"the Act"—see reg.2(1).
"adoption agency"—see *ibid.*
"statutory paternity pay (adoption)"—see *ibid.*

Entitlement to statutory adoption pay where there is more than one employer

25. Statutory adoption pay shall be payable to a person in respect of a week during any part of which he works only for an employer—
  (a) who is not liable to pay him statutory adoption pay; and
  (b) for whom he has worked in the week in which he is notified of being matched with the child.

Work during an adoption pay period

26.—(1) Where, in a case where statutory adoption pay is being paid to a person who works during the adoption pay period for an employer who is not liable to pay him statutory adoption pay and who does not fall within paragraph (b) of regulation 25, there shall be no liability to pay statutory adoption pay in respect of any remaining part of the adoption pay period.
  (2) In a case falling within paragraph (1), the person shall notify the person liable to pay statutory adoption pay within 7 days of the first day during which he works during the adoption pay period.
  (3) The notification contained in paragraph (2) shall be in writing if the person who has been liable to pay statutory adoption pay so requests.

Cases where there is no liability to pay statutory adoption pay

27.—(1) There shall be no liability to pay statutory adoption pay in respect of any week—
  (a) during any part of which the person entitled to it is entitled to statutory sick pay under Part 9 of the Act;
  (b) following that in which the person claiming it has died; or
  (c) subject to paragraph (2), during any part of which the person entitled to it is detained in legal custody or sentenced to a term of imprisonment (except where the sentence is suspended).
  (2) There shall be liability to pay statutory adoption pay in respect of any week during any part of which the person entitled to it is detained in legal custody where that person—
  (a) is released subsequently without charge;
  (b) is subsequently found not guilty of any offence and is released; or
  (c) is convicted of an offence but does not receive a custodial sentence.

DEFINITION

"the Act"—see reg.2(1).

[¹Working for not more than 10 days during an adoption pay period

27A. In the case where an employee does any work under a contract of service with his employer on any day for not more than 10 such days during his adoption pay period, whether consecutive or not, statutory adoption pay shall continue to be payable to the employee by the employer.]

AMENDMENT

1. Statutory Paternity Pay and Statutory Adoption Pay (General) and the Statutory Paternity Pay and Statutory Adoption Pay (Weekly Rates) (Amendment) Regulations 2006 (SI 2006/2236), reg.5 (October 1, 2006).

Statutory adoption pay and contractual remuneration

28. For the purposes of section 171ZP(4) and (5) of the Act, the payments which are to be treated as contractual remuneration are sums payable under a contract of service—
  (a) by way of remuneration;
  (b) for incapacity for work due to sickness or injury;
  (c) by reason of the adoption of a child.

DEFINITION

"the Act"—see reg.2(1).

Termination of employment before start of adoption pay period

29.—(1) Where the employment of a person who satisfies the conditions of entitlement to statutory adoption pay terminates for whatever reason (including dismissal) before the adoption pay period chosen in accordance with regulation 21 has begun, the period shall begin 14 days before the expected date of placement or, where the termination occurs on, or within 14 days before, the expected date of placement, on the day immediately following the last day of his employment.

(2) In a case falling within paragraph (1), the notice requirements set out in section 171ZL(6) of the Act and these Regulations shall not apply.

DEFINITION

"the Act"—see reg.2(1).

Avoidance of liability for statutory adoption pay

30.—(1) A former employer shall be liable to make payments of statutory adoption pay to a former employee in any case where the employee had been employed for a continuous period of at least 8 weeks and his contract of service was brought to an end by the former employer solely, or mainly, for the purpose of avoiding liability for statutory adoption pay.

(2) In a case falling within paragraph (1)—
  (a) the employee shall be treated as if he had been employed for a continuous period ending with the week in which he was notified of having been matched with the child for adoption; and
  (b) his normal weekly earnings shall be calculated by reference to his normal weekly earnings for the period of 8 weeks ending with the last day in respect of which he was paid under his former contract of service.

(SI 2002/2822, reg.31) (as amended)

Part 6

Statutory Paternity Pay and Statutory Adoption Pay: Provisions Applicable to both Statutory Paternity Pay and Statutory Adoption Pay

Introductory

31.—(1) Subject to paragraph (2), the provisions of regulations 32–47 below apply to statutory paternity pay payable under Part 12ZA of the Act and to statutory adoption pay payable under Part 12ZB of the Act.

(2) The provisions of regulation 44 only apply to statutory adoption pay.

Definition

"the Act"—see reg.2(1).

Treatment of persons as employees

32.—(1) [¹Subject to paragraph (1A),] in a case where, and in so far as, a person [¹. . .] is treated as an employed earner by virtue of the Social Security (Categorisation of Earners) Regulations 1978 he shall be treated as an employee for the purposes of Parts 12ZA and 12ZB of the Act, and in a case where, and in so far as, such a person is treated otherwise than as an employed earner by virtue of those Regulations, he shall not be treated as an employee for the purposes of Parts 12ZA and 12ZB of the Act.

[²(1A) Paragraph (1) shall have effect in relation to a person who—
(a) is under the age of 16; and
(b) would or, as the case may be, would not have been treated as an employed earner by virtue of the Social Security (Categorisation of Earners) Regulations 1978 had he been over that age,

as it has effect in relation to a person who is or, as the case may be, is not so treated.]

(2) A person who is in employed earner's employment within the meaning of the Act under a contract of apprenticeship shall be treated as an employee for the purposes of Parts 12ZA and 12ZB of the Act.

(3) A person who is in employed earner's employment within the meaning of the Act but whose employer—
(a) does not fulfil the conditions prescribed in regulation 145(1) of the Contributions Regulations in so far as that provision relates to residence or presence in Great Britain; or
(b) is a person who, by reason of any international treaty to which the United Kingdom is a party or of any international convention binding the United Kingdom—
    (i) is exempt from the provisions of the Act; or
    (ii) is a person against whom the provisions of the Act are not enforceable,

shall not be treated as an employee for the purposes of Parts 12ZA and 12ZB of the Act.

Statutory Paternity Pay and Statutory Adoption Pay Regulations 2002

AMENDMENTS

1. Employment Equality (Age) Regulations 2006 (SI 2006/1031), reg.49(1) and Sch.8, Pt 2, para.60 (October 1, 2006).
2. Employment Equality (Age) (Consequential Amendments) Regulations 2007 (SI 2007/825), reg.7 (April 6, 2007).

DEFINITIONS

"the Act"—see reg.2(1).
"Contributions Regulations"—see *ibid*.

Continuous employment

33.—(1) Subject to the following provisions of this regulation, where in any week a person is, for the whole or part of the week—
  (a) incapable of work in consequence of sickness or injury;
  (b) absent from work on account of a temporary cessation of work;
  (c) absent from work in circumstances such that, by arrangement or custom, he is regarded as continuing in the employment of his employer for all or any purposes,
and returns to work for his employer after the incapacity for or absence from work, that week shall be treated for the purposes of sections 171ZA, 171ZB and 171ZL of the Act as part of a continuous period of employment with that employer, notwithstanding that no contract of service exists with that employer in respect of that week.

(2) Incapacity for work which lasts for more than 26 consecutive weeks shall not count for the purposes of paragraph (1)(a).

(3) Where a person—
  (a) is an employee in an employed earner's employment in which the custom is for the employer—
    (i) to offer work for a fixed period of not more than 26 consecutive weeks;
    (ii) to offer work for such period on two or more occasions in a year for periods which do not overlap; and
    (iii) to offer the work available to those persons who had worked for him during the last or a recent such period, but
  (b) is absent from work because of incapacity arising from some specific disease or bodily or mental disablement,
then in that case paragraph (1) shall apply as if the words "and returns to work for his employer after the incapacity for or absence from work," were omitted and paragraph (4) shall not apply.

(4) Where a person is employed under a contract of service for part only of the relevant week within the meaning of subsection (3) of section 171ZL of the Act (entitlement to statutory adoption pay), the whole of that week shall count in computing a period of continuous employment for the purposes of that section.

DEFINITION

"the Act"—see reg.2(1).

Continuous employment and unfair dismissal

34.—(1) This regulation applies to a person in relation to whose dismissal an action is commenced which consists—

(SI 2002/2822, reg.34) (as amended)

  (a) of the presentation by him of a complaint under section 111(1) of the Employment Rights Act 1996;
  (b) of his making a claim in accordance with a dismissals procedure agreement designated by an order under section 110 of that Act; [1...]
  (c) of any action taken by a conciliation officer under section 18 of the Employment Tribunals Act 1996; [1or
  (d) of a decision arising out of the use of a statutory dispute resolution procedure contained in Schedule 2 to the Employment Act 2002 in a case where, in accordance with the Employment Act 2002 (Dispute Resolution) Regulations 2004, such a procedure applies.]

(2) If, in consequence of an action of the kind specified in paragraph (1), a person is reinstated or re-engaged by his employer or by a successor or associated employer of that employer, the continuity of his employment shall be preserved for the purposes of Part 12ZA or, as the case may be, Part 12ZB of the Act, and any week which falls within the interval beginning with the effective date of termination and ending with the date of reinstatement or re-engagement, as the case may be, shall count in the computation of his period of continuous employment.

(3) In this regulation—

  "successor" and "dismissal procedures agreement" have the same meanings as in section 235 of the Employment Rights Act 1996; and
  "associated employer" shall be construed in accordance with section 231 of the Employment Rights Act 1996.

AMENDMENT

1. Statutory Maternity Pay (General) and the Statutory Paternity Pay and Statutory Adoption Pay (General) (Amendment) Regulations 2005 (SI 2005/358), reg.4 (April 56, 2005).

DEFINITIONS

  "the Act"—see reg.2(1).
  "associated employer"—see para.(3).
  "dismissal procedures agreement"—see *ibid.*
  "successor"—see *ibid.*

Continuous employment and stoppages of work

35.—(1) Where, for any week or part of a week a person does not work because there is a stoppage of work due to a trade dispute within the meaning of section 35(1) of the Jobseekers Act 1995 at his place of employment, the continuity of his employment shall, subject to paragraph (2), be treated as continuing throughout the stoppage but, subject to paragraph (3), no such week shall count in the computation of his period of employment.

(2) Subject to paragraph (3), where during the stoppage of work a person is dismissed from his employment, the continuity of his employment shall not be treated in accordance with paragraph (1) as continuing beyond the commencement of the day he stopped work.

(3) The provisions of paragraph (1), to the extent that they provide that a week in which the stoppage of work occurred shall not count in the computation of a period of employment, and paragraph (2) shall not apply to a person who proves that at no time did he have a direct interest in the trade dispute in question.

Change of employer

5.84   **36.** A person's employment shall, notwithstanding a change of employer, be treated as continuous employment with the second employer where—
  (a) the employer's trade or business or an undertaking (whether or not it is an undertaking established by or under an Act of Parliament) is transferred from one person to another;
  (b) by or under an Act of Parliament, whether public or local and whenever passed, a contract of employment between any body corporate and the person is modified and some other body corporate is substituted as his employer;
  (c) on the death of his employer, the person is taken into employment of the personal representatives or trustees of the deceased;
  (d) the person is employed by partners, personal representatives or trustees and there is a change in the partners, or, as the case may be, personal representatives or trustees;
  (e) the person is taken into the employment of an employer who is, at the time he entered his employment, an associated employer of his previous employer, and for this purpose "associated employer" shall be construed in accordance with section 231 of the Employment Rights Act 1996;
  (f) on the termination of his employment with an employer he is taken into the employment of another employer and those employers are governors of a school maintained by a local education authority and that authority.

Reinstatement after service with the armed forces etc.

5.85   **37.** If a person who is entitled to apply to his employer under the Reserve Forces (Safeguard of Employment) Act 1985 enters the employment of that employer within the 6-month period mentioned in section 1(4)(b) of that Act, his previous period of employment with that employer (or if there was more than one such period, the last of those periods) and the period of employment beginning in that 6-month period shall be treated as continuous.

DEFINITION

  "the Act"—see reg.2(1).

Treatment of two or more employers or two or more contracts of service as one

5.86   **38.**—(1) In a case where the earnings paid to a person in respect of two or more employments are aggregated and treated as a single payment of earnings under regulation 15(1) of the Contributions Regulations, the employers of that person in respect of those employments shall be treated as one for the purposes of Part 12ZA or, as the case may be, Part 12ZB of the Act.

  (2) Where two or more employers are treated as one under the provisions of paragraph (1), liability for statutory paternity pay or, as the case may be, statutory adoption pay, shall be apportioned between them in such proportions as they may agree or, in default of agreement, in the proportions which the person's earnings from each employment bear to the amount of the aggregated earnings.

(SI 2002/2822, reg.38) (as amended)

(3) Where two or more contracts of service exist concurrently between one employer and one employee, they shall be treated as one for the purposes of Part 12ZA or, as the case may be, Part 12ZB of the Act, except where, by virtue of regulation 14 of the Contributions Regulations, the earnings from those contracts of service are not aggregated for the purposes of earnings-related contributions.

DEFINITIONS

"the Act"—see reg.2(1).
"Contributions Regulations"—see *ibid.*

Meaning of "earnings"

39.—(1) For the purposes of section 171ZJ(6) (normal weekly earnings for the purposes of Part 12ZA of the Act) and of section 171ZS(6) of the Act (normal weekly earnings for the purposes of Part 12ZB of the Act), the expression "earnings" shall be construed in accordance with the following provisions of this regulation.

(2) The expression "earnings" refers to gross earnings and includes any remuneration or profit derived from a person's employment except any payment or amount which is—
  (a) excluded from the computation of a person's earnings under regulation 25 of and Schedule 3 to, and regulation 123 of, the Contributions Regulations (payments to be disregarded) and regulation 27 of those Regulations (payments to directors to be disregarded) [¹(or would have been so excluded had he not been under the age of 16)];
  (b) a chargeable emolument under section 10A of the Act, except where, in consequence of such a chargeable emolument being excluded from earnings, a person would not be entitled to statutory paternity pay or, as the case may be, statutory adoption pay [¹(or where such a payment or amount would have been so excluded and in consequence he would not have been entitled to statutory paternity pay and statutory adoption pay had he not been under the age of 16)].

(3) For the avoidance of doubt, "earnings" includes—
[²(za) any amount retrospectively treated as earnings by regulations made by virtue of section 4B(2) of the Act;]
  (a) any sum payable in respect of arrears of pay in pursuance of an order for reinstatement or re-engagement under the Employment Rights Act 1996;
  (b) any sum payable by way of pay in pursuance of an order made under the Employment Rights Act 1996 for the continuation of a contract of employment;
  (c) any sum payable by way of remuneration in pursuance of a protective award under section 189 of the Trade Union and Labour Relations (Consolidation) Act 1992;
  (d) any sum payable by way of statutory sick pay, including sums payable in accordance with regulations made under section 151(6) of the Act;
  (e) any sum payable by way of statutory maternity pay;
  (f) any sum payable by way of statutory paternity pay;
  (g) any sum payable by way of statutory adoption pay.

5.87

Statutory Paternity Pay and Statutory Adoption Pay Regulations 2002

AMENDMENTS

1. Employment Equality (Age) Regulations 2006 (SI 2006/1031), reg.49(1) and Sch.8, Pt 2, para.61 (October 1, 2006).
2. Social Security, Occupational Pension Schemes and Statutory Payments (Consequential Provisions) Regulations 2007 (SI 2007/1154), reg.6 (April 6, 2007).

DEFINITIONS

"the Act"—see reg.2(1).
"Contributions Regulations"—see *ibid*.

Normal weekly earnings

5.88   **40.**—(1) For the purposes of Part 12ZA and Part 12ZB of the Act, a person's normal weekly earnings shall be calculated in accordance with the following provisions of this regulation.

(2) In this regulation—
"the appropriate date" means—
  (a) in relation to statutory paternity pay (birth), the first day of the 14th week before the expected week of the child's birth or the first day in the week in which the child is born, whichever is the earlier;
  (b) in relation to statutory paternity pay (adoption) and statutory adoption pay, the first day of the week after the week in which the adopter is notified of being matched with the child for the purposes of adoption;
"normal pay day" means a day on which the terms of a person's contract of service require him to be paid, or the practice in his employment is for him to be paid, if any payment is due to him; and
"day of payment" means a day on which the person was paid.

(3) Subject to paragraph (4), the relevant period for the purposes of sections 171ZJ(6) and 171ZS(6) is the period between—
  (a) the last normal pay day to fall before the appropriate date; and
  (b) the last normal pay day to fall at least 8 weeks earlier than the normal pay day mentioned in sub-paragraph (a),
including the normal pay day mentioned in sub-paragraph (a) but excluding that first mentioned in sub-paragraph (b).

(4) In a case where a person has no identifiable normal pay day, paragraph (3) shall have effect as if the words "day of payment" were substituted for the words "normal pay day" in each place where they occur.

(5) In a case where a person has normal pay days at intervals of or approximating to one or more calendar months (including intervals of or approximating to a year) his normal weekly earnings shall be calculated by dividing his earnings in the relevant period by the number of calendar months in that period (or, if it is not a whole number, the nearest whole number), multiplying the result by 12 and dividing by 52.

(6) In a case to which paragraph (5) does not apply and the relevant period is not an exact number of weeks, the person's normal weekly earnings shall be calculated by dividing his earnings in the relevant period by the number of days in the relevant period and multiplying the result by 7.

(7) In any case where a person receives a back-dated pay increase which includes a sum in respect of a relevant period, normal weekly earnings shall be calculated as if such a sum was paid in that relevant period even though received after that period.

(SI 2002/2822, reg.40) (as amended)

Definitions

"the Act"—see reg.2(1).
"adopter"—see *ibid*.
"the appropriate date"—see para.(2).
"day of payment"— see *ibid*.
"expected week"—see reg.2(1).
"normal pay day"—see para.(2).
"statutory paternity pay (adoption)"—see reg.2(1).
"statutory paternity pay (birth)"—see *ibid*.

Payment of statutory paternity pay and statutory adoption pay

41. Payments of statutory paternity pay and statutory adoption pay may be made in a like manner to payments of remuneration but shall not include payment in kind or by way of the provision of board or lodgings or of services or other facilities.

5.89

Time when statutory paternity pay and statutory adoption pay are to be paid

42.—(1) In this regulation, "pay day" means a day on which it has been agreed, or it is the normal practice between an employer or former employer and a person who is or was an employee of his, that payments by way of remuneration are to be made, or, where there is no such agreement or normal practice, the last day of a calendar month.

5.90

(2) In any case where—
(a) a decision has been made by an officer of the Board under section 8(1) of the Social Security Contributions (Transfer of Functions, etc.) Act 1999 as a result of which a person is entitled to an amount of statutory paternity pay or statutory adoption pay; and
(b) the time for bringing an appeal against the decision has expired and either—
   (i) no such appeal has been brought; or
   (ii) such an appeal has been brought and has been finally disposed of,
that amount of statutory paternity pay or statutory adoption pay shall be paid within the time specified in paragraph (3).

(3) Subject to paragraphs (4) and (5), the employer or former employer shall pay the amount not later than the first pay day after—
(a) where an appeal has been brought, the day on which the employer or former employer receives notification that it has been finally disposed of;
(b) where leave to appeal has been refused and there remains no further opportunity to apply for leave, the day on which the employer or former employer receives notification of the refusal; and
(c) in any other case, the day on which the time for bringing an appeal expires.

(4) Subject to paragraph (5), where it is impracticable, in view of the employer's or former employer's methods of accounting for and paying remuneration, for the requirement of payment referred to in paragraph (3) to be met by the pay day referred to in that paragraph, it shall be met not later than the next following pay day.

Statutory Paternity Pay and Statutory Adoption Pay Regulations 2002

(5) Where the employer or former employer would not have remunerated the employee for his work in the week in question as early as the pay day specified in paragraph (3) or (if it applies) paragraph (4), the requirement of payment shall be met on the first day on which the employee would have been remunerated for his work in that week.

DEFINITIONS

"the Board"—see reg.2(1).
"pay day"—see para.(1).

Liability of the Board to pay statutory paternity pay or statutory adoption pay

43.—(1) Where—
  (a) an officer of the Board has decided that an employer is liable to make payments of statutory paternity pay or, as the case may be, statutory adoption pay to a person;
  (b) the time for appealing against the decision has expired; and
  (c) no appeal against the decision has been lodged or leave to appeal against the decision is required and has been refused,
then for any week in respect of which the employer was liable to make payments of statutory paternity pay or, as the case may be, statutory adoption pay but did not do so, and for any subsequent weeks in the paternity pay period or, as the case may be, adoption pay period, the liability to make those payments shall, notwithstanding sections 171ZD and 171ZM of the Act, be that of the Board and not the employer.

(2) Liability to make payments of statutory paternity pay or, as the case may be, statutory adoption pay shall, notwithstanding sections 171ZD and 171ZM of the Act, be a liability of the Board and not the employer as from the week in which the employer first becomes insolvent until the end of the paternity pay or adoption pay period.

(3) For the purposes of paragraph (2), an employer shall be taken to be insolvent if, and only if—
  (a) in England and Wales—
    (i) he has been adjudged bankrupt or has made a composition or arrangement with his creditors;
    (ii) he has died and his estate falls to be administered in accordance with an order made under section 421 of the Insolvency Act 1986; or
    (iii) where an employer is a company or a limited liability partnership, a winding-up order [1. . .] is made or a resolution for a voluntary winding-up is passed (or, in the case of a limited liability partnership, a determination for a voluntary winding-up has been made) with respect to it [1or it enters administration], or a receiver or a manager of its undertaking is duly appointed, or possession is taken, by or on behalf of the holders of any debentures secured by a floating charge, of any property of the company or limited liability partnership comprised in or subject to the charge, or a voluntary arrangement proposed for the purposes of Part 1 of the Insolvency Act 1986 is approved under that Part of that Act;
  (b) in Scotland—

(i) an award of sequestration is made on his estate or he executes a trust deed for his creditors or enters into a composition contract;
(ii) he has died and a judicial factor appointed under section 11A of the Judicial Factors (Scotland) Act 1889 is required by that section to divide his insolvent estate among his creditors; or
(iii) where the employer is a company or a limited liability partnership, a winding-up order [1. . .] is made or a resolution for voluntary winding-up is passed (or, in the case of a limited liability partnership, a determination for a voluntary winding-up is made) with respect to it [1or it enters administration], or a receiver of its undertaking is duly appointed, or a voluntary arrangement proposed for the purposes of Part 1 of the Insolvency Act 1986 is approved under that Part.

AMENDMENT

1. Enterprise Act 2002 (Insolvency) Order 2003 (SI 2003/2096), art.5 and Sch.2, para.79 (September 15, 2003).

DEFINITIONS

"the Act"—see reg.2(1).
"the Board"—see reg.2(1).

Liability of the Board to pay statutory adoption pay in cases of legal custody or imprisonment

44. Where— 5.92
(a) there is liability to pay statutory adoption pay in respect of a period which is subsequent to the last week falling within paragraph (1)(c) of regulation 27; or
(b) there is liability to pay statutory adoption pay during a period of detention in legal custody by virtue of the provisions of paragraph (2) of that regulation,
that liability shall, notwithstanding section 171ZM of the Act, be that of the Board and not the employer.

DEFINITIONS

"the Act"—see reg.2(1).
"the Board"—see reg.2(1).

Payments by the Board

45. Where the Board become liable in accordance with regulation 43 or 44 to make payments of statutory paternity pay or, as the case may be, statutory adoption pay to a person, the first payment shall be made as soon as reasonably practicable after they become so liable, and payments thereafter shall be made at weekly intervals, by means of an instrument of payment or by such other means as appears to the Board to be appropriate in the circumstance of any particular case. 5.93

DEFINITION

"the Board"—see reg.2(1).

Persons unable to act

46.—(1) Where in the case of any person—
(a) statutory paternity pay or, as the case may be, statutory adoption pay is payable to him or he is alleged to be entitled to it;
(b) he is unable for the time being to act; and
(c) either—
  (i) no receiver has been appointed by the Court of Protection with power to receive statutory paternity pay or, as the case may be, statutory adoption pay on his behalf; or
  (ii) in Scotland, his estate is not being administered by any tutor, curator or other guardian acting or appointed in terms of law,

the Board may, upon written application to them by a person who, if a natural person, is over the age of 18, appoint that person to exercise, on behalf of the person unable to act, any right to which he may be entitled under Part 12ZA or, as the case may be, Part 12ZB of the Act and to deal on his behalf with any sums payable to him.

(2) Where the Board have made an appointment under paragraph (1)—
(a) they may at any time in their absolute discretion revoke it;
(b) the person appointed may resign his office after having given one month's notice in writing to the Board of his intention to do so; and
(c) the appointment shall terminate when the Board are notified that a receiver or other person to whom paragraph (1)(c) applies has been appointed.

(3) Anything required by Part 12ZA or 12ZB of the Act to be done by or to any person who is unable to act may be done by or to the person appointed under this regulation to act on his behalf, and the receipt of the person so appointed shall be a good discharge to the person's employer or former employer for any sum paid.

DEFINITIONS

"the Act"—see reg.2(1).
"the Board"—see reg.2(1).

Service of notices by post

47. A notice given in accordance with the provisions of these Regulations in writing contained in an envelope which is properly addressed and sent by prepaid post shall be treated as having been given on the day on which it is posted.

Social Security Contributions and Benefits Act 1992 (Application of Parts 12ZA and 12ZB to Adoptions from Overseas) Regulations 2003

(SI 2003/499) (AS AMENDED)

The Secretary of State, in exercise of the powers conferred on her by sections 171ZK and 171ZT of the Social Security Contributions and Benefits Act 1992 by this instrument, which contains only provision made by virtue of sections 2 and 4 of

(SI 2003/499) (as amended)

the Employment Act 2002 and is made before the end of the period of 6 months from the coming into force of those enactments, hereby makes the following Regulations—

ARRANGEMENT OF REGULATIONS

1. Citation, commencement and interpretation.
2. Application of Part 12ZA of the Act to adoptions from overseas.
3. Application of Part 12ZB of the Act to adoptions from overseas.

Schedule 1—Application of Part 12ZA of the Act to adoptions from overseas.
Schedule 2—Application of Part 12ZB of the Act to adoptions from overseas.

Citation, commencement and interpretation

1.—(1) These Regulations may be cited as the Social Security Contributions and Benefits Act 1992 (Application of Parts 12ZA and 12ZB to Adoptions from Overseas) Regulations 2003 and shall come into force, in so far as they apply powers to make regulations, on 10th March 2003, and for all other purposes on 6th April 2003.

(2) In these Regulations—

"adoption from overseas" means the adoption of a child who enters Great Britain from outside the United Kingdom in connection with or for the purposes of adoption which does not involve the placement of the child for adoption under the law of any part of the United Kingdom;

"the Act" means the Social Security Contributions and Benefits Act 1992.

GENERAL NOTE

These Regulations, made under provisions inserted into the SSCBA 1992 by the Employment Act 2002, apply Pts XIIZA and XIIZB of the 1992 Act, as modified by these Regulations, to adoptions from overseas. These are adoptions of children who enter Great Britain from outside the United Kingdom in connection with or for the purposes of adoption which does not involve the placement of a child for adoption under the law of any part of the United Kingdom. The relevant adoption law requirements are set out in the Adoption (Bringing Children into the United Kingdom) Regulations 2003 (SI 2003/1173). The regulations relating to statutory paternity pay and statutory adoption pay in connection with such overseas adoptions are the Statutory Paternity Pay (Adoption) and Statutory Adoption Pay (Adoptions from Overseas) Regulations 2003 (SI 2003/500).

Application of Part 12ZA of the Act to adoptions from overseas

2. Part 12ZA of the Act shall apply in relation to adoptions from overseas, with the modifications of sections 171ZB, 171ZE and 171ZJ of the Act specified in the second column of Schedule 1.

Application of Part 12ZB of the Act to adoptions from overseas

3. Part 12ZB of the Act shall apply in relation to adoptions from overseas, with the modifications of sections 171ZL and 171ZS of the Act specified in the second column of Schedule 2.

755

Social Security Contributions and Benefits Act 1992 Regulations 2003

SCHEDULE 1   **Regulation 2**

APPLICATION OF PART 12ZA OF THE ACT TO ADOPTIONS FROM OVERSEAS

5.101

Provision	Modification
Section 171ZB(2)	[¹. . .] In paragraph (a)(i), for "who is placed for adoption under the law of any part of the United Kingdom" substitute "who is adopted from overseas". In paragraph (a)(ii), for "a person with whom the child is so placed for adoption" substitute "an adopter of the child". [¹In paragraph (b), omit "ending with the relevant week".] In paragraph (d), for "the day on which the child is placed for adoption" substitute "the day on which the child enters Great Britain". In paragraph (e), for "a person with whom the child is placed for adoption" substitute "an adopter of the child".

Section 171ZB(3)	[¹For subsection (3) substitute—
	"(3) The references in subsection (2)(c) and (d) to the relevant week are to—
	  (a) the week in which official notification is sent to the adopter, or
	  (b) the week at the end of which the person satisfies the condition in subsection (2)(b), whichever is the later."]

Section 171ZB(6)	For "the placement for adoption of more than one child as part of the same arrangement" substitute "the adoption from overseas of more than one child as part of the same arrangement".
Section 171ZB(7)	Omit subsection (7).
Section 171ZE(3)	In paragraph (b), for "with the date of the child's placement for adoption" substitute "with the date of the child's entry into Great Britain".
Section 171ZE(10)	For subsection (10) substitute— "(10) Where more than one child is the subject of adoption from overseas as part of the same arrangement, and the date of entry of each child is different, the reference in subsection (3)(b) to the date of the child's entry into Great Britain shall be interpreted as a reference to the date of the entry of the first child to enter Great Britain".

Section 171ZJ(1)	In the appropriate places in the alphabetical order, insert—
	  "adopter", in relation to a child, means a person by whom the child has been or is to be adopted;"
	  "adoption from overseas" means the adoption of a child who enters Great Britain from outside the United Kingdom in connection with or for the purposes of adoption which does not involve the placement of the child for adoption under the law of any part of the United Kingdom, and the references to a child adopted from overseas shall be construed accordingly;"
	  "official notification" means written notification, issued by or on behalf of the relevant domestic authority, that it is prepared to issue a certificate to the overseas authority concerned with the adoption of the child, or has issued a certificate and sent it to that authority, confirming, in either case, that the adopter is eligible to adopt and has been assessed and approved as being a suitable adoptive parent;"
	  "relevant domestic authority" means—
	    (a) in the case of an adopter to whom the Intercountry Adoption (Hague Convention) Regulations 2003 apply

(SI 2003/499, Sch.1) (as amended)

Provision	Modification
	and who is habitually resident in Wales, the National Assembly of Wales;
	(b) in the case of an adopter to whom the Intercountry Adoption (Hague Convention) (Scotland) Regulations 2003 apply and who is habitually resident in Scotland, the Scottish Ministers;
	(c) in any other case, the Secretary of State".

AMENDMENT

1. Statutory Paternity Pay and Statutory Adoption Pay (Amendment) Regulations 2004 (SI 2004/488), reg.3(2) (April 6, 2004).

SCHEDULE 2   **Regulation 3**

APPLICATION OF PART 12ZB OF THE ACT TO ADOPTIONS FROM OVERSEAS

5.102

Provision	Modification
Section 171ZL(2)	[1. . .] In paragraph (a), for "with whom a child is, or is expected to be, placed for adoption under the law of any part of the United Kingdom" substitute "who is, or is expected to be, an adopter of a child from overseas". [¹In paragraph (b), omit "ending with the relevant week".]

Section 171ZL(3)	[¹For subsection (3) substitute—
	"(3) The reference in subsection (2)(d) to the relevant week is to—
	  (a) the week in which official notification is sent to the adopter, or
	  (b) the week at the end of which the person satisfies the condition in subsection (2)(b), whichever is the later."]

	[¹. . .]
Section 171ZL(4)	In paragraph (b), for "placed for adoption with him" substitute "adopted by him".
Section 171ZL(5)	For "the placement, or expected placement, for adoption of more than one child" substitute "the adoption, or expected adoption, from overseas of more than one child".
Section 171ZS(1)	In the appropriate places in the alphabetical order, insert— ""adopter", in relation to a child, means a person by whom a child has been or is to be adopted;" "adoption from overseas" means the adoption of a child who enters Great Britain from outside the United Kingdom in connection with or for the purposes of adoption which does not involve the placement of the child for adoption under the law of any part of the United Kingdom, and the reference to an adopter from overseas shall be construed accordingly;" "official notification" means written notification, issued by or on behalf of the relevant domestic authority, that it is prepared to issue a certificate to the overseas authority concerned with the adoption of the child, or has issued a certificate and sent it to that authority, confirming, in either case, that the adopter is eligible to adopt and has been assessed and approved as being a suitable adoptive parent;" "relevant domestic authority" means— (a) in the case of an adopter to whom the Intercountry Adoption (Hague Convention) Regulations 2003 apply

Provision	Modification
	and who is habitually resident in Wales, the National Assembly of Wales; (b) in the case of an adopter to whom the Intercountry Adoption (Hague Convention) (Scotland) Regulations 2003 apply and who is habitually resident in Scotland, the Scottish Ministers; (c) in any other case, the Secretary of State".

AMENDMENT

1. Statutory Paternity Pay and Statutory Adoption Pay (Amendment) Regulations 2004 (SI 2004/488), reg.3(3) (April 6, 2004).

Statutory Paternity Pay (Adoption) and Statutory Adoption Pay (Adoptions from Overseas) (Administration) Regulations 2003

(SI 2003/1192)

The Secretary of State, in exercise of the powers conferred on her by sections 7(1), 2(a) and (b), (4)(a), (b) and (c) and (5), 8(1) and (2)(a), (b) and (c), 10(1) and (2) and 51(1) of the Employment Act 2002 and sections 8(1)(f) and 25 of the Social Security Contributions (Transfer of Functions, etc.) Act 1999 and with the concurrence of the Commissioners of Inland Revenue, hereby makes the following Regulations:

ARRANGEMENT OF REGULATIONS

5.103
1. Citation and commencement.
2. Interpretation.
3. Application of the Statutory Paternity Pay and Statutory Adoption Pay (Administration) Regulations 2002 to adoptions from overseas.

Citation and commencement

5.104
1. These Regulations may be cited as the Statutory Paternity Pay (Adoption) and Statutory Adoption Pay (Adoptions from Overseas) (Administration) Regulations 2003 and shall come into force on 23rd May 2003.

GENERAL NOTE

5.105
These Regulations apply the Statutory Paternity Pay and Statutory Adoption Pay (Administration) Regulations 2002 (SI 2002/2820) to adoptions from overseas with the necessary modifications.

Interpretation

5.106
2. In these Regulations, "adoption from overseas" means the adoption of a child who enters Great Britain from outside the United Kingdom in connection with or for the purposes of adoption which does not involve the placement of the child for adoption under the law of any part of the United Kingdom.

(SI 2003/1192)

Application of the Statutory Paternity Pay and Statutory Adoption Pay (Administration) Regulations 2002 to adoptions from overseas

3.—(1) The Statutory Paternity Pay and Statutory Adoption Pay (Administration) Regulations 2002 shall apply in the case of adoptions from overseas with the modifications set out in the following paragraphs of this regulation.

(2) In regulation 2(1) (interpretation)—
(a) in the definition of "adopter", for the words "with whom the child is matched for adoption" substitute "by whom the child has been or is to be adopted";
(b) after the definition of "income tax quarter", insert—
"official notification" means written notification, issued by or on behalf of the relevant domestic authority, that it is prepared to issue a certificate to the overseas authority concerned with the adoption of the child, or has issued a certificate and sent it to that authority, confirming, in either case, that the adopter is eligible to adopt and has been assessed and approved as being a suitable adoptive parent";
(c) in the definition of "paternity leave", insert at the end "as modified in its application to adoptions from overseas by the Employment Rights Act 1996 (Application of Section 80B to Adoptions from Overseas) Regulations 2003"; and
(d) after the definition of "paternity pay period" insert—
"relevant domestic authority means:—
(a) in the case of an adopter to whom the Intercountry Adoption (Hague Convention) Regulations 2003 apply and who is habitually resident in Wales, the National Assembly for Wales;
(b) in the case of an adopter to whom the Intercountry Adoption (Hague Convention) (Scotland) Regulations 2003 apply and who is habitually resident in Scotland, the Scottish Ministers; and
(c) in any other case, the Secretary of State;".

(3) After regulation 2(2), insert—
"(3) References in these Regulations to provisions of Parts 12ZA and 12ZB of the Contributions and Benefits Act are to be construed as references to those provisions as modified by the Social Security Contributions and Benefits Act 1992 (Application of Parts 12ZA and 12ZB to Adoptions from Overseas) Regulations 2003."

(4) In regulation 11(3)(b)(ii) (time within which an employer is required to give decision that he has no liability to make payments), for "the end of the seven-day period that starts on the date on which the adopter is notified of having been matched with the child" substitute "the date on which the employer's evidence was provided, or, where not all of the evidence referred to in paragraph (1) was provided on one date, the date on which the last of the evidence was provided".

(5) Omit regulation 11(4).

Statutory Paternity Pay (Adoption) and Statutory Adoption Pay (Adoptions from Overseas) (Persons Abroad and Mariners) Regulations 2003

(SI 2003/1193)

The Secretary of State, in exercise of the powers conferred upon her by virtue of sections 171ZI, 171ZJ(1), 171ZR and 171ZS(1) of the Social Security Contributions and Benefits Act 1992 and with the concurrence of the Treasury, by this instrument, which contains only provision made by virtue of sections 2 and 4 of the Employment Act 2002 and is made before the end of the period of 6 months from the coming into force of those enactments, hereby makes the following Regulations:

ARRANGEMENT OF REGULATIONS

1. Citation and commencement.
2. Interpretation.
3. Application of the Statutory Paternity Pay and Statutory Adoption Pay (Persons Abroad and Mariners) Regulations 2002 to adoptions from overseas.

Citation and commencement

1. These Regulations may be cited as the Statutory Paternity Pay (Adoption) and Statutory Adoption Pay (Adoptions from Overseas) (Persons Abroad and Mariners) Regulations 2003 and shall come into force on 23rd May 2003.

GENERAL NOTE

These Regulations modify the application of the Statutory Paternity Pay and Statutory Adoption Pay (Persons Abroad and Mariners) Regulations 2002 (SI 2002/2821) as regards adoptions from overseas.

Interpretation

2. In these Regulations, "adoption from overseas" means the adoption of a child who enters Great Britain from outside the United Kingdom in connection with or for the purposes of adoption which does not involve the placement of the child for adoption under the law of any part of the United Kingdom.

Application of the Statutory Paternity Pay and Statutory Adoption Pay (Persons Abroad and Mariners) Regulations 2002 to adoptions from overseas

3.—(1) The Statutory Paternity Pay and Statutory Adoption Pay (Persons Abroad and Mariners) Regulations 2002 shall have effect in relation to adoptions from overseas with the modifications set out in the following paragraphs of this regulation.

(2) In regulation 1(2) (interpretation)—
(a) in the definition of "adopter", for "has the same meaning as it has in the General Regulations" substitute "means a person by whom the child has been or is to be adopted";
(b) after the definition of "the General Regulations", insert—
"official notification" means written notification, issued by or on behalf of the relevant domestic authority, that it is prepared to issue a certificate to the overseas authority concerned with the adoption of the child, or has issued a certificate and sent it to that authority, confirming, in either case, that the adopter is eligible to adopt and has been assessed and approved as being a suitable adoptive parent;
"relevant domestic authority" means—
(a) in the case of an adopter to whom the Intercountry Adoption (Hague Convention) Regulations 2003 apply and who is habitually resident in Wales, the National Assembly for Wales;
(b) in the case of an adopter to whom the Intercountry Adoption (Hague Convention) (Scotland) Regulations 2003 apply and who is habitually resident in Scotland, the Scottish Ministers; and
(c) in any other case, the Secretary of State;".
(c) for the definition of "statutory paternity pay (birth)" and "statutory paternity pay (adoption)" substitute—
"statutory paternity pay (adoption)" means statutory paternity pay payable in accordance with the provisions of Part 12ZA of the Act, where the conditions specified in section 171ZB(2) of the Act are satisfied;".
(3) For regulation (3), substitute—
"(3) References in these Regulations to provisions of Parts 12ZA and 12ZB of the Act are to be construed as references to those provisions as modified by the Social Security Contributions and Benefits Act 1992 (Application of Parts 12ZA and 12ZB to Adoptions from Overseas) Regulations 2003."
(4) In regulation 5(2) (entitlement to statutory paternity pay adoption))—
(a) in the first line, after "and who" insert ", in the week in which the adopter receives an official notification or completes 26 weeks' continuous employment with his employer, whichever is the later"; and
(b) in sub-paragraph (a), omit the words "in the week in which the adopter is notified of being matched with the child for the purposes of adoption".
(5) In regulation 6 (entitlement to statutory adoption pay)—
(a) in the first line, after "and who" insert ", in the week in which he receives an official notification or completes 26 weeks' continuous employment with his employer, whichever is the later"; and
(b) in paragraph (a), omit the words "in the week in which he is notified that he has been matched with the child for the purposes of adoption".

Statutory Paternity Pay and Statutory Adoption Pay (No.2) Regs 2003

Statutory Paternity Pay (Adoption) and Statutory Adoption Pay (Adoptions from Overseas) (No.2) Regulations 2003

(SI 2003/1194) (AS AMENDED)

The Secretary of State, in exercise of the powers conferred on her by sections 171ZB(2)(a), 171ZC(3)(a) to (d), (f) and (g), 171ZD(2) and (3), 171ZE(2)(a) and (b)(i), (3)(b), (7) and (8), 171ZG(3), 171ZJ(1), (3), (4), (7) and (8), 171ZL(8)(b) to (d), (f) and (g), 171ZM(2) and (3), 171ZN(2), (5) and (6), 171ZP(6), 171ZS(1), (3), (4), (7) and (8), and 175(4) of the Social Security Contributions and Benefits Act 1992, section 5(1)(g), (i) and (p) of the Social Security Administration Act 1992 and with the concurrence of the Commissioners of Inland Revenue in so far as such concurrence is required, by this instrument, which contains only provision made by virtue of sections 2, 4 and 53 and paragraphs 8 and 11 of Schedule 7 to the Employment Act 2002 and is made before the end of the period of 6 months from the coming into force of these enactments, hereby makes the following Regulations:

ARRANGEMENT OF REGULATIONS

General

5.113
1. Citation and commencement.
2. Interpretation and scope.
3. Application of the General Regulations to these Regulations.
4. Application.

Statutory paternity pay (adoption)

5. Conditions of entitlement to statutory paternity pay (adoption) in respect of adoptions from overseas: relationship with child and with adopter.
6. Period of payment of statutory paternity pay (adoption) in respect of adoptions from overseas.
7. Additional notice requirements for statutory paternity pay (adoption) in respect of adoptions from overseas.
8. Qualifying period for statutory paternity pay (adoption) in respect of adoptions from overseas.
9. Evidence of entitlement for statutory paternity pay (adoption) in respect of adoptions from overseas.
10. Entitlement to statutory paternity pay (adoption) where there is more than one employer in respect of adoptions from overseas.
11. Avoidance of liability for statutory paternity pay (adoption) in respect of adoptions from overseas.
12. Adoption pay period in respect of adoptions from overseas.

Statutory adoption pay

13. Adoption pay period in respect of adoptions from overseas where adoption is disrupted.
14. Additional notice requirements for statutory adoption pay in respect of adoptions from overseas.

15. Evidence of entitlement to statutory adoption pay in respect of adoptions from overseas.
16. Entitlement to statutory adoption pay in respect of adoptions from overseas where there is more than one employer.
17. Termination of employment and liability to pay statutory adoption pay in respect of adoptions from overseas.
18. Avoidance of liability for statutory adoption pay in respect of adoptions from overseas.
19. Revocation.

General

Citation and commencement

1. These Regulations may be cited as the Statutory Paternity Pay (Adoption) and Statutory Adoption Pay (Adoptions from Overseas) (No.2) Regulations 2003 and shall come into force on 30th May 2003.

GENERAL NOTE

These Regulations, made under provisions inserted into the SSCBA 1992 by the Employment Act 2002, make provision relating to statutory paternity pay and statutory adoption pay in respect of adoptions from overseas. They should be read together with the Social Security Contributions and Benefits Act 1992 (Application of Pts XIIZA and XIIZB to Adoptions from Overseas) Regulations 2003 (SI 2003/499), which provide for Pts XIIZA and XIIZB of the 1992 Act to have effect, with the modification prescribed in those Regulations, in relation to cases which involve adoption, but not the placement of a child for adoption under the law of any part of the United Kingdom. Regulation 19 of these (No.2) Regulations revokes the Statutory Pay (Adoption) and Statutory Adoption Pay (Adoptions from Overseas) Regulations 2003 (SI 2003/500), which came into force on April 6, 2003 and originally made provision for paternity and adoption pay in the case of adoptions from overseas. The (No.2) Regulations are virtually in identical form to the original set. The main difference is the correction of "employee" to read "employer" in reg.11 where it first appears, but a number of other minor drafting amendments have also been made.

Interpretation and scope

2.—(1) In these Regulations—
"the Act" means the Social Security Contributions and Benefits Act 1992;
"adopter", in relation to a child, means a person by whom the child has been or is to be adopted;
"adoption from overseas" means the adoption of a child who enters Great Britain from outside the United Kingdom in connection with or for the purposes of adoption which does not involve the placement of the child for adoption under the law of any part of the United Kingdom;
"the Application Regulations" means the Social Security Contributions and Benefits Act 1992 (Application of Parts 12ZA and 12ZB to Adoptions from Overseas) Regulations 2003;
"the Board" means the Commissioners of Inland Revenue;
"enter Great Britain" means enter Great Britain from outside the United Kingdom in connection with or for the purposes of adoption, and cognate expressions shall be construed accordingly;

"the General Regulations" means the Statutory Paternity Pay and Statutory Adoption Pay (General) Regulations 2002;

"official notification" means written notification, issued by or on behalf of the relevant domestic authority, that it is prepared to issue a certificate to the overseas authority concerned with the adoption of the child, or has issued a certificate and sent it to that authority, confirming, in either case, that the adopter is eligible to adopt, and has been assessed and approved as being a suitable adoptive parent;

"relevant domestic authority" means—
(a) in the case of an adopter to whom the Intercountry Adoption (Hague Convention) Regulations 2003 apply and who is habitually resident in Wales, the National Assembly for Wales;
(b) in the case of an adopter to whom the Intercountry Adoption (Hague Convention) (Scotland) Regulations apply and who is habitually resident in Scotland, the Scottish Ministers;
(c) in any other case, the Secretary of State;

"statutory paternity pay (adoption)" means statutory paternity pay payable in accordance with the provisions of Part 12ZA of the Act, as modified by the Application Regulations, where the conditions specified in section 171ZB(2) of the Act, as modified by the Application Regulations, are satisfied.

(2) References in these Regulations to the provisions of Parts 12ZA and 12ZB of the Act are to be construed as references to those provisions as modified by the Application Regulations.

(3) These Regulations apply to statutory paternity pay (adoption) and statutory adoption pay in respect of adoptions from overseas.

Application of the General Regulations to these Regulations

3.—(1) Subject to paragraph (2), the provisions of the General Regulations mentioned in paragraph (3) shall, in so far as they apply to statutory paternity pay (adoption) and statutory adoption pay, apply to adoptions from overseas.

(2) Any references to the provisions of Parts 12ZA or 12ZB of the Act in the regulations of the General Regulations mentioned in paragraph (3) shall be construed as references to those provisions as modified by the Application Regulations.

(3) The provisions of the General Regulations referred to in paragraph (1) are regulations 17 to 19, 26 to 28, 31 to 39, 41 to 47 and, subject to paragraph (4), regulation 40.

(4) In the General Regulations, the provisions of regulation 40 shall apply as if—

[1(a) in paragraph (2)(b), for "the week in which the adopter is notified of being matched with the child for the purposes of adoption" there were substituted—
"the week in which—
(i) official notification is sent to the adopter or
(ii) the person satisfies the condition in section 171ZB(2)(b) or 171ZL(2)(b) of the Act (26 weeks' continuous employment), whichever is the later;"]
(b) at the end of paragraph (2), there were added "'official notification' has the same meaning in the Statutory Paternity Pay (Adoption)

(SI 2003/1194, reg.3) (as amended)

and Statutory Adoption Pay (Adoptions from Overseas) (No.2) Regulations 2003".

AMENDMENT

1. Statutory Paternity Pay and Statutory Adoption Pay (Amendment) Regulations 2004 (SI 2004/488), reg.4 (April 6, 2004).

DEFINITIONS

"the Act—see reg.2(1).
"adopter"—see *ibid*.
"adoption from overseas"—see *ibid*.
"the Application Regulation"—see *ibid*.
"the General Regulations"—see *ibid*.
"official notification"—see *ibid*.
"statutory paternity pay (adoption)"—see *ibid*.

Application

4.—(1) Subject to the provisions of Part 12ZA of the Act (statutory paternity pay), the provisions of the General Regulations mentioned in paragraph (3) of regulation 3 and these Regulations, there is entitlement to statutory paternity pay (adoption) in respect of children who enter Great Britain on or after 6th April 2003.

(2) Subject to the provisions of Part 12ZB of the Act (statutory adoption pay), the provisions of the General Regulations mentioned in paragraph (3) of regulation 3 and these Regulations, there is entitlement to statutory adoption pay in respect of children who enter Great Britain on or after 6th April, 2003.

5.118

DEFINITIONS

"the Act"—see reg.2(1).
"enter Great Britain"—see *ibid*.
"the General Regulation"—see *ibid*.
"Part XIIZA"—see reg.(2).
"Pt XIIZB"—see *ibid*.
"statutory paternity pay (adoption)"—see reg.2(1).

Statutory paternity pay (adoption)

Conditions of entitlement to statutory paternity pay (adoption) in respect of adoptions from overseas: relationship with child and with adopter

5.—(1) The conditions prescribed under section 171ZB(2)(a) of the Act are that a person—
(a) is married to [¹, the civil partner] or the partner of a child's adopter (or in a case where there are two adopters, married to [¹, the civil partner] or the partner of the other adopter); and
(b) has, or expects to have, the main responsibility (apart from the responsibility of the child's adopter or, in a case where there are two adopters, together with the other adopter) for the upbringing of the child.

5.119

(2) For the purpose of paragraph (1), "partner" means a person (whether of a different sex or the same sex) who lives with the adopter and the child in an enduring family relationship but is not a relative of the adopter of a kind specified in paragraph (3).

(3) The relatives of a child's adopter referred to in the definition of "partner" in paragraph (2) are the adopter's parent, grandparent, sister, brother, aunt or uncle.

(4) References to relationships in paragraph (3)—
  (a) are to relationships of the full blood or half blood or, in the case of an adopted person, such of those relationships as would exist but for the adoption; and
  (b) include the relationship of a child with his adoptive, or former adoptive parents but do not include any other adoptive relationships.

AMENDMENT

1. Civil Partnership Act 2004 (Amendments to Subordinate Legislation) Order 2005 (SI 2005/2114), art.2(17) and Sch.17, para.6 (December 5, 2005).

DEFINITIONS

"the Act"—see reg.2(1).
"adopter"—see *ibid*.
"partner"—see para.(2).

Period of payment of statutory paternity pay (adoption) in respect of adoptions from overseas

5.120

6.—(1) Subject to notice under section 171ZC(1) of the Act, paragraph (92) and reg.8, a person entitled to statutory paternity pay (adoption) may choose the statutory paternity pay period to begin on—
  (a) the date on which the child enters Great Britain or, where the person is at work on that day, the following day; or
  (b) a pre-determined date, specified by the person, which is later than the date on which the child enters Great Britain.

(2) In a case where statutory paternity pay (adoption) is payable in respect of a child where the adopter has received official notification before 6th April 2003, the statutory paternity pay period shall begin on a predetermined date, later than the date of entry, specified by the person entitled to such pay in a notice under section 171ZC(1) of the Act, which is at least 28 days after the date on which that notice was given, unless the person liable to pay statutory paternity pay (adoption) agrees to the period beginning earlier.

(3) A person may choose for statutory paternity pay (adoption) to be paid in respect of a period of a week.

(4) A choice made in accordance with paragraph (1) is not irrevocable, but where a person subsequently makes a different choice in relation to the beginning of the statutory paternity pay period, section 171ZC(1) of the Act shall apply to it.

DEFINITIONS

"the Act"—see reg.2(1).
"adopter"—see *ibid*.
"enter Great Britain"—see *ibid*.
"official notification"—see *ibid*.
"statutory paternity pay (adoption)"—see *ibid*.

(SI 2003/1194, reg. 7) (as amended)

Additional notice requirements for statutory paternity pay (adoption) in respect of adoptions from overseas

7.—(1) Where a person gives notice under section 171ZC(1) of the Act he shall give further notice of the following matters to the person liable to pay him statutory paternity pay (adoption)—
  (a) the date on which official notification was received, within 28 days of that date, or within 28 days of his completion of 26 weeks of continuous employment with that person, whichever is the later;
  (b) the date on which the child enters Great Britain, within 28 days of entry.

(2) Where the child has not entered Great Britain on the expected date, the person shall, if he wishes to claim statutory paternity pay (adoption), give notice to the person liable to pay it, as soon as is reasonably practicable, that the period in respect of which statutory paternity pay is to be paid shall begin on a date different from that originally chosen by him.

(3) That date may be any date chosen in accordance with paragraph (1) of regulation 6 or specified in accordance with paragraph (2) of that regulation.

(4) Where it becomes known to that person that the child will not enter Great Britain, he shall notify the person who would have been liable to pay statutory pay (adoption), as soon as is reasonably practicable.

5.121

DEFINITIONS

"the Act"—see reg.2(1).
"enter Great Britain"—see *ibid*.
"official notification"—see *ibid*.
"statutory paternity pay (adoption)"—see *ibid*.

Qualifying period for statutory paternity pay (adoption) in respect of adoptions from overseas

8. The qualifying period for the purposes of section 171ZE(2) of the Act (period within which the statutory pay period must occur) is a period of 56 days beginning with the date the child enters Great Britain.

5.122

DEFINITIONS

"the Act"—see reg.2(1).
"enter Great Britain"—see *ibid*.

Evidence of entitlement for statutory paternity pay (adoption) in respect of adoptions from overseas

9.—(1) A person shall produce evidence of his entitlement to statutory paternity pay (adoption) in respect of adoptions from overseas by providing in writing to the person who will be liable to pay him statutory paternity pay (adoption) the declarations specified in paragraph (2) and the information specified in paragraph (3).

(2) The declarations referred to in para.(1) are as follows—
  (a) that he meets the conditions prescribed under section 171ZB(2)(a) of the Act and that it is not the case that statutory paternity pay (adoption) is not payable to him by virtue of the provisions of section 171ZE(4) of the Act;
  (b) that he has elected to receive statutory paternity pay (adoption), and not statutory adoption pay under Part 12ZB of the Act;
  (c) that official notification has been received.

5.123

(3) The information referred to in paragraph (1) is as follows—
(a) the name of the person claiming statutory paternity pay (adoption);
(b) the date on which it is expected that the child will enter Great Britain or, where the child has already entered Great Britain, that date;
(c) the date from which it is expected that the liability to pay statutory paternity pay (adoption) will begin;
(d) whether the period chosen in respect of which statutory paternity pay (adoption) is to be payable is a week.

(4) The declarations mentioned in paragraph (2) and information mentioned in paragraph (3) shall be provided to the person liable to pay statutory paternity pay (adoption) at least 28 days before the date mentioned in sub-paragraph (c) of paragraph (3) or, if that is not reasonably practicable, as soon as is reasonably practicable thereafter.

DEFINITIONS

"the Act"—see reg.2(1).
"adoption from overseas"—see *ibid.*
"enter Great Britain"—see *ibid.*
"official notification"—see *ibid.*
"Pt XIIZB"—see reg.2(2).
"statutory paternity pay (adoption)"—see reg.2(1).

Entitlement to statutory paternity pay (adoption) where there is more than one employer in respect of adoptions from overseas

10. Statutory paternity pay (adoption) shall be payable to a person in respect of a statutory pay week during any part of which he works only for an employer—
(a) who is not liable to pay him statutory paternity pay (adoption); and
(b) for whom he has worked in the week in which the adopter receives official notification.

DEFINITIONS

"adopter"—see reg.2(1).
"official notification"—see *ibid.*
"statutory paternity pay (adoption)"—see *ibid.*

Avoidance of liability for statutory paternity pay (adoption) in respect of adoptions from overseas

11.—(1) A former employer shall be liable to make payments of statutory paternity pay (adoption) to a former employee in any case where the employee has been employed for a continuous period of at least 8 weeks and his contract of service was brought to an end by the former employer solely, or mainly, for the purpose of avoiding liability for statutory paternity pay (adoption).

(2) In a case falling within paragraph (1)—
(a) the employee shall be treated as if he had been employed for a continuous period ending with the day the child enters Great Britain;
(b) his normal weekly earnings shall be calculated by reference to his normal weekly earnings for the period of 8 weeks ending with the last day in respect of which he was paid under his former contract of service.

(SI 2003/1194, reg.11) (as amended)

DEFINITIONS

"enter Great Britain"—see reg.2(1).
"statutory paternity pay (adoption)"—see *ibid*.

Statutory adoption pay

Adoption pay period in respect of adoptions from overseas

12.—(1) Subject to paragraph (2), a person entitled to statutory adoption pay may choose the adoption pay period to begin—
  (a) on the date on which the child enters Great Britain or, where the person is at work on that day, on the following day;
  (b) on the pre-determined date, specified by him, which is no later than 28 days after the date the child enters Great Britain.

(2) In a case where statutory adoption pay is payable in respect of a child where the adopter has received official notification before 6th April 2003, the statutory adoption pay period shall begin on a predetermined date, later than the date of entry, specified by the person entitled to such pay in a notice under section 171ZL(6) of the Act, which is at least 28 days after the date on which that notice was given, unless the person liable to pay statutory adoption pay agrees to the period commencing earlier.

(3) Where the choice made is that mentioned in sub-paragraph (b) of paragraph (1) or in a case where paragraph (2) applies, the adoption pay period shall, unless the employer agrees to the adoption pay period beginning earlier, begin no earlier than 28 days after notice under section 171ZL(6) of the Act has been given.

(4) Subject to regulation 13, the duration of any adoption pay period shall be a continuous period of 26 weeks.

(5) A choice made under paragraph (1), or a date specified under paragraph (2), is not irrevocable, but where a person subsequently makes a different choice or specifies a different date in relation to the beginning of the statutory adoption pay period, section 171ZL(6) of the Act shall apply to it.

5.126

DEFINITIONS

"the Act"—see reg.2(1).
"adopter"—see *ibid*.
"enter Great Britain"—see *ibid*.
"official notification"—see *ibid*.

Adoption pay period in respect of adoptions from overseas where adoption is disrupted

13.—(1) Where after a child enters Great Britain the child—
  (a) dies; or
  (b) ceases to live with the adopter,
the adoption pay period shall terminate in accordance with the provisions of paragraph (2).

(2) The adoption pay period shall, in a case falling within paragraph (1), terminate 8 weeks after the end of the week specified in paragraph (3).

5.127

(3) The week referred to in paragraph (2) is—
(a) in a case falling within paragraph (1)(a), the week during which the child dies;
(b) in a case falling within paragraph (1)(b), the week during which the child ceases to live with the adopter.
(4) For the purposes of paragraph (3), "week" means a period of 7 days beginning with Sunday.

DEFINITIONS

"adopter"—see reg.2(1).
"enter Great Britain"—see *ibid*.
"week"—see para.(4).

Additional notice requirements for statutory adoption pay in respect of adoptions from overseas

14.—(1) Where a person gives notice under section 171ZL(6) of the Act he shall give further notice of the following matters to the person liable to pay statutory adoption pay—
(a) the date on which official notification was received, within 28 days of that date, or within 28 days of his completion of 26 weeks of continuous employment, whichever is the later;
(b) the date on which the child enters Great Britain, within 28 days of entry.
(2) Where the child has not entered Great Britain on the expected date, the person shall, if he wishes to claim statutory adoption pay, give notice to the person liable to pay it, as soon as is reasonably practicable, that the period in respect of which statutory adoption pay is to be paid shall begin on a date different from that originally chosen by him.
(3) That date may be any date chosen in accordance with paragraph (1) of regulation 12 or specified in accordance with paragraph (2) of that regulation.
(4) Where it becomes known to the adopter that the child will not enter Great Britain, he shall notify the person who would have been liable to pay statutory adoption pay as soon as is reasonably practicable.

DEFINITIONS

"the act"—see reg.2(1).
"adopter"—see *ibid*.
"enter Great Britain"—see *ibid*.
"official notification"—see *ibid*.

Evidence of entitlement to statutory adoption pay in respect of adoptions from overseas

15.—(1) A person shall provide evidence of his entitlement to statutory adoption pay by providing, to the person who will be liable to pay it, a copy of the official notification and, in writing—
(a) the information specified in paragraph (2);
(b) a declaration that he has elected to receive statutory adoption pay, and not statutory paternity pay (adoption) under Part 12ZA of the Act;
(c) evidence, to be provided within 28 days of the child's entry into Great Britain, as to that date.

(SI 2003/1194, reg.15) (as amended)

(2) The information referred to in paragraph (1) is—
(a) the name and address of the person claiming statutory adoption pay;
(b) the date on which it is expected that the child will enter Great Britain or, where he has already done so, the date of entry.

(3) The information and declaration referred to in paragraph (1) shall be provided to the person liable to pay statutory adoption pay at least 28 days before the date chosen as the beginning of the adoption pay period in accordance with paragraph (1) of regulation 12 or specified in accordance with paragraph (2) of that regulation or, if that is not reasonably practicable, as soon as is reasonably practicable thereafter.

DEFINITIONS

"the Act"—see reg.2(1).
"enter Great Britain"—see *ibid*.
"official notification"—see *ibid*.
"Pt XIIZA"—see reg.2(2).
"statutory paternity pay (adoption)"—see reg.2(1).

Entitlement to statutory adoption pay in respect of adoptions from overseas where there is more than one employer

16. Statutory adoption pay shall be payable to a person in respect of a week during any part of which he works for an employer—
(a) who is not liable to pay him statutory adoption pay; and
(b) for whom he has worked in the week in which he receives official notification.

5.130

DEFINITION

"official notification"—see reg.2(1).

Termination of employment and liability to pay statutory adoption pay in respect of adoptions from overseas

17.—(1) Where the employment of a person who satisfies the conditions of entitlement to statutory adoption pay in respect of adoptions from overseas terminates for whatever reason (including dismissal) before the adoption pay period chosen or specified by that person in accordance with regulation 12 has begun, the period shall begin on a date chosen by that person which is at least 28 days after notice has been given and within 28 days of the date of the child's entry into Great Britain.

5.131

(2) Where the statutory adoption pay period has not commenced within a period of 6 months of the adopter's leaving his employer, liability to pay statutory adoption pay shall, notwithstanding section 171ZM(1) of the Act, pass to the Board.

(3) Where liability to pay statutory adoption pay has passed to the Board in accordance with paragraph (2) and the adopter, having started employment as an employed earner, becomes entitled to statutory adoption pay by virtue of that employment, the liability of the Board shall cease and section 171ZM(1) of the Act shall apply.

DEFINITIONS

"the Act"—see reg.2(1).
"adopter"—see *ibid*.

"adoption from overseas"—see *ibid*.
"the Board"—see *ibid*.

Avoidance of liability for statutory adoption pay in respect of adoptions from overseas

18.—(1) A former employer shall be liable to make payments of statutory adoption pay to a former employee in any case where the employee had been employed for a continuous period of at least 8 weeks and his contract of service was brought to an end by the former employer solely, or mainly, for the purpose of avoiding liability for statutory adoption pay.

(2) In a case falling within paragraph (1)—
  (a) the employee shall be treated as if he had been employed for a continuous period ending with the week in which he received official notification; and
  (b) his normal weekly earnings shall be calculated by reference to his normal weekly earnings for the period of 8 weeks ending with the last day in respect of which he was paid under his former contract of service.

DEFINITION

"official notification"—see reg.2(1).

Revocation

19. The Statutory Paternity Pay (Adoption) and Statutory Adoption Pay (Adoptions from Overseas) Regulations 2003 are hereby revoked.

PART VI

CHILD TRUST FUNDS

Child Trust Funds Act 2004 (Commencement No.1) Order 2004

(SI 2004/2422 (C.103))

The Treasury, in exercise of the powers conferred upon them by section 27 of the Child Trust Funds Act 2004, make the following Order:

ARRANGEMENT OF ARTICLES

1. Citation and interpretation
2. Commencement of certain provisions of the Act

Citation and interpretation

1.—(1) This Order may be cited as the Child Trust Funds Act 2004 (Commencement No.1) Order 2004.

(2) In this Order—

"account" means an account which (from the appointed day) is capable of being a child trust fund (within the meaning in the Act);

"the Act" means the Child Trust Funds Act 2004;

"the appointed day" means the day appointed under section 27 of the Act for the purposes of sections 8 and 9 of the Act.

6.1

Commencement of certain provisions of the Act

2. The following provisions of the Act shall come into force on 1st January 2005 for the purposes mentioned in relation to each provision:

6.2

Provision	*Purposes*
Section 1(3) of the Act	All purposes
Section 3(1) and (3) of the Act	All purposes (save that an account may only be a child trust fund from the appointed day)
Section 3(2), (4) to (9) and (12) of the Act	To allow accounts to be opened, and contracts with an account provider for their management to be signed, save that the account is only to be: (a) a child trust fund, or (b) subscribed to and operated, from the appointed day.
Section 5(1) and (2) of the Act	To ensure an orderly introduction of accounts, by issuing some vouchers before the appointed day.
Section 5(3) to (5) of the Act	Where a voucher has been issued before the appointed day under section 5(1) of the Act, to allow

775

Child Trust Funds Act 2004 (Commencement No.1) Order 2004

Provision	Purposes
	accounts to be opened, save that the account is only to be: (a) a child trust fund, or (b) subscribed to and operated, from that day.
Section 15(1), (2)(a) and (3) of the Act	So far as those provisions relate to the persons referred to in section 15(2)(a) of the Act
Section 17 of the Act	All purposes
Section 18 of the Act	All purposes
Section 20(1) (except paragraphs (b) and (c)), (2) to (6), (7) (except paragraph (c)), (8) and (9) of the Act	All purposes (except for the purposes of sections 6, 7, 9, 10 or 13 of the Act)
Section 21 of the Act	For the purposes of the provisions of section 20 of the Act which are commenced by this Order
Section 22(1) and (6) of the Act	All purposes
Section 23(1) to (3) of the Act	For the purposes of section 22(1) and (6) of the Act
Section 24(1) (except paragraph (c)), (2) and (3) of the Act	For the purposes of section 22(1) and (6) of the Act
Section 24(5) to (7) of the Act	All purposes

Child Trust Funds Act 2004 (Commencement No. 2) Order 2004

(SI 2004/3369 (C.158))

The Treasury, in exercise of the powers conferred upon them by section 27 of the Child Trust Funds Act 2004, make the following Order:

ARRANGEMENT OF ARTICLES

1. Citation and interpretation
2. Commencement of provisions of the Act

Citation and interpretation

6.3   **1.**—(1) This Order may be cited as the Child Trust Funds Act 2004 (Commencement No.2) Order 2004.
   (2) In this Order—
"the Act" means the Child Trust Funds Act 2004;

(SI 2004/3369 c.158, reg.1)

"the earlier Order" means the Child Trust Funds Act 2004 (Commencement No. 1) Order 2004.

Commencement of provisions of the Act

2.—(1) Sections 1 to 24 of the Act shall come into force on 6th April 2005, subject to the following paragraphs.

(2) Paragraph (1) does not apply to provisions brought into force for all purposes by the earlier Order.

(3) Section 23(1) of the Act shall come into force for all purposes on 1st January 2005.

(4) Where a provision of the Act (other than section 23(1)) was partially brought into force by the earlier Order, that provision shall come into force for all other purposes on 6th April 2005.

Child Trust Funds Regulations 2004

(SI 2004/1450) (AS AMENDED)

ARRANGEMENT OF REGULATIONS

PART 1

Introductory

1. Citation and commencement
2. Interpretation
3. Vouchers
4. Descriptions of accounts
5. Opening of account by responsible person or the child
6. Opening of account by Inland Revenue—(Revenue allocated accounts)
7. Government contributions

PART 2

Other requirements to be satisfied in relation to accounts

8. General requirements for accounts
9. Annual limit on subscriptions
10. Statements for an account
11. General investment rules
12. Qualifying investments for an account
13. Conditions for application by responsible person or the child to open an account (and changes to an account)
14. Account provider—qualifications and Board's approval
15. Account provider—appointment of tax representative
16. Account provider—withdrawal by Board of approval
17. Account provider—appeal against non-approval or withdrawal of Board's approval

777

18. Permitted withdrawals from an account
18A. Permitted withdrawals from an account where the child is terminally ill
19. Account provider ceasing to act (or ceasing to accept Revenue allocated accounts)
20. Account provider ceasing to qualify
21. Transfer of accounts to other account providers
22. Recoupment of Inland Revenue contributions to void accounts (and other accounts)
23. "Repair" of invalid accounts

PART 3

Tax and administration of accounts

24. Exemption from tax of account income and gains
25. Tax liabilities and reliefs—account provider to act on behalf of the named child
26. Repayments in respect of tax to account provider—interim tax claims
27. Repayments in respect of tax to account provider—annual tax claims
28. Account provider's tax claims—supplementary provisions
29. Assessments for withdrawing relief and recovering tax
30. Fortnightly claim and financial returns
31. Records to be kept by account provider
32. Returns of information by account provider
33. Information about "looked after children" from Local Authorities
33A. The Official Solicitor or Accountant of Court to be the person who has the authority to manage an account
34. Information to be provided to the Board
35. Inspection of records by officer of the Board
36. Capital gains tax—adaptation of enactments
37. Administration of tax in relation to accounts—supplementary
38. Application of the provisions of Chapter 2 of Part 13 of the Taxes Act to policies

Schedule — Stakeholder Accounts
Description of stakeholder account
Characteristics of stakeholder account etc
Stakeholder accounts—charges etc

The Treasury, in exercise of the powers conferred upon them by sections 3(1) to (5) and (7), 5(1), (4) and (5), 6, 7, 8(1), 9(2) and (10)(b), 11(1), 12(2), 13, 15, 16, 23(1) and 28(1) to (4) of the Child Trust Funds Act 2004, hereby make the following Regulations:

(SI 2004/1450, reg. 1) (as amended)

Part 1

Introductory

Citation and commencement

1. These Regulations may be cited as the Child Trust Funds Regulations 2004 and shall come into force for the purposes of—
   (a) issuing vouchers (see regulation 3),
   (b) completing account-opening formalities (see regulation 5),
   (c) applications under regulation 13 to open an account with effect from the appointed day,
   (d) applications under regulation 14 to be approved as an account provider to manage accounts from the appointed day,
   (e) regulation 17, so far as it relates to applications referred to in paragraph (d), and
   (f) making a fortnightly claim and financial return (see regulation 30),
on 1st January 2005, and for all other purposes on the appointed day.

Interpretation

2.—(1) In these Regulations—
(a) the following expressions have the meanings given in the Child Trust Funds Act 2004 ("the Act")—
"child"
"child trust fund"
"eligible child"
"Inland Revenue"
"Inland Revenue contributions" (see section 11(2) of the Act),
"parental responsibility" (see section 3(9) of the Act);
"relevant person" (see section 15(2) of the Act),
"responsible person", in relation to a child under 16 (see section 3(8) of the Act),
"the person entitled to child benefit in respect of the child" (see section 2(1)(a), (4) and (6) of the Act);
(b) except where the context otherwise requires—
"account" means a scheme of investment which (except in regulation 22(1)) qualifies as a child trust fund, other than in the cases of—
   (i) an account with a deposit-taker,
   (ii) a share or deposit account with a building society, or
   (iii) a deposit account with a person falling within section 840A(1)(b) of the Taxes Act, or a relevant European institution;
an "account investment" is an investment under the account which is a qualifying investment for an account within the meaning of regulation 12;
an "account provider" is a person who fulfils the conditions of these Regulations and is approved by the Board for the purpose of these Regulations as an account provider;
"appointed day" means the day appointed, under section 27 of the Act, for the purposes of sections 8 and 9 of the Act;

"assurance undertaking" has the meaning in Article 2 of the Council Directive of 5th November 2002 concerning life assurance (2002/83/EC);

[¹"Bank of England base rate" means the rate announced from time to time by the Monetary Policy Committee of the Bank of England as the official dealing rate, being the rate at which the Bank is willing to enter into transactions for providing short-term liquidity in the money markets;]

[³"the Board" means the Commissioners for Her Majesty's Revenue and Customs;]

"building society" means a building society within the meaning of the Building Societies Act 1986, or the Irish Building Societies Act 1989;

[⁴"building society bonus", except in regulation 24(a)(i), excludes any bonus, distribution of funds or the conferring of rights in relation to shares—

(a) in connection with an amalgamation, transfer of engagements or transfer of business of a building society, and

(b) mentioned in section 96 or 100 of the Building Societies Act 1986,

and "payment under a building society bonus scheme" shall be construed accordingly;]

"company", except in regulation 12(4)(a), means any body corporate having a share capital other than—

(i) an open-ended investment company, within the meaning given by section 236 of the Financial Services and Markets Act 2000,
(ii) a UCITS,
(iii) an industrial and provident society, or
(iv) a body corporate which is a 51 per cent. subsidiary of any industrial and provident society;

[²"credit union" means a society registered as a credit union under the Industrial and Provident Societies Act 1965 or the Credit Unions (Northern Ireland) Order 1985;]

"deposit-taker" has the meaning given by section 481(2) of the Taxes Act;

"the Director of Savings" has the same meaning as in the National Debt Act 1972;

"the Distance Marketing Directive" means Directive 2002/65/EC of the European Parliament and of the Council of 23rd September 2002, and includes any provisions by which an EEA State or the United Kingdom has transposed the Directive or has corresponding obligations in its domestic law, and "distance contract" has the meaning in that Directive;

"electronic communications" includes any communications by means of a telecommunication system (within the meaning in the Telecommunications Act 1984);

"EEA Agreement" means the Agreement on the European Economic Area signed at Oporto on 2nd May 1992, as adjusted by the Protocol signed at Brussels on 17th March 1993;

"EEA State" means a State, other than the United Kingdom, which is a Contracting Party to the EEA Agreement;

"European institution" means an EEA firm of the kind mentioned in paragraph 5(a), (b) or (c) of Schedule 3 to the Financial Services and Markets Act 2000 which is an authorised person for the purposes of that Act as a result of qualifying for authorisation under paragraph 12 of that Schedule;

"51 per cent. subsidiary" and "75 per cent. subsidiary" have the meanings given by section 838 of the Taxes Act;

"gains", except in regulations 22(1) to (3), 24(a)(ii), (iii) and (v), 37(5) and 38, means "chargeable gains" within the meaning in the 1992 Act;

"gilt-edged securities" has the meaning given by paragraphs 1 and 1A of Schedule 9 to the 1992 Act;

"incorporated friendly society" means a society incorporated under the Friendly Societies Act 1992;

"industrial and provident society" means a society registered or deemed to be registered under the Industrial and Provident Societies Act 1965 or under the Industrial and Provident Societies (Northern Ireland) Act 1969;

"investments under the account" has the same meaning as investments under a child trust fund in the Act;

investment trust" has the meaning given by section 842 of the Taxes Act, and references to the "eligible rental income" of an investment trust have the same meaning as in that section;

"the Management Act" means the Taxes Management Act 1970;

"market value" shall be construed in accordance with section 272 of the 1992 Act;

[3"the New Collective Investment Schemes Sourcebook" means the Sourcebook of that name made by the Financial Services Authority under the Financial Services and Markets Act 2000;

"non-UCITS retail scheme"—

(a) has the meaning in the New Collective Investment Schemes Sourcebook (that is, a scheme to which, or to whose authorised fund manager and depositary, Sections 5.1, 5.4 and 5.6 of that Sourcebook apply),

(b) includes a "recognised scheme" by virtue of section 270 or 272 of the Financial Services and Markets Act 2000, which would fall within paragraph (a) of this definition if it were an authorised fund, and

(c) includes a sub-fund of an umbrella which the terms of the scheme identify as a sub-fund which would fall within paragraph (a) or (b) of this definition if it were itself an authorised fund or a recognised scheme.

In this definition, expressions defined in the Glossary forming part of the Financial Services Authority Handbook have those defined meanings;]

"the 1992 Act" means the Taxation of Chargeable Gains Act 1992;

"notice" except in regulations 12(12) and 37(6)(a), means notice in writing;

[3"qualifying units in or shares of a non-UCITS retail scheme" means that—

(a) the instrument constituting the scheme secures that redemption of the units or shares in question shall take place no less frequently than bi-monthly (see Rule 6.2.16(6) of the New Collective Investment Schemes Sourcebook omitting the words "Except where (7) applies, and", read with Rule 6.3.4(1), whether or not those Rules apply to the scheme), and

(b) a provision for suspension of dealings in exceptional conditions in accordance with Rule 7.2 of that Sourcebook (or any foreign procedure which is a direct foreign equivalent of that Rule) shall not be treated as a provision contrary to paragraph (a) of this definition;]

"recognised stock exchange" has the same meaning as in section 841 of the Taxes Act;

"registered friendly society" has the meaning given by the Friendly Societies Act 1992 and includes any society that by virtue of section 96(2) of that Act is to be treated as a registered friendly society;

"relevant authorised person" has the same meaning as in section 333A(12) of the Taxes Act;

"relevant European institution" has the meaning given by section 326A(10) of the Taxes Act;

"security" means any loan stock or similar security of a company whether secured or unsecured;

"subscriptions" has the meaning in section 12(1) of the Act (but excluding Inland Revenue contributions and income or gains arising from investments under the account);

"tax" where neither income tax nor capital gains tax is specified means either of those taxes;

"the Taxes Act" means the Income and Corporation Taxes Act 1988;

"year", except in the expression "subscription year" in regulations 9, 21(5)(b) and 32(2)(b)(iv), means a year of assessment (within the meaning in section 832(1) of the Taxes Act, or section 288(1) of the 1992 Act, as the case may be);

(c) "authorised fund" means—
  (i) an authorised unit trust, or
  (ii) an open-ended investment company with variable capital incorporated in the United Kingdom in the case of which an authorisation order made by the Financial Services Authority under regulation 14 of the Open-Ended Investment Companies Regulations 2001 is in force;

"authorised unit trust" means a unit trust scheme in the case of which an authorisation order made by the Financial Services Authority under section 243 of the Financial Services and Markets Act 2000 is in force;

"the Collective Investment Schemes Sourcebook" means the sourcebook of that name made by the Financial Services Authority under the Financial Services and Markets Act 2000;

"depositary interest" means the rights of the person mentioned in paragraph (ii), under a certificate or other record (whether or not in the form of a document) acknowledging—
  (i) that a person holds relevant investments or evidence of the right to them, and
  (ii) that another person is entitled to rights in or in relation to those or identical relevant investments, including the right to receive such investments, or evidence of the right to them or the proceeds from such investments, from the person mentioned in paragraph (i),

where "relevant investments" means investments which are exclusively qualifying investments for an account falling within regulation 12(2)(a) to (i), and the rights mentioned in paragraph (ii) are exclusively rights in or in relation to relevant investments;

(SI 2004/1450, reg. 2) (as amended)

"fund of funds scheme" means—
  (i) an authorised fund which according to the terms of the scheme is a fund of funds scheme belonging to the category under that name established by the Financial Services Authority, and
  (ii) a part of an umbrella scheme which the terms of the scheme identify as a part that would belong to that category if it were itself an authorised fund;
"money market scheme" means—
  (i) an authorised fund which according to terms of the scheme is a money market scheme belonging to the category under that name established by the Financial Services Authority, and
  (ii) a part of an umbrella scheme which the terms of the scheme identify as a part that would belong to that category if it were itself an authorised fund;
"open-ended investment company", except in sub-paragraph (a), has the meaning given by subsection (10) of section 468 of the Taxes Act as that subsection is added in relation to open-ended investment companies by regulation 10(4) of the 1997 Regulations, and "shares" in relation to an open-ended investment company, includes shares of any class and of any denomination of a given class and, in relation to a part of an umbrella company, means shares in the company which confer for the time being rights in that part;
"securities scheme" means—
  (i) an authorised fund which according to the terms of the scheme is a securities scheme belonging to the category under that name established by the Financial Services Authority, and
  (ii) a part of an umbrella scheme which the terms of the scheme identify as a part which would belong to that category if it were itself an authorised fund;
"the 1997 Regulations" means the Open-ended Investment Companies (Tax) Regulations 1997;
"UCITS" means undertakings for collective investment in transferable securities within the meaning of Article 1 of Council Directive 85/611;
"umbrella scheme" means an authorised fund which according to the terms of the scheme is an umbrella scheme belonging to the category under that name established by the Financial Services Authority, and—
  (i) in the case of an authorised fund which is an authorised unit trust, references to a part of an umbrella scheme shall be construed in accordance with subsection (8) of section 468 of the Taxes Act, and, in relation to a part of an umbrella scheme, references to investments subject to the trusts of an authorised unit trust and to a unit holder shall be construed in accordance with subsection (9) of that section, and
  (ii) in the case of an authorised fund which is an open-ended investment company, references to a part of an umbrella scheme shall be construed in accordance with subsection (18) of section 468 of the Taxes Act as that subsection is added in relation to open-ended investment companies by regulation 10(4) of the 1997 Regulations, and, in relation to a part of an umbrella scheme, references to investments of the company shall be construed in accordance with subsection (12) of that section as so added;

"unit holder", except in relation to a part of an umbrella scheme, has the meaning given by subsection (6) of section 468 of the Taxes Act;
"unit trust scheme" has the meaning given by subsection (6) of section 468 of the Taxes Act;
"units", in relation to an authorised unit trust, means the rights or interests (however described) of the unit holders in that unit trust and, in relation to a part of an umbrella scheme, means the rights or interests for the time being of the unit holders in that part;
"warrant scheme" means—
- (i) an authorised fund which according to the terms of the scheme is a warrant scheme belonging to the category under that name established by the Financial Services Authority, and
- (ii) a part of an umbrella scheme which the terms of the scheme identify as a part that would belong to that category if it were itself an authorised fund.

(2) The table below indexes other definitions in these Regulations—

Term defined	Regulation
"the applicant"	5
"the commencement date"	7(8)
"description" of an account	4
"the disqualifying circumstances"	16
"first return period"	30(1)
"fortnightly period"	30(1)
"initial contribution"	7(1)
"interim tax claim"	26(2)
"local authority"	33(1)
"looked after child"	33(1)
"management agreement"	5
"the named child"	5 and 8(1)
"qualifying circumstances"	14
"qualifying investments for an account"	12
"registered contact"	8(1)(d)
"second return period"	30(1)
"special contribution"	7(1)
"subscription year"	9(2)
"supplementary contribution"	7(5)
"the termination event"	12(12)
"the transfer instructions"	8(2)(h)
"the internal transfer instructions"	8(2)(i)

AMENDMENTS

1. Child Trust Funds (Amendment) Regulations 2004 (SI 2004/2676), reg.3 (April 6, 2005).
2. Child Trust Funds (Amendment No.2) Regulations 2005 (SI 2005/909), reg.3 (April 6, 2005).
3. Child Trust Funds (Amendment No.3) Regulations 2005 (SI 2005/3349), reg.3 (December 27, 2005).
4. Child Trust Funds (Amendment No.3) Regulations 2006 (SI 2006/3195), reg.3 (January 1, 2007).

(SI 2004/1450, reg. 3) (as amended)

Vouchers

3.—(1) The voucher to be issued under section 5(1) of the Act shall contain the following particulars—
(a) the full name of the child,
(b) his date of birth,
(c) his unique reference number,
(d) the expiry date of the voucher, and
(e) the amount of the initial contribution (see regulation 7(1)),
and a statement that the voucher cannot be exchanged for money.

(2) The voucher shall be sent to the person who is entitled to child benefit in respect of the child (or, in the case of a child who is an eligible child because of section 2(3) of the Act, to a responsible person in relation to the child) by post.

(3) The expiry date [1. . .] shall be whichever is the earlier of—
(a) the date 12 months from the date of issue of the voucher, or
(b) where the child is over 17 years of age, the date on which he will attain the age of 18 years.

6.9

AMENDMENT

1. Child Trust Funds (Amendment) Regulations 2006 (SI 2006/199), reg.3 (February 7, 2006).

DEFINITIONS

"child"—see reg.2(1)(a).
"eligible child"—see *ibid.*
"responsible person"—see *ibid.*

Descriptions of accounts

4.—(1) An account may be of either of the following descriptions—

6.10

Stakeholder account

Where the account meets the characteristics and conditions in the Schedule to these Regulations.

Non-stakeholder account

Where any of those characteristics or conditions is not met.

(2) Accounts opened by the Inland Revenue (see regulation 6) must be stakeholder accounts.

DEFINITION

"account"—see reg.2(1)(b).

Opening of account by responsible person or the child

5.—(1) For the purposes of these Regulations, subject to [¹paragraphs (1A) and (2)], an account is opened for a child ("the named child") with an account provider on the date the last of the following conditions is satisfied (in any order), where "the applicant" means—
(a) if the named child is 16 or over, the child; and
(b) in any other case, a responsible person in relation to the named child.

6.11

785

Condition 1

The applicant gives the voucher relating to the named child to the account provider [¹not later than 7 days after its expiry date].

Condition 2

The applicant enters into an agreement with the account provider (the "management agreement") for the management of the account (see regulation 8(1) and (2)), which includes the application and declaration required by regulation 13.

Condition 3

Where that application is not in writing the applicant has agreed, or is treated as having agreed, the contents of the copy of the declaration required by regulation 13(3).

Condition 4

(a) In any case where the management agreement is a distance contract, the agreement must be an initial service agreement for the purposes of the Distance Marketing Directive, and contain the instructions required by regulation 8(1)(f), and

(b) in every case where there is any right to cancel (or automatic cancellation of) the management agreement, the period during which it may be exercised or occur has expired without that right being exercised or cancellation occurring.

(2) An account must satisfy the requirements that—

(a) no subscription to the account is accepted by the account provider until the account has been opened in accordance with paragraph (1); and

(b) where the account is so opened before the appointed day, it shall not be treated as open for the purpose of accepting subscriptions until the appointed day.

[¹(1A) The application to open the account must be made, and Condition 2 satisfied, not later than the expiry date of the voucher.]

AMENDMENT

1. Child Trust Funds (Amendment) Regulations 2006 (SI 2006/199), reg.4 (February 7, 2006).

DEFINITIONS

"account"—see reg.2(1)(b).
"account provider"—see *ibid.*
"appointed day"—see *ibid.*
"child"—see reg.2(1)(a).
"the Distance Marketing Directive"—see reg.2(1)(b).
"responsible person"—see reg.2(1)(a).
"subscriptions"—see reg.2(1)(b).

Opening of account by Inland Revenue—(Revenue allocated accounts)

6.—(1) The Board shall apply to open an account for a child to whom section 6 of the Act applies, by forwarding to an account provider the particulars which would be required for a voucher (see regulation 3), but omitting paragraph (1)(d) of that regulation.

(SI 2004/1450, reg.6) (as amended)

(2) The account provider shall immediately open a stakeholder account in the name of the child, which shall have the same effect as if a responsible person for the child (or the child if aged 16 or over) had entered into the account provider's standard management agreement for the stakeholder account in question, including the terms mentioned in Condition 2 of regulation 5(1) (but treating the reference to the application and declaration required by regulation 13 as a reference to the authorisation required by regulation 13(4)) and regulation 8(1)(f).

(3) The Inland Revenue shall maintain (and update from time to time) a list of account providers who have agreed to accept Revenue allocated accounts under this regulation, in the order of the date of their agreement, and the account provider shall be selected in rotation from the current list.

(4) Where the account provider offers two or more types of stakeholder account [2—
   (a) the account provider shall select the type or types to be used for the purposes of this regulation (subject to sub-paragraph (b)),
   (b) any type selected must be offered to the general public at the time of opening a Revenue allocated account of that type, and
   (c) if more than one type has been selected, the account to be opened shall be chosen by the account provider in rotation between the selected types of accounts.]

[¹(5) The Inland Revenue shall write to the person who is entitled to child benefit in respect of the child (or, in the case of a child who is an eligible child because of section 2(3) of the Act, to a responsible person in relation to the child) to inform them of the opening of the account and particulars of it.]

AMENDMENTS

1. Child Trust Funds (Amendment) Regulations 2004 (SI 2004/2676), reg.4 (April 6, 2005).
2. Child Trust Funds (Amendment No.3) Regulations 2005 (SI 2005/3349), reg.4 (December 27, 2005).

DEFINITIONS

"account"—see reg.2(1)(b).
"account provider"—see *ibid.*
"child"—see reg.2(1)(a).
"eligible child"—see *ibid.*
"responsible person"—see *ibid.*

Government contributions

7.—(1) The amounts of the contribution for the purposes of section 8(1) of the Act are set out in paragraphs (2) to (4), (the amounts set out in paragraphs (2) and (4)(a) to be known as the "initial contribution", and the amounts set out in paragraphs (3) and (4)(b) as the "special contribution").

(2) Where the child is an eligible child on the appointed day by virtue of section 2(1)(a) of the Act (by reason of a child benefit award), and—
   (i) was born after 31st August 2002 but before 6th April 2003, the amount is £277,
   (ii) was born between 6th April 2003 and 5th April 2004, the amount is £268, and

6.13

(iii) was born between 6th April 2004 and the day preceding the appointed day, the amount is £256.

(3) Where the child is an eligible child on the appointed day by virtue of section 2(1)(b) of the Act (by reason of being a child in the care of a local authority at that date) and—

    (i) was born after 31st August 2002 but before 6th April 2003, the amount is £554,

    (ii) was born between 6th April 2003 and 5th April 2004, the amount is £536, and

    (iii) was born between 6th April 2004 and the day preceding the appointed day, the amount is £512.

(4) Where the child [¹becomes an eligible child] on or after the appointed day and—

(a) is first an eligible child by virtue of section 2(1)(a) of the Act, the amount is £250, and

(b) is first an eligible child by virtue of section 2(1)(b) of the Act, the amount is £500.

(5) The amounts of the supplementary contribution for the purposes of section 9(2) of the Act (to be known as the "supplementary contribution") are set out in paragraphs (6) and (7).

(6) Where the child is an eligible child on the appointed day (and is a child to whom section 9 of the Act applies), the amount—

(a) if the commencement date was after 31st August 2002 but before 6th April 2003, is £266,

(b) if the commencement date was between 6th April 2003 and 5th April 2004, is £258,

(c) if the commencement date was between 6th April 2004 and the appointed day, is £250.

(7) Where the child becomes an eligible child after the appointed day (and is a child to whom section 9 of the Act applies), the amount is £250.

(8) The "commencement date", in relation to a child, means the first day for which child benefit was paid (under a decision mentioned in section 2(6) of the Act) in respect of the child, except that—

(a) where entitlement to child benefit is wholly excluded by a directly applicable Community provision, it means the date on which that exclusion took effect, and

(b) where the child was prevented from being an eligible child by virtue of section 2(5) of the Act, it means the date on which the child became an eligible child.

[¹(9) The Inland Revenue shall, following final determination of entitlement to child tax credit, write to the person who is entitled to child benefit in respect of the child (or, in the case of a child who is an eligible child because of section 2(3) of the Act, to a responsible person in relation to the child) to inform them that the supplementary contribution is being paid into the child's account.]

[²(10) A further contribution under section 10 of the Act of £250 is due for any child where—

(a) the commencement date (for child benefit: see paragraph (8)) in relation to that child is after 5th April 2005, and

(b) income support or income-based jobseeker's allowance was paid for that commencement date to a person whose applicable amount included an amount in respect of the child.

(SI 2004/1450, reg. 7) (as amended)

(11) On receipt of the further contribution from the Inland Revenue the account provider must credit the account held by the child with the amount of the payment.]

AMENDMENTS

1. Child Trust Funds (Amendment) Regulations 2004 (SI 2004/2676), reg.5 (April 6, 2005).
2. Child Trust Funds (Amendment) Regulations 2005 (SI 2005/383), reg.3 (April 6, 2005).

DEFINITIONS

"account"—see reg.2(1)(b).
"account provider"—see *ibid*.
"appointed day"—see *ibid*.
"child"—see reg.2(1)(a).
"eligible child"—see *ibid*.
"responsible person"—see *ibid*.

PART 2

OTHER REQUIREMENTS TO BE SATISFIED IN RELATION TO ACCOUNTS

General requirements for accounts

8.—(1) An account must satisfy the requirements that—
(a) it is the account for a single child ("the named child");
(b) the named child is or has been an eligible child;
(c) no child may hold more than one account;
(d) at any time—
   (i) where the named child is under 16, only a single responsible person in relation to the named child, or
   (ii) where the named child is 16 or over, only the child,
("the registered contact") may give instructions to the account provider with respect to its management;
(e) the account must at all times be managed in accordance with these Regulations by an account provider and, subject to regulation 6(2), under terms agreed and recorded in a management agreement made between the account provider and the registered contact (on behalf of the named child where appropriate); and
(f) the management agreement must include instructions to the provider as to the manner in which Inland Revenue contributions and any subscriptions made are to be invested under the account.

(2) Apart from other requirements of these Regulations the terms so agreed shall include the conditions that—
(a) the account investments shall be in the beneficial ownership of the named child;
(b) the title to all account investments, except those falling within regulation 12(2)(k), (l) or (m), shall be vested in the account provider or his nominee, subject to sub-paragraph (f);

(c) where a share certificate or other document evidencing title to an account investment is issued, it shall be held by the account provider or as he may direct, subject to sub-paragraph (f);

(d) in relation to qualifying investments falling within regulation 12(2)(a), (b) and (f) to (j), the account provider shall, if the registered contact so elects (and subject to any charge for the arrangement), arrange for the registered contact to receive a copy of the annual report and accounts issued to investors by every company, unit trust, open-ended investment company or other entity in which account investments are held;

(e) in relation to qualifying investments falling within regulation 12(2)(a), (b) and (f) to (j), the account provider shall, if the registered contact so elects (subject to any charge for the arrangement, and to any provisions made under any enactment), be under an obligation to arrange for the registered contact to be able—
  (i) to attend any meetings of investors in companies, unit trusts, open-ended investment companies and other entities in which account investments are held,
  (ii) to vote, and
  (iii) to receive, in addition to the documents referred to in sub-paragraph (d), any other information issued to investors in such companies, unit trusts, open-ended investment companies and other entities;

(f) if and so long as a person falling within regulation 14(2)(d)(iv) acts as account provider of an account, and the account investments include a policy of life insurance—
  (i) the title to all such policies shall be vested in the registered contact, and
  (ii) where a policy document or other document evidencing title to such policies of life insurance is issued, it shall be held by the registered contact;

(g) the account provider shall satisfy himself that any person to whom he delegates any of his functions or responsibilities under the management agreement is competent to carry out those functions or responsibilities;

(h) on the instructions of the registered contact ("the transfer instructions") and within such time as is stipulated by the registered contact in the transfer instructions, the whole of an account, with all rights and obligations of the parties to it, shall be transferred free of expense (except any incidental expenses) to another account provider subject to and in accordance with regulation 21;

[¹(ha) where the account is or has been transferred to the account provider by a transfer under regulation 21, that no charges or expenses are due in respect of that transfer, except in accordance with sub-paragraph (h);]

(i) where the account provider offers accounts of another description or type, on the instructions of the registered contact ("the internal transfer instructions") and within such time as is stipulated by the registered contact in the internal transfer instructions, the account shall become (free of expense, except any incidental expenses) an account of that other description or type (any necessary change in the investments being made accordingly); and

(j) the account provider shall notify the registered contact if by reason of any failure to satisfy the provisions of these Regulations an

(SI 2004/1450, reg. 8) (as amended)

account is or will become no longer exempt from tax by virtue of regulation 24.

(3) Where the transfer instructions or internal transfer instructions, or any new management agreement entered into by the registered contact with the account provider (or a new account provider) under regulation 8(1)(e), is a distance contract, the transfer or internal transfer shall only take effect once those contracts satisfy Condition 4 in regulation 5(1).

(4) The time stipulated in transfer instructions or internal transfer instructions shall be subject to any reasonable business period (not exceeding 30 days) of the account provider required for the practical implementation of the instructions.

(5) In this regulation, "incidental expenses" means stamp duty and other dealing costs of disposing of or acquiring investments.

AMENDMENT

1. Child Trust Funds (Amendment) Regulations 2004 (SI 2004/2676), reg.6 (April 6, 2005).

DEFINITIONS

"account"—see reg.2(1)(b).
"account investment"—see *ibid.*
"account provider"—see *ibid.*
"child"—see reg.2(1)(a).
"company"—see reg.2(1)(b).
"incidental expenses"—see reg.8(5).
"open-ended investment company"—see reg.2(1)(c).
"responsible person"—see reg.2(1)(a).
"subscriptions"—see reg.2(1)(b).
"tax"—see *ibid.*

Annual limit on subscriptions

9.—(1) Any person (including the child) may make subscriptions to a child's account, subject to paragraphs (2) and (3).

(2) Subscriptions to an account made during any subscription year, that is—
(a) the period beginning with the day on which the account is opened (or if opened before the appointed day, opened for the purpose of accepting subscriptions under regulation 5(2)(b)), and ending immediately before the child's next birthday, and
(b) any succeeding period of twelve months,

shall not in aggregate exceed the sum of £1,200.

(3) Where the aggregate of subscriptions in any year falls short of £1,200 or is nil, there shall be no addition to the amount for any succeeding year.

6.15

DEFINITIONS

"account"—see reg.2(1)(b).
"appointed day"—see *ibid.*
"child"—see reg.2(1)(a).
"subscriptions"—see reg.2(1)(b).

Statements for an account

10.—(1) The account provider must issue a statement for the account—
(a) annually, and

6.16

(b) where an account is transferred to another account provider under regulation 21, as at the transfer date.

(2) The statement date in the case of an annual statement must be—

(a) any date not more than [¹61] days before or after the named child's birthday, and

(b) not more than 12 months from the previous statement date.

(3) The statement shall be sent—

(a) where the named child is the registered contact, to the child,

(b) where a responsible person is the registered contact, to the named child care of the registered contact,

(c) where the Official Solicitor or Accountant of Court has been appointed under section 3(10) of the Act, to the Official Solicitor or Accountant of Court, on behalf of the child, and

(d) in any other case, to the named child,

within 30 days of the statement date.

(4) Statements shall include the following information—

(a) the full name of the child;

(b) his address;

(c) his date of birth;

(d) his unique reference number;

(e) the description of the account (see regulation 4);

(f) the name of the registered contact (if any);

(g) the statement date;

(h) the total market value of the investments under the account at the previous statement date (where the account provider held the account at the named child's previous birthday);

(i) the amount of any Government contributions [¹"(see regulation 7) received by the account provider], during the period between—

(i) the previous statement date referred to in paragraph (1)(a) or (b), or the opening of the account (whichever is the later), and

(ii) the statement date;

(j) the aggregate amount of subscriptions (if any) received during the period in sub-paragraph (i);

(k) the total amount of deductions (including management charges) made during the period in sub-paragraph (i);

(l) the total market value of the investments under the account at the statement date;

(m) the number or amount, description and market value of each of the investments under the account at the statement date;

(n) the basis used in calculating the market value of each investment under the account (together with a statement of any change from a basis used in the previous statement); and

(o) the exchange rate used where any investment is, or is denominated in, a currency other than sterling.

[¹(5) As an alternative to the information in paragraph (4)(k), the statement may include, in relation to any management charges or other incidental expenses deducted from the account during the period in paragraph (4)(i)—

(a) the rate, expressed as an annual percentage rate, at which, and the period in relation to which, such deductions were made, or

(b) where such deductions were made in relation to different periods at different rates—

(i) each rate, expressed as an annual percentage rate, at which those deductions were made; and
(ii) the period in relation to which they were made at that rate.]

AMENDMENT

1. Child Trust Funds (Amendment) Regulations 2004 (SI 2004/2676), reg.7 (April 6, 2005).

DEFINITIONS

"account"—see reg.2(1)(b).
"account provider"—see *ibid*.
"child"—see reg.2(1)(a).
"investments under the account"—see reg.2(1)(b).
"market value"—see *ibid*.
"responsible person"—see reg.2(1)(a).
"subscriptions"—see reg.2(1)(b).

General investment rules

11.—(1) All transactions by way of purchase by an account provider of investments under an account shall be made—
  (a) in the case of an authorised fund which is a dual priced unit trust, at the manager's price for the sale of the relevant class of units within the meaning of, and complying with the requirements of, rule 15.4.4 of the Collective Investment Schemes Sourcebook;
  (b) in the case of an authorised fund which is a single priced unit trust or an open-ended investment company, at the price of a unit or share within the meaning of, and complying with the requirements of, rule 4.3.11 of the Collective Investment Schemes Sourcebook; and
  (c) in the case of all other account investments, at the price for which those investments might reasonably be expected to be purchased in the open market.
(2) In paragraph (1)—
"a dual priced unit trust" means an authorised unit trust in respect of which the manager gives different prices for buying and selling units at the same time;
"a single priced unit trust" means an authorised unit trust in respect of which the manager gives the same price for buying and selling units at the same time.
(3) All other transactions by way of sale or otherwise by an account provider in investments under an account shall be made at the price for which those investments might reasonably be expected to be sold or otherwise transacted, as the case may be, in the open market.
(4) Investments, or rights in respect of investments, may not at any time—
  (a) be purchased or made otherwise than out of cash which an account provider holds under an account at that time; or
  (b) be purchased from—
    (i) the named child, or
    (ii) the spouse [³or civil partner] of the named child,
so as to become account investments under the account.
(5) Subject to paragraph (6), contributions, subscriptions and any other cash held by an account provider under an account shall be held only in sterling and be deposited in an account with a deposit-taker [¹(including for this

6.17

purpose a credit union)], or a deposit account or a share account with a building society, which is designated as a CTF account for the purposes of these Regulations only.

(6) An account provider who is a European institution, a relevant authorised person or an assurance undertaking may hold an account investor's cash subscription and other cash held under an account in the currency of the EEA State in which he has his principal place of business and may deposit such cash in an account, which is designated as mentioned in paragraph (5), with any person authorised under the law of that State to accept deposits.

AMENDMENTS

1. Child Trust Funds (Amendment No.2) Regulations 2005 (SI 2005/909), reg.4 (April 6, 2005).
2. Civil Partnership Act 2004 (Tax Credits, etc.) (Consequential Amendments) Order 2005 (SI 2005/2919), art.15 (December 5, 2006).

DEFINITIONS

"account"—see reg.2(1)(b).
"account investment"—see *ibid.*
"account provider"—see *ibid.*
"assurance undertaking"—see *ibid.*
"authorised fund"—see reg.2(1)(c).
"building society"—see reg.2(1)(b).
"child"—see reg.2(1)(a).
"Collective Investment Schemes Sourcebook"—see reg.2(1)(c).
"credit union"—see reg.2(1)(b).
"deposit taker"—see *ibid.*
"dual priced unit trust"—see reg.11(2).
"EEA State"—see reg.2(1)(b).
"European institution"—see *ibid.*
"investments under the account"—see *ibid.*
"open-ended investment company"—see reg.2(1)(c).
"relevant authorised person"—see reg.2(1)(b).
"single priced unit trust"—see reg.11(2).
"subscriptions"—see reg.2(1)(b).
"units"—see reg.2(1)(c).

Qualifying investments for an account

12.—(1) This regulation specifies the kind of investments ("qualifying investments for an account") which may be purchased, made or held under an account.

(2) Qualifying investments for an account to which paragraph (1) refers are—
   (a) shares, not being shares in an investment trust, issued by a company wherever incorporated and officially listed on a recognised stock exchange (see paragraph (3));
   (b) securities—
      (i) issued by a company wherever incorporated,
      (ii) which satisfy at least one of the conditions specified in paragraph (5), and
      (iii) in the case of securities of an investment trust, purchased or acquired by the account provider in circumstances where the investment trust satisfies the condition specified in paragraph (6);

(SI 2004/1450, reg. 12) (as amended)

 (c) gilt-edged securities;
 (d) any securities issued by or on behalf of a government of any EEA State;
 (e) any securities which, in relation to a security mentioned in sub-paragraph (d), would be a strip of that security if "strip" had the same meaning as in section 47 of the Finance Act 1942, with the omission of the words "issued under the National Loans Act 1968";
 (f) shares in an investment trust, listed in the Official List of the Stock Exchange (see paragraph (3)), in circumstances where the trust satisfies the condition specified in paragraph (6);
 (g) units in, or shares of, a securities scheme, warrant scheme or fund of funds scheme;
 (h) units in, or shares of, a money market scheme;
 (i) units in, or shares of, a UCITS;
 (j) a depositary interest;
 (k) cash deposited in a deposit account with a building society, or a person falling within section 840A(1)(b) of the Taxes Act [2(including for this purpose a credit union)] or a relevant European institution, subject to paragraph (8);
 (l) cash deposited in a share account with a building society, subject to paragraph (8);
 (m) policies of life insurance which satisfy the conditions specified in paragraphs (9) and (10);
 (n) any securities issued under the National Loans Act 1968—
  (i) for the purpose of or in connection with raising money under the auspices of the Director of Savings within the meaning of section 11(1)(a) of the National Debt Act 1972, and
  (ii) other than national savings certificates, premium savings bonds, national savings stamps and national savings gift tokens,
 which, according to the terms and conditions subject to which they are issued and purchased, are expressly permitted to be held under an account.
[3(o) arrangements falling within section 47 of the Finance Act 2005 (alternative finance arrangements) under which the person referred to in that section as Y is a financial institution;
 (p) arrangements falling within section 49 of that Act;
 (q) qualifying units in or shares of a non-UCITS retail scheme.]
 (3) An investment in shares fulfils the condition as to official listing in paragraph (2)(a) or (f) if—
 (a) in pursuance of a public offer, the account provider applies for the allotment or allocation to him of shares in a company or investment trust which are due to be admitted to such listing within 30 days of the allocation or allotment, and which, when admitted to such listing, would be qualifying investments for an account, and
 (b) the shares are not allotted or allocated to the account provider in the circumstances specified in paragraph (4).
 (4) The circumstances specified in this paragraph are where—
 (a) the allotment or allocation of the shares was connected with the allotment or allocation of—
  (i) shares in the company or investment trust of a different class, or
  (ii) rights to shares in the company or investment trust of a different class, or

795

(iii) shares or rights to shares in another company or investment trust, or
(iv) units in or shares in, or rights to units in or shares in, an authorised fund or a part of an umbrella scheme, or
(v) securities or rights to securities of the company or investment trust, or of another company or investment trust,

to the account provider, the registered contact or any other person; and

(b) the terms on which the first-mentioned shares in this paragraph were offered were significantly more favourable to the account provider or the named child than they would have been if their allotment or allocation had not been connected as described in sub-paragraph (a).

(5) The conditions specified in this paragraph are—
(a) that the shares in the company issuing the securities are listed on the official list of a recognised stock exchange;
(b) that the securities are so listed;
(c) that the company issuing the securities is a 75 per cent subsidiary of a company whose shares are so listed.

(6) The condition specified in this paragraph is that the investment trust has no eligible rental income, in its most recent accounting period to end before the date on which the shares in, or securities of, the investment trust first become investments under the account, provided that the shares or securities shall cease to be qualifying investments for an account if the investment trust has any eligible rental income, in subsequent accounting periods, during which the shares or securities are held.

(7) In paragraph (4)(a), "company" means any body corporate having a share capital.

(8) A deposit account or share account which is a qualifying investment for an account falling within paragraph (2)(k) or (l) must not be connected with any other investment, held by the named child or any other person, and for this purpose such an account is connected with an investment if—

(a) either was opened or acquired with reference to the other, or with a view to enabling the other to be opened or acquired on particular terms, or with a view to facilitating the opening or acquisition of the other on particular terms, and
(b) the terms on which the account was opened would have been significantly less favourable to the holder if the investment had not been acquired.

(9) The conditions specified in this paragraph are that—
(a) the insurance is on the life of the named child only;
(b) the terms and conditions of the policy provide—
   (i) that the policy may only be owned or held as a qualifying investment for an account which satisfies the provisions of these Regulations;
   (ii) that the policy shall automatically terminate if it comes to the notice of the account provider, in any manner, that the event specified in paragraph (11) has occurred in relation to the policy;
   (iii) for an express prohibition of any payment of the proceeds from the termination of the policy or a partial surrender of the rights conferred by the policy, to the named child (while he is still a child) [[1]except in accordance with regulation 18A (terminal illness)]; and

(iv) that the policy, the rights conferred by the policy and any share or interest in the policy or rights respectively, shall not be capable of assignment or (in Scotland) assignation, other than that they may be vested in the named child's personal representatives, and that the title to the policy may be transferred to a new account provider subject to and in accordance with regulations 8(2)(f) and 21;

(c) the policy evidences or secures a contract of insurance which—
   (i) falls within paragraph 1 or 3 of Part 2 of Schedule 1 to the Financial Services and Markets Act 2000 (Regulated Activities) Order 2001, or
   (ii) would fall within either of those paragraphs if the insurer were a company with permission under Part 4 of the Financial Services and Markets Act 2000 to effect or carry out contracts of insurance;

(d) the policy is not—
   (i) a contract to pay an annuity on human life,
   (ii) a personal portfolio bond within the meaning given by regulation 2(1) of the Personal Portfolio Bonds (Tax) Regulations 1999, or
   (iii) a contract, the effecting and carrying out of which constitutes "pension business" within the meaning given by section 431B(1) of the Taxes Act; and

(e) after the first payment in respect of a premium in relation to the policy has been made, there is no contractual obligation on any person to make any other such payment.

(10) The condition specified in this paragraph is that no sum may at any time, at or after the making of the insurance, be lent to or at the direction of the named child or registered contact by or by arrangement with the insurer for the time being responsible for the obligations under the policy.

(11) The event specified in this paragraph is that—

(a) there has been a breach of any of the conditions in paragraph (9) or (10), or any of those conditions was not satisfied at the date on which the insurance was made; and

(b) the breach or non-compliance cannot be remedied in accordance with regulation 23, or (in any other case), has not been remedied within a reasonable time.

(12) Where the event specified in paragraph (11) occurs in relation to a policy, the policy shall nevertheless be treated, for the purposes of these Regulations, excepting paragraphs (9)(b)(ii) and (11), and regulations 37(6) and 38, as if it had satisfied the conditions in paragraphs (9) and (10) during the period—

(a) commencing at the time when that specified event occurred, and

(b) ending immediately before—
   (i) the end of the final year in relation to the policy, within the meaning in section 546(4) of the Taxes Act, or
   (ii) the time at which that specified event came to the notice of the account provider,

whichever first occurs (the "termination event").

AMENDMENTS

1. Child Trust Funds (Amendment) Regulations 2004 (SI 2004/2676), reg.8 (April 6, 2005).

Child Trust Funds Regulations 2004

2. Child Trust Funds (Amendment No.2) Regulations 2005 (SI 2005/909), reg.5 (April 6, 2005).
3. Child Trust Funds (Amendment No.3) Regulations 2005 (SI 2005/3349), reg.5 (December 27, 2005).

DEFINITIONS

"account"—see reg.2(1)(b).
"account provider"—see *ibid*.
"authorised fund"—see reg.2(1)(c).
"building society"—see reg.2(1)(b).
"child"—see reg.2(1)(a).
"company"—see regs.2(1)(b) and 12(7).
"credit union"—see reg.2(1)(b).
"depositary interest"—see reg.2(1)(c).
"EEA State"—see reg.2(1)(b).
"European institution"—see *ibid*.
"fund of funds scheme"—see reg.2(1)(c).
"gilt-edged securities"—see reg.2(1)(b).
"investments under the account"—see *ibid*.
"investment trust"—see *ibid*.
"money market scheme"—see reg.2(1)(c).
"recognised stock exchange"—see reg.2(1)(b).
"relevant European institution"—see *ibid*.
"securities scheme"—see reg.2(1)(c).
"security"—see reg.2(1)(b).
"the Taxes Act"—see *ibid*.
"UCITS"—see reg.2(1)(c).
"umbrella scheme"—see *ibid*.
"units"—see *ibid*.
"warrant scheme"—see *ibid*.
"year"—see reg.2(1)(b).

Conditions for application by responsible person or the child to open an account (and changes to an account)

13.—(1) An application by a responsible person in relation to a child or the child if 16 or over, as the case may be, ("the applicant") to open an account for the child with an account provider must be made to the account provider in a statement which must satisfy the conditions specified in paragraphs (2) to (6).

(2) An application must specify the description of account applied for.

(3) An application must incorporate a declaration by the applicant that he—
   (a) is aged 16 years of age or over,
   (b) is—
       (i) (where the child is under 16) a responsible person in relation to the named child (that is, that he has parental responsibility [¹or, in Scotland, parental responsibilities] in relation to the child), or
       (ii) the child if 16 or over, and
   (c) is to be the registered contact for the account;
and where the application is not in writing, must authorise the account provider to record the terms of the declaration in a written declaration made on behalf of the applicant.

(SI 2004/1450, reg. 13) (as amended)

(4) The applicant must authorise the account provider (on behalf of the named child where appropriate)—
   (a) to hold the child's Inland Revenue contributions, subscriptions, account investments, interest, dividends and any other rights or proceeds in respect of those investments and cash, and
   (b) to make on his behalf any claims to relief from tax in respect of account investments,

and the authority must continue until a further application and declaration is made in accordance with paragraph (10).

(5) An application must contain—
   (a) the applicant's full name,
   (b) his address, including postcode,
   (c) the named child's full name [¹and date of birth],
   (d) his address, including postcode, and
   (e) the child's unique reference number on the voucher.

(6) There may be only one declaration and authorisation under paragraphs (3) to (5) in force for an account at any time.

(7) Except in the case—
   (a) of the death or incapacity of the registered contact,
   (b) where the registered contact cannot be contacted,
   (c) of the bringing to an end of a Court order, under which he is a responsible person for the named child,
   (d) of the named child attaining the age of 16 years,
   (e) where the Official Solicitor or Accountant of Court is appointed under section 3(10) of the Act, or
   (f) where a Court so orders,

any change in the identity of the registered contact shall require confirmation by the current registered contact that his declaration and authorisation under paragraphs (3)(c) and (4) is cancelled.

(8) An account provider must decline to accept an application if he has reason to believe that—
   (a) the voucher has expired, or is not or might not be genuine, or
   (b) the applicant has given untrue information in his application.

(9) Where the application is not in writing, the account provider shall make the written declaration referred to in paragraph (3), and notify the applicant of its contents, and such declaration shall take effect from the date on which the applicant agrees the contents (subject to any corrections), and if he neither agrees or disagrees with the contents within 30 days, he shall be treated as having agreed them.

(10) Where—
   (a) there is a change in the identity of the registered contact, the new registered contact, or
   (b) an account has been opened by the Inland Revenue under regulation 6 (Revenue allocated accounts) and a responsible person in relation to the child (or the child, if 16 or over) subsequently applies to the account provider to be the registered contact for the account, he,

shall make the application and declaration required by paragraphs (3) to (5).

[¹(11) Where the new registered contact is the Official Solicitor or the Accountant of Court, he shall make the declaration and authorisation required by paragraphs (3)(c) and (4) [²and shall be treated as a party to the existing management agreement for the account in question].]

AMENDMENTS

1. Child Trust Funds (Amendment) Regulations 2004 (SI 2004/2676), reg.9 (April 6, 2005).
2. Child Trust Funds (Amendment No.2) Regulations 2004 (SI 2004/3382), reg.3 (April 6, 2005).

DEFINITIONS

"account"—see reg.2(1)(b).
"account investment"—see *ibid*.
"account provider"—see *ibid*.
"child"—see reg.2(1)(a).
"parental responsibility"—see *ibid*.
"responsible person"—see *ibid*.
"subscriptions"—see reg.2(1)(b).
"tax"—see *ibid*.

Account provider—qualifications and Board's approval

6.20   **14.**—(1) This regulation specifies the circumstances ("qualifying circumstances") in which a person may be approved by the Board as an account provider.

(2) The qualifying circumstances are the following—
(a) the person must make an application to the Board for approval in a form specified by the Board;
(b) the person must undertake with the Board—
   (i) to either offer stakeholder accounts to the general public (whether or not accounts of another description are offered), or to fulfil the requirements in paragraph (3),
   (ii) to accept vouchers from any responsible person or the child if 16 or over (subject to [²paragraph (iia) and] regulation 13(8)),
   [³(iia) in the case of a credit union, to accept vouchers from any responsible person or the child if 16 or over, if the child to which the voucher relates is a member, or fulfils or is treated as fulfilling a qualification for admission to membership, of the credit union (subject to regulation 13(8))]
   (iii) where the person accepts Revenue allocated accounts, to allow instructions for their management to be made or given by post (whether or not other methods are allowed),
   (iv) to publicise (and up-date where appropriate) statements of the minimum amount which may be subscribed to an account on a single occasion, and the permitted means of payment of subscriptions,
   (v) to inform persons proposing to make subscriptions to an account (other than the named child) that the subscription is a gift to the child,
   (vi) to publicise (and up-date where appropriate) statements of the extent to which social, environmental or ethical decisions are taken into account in selecting, retaining or realising investments,
   (vii) that a child's unique reference number shall only be used for the purposes of the child's account (and of fulfilling the requirements of these Regulations with regard to that account), and
   (viii) that whether there is an initial contribution or special contribution to an account, whether there is a supplementary

(SI 2004/1450, reg.14) (as amended)

contribution to the account, and whether the account is a Revenue allocated account is information held for the purposes mentioned in paragraph (vii) only, and shall not be used for other purposes (including marketing other products);
(c) the person must demonstrate to the satisfaction of the Board that the person can correctly operate the procedures in regulation 30;
(d) an account provider must be—
   (i) an authorised person within the meaning of section 31(1)(a) or (c) of, or Schedule 5 to, the Financial Services and Markets Act 2000, who has permission to carry on one or more of the activities specified in Articles 14, 21, 25, 37, 40, 45, 51, 53 and (in so far as it applies to any of those activities) 64 of the Financial Services and Markets Act 2000 (Regulated Activities) Order 2001, but excluding any person falling within paragraph (iv) below;
[4[5(iia) in the case of a credit union, an authorised person within the meaning of section 31(1)(a) of the Financial Services and Markets Act 2000, who has permission to carry on one or more of the activities specified in Article 5 of the Financial Services and Markets Act 2000 (Regulated Activities) Order 2001;]
   (ii) a European institution which carries on one or more of those activities;
   (iii) a building society, a person falling within section 840A(1)(b) of the Taxes Act or a relevant European institution; or
   (iv) an insurance company within the meaning given by section 431(2) of the Taxes Act, an incorporated friendly society or a registered friendly society, or any other assurance undertaking;
(e) an account provider must not be prevented from acting as such by any requirement imposed under section 43 of the Financial Services and Markets Act 2000, or by any prohibition imposed by or under any rules made by the Financial Services Authority under that Act; and
(f) an account provider who—
   (i) is a European institution or a relevant authorised person and who does not have a branch or business establishment in the United Kingdom, or has such a branch or business establishment but does not intend to carry out all his functions as an account provider at that branch or business establishment, or
   (ii) falls within the expression "any other assurance undertaking" in sub-paragraph (d)(iv),
must fulfil one of the three requirements specified in regulation 15.

(3) The requirements in this paragraph are that the person provides to any potential applicant for a child trust fund ([1before commencement of completion of] any application under regulation 13)—
(a) a statement that a stakeholder account is available from a named alternative account provider who offers it on the terms in paragraph (2)(b)(i) (omitting the words from ", or to" to the end);
(b) a detailed description of that stakeholder account; and
(c) sufficient information (according to the method of communication used, and including documentation where appropriate) to put the potential applicant in the position to make an application to that alternative account provider, complying with regulation 13.

(4) The terms of the Board's approval may include conditions designed to ensure that the provisions of these Regulations are satisfied.

AMENDMENTS

1. Child Trust Funds (Amendment) Regulations 2004 (SI 2004/2676), reg.10 (April 6, 2005).
2. Child Trust Funds (Amendment No.2) Regulations 2005 (SI 2005/909), reg.6 (April 6, 2005).
3. Child Trust Funds (Amendment No.2) Regulations 2005 (SI 2005/909), reg.7 (April 6, 2005).
4. Child Trust Funds (Amendment No.2) Regulations 2005 (SI 2005/909), reg.8 (April 6, 2005).
5. Child Trust Funds (Amendment No.3) Regulations 2005 (SI 2005/3349), reg.6 (December 27, 2005).

DEFINITIONS

"account"—see reg.2(1)(b).
"account provider"—see *ibid*.
"applicant"—see reg.5.
"assurance undertaking"—see reg.2(1)(b).
"building society"—see *ibid*.
"child"—see reg.2(1)(a).
"child trust fund"—see *ibid*.
"company"—see reg.2(1)(b).
"credit union"—see *ibid*.
"European institution"—see *ibid*.
"incorporated friendly society"—see *ibid*.
"registered friendly society"—see *ibid*.
"relevant authorised person"—see *ibid*.
"relevant European institution"—see *ibid*.
"responsible person"—see reg.2(1)(a).
"subscriptions"—see reg.2(1)(b).
"the Taxes Act"—see *ibid*.

Account provider—appointment of tax representative

6.21   **15.**—(1) This regulation specifies the requirements mentioned in regulation 14(2)(f).

(2) The first requirement specified in this regulation is that—
(a) a person who falls within subsection (5) of section 333A of the Taxes Act is for the time being appointed by the account provider to be responsible for securing the discharge of the duties prescribed by paragraph (5) which fall to be discharged by the account provider, and
(b) his identity and the fact of his appointment have been notified to the Board by the account provider.

(3) The second requirement specified in this regulation is that there are for the time being other arrangements with the Board for a person other than the account provider to secure the discharge of such duties.

(4) The third requirement specified in this regulation is that there are for the time being other arrangements with the Board designed to secure the discharge of such duties.

(5) The duties prescribed by this paragraph are those that fall to be discharged by an account provider under these Regulations.

(6) The appointment of a person in pursuance of the first requirement shall be treated as terminated in circumstances where—

(SI 2004/1450, reg.15) (as amended)

(a) the Board have reason to believe that the person concerned—
  (i) has failed to secure the discharge of any of the duties prescribed by paragraph (5), or
  (ii) does not have adequate resources to discharge those duties, and
(b) the Board have notified the account provider and that person that they propose to treat his appointment as having terminated with effect from the date specified in the notice.

(7) Where, in accordance with the first requirement, a person is at any time responsible for securing the discharge of duties, the person concerned—
  (a) shall be entitled to act on the account provider's behalf for any of the purposes of the provisions relating to the duties;
  (b) shall secure (where appropriate by acting on the account provider's behalf) the account provider's compliance with and discharge of the duties; and
  (c) shall be personally liable in respect of any failure of the account provider to comply with or discharge any such duty as if the duties imposed on the account provider were imposed jointly and severally on the account provider and the person concerned.

DEFINITIONS

"account provider"—see reg.2(1)(b).
"notice"—see *ibid*.
"the Taxes Act"—see *ibid*.

Account provider—withdrawal by Board of approval

16.—(1) This regulation specifies the circumstances ("the disqualifying circumstances") in which the Board may by notice withdraw their approval of a person as an account provider in relation to an account.

(2) The disqualifying circumstances are that the Board have reason to believe—
  (a) that any provision of the Act or these Regulations, or any term of an undertaking given in accordance with regulation 14(2)(b) or condition under regulation 14(4), is not or at any time has not been satisfied, either in respect of an account managed by the account provider or otherwise; or
  (b) that a person to whom they have given approval to act as an account provider is not qualified so to act.

(3) The notice to which paragraph (1) refers shall specify—
  (a) the date from which the Board's approval is withdrawn; and
  (b) the disqualifying circumstances.

6.22

DEFINITIONS

"account"—see reg.2(1)(b).
"account provider"—see *ibid*.
"notice"—see *ibid*.

Account provider—appeal against non-approval or withdrawal of Board's approval

17. A person who has been notified of a decision by the Board not to approve that person as an account provider, or an account provider to whom notice of withdrawal of approval has been given under regulation 16, may

6.23

appeal against the decision by notice given to the Board within 30 days after the date of the notification or notice.

DEFINITIONS

"account provider"—see reg.2(1)(b).
"notice"—see *ibid.*

Permitted withdrawals from an account

6.24   **18.** Withdrawals from an account before the date on which the named child attains the age of 18 years may only be made—
   (a) by the account provider, to settle any management charges and other incidental expenses, which are due by or under the management agreement, or
   [¹(ab) in accordance with regulation 18A, or]
   (b) where the account provider is satisfied that the named child has died under that age.

AMENDMENT

1. Child Trust Funds (Amendment) Regulations 2004 (SI 2004/2676), reg.11 (April 6, 2005).

DEFINITIONS

"account"—see reg.2(1)(b).
"account provider"—see *ibid.*
"child"—see reg.2(1)(a).

[¹Permitted withdrawals from an account where the child is terminally ill

6.25   **18A.**—(1) A person with parental responsibility (or, in Scotland, parental responsibilities) for the named child (including a local authority, but excluding a person under 16), or the named child if 16 or over, may make a claim to the Board, for withdrawals from an account to be permitted in accordance with this regulation.
   (2) The claim shall be—
   (a) made in a manner prescribed by the Board, which shall include the giving of any consent necessary for the verification or consideration of the claim, and
   (b) accepted in either of the following cases:

Case 1

The child has been, or is, accepted by the Department for Work and Pensions as falling within section 72(5) of the Social Security Contributions and Benefits Act 1992 (special rules for terminally ill person's entitlement to care component of disability living allowance).

Case 2

Evidence that the named child is terminally ill has been supplied to the satisfaction of the Board.
   (3) The Board shall issue a letter to the claimant authorising withdrawals from the account under this regulation, and shall also notify the account provider.

(SI 2004/1450, reg.18A) (as amended)

(4) Once a claim has been accepted, withdrawals may be made by the registered contact (on behalf of the named child, where he is not the child) at any time—
(a) provided that, immediately following any withdrawal, a balance sufficient to keep the account open is maintained in the account, and
(b) excepting any transfer of a policy of life insurance (as opposed to the proceeds from such a policy).

(5) Where account investments are withdrawn in a form other than sterling currency, regulation 36(1)(b) shall apply (with any necessary modifications) to any such investment immediately before it is withdrawn.

(6) In this regulation, "terminally ill" has the meaning in section 66(2)(a) of the Social Security Contributions and Benefits Act 1992.]

AMENDMENT

1. Child Trust Funds (Amendment) Regulations 2004 (SI 2004/2676), reg.12 (April 6, 2005).

DEFINITIONS

"account"—see reg.2(1)(b).
"account investment"—see *ibid.*
"account provider"—see *ibid.*
"child"—see reg.2(1)(a).
"parental responsibility"—see *ibid.*

Account provider ceasing to act (or ceasing to accept Revenue allocated accounts)

19.—(1) A person shall give notice to the Board and to the registered contact of the account which he manages (or, if there is no registered contact, the named child) of his intention to cease to act as the account provider not less than 30 days before he so ceases so that his obligations to the Board under the account can be conveniently discharged at or about the time he ceases so to act, and the notice to the registered contact or the named child shall inform him of the right to transfer the account under regulation 21, and of his rights under regulation 20(3).

(2) A person shall also give notice to the Board of his intention to cease to accept further Revenue allocated accounts under regulation 6, not less than 30 days before he so ceases.

6.26

DEFINITIONS

"account"—see reg.2(1)(b).
"account provider"—see *ibid.*
"child"—see reg.2(1)(a).
"notice"—see reg.2(1)(b).

Account provider ceasing to qualify

20.—(1) A person shall cease to qualify as an account provider and shall notify the Board within 30 days of the relevant event in sub-paragraphs (a) to (f), of that relevant event, where—
(a) the person no longer fulfils the conditions of regulation 14;
(b) in the case of an individual, he becomes bankrupt, or the subject of a bankruptcy restrictions order or an interim bankruptcy restrictions order or, in Scotland, his estate is sequestrated;

6.27

(c) he makes any arrangement or composition with his creditors generally;
(d) in the case of a company, a resolution has been passed or a petition has been presented to wind it up;
(e) in the case of a building society, a person falling within section 840A(1)(b) of the Taxes Act or a relevant European institution—
  (i) it ceases to be a building society or to fall within section 840A(1)(b) of the Taxes Act or to be a relevant European institution, as the case may be;
  (ii) its directors have made a proposal under Part 1 of the Insolvency Act 1986 for a composition in satisfaction of its debts or a scheme of arrangement of its affairs; or
  (iii) a receiver or manager of its property has been appointed; or
(f) in the case of a European institution, a relevant authorised person or an assurance undertaking which falls within regulation 14(2)(d)(iv), action corresponding to any described in sub-paragraph (b) to (e) has been taken by or in relation to the institution, person or undertaking under the law of an EEA State.

(2) On giving the notice referred to in paragraph (1), the person shall also notify the registered contact (or, if there is no registered contact, the named child) of the right to transfer the account under regulation 21, and the notice shall inform the recipient of the rights under paragraph (3).

(3) Where a registered contact—
(a) receives a notice under paragraph (2), or regulation 19(1), and
(b) within 30 days of the sending of the notice, transfers the account to another account provider pursuant to regulation 21,

the period between the transferor ceasing to act or qualify as an account provider, and the transfer to the transferee, shall be ignored in determining whether the account has at all times been managed by an account provider.

DEFINITIONS

"account"—see reg.2(1)(b).
"account provider"—see *ibid*.
"assurance undertaking"—see *ibid*.
"building society"—see *ibid*.
"child"—see reg.2(1)(a).
"company"—see reg.2(1)(b).
"EEA State"—see *ibid*.
"European institution"—see *ibid*.
"notice"—see *ibid*.
"relevant authorised person"—see *ibid*.
"relevant European institution"—see *ibid*.
"the Taxes Act"—see *ibid*.

Transfer of accounts to other account providers

21.—(1) Where—
(a) arrangements are made by a registered contact to transfer the whole of the investments under an account from one account provider ("the transferor") to another account provider ("the transferee"), or
(b) the whole of the investments under an account are so transferred in consequence of an account provider ("the transferor") ceasing to act or to qualify as an account provider,

the transfer shall be treated as a transfer of the account.

(2) The account and its description under regulation 4 shall not be affected for the purposes of these Regulations by reason of the transfer, save that, where the registered contact specifies in accordance with paragraph (3)(a) an account of a different description, the account shall, on the transfer, become an account of that other description.

(3) The registered contact shall make—
  (a) the application required by regulation 13(2) (modified as if the words "applied for" were replaced with [¹ following the transfer]), and
  (b) the application and declaration required by regulation 13(3) to (5),
to the transferee.

[¹(3A) Where a registered contact applies in accordance with paragraph (3) to a potential transferee for a transfer under this regulation, specifying a stakeholder account offered by the transferee, the transferee shall not decline to accept that application (or the transfer in consequence of it) except where—
  (a) the transferee has reason to believe that the registered contact has given untrue information in his application;
  (b) the transferee demonstrates to the satisfaction of the Board that acceptance of transfers, or a class of transfers, during a particular period would jeopardise his ability to prevent any of the matters mentioned in regulation 16(2)(a); or
  (c) the transferor does not give the transferee the notice in accordance with paragraph (4).]

(4) The transferor shall on the date of the transfer give the transferee a notice containing the information specified in paragraph (5) and the declaration specified in paragraph (6).

(5) The information specified in this paragraph is—
  (a) as regards the named child—
    (i) his full name,
    (ii) his date of birth,
    (iii) his unique reference number;
  (b) as regards the account—
    (i) the description of the account,
    (ii) the date of the transfer,
    (iii) the total amount subscribed to the account during the period from the beginning of the subscription year in which the transfer takes place to the date of the transfer,
    (iv) any amount which has been claimed from the Board under regulations 26, 27 or 30 and which has not been paid at the date of the transfer;
  (c) the full name and address, including postcode, of the registered contact who has made the transfer arrangements.

(6) The declaration specified in this paragraph is a declaration by the transferor that—
  (a) he has fulfilled all his obligations to the named child, the Board or otherwise, which are imposed by these Regulations;
  (b) he has transferred to the transferee or his nominee all the account investments and that, where registration of any such transfer is required, he has taken the necessary steps to ensure that those account investments can be registered in the name of the transferee or nominee;
  (c) he will forward any further payment received in respect of those account investments to the transferee, on receipt of the payment, and

(d) the information contained in the notice is correct.

AMENDMENT

1. Child Trust Funds (Amendment) Regulations 2004 (SI 2004/2676), reg.13 (April 6, 2005).

DEFINITIONS

"account"—see reg.2(1)(b).
"account investment"—see *ibid.*
"account provider"—see *ibid.*
"child"—see reg.2(1)(a).
"eligible child"—see *ibid.*
"notice"—see reg.2(1)(b).

Recoupment of Inland Revenue contributions to void accounts (and other accounts)

22.—(1) Where—
(a) the named child has never been an eligible child (see regulation 8(1)(b)), or
(b) there is a breach of regulation 8(1)(c) in relation to an account,
the account is void, and the persons mentioned in paragraph (3) shall account to the Inland Revenue for Inland Revenue contributions paid in respect of the account, together with income and gains which have arisen in consequence of the crediting of any of those payments to the account.

(2) Where—
(a) the condition in section 9(5) of the Act was satisfied in relation to a child, but the determination under sections 18 to 21 of the Tax Credits Act 2002 has been overturned, or
(b) the condition in section 9(8) of the Act was satisfied in relation to a child, but it has subsequently been determined that payment of the relevant benefit or tax credit mentioned in that subsection should not have been made, or that the applicable amount or tax credit should not have included an amount or credit in respect of the child, [¹or
(c) the requirements of regulation 7(10) were satisfied in relation to a child, but it has subsequently been determined that payment of the relevant benefit mentioned in that provision should not have been made, or that the applicable amount should not have included an amount in respect of that child,]
the persons mentioned in paragraph (3) shall account to the Inland Revenue for any supplementary contribution [¹, or further contribution, as the case may be,] paid in respect of the account, together with income and gains which have arisen in consequence of the crediting of any such payment to the account.

(3) The persons mentioned in paragraphs (1) and (2) are—
(a) the account provider (to the extent that he has assets in his possession or control),
(b) the registered contact,
(c) the named child, and
(d) any person in whom the Inland Revenue contributions, income or gains, or any property directly or indirectly representing any of them, is vested (whether beneficially or otherwise)
and they shall be jointly and severally liable.

(SI 2004/1450, reg.22) (as amended)

(4) Where a person accountable under this regulation is notified by the Inland Revenue that an amount is due from him under it, that amount shall be treated for the purposes of Part 6 of the Management Act (collection and recovery) as if it were tax charged in an assessment on that person, and due and payable.

AMENDMENT

1. Child Trust Funds (Amendment) Regulations 2005 (SI 2005/383), reg.4 (April 6, 2005).

DEFINITIONS

"account"—see reg.2(1)(b).
"account provider"—see *ibid*.
"child"—see reg.2(1)(a).
"eligible child"—see *ibid*.
"the Management Act"—see reg.2(1)(b).
"tax"—see *ibid*.

"Repair" of invalid accounts

23.—(1) Except in the case of a breach of regulation 8(1)(b) or (c) (where no repair of an account is possible), it is an overriding requirement to be satisfied in relation to an account that the account provider and registered contact, as the case may be, take any steps necessary to remedy any breach of these Regulations.

(2) Where a breach is remedied as mentioned in paragraph (1), the account shall, to the extent of that breach, be treated as having been a valid account at all times, except for determining whether there has been a breach of these Regulations for the purposes of section 20 of the Act (penalties).

6.30

DEFINITIONS

"account"—see reg.2(1)(b).
"account provider"—see *ibid*.

PART 3

TAX AND ADMINISTRATION OF ACCOUNTS

Exemption from tax of account income and gains

24. Subject to compliance with these Regulations (and in particular regulation 9)—
   (a) no tax shall be chargeable on the account provider or his nominee, or on the named child or registered contact (on his behalf)—
      (i) in respect of interest, dividends, distributions or gains in respect of account investments [²(excluding any building society bonus)],
      [¹(ia) in respect of alternative finance return or profit share return paid by a financial institution (within the meanings in Chapter 5 of Part 2 of the Finance Act 2005);]
      [²(ib) in respect of a payment under a building society bonus scheme, so far as the payment is calculated by reference to account

6.31

Child Trust Funds Regulations 2004

investments (and if paid directly by the society into the account, the payment shall not count towards the subscription limit in regulation 9);]

(ii) on any annual profits or gains treated by section 714(2) of the Taxes Act as having been received by any of them in respect of account investments,

(iii) on an offshore income gain to which a disposal made by any of them of an account investment gives rise, which is treated by section 761(1) of the Taxes Act as constituting profits or gains,

(iv) on a profit realised by any of them from the discount on a relevant discounted security within the meaning of Schedule 13 to the Finance Act 1996, which is held as an account investment, or

(v) in respect of gains treated by section 541 of the Taxes Act as arising in connection with a policy of life insurance which is an account investment;

(b) losses accruing on any disposal of account investments shall be disregarded for the purposes of capital gains tax;

[³(ba) any gain or loss accruing on and attributable to a payment within paragraph (ib) of sub-paragraph (a) shall not be a chargeable gain or allowable loss for capital gains tax purposes;]

(c) section 349B(4) of the Taxes Act shall apply with the following modifications—

(i) for references to a plan manager, substitute references to an account provider,

(ii) for references to a plan, substitute references to an account, and

(iii) for the reference to [¹Chapter 3 of Part 6 of ITTOIA 2005], substitute a reference to the Act;

(d) a corresponding deficiency occurring at the end of the final year, within the meaning of section 549(1) of the Taxes Act, so far as it relates to a policy of life insurance which is an account investment, shall not be allowable as a deduction from the total income of the named child;

(e) relief in respect of tax shall be given in the manner and to the extent provided by these Regulations; and

(f) income arising from account investments shall not be regarded as income for any income tax purposes (including [¹section 629 of ITTOIA 2005]).

AMENDMENTS

1. Child Trust Funds (Amendment No.3) Regulations 2005 (SI 2005/3349), reg.7 (December 27, 2005).

2. Child Trust Funds (Amendment No.3) Regulations 2006 (SI 2006/3195), reg.4 (January 1, 2007).

3. Child Trust Funds (Amendment No.3) Regulations 2006 (SI 2006/3195), reg.5 (January 1, 2007).

DEFINITIONS

"account"—see reg.2(1)(b).
"account investment"—see *ibid*.
"account provider"—see *ibid*.
"child"—see reg.2(1)(a).

(SI 2004/1450, reg. 24) (as amended)

"gains"—see reg.2(1)(b).
"security"—see *ibid.*
"tax"—see *ibid.*
"the Taxes Act"—see *ibid.*
"year"—see *ibid.*

Tax liabilities and reliefs—account provider to act on behalf of the named child

25.—(1) An account provider may under these Regulations make tax claims, conduct appeals and agree on behalf of the named child (or of the registered contact in respect of the child) liabilities for and reliefs from tax in respect of an account.

(2) Tax claims shall be made to the Board in accordance with the provisions of regulations 26 and 27.

(3) Where any relief or exemption from tax previously given in respect of an account has by virtue of these Regulations become excessive, in computing the relief due on any claim there shall be deducted (so that amounts equal to that excess are set-off or repaid to the Board, as the case may be) notwithstanding that those amounts have been invested, any other amount of tax due to the Board by the account provider in respect of any tax liability in respect of account investments under an account including (but without prejudice to the making of an assessment under that Schedule) any amount falling due in respect of a liability under paragraph 3 or 4 of Schedule 23A to the Taxes Act.

6.32

DEFINITIONS

"account"—see reg.2(1)(b).
"account investment"—see *ibid.*
"account provider"—see *ibid.*
"child"—see reg.2(1)(a).
"tax"—see *ibid.*
"the Taxes Act"—see *ibid.*

Repayments in respect of tax to account provider—interim tax claims

26.—(1) Notwithstanding the provisions of any other enactment, the Board shall not be under an obligation to make any repayment in respect of tax under these Regulations earlier than the end of the month following the month in which the claim for the repayment is received.

(2) A claim for repayment in respect of tax which is not an annual claim ("interim tax claim") may be made only for a period of a month (or a number of months not exceeding six) beginning on the 6th day of the month and ending on the 5th day of the relevant following month.

(3) No claim for repayment may be made for the month ending 5th October or any subsequent month in a year until the annual claim due under regulation 27(2) in respect of an account for the preceding year has been duly made by the account provider and received by the Board.

(4) Where, on the occasion of a claim, there is due to the Board an amount in respect of tax, that amount shall be recoverable by the Board in the same manner as tax charged by an assessment on the account provider which has become final and conclusive.

(5) This regulation and regulation 27 shall not apply to any repayment in respect of tax on account investments falling within regulation 12(2)(m)

6.33

(life insurance), or on distributions and other rights or proceeds in respect of those investments.

DEFINITIONS

"account"—see reg.2(1)(b).
"account investment"—see *ibid*.
"account provider"—see *ibid*.
"tax"—see *ibid*.
"year"—see *ibid*.

Repayments in respect of tax to account provider—annual tax claims

27.—(1) An annual tax claim is a claim for repayment in respect of tax for a year and may not be made at any time more than six years after the end of the year.

(2) Where the account provider—
(a) has made at least one interim tax claim during a year, or
(b) wishes to reclaim tax, or there is due to the Board an amount in respect of tax, following the end of the year,
the account provider shall within six months after the end of the year make an annual tax claim to establish the total of tax repayments due under an account for that year.

(3) Where the aggregate of the repayments in respect of interim tax claims for the year shown by an annual tax claim exceeds the amount of tax repayable for the year shown on the claim, the account provider shall repay the amount of the excess to the Board with the claim.

(4) If an account provider fails to make the annual tax claim required under paragraph (2)(a) within the time limited, the Board may issue a notice to the account provider showing the aggregate of payments in respect of the interim tax claims for the year, and stating that the Board are not satisfied that the amount due to the account provider for that year exceeds the lower amount stated in the notice.

(5) If an annual tax claim is not delivered to the Board within 14 days after the issue of a notice under paragraph (4) the amount of the difference between the aggregate and the lower amount stated in the notice shall immediately become recoverable by the Board in the same manner as tax charged by an assessment on the account provider which has become final and conclusive.

(6) Where an annual tax claim has been made and the account provider subsequently discovers that an error or mistake has been made in the claim the account provider may make a supplementary annual claim within the time allowed in paragraph (1).

DEFINITIONS

"account"—see reg.2(1)(b).
"account provider"—see *ibid*.
"notice"—see *ibid*.
"tax"—see *ibid*.
"year"—see *ibid*.

Account provider's tax claims—supplementary provisions

28.—(1) Section 42 of the Management Act shall not apply to tax claims under these Regulations.

(SI 2004/1450, reg.28) (as amended)

(2) No appeal shall lie from the Board's decision on an interim tax claim.

(3) An appeal shall be to the Special Commissioners from the Board's decision on an annual tax claim, and the appeal shall be brought by giving notice to the Board within 30 days of receipt of notice of the decision.

(4) No payment or repayment made or other thing done on or in relation to an interim tax claim or a notice under regulation 27(4) shall prejudice the decision on an annual tax claim.

(5) The provisions contained in Part 5 of the Management Act (appeals and other proceedings) shall apply to an appeal under paragraph (3) above, and on appeal the Special Commissioners may vary the decision appealed against whether or not the variation is to the advantage of the appellant.

(6) All such assessments, payments and repayments shall be made as necessary to give effect to the Board's decision on an annual tax claim or to any variation of that decision on appeal.

(7) Claims under these Regulations shall be in such form and contain such particulars as the Board prescribe and, subject to regulation 32(1), shall be signed by the account provider, and forms prescribed for annual claims may require a report to be given by a person qualified for appointment as auditor of a company.

DEFINITIONS

"account provider"—see reg.2(1)(b).
"company"—see *ibid*.
"the Management Act"—see *ibid*.
"notice"—see *ibid*.
"tax"—see *ibid*.

Assessments for withdrawing relief and recovering tax

29.—(1) Where—   6.36
(a) any relief or exemption from tax given in respect of income or gains under an account is found not to be due or to be excessive, or
(b) the full amount of tax in respect of the income or gains under an account has not otherwise been fully accounted for and paid to the Board on behalf of the named child,

an assessment to tax may be made by the Board in the amount or further amount which in their opinion ought to be charged.

(2) An assessment to which paragraph (1) refers may be made on the account provider or on the registered contact (in respect of the child where the child is under the age of 16).

(3) If the assessment is made to recover tax in respect of income under an account it shall be made under Case VI of Schedule D.

(4) Sections 72 and 73 of the Management Act shall be modified in relation to accounts, so that—
(a) references to a parent or guardian include a reference to the registered contact for an account held by the named child, and
(b) references to an incapacitated person, in relation to Scotland, are to a person under the age of 16 years.

DEFINITIONS

"account"—see reg.2(1)(b).
"account provider"—see *ibid*.

"child"—see reg.2(1)(a).
"gains"—see reg.2(1)(b).
"the Management Act"—see *ibid*.
"tax"—see *ibid*.

Fortnightly claim and financial returns

6.37   **30.**—(1) In this regulation—
"fortnightly period" means a period—
   (a) beginning on the 1st, and ending on the 15th, day of a calendar month, or
   (b) beginning on the 16th, and ending on the last, day of a calendar month;
"first return period", in relation to account providers approved with effect from a date between 1st January 2005 and 28th February 2005, means the period beginning on the date on which the approval takes effect and ending on 28th February 2005;
"second return period", in relation to account providers approved with effect from a date between 1st January 2005 and 31st March 2005, means the period beginning on the later of 1st March 2005 and the date on which the approval takes effect, and ending on 31st March 2005;
"initial return period", in relation to account providers approved later, means the period—
   (a) beginning on the date on which the approval takes effect, or the appointed day (whichever is the later), and
   (b) ending simultaneously with the end of the current fortnightly period.
(2) The following provisions of this regulation apply to an account provider in relation to—
   (a) that provider's first, second or initial return period, and
   (b) each succeeding fortnightly period (other than succeeding a first return period),
during which, or during any part of which, he acted as an account provider.
(3) Within—
   (a) ten days of the end of a provider's first return period (if any), and
   (b) five days of the end of any other period mentioned in paragraph (2),
the account provider shall deliver by means of electronic communications to the Board, a return for that period, in a form specified by the Board.
(4) The return shall include a declaration of the information in paragraph (5), and a claim as mentioned in paragraph (6) (in each case, stated separately for each account, quoting the named child's unique reference number and date of birth).
(5) The information is that, during that period—
   (a) the account provider has opened an account in accordance with regulation 5 [^{2}. . .];
   (b) the account provider has opened a Revenue allocated account in accordance with regulation 6;
   (c) an account has been transferred to the account provider in accordance with regulation 21, and is held with the account provider at the end of the period; or
   (d) an account has been closed, due to the named child dying under the age of 18 (and the date of death).

(SI 2004/1450, reg.30) (as amended)

(6) The claim is—
(a) where paragraph (5)(a) or (b) applies, a claim for the initial contribution or special contribution due to the account in accordance with regulation 7(1) to (4); [¹. . .]
(b) where the Inland Revenue have informed the account provider that section 9 of the Act applies to the named child, a claim for the supplementary contribution due to the account in accordance with regulation 7(5) to (7) [¹; and
(c) where the Inland Revenue have informed the account provider that paragraph (10) of regulation 7 applies to the named child, a claim for the further contribution due to the account in accordance with that paragraph.]

(7) Paragraphs (5)(a) and (b) and (6)(a) and (b) shall apply notwithstanding any transfer of the account to another account provider under regulation 21, before the end of the period in question.

AMENDMENTS

1. Child Trust Funds (Amendment) Regulations 2005 (SI 2005/383), reg.5 (April 6, 2005).
2. Child Trust Funds (Amendment) Regulations 2006 (SI 2006/199), reg.4 (February 7, 2006).

DEFINITIONS

"account"—see reg.2(1)(b).
"account provider"—see *ibid.*
"appointed day"—see *ibid.*
"child"—see reg.2(1)(a).
"electronic communications"—see reg.2(1)(b).
"first return period"—see reg.30(1).
"fortnightly period"—see *ibid.*
"initial return period"—see *ibid.*
"second return period"—see *ibid.*

Records to be kept by account provider

31.—(1) An account provider shall at all times keep sufficient records in respect of an account to enable the requirements of these Regulations to be satisfied.

(2) In particular, an account provider shall produce (when required to do so by an officer of the Board) any—
(a) application made under regulation 13(1) or (10),
(b) voucher given to him,
(c) annual statement issued by him, and
(d) transfer notice given to him under regulation 21(4),
or electronic copies, within the period of 3 years from when it was made, issued or given (notwithstanding any transfer of the account under regulation 21).

DEFINITIONS

"account"—see reg.2(1)(b).
"account provider"—see *ibid.*
"notice"—see *ibid.*
"year"—see *ibid.*

6.38

Returns of information by account provider

6.39   **32.**—(1) An account provider shall within 60 days after the end of each year in which he acts as an account provider, and after ceasing to act or to qualify as an account provider, deliver by means of electronic communications to the Board a return for that year, or for the part of that year in which he so acted or qualified, in a form specified by the Board, which contains the information specified in paragraph (2).

(2) The information specified in this paragraph is information relating to each account in respect of which he acted as account provider, in the year or the part of the year for which the return is made, other than accounts transferred to another account provider under regulation 21 in that year or part of a year, as to—
- (a) as regards the named child—
    - (i) [¹. . .]
    - (ii) [¹. . .]
    - (iii) his unique reference number;
- (b) as regards each such account—
    - (i) whether or not the account is a stakeholder account,
    - (ii) whether or not there is a registered contact for the account,
    - (iii) the aggregate market value of the account investments held under the account, subject to paragraph (3), the value of each account investment being determined either as at 5th April in that year, or any other valuation date not falling earlier than 5th October in that year, and
    - (iv) the total amount of cash subscribed to the account, in the subscription year ending during the year or the part of the year for which the return is made.

(3) The reference in paragraph (2)(b)(iii) to market value shall be construed—
- (a) in the case of policies of life insurance, as a reference to their surrender value, and
- (b) as referring to separate values for—
    - (i) cash falling within regulation 12(2)(k) or (l), and
    - (ii) policies of life insurance and all other account investments.

(4) No claim for repayment, or repayment, may be made under regulations 26 and 27 until the returns which have become due under this regulation have been duly made by the account provider and received by the Board.

AMENDMENT

1. Child Trust Funds (Amendment No.2) Regulations 2005 (SI 2005/909), reg.9 (April 6, 2005).

DEFINITIONS

"account"—see reg.2(1)(b).
"account investment"—see *ibid*.
"account provider"—see *ibid*.
"child"—see reg.2(1)(a).
"electronic communications"—see reg.2(1)(b).
"market value"—see *ibid*.
"year"—see *ibid*.

(SI 2004/1450, reg.33) (as amended)

Information about "looked after children" from Local Authorities

33.—(1) In this regulation—
"local authority" includes an authority within the meaning of the Children (Northern Ireland) Order 1995;
"looked after and accommodated child", in Scotland, means a child who is—
  (a) both looked after, and provided with or placed in accommodation, by a local authority within the meaning of those expressions in Part 2 of the Children (Scotland) Act 1995, or
  (b) accommodated by a local authority under section 22 of that Act,
and related expressions shall be construed accordingly;
"looked after child"—
  (a) in England and Wales, has the meaning in section 22(1) of the Children Act 1989, extended to include a child accommodated by a local authority under section 17 of that Act, and
  (b) in Northern Ireland, means a child accommodated under Part 4 of the Children (Northern Ireland) Order 1995,
and related expressions shall be construed accordingly;
"return period" means a period—
  (a) beginning on the day immediately succeeding the appointed day, and ending one month after the appointed day, and
  (b) each succeeding period of one month.

(2) Within one month of the appointed day, every local authority shall deliver by means of electronic communications to the Board, a return in a form specified by the Board, which contains the information in paragraph (3) for every child who was—
  (a) looked after (in Scotland, looked after and accommodated) by the authority on the appointed day, and
  (b) born after 31st August 2002,
or a return stating that there were no such children.

(3) The information in this paragraph is a statement (prepared separately for each child) of—
  (a) the name of the local authority,
  (b) its address,
  (c) the unique identifier for the local authority,
  (d) the name of the local authority officer responsible for the return,
  (e) the child's full name, sex and date of birth,
  [³(ea) the full name and address of the child's mother, if known (or failing that, the same information for the child's father, if known), unless the local authority considers the child's situation to be particularly sensitive;]
  (f) the Home Office reference number, if any, of the child, and
  (g) either—
    (i) the full name and address of an individual who has parental responsibility (in Scotland, parental responsibilities) in relation to the child, or
    (ii) if paragraph (i) is considered inappropriate, a correspondence address for the child.

(4) Within [⁴ten] days of the end of each return period, every local authority shall deliver by means of electronic communications to the Board a return for that period in a form specified by the Board, covering every child—

(a) born after 31st August 2002, and
(b) who during that period has become a child looked after (in Scotland, looked after and accommodated) by that authority, for the first time since the appointed day,

or a return stating that there were no such children.

(5) After 31st August 2009, the return in paragraph (4) shall in addition cover every child who was looked after (in Scotland, looked after and accommodated) on his 7th birthday.

(6) The return in paragraph (4) shall consist of a statement (prepared separately for each child) of—
(a) the information in paragraph (3),
(b) the date on which the child first became a child looked after (in Scotland, looked after and accommodated) by that authority,
(c) where the child has also died during that period, the name and address of his personal representatives [1,

and where sub-paragraph (c) applies, the local authority shall also send a copy of the death certificate (or other documentary evidence of death) to the Board by post.]

[1(7) As an alternative to delivering the return required by paragraph (2) by means of electronic communications, the local authority may (until this paragraph is revoked) send the return to the Board by registered post.]

[2(8) Regulations 34 and 35 shall apply to local authorities, as if, in those regulations, for—
(a) "relevant person" there were substituted "local authority"; and
(b) references to an account or account investments there were substituted references to returns, forms or children mentioned in this regulation and regulation 33A,

so far as the Board may reasonably require information to be provided or records to be made available for the purposes of this regulation and regulation 33A.]

AMENDMENTS

1. Child Trust Funds (Amendment) Regulations 2004 (SI 2004/2676), reg.14 (April 6, 2005).
2. Child Trust Funds (Amendment No.2) Regulations 2004 (SI 2004/3382), reg.4 (April 6, 2005).
3. Child Trust Funds (Amendment No.2) Regulations 2006 (SI 2006/2684), reg.3 (October 31, 2006).
4. Child Trust Funds (Amendment No.2) Regulations 2006 (SI 2006/2684), reg.4 (October 31, 2006).

DEFINITIONS

"account"—see reg.2(1)(b).
"account investment"—see *ibid.*
"appointed day"—see *ibid.*
"child"—see reg.2(1)(a).
"electronic communications"—see reg.2(1)(b).
"local authority"—see reg.33(1).
"looked after and accommodated child"—see *ibid.*
"looked after child"—see *ibid.*
"parental responsibility"—see reg.2(1)(a).
"relevant person"—see *ibid.*
"return period"—see reg.33(1).

(SI 2004/1450, reg.33A) (as amended)

[¹The Official Solicitor or Accountant of Court to be the person who has the authority to manage an account

33A.—(1) Every local authority shall be under a duty to—
(a) identify any child born after 31st August 2002 and under 16, who falls within the circumstances specified in paragraph (2) and, for each such child,
(b) deliver a form (as part of the return required by regulation 33(2) or (4), as the case may be) in accordance with paragraph (3)(a).
(2) The circumstances specified are where—
(a) the child is looked after (in Scotland, looked after and accommodated) by the local authority, and
(b) at least one of the following conditions is satisfied.

Condition 1

There is no person, or no person other than the local authority, who has parental responsibility (in Scotland, parental responsibilities) for the child.

Condition 2

It is part of the care plan for the child that—
(a) the child will live indefinitely away from home (or his former home), and
(b) the child will not have face to face contact with any parent having parental responsibility (in Scotland, parental responsibilities) for the child.

Condition 3

An order has been made under section 34(4) of the Children Act 1989 or Article 53(4) of the Children (Northern Ireland) Order 1995, authorising the local authority to refuse to allow contact between the child and any person with parental responsibility (or, in Scotland, a supervision requirement made with a condition regulating contact under section 70(5)(b) of the Children (Scotland) Act 1995 that the child shall have no contact with a person with parental responsibilities), and there is no other individual with parental responsibility (in Scotland, parental responsibilities) for the child to act as registered contact.

Condition 4

The Court of Protection has—
(a) appointed a receiver for a person with parental responsibility for the child, or
(b) determined that such a person is a "patient" for the purposes of Part 7 of the Mental Health Act 1983,
and there is no other individual with parental responsibility for the child to act as registered contact.
In Scotland, in this Condition for—
(a) "Court of Protection" substitute "Sheriff",
(b) "receiver" substitute "guardian appointed under section 58 of the Adults with Incapacity (Scotland) Act 2000",

(c) the reference to a patient, substitute "incapable for the purposes of the Adults with Incapacity (Scotland) Act 2000," and
(d) "parental responsibility" substitute "parental responsibilities".

Condition 5

The child has been lost or abandoned, and there is no prospect for the foreseeable future of reunification of the child with a parent having parental responsibility (in Scotland, parental responsibilities) for the child.
In this Condition, "lost or abandoned"—
(a) in England and Wales, has the meaning in section 20(1)(b) of the Children Act 1989;
(b) in Northern Ireland, has the meaning in Article 21(1)(b) of the Children (Northern Ireland) Order 1995; and
(c) in Scotland, has the meaning in section 25(1)(b) of the Children (Scotland) Act 1995.

[²*Condition 6*

In England and Wales, an adoption agency or local authority has been authorised to place the child for adoption under section 19, or by a placement order under section 21, of the Adoption and Children Act 2002, or in Northern Ireland, an Order has been made under Article 17 or 18 of the Adoption (Northern Ireland) Order 1987 to free the child for adoption.]
(3) Where—
(a) the local authority (by a means authorised by regulation 33) delivers to the Board a form specified by the Board, giving particulars of the child and of the circumstances specified in paragraph (2) relevant to the child, and
(b) the Board (subject to checking and if necessary correcting the contents of the form) delivers it to the Official Solicitor (where the child is in England and Wales or Northern Ireland) or the Accountant of Court (where the child is in Scotland),
the Official Solicitor or Accountant of Court, as the case may be, shall be the person who has the authority to manage the child's account for the purposes of section 3(6)(b) of the Act.
(4) The Official Solicitor or Accountant of Court shall cease to be the person who has the authority to manage the child's account (and shall be discharged from the duties of registered contact) where—
(a) the child attains the age of 16,
(b) in any case where the child is under 16 and still looked after (in Scotland, looked after and accommodated) by a local authority—
 (i) the local authority confirms to the Official Solicitor or Accountant of Court that there is a named responsible person in relation to the child, who is able to be the registered contact for the child's account, and that none of the Conditions in paragraph (2) applies, and
 (ii) the Official Solicitor or Accountant of Court cancels his declaration and authorisation in accordance with regulation 13(7) and is replaced as registered contact by that responsible person, in accordance with regulation 13(10), or
(c) in any case where the child is under 16 and is not looked after (in Scotland, looked after and accommodated) by a local authority—

(SI 2004/1450, reg.33A) (as amended)

  (i) a responsible person for the child provides evidence to the satisfaction of the Official Solicitor or Accountant of Court, as the case may be, that he has parental responsibility for the child, and

  (ii) the Official Solicitor or Accountant of Court cancels his declaration and authorisation in accordance with regulation 13(7) and is replaced as registered contact by that responsible person, in accordance with regulation 13(10).

(5) A local authority shall, for the purposes of paragraph (4), confirm to the Official Solicitor or Accountant of Court, as the case may be—

 (a) whether the child is still looked after (in Scotland, looked after and accommodated) by the authority, and

 (b) the identity of the person or persons who had parental responsibility for the child at the date when he ceased to be looked after (in Scotland, looked after and accommodated) by the authority (or, at the option of the authority, any later date).

(6) Expressions defined in regulation 33 shall bear the same meanings in this regulation.]

AMENDMENTS

1. Child Trust Funds (Amendment No.2) Regulations 2004 (SI 2004/3382), reg.5 (April 6, 2005).
2. Child Trust Funds (Amendment No.2) Regulations 2006 (SI 2006/2684), reg.5 (October 31, 2006).

DEFINITIONS

 "account"—see reg.2(1)(b).
 "child"—see reg.2(1)(a).
 "parental responsibility"—see *ibid.*
 "responsible person"—see *ibid.*

Information to be provided to the Board

34. The Board may by notice require any relevant person to furnish them, within such time (not being less than 14 days) as may be provided in the notice, such information about any account or about any account investment (including copies of or extracts from any books or other records) as they may reasonably require for the purposes of these Regulations.

DEFINITIONS

 "account"—see reg.2(1)(b).
 "account investment"—see *ibid.*
 "notice"—see *ibid.*
 "relevant person"—see reg.2(1)(a).

Inspection of records by officer of the Board

35.—(1) The Board may by notice require any relevant person, within such time (not being less than 14 days) as may be provided in the notice, to make available for inspection at a place within the United Kingdom by an officer of the Board authorised for that purpose all documents (including books and other records) in his possession or under his control relating to any account or to any account investment.

(2) Where records are maintained by computer the person required to make them available for inspection shall provide the officer making the inspection with all the facilities necessary for obtaining information from them.

DEFINITIONS

"account"—see reg.2(1)(b).
"account investment"—see *ibid*.
"notice"—see *ibid*.
"relevant person"—see reg.2(1)(a).

Capital gains tax—adaptation of enactments

6.44   36.—(1) For the purposes of capital gains tax—
(a) any assets held by a named child as account investments shall be regarded as held by the child in a separate capacity from that in which he holds any other assets of the same description; and
(b) the named child shall be treated as having sold all the account investments, and as having reacquired them in his personal capacity, for a consideration equal to their market value, immediately before he attains the age of 18 years (and ceases to be a child).

(2) Sections 127 to 131 of the 1992 Act shall not apply in relation to qualifying investments falling within any of sub-paragraphs (a), (b), and (f) to (i) of regulation 12(2) which are held under an account if there is by virtue of any allotment for payment as is mentioned in section 126(2) of that Act a reorganisation affecting those assets.

DEFINITIONS

"account"—see reg.2(1)(b).
"account investment"—see *ibid*.
"child"—see reg.2(1)(a).
"market value"—see reg.2(1)(b).
"the 1992 Act"—see *ibid*.

Administration of tax in relation to accounts—supplementary

6.45   37.—(1) Nothing in these Regulations shall be taken to prejudice any powers conferred or duties imposed by or under any enactment in relation to the making of returns of income or gains, or for the recovery of tax, penalties or interest by means of an assessment or otherwise.

(2) Notwithstanding the provisions of these Regulations an account provider shall not be released from obligations under these Regulations in relation to an account except under conditions agreed in writing with and notified to that person by the Board.

(3) The provisions contained in the Management Act shall apply to any assessment under these Regulations as if it were an assessment to tax for the year in which, apart from these Regulations, the named child would have been liable (by reason of his ownership of the investments).

(4) No obligation as to secrecy imposed by statute or otherwise shall preclude the Board from disclosing to an account provider or registered contact that any provision of these Regulations has not been satisfied or that relief has been given or claimed in respect of investments under an account.

(SI 2004/1450, reg.37) (as amended)

(5) If—
(a) a chargeable event, within the meaning given by Chapter 2 of Part 13 of the Taxes Act, has happened in relation to a policy of life insurance which is an account investment, and
(b) the body by whom the policy was issued is satisfied that no gain is to be treated as chargeable to tax on the happening of the event by virtue of regulation 24(a)(v),

the body shall not be obliged to deliver the certificates mentioned in section 552(1) of that Act.

This paragraph does not prevent the operation of section 552(1) in a case to which regulation 38(1) applies.

(6) Where—
(a) it comes to the notice of the account provider, in any manner, that the event specified in regulation 12(11) has occurred in relation to a policy, and
(b) the account provider is not the insurer for the time being responsible for the obligations under the policy or, where the policy is not still in existence, the person who was the last such insurer,

the account provider shall, within 30 days of the event coming to his notice give notice to that insurer, specifying the event mentioned in sub-paragraph (a) and the termination event.

DEFINITIONS

"account"—see reg.2(1)(b).
"account investment"—see *ibid.*
"account provider"—see *ibid.*
"child"—see reg.2(1)(a).
"gains"—see reg.2(1)(b).
"the Management Act"—see *ibid.*
"notice"—see *ibid.*
"tax"—see *ibid.*
"the Taxes Act"—see *ibid.*
"year"—see *ibid.*

Application of the provisions of Chapter 2 of Part 13 of the Taxes Act to policies

38.—(1) This paragraph applies to a case where— 6.46
(a) the event specified in regulation 12(11) has occurred in relation to a policy of life insurance, and
(b) a termination event within the meaning in regulation 12(12) occurs in relation to that policy.

(2) Where—
(a) there is a case to which paragraph (1) applies, and
(b) a chargeable event in relation to the policy, within the meaning given by section 540 of the Taxes Act, has occurred prior to the time at which the termination event mentioned in paragraph (1)(b) occurs,

the named child shall cease to be, and shall be treated as not having been, entitled to relief from tax under regulation 24(a)(v), in respect of gains treated as arising on the occurrence of any chargeable event mentioned in sub-paragraph (b).

(3) The provisions of Chapter 2 of Part 13 of the Taxes Act shall apply, in a case to which paragraph (1) applies, to—

(a) the termination event mentioned in paragraph (1)(b), and
(b) any chargeable event mentioned in paragraph (2)(b),
with the modifications provided for in paragraphs (4) to (8) of this regulation, and the registered contact and the account provider shall account to the Board in accordance with this regulation for tax from which relief under regulation 24 has been given on the basis that the named child was so entitled, or in circumstances such that the named child was not so entitled.

(4) A termination of a policy of insurance pursuant to regulation 12(9)(b)(ii) shall be treated as the surrender in whole of the rights conferred by the policy, for the purposes of section 540(1)(a)(iii) of the Taxes Act.

(5) In section 547(5) of the Taxes Act, for the words after "total income" (where that expression first appears) substitute "that gain shall be chargeable to tax under Case VI of Schedule D".

(6) Relief under section 550 of the Taxes Act shall be computed as if paragraph (5) had not been enacted.

(7) In section 552 of the Taxes Act—
(a) in subsection (1)(b) for "policy holder" substitute "named child";
(b) in subsection (3)—
   (i) omit "(or, where the appropriate policy holder is a company, the corresponding financial year)";
   (ii) for "the name and address of the appropriate policy holder" substitute "the name and address of the named child";
   (iii) omit "and the corresponding financial year,";
(c) in subsection (5)—
   (i) for "the appropriate policy holder" substitute "the named child";
   (ii) omit sub-paragraph (b)(ii);
   (iii) omit paragraph (c);
   (iv) in paragraph (d) omit "except where paragraph (c) above applies,";
   (v) omit paragraph (f);
(d) in subsection (6)—
   (i) omit paragraph (b);
   (ii) for paragraph (c) substitute—
     "(c) if the event is a death, the period of three months beginning with the receipt of written notification of the death;";
   (iii) after paragraph (c) insert—
     "(d) if the event is—
       (i) a termination event, or
       (ii) a chargeable event preceding a termination event (as mentioned in regulation 38(2) of the Child Trust Funds Regulations 2004),
     the period of three months beginning with the date on which the insurer received notice under regulation 37(6) of those Regulations or, if earlier, actual notice of the termination event.";
(e) in subsection (7)—
   (i) in paragraph (a) omit ", or, where the policy holder is a company, the financial year,";
   (ii) omit paragraph (b);
   (iii) for paragraph (c) substitute—
     "(c) if the event is a death, the period of three months beginning with the receipt of written notification of the death;";

(SI 2004/1450, reg. 38) (as amended)

      (iv) after paragraph (c) insert—
          "(ca) if the event is—
              (i) a termination event, or
              (ii) a chargeable event preceding such a termination event (as mentioned in regulation 38(2) of the Child Trust Funds Regulations 2004,
          the period of three months beginning with the date on which the insurer received notice under regulation 37(6) of those Regulations or, if earlier, actual notice of the termination event."; and
      (v) in paragraph (d) after "paragraph (c)" insert "or (ca)";
(f) in subsection (8)—
      (i) in paragraph (b) for "policy holder" substitute "named child in respect";
      (ii) in paragraph (c) omit the words from "or" to the end;
(g) in subsection (9) omit "or financial year" in each place where they occur;
(h) in subsection (10)—
      (i) before the definition of "amount" insert—
          " 'named child' has the same meaning as in the Child Trust Funds Regulations 2004;";
      (ii) omit the definitions of "appropriate policy holder" and "financial year";
      (iii) for the definition of "the relevant year of assessment" substitute—
          " 'the relevant year of assessment', in the case of any gain, means the year of assessment to which the gain is attributable;"; and
      (iv) after the definition of "section 546 excess" insert—
          " 'termination event' has the same meaning as in the Child Trust Funds Regulations 2004;"; and
      (v) omit subsection (11).

(8) In section 552ZA of the Taxes Act—
(a) in subsection (2)(b) omit the words "or an assignment"; and
(b) omit subsections (3) and (4).
(9) The account provider shall account for and pay income tax at the lower rate in force for the year in which the termination event, or the chargeable event mentioned in paragraph (2)(b) occurred, as the case may be, and any amount so payable—
    (a) may be set off against any repayment in respect of tax due under regulation 26 or 27 and subject thereto,
    (b) shall be treated as an amount of tax due not later than 6 months after the end of the year in which the event specified in regulation 12(11) came to the notice of the account provider, and
    (c) shall be payable without the making of an assessment.
(10) Where tax is charged in accordance with paragraph (3)(a) or (b)—
(a) an assessment to income tax at the lower rate in force for the relevant year may be made on the account provider or on the registered contact (on behalf of the named child), and
(b) an assessment to income tax at the higher rate within the meaning of section 832(1) of the Taxes Act, for that year, may be made on the registered contact (on behalf of the named child) within five years after the 31st January next following that year, and regulation 29 shall not apply.

DEFINITIONS

"account provider"—see *ibid*.
"child"—see reg.2(1)(a).
"company"—see reg.2(1)(b).
"notice"—see *ibid*.
"tax"—see *ibid*.
"the Taxes Act"—see *ibid*.
"year"—see *ibid*.

SCHEDULE

STAKEHOLDER ACCOUNTS

Description of stakeholder account

6.47   1. An account is a stakeholder account where it has the characteristics and complies with the conditions set out in paragraph 2.

Characteristics of stakeholder account etc

6.48   2.—(1) A stakeholder account must have the characteristics set out in sub-paragraph (2) and must comply with the conditions set out in sub-paragraphs (3) to (5).
(2) The characteristics of a stakeholder account are—
   (a) the account does not directly hold investments of any of the following kinds—
      (i) those referred to in regulation 12(2)(f) (shares in an investment trust);
      (ii) securities of an investment trust;
      (iii) rights in with-profits endowment policies;
      (iv) rights, under a contract of insurance, in a with-profits fund;
      (v) units or shares in a relevant collective investment scheme unless it is a requirement of that scheme that the purchase and sale price of those units or shares shall, at any given time, not differ from each other and that the price must be made available to the public on a daily basis;
      (vi) rights under a contract of insurance which are expressed as shares in funds held by the insurer unless it is a requirement of the contract of insurance that the purchase and sale price of those shares shall, at any given time, not differ from each other and that the price must be made available to the public on a daily basis;
      [¹(via) shares referred to in regulation 12(2)(a) (shares issued by a company wherever incorporated and officially listed on a recognised stock exchange)]
      (vii) depositary interests, where the investments concerned are investments of any of the kinds listed above in this paragraph;
   (b) [¹the requirement is fulfilled that] the account provider, and any relevant person, [¹. . .] ensure that, subject to the other provisions of this paragraph, the account has exposure to equities [¹. . .];
   [¹(ba) interest accrues on investments referred to in regulation 12(2)(k) and (l) (cash deposited in a deposit account or in a share account) on a daily basis at a rate that is not less than the Bank of England base rate minus 1 per cent per annum [³, except where cash is held temporarily on deposit in the course of dealing in investments under the account];
   [²(baa) when the Bank of England base rate increases, the interest rate on investments referred to in regulation 12(2)(k) and (l) (cash deposited in a deposit account or in a share account) must be raised within one month of the date of that increase;]
   (bb) in relation to qualifying investments which are securities (other than in an investment trust) or a depositary interest where the relevant investments (within the meaning in that definition) are such securities, the requirement is fulfilled that—
      (i) the securities fall within regulation 12(2)(c) [², (d) or (e)], or
      (ii) where the securities fall within regulation 12(2)(b) [². . .] or (n), the contract under which the securities are or have been acquired, or any other transaction entered into by the registered contact or any other person, has the effect that the named child is not exposed, or not exposed to a significant extent, to the risk of loss from fluctuations in the value of the securities exceeding 20% of the capital consideration paid or payable for the acquisition of those securities, during the period when the securities in question are held in the account.]

(c) [¹the requirement is fulfilled that] the account provider and any relevant person [¹. . .] have regard to—
  (i) the need for diversification of investments of the account, in so far as is appropriate to the circumstances of the account; and
  (ii) the suitability for the purposes of the account of any investment, investment strategy or investment option proposed; and
(d) except where otherwise instructed by the registered contact, the account is subject to lifestyling.

(3) The account provider must permit payment of subscriptions to the account by—
(a) cheque;
(b) direct debit;
(c) standing order;
(d) direct credit (other than standing order).

[¹For the purposes of this sub-paragraph, those means of payment do not include payments by cash, credit card or debit card or any combination including a payment by cash, credit card or debit card.]

(4) The minimum amount which may be subscribed to the account on a single occasion is £10 except where the account provider permits a smaller amount.

(5) Deductions from the account may only be made in the circumstances, and to the extent, set out in paragraph 3.

(6) In this paragraph—

"equities" means shares issued by a company wherever incorporated and officially listed on a recognised stock exchange;

"insurer" means—
  (a) a person who has permission under Part 4 of the Financial Services and Markets Act 2000 to effect or carry out contracts of insurance, or
  (b) an EEA firm of the kind mentioned in paragraph 5(d) of Schedule 3 to that Act, which has permission under paragraph 15 of that Schedule (as a result of qualifying for authorisation under paragraph 12 of that Schedule) to effect or carry out contracts of insurance;

"lifestyling" means the process beginning from a date on or before the child is 13 years of age, or from when the account is opened, whichever is later, and continuing until the child is 18 years of age, by which the account provider, and any relevant person, adopts an investment strategy which aims progressively to minimise the variation or potential variation in capital value of the account caused by market conditions from time to time;

"relevant collective investment scheme" means an authorised unit trust scheme, an authorised open-ended investment company or a recognised scheme, as the case may be, as defined in section 237(3) of the Financial Services and Markets Act 2000;

"relevant person" means any person to whom the account provider has delegated any of his functions or responsibilities under the management agreement; and

"with-profits fund" means a fund maintained by an insurer in respect of a particular part of its long-term business for which—
  (a) separate accounting records are maintained by the insurer in respect of all income and expenditure relating to that part of its business; and
  (b) the benefits payable in respect of policies allocated to that fund are determined partly by reference to a discretion exercisable by any person.

(7) In this paragraph, the definitions of "contract of insurance" and "insurer" must be read with—
(a) section 22 of the Financial Services and Markets Act 2000,
(b) any relevant order made under that section, and
(c) Schedule 2 to that Act.

Stakeholder accounts—charges etc

3.—(1) Deductions from a stakeholder account may only be made to the extent set out in this paragraph.

(2) Subject to sub-paragraph (5), charges for the management of, and other expenses in connection with, a stakeholder account may be recovered from the account to the extent that they do not exceed whichever is the greater of—
(a) 3/730 per cent of the value of the child's rights in the account for each day on which the account is held; or

6.49

(b) 3/730 per cent of the value of the investments under the account for each day on which the account is held.

(3) For the purposes of sub-paragraph (2)—
   (a) the frequency, which must be daily, weekly or monthly, with which rights or investments are to be valued; and
   (b) where valuation is to take place weekly or monthly, the day of the week or, as the case may be, the date in the month on which it is to take place,

must be specified in advance in writing by the account provider to the registered contact, and the specification may not be amended during the period of 12 months after the date on which it is made.

(4) When calculating the value of a child's rights or of investments for the purposes of sub-paragraph (2), where the account provider has specified under sub-paragraph (3) that they are to be valued weekly or monthly—
   (a) where they are to be valued weekly, they are to be valued on such day of the week ("the specified day") as has been so specified by the account provider (except that, where that day is not a working day, the rights are to be valued on the next working day), and the value of the rights on each subsequent day prior to the next specified day is to be taken to be the value of the rights on the previous specified day; and
   (b) where they are to be valued monthly, they are to be so valued on such date in each month ("the specified date") as has been so specified by the account provider (except that, where that date is not a working day, the rights are to be valued on the next working day), and the value of the rights on each subsequent day prior to the next specified date is to be taken to be the value of the rights on the previous specified date.

(5) The following charges and expenses may be deducted in full from the account and are not subject to and do not count towards the limit provided for in sub-paragraph (2)—
   (a) any stamp duty, stamp duty reserve tax [[1], value added tax] or other charges [[1](including any dilution levy)] incurred by the account provider directly or indirectly in the sale or purchase of investments held under the account;
   [[1](aa) where any amount of tax is paid or anticipated to be payable in respect of income received or capital gains realised by the account provider in respect of investments held for the purposes of the account, the amount so deducted or anticipated;]
   (b) any charges or expenses incurred by the account provider directly or indirectly in complying with an order of the court or any other requirements imposed by law; and
   (c) expenses incurred by the account provider in complying with its obligations under regulation 8(2)(d) and (e).

(6) Valuations for the purpose of sub-paragraph (2) shall be after the deduction of any charges or expenses properly deducted from the account under sub-paragraph (5).

AMENDMENTS

1. Child Trust Funds (Amendment) Regulations 2004 (SI 2004/2676), reg.15 (April 6, 2005).

2. Child Trust Funds (Amendment No.2) Regulations 2004 (SI 2004/3382), reg.6 (April 6, 2005).

3. Child Trust Funds (Amendment No.2) Regulations 2006 (SI 2006/2684), reg.6 (October 31, 2006).

DEFINITIONS

"account"—see reg.2(1)(b).
"account provider"—see *ibid.*
"Bank of England base rate"—see *ibid.*
"child"—see reg.2(1)(a).
"company"—see reg.2(1)(b).
"contract of insurance"—see para.2(7).
"depositary interest"—see reg.2(1)(c).
"equities"—see para.2(6).
"insurer"—see *ibid.*, and para.2(7).
"investments under the account"—see reg.2(1)(b).
"investment trust"—see *ibid.*
"lifestyling"—see para.2(6).

"open-ended investment company"—see reg.2(1)(c).
"recognised stock exchange"—see reg.2(1)(b).
"relevant collective investment scheme"—see para.2(6).
"relevant person"—see reg.2(1)(a) and para.2(6).
"subscriptions"—see reg.2(1)(b).
"tax"—see *ibid*.
"units"—see reg.2(1)(c).
"with-profits fund"—see para.2(6).

Child Trust Funds (Insurance Companies) Regulations 2004

(SI 2004/2680)

The Treasury, in exercise of the powers conferred upon them by section 333B of the Income and Corporation Taxes Act 1988 as extended by section 14(1) of the Child Trust Funds Act 2004, hereby make the following Regulations:

6.50

ARRANGEMENT OF REGULATIONS

1. Citation and commencement
2. Interpretation
3. Child trust fund business
4.–17. Modifications of the Taxes Act
18.–19. Modification of the Taxation of Chargeable Gains Act 1992
20.–21. Modification of the Capital Allowances Act 2001
22. Amendments to the Insurance Companies Regulations

Citation and commencement

1. These Regulations may be cited as the Child Trust Funds (Insurance Companies) Regulations 2004 and shall come into force on the day appointed under section 27 of the Child Trust Funds Act 2004, for the purposes of sections 8 and 9 of that Act.

6.51

Interpretation

2. In these Regulations—
"child trust fund business" has the meaning given by regulation 3;
"individual savings account business" has the meaning given in the Insurance Companies Regulations;
"the Insurance Companies Regulations" means the Individual Savings Account (Insurance Companies) Regulations 1998;
"the principal Regulations" means the Child Trust Funds Regulations 2004;
"the Taxes Act" means the Income and Corporation Taxes Act 1988.

6.52

Child trust fund business

3. For the purposes of these Regulations "child trust fund business", in relation to an insurance company, means so much of that company's

6.53

life assurance business as is referable to any policy of life insurance, or to the reinsurance of liabilities under any such policy, where the policy is, on the date on which the insurance is made, a qualifying investment for an account within the meaning of regulation 12 of the principal Regulations.

Modifications of the Taxes Act

4. Regulations 5 to 17 specify modifications of provisions of the Taxes Act so far as concerns the child trust fund business (and, in the case of regulations 11(b) and (c), 13 and 14, the individual savings account business) of insurance companies.

5. In section 431(2) insert at the appropriate place the following definition—
 "'child trust fund business' has the meaning given by regulation 3 of the Child Trust Funds (Insurance Companies) Regulations 2004;".

6. In both of sections 431C(1) and 431D(1) after "pension business" insert ", child trust fund business".

7. In section 431F after "pension business," insert "child trust fund business,".

8. In section 432A(2) (as modified by the Insurance Companies Regulations) after paragraph (aa) insert—
 "(ab) child trust fund business;".

9. In section 432AA(4) (as modified by the Insurance Companies Regulations) after paragraph (aa) insert—
 "(ab) child trust fund business;".

10. In both of sections 432C(1) and 432D(1) after "pension business," insert "child trust fund business,".

11. In section 436—
 (a) after the words "pension business", in each place where they occur, insert "or child trust fund business";
 (b) in subsection (1)(a) for "that business" substitute "the business of each such category".
 (c) after subsection (3)(c) insert—
  "(ca) there may be set off (so far as it has not been set off under paragraph (c)), against the profits of child trust fund business any loss, to be computed on the same basis as the profits, which has arisen from individual savings account business, in the same or any previous accounting period;
  (cb) there may be set off (so far as it has not been set off under paragraph (c)), against the profits of individual savings account business any loss, to be computed on the same basis as the profits, which has arisen from child trust fund business, in the same or any previous accounting period;".

12. In section 438(1) add at the end "or child trust fund business".

13. In section 440(4)(a) add at the end, "individual savings account business or child trust fund business, or assets linked to any of those categories but not to any other category of business".

14. In section 440A(2)(a)(i) after "pension business" insert ", individual savings account business or child trust fund business or any of those categories of business".

15. In section 466(2) insert at the appropriate place the following definition—

(SI 2004/2680, reg. 15)

" 'child trust fund business' shall be construed in accordance with section 431(2);".

16. In section 755A (as modified by the Insurance Companies Regulations) after paragraph (aa) in each of subsections (4) and (13) insert—
"(ab) child trust fund business,".

17. In paragraph 5(5) of Schedule 19AA after "pension business," insert "child trust fund business,".

Modification of the Taxation of Chargeable Gains Act 1992

18. Regulation 19 specifies a modification of section 212 of the Taxation of Chargeable Gains Act 1992 so far as concerns child trust fund business of insurance companies.

19. In section 212(2) after "pension business" insert, "child trust fund business".

Modification of the Capital Allowances Act 2001

20. Regulation 21 specifies a modification of section 256 of the Capital Allowances Act 2001 so far as concerns child trust fund business of insurance companies.

21. In section 256(3)(a) after "pension business" insert, "child trust fund business".

Amendments to the Insurance Companies Regulations

22. Regulations 13(b), 15 and 16 of the Insurance Companies Regulations (which are superseded by regulations 11(b), 13 and 14 of these Regulations) shall cease to have effect.

GENERAL NOTE

These Regulations make various technical modifications to revenue law provisions. They provide for the exemption from corporation tax of income and gains made by an insurance company providing child trust funds, so far as they relate to the company's child trust fund business. They also provide for the profit from operating child trust fund business to be taxed in the same way as profits from the company's Individual Savings Account (ISA) business, and for losses arising one category to be set off against profits from the other.

The Child Trust Funds (Non-tax Appeals) Regulations 2005

(SI 2005/191)

Made   *3 February 2005*
Laid before Parliament   *4 February 2005*
Coming into force   *25 February 2005*

The Treasury, in exercise of the powers conferred upon them by sections 23(1), 24(5) and 28(1) to (4) of the Child Trust Funds Act 2004, make the following Regulations:

The Child Trust Funds (Non-Tax Appeals) Regulations 2005

Citation, commencement and duration

6.60   **1.**—(1) These Regulations may be cited as the Child Trust Funds (Non-tax Appeals) Regulations 2005 and shall come into force on 25 February 2005.

(2) These Regulations shall cease to have effect on the day appointed by Order made under section 24(1) of the Child Trust Funds Act 2004 (temporary modifications).

Interpretation

6.61   **2.** *Omitted.*

Prescribed manner of notice of appeal

6.62   **3.**—(1) The prescribed manner of giving notice of appeal to the Inland Revenue under section 23(1) of the Child Trust Funds Act 2004 is as follows.

(2) The notice must—
(a) be given in writing,
(b) contain sufficient information to identify the appellant and the decision against which the appeal is being made, and
(c) be signed by or on behalf of the appellant.

(3) In paragraph (2)(a) "writing" includes writing produced by electronic communications if those electronic communications are approved by the Commissioners of Inland Revenue.

(4) In paragraph (2)(c) "signed", where the notice is in writing produced by electronic communications, means authenticated in any manner approved by those Commissioners.

DEFINITIONS

"Inland Revenue"—see Child Trust Funds Act 2004, s.29, but see the note below.
"signed"—see para.(4).
"writing"—see para.(3).

GENERAL NOTE

6.63   For what amounts to a signature, see the annotation to reg.2 of the Tax Credits (Notice of Appeal) Regulations 2002. Also, see para.(4) for signatures on electronic documents.

The functions of the Commissioners of Inland Revenue have been transferred to the Commissioners for Her Majesty's Revenue and Customs (Commissioners for Revenue and Customs Act 2005, s.5(2)(a)).

6.64   **4.–15.** *Omitted.*

General Commissioners (Jurisdiction and Procedure) (Amendment) Regulations 2005

(SI 2005/340)

6.65   The Lord Chancellor, in exercise of the powers conferred upon him by section 56B of the Taxes Management Act 1970, after consultation with the Council on

(SI 2005/340)

Tribunals in accordance with section 8 of the Tribunal and Inquiries Act 1992 and with the consent of the Scottish Ministers, hereby makes the following Regulations:

ARRANGEMENT OF REGULATIONS

1. Citation, commencement and interpretation
2. Amendment to the General Commissioners (Jurisdiction and Procedure) Regulations 1994

Citation, commencement and interpretation

1.—(1) These Regulations may be cited as the General Commissioners (Jurisdiction and Procedure) (Amendment) Regulations 2005 and shall come into force on the 14th March 2005.

(2) Any reference to a regulation by number alone means the regulation so numbered in the General Commissioners (Jurisdiction and Procedure) Regulations 1994.

Amendments to the General Commissioners (Jurisdiction and Procedure) Regulations 1994

2. In regulation 2 in the definition of "proceedings" after paragraph (g) insert—

"(h) any appeal to the General Commissioners under regulations made under section 13 of the Child Trust Funds Act 2004 or any appeal to the General Commissioners under section 22 of that Act;".

3. *[Omitted]*.

GENERAL NOTE

These Regulations amend the General Commissioners (Jurisdiction and Procedure) Regulations 1994 (SI 1994/1812) so as include "tax appeals" made pursuant to ss.13 and 22 of the Child Trust Funds Act 2004 within the definition of "proceedings" in reg.2 of the 1994 Regulations.

Special Commissioners (Jurisdiction and Procedure) (Amendment) Regulations 2005

(SI 2005/341)

The Lord Chancellor, in exercise of the powers conferred upon him by section 56B of the Taxes Management Act 1970, after consultation with the Council on Tribunals in accordance with section 8 of the Tribunal and Inquiries Act 1992 and with the consent of the Scottish Ministers, hereby makes the following Regulations:

ARRANGEMENT OF REGULATIONS

1. Citation, commencement and interpretation
2. Amendment to the Special Commissioners (Jurisdiction and Procedure) Regulations 1994

Special Commissioners (Jurisdiction and Procedure) (Amendment) Regs 2005

Citation, commencement and interpretation

6.70   **1.**—(1) These Regulations may be cited as the Special Commissioners (Jurisdiction and Procedure) (Amendment) Regulations 2005 and shall come into force on the 14th March 2005.

(2) Any reference to a regulation by number alone means the regulation so numbered in the Special Commissioners (Jurisdiction and Procedure) Regulations 1994.

Amendment to the Special Commissioners (Jurisdiction and Procedure) Regulations 1994

6.71   **2.** In regulation 2 in the definition of "proceedings" after paragraph (n) insert—

"(o) any appeal to the Special Commissioners under regulations made under section 13 of the Child Trust Funds Act 2004 or any appeal to the Special Commissioners under section 22 of that Act;".

GENERAL NOTE

6.72   These Regulations amend the Special Commissioners (Jurisdiction and Procedure) Regulations 1994 (SI 1994/1811) to include "tax appeals" made pursuant to ss.13 or 22 of the Child Trust Funds Act 2004 within the definition of "proceedings" in that reg.2 of the 1994 Regulations.

The Child Trust Funds (Appeals) Regulations 2005

(SI 2005/990)

Made   *24th March 2005*
Coming into force in accordance with regulation 1(1)

6.73   Whereas a draft of this instrument was laid before Parliament in accordance with section 80(1) of the Social Security Act 1998 and approved by resolution of each House of Parliament.

Now therefore, the Secretary of State for Work and Pensions, in exercise of the powers conferred upon him by sections 7(6) and (7), 12(7), 14(10)(a) and (11), 16(1) and (3)(a), 28(1), 79(1) and (4) to (7) and 84 of, and paragraphs 7, 11 and 12 of Schedule 1 to, and paragraphs 1 to 6 of Schedule 5 to, the Social Security Act 1998, after consultation with the Council on Tribunals in accordance with section 8 of the Tribunals and Inquiries Act 1992, hereby makes the following Regulations:

Citation, commencement, duration and interpretation

6.74   **1.**—(1) These Regulations may be cited as the Child Trust Funds (Appeals) Regulations 2005 and shall come into force on the day after they are made.

(2) These Regulations shall cease to have effect on such day as is appointed by order made under section 24(1) of the Child Trust Funds Act 2004.

(3) In these Regulations, unless the context otherwise requires—

(SI 2005/990, reg.1)

"the Act" means the Social Security Act 1998;
"the 2004 Act" means the Child Trust Funds Act 2004;
"appeal" means an appeal under section 22 of the 2004 Act to an appeal tribunal;
"the Board" means the Commissioners of Inland Revenue;
"the clerk to the appeal tribunal" means a clerk assigned to the appeal tribunal in accordance with regulation 7;
"decision notice" has the meaning given in regulation 18(1) and (2);
"financially qualified panel member" means a person appointed to the panel constituted under section 6 of the Act who satisfies the requirements of paragraph 4 of Schedule 3 to the Social Security and Child Support (Decisions and Appeals) Regulations 1999 (financial qualifications);
"legally qualified panel member" means a person appointed to the panel constituted under section 6 of the Act who satisfies the requirements of paragraph 1 of Schedule 3 to the Social Security and Child Support (Decisions and Appeals) Regulations 1999 (legal qualifications);
"notification period" has the meaning given in regulation 3;
"party to the proceedings" means the Board and any person who brings an appeal;
"the President" means the President of appeal tribunals appointed under section 5 of the Act.

(4) In these Regulations any reference to the chairman of the appeal tribunal shall, in the case of an appeal tribunal which has only one member, include reference to that member.

GENERAL NOTE

Para. (3)—"the Board"
The functions of the Commissioners of Inland Revenue have been transferred to the Commissioners for Her Majesty's Revenue and Customs (Commissioners for Revenue and Customs Act 2005, s.5(2)(a)).

6.75

Service of notices or documents

2. Where by any provision of these Regulations—

6.76

(a) any notice or other document is required to be given or sent to the clerk to the appeal tribunal or to the Board, that notice or document shall be treated as having been so given or sent on the day that it is received by the clerk to the appeal tribunal or by the Board, and

(b) any notice or other document is required to be given or sent to any person other than the clerk to the appeal tribunal or the Board, that notice or document shall, if sent to that person's last known address, be treated as having been given or sent on the day that it was posted.

DEFINITIONS

"the Board"—see reg.1(3), but see also the note below.
"the clerk to the appeal tribunal"—*ibid*.

GENERAL NOTE

The functions of the Commissioners of Inland Revenue ("the Board") have been transferred to the Commissioners for Her Majesty's Revenue and Customs (Commissioners for Revenue and Customs Act 2005, s.5(2)(a)).

6.77

Disputes about notices of appeal

3. Where a dispute arises as to whether notice of an appeal was given to the Board within the period of thirty days specified in section 23(1) of the 2004 Act ("the notification period") the dispute shall be referred to, and be determined by, a legally qualified panel member.

DEFINITIONS

"the 2004 Act"—see reg.1(3).
"the Board"—*ibid.*, but see also the note below.
"legally qualified panel member"—*ibid.*

GENERAL NOTE

The functions of the Commissioners of Inland Revenue ("the Board") have been transferred to the Commissioners for Her Majesty's Revenue and Customs (Commissioners for Revenue and Customs Act 2005, s.5(2)(a)).

Late appeals

4.—(1) Where the conditions specified in paragraphs (2) to (8) are satisfied, an appeal may be brought within a period of one year after the expiration of the notification period.

(2) An application to bring a late appeal under this regulation shall be made in writing, signed by or on behalf of the appellant and sent to the Board and it shall include sufficient information to determine—
  (a) the identity of the appellant;
  (b) whether the appellant is a relevant person within the meaning of section 22(3) of the 2004 Act or a personal representative of a child in accordance with section 22(5), if the appellant is appealing in either capacity;
  (c) the subject of the appeal to which the application relates;
  (d) the decision against which the appeal is being made; and
  (e) the grounds on which the applicant seeks time to appeal, including details of any relevant special circumstances for the purposes of paragraph (4).

(3) An application to bring a late appeal under this regulation shall be determined by a legally qualified panel member, except that where the Board consider that the conditions in paragraphs (4)(b) to (8) are satisfied, the Board may grant the application.

(4) An application to bring a late appeal shall not be granted unless—
  (a) the panel member is satisfied that, if the application is granted, there are reasonable prospects that the appeal will be successful; or
  (b) the panel member is, or the Board are, satisfied that it is in the interests of justice for the application to be granted.

(5) For the purposes of paragraph (4) it is not in the interests of justice to grant an application unless the panel member is, or the Board are, as the case may be, satisfied that—
  (a) the special circumstances specified in paragraph (6) are relevant to the application; or
  (b) some other special circumstances exist which are wholly exceptional and relevant to the application,

and as a result of those special circumstances, it was not practicable for the appeal to be brought within the notification period.

(SI 2005/990, reg.4)

(6) For the purposes of paragraph (5)(a), the special circumstances are that—
  (a) the applicant or a partner or dependant of the applicant has died or suffered serious illness;
  (b) the applicant is not resident in the United Kingdom; or
  (c) normal postal services were disrupted.

(7) In determining whether it is in the interests of justice to grant the application, regard shall be had to the principle that the greater the amount of time that has elapsed between the expiration of the notification period and the making of the application to bring a late appeal, the more compelling should be the special circumstances on which the application is based.

(8) In determining whether it is in the interests of justice to grant an application, no account shall be taken of the following—
  (a) that the applicant or any person acting for him was unaware of or misunderstood the law applicable to his case (including ignorance or misunderstanding of the notification period); or
  (b) that a Social Security Commissioner or a court has taken a different view of the law from that previously understood and applied.

(9) An application under this regulation for a late appeal which has been refused may not be renewed.

(10) The panel member who determines an application under this regulation shall record a summary of his decision in such written form as has been approved by the President.

(11) As soon as practicable after the decision is made a copy of the decision shall be sent or given to every party to the proceedings.

DEFINITIONS

"the 2004 Act"—see reg.1(3).
"appeal"—*ibid.*
"the Board"—*ibid.*, but see also the note below.
"legally qualified panel member"—*ibid.*
"notification period"—*ibid.*
"party to the proceedings"—*ibid.*
"the President"—*ibid.*

GENERAL NOTE

See the note to reg.5 of the Tax Credit (Appeals) (No.2) Regulations 2002.   6.81
The functions of the Commissioners of Inland Revenue ("the Board") have been transferred to the Commissioners for Her Majesty's Revenue and Customs (Commissioners for Revenue and Customs Act 2005, s.5(2)(a)).

Death of a party to an appeal

5. In any proceedings relating to an appeal under section 22(2), (4), (5) or (6) of the 2004 Act, on the death of a party to the proceedings (other than the Board) the personal representative of the person who has died may represent him at any hearing.   6.82

DEFINITIONS

"the 2004 Act"—see reg.1(3).
"appeal"—*ibid.*
"the Board"—*ibid.*, but see also the note below.
"party to the proceedings"—*ibid.*

The Child Trust Funds (Appeals) Regulations 2005

General Note

6.83   The functions of the Commissioners of Inland Revenue ("the Board") have been transferred to the Commissioners for Her Majesty's Revenue and Customs (Commissioners for Revenue and Customs Act 2005, s.5(2)(a)).

Composition of appeal tribunals

6.84   **6.**—(1) Subject to paragraphs (2) and (3), an appeal tribunal for the purposes of these Regulations shall consist of one legally qualified panel member.

(2) An appeal tribunal shall consist of a financially qualified panel member and a legally qualified panel member where the appeal may require consideration by members of the appeal tribunal of financial issues which are, in the opinion of the President, difficult and which relate to the administration of a child trust fund.

(3) The President may determine that the appeal tribunal shall include such an additional member drawn from the panel constituted under section 6 of the Act as he considers appropriate for the purposes of providing further experience for that additional panel member or for assisting the President in the monitoring of standards of decision making by panel members.

Definitions

"appeal"—see reg.1(3).
"appeal tribunal"—see s.39(1) of the Social Security Act 1998, as applied by reg.14 of the Child Trust Funds (Non-tax Appeals) Regulations 2005.
"financially qualified panel member"—see reg.1(3).
"legally qualified panel member"—*ibid.*
"the President"—*ibid.*

Clerk to an appeal tribunal

6.85   **7.** For the purposes of an appeal the Secretary of State shall assign a clerk to service each appeal tribunal and the clerk so assigned shall be responsible for summoning members of the panel constituted under section 6 of the Act to serve on the tribunal.

Definitions

"the Act"—see reg.1(3).
"appeal tribunal"—see s.39(1) of the Social Security Act 1998, as applied by reg.14 of the Child Trust Funds (Non-tax Appeals) Regulations 2005.

Consideration and determination of appeals

6.86   **8.**—(1) The procedure in connection with the consideration and determination of an appeal shall, subject to the following provisions of these Regulations, be such as a legally qualified panel member shall determine.

(2) A legally qualified panel member may give directions requiring a party to the proceedings to comply with any provision of these Regulations and may at any stage of the proceedings, either of his own motion or on a written application made to the clerk to the appeal tribunal by any party to the proceedings, give such directions as he may consider necessary or desirable for

the just, effective and efficient conduct of the proceedings and may direct any party to the proceedings to provide such particulars or to produce such documents as may be reasonably required.

(3) Where a clerk to the appeal tribunal is authorised to take steps in relation to the procedure of the tribunal he may give directions requiring any party to the proceedings to comply with any provision of these Regulations.

DEFINITIONS

"appeal"—see reg.1(3).
"the clerk to the appeal tribunal"—*ibid*.
"legally qualified panel member"—*ibid*.
"party to the proceedings"—*ibid*.

GENERAL NOTE

See the note to reg.11 of the Tax Credits (Appeals) (No.2) Regulations 2002. If an appellant is given due warning, an appeal may be struck out under reg.13(1)(b) for failure to comply with a direction.

6.87

Choice of hearing

9.—(1) Where an appeal is made to an appeal tribunal the appellant and any other party to the proceedings shall notify the clerk to the appeal tribunal, on a form approved by the Secretary of State, whether he wishes to have an oral hearing or whether he is content for the appeal to proceed without an oral hearing.

6.88

(2) The form shall include a statement informing the appellant that, if he does not notify the clerk to the appeal tribunal as required by paragraph (1) within the period specified in paragraph (3), the appeal may be struck out in accordance with regulation 13(1).

(3) Notification in accordance with paragraph (1)—
  (a) if given by the appellant, must be given or sent to the clerk to the appeal tribunal within 14 days of the date on which the form is issued to him; or
  (b) if given by the Board, must be given or sent to the clerk to the appeal tribunal within 14 days of the date on which the form is issued to the appellant,
or within such longer period as the clerk may direct.

(4) Where an oral hearing is requested in accordance with paragraphs (1) and (3) the appeal tribunal shall hold an oral hearing unless the appeal is struck out under regulation 13(1).

(5) The chairman of the appeal tribunal may of his own motion direct that an oral hearing of the appeal be held if he is satisfied that such a hearing is necessary to enable the appeal tribunal to reach a decision.

DEFINITIONS

"appeal"—see reg.1(3).
"appeal tribunal"—see s.39(1) of the Social Security Act 1998, as applied by reg.14 of the Child Trust Funds (Non-tax Appeals) Regulations 2005.
"the Board"—see reg.1(3), but see also the note below.
"the clerk to the appeal tribunal"—*ibid*.
"party to the proceedings"—*ibid*.

GENERAL NOTE

6.89 See the note to reg.12 of the Tax Credits (Appeals) (No.2) Regulations 2002.
The functions of the Commissioners of Inland Revenue ("the Board") have been transferred to the Commissioners for Her Majesty's Revenue and Customs (Commissioners for Revenue and Customs Act 2005, s.5(2)(a)).

Withdrawal of appeal

6.90 **10.**—(1) At any time before an appeal is determined it may be withdrawn by the appellant either—
  (a) at an oral hearing; or
  (b) by giving notice in writing of withdrawal to the clerk to the appeal tribunal.

(2) If an appeal is withdrawn in accordance with paragraph (1)(a), the clerk to the appeal tribunal shall send a notice in writing to any party to the proceedings who is not present when the appeal is withdrawn informing him that the appeal has been withdrawn.

(3) If an appeal is withdrawn in accordance with paragraph (1)(b), the clerk to the appeal tribunal shall send a notice in writing to every party to the proceedings informing him that the appeal has been withdrawn.

DEFINITIONS

"appeal"—see reg.1(3).
"the clerk to the appeal tribunal"—*ibid*.
"party to the proceedings"—*ibid*.

GENERAL NOTE

6.91 See the note to reg.13 of the Tax Credits (Appeals) (No.2) Regulations 2002.

Summoning of witnesses and administration of oaths

6.92 **11.**—(1) The chairman of the appeal tribunal may by summons, or in Scotland, by citation, require any person in Great Britain to attend as a witness at a hearing of an appeal at such time and place as shall be specified in the summons or citation and, subject to paragraph (2), at the hearing to answer any question or produce any documents in his custody or under his control which relate to any matter in question in that appeal but—
  (a) no person shall be required to attend in obedience to such summons or citation unless he has been given at least 14 days' notice of the hearing or, if less than 14 days' notice is given, he has informed the tribunal that the notice given is sufficient; and
  (b) no person shall be required to attend and give evidence or to produce any document in obedience to such summons or citation unless the necessary expenses of attendance are paid or tendered to him.

(2) No person shall be compelled to give any evidence or produce any document or other material that he could not be compelled to give or produce on a trial of an action in a court of law in that part of Great Britain where the hearing takes place.

(3) In exercising the powers conferred by this regulation, the chairman of the appeal tribunal shall take into account the need to protect any matter

(SI 2005/990, reg.11)

that relates to intimate personal or financial circumstances, is commercially sensitive, consists of information communicated or obtained in confidence or concerns national security.

(4) Every summons or citation issued under this regulation shall contain a statement to the effect that the person in question may apply in writing to a legally qualified panel member to vary or set aside the summons or citation.

(5) The chairman of the appeal tribunal may require any witness, including a witness summoned under the powers conferred by this regulation, to give evidence on oath or affirmation and for that purpose there may be administered an oath or affirmation in due form.

DEFINITIONS

"appeal"—see reg.1(3).
"appeal tribunal"—see s.39(1) of the Social Security Act 1998, as applied by reg.14 of the Child Trust Funds (Non-tax Appeals) Regulations 2005.

GENERAL NOTE

See the note to reg.15 of the Tax Credits (Appeals) (No.2) Regulations 2002. 6.93

Confidentiality in appeals

12.—(1) In the circumstances prescribed in paragraph (2), for the purposes of paragraph 7 of Schedule 1 to the Act (confidentiality), in an appeal the prescribed material is— 6.94
  (a) the address of the eligible child within the meaning of section 2 of the 2004 Act and, in relation to an appeal under of 22(2) of that Act, the address of any relevant person within the meaning of section 22(3); and
  (b) information the use of which could reasonably be expected to lead to the location of any person specified in sub-paragraph (a).

(2) Paragraph (1) applies where a relevant person within the meaning of section 22(3) of the 2004 Act, or a local authority with parental responsibility within the meaning of section 3(9) of that Act in relation to the eligible child, notifies the Board—
  (a) when notice of appeal is given to the Board under section 23(1) of that Act; or
  (b) in response to an enquiry by the Board if notification is within 14 days of the enquiry,
that he or it would like the information specified in paragraph (1) to remain confidential.

DEFINITIONS

"the 2004 Act"—see reg.1(3).
"appeal"—*ibid*.
"the Board"—*ibid*., but see also the note below.

GENERAL NOTE

The functions of the Commissioners of Inland Revenue ("the Board") have been transferred to the Commissioners for Her Majesty's Revenue and Customs (Commissioners for Revenue and Customs Act 2005, s.5(2)(a)). 6.95

Appeals which may be struck out

6.96 **13.**—(1) Subject to paragraphs (2) and (3), an appeal may be struck out by the clerk to the appeal tribunal—
  (a) for want of prosecution including an appeal not made within the time specified in section 23(1) of the 2004 Act and regulation 4;
  (b) for failure of the appellant to comply with a direction given under these Regulations where the appellant has been notified that failure to comply with the direction could result in the appeal being struck out; or
  (c) for failure of the appellant to notify the clerk to the appeal tribunal, in accordance with regulation 9, whether or not he wishes to have an oral hearing of his appeal.

(2) Where the clerk to the appeal tribunal determines to strike out the appeal, he shall notify the appellant that his appeal has been struck out and of the procedure for reinstatement of the appeal as specified in regulation 14.

(3) The clerk to the appeal tribunal may refer any matter for determination under this regulation to a legally qualified panel member for decision by the panel member rather than the clerk to the appeal tribunal.

Definitions

"the 2004 Act"—see reg.1(3).
"appeal"—*ibid*.
"the clerk to the appeal tribunal"—*ibid*.
"legally qualified panel member"—*ibid*.

Reinstatement of struck out appeals

6.97 **14.**—(1) The clerk to the appeal tribunal may reinstate an appeal which has been struck out in accordance with regulation 13(1)(c) where—
  (a) the appellant has made representations to him or, as the case may be, further representations in support of his case with reasons why he considers that his appeal should not have been struck out;
  (b) the representations are made in writing within one month of the order to strike out the appeal being issued; and
  (c) the clerk is satisfied in the light of those representations that there are reasonable grounds for reinstating the appeal,
but if the clerk is not satisfied that there are reasonable grounds for reinstatement a legally qualified panel member shall consider whether the appeal should be reinstated in accordance with paragraph (2).

(2) A legally qualified panel member may reinstate an appeal which has been struck out in accordance with regulation 13 where—
  (a) the appellant has made representations or, as the case may be, further representations in support of his case with reasons why he considers that his appeal should not have been struck out, to the clerk to the appeal tribunal, in writing within one month of the order to strike out the appeal being issued, and the panel member is satisfied in the light of those representations that there are reasonable grounds for reinstating the appeal;
  (b) the panel member is satisfied that the appeal is not an appeal which may be struck out under regulation 13; or
  (c) the panel member is satisfied that notwithstanding that the appeal is one which may be struck out under regulation 13, it is not in the interests of justice for the appeal to be struck out.

(SI 2005/990, reg.14)

DEFINITIONS

"appeal"—see reg.1(3).
"the clerk to the appeal tribunal"—*ibid*.
"legally qualified panel member"—*ibid*.

Procedure at oral hearings

15.—(1) Subject to regulations 16, 17 and 20, the procedure for an oral hearing shall be such as the chairman of the appeal tribunal shall determine.

(2) Except where paragraph (4) applies, not less than 14 days' notice (beginning with the day on which notice is given and ending on the day before the hearing of the appeal is to take place) of the time and place of any oral hearing of an appeal shall be given to every party to the proceedings.

(3) If such notice has not been given to a person to whom it should have been given under the provisions of paragraph (2) the hearing may proceed only with the consent of that person.

(4) Any party to the proceedings may waive his right under paragraph (2) to receive not less than 14 days' notice of the time and place of any oral hearing by giving notice to the clerk to the appeal tribunal.

(5) If a party to the proceedings to whom notice has been given under paragraph (2) fails to appear at the hearing the chairman of the appeal tribunal may, having regard to all the circumstances including any explanation offered for the absence—
   (a) proceed with the hearing notwithstanding his absence; or
   (b) give such directions with a view to the determination of the appeal as he may think proper.

(6) If a party to the proceedings has waived his right to be given notice under paragraph (2) the chairman of the appeal tribunal may proceed with the hearing notwithstanding his absence.

(7) An oral hearing of an appeal shall be in public except where the chairman of the appeal tribunal is satisfied that it is necessary to hold the hearing, or part of the hearing, in private—
   (a) in the interests of national security, morals, public order or children;
   (b) for the protection of private or family life of one or more parties to the proceedings; or
   (c) in special circumstances, because publicity would prejudice the interests of justice.

(8) At an oral hearing—
   (a) any party to the proceedings shall be entitled to be present and be heard; and
   (b) the following persons may be present by means of a live television link—
       (i) a party to the proceedings or his representative or both; or
       (ii) where an appeal tribunal consists of more than one member, a tribunal member other than the chairman,
provided that the chairman of the appeal tribunal gives permission.

(9) A person who has the right to be heard at a hearing may be accompanied and may be represented by another person whether having professional qualifications or not and, for the purposes of the proceedings at the hearing, any such representative shall have all the rights and powers to which the person whom he represents is entitled.

6.98

The Child Trust Funds (Appeals) Regulations 2005

(10) The following persons shall also be entitled to be present at an oral hearing (whether or not it is otherwise in private) but shall take no part in the proceedings—
   (a) the President;
   (b) any person undergoing training as a chairman or member of an appeal tribunal or as a clerk to an appeal tribunal;
   (c) any person acting on behalf of the President in the training or supervision of panel members or in the monitoring of standards of decision-making by panel members;
   (d) with the leave of the chairman of the appeal tribunal, any other person; and
   (e) a member of the Council on Tribunals or of the Scottish Committee of the Council on Tribunals.

(11) Nothing in paragraph (10) affects the rights of—
   (a) any person mentioned in sub-paragraphs (a) and (b) of that paragraph where he is sitting as a member of a tribunal or acting as its clerk; or
   (b) the clerk to the tribunal,
and nothing in this regulation prevents the presence at an oral hearing of any witness or of any person whom the chairman of the appeal tribunal permits to be present in order to assist the appeal tribunal or the clerk.

(12) Any person entitled to be heard at an oral hearing may address the tribunal, may give evidence, may call witnesses and may put questions directly to any other person called as a witness.

(13) For the purpose of arriving at its decision an appeal tribunal shall, and for the purpose of discussing any question of procedure may, notwithstanding anything contained in these Regulations, order all persons not being members of the tribunal, other than the person acting as clerk to the appeal tribunal, to withdraw from the hearing except that—
   (a) a member of the Council on Tribunals or of the Scottish Committee of the Council on Tribunals, the President or any other person mentioned in paragraph (10)(c); and
   (b) with the leave of the chairman of the appeal tribunal, any person mentioned in paragraph (10)(b) or (d),
may remain present at any such sitting.

(14) In this regulation "live television link" means a live television link or other facilities which allow a person who is not physically present at an oral hearing to see and hear proceedings and be seen and heard by those physically present.

DEFINITIONS

"appeal"—see reg.1(3).
"appeal tribunal"—see s.39(1) of the Social Security Act 1998, as applied by reg.14 of the Child Trust Funds (Non-tax Appeals) Regulations 2005.
"the clerk to the appeal tribunal"—see reg.1(3).
"live television link"—see para.(14).
"party to the proceedings"—see reg.1(3).
"the President"—*ibid.*

GENERAL NOTE

6.99   See the note to reg.18 of the Tax Credits (Appeals) (No.2) Regulations 2002.

(SI 2005/990, reg.16)

Manner of providing expert assistance

16.—(1) Where an appeal tribunal requires one or more experts to provide assistance to it in dealing with a question of fact of special difficulty under section 7(4) of the Act, such an expert shall, if the chairman of the appeal tribunal so requests, attend at the hearing and give evidence.

(2) If the chairman of the appeal tribunal considers it appropriate, the expert shall enquire into and provide a written report on the question to be dealt with in accordance with paragraph (1).

(3) A copy of any written report received from an expert in accordance with paragraph (2) shall be supplied to every party to the proceedings.

DEFINITIONS

"appeal tribunal"—see s.39(1) of the Social Security Act 1998, as applied by reg.14 of the Child Trust Funds (Non-tax Appeals) Regulations 2005.
"party to the proceedings"—see reg.1(3).

GENERAL NOTE

See the note to reg.19 of the Tax Credits (Appeals) (No.2) Regulations 2002.

Postponement and adjournment

17.—(1) Where a person to whom notice of an oral hearing is given wishes to request a postponement of that hearing he shall do so in writing to the clerk to the appeal tribunal stating his reasons for the request, and the clerk may grant or refuse the request as he thinks fit or may pass the request to a legally qualified panel member who may grant or refuse the request as he thinks fit.

(2) Where the clerk to the appeal tribunal or the panel member, as the case may be, refuses a request to postpone the hearing he shall—
  (a) notify in writing the person making the request of the refusal; and
  (b) place before the appeal tribunal at the hearing both the request for the postponement and notification of its refusal.

(3) A panel member or the clerk to the appeal tribunal may of his own motion at any time before the beginning of the hearing postpone the hearing.

(4) An oral hearing may be adjourned by the appeal tribunal at any time on the application of any party to the proceedings or of its own motion.

DEFINITIONS

"appeal tribunal"—see s.39(1) of the Social Security Act 1998, as applied by reg.14 of the Child Trust Funds (Non-tax Appeals) Regulations 2005.
"the clerk to the appeal tribunal"—see reg.1(3).
"legally qualified panel member"—*ibid*.
"party to the proceedings"—*ibid*.

GENERAL NOTE

See the note to reg.20 of the Tax Credits (Appeals) (No.2) Regulations 2002.

Decisions of appeal tribunals

18.—(1) Every decision of an appeal tribunal shall be recorded in summary by the chairman of the appeal tribunal and shall be referred to as a decision notice.

The Child Trust Funds (Appeals) Regulations 2005

(2) The decision notice specified in paragraph (1) shall be in such written form as shall have been approved by the President and shall be signed by the chairman of the appeal tribunal.

(3) As soon as may be practicable after an appeal has been decided by an appeal tribunal, a copy of the decision notice shall be sent or given to every party to the proceedings who shall also be informed of—

(a) his right under paragraph (4); and
(b) the conditions governing appeals to a Social Security Commissioner.

(4) Subject to paragraph (5), a party to the proceedings may apply in writing to the clerk to the appeal tribunal for a statement of the reasons for the tribunal's decision within one month of the sending or giving of the decision notice to every party to the proceedings or within such longer period as may be allowed in accordance with regulation 19.

(5) Where—

(a) the decision notice is corrected in accordance with regulation 21; or
(b) an application under regulation 22 for the decision to be set aside is refused for reasons other than a refusal to extend the time for making the application,

the period specified in paragraph (4) shall run from the date on which notice of the correction or the refusal of the application for setting aside is sent to the applicant.

(6) Following the application made under paragraph (4), the chairman of the appeal tribunal shall record a statement of the reasons and a copy of that statement shall be given or sent to every party to the proceedings as soon as may be practicable.

(7) If the decision is not unanimous, the decision notice specified in paragraph (1) shall record that one of the members dissented and the statement of reasons referred to in paragraph (6) shall include the reasons given by the dissenting member for dissenting.

DEFINITIONS

"appeal"—see reg.1(3).
"appeal tribunal"—see s.39(1) of the Social Security Act 1998, as applied by reg.14 of the Child Trust Funds (Non-tax Appeals) Regulations 2005.
"the clerk to the appeal tribunal"—see reg.1(3).
"decision notice"—*ibid*.
"party to the proceedings"—*ibid*.
"the President"—*ibid*.

GENERAL NOTE

6.105 See the note to reg.21 of the Tax Credits (Appeals) (No.2) Regulations 2002.

Late applications for statements of reasons of tribunal decisions

6.106 **19.**—(1) The time for making an application for the statement of reasons for an appeal tribunal's decision may be extended where the conditions specified in paragraphs (2) to (8) are satisfied, but, subject to regulation 18(5), no application shall in any event be brought more than three months after the date of the sending or giving of the notice of the decision of the appeal tribunal.

(2) An application for an extension of time under this regulation shall be made in writing and shall be determined by a legally qualified panel member.

(3) An application under this regulation shall contain particulars of the grounds on which the extension of time is sought, including details of any relevant special circumstances for the purposes of paragraph (4).

(4) The application for an extension of time shall not be granted unless the panel member is satisfied that it is in the interests of justice for the application to be granted.

(5) For the purposes of paragraph (4) it is not in the interests of justice to grant the application unless the panel member is satisfied that—
  (a) the special circumstances specified in paragraph (6) are relevant to the application; or
  (b) some other special circumstances are relevant to the application,
and as a result of those special circumstances it was not practicable for the application to be made within the time limit specified in regulation 18(4).

(6) For the purposes of paragraph (5)(a), the special circumstances are that—
  (a) the applicant or a partner or dependant of the applicant has died or suffered serious illness;
  (b) the applicant is not resident in the United Kingdom; or
  (c) normal postal services were disrupted.

(7) In determining whether it is in the interests of justice to grant the application, the panel member shall have regard to the principle that the greater the amount of time that has elapsed between the expiration of the time within which the application for a copy of the statement of reasons for a tribunal's decision is to be made and the making of the application for an extension of time, the more compelling should be the special circumstances on which the application is based.

(8) In determining whether it is in the interests of justice to grant the application, no account shall be taken of the following—
  (a) that the person making the application or any person acting for him was unaware of, or misunderstood, the law applicable to his case (including ignorance or misunderstanding of the time limits imposed by these Regulations); or
  (b) that a Social Security Commissioner or a court has taken a different view of the law from that previously understood and applied.

(9) An application under this regulation for an extension of time which has been refused may not be renewed.

(10) The panel member who determines an application under this regulation shall record a summary of his determination in such written form as has been approved by the President.

(11) As soon as practicable after the determination is made, notice of the determination shall be sent or given to every party to the proceedings.

(12) Any person who under paragraph (11) receives notice of the determination may, within one month of the determination being sent to him, apply in writing for a copy of the reasons for that determination and a copy shall be supplied to him.

DEFINITIONS

"appeal tribunal"—see s.39(1) of the Social Security Act 1998, as applied by reg.14 of the Child Trust Funds (Non-tax Appeals) Regulations 2005.
"legally qualified panel member"—see reg.1(3).
"party to the proceedings"—*ibid.*
"the President"—*ibid.*

GENERAL NOTE

6.107 See the note to reg.22 of the Tax Credits (Appeals) (No.2) Regulations 2002.

Record of tribunal proceedings

6.108 **20.**—(1) A record of the proceedings at an oral hearing, which is sufficient to indicate the evidence taken, shall be made by the chairman of the appeal tribunal in such medium as he may direct.
(2) The clerk to the appeal tribunal shall preserve—
(a) the record of proceedings;
(b) the decision notice; and
(c) any statement of the reasons for the tribunal's decision,
for the period specified in paragraph (3).
(3) That period is six months from the date of—
(a) the decision made by the appeal tribunal;
(b) any statement of reasons for the tribunal's decision;
(c) any correction of the decision in accordance with regulation 21;
(d) any refusal to set aside the decision in accordance with regulation 22; or
(e) any determination of an application under regulation 25 for leave to appeal against the decision,
or until those documents are sent to the office of the Social Security Commissioners in connection with an appeal against the decision, or an application to a Social Security Commissioner for leave to appeal, if either occurs within the six months.
(4) Any party to the proceedings may within the period specified in paragraph (3) apply in writing for a copy of the record of proceedings and a copy shall be supplied to him.

DEFINITIONS

"appeal tribunal"—see s.39(1) of the Social Security Act 1998, as applied by reg.14 of the Child Trust Funds (Non-tax Appeals) Regulations 2005.
"the clerk to the appeal tribunal"—see reg.1(3).
"decision notice"—*ibid.*
"party to the proceedings"—*ibid.*

GENERAL NOTE

6.109 See the note to reg.23 of the Tax Credits (Appeals) (No.2) Regulations 2002.

Correction of accidental errors

6.110 **21.**—(1) The clerk to the appeal tribunal or a legally qualified panel member may at any time correct accidental errors in the notice of any decision of an appeal tribunal made under the 2004 Act.
(2) A correction made to a decision notice shall be deemed to be part of the decision notice and written notice of it shall be given as soon as practicable to every party to the proceedings.

DEFINITIONS

"the 2004 Act"—see reg.1(3).
"appeal tribunal"—see s.39(1) of the Social Security Act 1998, as applied by reg.14 of the Child Trust Funds (Non-tax Appeals) Regulations 2005.
"the clerk to the appeal tribunal"—see reg.1(3).

"decision notice"—*ibid*.
"legally qualified panel member"—*ibid*.
"party to the proceedings"—*ibid*.

GENERAL NOTE

See the note to reg.24 of the Tax Credits (Appeals) (No.2) Regulations 2002.

Setting aside decisions on certain grounds

22.—(1) On an application made by a party to the proceedings, a decision of an appeal tribunal made on an appeal may be set aside by a legally qualified panel member in a case where it appears just to set the decision aside on the ground that—
   (a) a document relating to the proceedings in which the decision was made was not sent to, or was not received at an appropriate time by, a party to the proceedings or the party's representative or was not received at an appropriate time by the person who made the decision;
   (b) a party to the proceedings in which the decision was made or the party's representative was not present at a hearing relating to the proceedings.
(2) In determining whether it is just to set aside a decision on the ground set out in paragraph (1)(b), the panel member shall determine whether the party making the application gave notice that he wished to have an oral hearing, and if that party did not give such notice the decision shall not be set aside unless that member is satisfied that the interests of justice manifestly so require.
(3) An application under this regulation shall—
   (a) be made within one month of the date on which—
      (i) a copy of the decision notice is sent or given to the parties to the proceedings in accordance with regulation 18(3); or
      (ii) the statement of the reasons for the decision is given or sent in accordance with regulation 18(6),
      whichever is the later;
   (b) be in writing and signed by a party to the proceedings or, where the party has provided written authority to a representative to act on his behalf, that representative;
   (c) contain particulars of the grounds on which it is made; and
   (d) be sent to the clerk to the appeal tribunal.
(4) Where an application to set aside a decision is entertained under paragraph (1), every party to the proceedings shall be sent a copy of the application and shall be afforded a reasonable opportunity of making representations on it before the application is determined.
(5) Where a legally qualified panel member refuses to set aside a decision he may treat the application to set aside the decision as an application under regulation 18(4) for a statement of the reasons for the tribunal's decision, subject to the time limits set out in regulation 18(4) and (5).
(6) Notice in writing of a determination on an application to set aside a decision shall be sent or given to every party to the proceedings as soon as may be practicable and the notice shall contain a statement giving the reasons for the determination.
(7) The time within which an application under this regulation must be made may be extended by a period not exceeding one year where the conditions specified in paragraphs (8) to (12) are satisfied.

(8) An application for an extension of time shall be made in accordance with paragraph (3)(b) to (d), shall include details of any relevant special circumstances for the purposes of paragraph (10) and shall be determined by a legally qualified panel member.

(9) An application for an extension of time shall not be granted unless the panel member is satisfied that—
 (a) if the application is granted there are reasonable prospects that the application to set aside will be successful; and
 (b) it is in the interests of justice for the application for an extension of time to be granted.

(10) For the purposes of paragraph (9) it is not in the interests of justice to grant an application for an extension of time unless the panel member is satisfied that—
 (a) the special circumstances specified in paragraph (11) are relevant to the application; or
 (b) some other special circumstances exist which are wholly exceptional and relevant to that application,
and as a result of those special circumstances, it was not practicable for the application to set aside to be made within the time limit specified in paragraph (3)(a).

(11) For the purposes of paragraph (10)(a), the special circumstances are that—
 (a) the applicant or a partner or dependant of the applicant has died or suffered serious illness;
 (b) the applicant is not resident in the United Kingdom; or
 (c) normal postal services were disrupted.

(12) In determining whether it is in the interests of justice to grant an application for an extension of time, the panel member shall have regard to the principle that the greater the amount of time that has elapsed between the expiry of the time within which the application to set aside is to be made and the making of the application for an extension of time, the more compelling should be the special circumstances on which the application for an extension is based.

(13) An application under this regulation for an extension of time which has been refused may not be renewed.

DEFINITIONS

"appeal"—see reg.1(3).
"appeal tribunal"—see s.39(1) of the Social Security Act 1998, as applied by reg.14 of the Child Trust Funds (Non-tax Appeals) Regulations 2005.
"the clerk to the appeal tribunal"—see reg.1(3).
"decision notice"—*ibid*.
"legally qualified panel member"—*ibid*.
"party to the proceedings"—*ibid*.

GENERAL NOTE

6.113 See the note to reg.25 of the Tax Credits (Appeals) (No.2) Regulations 2002.

Provisions common to regulations 21 and 22

6.114 **23.**—(1) There shall be no appeal against a correction made under regulation 21 or a refusal to make such a correction or against a determination made under regulation 22.

(SI 2005/990, reg. 23)

(2) Nothing in regulation 21 or 22 shall be construed as derogating from any power to correct errors or set aside decisions which is exercisable apart from these Regulations.

Service of decision notice by electronic mail

24. For the purposes of the time limits in regulations 18 to 22, a properly addressed copy of a decision notice sent by electronic mail is effective from the date it is sent.

6.115

DEFINITION

"decision notice"—see reg.1(3).

Application for leave to appeal to a Commissioner from an appeal tribunal

25.—(1) Subject to paragraph (2), an application for leave to appeal to a Social Security Commissioner from a decision on an appeal shall—
   (a) be sent to the clerk to the appeal tribunal within the period of one month of the date of the applicant being sent a written statement of the reasons for the decision against which leave to appeal is sought;
   (b) be in writing and signed by the applicant or, where he has provided written authority to a representative to make the application on his behalf, by that representative;
   (c) contain particulars of the grounds on which the applicant intends to rely;
   (d) contain sufficient particulars of the decision of the appeal tribunal to enable the decision to be identified; and
   (e) if the application is made late, contain the grounds for seeking late acceptance.

6.116

(2) Where after the written statement of the reasons for the decision has been sent to the parties to the proceedings—
   (a) the decision notice is corrected in accordance with regulations 21; or
   (b) an application under regulation 22 for the decision to be set aside is refused for reasons other than a refusal to extend the time for making the application,
the period specified in paragraph (1)(a) shall run from the date on which notice of the correction or the refusal of the application for setting aside is sent to the applicant.

(3) Where an application for leave to appeal to a Social Security Commissioner is made by the Board, the clerk to an appeal tribunal shall, as soon as may be practicable, send a copy of the application to every other party to the proceedings.

(4) A person determining an application for leave to appeal to a Social Security Commissioner shall record his determination in writing and send a copy to every party to the proceedings.

(5) Where there has been a failure to apply for leave to appeal within the period of time specified in paragraph (1)(a) or (2) but an application is made within one year of the last date for making an application within that period, a legally qualified panel member may, if for special reasons he thinks fit, accept and proceed to consider and determine the application.

(6) Where an application for leave to appeal against a decision of an appeal tribunal is made—

(a) if the chairman of the appeal tribunal when the decision was given was a fee-paid legally qualified panel member, the application may be determined by a salaried legally qualified panel member; or
(b) if it is impracticable, or would be likely to cause undue delay, for the application to be determined by whoever was the chairman of the appeal tribunal when the decision was given, the application may be determined by another legally qualified panel member.

DEFINITIONS

"appeal"—see reg.1(3).
"appeal tribunal"—see s.39(1) of the Social Security Act 1998, as applied by reg.14 of the Child Trust Funds (Non-tax Appeals) Regulations 2005.
"the Board"—see reg.1(3), but see also the note below.
"the clerk to the appeal tribunal"—*ibid*.
"decision notice"—*ibid*.
"legally qualified panel member"—*ibid*.
"party to the proceedings"—*ibid*.

GENERAL NOTE

6.117

See the note to reg.27 of the Tax Credits (Appeals) (No.2) Regulations 2002.
The functions of the Commissioners of Inland Revenue ("the Board") have been transferred to the Commissioners for Her Majesty's Revenue and Customs (Commissioners for Revenue and Customs Act 2005, s.5(2)(a)).

The Social Security Commissioners (Procedure) (Child Trust Funds) Regulations 2005

(SI 2005/1031)

Made   24th March 2005
Coming into force in accordance with regulation 1(1)

ARRANGEMENT OF REGULATIONS

PART I

GENERAL PROVISIONS

6.118

1. Citation, commencement and duration
2. Interpretation
3. General powers of a Commissioner
4. Transfer of proceedings between Commissioners
5. Delegation of functions to authorised officers
6. Manner of and time for service of notices, etc.
7. Funding of legal services

(SI 2005/1031)

Part II

Applications for Leave to Appeal and Appeals

8. Application of this Part
9. Application to a Commissioner for leave to appeal
10. Notice of application to a Commissioner for leave to appeal
11. Determination of application
12. Notice of appeal
13. Time limit for appealing
14. Acknowledgement of a notice of appeal and notification to each respondent

Part III

Procedure

15. Representation
16. Respondent's written observations
17. Written observations in reply
18. Directions, further particulars and observations
19. Non-disclosure of medical evidence
20. Requests for hearings
21. Hearings
22. Summoning of witnesses
23. Withdrawal of applications for leave to appeal and appeals
24. Irregularities

Part IV

Decisions

25. Determinations and decisions of a Commissioner
26. Correction of accidental errors in decisions
27. Setting aside decisions on certain grounds
28. Provisions common to regulations 26 and 27

Part V

Applications for Leave to Appeal to the Appellate Court

29. Application to a Commissioner for leave to appeal to the Appellate Court

The Lord Chancellor, in exercise of the powers conferred upon him by sections 14, 15, 16, 28, 79(2) and 84 of, and Schedules 4 and 5 to, the Social Security Act 1998 as applied and modified by the Child Trust Funds (Non-tax Appeals) Regulations 2005, after consultation with the Scottish Ministers, and with the

The Social Security Commissioners (Child Trust Funds) Regs 2005

Council on Tribunals in accordance with section 8 of the Tribunals and Inquiries Act 1992, makes the following Regulations, a draft of which has, in accordance with section 80(1) of the Social Security Act 1998, been laid before and approved by resolution of each House of Parliament:

PART I

GENERAL PROVISIONS

Citation, commencement and duration

6.119   **1.**—(1) These Regulations may be cited as the Social Security Commissioners (Procedure) (Child Trust Funds) Regulations 2005 and shall come into force on the day after the day on which they are made.

(2) These Regulations shall cease to have effect on such day as is appointed by order made under section 24(1) of the Child Trust Funds Act 2004 (temporary modifications).

Interpretation

6.120   **2.** In these Regulations—

"the 1998 Act" means the Social Security Act 1998, as applied and modified by the Child Trust Funds (Non-tax Appeals) Regulations 2005;

"the 2004 Act" means the Child Trust Funds Act 2004;

"appeal" means an appeal which by virtue of section 24 of the 2004 Act is from an appeal tribunal to a Social Security Commissioner;

"appeal tribunal" means an appeal tribunal constituted under Chapter 1 of Part 1 of the Social Security Act 1998;

"authorised officer" means an officer authorised by the Lord Chancellor, or in Scotland by the Secretary of State, in accordance with paragraph 6 of Schedule 4 to the 1998 Act;

"chairman" means—
  (i) the person who was the chairman or the sole member of the appeal tribunal which gave the decision against which leave to appeal is being sought; or
  (ii) any other person authorised to deal with applications for leave to appeal to a Commissioner against that decision under section 14(10)(a) of the 1998 Act;

"funding notice" means the notice or letter from the Legal Services Commission confirming that legal services are to be funded;

"legal aid certificate" means the certificate issued by the Scottish Legal Aid Board confirming that legal services are to be funded;

"legally qualified" means being a solicitor or barrister, or in Scotland, a solicitor or advocate;

"Legal Services Commission" means the Legal Services Commission established under section 1 of the Access to Justice Act 1999;

"live television link" means a television link or other audio and video facilities which allow a person who is not physically present at an oral hearing to see and hear proceedings and be seen and heard by all others who are present (whether physically present or otherwise);

"office" means an Office of the Social Security Commissioners;
"party" means a party to the proceedings;
"penalty appeal" means an appeal against a decision under section 21 of the 2004 Act which by virtue of section 24(2) of that Act lies to a Commissioner;
"proceedings" means any proceedings before a Commissioner, whether by way of an application for leave to appeal to, or from, a Commissioner, or by way of an appeal, or otherwise;
"respondent" means—
  (i) any party to the appeal other than the applicant or appellant;
  (ii) any other person taking part in the proceedings at the direction or with the leave of a Commissioner;
"Scottish Legal Aid Board" means the Scottish Legal Aid Board established under section 1 of the Legal Aid (Scotland) Act 1986;
"summons", in relation to Scotland, corresponds to "citation" and regulation 22 shall be construed accordingly.

General powers of a Commissioner

3.—(1) Subject to the provisions of these Regulations, a Commissioner may adopt any procedure in relation to proceedings before him.

(2) A Commissioner may—
(a) extend or abridge any time limit under these Regulations (including, subject to regulations 9(3) and 13(3), granting an extension where the time limit has expired);
(b) expedite, postpone or adjourn any proceedings.

(3) Subject to paragraph (4), a Commissioner may, on or without the application of a party, strike out any proceedings for want of prosecution or abuse of process.

(4) Before making an order under paragraph (3), the Commissioner shall send notice to the party against whom it is proposed that it should be made giving him an opportunity to make representations why it should not be made.

(5) A Commissioner may, on application by the party concerned, give leave to reinstate any proceedings which have been struck out in accordance with paragraph (3) and, on giving leave, he may give directions as to the conduct of the proceedings.

(6) Nothing in these Regulations shall affect any power which is exercisable apart from these Regulations.

DEFINITIONS

"Commissioner"—see s.39(1) of the Social Security Act 1998, as applied by reg.14 of the Child Trust Funds (Non-tax Appeals) Regulations 2005.
"party"—see reg.2.
"proceedings"—*ibid.*

Transfer of proceedings between Commissioners

4. If it becomes impractical or inexpedient for a Commissioner to continue to deal with proceedings which are or have been before him, any other Commissioner may rehear or deal with those proceedings and any related matters.

Definitions

"Commissioner"—see s.39(1) of the Social Security Act 1998, as applied by reg.14 of the Child Trust Funds (Non-tax Appeals) Regulations 2005.
"proceedings"—*ibid*.

Delegation of functions to authorised officers

6.123   **5.**—(1) The following functions of the Commissioners may be exercised by legally qualified authorised officers, to be known as legal officers to the Commissioners—

(a) postponing a hearing under regulation 3;
(b) extending or abridging time, directing expedition, giving notices, striking out and reinstating proceedings under regulation 3;
(c) giving directions under regulation 6;
(d) giving directions under regulation 18;
(e) determining requests for or directing hearings under regulation 20;
(f) summoning witnesses, and setting aside a summons made by a legal officer, under regulation 22;
(g) giving leave to withdraw or reinstate applications or appeals under regulation 23;
(h) waiving irregularities under regulation 24 in connection with any matter being dealt with by a legal officer.

(2) Any party may, within 14 days of being sent notice of the direction or order of a legal officer, make a written request to a Commissioner asking him to reconsider the matter and confirm or replace the direction or order with his own, but, unless ordered by a Commissioner, a request shall not stop proceedings under the direction or order.

Definitions

"appeal"—see reg.2.
"authorised officer"—*ibid*.
"Commissioner"—see s.39(1) of the Social Security Act 1998, as applied by reg.14 of the Child Trust Funds (Non-tax Appeals) Regulations 2005.
"legally qualified"—see reg.2.
"party"—*ibid*.
"proceedings"—*ibid*.
"summons"—*ibid*.

Manner of and time for service of notices, etc.

6.124   **6.**—(1) A notice to or document for any party shall be deemed duly served if it is—

(a) delivered to him personally;
(b) properly addressed and sent to him by prepaid post at the address last notified by him for this purpose, or to his ordinary address;
(c) subject to paragraph (2), sent by e-mail; or
(d) served in any other manner a Commissioner may direct.

(2) A document may be served by e-mail on any party if the recipient has informed the person sending the e-mail in writing—

(a) that he is willing to accept service by e-mail;
(b) of the e-mail address to which the documents should be sent; and
(c) if the recipient wishes to so specify, the electronic format in which documents must be sent.

(SI 2005/1031, reg.6)

(3) A notice to or other document for a Commissioner shall be—
(a) delivered to the office in person;
(b) sent to the office by prepaid post;
(c) sent to the office by fax; or
(d) where the office has given written permission in advance, sent to the office by email.

(4) For the purposes of any time limit, a properly addressed notice or other document sent by prepaid post, fax or e-mail is effective from the date it is sent.

DEFINITIONS

"Commissioner"—see s.39(1) of the Social Security Act 1998, as applied by reg.14 of the Child Trust Funds (Non-tax Appeals) Regulations 2005.
"office"—see reg.2.
"party"—*ibid*.

Funding of legal services

7. If a party is granted funding of legal services at any time, he shall—   6.125
(a) where funding is granted by the Legal Services Commission, send a copy of the funding notice to the office;
(b) where funding is granted by the Scottish Legal Aid Board, send a copy of the legal aid certificate to the office; and
(c) notify every other party that funding has been granted.

DEFINITIONS

"funding notice"–see reg.2.
"legal aid certificate"—*ibid*.
"Legal Services Commission"—*ibid*.
"office"—*ibid*.
"party"—*ibid*.
"Scottish Legal Aid Board"—*ibid*.

GENERAL NOTE

See the note to reg.6A of the Social Security Commissioners (Procedure) (Tax   6.126
Credits Appeals) Regulations 2002.

PART II

APPLICATIONS FOR LEAVE TO APPEAL AND APPEALS

Application of this Part

8. In this Part—   6.127
(a) regulations 9, 10, and 11 apply to appeals other than penalty appeals;
(b) regulations 12, 13 and 14 apply to all appeals.

DEFINITIONS

"appeal"—see reg.2.
"penalty appeal"—*ibid*.

857

Application to a Commissioner for leave to appeal

6.128

9.—(1) An application to a Commissioner for leave to appeal against the decision of an appeal tribunal may be made only where the applicant has sought to obtain leave from the chairman and leave has been refused or the application has been rejected.

(2) Subject to paragraph (3) an application to a Commissioner shall be made within one month of notice of the refusal or rejection being sent to the applicant by the appeal tribunal.

(3) A Commissioner may for special reasons accept a late application or an application where the applicant failed to seek leave from the chairman within the specified time, but did so on or before the final date.

(4) In paragraph (3) the final date means the end of a period of 13 months from the date on which the decision of the appeal tribunal or, if later, any separate statement of the reasons for it, was sent to the applicant by the appeal tribunal.

DEFINITIONS

"appeal tribunal"—see reg.2.
"chairman"—*ibid.*
"Commissioner"—see s.39(1) of the Social Security Act 1998, as applied by reg.14 of the Child Trust Funds (Non-tax Appeals) Regulations 2005.
"final date"—see para.(4).

GENERAL NOTE

6.129

See the note to reg.7 of the Social Security Commissioners (Procedure) (Tax Credits Appeals) Regulations 2002.

Notice of application to a Commissioner for leave to appeal

6.130

10.—(1) An application to a Commissioner for leave to appeal shall be made by notice in writing, and shall contain—
(a) the name and address of the applicant;
(b) the grounds on which the applicant intends to rely;
(c) if the application is made late, the grounds for seeking late acceptance; and
(d) an address for sending notices and other documents to the applicant.

(2) The notice in paragraph (1) shall have with it copies of—
(a) the decision against which leave to appeal is sought;
(b) if separate, the written statement of the appeal tribunal's reasons for it; and
(c) the notice of refusal or rejection sent to the applicant by the appeal tribunal.

(3) Where an application for leave to appeal is made by the Board, it shall send each respondent a copy of the notice of application and any documents sent with it when they are sent to the Commissioner.

DEFINITIONS

"appeal tribunal"—see reg.2.
"the Board"—see s.39(1) of the Social Security Act 1998, as applied by reg.14 of the Child Trust Funds (Non-tax Appeals) Regulations 2005, but see also the note below.
"Commissioner"—*ibid.*

(SI 2005/1031, reg.10)

GENERAL NOTE

See the note to reg.8 of the Social Security Commissioners (Procedure) (Tax Credits Appeals) Regulations 2002.

The functions of the Commissioners of Inland Revenue ("the Board") have been transferred to the Commissioners for Her Majesty's Revenue and Customs (Commissioners for Revenue and Customs Act 2005, s.5(2)(a)).

6.131

Determination of application

11.—(1) The office shall send written notice to the applicant and each respondent of the determination of an application for leave to appeal to a Commissioner.

6.132

(2) Subject to a direction by a Commissioner, on an application under regulation 9—
   (a) notice of appeal shall be deemed to have been sent on the date when notice of the determination is sent to the applicant; and
   (b) the notice of application shall be deemed to be a notice of appeal sent under regulation 12.

(3) If a Commissioner grants an application for leave to appeal he may, with the consent of the applicant and each respondent, treat and determine the application as an appeal.

DEFINITIONS

"appeal"—see reg.2.
"Commissioner"—see s.39(1) of the Social Security Act 1998, as applied by reg.14 of the Child Trust Funds (Non-tax Appeals) Regulations 2005.
"office"—*ibid*.
"respondent"—*ibid*.

Notice of appeal

12.—(1) Subject to regulation 11(2), an appeal shall be made by notice in writing and shall contain—
   (a) the name and address of the appellant;
   (b) where applicable, the date on which the appellant was notified that leave to appeal had been granted;
   (c) the grounds on which the appellant intends to rely;
   (d) if the appeal is made late, the grounds for seeking late acceptance; and
   (e) an address for sending notices and other documents to the appellant.

6.133

(2) The notice in paragraph (1) shall have with it copies of—
   (a) the notice informing the appellant that leave to appeal has been granted;
   (b) the decision against which leave to appeal has been granted;
   (c) if separate, the written statement of the appeal tribunal's reasons for it.

DEFINITIONS

"appeal"—see reg.2.
"appeal tribunal"—*ibid*.

GENERAL NOTE

As reg.11(2) is almost invariably applied when a Commissioner grants leave, this regulation usually applies only to penalty appeals.

6.134

Time limit for appealing

13.—(1) In the case of a penalty appeal, the notice of appeal shall not be valid unless it is sent to a Commissioner within one month of the decision of the appeal tribunal being sent to the applicant.

(2) For all other appeals, a notice of appeal shall not be valid unless it is sent to a Commissioner within one month of the date on which the appellant was sent written notice that leave to appeal had been granted.

(3) A Commissioner may for special reasons accept late notice of appeal.

DEFINITIONS

"appeal"—see reg.2.
"appeal tribunal"—*ibid.*
"Commissioner"—see s.39(1) of the Social Security Act 1998, as applied by reg.14 of the Child Trust Funds (Non-tax Appeals) Regulations 2005.
"penalty appeal"—see reg.2.

GENERAL NOTE

Para. (1)
In his *Practice Memorandum No.6*, the Chief Social Security Commissioner states that, where, either on the tribunal's own initiative or following a request made within the time allowed by regs 18(4) and 19 of the Child Trust Funds (Appeals) Regulations 2005, a statement of reasons for a tribunal's decision is sent to the appellant separately from the decision notice, the statement of reasons will be treated as "the decision of the appeal tribunal" for the purposes of the time limit for appealing in penalty proceedings.

Para. (2)
In practice, this paragraph applies only when a tribunal chairman has granted leave to appeal, because a person granted leave to appeal by a Commissioner is almost invariably deemed to have appealed under reg.11(2).

Acknowledgement of a notice of appeal and notification to each respondent

14. The office shall send—
(a) to the appellant, an acknowledgement of the receipt of the notice of appeal;
(b) to each respondent, a copy of the notice of appeal.

DEFINITIONS

"appeal"—see reg.2.
"office"—*ibid.*
"respondent"—*ibid.*

(SI 2005/1031, reg.15)

Part III

Procedure

Representation

15. A party may conduct his case himself (with assistance from any person if he wishes) or be represented by any person whom he may appoint for the purpose.

6.138

Definition

"party"—see reg.2.

General Note

See the note to reg.13 of the Social Security Commissioners (Procedure) (Tax Credits Appeals) Regulations 2002.

6.139

Respondent's written observations

16.—(1) A respondent may submit to a Commissioner written observations on an appeal within one month of being sent written notice of it.

(2) Written observations shall include—
  (a) the respondent's name and address and address for sending documents;
  (b) a statement as to whether or not he opposes the appeal; and
  (c) the grounds upon which the respondent proposes to rely.

(3) The office shall send a copy of any written observations from a respondent to every other party.

(4) Where there is more than one respondent, the order of and time for written observations shall be as directed by a Commissioner under regulation 18.

6.140

Definitions

"appeal"—see reg.2.
"Commissioner"—see s.39(1) of the Social Security Act 1998, as applied by reg.14 of the Child Trust Funds (Non-tax Appeals) Regulations 2005.
"office"—see reg.2.
"party"—*ibid*.
"respondent"—*ibid*.

General Note

See the note to reg.15 of the Social Security Commissioners (Procedure) (Tax Credits Appeals) Regulations 2002.

6.141

Written observations in reply

17.—(1) Any party may submit to a Commissioner written observations in reply within one month of being sent written observations under regulation 16.

(2) The office shall send a copy of any written observations in reply to every other party.

6.142

(3) In the case of an appeal other than a penalty appeal, where—
(a) written observations have been received under regulation 16; and
(b) each of the Board and the appellant expresses the view that the decision appealed against was erroneous in point of law,
a Commissioner may make an order under section 14(7) of the 1998 Act setting aside the decision and may dispense with the procedure in paragraphs (1) and (2).

DEFINITIONS

"the 1998 Act"—see reg.2.
"appeal"—*ibid*.
"the Board"—see s.39(1) of the Social Security Act 1998, as applied by reg.14 of the Child Trust Funds (Non-tax Appeals) Regulations 2005, but see also the note below.
"Commissioner"—*ibid*.
"office"—see reg.2.
"party"—*ibid*.
"penalty appeal"—*ibid*.

GENERAL NOTE

6.143 See the note to reg.15 of the Social Security Commissioners (Procedure) (Tax Credits Appeals) Regulations 2002.

Directions, further particulars and observations

6.144 **18.**—(1) Subject to paragraph (2), where a Commissioner considers that an application or appeal made to him gives insufficient particulars to enable the question at issue to be determined, he may direct the party making the application or appeal, or any respondent, to furnish any further particulars which may reasonably be required.

(2) No person shall be compelled to give any evidence or produce any document or other material that he could not be compelled to give or produce on a trial of an action in a court of law in that part of Great Britain where the hearing takes place.

(3) A Commissioner may, before determining the application or appeal, direct the appeal tribunal to submit a statement of such facts or other matters as he considers necessary for the proper determination of that application or appeal.

(4) At any stage of the proceedings, a Commissioner may, on or without an application, give any directions as he may consider necessary or desirable for the efficient despatch of the proceedings.

(5) Without prejudice to regulations 16 and 17, or to paragraph (4), and subject to paragraph (2), a Commissioner may direct any party before him, to make any written observations as may seem to him necessary to enable the question at issue to be determined.

(6) An application under paragraph (4) shall be made in writing to a Commissioner and shall set out the direction which the applicant seeks.

(7) Unless a Commissioner shall otherwise determine, the office shall send a copy of an application under paragraph (4) to every other party.

DEFINITIONS

"appeal"—see reg.2.
"appeal tribunal"—*ibid*.

(SI 2005/1031, reg.18)

"Commissioner"—see s.39(1) of the Social Security Act 1998, as applied by reg.14 of the Child Trust Funds (Non-tax Appeals) Regulations 2005.
"office"—see reg.2.
"party"—*ibid.*
"proceedings"—*ibid.*
"respondent"—*ibid.*

GENERAL NOTE

Case management directions are usually issued when leave to appeal is granted by a Commissioner or upon receipt of an appeal. Such directions often shorten the procedure required under regs 16 and 17 (see the note to reg.15 of the Social Security Commissioners (Procedure) (Tax Credits Appeals) Regulations 2004). However, case management directions may be issued at any stage of the proceedings. They commonly require submissions to be made on specific issues or for specific written or documentary evidence to be produced. For the power to issue a summons requiring attendance in person, see reg.22.

6.145

Non-disclosure of medical evidence

19.—(1) Where, in any proceedings, there is before a Commissioner medical evidence relating to a person which has not been disclosed to that person and in the opinion of the Commissioner the disclosure to that person of that evidence would be harmful to his health, such evidence shall not be disclosed to that person.

6.146

(2) Evidence such as is mentioned in paragraph (1) shall not be disclosed to any person acting for or representing the person to whom it relates, unless the Commissioner considers that it is in the interests of the person to whom the evidence relates to disclose it.

(3) Non-disclosure under paragraphs (1) or (2) does not preclude the Commissioner from taking the evidence concerned into account for the purpose of the proceedings.

DEFINITIONS

"Commissioner"—see s.39(1) of the Social Security Act 1998, as applied by reg.14 of the Child Trust Funds (Non-tax Appeals) Regulations 2005.
"proceedings"—see reg.2.

GENERAL NOTE

See the note to reg.14 of the Tax Credits (Appeals) (No.2) Regulations 2002. However, it is difficult to see how harmful medical evidence could be relevant to a child trust fund appeal and the Child Trust Funds (Appeals) Regulations 2005 do not include a similar provision for child trust fund appeals before tribunals.

6.147

Requests for hearings

20.—(1) Subject to paragraphs (2) to (5), a Commissioner may determine any proceedings without a hearing.

6.148

(2) In the case of a penalty appeal, where a request for a hearing is made by the party on whom the penalty has been imposed, a Commissioner shall grant the request.

(3) Where a request for a hearing is made by any party other than as provided by paragraph (2), a Commissioner shall grant the request unless he is satisfied that the proceedings can properly be determined without a hearing.

The Social Security Commissioners (Child Trust Funds) Regs 2005

(4) Where a Commissioner refuses a request for a hearing, he shall send written notice to the person making the request, either before or at the same time as making his determination or decision.

(5) A Commissioner may, without an application and at any stage, direct a hearing.

DEFINITIONS

"Commissioner"—see s.39(1) of the Social Security Act 1998, as applied by reg.14 of the Child Trust Funds (Non-tax Appeals) Regulations 2005.
"party"—see reg.2.
"penalty appeal"—*ibid*.
"proceedings"—*ibid*.

GENERAL NOTE

6.149   See the note to reg.18 of the Social Security Commissioners (Procedure) (Tax Credits Appeals) Regulations 2002.

Hearings

6.150   **21.**—(1) This regulation applies to any hearing of an application or appeal to which these Regulations apply.

(2) Subject to paragraph (3), the office shall give reasonable notice of the time and place of any hearing before a Commissioner.

(3) Unless all the parties concerned agree to a hearing at shorter notice, the period of notice specified under paragraph (2) shall be at least 14 days before the date of the hearing.

(4) If any party to whom notice of a hearing has been sent fails to appear at the hearing, the Commissioner may proceed with the case in that party's absence, or may give directions with a view to the determination of the case.

(5) Any hearing before a Commissioner shall be in public, unless the Commissioner for special reasons directs otherwise.

(6) Where a Commissioner holds a hearing the following persons shall be entitled to be present and be heard—
   (a) the person making the application or appeal;
   (b) any respondent;
   (c) with the leave of the Commissioner, any other person.

(7) Subject to the direction of a Commissioner—
   (a) any person entitled to be present and be heard at a hearing; and
   (b) any representatives of such a person,
may be present by means of a live television link.

(8) Any provision in these regulations which refers to a party or representative being present is satisfied if the party or representative is present by means of a live television link.

(9) Any person entitled to be heard at a hearing may address the Commissioner and—
   (a) in the case of a penalty appeal, the party on whom the penalty has been imposed may give evidence, call witnesses and put questions directly to any other person called as a witness;
   (b) in all other cases, a person entitled to be heard may with the leave of the Commissioner, give evidence, call witnesses and put questions directly to any other person called as a witness.

(SI 2005/1031, reg.21)

(10) Nothing in these Regulations shall prevent a member of the Council on Tribunals or of the Scottish Committee of the Council in his capacity as such from being present at a hearing before a Commissioner which is not held in public.

DEFINITIONS

"appeal"—see reg.2.
"Commissioner"—see s.39(1) of the Social Security Act 1998, as applied by reg.14 of the Child Trust Funds (Non-tax Appeals) Regulations 2005.
"live television link"—see reg.2.
"office"—*ibid.*
"party"—*ibid.*
"penalty appeal"—*ibid.*
"respondent"—*ibid.*

Summoning of witnesses

22.—(1) Subject to paragraph (2), a Commissioner may summon any person to attend a hearing as a witness, at such time and place as may be specified in the summons, to answer any questions or produce any documents in his custody or under his control which relate to any matter in question in the proceedings.

(2) A person shall not be required to attend in obedience to a summons under paragraph (1) unless he has been given at least 14 days' notice before the date of the hearing or, if less than 14 days, has informed the Commissioner that he accepts such notice as he has been given.

(3) Upon the application of a person summoned under this regulation, a Commissioner may set the summons aside.

(4) A Commissioner may require any witness to give evidence on oath and for this purpose an oath may be administered in due form.

DEFINITIONS

"Commissioner"—see s.39(1) of the Social Security Act 1998, as applied by reg.14 of the Child Trust Funds (Non-tax Appeals) Regulations 2005.
"proceedings"—see reg.2.
"summons"—*ibid.*

GENERAL NOTE

See the note to reg.15 of the Tax Credits (Appeals) (No.2) Regulations 2002.

Withdrawal of applications for leave to appeal and appeals

23.—(1) At any time before it is determined, an applicant may withdraw an application to a Commissioner for leave to appeal against a decision of an appeal tribunal by giving written notice to a Commissioner.

(2) At any time before the decision is made, the appellant may withdraw his appeal with the leave of a Commissioner.

(3) A Commissioner may, on application by the party concerned, give leave to reinstate any application or appeal which has been withdrawn in accordance with paragraphs (1) and (2) and, on giving leave, he may make directions as to the conduct of the proceedings.

The Social Security Commissioners (Child Trust Funds) Regs 2005

DEFINITIONS

"appeal"—see reg.2.
"appeal tribunal"—*ibid.*
"Commissioner"—see s.39(1) of the Social Security Act 1998, as applied by reg.14 of the Child Trust Funds (Non-tax Appeals) Regulations 2005.
"party"—see reg.2.
"proceedings"—*ibid.*

GENERAL NOTE

6.154
Note that a Commissioner's approval is not required if an application for leave to appeal is to be withdrawn, whether it is an application for leave to appeal to a Commissioner or an application for leave to appeal to the Court of Appeal or Court of Session (see reg.29(3)).

Irregularities

6.155
24. Any irregularity resulting from failure to comply with the requirements of these Regulations shall not by itself invalidate any proceedings, and the Commissioner, before reaching his decision, may waive the irregularity or take steps to remedy it.

DEFINITIONS

"Commissioner"—see s.39(1) of the Social Security Act 1998, as applied by reg.14 of the Child Trust Funds (Non-tax Appeals) Regulations 2005.
"proceedings"—see reg.2.

PART IV

DECISIONS

Determinations and decisions of a Commissioner

6.156
25.—(1) The determination of a Commissioner on an application for leave to appeal shall be in writing and signed by him.

(2) The decision of a Commissioner on an appeal shall be in writing and signed by him and, unless it was a decision made with the consent of the parties or an order setting aside a tribunal's decision under section 14(7) of the 1998 Act, he shall include the reasons.

(3) The office shall send a copy of the determination or decision and any reasons to each party.

(4) Without prejudice to paragraphs (2) and (3), a Commissioner may announce his determination or decision at the end of a hearing.

DEFINITIONS

"the 1998 Act"—see reg.2.
"appeal"—*ibid.*
"Commissioner"—see s.39(1) of the Social Security Act 1998, as applied by reg.14 of the Child Trust Funds (Non-tax Appeals) Regulations 2005.
"Commissioner"—*ibid.*
"office"—see reg.2.
"party"—*ibid.*

(SI 2005/1031, reg.25)

GENERAL NOTE

See the note to reg.23 of the Social Security Commissioners (Procedure) (Tax Credits Appeals) Regulations 2002.

6.157

Correction of accidental errors in decisions

26.—(1) Subject to regulations 4 and 28, the Commissioner who gave the decision may at any time correct accidental errors in any decision or record of a decision.

(2) A correction made to, or to the record of, a decision shall become part of the decision or record, and the office shall send a written notice of the correction to any party to whom notice of the decision has been sent.

6.158

DEFINITIONS

"Commissioner"—see s.39(1) of the Social Security Act 1998, as applied by reg.14 of the Child Trust Funds (Non-tax Appeals) Regulations 2005.
"office"—see reg.2.
"party"—*ibid*.

GENERAL NOTE

See the note to reg.24 of the Tax Credits (Appeals) (No.2) Regulation 2002.

6.159

Setting aside decisions on certain grounds

27.—(1) Subject to regulations 4 and 28, on an application made by any party, the Commissioner who gave the decision in proceedings may set it aside where it appears just to do so on the ground that—

(a) a document relating to the proceedings was not sent to, or was not received at an appropriate time by, a party or his representative or was not received at an appropriate time by the Commissioner; or

(b) a party or his representative was not present at a hearing before the Commissioner.

(2) An application under this regulation shall be made in writing to a Commissioner within one month from the date on which the office gave written notice of the decision to the party making the application.

(3) Unless the Commissioner considers that it is unnecessary for the proper determination of an application made under paragraph (1), the office shall send a copy of it to each respondent, who shall be given a reasonable opportunity to make representations on it.

(4) The office shall send each party written notice of a determination of an application to set aside a decision and the reasons for it.

6.160

DEFINITIONS

"Commissioner"—see s.39(1) of the Social Security Act 1998, as applied by reg.14 of the Child Trust Funds (Non-tax Appeals) Regulations 2005.
"office"—see reg.2.
"party"—*ibid*.
"proceedings"—*ibid*.
"respondent"—*ibid*.

GENERAL NOTE

See the note to reg.25(1) of the Tax Credits (Appeals) (No.2) Regulations 2002. Note that an unsuccessful application for a decision to be set aside does not

6.161

prejudice the possibility of an appeal, provided the application was not late (see reg.29(2)(b) below).

Provisions common to regulations 26 and 27

28.—(1) In regulations 26 and 27, the word "decision" shall include determinations of applications for leave to appeal, orders setting aside tribunal decisions under section 14(7) of the 1998 Act and decisions on appeals.

(2) There shall be no appeal against a correction or a refusal to correct under regulation 26 or a determination given under regulation 27.

DEFINITIONS

"the 1998 Act"—see reg.2.
"appeal"—*ibid*.

PART V

APPLICATIONS FOR LEAVE TO APPEAL TO THE APPELLATE COURT

Application to a Commissioner for leave to appeal to the Appellate Court

29.—(1) Subject to paragraph (2), an application to a Commissioner under section 15 of the 1998 Act for leave to appeal against a decision of a Commissioner shall be made in writing, stating the grounds of the application, within three months from the date on which the applicant was sent written notice of the decision.

(2) Where—
(a) any decision or record of a decision is corrected under regulation 26; or
(b) an application for a decision to be set aside under regulation 27 is refused for reasons other than that the application was made outside the period specified in regulation 27(2),

the period specified in paragraph (1) shall run from the date on which written notice of the correction or refusal of the application to set aside is sent to the applicant.

(3) Regulations 23(1) and 23(3) shall apply to an application to a Commissioner for leave to appeal from a Commissioner's decision as they apply to the proceedings in that regulation.

DEFINITIONS

"the 1998 Act"—see reg.2.
"Commissioner"—see s.39(1) of the Social Security Act 1998, as applied by reg.14 of the Child Trust Funds (Non-tax Appeals) Regulations 2005.
"proceedings"—see reg.2.

GENERAL NOTE

See the note to reg.27 of the Social Security Commissioners (Procedure) (Tax Credits Appeals) Regulations 2002.

PART VII

HMRC CODES OF PRACTICE AND GUIDANCE

NOTE

HMRC publishes manuals, guides and forms dealing with all parts of the law under its management. For a full list of those dealing with tax credits go to the HMRC website at *http://www.hmrc.gov.uk/leaflets/credt.htm*. For the guidance manuals issued to staff go to *http://www.hmrc.gov.uk/taxcredits/manuals-legislation.htm*. For the forms in the TC series, go to *http://www.hmrc.gov.uk/menus/tax_credits.htm*.

All the guides are official publications. But none in this field carry the force of law. Nonetheless some of them are particularly important as they set out the terms on which HMRC exercises discretions (for example as to overpayments and penalties). They also detail the administrative procedures and standards that HMRC sets itself. The key guides to the way in which HMRC deals with overpayments and penalties are set out in this volume. They are marked in bold in the following list of leaflets:

Changes of circumstances	General guidance on the new regime for reporting changes (September 2006)
WTC1	Child Tax Credit and Working Tax Credit. An introduction (October 2004, currently being updated)
WTC2	Child Tax Credit and Working Tax Credit— a guide (May 2005, currently being updated)
WTC5	Help with the costs of childcare—information for parents and childcare providers (November 2006)
WTC6	Child Tax Credit and Working Tax Credit Other types of help you may be able to get (November 2006)
WTC7	**Tax Credits penalties What happens at the end of a check (April 2007)**
WTC/AP	Child Tax Credit and Working Tax Credit: how to appeal against a tax credit decision or award (October 2004)
WTC/FS1	Tax credits enquiry (April 2007)
WTC/FS2	Tax credits examinations (April 2007)
WTC/FS3	Tax credits formal request for information (May 2006)
WTC/FS4	Tax credits meetings (May 2006)
COP26	**Code of Practice 26: What happens if we have paid you too much tax credit? (March 2006)**

The following leaflets have been withdrawn from current use and are archived on the HMRC site: WTC3, WTC4, COP23 (Child Tax Credit and

Working Tax Credit local office examination), COP27 (Child Tax Credit and Working Tax Credit local office enquiries).

The key standard forms are available to download from the site above. They are:

TC600	Tax Credits claim form
TC602	Checking a tax credits award
TC603R	Tax Credits renewal pack
TC603RD	Tax Credits renewal and annual declaration
TC689	Authority for intermediary to act
TC846	Request to reconsider recovery of overpaid tax credits

The standard manuals issued to staff are:

CCM	New Tax Credits Claimant Compliance Manual
NTC Manual	Clerical procedures
TCTM	Tax Credits Technical Manual

All are available on the site above (although some paragraphs are withheld under the Freedom of Information Act exemptions).

LEAFLET WTC 7

TAX CREDITS PENALTIES

WHAT HAPPENS AT THE END OF A CHECK (APRIL 2007)

Introduction

When you make a claim for Child Tax Credit or Working Tax Credit you are responsible for making sure that the information on your claim form is correct.

This leaflet is for anyone who may get charged a penalty after we have carried out a check on their tax credits claim. It does not tell you everything about penalties, but it does tell you what is likely to happen and what you can do if we charge you a penalty.

Information about how and why we carry out tax credits checks is in Factsheets WTC/FS1 and WTC/FS2. We give these to claimants when we start a check. They are also available at *http://www.hmrc.gov.uk/leaflets/credit.htm*

7.1

Why we charge penalties

We charge penalties to

- encourage people to take care and make sure their claims are correct
- stop claimants from supplying incorrect information, and
- penalise those who try to defraud the system.

7.2

Your penalty

You may be liable to a penalty if

- we find that you have not told us about a change in your circumstances that results in a tax credits overpayment, or
- you have supplied incorrect information about your tax credits claim.

7.3

Not telling us about a change in circumstances

If you do not tell us about the following changes in your circumstances we can charge you a maximum penalty of up to £300.

You must tell us if

- you marry or become a civil partner or part of a couple who live together as husband and wife or as civil partners
- you stop being part of a married couple or civil partnership or a couple living together as husband and wife or as civil partners
- your average weekly childcare costs go down by £10 a week or more for four weeks in a row

7.4

- you stop paying childcare costs
- you or your partner leave the country for more than eight weeks. This is extended to 12 weeks if you go, or stay abroad because you, or a member of your family, is ill or has died
- your usual working hours change so that you work
  — less than 16 hours a week, or
  — less than 30 hours a week,

  For couples with children it is your joint working hours that count towards the 30 hours
- one of your children leaves the family and moves to live with someone else. This includes a child who has been
  — taken into care or fostered to another family
  — found guilty by a court and sentenced to custody or detention for a period of four months or more
- a child or young person you are responsible for stops qualifying for support, for example they
  — leave non-advanced full-time education or approved training before they reach 20
  — start to have their training provided under a contract of employment
  — stop being registered with a careers service, or the Connexions Service or equivalent
  — start to claim Income Support, Incapacity Benefit, incomebased Jobseeker's Allowance, Child Tax Credit or Working Tax Credit in their own right
- a child or qualifying young person dies
- you have been on strike for more than 10 days.

Usually it will be obvious when there has been a change, and you must tell us **within one month** of the date the change happened.

For example, you change your job on 8 May 2007 and instead of working 35 hours a week you now work 25 hours a week. You must tell us about this by 8 June 2007.

Sometimes it might not be clear exactly when there has been a change, so you must tell us **within one month** of the date you realise that the change has happened.

For example, the exact number of hours you work each week varies as you often work some overtime as well as your standard hours of 26 hours a week. Most weeks you work more than four hours overtime a week so your usual hours are more than 30 hours a week. However, the amount of overtime available varies and you do not always work all the overtime available. On 7 September 2007 when looking back you realise that your usual hours are now less than 30 hours a week and have been since 20 August 2007. You must tell us about this by 6 October 2007.

Tax Credits Penalties

Week starting Monday	Overtime offered	Overtime worked	Actual hours worked	Usual hours
18/6	14	14	40	30+
25/6	10	10	36	30+
2/7	6	4	30	30+
9/7	1	1	27	30+
16/7	10	10	36	30+
23/7	3	3	29	30+
30/7	14	14	40	30+
6/8	0	0	26	30+
13/8	4	4	30	30+
20/8	2	2	28	16–30
27/8	0	0	20.8*	16–30
3/9	1	1	27	16–30

* Didn't work the Bank Holiday

The date the change happened and the date you first became aware of the change are matters of fact. If you do not agree with our decision to charge a penalty please discuss it with us and we will consider what you say. If we still think that you did not tell us in time you can ask the Appeals Tribunal to decide (see "Your rights" on page 7[1]).

Reasonable excuse

We will not charge you a penalty if you have a reasonable excuse for not telling us about a change in your circumstances.

7.5

What is a reasonable excuse?

A reasonable excuse might be that

7.6

- you had a serious illness that prevented you from sending the information
- we received your notification late because of an unexpected postal dispute

A reasonable excuse is not that

- you have been too busy to tell us about a change in circumstances
- you did not know you had to tell us about a change in circumstances.

Please tell us if you think you have a reasonable excuse and we will consider what you say.

Whether your excuse is reasonable is a matter of law. If we do not agree that your excuse is reasonable you can ask the Appeals Tribunal to decide (see page 8).

Supplying incorrect information

We can charge you a penalty of up to £3000 if you have negligently not taken care to make sure any information you sent us was correct.
This includes the information you give

7.7

[1] Please see para.7.19, below.

- in your claim
- on any notification of a change in circumstances, and
- in response to a particular request for information during our checks.

We will explain why we believe that you have been negligent. If you do not accept our explanation you can ask the Appeals Tribunal to decide (see "Your rights" on page 7[1]).

What is negligence?

7.8 Negligence is not taking reasonable care.
A careful person would

- make a complete and correct claim to the best of their knowledge and belief
- read the notes supplied with the claim that relate to their own circumstances
- ask for help if they are unable to cope with the claim or declaration themselves.

Plain carelessness can be negligence

7.9 We will not consider you negligent if you have had wrong advice given to you by for example an HMRC Enquiry Centre, Job Centre Plus or an adviser such as the Citizens Advice Bureau.

Couples

7.10 If you have made a joint claim with your partner, you are both responsible for the information you provide in your claim.
We will charge you a penalty as a couple where

- either of you could have told us about any change in circumstances, or
- you were both responsible for supplying incorrect information.

If the incorrect information relates to one partner—and the other person could not have reasonably known that it was not correct—we will only charge the penalty on that partner.

The maximum penalty for a joint claim is no more than the maximum penalty for an individual claim.

Paying your penalty

7.11 We will contact you if we think that you have become liable to a penalty. We can do this

- by phone
- in a meeting, or
- in writing.

We will explain why we are charging you a penalty and tell you the maximum amount chargeable. We will always consider a lesser penalty and we will discuss this with you.

[1] Please see para.7.19, below.

The amount of your penalty

When working out the amount of the penalty reduction, we will take into account

- the amount of tax credits over-claimed
- whether you have been liable for tax credits penalties before, and
- the extent to which you co-operate with us in providing information to establish your proper entitlement to tax credits and to bring our check to a close.

If you do not understand our explanation of the penalty, you can ask us to put it in writing so that you can seek independent advice.

If you agree with the penalty

We will discuss the arrangements for payment covering

- any overpaid tax credits
- any interest due, and
- the penalty.

Depending on your circumstances, you can pay either in a lump sum or in instalments.

Arranging payment

Once we have agreed the arrangements we will ask you to sign a letter that sets out

- the total amount you have to pay, and
- the final date for payment, or the number of instalments and when they are due.

We will send you a final letter accepting the arrangement. This exchange of letters is a legally binding contract. If you refuse to pay, we will take legal action to recover any money you owe.

If you disagree with the penalty

You should let us know. We will listen to what you have to say. If we cannot agree, we will issue a penalty notice so that you can appeal or appoint a representative to appeal for you.

Interest

We may charge you interest if we have overpaid tax credits because of negligence on your part. We also charge interest on any penalties that you pay late.

Co-operation

The extent to which you co-operate and provide us with information is entirely up to you. You should remember that the level of your co-operation could affect the amount of any penalty.

877

If you are not sure whether to give us the information, or if you are reluctant to co-operate, we suggest you get independent advice before deciding what to do. We may decide to reduce or stop your current tax credits payments based on the information we hold.

Help

7.18 You can get help from your nearest Citizens Advice Bureau. You will find them in *The Phone Book*.

Your rights

7.19 You have the right to appeal if we

- ask you to pay penalties or interest, or
- amend your award.

You can find out more information about how to appeal by reading our leaflet WTC/AP *"How to appeal against a tax credits decision or award"*, which you can get from any HM Revenue & Customs Enquiry Centre or online at *http://www.hmrc.gov.uk/leaflets/wtc_ap.pdf* We will not treat your right of appeal as non co-operation.

Appeals Tribunal

7.20 If we do not agree with your appeal we will send your claim to an independent Unified Appeals Tribunal. They will listen to both of us and decide whether you will have to pay the penalty and how much you will have to pay.

If you disagree with the Appeals Tribunal's decision, you can appeal to the Social Security Commissioners. You will be sent information on how to do this with the Appeal Tribunal's decision notice.

Customer Service

HM Revenue & Customs commitment

7.21 We aim to provide a high quality service with guidance that is simple, clear and accurate.

We will

- be professional and helpful
- act with integrity and fairness, and
- treat your affairs in strict confidence within the law.

We aim to handle your affairs promptly and accurately so that you receive or pay only the right amount due.

Putting things right

7.22 If you are not satisfied with our service, please let the person dealing with your affairs know what is wrong. We will work as quickly as possible to put things right and settle your complaint.

If you are still unhappy, ask for your complaint to be referred to the Complaints Manager.

Customers with particular needs

We offer a range of facilities for customers with particular needs, including   7.23

- wheelchair access to nearly all HMRC Enquiry Centres
- help with filling in forms
- for people with hearing difficulties
    — BT Typetalk
    — Induction loops.

We can also arrange additional support, such as

- home visits, if you have limited mobility or caring responsibilities and cannot get to one of our Enquiry Centres
- services of an interpreter
- sign language interpretation
- leaflets in large print, Braille and audio.

For complete details please go online at *http://www.hmrc.gov.uk/enq* or contact us. You will find us in *The Phone Book* under HM Revenue & Customs.

GENERAL NOTE

This leaflet was issued in April 2007. The final part of the leaflet, "Further information" has not been included.   7.24

CODE OF PRACTICE 26

WHAT HAPPENS IF WE HAVE PAID YOU TOO MUCH TAX CREDIT?

Introduction

7.25 Tax credits are based on your household income and personal circumstances for the whole of the tax year (6 April to 5 April). If you tell us about a change in your income or circumstances, we work out the revised amount of tax credits for that tax year. If the changes mean you are due less tax credits for that tax year, you may have an overpayment.

In this leaflet, unless we say otherwise, we use the word "overpayment" for

- an amount owed to us after the end of the tax year. This we normally recover in the following tax year, or
- an amount paid to you which we find during the tax year is likely to exceed your entitlement. This we normally recover through an in-year reduction to tax credit payments to help avoid an overpayment at the end of the tax year.

If you need help, contact us. If you would like independent help, you can ask a friend, a professional adviser or an organisation like Citizens Advice to help you. You can ask them to talk to us on your behalf, but we cannot do this without your permission. Call us and we will tell you how to give your permission.

Asking for more time to pay

7.26 Call us on 0845 300 3900. We will ask you for more information about your circumstances before deciding whether to further reduce the rate at which we recover an overpayment (See the next question for details of the information we will ask you about).

We may offer an option for extending the period over which you pay back the overpayment by changing the rate at which you pay it back. If we do increase your payments to help you budget, it will take you longer to pay off the overpayment.

In exceptional circumstances, we may write off all or part of an overpayment if it would cause you or your family hardship to pay it back.

Call us on 0845 302 1429 as soon as possible so we can make arrangements for you to pay back in equal instalments over 12 months.

If you need a longer period, please let us know when you call. We will want to know

- your family circumstances, in particular young children, and anyone chronically ill or disabled
- your income now and in the future
- your living expenses, (for example, rent, gas or electricity bills)
- your savings, investments and other assets
- your other debts, (for example, mortgage repayments)

What happens if we have paid you too much tax credit?

- how long it will take you to pay back the overpayment
- any earlier payments to us.

When we have all your information, we may offer you a longer repayment period, or we may delay starting to collect the overpayment from you.

In exceptional circumstances, we may write off all or part of an overpayment if it would cause you or your family hardship to pay it back.

Disagreeing with recovery of an overpayment

Make sure 7.27

- you have all the information about your tax credits award before you contact us, and
- that you want to dispute recovery of the overpayment—not just ask for more time to pay.

For us to write off an overpayment you must be able to show that the overpayment happened because

- we made a mistake, and
- it was reasonable for you to think your payments were right.

This means that you must have checked your award notice when you received it.

If you ask us to reconsider our decision to recover an overpayment, amongst other things, we will

- check whether our calculations are correct, and that they were based on the information that you gave us
- check whether we instructed your employer to pay the wrong amount of Working Tax Credit
- check whether we delayed using the information you provided
- look for any incorrect or missing details on your award notices that we would have expected you to spot and to tell us about, and
- consider your reasons for believing that your payments were right.

We will take the same approach where another government department made the mistake that led to the overpayment. We would consider whether it was reasonable for you to think your payments were right, following the mistake by the other government department.

But if you want help paying back the overpayment as it will cause you financial difficulties, see the section "Asking for more time to pay" on page 2[1].

If one of our Helpline advisers, or a letter from us, wrongly tells you that your award is correct even though you contacted us

- to tell us your award notice was wrong, or
- to tell us about an unexplained change to your payments, or
- to question how we had worked out your entitlement, and

an overpayment then occurs, we will not seek recovery of that overpayment.

[1] Please see para.7.26, above.

881

What happens if we have paid you too much tax credit?

We will usually check that you provided full information about your circumstances and income when you spoke to the Helpline so they could give you the correct advice. So please tell us the date and time you telephoned us when you complete form TC846—*Request to reconsider recovery of overpaid tax credits* to say why you disagree with recovery of the overpayment.

We expect you at least to have checked that the following details on your award notices were correct (whether at the start of the award period, during the year or when the final award notice comes).

- whether the award is for you as an individual or as part of a couple
- the hours you work
- whether you receive Income Support or income-based Jobseeker's Allowance or Pension Credit
- whether you, or anyone in your household, has a disability element
- the number and age of any children in your household
- childcare costs
- your total household income for the period shown on the award notice.

You should also have checked the amounts going into your bank account. We would expect you to tell us if you received any payments that did not match what was shown on the award notices during the period that the overpayment arose.

We expect you to contact us to let us know about any incorrect information for your circumstances on the day the notice was issued. If you have a change to your circumstances or income, we expect you to contact us again.

We expect you to check that your final award notice correctly shows the details for that tax year.

If there is a dispute regarding an overpayment, we may check our call records to make sure that you contacted us to let us know of any changes or mistakes.

We will normally ask you to pay back the overpayment. If you had received an award notice that you did not understand, we would normally expect you, or someone on your behalf, to ask for advice.

We expect you to check that the personal details on your award notice are correct and that the payments you receive in your bank account match those shown on the award notice. If exceptional circumstances—for example bereavement of a close relative or a serious illness—prevented you from doing this, tell us the reasons when you complete form TC846. We will then consider your reasons with the rest of the information you provide.

Complete form TC846 and return it to the Tax Credit Office. If you didn't get a copy of the form with this leaflet, you can get it from *http://www.hmrc.gov.uk/menus/tax_credits.htm* or by calling us on 0845 300 3900.

We will suspend recovery of the overpayment when we receive the form TC846 or a written dispute from you. We will write to you confirming that we are suspending recovery and telling you what happens next. We will decide whether you must pay back all or only part of the overpayment. We will give you this decision, along with our reasons, in writing. If we decide

What happens if we have paid you too much tax credit?

that part or all of the overpayment should be recovered after reviewing the information that you provide, we will start recovery again.

If there is some new relevant information that you can provide, and you are unhappy with a decision to recover the overpayment, please write to us at the address at the back of this leaflet, as soon as possible. We will suspend recovery of the overpayment again while we review the information you give us.

If there is no new relevant information and you are still unhappy with the decision, you may wish to consider referring the matter to the Adjudicator or the Parliamentary Ombudsman.

Alternatively, you may wish to contact a professional adviser or an organisation like Citizens Advice to consider what options are open to you to dispute the recovery, including any through the courts.

Causes of overpayments

An overpayment can happen if, for example   7.28

- you delay telling us about a change in your circumstances, or
- we delay recording the change of circumstance that you told us about, or
- your income as a whole for a tax year up to and including 2005–2006 is £2,500 more than your income in the previous tax year, or
- your income as a whole for a tax year from 2006–2007 onwards is £25,000 more than your income in the previous tax year, or
- your award was not based on the right details, or
- you receive provisional payments based upon incorrect information about your personal circumstances, or
- you fail to renew your award on time whereby any provisional payments you received are recoverable.

If you want help understanding what may have caused your overpayment, call us on 0845 300 3900.

Paying back overpayments

We will collect it back by one of the following methods   7.29

- if you are still receiving tax credit payments as the same household for which the overpayment arose, we will automatically reduce the amount we pay you (see the next question), or
- if you are no longer entitled to tax credits, we will ask you to make a direct payment to us, or
- if your tax credit award has ended as your household has changed, we will ask you to make a direct payment to us. We will do this even if you are receiving another award of tax credits for a new household you are part of.

We automatically reduce your payments to recover a previous year's overpayment. The maximum recovery rate depends on your current tax credit award as follows

What happens if we have paid you too much tax credit?

Tax credit award	Maximum recovery rate
An award with no reduction due to income	10%
An award of the family element of Child Tax Credit only	100%
All other awards—For example, those entitled to Child Tax Credit above the family element, or Working Tax Credit below the maximum	25%

Phone us on 0845 300 3900 if you want help understanding which recovery rate applies to you.

If the reduced payments cause you financial difficulties, see the section "Asking for more time to pay" on page 2[1]. If you dispute recovery of the overpayment, because it arose due to a mistake by us, see the section "Disagreeing with recovery of an overpayment" on page 3[2].

Your tax credit payments can go up or down if your circumstances or your income change during the tax year.

After you tell us about a change in your circumstances or a change in your income, we work out the new amount of tax credit payments you are due and issue a new award notice. If the changes mean you are awarded less tax credits, we automatically

- reduce your payments, or
- stop paying you tax credits for the rest of the year, if we have already paid you as much as, or more than, you are entitled to.

We may also reduce your payments further to help avoid an overpayment after the end of the tax year. This would only be up to the maximum amounts as set out in the last question.

If you tell us about a change of circumstances and we find you are not entitled to tax credits at all, we will stop paying you tax credits for the rest of the year.

Joint claims

7.30 Because you and your partner must make a joint claim for tax credits, we can ask either of you to pay back an overpayment on the joint claim, even if you and your former partner have now split up.

Our first step will be to ask both of you jointly to pay us the money. We will send letters to both of you showing the total amount due. Where we do not have an address for one of you, we will make every effort to trace him or her.

You can ask us to consider whether there should be a difference between what you and your former partner are asked to repay. We will take into account the circumstances, income and expenses of each of you in reaching a decision. Where, for example, you ask us to consider a difference between your and your former partner's ability to pay, we may ask

- each of you to pay us different amounts of the overpayment, or
- one of you to pay us the full amount.

[1] Please see para.7.26, above.
[2] Please see para.7.27, above.

What happens if we have paid you too much tax credit?

In law, both partners are jointly responsible to pay the full amount unless we send out new notices saying otherwise.

Appeal rights

You can appeal against your Child Tax Credit or Working Tax Credit award if you do not feel it has been calculated correctly and any penalty we have imposed in connection with your tax credits claim. We will always tell you if you have a right of appeal on the notice that sets out the decision.

If you want more information, please read our leaflet WTC/AP "*How to appeal against a tax credits decision or award.*" This is available on our website at *http://www.hmrc.gov.uk/leaflets/wtc_ap.htm* or by calling 0845 900 0404 or from any HMRC Enquiry Centre.

You cannot appeal against our decision to recover an overpayment although you may have other options available to you, see the section "*What can I do if you still think the overpayment should be recovered?*" on page 5.

7.31

Contacting us

- Call us between 8am and 8pm, seven days a week

Helpline	0845 300 3900
Minicom/Textphone	0845 300 3909
If you prefer to speak in Welsh	0845 302 1489

    If you are living overseas and cannot get through on the Helpline number shown, please call 00 44 289 0808 316

- Visit any HMRC Enquiry Centre—you may need to make an appointment to see an adviser

- Write to

    Tax Credit Office

    Preston

    PR1 0SB.

7.32

Customer Service

We aim to provide a high quality service with guidance that is simple, clear and accurate.

We will

- be professional and helpful
- act with integrity and fairness, and
- treat your affairs in strict confidence within the law.

We aim to handle your affairs promptly and accurately so that you receive or pay only the right amount due.

If you are not satisfied with our service, please let the person dealing with your affairs know what is wrong. We will work as quickly as possible to put things right and settle your complaint.

7.33

What happens if we have paid you too much tax credit?

If you are still unhappy, ask for your complaint to be referred to the Complaints Manager.

We offer a range of facilities for customers with particular needs, including

- wheelchair access to nearly all HMRC Enquiry Centres
- help with filling in forms
- for people with hearing difficulties
    — BT Typetalk
    — Induction loops.

We can also arrange additional support, such as

- home visits, if you have limited mobility or caring responsibilities and cannot get to one of our Enquiry Centres
- services of an interpreter
- sign language interpretation
- leaflets in large print, Braille and audio.

For complete details please

- go online at *http://www.hmrc.gov.uk/enq*, or
- contact us. You will find us in *The Phone Book* under HM Revenue & Customs.

INDEX

LEGAL TAXONOMY
FROM SWEET & MAXWELL

This index has been prepared using Sweet and Maxwell's Legal Taxonomy. Main index entries conform to keywords provided by the Legal Taxonomy except where references to specific documents or non-standard terms (denoted by quotation marks) have been included. These keywords provide a means of identifying similar concepts in other Sweet & Maxwell publications and online services to which keywords from the Legal Taxonomy have been applied. Readers may find some minor differences between terms used in the text and those which appear in the index. Suggestions to *sweetandmaxwell.taxonomy@thomson.com*.

(All references are to paragraph number)

50-plus element
working tax credit, 2.80–2.81
Accounting date
trading income, 1.658
Adjournments
child trust funds (appeals), 6.102–6.103
tax credits (appeals), 2.414–2.415
Administration
see **Administrative requirements**
Administration of oaths
child trust funds (appeals), 6.92–6.93
tax credits (appeals), 2.401–2.402
Administrative requirements (statutory adoption pay)
adoption from overseas, 5.103–5.107
determination of entitlement issues
application, 5.30
form of application, 5.31
employers' records
generally, 5.26
inspection, 5.27
funding of liabilities
application to Revenue, 5.21
date of payment of contributions, 5.24
generally, 5.20
method, 5.22–5.23
overpayments, 5.25
provision of information, 5.32
Administrative requirements (statutory maternity pay)
employer's records
maintenance, 4.45
production, 4.46
expected week of confinement, 4.39
notice of absence from work, 4.40
notification of employment after confinement, 4.41
provision of information
claims for other benefits, 4.44
determination of questions, 4.42–4.43

Administrative requirements (statutory paternity pay)
adoption from overseas, 5.103–5.107
determination of entitlement issues
application, 5.30
form of application, 5.31
employers' records
generally, 5.26
inspection, 5.27
funding of liabilities
application to Revenue, 5.21
date of payment of contributions, 5.24
generally, 5.20
method, 5.22–5.23
overpayments, 5.25
provision of information, 5.32
Administrative requirements (tax credits)
definitions, 2.363
general note, 2.361
forwarding of claims, 2.366
holding of claims, 2.366
provision of information
by authorities, 2.365
to authorities, 2.364
recording of claims, 2.366
statutory provision, 1.348–1.349
Adopters
annual payments, 1.712
Adoption
statutory paternity pay
see also **Statutory paternity pay**
conditions of entitlement, 5.57–5.58
evidence of entitlement, 5.62
notice requirements, 5.60
payment period, 5.59
qualifying period, 5.61
statutory provisions, 1.77–1.78
treatment of more than one employer, 5.63
working tax credit, 2.37–2.40

887

Index

Adoption from overseas
and **Overseas adoption**
Adoption pay
see **Statutory adoption pay**
Advance claims
generally, 2.286–2.287
working tax credit, 2.288–2.289
"Advance funding"
statutory maternity pay, 4.86
Age
statutory pay, 1.116
Agency workers
employment income, 1.425
Air crew
statutory adoption pay, 1.110–1.111
statutory maternity pay, 1.69
statutory paternity pay, 1.91–1.92
statutory sick pay
  definitions, 3.49, 3.55–3.56, 3.62
  general note, 3.46
  statutory provision, 1.56
  time for compliance, 3.64
Amendments
claims, 2.281
Amendments (tax returns)
Revenue, by
  during enquiry, 1.10
  generally, 1.7
taxpayer, by
  during enquiry, 1.9
  generally, 1.6
Amount treated as income of settlor
settlements
  charge to tax, 1.696–1.696
  income charged, 1.699
  person liable, 1.700
  "settlement", 1.698
Annual payments
adopters, to, 1.712
employment insurance payments, 1.710–1.711
foreign maintenance payments, 1.705
health insurance payments, 1.710–1.711
pension income, 2.131
periodical payments of personal injury damages
  compensation awards, 1.707
  generally, 1.706
  persons entitled, 1.708
  trusts, from, 1.709
Annual reports
tax credits, 1.330–1.331
Annual review
tax credits, 1.332–1.333
Annuities
life annuity payments
  charge to tax, 1.689
  income charged, 1.691
  meaning, 1.690
  person liable, 1.692
pension income, 2.131–2.132

Appeal notices
child trust funds (appeals)
  acknowledgment, 6.137
  disputes concerning, 6.78–6.79
  generally, 6.133–6.134
  notification, 6.137
  prescribed form, 6.62–6.63
  service, 6.76–6.77
  signature, 6.62–6.63
  statutory provision, 1.611
  time limits, 6.135–6.136
tax credits (appeals)
  acknowledgment, 2.462–2.463
  generally, 2.457–2.458
  notification, 2.462–2.463
  prescribed form, 2.368–2.369
  time limits, 2.459–2.461
Appeals
child care providers approval scheme, 2.588
child trust funds, and
  see also **Appeals (child trust funds)**
  appealable decisions, 1.609–1.610
  exercise of right, 1.611–1.615
  general regulations, 6.73–6.117
  jurisdiction, 6.65–6.72
  notice of appeal, 6.59–6.64
  penalties, 1.605–1.608
  procedure regulations, 6.118–6.164
  temporary modifications, 1.616–1.617
late appeals
  child trust funds (appeals), 6.80–6.81
  tax credits (appeals), 2.379–2.384
tax returns, 1.19–1.21
tax credits
  see also **Appeals (tax credits)**
  appealable decisions, 1.324–1.325
  exercise of right, 1.326–1.329
  general regulations, 2.370–2.437
  notice of appeal, 2.367–2.369
  procedure regulations, 2.438–2.491
  temporary modifications, 1.358–1.362
verification of claims, 2.366
Appeals (child trust funds)
adjournment, 6.102–6.103
administration of oaths, 6.92–6.93
appeals tribunal
  Clerk, 6.85
  composition, 6.84
  constitution, 1.151–1.152
  decisions, 6.104–6.105
  panel for appointment, 1.149–1.150
  President, 1.147–1.148
appeals tribunal, to
  generally, 1.153–1.155
  redetermination, 1.156–1.157
  supplementary provisions, 1.177–1.180
appealable decisions, 1.609–1.610
application for leave to appeal to appellate court, 6.163–6.164
application for leave to appeal to Commissioner
  determination, 6.132

888

Index

Appeals (child trust funds)—*cont.*
application for leave to appeal to Commissioner—*cont.*
  general regulations, under, 6.116–6.117
  generally, 6.128–6.129
  notice, 6.130–6.131
  withdrawal, 6.153–6.154
assessment of tax returns, 1.20–1.21
choice of hearing, 6.88–6.89
Clerk to appeals tribunal, 6.85
Commissioner, to
  application for leave to appeal, 6.116–6.117
  decisions, 6.156–6.162
  delegation of functions, 6.123
  general powers, 6.121
  statutory provisions, 1.158–1.164
  transfer of proceedings, 6.122
confidentiality, 6.94–6.95
consideration, 6.86–6.87
correction of errors
  Commissioner, by, 6.158–6.159
  generally, 6.110–6.111
  service by electronic mail, 6.115
  statutory provision, 1.169
  supplementary provisions, 6.114
Court of Appeal, to
  application for leave to appeal, 6.163–6.164
  statutory provision, 1.165–1.166
death of party, 6.82–6.83
decisions of appeals tribunal
  generally, 6.104–6.105
  service by electronic mail, 6.115
decisions of Board, 1.196–1.197
decisions of Commissioner
  correction of errors, 6.158–6.159
  generally, 6.156–6.157
  setting aside, 6.160–6.161
  supplementary provisions, 6.162
definitions
  general, 1.175–1.176
  general regulations, 6.74–6.75
  Part II, for, 1.170
  procedure regulations, 6.120
delegation of functions to authorised officers, 6.123
determination, 6.86–6.87
directions, 6.144–6.145
error correction
  Commissioner, by, 6.158–6.159
  generally, 6.110–6.111
  service by electronic mail, 6.115
  statutory provision, 1.169
  supplementary provisions, 6.114
exercise of right
  generally, 1.198–1.203, 1.611–1.615
  regulations, 1.204–1.205
expert assistance, 6.100–6.101
finality of decisions, 1.168
funding of legal services, 6.125–6.126
further particulars, 6.144–6.145
General Commissioners, 6.65–6.68

Appeals (child trust funds)—*cont.*
general regulations
  citation, 6.74
  commencement, 6.74
  definitions, 6.74–6.75
  duration, 6.74
  general provisions, 6.76–6.117
  recitals, 6.73
hearings
  generally, 6.150
  oral hearings, 6.98–6.99
  requests, 6.148–6.149
irregularities, 6.155
jurisdiction
  General Commissioners, 6.65–6.68
  Special Commissioners, 6.69–6.72
late appeals, 6.80–6.81
medical evidence
  non-disclosure, 6.146–6.147
notice of appeal
  acknowledgment, 6.137
  disputes concerning, 6.78–6.79
  generally, 6.133–6.134
  notification, 6.137
  prescribed form, 6.62–6.63
  service, 6.76–6.77
  signature, 6.62–6.63
  statutory provision, 1.611
  time limits, 6.135–6.136
oaths, 6.92–6.93
observations
  directions, 6.144–6.145
  reply, in, 6.142–6.143
  respondent, by, 6.140–6.141
oral hearings
  adjournment, 6.102–6.103
  expert assistance, 6.100–6.101
  generally, 6.98–6.99
  postponement, 6.102–6.103
  record of proceedings, 6.108–6.109
penalties, 1.605–1.608
point of law, on, 1.165–1.166
postponement, 6.102–6.103
procedure
  generally, 1.167
  regulations, 1.187
procedure regulations
  arrangement, 6.118
  citation, 6.119
  commencement, 6.119
  definitions, 6.120
  duration, 6.119
  general provisions, 6.121–6.164
record of proceedings
  generally, 6.108–6.109
  service by electronic mail, 6.115
Regulations
  general, 6.73–6.117
  jurisdiction, 6.65–6.72
  notice of appeal, 6.59–6.64
  procedure, 6.118–6.164
reinstatement, 6.97
representation, 6.138–6.139

889

Index

Appeals (child trust funds)—*cont.*
requests for hearings, 6.148–6.149
respondent's observations, 6.140–6.141
service of notices or documents
  electronic mail, by, 6.115
  generally, 6.76–6.77
  manner and time, 6.124
setting aside of decisions
  Commissioner, by, 6.160–6.162
  generally, 6.112–6.113
  service by electronic mail, 6.115
  statutory provision, 1.169
  supplementary provisions, 6.114
Social security commissioners
  appointment, 1.181
  certificates, 1.185
  delegation of functions, 1.184
  jurisdiction, 6.65–6.72
  remuneration, 1.182
  supplemental, 1.186
  tenure, 1.183
Special Commissioners, 6.69–6.72
statement of reasons
  generally, 6.104–6.105
  late applications, 6.106–6.107
  service by electronic mail, 6.115
striking out
  grounds, 6.96
  reinstatement, 6.97
temporary modifications, 1.616–1.617
time limits
  extension, 6.80–6.81
  generally, 6.135–6.136
transfer of proceedings to Commissioner, 6.122
withdrawal
  general regulations, under, 6.90–6.91
  generally, 6.153–6.154
witness summonses
  general regulations, under, 6.92–6.93
  generally, 6.151–6.152
written observations
  directions, 6.144–6.145
  reply, in, 6.142–6.143
  respondent, by, 6.140–6.141

Appeals (tax credits)
adjournment, 2.414–2.415
administration of oaths, 2.401–2.402
appeals tribunal, to
  Clerks, 2.392
  composition, 2.390–2.391
  decisions, 2.416–2.437
  generally, 1.153–1.155
  redetermination, 1.156–1.157
appealable decisions, 1.324–1.325
applications for leave to appeal to appellate court, 2.490–2.491
applications for leave to appeal to Commissioner
  determination, 2.456
  general regulations, under, 2.434–2.437
  generally, 2.448–2.452
  introductory, 2.447

Appeals (tax credits)—*cont.*
applications for leave to appeal to Commissioner—*cont.*
  notice, 2.453–2.455
  withdrawal, 2.480–2.481
assessment of tax returns, 1.20–1.21
choice of hearing, 2.395–2.396
Clerks to appeals tribunal, 2.392
Commissioner, to
  application for leave to appeal, 2.447–2.456
  decisions, 2.483–2.489
  delegation of functions, 2.443
  general powers, 2.441
  statutory provisions, 1.158–1.164
  transfer of proceedings, 2.442
consideration, 3.432–2.394
correction of errors
  Commissioner, by, 2.485–2.486
  generally, 2.426–2.427
  service by electronic mail, 2.432
  statutory provision, 1.169
  supplementary provisions, 2.431
Court of Appeal, to
  applications for leave to appeal, 2.490–2.491
  generally, 1.165–1.166
death of party, 2.389
decisions of appeals tribunal, 2.416–2.421
decisions of Board, 1.198–1.203
decisions of Commissioner
  correction of errors, 2.485–2.486
  generally, 2.483–2.484
  setting aside, 2.487–2.488
  supplementary provisions, 2.489
definitions
  general regulations, 2.371–2.372
  procedure regulations, 2.440
  statutory provision, 1.170
delegation of functions, 2.443
determination, 2.393–2.394
directions
  applications, 2.387–2.388
  death of party, 2.389
  determination of applications, 2.393–2.394
  withdrawal of applications, 2.397–2.398
error correction
  generally, 2.426–2.427
  service by electronic mail, 2.432
  statutory provision, 1.169
  supplementary provisions, 2.431
exercise of right
  generally, 1.326–1.329
  other persons, 2.375–2.376
expert assistance, 2.412–2.413
extensions of time
  applications, 2.385–2.386
  generally, 2.379–2.384
funding legal services, 2.445–2.446
further directions, 2.470–2.472

Index

Appeals (tax credits)—*cont.*
general regulations
  appeals tribunal, 2.390–2.392
  decisions, 2.416–2.437
  general matters, 2.375–2.389
  procedure, 2.393–2.415
  service of notices, 2.373–2.374
hearings
  choice, 2.395–2.396
  generally, 2.477
  oral, 2.406–2.415
  requests, 2.475–2.476
irregularities, 2.481–2.482
late appeals, 2.379–2.384
medical evidence, non-disclosure of
  general regulations, under, 2.399–2.400
  generally, 2.473–2.474
notice of appeal
  acknowledgment, 2.462–2.463
  generally, 2.457–2.458
  notification, 2.462–2.463
  prescribed form, 2.368–2.369
  time limits, 2.459–2.461
oaths, 2.401–2.402
observations
  directions, 2.470–2.472
  reply, in, 2.468–2.469
  respondent, by, 2.466–2.467
oral hearings
  adjournment, 2.414–2.415
  expert assistance, 2.412–2.413
  generally, 2.406–2.411
  postponement, 2.414–2.415
penalty proceedings
  determination, 2.393–2.394
  withdrawal, 2.397–2.398
point of law, on, 1.165–1.166
postponement, 2.414–2.415
procedure
  generally, 1.167
  regulations, 1.187
procedure regulations
  appeal procedure, 2.464–2.482
  applications for leave to appeal, 2.447–2.463
  applications for leave to appeal to appellate court, 2.490–2.491
  Commissioner's powers, 2.441
  decisions, 2.483–2.489
  delegation of functions, 2.443
  funding of legal services, 2.445–2.446
  service of notices, 2.444
  transfer of proceedings, 2.442
record of proceedings
  generally, 2.424–2.425
  service by electronic mail, 2.432
Regulations
  general, 2.370–2.437
  notice of appeal, 2.367–2.369
  procedure, 2.438–2.491
reinstatement, 2.405
representation, 2.464–2.465
requests for hearings, 2.475–2.476

Appeals (tax credits)—*cont.*
respondent's written observations, 2.466–2.467
right of appeal
  decisions of Board, 1.198–1.203
  generally, 1.326–1.329
  other persons, 2.375–2.376
service of notices
  electronic mail, by, 2.432
  generally, 2.373–2.374
  manner and time, 2.444
setting aside of decisions
  Commissioner, by, 2.487–2.489
  generally, 2.428–2.430
  service by electronic mail, 2.432
  statutory provision, 1.169
  supplementary provisions, 2.431
Social security commissioners
  appointment, 1.181
  certificates, 1.185
  delegation of functions, 1.184
  remuneration, 1.182
  supplemental, 1.186
  tenure, 1.183
statement of reasons
  generally, 2.419
  late applications, 2.422–2.423
  service by electronic mail, 2.432
striking out
  grounds, 2.403–2.404
  reinstatement, 2.405
temporary modifications, 1.358–1.362
time limits
  extension, 2.379–2.386
  generally, 2.377–2.378
transfer of proceedings, 2.442
withdrawal, 2.480–2.481
witness summonses
  general regulations, under, 2.401–2.402
  generally, 2.478–2.479
written observations
  directions, 2.470–2.472
  reply, in, 2.468–2.469
  respondent, by, 2.466–2.467

Appeals tribunal (child trust funds)
appeals to
  generally, 1.153–1.155
  redetermination, 1.156–1.157
  supplementary provisions, 1.177–1.180
Clerk, 6.85
composition, 6.84
constitution, 1.151–1.152
decisions, 6.104–6.105
panel for appointment, 1.149–1.150
President, 1.147–1.148

Appeals tribunal (tax credits)
appeals to
  generally, 1.153–1.155
  redetermination, 1.156–1.157
Clerks, 2.392
composition, 2.390–2.391
decisions, 2.416–2.437

Index

Applications (permission to appeal to appellate court)
child trust funds (appeals), 6.163–6.164
tax credits (appeals), 2.490–2.491
Applications (permission to appeal to Commissioner)
child trust funds (appeals)
  determination, 6.132
  general regulations, under, 6.116–6.117
  generally, 6.128–6.129
  notice, 6.130–6.131
  withdrawal, 6.153–6.154
tax credits (appeals)
  determination, 2.456
  general regulations, under, 2.434–2.437
  generally, 2.448–2.452
  introductory, 2.447
  notice, 2.453–2.455
  withdrawal, 2.480–2.481
Approval of Child Care Providers Scheme
see **Childcare Approval Scheme**
Aspect enquiries
amendment by taxpayer, 1.9
completion, 1.12
correction by Revenue, 1.10
notice, 1.8
Assault
officers of Revenue and Customs, 1.745
Assignment
tax credits, 1.340–1.341
Asylum seekers
definitions, 2.500
exclusion from entitlement, 2.501–2.510
general note, 2.507
modifications of Act, 2.511–2.512
statutory provision, 1.334–1.335
transitional relief, 2.513–2.514
Attendance allowance
social security income, 2.145
"Avoidance of liability"
statutory adoption pay
  adoption from overseas, 5.132
  generally, 5.78
statutory maternity pay, 4.6–4.7
statutory paternity pay
  adoption from overseas, 5.125
  generally, 5.67
statutory sick pay, 3.10

Back to work bonus
social security income, 2.145
Bad debts
trading income, 1.650
Bankruptcy
tax credits, 1.340–1.341
Basic element (working tax credit)
adoption, 2.37–2.40
ceasing to undertake work, 2.51–2.52
childbirth, 2.37–2.40
gaps between jobs, 2.53–2.54
ill health, 2.41–2.42
pay in lieu of notice, 2.49–2.50

Basic element (working tax credit)—*cont.*
qualifying remunerative work, and
  excepted activities, 2.35
  generally, 2.25–2.31
  hours worked, 2.36
  minimum level of continuity, 2.33
  remunerative work, 2.34
  routes to entitlement, 2.32
seasonal work, 2.43–2.44
strike periods, 2.45–2.46
suspension from work, 2.47–2.48
term-time work, 2.43–2.44
working less than 16 hours a week, 2.51–2.52
"Basis periods"
accounting date, 1.658
normal rules, 1.659
professions and vocations, 1.657
"Benefits code"
see also **Employment income**
see also **Taxable benefits**
definitions, 1.430
dispensations, 1.429
meaning, 1.427
relationship with earnings, 1.428
Bereavement payment
social security income, 2.145
"Betting winnings"
investment income, 2.156
Birth
evidence
  statutory paternity pay, 5.54–5.55
  tax credits, 2.324
statutory paternity pay
  conditions of entitlement, 5.48–5.50
  evidence of entitlement, 5.54–5.55
  notice requirements, 5.52
  payment period, 5.51
  qualifying period, 5.53
  statutory provisions, 1.72–1.76/1
  treatment of more than one employer, 5.56
tax credits, 2.324
working tax credit, 2.37–2.40
Board of Inland Revenue
see **Commissioners of Inland Revenue**
"Breach of regulations"
statutory maternity pay, 1.135–1.136
statutory sick pay, 1.135–1.136
Building societies (dividends)
savings and investment income, 1.681
Business entertainment
trading income, 1.652

Capital expenditure
trading income, 1.648
Capital gains
generally, 2.103
Capital receipts
trading income, 1.655
"Capital rule"
generally, 2.103

Index

Car fuel benefits
  calculation of cash equivalent, 1.462
  nil cash equivalent, 1.463
  treatedment as earnings, 1.461
Carers
  remunerative work, 2.35
Carer's allowance
  social security income, 2.147
Cash vouchers
  see **Vouchers**
"Ceasing to undertake work"
  working tax credit, 2.51–2.52
Change of circumstances (tax credits)
  advance, in, 2.319
  amendment, 2.312
  childcare element (working tax credit), 2.76–2.77
  civil partnerships, 2.259
  date of, 2.313–2.318
  decrease of rate, 2.307–2.308
  definitions, 2.207
  discretionary, 1.248
  evidence of birth or adoption, 2.324
  failure to report, 1.250
  generally, 1.243–1.244
  increase of maximum rate, 2.305–2.306
  mandatory, 1.246
  method, 2.309–2.310
  person acting on behalf of another, by, 2.320–2.323
  relevant changes, 1.245
  relevant person, 2.311
"Change of employer"
  statutory maternity pay, 4.25
Charge to tax (income tax)
  emoluments (offices and employment)
    see also **Employment income**
    see also **Pension income**
    see also **Social security income**
    general note, 1.407
  employment income
    see also **Employment income**
    agency workers, 1.425
    deductions from earnings, 1.461–1.472
    earnings, 1.426
    "employment", 1.414–1.415
    exemptions, 1.456–1.460
    general note, 1.407
    introductory provision, 1.412–1.413
    nature, 1.417–1.419
    office-holders, 1.416
    operation, 1.420–1.424
    taxable benefits, 1.427–1.455
  general note
    ITA 2007, 1.750
    ITEPA 2003, under, 1.407
  general rule
    ITA 2007, 1.753–1.755
    ITTOIA 2005, 1.626–1.627
    ITEPA 2003, under, 1.410
  miscellaneous income
    see also **Miscellaneous income**

Charge to tax (income tax)—*cont.*
  miscellaneous income—*cont.*
    income not otherwise charged, 1.701
    settlements, 1.696–1.700
  pension income
    see also **Pension income**
    amount charged, 1.476
    general note, 1.474
    general rules, 1.478–1.482
    introductory provision, 1.473
    nature of charge, 1.475
    person liable to tax, 1.477
    social security pensions, 1.483–1.486
  property income
    see also **Property income**
    generally, 1.668
    income charged, 1.670
    person liable, 1.671
    territorial scope, 1.669
  savings and investments income
    see also **Savings and investments income**
    dividends from non-resident UK companies, 1.686
    dividends from UK resident companies, 1.683
    interest, 1.678
    purchased life annuity payments, 1.689
  Schedule E (offices and employment emoluments)
    see also **Employment income**
    see also **Pension income**
    see also **Social security income**
    general note, 1.407
  social security income
    see also **Social security income**
    amount charged, 1.493
    definitions, 1.525–1.526
    exempt benefits, 1.502–1.517
    foreign benefits, 1.521–1.524
    general note, 1.488
    introductory provision, 1.487
    nature of charge, 1.489–1.490
    person liable to tax, 1.494
    taxable benefits, 1.495–1.501
    wholly exempt benefits, 1.518–1.520
  trading income
    see also **Trading income**
    generally, 1.633
    income charged, 1.635
    person liable, 1.636
    territorial scope, 1.634
Charitable work
  see **Voluntary work**
"Cheque vouchers"
  meaning, 1.440
"Child"
  childcare element (working tax credit), 22.72–2.73
Child benefit
  social security income, 2.145
Child maintenance
  see **Child support**

Index

Child maintenance bonus
  social security income
    income support, 1.505
    jobseeker's allowance, 1.510
Child support
  disregards, 2.176
Child tax credit
  administrative arrangements
    definitions, 2.363
    general note, 2.361
    provision of information, 2.364–2.365
    recording, etc. of claims, 2.366
    statutory provisions, 1.348–1.349
  age of child, 2.205–2.206
  annual reports, 1.330–1.331
  annual review, 1.332–1.333
  appeals
    see also **Appeals (tax credits)**
    appealable decisions, 1.324–1.325
    exercise of right, 1.326–1.329
    general regulations, 2.370–2.437
    notice of appeal, 2.367–2.369
    procedure regulations, 2.438–2.491
    temporary modifications, 1.358–1.362
  approval of child care providers scheme
    appeals, 2.588
    approved criteria, 2.584
    approved person, 2.583
    approved system, 2.585
    criteria, 2.584
    definitions, 2.579
    fees, 2.589
    period of approval, 2.587
    qualifying child care, 2.582
    Regulations, 2.578–2.590
    requirements, 2.581
    specified body, 2.580
    system, 2.585
  assignment, 1.340–1.341
  bankruptcy, 1.340–1.341
  changes of circumstances
    advance, in, 2.319
    amendment, 2.312
    automatic, 1.249
    civil partnerships, 2.259
    date of, 2.313–2.318
    decrease of rate, 2.307–2.308
    definitions, 2.207
    discretionary, 1.248
    failure to report, 1.250
    generally, 1.243–1.244
    increase of maximum rate, 2.305–2.306
    mandatory, 1.246
    method, 2.309–2.310
    person acting on behalf of another, by, 2.320–2.323
    relevant changes, 1.245
    relevant person, 2.311
  child care providers scheme
    appeals, 2.588
    approved criteria, 2.584
    approved person, 2.583
    approved system, 2.585

Child tax credit—*cont.*
  child care providers scheme—*cont.*
    criteria, 2.584
    definitions, 2.579
    fees, 2.589
    period of approval, 2.587
    qualifying child care, 2.582
    Regulations, 2.578–2.590
    requirements, 2.581
    specified body, 2.580
    system, 2.585
  claims
    see also **Claims**
    definitions, 2.275–2.276
    generally, 2.277–2.303
    statutory provisions, 1.231–1.240
  Codes of Practice
    overpayments, 7.24–7.32
  Crown employment, 1.338–1.339
  death of child, after, 2.209–2.210
  decisions
    discovery, on, 1.290–1.292
    final decision, 1.286–1.287
    final notice, 1.284–1.285
    information requirements, 1.295–1.296
    initial decision, 1.276–1.279
    notice of, 1.297–1.298
    official error, subject to, 1.293–1.294
    other revised decisions, 1.282–1.283
    power to enquire, 1.288–1.289
    revision after notifications, 1.280–1.281
  definitions
    regulations, in, 2.185–2.186
    statute, in, 1.346–1.347
  determination of rate
    cut-off provisions, 2.268–2.269
    full year periods, 2.266
    generally, 2.251–2.265
    introduction, 2.225–2.226
    short periods, 2.267
  development of system, 1.223
  disabled child, 2.213–2.214
  disclosure of information, 1.350–1.351
  duration, 1.241–1.242
  entitlement, 1.258–1.260
  evidence of birth or adoption, 2.324
  failure to comply with requirements, 1.312–1.313
  failure to make correct payments, 1.314–1.315
  forwarding of claims, 2.366
  fraud, and
    generally, 1.318–1.319
    powers relating to documents, 1.320–1.321
  functions of Commissioners, 1.229–1.230
  holding of claims, 2.366
  inalienability, 1.340–1.341
  income test
    see also **Income test**
    calculation, 2.115–2.120
    definitions, 2.113–2.114
    disregards, 2.175–2.182

Index

Child tax credit—*cont.*
  income test—*cont.*
    employment income, 2.121–2.130
    foreign income, 2.161–2.162
    general note, 2.101–2.111
    investment income, 2.155–2.158
    miscellaneous income, 2.173–2.174
    notional income, 2.163–2.172
    pension income, 2.131–2.137
    property income, 2.159–2.160
    social security income, 2.144–2.150
    statutory provision, 1.251–1.257
  income thresholds, 2.218–2.220
  incorrect statements, 1.309–1.311
  interest
    definitions, 2.495
    general note, 2.494
    overpayments, on, 2.496
    prescribed rate, 2.497
    statutory provision, 1.322–1.323
    student income, 2.151–2.154
    trading income, 2.138–2.143
  maximum rate
    generally, 2.211–2.212
    statutory provision, 1.261–1.263
  means testing, 2.101
  Northern Ireland, 1.363–1.364
  notices by Board, 1.342–1.343
  notices to provide information
    childcare provider, to, 2.326
    dates to be specified, 2.327
    definitions, 2.272
    electronic communications, 2.273–2.274
    employers, to, 2.325
    s.17 TCA 2002, under, 2.328–2.331
  notification of change of circumstances
    advance, in, 2.319
    amendment, 2.312
    automatic, 1.249
    civil partnerships, 2.259
    date of, 2.313–2.318
    decrease of rate, 2.307–2.308
    definitions, 2.207
    discretionary, 1.248
    evidence of birth or adoption, 2.324
    failure to report, 1.250
    generally, 1.243–1.244
    increase of maximum rate, 2.305–2.306
    mandatory, 1.246
    method, 2.309–2.310
    person acting on behalf of another, by, 2.320–2.323
    relevant changes, 1.245
    relevant person, 2.311
  official errors
    definitions, 2.536–2.537
    general note, 2.539
    generally, 2.538
  overpayments
    Code of Practice, 7.24–7.32
    generally, 1.303–1.304
    recovery, 1.305–1.306, 2.355

Child tax credit—*cont.*
  payment
    employees' rights, 1.301–1.302
    generally, 1.299–1.300
  payment by Revenue and Customs
    amount, 2.353–2.354
    bank account requirement, 2.358–2.359
    definitions, 2.335
    general note, 2.333
    joint claims, for, 2.336–2.341
    method, 2.356–2.357
    person acting on behalf of another, for, 2.342–2.343
    postponement, 2.351–2.352
    recovery of overpayments, 2.355
    renewal claims, 2.344–2.345
    single payments, 2.349–2.350
    timing, 2.346–2.348
  penalties
    determination, 1.369
    failure to comply with requirements, 1.312–1.313
    failure to make correct payments, 1.314–1.315
    generally, 1.374–1.377
    Guidance, 7.1–7.23
    incorrect statements, etc., 1.309–1.311
    mitigation, 1.371
    proceedings before Commissioners, 1.370
    recovery, 1.373
    supplementary, 1.316–1.317
    time limits, 1.372
  period of award, 1.241–1.242
  persons subject to immigration control
    definitions, 2.500
    exclusion from entitlement, 2.501–2.510
    general note, 2.507
    modifications of Act, 2.511–2.512
    statutory provision, 1.334–1.335
    transitional relief, 2.513–2.514
  polygamous marriages
    definitions, 2.548–2.549
    general note, 2.546
    modification of Regulations, 2.551–2.557
    modification of TCA 2002, 2.550
    statutory provision, 1.336–1.337
  provision of information
    authorities, by, 2.365
    authorities, to, 2.364
    functions relating to employment, 2.565, 2.577
    functions relating to health, 2.542–2.544, 2.561, 2.575
    functions relating to training, 2.565, 2.577
  qualifying young person
    definition, 2.185
    maximum age, 2.207–2.208

895

Index

Child tax credit—*cont.*
  rate, 1.274–1.275
  recording of claims, 2.366
  recovery of overpayments
    generally, 1.305–1.306
    method, 2.355
  residence requirements
    Crown servants posted overseas, 2.529–2.531
    definitions, 2.517–2.518
    ordinary residence, 2.522–2.525
    person treated as not being in UK, 2.519–2.526
    temporary absence from UK, 2.527–2.528
    transitional provision, 2.532–2.533
  responsibility for child
    competing claims, 2.195–2.196
    excepted cases, 2.197–2.203
    generally, 2.187–2.193
    normally living with test, 2.194
    special case, 2.204
  severely disabled child, 2.213–2.214
  statutory provisions
    see also **Tax credits**
    appeals, 1.324–1.329
    child tax credit, 1.258–1.263
    decisions, 1.276–1.298
    fraud, 1.318–1.321
    generally, 1.227–1.257
    interest, 1.322–1.323
    payment, 1.299–1.308
    penalties, 1.309–1.317
    rate, 1.274–1.275
    supplementary, 1.330–1.347
    working tax credit, 1.264–1.273
  transitional provisions, 2.566–2.569
  underpayments, 1.307–1.308
  use of information, 1.350–1.351
  verification of claims, 2.366
Child Tax Credit Regulations 2002
  arrangement of Regulations, 2.183
  citation, 2.184
  commencement, 2.184
  definitions, 2.185–2.186
  effect, 2.184
  general provisions, 2.187–2.214
  modifications to, 2.551
Child trust funds
  account providers
    approval, 1.546–1.548
    ceasing to act, 6.26
    ceasing to qualify, 6.27
    generally, 1.546
    introduction, 1.528
    provision of information, 1.594–1.595
    qualifying circumstances, 6.20–6.23
    types of account, 1.547–1.549
    withdrawal of approval, 6.22
  appeals
    see also **Child trust funds (appeals)**
    appealable decisions, 1.609–1.610
    exercise of right, 1.611–1.615

Child trust funds—*cont.*
  appeals—*cont.*
    general regulations, 6.73–6.117
    jurisdiction, 6.65–6.72
    notice of appeal, 6.59–6.64
    penalties, 1.605–1.608
    procedure regulations, 6.118–6.164
    temporary modifications, 1.616–1.617
  approval of account providers
    appeals, 6.23
    appointment of tax representative, 6.21
    disqualifying circumstances, 6.22
    generally, 1.546–1.548
    qualifying circumstances, 6.20
    withdrawal, 6.22
  assignment of investments, 1.554–1.555
  background, 1.528
  bankruptcy of child, 1.554–1.555
  capital gains tax
    adaptation of enactments, 6.44
    generally, 1.590–1.591
  characteristics
    eligible child, 1.535–1.543
    introduction, 1.530–1.534
    requirements to be satisfied, 1.544–1.553
  charge over investments, 1.554–1.555
  child benefit, 1.537
  child in care, 1.538
  Commissioners of Inland Revenue, and
    General Commissioners, 6.57–6.60
    Special Commissioners, 6.61–6.64
  contributions
    further, 1.581–1.585
    generally, 6.13
    initial, 1.571–1.572
    non-monetary subscriptions, 1.588–1.589
    recoupment, 1.586–1.587
    supplementary, 1.573–1.580
  corporation tax, 1.592–1.593
  date of birth, 1.537
  death of child, and
    payments to parent, 1.601–1.602
    withdrawal of fund, 1.549
  descriptions of accounts, 6.10
  eligible child
    meaning, 1.535–1.543
    opening of fund, 1.556–1.561
  further contributions, 1.581–1.585
  general note, 1.528
  generally, 1.530–1.534
  HM Revenue and Customs
    opening of fund, 1.562–1.568
    status and role, 1.534
  inalienability, 1.554–1.555
  income tax, 1.590–1.591
  information
    account providers, from, 1.594–1.595
    child in care of authority, about, 1.596–1.597
    disclosure of, 1.600
    use of, 1.598–1.599

Index

Child trust funds—*cont.*
  initial contributions, 1.571–1.572
  insurance companies, 6.50–6.58
  invalid accounts, repair of, 6.30
  investment rules
    generally, 6.17
    qualifying investments, 6.18
  jurisdiction of Commissioners
    General Commissioners, 6.57–6.60
    Special Commissioners, 6.61–6.64
  looked after child
    authority to manage account, 6.41
    generally, 1.538
    information from local authorities, 6.40
  management of, 1.551
  meaning, 1.530–1.534
  migrant workers' children, 1.540
  Northern Ireland, 1.618
  objectives, 1.528
  opening by eligible child
    conditions for application, 6.19
    generally, 6.11
    statutory provision, 1.556–1.561
  opening by HM Revenue and Customs
    generally, 6.12
    statutory provision, 1.562–1.568
  opening by responsible person
    conditions for application, 6.19
    generally, 6.11
    statutory provision, 1.556–1.561
  parental responsibility, 1.544
  penalties
    appeals, 1.605–1.608
    decisions, 1.605–1.608
    generally, 1.603–1.604
    mitigation, 1.605–1.608
    recovery, 1.605–1.608
  recoupment of IR contributions
    generally, 6.29
    statutory provision, 1.586–1.587
  repair of invalid accounts, 6.30
  repayments of tax to account provider
    annual claims, 6.34
    interim claims, 6.33
  requirements to be satisfied
    generally, 6.14
    statutory provision, 1.544–1.553
  residence, 1.540–1.541
  responsible person
    meaning, 1.552–1.553
    opening of fund, 1.556–1.561
  revenue allocated accounts
    account provider ceases to accept, where, 6.26
    generally, 6.12
    statutory provision, 1.562–1.568
  Revenue and Customs
    opening of fund, 1.562–1.568
    status and role, 1.534
  stakeholder accounts
    characteristics, 6.48
    charges, 6.49

Child trust funds—*cont.*
  stakeholder accounts—*cont.*
    description, 6.47
    generally, 6.10
  statements of account, 6.15
  subscription limits
    generally, 6.15
    statutory provision, 1.588–1.589
  supplementary contributions, 1.573–1.580
  tax
    account provider to act on behalf of named child, 6.32
    administration, 6.45
    application of Taxes Act, 6.46
    assessment for withdrawal of relief, 6.36
    capital gains tax, 1.590–1.591
    corporation tax, 1.592–1.593
    fortnightly claims, 6.37
    generally, 6.31
    income tax, 1.590–1.591
    information about looked after children, 6.40–6.41
    information to be provided to Board, 6.42
    inspection of records, 6.43
    records, 6.38
    repayments to account provider, 6.33–6.35
    returns of information, 6.39
    tax returns, 6.37
  transfers
    account provider ceases to act, where, 6.26
    account provider ceases to qualify, where, 6.27
    other providers, to, 6.28
    statutory provision, 1.569–1.570
  vouchers
    generally, 6.9
    statutory provision, 1.557–1.558
  withdrawals from fund
    child is terminally ill, where, 6.25
    permitted, 6.24
    statutory provision, 1.549

Child Trust Funds Act 2004
  arrangement of sections, 1.527
  commencement
    introduction, 1.529
    Order No.1, 6.1–6.2
    Order No.2, 6.3–6.4
  extent, 1.529
  general note, 1.528
  general provisions, 1.530–1.617
  supplementary, 1.618–1.624

Child trust funds (appeals)
  adjournment, 6.102–6.103
  administration of oaths, 6.92–6.93
  appeals tribunal
    Clerk, 6.85
    composition, 6.84
    constitution, 1.151–1.152
    decisions, 6.104–6.105

Child trust funds (appeals)—*cont.*
  appeals tribunal—*cont.*
    panel for appointment, 1.149–1.150
    President, 1.147–1.148
  appeals tribunal, to
    generally, 1.153–1.155
    redetermination, 1.156–1.157
    supplementary provisions, 1.177–1.180
  appealable decisions, 1.609–1.610
  application for leave to appeal to appellate court, 6.163–6.164
  application for leave to appeal to Commissioner
    determination, 6.132
    general regulations, under, 6.116–6.117
    generally, 6.128–6.129
    notice, 6.130–6.131
    withdrawal, 6.153–6.154
  assessment of tax returns, 1.20–1.21
  choice of hearing, 6.88–6.89
  Clerk to appeals tribunal, 6.85
  Commissioner, to
    application for leave to appeal, 6.116–6.117
    decisions, 6.156–6.162
    delegation of functions, 6.123
    general powers, 6.121
    statutory provisions, 1.158–1.164
    transfer of proceedings, 6.122
  confidentiality, 6.94–6.95
  consideration, 6.86–6.87
  correction of errors
    Commissioner, by, 6.158–6.159
    generally, 6.110–6.111
    service by electronic mail, 6.115
    statutory provision, 1.169
    supplementary provisions, 6.114
  Court of Appeal, to
    application for leave to appeal, 6.163–6.164
    statutory provision, 1.165–1.166
  death of party, 6.82–6.83
  decisions of appeals tribunal
    generally, 6.104–6.105
    service by electronic mail, 6.115
  decisions of Board, 1.196–1.197
  decisions of Commissioner
    correction of errors, 6.158–6.159
    generally, 6.156–6.157
    setting aside, 6.160–6.161
    supplementary provisions, 6.162
  definitions
    general, 1.175–1.176
    general regulations, 6.74–6.75
    Part II, for, 1.170
    procedure regulations, 6.120
  delegation of functions to authorised officers, 6.123
  determination, 6.86–6.87
  directions, 6.144–6.145
  error correction
    Commissioner, by, 6.158–6.159
    generally, 6.110–6.111

Child trust funds (appeals)—*cont.*
  error correction—*cont.*
    service by electronic mail, 6.115
    statutory provision, 1.169
    supplementary provisions, 6.114
  exercise of right
    generally, 1.198–1.203, 1.611–1.615
    regulations, 1.204–1.205
  expert assistance, 6.100–6.101
  finality of decisions, 1.168
  funding of legal services, 6.125–6.126
  further particulars, 6.144–6.145
  General Commissioners, 6.65–6.68
  general regulations
    citation, 6.74
    commencement, 6.74
    definitions, 6.74–6.75
    duration, 6.74
    general provisions, 6.76–6.117
    recitals, 6.73
  hearings
    generally, 6.150
    oral hearings, 6.98–6.99
    requests, 6.148–6.149
  irregularities, 6.155
  jurisdiction
    General Commissioners, 6.65–6.68
    Special Commissioners, 6.69–6.72
  late appeals, 6.80–6.81
  medical evidence
    non-disclosure, 6.146–6.147
  notice of appeal
    acknowledgment, 6.137
    disputes concerning, 6.78–6.79
    generally, 6.133–6.134
    notification, 6.137
    prescribed form, 6.62–6.63
    service, 6.76–6.77
    signature, 6.62–6.63
    statutory provision, 1.611
    time limits, 6.135–6.136
  oaths, 6.92–6.93
  observations
    directions, 6.144–6.145
    reply, in, 6.142–6.143
    respondent, by, 6.140–6.141
  oral hearings
    adjournment, 6.102–6.103
    expert assistance, 6.100–6.101
    generally, 6.98–6.99
    postponement, 6.102–6.103
    record of proceedings, 6.108–6.109
  penalties, 1.605–1.608
  point of law, on, 1.165–1.166
  postponement, 6.102–6.103
  procedure
    generally, 1.167
    regulations, 1.187
  procedure regulations
    arrangement, 6.118
    citation, 6.119
    commencement, 6.119
    definitions, 6.120

898

Index

Child trust funds (appeals)—*cont.*
procedure regulations—*cont.*
  duration, 6.119
  general provisions, 6.121–6.164
record of proceedings
  generally, 6.108–6.109
  service by electronic mail, 6.115
Regulations
  general, 6.73–6.117
  jurisdiction, 6.65–6.72
  notice of appeal, 6.59–6.64
  procedure, 6.118–6.164
reinstatement, 6.97
representation, 6.138–6.139
requests for hearings, 6.148–6.149
respondent's observations, 6.140–6.141
service of notices or documents
  electronic mail, by, 6.115
  generally, 6.76–6.77
  manner and time, 6.124
setting aside of decisions
  Commissioner, by, 6.160–6.162
  generally, 6.112–6.113
  service by electronic mail, 6.115
  statutory provision, 1.169
  supplementary provisions, 6.114
Social security commissioners
  appointment, 1.181
  certificates, 1.185
  delegation of functions, 1.184
  jurisdiction, 6.65–6.72
  remuneration, 1.182
  supplemental, 1.186
  tenure, 1.183
Special Commissioners, 6.69–6.72
statement of reasons
  generally, 6.104–6.105
  late applications, 6.106–6.107
  service by electronic mail, 6.115
striking out
  grounds, 6.96
  reinstatement, 6.97
temporary modifications, 1.616–1.617
time limits
  extension, 6.80–6.81
  generally, 6.135–6.136
transfer of proceedings to Commissioner, 6.122
withdrawal
  general regulations, under, 6.90–6.91
  generally, 6.153–6.154
witness summonses
  general regulations, under, 6.92–6.93
  generally, 6.151–6.152
written observations
  directions, 6.144–6.145
  reply, in, 6.142–6.143
  respondent, by, 6.140–6.141
Child Trust Funds (Appeals) Regulations 2005
citation, 6.74
commencement, 6.74

Child Trust Funds (Appeals) Regulations 2005—*cont.*
definitions, 6.74–6.75
duration, 6.74
general provisions, 6.76–6.117
recitals, 6.73
Child Trust Funds (Insurance Companies) Regulations 2004
arrangement of regulations, 6.50
citation, 6.51
commencement, 6.51
definitions, 6.52
general provisions, 6.53–6.58
Child Trust Funds (Non-tax Appeals) Regulations 2005
citation, 6.60
commencement, 6.60
definitions, 6.61
general provisions, 6.62–6.64
recitals, 6.59
Child Trust Funds Regulations 2004
arrangement of regulations, 6.5
citation, 6.6
commencement, 6.6
definitions, 6.7–6.8
general provisions, 6.9–6.46
schedule, 6.47–6.49
Childbirth
see **Birth**
Childcare
see also **Approval of Child Care Providers Scheme**
employer-contracted and provided
  "care", 1.459
  "child", 1.459
  employer-contracted, 1.458
  employer-provided, 1.456–1.457
  introductory note, 1.413
  "parental responsibility", 1.459
  "qualifying child care", 1.460
  regulations, 2.128
notice to provide information by provider, 2.326
Childcare Approval Scheme
appeals, 2.588
approved criteria, 2.584
approved person, 2.583
approved system, 2.585
criteria, 2.584
definitions, 2.579
fees, 2.589
period of approval, 2.587
qualifying child care, 2.582
Regulations
  application, 2.578
  citation, 2.578
  commencement, 2.578
  definitions, 2.579
  general provisions, 2.580–2.589
  revocation and saving, 2.590
requirements, 2.581
specified body, 2.580
system, 2.585

Index

Childcare element (working tax credit)
  calculation of childcare charges, 2.74–2.75
  change of circumstances, 2.76–2.77
  "child", 2.72–2.73
  "childcare", 2.72–2.73
  generally, 2.69–2.71
  incapacitation, 2.71
  payment by Revenue and Customs, 2.336–2.337
  qualifying young persons, 2.73
  "relevant childcare charges", 2.72–2.73
  statutory provision, 1.272–1.273
"Childcare providers"
  notice to provide information, 2.326
Childcare vouchers
  meaning, 1.440
Children
  childcare element (working tax credit), 22.72–2.73
Christmas bonus
  social security income, 2.145
Civil partners
  references in Income Tax Acts, 1.767
Civil partnerships
  tax credits, 2.259
Civil penalties
  see **Penalties**
CJD
  see **Creuzfeld-Jakob Disease**
Claims
  administrative arrangements
    definitions, 2.363
    general note, 2.361
    provision of information, 2.364–2.365
    recording, etc. of claims, 2.366
  advance, in
    generally, 2.286–2.287
    working tax credit, 2.288–2.289
  amendment, 2.281
  conditional, 2.296
  dead applicants, on behalf of
    generally, 2.297–2.298
    joint claims, for, 2.299–2.300
  deeming provision
    final notice, in response to, 2.292–2.293
    one member of couple on behalf of both, 2.294–3.349
    revenue final notice, in response to, 2.290–2.291
  definitions
    generally, 2.272
    relevant date, 2.275–2.276
  disability element of WTC, 2.284–2.285
  electronic communications, 2.273–2.274
  forwarding of, 2.366
  holding of, 2.366
  method, 2.277–2.280
  person acting on behalf of another, by
    generally, 2.301
    other appointed persons, 2.302–2.303
  polygamous marriages, 2.554

Claims—*cont.*
  provision of information
    by authorities, 2.365
    to authorities, 2.364
  recording, 2.366
  statutory provisions
    generally, 1.231–1.238
    supplementary, 1.239–1.240
  time limits, 2.282–2.283
  verification, 2.366
Clerical errors
  child trust funds (appeals)
    Commissioner, by, 6.158–6.159
    generally, 6.110–6.111
    service by electronic mail, 6.115
    statutory provision, 1.169
    supplementary provisions, 6.114
  tax credits (appeals)
    Commissioner, by, 2.485–2.486
    generally, 2.426–2.427
    service by electronic mail, 2.432
    statutory provision, 1.169
    supplementary provisions, 2.431
  tax returns
    during enquiry, 1.10
    generally, 1.7
Clerks (appeals tribunal)
  child trust funds (appeals), 6.85
  tax credits (appeals), 2.392
Closure notices
  tax return enquiries, 1.12
Codes of practice
  overpayments, 7.24–7.32
Cohabitation
  references in Income Tax Acts, 1.76
Commissioners for Revenue and Customs
  administration of taxes, 1.3
  appointment, 1.732
  assault, 1.745
  child trust funds, and
    appeals, 6.121
    General Commissioners, 6.57–6.60
    Special Commissioners, 6.61–6.64
  child trust funds (appeals)
    application for leave to appeal, 6.116–6.117
    decisions, 6.156–6.162
    delegation of functions, 6.123
    general powers, 6.121
    statutory provisions, 1.158–1.164
    transfer of proceedings, 6.122
  conduct of proceedings, 1.739
  decisions
    amendment of existing legislation, 1.210–1.211
    appeals, 1.196–1.211
    definitions, 1.212–1.215
    generally, 1.190–1.191
    matters arising, 1.206–1.207
    regulations, 1.192–1.193
    Secretary of State's delegated functions, 1.208–1.209

Index

Commissioners for Revenue and Customs—*cont.*
  decisions—*cont.*
    supersession of earlier decisions, 1.194–1.195
    tax credits, 1.276–1.298
    verification of claims, 2.366
    variation of earlier decisions, 1.194–1.195
  declaration of confidentiality, 1.734
  former Inland Revenue matters
    generally, 1.737
    schedule, 1.748
  freedom of information, 1.743
  functions
    ancillary powers, 1.738
    conduct of proceedings, 1.739
    exercise by officers, 1.740
    former Inland Revenue matters, 1.737
    generally, 1.229–1.230
    initial, 1.736
  general note, 1.731
  information
    confidentiality, 1.742
    freedom of information, 1.743
    use, 1.741
  initial functions, 1.736
  ITEPA 2003, 1.409
  notices
    tax credits, 1.342–1.343
  obstruction, 1.744
  offences
    assault, 1.745
    obstruction, 1.744
    power of arrest, 1.746
  payments
    amount, 2.353–2.354
    bank account requirement, 2.358–2.359
    definitions, 2.335
    general note, 2.333
    joint claims, for, 2.336–2.341
    method, 2.356–2.357
    person acting on behalf of another, for, 2.342–2.343
    postponement, 2.351–2.352
    recovery of overpayments, 2.355
    renewal claims, 2.344–2.345
    single payments, 2.349–2.350
    timing, 2.346–2.348
  resignation, 1.732
  responsibility for certain taxes, 1.3
  staff appointments, 1.733
  supply of information
    statutory adoption pay, 1.392
    statutory paternity pay, 1.392
  tax credits
    appeals, 2.441
    functions, 1.229–1.230
    notices, 1.342–1.343
  tax credits (appeals)
    application for leave to appeal, 2.447–2.456

Commissioners for Revenue and Customs—*cont.*
  tax credits (appeals)—*cont.*
    decisions, 2.483–2.489
    delegation of functions, 2.443
    general powers, 2.441
    statutory provisions, 1.158–1.164
    transfer of proceedings, 2.442
  transfer of property, 1.747
  use of information
    statutory adoption pay, 1.394
Commissioners for Revenue and Customs Act 2005
  arrangement of sections, 1.730
  consequential amendments, 1.747
  general provisions, 1.732–1.746
  introduction, 1.731
  schedule, 1.748
Commissioners of Inland Revenue
  see **Commissioners for Revenue and Customs**
Compensation of employers (statutory maternity pay)
  additional payment to small employers, 4.84
  advance funding, 4.86
  date of payment of contributions, 4.89
  definitions
    generally, 4.81
    "small employer", 4.83
  general note, 4.82
  method
    deduction from payments to Revenue, 4.87
    payments to employer by Revenue, 4.88
  overpayments, 4.90
  prescribed amount, 4.85
Compensation of employers (statutory sick pay)
  amount, 3.86
  definitions, 3.83
  general note, 3.84
  generally, 3.85
  method, 3.86–3.88
"Conditional claims"
  generally, 2.296
Confidentiality
  child trust funds (appeals), 6.94–6.95
"Continental shelf employees"
  statutory adoption pay
    adoption from overseas, 5.108–5.112
    definitions, 5.34
    general note, 5.35
    generally, 5.43
  statutory maternity pay
    definitions, 4.62
    general note, 4.63
    generally, 4.71
    statutory provisions, 1.69
  statutory paternity pay
    adoption from overseas, 5.108–5.112
    definitions, 5.34
    general note, 5.35
    generally, 5.43

901

Index

"**Continental shelf employees**"—*cont.*
  statutory paternity pay—*cont.*
    statutory provisions, 1.91–1.92
  statutory sick pay
    definitions, 3.50, 3.57, 3.63
    general note, 3.46
    statutory provision, 1.56
    time for compliance, 3.64
Continuity of employment
  statutory adoption pay
    change of employer, 5.84
    generally, 5.81
    reinstatement after service with armed forces, 5.85
    stoppages of work, 5.83
    unfair dismissal, 5.82
  statutory maternity pay
    change of employer, 4.25
    generally, 4.21
    stoppages of work, 4.23–4.24
    unfair dismissal, 4.22
  statutory paternity pay
    change of employer, 5.84
    generally, 5.81
    reinstatement after service with armed forces, 5.85
    stoppages of work, 5.83
    unfair dismissal, 5.82
Continuous employment
  see **Continuity of employment**
Contracting out
  statutory adoption pay, 1.104–1.105
  statutory paternity pay, 1.85–1.86
"**Contractual remuneration**"
  statutory adoption pay
    generally, 5.76
    statutory provision, 1.106–1.107
  statutory maternity pay
    generally, 4.33
    statutory provision, 1.131
  statutory paternity pay
    generally, 5.66
    statutory provision, 1.87–1.88
  statutory sick pay, 1.123
Contribution-based jobseekers' allowance
  social security income, 2.145
"**Correction of errors**"
  child trust funds (appeals)
    Commissioner, by, 6.158–6.159
    generally, 6.110–6.111
    service by electronic mail, 6.115
    statutory provision, 1.169
    supplementary provisions, 6.114
  tax credits (appeals)
    Commissioner, by, 2.485–2.486
    generally, 2.426–2.427
    service by electronic mail, 2.432
    statutory provision, 1.169
    supplementary provisions, 2.431
  tax returns
    during enquiry, 1.10
    generally, 1.7

Council tax benefit
  social security income, 2.145
Court of Appeal
  child trust funds (appeals)
    application for leave to appeal, 6.163–6.164
    statutory provision, 1.165–1.166
  tax credits (appeals)
    applications for leave to appeal, 2.490–2.491
    generally, 1.165–1.166
Credit tokens
  application of provisions, 1.442
  benefit treated as earnings, 1.444
  disregard for money, goods or services obtained, 1.445
  meaning, 1.443
"**Creuzfeldt-Jakob disease**"
  investment income, 2.157
Crime prevention (fraud)
  statutory adoption pay
    generally, 1.390–1.391
    procedure and appeals, 1.397–1.405
  statutory paternity pay
    generally, 1.390–1.391
    procedure and appeals, 1.397–1.405
  tax credits
    generally, 1.318–1.319
    powers relating to documents, 1.320–1.321
    supply of information by tax authorities, 1.138–1.139
Crown employees
  overseas employees
    generally, 2.529–2.530
    partners, 2.531
  statutory adoption pay, 1.108–1.109
  statutory maternity pay, 1.68
  statutory paternity pay, 1.89–1.90
  statutory sick pay, 1.55
  tax credits, 1.338–1.339
Crown servants (overseas employees)
  generally, 2.529–2.530
  partners, 2.531

Death
  child tax credit, 2.209–2.210
  child trust funds (appeals), 6.82–6.83
  statutory maternity pay, 4.20
  tax credits (appeals), 2.389
  tax credits
    generally, 2.297–2.298
    joint claims, for, 2.299–2.300
    working tax credit, 2.82–2.83
"**Debts incurred and later released**"
  trading income, 1.656
Decisions (appeals tribunal)
  child trust funds (appeals)
    generally, 6.104–6.105
    service by electronic mail, 6.115
  tax credits (appeals), 2.416–2.421

Index

Decisions (Commissioners of Inland Revenue)
amendment of existing legislation, 1.210–1.211
appeals
  exercise of right, 1.198–1.203
  generally, 1.196–1.197
  regulations, 1.204–1.205
child trust funds (appeals)
  correction of errors, 6.158–6.159
  generally, 6.156–6.157
  setting aside, 6.160–6.161
  supplementary provisions, 6.162
definitions, 1.212–1.215
generally, 1.190–1.191
matters arising, 1.206–1.207
regulations, 1.192–1.193
Secretary of State's delegated functions, 1.208–1.209
supersession of earlier decisions, 1.194–1.195
tax credits
  correction of errors, 2.485–2.486
  discovery, on, 1.290–1.292
  final decision, 1.286–1.287
  final notice, 1.284–1.285
  generally, 2.483–2.484
  information requirements, 1.295–1.296
  initial decision, 1.276–1.279
  notice of, 1.297–1.298
  official error, subject to, 1.293–1.294
  other revised decisions, 1.282–1.283
  power to enquire, 1.288–1.289
  revision after notifications, 1.280–1.281
  setting aside, 2.487–2.488
  supplementary provisions, 2.489
verification of claims, 2.366
variation of earlier decisions, 1.194–1.195

Deductions
application of provisions, 1.461
"deductibility provisions", 1.466
employment income, 2.128
expenses, 1.469
expenses paid by employee
  effect of reimbursement, 1.468
  generally, 1.467
general rules
  double deductions, 1.464
  income from which be made, 1.462
  maximum amount, 1.463
  order for making, 1.465
pension income, 2.135
regulations, 2.128
social security income, 2.148
trading income
  bad debts, 1.650
  business entertainment and gifts, 1.652
  capital expenditure, 1.648
  doubtful debts, 1.650
  generally, 2.141
  professions and vocations, 1.647
  relationship between rules, 1.646
  social security contributions, 1.653

Deductions—*cont.*
trading income—*cont.*
  unconnected losses, 1.649
  unpaid remuneration, 1.651
  wholly and exclusively rules, 1.649
travel expenses
  necessary attendance, for, 1.471
  performance of duties, in, 1.470
  "workplace", 1.472

"Deemed income from capital"
generally, 2.103

Delegation
child trust funds (appeals), 6.123
tax credits (appeals), 2.443

"Depriving self of income to secure entitlement"
notional income, 2.167–2.168

Detention
statutory maternity pay, 4.16–4.17
statutory paternity pay, 5.92
statutory sick pay, 3.8

"Determination of rate"
child tax credit
  full year periods, 2.266
  generally, 2.251–2.265
  short periods, 2.267
cut-off provisions, 2.268–2.269
generally, 2.225–2.226
working tax credit
  full year periods, 2.243–2.249
  generally, 2.227–2.242
  short periods, 2.250

Directions
child trust funds (appeals), 6.144–6.145
tax credits (appeals)
  applications, 2.387–2.388
  death of party, 2.389
  determination of applications, 2.393–2.394
  withdrawal of applications, 2.397–2.398

Disability element (working tax credit)
Cases A to G, 2.58
date of claim, 2.284–2.285
generally, 2.55–2.57
initial claims, 2.59–2.60
relevant disabilities, 2.86–2.98
"training for work", 2.61–2.62

"Disability periods"
working tax credit, 2.41–2.42

Disability living allowance
social security income, 2.145

Disability pension
see **Pension income**

Disability working allowance
working tax credit, 2.56

"Disabled child"
child tax credit, 2.213–2.214

Disabled persons tax credit
social security income, 2.145

"Disabled person's vehicle maintenance grant"
other income, 1.716

903

Index

Disclosure (*information*)
  statutory maternity pay, 1.143
  statutory sick pay, 1.141
  tax credits, 1.350–1.351
Discretionary payments
  disregards, 2.176
  social security income, 2.145
Disregards
  conditional exclusions, 2.181
  employment income, 2.122
  generally, 2.175–2.179
  investment income, 2.156
  partial disregard, 2.182
  pension income, 2.132
  social security income, 2.145
  student income, 2.153–2.154
  total disregard, 2.180
Divided contracts
  statutory adoption pay
    general note, 5.10
    generally, 5.72
    lapse of election, 5.15
    notification of election, 5.12
    provision of information, 5.13
    relevant employer, 5.14, 5.86
  statutory maternity pay
    generally, 4.10
    relevant employer, 4.31–4.32
  statutory maternity pay (National Health Service)
    lapse of election, 4.79
    notification of election, 4.76
    provision of information, 4.77
    treatment of more than one contract as one, 4.75
    treatment of two or more employers as one, 4.78
  statutory paternity pay
    adoption of child, on, 5.63
    birth of child, on, 5.56
    general note, 5.10
    lapse of election, 5.15
    notification of election, 5.12
    provision of information, 5.13
    relevant employer, 5.14, 5.86
  statutory sick pay
    generally, 3.40
    relevant employer, 3.38–3.39
  statutory sick pay (National Health Service)
    lapse of election, 3.81
    notification of election, 3.78
    provision of information, 3.79
    treatment of more than one contract as one, 3.77
    treatment of two or more employers as one, 3.80
Dividends
  non-resident UK companies, from
    charge to tax, 1.686
    income charged, 1.687
    person liable, 1.688
  savings and investment income, 1.48

Dividends—*cont.*
  UK resident companies, from
    charge to tax, 1.683
    income charged, 1.684
    introduction, 1.682
    person liable, 1.685
"Doubtful debts"
  trading income, 1.650

Earnings
  employment income, 1.426
  statutory adoption pay
    generally, 5.87
    normal weekly earnings, 5.88
  statutory maternity pay
    generally, 4.34
    normal weekly earnings, 4.35–4.36
  statutory paternity pay
    generally, 5.87
    normal weekly earnings, 5.88
  statutory sick pay
    excepted payments, 3.35
    generally, 3.34
    normal weekly earnings, 3.36–3.37
Education maintenance allowance
  disregards, 2.176
"Eileen Trust"
  tax credits, 2.157
Electronic communications
  claims and notifications, 2.273–2.274
Employed earners
  see **Employees**
Employees
  statutory maternity pay, 4.30
  statutory paternity pay, 5.80
Employer-contracted childcare
  see **Childcare**
Employers
  notice to provide information, 2.325
  payment of WTC, 2.333
  provision of information, and
    statutory maternity pay, 1.144
    statutory sick pay, 1.142
Employment records
  statutory adoption pay
    generally, 5.26
    inspection, 5.27
  statutory maternity pay
    maintenance, 4.45
    production, 4.46
  statutory paternity pay
    generally, 5.26
    inspection, 5.27
  statutory sick pay
    maintenance, 3.26
    production, 3.27
Employment Act 2002
  arrangement of sections, 1.378
  general note, 1.379
  general provisions
    maternity, 1.396
    paternity and adoption, 1.380–1.395
    schedule, 1.397–1.405

Index

"Employment contract terminated to avoid liability"
  statutory maternity pay, 4.6–4.7
  statutory sick pay, 3.10
"Employment functions"
  provision of information, and general note, 2.563
  generally, 2.565, 2.577
Employment income
  agency workers, 1.425
  benefits code
    definitions, 1.430
    dispensations, 1.429
    meaning, 1.427
    relationship with earnings, 1.428
  car fuel
    benefit treated as earnings, 1.461
    calculation of cash equivalent, 1.462
    nil cash equivalent, 1.463
  cash vouchers
    application of provisions, 1.434–1.435
    benefit treated as earnings, 1.438
    disregard for money, goods or services obtained, 1.445
    meaning, 1.436
    sickness-benefits related, 1.437
  charge to tax
    agency workers, 1.425
    "employment", 1.414–1.415
    exemptions, 1.413
    introductory provision, 1.412–1.413
    nature, 1.417–1.419
    office-holders, 1.416
    operation, 1.420–1.424
  credit tokens
    application of provisions, 1.442
    benefit treated as earnings, 1.444
    disregard for money, goods or services obtained, 1.445
    meaning, 1.443
  deductions from earnings
    application of provisions, 1.461
    "deductibility provisions", 1.466
    expenses, 1.469
    expenses paid by employee, 1.467–1.468
    general rules, 1.462–1.465
    regulations, 2.128
    travel expenses, 1.470–1.472
  definitions
    "employment", 1.414–1.415
    "employment income", 1.418
    "exempt income", 1.419
    "general earnings", 1.418
    "net taxable earnings", 1.422
    "net taxable specific income", 1.423
    "paid", 1.432
    "put at disposal", 1.432
    "specific employment income", 1.418
    "taxable earnings", 1.421
    "taxable specific income", 1.421
  differences from tax assessments, 2.127
  disregarded payments, 2.122

Employment income—*cont.*
  earnings, 1.426
  employer-contracted and provided childcare
    "care", 1.459
    "child", 1.459
    definitions, 1.459–1.460
    employer-contracted, 1.458
    employer-provided, 1.456–1.457
    introductory note, 1.413
    "parental responsibility", 1.459
    "qualifying child care", 1.460
    regulations, 2.128
  "employment", 1.414–1.415
  employment-related benefits
    cash equivalent treated as earnings, 1.448
    cost of benefit, 1.449
    excluded benefits, 1.447
    meaning, 1.446
  exemptions
    "care", 1.459
    "child", 1.459
    definitions, 1.459–1.460
    employer-contracted childcare, 1.458
    employer-provided childcare, 1.456–1.457
    introductory note, 1.413
    "parental responsibility", 1.459
    "qualifying child care", 1.460
    regulations, 2.128
  expenses payments
    definitions, 1.432
    relevant sums, 1.431
    sums treated as earnings, 1.433
  general note
    regulations, 2.123
    statutory provisions, 1.407
  generally, 2.121
  identity of taxpayer, 2.129
  lower-paid employment
    calculation of earnings rate, 1.454
    excluded provisions of benefits code, 1.452
    extra amounts relating to car, 1.455
    meaning, 1.453
  meaning, 1.418
  minor benefits, 1.450–1.451
  nature, 2.126
  nature of charge to tax
    definitions, 1.418–1.419
    generally, 1.417
  non-cash vouchers
    application of provisions, 1.439
    benefit treated as earnings, 1.441
    disregard for money, goods or services obtained, 1.445
    meaning, 1.440
  office-holders, 1.416
  operation of tax charge
    amount of income charged, 1.420
    definitions, 1.421–1.423
    person liable to tax, 1.424

905

Employment income—*cont.*
  scope, 2.124
  self-employment, 2.125
  sickness-benefits related vouchers, 1.437
  statutory provisions
    charge to tax, 1.412–1.425
    deductions from earnings, 1.461–1.472
    earnings, 1.426
    general note, 1.407
    taxable benefits, 1.427–1.455
  taxable benefits
    benefits code, 1.427–1.430
    cash vouchers, 1.434–1.438
    credit tokens, 1.442–1.445
    expenses payments, 1.431–1.433
    lower-paid employees, 1.452–1.455
    minor benefits, 1.450–1.451
    non-cash vouchers, 1.439–1.441
    residual liability, 1.446–1.449
    vouchers, 1.434–1.441
  time of calculation, 2.130
  travel expenses
    necessary attendance, for, 1.471
    performance of duties, in, 1.470
    "workplace", 1.472
  vouchers
    cash vouchers, 1.434–1.438
    non-cash vouchers, 1.439–1.441
"Employment insurance payments"
  annual payments, 1.710–1.711
Employment records
  statutory adoption pay
    generally, 5.26
    inspection, 5.27
  statutory maternity pay
    maintenance, 4.45
    production, 4.46
  statutory paternity pay
    generally, 5.26
    inspection, 5.27
  statutory sick pay
    maintenance, 3.26
    production, 3.27
"Employment-related benefits"
  cash equivalent treated as earnings, 1.448
  cost of benefit, 1.449
  excluded benefits, 1.447
  meaning, 1.446
Employment zones
  disregards, 2.176
  remunerative work, 2.35
Enforcement
  statutory maternity pay
    breach of regulations, 1.135–1.136
    fraud, 1.137
    negligence, 1.137
  statutory sick pay
    breach of regulations, 1.135–1.136
    fraud, 1.137
    negligence, 1.137
Enquiries into tax returns
  see **Tax enquiries**

Entitlement
  statutory adoption pay
    determination of issues, 5.30–5.31
    evidence, 5.71
    provision of information, 5.28–5.29
    statutory provisions, 1.98–1.99
  statutory maternity pay
    evidence, 4.58
    generally, 1.58–1.59
  statutory paternity pay
    adoption of child, on, 5.57–5.63
    birth of child, on, 5.48–5.56
    determination of issues, 5.30–5.31
    evidence, 5.48–5.50, 5.57–5.58
    provision of information, 5.28–5.29
    statutory provisions, 1.72–1.80
  statutory sick pay
    employer's liability, 1.32–1.31
    evidence, 3.66–3.74
    general note, 1.31
    limitations, 1.48–1.49
    qualifying conditions, 1.32–1.47
Error by officials
  see **Official errors**
Errors
  see **Correction of errors**
"Evaluation studies"
  generally, 2.571
  Northern Ireland, 2.573
Evidence (entitlement)
  see also **Medical evidence**
  statutory adoption pay, 5.71
  statutory maternity pay, 4.58
  statutory paternity pay
    adoption of child, on, 5.57–5.58
    birth of child, on, 5.48–5.50
  statutory sick pay
    definitions, 3.66
    form of doctor's statement, 3.69–3.72
    form of special statement, 3.73–3.74
    general note, 3.67
    information required, 3.68
Ex gratia **payments**
  social security income, 2.145
Exempt income
  annual payments
    adopters, to, 1.712
    employment insurance payments, 1.710–1.711
    foreign maintenance payments, 1.705
    health insurance payments, 1.710–1.711
    periodical payments of personal injury damages, 1.706–1.709
  employment income, 1.419
  employment insurance payments, 1.710–1.711
  foreign maintenance payments, 1.705
  general disregard, 1.717
  health insurance payments, 1.710–1.711
  introduction, 1.626
  overview, 1.704
  payments to adopters, 1.712

Exempt income—*cont.*
  periodical payments of personal injury damages
    compensation awards, 1.707
    generally, 1.706
    persons entitled, 1.708
    trusts, from, 1.709
  statutory overview, 1.628
  tax credits
    employment income, 2.128
    pension income, 2.135
    social security income, 2.148
    trading income, 2.141
"Expected week of confinement"
  statutory maternity pay, 4.39
Expenses
  definitions, 1.432
  relevant sums, 1.431
  sums treated as earnings, 1.433
Experts
  child trust funds (appeals), 6.100–6.101
  tax credits (appeals), 2.412–2.413
Extensions of time
  child trust funds (appeals), 6.80–6.81
  tax credits (appeals)
    applications, 2.385–2.386
    generally, 2.379–2.384

"Failure to comply with requirements"
  statutory adoption pay, 1.388–1.389
  statutory paternity pay, 1.388–1.389
  tax credits, 1.312–1.313
"Failure to make correct payments"
  tax credits, 1.314–1.315
Farming
  trading income, 1.637
Fees
  child care providers approval scheme, 2.589
Finality (decisions)
  child trust funds (appeals), 1.168
  tax credits appeals, 1.168
50-plus element
  working tax credit, 2.80–2.81
Foreign income
  introduction, 1.626
  social security income
    application of provisions, 1.521–1.522
    person liable to tax, 1.524
    taxable income, 1.523
  statutory overview, 1.628
  tax credits, 2.161–2.162
"Foreign maintenance payments"
  annual payments, 1.705
"Former Inland Revenue matters"
  generally, 1.737
  schedule, 1.748
Foster-care relief
  definitions
    foster-care receipts, 1.726
    providing foster care, 1.727
  overview, 1.724
  qualifying person, 1.725
  trading income, 1.639

"Forwarding claims"
  administrative arrangements, 2.366
Fraud
  penalties
    statutory maternity pay, 1.137
    statutory sick pay, 1.137
  tax returns, 1.18
Fraud prevention
  see **Crime prevention (fraud)**
Freedom of information
  Her Majesty's Revenue and Customs, 1.743
Funding of legal services
  see **Legal advice and funding**
Funding of liabilities
  statutory adoption pay
    application to Revenue, 5.21
    date of payment of contributions, 5.24
    generally, 5.20
    method, 5.22–5.23
    overpayments, 5.25
  statutory paternity pay
    application to Revenue, 5.21
    date of payment of contributions, 5.24
    generally, 5.20
    method, 5.22–5.23
    overpayments, 5.25
"Further particulars"
  child trust funds (appeals), 6.144–6.145
  tax credits (appeals), 2.470–2.472

Gambling
  investment income, 2.156
"Gaps between jobs"
  working tax credit, 2.53–2.54
General Commissioners
  child trust funds (appeals), 6.65–6.68
"General earnings"
  employment income, 1.418
Generally accepted accounting practice
  trading income, 1.641
Gifts
  trading income, 1.652
Guardian's allowance
  social security income, 2.145

Haemophilia
  investment income, 2.157
Health
  provision of information, and
    definitions, 2.543
    general note, 2.542
    generally, 2.544, 2.561
    Northern Ireland, 2.575
"Health insurance payments"
  annual payments, 1.710–1.711
Hearings
  child trust funds (appeals)
    choice, 6.88–6.89
    generally, 6.150
    oral hearings, 6.98–6.99
    requests, 6.148–6.149

Hearings—*cont.*
  tax credits (appeals)
    choice, 2.395–2.396
    generally, 2.477
    oral, 2.406–2.415
    requests, 2.475–2.476
HM Revenue and Customs
  see **Revenue and Customs**
"Holding claims"
  administrative arrangements, 2.366
"Hours worked"
  qualifying remunerative work, 2.36
Housing benefit
  social security income, 2.145

"Identity of taxpayer"
  see also **Income test**
  employment income, 2.129
  pension income, 2.136
  social security income, 2.149
  trading income, 2.142
Ill health
  working tax credit, 2.41–2.42
Immigrants
  definitions, 2.500
  exclusion from entitlement, 2.501–2.510
  general note, 2.507
  modifications of Act, 2.511–2.512
  polygamous marriages, 2.557
  statutory provision, 1.334–1.335
  transitional relief, 2.513–2.514
Immigration control
  see **Immigrants**
Imprisonment
  statutory maternity pay, 4.16–4.17
  statutory paternity pay, 5.92
  statutory sick pay, 3.8
"Inalienability"
  tax credits, 1.340–1.341
"Incapacitation"
  childcare element (working tax credit), 2.71
Incapacity benefit
  social security income
    long-term, 1.502
    short-term, 1.503
  statutory maternity pay
    generally, 4.37
    statutory provision, 1.130
  statutory sick pay, 1.124–1.125
  working tax credit, 2.145
Incapacity for work
  statutory sick pay
    notification, 3.15
    persons deemed incapable, 3.4–3.5
    persons unable to act, 3.22–3.23
  working tax credit, 2.41–2.42
Income
  calculation, 2.115–2.120
  capital, 2.103
  deemed income from capital, 2.103
  definitions, 2.113–2.114

Income—*cont.*
  disregards
    conditional exclusions, 2.181
    generally, 2.175–2.179
    partial disregard, 2.182
    total disregard, 2.180
  employment income
    deductions, 2.128
    differences from tax assessments, 2.127
    disregarded payments, 2.122
    exemptions, 2.128
    general note, 2.123
    generally, 2.121
    identity of taxpayer, 2.129
    nature, 2.126
    scope, 2.124
    self-employment, 2.125
    time of calculation, 2.130
  foreign income, 2.161–2.162
  general note
    change in approach, 2.103
    cross-references, 2.111
    differences from tax assessments, 2.104
    introduction, 2.101
    questions to be decided, 2.105–2.110
    Tax Law Rewrite Project, 2.102
  investment income
    disregarded payments, 2.156
    general note, 2.158
    generally, 2.155
    very severe disablement payments, 2.157
  miscellaneous income, 2.173–2.174
  not otherwise charged
    charge to tax, 1.701
    income charged, 1.702
    person liable, 1.703
  notional income
    depriving self of income to secure entitlement, 2.167–2.168
    entitlement to sums, 2.169–2.170
    generally, 2.163–2.164
    provision of services for less than full earnings, 2.171–2.172
    sums treated as income under Taxes Acts, 2.165–2.166
  pension income
    deductions, 2.135
    disregarded payments, 2.132
    exemptions, 2.135
    general note, 2.133
    generally, 2.131
    identity of taxpayer, 2.136
    relevant income, 2.134
    time of calculation, 2.137
  polygamous marriages, 2.553
  property income, 2.159–2.160
  social security income
    deductions, 2.148
    disregarded payments, 2.145
    exemptions, 2.148
    general note, 2.146
    generally, 2.144

Index

Income—*cont.*
  social security income—*cont.*
    identity of taxpayer, 2.149
    relevant income, 2.147
    time of calculation, 2.150
  statutory provision, 1.251–1.257
  student income
    disregarded payments, 2.153–2.154
    generally, 2.151–2.152
  tax-exempt savings, 2.103
  thresholds
    definitions, 2.217
    generally, 2.218–2.220
  trading income
    deductions, 2.141
    exemptions, 2.141
    general note, 2.139
    generally, 2.138
    identity of taxpayer, 2.142
    relevant income, 2.141
    self-employment, 2.140
    time of calculation, 2.143
  voluntary work, 2.170–2.171

"Income not otherwise charged"
  charge to tax, 1.701
  income charged, 1.702
  person liable, 1.703

Income support
  generally, 2.221–2.222
  income test, 2.107
  social security income
    amount in excess of taxable maximum, 1.506
    child maintenance bonus, 1.505
    definitions, 1.508–1.509
    general rule, 1.504
    generally, 2.145
    taxable maximum, 1.507
    trade disputes, 1.504

Income tax
  assessment, 2.104
  charge to tax, 1.753–1.755
  definitions
    civil partners, 1.767
    "company", 1.766
    general list, 1.765
    living together, 1.767
    married persons, 1,767
    overview, 1.764
  employment income, 1.412–1.472
  exempt income, 1.704–1.717
  foster-care relief, 1.724–1.727
  general note
    ITA 2007, 1.750
    ITEPA 2003, 1.407
    ITTOIA 2005, 1.626–1.627
  general provisions, 1.728–1.729
  individuals in UK for temporary purpose
    employment income, 1.760
    foreign income, 1.759
  individuals temporarily abroad, 1.756–1.757
  individuals working abroad, 1.758

Income tax—*cont.*
  jointly held property
    declarations of unequal beneficial interests, 1.763
    generally, 1.761–1.762
  miscellaneous income, 1.693–1.703
  overview
    ITA 2007, 1.751–1.752
    ITEPA 2003, 1.410–1.411
    ITTOIA 2005, 1.628–1.629
  pension income, 1.473–1.486
  property income, 1.660–1.672
  rent-a-room relief, 1.718–1.723
  residence
    individuals in UK for temporary purpose, 1.759–1.760
    individuals temporarily abroad, 1.756–1.757
    individuals working abroad, 1.758
  returns
    see also **Tax returns**
    generally, 1.4–1.32
  savings and investment income, 1.673–1.692
  social security income, 1.487–1.524
  trading income, 1.630–1.659

Income Tax Act 2007
  see also **Income tax**
  arrangement of sections, 1.749
  definitions, 1.764–1.767
  general note, 1.750
  general provisions
    charge to tax, 1.753–1.755
    jointly held property, 1.761–1.763
    overview, 1.751–1.752
    residence, 1.756–1.760

Income tax (charge to tax)
  emoluments (offices and employment)
    see also **Employment income**
    see also **Pension income**
    see also **Social security income**
    general note, 1.407
  employment income
    see also **Employment income**
    agency workers, 1.425
    deductions from earnings, 1.461–1.472
    earnings, 1.426
    "employment", 1.414–1.415
    exemptions, 1.456–1.460
    general note, 1.407
    introductory provision, 1.412–1.413
    nature, 1.417–1.419
    office-holders, 1.416
    operation, 1.420–1.424
    taxable benefits, 1.427–1.455
  general note
    ITA 2007, 1.750
    ITEPA 2003, under, 1.407
  general rule
    ITA 2007, 1.753–1.755
    ITTOIA 2005, 1.626–1.627
    ITEPA 2003, under, 1.410

Income tax (charge to tax)—*cont.*
miscellaneous income
see also **Miscellaneous income**
income not otherwise charged, 1.701
settlements, 1.696–1.700
pension income
see also **Pension income**
amount charged, 1.476
general note, 1.474
general rules, 1.478–1.482
introductory provision, 1.473
nature of charge, 1.475
person liable to tax, 1.477
social security pensions, 1.483–1.486
property income
see also **Property income**
generally, 1.668
income charged, 1.670
person liable, 1.671
territorial scope, 1.669
savings and investments income
see also **Savings and investments income**
dividends from non-resident UK companies, 1.686
dividends from UK resident companies, 1.683
interest, 1.678
purchased life annuity payments, 1.689
Schedule E (offices and employment emoluments)
see also **Employment income**
see also **Pension income**
see also **Social security income**
general note, 1.407
social security income
see also **Social security income**
amount charged, 1.493
definitions, 1.525–1.526
exempt benefits, 1.502–1.517
foreign benefits, 1.521–1.524
general note, 1.488
introductory provision, 1.487
nature of charge, 1.489–1.490
person liable to tax, 1.494
taxable benefits, 1.495–1.501
wholly exempt benefits, 1.518–1.520
trading income
see also **Trading income**
generally, 1.633
income charged, 1.635
person liable, 1.636
territorial scope, 1.634
Income Tax (Earnings and Pensions) Act 2003 (ITEPA)
see also **Income tax**
arrangement of sections, 1.406
definitions, 1.525–1.526
general note
CRCA 2005, 1.409
interpretation, 1.408
introduction, 1.407

Income Tax (Earnings and Pensions) Act 2003 (ITEPA)—*cont.*
general provisions
employment income, 1.412–1.472
overview, 1.410–1.411
pension income, 1.473–1.486
social security income, 1.487–1.524
Income tax (tax returns)
amendment by taxpayer
during enquiry, 1.9
generally, 1.6
appeals, 1.28–1.25
assessment
appeals, 1.19–1.25
discovery of loss of tax, on, 1.13
loss, etc., 1.27
relief for excessive assessments, 1.14–1.15
time limits, 1.16–1.18
want of form, 1.28
closure notices, 1.12
correction by Revenue
during enquiry, 1.10
generally, 1.7
definitions, 1.29
destruction, etc., 1.23
enquiry
amendment by taxpayer, 1.9
completion, 1.12
correction by Revenue, 1.10
notice, 1.8
fraudulent conduct, 1.18
generally, 1.4
loss, etc., 1.27
negligent conduct, 1.18
notice of enquiry, 1.8
penalties, 1.26
records, 1.11
relief for excessive assessments
double assessment, 1.14
error, 1.15
self-assessment, 1.5
time limits
fraudulent conduct, 1.18
income received after year for which assessable, 1.17
negligent conduct, 1.18
ordinary period, 1.16
want of form, 1.28
Income Tax (Trading and Other Income) Act 2005
see also **Income tax**
arrangement of sections, 1.625
general note, 1.626–1.627
general provisions
exempt income, 1.704–1.717
foster-care relief, 1.724–1.727
general rules, 1.728–1.729
miscellaneous income, 1.693–1.703
overview, 1.628–1.629
property income, 1.660–1.672
rent-a-room relief, 1.718–1.723

910

Income Tax (Trading and Other Income) Act 2005—*cont.*
　general provisions—*cont.*
　　savings and investment income, 1.673–1.692
　　trading income, 1.630–1.659
"Income test"
　calculation, 2.115–2.120
　capital, 2.103
　deemed income from capital, 2.103
　definitions, 2.113–2.114
　disregards
　　conditional exclusions, 2.181
　　generally, 2.175–2.179
　　partial disregard, 2.182
　　total disregard, 2.180
　employment income
　　deductions, 2.128
　　differences from tax assessments, 2.127
　　disregarded payments, 2.122
　　exemptions, 2.128
　　general note, 2.123
　　generally, 2.121
　　identity of taxpayer, 2.129
　　nature, 2.126
　　scope, 2.124
　　self-employment, 2.125
　　time of calculation, 2.130
　foreign income, 2.161–2.162
　general note
　　change in approach, 2.103
　　cross-references, 2.111
　　differences from tax assessments, 2.104
　　introduction, 2.101
　　questions to be decided, 2.105–2.110
　　Tax Law Rewrite Project, 2.102
　investment income
　　disregarded payments, 2.156
　　general note, 2.158
　　generally, 2.155
　　very severe disablement payments, 2.157
　miscellaneous income, 2.173–2.174
　notional income
　　depriving self of income to secure entitlement, 2.167–2.168
　　entitlement to sums, 2.169–2.170
　　generally, 2.163–2.164
　　provision of services for less than full earnings, 2.171–2.172
　　sums treated as income under Taxes Acts, 2.165–2.166
　pension income
　　deductions, 2.135
　　disregarded payments, 2.132
　　exemptions, 2.135
　　general note, 2.133
　　generally, 2.131
　　identity of taxpayer, 2.136
　　relevant income, 2.134
　　time of calculation, 2.137
　polygamous marriages, 2.553
　property income, 2.159–2.160

"Income test"—*cont.*
　social security income
　　deductions, 2.148
　　disregarded payments, 2.145
　　exemptions, 2.148
　　general note, 2.146
　　generally, 2.144
　　identity of taxpayer, 2.149
　　relevant income, 2.147
　　time of calculation, 2.150
　statutory provision, 1.251–1.257
　student income
　　disregarded payments, 2.153–2.154
　　generally, 2.151–2.152
　tax-exempt savings, 2.103
　thresholds, 2.218–2.220
　trading income
　　deductions, 2.141
　　exemptions, 2.141
　　general note, 2.139
　　generally, 2.138
　　identity of taxpayer, 2.142
　　relevant income, 2.141
　　self-employment, 2.140
　　time of calculation, 2.143
　voluntary work, 2.170–2.171
"Income thresholds"
　definitions, 2.217
　generally, 2.218–2.220
Incorrect statements
　see **Misstatements**
Individual savings accounts
　income test, 2.103
　investment income, 2.156
Industrial injuries benefits
　social security income, 2.145
Information
　administrative arrangements, and
　　by authorities, 2.365
　　to authorities, 2.364
　employers, by
　　statutory maternity pay, 1.144
　　statutory sick pay, 1.142
　functions relating to employment
　　general note, 2.563
　　generally, 2.565, 2.577
　functions relating to health
　　definitions, 2.543
　　general note, 2.542
　　generally, 2.544, 2.561
　　Scotland, 2.575
　functions relating to training
　　general note, 2.563
　　generally, 2.565, 2.577
　Secretary of State, by
　　statutory maternity pay, 1.143
　　statutory sick pay, 1.141
　statutory adoption pay
　　entitlement, as to, 5.28–5.29
　　generally, 5.32
　statutory maternity pay, 4.40
　　claims for other benefits, 4.44
　　determination of questions, 4.42–4.43

Index

Information—*cont.*
statutory paternity pay
entitlement, as to, 5.28–5.29
generally, 5.32
statutory sick pay
employee to Secretary of State, by, 3.28–3.29
employer to employee, by, 3.30–3.31
tax authorities, by
contributions purposes, for, 1.140
fraud prevention, for, 1.138–1.139
tax credits
generally, 2.571
Northern Ireland, 2.573
Inland Revenue
see **Revenue and Customs**
Insolvency (employers)
statutory sick pay, 3.20
Intensive Activity Period
remunerative work, 2.35
Intercountry adoption
pay period, 5.126–5.127
statutory adoption pay
administration, 5.103–5.107
application of General Regulations 2002, 5.117
application of SSCBA 1992, 5.96–5.102
avoidance of liability, 5.132
continental shelf employees, 5.108–5.112
definitions, 5.116
evidence of entitlement, 5.129
general note, 5.115
mariners, 5.108–5.112
notice requirements, 5.128
pay period, 5.126–5.127
persons abroad, 5.108–5.112
termination of employment, 5.131
treatment of more than one employer, 5.130
statutory sick pay
administration, 5.103–5.107
application of General Regulations 2002, 5.117
application of SSCBA 1992, 5.96–5.102
avoidance of liability, 5.125
conditions of entitlement, 5.119
continental shelf employees, 5.108–5.112
definitions, 5.116
evidence of entitlement, 5.123
general note, 5.115
mariners, 5.108–5.112
notice requirements, 5.121
pay period, 5.120
persons abroad, 5.108–5.112
qualifying period, 5.122
treatment of more than one employer, 5.124
Interest
charge to tax, 1.678
income charged, 1.679

Interest—*cont.*
person liable, 1.680
tax credits
definitions, 2.495
general note, 2.494
generally, 1.322–1.323
overpayments, on, 2.496
prescribed rate, 2.497
territorial scope, 1.677
trading income, 1.645
"Interruption of employment"
statutory sick pay, 3.25
Investment income
building society dividends, 1.681
dividends from non-resident UK companies
charge to tax, 1.686
income charged, 1.687
person liable, 1.688
dividends from UK resident companies
charge to tax, 1.683
income charged, 1.684
introduction, 1.682
person liable, 1.685
general note, 1.674
interest
charge to tax, 1.678
income charged, 1.679
person liable, 1.680
territorial scope, 1.677
introduction, 1.626
overview, 1.673
priority rules
generally, 1.675–1.676
introduction, 1.629
purchased life annuity payments
charge to tax, 1.689
income charged, 1.691
meaning, 1.690
person liable, 1.692
statutory overview
introduction, 1.628
priority rules, 1.629
tax credits
disregarded payments, 2.156
general note, 2.158
generally, 2.155
very severe disablement payments, 2.157
territorial scope of charge, 1.677
Irregularities
child trust funds (appeals), 6.155
tax credits (appeals), 2.481–2.482
ISAs
see **Individual investment accounts**

Jobseekers' allowance
child maintenance bonus, 1.510
generally, 2.221–2.222
income test, 2.107
Intensive Activity Period, 2.35
social security income
amount in excess of taxable maximum, 1.511

Index

Jobseekers' allowance—*cont.*
  social security income—*cont.*
    child maintenance bonus, 1.510
    definitions, 1.515
    generally, 2.145
    taxable maximum, 1.512–1.514
  taxable maximum
    amount in excess of, 1.511
    contribution-based JSA, 1.514
    definitions, 1.515
    general, 1.512
    income-based JSA, 1.513
Joint property
  declarations of unequal beneficial interests, 1.763
  generally, 1.761–1.762
Jurisdiction
  child trust funds (appeals)
    General Commissioners, 6.65–6.68
    Special Commissioners, 6.69–6.72

"Late appeals"
  child trust funds (appeals), 6.80–6.81
  tax credits (appeals), 2.379–2.384
Legal advice and funding
  child trust funds (appeals), 6.125–6.126
  tax credits (appeals), 2.445–2.446
"Life annuity payments"
  charge to tax, 1.689
  income charged, 1.691
  meaning, 1.690
  person liable, 1.692
Linking periods
  statutory sick pay. 3.6–3.7
"Living away from home allowance"
  disregards, 2.176
"Living together"
  references in Income Tax Acts, 1.767
Lone-parent element
  working tax credit, 2.67–2.68
"Lottery winnings"
  investment income, 2.156
"Lower-paid employment"
  calculation of earnings rate, 1.454
  excluded provisions of benefits code, 1.452
  extra amounts relating to car, 1.455
  meaning, 1.453

Maintenance
  disregards, 2.176
Mariners
  see **Seafarers**
"Market gardening"
  trading income, 1.637
Married persons
  see **Spouses**
Maternity allowance
  statutory maternity pay, 4.38
  working tax credit, 2.145
Maternity pay
  and **Statutory maternity pay**
"Macfarlane Trust"
  tax credits, 2.157

Means testing
  capital, 2.103
  general rule, 2.101
Medical evidence
  child trust funds (appeals)
    non-disclosure, 6.146–6.147
  maternity
    definitions, 4.57
    evidence of pregnancy and confinement, 4.58
    form of certificate, 4.59–4.60
  sickness
    definitions, 3.66
    doctor's statement, 3.69–3.72
    general note, 3.67
    information required, 3.68
    special statement, 3.73–3.74
  tax credits (appeals)
    general regulations, under, 2.399–2.400
    generally, 2.473–2.474
"Milk tokens"
  social security income, 2.145
"Miscellaneous income"
  amount treated as income of settlor
    settlements, 1.696–1.700
  income not otherwise charged
    charge to tax, 1.701
    income charged, 1.702
    person liable, 1.703
  introduction, 1.626
  overview, 1.693
  priority rules
    generally, 1.694–1.695
    introduction, 1.629
  settlements
    charge to tax, 1.696–1.697
    income charged, 1.699
    person liable, 1.700
    "settlement", 1.698
  statutory overview
    introduction, 1.628
    priority rules, 1.629
  tax credits
    general note, 2.174
    generally, 2.173
  territorial scope, 1.696
Misstatements
  statutory adoption pay, 1.390–1.391
  statutory paternity pay, 1.390–1.391
  tax credits, 1.309–1.311
Mistakes
  see **Clerical errors**
Mobility supplement
  see **War pensioner's mobility supplement**

National insurance contributions
  trading income, 1.653
National savings
  income test, 2.103
Negligence
  statutory maternity pay, 1.137

Index

Negligence—*cont.*
  statutory sick pay, 1.137
  tax returns, 1.18
"Net taxable earnings"
  employment income, 1.422
"Net taxable specific income"
  employment income, 1.423
New Deal
  disregards, 2.176
NHS employees (divided contracts)
  statutory maternity pay
    lapse of election, 4.79
    notification of election, 4.76
    provision of information, 4.77
    treatment of more than one contract as one, 4.10, 4.75
    treatment of two or more employers as one, 4.31–4.32, 4.78
  statutory paternity pay
    general note, 5.10
    lapse of election, 5.15
    notification of election, 5.12
    provision of information, 5.13
    relevant employer, 5.14
  statutory sick pay
    generally, 3.40
    lapse of election, 3.81
    notification of election, 3.78
    provision of information, 3.79
    relevant employer, 3.38–3.39
    treatment of more than one contract as one, 3.77
    treatment of two or more employers as one, 3.80
"Non-cash vouchers"
  application of provisions, 1.439
  benefit treated as earnings, 1.441
  disregard for money, goods or services obtained, 1.445
  meaning, 1.440
"Normal working earnings"
  statutory adoption pay
    "earnings", 5.87
    generally, 5.88
  statutory maternity pay
    "earnings", 4.34
    generally, 4.35–4.36
  statutory paternity pay
    "earnings", 5.87
    generally, 5.88
"Normal working weeks"
  statutory maternity pay
    generally, 4.27–4.28
    "week", 4.29
"Normally living with test"
  child tax credit, 2.194
Northern Ireland
  tax credits
    evaluation and statistical studies, 2.572–2.573
    generally, 1.363–1.364

Notices
  absence from work
    statutory maternity pay, 4.40
  child trust funds (appeals)
    acknowledgment, 6.137
    disputes concerning, 6.78–6.79
    generally, 6.133–6.134
    notification, 6.137
    prescribed form, 6.62–6.63
    service, 6.76–6.77
    signature, 6.62–6.63
    statutory provision, 1.611
    time limits, 6.135–6.136
  enquiries in returns, 1.8
  provision of information
    childcare provider, to, 2.326
    dates to be specified, 2.327
    definitions, 2.272
    electronic communications, 2.273–2.274
    employers, to, 2.325
    s.17 TCA 2002, under, 2.328–2.331
  tax credits, 1.342–1.343
  tax credits (appeals)
    acknowledgment, 2.462–2.463
    generally, 2.457–2.458
    notification, 2.462–2.463
    prescribed form, 2.368–2.369
    time limits, 2.459–2.461
  tax returns, 1.8
Notification
  change of circumstances
    see also **Notification (change of circumstances)**
    definitions, 2.272
    electronic communications, 2.273–2.274
    generally, 2.305–2.324
    polygamous marriages, 2.554
  employment after confinement, 4.41
  incapacity for work, 3.15
  statutory maternity pay, 4.41
  statutory sick pay, 3.15
Notification (change of circumstances)
  advance, in, 2.319
  amendment, 2.312
  date
    disability element of CTC, 2.317–2.318
    disability element of WTC, 2.315–2.316
    increase of maximum rate, 2.313–2.314
  decrease of rate, 2.307–2.308
  definitions
    generally, 2.272
    notification date, 2.207
  disability element of CTC, 2.317–2.318
  disability element of WTC, 2.315–2.316
  electronic communications, 2.273–2.274
  evidence of birth or adoption, 2.324
  increase of maximum rate, and
    date of notification, 2.313–2.314
    general rule, 2.305–2.306
    method, 2.309–2.310

Notification (change of circumstances)—*cont.*
person acting on behalf of another, by
generally, 2.320–2.321
other appointed persons, 2.322–2.323
polygamous marriages, 2.554
relevant person, 2.311

Notional income
depriving self of income to secure entitlement, 2.167–2.168
entitlement to sums, 2.169–2.170
generally, 2.163–2.164
provision of services for less than full earnings, 2.171–2.172
sums treated as income under Taxes Acts, 2.165–2.166

Oaths
child trust funds (appeals), 6.92–6.93
tax credits (appeals), 2.401–2.402

Observations
child trust funds (appeals)
directions, 6.144–6.145
reply, in, 6.142–6.143
respondent, by, 6.140–6.141
tax credits (appeals)
directions, 2.470–2.472
reply, in, 2.468–2.469
respondent, by, 2.466–2.467

Obstruction
officers of Revenue and Customs, 1.744

Officeholders
employment income, 1.416

Officers of Revenue and Customs
see **Revenue and Customs officers**

"Official errors"
definitions, 2.536–2.537
general note, 2.539
generally, 2.538

Offshore workers
statutory adoption pay
adoption from overseas, 5.108–5.112
definitions, 5.34
general note, 5.35
generally, 5.43
statutory maternity pay
definitions, 4.62
general note, 4.63
generally, 4.71
statutory provisions, 1.69
statutory paternity pay
adoption from overseas, 5.108–5.112
definitions, 5.34
general note, 5.35
generally, 5.43
statutory provisions, 1.91–1.92
statutory sick pay
definitions, 3.50, 3.57, 3.63
general note, 3.46
statutory provision, 1.56
time for compliance, 3.64

Oral hearings
child trust funds (appeals)
adjournment, 6.102–6.103
expert assistance, 6.100–6.101
generally, 6.98–6.99
postponement, 6.102–6.103
record of proceedings, 6.108–6.109
tax credits (appeals)
adjournment, 2.414–2.415
expert assistance, 2.412–2.413
generally, 2.406–2.411
postponement, 2.414–2.415

Ordinary residence
Crown servants posted overseas
generally, 2.529–2.530
partners, 2.531
definitions, 2.517–2.518
meaning, 2.522–2.525
person treated as not being in UK, 2.519–2.526
temporary absence from UK, 2.527–2.528
transitional provision, 2.532–2.533

Overpayments
Code of Practice, 7.24–7.32
interest, 2.496
statutory adoption pay, 5.25
statutory maternity pay, 4.90
statutory paternity pay, 5.25
tax credits
generally, 1.303–1.304
recovery, 1.305–1.306, 2.355

Overseas adoptions
see **Intercountry adoption**

Overseas employees
Crown servants
generally, 2.529–2.530
partners, 2.531

"Paid"
employment income, 1.432

Partnership income
introduction, 1.626
statutory overview, 1.628

Paternity pay
and **Statutory paternity pay**

Payments in lieu of notice
working tax credit, 2.49–2.50

"Pay period"
overseas adoptions, 5.126–5.127
statutory adoption pay
disrupted adoption, 5.69
generally, 5.68
statutory provision, 1.102–1.103
treatment of more than once contract, 5.70
statutory maternity pay
generally, 4.4–4.5
statutory provision, 1.60–1.61
statutory paternity pay
adoption of child, on, 5.59
birth of child, on, 5.51
statutory provision, 1.83–1.84

915

"Pay period"—*cont.*
  work during
    statutory adoption pay, 5.73
    statutory paternity pay, 5.64
Payments (employers) (statutory adoption pay)
  funding
    application to Revenue, 5.21
    date of payment of contributions, 5.24
    generally, 5.20
    method, 5.22–5.23
    overpayments, 5.25
  generally, 5.89
  period
    adoption of child, on, 5.59
    birth of child, on, 5.51
  persons acting on behalf of another, to, 5.94
  timing, 5.90
Payments (employers) (statutory maternity pay)
  funding
    additional payment to small employers, 4.84
    advance funding, 4.86
    date of payment of contributions, 4.89
    deduction from payments to Revenue, 4.87
    definitions, 4.81
    general note, 4.82
    overpayments, 4.90
    payments to employer by Revenue, 4.88
    prescribed amount, 4.85
    "small employer", 4.83
  generally, 4.47
  persons acting on behalf of another, to, 4.52–4.53
  rounding, 4.48
  Secretary of State, by, 4.50–4.51
  timing, 4.49
Payments (employers) (statutory paternity pay)
  funding
    application to Revenue, 5.21
    date of payment of contributions, 5.24
    generally, 5.20
    method, 5.22–5.23
    overpayments, 5.25
  generally, 5.89
  period
    adoption of child, on, 5.59
    birth of child, on, 5.51
  persons acting on behalf of another, to, 5.94
  timing, 5.90
Payments (employers) (statutory sick pay)
  funding
    amount, 3.86
    definitions, 3.83
    general note, 3.84
    generally, 3.85
    method, 3.86–3.88

Payments (employers) (statutory sick pay)—*cont.*
  liability of Secretary of State, 3.18–3.19
  method, 3.16
  Secretary of State, by, 3.21
  statements relating to, 3.32
  time limits, 3.17
Payments (Revenue and Customs)
  see also **Payments (Revenue and Customs) (tax credits)**
  statutory adoption pay
    generally, 5.93
    liability, 5.91
  statutory maternity pay, 4.88
  statutory paternity pay
    generally, 5.93
    liability, 5.91
Payments (Revenue and Customs) (tax credits)
  amount, 2.353–2.354
  bank account requirement, 2.358–2.359
  child care element of WTC, 2.336–2.337
  definitions, 2.335
  general note, 2.333
  introduction, 2.333
  joint claims, for
    child tax credit, 2.336–2.337
    child care element of WTC, 2.336–2.337
    death of one of couple, 2.340–2.341
    working tax credit, 2.338–2.339
  method, 2.356–2.357
  person acting on behalf of another, for, 2.342–2.343
  polygamous marriages, 2.555
  postponement, 2.351–2.352
  recovery of overpayments
    generally, 1.305–1.306
    method, 2.355
  renewal, on, 2.344–2.345
  single payments, 2.349–2.350
  timing
    bank account, 2.346–2.347
    other than to bank account, 2.348
  working tax credit, and
    generally, 2.338–2.339
    introduction, 2.333
Penalties
  child trust funds
    appeals, 1.605–1.608
    decisions, 1.605–1.608
    generally, 1.603–1.604
    mitigation, 1.605–1.608
    recovery, 1.605–1.608
  statutory adoption pay
    appeals, 1.399
    definitions, 1.405
    determination, 1.397–1.398
    failure to comply, 1.388–1.389
    fraud, 1.390–1.391
    incorrect statements, 1.390–1.391
    interest, 1.404
    mitigation, 1.402

Index

Penalties—*cont.*
  statutory adoption pay—*cont.*
    proceedings before Commissioners, 1.400
    proceedings before court, 1.401
    time limits, 1.403
  statutory maternity pay
    breach of regulations, 1.135–1.136
    fraud, 1.137
    negligence, 1.137
  statutory paternity pay
    appeals, 1.399
    definitions, 1.405
    determination, 1.397–1.398
    failure to comply, 1.388–1.389
    fraud, 1.390–1.391
    incorrect statements, 1.390–1.391
    interest, 1.404
    mitigation, 1.402
    proceedings before Commissioners, 1.400
    proceedings before court, 1.401
    time limits, 1.403
  statutory sick pay
    breach of regulations, 1.135–1.136
    fraud, 1.137
    negligence, 1.137
  tax credits
    determination, 1.369, 2.393–2.394
    failure to comply with requirements, 1.312–1.313
    failure to make correct payments, 1.314–1.315
    Guidance, 7.1–7.23
    incorrect statements, etc., 1.309–1.311
    mitigation, 1.371
    proceedings before Commissioners, 1.370
    recovery, 1.373
    supplementary, 1.316–1.317
    time limits, 1.372
    withdrawal, 2.397–2.398
  tax returns, 1.22
Pension income
  annual payments, 2.131
  charge to tax
    amount charged, 1.476
    nature, 1.475
    person liable to tax, 1.477
  deductions, 2.135
  disregarded payments, 2.132
  exemptions, 2.135
  general note
    regulations, 2.133
    statutory provisions, 1.474
  general rules
    application of provisions, 1.478–1.479
    "pension", 1.480
    person liable to tax, 1.482
    taxable pension income, 1.481
  generally, 2.131
  identity of taxpayer, 2.136
  relevant income, 2.134

Pension income—*cont.*
  state retirement pension
    application of provisions, 1.483–1.484
    person liable to tax, 1.486
    taxable pension income, 1.485
  statutory provisions
    charge to tax, 1.475–1.477
    general note, 1.474
    general rules, 1.478–1.482
    introductory provision, 1.473
    social security pensions, 1.483–1.486
  time of calculation, 2.137
Periodical payments (personal injury)
  compensation awards, 1.707
  generally, 1.706
  persons entitled, 1.708
  trusts, from, 1.709
Personal allowances
  income test, 2.104
Personal equity plans
  investment income, 2.156
Personal injury (damages)
  exempt income
    compensation awards, 1.707
    generally, 1.706
    persons entitled, 1.708
    trusts, from, 1.709
  interest, 1.713
"Persons abroad"
  statutory adoption pay
    absent from Great Britain, 5.38
    adoption from overseas, 5.108–5.112
    definitions, 5.34
    general note, 5.35
    has worked in other EEA States, 5.39
    in other EEA States, 5.37
    time for compliance, 5.41
  statutory maternity pay
    absent from Great Britain, 4.65
    definitions, 4.62
    "employee", 4.66
    general note, 4.63
    in other Member States, 4.64
    time for compliance, 4.69
    women who worked in the EC, 4.68
  statutory paternity pay
    absent from Great Britain, 5.38
    adoption from overseas, 5.108–5.112
    definitions, 5.34
    general note, 5.35
    has worked in other EEA States, 5.39
    in other EEA States, 5.37
    time for compliance, 5.41
  statutory sick pay
    absent from Great Britain, 3.52–3.53
    definitions, 3.47–3.58
    employees, 3.59
    general note, 3.46
    persons abroad, 3.59–3.60
    in other Member States, 3.51
    time for compliance, 3.64

Index

"Persons subject to immigration control"
definitions, 2.500
exclusion from entitlement, 2.501–2.510
general note, 2.507
modifications of Act, 2.511–2.512
polygamous marriages, 2.557
statutory provision, 1.334–1.335
transitional relief, 2.513–2.514

Pilots
statutory adoption pay, 1.110–1.111
statutory maternity pay, 1.69
statutory paternity pay, 1.91–1.92
statutory sick pay
  definitions, 3.49, 3.55–3.56, 3.62
  general note, 3.46
  statutory provision, 1.56
  time for compliance, 3.64

"Points of law"
child trust funds (appeals), 1.165–1.166
tax credits (appeals), 1.165–1.166

Polygamy (tax credits)
amendment of Regulations, 2.551–2.557
amendment of TCA 2002, 2.550
definitions, 2.548–2.549
general note, 2.546
statutory provision, 1.336–1.337

Postponement
hearings
  child trust funds (appeals), 6.102–6.103
  tax credits (appeals), 2.414–2.415
payments, 2.351–2.352

"Premium bonds"
income test, 2.103

Professional representation
child trust funds (appeals), 6.138–6.139
tax credits (appeals), 2.464–2.465

Professions
basic rules, 1.640
basis periods, 1.657
receipts, 1.647
rules restricting deductions, 1.647

Property income
calculation of profits, 1.672
charge to tax
  generally, 1.668
  income charged, 1.670
  person liable, 1.671
  territorial scope, 1.669
generating income from land, 1.667
introduction, 1.626
overseas property business, 1.666
overview, 1.660–1.661
priority rules
  generally, 1.662–1.663
  introduction, 1.629
profits
  generally, 1.668
  income charged, 1.670
  person liable, 1.671
  territorial scope, 1.669

Property income—*cont.*
property businesses
  introduction, 1.664–1.667
  profits, 1.668–1.672
statutory overview
  introduction, 1.628
  priority rules, 1.629
tax credits
  general note, 2.160
  generally, 2.159
UK property business, 1.665

Provision of information
administrative arrangements, and
  by authorities, 2.365
  to authorities, 2.364
employers, by
  statutory maternity pay, 1.144
  statutory sick pay, 1.142
functions relating to employment
  general note, 2.563
  generally, 2.565, 2.577
functions relating to health
  definitions, 2.543
  general note, 2.542
  generally, 2.544, 2.561
  Scotland, 2.575
functions relating to training
  general note, 2.563
  generally, 2.565, 2.577
Secretary of State, by
  statutory maternity pay, 1.143
  statutory sick pay, 1.141
statutory adoption pay
  Board, by, 1.392
  entitlement, as to, 5.28–5.29
  generally, 5.32
  Secretary of State, by, 1.393
statutory maternity pay, 4.40
  claims for other benefits, 4.44
  determination of questions, 4.42–4.43
statutory paternity pay
  Board, by, 1.392
  entitlement, as to, 5.28–5.29
  generally, 5.32
  Secretary of State, by, 1.393
statutory sick pay
  employee to Secretary of State, by, 3.28–3.29
  employer to employee, by, 3.30–3.31
tax authorities, by
  statutory adoption pay, 1.392–1.393
  statutory paternity pay, 1.392–1.393
  tax credits, 1.138–1.140
tax credits
  contributions purposes, for, 1.140
  fraud prevention, for, 1.138–1.139
  generally, 2.571
  Northern Ireland, 2.573

"Purchased life annuity payments"
charge to tax, 1.689
income charged, 1.691
meaning, 1.690
person liable, 1.692

Index

"Put at disposal"
employment income, 1.432

"Qualifying days"
statutory sick pay
  generally, 3.11–3.13
  statutory provision, 1.46–1.47
Qualifying periods
statutory paternity pay
  adoption of child, on, 5.61
  birth of child, on, 5.53
"Qualifying remunerative work"
excepted activities, 2.35
generally, 2.25–2.31
hours worked, 2.36
minimum level of continuity, 2.33
remunerative work, 2.34
routes to entitlement, 2.32
"Qualifying young persons"
definition, 2.185
maximum age, 2.207–2.208
working tax credit, and
  childcare element, 2.73
  death, 2.82–2.83

Reasons
child trust funds (appeals)
  generally, 6.104–6.105
  late applications, 6.106–6.107
  service by electronic mail, 6.115
tax credits (appeals)
  generally, 2.419
  late applications, 2.422–2.423
  service by electronic mail, 2.432
Receipts
basic rules, 1.643–1.644
capital receipts, 1.655
debts incurred and later released, 1.656
professions and vocations, 1.654
Recording of proceedings
child trust funds (appeals)
  generally, 6.108–6.109
  service by electronic mail, 6.115
tax credits (appeals)
  generally, 2.424–2.425
  service by electronic mail, 2.432
Records
administrative arrangements
  claims, 2.366
statutory adoption pay
  generally, 5.26
  inspection, 5.27
statutory maternity pay
  maintenance, 4.45
  production, 4.46
statutory paternity pay
  generally, 5.26
  inspection, 5.27
statutory sick pay
  maintenance, 3.26
  production, 3.27

Recovery of payments (overpayments)
statutory maternity pay
  payments to employer by Revenue, from, 4.88
  payments to Revenue, from, 4.87
tax credits
  generally, 1.305–1.306
  method, 2.355
Recovery of payments (statutory maternity pay)
additional payment to small employers, 4.84
advance funding, 4.86
date of payment of contributions, 4.89
definitions
  generally, 4.81
  "small employer", 4.83
general note, 4.82
method
  deduction from payments to Revenue, 4.87
  payments to employer by Revenue, 4.88
overpayments, 4.90
prescribed amount, 4.85
Recovery of payments (statutory sick pay)
amount, 3.86
definitions, 3.83
general note, 3.84
generally, 3.85
method, 3.86–3.88
statutory provisions, 1.51–1.53
Reinstatement
service with armed services
statutory maternity pay, 4.26
Reinstatement of applications
child trust funds (appeals), 6.97
tax credits (appeals), 2.405
"Relevant income"
generally, 2.223–2.224
Rent-a-room relief
definitions
  rent-a-room amount, 1.722
  rent-a-room receipts, 1.720
  residence, 1.721
individual's limit, 1.723
introduction, 1.626
overview, 1.718
qualifying person, 1.719
statutory overview, 1.628
trading income, 1.639
Representation
see **Professional representation**
Residence
Crown servants posted overseas
  generally, 2.529–2.530
  partners, 2.531
definitions, 2.517–2.518
individuals in UK for temporary purpose
  employment income, 1.760
  foreign income, 1.759
individuals temporarily abroad, 1.756–1.757

919

Index

Residence—*cont.*
  individuals working abroad, 1.758
  ordinary residence, 2.522–2.525
  person treated as not being in UK, 2.519–2.526
  polygamous marriages, 2.556
  temporary absence from UK, 2.527–2.528
  transitional provision, 2.532–2.533
Respondent's observations
  see **Observations**
"Responsibility for child"
  competing claims, 2.195–2.196
  excepted cases, 2.197–2.203
  generally, 2.187–2.193
  normally living with test, 2.194
  special case, 2.204
Returns of income
  see **Tax returns**
Revenue and Customs
  Commissioners
    appointment, 1.732
    declaration of confidentiality, 1.734
    functions, 1.736–1.740
    staff appointments, 1.733
  conduct of proceedings, 1.739
  confidentiality, 1.742
  former Inland Revenue matters
    generally, 1.737
    schedule, 1.748
  freedom of information, 1.743
  functions
    ancillary powers, 1.738
    conduct of proceedings, 1.739
    exercise by officers, 1.740
    former Inland Revenue matters, 1.737
    initial, 1.736
  general note, 1.731
  information
    confidentiality, 1.742
    freedom of information, 1.743
    use, 1.741
  initial functions, 1.736
  ITEPA 2003, 1.409
  obstruction, 1.744
  offences
    assault, 1.745
    obstruction, 1.744
    power of arrest, 1.746
  officers
    appointment, 1.733
    assault, 1.745
    declaration of confidentiality, 1.734
    exercise of functions, 1.740
  payments by
    see also **Revenue and Customs (payments)**
    general note, 2.333
    generally, 2,421–2.359
    introduction, 2.333
    ˙ignation, 1.732
    ˋsfer of property, 1.747

Revenue and Customs officers
  assault, 1.745
  declaration of confidentiality, 1.734
  exercise of Commissioners functions, 1.740
  generally, 1.733
  obstruction, 1.744
Revenue and Customs (payments)
  amount, 2.353–2.354
  bank account requirement, 2.358–2.359
  child care element of WTC, 2.336–2.337
  definitions, 2.335
  general note, 2.333
  introduction, 2.333
  joint claims, for
    child tax credit, 2.336–2.337
    child care element of WTC, 2.336–2.337
    death of one of couple, 2.340–2.341
    working tax credit, 2.338–2.339
  method, 2.356–2.357
  person acting on behalf of another, for, 2.342–2.343
  postponement, 2.351–2.352
  recovery of overpayments
    generally, 1.305–1.306
    method, 2.355
  renewal, on, 2.344–2.345
  single payments, 2.349–2.350
  timing
    bank account, 2.346–2.347
    other than to bank account, 2.348
  working tax credit, and
    generally, 2.338–2.339
    introduction, 2.333
Rounding
  statutory adoption pay, 5.6–5.7
  statutory maternity pay, 4.48
  statutory paternity pay, 5.6–5.7

Savings income
  building society dividends, 1.681
  dividends from non-resident UK companies
    charge to tax, 1.686
    income charged, 1.687
    person liable, 1.688
  dividends from UK resident companies
    charge to tax, 1.683
    income charged, 1.684
    introduction, 1.682
    person liable, 1.685
  general note, 1.674
  interest
    charge to tax, 1.678
    income charged, 1.679
    person liable, 1.680
    territorial scope, 1.677
  introduction, 1.626
  overview, 1.673
  priority rules
    generally, 1.675–1.676
    introduction, 1.629

Index

Savings income—*cont.*
  purchased life annuity payments
    charge to tax, 1.689
    income charged, 1.691
    meaning, 1.690
    person liable, 1.692
  statutory overview
    introduction, 1.628
    priority rules, 1.629
  territorial scope of charge, 1.677
"Schedules"
  see also **Income tax**
  ITEPA 2003, 1.407
  ITTOIA 2005, 1.626
Scholarship income
  other income, 1.715
  tax credits, 2.153–2.154
Seafarers
  statutory adoption pay
    definitions, 5.34
    general note, 5.35
    generally, 5.42
  statutory maternity pay
    adoption from overseas, 5.108–5.112
    definitions, 4.62
    general note, 4.63
    generally, 4.70
    statutory provisions, 1.69
  statutory paternity pay
    definitions, 5.34
    general note, 5.35
    generally, 5.42
    statutory provisions, 1.91–1.92
  statutory sick pay
    adoption from overseas, 5.108–5.112
    definitions, 3.47–3.48, 3.54, 3.61
    general note, 3.46
    statutory provision, 1.56
    time for compliance, 3.64
Seasonal workers
  working tax credit, 2.53–2.54
Second-adult element
  working tax credit, 2.65–2.66
Self assessment
  tax returns, 1.5
Self-employment
  employment income, 2.125
  trading income, 2.140
Service (notices)
  child trust funds (appeals)
    electronic mail, by, 6.115
    generally, 6.76–6.77
    manner and time, 6.124
  statutory adoption pay, 5.95
  statutory paternity pay, 5.95
  tax credits (appeals)
    electronic mail, by, 2.432
    generally, 2.373–2.374
    manner and time, 2.444
Setting aside (decisions)
  child trust funds (appeals)
    Commissioner, by, 6.160–6.162
    generally, 6.112–6.113

Setting aside (decisions)—*cont.*
  child trust funds (appeals)—*cont.*
    service by electronic mail, 6.115
    statutory provision, 1.169
    supplementary provisions, 6.114
  tax credits (appeals)
    Commissioner, by, 2.487–2.489
    generally, 2.428–2.430
    service by electronic mail, 2.432
    statutory provision, 1.169
    supplementary provisions, 2.431
Settlements
  charge to tax, 1.696–1.697
  income charged, 1.699
  person liable, 1.700
  "settlement", 1.698
Severe disability element
  working tax credit, 2.78–2.79
Severe disablement allowance
  investment income, 2.157
  social security income, 2.145
"Severely disabled child"
  child tax credit, 2.213–2.214
Sick pay
  see also **Statutory sick pay**
Sickness benefits (vouchers)
  taxable benefits, 1.437
"Sickness periods"
  working tax credit, 2.41–2.42
Social fund
  social security income, 2.145
Social Security Act 1998
  amendments, 1.145
  arrangement of sections, 1.146
  definitions, 1.170, 1.175–1.176
  general provisions, 1.147–1.169
  Parliamentary control of regulations, 1.173–1.174
  regulations and orders, 1.171–1.172
  schedules, 1.177–1.187
  supplementary provisions, 1.170–1.176
Social Security Administration Act 1992
  arrangement of sections, 1.132
  general provisions
    claims and payments, 1.133–1.134
    enforcement, 1.135–1.137
    information, 1.138–1.144
Social security administration (statutory adoption pay)
  adoption from overseas, 5.103–5.107
  determination of entitlement issues
    application, 5.30
    form of application, 5.31
  employers' records
    generally, 5.26
    inspection, 5.27
  funding of liabilities
    application to Revenue, 5.21
    date of payment of contributions, 5.24
    generally, 5.20
    method, 5.22–5.23
    overpayments, 5.25
    provision of information, 5.32

Social security administration (statutory maternity pay)
employer's records
  maintenance, 4.45
  production, 4.46
expected week of confinement, 4.39
notice of absence from work, 4.40
notification of employment after confinement, 4.41
provision of information
  claims for other benefits, 4.44
  determination of questions, 4.42–4.43

Social security administration (statutory paternity pay)
adoption from overseas, 5.103–5.107
determination of entitlement issues
  application, 5.30
  form of application, 5.31
employers' records
  generally, 5.26
  inspection, 5.27
funding of liabilities
  application to Revenue, 5.21
  date of payment of contributions, 5.24
  generally, 5.20
  method, 5.22–5.23
  overpayments, 5.25
provision of information, 5.32

Social security commissioners
child trust funds (appeals)
  appointment, 1.181
  certificates, 1.185
  delegation of functions, 1.184
  jurisdiction, 6.65–6.72
  remuneration, 1.182
  supplemental, 1.186
  tenure, 1.183
tax credits appeals, and
  appointment, 1.181
  certificates, 1.185
  delegation of functions, 1.184
  remuneration, 1.182
  supplemental, 1.186
  tenure, 1.183

Social security commissioners (Procedure) (Child Trust Funds) Regulations 2005
arrangement of Regulations, 6.118
citation, 6.119
commencement, 6.119
definitions, 6.120
duration, 6.119
general provisions
  appeal procedure, 6.138–6.155
  applications for leave to appeal, 6.127–6.137
  applications for leave to appeal to appellate court, 6.164–6.164
  Commissioner's powers, 6.121
  decisions, 6.156–6.162
  delegation of functions, 6.123

Social security commissioners (Procedure) (Child Trust Funds) Regulations 2005—*cont.*
general provisions—*cont.*
  funding of legal services, 6.125–6.126
  service of notices, 6.124
  transfer of proceedings, 6.122

Social security commissioners (Procedure) (Tax Credits Appeals) Regulations 2002
arrangement of, 2.438
citation, 2.439
commencement, 2.439
definitions, 2.440
duration, 2.439
general provisions
  appeal procedure, 2.464–2.482
  applications for leave to appeal, 2.447–2.463
  applications for leave to appeal to appellate court, 2.490–2.491
  Commissioner's powers, 2.441
  decisions, 2.483–2.489
  delegation of functions, 2.443
  funding of legal services, 2.445–2.446
  service of notices, 2.444
  transfer of proceedings, 2.442

Social security contributions
see **National insurance contributions**

Social Security Contributions and Benefits Act 1992
application, 1.115
arrangement of sections, 1.30
definitions, 1.116–1.117
general note, 1.31
general provisions
  statutory adoption pay, 1.97–1.114
  statutory maternity pay, 1.58–1.70
  statutory paternity pay, 1.71–1.96
  statutory sick pay, 1.32–1.57
modifications to
  adoptions from overseas, 5.96–5.102
  dismissal for reasons of pregnancy, 4.94–4.95
schedules, 1.118–1.131

Social Security Contributions (Transfer of Functions, etc.) Act 1999
arrangement of sections, 1.189
definitions, 1.215
general provisions, 1.190–1.213
long title, 1.188
miscellaneous provisions, 1.214–1.216

Social security income
charge to tax
  amount charged, 1.493
  definitions, 1.491–1.492
  nature of charge, 1.489–1.490
  person liable to tax, 1.494
child maintenance bonus
  income support, 1.505
  jobseeker's allowance, 1.510
deductions, 2.148
disregarded payments, 2.145

Index

Social security income—*cont.*
exemptions
  generally, 2.148
  incapacity benefit, 1.502–1.503
  income support, 1.504–1.509
  increases in respect of children, 1.510
  jobseeker's allowance, 1.510–1.515
foreign benefits, 1.521–1.524
general note
  regulations, 2.146
  statutory provisions, 1.488
generally, 2.144
identity of taxpayer, 2.149
incapacity benefit
  long-term, 1.502
  short-term, 1.503
income support
  amount in excess of taxable maximum, 1.506
  child maintenance bonus, 1.505
  definitions, 1.508–1.509
  general rule, 1.504
  taxable maximum, 1.507
  trade disputes, 1.504
jobseeker's allowance
  amount in excess of taxable maximum, 1.511
  child maintenance bonus, 1.510
  definitions, 1.515
  taxable maximum, 1.512–1.514
relevant income, 2.147
statutory provisions
  charge to tax, 1.489–1.494
  exempt benefits, 1.502–1.517
  foreign benefits, 1.521–1.524
  general note, 1.488
  introductory provision, 1.487
  taxable benefits, 1.495–1.501
  wholly exempt benefits, 1.518–1.520
Table A benefits, 1.495–1.497
Table B benefits, 1.518–1.520
taxable benefits
  exemptions, 1.502–1.517
  person liable to tax, 1.500–1.501
  Table A, 1.495–1.497
  taxable income, 1.498–1.499
taxable foreign benefits
  application of provisions, 1.521–1.522
  person liable to tax, 1.524
  taxable income, 1.523
time of calculation, 2.150
wholly exempt benefits, 1.518–1.520
Social security pensions
see **Pension income**
see **State retirement pension**
Special Commissioners
child trust funds (appeals), 6.69–6.72
"Specific employment income"
employment income, 1.418
"Sports award"
remunerative work, 2.35
Spouses
references in Income Tax Acts, 1.767

State pension credit
generally, 2.222
income test, 2.107
State retirement pension
see also **Pension income**
application of provisions, 1.483–1.484
person liable to tax, 1.486
taxable pension income, 1.485
Statements of reasons
child trust funds (appeals)
  generally, 6.104–6.105
  late applications, 6.106–6.107
  service by electronic mail, 6.115
tax credits (appeals)
  generally, 2.419
  late applications, 2.422–2.423
  service by electronic mail, 2.432
Statistical evidence
generally, 2.571
Northern Ireland, 2.573
Statutory adoption pay
administration
  determination of entitlement issues, 5.28–5.31
  employers' records, 5.26–5.27
  funding of liabilities, 5.20–5.25
  provision of information, 5.32
  statutory provision, 1.380–1.387
adoption without placement, 1.113–1.114
avoidance of liability, 5.78
benefits, 1.106–1.107
continental shelf employees
  definitions, 5.34
  general note, 5.35
  generally, 5.43
  statutory provision, 1.110–1.111
continuous employment
  change of employer, 5.84
  generally, 5.81
  reinstatement after service with armed forces, 5.85
  stoppages of work, 5.83
  unfair dismissal, 5.82
contracting out restrictions, 1.104–1.105
contractual remuneration, and
  generally, 5.76
  statutory provision, 1.110–1.111
Crown employment, 1.108–1.109
definitions, 1.112
determination of entitlement issues
  application, 5.30
  form of application, 5.31
divided contracts
  general note, 5.10
  lapse of election, 5.15
  notification of election, 5.12
  provision of information, 5.13
  relevant employer, 5.14
earnings, 5.87
employed earners, 5.80
employer's liability
  funding, 1.381–1.382
  generally, 1.100–1.101

Statutory adoption pay—*cont.*
  employers' records
    generally, 5.26
    inspection, 5.27
  entitlement
    determination of issues, 5.30–5.31
    provision of information, 5.28–5.29
    statutory provisions, 1.98–1.99
  evidence of entitlement, 5.71
  excepted cases, 5.74
  failure to comply, 1.388–1.389
  fraud
    generally, 1.390–1.391
    procedure and appeals, 1.397–1.405
  funding of liabilities
    application to Revenue, 5.21
    date of payment of contributions, 5.24
    generally, 5.20
    method, 5.22–5.23
    overpayments, 5.25
  general note, 1.97
  incorrect statements, 1.390–1.391
  information
    power to require, 1.386–1.387
    supply, 1.392–1.393
    use by Board, 1.394
  liability of Revenue, 5.91
  mariners
    definitions, 5.34
    general note, 5.35
    generally, 5.42
    statutory provision, 1.110–1.111
  NHS employees
    general note, 5.10
    lapse of election, 5.15
    notification of election, 5.12
    provision of information, 5.13
    relevant employer, 5.14
  normal weekly earnings
    earnings, 5.87
    generally, 5.88
  notice requirements, 5.70
  overseas adoptions
    administration, 5.103–5.107
    application of General Regulations 2002, 5.117
    application of SSCBA 1992, 5.96–5.102
    avoidance of liability, 5.132
    continental shelf employees, 5.108–5.112
    definitions, 5.116
    evidence of entitlement, 5.129
    general note, 5.115
    mariners, 5.108–5.112
    notice requirements, 5.128
    pay period, 5.126–5.127
    persons abroad, 5.108–5.112
    termination of employment, 5.131
    treatment of more than one employer, 5.130

Statutory adoption pay—*cont.*
  pay period
    disrupted adoption, 5.69
    generally, 5.68
    statutory provision, 1.102–1.103
    treatment of more than once contract, 5.70
  payment
    generally, 5.89
    liability of Revenue, 5.91
    persons acting on behalf of another, to, 5.94
    Revenue, by, 5.93
    statutory provisions, 1.383–1.384
    timing, 5.90
  penalties
    appeals, 1.399
    definitions, 1.405
    determination, 1.397–1.398
    failure to comply, 1.388–1.389
    fraud, 1.390–1.391
    incorrect statements, 1.390–1.391
    interest, 1.404
    mitigation, 1.402
    proceedings before Commissioners, 1.400
    proceedings before court, 1.401
    time limits, 1.403
  persons abroad
    absent from Great Britain, 5.38
    definitions, 5.34
    general note, 5.35
    has worked in other EEA States, 5.40
    in other EEA States, 5.37
    time for compliance, 5.41
  provision of information
    entitlement, as to, 5.28–5.29
    generally, 5.32
  rate, 1.102–1.103
  relationship with benefits, 1.106–1.107
  rounding, 5.6–5.7
  service of notices, 5.95
  special classes of person, 1.110–1.111
  statutory provisions
    administration, 1.380–1.387
    adoption without placement, 1.113–1.114
    contracting out restrictions, 1.104–1.105
    Crown employment, 1.108–1.109
    definitions, 1.112
    employer's liability, 1.100–1.101
    entitlement, 1.98–1.99
    general note, 1.97
    information, 1.392–1.394
    pay period, 1.102–1.103
    penalties, 1.388–1.391
    rate, 1.102–1.103
    relationship with benefits, 1.106–1.107
    relationship with remuneration, 1.106–1.107
    special classes of person, 1.110–1.111
    supplementary, 1.112

Index

Statutory adoption pay—*cont.*
supply of information
  Board, by, 1.392
  Secretary of State, by, 1.393
ten days or less working in pay period, 5.75
termination of employment before start of period, 5.77
treatment of more than once contract
  general note, 5.10
  generally, 5.72
  lapse of election, 5.15
  notification of election, 5.12
  provision of information, 5.13
  relevant employer, 5.14, 5.86
weekly rates
  general note, 5.3
  generally, 5.5
  rounding, 5.6–5.7
work during pay period, 5.73
working tax credits
  social security income, 2.145
working 10 days or less in pay period, 5.75
Statutory Adoption Pay (Administration) Regulations 2002
application
  Adoption from Overseas Regulations, to, 5.103–5.107
arrangement of Regulations, 5.16
citation, 5.17
commencement, 5.17
definitions, 5.19
general note, 5.18
general provisions, 5.20–5.32
Statutory Adoption Pay (Adoption from Overseas) (No.2) Regulations 2003
application, 5.118
arrangement of Regulations, 5.113
citation, 5.114
commencement, 5.114
definitions, 5.116
general note, 5.115
general provisions, 5.126–5.132
revocation provision, 5.133
Statutory Adoption Pay (General) Regulations 2002
application
  Adoption from Overseas (No.2) Regulations, to, 5.117
  generally, 5.47
arrangement of Regulations, 5.44
citation, 5.45
commencement, 5.45
definitions, 5.46
general provisions, 5.68–5.95
Statutory Adoption Pay (NHS Employees) Regulations 2002
arrangement of Regulations, 5.8
citation, 5.9
commencement, 5.9
definitions, 5.9
general note, 5.10
general provisions, 5.11–5.15

Statutory Adoption Pay (Persons Abroad and Mariners) Regulations 2002
application
  Adoption from Overseas (No. 2) Regulations, to, 5.108–5.112
arrangement of Regulations, 5.33
citation, 5.34
commencement, 5.34
definitions, 5.34
general note, 5.35
general provisions, 5.36–5.43
Statutory Adoption Pay (Weekly Rates) Regulations 2002
arrangement of Regulations, 5.1
citation, 5.2
commencement, 5.2
general note, 5.3
general provisions, 5.4–5.7
Statutory maternity pay
administration
  employer's records, 4.45–4.46
  expected week of confinement, 4.39
  notice of absence from work, 4.40
  notification of employment after confinement, 4.41
  provision of information, 4.42–4.44
avoidance of liability, 4.6–4.7
benefits, and
  generally, 1.66–1.67
  miscellaneous provision, 1.129–2.185
breach of regulations, 1.135–1.136
change of employer, 4.25
civil penalties
  breach of regulations, 1.135–1.136
  fraud, 1.137
  negligence, 1.137
compensation of employerss
  additional payment to small employers, 4.84
  advance funding, 4.86
  date of payment of contributions, 4.89
  deduction from payments to Revenue, 4.87
  definitions, 4.81
  general note, 4.82
  overpayments, 4.90
  payments to employer by Revenue, 4.88
  prescribed amount, 4.85
  "small employer", 4.83
continental shelf employees
  definitions, 4.62
  general note, 4.63
  generally, 4.71
  statutory provisions, 1.69
continuous employment
  change of employer, 4.25
  generally, 4.21
  stoppages of work, 4.23–4.24
  unfair dismissal, 4.22
contractual remuneration, as
  generally, 4.33
  statutory provision, 1.131

925

Statutory maternity pay—*cont.*
　Crown employment, 1.68
　death of woman, 4.20
　definitions
　　"earnings", 4.34
　　"employee", 4.30
　　generally, 4.2–4.3
　　statutory provisions, 1.70
　　"week", 4.29
　detention in custody, 4.16–4.17
　determination of entitlement
　　application, 3.93
　　definitions, 3.92
　　procedure, 3.94
　divided contracts (general Regulations)
　　treatment of more than one contract as one, 4.10
　　treatment of two or more employers as one, 4.31–4.32
　divided contracts (NHS Regulations)
　　lapse of election, 4.79
　　notification of election, 4.76
　　provision of information, 4.77
　　treatment of more than one contract as one, 4.75
　　treatment of two or more employers as one, 4.78
　employee, 4.30
　employee's duties, 1.134
　employer's records
　　maintenance, 4.45
　　production, 4.46
　employment contract terminated to avoid liability, 4.6–4.7
　enforcement
　　breach of regulations, 1.135–1.136
　　fraud, 1.137
　　negligence, 1.137
　entitlement, 1.58–1.59
　expected week of confinement, 4.39
　fraud, 1.137
　funding of employers' liabilities, 1.64–1.65
　imprisonment, 4.16–4.17
　incapacity benefit, and
　　generally, 4.37
　　statutory provision, 1.130
　information
　　disclosure by Secretary of State, 1.143
　　employers, by, 1.144
　liability of Secretary of State to pay
　　generally, 4.12–4.13
　　statutory provision, 1.58–1.59
　mariners
　　definitions, 4.62
　　general note, 4.63
　　generally, 4.70
　　statutory provisions, 1.69
　maternity allowance, 4.38
　medical evidence
　　definitions, 4.57
　　evidence of pregnancy and confinement, 4.58

Statutory maternity pay—*cont.*
　medical evidence—*cont.*
　　form of certificate, 4.59–4.60
　　modification of provisions, 4.8–4.9
　　national health service employees
　　　lapse of election, 4.79
　　　notification of election, 4.76
　　　provision of information, 4.77
　　　treatment of more than one contract as one, 4.75
　　　treatment of two or more employers as one, 4.78
　negligence, 1.137
　normal working earnings
　　"earnings", 4.34
　　generally, 4.35–4.36
　normal working weeks
　　generally, 4.27–4.28
　　"week", 4.29
　notice of absence from work, 4.40
　notification of employment after confinement, 4.41
　offences, 4.54–4.55
　pay period
　　generally, 4.4–4.5
　　statutory provision, 1.60–1.61
　payment
　　generally, 4.47
　　persons acting on behalf of another, to, 4.52–4.53
　　rounding, 4.48
　　Secretary of State, by, 4.50–4.51
　　timing, 4.49
　persons abroad
　　absent from Great Britain, 4.65
　　definitions, 4.62
　　"employee", 4.66
　　general note, 4.63
　　in other Member States, 4.64
　　time for compliance, 4.69
　　women who worked in the EC, 4.68
　persons acting on behalf of another, to, 4.52–4.53
　provision of information
　　claims for other benefits, 4.44
　　determination of questions, 4.42–4.43
　rate
　　generally, 4.11
　　statutory provision, 1.62–1.63
　recovery of payments, 1.64–1.65
　reinstatement after service with armed services, 4.26
　relationship with benefits
　　generally, 1.66–1.67
　　miscellaneous provision, 1.129–2.185
　rounding fractional amounts, 4.48
　special classes of persons, 1.69
　statutory provisions
　　Crown employment, 1.68
　　definitions, 1.70
　　entitlement, 1.58–1.59
　　pay period, 1.60–1.61
　　rate, 1.62–1.63

Index

Statutory maternity pay—*cont.*
statutory provisions—*cont.*
recovery of payments, 1.64–1.65
relationship with benefits,
1.66–1.67
special classes of persons, 1.69
stoppages of work, 4.23–4.24
ten days or less work in pay period,
4.18–4.19
treatment of more than one contract of service
generally, 4.10
NHS employees, 4.75
relevant employer, 4.31–4.32
unfair dismissal, 4.22
work after confinement, 4.14–4.15
working tax credits
social security income, 2.145
working 10 days or less in pay period,
4.18–4.19
Statutory Maternity Pay (Compensation of Employers) and Miscellaneous Amendment Regulations 1994
arrangement of Regulations, 4.80
citation, 4.81
commencement, 4.81
definitions, 4.81
general note, 4.82
general provisions, 4.83–4.90
revocations, 4.91
Statutory Maternity Pay (Decisions) Regulations 1999
arrangement of Regulations, 3.91
citation, 3.92
commencement, 3.92
definitions, 3.92
general provisions, 3.93–3.94
revocation, 3.95
Statutory Maternity Pay (General) Regulations 1986
amendments to
2000 Regulations, 4.92–4.98
arrangement of Regulations, 4.1
citation, 4.2
commencement, 4.2
definitions, 4.2–4.3
general provisions
administration, 4.39–4.46
employee, 4.30
entitlement, 4.4–4.20
miscellaneous, 4.30–4.38
normal working weeks, 4.27–4.29
offences, 4.54–4.55
payment, 4.47–4.53
Statutory Maternity Pay (Medical Evidence) Regulations 1987
arrangement of Regulations, 4.56
citation, 4.57
commencement, 4.57
definitions, 4.57
general provisions, 4.58
schedule, 4.59–4.60

Statutory Maternity Pay (National Health Service Employees) Regulations 1991
arrangement of Regulations, 4.73
citation, 4.74
commencement, 4.74
definitions, 4.74
general provisions, 4.75–4.79
Statutory Maternity Pay (Persons Abroad and Mariners) Regulations 1987
arrangement of Regulations, 4.61
citation, 4.62
commencement, 4.62
definitions, 4.62
general note, 4.63
general provisions, 4.64–4.72
Statutory paternity pay
administration
determination of entitlement issues,
5.28–5.31
employers' records, 5.26–5.27
funding of liabilities, 5.20–5.25
provision of information, 5.32
statutory provision, 1.380–1.387
adoption of child, on
conditions of entitlement, 5.57–5.58
evidence of entitlement, 5.62
notice requirements, 5.60
payment period, 5.59
qualifying period, 5.61
statutory provisions, 1.77–1.78
treatment of more than one employer,
5.63
adoption without placement, 1.95–1.96
avoidance of liability, 5.67
birth of child, on
conditions of entitlement, 5.48–5.50
evidence of entitlement, 5.54–5.55
notice requirements, 5.52
payment period, 5.51
qualifying period, 5.53
statutory provisions, 1.72–1.76/1
treatment of more than one employer,
5.56
conditions of entitlement
adoption of child, on, 5.57–5.58
birth of child, on, 5.48–5.50
continental shelf employees
definitions, 5.34
general note, 5.35
generally, 5.43
continuous employment
change of employer, 5.84
generally, 5.81
reinstatement after service with armed forces, 5.85
stoppages of work, 5.83
unfair dismissal, 5.82
contractual remuneration, and
generally, 5.66
statutory provision, 1.87–1.88
definitions, 1.93–1.94

927

Index

Statutory paternity pay—*cont.*
  detention in custody, 5.92
  determination of entitlement issues
    application, 5.30
    form of application, 5.31
  divided contracts
    general note, 5.10
    lapse of election, 5.15
    notification of election, 5.12
    provision of information, 5.13
    relevant employer, 5.14
  earnings, 5.87
  employed earners, 5.80
  employer's liability, 1.81–1.82
  employers' records
    generally, 5.26
    inspection, 5.27
  entitlement
    adoption of child, on, 5.57–5.63
    birth of child, on, 5.48–5.56
    determination of issues, 5.30–5.31
    provision of information, 5.28–5.29
    statutory provisions, 1.72–1.80
  evidence of entitlement
    adoption of child, on, 5.57–5.58
    birth of child, on, 5.48–5.50
  excepted cases, 5.65
  failure to comply, 1.388–1.389
  fraud
    generally, 1.390–1.391
    procedure and appeals, 1.397–1.405
  funding of liabilities
    application to Revenue, 5.21
    date of payment of contributions, 5.24
    generally, 5.20
    method, 5.22–5.23
    overpayments, 5.25
  imprisonment, 5.92
  incorrect statements, 1.390–1.391
  information
    power to require, 1.386–1.387
    supply, 1.392–1.393
    use by Board, 1.394
  liability of Revenue to pay
    detention in custody, 5.92
    generally, 5.91
    imprisonment, 5.92
  mariners
    definitions, 5.34
    general note, 5.35
    generally, 5.42
  NHS employees
    general note, 5.10
    lapse of election, 5.15
    notification of election, 5.12
    provision of information, 5.13
    relevant employer, 5.14
  normal weekly earnings
    earnings, 5.87
    generally, 5.88
  notice requirements
    adoption of child, on, 5.60

Statutory paternity pay—*cont.*
  notice requirements—*cont.*
    birth of child, on, 5.52
    statutory provisions, 1.79–1.80
  overseas adoptions
    administration, 5.103–5.107
    application of General Regulations 2002, 5.117
    application of SSCBA 1992, 5.96–5.102
    avoidance of liability, 5.125
    conditions of entitlement, 5.119
    continental shelf employees, 5.108–5.112
    definitions, 5.116
    evidence of entitlement, 5.123
    general note, 5.115
    mariners, 5.108–5.112
    notice requirements, 5.121
    pay period, 5.120
    persons abroad, 5.108–5.112
    qualifying period, 5.122
    treatment of more than one employer, 5.124
  pay period
    adoption of child, on, 5.59
    birth of child, on, 5.51
    statutory provision, 1.83–1.84
  payment
    generally, 5.89
    liability of Revenue, 5.91
    persons acting on behalf of another, to, 5.94
    Revenue, by, 5.93
    timing, 5.90
  penalties
    appeals, 1.399
    definitions, 1.405
    determination, 1.397–1.398
    failure to comply, 1.388–1.389
    fraud, 1.390–1.391
    incorrect statements, 1.390–1.391
    interest, 1.404
    mitigation, 1.402
    proceedings before Commissioners, 1.400
    proceedings before court, 1.401
    time limits, 1.403
  persons abroad
    absent from Great Britain, 5.38
    definitions, 5.34
    general note, 5.35
    has worked in other EEA States, 5.39
    in other EEA States, 5.37
    time for compliance, 5.41
  provision of information
    entitlement, as to, 5.28–5.29
    generally, 5.32
  qualifying period
    adoption of child, on, 5.61
    birth of child, on, 5.53
  rate, 1.83–1.84
  rounding, 5.6–5.7

Index

Statutory paternity pay—*cont.*
service of notices, 5.95
special classes of persons, 1.91–1.92
statutory provisions
  administration, 1.380–1.387
  adoption without placement,
    1.95–1.96
  contracting out restrictions,
    1.85–1.86
  Crown employment, 1.89–1.90
  definitions, 1.93–1.94
  employer's liability, 1.81–1.82
  entitlement, 1.72–1.80
  general note, 1.71
  information, 1.392–1.394
  pay period, 1.83–1.84
  penalties, 1.388–1.391
  rate, 1.83–1.84
  relationship with contractual
    remuneration, 1.87–1.88
  special classes of persons, 1.91–1.92
  supplementary, 1.93
supply of information
  Board, by, 1.392
  Secretary of State, by, 1.393
treatment of more than once contract
  adoption of child, on, 5.63
  birth of child, on, 5.56
  general note, 5.10
  lapse of election, 5.15
  notification of election, 5.12
  provision of information, 5.13
  relevant employer, 5.14, 5.86
weekly rates
  general note, 5.3
  generally, 5.4
  rounding, 5.6–5.7
work during pay period, 5.64
working tax credits
  social security income, 2.145

**Statutory Paternity Pay
(Administration) Regulations
2002**
application
  Adoption from Overseas Regulations,
    to, 5.103–5.107
arrangement of Regulations, 5.16
citation, 5.17
commencement, 5.17
definitions, 5.19
general note, 5.18
general provisions, 5.20–5.32

**Statutory Paternity Pay (Adoption
from Overseas) (No.2)
Regulations 2003**
application, 5.118
arrangement of Regulations, 5.113
citation, 5.114
commencement, 5.114
definitions, 5.116
general note, 5.115
general provisions, 5.119–5.125
revocation provision, 5.133

**Statutory Paternity Pay (General)
Regulations 2002**
application
  Adoption from Overseas (No.2)
    Regulations, to, 5.117
  generally, 5.47
arrangement of Regulations, 5.44
citation, 5.45
commencement, 5.45
definitions, 5.46
general provisions
  adoption, 5.57–5.63
  birth, 5.48–5.56
  common provisions, 5.64–5.67
  miscellaneous, 5.79–5.95

**Statutory Paternity Pay (NHS
Employees) Regulations 2002**
arrangement of Regulations, 5.8
citation, 5.9
commencement, 5.9
definitions, 5.9
general note, 5.10
general provisions, 5.10–5.15

**Statutory Paternity Pay (Persons
Abroad and Mariners)
Regulations 2002**
application
  Adoption from Overseas (No.2)
    Regulations, to, 5.108–5.112
arrangement of Regulations, 5.33
citation, 5.34
commencement, 5.34
definitions, 5.34
general note, 5.35
general provisions, 5.36–5.43

**Statutory Paternity Pay (Weekly Rates)
Regulations 2002**
arrangement of Regulations, 5.1
citation, 5.2
commencement, 5.2
general note, 5.3
general provisions, 5.4–5.7

Statutory sick pay
air crew
  definitions, 3.49, 3.55–3.56, 3.62
  general note, 3.46
  statutory provision, 1.56
  time for compliance, 3.64
avoidance of liability, 3.10
benefits, and
  generally, 1.54
  miscellaneous provisions,
    1.122–1.128
breach of regulations, 1.135–1.136
calculation of limit, 3.14
civil penalties
  breach of regulations, 1.135–1.136
  fraud, 1.137
  negligence, 1.137
compensation of employers
  amount, 3.86
  definitions, 3.83
  general note, 3.84

Index

Statutory sick pay—*cont.*
  compensation of employers—*cont.*
    generally, 3.85
    method, 3.86–3.88
  continental shelf employees
    definitions, 3.50, 3.57, 3.63
    general note, 3.46
    statutory provision, 1.56
    time for compliance, 3.64
  contractual remuneration, 1.123
  Crown employment, 1.55
  definitions
    earnings, 3.34
    employee, 3.33
    generally, 3.2–3.3
    statutory provisions, 1.57
  detention in custody. 3.8
  determination of entitlement
    application, 3.93
    definitions, 3.92
    procedure, 3.94
  divided contracts (general Regulations)
    generally, 3.40
    relevant employer, 3.38–3.39
  divided contracts (NHS Regulations)
    lapse of election, 3.81
    notification of election, 3.78
    provision of information, 3.79
    treatment of more than one contract as one, 3.77
    treatment of two or more employers as one, 3.80
  earnings
    excepted payments, 3.35
    generally, 3.34
    normal weekly earnings, 3.36–3.37
  employee's duties, 1.133
  employer's liability, 1.32–1.31
  employment contract terminated to avoid liability, 3.10
  enforcement
    breach of regulations, 1.135–1.136
    fraud, 1.137
    negligence, 1.137
  entitlement
    employer's liability, 1.32–1.31
    general note, 1.31
    limitations, 1.48–1.49
    qualifying conditions, 1.32–1.82
  fraud, 1.137
  general note, 1.31
  imprisonment, 3.8
  incapacity benefit, 1.124–1.125
  information
    disclosure by Secretary of State, 1.141
    employers, by, 1.142
  insolvency of employer, 3.20
  interruption of employment
    excepted days, 3.25
  limitations on entitlement, 1.48–1.49
  linking periods of incapacity. 3.6–3.7

Statutory sick pay—*cont.*
  mariners
    definitions, 3.47–3.48, 3.54, 3.61
    general note, 3.46
    statutory provision, 1.56
    time for compliance, 3.64
  maximum entitlement, 3.9
  medical evidence
    definitions, 3.66
    form of doctor's statement, 3.69–3.72
    form of special statement, 3.73–3.74
    general note, 3.67
    information required, 3.68
  method of payment, 3.16
  national health employees
    lapse of election, 3.81
    notification of election, 3.78
    provision of information, 3.79
    treatment of more than one contract as one, 3.77
    treatment of two or more employers as one, 3.80
  negligence, 1.137
  notification of incapacity for work
    generally, 3.15
    statutory provisions, 1.49
  offences, 3.42–3.43
  payment
    liability of Secretary of State, 3.18–3.19
    method, 3.16
    Secretary of State, by, 3.21
    statements relating to, 3.32
    time limits, 3.17
  percentage threshold
    definitions, 3.83
    general note, 3.84
    generally, 3.85–3.88
  persons abroad
    absent from Great Britain, 3.52–3.53
    definitions, 3.47–3.58
    employees, 3.59
    general note, 3.46
    persons abroad, 3.59–3.60
    in other Member States, 3.51
    time for compliance, 3.64
  persons deemed incapable of work, 3.4–3.5
  persons unable to act, 3.22–3.23
  provision of information
    employee to Secretary of State, by, 3.28–3.29
    employer to employee, by, 3.30–3.31
  qualifying conditions
    period of entitlement, 1.39–1.45
    period of incapacity for work, 1.32–1.38
    qualifying days, 1.46–1.47
  qualifying days
    generally, 3.11–3.13
    statutory provisions, 1.46–1.47
  rate of payment, 1.50
  records
    maintenance, 3.26
    production, 3.27

Index

Statutory sick pay—*cont.*
  recovery of statutory sick pay
    amount, 3.86
    definitions, 3.83
    general note, 3.84
    generally, 3.85
    method, 3.86–3.88
    statutory provisions, 1.51–1.53
  relationship with benefits
    generally, 1.54
    miscellaneous provisions, 1.122–1.128
  rounding fractional amounts, 3.24
  special classes of person, 1.56
  statutory provisions
    Crown employment, 1.55
    definitions, 1.57
    employer's liability, 1.32–1.31
    general note, 1.31
    limitations on entitlement, 1.48–1.49
    qualifying conditions, 1.33–1.47
    rates of payment, 1.50
    recovery of payments, 1.51–1.53
    relationship with benefits, 1.54
    special classes of person, 1.56
  time limits for payment, 3.17
  treatment of two or more contracts as one
    generally, 3.40
    NHS employees, 3.77
    relevant employer, 3.38–3.39
  unemployability supplement, 1.126
Statutory Sick Pay (Decisions) Regulations 1999
  arrangement of Regulations, 3.91
  citation, 3.92
  commencement, 3.92
  definitions, 3.92
  general provisions, 3.93–3.94
  revocation, 3.95
Statutory Sick Pay (General) Regulations 1982
  arrangement of Regulations, 3.1
  citation, 3.2
  commencement, 3.2
  definitions, 3.2–3.3
  general provisions, 3.4–3.43
Statutory Sick Pay (Mariners, Air crew and Person Abroad) Regulations 1982
  arrangement of Regulations, 3.44
  citation, 3.45
  commencement, 3.45
  definitions, 3.45
  general note, 3.46
  general provisions, 3.47–3.64
Statutory Sick Pay (Medical Evidence) Regulations 1985
  arrangement of Regulations, 3.65
  citation, 3.66
  commencement, 3.66
  definitions, 3.66
  general note, 3.67
  general provisions, 3.68
  schedules, 3.69–3.74

Statutory Sick Pay (NHS Employees) Regulations 1985
  arrangement of Regulations, 3.75
  citation, 3.76
  commencement, 3.76
  definitions, 3.76
  general provisions, 3.77–3.81
Statutory Sick Pay Percentage Threshold Order 19995
  arrangement of Regulations, 3.82
  citation, 3.83
  commencement, 3.83
  consequential amendments, 3.90
  definitions, 3.83
  general note, 3.84
  general provisions, 3.85–3.88
  repeals, 3.89
  revocations, 3.89
"Stoppages of work"
  statutory maternity pay, 4.23–4.24
Strikes
  statutory maternity pay, 4.23–4.24
  working tax credit, 2.45–2.46
Striking out
  child trust funds (appeals)
    grounds, 6.96
    reinstatement, 6.97
  tax credits (appeals)
    grounds, 2.403–2.404
    reinstatement, 2.405
Student income
  disregarded payments, 2.153–2.154
  generally, 2.151–2.152
Student loans
  other income, 1.714
  tax credits, 2.153–2.154
Supersession (decisions)
  decisions of Board, 1.194–1.195
Supply of information
  see **Provision of income**
Suspension from work
  working tax credit, 2.47–2.48

"Table A benefits"
  social security income, 1.495–1.497
"Table B benefits"
  social security income, 1.518–1.520
Tax credits
  see also **Child tax credit**
  see also **Working tax credit**
  administrative arrangements, 1.348–1.349
  annual reports, 1.330–1.331
  annual review, 1.332–1.333
  appeals
    see also **Tax credits (appeals)**
    appealable decisions, 1.324–1.325
    exercise of right, 1.326–1.329
    general regulations, 2.370–2.437
    notice of appeal, 2.367–2.369
    procedure regulations, 2.438–2.491
    temporary modifications, 1.358–1.362
  assignment, 1.340–1.341
  bankruptcy, 1.340–1.341

931

Index

Tax credits—cont.
changes of circumstances
  automatic notification, 1.249
  discretionary notification, 1.248
  failure to report, 1.250
  generally, 1.243–1.244
  mandatory notification, 1.246
  relevant changes, 1.245
child tax credit
  entitlement, 1.258–1.260
  general note, 1.221
  maximum rate, 1.261–1.263
civil partnerships, 2.259
claims
  generally, 1.231–1.238
  supplementary, 1.239–1.240
Codes of Practice
  overpayments, 7.24–7.32
Crown employment, 1.338–1.339
decisions
  discovery, on, 1.290–1.292
  final decision, 1.286–1.287
  final notice, 1.284–1.285
  information requirements, 1.295–1.296
  initial decision, 1.276–1.279
  notice of, 1.297–1.298
  official error, subject to, 1.293–1.294
  other revised decisions, 1.282–1.283
  power to enquire, 1.288–1.289
  revision after notifications, 1.280–1.281
definitions, 1.346–1.347
development of system, 1.223
disclosure of information, 1.350–1.351
duration, 1.241–1.242
evaluation studies
  generally, 2.571
  Northern Ireland, 2.573
failure to comply with requirements, 1.312–1.313
failure to make correct payments, 1.314–1.315
fraud, and
  generally, 1.318–1.319
  powers relating to documents, 1.320–1.321
functions of Board, 1.229–1.230
general note
  child tax credit, 1.221
  future developments, 1.226
  generally, 1.219
  problems with Act, 1.225
  scheme of Act, 1.218
  statutory basis, 1.220
  working tax credit, 1.222
generally, 1.227–1.228
inalienability, 1.340–1.341
income test, 1.251–1.257
incorrect statements, etc., 1.309–1.311
interest, 1.322–1.323
Northern Ireland
  evaluation and statistical studies, 2.572–2.573
  generally, 1.363–1.364

Tax credits—cont.
notices by Board, 1.342–1.343
overpayments
  Code of Practice, 7.24–7.32
  generally, 1.303–1.304
  recovery, 1.305–1.306
payment
  employees' rights, 1.301–1.302
  generally, 1.299–1.300
penalties
  determination, 1.369
  failure to comply with requirements, 1.312–1.313
  failure to make correct payments, 1.314–1.315
  Guidance, 7.1–7.23
  incorrect statements, etc., 1.309–1.311
  mitigation, 1.371
  proceedings before Commissioners, 1.370
  recovery, 1.373
  supplementary, 1.316–1.317
  time limits, 1.372
period of award, 1.241–1.242
persons subject to immigration control, 1.334–1.335
polygamous marriages, 1.336–1.337
provision of information
  evaluation studies, 2.571
  statistical studies, 2.571
rate, 1.274–1.275
statistical studies
  generally, 2.571
  Northern Ireland, 2.573
underpayments, 1.307–1.308
use of information, 1.350–1.351
working tax credit
  childcare element, 1.272–1.273
  entitlement, 1.264–1.269
  general note, 1.222
  maximum rate, 1.270–1.271
Tax Credits Act 2002
arrangement of sections, 1.217
commencement
  generally, 1.354–1.355
  introduction, 1.224
  Order No. 3, 2.1–2.7
  Order No. 4, 2.8–2.11
consequential amendments, 1.344–1.345
definitions
  general, 1.367–1.368
  tax credits, 1.346–1.347
general note, 1.218–1.226
general provisions, 1.227–1.347
modifications
  persons subject to immigration control, 2.511–2.512
  polygamous marriages, 2.550
Northern Ireland, 1.363–1.364
Parliamentary control, 1.366
regulations, orders and schemes, 1.365

Index

Tax Credits Act 2002—*cont.*
  repeals
    generally, 1.352–1.353
    Order No. 3, 2.7
  savings
    generally, 1.356–1.357
    Order No. 3, 2.4
  schedule, 1.369–1.373
  supplementary provisions, 1.348–1.351
  tax credits
    appeals, 1.324–1.329
    child tax credit, 1.258–1.263
    decisions, 1.276–1.298
    fraud, 1.318–1.321
    generally, 1.227–1.257
    interest, 1.322–1.323
    payment, 1.299–1.308
    penalties, 1.309–1.317
    rate, 1.274–1.275
    supplementary, 1.330–1.347
    working tax credit, 1.264–1.273
  temporary modifications, 1.358–1.362
  transitional provisions
    child tax credit, 2.566–2.569
    generally, 1.356–1.357
    Order No. 3, 2.5–2.6
    Order 2005, 2.12–2.18
    tax year 2003/04, 2.4–2.5

Tax Credits (Administrative Arrangements) Regulations 2002
  arrangement of Regulations, 2.360
  citation, 2.362
  commencement, 2.362
  definitions, 2.363
  general note, 2.361
  general provisions, 2.364–2.366

Tax credits (appeals)
  adjournment, 2.414–2.415
  administration of oaths, 2.401–2.402
  appeals tribunal, to
    Clerks, 2.392
    composition, 2.390–2.391
    decisions, 2.416–2.437
    generally, 1.153–1.155
    redetermination, 1.156–1.157
  appealable decisions, 1.324–1.325
  applications for leave to appeal to appellate court, 2.490–2.491
  applications for leave to appeal to Commissioner
    determination, 2.456
    general regulations, under, 2.434–2.437
    generally, 2.448–2.452
    introductory, 2.447
    notice, 2.453–2.455
    withdrawal, 2.480–2.481
  assessment of tax returns, 1.20–1.21
  choice of hearing, 2.395–2.396
  Clerks to appeals tribunal, 2.392
  Commissioner, to
    application for leave to appeal, 2.447–2.456
    decisions, 2.483–2.489

Tax credits (appeals)—*cont.*
  Commissioner, to—*cont.*
    delegation of functions, 2.443
    general powers, 2.441
    statutory provisions, 1.158–1.164
    transfer of proceedings, 2.442
  consideration, 3.432–2.394
  correction of errors
    Commissioner, by, 2.485–2.486
    generally, 2.426–2.427
    service by electronic mail, 2.432
    statutory provision, 1.169
    supplementary provisions, 2.431
  Court of Appeal, to
    applications for leave to appeal, 2.490–2.491
    generally, 1.165–1.166
  death of party, 2.389
  decisions of appeals tribunal, 2.416–2.421
  decisions of Board, 1.198–1.203
  decisions of Commissioner
    correction of errors, 2.485–2.486
    generally, 2.483–2.484
    setting aside, 2.487–2.488
    supplementary provisions, 2.489
  definitions
    general regulations, 2.371–2.372
    procedure regulations, 2.440
    statutory provision, 1.170
  delegation of functions, 2.443
  determination, 2.393–2.394
  directions
    applications, 2.387–2.388
    death of party, 2.389
    determination of applications, 2.393–2.394
    withdrawal of applications, 2.397–2.398
  error correction
    generally, 2.426–2.427
    service by electronic mail, 2.432
    statutory provision, 1.169
    supplementary provisions, 2.431
  exercise of right
    generally, 1.326–1.329
    other persons, 2.375–2.376
  expert assistance, 2.412–2.413
  extensions of time
    applications, 2.385–2.386
    generally, 2.379–2.384
  funding legal services, 2.445–2.446
  further directions, 2.470–2.472
  general regulations
    appeals tribunal, 2.390–2.392
    decisions, 2.416–2.437
    general matters, 2.375–2.389
    procedure, 2.393–2.415
    service of notices, 2.373–2.374
  hearings
    choice, 2.395–2.396
    generally, 2.477
    oral, 2.406–2.415
    requests, 2.475–2.476
  irregularities, 2.481–2.482

933

Tax credits (appeals)—*cont.*
late appeals, 2.379–2.384
medical evidence, non-disclosure of
general regulations, under, 2.399–2.400
generally, 2.473–2.474
notice of appeal
acknowledgment, 2.462–2.463
generally, 2.457–2.458
notification, 2.462–2.463
prescribed form, 2.368–2.369
time limits, 2.459–2.461
oaths, 2.401–2.402
observations
directions, 2.470–2.472
reply, in, 2.468–2.469
respondent, by, 2.466–2.467
oral hearings
adjournment, 2.414–2.415
expert assistance, 2.412–2.413
generally, 2.406–2.411
postponement, 2.414–2.415
penalty proceedings
determination, 2.393–2.394
withdrawal, 2.397–2.398
point of law, on, 1.165–1.166
postponement, 2.414–2.415
procedure
generally, 1.167
regulations, 1.187
procedure regulations
appeal procedure, 2.464–2.482
applications for leave to appeal, 2.447–2.463
applications for leave to appeal to appellate court, 2.490–2.491
Commissioner's powers, 2.441
decisions, 2.483–2.489
delegation of functions, 2.443
funding of legal services, 2.445–2.446
service of notices, 2.444
transfer of proceedings, 2.442
record of proceedings
generally, 2.424–2.425
service by electronic mail, 2.432
Regulations
general, 2.370–2.437
notice of appeal, 2.367–2.369
procedure, 2.438–2.491
reinstatement, 2.405
representation, 2.464–2.465
requests for hearings, 2.475–2.476
respondent's written observations, 2.466–2.467
right of appeal
decisions of Board, 1.198–1.203
generally, 1.326–1.329
other persons, 2.375–2.376
service of notices
electronic mail, by, 2.432
generally, 2.373–2.374
manner and time, 2.444
setting aside of decisions
Commissioner, by, 2.487–2.489

Tax credits (appeals)—*cont.*
setting aside of decisions—*cont.*
generally, 2.428–2.430
service by electronic mail, 2.432
statutory provision, 1.169
supplementary provisions, 2.431
Social security commissioners
appointment, 1.181
certificates, 1.185
delegation of functions, 1.184
remuneration, 1.182
supplemental, 1.186
tenure, 1.183
statement of reasons
generally, 2.419
late applications, 2.422–2.423
service by electronic mail, 2.432
striking out
grounds, 2.403–2.404
reinstatement, 2.405
temporary modifications, 1.358–1.362
time limits
extension, 2.379–2.386
generally, 2.377–2.378
transfer of proceedings, 2.442
withdrawal, 2.480–2.481
witness summonses
general regulations, under, 2.401–2.402
generally, 2.478–2.479
written observations
directions, 2.470–2.472
reply, in, 2.468–2.469
respondent, by, 2.466–2.467

Tax Credits (Appeals) (No. 2) Regulations 2002
arrangement of Regulations, 2.370
citation, 2.371
commencement, 2.371
definitions, 2.371–2.372
duration, 2.371
general provisions
appeals tribunal, 2.390–2.392
decisions, 2.416–2.437
general matters, 2.375–2.389
procedure, 2.393–2.415
service of notices, 2.373–2.374

Tax Credits (Approval of Child Care Providers) Scheme 2005
appeals, 2.588
approved criteria, 2.584
approved person, 2.583
approved system, 2.585
criteria, 2.584
definitions, 2.579
fees, 2.589
period of approval, 2.587
qualifying child care, 2.582
Regulations
application, 2.578
citation, 2.578
commencement, 2.578
definitions, 2.579

Index

Tax Credits (Approval of Child Care Providers) Scheme 2005—*cont.*
Regulations—*cont.*
general provisions, 2.580–2.589
revocation and saving, 2.590
requirements, 2.581
specified body, 2.580
system, 2.585

Tax Credits (Claims and Notifications) Regulations 2002
arrangement of Regulations, 2.270
citation, 2.271
commencement, 2.271
definitions, 2.272
effect, 2.271
general provisions
  claims, 2.275–2.303
  electronic communications, 2.273–2.274
  final decisions, 2.328–2.331
  notice to provide information, 2.325–2.327
  notifications, 2.304–2.324
modifications to, 2.554

Tax Credits (Definition and Calculation of Income) Regulations 2002
arrangement of Regulations, 2.100
citation, 2.112
commencement, 2.112
definitions, 2.113–2.114
effect, 2.112
general note
  change in approach, 2.103
  cross-references, 2.111
  differences between calculations and tax assessments, 2.104
  introduction, 2.101
  questions to be decided, 2.105–2.110
  Tax Law Rewrite Project, 2.102
general provisions
  disregards, 2.175–2.182
  income, 2.115–2.174
modifications to, 2.553

Tax Credits (Immigration) Regulations 2003
arrangement of Regulations, 2.498
citation, 2.499
commencement, 2.499
definitions, 2.500
general provisions, 2.501–2.514
modifications to, 2.557

Tax Credits (Income Thresholds and Determination of Rates) Regulations 2002
arrangement of Regulations, 2.215
citation, 2.216
commencement, 2.216
definitions, 2.217
effect, 2.216
general provisions, 2.218–2.269

Tax Credits (Interest Rate) Regulations 2003
arrangement of Regulations, 2.492

Tax Credits (Interest Rate) Regulations 2003—*cont.*
citation, 2.493
commencement, 2.493
definitions, 2.495
general note, 2.494
general provisions, 2.496–2.497

Tax Credits (Notice of Appeal) Regulations 2002
citation, 2.367
commencement, 2.367
general provisions, 2.368–2.369

Tax Credits (Official Error) Regulations 2003
arrangement of Regulations, 2.534
citation, 2.535
commencement, 2.535
definitions, 2.536–2.537
general note, 2.539
general provision, 2.538

Tax Credits (Payments by the Commissioners) Regulations 2002
arrangement of Regulations, 2.332
citation, 2.334
commencement, 2.334
definitions, 2.335
effect, 2.334
general note, 2.333
general provisions, 2.336–2.359
modifications to, 2.555

Tax Credits (Polygamous Marriages) Regulations 2003
arrangement of Regulations, 2.545
citation, 2.547
commencement, 2.547
definitions, 2.548–2.549
effect, 2.547
general note, 2.546
general provision, 2.550–2.557

Tax Credits (Provision of Information) (Evaluation and Statistical Studies) Regulations 2003
citation, 2.570
commencement, 2.570
general provision, 2.571

Tax Credits (Provision of Information) (Evaluation and Statistical Studies) (Northern Ireland) Regulations 2004
citation, 2.572
commencement, 2.572
general provision, 2.573

Tax Credits (Provision of Information) (Functions Relating to Employment and Training) Regulations 2003
arrangement of Regulations, 2.562
citation, 2.564
commencement, 2.564
general note, 2.563
general provision, 2.565

Index

Tax Credits (Provision of Information) (Functions Relating to Employment and Training) Regulations 2005
citation, 2.576
commencement, 2.576
general provision, 2.577

Tax Credits (Provision of Information) (Functions Relating to Health) Regulations 2003
arrangement of Regulations, 2.540
citation, 2.541
commencement, 2.541
definitions, 2.543
general note, 2.542
general provision, 2.544

Tax Credits (Provision of Information) (Functions Relating to Health) (Scotland) Regulations 2004
citation, 2.574
commencement, 2.574
general provision, 2.575

Tax Credits (Provision of Information) (Functions Relating to Health) (No.2) Regulations 2003
arrangement of Regulations, 2.558
citation, 2.560
commencement, 2.560
general note, 2.559
general provision, 2.561

Tax Credits (Residence) Regulations 2003
arrangement of Regulations, 2.515
citation, 2.516
commencement, 2.516
definitions, 2.517–2.518
general provisions, 2.519–2.531
modifications to, 2.556
transitional provision, 2.532–2.533

Tax enquiries
amendment by taxpayer, 1.9
completion, 1.11
correction by Revenue, 1.10
notice, 1.8

"Tax-exempt savings"
income test, 2.103
voluntary work, 2.170–2.171

"Tax Law Rewrite Project"
calculation of income, 2.102

Tax returns
amendment by taxpayer
during enquiry, 1.9
generally, 1.6
appeals, 1.28–1.25
assessment
appeals, 1.19–1.25
discovery of loss of tax, on, 1.13
loss, etc., 1.27
relief for excessive assessments, 1.14–1.15
time limits, 1.16–1.18
want of form, 1.28
closure notices, 1.12

Tax returns—*cont.*
correction by Revenue
during enquiry, 1.10
generally, 1.7
definitions, 1.29
destruction, etc., 1.23
enquiry
amendment by taxpayer, 1.9
completion, 1.12
correction by Revenue, 1.7
notice, 1.8
fraudulent conduct, 1.18
generally, 1.4
loss, etc., 1.27
negligent conduct, 1.18
notice of enquiry, 1.8
penalties, 1.26
records, 1.11
relief for excessive assessments
double assessment, 1.14
error, 1.15
self-assessment, 1.5
time limits
fraudulent conduct, 1.18
income received after year for which assessable, 1.17
negligent conduct, 1.18
ordinary period, 1.16
want of form, 1.28

Taxable benefits
benefits code
definitions, 1.430
dispensations, 1.429
meaning, 1.427
relationship with earnings, 1.428
car fuel
benefit treated as earnings, 1.461
calculation of cash equivalent, 1.462
nil cash equivalent, 1.463
cash vouchers
application of provisions, 1.434–1.435
benefit treated as earnings, 1.438
disregard for money, goods or services obtained, 1.445
meaning, 1.436
sickness-benefits related, 1.437
credit tokens
application of provisions, 1.442
benefit treated as earnings, 1.444
disregard for money, goods or services obtained, 1.445
meaning, 1.443
employment-related benefits
cash equivalent treated as earnings, 1.448
cost of benefit, 1.449
excluded benefits, 1.447
meaning, 1.446
expenses payments
definitions, 1.432
relevant sums, 1.431
sums treated as earnings, 1.433

Index

Taxable benefits—*cont.*
 foreign benefits
  application of provisions, 1.521–1.522
  person liable to tax, 1.524
  taxable income, 1.523
 general note
  regulations, 2.123
  statutory provisions, 1.407
 lower-paid employment
  calculation of earnings rate, 1.454
  excluded provisions of benefits code, 1.452
  extra amounts relating to car, 1.455
  meaning, 1.453
 minor benefits, 1.450–1.451
 non-cash vouchers
  application of provisions, 1.439
  benefit treated as earnings, 1.441
  disregard for money, goods or services obtained, 1.445
  meaning, 1.440
 sickness-benefits related vouchers, 1.437
 social security income
  exemptions, 1.502–1.517
  person liable to tax, 1.500–1.501
  Table A, 1.495–1.497
  taxable income, 1.498–1.499
 vouchers
  cash vouchers, 1.434–1.438
  non-cash vouchers, 1.439–1.441
Taxable income
 employment income, 1.421
"Taxable maximum"
 income support
  amount in excess of, 1.506
  general, 1.507
 jobseeker's allowance, and
  amount in excess of, 1.511
  contribution-based JSA, 1.514
  definitions, 1.515
  general, 1.512
  income-based JSA, 1.513
"Taxable specific income"
 employment income, 1.421
Taxes Management Act 1970
 arrangement of sections, 1.1
 definitions, 1.29
 general note, 1.2
 general provisions
  administration, 1.3
  appeals, 1.19–1.25
  assessment and claims, 1.12–1.18
  penalties, 1.26
  records, 1.11
  returns of income and gains, 1.4–1.10
 miscellaneous provisions
  documents, 1.27–1.28
"Temporary absence from United Kingdom"
 residence requirements, 2.527–2.528
"Term-time work"
 working tax credit, 2.43–2.44

Territorial waters
 statutory pay, 1.115
TESSAs
 investment income, 2.156
30-hour element
 working tax credit, 2.63–2.64
Time
 see also **Time limits**
 calculation of income
  employment income, 2.130
  pension income, 2.137
  social security income, 2.150
  trading income, 2.143
Time limits
 child trust funds (appeals)
  extension, 6.80–6.81
  generally, 6.135–6.136
 claims, 2.282–2.283
 statutory sick pay, 3.17
 tax credits (appeals)
  extension, 2.379–2.386
  generally, 2.377–2.378
 tax credits, 2.282–2.283
"Top-up payments"
 disregards, 2.176
Trading income
 accounting date, 1.658
 bad debts, 1.650
 basic rules
  calculation of losses, 1.642
  deductions, 1.646
  GAAP, 1.641
  interest, 1.645
  professions and vocations, 1.640
  receipts and expenses, 1.643–1.644
 basis periods
  accounting date, 1.658
  normal rules, 1.659
  professions and vocations, 1.657
 business entertainment and gifts, 1.652
 calculation of losses, 1.642
 capital expenditure, 1.648
 capital receipts, 1.655
 charge to tax
  generally, 1.633
  income charged, 1.635
  person liable, 1.636
  territorial scope, 1.634
 debts incurred and later released, 1.656
 deductions
  relationship between rules, 1.646
  rules restricting, 1.647–1.653
 doubtful debts, 1.650
 farming, 1.637
 foster-care relief, 1.639
 generally accepted accounting practice, 1.641
 income treated as trade profits
  charge to tax, 1.633–1.636
  starting and cessation, 1.638
 interest, 1.645
 introduction, 1.626
 market gardening, 1.637

937

Index

Trading income—*cont.*
  overview, 1.630–1.631
  priority rules
    generally, 1.632
    introduction, 1.629
  professions and vocations
    basic rules, 1.640
    basis periods, 1.657
    receipts, 1.647
    rules restricting deductions, 1.647
  receipts
    basic rules, 1.643–1.644
    capital receipts, 1.655
    debts incurred and later released, 1.656
    professions and vocations, 1.654
  rent-a-room relief, 1.639
  rules restricting deductions
    bad debts, 1.650
    business entertainment and gifts, 1.652
    capital expenditure, 1.648
    doubtful debts, 1.650
    professions and vocations, 1.647
    social security contributions, 1.653
    unconnected losses, 1.649
    unpaid remuneration, 1.651
    wholly and exclusively rules, 1.649
  social security contributions, 1.653
  statutory overview
    introduction, 1.628
    priority rules, 1.629
  tax credits
    deductions, 2.141
    exemptions, 2.141
    general note, 2.139
    generally, 2.138
    identity of taxpayer, 2.142
    relevant income, 2.141
    self-employment, 2.140
    time of calculation, 2.143
  trade profits
    basic rules, 1.640–1.646
    basis periods, 1.657–1.659
    income treated as, 1.633–1.638
    receipts, 1.654–1.656
    rules restricting deductions, 1.647–1.653
  unconnected losses, 1.649
  unpaid remuneration, 1.651
  wholly and exclusively rules, 1.649
Training
  provision of information, and
    general note, 2.563
    generally, 2.565, 2.577
  remunerative work, 2.35
  working tax credit, 2.61–2.62
Training allowance
  remunerative work, 2.35
"Training for work"
  disability element (working tax credit), 2.61–2.62
"Training grants"
  disregards, 2.177

Transfer of assets
  Revenue and Customs, 1.747
Transfer of proceedings
  child trust funds (appeals), 6.122
  tax credits (appeals), 2.442
"Transport vouchers"
  meaning, 1.440
Travelling expenses
  disregards, 2.176–2.177
  necessary attendance, for, 1.471
  performance of duties, in, 1.470
  "workplace", 1.472
"Treatment of more than one contract"
  statutory adoption pay
    general note, 5.10
    generally, 5.72
    lapse of election, 5.15
    notification of election, 5.12
    provision of information, 5.13
    relevant employer, 5.14, 5.86
  statutory maternity pay
    generally, 4.10
    relevant employer, 4.31–4.32
  statutory paternity pay
    adoption of child, on, 5.63
    birth of child, on, 5.56
    general note, 5.10
    lapse of election, 5.15
    notification of election, 5.12
    provision of information, 5.13
    relevant employer, 5.14, 5.86
  statutory sick pay
    generally, 3.40
    relevant employer, 3.38–3.39

"Unconnected losses"
  trading income, 1.649
Underpayments
  tax credits, 1.307–1.308
Unemployability supplement
  statutory sick pay, 1.126
Unfair dismissal
  statutory maternity pay, 4.22
"Unpaid remuneration"
  trading income, 1.651

Variation
  decisions of Board, 1.194–1.195
Vehicle maintenance grant
  see **Disabled person's vehicle maintenance grant**
Verification
  claims, 2.366
Vocations
  see **Professions**
Voluntary work
  income test, 2.170–2.171
  remunerative work, 2.35
Vouchers
  cash
    application of provisions, 1.434–1.435
    benefit treated as earnings, 1.438

Index

Vouchers—*cont.*
cash—*cont.*
disregard for money, goods or services obtained, 1.445
meaning, 1.436
sickness-benefits related, 1.437
child trust funds
generally, 6.9
statutory provision, 1.557–1.558
non-cash
application of provisions, 1.439
benefit treated as earnings, 1.441
disregard for money, goods or services obtained, 1.445
meaning, 1.440
sickness benefits related, 1.437

War pensioner's mobility supplement
pension income, 2.132

"Weekly rates"
statutory adoption pay
general note, 5.3
generally, 5.4
rounding, 5.6–5.7
statutory paternity pay
general note, 5.3
generally, 5.4
rounding, 5.6–5.7

Welfare food
milk tokens, 2.145

"Wholly and exclusively"
trading income, 1.649

"Wholly exempt benefits"
social security income, 1.518–1.520

Widowed mother's allowance
social security income, 2.147

Widowed parent's allowance
social security income, 2.147

"Winnings"
investment income, 2.156

Withdrawal
child trust funds (appeals)
general regulations, under, 6.90–6.91
generally, 6.153–6.154
tax credits (appeals), 2.480–2.481

Witness summonses
child trust funds (appeals)
general regulations, under, 6.92–6.93
generally, 6.151–6.152
tax credits (appeals)
general regulations, under, 2.401–2.402
generally, 2.478–2.479

"Work after confinement"
statutory maternity pay, 4.14–4.15

"Work during pay period"
statutory adoption pay, 5.73
statutory paternity pay, 5.64

"Working less than 16 hours a week"
working tax credit, 2.51–2.52

Working tax credit
administrative arrangements
definitions, 2.363
general note, 2.361

Working tax credit—*cont.*
administrative arrangements—*cont.*
provision of information, 2.364–2.365
recording, etc. of claims, 2.366
statutory provision, 1.348–1.349
adoption, 2.37–2.40
annual reports, 1.330–1.331
annual review, 1.332–1.333
appeals
see also **Appeals (tax credits)**
appealable decisions, 1.324–1.325
exercise of right, 1.326–1.329
general regulations, 2.370–2.437
notice of appeal, 2.367–2.369
procedure regulations, 2.438–2.491
temporary modifications, 1.358–1.362
approval of child care providers scheme
appeals, 2.588
approved criteria, 2.584
approved person, 2.583
approved system, 2.585
criteria, 2.584
definitions, 2.579
fees, 2.589
period of approval, 2.587
qualifying child care, 2.582
Regulations, 2.578–2.590
requirements, 2.581
specified body, 2.580
system, 2.585
assignment, 1.340–1.341
bankruptcy, 1.340–1.341
basic element
adoption, 2.37–2.40
ceasing to undertake work, 2.51–2.52
childbirth, 2.37–2.40
gaps between jobs, 2.53–2.54
ill health, 2.41–2.42
pay in lieu of notice, 2.49–2.50
qualifying remunerative work, 2.25–2.34
seasonal work, 2.43–2.44
strike periods, 2.45–2.46
suspension from work, 2.47–2.48
term-time work, 2.43–2.44
working less than 16 hours a week, 2.51–2.52
capital rule, 2.103
carers, 2.35
ceasing to undertake work, 2.51–2.52
change of circumstances
advance, in, 2.319
amendment, 2.312
automatic, 1.249
date of, 2.313–2.318
decrease of rate, 2.307–2.308
definitions, 2.207
discretionary, 1.248
evidence of birth or adoption, 2.324
failure to report, 1.250
generally, 1.243–1.244
increase of maximum rate, 2.305–2.306
mandatory, 1.246

939

Index

Working tax credit—*cont.*
  change of circumstances—*cont.*
    method, 2.309–2.310
    person acting on behalf of another, by, 2.320–2.323
    relevant changes, 1.245
    relevant person, 2.311
  charitable work, 2.35
  child care providers
    appeals, 2.588
    approved criteria, 2.584
    approved person, 2.583
    approved system, 2.585
    criteria, 2.584
    definitions, 2.579
    fees, 2.589
    period of approval, 2.587
    qualifying child care, 2.582
    Regulations, 2.578–2.590
    requirements, 2.581
    specified body, 2.580
    system, 2.585
  childbirth, 2.37–2.40
  childcare element
    calculation of childcare charges, 2.74–2.75
    change of circumstances, 2.76–2.77
    "child", 2.72–2.73
    "childcare", 2.72–2.73
    generally, 2.69–2.71
    incapacitation, 2.71
    qualifying young persons, 2.73
    "relevant childcare charges", 2.72–2.73
    statutory provisions, 1.272–1.273
  claims
    see also **Claims**
    definitions, 2.275–2.276
    generally, 2.277–2.303
    statutory provision, 1.231–1.240
  Codes of Practice
    overpayments, 7.24–7.32
  conditions of entitlement
    basic element, 2.25–2.62
    childcare element, 2.69–2.77
    death of child, after, 2.82–2.83
    disability element, 2.55–2.62
    50-plus element, 2.80–2.81
    lone-parent element, 2.67–2.68
    second-adult element, 2.65–2.66
    severe disablement, 2.78–2.79
    30-hour element, 2.63–2.64
  Crown employment, 1.338–1.339
  death of child, after, 2.82–2.83
  decisions
    discovery, on, 1.290–1.292
    final decision, 1.286–1.287
    final notice, 1.284–1.285
    information requirements, 1.295–1.296
    initial decision, 1.276–1.279
    notice of, 1.297–1.298
    official error, subject to, 1.293–1.294
    other revised decisions, 1.282–1.283

Working tax credit—*cont.*
  decisions—*cont.*
    power to enquire, 1.288–1.289
    revision after notifications, 1.280–1.281
  definitions
    regulations, in, 2.32
    statute, in, 1.346–1.347
  determination of rate
    cut-off provisions, 2.268–2.269
    full year periods, 2.243–2.249
    generally, 2.227–2.242
    introduction, 2.225–2.226
    short periods, 2.250
  development of system, 1.223
  disability element
    Cases A to G, 2.58
    generally, 2.55–2.57
    initial claims, 2.59–2.60
    relevant disabilities, 2.86–2.98
    "training for work", 2.61–2.62
  disability periods, 2.41–2.42
  disability work allowance, 2.56
  disclosure of information, 1.350–1.351
  duration, 1.241–1.242
  elements of credit
    basic element, 2.25–2.62
    childcare element, 2.69–2.77
    death of child, after, 2.82–2.83
    disability element, 2.55–2.62
    50-plus element, 2.80–2.81
    generally, 2.23–2.24
    lone-parent element, 2.67–2.68
    second-adult element, 2.65–2.66
    severe disability element, 2.78–2.79
    30-hour element, 2.63–2.64
  employment zone programme, 2.35
  entitlement, 1.264–1.269
  excepted activities, 2.35
  failure to comply with requirements, 1.312–1.313
  failure to make correct payments, 1.314–1.315
  50-plus element, 2.80–2.81
  fraud, and
    generally, 1.318–1.319
    powers relating to documents, 1.320–1.321
  forwarding of claims, 2.366
  functions of Board, 1.229–1.230
  gaps between jobs, 2.53–2.54
  general note, 1.222
  holding of claims, 2.366
  hours worked, 2.36
  ill health, 2.41–2.42
  inalienability, 1.340–1.341
  incapacity for work, 2.41–2.42
  income test
    see also **Income test**
    calculation, 2.115–2.120
    definitions, 2.113–2.114
    disregards, 2.175–2.182
    employment income, 2.121–2.130
    foreign income, 2.161–2.162

Index

Working tax credit—*cont.*
income test—*cont.*
general note, 2.101–2.111
investment income, 2.155–2.158
miscellaneous income, 2.173–2.174
notional income, 2.163–2.172
pension income, 2.131–2.137
property income, 2.159–2.160
social security income, 2.144–2.150
statutory provision, 1.251–1.257
student income, 2.151–2.154
trading income, 2.138–2.143
income thresholds, 2.218–2.220
incorrect statements, etc., 1.309–1.311
Intensive Activity Period, 2.35
interest
definitions, 2.495
general note, 2.494
overpayments, on, 2.496
prescribed rate, 2.497
statutory provision, 1.322–1.323
lone-parent element, 2.67–2.68
maximum rate
amount, 2.99
generally, 2.84–2.85
statutory provision, 1.270–1.271
means testing, 2.101
minimum level of continuity, 2.33
Northern Ireland, 1.363–1.364
notices by Board, 1.342–1.343
notices to provide information, and
childcare provider, to, 2.326
dates to be specified, 2.327
definitions, 2.272
electronic communications, 2.273–2.274
employers, to, 2.325
s.17 TCA 2002, under, 2.328–2.331
notification of change of circumstances
advance, in, 2.319
amendment, 2.312
automatic, 1.249
date of, 2.313–2.318
decrease of rate, 2.307–2.308
definitions, 2.207
discretionary, 1.248
evidence of birth or adoption, 2.324
failure to report, 1.250
generally, 1.243–1.244
increase of maximum rate, 2.305–2.306
mandatory, 1.246
method, 2.309–2.310
person acting on behalf of another, by, 2.320–2.323
relevant changes, 1.245
relevant person, 2.311
official errors
definitions, 2.536–2.537
general note, 2.539
generally, 2.538
overpayments
Code of Practice, 7.24–7.32
generally, 1.303–1.304
recovery, 1.305–1.306

Working tax credit—*cont.*
pay in lieu of notice, 2.49–2.50
payment
employees' rights, 1.301–1.302
generally, 1.299–1.300
payment by Revenue and Customs
child care element, 2.336–2.337
generally, 2.338–2.339
introduction, 2.333
penalties
determination, 1.369
failure to comply with requirements, 1.312–1.313
failure to make correct payments, 1.314–1.315
Guidance, 7.1–7.23
incorrect statements, etc., 1.309–1.311
mitigation, 1.371
proceedings before Commissioners, 1.370
recovery, 1.373
supplementary, 1.316–1.317
time limits, 1.372
period of award, 1.241–1.242
persons subject to immigration control
definitions, 2.500
exclusion from entitlement, 2.501–2.510
general note, 2.507
modifications of Act, 2.511–2.512
statutory provision, 1.334–1.335
transitional relief, 2.513–2.514
polygamous marriages
definitions, 2.548–2.549
general note, 2.546
modification of Regulations, 2.551–2.557
modification of TCA 2002, 2.550
statutory provision, 1.336–1.337
provision of information
authorities, by, 2.365
authorities, to, 2.364
functions relating to employment, 2.565, 2.577
functions relating to health, 2.542–2.544, 2.561, 2.575
functions relating to training, 2.565, 2.577
qualifying remunerative work
excepted activities, 2.35
generally, 2.25–2.31
hours worked, 2.36
minimum level of continuity, 2.33
remunerative work, 2.34
routes to entitlement, 2.32
qualifying young persons
childcare element, 2.73
death, 2.82–2.83
rate, 1.274–1.275
recording of claims, 2.366
remunerative work, 2.34

941

Index

Working tax credit—*cont.*
residence requirements
Crown servants posted overseas, 2.529–2.531
definitions, 2.517–2.518
ordinary residence, 2.522–2.525
person treated as not being in UK, 2.519–2.526
temporary absence from UK, 2.527–2.528
routes to entitlement, 2.32
seasonal work, 2.43–2.44
second-adult element, 2.65–2.66
severe disability element, 2.78–2.79
sickness, 2.41–2.42
sports award, 2.39
statutory provisions
see also **Tax credits**
appeals, 1.324–1.329
child tax credit, 1.258–1.263
decisions, 1.276–1.298
fraud, 1.318–1.321
generally, 1.227–1.257
interest, 1.322–1.323
payment, 1.299–1.308
penalties, 1.309–1.317
rate, 1.274–1.275
supplementary, 1.330–1.347
working tax credit, 1.264–1.273
strike periods, 2.45–2.46
suspension from work, 2.47–2.48

Working tax credit—*cont.*
term-time work, 2.43–2.44
30-hour element, 2.63–2.64
training allowance, 2.58
underpayments, 1.307–1.308
use of information, 1.350–1.351
verification of claims, 2.366
voluntary work, 2.35
working less than 16 hours a week, 2.51–2.52
Working Tax Credit (Entitlement and Maximum Rate) Regulations 2002
arrangement of Regulations, 2.19
citation, 2.20
commencement, 2.20
definitions, 2.22
effect, 2.20–2.21
general note, 2.21
general provisions
conditions of entitlement, 2.25–2.83
elements of credit, 2.23–2.24
maximum rate, 2.84–2.85
modifications to, 2.552
schedules
disabilities, 2.86–2.98
maximum rates, 2.99
Working Tax Credit (Payment by Employers) Regulations 2002
general note, 2.333
"Wounds pension"
pension income, 2.132